BRUCE CATTON'S
CIVIL WAR

ABOUT THE AUTHOR

BRUCE CATTON was born in Petoskey, Michigan, in 1899. The son of a Congregationalist minister, he became a journalist, spending the years 1920–1926 writing for the *Cleveland News, Boston American,* and *Cleveland Plain Dealer.* From 1926 until 1941 Catton worked for the Newspaper Enterprise Association, writing editorials, book reviews, and as a Washington correspondent.

In 1942 during WW II he became the Director of Information for the War Production Board, and later he held similar posts in the Department of Commerce and the Department of the Interior. His experiences as a federal employee prepared him to write *War Lords of Washington* in 1948.

Catton is best known for his popular historical works on the Civil War, especially his trilogy: *Mr. Lincoln's Army* (1951), *Glory Road* (1952), and *A Stillness at Appomattox* (1953). The last volume won both the 1954 Pulitzer Prize and the 1954 National Book Award. Catton has written other books on the Civil War including *The Hallowed Ground, The Coming Fury,* and *Terrible Swift Sword.* Bruce Catton died in 1978.

BRUCE CATTON'S
CIVIL WAR

Three Volumes in One

Mr. Lincoln's Army

Glory Road

A Stillness at Appomattox

THE FAIRFAX PRESS
New York

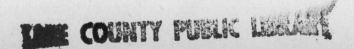

This volume contains the complete and unabridged texts of the
original editions. They have been completely reset for this volume.

Copyright © 1984 by William B. Catton

This Omnibus edition was previously published in separate
volumes under the titles:
Mr. Lincoln's Army copyright MCMLI, © MCMLXII by
Bruce Catton
Glory Road copyright MCMLII by Bruce Catton
A Stillness at Appomattox copyright MCMLIII by Bruce Catton

This 1984 edition is published by Fairfax Press, distributed
by Crown Publishers, Inc., by arrangement with Doubleday &
Company, Inc.

Manufactured in the United States of America

Library of Congress Cataloging in Publication Data

Catton, Bruce, 1899–1978
    Bruce Catton's Civil War.

    Bibliography: p.
    Includes index.
    Contents: Mr. Lincoln's army—Glory road—A
stillness at Appomattox.
    1. United States–History–Civil War, 1861–1865 –
Campaigns.   2. United States–History–Civil War, 1861–
1865 – Regimental histories.   3. United States.   Army of
the Potomac.   I. Title.
E470.2.C358   1984   973.7   84-8166

ISBN: 0-517-447711

h g f e d c b a

CONTENTS

MR. LINCOLN'S
ARMY

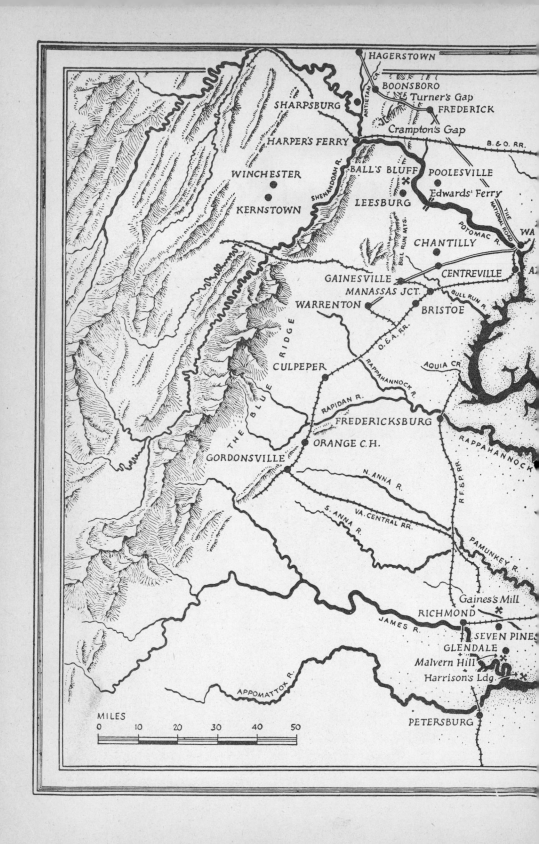

HAGERSTOWN

BOONSBORO
Turner's Gap
FREDERICK
Crampton's Gap

ANTIETAM CR.

SHARPSBURG

HARPER'S FERRY

B. & O. RR.

WINCHESTER

BALL'S BLUFF
POOLESVILLE
Edwards' Ferry

SHENANDOAH R.

LEESBURG

KERNSTOWN

CHANTILLY

WA

NATIONAL ROAD

POTOMAC R.

THE

BULL RUN MTS.

GAINESVILLE
MANASSAS JCT.
WARRENTON

CENTREVILLE

AZ

BRISTOE

BULL RUN R.

O. & A. RR.

CULPEPER

RAPPAHANNOCK R.

AQUIA CR.

RAPIDAN R.

THE BLUE RIDGE

FREDERICKSBURG

RAPPAHANNOCK

ORANGE C.H.

GORDONSVILLE

N. ANNA R.

S. ANNA R.

VA. CENTRAL RR.

RF. & P. RR.

PAMUNKEY R.

Gaines's Mill

RICHMOND

JAMES R.

SEVEN PINES
GLENDALE
Malvern Hill
Harrison's Ldg.

APPOMATTOX R.

MILES
0   10   20   30   40   50

PETERSBURG

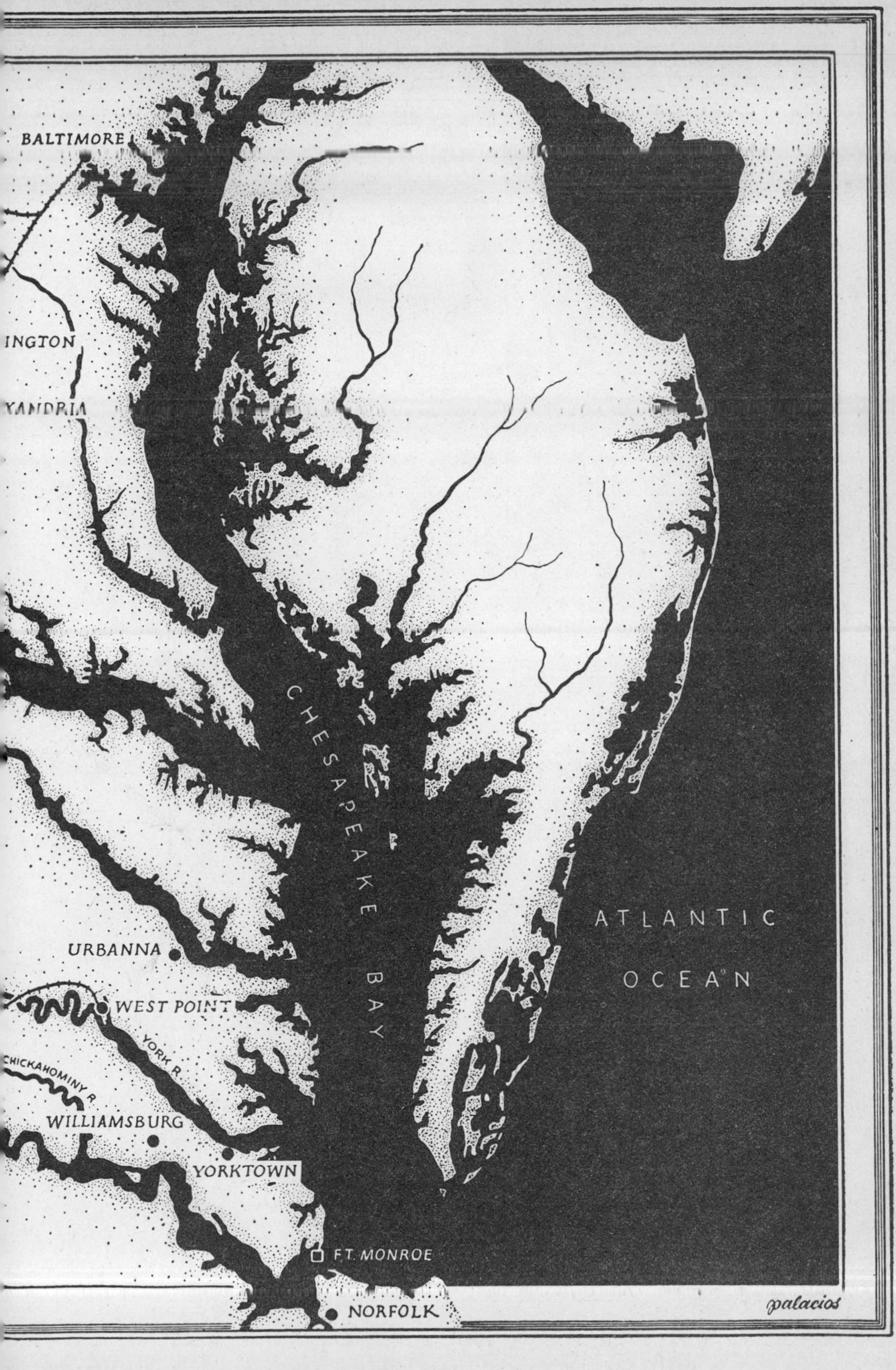

BALTIMORE
INGTON
XANDRIA
CHESAPEAKE BAY
ATLANTIC OCEAN
URBANNA
WEST POINT
YORK R.
CHICKAHOMINY R.
WILLIAMSBURG
YORKTOWN
FT. MONROE
NORFOLK
palacios

To Cherry

ONE

Picture-Book War

1. THERE WAS TALK OF TREASON

THE ROWBOAT SLID out on the Potomac in the hazy light of a hot August morning, dropped down past the line of black ships near the Alexandria wharves, and bumped to a stop with its nose against the wooden side of a transport. Colonel Herman Haupt, superintendent of military railroads, a sheaf of telegrams crumpled in one hand, went up the Jacob's ladder to the deck—clumsily, as was to be expected of a landsman, but rapidly, for he was an active man—and disappeared into a cabin. A moment later he returned, and as he came down the ladder he was followed by a short, broad-shouldered, sandy-haired man, deeply tanned by the sun of the Virginia peninsula, with thin faint lines of worry between his eyes: Major General George Brinton McClellan, commander of the Army of the Potomac, which had been coming up from the south by water for a week and more and which at the moment was scattered all the way from Alexandria to the upper Rappahannock, most of it well out of the general's reach and all of it, as he suspected, soon to be out from under his authority.

There was an air about this youthful general—an air of far-off bugles, and flags floating high, and troops cheering madly, as if the picture of him which one hundred thousand soldiers had created had somehow become real and was now an inseparable part of his actual appearance. He could look jaunty and dapper after a day in the saddle, on muddy roads, in a driving rainstorm; like a successful politician, he lived his part, keeping himself close to the surface so that every cry and every gesture of the men who adored him called him out to a quick response that was none the less genuine for being completely automatic. It was impossible to see him, in his uniform with the stars on his shoulders, without also seeing the army—"my army," he called it proudly, almost as if it were a personal possession, which was in a way the case: he had made it, he had given it shape and color and spirit, and in his mind and in the minds of the men he commanded the identification was complete.

He sat in the stern of the rowboat, beside the superintendent of military railroads, and he was silent as the boat went back upstream to the landing. The docks and the river front were a confusion of steamboats and barges and white-topped wagons and great stacks of boxed goods and equipment, and the quaint little town itself was lost in a restless, lounging concourse of soldiers: loose fringes of a moving army, convalescents and strays and detailed men, and here and there a regiment moving off with cased flags at route step toward some outlying camp. From this same town the general had set out, nearly five months ago, to take his army down to the swamps and forests below Richmond and win the war; he had known in his heart that he was destined to save the country, and the army had gone forth with unstained uniforms and gleaming rifle barrels, and with proud flags that had never touched the ground.

But nothing had worked quite the way he had expected. The Army of the Po-

5

tomac, made in his own image, had spent some months on the Virginia peninsula—that long neck of land which runs southeast between the James and the York rivers, and which the army remembered as composed chiefly of mud, mosquitoes, and steaming heat, with a great tangle of gloomy forests infested by lean and hairy men with rifles who uttered shrill, nerve-splitting screams as they came forward endlessly to the attack. The luck of the army and the general had been all bad. Many battles had been fought, and while no great defeat had been suffered there had been a weary retreat from in front of Richmond to a dismal camp far down the river. The general considered that this retreat had been a masterful accomplishment, but the government considered it sheer disaster, and it was trying now—in August 1862—to strike the southern Confederacy with another instrument.

This new instrument, as McClellan was frank to state, had been poorly chosen. Scattered fragments of commands had been swept together and entrusted to a self-confident soldier from the Western armies, General John Pope, and Pope had been sent down into Virginia overland, following the line of the Orange and Alexandria Railroad to the Rappahannock River. Leaving McClellan and his army to swelter in their camp on the James, the Rebels had promptly concentrated against Pope's army and had been giving him a bad time of it—so bad, indeed, that McClellan's army was now being pulled back to Washington and was being forwarded to Pope by bits and pieces. McClellan was not being sent forward with it; and this morning, as he passed through the sprawling base of supplies, where white door fronts of the colonial era looked down on muddy streets churned by endless wagon trains, it seemed likely that he would presently be a general without an army.

The general went with the colonel to the colonel's office. They were both West Pointers, and when the war broke out they had both been railroad men, and they could talk the same language. As soon as they were seated Haupt gave McClellan such news as he had. None of it was good. Seen thus, from behind the lines, the war was untidy, misdirected, discouraging.

Enemy forces, said Haupt, were across the railroad line at Manassas Junction. It had been thought at first that these were merely a handful of roving cavalry—cavalry had descended on the railroad a few days earlier, farther down the line at Catlett's—but it was beginning to be clear now that they were more important than that. A New Jersey brigade had gone forward to restore the situation and had run into rifle and artillery fire too heavy to come from any cavalry; had, as a matter of fact, been most distressingly cut to pieces. Two Ohio infantry regiments were holding on where the railroad crossed Bull Run, but they were obviously in grave danger and would probably have to come back. Confederates apparently were either on or near the railroad this side of them, between Bull Run and Alexandria; the bridge over Pohick Creek near Burke's Station, only thirteen miles out, was rumored to have been burned, and the telegraph line had been cut. Nor was it just the two Ohio regiments that were in peril. The seizure of Manassas Junction meant that General Pope was out of forage for his horses and rations for his men.

Colonel Haupt did not know where Pope was, and it seemed that the War Department did not know either. It was bombarding Haupt with inquiries and had evidently developed the jitters—McClellan saw a wire complaining that there had been "great neglect and carelessness" on the Manassas plain. To McClellan that seemed obvious. He did not admire General Pope, either as a man or as a soldier, and his present prospect of forwarding his own troops to Pope at a time when Pope's position was unknown and the road leading in his direction was blocked by Rebel soldiers was not one that McClellan could think about with any pleasure.

Clearly, this was no time for an army commander or a superintendent of military railroads to sit holding his thumbs. With the plight of Pope's army and the dire fix of those two Ohio regiments Colonel Haupt had no direct concern, except that it was up to him to get the railroad back in working order so that these and other troops could be fed, supplied, and, if necessary, transported; and for this he had a plan of action, which he now asked McClellan to approve. A wrecking and construction train, ready to go forward and repair damaged tracks and bridges, was standing on a siding with steam up. Also ready was a freight train loaded with forage and rations. Haupt proposed to send out ahead of these a train of flatcars carrying a battery of field artillery and a few hundred sharpshooters. This could go as far as the condition of the track permitted, and the guns and riflemen could then advance by road and clear out such Rebel marauders as might be in the vicinity. The wrecking train could then get the bridges repaired in short order—Haupt kept a stock of prefabricated bents and stringers on hand, ready for just such emergencies as this, and if they had to, his construction gangs could build a bridge with timber from torn-down farmhouses along the right of way—and when that had been done the supply trains could be leapfrogged through with subsistence for Pope's army.

The thin lines between McClellan's eyes deepened slightly and he shook his head slowly. He could not approve the plan. It would be attended with risk. Haupt was primarily a railroad man; any kind of expedient was all right, for him, if it just gave him a chance to put his track gangs on the job and get the line opened up again. Also, there was not, inherently, any very great difference between a Rebel army and a spring freshet on a Pennsylvania mountain river—both broke up a railroad, and when the damage had been done one went out and fixed it as quickly as possible. But McClellan's mind was full of the mischances that can befall troops which are incautiously thrust out into enemy territory; he repeated that he could not approve. Haupt was irritated. All military operations, he said, were attended with risk, as far as he could see, and the risk here did not seem to be excessive. Surely, if the advance guard were properly handled, nothing very disastrous could happen. The trains could be kept safely in the rear while the skirmishers went forward. If the enemy were found in force, the men could retire to their train and the whole expedition could quickly be brought back out of harm's way.

McClellan shook his head again. The situation was too obscure. Enemy troops, possibly in very substantial numbers, appeared to be between Pope's army and Washington; the first thing to do was to arrange the troops actually present in such a way that the capital itself would be safe. Then preparations could be made for an advance in force. Meanwhile—the general had grown pale beneath his tan and appeared genuinely unwell—did the colonel have any brandy and water? The colonel did. McClellan took it and seemed revived, borrowed a scratch pad, and wrote a telegram to the War Department, reporting that he was ashore in Alexandria and describing the situation as he had found it. Then he departed.

Left to himself, Haupt fumed and pondered, and wished that he had not succeeded in finding McClellan at all. Earlier in the morning he had telegraphed his proposal to General Henry W. Halleck, commander, under the President, of the armies of the United States. Halleck, who never made a decision himself if it could possibly be passed along to someone else, had replied: "If you can see Gen. McClellan, consult him. If not, go ahead as you propose." Haupt had now seen General McClellan and he wished he hadn't; if he had only missed him, the expedition could be under way by now.

Although he had been trained as a soldier—he had been graduated from West Point in 1835, in the same class with George Gordon Meade—Haupt was essentially a civilian. Resigning his commission shortly after graduation, he had gone into railroad work, had built a good part of the Juniata division of the Pennsylvania Railroad, and had become, successively, division superintendent and chief engineer for that line. He had been brought into the army, somewhat against his will, as a railroad and construction expert, and he was admired in high places. President Lincoln liked to tell about the marvelous bridge Haupt had built "out of beanpoles and cornstalks" down on the Aquia Creek line out of Fredericksburg. Haupt actually belonged in the next century; as it was, in the Civil War most generals failed to appreciate him. He was used to direct action, and generals irritated him. His present job gave them many occasions to do this, and they never seemed to miss a chance. Three days ago, for example, Haupt had bestirred himself to assemble trains to send General Joe Hooker's division forward to Pope. He got the trains lined up, Hooker's troops were at hand ready to go aboard, but Hooker himself had vanished—presumably to seek the flesh-pots in Washington. Haupt telegraphed to his good friend and brother railroad man, P. H Watson, Assistant Secretary of War. Back came Watson's reply:

"General Hooker was in Alexandria last night, but I will send to Willard's and see if he is there. I do not know any other place that he frequents. Be as patient as possible with the generals; some of them will trouble you more than they do the enemy."[1]

That was a judgment with which Haupt was ready to agree. He had no sooner got Hooker out of his hair than General Samuel D. Sturgis got into it. Sturgis showed up with a division of troops, demanding immediate transportation to the front. To make sure that his request for transportation got top priority Sturgis had moved his soldiers out and had seized the railroad—or that part of it which lay within his reach, which was enough to tie up the entire line—swearing that no trains would go anywhere until his division had been moved. Haupt tried to reason with him, but it was no go—Haupt was a colonel and Sturgis was a general, and Sturgis would not listen. Sturgis had the rank and he had the soldiers, and for the moment he had the railroad, too, and no temporary colonel was going to tell him what to do.

Haupt had had to go through that sort of thing before. General Pope had had similar ideas when he first took command in northern Virginia, announcing that his own quartermaster would control the movement of railroad cars just as he ran the wagon trains, and informing Haupt that his function was to do as he was told. Within two weeks the line had got into such a snarl that no trains could move in any direction. Pope came to see that it took a railroad man to run a railroad—he could get a point now and then if it was obvious enough, could John Pope, for all his bluster—and he was glad to hand the road back to Colonel Haupt: particularly so since Haupt by this time had got from the Secretary of War an order giving him complete and unqualified control over the railroad and everything on it, regardless of the orders any army commander might issue. Haupt, therefore, was ready to take Sturgis in his stride; but Sturgis had troops and guns and swore he would use them. Furious, Haupt telegraphed Halleck, getting in return a bristling order which specifically authorized him, in the name of the general-in-chief, to put Sturgis under arrest if there was any more funny business. Haupt summoned Sturgis to his office. Sturgis came, rather elevated with liquor, accompanied by his chief of staff.

Haupt showed Halleck's order and explained that he was getting all sorts of troops and supplies forward to General Pope and that Sturgis would simply have to wait his turn. Sturgis was not impressed, and he somehow got the idea that the order Haupt was exhibiting had been issued by General Pope.

"I don't care for John Pope one pinch of owl dung," said Sturgis solemnly—a sentiment which had its points but was hardly germane. Patiently Haupt explained: this order was not from Pope, it was from Halleck, who held the power to bind and to loose. Sturgis shook his head and repeated his judgment of Pope, savoring the sentence as if the thought had been bothering him for a long time. Haupt fluttered the order at him and went over it a third time. Sturgis, his needle stuck in one groove, repeated:

"I don't care for John Pope—"

His chief of staff tugged at his sleeve to stop him, and hastily and earnestly whispered in his ear. Sturgis blinked, finally got the point, and rose to his feet ponderously.

"Well, then," he said—with what, all things considered, might be called owlish dignity, "*take* your damned railroad."

So that had been settled, and Sturgis had awaited his turn. But the episode had tied up the railroad for the better part of a day and had canceled the movement of four troop trains. Haupt was more than ready to agree with Assistant Secretary Watson about the generals.

Anyway, that was over. Now there was the problem of reopening Pope's supply line. Pope's soldiers must be getting hungry; and besides, with the outer end of the line gone, the Alexandria yards were clogged with loaded freight cars that had no place to go. Across the river, in Washington, the Baltimore and Ohio was complaining that boxcars consigned to Pope's army were filling the tracks on Maryland Avenue; the available B. & O. engines were too heavy to go over the Long Bridge; would Colonel Haupt please send an engine over from Alexandria and get them, so that the B. & O. could go on with its regular work? This Haupt could by no means do, having more cars in Alexandria now than he could handle. The B. & O. needled the War Department, which sent plaintive messages; and the day wore on, and the situation did not improve. Haupt reflected that he was, after all, in charge of the railroad, and that somewhere off to the southwest there was an army that greatly needed supplies. He determined to go ahead on his own hook. After dark he sent a message to McClellan—who by now had established his headquarters on shore—notifying him that at four in the morning he would start his construction train forward, followed by the subsistence train. Would McClellan at least let him have two hundred soliders to go along as train guard? If the men did not report, Haupt added, the trains would go ahead without them.

He got no answer. At midnight he gave up on McClellan, got on his horse, and set out to appeal to the first general he saw—any general, just so long as he had a few troops to spare and was willing to loan a few of them to help open a vital railway line.

By good luck the first general Haupt found was Winfield Scott Hancock, a brigade commander in the Army of the Potomac, recently back from the peninsula, where in spite of the fact that his brigade had not had too much fighting to do he had somehow marked both it and himself as men who would be very useful indeed before the war was over. Late as it was, Hancock had only just gone to bed. He liked to do all his paper work around midnight and had a habit, whenever he encountered a report that was in any way faulty, of having the author hauled out of bed at once and brought to brigade headquarters to receive a dressing-down that was usually loud enough to arouse the nearby regiments. This trait was a trial to Hancock's staff, but it meant that most reports by now were letter-perfect before they ever reached the general.

Hancock was a direct actionist, who both looked and acted like a soldier—a burly, handsome man, who somehow managed always to be wearing a clean white shirt even when the army had been in the field for weeks, and who, in an army where the officers were notably profane, was outstanding for the vigor, range, and effectiveness of his cursing. His men liked to tell how, at the battle of Williamsburg, he had galloped up, outdistancing his staff, to order his troops to the charge—"the air was blue all around him," one of them recalled admiringly. There was a great breezy vigor and bluffness about the man. Earlier in the war, when his brigade was still in training, his men had taken to killing and eating the sheep of farmers near camp, and Hancock had determined to stop it. One afternoon, riding the lines near his camp, he had seen a knot of soldiers in a meadow, bending over the body of a sheep. Putting his horse to the fence, he galloped up, shouting mightily, and the men of course scattered—all except one who tarried too long and whom Hancock, flinging himself from his saddle, seized with strong hands.

"Now, you scoundrel, don't tell me you didn't kill that sheep—I saw you with my own eyes!" roared the general. Just then the sheep, not yet knifed, realized that it was no longer being held and sprang to its feet and scampered nimbly away. Hancock stared at the rocketing sheep, looked blankly at the quaking soldier in his hands—and then threw his head back and made the meadow ring with shouts of laughter.[3]

It was this Hancock whom Haupt found on his midnight quest for troops. Hancock heard his story and immediately detailed the men for him, and early in the morning Haupt's trains went lurching off into Virginia. By ten in the morning Haupt was notified that the bridge near Burke's Station had been rebuilt. He also learned that enemy troops were still somewhere in the vicinity of Manassas in very great strength; the head of the construction gang had been told that Lee himself was with them. A little later trains came steaming back from Fairfax Station loaded with wounded men.

For the moment this was all the news there was. Haupt's line of track went off into the darkness where moved shadowy forces made large by rumor. For all anyone knew, Lee and his whole army might be between Pope and Washington. McClellan picked up a report that 120,000 Confederates were moving toward Arlington and the Chain Bridge, bent on the capture of Washington and Baltimore. Halleck sagely remarked that the thing to be afraid of at that moment was the danger that Rebel cavalry might dash forward by night and enter the city— "Rebel cavalry" in those days being terrifying words, since the plow hands and mechanics whom the Federals were earnestly trying to turn into cavalrymen were no match at all for Jeb Stuart's incomparable troopers.

McClellan sent four infantry regiments out to the works at Upton's and Munson's hills, covering the main highway in from Centreville, and instructed them to hold the lines there at all hazards. The two divisions of Franklin's army corps, just disembarked, loitered about Alexandria waiting for orders; Halleck and McClellan agreed that they ought to go forward to aid Pope, but nobody knew quite where Pope was to be found, and anyway, Franklin had no horses to pull his artillery and no wagon train to carry food and ammunition, and there seemed to be no cavalry at hand to scout the road for him. Haupt darkly remarked to himself that a march of twenty-five miles would put Franklin in the fortified lines at Centreville, which would surely be within reaching distance of Pope, and felt that Franklin's men could carry on their backs enough food and ammunition to take them that far. Besides, Haupt seriously doubted that there was anything hostile this side of Centreville which could hurt a whole army corps. But nobody asked Haupt's opinion, McClellan and Halleck began to bicker fruitlessly about the advance, and Franklin's troops stayed where they were.

The next day was August 29, and outposts reported hearing the rumble of gunfire from beyond Centreville. Somewhere off in the outer darkness the armies apparently had collided. Later in the day Haupt was able to confirm this. Sitting at the end of the railway telegraph line, he got a mesage from Pope himself—in Centreville, by now—and Pope seemed to be in good spirits, reporting that he was engaged with sixty thousand Confederates, that Joe Hooker was driving them handsomely, and that McDowell and Sigel were cutting off the enemy's retreat. McClellan ordered Franklin to move forward, telling him: "Whatever may happen, don't allow it to be said that the Army of the Potomac failed to do its utmost for the country"—a remark which is a complete tip-off to the strange jealousies, rivalries, and antagonisms that were besetting the high command just then. The troops started to move that morning, Franklin remaining behind in an attempt to get supply wagons, of which he finally rounded up a scant twenty; then McClellan began to have second thoughts, wired Halleck that he did not think Franklin's men were in shape to accomplish much if they ran into serious resistance along the road, and finally ordered Franklin to halt at Annandale, seven miles out. Haupt had his railroad open as far as the Bull Run Bridge and was pushing supplies forward as fast as the trains could move.

As far as Haupt could see, things were on the mend. Pope was in touch with Washington and with his supply line again, his wagons were moving the stores up from Fairfax Station to Centreville, and the fighting seemed to be going favorably. But on the following day the luckless railroad man entered into a full-fledged nightmare, which was visited on him by order of the Secretary of War, Mr. Edwin M. Stanton.

Stanton, with his pudgy, bustling figure, his scraggly beard, and his hot little eyes, was prone to disastrous impulses when the going got tough, and he gave way to one on the thirtieth of August, 1862. Late the night before, Pope reported having fought a heavy battle in which he had lost ten thousand men and the enemy twice that many. The Confederates, he assured the Secretary, were in full retreat and he was about to pursue with vigor, which was all to the good. But Stanton, reflecting on those ten thousand casualties—plus the Rebel wounded, who must be tended for humanity's sake—suddenly concluded that the wounded would never in the world be cared for unless he departed swiftly from regular channels, and he immediately departed therefrom with restless energy. He publicly issued an invitation to government clerks, private citizens, and all the sundry to volunteer as nurses and stretcher-bearers for the wounded out beyond Centreville. Simultaneously he ordered Haupt to stop whatever he was doing and prepare to transport his volunteer brigade to the field at once. (He also rounded up all the hacks and carriages he could find in Washington and sent them off to Centreville by road, but that did not affect Haupt; it just clogged the highway that Pope's men had to use.) Shortly thereafter scores and hundreds of civilians began to pour into Alexandria demanding transportation. Most of them were drunk, and those who were not were carrying bottles of whisky and obviously would be drunk before very long.

Haupt's head swam at the thought of dumping this howling mob down on a battlefield. Orders were orders, to be sure, but he was enough of an army man to know that there are ways and ways of rendering obedience. He delayed the train as long as he could; then, when he finally sent it off, he wired the officer in command at Fairfax Station to arrest all who were drunk. Also, he bethought himself that while he had been ordered to take this mob out he had not been ordered to bring it back, so as soon as the train had been unloaded he had it hauled back to Alexandria.

"Those who were sober enough straggled off as soon as it was light enough to see, and wandered around until all whisky and provisions became exhausted, when they returned to the station to get transportation back," Haupt wrote later. "In this, most of them were disappointed."

It seemed cruel, he added, to make these people walk all the way back to Washington in the rain, but it was better to do that than to ignore the wounded; besides, his opinion of the volunteer nurses was not high—"generally it was a hard crowd and of no use whatever on the field." He learned later that some of the men bribed army ambulance drivers to leave the wounded and carry the civilians back to Washington.[4]

And as this affair began to be straightened out the news from the front abruptly became worse. Having announced that he had won a great victory, Pope was slow to report bad news, but the news came trickling back anyway. One of the first to get the drift was General Jacob Cox, an Ohioan who had gone to the lines at Upton's Hill in command of the four regiments McClellan had sent out to hold the ground "at any hazard." On the morning of August 30, Cox saw the ambulances coming in from Centreville, accompanied by the walking wounded. These were men who had left the field the night before, and their impression was that they had won the battle and that the enemy was in retreat. Cox noticed that the sound of the firing, which he had been hearing all the previous day, was not nearly so loud. Adding that to the reports from the wounded men, he assumed that Pope was pursuing the foe and that the gunfire came from rear-guard actions—an assumption which Pope himself held until he finally reached the point at which further delusion was impossible. During the afternoon, however, Cox could hear that the sound of the firing was getting louder—much louder and much heavier, with long, sustained, reverberating rolls of gunfire in which the individual shots could no longer be distinguished. Toward evening the pathetic parade of wounded was coming in greater numbers. It was accompanied by stragglers, and by dark the evidence of a disastrous defeat was all too visible.[5] The spirits of the soldiers in the camps around Alexandria, which had been raised mightily by the early report of a victory, began to sag, and the provost marshal notified the War Department that he needed more men if he was to preserve order—"we are being overrun with straggling officers and men." The colonel of the 55th New York Infantry, landing at the Alexandria wharves next morning, noted an air of great depression as soon as he stepped ashore. Nobody knew just what had happened, but all sorts of rumors were afloat; he found the word "treason" being used freely.

Treason: betrayal, treachery, a will to lose when the means to win are at hand; a dark, frightening word, coming up out of the shadows, carrying fear and distrust and panic unreason with it, so that the visible enemies in gray and butternut off toward the Bull Run Mountains seemed less to be feared than those who might be standing, all unsuspected, at one's elbow. The word was used everywhere: in the President's Cabinet, in the War Department, in the tents of the generals, and—most disastrously of all—in the ranks of the tired army that was plodding back toward Washington. All of the disillusionment which began when the army was repulsed before Richmond, all of the sudden war-weariness which had come so soon to a land that had been long at peace, all of the bewilderment felt by men who saw themselves striking ineffectually at targets that mysteriously shifted and dissolved as one struck—all of this, welling up in the hearts of men who had done their best to no avail, began to find expression in that word. There had been betrayal: of high hopes and noble purposes, of all the army meant to itself and to the country. The country had suffered more than a defeat. What was happening now was the beginning of disintegration.

2. WE WERE NEVER AGAIN EAGER

In the end it would become an army of legend, with a great name that still clangs when you touch it. The orations, the brass bands and the faded flags of innumerable Decoration Day observances, waiting for it in the years ahead, would at last create a haze of romance, deepening spring by spring until the regiments and brigades became unreal—colored-lithograph figures out of a picture-book war, with dignified graybeards bemused by their own fogged memories of a great day when all the world was young and all the comrades were valiant.

But the end of August in the year 1862 was not the time for taking a distant and romantic view of things. The Army of the Potomac was not at that moment conscious of the formation of legends; it was hungry and tired, muddy and ragged, sullen with the knowlege that it had been shamefully misused, and if it thought of the future at all it was only to consider the evil chances which might come forth during the next twenty-four hours. It was in a mood to judge the future by the past, and the immediate past had been bad. The drunken generals who had botched up supply lines, the sober generals who had argued instead of getting reinforcements forward, the incredible civilians who had gone streaming out to a battelfield as to a holiday brawl, the incompetents who thought they were winning when they were losing were symbols of a betrayal that was paid for in suffering and humiliation by the men who were discovering that they had enlisted to pay just such a price for other men's errors.

The army had developed a high spirit down on the peninsula in spite of its troubles; a certain cockiness, even, a feeling that it knew of no other soldiers who were quite as good, plus a deep certainty that there was no general anywhere who could be trusted as much as its own commander, General McClellan. But this spirit was dissolving and the certainty was being mocked; and as it plodded on toward the fortified lines at Alexandria it was on the verge of ceasing to be an army at all. Men drifted off through the fields or formed little knots about campfires in the woods and farmyards. The winding columns on the roads stretched as they moved, the head of each column moving just a little faster than the tail. There was no panic, as there had been a year earlier after the first fight at Bull Run, when what had been thought to be an army simply melted into a frantic mob. Save for a bad hour or so at the Bull Run Bridge on the night of August 30, there had been no headlong rush to get away. But the miracle of the spirit which takes thousands of young men, ties them together in strange self-forgetfulness, and enables them to walk steadfastly and without faltering into the certainty of pain and death was wearing very thin. Bickerings and blunderings had sapped its power; where the men went now they went sullenly and only because they must. It would take little more to cause the men to realize that "must" had force only so long as they consented to it.

The army had been gay when it went out. The point that is so easy to overlook nowadays, when all of the illusions about war have been abraded to dust, is that those young men went off to war eagerly and with light hearts, coveting the great adventure which they blithely believed lay just ahead. They went to war because they wanted to go, every man of them, and the obvious fact that in their innocence they did not have the remotest idea what the reality was going to be like does not change the fact. The bounty jumpers and the drafted men had not yet appeared. This was the army of the nation's youth, consciously trying to live up to its own conception of bravery, convinced that a soldier marched forward into high romance; an army with banners that postured pathetically and sincerely as it followed its own boyish vision.

That posturing was of the very essence of the army's spirit, and it caused things to happen that could not happen in the armies of today. We read, for instance, of the father and son who enlisted together in a regiment of Massachusetts infantry. In the fighting at Bull Run the son was killed, and a comrade took the news to the father in the midst of the action. "Well," said the father grimly, "I would rather see him shot dead, as he was, than see him run away." And there is a glimpse of a New York regiment holding the line in another battle under heavy fire. The colonel of an adjoining regiment came over to report that this New York outfit was an especial target because its colors were being held too high: lower them a bit and the fire wouldn't be so costly. The colonel of the New York regiment—himself the most conspicuous target of all, riding slowly back and forth on horseback in rear of his men, who were lying behind a rail fence—looked at the waving flag and said: "Let it wave high. It is our glory." Then there was the colonel of another New York regiment, mortally wounded in a charge, who ordered his men to lift him and prop him up against a tree facing the firing. This done, at whatever cost in pain to the dying man, he said faintly: "Tell Mother I died with my face to the enemy"—and, the message duly noted, died.[1]

The spirit of the first campaign these soldiers made comes down to us in a journal written by young Captain George Freeman Noyes, a pea-green but ardent officer on General Abner Doubleday's staff, who found himself making a night march up the Rappahannock when Pope was concentrating his army against Stonewall Jackson early in August. Wrote Captain Noyes:

"And so over a heavily-wooded, rolling country, through roads arched with foliage, the moonlight filling them with fantastic shapes and shadows, we pursued our romantic way. The peculiar quiet of the hour, and the weird influence of the forest scenery, with patches of moonlight flung in here and there among the prevailing shadow, every turn of the road seemingly a narrow pass over which giant and grotesque trees stood guard to oppose our progress, added mystic significance to those reflections which our anticipated battle naturally awakened. No longer Yankee soldiers of the nineteenth century, we were for the nonce knights of the ancient chivalry."[2]

Those fanciful old ideas about the glory of a waving flag, the shame of running from danger, the high importance of dying with one's face to the foe—since that war they have come to seem as out of date as the muzzle-loaders that were used for weapons in those days. The American soldier of later, more sophisticated eras may indeed die rather than retreat, and do it as courageously as any, but he never makes a song about it or strikes an attitude. His heroism is without heroics, and fine phrases excite his instant contempt, because he knows even before he starts off to war that fine phrases and noble attitudes and flags waving in death's own breeze are only so many forms of a come-on for the innocent; nor does he readily glimpse himself as a knight of the ancient chivalry. But in the 1860s the gloss had not been worn off. Young men then went to war believing all of the fine stories they had grown up with; and if, in the end, their disillusion was quite as deep and profound as that of the modern soldier, they had to fall farther to reach it.

The fall was acutely painful, and it was taking place rapidly in the late summer of 1862. The easiest way to see what was going on—in the soldiers' emotions, and in the war itself—is to follow briefly the career of the Black Hat Brigade, which was to become famous.

This outfit was made up of the 2nd, 6th, and 7th Wisconsin regiments and the 19th Indiana—Western troops in an army predominantly of Easterners—and it was assembled in Fredericksburg in the spring and put under the command of young John Gibbon, lately jumped to a brigadier's commission from his position as captain of regular artillery. Gibbon was a West Pointer—a lean, sharp-nosed, bearded man with a habit of blunt speech, who was quietly sorry to have to leave his guns and his tough regulars, where he felt at home, for infantry and volunteers, where he felt strange. He had served on the Western plains under Albert Sidney Johnston before the war; came from North Carolina, had three brothers in the Confederate Army, but for his part had elected to stand by the Union.

Rather to his surprise, he found that he liked his new command, and he wrote that all the men needed was discipline and drill to make first-class soldiers: a judgment that was to be vindicated, for these Westerners turned out to be fighters as good as any the army ever possessed. Gibbon applied the drill and discipline, discovered that volunteers were unlike regulars—praise and the promise of reward were more effective than the fear of punishment which the regulars required—and to tone up their morale he saw to it that they were outfitted, beyond regulations, with black felt hats and white gaiters; hence their nickname, the Black Hat Brigade.

The first combat veterans the boys encountered—Shields's division, down from the Shenandoah Valley after a bloody fight with Stonewall Jackson—jeered at them for bandbox soldiers, but the Westerners retorted that they would rather wear leggings than be lousy like some people, and anyway, they liked their own natty appearance. Like all new troops in that army, when they started cross-country marching in the hot summer they threw their coats and blankets in the nearest ditches, knowing that they could draw new ones, and no questions asked, from the regimental quartermasters. This pained Gibbon's regular-army soul, and he forced the company commanders to receipt for the issue of clothing thereafter, and compelled them to make regular returns on the requisitions, under penalty of drawing no pay. The brigade carried its coats and blankets henceforward: a thing which caused muttering at first, but morale was high and Gibbon made the men feel like soldiers, and the muttering died away.[3]

So far the war had been a romantic frolic for these boys. They liked to remember the period of training around Washington, when they had been camped along a stream on the far side of which were home-state neighbors, the 5th Wisconsin. The 5th belonged to General Hancock's brigade, and Hancock had a bull voice that could be heard halfway to Richmond, and the 5th was commanded by a Colonel Cobb, very much of a leading citizen back home but strictly an amateur soldier here like all the rest of them. One day when Hancock was drilling his brigade Colonel Cobb got mixed up and took his regiment off the wrong way in some evolution, and the delighted Wisconsin boys across the river could hear Hancock roar: "Colonel Cobb! Where in the damnation are you going with your battalion?" Thereafter, as long as they were neighbors, it struck the Black Hat Brigade as amusing to go down to the riverbank in the still of the evening and chant in unison: "Colonel Cobb! Where in the damnation are you going with your battalion?"

They had worked out a gag for rainy days, when it was too muddy to drill and all hands were snuggled under their pup tents trying to keep dry and were afflicted by boredom. Some private possessed of a great voice would sing out: "When our army marched down to Bull Run, what did the big bullfrog say?" And hundreds of men would croak: "Big thing! Big thing!" ("Big thing" was Civil War slang for any notable event or achievement—a great battle, promotion to a corporal's chevrons, a two-week furlough, the theft of a crock of apple butter, or anything else worth talking about.) Then the leader would call: "And when our army came back from Bull Run, what did the little frogs say?" To which the answer in unmelodious screeching trebles, was: "Run, Yank! Run, Yank!" And to close it, the question was: "What does the Bully Sixth say?" The answer, in deep pinewoods bass: "Hit 'em again! Hit 'em again!"

The whole brigade took a queer, perverse pride in the regimental band of the 6th Wisconsin—not because it was so good, but because it was so terrible. It was able to play only one selection, something called "The Village Quickstep," and its dreadful inefficiency (the colonel referred to it in his memoirs as "that execrable band") might have been due to the colonel's quaint habit of assigning men to the band not for musical ability but as punishment for misdemeanors—or so, at least, the regiment stoutly believed. The only good thing about the band was its drum major, one William Whaley, who was an expert at high and fancy twirling of his baton. At one review, in camp around Washington, the brigade had paraded before McClellan, who had been so taken with this drum major's "lofty pomposity" (as a comrade described it) that he took off his cap in jovial salute—whereupon the luckless Whaley, overcome by the honor, dropped his baton ignominiously in the mud, so that his big moment became a fizzle.[4]

At the end of July the brigade moved out of its camp at Fredericksburg and tramped up the Rappahannock to join Pope—the same movement which led Captain Noyes to see knights of the ancient chivalry marching along the moonlit roads. The men were impatient. They belonged to General Irvin McDowell's corps, and they had been sorely disappointed because orders to go to Richmond and join McClellan's forces there had been canceled at the last minute. Now they looked ahead to action, for it was believed that Pope would plunge at once into battle. Reaching the point of concentration, they did a geat deal of marching and countermarching and heard the rumble of artillery duels from afar, and once or twice long-range shells fell among them, but they got into no fighting. And finally they found themselves, with the three other brigades in the division of General Rufus King, trudging off to the northeast on the Warrenton turnpike, heading in the directin of Centreville. Along the way they captured their first prisoner—a straggler from Stonewall Jackson's corps, who had had his fill of fighting and surrendered willingly enough, but who was an authentic armed Rebel for all that. This lanky soldier looked with interest at the full packs carried by Gibbon's boys and remarked: "You uns is like pack mules—we uns is like race horses. All Old Jackson gave us was a musket, a hundred rounds, and a gum blanket, and he druv us like hell."

The men did not know exactly where they were going, but they understood vaguely that Old Jackson was somewhere up ahead; it looked as if they would get into a sure-enough fight this time, and their spirits rose. To be sure, if they were being hurried into action their course was obstructed by numerous mixups. They had got into Warrenton at dusk, hungry, their rations exhausted, and were met by General McDowell in person, who regretted that they could not have any supper but ordered them to move out on the turnpike at once: this was a forced march, no time to draw rations, they had to keep moving. So they started on, found the road blocked by stalled wagon trains, and made a supperless bivouac two miles from Warrenton. The next day they were led down a country lane and thrown into line of battle on some deserted farm, and held there for several hours in complete solitude, before they were recalled and taken back to the main highway; and there they were halted again, to butcher some of their beef cattle and make a leisurely meal. But the men had been soldiers long enough to understand that that sort of thing just went with army life, and their enthusiasm was undimmed. At last, after an afternoon in which they had heard occasional sputters of musket fire far ahead, they went tramping along the pike a mile or two out of the little hamlet of Gainesville, the brigade well closed up, General Gibbon riding at the head, a mile of empty road in front and behind separating it from the rest of the division. It was getting on toward sunset, and the trees on the left of the road were casting long cool shadows. A regimental band was playing a quickstep—one hopes, somehow, that it was the band of the 6th Wisconsin—and the boys were enjoying the war.

The road led straight ahead, like a white dusty arrow, and General Gibbon trotted on in advance to the top of a little rise, where he pulled up to see if he could see anything of the leading brigade. It had vanished, and Gibbon glanced off to the west, to the left of the road. The ground was more or less open there, and it rose in a long, gentle slope; and as Gibbon looked he saw several slim columns of horse—roving cavalry, most likely, he told himself—come trotting out of a grove on the hillside, half a mile away. He was just beginning to speculate whether this cavalry was Federal or Confederate when all the little columns swerved simultaneously, presenting their flanks. At sight of this familiar maneuver something clicked in the mind of this young general who had always been a gunner: that wasn't cavalry at all, it was field artillery going into battery!

Gibbon sent an aide galloping back to the rear of the column to bring up the brigade artillery—Battery B, 4th U.S., the one Gibbon himself had commanded before he became a brigadier of infantry. The aide had hardly started when six shells came screaming over the road, to burst in the woods off to the right. The colonels of the four infantry regiments, without waiting for orders, swung their men into line facing to the west and got them off the road and had them lie down under cover of a low bank. Battery B came clattering madly up the pike in a cloud of dust, while another salvo from the hostile battery crashed into the treetops. As he cantered into a field west of the road to post the guns Gibbon noticed with approval that his soldiers, although they had been taken completely by surprise, did not seem to be nervous. Perhaps half a dozen men, out of more than eighteen hundred present, had scurried hastily off into the woods when the first shells came over, but they were coming back now with shamefaced grins to rejoin their comrades. Battery B came up, the men tore down a rail fence to make a gateway, and the guns went lumbering into the field beside

Gibbon, swinging around and unlimbering with the sure precision of the regulars. In a moment counterbattery fire had been opened.

Up to this point nothing had been seen of the enemy but his six guns. The natural supposition was that they were horse artillery attached to Jeb Stuart's cavalry, engaged in cavalry's favorite practice of harassing infantry on the march. The logical thing to do was to shake a line of infantry out to chase the guns away, and this—after a quick study of the ground in front—Gibbon proceeded to do. The 2nd Wisconsin and 19th Indiana moved forward from behind the protecting bank, broke through a little belt of bushes and scrub trees, and started out across the field to make the Rebel battery cease and desist. The whole thing was done with earnest care, just as it had been done on the drill ground so many times: colonel and lieutenant colonel of each regiment full of business, carefully sighting the lines of direction, sending guides forward, fussing mightily about alignment, trying their level best to do it all regular-army style—doing it just a little self-consciously, one gathers, because General Gibbon came riding over from the guns to watch, and the general was a regular, and this was the first time under fire. The lines were formed presently and the men went forward, a fringe of skirmishers in advance, and they came to the top of a low ridge. The Confederate artillery suddenly ceased firing, and a line of gray-clad skirmishers rose from the grass in front of the guns and began a pop-pop of small-arms fire. Then, from the woods beyond, a great mass of Confederate infantry emerged, coming down the slope to give the Westerners their first trial by combat, red battle flags with the starred blue cross snapping in the evening breeze—Stonewall Jackson's men, whose measured conviction it was that they could whip any number of Yankees at any time and place, and whose record gave them tolerably good reason for the belief.

And a long, tearing crackle of musketry broke over the shadowed field, and the Wisconsin and Indiana boys learned what it was like to fight. Gibbon, who had thought he was quelling impudent horse artillery, went spurring back to bring up his other two regiments, couriers galloped down the road to ask for help from the other brigades, and presently the 6th Wisconsin came up to take position at the right of the line. Many years later its colonel recalled with pride the military precision with which his regiment deployed for action under fire. Gibbon threw the 7th Wisconsin in where the 2nd was fighting, and the battle was on.

It was a strange battle—a straightaway, slam-bang, stand-up fight with no subtleties and no maneuvering, no advancing and no retreating. Some of the Confederates found cover around a little farmhouse, and the 6th Wisconsin got some protection because the ground sagged in an almost imperceptible little hollow right where it was posted, so that most of the bullets that came its way went overhead. But for the most part the men did not seek cover—did not even lie down on the ground, which was the way many fire fights took place in those days, but simply stood facing each other in even, orderly ranks, as if they were on parade awaiting inspection, and volleyed away at the murderous range of less than one hundred yards.

On the right, Battery B fired rapidly and accurately, and some other brigade had brought another battery into action off on the left, and before long General Doubleday sent up the 56th Pennsylvania and the 76th New York—virgin regiments, like those of Gibbon—to join in the fight; and this amazing combat of two dress-parade battle lines at point-blank range sent its echoes resounding across the Manassas plain, while a dense cloud of acrid smoke went rolling up the evening sky. Years later General Gibbon remarked that he heard, that evening, the heaviest musket fire he heard during the entire war.

The fight lasted for an hour and a half. When it ended both sides were exactly where they were when it began, except that a Confederate brigade which tried a

flanking movement around the Federal right had got tangled up in a ravine full
of underbrush, in the smoky dusk, and couldn't find its way out, while the 19th
Indiana had been edged off to the left rear to cope with what looked like a flank
attack from that direction. Gibbon was proud of the way his Hoosiers managed
this maneuver while under fire. Toward evening, with the Confederate fieldpieces out of action, Stuart's incredible artillerist, John Pelham, brought a section of guns up to within seventy paces of Gibbon's line and opened fire,
without any visible effect whatever except to add to the total of killed and
maimed.

Night came at last, mercifully, and put an end to it, the rival battle lines
slowly drew apart, and, as General Gibbon wrote, "everything except the groans
of the wounded quieted down." The Black Hat boys could call themselves veterans now; they had had their baptism of fire—baptism by total immersion, one
might say. The 2nd Wisconsin—which, over the length of the war, was to win
the terrible distinction of having a higher percentage of its total enrollment
killed in action than any other regiment in the United States Army—had taken
500 men into this fight and left 298 of them dead or wounded on the field; it got
a leg on the record that evening. The 7th Wisconsin and the 19th Indiana had
lost nearly as heavily. The 6th Wisconsin had been lucky by comparison, losing
72 men out of 504 engaged. A regimental historian wrote later that to the end of
the war this brigade was always ready for action, "but we were never again
eager."

All in all, more than a third of the Federal soldiers who went into action that
evening had been shot. Over on the Confederate side, though the Federals
didn't know it at the time, the story was about the same. The famous Stonewall
brigade had lost 33 per cent of its numbers, the 21st Georgia had lost 173 out of
242 in action, and two division commanders had gone down, one of them the
famous General Dick Ewell. Next morning one of Jeb Stuart's staff officers
came out to take a casual look at the scene of action. "The lines were well
marked by the dark rows of bodies stretched out on the broomsedge field, lying
just where they had fallen, with their heels on a well-defined line," he wrote.
"The bodies lay in so straight a line that they looked like troops lying down to
rest. On each front the edge was sharply defined, while towards the rear it was
less so. Showing how men had staggered backward after receiving their death
blow."[5]

The Federals drew a line of battle in the woods next to the turnpike, sent out
parties to bring in as many of the wounded as possible, established crude field
hospitals under the trees, and in general tried to catch their breath. A staff officer, coming up the pike from the rear, found a campfire blazing in the road, with
the generals grouped around it, staff officers seated outside the inner circle, orderlies holding the reins of saddled horses still farther out, the firelight gleaming
on tanned faces, a ribbon of wood smoke climbing up out of the glow to disappear in the arching branches above. The brigadiers were assembled and the division commander, General King, who had been taken ill that afternoon and
had had to seek shelter back at Gainesville and so had not been present during
the fight, came up to join them, weak and pale. His division was part of
McDowell's corps, but nobody could find McDowell, who had ridden off in
midafternoon to seek General John Pope in the vicinity of Manassas and who, it
developed later, had got completely lost in the woods and found neither Pope
nor anyone else until the next day. Since neither King nor McDowell had been
around while the fighting was going on, the battle had really been fought under
nobody's direction—except Gibbon's and he was responsible only for his own
brigade. Now that the generals were in council nobody knew quite what to do,
for King's original orders were to march to Centreville, and it was painfully obvious that before he could do that he would have to drive Stonewall Jackson out
of the way, which was clearly too much of a task for any single division.

In the end it was agreed that the command had better withdraw in the direction of Manassas Junction, which lay several miles to the east, and it was so ordered. Sometime after midnight the tired troops withdrew and tramped silently off down a country road in the blackness, all the gay banter of their earlier marches quite forgotten; and in a cloudy dawn they dropped down in a field near Manassas to get a little sleep, while the staff hurried off to try to find Pope, McDowell, or somebody who could tell them what the brigade was supposed to do next.

The soldiers didn't get much sleep. Orders came in presently: Fitz-John Porter and his V Corps from the Army of the Potomac were coming up and would be backtracking along the road toward Gainesville, and King's division—now commanded by General John Hatch, for King's illness had put him out—would go with them. So the men drew up in marching order by the roadside, and pretty soon the head of Porter's corps came along, marching with an indefinable swagger even in the informal route step of the cross-country hike, and the young Westerners cheered mightily in boyish hero worship—this was the Army of the Potomac, these were veterans of the fabulous fighting around Richmond, McClellan's men were joining Pope's, and everything would be all right now.

Porter's men received the cheers with high disdain. They included a solid division of regulars, plus some volunteer regiments which had acquired much esprit de corps, which means that they looked down on practically all soldiers who did not belong to their own outfit. They had taken the worst the Confederates had to give at Gaines's Mill, and at Malvern Hill they had seen the furious Southern assault waves break up in a swirling foam of bloody repulse on the hard rock of massed artillery and rifle fire, and their immeasurable contempt for John Pope was quite broad enough to include all of his troops. They called out loftily: "Get out of the way, straw-feet—we're going to go up to show you how to fight." ("Straw-foot" was the Civil War term for rookie. The idea was that some of the new recruits were of such fantastic greenness that they did not know the left foot from the right and hence could not be taught to keep time properly or to step off on the left foot as all soldiers should. The drill sergeants, in desperation, had finally realized that these green country lads did at least know hay from straw and so had tied wisps of hay to the left foot and straw to the right foot and marched them off to the chant of "Hay-foot, straw-foot, hay-foot, straw-foot." Hence: straw-foot—rookie, especially a dumb rookie.) Gibbon's boys were hurt—after last evening they felt entitled to join any brotherhood whose entry fee was courage under fire—and they yelled back: "Wait until you've been where we've been—that'll take some of the slack out of your pantaloons"; but they still admired those hard veterans and were glad to be with them. After a while they swung into column and followed the V Corps along the road, heading back toward what they had just marched away from—perfectly ready to fight again, but not hankering for it any longer.

3. YOU MUST NEVER BE FRIGHTENED

If any of Gibbon's boys had had the speculative bent to sit down and figure out just what their prodigious valor had bought for the Union cause, a most dismaying fact would have come to light. The chief result of that desperate fight in the meadow was that the befuddlement of General John Pope became complete instead of only partial.

General Pope had been having his troubles for some time. He had not been entirely sure where his own army was, and he had not in the least known where the enemy was, and he had been frantically trying to use the one to find the other. For several days he had been holding the line of the Rappahannock, guarding the fords, dueling with his artillery whenever Rebel forces showed themselves on the far side of the river, sending his cavalry dashing about with vast energy, and he had about concluded that a great battle would be fought soon in the vicinity of Warrenton. It would be a desperate encounter, because he was outnumbered, or at least believed that he was. As he understood the top strategy in Washington, he was supposed to hold the line at all costs until McClellan's army could join him, whereupon General Halleck would ride down from Washington and take active command in the field of both Pope and his troops and McClellan and his—Pope and McClellan then becoming, as Pope believed, wing commanders under the general-in-chief.

Pope was deceived in this belief: the last thing Halleck wanted was to command troops in the field against Robert E. Lee; but at the moment no one but Halleck knew this. So on August 26 Pope had been drawing his forces together near Warrenton, spattering the landscape with galloping couriers, as he called outlying divisions to his rendezvous. From McClellan's army, grumpily returning from the peninsula, Fitz-John Porter and the V Corps were coming up the river from Fredericksburg, and General Ambrose Burnside and the IX Corps had landed at Aquia Creek and presumably were making their way to him overland, while the rest of McClellan's men were coming in via Alexandria. A few days more and the reunion would be complete and the responsibility would pass from his shoulders.

But then things started to happen. First Stonewall Jackson disappeared from Pope's front. He was detected marching off to the northwest, and it seemed likely he was heading for his old haunts in the Shenandoah Valley, but on second thought Pope considered a flank attack on his lines at Warrenton probable, and he sent out new orders to hurry the concentration. Then, after dark, the telegraph wire to Washington went dead, and it appeared that Confederate cavalry was up to its old trick of jumping the supply lines. Joe Hooker—who had at last caught his train and got to the front—was ordered to take his division up the railroad and attend to it. Next day it developed that it was Jackson, not cavalry, on the suppy line, and the tired couriers galloped off with new orders: concentration at Gainesville, now, with the cavalry under Buford swinging west through Thoroughfare Gap to see what had become of the rest of Lee's army. Toward evening Hooker collided with Confederate infantry at Bristoe Station and chased it north across Broad Run after a sharp fight, and orders were changed once more: the army will concentrate at Manassas, Jackson has delivered himself into our hands, and if we move fast we shall "bag the whole crowd."

Pope rode in haste to Bristoe, set out next morning for Manassas, lost Jackson's trail, and changed orders still further: concentrate at Centreville now, Jackson is somewhere near here, if we are alert we can destroy him. And finally, late that night, Pope got news of the fight Gibbon and Doubleday had stumbled into near Gainesville, and the picture became very clear to him—or so he thought. Jackson, having raided the Union supply depot, was trying desperately to get away. King's division had intercepted his retreat and rebuffed him (as Pope conceived), and Jackson was caught squarely between the two wings of the Union Army and could be crushed the very next day. Pope sat down at Centreville, to which place he had by now gyrated, sent jubilant messages to Washington, and made ready for his apotheosis: triumph, confusion to the enemies of the Republic, and a brilliant demonstration that Pope had the secret of victory which McClellan lacked.

The only trouble with this picture was that it was completely false. Jackson was not trapped and he was not trying to get away. On the contrary, he very much wanted to stay and fight, and while Pope's troops had been countermarching so feverishly he had found a good position near the old Bull Run battlefield, had established himself there, and had waited to be discovered. Pope being quite unable to find him, Jackson had moved out to give a prod to the first

Union troops that came within reach—King's division—as a means of calling attention to his whereabouts. Jackson's primary mission was not simply to loot and destroy Pope's base of supplies, enjoyable though that task had been. General Lee had determined that Pope must be beaten ("suppressed" was his contemptuous word for it) before all of McClellan's army could join him, and he had reached out with the long, muscular arm of Stonewall Jackson to pin the Northerner down on some good fighting ground suitably remote from the Rappahannock. Now, with Pope rushing to fall on Jackson, Lee was coming up with all speed. Pope, who believed himself to be casting a cunning net, was walking straight into one.

The soldiers whom General Pope was bringing up to Bull Run were by no means happy. Knowing nothing of the high strategy involved, they were perfectly aware that they had been marched back and forth to no good purpose for the better part of a week, and they had been around long enough to understand that this meant the high command was confused and jittery. They had outmarched their supplies, in all the confusion, and most of them were hungry, and the shuttling back and forth, up hill and down dale, had brought many to the point of exhaustion. The cavalry was deadbeat: some detachments came in from outpost duty on foot, leading horses that were too worn to carry weight even at a walk. The colonel of one regiment reported that his men had not had their coats off for three weeks, and in many squadrons there were not half a dozen men who could get their horses up to a trot.

To make things worse, what Pope was commanding was not an army but simply a thrown-together collection of troops. Technically, Pope's army—named, for its brief life, the Army of Virginia—consisted of three army corps: those of Franz Sigel, Nathaniel P. Banks, and Irvin McDowell. Sigel's men included a large number of German regiments—immigrants, for the most part, who had had German army training and should have been first-rate soldiers, but who somehow seemed to lose their effectiveness under the loose discipline of the American volunteer army. They had originally belonged to the famous but unmilitary General John Charles Frémont, who had ingloriously led them to failure in the mountain country to the west. Their morale was low, and Sigel was by no means the man who could pull them together. Banks was a political general—a distinguished Massachusetts businessman and politician, former Republican Speaker of the House of Representatives, a man who, by the strange custom of that war, was "entitled" to a major general's commission because of his importance as a political leader and a public figure. He was a good man and devoted to the cause, but he was no soldier; up in the valley Stonewall Jackson had routed him and run rings around him, and the Confederates had consumed his stores so regularly that they derisively dubbed him "Old Jack's commissary general." He had first-rate soldiers in his command—Easterners, mostly, with a fair number of Ohioans and a sprinkling from Indiana and Wisconsin—and they would do well if they ever got competent leadership.

McDowell was the only real soldier in the group, and he commanded excellent troops. King's division, now led by Hatch and later to go to Doubleday, contained some of the best soldiers in the army, and John Reynolds led a solid division of Pennsylvanians, who were good men under a good general. Ricketts, commanding the third division, had been an artillerist at the first battle of Bull Run. His division included a number of men who had fought well under poor leaders in the valley. All in all, this army corps was basically as good as any in either army, but it suffered from the fact that McDowell, a good man and a capable general, was one of those soldiers born to bad luck. Nothing ever went right for him. The aura of failure, born of that first fight at Bull Run, trailed after him. The men disliked him violently—even a special hat which he had devised for his summer comfort, a cool but rather weird-looking contrivance of bamboo and cloth, they chalked up as a point against him—and for some unaccountable reason they widely believed that he was in cahoots with the enemy. He and McClellan disliked each other, and McClellan blamed him for not coming down from Fredericksburg to help him during the Seven Days' fighting, although McDowell himself had protested against the administration strategy that had held him north of the Rappahannock and considered that his proper place was with the army on the Chickahominy.

Pope made McDowell his first lieutenant and leaned on him heavily, but cursed him behind his back ("God damn McDowell! He's never where I want him!" Pope had cried on the eve of the battle), and Pope ignored him when McDowell gave him the advice that might have saved him from the snare Lee and Jackson were setting. A staff officer in King's division wrote after his first meeting with him: "I liked McDowell's looks; he seemed to me strong, self-contained, ready for responsibility and able to sustain it. I had yet to learn how much his too frequent forgetfulness of the courtesy due even to a common soldier was to impair his usefulness and injure his popularity."[1] And a young officer of engineers who dined with McDowell late in 1861 left the following appraisal:

"He was at that time in the full flush of mature manhood, fully six feet tall, deep chested, strong limbed, clear eyed, and in every respect a fine and impressive soldier, but at dinner he was such a Gargantuan feeder and so absorbed in the dishes before him that he had but little time for conversation. While he drank neither wine nor spirits, he gobbled the larger part of every dish within reach, and wound up with an entire watermelon, which he said was 'monstrous fine!' . . . As we rode back to the city in the afternoon, McPherson"—later General James B. McPherson, commander of the Army of the Tennessee—"and I discussed him freely, and, allowing him every professional qualification, we agreed that no officer who was so great a gourmand as he could by any chance prove to be a great and successful leader of men."[2]

That, then, was Pope's army; some poor soldiers and some good ones, led by two corps commanders who ought to have been back in civilian life and a third who had neither the luck to win victories nor the touch to make men respond to his leadership. In addition, Pope had received two army corps from the Army of the Potomac. One was under the command of General S. P. Heintzelman, a stout old regular with an engaging, knobby-cheeked face surmounted by a fuzz of whiskers. He had plenty of energy—had gone up in one of the newfangled observation balloons on the peninsula to see for himself what the enemy was up to; was blunt in speech, with a nasal twang to his voice, and somehow just missed being an effective corps commander. Heintzelman brought two of the best combat divisions in the army with him. One was Joe Hooker's: Hooker was an intemperate man, in several senses of the word, and he never got along with any of his superior officers, but he at least liked to fight and had driving energy. The other division was led by Phil Kearny, who was all flame and color and ardor, with a slim, twisted streak of genius in him.

Kearny had probably seen more fighting than any man on the field. He had served in Mexico as a cavalry captain; had remarked, in youthful enthusiasm, that he would give an arm to lead a cavalry charge against the foe. He got his wish, at the exact price offered, a few days later, leading a wild gallop with flashing sabers and losing his left arm. He once told his servant: "Never lose an arm; it makes it too hard to put on a glove." When General Oliver Otis Howard lost his right arm in the fighting at Seven Pines, Kearny visited him in hospital and said consolingly: "General, I am sorry for it, but you must not mind it: the ladies will not think the less of you." To which sobersides Howard returned his one recorded wisecrack: "There is one thing we can do, General; we can buy our gloves together." Kearny smiled gaily and cried, "Sure enough," and the two men had shaken on it with the hands they had left.

Kearny had served in the French Army in Algiers and northern Italy and had fought at Magenta and Solferino. A French officer wrote that Kearny "went under fire as on parade, with a smile on his lips." It was reported that in some battle on the peninsula a colonel whom he ordered forward into action asked him just where he should put his men and received the reply: "Oh, anywhere, Colonel—you'll find lovely fighting all along the line." Winfield Scott had called him "the bravest man I ever saw, and a perfect soldier," and nobody who had followed him would dispute the point. He hated McClellan and he hated Pope, and he had the knack of making his troops feel that they were the finest soldiers on the planet. He had invented the "Kearny patch," a red lozenge of flannel which every man in his command wore on his cap, so that the outfit became known as the "red diamond division" and wore its badge with vast pride. When a new regiment joined the division, the soldiers looked on it with reserve until it had proved its bravery in combat; then, a survivor wrote, they agreed that this new regiment "was worthy of the red diamond division." Later in the war Kearny's device was taken up at headquarters, and a special patch was made for each army corps. The shoulder patches worn by American soldiers in subsequent wars were direct descendants of Phil Kearny's morale builder.[3]

Kearny and Hooker might be hard to manage, and Heintzelman might offer negligible qualities of leadership, but those two divisions would fight furiously wherever they were put: Pope could be sure of that. The same thing was true of the army corps brought in by Fitz-John Porter: two divisions, one of regulars, one of volunteers, superb soldiers who had fully proved their fighting qualities, with a corps commander who might well have been the best officer then in the army. Porter was well-born—a New Hampshire man, nephew of the Commodore David Porter who was a hero of the War of 1812, and a cousin of the Captain David Dixon Porter who was Farragut's right-hand man on the Mississippi—and he was an intimate friend of McClellan, who let him fight both Gaines's Mill and Malvern Hill in his own way. He was handsome, soldierly-looking, perhaps just a shade arrogant. He had nothing but contempt for Pope and he expressed his contempt freely, both verbally and in writing, a fact which later had tragic results. He was one of the few soldiers of that bewhiskered era who could wear a full beard and still look trim and dapper.

Lastly, Pope had just been joined by General Jesse Reno, a stocky, capable soldier who brought one slim division and two brigades of another from Burnside's corps; men who technically belonged to McClellan but who had been on an expedition along the Carolina coast and had not fought in front of Richmond. They had done well in the Carolinas, and Burnside was not at the moment with them—a considerable advantage, though no one realized it at the time.

All of these troops Pope was frantically summoning to overwhelm Jackson. If battles were fought on a simple basis of counting numbers, he had more than enough to do the job, but battles aren't settled that way. Pope's handicaps outweighed any conceivable advantage numbers might give him. Pope's own men were discouraged because they had never had good top leadership and saw no reason to believe they were getting it now. The men from the Army of the Potomac were battle-tried and considered themselves fighters every bit as good as any Confederates they were apt to meet, but they were deeply dejected by their transfer to Pope, and they had no higher opinion of him than McClellan had. This was largely Pope's own fault. He had celebrated his assumption of command by issuing an incredibly bombastic address to the troops, announcing that out West where he came from he was used to looking upon the backs of his enemies, and asserting that the army would henceforth stop worrying about bases of supply, lines of retreat, and so on, and simply go ahead and win battles. This was just asking for trouble and everybody knew it, and the Federal soldiers jeered at the message quite as much as did the Confederates. After the war Pope told a friend that Secretary Stanton had written the address and induced him to issue it. Even if that explanation is true (and Pope makes a poor witness) it doesn't exculpate him: the difference between the stupidity of a man who would write such a screed in the first place and the stupidity of a man who would issue it in his own name after someone else wrote it is a difference only in degree.

So the men Pope brought up to the Warrenton turnpike on the twenty-ninth of August were men who expected the worst and knew they were entitled to expect it. Whatever bravery and endurance could do to redeem the mistakes of the general in command would be done, but unless the soldiers' luck was in, for a change, it would not be enough. And their luck was not in. From first to last the Army of the Potomac was unlucky. It fought for four years, and it took more killing, proportionately, than any army in American history, and its luck was always out; it did its level best and lost; when it won the victory was always clouded by a might-have-been, and when at last the triumph came at Appomattox there were so very, very many of its men who weren't there to see it.

Pope fought his battle about as one might expect: with great energy, but defective judgment. Jackson, whose position he had finally discovered, was lined up behind an unfinished railroad embankment north of the turnpike, a position as good as a fort; and Jackson was quite happy to let Pope wear the Federal army out while he waited for Lee to join him. As soon as it was light enough to fight Pope began to oblige him. Sigel's Germans attacked first and were repulsed. Then Hooker drove for the center of the line and got a brigade up on the embankment, where Northern and Southern boys fought desperately with bayonets and clubbed muskets before the Northerners were driven down. Now Phil Kearny came in through the woods to smash at A. P. Hill, at the left end of Jackson's line—bent him back and forced him to call for reinforcements, but, like Hooker, found the task too much for him and had to pull out. Kearny sat his horse in the woods and watched his beaten boys returning; saw the 3rd Michigan, which had had ruinous losses, and wept as the regiment went by, crying, "Oh, what has become of my gallant old Third?"[4] Reynolds sent his Pennsylvanians in, but Jackson had too much artillery for them and they, too, were rebuffed; and after twilight Hatch's division collided with Hood's Texans along the highway and had to retreat in the darkness after a savage and confused encounter. A major in Hatch's 76th New York, unhorsed and wounded, came limping back and met disorganized troops in the dark and tried to rally them, only to find himself a prisoner of war: the men belonged to the 2nd Mississippi and wore the Rebel gray.

Meanwhile, off to the left, Porter was coming up with his men. Pope thought Porter had a clear road ahead that would put him on Jackson's flank and roll up his lines for keeps, and ordered him to attack and win the day. But Porter discovered that his clear road was most effectively blocked by thirty thousand sinewy Confederates under James Longstreet, who had silently filed into line of battle around noon, all unseen, and who were now lying in wait, fairly aching to be attacked. Longstreet was a counterpuncher, and a deadly one, and he wanted nothing on earth that day quite so much as to receive an attack by Porter, whom he outnumbered three to one. Porter, sensibly enough, notified Pope of this obstruction and sat tight. But Pope simply refused to believe him. His calculations (made God knows how) had convinced him that Longstreet couldn't possibly reach the field for another twenty-four hours, and he sent back word that Porter was wrong—there was nothing whatever in front of him, the way to Jackson's unguarded flank was wide open, Porter must attack at once. In the end, the attack was not made—to the salvation of the army and the personal ruin of Fitz-John Porter—and long after dark Pope sullenly recalled Porter and his men and brought them up to the main line along the highway.

When morning came Pope gave way to his final, most disastrous delusion. The Texans whom Hatch had bumped into the night before had withdrawn along toward midnight, and Jackson had pulled back his own men in one or two places to make his alignment more compact and had his troops snugly concealed in the woods back of the railroad embankment. Pope was persuaded by all of this that Jackson was in full retreat, and he triumphantly notified Washington that he had won a great victory, and ordered an immediate pursuit, horse, foot, and guns. He had his headquarters on an open knoll and he stood there this morning with his generals, puffing a cigar, overflowing with good humor, exchanging jokes and congratulations, while a small regiment of orderlies stood in the background holding the generals' horses and the breeze whipped the flags and pennants. McDowell was to be in general charge of the pursuit, and Porter, whose troops were fresh, was to lead; Hatch and Reynolds would follow him, while Hooker and Kearny would go along on a parallel road a couple of miles to the north. Orders were to press the enemy vigorously all day. In vain Porter tried to convince Pope that there was an ominous congregation of Rebels off to the south of the highway, with nothing to indicate that they had departed. When Pope made up his mind it stayed made up, and there was no room in it this morning for anything but the conviction that the enemy was in flight. So the troops were wheeled around and got into formation, the artillery came rumbling up, and the pursuit began.

It was probably the briefest pursuit in history. The skirmish lines that went combing through the meadows and groves very quickly discovered that something was still waiting behind that railway embankment. Under Pope's concept of things, that could be nothing more than a rear guard, left there to fight a delaying action while the main body got safely away. So Porter, with deep misgivings, pulled his men out into a battle line on the north side of the road and sent them forward, through a tangle of little hillocks and gullies, across a quiet country road, and on up a gradual rise toward the embankment and the silent woods behind it. Reynolds was under orders to follow him, fanning his troops out on the south side of the turnpike just in case there should be a few Rebels in that area, but now it looked as if Porter might need help, so Reynolds was called in to lend a hand on the right, and Porter's left was quite exposed. To give it a little protection, Porter pulled the 5th and 10th New York out of Sykes's division and sent them, with a battery of regular artillery, to a little hill south of the highway. His men went on, while Hatch formed line farther to the right, and the generals on the hill waited in quiet confidence.

A few Confederate batteries were in sight (part of the rear guard, judged Pope; harbingers of coming trouble, thought Porter) and they opened on Porter's lines, Union batteries replying immediately. The staccato bursts of fire from the skirmishers came more frequently as the advance continued, and the artillery fire on both sides became heavier and heavier. Then suddenly the whole railway embankment sparkled and glistened as the sunlight was reflected off polished rifle barrels, and Stonewall Jackson's massed troops came out of the woods to take their places on the firing line. A gigantic tumult of musketry filled the air, and Federals and Confederates exchanged long, crashing volleys at close range, and instead of a rear-guard action there was a full-dress battle. Jackson's men burned the slope with rifle fire, and on a hill to the southwest new batteries unlimbered, to rake Porter's battle lines with heavy salvos—a deadly enfilade fire that cut the support lines to pieces and left the advance isolated and helpless. The troops in front crumbled and fell back, rallied on the fragments in the rear, and went forward again, drifted back anew, and then drove ahead a third time.

It came to hand-to-hand fighting in places, and at one spot the Confederates ran out of ammunition and threw heavy stones down the bank on the heads of the Federals who were scrambling up. Everywhere there was a smother of battle smoke, the yells of the soldiers, and a tremendous uproar of gunfire. One Northern column came up led by an officer on horseback who rode two dozen paces in front, in defiance of regulations (mounted officers were supposed to ride in rear of the troops in all columns of assault). He rode straight for the embankment, looking neither to the right nor the left, sword held high, the storm of bullets somehow missing him, and put his horse up the steep slope and got clear to the top. For one agonizing, dramatic moment he was poised there, still facing to the front, all alone on the deadly sky line that his men could not reach, central figure in an unbelievable tableau. From the hard Southern fighters to the right and left there went up one spontaneous cry—*"Don't kill him!"* Then the smoke-fog covered the bank, and the crash of the rifles swept along the line, and when the smoke drifted away the horse and rider were dead at the top of the bank.

Off to Porter's right Hatch sent in his brigades in a deep column. The first line got to the embankment, broke, and came flying back. Gibbon was dashing about on foot, his revolver out, shouting: "Stop those stragglers—make them fall in—shoot them if they don't!" while a Wisconsin regiment crouched with fixed bayonets, ready to impale the fugitives if they went any farther. The rout was stopped, the attack went ahead again, and a skirmish line, strengthened almost to the weight of a line of battle, got on the embankment but could not stay there. From the left, Rebel artillery sent solid shot straight along the front. "A solid shot will plow into the ground, spitefully scattering the dirt," a survivor recalled afterward, "and bound a hundred feet into the air, looking as it flies swiftly like an India-rubber playing ball."[5]

Abner Doubleday brought his brigade into action. He had heard the first shot of the entire war—indeed, it had been fired at him personally, in a manner of speaking, since he had been a captain of artillery in Fort Sumter in the spring of 1861—and it was reported that Doubleday himself had sighted the gun which fired the first Union shot in reply. He had got his star when the Sumter garrison came north after the surrender, and now he was leading his troops in a desperate fight. One has to chuckle, just a little, thinking about Doubleday. The generals of that army, the good ones and the bad ones alike, were intensely jealous of fame and distinction. Here was Doubleday, strictly an average general, never making any great mistakes but never winning any great laurels either—when Reynolds was killed at Gettysburg the following year Meade took good care not to turn his corps over to Doubleday, the ranking division commander. It is fascinating to wonder what the other generals would have said if they could have known that in the end Doubleday was going to be one of the most famous of them all—not for his war record, but for his alleged connection with the origin of the game of baseball, which the soldiers were just then beginning to play in their off hours.

"Our lines were in the open fields in front of a strip of woods," a Wisconsin soldier wrote. "The Rebel musketry fire was pouring from the woods upon our men who were closing together and rallying under the attack. Regiments would sweep splendidly forward into the front line, fire a crashing volley into the woods, and then work with great energy. But they quickly withered away until there would appear to be a mere company crowding around the colors."[6]

Joe Hooker, who seemed to be ranking officer on that part of the field, trotted up at last on his white horse, looked the hopeless situation over, and ordered a retirement. The blue line drew back, step by step, still facing to the front; and as it did so the Confederates came out from behind the embankment and followed them, step by cautious step, neither side firing. When the Federal line halted, the Confederates would halt and lie down, holding their muskets ready; when the Federals stepped back again, the Confederates would get up and step after them—a strange, silent, queerly ominous advance and retreat, with the crash of battle sounding loudly beyond the woods to right and to left.

Porter's men were beaten and fell back, and Hatch's trooops were beaten and fell back. Longstreet brought his men out of their concealment—it was time to disillusion John Pope at last—and drove them forward in a long charge along the turnpike and over the hills and fields to the south. And Reynolds's Pennsylvanians had been taken off to the right, so that there was nobody in front of Longstreet's thirty thousand but one battery of regular artillery and Porter's two volunteer regiments of infantry, isolated on a knoll behind a farmhouse, and they were not nearly enough.

These two regiments belonged to Sykes's division. Except for them the division was composed solidly of regulars, and when they had first been brigaded with it the volunteers had not known quite how to act. They remembered how General Sykes, cold and unemotional, with a fine bushy beard and a crusty regular-army manner, had greeted them when they had joined his command. He had them lined up on parade and read to them McClellan's order which made them part of his division. Then he said, "You have heard what our commander-in-chief General McClellan says. I only add that if there is any hard work to be done you have got to do it." The soldiers gulped, then gave three cheers, and after that they belonged to the family.[7]

Right now they belonged to a forlorn hope. The 10th New York had been placed in front as a heavy skirmish line, and Longstreet's advance rolled over it and crumpled it and ground it aside (one participant remembered "a fat little major" in the 10th whacking the Federals with the flat of his sword to hold them to their work) and came on up the hill to capture the battery. The 5th New York were dressed as Zouaves—bright red baggy pants, white canvas leggings, broad red sash at the waist, short blue jacket, tasseled red caps; it appears that they were the soldiers who had taunted Gibbon's boys the day before. They hung on now long enough to let the regulars get the guns away, and then they retired—what was left of them, anyway. In their brief fight they had lost 124 men killed and 223 wounded out of 490 present—the highest percentage of loss, in killed, suffered by any Federal regiment in one battle during the entire war. As they pulled out they could see Sykes's regular battalions, north of the pike, wheeling out of line and into column under a merciless fire as only the regulars could do. Whatever else might happen, Porter's men had lived up to the boast they had made to the Black Hat Brigade: they had shown any and all straw-feet how to fight.

Pope and McDowell saw the danger now and worked frantically to get protection over on the left. Some of Sigel's men were sent there, and they took with them a battery of mountain howitzers—funny little guns that were carried into action on the backs of mules, to be taken down and assembled on diminutive gun carriages when it was time to fight. Some of Hooker's boys saw these howitzers for the first time that day as Sigel's Germans took them forward into action, and they jeered loudly and asked what in the world sort of battery that was. "The shackass battery, by Gott—get out mit der way or we blow your hets off!" cried the Germans.

Ricketts sent a couple of brigades over from the far right, and they took possession of a little swale beside the Germans and slugged it out with Hood's Texans. In one of these brigades was the 12th Massachusetts, a kid-glove regiment commanded by Colonel Fletcher Webster, son of the great Daniel. This outfit had left Boston a year earlier amid impressive ceremonies, carrying an elaborate flag of white silk presented by "the ladies of Boston," the silk being edged in blue and gold and bearing the coat of arms of Massachusetts on one side and on the other a quotation from the famous orator—"Not a stripe erased or polluted, not a single star obscured."

In addition to a fancy flag and the admiration of the ladies of Boston, the 12th Massachusetts had brought a song to war—a fine, swinging song with a deep roll of tramping feet and ruffled drums in it, a song to which a woman later gave tremendous words, so that it lives on as the nation's greatest battle hymn, with something in it that goes straight down to the deepest emotions of the country's heart. During its training-camp days the 12th had been stationed at Fort Warren, in Boston Harbor, where the 2nd U.S. Infantry was also stationed; and the regulars had picked up a snappy tune—a camp-meeting revival hymn, written in Charleston, South Carolina, around 1850, entitled "Say Brothers Will We Meet You Over on the Other Shore?" What a battalion of U.S. regulars was doing knowing a gospel hymn is beyond imagination, but they did know it, and because it was a fine song to march to they had fitted new words to it: "John Brown's body lies a-mouldering in the grave . . . and we go marching on." The 12th liked the song and learned to sing it, and they had a fine band to provide the accompaniment. There was a big review on Boston Common on a bright summer afternoon, with Edward Everett delivering an oration, and a feminine committee presenting the silk flag, and an open-air dinner on the Beacon Street mall afterward. When the dinner had been eaten the regiment paraded back to Fort Warren, going down State Street singing the John Brown song with the band at the head of the column, and the war was all youth and music and bright flags and heroism.

A few days later they marched through Boston to take the train for Washington, and again they sang the song. When they got to New York they had a big parade up Broadway, and thousands of people lined the sidewalks and leaned out of the windows and heard the John Brown song for the first time—1,040 young men singing it, with a brass band playing and a great roll of drums and all the feet rhythmically tramping on the pavement. And in Washington they sang it again, and in no time at all the song was famous from the seacoast to the Mississippi Valley, and all the troops around Washington were singing it. Then one afternoon Julia Ward Howe sat in a carriage, heard a marching brigade singing it—the Black Hat boys claim it was their brigade, which is as it may be—and regretted that so fine a tune did not have better words. Early next morning she sat by an open window and wrote the mighty battle hymn, which has been a heritage of Americans ever since. And the 12th Massachusetts had started it all—or, if one goes back farther, the workaday 2nd regiment of regulars, aided by a pious hymnographer from the deepest south.[8]

But the dandy 12th was a long way from the ladies of Boston now, and Colonel Webster was killed, and the 12th was finally forced back, along with the rest of Ricketts's men and the Germans. For whatever it might be worth to them, they had at least made Confederate John B. Hood pause and call for help before they retreated—a thing not too many Union troops were able to do, then or at any other time.

Dusk came, and the field dissolved in a blur of retreating regiments, bewildered stragglers, defiant batteries firing canister to stay the advancing Confederates, and heavy waves of assault crashing against the last hills this side of Bull Run Bridge, over which the entire army had to retreat. John Gibbon found himself on one of these hills, bringing his brigade and steady old Battery B back step by step in such fine order that General McDowell, riding up, told him to take charge of the whole rear guard and be last man over the bridge. McDowell rode away and Phil Kearny came up, furious with the shame of defeat.

"I suppose you appreciate the condition of affairs here, sir?" said Kearny savagely. Gibbon looked at him inquiringly. "It's another Bull Run, sir, it's another Bull Run!"

Gibbon hoped it was not as bad as that.

"Perhaps not," said Kearny. "Reno is keeping up the fight. He is not stampeded. I am not stampeded. You are not stampeded. That is about all, sir, my God, that's about all!"[9]

The sun went down, and in the twilight the air was so full of smoke that the Union Army could not see the men who had beaten it. But the bullets and the shell kept coming, and the rear guard hung on and let the wreckage stream back across the bridge, and the Pennsylvanians and Sykes's regulars and some of Sigel's Germans stayed grimly on the Henry House Hill, where Stonewall Jackson had won his nickname the summer before, and at last it was time to go. Gibbon's men got across, finally, and formed line of battle along the far side of the stream, but there was no further pursuit. The battle was over. Hungry Federals scrabbled among the wreckage of overturned wagons near the bridge to collect hardtack.

Late that night Phil Kearny overtook his headquarters wagon and sat down to write out his report. He had a writing pad on his knee, and since he had but one arm an aide stood by, steadying the pad with one hand. The aide was young, and what he had been through that day had shaken him, and he trembled, making the pad quiver. Kearny looked up and asked him what was the matter. Frankly the youngster confessed that he was afraid.

Kearny gave him a long, sober look.

"You must never be frightened of anything," he said.[10]

4. MAN ON A BLACK HORSE

The stone bridge and the road leading across it were a tangle of lost soldiers, sutlers' wagons, jolting guns and caissons, and weary regiments and brigades striving to keep some sort of formation as they forced their way through the confusion. A dozen long wagon trains were trying to get on the road simultaneously—some of them had been called from Centreville that morning, when the army thought it was going to pursue someone, and they arrived just in time to turn around and join in the flight—and there was a huge traffic jam. The sutlers' wagons seemed to be an especial problem; their drivers were almost frantic in their desire to get on the road and be gone, for in a jam like this, with discipline loosened, everybody hungry, and pitch-darkness prevailing, the soldiers were all too likely to consider them fair game and start indiscriminate looting. Now and then one of these wagons would succeed in getting on the highway and the driver would force his distracted horses to a gallop, careening ahead through infantry detachments and sending the men flying, and winding up, as likely as not, in a ditch.

In the grass and briars off the road there were little groups of men gathered about flags—each group the nucleus of some lost regiment trying to reassemble—and over all the noise of the retreat could be heard the cries of these men, plaintively chanting their regimental numbers: "Twenty-fourth New York! . . . Third Maine—Third Maine! . . . Bucktails!" Acrid smoke tainted the night air, and as the darkness deepened a steady rain set in. A soldier in the 27th New York remembered that his regiment was drawn square across the road with fixed bayonets to halt the flood; but blows, bayonets and threats were of no avail—"the disorganized and demoralized mob rushed recklessly around our flanks."[1] Later, he added, the disorder subsided, and the regiments marched by in more regular order. A war correspondent who had witnessed the headlong departure from the field after the first battle of Bull Run insisted that there was "little or none" of the panic that attended the first retreat, and felt that, all things considered, this retreat was fairly orderly; but it stood out in the memory of the men who had to live through it as one of the gloomiest, most miserable nights of the war.

And if there was no sustained panic there was a smoldering, unreasoning anger, and there was ugly talk. Luckless General McDowell sat his horse and watched the army struggle past, and as they went by men called out "Traitor!" and "Scoundrel!" A private in the 11th Massachusetts, from Hooker's division, turned to another and growled: "How guilty he looks, with that basket on his head!" This was in reference to poor McDowell's fancy summer headpiece. In the surviving photographs it does look somewhat like a battered coal scuttle, but the men's objections were not based on aesthetic grounds; somehow the army had acquired the remarkable conviction that for an obscure and traitorous purpose McDowell had designed this hat as a distinguishing mark for the enemy to see and recognize. As they trudged along the road the men of the 11th told each other how a brigadier in Hooker's division, meeting a non-com who was staggering wounded to the rear during the heat of the day's combat, had asked how things were going up front.

"We're holding our own now, but McDowell has charge of the left," said the non-com.

"Then God save the left!" said the brigadier bitterly.

At one stage during the battle, the men insisted, one of McDowell's regiments fired a random volley and then turned and ran for the rear, shouting to its officers: "You can't play it on us!" A diarist explained: "General McDowell was viewed as a traitor by a large majority of the officers and men . . . and thousands of soldiers firmly believed that their lives would be purposely wasted if they obeyed his orders in the time of the conflict." A stout partisan of Joe Hooker, this writer added: "General Pope acted like a dunderpate during the day, and scorning the wise advice of abler generals like Hooker and Kearny allowed General McDowell to maneuver the troops upon the field." One man was heard to say during the retreat: "I would sooner shoot MdDowell than Jackson." Some uniformed reader of Horace Greeley, passing General Pope, sang out: "Go west, young man, go west!" A member of the Black Hat Brigade noted that "open sneering at General Pope was heard on all sides," and a veteran of the 3rd Wisconsin, in Banks's corps, wrote that "the feeling was strong in the army against Pope and McDowell," adding: "All knew and felt that as soldiers we had not had a fair chance."[2]

The one chuckle anyone recorded for that dreary evening came early in the proceedings, when a pallid artillery officer, groaning with pain from a wound, was being carried to the rear on a stretcher. Suddenly a covey of shells sailed low overhead and burst a few yards beyond. With one bound the disabled officer leaped from the stretcher and ran to the rear on nimble and undamaged legs, his stretcher-bearers running after him but quite unable to overtake him, while the troops along the road whooped derisively.

Somehow the army got back to Centreville and began to sort itself out behind the entrenchments there in the cheerless dawn of a chilly, rainy morning. Franklin's corps came up from Alexandria at last and moved down the road to form line of battle along Cub Run, a small stream that cuts across the highway halfway between Centreville and Bull Run Bridge. Pope recovered his powers of undaunted speech and wired Halleck that the enemy was badly whipped, concluding bravely: "Do not be uneasy. We will hold our own here." But this was too obviously a whistle to keep up his own courage to be believed, and anyway, General Lee had no intention whatever of attacking him behind his entrenchments. Instead, Lee sent Jackson's men slipping around to the north through the drizzle, striking for a road that would put them once again in Pope's rear. The exhausted Union cavalry detected the move and notified Pope, and Kearny and Reno hauled their men out of the muddy camp and started back toward Washington, turning sharply to the left when they reached the Little River turnpike, to thwart the move.

Next afternoon there was a wild, brief, and bloody fight near the country house of Chantilly, with a mad, gusty wind and a driving rain, and an overpowering thunderstorm which made so much noise that the gunfire itself could not be heard at Centreville, three miles away. Jackson was repulsed, and Phil Kearny—galloping through the dark wood with the lightning gleaming on the wet leaves, his sword in his hand and the bridle reins held in his teeth—rode smack into a line of Confederate infantry and was shot to death. The Confederates took his dead body to a farmhouse and laid it out with decent care, and A. P. Hill came to pay his tribute to the stout warrior his men had killed. Lee later sent the body through the lines in an ambulance under a flag of truce, "thinking that the possession of his remains may be a consolation to his family." The boys of Kearny's battle-torn 3rd Michigan Regiment wept unashamedly when they heard the news.

Also killed in this fight was General Isaac Stevens, division commander under Reno: a little swarthy man who had come out of West Point years earlier to be an engineer officer, left the army to become governor of Washington Territory and was beginning to be recognized as a soldier of more than ordinary ability and promise.

This fight might have developed into something fairly big if it had not been for the storm. Pope had two fresh army corps at hand—Franklin's and Sumner's, which had arrived this day—and an opportunity to handle Jackson's men pretty roughly appears to have been developing. But it was just naturally too stormy to fight that evening. Most of the men's cartridges were wet ("If your guns won't go off, neither will the enemy's," Jackson sternly told a brigadier who wanted to leave the line), and the rain was coming into the men's faces so hard they couldn't see each other, and anyway, Pope had finally been persuaded that he was licked. So the armies drew apart, and the Federals evacuated the bleak bivouac at Centreville—leaving fires burning smokily in the rain to deceive lurking Rebels—and moved back toward the lines around Alexandria.

This was the final, formal admission that the campaign had ended in flat failure. The rain kept coming down, the men knew Phil Kearny was dead, and the mood of hopeless depression deepened.

The 55th New York, just up from the peninsula—the same whose colonel, landing at Alexandria, had heard much talk of treason—was sent up against the tide on some obscure mission requiring its presence at Fairfax Courthouse. The colonel left his record of what they got into on the day of the action at Chantilly:

"Soon the road became a mud hole, in which one could with difficulty direct his steps by the flashes of lightning. Disorder began to affect the ranks. The soldiers advanced painfully through the sticky earth, from which they could hardly lift their feet. The middle of the road was soon monopolized by an interminable file of wagons, retreating toward Alexandria. Mingled with them were batteries of artillery, which, endeavoring to pass by the wagons, blocked the road. The orders of officers, the cries of the teamsters, the oaths of the soldiers, were mingled with peals of thunder. All this produced a deafening tumult, in the midst of which it was difficult to recognize each other, and from the confusion of which we could not free ourselves without leaving behind us a large number of stragglers."

At Fairfax Courthouse it was a great deal worse, and there was a miserable, rain-soaked confusion: "By the light of the fires kindled all around in the streets, in the yards, in the fields, one could see a confused mass of wagons, ambulances, caissons, around which thousands of men invaded the houses, filled up the barns, broke down the fences, dug up the gardens, cooked their suppers, smoked, or slept in the rain. These men belonged to different corps. They were neither sick nor wounded; but, favored by the disorder inseparable from defeat, they had left their regiments at Centreville, to mingle with the train escorts, or had come away, each by himself, hurried on by the fear of new combats; stragglers and marauders, a contemptible multitude, whose sole desire was to flee from danger."

Nor was this the worst. What the colonel had run into so far was simply what might be called the advance guard of the retreat: the walking wounded, the fainthearts, and the honestly bewildered, pushed ahead by the army as it made its own progress to the rear. Next day the main body began to come through. During the daytime it was fairly orderly, but when evening came everything seemed to disintegrate.

"Those who for eight days had done nothing but march and fight were worn out with fatigue," the colonel noted. "Everyone knew that the enemy was no longer at our heels. No salutary fear kept them in the ranks and many gave way to the temptation to take a few hours rest. They lighted great fires, whose number became greater and greater, so that at a few leagues from Alexandria the whole country appeared to be illuminated. There was everywhere along the road the greatest confusion. Infantry and cavalry, artillery and wagons, all hurried on pell mell, in the midst of rallying cries of officers and calls and oaths of the men."[3]

One-armed General Howard, rejoining the troops after recovery from his wound just in time to take part in the retreat after Chantilly, wrote dolefully: "Who will ever forget the straggling, the mud, the rain, the terrible panic and loss of life from random firing, and the hopeless feeling—almost despair—of that dreadful night march!"[4]

An Irish private, clumping through the mud, growled an all-inclusive complaint at the hardships of army life. A comrade scoffed at him: 'You're just sore because you aren't a general and can't ride a horse."

"No," said the Irishman stoutly. "It's because it's meself that is obliged to associate with such fools as yourself and Gineral Pope."

An officer of Porter's regulars noted that "everyone you met had an unwashed, sleepy, downcast aspect, and looked as if he would like to hide his head somewhere from all the world." At each halt men would drop by the road and fall sound asleep, and each time it became harder and harder to rouse the men and get them to take their places in the ranks when the march was resumed. Some stragglers were still trying ineffectually to find their regiments; others had given up and were slouching along without their weapons, neither knowing nor caring where their regiments were. Men who went into bivouac around Fairfax Station found that the fields had turned into marshes, although the rain, fortunately, had stopped at last. Far away to the northwest there was heard the rumble of gunfire as some collision of outposts brought isolated batteries into action. Closer at hand, Jeb Stuart's troopers were harassing the rear guard—Banks's corps, which had been guarding stores at Bristoe Station during the Bull Run fight and which had been ordered to destroy locomotives and cars, burn all supplies, and come hiking back to Alexandria. It came up to take position in rear of the army, its spirits sagging to zero. General George H. Gordon, commanding a brigade in this corps, noted that when supplies were issued at Fairfax on September 2, the divisions of Hooker and Kearny together drew only 5,000 rations. Between them they had taken more than 10,000 men into action at Bull Run and had suffered a joint total of 1,500 casualties; fully 3,500 men, then, had gone absent without leave—and this from two of the crack divisions of the army. Gordon also noted an Ohio cavalry regiment numbering just under 600 men which was short 448 horses.

In all the accounts of this retreat there is a great deal about the mud, the hunger, and the weariness of men who had marched and fought until they were utterly exhausted. Yet those were not in fact the really important troubles. A few miles away to the north and west, taking a day's rest in the fields near the Potomac before striking across the river for further adventures, was Lee's Army of Northern Virginia. It had marched just as far and just as hard, and had gone just as hungry, and had fought just as much. In proportion it was even beginning to suffer as much from straggling, owing to a complex of reasons ranging all the way from lack of shoes to inability to understand the rationale of invasion. But this army was lighthearted and full of enthusiasm. It was well led and knew it, and it had absorbed the notion that there were no Yankees anywhere whom it could not whip. While Pope was sadly wiring Halleck that "there is an intense idea among [the troops] that they must get behind the entrenchments," and one of Colonel Haupt's aides was sending back word that "the volunteers are much demoralized and ready to stampede," the Confederates were looking ahead to new campaigns with high confidence.

It wasn't hardships that had got the Federals down, although they had had hardships and to spare. It was what had seeped down to the men in the ranks from the hatred, suspicion, and confusion in high places, the wastage which the men had seen for themselves and had themselves been a part of, the heart-numbing realization that what ought to be the Republic's finest army had been shockingly and irretrievably mishandled. The very best that ardent young spirits could give of bravery and endurance had been given, and it had all been to no purpose. Porter's men, teaching the straw-feet how to fight; Gibbon's young Westerners, proving their manhood by standing up toe to toe with their enemies until night came down to make fighting impossible; the Pennsylvanians and the regulars and the Germans, hanging on in the dusk around the Henry House Hill to keep open the last line of retreat—all of these had done as well as any soldiers could do on any field, and all of them knew that it had been futile. They were learning the reality of war, these youngsters, getting face to face with the sickening realization that men get killed uselessly because their generals are stupid, so that desperate encounters where the last drop of courage has been given serve the country not at all and make a patriot look a fool.

And then, at the last minute of despair, the unbelievable happened.

The head of the leading column of the retreat was coming in on the Fairfax road, near the forts on Munson's Hill, on the afternoon of September 2. The sun had finally come out, and the roads had dried enough so that a long, lazy cloud of dust hung in the air above the marching men. Pope and McDowell rode in the lead, their uniforms gray with the dust, their beards powdered. Their mounted staff officers and orderlies followed them, and after a brief interval came Hatch's division with an endless shuffle-shuffle of dragging feet, each man staring dully at the back of the man in front, nobody saying a word. Out into the road ahead, coming toward them, rode a little knot of horsemen, trotting forward confidently; the man in front rode a great black horse and had a bright yellow sash about his waist and was erect and dapper in the saddle, and as he came up to the two generals his hand flipped up to the visor of his cap in a salute that had all the gaiety and snap of the youthful, confident army these men had once been and had all but forgotten. General Hatch, looking ahead, stiffened as he saw it—there was only one man in the army who saluted in just that way—and he cantered ahead suddenly to see and hear for himself. He got there just in time to listen as General McClellan told Pope and McDowell that by order of the President he was assuming command of the troops.

The two generals impassively returned the salute. McClellan gave a few directions about the positions the troops should take when they reached the fortifications. On the horizon there was a dull bump-bump of gunfire, and McClellan asked what that might be. Pope answered that it was probably some attack on Sumner's corps, coming up as flank guard; meanwhile, did General McClellan object if Pope and McDowell rode on in to Washington? McClellan replied that he had not an objection in the world, but for himself he was going to ride to the sound of the firing and see what was going on in the way of fighting. . . . One gathers that the interchange did McClellan a great deal of good.

Hatch had heard all that he needed to hear. He had a score to settle with Pope, whom he hated. When Pope had first come east, Hatch had been in command of the cavalry attached to Banks's corps, and when Pope had made his first thrust down to the Rapidan, Hatch had been ordered to go in advance to seize the important railroad junction of Gordonsville and destroy Rebel supplies and connections there. The march had been delayed; while Hatch waited for infantry and artillery to go with him, the delay gave the enemy time to occupy Gordonsville in force, and the move had been a failure. A few days later Pope ordered him to try again, this time taking cavalry alone and cutting the railroad line from Gordonsville to Charlottesville. Hatch crossed the Blue Ridge in a pelting rain, got mired in muddy mountain roads, and came stumbling back a few days later, his mission unaccomplished; Pope gave him an angry dressing-down, relieved him of his command, and sent him to King's division to lead a brigade of infantry. Hatch felt that he had been unfairly treated. Now was his chance to get even.

He trotted back the few yards that separated the generals from the head of his own infantry. In a loud voice—easily to be heard by Pope and McDowell—he shouted: "Boys, McClellan is in command of the army again! Three cheers!"[5]

There was a brief, stunned silence; then a wild, hysterical yell went up from the soldiers. Hats, caps, and knapsacks were tossed into the air. The roar swept back along the column as men to the rear heard the news, and the men still farther back joined in without waiting to be told: they knew there was only one man alive who could make the army cheer like that. The cheering did not stop; men capered, thumped each other on the back, yelled themselves into hoarseness. Far back down the highway, out of sight, went the noise, officers joining with the men. One of Hatch's staff came spurring back to John Gibbon and gave him the news. As an old regular, Gibbon took it as just another camp rumor and said so. No, insisted the officer, this time it was true: he himself had *seen* McClellan, just up the road, giving orders to Pope and McDowell. Gibbon swung in his saddle and raised his own voice: "Men, General McClellan is in command of the army!" The air was filled with tumult. Men broke ranks, danced, howled, laughed hysterically, wept; and, Gibbon wrote later, "the weary, fagged men went into camp cheerful and happy, to talk over their rough experience of the past three weeks and speculate as to what was ahead."[6]

It was a big army and it covered a lot of ground, and it took time for the word to get around. Sykes's regulars, pushing on to get into the lines before midnight, were still on the road by starlight. They had fallen out for a short breather, and the dead-exhausted men had dropped in their tracks and were dozing. Two officers stood by their horses, looking ahead in the darkness, and saw a few horsemen approaching. One of the officers gaped: if he didn't know better, he said, he would say one of those riders was McClellan. This, said the other officer, was nonsense. McClellan had been relieved days ago, and anyhow, what would he be doing out here, at this time of night, without an escort? The first officer continued to stare, hope rising. Then some other officer saw, and recognized; and over the silent roadway, where men slept in the dust under the stars, he raised a strong, clear voice that could shout orders above the din of battle: "Colonel! Colonel! General McClellan is here!"

Ten seconds later every man was on his feet, sending a long cheer up to the night sky; "such a hurrah," a participant wrote later, "as the Army of the Potomac had never heard before. Shout upon shout went out into the stillness of the night; and as it was taken up along the road and repeated by regiment, brigade, division and corps, we could hear the roar dying away in the distance. The effect of this man's presence upon the Army of the Potomac—in sunshine or rain, in darkness or in daylight, in victory or defeat—was electrical, and too wonderful to make it worth while attempting to give a reason for it."[7]

The men who were there that night seem to have spent the rest of their lives trying to make people who were not there understand what it was like. About all they could say was that there was mad cheering and hysterical happiness and a sudden feeling that everything was going to be all right, so that every man forgot that he was tired and hungry and dirty, forgot that he had been miserably beaten, and looked forward with a bright certainty that all mistakes would presently be redeemed. And it is clear that some sort of miracle had happened; the most amazing and dramatic one, perhaps, in American military history, with an entire army completely transformed between the hot dust of midafternoon and the quiet coolness of starlight. But exactly why this miracle took place, and precisely what it was that this man did to make the soldiers love him as no general in the army's history was ever loved—this they could not seem to tell, probably because they did not quite know themselves. One veteran, trying to explain, finally let it go by saying: "The love borne by soldiers to a favorite chief, if it does not surpass, is more unreasoning than the love of woman."[8]

Whatever it was, there it was: an intangible, like so many of the important things in the life of an army, or a nation, or a man, indefinable but of tremendous power. The men who cheered and exulted and went gladly forth to the bloodiest field of all because they saw this man at the head of the column are all gone, and the man himself, with the hatred and the adoration that he inspired, is gone with them, and the cheers and the gunfire of that army echo far off, in old memories, unreal and ghostlike, the passion and the violence all filtered out, leaving the inexplicable picture of an army transfigured. And it seems that this man, with his yellow sash and his great black horse and his unforgettable air of parade-ground trimness and dash, somehow was in his own person the soldier every soldier had longed to be, the embodiment of the gaiety that had been lost and the hope that had been given up. He was what the army and the impossible, picture-book war itself had meant back in the army's youth when innocence had not yet died. And when he came back men split their throats with cheering, and tilted their battle flags proudly forward, and forgot that they had been starved and misused, and became a great army once more and went off to define the shape and purport of the war on the sunlit fields and glades that were waiting for them around a little Dunker church in the Maryland hills.

TWO

The Young General

1. A GREAT WORK IN MY HANDS

HE WAS TRUSTED to the point of death by one hundred thousand fighting men, but he himself always had his lurking doubts. The soldiers firmly believed that where he was everything was bound to be all right. They would gladly awaken from the deepest sleep of exhaustion to go and cheer him because they felt that way. After Malvern Hill an entire division, underfed for days, deserted the sputtering campfires where in a gloomy rain it was cooking the first hot meal of the week, in order to splash through the mud and hurrah as he galloped down the road, and felt satisfied even though all the fires went out and breakfast was sadly delayed. But it seems that McClellan was never quite convinced. An uncertainty tormented him. It was almost as if some invisible rider constantly followed him, in the brightly uniformed staff that rode with him, and came up abreast every now and then to whisper: "But, General, are you *sure?*" Every man tried to live up to his own picture of himself. McClellan's picture was glorious, but one gathers that he was never quite confident that he could make it come to life.

Perhaps this was partly because too much had happened to him too soon. Long afterward he remarked: "It probably would have been better for me personally had my promotion been delayed a year or more"; and he was probably quite right. Fame came early, and it came like an explosion, touched off before he had had a chance to get set for it. He found himself at the top of the ladder almost before he started to climb, and the height was dizzying. One day he was leading a diminutive army of volunteers in an obscure campaign far back in the wild mountains; the next day—almost literally, the next day—he was the savior of his country, with President and Congress piling a prodigious load on his shoulders, and with every imaginable problem arising from the most confusing and pressing of wars seemingly coming straight to him, and to him alone, for solution. He bore himself with a confident air and he said calmly, "I can do it all," but somewhere far down inside there was a corroding unease.

He was thirty-five when the war started. A West Point graduate, he had done well as a young subaltern in the Mexican War, and later he had been sent to the Crimea by the War Department to watch the British and the French fight the Russians. Then, with the rank of captain, he had resigned from the army to go into business. A capable engineer, by the spring of 1861 he had become a ten-thousand-dollar-a-year railroad president, and he was working in Cincinnati when Fort Sumter fell and the war began. The war reached out for him without delay.

It began with the governors. State governors were of great importance in the war machinery of that era—considerably more important than the War Department itself, at first. Under the law, all volunteer regiments were raised, officered, and trained by the state authorities, and the regiments were sworn into Federal service only after they had been completely organized in the states. This threw a heavy load on the governors—men of peace and politics, whose military staffs consisted of militia colonels and brigadiers, ardent persons but utterly ignorant of any warlike activity beyond a peacetime militia muster. The governors, as a result, were frantic to get a few West Pointers around them, and a retired army officer with an excellent record, like McClellan, was an obvious prize. So by mid-April, McClellan, who was a Pennsylvanian by birth, had received a message from Governor Andrew G. Curtin of Pennsylvania, inviting him to come to Harrisburg at once and take charge of the Pennsylvania troops. He wound up his business affairs in Cincinnati as quickly as he could and took off for Harrisburg, stopping at Columbus en route to see Ohio's Governor William Dennison, who wanted his advice. The stopover made all the difference.

McClellan appeared at Dennison's office, wearing civilian garb and a soft felt hat, impressing the governor and his advisers as a quiet, modest, self-possessed man and looking, as one of them remarked, exactly like what he was—"a railway superintendent in his business clothes." The governor explained what he was up against. He had what looked like the impossible job of getting ten thousand men ready for the field, and there was no one around who knew the first thing about the military arts. The state arsenal contained nothing in the way of equipment but a few boxes of ancient smoothbore muskets, badly rusted, plus a couple of brass six-pounder fieldpieces, somewhat honeycombed from the firing of salutes and devoid of any auxiliary equipment except for a pile of mildewed harness. The recruits were already beginning to show up—a few companies, gaudy in old-style militia uniforms, had got to town and were sleeping in uncomfortable elegance in the legislative chambers in the statehouse—and so far the state had not even picked a site for a training camp. Under these circumstances the governor had no intention of letting a good West Pointer slip through his fingers, and he then and there offered McClellan the command of Ohio's troops—the command of them, plus the task of getting them housed, fed, clad, trained, and organized. McClellan promptly accepted, moved into an office in the statehouse, and got down to work, a major general of volunteers.[1]

It is interesting to speculate about the difference there would have been in McClellan's career had he gone on to Harrisburg and taken command of the Pennsylvania troops instead of staying in Ohio. Fame would have come much more slowly, and he would have had a chance to adjust himself to it. Pennsylvania sent a solid division down to Washington shortly after Bull Run. It was the division McClellan would have commanded had he gone to Harrisburg; it contained good men and had some first-class officers, and it was just the right organization to build a solid reputation for its commanding general—it brought George G. Meade up to the command of the Army of the Potomac in 1863, after giving him plenty of time to prove himself and to find himself in battle. What would McClellan's luck have been with that division? No immediate limelight, comparative obscurity during the army's early days—what would have become of him, anyway?

(Another might-have-been: there came to McClellan's Ohio headquarters one day that spring a former infantry captain, somewhat seedy, presenting himself as a one-time acquaintance of the general looking for work; name of U. S. Grant. Was there a place for him, perhaps, on McClellan's staff? The general was away that day, and Grant was told to come back later. Instead of coming back Grant went west and finally wangled command of a regiment of Illinois volunteers. McClellan would have given him a staff job if he had seen him. What, one wonders, would Grant's future have been in that case?)

Well, the might-have-beens didn't happen. McClellan never did go to Harrisburg, command of the Pennsylvanians went to someone else, and if McClellan himself ever mused about it in later years there is no record of it. What did happen was that as soon as he got his Ohio regiments mustered into United States service he found himself holding one of the key jobs in the whole army. Ohio was on the frontier. The western part of Virginia was just across the river and the Confederates had sent troops deep into the mountains. It was correctly supposed in Washington that this part of Virginia was strongly Unionist—the Confederate commander, getting no recruits, complained that the inhabitants were full of "an ignorant and bigoted Union sentiment"—and it seemed important to drive the Confederates out. Also, the Rebels were cutting the Baltimore and Ohio railway, main traffic artery from the capital to the West. So McClellan, by the end of May, found himself across the Ohio River, commanding a substantial little force of sixteen Ohio regiments, nine from Indiana, and two newly organized regiments of Unionist Virginians from Parkersburg and Wheeling, together with twenty-four guns. He moved carefully up into the mountains, found two Confederate detachments drawn up in the passes, attacked one and caved it in, causing the other to retreat posthaste, and moved on to the town of Beverly, taking prisoners, securing everything west of the Alleghenies for the Union, and making possible the eventual formation of the state of West Virginia.

It had been neatly done, it was the North's first feat of arms, and the country rejoiced at the news—the more so, perhaps, because it looked like a good deal more of an achievement than it actually was. McClellan always knew how to make his soldiers take pride in their own deeds, and he gave it to them strong after they marched into Beverly, congratulating them in an official order which told them that they had "annihilated two armies, commanded by educated and experienced soldiers, entrenched in mountain fastnesses fortified at their leisure." This was all right, and it was the sort of thing that built up morale; but the "two armies" had in fact been separate parts of one ill-equipped, untrained force that hardly numbered forty-five hundred men all told, and the "annihilation" consisted in the retreat of this force and the loss by it of about a thousand men. The order was reprinted in the North, together with McClellan's dispatches to the War Department, which were somewhat less flamboyant but which still made the conquest look like something out of Napoleon's campaign in northern Italy. Also reprinted, and widely admired, was the address McClellan had issued to his soldiers just before the battle: "Soldiers! I have heard that there was danger here. I have come to place myself at your head and to share it with you. I fear now but one thing—that you will not find foemen worthy of your steel. I know that I can rely upon you."

All of this, remember, was happening in the early summer of 1861, when the war was still spanking new and people were hungry for heroes and for victories, and when the country was ready to take a general at his own evaluation. Some of McClellan's officers, to be sure, were just a bit baffled. One of his brigadiers wrote that McClellan's dispatches and proclamations seemed to have been written by "quite a different person from the sensible and genial man we knew in daily life and conversation" and remarked that the young major general appeared to be "in a morbid condition of mental exaltation."[2] But in the country at large it went over big; and just then, before anybody had forgotten about it, the news came in of the humiliating disaster at Bull Run, with untrained regiments legging it all the way back to Washington, and carriageloads of distinguished sight-seers contributing to the rout. Everybody had been chanting, "On to Richmond"; now came the realization that the war was not going to be a gay parade of triumphant militia regiments, whose bright uniforms and martial bearing would make up for any deficiencies in military experience and leadership. The war was going to be long, mean, and bloody, and above all else there was needed a really competent general who could turn the volunteer forces into an army.

To be sure, Lincoln had at his elbow Lieutenant General Winfield Scott, the hero of two wars; but Scott was old and nearly senile, he was too fat and infirm to mount a horse or even to review his troops, let alone lead them into action, and his great reputation and his stout old heart were all he could place at the government's disposal. Inevitable, then, that everyone should look at McClellan. His achievement in western Virginia took on an added shine when measured against Bull Run. His troops had not fled in terror after a few random volleys; they had gone into action coolly, scaling lofty mountains and annihilating two armies. This man knew what he wa doing, and knew how to make people believe that he knew what he was doing, which was even more important just then; and the very depth of the country's shame and disappointment at Bull Run helped to lift McClellan to the peak. Overnight he was called to Washington and invested with the command.

No American general ever came to high command under circumstances quite like these. He was thirty-five, and it was just three months since he had sat in Governor Dennison's office and received the tender of command of Ohio's volunteers. Now he was in Washington, with the safety of the entire nation on his shoulders; and before he had even started on this new job he was being universally acclaimed as a genius, with a fanfare that built his brief Virginia campaign up into an achievement that would stand comparison with the records of the great captains of history. He was "the young Napoleon" to one and all—even to himself, apparently, for he permitted himself to be photographed in the traditional Napoleonic pose, one arm folded behind his back, the other hand thrust into his coat front, a look of intense martial determination on his face. In a letter home, written the day after he reached Washington, McClellan sounds like a man who can hardly believe that what is happening to him is real: "I find myself in a new and strange position here: President, cabinet, Gen. Scott, and all deferring to me. By some strange operation of magic I seem to have become the power of the land." A few days later he went to Capitol Hill, to argue for a new law permitting him to appoint aides to his staff from civil life if he chose. The experience among the lawmakers was giddying—all experiences were, from the height he occupied just then—and he unburdened himself in another letter to his wife:

"I went to the Senate to get it through, and was quite overwhelmed by the congratuations I received and the respect with which I was treated. I suppose half a dozen of the oldest made the remark I am becoming so much used to: "Why, how young you look, and yet an old soldier!" It seems to strike everybody that I look young. They give me my way in everything, full swing and unbounded confidence. All tell me that I am held responsible for the fate of the nation, and that all its resources shall be placed at my disposal. It is an immense task that I have on my hands, but I believe I can accomplish it."

And he added, bemused: "Who would have thought, when we were married, that I should so soon be called upon to save my country?"

He *was* young, for a conquering hero, and it was only natural that he himself should have been impressed by his own eminence. And yet, in these letters to the young wife he had married little more than a year earlier, one presently begins to find something more than the natural blinking of a man who is dazzled by his own good fortune; something more than the artless self-congratulation a man is entitled to indulge in when he brags innocently to the wife of his bosom. It gets said too often. There is too much lingering on the adoration other men feel for him, on the wild enthusiasm he arouses, on the limitless power and responsibility that are his. The perplexity of the brigadier in western Virginia becomes understandable: this man, utterly winning and modest and soft-spoken in all his personal contacts, simply could not, down inside, look long enough at the great figure he was becoming, could not get enough of the savor of admiration and love that were coming to him. Over and over, from the day he left Ohio for the expedition into the lonely mountains to his final days in the army, there is this same note. What buried sense of personal inadequacy was gnawing at this man that he had to see himself so constantly through the eyes of men and women who looked upon him as a hero out of legend and myth?

Early in June, before the great weight of national command had been placed upon him, he was writing his wife of the huge crowds that met him at every stop in Ohio—"gray-haired old men and women, mothers holding up their children to take my hand, girls, boys, all sorts, cheering and crying God bless you! . . . I could hear them say, 'He is our own general'; 'Look at him, how young he is'; '*He* will thrash them'; 'He'll do,' etc., etc., ad infinitum." In western Virginia there was more of the same: "It is a proud and glorious thing to see a whole people here, simple and unsophisticated, looking up to me as their deliverer from tyranny." The weight of his own duties impressed him while he still commanded this detached force on the slope of the Alleghenies: "I realize now the dreadful responsibility on me—the lives of my men, the reputation of the country, and the success of the cause." And he himself must do it all. From Grafton he wrote that "everything here needs the hand of the master and is getting it fast"; and, a little later, "I don't feel sure that the men will fight very well under anyone but myself; they have confidence in me, and will do anything that I put them at."

On his first day in Washington he was saying confidently: "I see already the main causes of our recent failure; I am sure that I can remedy these, and am confident that I can lead these armies of men to victory once more." He had already, in less than twenty-four hours, had to refuse dinner invitations from General Scott and from four cabinet ministers; a few days later he dined at the White House, guest of the President, with the British and French ministers and assorted senators present, reported that the dinner was "rather long and rather tedious, as such things generally are." Scott, the aging general-in-chief, had become a nuisance within a week and would have to be quietly by-passed. "I am leaving nothing undone to increase our force; but the old general always comes in the way. . . . I have to fight my way against him. Tomorrow the question will probably be decided by giving me absolute control independently of him. I sup-

pose it will result in enmity on his part against me; but I have no choice. The
people call upon me to save the country. I must save it, and cannot respect anything that is in the way."

Undeniably, Scott was an obstacle, a querulous fuss-budget, his greatness
only a memory. It would be inadvisable, he held, for the young general to organize the forces about Washington as an *army:* the regulations said McClellan
commanded the departments of Washington and northeastern Virginia, with all
the troops that lay therein, and that was sufficient. Inadvisable, too, to organize
the new levies into divisions. He, Scott, had simply had brigades in the army he
took to Mexico City, and what was adequate then would be adequate now. Nor
should regular-army officers be encouraged, or even permitted, to leave their
own assignments in order to command volunteers; the hard core of regular
troops was needed and the volunteer army must be grouped around it, and the
strength of the regulars could not be diluted by sending the officers out into the
new regiments and brigades. And so on and on; McClellan was entirely right—
the job could not be done unless he could find a way around the old gentleman.

Furthermore, McClellan's boast was justified: the people *were* calling upon
him to save the country, and he *did* see "the main causes of our failure" very
clearly and was moving effectively to cure them. He began, simply enough, by
getting the disorganized officers and men off the streets and into camp. The regulars who were available he formed into a provost guard, with a tough colonel to
take charge of scouring out the bars and herding the uniformed wanderers back
to their regiments. On the Washington side of the river, camps were set up to
receive the new levies as they came in from the states, and provisional brigades
were established to complete their training and discipline. More seasoned regiments were sent across to camps on the Virginia side, where they could help
protect the capital while they were being turned into fully disciplined troops.
Lines were traced for a complete ring of fortifications encircling Washington in
a line thirty-three miles long; enclosed forts on commanding hills, protected
batteries covering the intervals, chains of rifle pits in between, with particular
attention to the approaches on the Virginia side. Confederate Joe Johnston had
pushed his outposts up to within half a dozen miles of the river; McClellan had
no intention of trying to push him back just yet, but he made certain that the
enemy could not get any closer.

After a week he was able to report proudly: "I have Washington perfectly
quiet now; you would not know that there was a regiment here." No soldier was
allowed to leave his camp without a pass, and passes were made hard to get.
Similarly, civilians were prevented from visiting the camps without passes and
were kept from crossing the bridges to the Virginia side unless they had legitimate business there. The bewildered men in uniform who had been disconso-
lately idling on the streets and in their tents suddenly discovered that they were
going to be soldiers after all; they were kept busy, things moved with snap and
order, there seemed to be a reason for the routine that had descended upon their
lives.

The most incompetent and unfit of the regimental officers were weeded out
by hastily organized selection boards. These selection boards were badly
needed. The great weakness of this army lay in its officer corps, and the big
problem of the high command always was to find officers who were worthy of
the men they were leading. Later, as the test of battle helped to weed out the obvious misfits, and as hard experience developed qualities of natural leadership in
others, this problem became simpler, but in the beginning it occasionally
seemed beyond solution. The officers were in most cases as ignorant as the men
they led, and they were usually ten times harder to handle. A few of them saw
their own inadequacy and eliminated themselves, like the sixty-year-old Maine
colonel who, learning that a selection board had been set up, came before it voluntarily and asked to be relieved. He had enjoyed militia work for forty years,

he said artlessly, but he was finding actual warfare a different proposition and he felt that he was too old to learn; he would send in his resignation at once if they would suspend proceedings and spare him the humiliation of being officially weeded out.[3]

An idea of the size of the officer problem can be had from a glimpse at the diary of a member of the 75th New York, which regiment stopped over in Baltimore while on the way to Washington that summer. This man wrote despondently: "Tonight, not 200 men are in camp. Capt. Catlin, Capt. Hulburt, Lt. Cooper and one or two other officers are under arrest. A hundred men are drunk, a hundred more are at houses of ill fame, and the balance are everywhere. . . . Col. Alford is very drunk all the time now."[4]

A diarist in the 11th Massachusetts told of one colonel who put the regimental chaplain in charge of his cooking arrangements and held him so strictly accountable for the quality of the meals that the poor man had no time for his priestly duties. After one particularly bad meal the colonel called the chaplain before him and barked: "If you don't cook a better dinner than this tomorrow, I'll have you tied to the flagstaff next Sunday and make you preach to the regiment for two hours!" As a result, the chaplain spent so much time in the kitchen the next day that he was unable to officiate at a funeral, and the services had to be read by the regimental surgeon. The diarist added sadly that colonels who didn't insist on having regular devotional services usually failed to hold the respect of their men.[5]

There was a happy-go-luckly informality about the men in charge of some of these new regiments. The 19th Maine, being Yankees, sought to turn an honest penny by laying in a stock of fruit and flour and baking pies, which the regiment sold in surrounding camps. A sergeant in a Massachusetts regiment, being offered a pie by one such, asked the price. Twenty-five cents, he was told. "I won't pay it," he said promptly, being a Yankee himself. "Your colonel was just through here selling them for twenty cents."[6]

Somehow these officers were either taught their business or eliminated. The selection boards weeded out more than three hundred, but they couldn't begin to reach them all, deep questions of local politics being bound up in most of the original appointments; state governors were touchy, and the administration hated to offend them. But what a selection board couldn't do a good brigadier general could. Phil Kearny, for instance, got his regiments up to snuff in short order. The day he was assigned to his brigade he found most of the men lawlessly stripping an adjacent apple orchard. He immediately called in the field officers of his regiments and gave them a terrific blowing up in his crispest regular-army style. The officers, as freeborn Americans who weren't used to being talked to that way, answered back with heat; so Kearny switched his tactics, turned on the charm instead, took all the officers to an elaborate dinner party, transformed them into a little band of brothers before they knew quite what was happening, and by midnight had them all agreeing that for the honor of the brigade and their own heroic souls they would thereafter enforce discipline in the strictest military style. They did, too.

All up and down the line the volunteers began to find that this was an army, not just a disorganized aggregration of soliders. Someone took the trouble to inspect the camps and teach the colonels how to lay them out so they were neat, tidy, and sanitary. The supply system was reorganized and the men ate regularly; regimental sick lists declined as sanitation and meals improved and soldiers were taught how to pitch their tents so that the first shower would not flood everything they contained, and the dreary discouragement that devitalized homesick boys began to lift. Regimental commanders found themselves answerable to brigadiers who inspected camp and drill ground and insisted on good performance—and who, when performance was not good, knew enough about their jobs to show how it could be improved. Brigades, in turn, were formed into divisions, with regular-army officers riding herd on them. The War Department was still buying quantities of amazingly shoddy goods—the tents were skimpy and leaky, many of the fine new uniforms lost their shape and color almost overnight, the New England boys noted that the shoes were poorly made and would never last, and the arms that were issued were sadly imperfect—but at least the stuff was coming in and being distributed. The air of the holiday militia outing was gone.

Then there were the reviews—reviews of regiments, of brigades, of divisions—with regimental officers nervously inspecting arms and equipments beforehand, with the bands zealously blaring out marching tunes, and with the new soldiers proudly performing their recently learned maneuvers on the smooth turf, while the flags streamed in the breeze and admiring civilians stood about the reviewing stand, the ladies bright with their hooped skirts and sunshades . . . and always, as the crowning feature, the young general himself, galloping down the lines on his great black charger at a pace his staff could never quite maintain, seeing everything, demanding good performance, and then glowing with happy pride when it was given. They cheered as he went by—how could they help it, when he was the living symbol of their regained self-respect?—and they cheered afresh when he acknowledged their cheers. Wrote one of his officers:

"He had a taking way of returning such salutations. He went beyond the formal military salute, and gave his cap a little twirl, which with his bow and smile seemed to carry a little of personal good fellowship even to the humblest private soldier. If the cheer was repeated he would turn in his saddle and repeat the salute. It was very plain that these little attentions to the troops took well, and had no doubt some influence in establishing a sort of comradeship between him and them."[7]

Not that there was any familiarity or easygoing softness in the relations between general and soldiers. There was a vast gulf fixed, then as now, between the major general commanding and the humble private, and McClellan did not narrow it. He did not live in camp, but stayed in the heart of Washington, in a fine big house where he gave elaborate dinner parties to glittering people, and wherever he went he was trailed by his staff, including two genuine French princes, and a trim cavalry escort. The troops did not see him during their workaday routine; when he came on the scene it was always a special event, surrounded by all of the formalities. He could apply a severe discipline when it seemed necessary. The 2nd Maine Regiment refused to turn out for duty one day in August. Camped near it were some ninety-day regiments whose time had expired, and they were going home, and the boys in the 2nd Maine, although they had enlisted for three years, felt that they ought to go home too—the war was going to last much longer than they had expected; if it was fair for one regiment to leave, why wasn't it fair for all? McClellan came down on them quietly but hard, and sixty-three men were presently shipped off to the dreaded fortress of Dry Tortugas—a frowning pile of masonry on a desolate sand key in the Gulf of Mexico, originally built as "the Gibraltar of the new world" but now used as a disciplinary barracks for hard cases—to break rocks for the rest of the war.

With another somewhat similar case McClellan tried a different tack. The 79th New York was a former militia regiment; called itself the "Highlanders," came to Washington in the bare-kneed glory of kilts, and had a crusty Scottish colonel named Cameron. It had been at Bull Run, where its colonel had been killed; it had long since abandoned kilts for the regulation sky-blue pants, and it was fed up with military life. Also, it was brigaded under William Tecumseh Sherman, who was a hard man and who at that time seems to have had something to learn about the way to handle volunteer troops. So one morning the 79th refused to do duty and demanded an adjustment of its grievances. McClellan rounded up a battalion of regular infantry, plus a squadron of regular cavalry and a battery of regular artillery—hard-boiled Indian fighters from the plains, filled with strong disdain for volunteer soldiers—and lined them up facing the 79th, firearms loaded and ready for use; whereupon the 79th was invited to stop being mutinous and return to duty. The New Yorkers blinked at the ominous array in front of them. These regulars, clearly, were perfectly willing to shoot volunteers if ordered, and the officer in charge had a frosty glint in his eye. The 79th had had no notion that it was committing mutiny; it was just exercising its democratic right of protest, as American citizens always did; but if the major general commanding saw it differently, what with all those regulars, why . . . So the 79th returned to duty, and nobody was shot, and McClellan took the regimental colors away and kept them in his own office, restoring them a month later with a neat little flourish and the comment that the Highlanders had redeemed themselves by good conduct.

So McClellan was able to write to his wife truthfully: "I have restored order very completely already." Things were looking up, and the young general wrote, "I shall carry this thing *en grand* and crush the Rebels in one campaign. I flatter myself that Beauregard has gained his last victory." And how could he help feeling that way, when he drank daily of the adulation of his men? "You have no idea how the men brighten up now when I go among them. I can see every eye glisten. Yesterday they nearly pulled me to pieces in one regiment. You never heard such yelling."

Yet the Rebels were menacing, and there was cause for deep worry. Behind their fortified lines at Centreville and Manassas, who knew what dark plans were afoot? Washington was ill defended; "If Beauregard does not attack tonight I shall regard it as a dispensation of Providence." And in mid-August: "I cannot get one minute's rest during the day, and sleep with one eye open at night, looking out sharply for Beauregard, who, I think, has some notion of making a dash in this direction." Next day the danger seemed even worse: "I am here in a terrible place; the enemy have from three to four times my force; the President, the old general, cannot or will not see the true state of affairs."

It was very disturbing; especially so since the danger actually existed almost exclusively in the mind of the commanding general. The Confederates were well dug in near the site of their old Bull Run victory, but Joseph E. Johnston, their commander, and his flamboyant second-in-command, the famous Pierre Gustave Toutant Beauregard—something of a young Napoleon himself, in ardent Southern esteem—were asking nothing more than that the Yankees would leave them alone for a few months. They had perhaps thirty thousand men with them—about a quarter of the number McClellan believed them to have—and their troubles in respect to organization, discipline, and leadership were quite as pressing as those of the Federals, if not a little more so, the Southern private being a rugged individualist not readily amenable to military rule. The lone Southerner who was talking in terms of an offensive in those days was the dour and warlike Stonewall Jackson, who figured that the North was still badly off balance and could be had even by untrained troops; but Jackson had not yet become famous, and his voice went unheard, and neither Johnston nor Beauregard was even dreaming of offensive action. Not until October would Johnston suggest an advance, and then he conditioned the suggestion with the stipulation that he be heavily reinforced. Reinforcements being denied, he dropped the idea. He was heavily outnumbered and he was perfectly well aware of it, even though McClellan saw him as having "three or four times my force." While Johnston was trying to get his own disorganized battalions into something resembling military shape, McClellan was anxiously writing: "I have scarcely slept one moment for the last three nights, knowing well that the enemy intend some movement and fully recognizing our own weakness."

But if there were anxiety, unease, and a deep awareness of weakness at GHQ in Washington, there was also that dazzling glimpse of greatness, the echo of strange promises of future fame loftier than any other American had ever had, mysterious whispers that could hardly be described even in the privacy of a letter to the general's own wife. On the ninth of August, 1861, McClellan was writing home:

"I receive letter after letter, have conversation after conversation, calling on me to save the nation, alluding to the presidency, dictatorship, etc. As I hope one day to be united with you forever in Heaven, I have no such aspiration. I would cheerfully take the dictatorship and agree to lay down my life when the country is saved. I am not spoiled by my unexpected new position. I feel sure that God will give me the strength and wisdom to preserve this great nation; but I tell you, who share all my thoughts, that I have no selfish feeling in this matter. I feel that God has placed a great work in my hands."

To which one can only remark that for a newcomer this young general had certainly been getting around. He had been in Wasington less than a fortnight, and barely four months ago he had been an obscure Ohio civilian; but already there was talk of the presidency, and people were telling him he should become a dictator. It was a moment of infinite possibilities, the entire country was at his disposal, he could do as he liked with it: he would spurn the dictatorship, he would gladly lay down his life after taking the dictatorship, with God's help he would preserve the nation; and all the while, never to be forgotten, he could get those dark glimpses of unfathomable Rebel strength and schemings across the river, coiling and uncoiling in the dim light in movements of infinite menace. Secure in his own nutshell, he was king of infinite space. But there were those bad dreams.

2. AYE, DEEM US PROUD

The war was very pleasant for a while, in the fall of 1861, for the soldiers who were guarding the line of the Potomac above Washington. The Maryland countryside there is open and gently rolling, with blue mountain ranges breaking the sky line to the west and with long vistas of cornfield and pasture and wood lot stretching away south to the river and beyond. The weather was mild and bright, and the business of learning how to be a soldier was engrossing and even rather exciting. Across the river there were unknown numbers of Confederates, whose pickets were often seen and frequently heard from in exchanges of long-range rifle fire. The 15th Massachusetts, picketing the shore near Edwards' Ferry, some fifteen miles upstream from the capital, felt that it was well acquainted with the Mississippi outfit on the other side. Northern boys and Southern boys used to exchange gossip across the river, and they finally agreed that "the shooting of pickets is all nonsense"—an agreement to which the Massachusetts soldiers came the more readily, as one of their number admitted, because they were armed with old smoothbore muskets which would barely carry across the stream, while the Southerners had rifles. One day a Mississippian crossed the river in a leaky skiff and had dinner with a knot of Massachusetts soldiers on the bank.[1]

Permanent camps were laid out, and soldiering was not too uncomfortable most of the time. There was a great deal to learn—about the war, about the people who lived in a state where human beings were owned as slaves. Boys in the 27th Indiana felt that they had come to a foreign land; styles of architecture and methods of farming were different, here in Maryland, than they were back along the Wabash, and even the language seemed strange. The money, for instance, was spoken of in terms of sixpences and shillings, and the Hoosiers learned they weren't understood when they said "quarter" and "dime." The 21st Massachusetts found that the thrift and neatness of New England farms were not visible here, and the colored field hands seemed shockingly ragged, ignorant, and shiftless. To this abolitionist regiment, slavery seen at first hand was abhorrent. A little earlier, at Annapolis, a fugitive slave came into camp and was hidden, and after dark the soldiers stole a rowboat, fixed the slave up with hardtack and salt pork, and helped him steal off north by water. It developed that the slave was owned by the governor of Maryland, no less, and there were repercussions—Lincoln and the governor being engaged just then in a delicate game to keep Maryland in the Union, and the governor's good will being important.[2] The slavery issue, indeed, was beginning to disturb a number of the Northern soldiers. By the end of September, Brigadier General Charles P. Stone, commanding the division which held this part of the Potomac, felt it necessary to issue general orders admonishing all hands "not to incite and encourage insubordination among the colored servants in the neighborhood of the camps."

In general, the Western troops were less disturbed than the New Englanders. To the Westerners, this war was being fought to restore the Union; to the New Englanders, the abolition of human slavery was mixed up in it too, and freedom was an all-embracing idea that included black men as well as white. Sentiment back home was strongly abolitionist, and it was felt in camp. Shortly after General Stone issued his warning, two fugitive slaves sought refuge within the lines of the 20th Massachusetts. Obedient to the general's orders, a young officer took a squad, hauled the slaves out of hiding, and returned them to their owner. The regiment was a bit upset, and some of the men wrote home about it. Shortly afterward the colonel of the regiment received a stern letter from John A. Andrew, the governor of Massachusetts, officially reprimanding the young officer for returning the slaves and rebuking the colonel for countenancing it.

The colonel was William R. Lee, a doughty old West Pointer, one of whose classmates at the Academy had been a brilliant, ramrod-straight young Southerner named Jefferson Davis. Lee had simply been obeying orders, and he passed the governonr's rebuke along to General Stone, who wrote the governor a sharp letter: this regiment was in United State service now and the governor had no business meddling with discipline, the young lieutenant and the colonel had properly done what they were told to do and were not subject to reprimand from any governor, and would the governor in future please keep his hands off? Governor Andrew, an executive whose strong support of the administration's war program in the dark days just after Fort Sumter fell had been an extremely important factor, was the last man in America to take a letter like that meekly, and he replied with some heat. The correspondence became rather extensive and passionate, and Governor Andrew finally passed it all along to the senior senator from Massachusetts, Charles Sumner, who denounced General Stone on the floor of the Senate. The general, in turn, wrote to Sumner in terms so bitter that it almost seemed as if he were challenging the senator to duel.

General Stone was getting in a bit over his head here, with the war still in its swaddling clothes, and with both of these Massachusetts statesmen being men of vast influence with the administration. As a soldier, General Stone felt that he was on solid ground—as, in fact, he unquestionably was. Stone might have been influenced, too, by the fact that he himself had more or less of a stand-in at the White House. Early in 1861 he had been commissioned as a colonel by James Buchanan, made inspector general of the District of Columbia, and given responsibility for maintaining order and preventing any secessionist putsch before and during the inauguration of Abraham Lincoln. He used to remark that he was the very first man mustered in to defend the country against rebellion. Lincoln had seen a good bit of him and had learned to trust him; indeed, if there was any substance to the story of secessionist plots to prevent the inauguration—and to the end of his days Stone believed that there was a great deal of substance to it—Lincoln had trusted him with his life. Now Stone was a brigadier commanding a division, he had the strong support of General McClellan, and he was quite willing to bark back at a senator, a governor, or anyone else if he had to do it to maintain discipline.

The flare-up over slavery, however, was not yet ready to come to a head. What was important now was perfecting the drill and training of the troops and guarding the line of the Potomac. Joe Johnston had a substantial outpost at Leesburg, over on the Virginia side, just a few miles away, and the commanding general was suspicious and wanted a good watch kept. Meanwhile, the boys still had a good deal to learn. There was a little trouble in the 15th Massachusetts over ambulance drill. The 15th had a nice twenty-four-piece band, and the bandsmen discovered that when they weren't tootling on their instruments they were ambulance men, required to put in at least one hour every day learning how to apply tourniquets, how to carry stretchers so as to give a wounded man the minimum of discomfort, how to get a casualty from a stretcher into an ambulance, and so on. They objected bitterly, refusing to turn out for drill and announcing, somewhat vaingloriously, that they would die before they would do any such duty. The colonel took them at their word; he had them locked in the stockade under guard and informed them that they would get food and water when they decided to obey orders, but not before. The bandsmen presently recanted.

In their sister regiment, Colonel Lee's 20th, it was discovered that city-bred Bay Staters had got a long way from the old tradition of the minuteman with his ever-ready rifle. The regiment was turned out for target practice and the colonel found that most of the boys simply pointed their rifles in the general direction of the target, shut both eyes tightly, and hauled back on the trigger. This had to be fixed, and was. . . . The artillery needed teaching too. Here and there, on hills commanding the river, was a battery posted to foil Rebel cavalry, which was believed to be exceedingly daring and dangerous, and the battery commanders took alarm easily, smiting the Virginia hills and fields with solid shot whenever anything suspicious appeared. It is recorded that one battery gleefully reported that it had bombarded and gloriously routed a whole regiment of Rebel cavalry, only to find a bit later that it had been disrupting a colored funeral procession.

There were practice marches to be made, too, by troops which were full of enthusiasm for war but which did not quite see the point of some of war's training-camp maneuvers. The 55th New York, for instance, a regiment composed largely of Frenchmen recruited on Manhattan Island, with non-coms who had served in the French Army, had a comfortable camp at Tennallytown, on the edge of Washington, and hiked far upriver in a cold, drizzling rain. The regiment countermarched, at last, and finally took position on a comfortless hilltop in plain sight of its own snug camp, which was no more than a mile away; and here, with the rain coming down harder and colder, the men were ordered to bivouac for the night. They muttered angrily: What point in sleeping here, shelterless, in the rain, when they could regain their own camp in another half-hour? A sergeant, veteran of the Crimea and Algiers, ruffled his Gallic mustachios and spoke soothingly. "Bah!" he said. "This is but to season the conscripts. We shall see many worse days than this." (He was quite right about seeing worse days; the 55th New York was to get so badly shot up within a year it had to lose its independent existence and be consolidated with another regiment.)[3]

So the boys learned the ways of soldiering, and bumped against the hard edges of the slavery problem, and enjoyed the lovely landscape and the good weather and the relatively harmless thrills of long-range picket firing at Johnny Reb. The New Englanders discovered that the 1st Minnesota, posted near them along the river, made good neighbors; the Minnesota regiment had several companies of lumberjacks from the north woods and the lumberjacks were mostly recent migrants from the forests of Maine, so that the outfit had something of a down-East flavor. The Minnesotans were enjoying the war at the moment; had built bake ovens so that they could have soft bread instead of hard-tack, bought fruit and sweet potatoes from the Maryland farmers, and wrote home that they were living "like princes and fighting cocks." Their picket post was on a tree-shaded hill overlooking the Potomac, and they got rope and put up a swing there and swung in it while keeping an eye open for invaders, and made friends, long-range, with the Rebels on the opposite shore. Their colonel, just then, was a man with the surpassingly warlike name of Napoleon Jackson Tecumseh Dana, soon to be promoted to a brigadier's commission.[4]

The 20th Massachusetts considered itself tolerably well seasoned. It could laugh, in mid-October, at its greenhorn nervousness of early September, when it marched up from Washington, bivouacked dead-tired in the dark, and sprang to arms in a wild panic because of a sudden, unearthly noise that shattered the midnight stillness: the braying of teams of army mules tethered in the next field. Colonel Lee was happily writing to Governor Andrew that General Stone (whatever his defects might be on the slavery issue) had promised the 20th that "we would not be deprived of our due share of active service." He related, too, the great pride the regiment felt in the fine equipment its state had provided. The general had asked if the regiment had everything it needed, and Colonel Lee had replied: "My regiment, sir, came from Massachusetts!" The governor could take a bow on that one; right after Fort Sumter he had sent an agent to England to buy arms, and the 20th had been equipped from the start with En-field rifles, the regulation British army musket.[5]

Along toward the end of October the general was able to make good his promise to the 20th Massachusetts. A colored teamster who had deserted the 13th Mississippi at Leesburg was brought into camp with a tale to tell, which was that the Confederates at Leesburg had sent all their baggage back to Joe Johnston's lines at Manassas and expected to retreat very soon, fearing that the Yankees over in Maryland heavily outnumbered them and planned aggression. Right at this time McClellan sent a division up the river on the Virginia side, halting it at Dranesville, a village some ten miles southeast of Leesburg, to see what the Rebels might be up to; and to General Stone he sent word of this move, suggesting that the general might make a small reconnoissance of his own. The suggestion was a bit vague, and General Stone interpreted it liberally; crossed a regiment or two at Edwards' Ferry and sent others three miles upstream to make a crossing at Harrison's Island, figuring that a slight demonstration there might make the enemy evacuate Leesburg.

The 20th Massachusetts thus found itself making a night march, and at midnight it was down to the bank of the dark river, the men waiting their turn to get into three small boats to be ferried over the water. There was much confusion and waiting; nobody in particular seemed to be in charge of anything, and the boats were ridiculously inadequate, having a combined capacity of only twenty-five men. But by the time the sky was beginning to get light in the east, most of the 20th was roosting on the flat, uninteresting length of Harrison's Island, peering at the 150-yard channel that separated the island from the Virginia shore. There was a high, wooded bluff over there—Ball's Bluff, it was called—and the boys of the 20th learned that five companies of the 15th Massachusetts had crossed the evening before and were up to something beyond the rim of the hill. At dawn two companies of the 20th, accompanied by Colonel Lee himself, went across, found their way up the bluff by a roundabout cow path, and joined the 15th in an open glade on the heights. During the morning the rest of the regiment joined them.

Nothing much appeared to be happening, nor did there seem to be an especial point to the proceedings. Colonel Charles Devens, the Boston lawyer who had become colonel of the 15th and who was ultimately to develop into quite a soldier, had taken a few of his men nearly to Leesburg, in the early dawn, without discovering any Rebel camp. Then, a little later, he had brushed into some Confederate outposts, and there had been a desultory exchange of random shots. Now he was back in the glade, reinforcements were coming up, and it looked as if there might be a fight sooner or later. The Confederates were off in the woods; nobody knew just where they were or how strong they were, but the pickets were doing a little shooting. Devens had sent back all the news he had to General Stone, who had messaged him to hang on: he was sending Colonel Edward D. Baker over to take charge, with additional troops.

Presently Colonel Baker appeared. He was a man of some fame, with a streak of romance in him, an intimate friend of President Lincoln, a man who had roamed to far places and loved the swing of poetry and the ring of great words. A veteran of the Mexican War, he had gone to California and had become a man of considerable note in gold-rush San Francisco. In 1860 he had moved to Oregon, winning election there to the United States Senate, and he had introduced Lincoln to the crowd at the inauguration ceremonies in March, riding with him in his carriage as his chosen companion. He told the Senate that spring: "I want sudden, bold, forward, determined war," and he set out to get it personally, raising and becoming colonel of the 71st Pennsylvania—a Philadelphia regiment which, as compliment to its colonel, was then known as "the California regiment," although Baker by now was officially an Oregonian. He went off to war gaily, and to a friend he quoted: "Press where ye see my white plume shine amidst the ranks of war." Now he was here on Ball's Bluff in charge of an advance against the enemy. He had been delayed getting here; bringing his regiment up on the Maryland side, he had been dismayed by the lack of boats and had spent an hour or more getting an old flatboat out of the canal, nearby, into the river so that more men could be carried. He had a couple of guns coming up, and he was ready to fight.

The fight was beginning to develop. The Confederates were gathering in the surrounding woods in some strength, and when Baker came up to the 20th Massachusetts he shook Colonel Lee's hand and said briskly, "I congratulate you, sir, on the prospect of a battle." Turning to the soldiers, he called out, "Boys, you want to fight, don't you?" Quite sincerely the boys cheered, and yelled that they did. Baker hurried back to the edge of the bluff, where there was a great deal of trouble getting the guns up, and the boys of the 20th peeled off their overcoats—fancy gray coats with billiant linings of red silk: the Bay State had equipped them nobly—and hung them on the trees and got ready to fight. From the woods in front of them there came a ragged volley, which hurt no one—in the uncertain shadows the Rebels seem to have mistaken the line of hanging overcoats for soldiers, and the empty coats were liberally peppered. Then there began a noisy uproar of earnest file firing and the battle was on; the heavy smoke drifted across the little clearing like a rank fog, and the 20th Massachusetts began to fire back. Men were hit now, and there was a high nervous tension in this green regiment. The Rebels began to be visible through the trees and the smoke. A Massachusetts private saw a Confederate officer on a big horse and drew a bead on him. Unaccountably, when he tried to pull the trigger nothing happened. He lowered his musket and stared stupidly at his right hand; the trigger finger had been neatly removed by a bullet, and he had not even felt it. Off to the left the two guns were finally put into position and began to bang.

Colonel Baker went back to the edge of the bluff. His own regiment had come up and was in line, and another one was scrambling up—the 42nd New York, widely known as the Tammany Regiment, led by Colonel Milton Cogswell. Baker waved to him and came close enough to sing out an adaptation of a couple of lines from Scott's *Lady of the Lake*—

"One blast upon your bugle horn
Is worth a thousand men"—

and asked Cogswell how he liked the looks of things. Cogswell, who was a West Pointer, didn't like it much. The confusion around the river crossing seemed inexcusable, with no one in charge of the boats and no sort of order being maintained; a knack for quoting poetry while under fire seemed a poor substitute for executive ability, and it struck him that the force on the bluff was in a desperately bad spot, with the Confederates shooting down at them from higher ground in the woods and with no intelligent plan of battle being followed. The two guns were silent, sharpshooters having knocked off the gunners; Colonel Lee himself was helping with the loading for a time. On its final discharge one gun recoiled back to the edge of the bluff and toppled over. Baker hurried to the right of the line, exhorting everyone to hold on. A swift mental calculation had shown him that with the few boats available it would take three hours to get everybody back across the river, and it seemed better to stay and fight. Nobody knows what sort of tactics he might have devised to continue the battle, because just as that moment he fell dead with a Rebel bullet in his heart.

After that everything began to go to pieces. Cogswell led an abortive assault off to the left, in an attempt to cut an opening so that the command could go downstream on the Virginia side to join the troops that had crossed at Edwards' Ferry. The assault crumbled almost before it began, and there was nothing left but to try to get down the bluff and cross the river.

So there was a wild scramble down the steep hill in the dusk, with exultant Confederates following closely to the brow of the hill and shooting down at the fugitives. The 15th Massachusetts held them off for a while with a skirmish line, but finally they had to go, and a detachment from the Tammany Regiment which tried to take their place fared no better. Pretty soon everyone was on the beach, and it was almost dark, and musket fire was coming down heavily from the bluff, and there were only four boats—two of them the merest skiffs—to carry upward of a thousand men across a wide river. The big flatboat that Colonel Baker had horsed out of the canal earlier in the day was loaded down until it was almost awash, and then it set out, with men standing on each side to pole it along.

Rifle fire followed it—so many bullets were splashing in the water, a soldier wrote, that the river was "as white as in a great hail storm"—and presently a couple of the men who were poling were shot and fell heavily on the gunwale, tilting the overloaded boat so that water came rushing over the side and it capsized. Thirty or forty men were drowned, and the boat floated away in the darkness, bottom-side up. The two skiffs disappeared and were seen no more. The one remaining craft, a sheet-metal lifeboat, was punctured by bullets and sank in midstream, and all hands were marooned. A few men found a neck-deep ford to Harrison's Island and made their escape that way. Others took off their clothing and swam, an officer warning them to throw their rifles into the river so that the Rebels couldn't have them. The rest were taken prisoner.

Next day, when what was left of the command assembled on the Maryland side and counted noses, they found that more than nine hundred men had been lost—some two hundred or more shot, the remainder captured. Colonel Lee, Colonel Cogswell, and the major of the 20th Massachusetts, Paul Joseph Revere, descendant of the Revolutionary rider, went off to Libby Prison in Richmond. Among the wounded left on the Virginia shore was a young first lieutenant of the 20th's Company A, Oliver Wendell Holmes, Jr. And Colonel Baker, the friend of Abraham Lincoln and the hero of the United States Senate, was dead.

Which meant that there was going to be a post-mortem, and a big one. If the nation had known as much then as it knew two years later about the war and loss and the mischances of the battlefield, the dark little tragedy might not have aroused such an uproar. But the war was still new, and Baker's death meant that a bright flame had suddenly been snuffed out, and the confusion and mishandling that had caused the defeat seemed to cry aloud for investigation. This was no Bull Run, where defeat had obviously been due to the greenness of the troops. The men who fought here had fought well enough, but it was inescapably clear that there had not been any very good reason for their crossing the river in the first place, and that, once they had gone across, no one had known what to do with them. Baker was dead, and his own brave but incompetent efforts were not to be criticized, but there was angry criticism and to spare piling up for somebody.

Somehow the spotlight stayed on this affair. The papers told how Colonel Devens paraded what was left of the 15th Massachusetts a few days after the fight and gave them a brief pep talk, asking them if they were ready to meet their "traitorous foes" once more: "Would you go next week? Would you go tomorrow? Would you go at this moment?" To which, of course, the emotional youngsters replied with a wild shout of "Yes!"[6] From beyond the enemy lines it was reported that the Confederates had said that fewer of the Massachusetts officers would have been killed had they not been too proud to surrender—which inspired Union Brigadier General Lander, a regular-army officer to whose brigade the Massachusetts regiments actually belonged, to write a poem, beginning:

> Aye, deem us proud, for we are more
> Than proud of all our mighty dead . . .

It went on for eight full stanzas. The anthologies no longer carry it, but it must come close to winning the distinction of being the best threnody ever written by a brigadier general in the United States Army; and it drew plenty of attention at the time.

Furthermore, public attention was painfully focused on Colonel Lee and Major Revere. The United States Navy had just captured a Confederate privateer, and it was announced that since the Confederacy was not a legitimate nation her so-called privateersmen were in fact pirates and would be hanged as such; and the government at Richmond promptly replied that if these privateers were hanged an equal number of Federal army officers, chosen by lot from among the prisoners at Richmond, would be hanged in reprisal. The lot fell on Lee and Revere, among others, and they were lodged in condemned cells. A captured sergeant from the 20th Massachusetts talked to Lee just before he was locked up: did the colonel have any message for his old regiment? Colonel Lee was reputed to be the oldest officer in the army, except for General Sumner, and he was deeply affected by emotion. "Tell the men—" he began. He stopped and cleared his throat heavily; when emotion takes an old soldier it usually takes him hard. "Tell the men their colonel died like a brave man." The message got back and was printed. Agonized attention fell on the officers waiting for death—until at last the Lincoln administration decided that nothing was to be gained by getting into a hanging contest with Jefferson Davis, and let it be known that the privateersmen would be treated as regular prisoners of war, after all. In time Lee and Revere were exchanged and came north, and Lee later became a brigadier.

But if concern over the possible hanging of prisoners was ended, there was no quick ending for the concern over the tragedy of Ball's Bluff. The state of Massachusetts had seen her sons sacrificed to no purpose and had influential spokesmen in Washington; also, the state of Massachusetts—through her governor and her senior senator—had already had trouble with this General Stone who was responsible for the whole Ball's Bluff business in the first place. Stone was a pro-slavery man—or at least he was not anti-slavery, and that might be much the same thing—and there were queer stories afloat. He went out of his way to protect Rebel property—*Rebel* property, the property of men who were trying to destroy the government. There had been flags of truce between his headquarters and Confederate headquarters across the river. Mysterious messengers had been seen going and coming; there was a question about passes that had been issued, allowing Southern sympathizers to go through the lines: was not this general actually in league with rebellion? Might it not be that the regiments sent across the river into a deadly trap had been designedly sacrificed? Should not Congress look into it: Congress, whose own hero had been slain in this affair? Should not Congress be alert to make sure that there was no sympathy with treason in high places in the army?

Congress should. Congress acted accordingly. And there grew out of all of this a new force in government, a force which was to have a great effect, for good or for evil, on the way the war was run and on the men who ran it: the Joint Committee on the Conduct of the War, with the bitter-end anti-slavery radical Republicans in complete control and with Senator Ben Wade of Ohio as chairman. Wade was as tough as Allegheny nails, and he hated slavery and all of slavery's spokesmen; had brought his rifle to Washington when he was elected to the Senate, daring the fire-eating Southerners to challenge him to duel, and had given back bitterness for bitterness, hatred for hatred, on the floor of the Senate, doing all that one man might do to make the coming conflict a war to the knife, utterly determined now that it should be a war to end slavery and destroy the slave-owning class as well as a war to save the Union.

The committee held hearings and broke General Stone. A mass of vague and mysterious evidence was collected—indefinite, unanswerable, and damning—and it was passed along to the War Department, accompanied by strong subsurface pressure. The evidence was just strong enough so that McClellan himself could not save Stone, just strong enough to make Lincoln, who had trusted Stone so deeply, admit that there seemed to be grounds for action; and Stone was removed from his command and locked up for long months in Fort Lafayette in New York Harbor. No formal charge was ever placed against him. He could not answer his accusers because he never knew quite what he was accused of; he could not be brought to trial because nobody else knew either. He was simply encased in a cloud of doubt and suspicion. One day he was a general in charge of a division, honored among men, and the next day he was a prisoner in a cell, walled away from the world. Months later he was quietly released; many months after that, when Grant came to the top command, he was given a combat assignment again, heading a brigade in the Army of the Potomac. But for the moment he was completely ruined.[7]

And this, if anybody had bothered to see it that way, was more than just a rough deal for General Stone. It was a flaming portent in the sky for all soldiers who might come to command in the armies of the Union: the civil authority was going to ride herd on the generals, and woe unto the man in shoulder straps who failed to please it. A new and unlooked-for complication was entering the ancient science of war. It was not going to be enough for a general simply to have military ability. He would have to show that his heart was in the cause, and the definition of "the cause" was going to be in the hands of men who had ideas never taught at West Point.

3. I DO NOT INTEND TO BE SACRIFICED

That was the point General McClellan never quite understood. How could he? No general had ever had to understand anything of the kind before. He was not merely the commander of an army in a nation at war; he was the central figure in a risky new experiment which involved nothing less than working out, under fire, the relationships that must exist between a popular government and its soldiers at a time when the popular government is fighting for its existence.

Nothing in the country's previous history shed any light on the problem. The Revolution itself had simply been a great act of creation—an inspiration, from which both sides could draw equally, but not an object lesson. Eighteen-twelve and Mexico had hardly been more than episodes—sudden, angry outbursts of the energy of growth and development, absorbing enough but bringing no problems that could not for the most part be left to the regular military establishments. But this war was different. It went all the way to the heart and it could not be left to the regulars. Nobody had yet discovered how a democracy puts all its power and spirit under the discipline of an all-consuming war and at the same time continues to be a democracy. Here was where everybody was going to find out, and the only safe prediction was that it was going to be a tough time for soldiers.

One thing, to be sure, had been made clear: no simple outpouring of undisciplined and untrained men was going to win. Bull Run had taught that much. The tradition of Lexington and Concord no longer applied. The embattled farmer, leaving his plow in the furrow and taking his musket from the wall to go out and whip the King's soldiers, had to sign up for three years now, and the bark of the drill sergeant—heard all day long on every field around Washington—was the audible symbol of the fact that until the war ended the freeborn American was going to be taking orders. That fact had been accepted, the young general had it well in hand, and everybody was happy about the way he was doing his job. But what came next?

What came next was the fact that nobody trusted anybody, which put a terrible new factor into the military equation: an unknown, packed with explosive force.

By all standards of military common sense, General Stone had been quite right in squelching Governor Andrew, and the governor had been absurdly wrong. But military common sense wasn't enough now, unless it was linked to an understanding of the overwhelming pressures which could be created by purely political considerations. Right though he might have been, according to the books, General Stone had in fact been wrong. By the purely pragmatic test—how does a general act so that he can get his job done?—he had made a huge mistake. He might have been perfectly correct in insisting that the civil authority must not reach inside the military machine to interfere with the discipline, but in the end the civil authority did reach into the machinery long enough to pluck General Stone out of it. That was doubtless very unjust, but it was the way things were and it behooved every general to take the fact into account. The war could be won without generals like General Stone, worthy as the man was, but it could not be won without war governors like John Andrew, wrongheaded and obstreperous though such men might frequently be.

There was also the Cabinet. Specifically, there were men like the honorable Salmon Portland Chase, Secretary of the Treasury and a power in the land. Secretary Chase was not a particularly lovable character; he was humorless and more than slightly sanctimonious and he was cursed with a burning, self-centered ambition which he could always justify somehow, to himself, as a simple passion for God's own righteousness, with which he identified his every motive. He was away outside the field of military operations, his concern being—in theory, at least—exclusively with currency and loans and taxation and the ins and outs of wartime finance. But he was also a man the generals had to reckon with. He was not in the Cabinet because he was a genius of finance; he was in there because he was a power in politics, leader of a certain group in the electorate, spokesman for an important number of the American people. He concerned himself directly and immediately with military matters, and when he raised his voice on those subjects it was listened to. So McClellan found himself, rather against his will, closeted with the Secretary of the Treasury now and then, explaining military plans to him and listening, with such grace as he could muster, to the military ideas the Secretary had evolved.

There is something almost grotesque, to modern eyes, in the recorded spectacle of Chase solemnly bending over a map of Virginia and with pudgy forefinger tracing the proper line of operations for the Army of the Potomac. But it is quite beside the point to say that Chase should not have been bothering his head about such matters. There he was, one essential element in the government of the country, embodying a popular voice which might indeed be tragically confused but which had to be heard if the country was to be held together. He was a part of the unknown new factor in the problem which the young general had to solve, and there was no sense in simply complaining that he ought not be in it at all: he *was* in it and he was going to stay in, and that was that.

Then there was such a man as Edwin M. Stanton, the prominent lawyer and Democratic politician, recently Attorney General in the dying months of Buchanan's administration, who was entering the intimate circle around the young general as a species of unofficial legal counselor, and who a little later was to become Secretary of War. Mr. Stanton was irascible, with a nature which was a singular blend of a habit of blunt speech and a fondness for devious intrigue. He had hard eyes behind steel-rimmed spectacles and he had a talent for savage criticism—a man who could plunge into sudden pessimism so deep as to resemble abject panic, but who could also drive for a chosen goal with uncommon ruthlessness. Right now he was deeply disgusted with everything the Lincoln administration was doing—with Lincoln himself, whom he spoke of bitterly as "the original gorilla," and with all of Lincoln's official family, which he suspected would be turned out of office before long by the arrival in Washington of Jefferson Davis and his minions. He was complaining that the administration was trying to give a strict Republican-party cast to the war; a complaint which comes very strangely from the man who, a few months later, was bending every effort to have the war conducted by the most extreme Republican principles. He was also urging McClellan to ignore the cackling politicians and make himself dictator. Of McClellan he wrote despondently to Mr. Buchanan: "If he had the ability of Caesar, Alexander or Napoleon, what can he accomplish? Will not Scott's jealousy, cabinet intrigues, Republican interference, thwart him at every step?"[1]

With this McClellan unquestionably would have agreed; most particularly with reference to General Scott. Scott was in the way, and it was clear that he would have to go. He belonged to an earlier day, and he was now hardly more than a great reputation bearing up a showy uniform. McClellan was pointedly keeping him in ignorance of the number and assignments of the new troops that were arriving, even though the old general was, at least nominally, the commander of the country's armies. McClellan also was conferring with senators and cabinet members about matters which legally fell within Scott's purview. Painfully Scott confessed that "I have become an incumbrance to the army as well as to myself"—for he was, as he wrote, "broken down by many particular hurts, besides the general infirmities of age"—and he could see that it was time for him to leave and let a younger man take over. He hoped that the younger man might be Henry Halleck, who had written military textbooks and who could put down on paper elaborate and beautifully reasoned treatises on strategy, and who was casually but on the whole respectfully known in the army as "Old Brains." But the White House was cool to the idea. General Scott had to admit that McClellan seemed to be in line for the place; had to admit, also, that he unquestionably had "very high qualifications for military command"; and so in mid-August the old general finally requested that he, Winfield Scott, be placed on the retired list.

The President went to him and tried to talk him out of it, and when he failed the application was simply pigeonholed, and Scott stayed on for a time as a pathetic supernumerary, ignored and absentmindedly honored for what he used to be. It hurt the old man acutely, for he was intensely vain; but Scott wrote that no matter how or where he spent the rest of his life, "my frequent and latest prayer will be, 'God save the Union.' "[2] And at last, in November, a couple of weeks after the Ball's Bluff disaster, Scott's plea for retirement was accepted, and McClellan got up in the half-light of a rainy morning to go clattering down to the station with his mounted escort to see the old man off. There they stood on the wet platform, formally bidding each other Godspeed, the worn-out old soldier, grotesque with his feeble fat body bulging in its uniform, and the dapper youngster, erect and confident, with the lesser brass standing at attention all around; and McClellan himself felt the force of the contrast. "It may be," he wrote to his wife, "that at some distant day I, too, shall totter away from Washington, a worn-out soldier, with naught to do but make my peace with God. The sight of this morning was a lesson to me which I hope not soon to forget. I saw there the end of a long, active and ambitious life, the end of the career of the first soldier of his nation; and it was a feeble old man scarce able to walk; hardly anyone there to see him off but his successor. Should I ever become vainglorious and ambitious, remind me of that spectacle."

It was to be just a year, plus three or four days, before McClellan himself would take the train out of Washington to retirement. But for the moment that day was deeply hidden in the future, and there were the problems of the present to worry about. And while McClellan took Scott's high place and became general of all the country's armies, his most pressing problems seemed to be chiefly two: the presence of General Joe Johnston's army in Centreville and Manassas, with outposts so far north that Confederate pickets could see the unfinished dome of the Capitol, and the existence along the Potomac River of highly effective Rebel batteries of artillery.

These latter created an immediate pinch. During the weeks before Bull Run the Confederates had edged forward to the river below Washington and had put up fortifications at three places—at Quantico, at Mathias Point, and at Aquia Creek, northern terminus of the Richmond, Fredericksburg and Potomac Railroad. In addition, they had removed all lights, buoys and channel markers from the stream. Nobody much came down to molest them, and they had plenty of time that summer to make the positions strong and to mount heavy guns; and by early autumn the Lincoln administration was forced to realize that the capital was effectively blockaded as far as its water approach was concerned. To be sure, the railroad line was open, and troops and supplies could come in freely; but the water route was closed—warships could run the gauntlet without too much trouble, but merchant vessels couldn't—and this was not only a big nuisance but a flaming humiliation as well. While Secretary Seward was assuring European nations that the Federal government was getting the insurrection well under control, the uncomfortable fact remained that the government could not open the waterway to its own capital.

The navy did what it could to restore the situation, without effect. It simply had no good ships to spare for operations on the Potomac. Practically everything that would float and carry a gun was needed on the blockade, or on the inland rivers, or on the high seas hunting commerce destroyers. At the beginning of the summer the navy's Potomac flotilla consisted of one small side-wheel steamer and two converted tugs, the three mounting a total of seven light guns. In June this hopeful little squadron steamed down to attack the works at Aquia Creek, retiring after a five-hour bombardment in which a good deal of powder was burned and a grand racket created but in which nobody on either side was hurt. Later in the month, stiffened by the arrival of the U.S.S. *Pawnee*—which was at least a regular warship, although only a second-class sloop—the navy returned to the fray, going down to Mathias Point and sending a landing party ashore, under the cover of gunfire, to seize the works and spike the batteries. This was playing into the Rebels' hands; they had infantry there, brought it up, drove the landing party off, and killed Commander James H. Ward, who had charge of the venture. After that the batteries were allowed to stay there undisturbed. In February of 1862, when the navy began mounting the expedition that was to capture New Orleans, David Dixon Porter came under fire while going downstream in the ex-revenue cutter *Harriet Lane,* which took a round shot through one of her paddle wheels.[3]

Clearing the Potomac, then, was up to the army—which of course meant that it was up to McClellan. McClellan pointed out, sensibly enough, that the existence of the Rebel batteries along the Potomac depended on Johnston and his army at Centreville and Manassas; as long as Johnston stayed there they would remain, but they would go automatically when he retreated. The Manassas–Centreville stronghold was the real objective, then. The young general would presently put his army in motion and clear this stronghold out?

He would. Riding out in the Virginia countryside with McDowell, McClellan used to gesture toward the eastern end of the Confederate line at Manassas and say, "We shall strike them there." He eased some troops forward a few miles "by way of getting elbow-room" and wrote confidently to his wife: "The more room I get the more I want, until by and by I suppose I shall be so insatiable as to think I cannot do with less than the whole state of Virginia." Joe Hooker, who had his division in training over on the eastern shore of Maryland, was lined up to prepare for a river crossing that would clear the Virginia shore of all graycoats. But McClellan refused to be precipitate about it. The lines around Centreville and Manassas were strong. The army's secret service assured McClellan that Johnston had something like ninety thousand men behind those entrenchments—men well drilled and well armed, and all athirst for Yankee blood. The more McClellan thought about it, the less did a frontal assault on those lines appeal to him.

He was in this mood when he took over Scott's job and became responsible for the strategy of the entire war; and a day or so after that he attended a cabinet meeting, sitting alone and somewhat silent at one end of the long council table. At the meeting this day was a young colonel of the 9th New York, one Rush Hawkins, who had just come back from the expedition which had seized Hatteras Inlet on the Carolina coast, and who was making a report on the situation there. When the meeting ended McClellan beckoned Hawkins to his side and began to ask questions, not about Hatteras but about conditions around Norfolk and Hampton Roads. Hawkins was all primed; he had been telling old General Wool, who was in command at Fortress Monroe, that what the government ought to do was land an army at the tip of the Virginia peninsula and move on Richmond from the east, and he quickly sketched out a rough map of the terrain, showing where the roads led and pointing out how gunboats could provide transportation and flank protection for an invading army by steaming up the York and James rivers.

McClellan pumped him dry and pocketed his sketch map. The young colonel's idea meshed with an idea of his own—was it really necessary to attack the Confederate fortifications at Manassas at all? The North had sea power and the South did not; despite the batteries along the Potomac, a properly convoyed fleet of transports could ascend and descend the river at any time. Why not take the army down the bay by water, land somewhere east of Richmond just as Hawkins was suggesting, and move in on the Confederate capital from that direction, completely by-passing Joe Johnston and his defensive works? The move would compel Johnston to retreat at once. Unless he retreated swiftly, the Federal army might even get to Richmond before he did. In any case, it could get clear to the gates of the Rebel capital without a contest and could fight its great battle there where victory would be decisive.

McClellan developed this idea. The President, the Cabinet, and the newspapers were calling for action—open the Potomac, drive Johnston out of northern Virginia—but McClellan at length concluded that his new plan was sounder; and by early December, in reply to a note from Lincoln, he wrote that "I have now my mind actually turned toward another plan of campaign that I do not think at all anticipated by the enemy nor by many of our own people."

This meant delay. It would take time to round up enough shipping for an amphibious venture of this magnitude—for McClellan proposed to move on Richmond with an army of at least 150,000 men—and there were innumerable details to get in shape. McClellan began to see that it would be spring, at the earliest, before he could move. This meant that the people and the administration would have to be patient. It was a bad time to call for patience. Ball's Bluff seemed to call for action—not merely for revenge, although that would be welcome, but for an advance that would relieve the North of the shame of having impudent Rebel hordes camped almost within gunshot of the capital, ready to gobble up any detachment that ventured to cross the river. By the end of October the navy had formally reported that the Potomac would have to be considered closed to water traffic, except for movements made under the protection of heavy warships.

And this, in turn, meant that the young general's place was beginning to be difficult. He was still the predestined hero chosen to save the Republic, and the cheers of his men continued to echo across the hills when he rode about the lines; but he was learning that much is expected of the man to whom much has been given, and his temper was beginning to wear ragged. There was a flaw in the arrangement somewhere. He saw the problem so clearly, and he had promised the country that the war would be "short, sharp and decisive," and he had worked a great transformation in the capital and in the army that protected it; yet there was a growing note of criticism, the President and his Cabinet seemed to be more and more impatient, and the clear strategic plans that were so simple to a trained soldier had to be explained, and justified, and explained afresh to men who did not understand what he was talking about and who could by no means be trusted to keep their mouths shut when they were entrusted with classified information.

This fall the young general was writing to his wife: "I can't tell you how disgusted I am becoming with these wretched politicians," and "this getting ready is slow work with such an administration. I wish I were well out of it." The note recurred, as the months wore away: "I am becoming daily more disgusted with this administration—perfectly sick of it. If I could with honor resign I would quit the whole concern tomorrow; but so long as I can be of any real use to the nation in its trouble I will make the sacrifice. No one seems able to comprehend my real feeling—that I have no ambitious feelings to gratify, and only wish to serve my country in its trouble." He was no longer telling proudly about multiple dinner invitations from members of the Cabinet. Instead: "When I returned yesterday, after a long ride, I was obliged to attend a meeting of the cabinet at eight p.m., and was bored and annoyed. There are some of the greatest geese in the cabinet I have ever seen—enough to tax the patience of Job."

There was never-failing consolation in the adoration of the army: " 'Our George' they have taken it into their heads to call me. I ought to take good care of these men, for I believe they love me from the bottom of their hearts; I can see it in their faces when I pass among them." But the army, unfortunately, was not all: "I appreciate all the difficulties in my path: the impatience of the people, the venality and bad faith of the politicians, the gross neglect that has occurred in obtaining arms, clothing, etc." There were matters of state to worry about also: "This unfortunate affair of Mason and Slidell has come up and I shall be obliged to devote the day to endeavoring to get our government to take the only prompt and honorable course of avoiding a war with England and France. . . . It is sickening in the extreme, and makes me feel heavy at heart, when I see the weakness and unfitness of the poor beings who control the destinies of this great country."

Something—it may be remarked—seems to have been going to the young general's head right about then. The famous Mason and Slidell incident had indeed created a regrettable moment of crisis, and the country could have had a full-dress war with England just by asking for it, in December of 1861. But neither Lincoln nor Seward had the remotest notion of letting the dispute boil over into war—"One war at a time," Lincoln kept saying—and the dispute was settled smoothly, at some cost to inflamed national pride. McClellan was simply deluding himself if he thought that it was at any time necessary for him to needle either the President or the Secretary of State into sensible behavior.

For that matter, if McClellan felt obliged to guide the President on foreign policy he was hardly taking the most tactful path to gain his end. It was just at this time—when the danger of war with England had suddenly become real and imminent, when the administration was irritably asking when the army would take the offensive, and when the Potomac River shipping was stagnating at the wharves because of the defiant Rebel batteries downstream—that McClellan chose to deliver his famous snub to the President: came back to his house one evening, was told the President was in the parlor waiting to see him, and calmly went upstairs and got into bed, leaving the President to cool his heels as he might please. At about the same time he was writing to his wife: "I have not been at home for some three hours, but am concealed at Stanton's to dodge all enemies in the shape of 'browsing' presidents, etc." A few months later, when the unpredictable Stanton had become Secretary of War and great enmity had arisen between general and Secretary, McClellan was to complain that Stanton insulated him from the White House and kept him from seeing the President. If Stanton did do that when his time came, he at least had something to work on.

Not that McClellan did not have many things on his mind. The whole load had been placed upon him. He had said confidently, "I can do it all," and he was overworking himself with relentless energy, but the load was crushing. He saw himself at times as a man held back by civilian incompetence; "The people think me all-powerful. Never was there a greater mistake. I am thwarted and deceived by these incapables at every turn." And while Lincoln had the impression that an advance on Manassas was prevented only by McClellan's hesitation, McClellan was writing: "I am doing all I can to get ready to move before winter sets in, but it now begins to look as if we were condemned to a winter of inactivity. If it is so the fault will not be mine: there will be that consolation for my conscience, even if the world at large never knows it."

McClellan was beginning to realize, too, that as general-in-chief of the armies he had some sort of responsibility in regard to the slavery issue. He was moved to deep reflections on the evils of slavery when he read the reports from the expedition that had captured Port Royal, South Carolina, late that fall. As the troops seized portions of the Carolina coast, great numbers of slaves came wandering into the Union lines with their simple possessions tied up in bundles—infinitely wistful and confused, not knowing what was happening but sensing, somehow, that a great day of change had arrived. There was something in this spectacle "inexpressibly mournful" to the young general as he sat at headquarters late at night and poured out his inmost thoughts to his young wife. He wrote: "When I think of some of the features of slavery I cannot help shuddering. Just think for one moment, and try to realize that at the will of some brutal master you and I might be separated forever! It is horrible; and when the day of adjustment comes I will, if successful, throw my sword into the scale to force an improvement in the condition of these poor blacks." And then the young general, so deeply moved with a sincere, fundamental emotion, added the towering anticlimax: "I do think that some of the rights of humanity ought to be secured to the negroes. There should be no power to separate families, and the right of marriage ought to be secured to them."

But these moments of self-communion, bringing the bright vision of an all-powerful young conqueror using his great victory to right profound wrongs, were after all relatively few. The more immediate concerns left little room for them. Washington had become antagonistic to him. There was afoot a subtle, implacable hostility, born of villainy, moving below the surface to thwart the man who would save the country. Matters were not going right, and it was because there were men in high places who did not want matters to go right. Very late at night, worn by a hard day, McClellan told his wife: ". . . the necessity for delay has not been my fault. I have a set of men to deal with unscrupulous and false; if possible they will throw whatever blame there is on my shoulders, and I do not intend to be sacrificed by such people. I still trust that the all-wise Creator does not intend our destruction, and that in His own good time He will free the nation from the men who curse it, and will restore us to his favor." Specifically who might these men be? They are not named, they are just there, the men who try to talk strategy to a soldier, who insist on a quick stab at Manassas (where overwhelming foes lie in wait) instead of easily agreeing that it is more sensible to wait and go round by the peninsula; the men who want the Potomac opened at once; the frock-coated politicians who think they are somebodies even though there is a great war to be fought, who commission ignorant civilians like themselves as generals and entrust troops to them, who sometimes quite openly do not want or expect a soldier to succeed unless he sees political issues as they do.

The effect of all this was to drive McClellan deeper in on himself—this sensitive, immeasurably introspective man, whose high confidence rested on a dark substratum of doubt, where every problem, every venture, had to be given prolonged study to make sure that inexplicable dangers were not attached to it. The army was not only the instrument he had created and was ready to use; it was his refuge as well, ready with cheers and understanding to dispel those queer twinges of self-distrust that could come up even without the nagging criticism of ignorant politicians. To this nagging he could oppose obstinacy. He would handle the army according to purely military principles, and he would not be hurried.

He presented at last his plan for taking the army down the river by water (in the spring, when warm weather and the end of winter damp had made passable the execrable unpaved roads of Virginia), and there was endless to-do about it. Typhoid fever laid him up for a while. Lincoln came to see him while he was convalescing, and once again couldn't seem to get admitted to the presence; Lincoln then called into council General McDowell and General William Franklin, explaining that he had to talk to somebody, and remarking that if General McClellan did not intend to use the army he would like to borrow it for a time. Recovering, McClellan found himself involved with a good part of the Cabinet, plus the two generals, discussing matters of strategy. He froze McDowell with icy politeness when McDowell tried to express his embarrassment at having been called into consultation over the head of the army commander, and listened in noncommittal silence while Secretary Seward, slouching in his chair, said he didn't particularly care whether the army beat the Confederates at Manassas or at the gates of Richmond, just so long as it beat them somewhere. When Secretary Chase asked him bluntly if he actually did plan to do anything definite with the army, and if so when he proposed to do it, McClellan was equally blunt: said that he had a plan, with a perfectly good time element in it, and if the President ordered him to spill it in public he would do so, but that if he were not so ordered he would prefer to keep quiet, feeling that it would be well to have as few civilians as possible know about secrets of strategy. Whereupon, amid some hemming and hawing, Lincoln adjourned the meeting.

They had come quite a distance now from the day when Republican senators were flocking around the general with throat noises of admiration, saying, "How young he is!"; quite a distance from the day when four separate cabinet ministers craved the general's presence at dinner, and all criticism was suspended while the young soldier had a free hand. And it was all dreadfully complicated by the fact that suspicion and fear—perfectly natural, considering that the country was at war with itself—had been turned loose in the capital. That operated to intensify the handicap which, under any circumstances, must rest on the shoulders of a democracy's general. Of necessity, a democracy deeply distrusts its army, and in all ordinary times it wears its distrust openly on its sleeve—especially a democracy like that of 1861, which was still brash and crude and wore its hat in the parlor. But when a democracy goes to war in a big way it is suddenly compelled to rely on its army for its very existence. Then its instinct for self-preservation forces it to watch the army very carefully, to be excessively critical, to demand illogical and sometimes impossible things, and to be savage if they are not quickly done. And it is up to the general in command to realize all of this. A capacity for getting along with the civil authorities is just as essential a part of his equipment as is the ability to plan campaigns and win battles. (McClellan's opposite number, Robert E. Lee, could have told him about that: Lee had this capacity to his very finger tips.)[4]

And this capacity for getting along with the civilians does not consist merely in an ability to butter people up gracefully, to suffer fools in council with patience, and to yes the ignorant officeholders along. What it really means is that the general must understand that he is not a free agent and cannot hope to become one. He has to work within the limitations imposed by the fact that he is working for a democracy, which means that at times he must modify or abandon the soundest military plan and make do with a second-best. McClellan's experience in that difficult autumn and winter of inaction provides an illustration.

The administration desperately wanted him to drive the Confederates out of northern Virginia and open the Potomac waterway. For perfectly sound military reasons McClellan refused. What never entered his head was the fact that his own ability to command the army and to control the war was going to depend, at least in part, on the readiness with which he satisifed the administration's demands. In the long run this civilian voice was going to be heard, whether or no; if the general would not listen, there would eventually be a general there who would.

It was the same in the matter of appointing corps commanders. An army as big as the Army of the Potomac could not operate very well with the division as the largest administrative unit. The divisions had to be grouped into army corps, and generals had to be named to command those corps. Lincoln and his Cabinet, spurred by a bookish understanding of this, kept pressing McClellan to set the corps up and appoint the commanders. McClellan kept refusing; he would name corps commanders, he said, only after the test of battle had shown him which generals were best qualified for those important jobs. Which was all right—except that one morning he came down to work and found that the President had officially appointed the corps commanders himself. McClellan complained bitterly about it, as well he might; but he never saw that he really had himself to blame. The administration's insistence on having corps commanders appointed meant that corps commanders were going to be appointed—if not by the major general commanding, then by someone else. This was probably wrong, but it was one of the facts of life which the major general commanding needed to assimilate.

But by midwinter, in spite of all disputes and misunderstandings, the War Department was collecting steamers, ferryboats, tugs, canal barges, schooners—

anything that would carry men or supplies—and making ready for the great descent of the Potomac, for McClellan had finally made his point. Richmond was to be attacked from the east, and a tremendous amphibious operation was to be launched. There was a stir in the far-flung camps. Discipline was good, spirits were high; the new system of corps command was creaking somewhat, but it was working. With profound relief McClellan looked forward to getting out of the capital, away from the scheming politicians, out into the field with his soldiers. To his wife he wrote: "If I can get out of this scrape you will never catch me in the power of such a set again."

And a young officer in the 7th Maine wrote home: "We have no baggage with us but our blankets. I enjoy this kind of life immensely. We expect to be in Richmond in a fortnight."[5]

THREE

The Era of Suspicion

1. BUT YOU MUST ACT

THE POINT THAT is so easy to overlook nowadays is that the men of the 1860s were living in the center of a fiery furnace. It was not a tidy, clear-cut war against some foreign nation that was being waged. It was a *civil* war, a war not between men of two nations but between men of two beliefs, two philosophies, two ways of considering human society and its structure and purpose. The opposing beliefs were not sharply defined and clear so that no man could mistake which camp he belonged in. On the contrary, there were a dozen gradations of belief leading from one to the other, and a man might belong in one camp on one issue and in the other camp on another; and the very word "loyalty" might mean loyalty to a flag, to a cause, or to a belief in some particular social and political theory, and "treason" might mean disloyalty to any of these. Indeed, the war was peculiarly and very bitterly a war of the tragically modern kind, in which loyalties and disloyalties do not follow the old patterns even though those patterns may be the only ones men can use when they try to formulate their loyalty. And so that generation was deprived of the one element that is essential to the operation of a free society—the ability to assume, in the absence of good proof to the contrary, that men in public life are generally decent, honorable, and loyal. Because that element was lacking, the wisest man could be reasonable with only part of his mind; a certain area had to be given over to emotions which were all the more mad and overpowering because he shared them with everyone else.

Hence the Civil War was fought and directed in an air of outright melodrama. It was stagy and overdone, and the least inhibited theatrical director nowadays would throw out large parts of the script on the simple ground that it was too wild to be credible—but it was all real, the villainies and dangers were all visible, and the worst things anyone could imagine seemed quite as likely as not to be completely true. The confused soldiers who imagined that General

McDowell wore a fancy hat in order to have traitorous communion with the Rebels were not out of their minds; they were simply applying, on their own level, the same sort of panic suspicion that was besetting their elders. All the way through there were two lines of action going on: the visible one, out in the open, where there were flags and rumbling guns and marching men to be seen, and the invisible one which affected and colored all the rest. Sunlight and death were upon the earth in the spring of 1862, and no one was wholly rational.

On the surface, everything was fine. Nearly two hundred thousand young men had been drilled, disciplined, clothed, armed, and equipped. They innocently thought themselves veterans. They had roughed it for a whole autumn and winter under canvas, knew what it was like to sleep on bare ground in the rain, had learned the intricate, formalized routines by which marching columns transformed themselves into battle lines, and they had been brought to a razor edge of keenness. The great unpredictable that lay ahead of them seemed a bright adventure, for in the 1860s cynicism was not a gift which came to youth free, in advance; it had to be earned, and all illusions had to be lost the hard way. Day by day the new divisions got ready for the great move southward, discarding surplus gear, preparing wagon trains for cross-country movement. The roads and docks and warehouses along the Potomac were full of bustle and hustle, and the empty transports lay waiting on the bright water.

But beneath this enthusiasm and eager hope there were doubt and bickering, and the men who knew the most were the men who worried the most. A cloud somewhat larger than a man's hand lay upon the sky: symbolized, as winter died, by a very literal cloud of black, oily smoke rising from the burning supply depots of the Confederate encampments around Centreville and Manassas. Confederate Joe Johnston, meditating on the fact that McClellan had three times his numbers, had decided not to wait to be pushed. He put the torch to all the goods he could not move—a million pounds of bacon, along with much else, went to the flames—and he pulled his army out of its entrenchments, marching back to a safer post behind the Rappahannock River. And while this retreat was, in a way, what everybody had been hoping for—Rebel vedettes could no longer gaze insolently down on the capital city, and the troublesome batteries along the Potomac were all evacuated, leaving the waterway clear—the move took the high command by surprise. It might be cause for joy, but it was also very disturbing.

To General McClellan, among others. In the elaborate chess game that was just beginning he had worked out a clever sequence of moves, and this retreat joggled the board and displaced the men. McClellan had planned to float his army down to the mouth of the Rappahannock, landing at a town called Urbanna, some sixty miles due east of Richmond. That would put him in Johnston's rear, the Confederate Army would have to retreat in hot haste—and, being so hasty, very likely in considerable disorder—and the Federal army would be where it could cut off this retreat and bring on a battle under highly favorable circumstances. But now Johnston was not where he had been, and the Urbanna move was no good. Committed to the water route, at the cost of long, infinitely difficult wrangles with President and Cabinet, McClellan realized that he would have to go to Fortress Monroe and make his way up the long peninsula between the York and James rivers.

In a way, that was all right. His flanks and his supply line would be protected, and he had been informed that the peninsular highways were sandy, and hence readily passable in wet weather—a thumping bit of misinformation, if ever there was one. But it meant a slow, slogging drive, no chance to cut off the Rebel army, and a big, stand-up fight before Richmond was reached. He had written earlier that the move via the peninsula was "less brilliant." Still, he greatly preferred it to the overland route, which was what Lincoln and his Cabinet wanted: the route straight down the railroad track, supply line getting longer each day and cruelly tempting the Rebel cavalry raiders, and all sorts of mischance possible as the army got deeper into enemy territory.

There had been trouble about that; much trouble, the end of which was not yet. Out of it had come a singular episode—fantastic, reflecting the temper of the times and the strange character of the war they were fighting. It happened, oddly, on the very day General Johnston started his gray columns south out of Manassas, when Lincoln sent for McClellan early in the morning and asked him to come to the White House. When McClellan got there he found the President sober, somewhat distraught. There was, said Lincoln, an ugly matter to talk about. It seemed to be so ugly that Lincoln hardly knew how to begin; McClellan finally had to prompt him by suggesting that, the uglier the matter was, the better it would be to speak about it frankly and openly. So Lincoln got into it.

People had been telling him, said the President, that there was much more to McClellan's plan of campaign than met the eye. The big objection to taking the army down the bay by water had always been the fear that Washington would be left uncovered, defenseless against a sudden Rebel stab—and a successful stab into the heart of the capital would mean the end of everything, the Southern Confederacy a real nation, the mystic union of the states dissolved forever. Now, the President went on, it was being alleged, by men whose suspicions had to be taken into account, that McClellan was planning to leave the capital unprotected on purpose—that he was inviting the Rebel stab, that he wanted the Confederacy to win, that he was moving according to stealthy and treasonous design.

McClellan sprang to his feet. He could permit no one, he said, to couple his name with the word "treason." Years later he wrote that he spoke "in a manner not altogether decorous toward the chief magistrate." The President, said the general hotly, would have to retract that expression. Lincoln tried to soothe him; the expression was not his, he was merely telling McClellan what others were saying. For his part, he did not for a moment believe that McClellan had any traitorous intent. (Which should have been fairly obvious; otherwise, he was simply an imbecile to retain him in command of the army.) McClellan's feathers, having been thoroughly ruffled, were slow in settling back into place. He remarked that the President might well be careful thereafter in his use of language. Again Lincoln insisted that the offensive accusation was not his; according to McClellan, Lincoln apologized, and the general finally took his leave, wondering how "a man of Mr. Lincoln's intelligence could give ear to such abominable nonsense."

Abominable nonsense it surely was. Lincoln was no fool and McClellan was no knave, but they sat in the White House and this monstrous accusation that the commander of the nation's armies was a traitor had to be taken up and considered, dark suspicion being the order of the day. What a change had taken place since the great days of the previous July when all anybody wanted was to entrust the country's fate to the young general from the West; what an unendurable tension must have been in the air, to make such an interview possible!

Yet McClellan seems to have missed the real point. He left the White House feeling that Lincoln himself more than half believed the charge, and he was naturally full of deep resentment. But somehow he never realized that the mere existence of this calumny must profoundly affect his own course of action. Here again was that unknown quantity in the military equation he had to solve, and there was nothing in the West Point textbooks to prepare him for it. How does a general beginning a great campaign act, when the men he must report to suspect that he wants to lose rather than to win?

The one thing that is obvious is that such a general does not act the way generals ordinarily act. For McClellan was not a general out of the military histories, solving according to the best scientific principles the problem which the civil power had handed him; he was a man living and working in an era so desperately beset that "abominable nonsense" could be believed by responsible public officials. What might be permitted to a general in another era would not be permitted to him. The existence of the deep and terrible suspicion and uncertainty which lay back of Lincoln's summons to the White House would have to be as much a factor in McClellan's calculations as would the strategic plans of General Joseph E. Johnston. Lincoln had tried to tip him off, and McClellan could see only that a great injustice was being done.

Events were not kind to him in the days immediately after the interview. Johnston's retreat became known. McClellan marched his troops down to Centreville and Manassas, partly for pursuit, in case the Confederate withdrawal offered an opening to strike, and partly to give the army practice in cross-country movements. Viewed by a military eye, the defensive works which Johnston had evacuated were indeed strong; but in the gun emplacements there remained large numbers of harmless wooden cannon—trimmed logs, painted black and upended over wagon wheels, menacing-looking from a distance but incapable of killing Union soldiers. Whether these Quaker guns had been there all the time or had simply been put in place by the wily Confederate leader (a man fertile in deceptive expedients) to cover the withdrawal, no one knew—or much cared: for the obvious fact was that in nearly eight months of command McClellan had never got his troops close enough to Johnston's lines to find out whether Johnston's guns would shoot or not. The story of the wooden guns went all across the land, and there was an uproar: so *this* was the danger that had kept the great Federal army immobile all fall and winter. Proper military caution was made to look like plain timidity. It was unfair, but there was no help for it; and the men who doubted McClellan's desire to win a victory had one more item to record against him.

None of this depressed the army itself. The boys enjoyed the march, even though they had strong remarks to make about the depth of the Virginia mud; and while they were innocently eager to go into action they were willing to agree that the general who kept them from assaulting the wicked entrenchments around Manassas had done them a good turn. McClellan deftly reminded them of this in a spirited address issued at Fairfax Courthouse in mid-March. After telling the soldiers that he was about to take them "where you all wish to be— the decisive battlefield," and remarking that the time of inaction was over, he declaimed:

"I am to watch over you as a parent over his children; and you know that your general loves you from the depths of his heart. It shall be my care, as it has ever been, to gain success with the least possible loss; but I know that, if it is necessary, you will willingly follow me to our graves for our righteous cause. . . . I shall demand of you great, heroic exertions, rapid and long marches, desperate combats, privations perhaps. We will share all these together; and when this sad war is over we will return to our homes, and feel that we can ask no higher honor than the proud consciousness that we belonged to the Army of the Potomac."[1]

The army was definitely going to move. With the Manassas line evacuated, it was going to go to the peninsula rather than to Urbanna, and the transports had been assembled. Lincoln was deeply dubious about the move, and he laid down as the unalterable guiding principle that, no matter where the army went or what it did, Washington must not for one minute be left unprotected. The steps he took to make certain of that point were not especially pleasing to McClellan. He first removed McClellan from the command of all the armies and limited him to command of the Army of the Potomac. (There may be some reason to suppose that this was simply a precautionary measure—that Lincoln intended to have a long look at McClellan in actual field operations and was ready to restore him to supreme command if everything went well. No one was named to the vacated job for some months. McClellan, of course, could see it only as a demotion, and it rankled.)² As a second step, having stipulated that the capital must at all costs be left secure, Lincoln called a council of McClellan and his corps commanders—those new corps commanders, in whose selection McClellan had had no voice—and asked them what force they, as military men, thought adequate to insure such security.

The assembled generals, after taking thought, reported that forty thousand men "in and about Washington" would be adequate. Lincoln accepted this figure, stipulating in addition that a substantial guard must also be left in the neighborhood of Manassas, to keep the Confederates from reoccupying their abandoned works. This was agreed to. There were men enough to provide this force and still leave McClellan ample means for his campaign on the peninsula. But while the men were going aboard ship and the first of the transports were dropping down the Potomac, high strategy began to get all snarled up in a question of arithmetic, and the way was paved for failure.

The plan was somewhat complicated. McClellan was going to take upward of a hundred thousand men down to Fortress Monroe for the march up the peninsula. In addition, McDowell, commanding one corps of the army, was to assemble thirty thousand-odd at Fredericksburg, whence he could take them down to join McClellan whenever McClellan summoned him. Up in the Shenandoah Valley there was General Banks, whose primary function was to keep the Rebels from cutting the line of the Baltimore and Ohio and erupting into Pennsylvania. Banks had more men than he needed, the situation in the valley being quiet, so he was instructed to leave part of his men there and bring the bulk of them over to Manassas. Farther west, in the mountain country where McClellan made his first reputation, there was General John Charles Frémont, the famous "Pathfinder" of California, the darling of the abolitionists, and a hero of all ardent Republicans.

Lincoln was already aware of Frémont's irritating eagerness to make high policy for the administration, and he knew that he was hopelessly inept as an administrator, but he had not yet discovered that the man was also completely incompetent as a soldier; and Frémont's mission was to slide southwest through the mountains in the general direction of eastern Tennessee, where there was strong Unionist sentiment that seemed worth cultivating and where there was also an important Confederate railway line that might profitably be seized. To give Frémont added strength, and also to put under his congenial command more of the German regiments in which antislavery sentiment ran so strong, Lincoln detached Blenker's division from McClellan and sent it west; he admitted to McClellan that political pressure which he felt unable to resist was chiefly responsible for this, and McClellan bitterly wrote it down as a sign that the President was weak-willed.

Everybody was beginning to move. Banks was bringing the larger part of his force east over the Blue Ridge, to take station at Manassas; McDowell was grouping his own divisions and preparing for the advance; the leading elements of the Army of the Potomac were going ashore at Fortress Monroe—going down from the ships on long, floating bridges and jumping into waist-deep water to wade the last few yards—and if the administration was making things difficult for McClellan, it was at least satisfied with the layout. And just then Stonewall Jackson upset the entire schedule.

What Jackson actually did, measured by any quantitative standard, was not really very important. He commanded fewer than four thousand men at that time, and he had them camped in the Shenandoah Valley to keep an eye on the Yankee invader. He got wind of Banks's move eastward, underestimated the numbers Banks was leaving behind, and moved boldly forward to the attack, hitting Shields's division at Kernstown, a few miles south of Winchester, one afternoon late in March. Since Shields had twice as many men as had been supposed, Jackson was roundly whipped and he had to retreat up the valley after a savage little battle which Shields's boys recalled later with vast pride—theirs was the only outfit in the Union Army which could say it had licked Stonewall Jackson in open fight. As a military spectacle this battle of Kernstown was notable chiefly because it showed what an iron-hard man Jackson was: he cashiered his best general afterward for withdrawing his men without orders. To be sure, the men were totally out of ammunition and were badly outnumbered, and the withdrawal was just plain common sense, but that made no difference: the retreat hadn't been ordered at headquarters, and anyhow, as Jackson sternly remarked, the men could have stayed and used their bayonets. This was rough on the general who got cashiered, but it had a notably stimulating effect on all other generals who served under Jackson thereafter.[3]

Seemingly, all that had happened was that Jackson had made an ill-advised attack and had been beaten. But the effects, by a round-about route, were felt afar off. Both McClellan and Banks agreed that if Jackson was strong enough to attack Shields he had better be watched pretty carefully, since the Rebels obviously had more men in the valley than had been supposed—neither general dreaming that Jackson had made his attack with so small a force. So it was decided that Banks must keep his entire command in the Shenandoah Valley; a strategic area of considerable sensitivity; and troops were drawn from the fortifications around Washington to occupy the Manassas-Centreville line which had originally been designated for Banks. That done, McClellan took a last look around, concluded that everything was under control, wrote a final note to the War Department showing how the troops which he was not taking with him were disposed, and set off for Fortress Monroe.

Now the dispositions he had made, as revised because of the battle of Kernstown, were certainly adequate to give Washington the protection Lincoln had insisted on. As a military man McClellan could honestly feel that he had done all that was required. But he wasn't called on to satisfy military men on this point; he had to satisfy politicians who were more than ready to see spooks under the bed, and from their point of view he had left himself wide open to the charge of ignoring his instructions—this general whom the Secretary of War and the administration leaders on Capitol Hill had already accused of treasonous intent. The actual figures are a bit dull, but they need to be looked at for a moment:

McClellan had left some seventy-three thousand men behind, as his note showed. Banks in the Shenandoah had slightly more than thirty-five thousand, some eighteen thousand were at Manassas and Warrenton, thirteen hundred or so were along the Potomac downstream from Washington, and there were approximately eighteen thousand in the Washington garrison. Total, seventy-three thousand and odd—enough, surely, to carry out the letter of his instructions?

Not to Lincoln's eyes, which were the eyes that had to be satisfied. To begin with, some ten thousand of these men were Blenker's Germans, bound west to serve with Frémont and hence out of calculation as far as the defense of Washington was concerned. In addition, when he figured the strength of Manassas and Washington, McClellan had included certain troops which were due to come in soon from the state capitals but which had not yet arrived; what Lincoln soon discovered was that there were actually less than thirteen thousand in the Washington garrison, almost all of them untrained men. As far as he could see, instead of the forty thousand men who were to be left "in and about Washington" there were only these almost useless thirteen thousand, plus the handful downstream, plus the troops at Manassas and Warrenton. All in all, after carefully counting heads, Lincoln could find fewer than twenty-eight thousand soldiers in and near the capital.

To this, of course, McClellan would have replied that the thirty-five thousand under Banks in the Shenandoah should properly be added, since they were near enough and strong enough to make their presence felt. But it was asking a little too much to expect Lincoln and the Cabinet to see it that way under the conditions then prevailing. To civilian eyes the force in the Shenandoah was a long way off. No one in Washington could forget that the Union had had a fairly strong army in the Shenandoah when McDowell was beaten at Bull Run: its presence in the valley had not served to protect Washington in July 1861, and an unmilitary President and Cabinet could hardly be blamed for feeling that things might be no different in April of 1862. Add it up any way he tried, the President could only conclude that McClellan had not done what he had been told to do. The capital was not properly defended.

The reaction to this was immediate. McClellan had barely started up the peninsula when he was officially notified that McDowell's corps at Fredericksburg had been withdrawn from his command and would get its orders hereafter direct from Washington.

Which meant that his campaign started under a great handicap. McClellan himself got off the boat at Fortress Monroe on April 2 and found that he had on hand—disembarked, equipped, and ready to go—some fifty-eight thousand men: five infantry divisions, a scattering of cavalry, and a hundred guns. He at once started them up the roads toward Yorktown, with instructions that the rest of the army was to follow as soon as it arrived. The first thing he discovered was that someone had steered him wrong about those sandy roads on the peninsula. Instead of being sandy they were uniformly of pure gumbo mud, with hollow crowns so that they collected whatever water might be coming down; and the weather turned rainy, so that the roads quickly became bottomless beyond anything in anybody's imagination. Guns and wagons sank to the axles and beyond. One officer wrote later that he saw a mule sink completely out of sight, all but its ears, in the middle of what was suppposed to be a main road. He added that it was a rather small mule.[4]

McClellan's next discovery was that the Rebels had dug a line of entrenchments running completely across the peninsula from Yorktown, on the York River, to the mouth of Warwick Creek, on the James. Emplaced in these lines they had several dozen heavy naval guns (acquired a year earlier through capture of the United States navy yard at Norfolk) plus a number of fieldpieces, and they appeared to have all the infantry they needed. The approaches to this line led through swamps and tangled woodlands, and every foot of road would have to be corduroyed before guns could be brought up. Bewiskered old General Heintzelman, leading the advance, reported—somewhat hastily, it would seem—that a direct assault was out of the question. McClellan decided there would have to be a siege. Under his original plans he would simply have brought McDowell down from the north to take the Rebel works in the rear, thereby forcing their immediate evacuation, but McDowell was no longer his to command. To get past these lines McClellan would have to go straight over them, and that appeared to be a matter for the slow, methodical, step-by-step process of digging parallels, moving up heavy guns, and getting everything ready to blast the Rebel works off the face of the earth by sheer weight of gunfire.

Concerning which there was to be great argument, then and thereafter. When McClellan got his first look at the Yorktown lines, the Confederate force there was under command of General John B. Magruder, who had no more than twelve thousand men and who felt the lines to be faulty both in design and in construction. Magruder was never especially distinguished as a combat general, but in his idle moments he had considerable talent as an amateur actor, and he now called on this theatrical ability to help him. He marched a couple of regiments through a clearing, in sight of the Federal advance guard, double-quicked them around a little forest out of sight, and then marched them through the clearing again—over and over, like a stage manager using a dozen adenoidal spear carriers to represent Caesar's legions. The device worked, and Heintzelman reported the Rebels present in great strength and with many more coming up.

Joe Johnston, hastening down in advance of his own troops to have a look at the situation, appreciated the dodge but felt it could hardly be relied on forever. He galloped back to Richmond in dismay to report that the lines were quite untenable: McClellan could get through or around them any time he wanted to make a real push, to put the whole Confederate Army there would simply be to put it in a trap, best to evacuate at once and prepare to fight near Richmond. Davis and Lee overruled him, on the ground that McClellan's advance must be delayed as long as possible. Evacuation would mean the fall of Norfolk, and that would mean the loss of the famous ironclad *Virginia* (ex-*Merrimac*), which drew too much water to come up James River to Richmond and was too unseaworthy to go out beyond the Virginia capes into the open ocean. Also—and far more important, the entire Confederate Army was about to undergo complete reorganization. The men had originally enlisted for twelve months, and their terms were just now expiring. Conscription was going into effect and none of the manpower would actually be lost, but for some weeks there would be complete turmoil, not to say chaos, with officers being shifted or replaced all over the lot and with every regiment having a grand reshuffle. It would be almost impossible to maneuver or to fight in the open until that was over. So Johnston, much against his will, took his army down to Yorktown to stave off the advance as long as he could. When he got it there his pessimism deepened; to Lee, in Richmond, he wrote that "no one but McClellan could have hesitated to attack." But the attack was not made. Instead there was a gradual, painstaking building up of Federal strength in preparation for a final, overwhelming artillery bombardment. Johnston knew that when this assault came he would have to leave, but mercifully (to his eyes) the assault was long in coming.

Lincoln and his Cabinet knew nothing of Johnston's trepidation or of the disorganized condition of the Confederate Army. What they did know was that McClellan's army was simply sitting down before the enemy's works, waiting. They had already begun to suspect that McClellan was a general who moved very slowly; now, knowing little or nothing of the obstacle in front of him, knowing only that weeks were passing without an advance, they found suspicion hardening to certainty. This was hard to bear; for men who already doubted McClellan's good faith and loyalty it was quite impossible to bear in silence. The clamor against McClellan deepened, became a clamor against Lincoln for keeping him in command. Lincoln tried to give McClellan an understanding of this increasing pressure as a factor which McClellan would have to keep constantly in mind when he made his plans; tried to show him that it was a pressure which, political conditions being what they so regettably were, even the President of the United States might finally be unable to resist. On April 9 Lincoln wrote him: "And once more let me tell you, it is indispensable to *you* that you strike a blow. I am powerless to help this." He concluded the letter by assuring McClellan that he would sustain him as far as he could: "but," he added, "you must act."

This was easy enough to order from Washington. McClellan might be pardoned for feeling that he was being second-guessed in an unconscionable manner by men who knew nothing about what he was really up against. To say "Strike a blow!" was simple enough; actually striking it meant sending young men through swamps and almost impassable second-growth timber against enemies amply protected by heavy earthworks, and even at this date it is not easy to say that such an attack would have won. The men of the Army of the Potomac were to learn that when the Army of Northern Virginia was once properly dug in, on ground where it proposed to linger, it could be uncommonly hard to move. Joe Johnston might have been wrong and McClellan might have been right. The trouble was that being right wasn't quite enough. Nothing was going to satisfy Washington except results, and Washington was not going to wait too long for them, either. Nobody was going to be reasonable about anything.

2. THE VOICE OF CAUTION

In the end, the big show at Yorktown never came off. The army waited in front of the Rebel lines for a month, nerving itself for the great test; and then one morning the pickets sent back word that the enemy trenches were all empty. Patrols went groping forward and confirmed the news: nobody there, nothing left but a few dozen heavy guns which the Confederates had been unable to move—not wooden guns this time, as at Manassas, but sure-enough cannon of the navy model, too heavy and cumbersome to be taken along by an army that proposed to make speed on the retreat. McClellan had finally completed his approaches, and his siege guns and heavy mortars were all in position. In one more day he would have been ready to open a shattering bombardment, and Johnston had decided not to wait for him.

So instead of the great drama of a ten-mile cannonade and a mighty assault by storming battle lines extending beyond vision, what the army got was a floundering pursuit and a nasty, confused rear-guard action in damp thickets and flat, dismal fields, where reality was limited to the actions of the nearest dozen comrades, where men fell killed or maimed without seeing the enemies who struck them, and where it was quite impossible for most of the men to get any sort of idea of what was actually going on.

The troops got across the empty entrenchments and moved up the unspeakable roads, with a dull rain coming down, over a soggy level country of soaked fields and gloomy woods and scattered farms, none of them like the familiar green farms of home; and far up ahead the men heard the noise of fighting, and the roads were hopelessly clogged with mired wagon trains, and Phil Kearny came galloping up to force a way for his troops. He stormed mightily, put two officers of the train guard under arrest, demanded that the wagons be tipped over off the road or burned where they stood—he was ordered up to fight and he would have the road regardless. Admiring, the soldiers listened while he roared: "I will show you what fire *feels* like unless you set the torch to your goddamned cowardly wagons!"[1] And his men finally got by the tangle, passing open fields, wherein huge bodies of troops were unaccountably standing quite idle, and went plodding unevenly forward until they got up within range; and there, in the obscuring haze of smoke, the boys formed line as well as they could and blazed away in the general direction of the bursts of rifle fire that were coming out of the woods and fields a couple of hundred yards away.

Some of them were formed out in the open and some in dense forest, full of fallen trees and bothersome underbrush; the enemy was a more or less invisible presence—an area, like a hazy, indistinct wood lot, or a smoky line of rail fence with briars grown up around it, from which came little spitting streaks of flame, and whistling bullets that made an unnerving noise. The 55th New York, with its baggy red French pants quite rain-soaked, got into a stretch of timber where the soldiers could hear the Rebels but could seldom see them. They stayed there for three hours, firing as fast as they could load, using up sixteen thousand rounds of ammunition, and—as the colonel discovered later, when he went out to examine the ground in front of them—killing just fifteen Confederates. The colonel made a rough calculation and figured that perhaps a hundred and fifty more of the enemy, at a maximum, had been wounded: where had all those bullets gone, anyhow?

Hooker's men discovered that the neat, formal battle lines of the training camp didn't seem to make their appearance in actual combat. Instead everybody got behind a tree or a stump or a boulder if he could possibly manage it.

One private, thus protected, called out to a buddy: "Why don't you get behind a tree?" and heard the buddy shout: "Confound it! There ain't enough for the officers!" Men of the 5th New York went up to the front through a little cemetery where were buried Confederate soldiers who had died during the preceding winter. The little burying ground was full of graves, but over the gate someone had tacked a sign: "Come along, Yank, there's room outside to bury you."[2]

The firing at last died down and the Rebels drew off. It was only a rear-guard action, after all, and Joe Johnston had no intention of keeping his men there to make a finish fight of it. Then the Federals at the front heard a great cheering behind them, and they knew what caused it and joined in it lustily; and there, spattering across the damp fields, came General McClellan, blue coat all stained with mud, a glazed covering over his cap, his staff riding furiously in a vain effort to keep up with him. McClellan rode all along the lines, each regiment got a chance to cheer, and night came down on the army's first battlefield.

Among the higher echelons the battle gave rise to grumblings. Heintzelman, who had command of the advance, asserted that Sumner was on the field with thirty thousand men and failed to get any of them into action, and the two generals argued the matter hotly. McClellan, coming up as the fight ended, got the idea that most of the fighting had been done by Hancock's brigade, which had indeed done well, though it got into the action late. He built his dispatch around that part of the battle, telegraphing Stanton that "Hancock was superb," and thereby roused the anger of Hooker and Kearny, whose troops had suffered far more than had Hancock's, and who felt that the major general commanding was purposely slighting them. But in the end that was straightened out, and the army went toiling on up the peninsula, while Johnston pulled his own troops close to Richmond and made ready for a finish fight.

The men were beginning to get their officers sorted out by now. Hooker and Kearny were already known to the whole army. They had fire, ardor, the quality which writers of that generation called "dash"; like McClellan, they insisted that members of their staff be brightly uniformed and excellently mounted, and they made their rounds as McClellan made his, with a fine brave clattering and show, very martial and stimulating for the young soldiers to see. They built high morale in their troops. Hooker's division, going into action in this rear-guard fight at Williamsburg, saw a regiment of cavalry stringing out its mounted line in the rear, according to army custom, to check stragglers and round up laggards. Angrily the men set up the shout: "Hooker's men don't need any cavalry to make *them* stay in front!"

All kinds of stories were beginning to cluster about Kearny. His headquarters wagon carried a fancy carpet for his tent, a special camp bed imported from Europe, and a huge stock of imported wines and brandies; and he had a field kitchen on wheels, on the French army model, which always kept up with his headquarters so that he could have hot meals. (Kearny was independently wealthy and could afford such frills.) Officers of the New Jersey brigade claimed that he had happened along once just as they had taken over a planter's house for brigade headquarters. They found in the parlor a decanter of whisky which they hesitated to drink, fearing that it had been poisoned—army rumor said that was a favorite Rebel trick. Kearny listened as they explained their fears, then poured out a thumping major general's dose and drank it down. "If I'm not dead in fifteen minutes," he said, turning to mount his horse, "go ahead and drink all you want."[3]

The men were getting acquainted with Edwin V. Sumner, too; a tough old man with white hair and beard, who had been in the army since 1819 and had a tremendous booming voice. They called him "Bull Sumner," or "The Bull of the Woods," and liked him even though he was a great martinet, with old-army ideas about discipline. He was a formidable-looking general, now in command of an army corps, always erect and proud in the saddle, and he never quite real-

ized that the army was any different now than it had been before the war, when
he spent almost forty years in slow progress from second lieutenant to colonel.
Youthful Major Thomas Hyde of the 7th Maine was sent to deliver some report
to him one day; Sumner looked him over from head to foot and finally burst out:
"You a major? My God, sir, you will command the armies of the United States
at my age, sir!"[4] After one searing fight the 66th New York showed up under
temporary command of a second lieutenant, who happened to be the senior
surviving officer. Sumner looked at the boy and instead of seeing the frightfully
cut-up regiment he saw only that a shavetail had a colonel's job. He shook his
head and said: "If I had found myself, when a second lieutenant, in command of
so fine a regiment, I would have considered my fortune made."[5] He was still the
cavalry colonel of the Indian-fighting plains army, with all the defects and virtues which that implies; not qualified for proper corps command, but a fine old
smoothbore for all that.

Then there was Heintzelman, another corps commander, very much like
Sumner in many ways; an old-timer, an Indian fighter from the plains, rugged
and stiff and hard, still a regimental officer at heart, brave enough for a dozen
men but unfitted for any problem of leadership that extended beyond men he
could reach with his own voice. Like Sumner, he could put Johnny-come-lately
officers in their place. When Oliver Otis Howard first reported to him, proudly
bringing in his new 3rd Maine Regiment, Heintzelman looked the men over and
said to Howard: "You have a fine regiment; they march well and they give
promise for the future; but they are not well drilled—poor officers but good-
looking men!"[6] Heintzelman had been in the middle of the fighting at the first
battle of Bull Run, where he had been badly wounded.

The Pennsylvania troops were beginning to know George Gordon Meade,
even though he was as yet only a brigadier, and a new one to boot. He was a tall,
grizzled man with a fine hawk's nose and a perfectly terrible temper, which
would lash out furiously at any officer who failed to do his job. A war correspondent considered that Meade, on horseback, looked "like a picture of a hel-
meted knight of old"; one of his staff complained that he rode "in a most
aggravating way, neither at a walk nor a gallop but at sort of an amble." He was
notably cool under fire; sat his horse with his staff, one time, surveying the situation through glasses, while Rebel bullets whizzed wickedly all around and the
staff earnestly wished the general would finish his reconnoissance so they could
get out of there; lowered his glass at last, took in the staff's nervousness, and remarked sardonically that maybe they had better leave—"This is pretty hot; it
may kill some of our horses." He lacked the ability to inspire troops; once remarked, without any rancor, that he had heard his men call him "a damned
goggle-eyed old snapping turtle." He never drew the kind of cheers that Hooker
and Kearny always got, but he kept his command in good shape and had a
sharp eye for details. He was wholly admirable as a man, with no trace of self-
seeking; would reach high place in the army, do his hard job to the best of his
ability, and indulge in no argument or complaint when promotion and praise finally missed him.[7]

One by one the officers were beginning to stand out, for this virtue or that. Already noticeable was an extremely junior second lieutenant on McClellan's
staff, to which he had recently graduated from Kearny's: a broad-shouldered
six-footer with a slim waist and muscular legs, fresh out of West Point, known as
one of the finest horsemen in the army—George Armstrong Custer, who was to
survive hot actions of this war only to die under the guns of the Sioux on the
Montana hills. Custer was familiarly known as "Cinnamon" because of the cin-
namon-flavored hair oil he used so liberally; wore long glistening curls and a
show-off uniform with a tight hussar jacket and black trousers trimmed with
gold lace, and looked, as another staff member remarked, "like a circus rider
gone mad." Like Confederate George Pickett, who also wore curls, and Jeb

Stuart, who was also a show-off, he was all soldier. He first impressed himself on McClellan's attention when the general, accompanied by his gilded staff, rode up to the bank of the Chickahominy for the first time and remarked, "I wish I knew how deep it is." The staff exchanged glances, looked thoughtfully at the dark water, began to make estimates. Custer spurred up to the bank, muttering "I'll damn soon show him," and rode his floundering horse out to the middle of the river, where he turned in his saddle and called out, "That's how deep it is, General."[8]

But standing out above all these, of course, was McClellan. He had become the general who could do no wrong, in the soldiers' eyes, and they blithely over-looked things that would have earned bleak hatred for any other general. Officers of an anti-slavery cast noted suspiciously that McClellan took uncommon pains to protect Rebel property from the moment the army landed on the peninsula. One of them complained bitterly that provost guards were to be found protecting every farmhouse, stable, kitchen garden, and well, and asserted that they stood guard even over the rail fences, regarded by soldiers as prime material for campfires. "I have seen our men," protested this officer, waxing warm, "covered with dust and overcome by the heat, try in vain to get water from wells overflowing, from which stringent orders drove them away because the supply of water for a Rebel family might be diminished. I have also seen them, covered with mud and shivering with the rain, prevented by orders of the general-in-chief from warming themselves with the fence rails of dry wood which were ready at their hands, because the cattle of a Rebel farmer might get out and eat the grass in his fields while he was rebuilding his fences."[9] Another officer noted indignantly that the farmers admitted that McClellan protected their property against the men of his army better than Johnston had protected it against the Confederates.

But somehow all of this made no difference whatever. Up around Fredericksburg, at that time, General McDowell was winning the lasting enmity of his own soldiers by his care to protect civilian property; here was McClellan, right in the presence of the enemy, doing the same thing and rising even higher in popularity. How account for it? How, except by saying that one man had the magic touch and the other lacked it. But the magic touch is not entirely a mystery, even so. McClellan took extraordinary pains to make his men feel that they were good soldiers and that the commanding general knew they were good and was grateful to them for it. After the fight at Williamsburg he was prompt to visit the regiments which had been engaged and thank them for their fine work. In one newspaper dispatch we see him visiting, in succession, the 5th Wisconsin, the 7th Maine, and the 33rd New York, making a brief, graceful little speech to each: "I have come to thank you for your bravery and good conduct in the action of yesterday. . . . You acted like veterans! Veterans of many battles could not have done better!"

Then there was the time, a few days later, when the 4th Michigan, plus a squadron of cavalry and a few engineer troops, made a reconnoissance across the Chickahominy and collided with Rebel troops, driving them off and losing some eight men in killed and wounded while doing it. McClellan visited the regiment as soon as it got back to camp; in front of the men he shook hands with the colonel and congratulated him, shook hands also with the captain who had been mentioned for gallant conduct. Then he turned to the men themselves, not with a little speech this time but with an easy, friendly comradeship. "How do you feel, boys?" There was a quick chorus of "We feel bully, General!" Still casual, McClellan asked them: "Do you think anything can stop you from going to Richmond?" And the regiment yelled "No!" in a shout that Jefferson Davis might almost have heard, off beyond the swamps in the Confederate capital; and McClellan gave the men his gay little salute and galloped away, leaving the Michigan boys feeling almost as if they had married him.[10]

And if there is a mystery in the way McClellan's men could ignore his care to protect Rebel property while McDowell's men found the same care unforgivable when McDowell displayed it, there is equal mystery in the way those actions were regarded back in Washington. The anti-slavery Republicans, already suspecting that McClellan proposed to sell out the Union, found in his protection of Confederate civilian property strong corroboration of their suspicion. Yet McDowell, who was doing exactly the same thing, was the chosen hero of these men. They rejoiced when he was taken out from under McClellan's command and would have liked to see him in McClellan's place; to their minds he was the shining example of what a general ought to be. Again, the answer, to an extent, may be much the same in reverse: one general had the touch for dealing with political persons at the capital, and the other general did not.

Indeed, that queer riddle of what a general could and could not do goes even farther. At the time when McClellan was slowly pursuing Johnston up to the edge of Richmond, General Halleck, out in the Mississippi Valley, was pursuing General Beauregard, who was retreating down into northern Mississippi after the dreadful, mangling fight at Shiloh. McClellan was pursuing very cautiously. His reasons might have been good or they might have been bad; in any case, his pursuit was slow, which was a damning mark against him with Secretary Stanton and the radical group in Congress. Halleck, who had more of a numerical superiority over Beauregard than McClellan had over Johnston, was edging forward with a sluggish deliberation that made McClellan's advance look precipitate, averaging hardly a mile a day and entrenching up to the ears every evening. Yet Halleck, like McDowell, was a hero to Stanton and his crowd, rising in favor daily, destined before long to be brought to the capital as supreme commander. McClellan's hesitation was proof of his disloyalty; Halleck's hesitation, twice as pronounced and far less justified, was simply ignored—by everyone except Lincoln, who felt that both men ought to hurry a little more.

All of this proves nothing much except that the nation was running a high fever and had a touch of delirium now and then. But the effects were tragic, for in the end it was those amateur soldiers down among the Chickahominy swamps who were going to have to pay for it. The relations between a general and his superiors can't be poisoned in just one direction; the poison works both ways, and if the radicals believed McClellan to be a villain, McClellan returned the sentiment with interest. His letters to his wife no longer showed merely the irritation and nervous strain of a young general who was being crowded a little too hard; they reflected downright fury, coupled with a conviction that the civilians who were working against him were scoundrels. The detachment of McDowell's corps was "the most infamous thing that history has recorded." When the President urged McClellan to break the Confederate lines, "I was much tempted to reply that he had better come and do it himself." Long before the siege of Yorktown ended he was writing: "Don't worry about the wretches; they have done nearly their worst, and can't do much more. I am sure that I will win in the end, in spite of all their rascality. History will present a sad record of these traitors who are willing to sacrifice the country and its army for personal spite and personal aims." He spoke of his predicament—a man with "the Rebels on one side, and the abolitionists and other scoundrels on the other"—and a few days later wrote that "those hounds in Washington are after me again."

The main collison with the Confederate Army had not yet taken place. Yet already there had developed this amazing situation: the Secretary of War, plus leading administration senators, believed the general commanding the army to be a traitor who would rather lose than win, and the general, in his turn, believed that *they* were traitors who would rather see the country lose than permit him to win. That word "treason," so rare in American history, was dancing back and forth like a tennis ball. Misunderstanding between the home office and the man in the field had become complete; had developed a breach not to be healed, with hatred and anger and terrible suspicions that would be incredible were they not all part of the record. Like a steaming, choking fog, this atmosphere hung over the army, poisoning its chances, staining its banners. Whoever was most at fault, this heavy intangible lay across the army's path, ready to take the lives of boys who had had no part in it and who would die not knowing that it existed.

Now there could be only one road to salvation for McClellan, for his soldiers, and for the country itself. McClellan had to win. Victory in front of Richmond would swallow up everything, leaving the hot accusations and recriminations as dry bones which the historians might pick over at their convenience. The weight that rested on the broad shoulders of the young general was heavier than he knew. For if the war itself was the supreme test of democratic institutions—"testing whether . . . any nation so conceived and so dedicated can long endure"—the fighting of it was testing the qualities of democracy's leaders. The unfathomable strength of the country had been placed at these leaders' disposal. If that strength could be used properly, the war could be won quickly and the country would be spared much suffering. If it could not, if leadership failed to measure up, then the people themselves would have to carry the whole load, and everything they had hoped for in this bright land of promise would depend on their finding within themselves enough endurance and heroism and patience to meet the unimaginable agony which their leaders had been unable to spare them.

To which it may be said that McClellan did the best he could and that he worked under terrible handicaps, some of which he created himself. One of them—in some ways, considering his own inner nature, the most damaging of all—was a matter of detail: selection of the wrong man to run G-2, Army Intelligence—Army Secret Service, as they called it in those days.

G-2 was handled by a short, stocky, bearded man who was known around headquarters as Major E. J. Allen, and who in reality was Allen Pinkerton, famous head of a famous detective agency in Chicago. First of the country's great private detectives, Pinkerton had genuine talent, coupled with a certain flair for publicity; he had handled many jobs for railroads, as a railroad man McClellan had known him before the war, and when McClellan became a major general he called in Pinkerton and put him in charge of military intelligence, espionage and counterespionage alike. Pinkerton built up quite an organization, and in the long run what McClellan knew about the Confederate Army that was facing him was mostly what Pinkerton told him.

As it turned out, Pinkerton was a fine man for running down train robbers and absconding bank cashiers but was completely miscast as chief of military intelligence. He had energy, courage, administrative ability, and imagination—too much imagination, perhaps, for he was operating in an era when a fine hairline separated the ridiculously false from the frighteningly true. Early in 1861, while he was still in civil life, he had gone into Maryland at the bidding of the president of the Philadelphia, Wilmington and Baltimore Railroad, who had heard of secessionist plots to sabotage the railroad leading to Washington and wanted to find out about them. Pinkerton planted operatives in Baltimore, Havre de Grace, Perryville, and other places, and presently reported that he had discovered not merely a plan to sabotage the railroad but a widespread plot to kill Abraham Lincoln before his inauguration.

Pinkerton's men lived with this plot; after the war, in his memoirs, Pinkerton told how they got into secret societies, mingled freely with secession-minded Baltimore blue-bloods, cultivated beautiful friendships with Baltimore belles "under the witching spell of music and moonlit nature," and uncovered a far-reaching, elaborately detailed conspiracy for assassination. It is something of a comedown to find that the leader of this conspiracy was a barber in a Baltimore hotel—the build-up about Southern aristocrats leads one to expect a Virginia Carter, at the very least—but so it was. One of Pinkerton's men sat in on a secret meeting where men drew lots to see who would actually do the killing, another one came up with information about plans for cutting telegraph wires and destroying railroad bridges (presumably so that the North could neither learn of the assassination nor do anything about it after it had happened), and Pinkerton submitted a full report while Lincoln was on his way east.

The report caused much excitement, quite naturally: it was either a perfect script for a theatrical thriller or an astounding revelation of deadly plotting which simply had to be frustrated. As a final result Lincoln changed his plans: slipped quietly out of Harrisburg and came into Washington by sleeping car a day ahead of time, thereby arousing much derision and criticism.

Lincoln seems never to have been quite certain whether Pinkerton had saved his life or induced him to make a fool of himself, and nobody since then has been able to be quite certain about it either. The plot itself, as Pinkerton described it in his book, has a wildly improbable sound, with the conspirators behaving in an impossibly stagy manner; but just as one concludes that the thing simply could not have been true, there comes the recollection that when the 6th Massachusetts Infantry passed through Baltimore just after Fort Sumter there was precisely the kind of riot that Pinkerton's men had mentioned as a projected stage setting for the murder of Lincoln: a riot in which angry men fired real guns and in which both soldiers and citizens of Baltimore were killed. Also, in 1865, a plot quite as harebrained as anything Pinkerton's men reported did result in Lincoln's death. Men were living in the center of a lurid and improbable melodrama in those days, and if it was fantastic, it was very real; just as the tale strains credulity to the breaking point somebody is killed—by pistol or by knife or by hangman's noose. They might have exaggerated their stage effects in a most inartistic manner, but their guns were not loaded with blank cartridges.

At any rate, Pinkerton took over McClellan's military intelligence problem and applied real ingenuity to the job. His men went fanning out behind the Confederate lines to some purpose; one of them actually got in with Confederate Secretary of War Judah Benjamin, in the days before McClellan took his army down to the peninsula, and carried a pass signed by that official and became a member of a Rebel counterespionage outfit that was trying to catch Yankee spies. Each of Pinkerton's men carried a pass through the Union lines written in invisible ink which became visible only on exposure to sunlight. They got in touch with a secret organization of colored men in Richmond, the Loyal League, who met in cellars and attics and whose password was "Friends of Uncle Abe," and who helped the Union operatives in and out of the Rebel capital. One agent even joined a Confederate spy team and became a courier, carrying messages back and forth between Richmond and Baltimore—the messages, of course, all being copied for McClellan before delivery. Timothy Webster, the greatest of Pinkerton's spies, was finally caught and hanged. Other spies disappeared, as spies do in wartime; but all in all they had perfected a genuinely remarkable system for getting forbidden information out of Richmond.

But the incomprehensible part about it all is that with this elaborate espionage network, operated by experts and staffed by brave and intelligent men, the information that was brought to McClellan was so disastrously wrong. Disastrously, because it made the Rebel armies appear more than twice as large as they really were and because McClellan believed it and acted on it. Pinkerton's spy system was well organized, bold, successful—and McClellan would have been infinitely better off if he had had no spy system whatever.

While McClellan was waiting in front of Yorktown, Pinkerton proudly gave him a report showing that Joe Johnston had from 100,000 to 120,000 men in line against him. This information, he said, came from "officers of their army and from persons connected with their commissary department," where they were issuing 119,000 daily rations—the only instance in history, probably, where the Confederates were accused of overfeeding their men. Pinkerton added that it was safe to assume that his estimate was under rather than over the real figure. Now the only trouble with that was that Johnston at the time had barely 50,000 men on the peninsula. He was shockingly outnumbered and he knew it, and the only hope that he could see was for Davis to strip the Southern coast line bare of troops, no matter what the cost locally, and reinforce him with every available man so that he might be brought near enough to McClellan's numbers to have some chance of fighting a successful battle.

Some six weeks later, on the eve of the fateful Seven Days' Battles in front of Richmond, Pinkerton assured McClellan that Lee had more than 180,000 men facing him; probably many more, since the agents had actually identified 200 regiments of infantry and cavalry, eight battalions of independent troops, five battalions of artillery, twelve companies of independent infantry and cavalry, and forty-six additional companies of artillery, and the Rebels undoubtedly had many other outfits present whose designations could not be learned. After the fighting was over, Pinkerton reported that he was satisfied the Rebels had at least 200,000 men in the battles, of whom 40,000 were casualties. Long after the war Pinkerton continued to insist on the accuracy of his figures; he had obtained them, he said, "from prisoners of war, contrabands, loyal southerners, deserters, blockade-runners and from actual observations by trustworthy scouts."

So to all the other handicaps that beset him—distrust at the War Department, troops withheld, strategic plans countermanded—McClellan had his final, ruinous handicap to contend with: heavily outnumbering his opponent, he was led to believe that his opponent heavily outnumbered him. He and his staff took Pinkerton's word as gospel. This was hard to do sometimes; McClellan's headquarters had a fairly accurate count on the number of divisions in the Confederate Army, and that number could not conceivably account for the vast hordes of men supposed to be present. But instead of questioning Pinkerton's figures, headquarters simply assumed that those divisions were "grand divisions"—oversized groupings of two or more army crops, such as Burnside set up later at Fredericksburg—and continued to believe that from 180,000 to 200,000 armed Rebels were in front of them.

It was just tragic that this had to happen to McClellan, of all generals; for this man must always listen, at the last, to the voice of caution, the subconscious warning that action may bring unlooked-for perils, the lurking fear that maybe some contingency has not been calculated. Before he can act, everything must be ready, every preparation must be made, every possible mischance must be provided for. Now, with his own career and the nation's fate balanced on a knife's edge, with Lincoln quietly warning him that he must at all costs *do* something, there is this final deterrent: conducting an offensive campaign deep in enemy territory, he finds himself to be dreadfully outnumbered—so much so that only a very great daring would make an offensive possible at all. Almost everything he did and failed to do in this campaign can be explained by that one fact.

3. TOMORROW NEVER COMES

With all of these difficulties of espionage, counting numbers, and weighing risks, the men in the ranks had nothing to do. They never even saw their own army all in a mass, to say nothing of the enemy's. In this broken, wooded country the Rebels were usually visible, even in battle, only as small detachments. The men could see that they were edging up toward Richmond. Heintzelman's corps was close enough so that the men could hear the church bells ringing in the capital, and if progress looked slow to people back in Washington, it seemed fast enough to the men who had to tramp along the bottom-less roads.

There had been too much rain, and in the lowlands the humid heat was an oppressive weight to boys from the North, and a general air of weather-beaten tarnish began to appear on brigades that had been natty and polished when they came off the transports. Officers who had been bright with gold-embroidered shoulder straps, red sashes, and plumed felt hats became more somber-looking; many of them bought privates' uniforms and sewed the insignia of rank on the shoulders, having learned that in a fight or on the picket lines the enemy believed in picking off the officers first. Regiments that had worn fancy leggings or gaiters began to discard them, the men finding that it was more comfortable to roll the trouser leg snug at the ankle and haul the gray regulation sock up over it. Paper collars had disappeared, and the men in the Zouave regiments, which wore gay red pants and yellow sashes, topped by Turkish-style fezzes, began to wonder if these uniforms were not both unduly conspicuous on the firing line and excessively hard to keep neat.

When the actual fighting came it was desperately confused, and even the generals seem to have had trouble understanding what was happening. Finding McClellan with part of his army south of the Chickahominy and part of it north, Joe Johnston waited for a heavy rain to swell the river and make passage between the two wings more difficult, and then fell hard on the part that was south of the river. The battle of Seven Pines, or Fair Oaks, which resulted was bloody enough, with five or six thousand casualties on each side, but it was indecisive. The diaries and memoirs of the men who fought in it cannot be put together to make a picture of anything but a series of savage combats in wood and swamp, where wounded Confederates drowned in stagnant pools and wounded Federals were burned when powder flashes set fire to dead leaves and underbrush insufficiently dampened by rain; and there seemed to be no tactical plans other than a simple urge to get the men up into places where they could shoot at each other.

Things went badly, and Bull Sumner was ordered to bring his corps over from the north side and get into the fight. He marched his men up to the flooded river to find that the makeshift bridge the engineers had built was ready to float off downstream—center part loose from its underpinning, foaming water all about, engineer officer coming up to tell him that the bridge was unsafe and it was impossible to use it. Sumner roared: "Impossible? Sir, I tell you I *can* cross! I am ordered!" And cross he did, too, although his men waded knee-deep in water that swirled over the planking. The muddy roads on the south side were so soupy that his artillery almost sank out of sight, and the gunners worked up to their waists in mud and water to inch the guns along. When they finally got them into action, each recoil drove the wheels down into the soft ground nearly to the hub caps.[1] Sumner sent the 5th New Hampshire in on a counterattack after a Confederate charge had been repulsed. The regiment's colonel, a former newspaper editor named E. E. Cross, who had lived in the Far West and had fought both Mexicans and Indians, exhorted the men: "Charge 'em like hell, boys—show 'em you *are* damned Yankees!" As the regiment advanced, Cross fell wounded. He propped himself up on an elbow, and when some of the men came over to help him he told them: "Never mine me—whip the enemy first and take care of me afterward."[2]

General William H. French, stout and apoplectic, with a face so red that he always looked as if his collar were choking him, set out to gallop boldly along the line of his brigade as it prepared to go into action, and dropped completely out of sight in muddy water when his horse bounced into what had been thought to be a mere surface puddle. The general came up blowing and swearing mightily, while the brigade shouted with laughter. A lieutenant in the 57th New York was told by his colonel to lead his company off through the wood to get an enfilade fire on a Confederate detachment in front. He did so, and the Rebels withdrew, new troops being, as Longstreet indelicately remarked, "as sensitive about the flanks as a virgin." When the metropolitan papers came to camp a few days later the lieutenant discovered that this modest little exploit had become a grand charge, led by a general, which had driven the enemy with great slaughter. Reflecting on the way a small story can become great, the lieutenant wrote: "If the history of past ages is as much tainted as the history we are now making—then alas poor Yorick!"[3] Toward the end of the battle, some anonymous Federal put a bullet through Joe Johnston's shoulder, and a moment later a shell fragment hit the general in the chest and unhorsed him: and thus the one significant result of the battle—its significance not guessed at the time—was that Robert E. Lee became commander of the Army of Northern Virginia.

After the battle things were about as they had been, except that a horrible stench hung over the whole broad valley. McClellan felt that the attack had been intelligently conceived—"It is the only smart thing Joe Johnston has yet attempted. It was *very* smart," he was quoted as saying—and he busied himself getting the roads improved so that heavy guns could be moved up, while he saw to it that his lines were protected by proper entrenchments, and he moved more and more of the army over to the south side of the river. He had each division lined up for dress parade a few days after the battle, and a stirring order from himself was read to the men:

"Soldiers of the Army of the Potomac! I have fulfilled at least a part of my promise to you. You are now face to face with the Rebels, who are held at bay in front of their capital. The final and decisive battle is at hand. Unless you believe your past history, the result cannot be for a moment doubtful." The proclamation went on and on, assuring the soldiers that they were better fighters than their enemies, and concluding: "Soldiers! I will be with you in this battle and share its dangers with you. Our confidence in each other is now founded upon the past. Let us strike the blow which is to restore peace and union to this distracted land. Upon your valor, discipline and mutual confidence the result depends."[4]

It is written that the soldiers cheered when they heard these fine words, and they probably did—although during the next fortnight or so there seemed to be very little in their general situation to cause much cheering. The weather was muggy and enervating, the mosquitoes were a trial, sick lists grew dolefully long as malaria and other complaints appeared, and there was no escape whatever from the frightful smell. Many dead had gone unburied in the swamps and thickets, others had been given a mere covering of earth which the rains quickly washed away, and anyway, nobody had warned these boys that one of the worst things about war is the way it stinks. All an individual soldier could see was the uninspiring acre or so in his immediate vicinity, and the adventure and excitement of war seemed to have shrunk to sullen endurance of boredom and acute physical discomfort.

But morale did not sag as much as might be supposed. McClellan's prose might be purple, but it did create self-esteem. The men felt that they had done well at Williamsburg, and Seven Pines had been twice as big a fight and they had got through it all right; they had passed the test of battle and nobody had ever licked them, and they began to feel that they were seasoned old soldiers. They had learned about artillery fire, which was so terrifying to new troops and, for that matter, not exactly pleasant to old ones. Shell and solid shot fired by smoothbore cannon were perfectly visible in flight and always seemed to be coming right at the observer: a completely unnerving thing until one got used to it. Spent shot, rolling along the ground, was deceptively dangerous; it looked harmless but wasn't, and some of Hooker's men told how an officer had put his foot out to stop such a ball and had lost his leg thereby. Shells were unpredictable. One man had picked up a dud and it had exploded in his hands—yet by some freak he was not badly hurt; at other times one shellburst might kill half a dozen men. A boy in a New Jersey regiment wrote that going under fire for the first time was pretty terrible: some of the men in his company, he said, were so scared they simply fell to the ground as if shot, picking themselves up sheepishly a bit later as nerve returned. He recalled one boy who went up to the firing line like a man in a trance, moaning over and over: "O Lord, dear good Lord!"

Regiments which were still equipped with the old Harper's Ferry muskets were disgusted with these weapons: ancient flintlocks which had been altered to percussion firing, with a rifled tube inserted in the barrel. They had a tremendous kick and were considered almost as dangerous to the user as to his target. Members of the Pennsylvania Bucktails—the 13th Pennsylvania, recruited in the Northern mountains and used to good rifles—found that the kick arose from the fact that the original bore of the musket was deeper than the tube; they remedied matters by ramming two or three dimes solidly down the bottom of the barrel, filling the chamber and preventing "back action."

The Frenchmen of the 55th New York, who knew things about cookery that most of the American boys did not know, felt that there were worse places to camp than the Chickahominy Valley. The place was full of bullfrogs, and the regimental mess reveled in frogs' legs "as large as and more delicate than the legs of chicken." The venturesome Frenchmen also learned that the blacksnakes found in the swamps were good to eat, although the other regiments were slow to copy them. A number of the generals, gifted with some political awareness, took the trouble to write to the state governors, telling them how well their troops had behaved.

New troops came in. McDowell's corps was still an independent command, but McCall's divison was detached from it and joined McClellan via Fortress Monroe, while a division under General William B. Franklin came along a bit later. McClellan got permission to form a couple of new army corps and name the commanders himself, Porter and Franklin getting the posts; now he at least had two corps commanders of his own selection, and he began to feel encouraged. Day by day he got his lines closer in toward Richmond, bringing up the heavy guns that were to have blasted Joe Johnston at Yorktown, defending himself every step of the way with earthworks.

Lee concluded that McClellan's attack would be a matter of regular approaches and siege guns, as at Yorktown, and confessed that the Confederates could not play that sort of game. Longstreet wrote long afterward that the Yankee plan was sound "and would have been a success if the Confederates had consented to such a program." McClellan kept Porter and his new corps north of the river—McDowell was under orders to march down from Fredericksburg and join him, and it was important to extend a hand to him. A little later Stonewall Jackson erupted again in the Shenandoah Valley, and McDowell was held back on panicky orders from Washington, and Porter's corps was left extending its welcoming hand into empty space. Once again McClellan felt betrayed; but the long rainy spell had ended, and the sun was drying the roads, and the prospects for an advance looked good.

Indeed, McClellan was whistling quite a hopeful tune just then. A week after the Seven Pines fight he wired Secretary Stanton that he would be "in perfect readiness to move forward and take Richmond the moment McCall reaches here and the ground will admit the passage of artillery." Three days later he assured the Secretary: "I shall attack as soon as the weather and the ground will permit." Four days after that he wired: "After tomorrow we shall fight the Rebel army as soon as Providence will permit."

Nor was this just his official version. To his wife McClellan wrote with equal confidence. In mid-June, a few days after McCall's division had checked in, he assured her that he would begin his advance "on Tuesday or Wednesday," when the roads would be thoroughly dry and all the temporary bridges over the river would be complete. He gave her a peek at his strategy; as Lee and Longstreet had suspected, he would try to get his heavy artillery far enough forward to blast an opening for his troops, driving the Rebels from their trenches by gunfire, moving his soliders up to the abandoned works, bringing the siege guns up close again, shelling the city, and then making a final assault. He was confident because of the soundness of his plans and because of the ardor of his men: "I think there is scarcely a man in this whole army who would not give his life for me, and willingly do whatever I ask.... I think I can so use our artillery as to make the loss of life on our side comparatively small." Two days later he was writing that "we shall soon be on the move," and four days after that he confided that he would strike his first great blow "within a couple of days." Two days after this letter he wrote: "I expect to be able to take a decisive step in advance day after tomorrow."

Day after tomorrow was slow in coming. For more than a fortnight the opening of the grand assault was always just a day or two ahead; and always there were additional last-minute preparations to make, final repairs to be put on the roads and the bridges, new dispositions to be made in the arrangement of the waiting troops. He believed that he was outnumbered, even with the reinforcements; Pinkerton's reports on Lee's overwhelming strength were detailed and explicit. Everything must be completely ready before the army can move, the last perfecting touch must be added, when the fight begins there must be nothing left to chance. And this was not only because of the overmatching strength of the enemy. There was Washington to think of; men there were trying to wreck the country, and if anything went wrong in the army the nation's ruin would be complete.

McClellan went into detail on this subject in a letter to his wife. The grapevine told him that Secretary Stanton and Secretary Chase had quarreled, and that McDowell—whom, by this time, McClellan had written down as a conniving schemer who wanted the top command for himself—had given up his old alliance with Chase and was now cultivating the Secretary of War. Sadly (and, heaven knows, understandably enough) McClellan wrote: "Alas! poor country that should have such rulers." He added: "When I see such insane folly behind me I feel that the final salvation of the country demands the utmost prudence on my part, and that I must not run the slightest risk of disaster, for if anything happened to this army our cause would be lost." A day or two earlier he had written her that recent messages from Lincoln and Stanton had quite an amiable tone, but he added acidly: "I am afraid that I am a little cross at them, and that I do not quite appreciate their sincerity and good feeling. *Timeo Danaos et dona ferentes.* How glad I will be to get rid of the whole lot!"

From all of which it is clear that the whole miserable combination of sorry circumstances—estrangement from his superiors, false reports from his intelligence section, and dreadful suspicion and enmity clouding all the channels between army headquarters and Washington—had piled up too much of a load for this man's army to carry. The great assault on Richmond must be delayed to the last moment because caution, above all other qualities, is the one great essential: caution in the face of powerful foes in front, caution because of treachery and foul conspiracy in the rear. Everything that had been building up through nine long months of disillusionment, every paralyzing force created by the willingness of public men to believe the worst of their fellows, was pressing on him now to make him wary, to compel him to think twice and thrice before taking a step, to people the starless darkness of imagination with just-discernible dangers that must be prepared for in advance. One false move and the country itself is lost! No wonder that tomorrow never quite comes, that there is always a final safeguard to erect.

And while all of this was going on, Lee, half a dozen miles away, was exerting all his strategy to keep McClellan immobile, with Porter's corps extended helplessly north of the river, until by the use of every possible expedient the Rebel army could be made strong enough to hit that one weak spot. McClellan could not be attacked south of the river—his works there were too strong, Lee's num-

bers were too few—but at all costs he must be kept from asserting the initiative
and beginning his remorseless siege-gun advance, for if that were once well
begun Richmond would inevitably be lost. And so while McClellan waited and
made ready (he was writing: "I have a kind of presentiment that tomorrow will
bring forth *something-what*, I do not know"), Lee brought Jackson down from
the valley and with an audacity that still looks breath-taking assembled three
fourths of his outnumbered army on the north side of the Chickahominy to assault the troops of Fitz-John Porter.

Lee was barely in time. Even while he was grouping his forces for the grand
attack, McClellan was at last beginning to move. Orders filtered downward,
from army to corps to division; and on the morning of June 25, Kearny's and
Hooker's men left their knapsacks in camp, formed line of battle, and started
out toward the Rebel capital.

They passed the advance entrenchments along the old Williamsburg road,
where the Seven Pines fighting had centered, and set out across the gloomy
country in a drizzling rain. There was a broad open field, and on the far side
there was a stretch of timber, with the ground all swampy underfoot, the black
tree trunks coming up in damp twilight out of dead pools and spongy earth. At
the near side of this wood the infantry halted, and the guns in the rear opened
up and raked the timber. Rebel batteries off in the distance answered back, and
for a time there was a spirited artillery duel, noisy but not doing much harm to
either side. Then the gunfire died away, the soldiers moved forward into the
wood, and the skirmish line began to shoot at the Rebel pickets and waited for
the main line to come up; and there was a slow, mean fire fight in the wood,
where wounded men had to be propped up against trees or stumps, while they
waited for the stretcher-bearers, lest they drown. In the end the Rebels withdrew—they were not present in any great strength—and the Northerners
cleared the wood and got to the far edge, where they looked out upon a broad
clearing which held the dark earthworks of Lee's main line of defense. The
drizzly afternoon wore away and word came to dig in; the new line was a mile or
more in advance of the old one, and it looked as if the big push for Richmond
had begun.

But next day everything slowed down. The Confederate Army seemed to be
in a high state of nervous irritability. The Yankee picket line had to be
strengthened until it had almost the weight of a regular skirmish line; here and
there, up and down the front, little detachments of Rebels would attack in a
rush, drawing off again when the fire got hot. All along the line, throughout the
day, there would be sudden bursts of artillery fire as Confederate batteries
sprang into unexpected activity, fired a dozen rounds, and then subsided into silence. Nothing ever quite developed into a real battle, but it was not what could
be called quiet, either.

Through gaps in the trees, in the rare spots where one could get a look into the
distance, lines of marching troops could be seen. There was an ominous sense
that something was building up, as if thunderheads were piling high on the
horizon, about to break forth with wild lightning. Off to the north, muffled by
distance and dead air, there was a steady rumble of gunfire during the afternoon
and evening, but three quarters of the army was south of the river and the boys
had their minds on what was right in front of them; what was going on north of
the river didn't sound much different from what was going on right here, except
that there were fewer breaks in it. The men spent an uneasy night on the line; a
number of regimental bands were kept playing long after dark, the brisk tunes
dying away in the somber pine flats. Some of the men heard vague talk of a victory won north of the river.

Next day there was more of the same, with a slightly increased tempo. The
outposts in front of Hooker's division could hear a good deal of frenzied activity
beyond the Rebel picket posts. Southern officers were shouting constantly, ap-

parently trying to get large bodies of troops formed up and moved; the Northerners could hear repeated commands—"From the right of companies to rear in a column. . . . Right face. . . . Don't get into a dozen ranks there. . . . Why don't they move forward?" Something big was in the wind; yet afterward the outposts remembered that they had been mildly puzzled: with all that shouting and maneuvering going on, they didn't seem to hear the actual tramp of marching men.[5]

At the various headquarters the men noticed a good deal of coming and going, with aides and mounted orderlies constantly galloping in and galloping out. To the northward, as the afternoon of June 27 wore away, a huge cloud of dirty white smoke went rolling up the sky, and the men who saw it wagged their heads: lots of guns being fired over there across the river, to make all that smoke. The atmosphere was heavy, and for some reason it affected the acoustics; in places the roar of that battle could be heard plainly, in other places there was no noise at all, even though the firing was abnormally heavy and was taking place only a few miles away. Along in mid-afternoon Slocum's division of Franklin's corps was pulled out of camp and was sent hiking along the miserable woods roads to the Chickahominy bridges. In this division was the 16th New York, gay and bright with a fancy touch to its uniforms; the colonel's wife had sent down a huge bale of brand-new straw hats, one for each man, and the whole regiment was wearing them. A few days later it was noticed that every straw hat was gone. The men found that when they got into action—which they did, as soon as they crossed the river—the hats turned them into perfect targets, and they lost 228 men before they discarded them.

And still nothing much actually seemed to happen south of the river. When night came word trickled back that there had been a terrible big fight over on the north side; but on the south side, although they had been right on the edge of an all-out battle for two days, it never quite developed. The Rebel lines continued to bristle, and in one or two spots the Confederates came out with what looked like pretty serious assaults (although it did seem that they were repulsed rather easily) and the Rebel artillery was ready to make a nuisance of itself at a moment's notice all along the front. And then next morning there was more galloping and coming and going than ever, around corps and division and brigade headquarters, and great black clouds of smoke went up as men set fire to various supply dumps. While the boys were puzzling over this, they were marched up to wagon trains and told to load up with salt pork, hardtack, coffee, and the like; and they noticed that instead of having definite quantities measured out for them, the way it usually happened, they were simply given all they could put in their haversacks. The 5th New York was directed to wagons containing the brigade's knapsacks; instead of being allowed to look for their own, the men were told to take the first ones they came to and be quick about it, and as soon as every man had one, provost guards set fire to the rest. The 4th New Jersey, to its amazement, got sudden orders to dig pits and bury all knapsacks. Up and down the camps the men began to look at each other and mutter: "It's a big skedaddle."

It was. By a painfully narrow margin Lee had beaten McClellan to the punch. Leaving twenty thousand men on the south side of the river—twenty thousand to face some seventy thousand Federals—he had marched everybody else to the north side for a vicious attack on Porter's isolated corps. The first blow, struck at Mechanicsville on the afternoon of June 26, had been rebuffed, but the next day Lee threw fifty-seven thousand men at Porter's new lines back of Boatswain's Swamp, near Gaines's Mill, and after a crunching, grinding struggle in which some Confederate brigades were all but torn apart he broke the lines and drove Porter back across the river, forcing McClellan to order a retreat.

The ominous noises which the Federals south of the river had been hearing in their front throughout the two days were simply the contribution of the Confed-

eracy's distinguished amateur actor, General Magruder, who was having just
the kind of time for himself he had had at Yorktown. Magruder had been exceedingly nervous. His twenty thousand men were all that stood between
McClellan and Richmond for forty-eight hours, and Magruder was very much
aware that if the Yankees once caught on there was little he could do to keep
them from rolling right over him and going into the capital. So he had played
the old Yorktown game with every variation he could think of. Regiments had
gone out into open spaces to march and countermarch and look numerous; officers had stood in the woods, shouting commands to completely imaginary brigades; picket lines and patrols and advanced batteries had been kept
effervescently active, as if making final preparation for a huge attack. In the end,
it had worked.

It had worked, partly because Magruder skillfully imposed on the Union
commanders facing him—or on most of them, at any rate—and partly because
McClellan and his corps commanders were already convinced that Lee had
close to two hundred thousand men on the field, so that it was possible for him
(as it seemed to them) to use sixty thousand or more to crush Porter north of the
river and still retain overwhelming numbers on the south side. Pinkerton's fantastic reports, believed like the writ of the true faith, were worth a couple of
army corps to the Confederacy that week. Heintzelman, under whom the preparatory advance had been made on June 25, had been worried all along; told
McClellan that night that he hardly thought he could hold his advanced position unless he could be reinforced, and when the attack on Porter was at its
height and McClellan messaged his corps commanders to see if they could possibly spare any men, Heintzelman replied that in a pinch he could send two brigades, "but the men are so worn out I fear they would not be in a condition to
fight after making a march of any distance." Sumner had been imposed on
equally; his messages back to army headquarters told about "sharp shelling" all
along his lines and predicted a heavy attack on his right. Franklin notified the
commanding general that the enemy was "massing heavy columns" in his front,
and the remaining corps commander, Erasmus Keyes (who was to drop into
military oblivion at the end of this campaign), reported it would take all the men
he had to hold his position.

McClellan stayed in his headquarters tents, pitched under trees on a pleasant
hill by a farmhouse a mile or more south of the river, his uniform coat folded
over a camp chair, standing in the open now and then to listen to the firing, tot-
ting up the reports from his subordinates. The situation on both sides of the
river, he wrote, was so ominous that he could not tell where the real assault was
going to be made; at night he wired Stanton that he was "attacked by greatly
superior numbers on this side."

He did not visit the battlefield. Indeed, in all of the great fights which the
Army of the Potomac had while under his command, McClellan stayed close to
headquarters. His physical courage was high enough—many of his soldiers have
commented on his extreme coolness when making reconnoissance under fire—
but there seems to have been in him a deep, instinctive shrinking from the sight
of bloodshed and suffering, an emotional reaction to the horrors of the front
lines that was more than he could stand. He wrote to his wife, about this time,
that "every poor fellow that is killed or wounded haunts me," and the army's
profound confidence that McClellan was anxious to spare his men's lives was
solidly based on fact. He was anxious to spare them, and when he had to send
them to their deaths he did not like to watch it. So, in any case, he remained at
headquarters, where he took counsel of his caution: dangerous to send heavy reinforcements north of the river lest the lines to the south be broken; dangerous
to strike boldly for Richmond, on the south side, lest disaster take place on the
north; hold on, then, as well as may be, on both banks, make Porter's fight a
holding and delaying action, withdraw to some good point on the James River,

get reinforcements, refit, and prepare for a new offensive at a later date. On the night the Gaines's Mill fight ended McClellan called in his corps commanders and gave orders for the retreat.

The corps commanders agreed that this was the only thing to do. Not so the two firebrand division commanders who held the lines nearest Richmond, Phil Kearny and Joe Hooker. They were indignant at the news, for it appears that Magruder had not fooled them very much; they knew the Rebel lines in front of them were thin and they believed they could and should be broken at once. They pressured their corps commander, Heintzelman, and late in the evening dragooned him into taking them to see McClellan, accompanied by a few of their brigade commanders. At the headquarters tent Kearny demanded permission to make an attack at once. He and Hooker, he said, could march straight into Richmond: if the general felt that they couldn't stay there (the disaster north of the river had broken the army's supply line) they could at least free the fourteen thousand Union prisoners of war in the city, disrupt all of Lee's stategic plans, and get back safely. Hooker agreed; in his opinion one division could do the job, but to play safe they might use two—let Kearny make the attack with his division and let Hooker support him with his. Heintzelman, under pressure, said that he felt the generals' proposal was sound.

McClellan was unmoved and insisted that the retreat must take place as ordered. Fiery Kearny was indignant; a staff officer who was present wrote later that Kearny denounced McClellan "in language so strong that all who heard it expected he would be placed under arrest until a general court martial could be held, or at least he would be relieved of his command." That didn't happen, however, McClellan apparently feeling that the thing to do with Kearny was to let him blow off steam every now and then, and the officers went back to their posts.[6]

So the retreat was made. It was handled, the books say, with consummate skill. Lee never could quite find the opening he needed to turn the withdrawal into a rout, and if the general situation gave him a chance to destroy the invading army, McClellan prevented him from taking advantage of it. But to the soldiers themselves the picture was never clear. They had no maps; they only knew that after spending some weeks in their fortified lines they were on the march again, in a confused country where none of the narrow, winding roads appeared to lead anywhere in particular, and there seemed to be a good deal of fighting mixed in with all the marching.

A member of the 40th New York wrote that, when his regiment was pulled out of the line and marched off to become part of the rear guard, the men thought for quite a time that they were actually advancing on Richmond to capture the place and end the war. The 1st Minnesota found itself drawn up in a field near a country railroad station, supporting a Rhode Island battery. A Confederate battle line emerged from a wood a mile away and advanced to the attack. Old General Sumner came galloping up, his white head bare in the wind, his hat clenched in one fist; he put the 5th New Hampshire and the 88th New York in beside the Westerners, and they went out into the field and drove the Rebels back. A little later a brigade of New York troops charged and captured a section of a Rebel battery, spiking the guns when they found they couldn't get them away. Then, after dark, the Federals moved off down a road through a swamp. Long afterward they learned that they had had a part in the battle of Savage Station, in which the army's retreat was effectively protected, but at the time it was just a fight; and if the rest of the army was in retreat, the fact was not especially evident to the high private.

Indeed, old man Sumner himself got a little mixed up about it. When evening came he felt that he had won a victory, and when orders came to withdraw he cried: "I never leave a victorious field—why, if I had twenty thousand more men I could crush this rebellion." Staff pointed out that McClellan's orders to withdraw were explicit, and Sumner finally obeyed, complaining: "General McClellan did not know all the circumstances when he wrote that note. He did not know that we would fight a battle and gain a victory."[7]

The 15th Massachusetts knew a retreat was going on, but had fun anyway: their job was to destroy supplies that couldn't be moved, and they had a freight train of ammunition to get rid of. The railroad bridge over the river had been wrecked, so they simply set the train on fire, started it moving toward the ruined bridge, and sat back to enjoy a grand combination of train wreck, bonfire, and Fourth of July fireworks.

Night came on, and two weary batteries of regular artillery—Batteries A and C, 4th U.S.—went to sleep in a wood, dead-tired. Next morning the skipper of the two batteries, Captain George W. Hazzard, heard bugles sounding reveille from fields which he knew had been unoccupied the night before. He got up to look about—Rebels all around him, no sign of any Union troops anywhere. He gave hurried orders: hitch up quickly but quietly and get the guns away before the Rebels catch on, move at a walk so as not to make any more noise than can be helped. He finally rejoined the army, bringing with him a battalion of infantry stragglers who, like the artillerymen, had gone to sleep in the wood ignorant that the army was pulling out. A similar adventure befell three infantry regiments—104th Pennsylvania and 56th and 100th New York, which fought in front of Savage Station and weren't notified that everybody else was leaving. They were nearly captured, made an all-night march along bewildering roads, got entirely lost, and at last came stumbling into camp three days later, mad enough to bite the heads off nails. It was reported that they were the only regiments in the army which failed to cheer McClellan after the army was safely back on the James River.

That same night Colonel William Averell of cavalry came riding up to McClellan's field headquarters all excited: the roads between the army and Richmond were empty and the army might go there unopposed. McClellan smiled grimly and shook his head; the roads would be full enough tomorrow—which was entirely correct, since Lee was bringing every man he had to press the retreat, and the moment for a counterblow had passed. To Averell, McClellan added: "If any army can save this country it will be the Army of the Potomac, and it must be saved for that purpose."[8]

Next day there was bitter fighting late in the afternoon around a crossroads settlement named Glendale, where Lee led Longstreet's and A. P. Hill's division up to the middle of McClellan's long column and tried to break it in half. The worst of the fighting fell to McCall's Pennsylvania division, which met Longstreet's attack head-on, and there was deadly hand-to-hand fighting around a Union battery, with Northern and Southern boys savagely braining each other with clubbed muskets, driving bayonets into human flesh. A Confederate officer slew two gunners with his sword, went down when three Federals fell on him with bayonets. Captain Hazzard, who had been left behind the night before, was killed, and General McCall was taken prisoner, and the Pennsylvanians finally broke and went to the rear fast. Going back, they met Hooker's division coming up. A Pennsylvania colonel, riding to the rear faster than the soldiers thought necessary, tearfully implored the oncoming troops to "hurry up and save my poor men." Hooker's boys jeered at him, yelling: "Dry up, you old fool—pull your eagles off—go home to your mother."[9]

The 1st Minnesota was one of the regiments sent in to repair the break. Sumner came riding up as they formed their battle line; reining up in front of them, he called out: "Boys, I may not see all of you again, but I know you'll hold that line." Then he waved his hat, and they moved forward. Kearny, holding on over to the right and looking for any help he could get—both Longstreet and Hill were attacking now, and the safety of the whole army was in the balance—sent staff officers back to bring up the first troops they found. These turned out to be General George Taylor's brigade—1st, 2nd, 3rd, and 4th New Jersey, which used to be Kearny's own: the same which had been lawlessly robbing an orchard when Kearny first took command, disciplined by his own hand, still fa mous foragers. (Kearny once told Lincoln, in effect: If you really want to capture Richmond, put a hen house and a peach orchard on the far side and the New Jersey brigade on this side—they'll get through all the fortifications of Richmond to get the hens and the peaches.)

Staff officers pulled up, all in a lather: General Kearny had lost a battery and wanted the old brigade to help him get it back—would they come? Brigade let out a yell and swung into line almost before the orders could be given; swarmed across a field, chased assorted Rebels out of a sunken road, and recaptured the guns, boasting afterward that they got there before Kearny's own men arrived. . . . It was this brigade's General Taylor, incidentally, who had been momentarily confused at Gaines's Mill a couple of days earlier. He had led his brigade up as reinforcement and was met by one of the French princes serving on McClellan's staff, loaned that day to Fitz-John Porter and riding to Taylor with Porter's orders. In the excitement of the fight the young prince began shouting the orders in French, of which Taylor knew not a word. Turning to his staff, Taylor demanded: "Who the devil *is* he, and what does he want?" A staff officer who could speak French finally showed up, and the puzzle was straightened out. . . . Somewhere in this Glendale fight was another Union battery which the Rebels attempted to capture. As the Southerners advanced, the battery commander told his men to stand firm; a grim Yankee gunner, looking at the tattered foe, remarked: "I ain't goin' to git from no such ragged fellers as they be," and the battery held its ground.

After the Glendale fight there was more marching. The army was continuing its retreat to the James River, where gunboats and fleets of supply steamers promised safety; but to the soldiers it was just another night march rather than a retreat. They had been hurt badly at Glendale, but when the line was broken they had restored it, and at the end of the day the Rebels had been beaten back, and the men felt they had done well. They were confirmed in this opinion next day, when part of the army and most of the artillery lingered on Malvern Hill, where Lee's last attempt to destroy the Army of the Potomac was decisively repulsed. This fight was a field day for the gunners; Rebel artillery couldn't seem to get into position to do much damage, the roads being few and Lee's staff work defective, and solid rows of Union fieldpieces, lined up hub to hub at the top of a long slope, broke the charging Confederate infantry to bits. The Confederate General D. H. Hill noted after the battle that more than half of all the casualties Lee's army suffered that day were caused by artillery fire—an unprecedented thing for that war, where the infantry musket was the big killer.

Rain set in again during the night, and in the early morning Colonel Averell, who had the rear guard, found his little command alone on the broad hilltop. Behind him, in the low country where the muddy lanes led to the banks of the James, the army and its heavy wagon trains were struggling along to the most cheerless of camps, with the dark gunboats anchored offshore. In front of him there was a heavy mist, blotting out the terrible slope where the battle had been fought. In the mist he could see nothing, but out of it came a pulsating, endless wave of pitiful sound—the agonized cry of moaning of thousands of wounded boys who had been lying on the ground, unattended, all night long. By and by the sun came up and the mist thinned, and presently he could see the battleground, one of the most horrible sights of the war. Five thousand men lay there, covering the ground like a ragged carpet that lived and made incoherent sounds and, here and there, moved dreadfully. "A third of them were dead or dying," he wrote, "but enough of them were alive and moving to give the field a singular crawling effect." The ambulance parties came out to do what they could for the mangled men, and at the one side of the field Stonewall Jackson had details out hastily burying the dead; he expected to have to fight over that ground and he felt it would hurt morale to make his men advance past so many corpses. And Averell finally recalled his rear guard and went down the reverse slope of the hill to join the rest of the army in the new camp at Harrison's Landing.[10]

4. PILLAR OF SMOKE

It was either the end of everything or a new beginning. The fields by the river were sodden, and the sky kept dripping rain as if the bottom had fallen out of all the clouds, and the fine hopes of a year of unlimited promise had been ground under in mud and bloodshed and the nameless horrors of the battlefields. Weary with a week in the saddle and with the unutterable loneliness and weight of command, McClellan took over the house and grounds of Berkeley Plantation for his headquarters. The house was a fine one, spaciously built of brick in the colonial days, but he did not care to occupy it. Ambulance details had got there ahead of him, and it was filled with desperately wounded men—"a gruesome place," one officer confessed after visiting it—and the commanding general's tents were pitched on the lawn some rods away from the dwelling.

Lee had failed in his big effort to surround and demolish this army. It was safe here on the river, with gunboats on guard in the stream and with a fleet of transports and supply steamers ready to bring new men and equipment. Yet the army was isolated, just the same; in the war, but curiously out of it for the moment, as if it had been stranded here on the mud flats by some strange ebb tide, damaged by wind and wave, inert, its future wholly problematical. For it was an army which, by now, drew its spirit and its tone from its commander, and its commander was walled away from the world. It was not for nothing that he identified himself, in the purple prose of his army proclamations, with the lives and well-being of his men. The seven days of fighting which had torn the army so cruelly had torn him in the same way. The emotional tension thus created in him had led to a blind and angry reaction: the army had suffered; suffering, it had failed; the failure could only be due to betrayal by those who should have supported it. At any cost, its commander must show that the cause of this suffering was not himself. In the heat of this feeling he had sent Secretary Stanton a passionate telegram after the fight at Gaines's Mill—a strange, taut message, explaining how evil the fortunes of the day had been and bitterly disclaiming any responsibility for the defeat. With only ten thousand more men, he cried, he could yet gain the victory; the battle just fought would have been so different if Washington had not held back the few reinforcements he had asked for. He continued:

"I feel too earnestly tonight. I have seen too many dead and wounded comrades to feel otherwise than that the government has not sustained this army. If you do not do so now the game is lost."

And then the final, bitter sentences, calculated to burn all bridges—or, conceivably, not calculated at all, just slipping out like a cry of unendurable passion:

"If I save this army now, I tell you plainly that I owe no thanks to you or to any other persons in Washington. You have done your best to sacifice this army."

Passionate or cold, McClellan was a man of clear intelligence and he knew as well as anyone that an army commander does not say that to the Secretary of War, and through him to the President, without forcing a showdown. Everything said and done in Washington, after this message, would be judged by McClellan in light of the fact that those words had been spoken. Presumably he would be cashiered; if not, it could only mean that Washington was knuckling under and was tacitly confessing its guilt as well—continuing him in command

and leaving so flat an accusation unanswered! But what McClellan never knew was that neither Lincoln nor Stanton ever saw that bitter, accusing conclusion until many months later. A War Department functionary, decoding dispatches from army headquarters and preparing them for the Secretary, found his eyes popping out when he read those two closing sentences. Shocked to the bottom of his orderly governmental soul, he simply deleted them, and the general's dispatch went spiraling upward through the hierarchy with the damning charge omitted. Irascible Stanton did not see it until long after he and McClellan had ceased to be problems to each other.

Meanwhile, the general was more than ever thrown in on the army. He might draw supplies from Washington, might even get reinforcements—he was telling the War Department that he needed fully a hundred thousand fresh soldiers—but he could not get emotional support from that source any longer. That could come only from the soldiers. To his wife, on the day the dejected army filed into the lines at Harrison's Landing, he wrote that "the dear fellows cheer me as of old as they march to certain death, and I feel prouder of them than ever," and he confessed that it was only among the troops that he felt at home. Describing the week of fighting and marching, he wrote: "You can't tell how nervous I became; everything seemed like the opening of artillery, and I had no rest, no peace, except when in front with my men. The duties of my position are such as often to make it necessary for me to remain in the rear. It is an awful thing." But the men never failed. He rode among them and "they began to cheer as usual, and called out that they were all right and would fall to the last man for 'Little Mac.' "

So he tried to give the army the reassurance which the army gave him. Independence Day came three days after the army reached the river. To the troops McClellan issued a stirring proclamation: "Under every disadvantage of numbers, and necessarily of position also, you have in every conflict beaten back your foes with enormous slaughter. That your conduct ranks you among the celebrated armies of history, no one will ever question; then each of you may always say with pride, 'I belonged to the Army of the Potomac.' "[1]

It must be admitted that when it first reached camp the army did not feel particularly heroic or distinguished. The flat fields around Harrison's Landing struck it as a poor place for a camp. Most of the ground was growing wheat, which was cut down and laid to serve as bedding under the shelter tents. It didn't work very well. The ground turned into semi-liquid mud, the tent pins wouldn't hold, the soggy straw either floated away or was mashed out of sight, and worn-out men awoke to find themselves lying in mud puddles with clammy canvas collapsed on top of them. (Some of them did, anyway: many others had had to abandon tent-and-blanket rolls during the retreat and had nothing whatever to sleep on or under.) The 8th Ohio, coming down from the north in a reinforcement brigade and reaching the landing the day after camp had been made, thought at first that the whole country had been flooded. "It was almost as muddy," wrote one soldier, "as if the waters of the deluge had just retreated from the face of the earth."[2]

Nobody had had much to eat for several days, what with the constant fighting and marching, and it was hard to find wood for fires here—or, while the rain lasted, to make fires burn if wood could be found. There was great confusion at first, with men separated from their commands, and brigades and divisons were all split up and intermingled. While they were trying to sort themselves out an obnoxious battery of Confederate horse artillery popped up on a low ridge north of the camp and began flinging shells down on the plain. The men swore wearily, a brigade went up to drive the guns away, and the high command—almost as punch-drunk momentarily as the men themselves—got some field fortifications built along the ridge so that further disturbances of the peace could be held away.

It was right at this time, too, that the army as a whole made a horrifying discovery about itself. It was lousy.

The men were ashamed when they discovered it, until they found that everybody was in the same boat; then they accepted it as one of the miserable facts of army life and made jokes about it. One man declared that in the Glendale fight he had seen a high officer dramatically calling a brigade to the charge—posing bravely on his horse, his right hand holding his sword high, while with his left hand he busily and unconsciously kept scratching himself. The surgeon of the 57th New York would not believe it when the colonel told him the regiment was infested; said it must be just a few of the men, careless fellows, no doubt, who didn't bother to keep clean. The colonel, probably wondering how anyone could be expected to keep clean in a solid week of unbroken fighting and marching, exploded at him: "The whole army is lousy! I am lousy, you are lousy, General McClellan is lousy!"[3] The army got some relief as supply ships came up. New clothing was distributed, and details were formed to collect and burn verminous underwear and uniforms.

The heat was oppressive. Mosquitoes seemed even worse here than they had been around Richmond. The camp stank horribly: too many men were crowded into too small an area, the pits that were dug for refuse never seemed quite adequate, the latrines were an abomination. There was a plague of flies, and the drinking water (obtained, for the most part, by digging shallow wells) was unpleasantly warm and muddy, and was beyond all question tainted. A new surgeon arrived to join the 5th New Hampshire just at this time, and he wrote feelingly of the impression made by what he saw: "The barefooted boys, the sallow men, the threadbare officers and seedy generals, the diarrhea and dysentery, the yellow eyes and malarious faces, the beds upon the bare earth in the mud, the mist and the rain." All of this, he confessed, instantly destroyed his "pre-conceived ideas of knight-errantry."[4]

Fresh provisions came down from the North, which was a help; cabbages, tomatoes, and potatoes were welcome, although the men were not entirely sure that fresh beef was much better than salt pork—the butchers were inexpert and hasty, carcasses were usually cut up while lying on the ground, and the meat had a way of being sandy by the time it got to the company cooks. In any case, the cooks rarely knew of any way to cook beef except by boiling it. The one good feature about the place, the men agreed, was that they could bathe in James River.

But even though Harrison's Landing was a miserable camp, where the regimental sick lists kept lengthening and tired boys had enough unwanted leisure to remember that they were homesick, the army was not altogether discouraged. It had learned things about war that it had never dreamed of, to be sure, but as the men compared notes on what they had been through it seemed to them that they had done very well indeed. They could not understand just why they had had to retreat, and it was a disappointment not to be in Richmond; but every battle, when they looked back on it, seemed to have been no worse than a draw, and Malvern Hill they rightly considered a distinct victory. If some of them felt that so fine a victory ought to have been followed up by an advance on Richmond, they concluded after talking it over that Little Mac knew what he was doing and that they could safely leave all such problems to him.

Had they known it, as stout a friend of McClellan as Fitz-John Porter himself believed that the retreat after Malvern Hill was a mistake; a determined advance next day, he thought, would have pushed Lee aside and opened the way to Richmond. Phil Kearny, who had long since come to dislike McClellan intensely—he still thought McClellan had slighted him in his dispatches describing the battle of Williamsburg, and anyway, McClellan just wasn't the type that hot-blooded Kearny could admire—was violent in his criticism. When the order to retreat reached him at the end of the battle, he cried out: "I, Philip Kearny, an old soldier, enter my solemn protest against this order for retreat. We ought instead of retreating to follow up the enemy and take Richmond. And in full view of all the responsibility of such a declaration, I say to you all, such an order can only be prompted by cowardice or treason."[5]

Kearny's remarks were to get back to Washington in time, but they did not circulate among the enlisted men. With them McClellan's name still had the old magic. The 3rd Michigan, which was one of Kearny's regiments, was making a despairing effort to boil coffee on one of the first mornings in camp. Fires wouldn't burn in the rain, and men were gathered around trying to hold blankets, overcoats, and what not over the smoldering embers, when McClellan came riding by. The men dropped everything and ran over to cluster around him and shout, and when he could make himself heard he quietly told them that he knew things had been tough but that everything was going to be all right from now on: they were fine soldiers, they had given the Rebels more than they had received, and they'd take Richmond yet. The boys cheered and went back to their fires, got them going somehow, drank their coffee, and felt better. Talking things over after they had finished their coffee and had their pipes lighted, they agreed that they were quite a regiment and the army was quite an army; they had marched all night and fought all day for a week, most of the time they had whipped the enemy—who could have done better than that? And as for McClellan: he was still the man.[6]

New uniforms were issued, and there were reviews: a grand series of reviews, presently, with President Lincoln himself on hand to sit on his horse, lanky and ungainly, beside McClellan to watch the men march past. A boyish lieutenant on the staff of General Taylor, of the New Jersey brigade, hadn't managed to get in on the issue of new uniforms. His pants were unspeakably ragged and dirty—he confessed that he had not had them off for upward of a week—and he was excused from the review. That evening he went to General Taylor's tent on business, entered, and found Lincoln himself there, chatting with Taylor. Abashed, he tried to withdraw; no man in pants like this had any business lingering in the presence of the President of the United States. But Lincoln told him not to leave and asked Taylor to introduce him. Taylor did so, explaining about the regrettable pants worn out in the country's hard service. Lincoln shook hands, rested his left hand on the boy's shoulder, and said: "My son, I think your country can afford to get you a new pair of breeches."[7]

Lincoln hadn't come all the way down from Washington just to review troops, of course, nor did he spend much time chatting with brigade commanders. He was there primarily to see McClellan and to find out for himself, if possible, just what could be done next with the Army of the Potomac. The war was approaching an unexpected crisis, and much more had been lost than a few square miles of swampland along the Chickahominy. What was fast disappearing was the last chance for a relatively short war; going with it, or soon to go, was the high hope and confidence with which the country had faced the summer's fighting. Unless the war could be won quickly it would become a new kind of war, creating its own objectives, exacting a fearful price; no longer an affair of esprit de corps and hero worship and the élan of highhearted volunteer fighters, but a long, brutal, grinding, and totally unpredictable struggle to which all the agony and heartbreak of the Seven Days' fighting would be only a prelude.

The sky had been so bright that spring, and final victory had not appeared to be far away. In the West, Kentucky and most of Tennessee were safe and New Orleans was taken, and it looked as if the whole length of the Mississippi would soon be open. In the East, amphibious expeditions had seized much of the Confederacy's coast line, and McClellan's army had seemed ready to drive straight through to Richmond. Secretary Stanton had been so encouraged in April that he had blithely closed all of the recruiting offices, which was a black item against him in McClellan's book. Now the brightness was gone and dark clouds were climbing up the sky. The armies in the West were stalled—no actual repulse anywhere, but no victories, either. Every detail of the Virginia campaign had gone awry, and men were thankful because the Army of the Potomac had not actually been destroyed. John Pope had been brought on from the West to make an army out of the scattered commands north of the Rappahannock— McDowell's, Sigel's, and Banks's—but McClellan's army still represented most of the muscle, and it was the big question mark. What could it do now? Or, considering that it was McClellan's army, what *would* it do? Lincoln had to find out.

When the bad news first came in from in front of Richmond, Lincoln had been consoling. In his first message to McClellan he told him: "Maintain your ground if you can, but save the army at all events, even if you fall back to Fort Monroe. We still have strength enough in the country, and will bring it out." Next day he wired McClellan: "If you think you are not strong enough to take Richmond just now, I do not ask you to just now," and promised reinforcements; a new levy of three hundred thousand volunteers was to be raised at once. On the following day he wired that he was satisfied that "yourself, officers and men have done the best you could" and conveyed "ten thousand thanks for it." A day later he repeated his acknowledgment of "the heroism and skill of yourself, officers and men" and assured McClellan: "If you can hold your present position we shall hive the enemy yet." In a letter Lincoln went into detail about reinforcements, again urged the general to hold on and make his army safe, and added in a postscript: "If at any time you feel able to take the offensive, you are not restrained from doing so." Confidently McClellan replied: "Alarm yourself as little as possible about me, and don't lose confidence in this army."

So far, so good; President and general seemed to understand one another. Now the President was on the ground to talk things over.

Yet how could they talk, those two men, even with incalculable matters depending on their coming to agreement? We know both of them by now; we have had two generations to study them and find out what they really meant. But they could never see each other clearly. Too many shadows lay between them. On each man was a pressure; in each man was an ignorance which kept him from understanding just what the other man's pressure was like—ignorance of politics, for the one, and of military affairs, for the other. Behind each man, subtly influencing him, were the suspicions his colleagues held, including on each side the dim half belief that perhaps the other man did not really wish a speedy end to the war. (Among the "war Democrats," who had no use for anti-slavery agitation, was the feeling that the Republicans did not want the war to end until it could be made into an instrument to crush slavery. Among the Republicans was the conviction that men like McClellan wanted the war to drag out into an indecisive peace-without-victory which would leave slavery intact. These two feelings were in the backgrounds of the President and the general who were to confer with each other.)

McClellan had bluntly accused the administration of infamous conduct. He had not been rebuked for it. He had had nothing from Washington since then but kind words. How could he interpret that, except as clear proof that there *was* infamous conduct in Washington and that the authors of it—the men who gave him his orders—felt so guilty that they dared not resent his angry words? He had invited them to cashier him and they had not done it; instead, Stanton had sent a note assuring him that "you have never had from me anything but the most confiding integrity," followed by another asserting: "No man had ever a truer friend than I have been to you and shall continue to be. You are seldom absent from my thoughts, and I am ready to make any sacrifice to aid you."

And Lincoln? Among his trusted cabinet members was Gideon Welles, the

Secretary of the Navy, who has been described as an irascible Santa Claus with his stern face and his bushy white whiskers, and who was eminently level-headed, taking no part in the frantic factional efforts to tell Lincoln how to run the war. Welles had visited McClellan on the peninsula shortly after Yorktown fell and had had a long and oddly revealing talk with him. McClellan had confided his great desire to capture Charleston, South Carolina, a city which he would like "to demolish and annihilate." (The general must have been really worked up that day. It is impossible to imagine him demolishing and annihilating any city: for better or for worse, he completely lacked the Sherman touch.) In his diary—that marvelous depository for acid comments—Welles went on with the tale:

"He detested, he said, both South Carolina and Massachusetts, and should rejoice to see both states extinguished. Both were and always had been ultra and mischievous, and he could not tell which he hated most. These were the remarks of the general-in-chief at the head of our armies then in the field, and when as large a proportion of his troops were from Massachusetts as from any state in the Union, while as large a proportion of those who were opposed, who were fighting the Union, were from South Carolina as from any state. He was leading the men of Massachusetts against the men of South Carolina, yet he, the general, detests them alike."[8]

It is easy enough at this day to see McClellan's outburst as a variant of "a plague on both your houses," directed at the fire-eaters of North and South alike, and it is hard to get very disturbed about it. But there was a war on then, and a detached attitude was hard to come by, and, as Welles said, that *was* an odd way for a Northern general to talk. A Northern newspaper correspondent, summing up the Seven Days' Battles, had written that "Massachusetts mourns more dead soldiers, comparatively, than any state's quota in the Army of the Potomac." It is fair to assume that Welles had told Lincoln about McClellan's words. Would not those words inevitably get in between the two men as they talked about the future course of the war?

If those words wouldn't, there were others that would. Phil Kearny had been free in his comments. His insistence that he could march his own division into Richmond, after Lee struck his first blow north of the Chickahominy, and his angry denunciation of McClellan for ordering a retreat were by no means army secrets. Brigadier General Hiram G. Berry, who commanded one of Kearny's brigades, had been present when Kearny sounded off, and Berry, who came from Maine, was in steady confidential correspondence with Vice-President Hannibal Hamlin. Even earlier, Kearny had been writing to a friend in the North that "McClellan is a dirty, sneaking traitor," and was suggesting that back of McClellan's strategy "there is either positive treason or at least McClellan or the few with him are devising a game of politics rather than war." At this distance it is fairly easy to recognize Kearny as a tolerably familiar type in the long history of the American Army—the ardent, hard-fighting, distinguished soldier who just has to blow off at the mouth every now and then. But Lincoln was conferring with McClellan in 1862, and all he could be expected to see was that the most slashing fighter in the army was doubting the loyalty of his commanding general.

And Lincoln was in the mood to heed the words of a hard fighter. At bottom his whole problem was summed up in the fact that the North had the power to win the war but lacked the slugging, driving generals who would use that power. He could form his own judgments of men, and he was not persuaded by all the whispers about McClellan's loyalty; what did bother him about McClellan, from first to last, was McClellan's reluctance to crowd the enemy into a corner and punch until somebody dropped. Perhaps the most revealing remark Lincoln ever made about his relationship with McClellan was one concerning an entirely different general. Earlier that spring Grant fought the battle of Shiloh—fought it inexpertly, suffering a shameful surprise, losing many men who need not have been lost. There was a great clamor against him, he was denounced as an incompetent and a drunkard, and tremendous political pressure was put on Lincoln to remove him. A. K. McClure, the Pennsylvania politician who was intimate with Lincoln, was convinced that Lincoln, as a matter of practical politics, "could not sustain himself if he attempted to sustain Grant," and late one night he went to the White House to argue the point. He told Lincoln "with all the earnestness I could command" that he simply must get rid of Grant. Then, as McClure described it: "Lincoln remained silent for what seemed a very long time. He then gathered himself up in his chair and said in a tone of earnestness that I shall never forget: *'I can't spare this man; he fights.'* " Lincoln had warned McClellan that there were political pressures which even the President could not resist; but to uphold a fighting general he was ready to resist any pressure whatever.[9]

However all of that may be, Lincoln and McClellan had their conference. And McClellan there made his crowning mistake. Having failed to understand that political considerations could modify the best plans of the best military men in a democracy at war, he suddenly switched from military planning to political planning—with disastrous results.

Here he was, barely a week after the battle of Malvern Hill, with the whole future of the war depending on the speed and energy with which the army could be repaired and thrown into a new campaign, with all of the involved problems growing out of that fact resting chiefly on himself for solution, with his own career, the fate of the army, and the safety of the country itself depending on what might come out of his talks with the President: and to the President he gave, not a plan for renewing the fighting, but a long letter telling him how he should shape the policy of the war.

It was his desire, McClellan wrote, to expound his views regarding the rebellion, even though those views "do not strictly relate to the situation of this army or strictly come within the scope of my official duties." But the policy he was arguing for must be adopted by the President and put promptly into effect "or our cause will be lost." It was a policy, he said, both "constitutional and conservative," which would "receive the support of almost all truly loyal men" and which, it might be hoped, would even "commend itself to the favor of the Almighty."

Specifically: "neither confiscation of property, political executions of persons, territorial organization of states or forcible abolition of slavery should be contemplated for a moment." In the fighting, Federal armies should protect private property and unarmed persons, and there should be no "offensive demeanor by the military toward citizens"; there should be no military arrests, except in areas where actual fighting was going on, and where military government was set up it should be confined to preserving order and protecting political rights. Military power should never be used to interfere "with the relations of servitude"; if contraband slaves were pressed into service, the rights of their owners to compensation should be recognized. Unless some such policy as this were adopted, the effort to get new recruits for the army would fail; and if the government should adopt "radical views" on the slavery issue, the existing armies would disintegrate.

To put through such a policy, McClellan added, the President would need a sympathetic general-in-chief for the armies. He did not ask that place for himself but would willingly serve "in such position as you may assign me."

Now it is probably true that at least a part of this letter was aimed at the egregious General Pope, who had celebrated the assumption of his new command by issuing ferocious orders regarding the treatment of Rebel civilians within his lines—orders so unduly restrictive that the government quietly let them become a dead letter. To that extent McClellan was on sound ground. But there can be no doubt whatever that the final effect of the letter was to convince Lincoln that McClellan was not the general he could use to win the war.

For two reasons.

To begin with, Lincoln was reluctantly concluding that the war could not be won on the first simple flush of enthusiasm for saving the Union. That would remain the one dominant motive, to be sure: he was presently to write his famous letter to Horace Greeley declaring that he would save the Union in any way he could, whether by freeing no slaves, by freeing just a few, or by freeing all. It was a motive to which he had remained true despite tremendous pressure from his own party. He had disciplined General Frémont, first presidential candidate of the Republican party, for issuing a premature proclamation of emancipation. He had rebuked former Secretary of War Cameron when that slippery individual, deep in trouble because of slovenly administration of his office, tried to wrap the anti-slavery cloak about his bent shoulders. He had disavowed the act of General David Hunter, another hero of the abolitionists, who tried to proclaim abolition along the Southern seacoast that spring. Painfully and patiently he had tried to bring forth some solution for the terrible slavery problem aside from outright, forcible emancipation. He had persuaded a reluctant Congress to adopt a joint resolution for compensated emancipation; there had been something fairly pathetic in his appeal to the people of the slave states to support such a settlement—"I do not argue; I beseech you to make the arguments for yourselves. You cannot, if you would, be blind to the signs of the times."

But the sands were running out. By the end of the first week of July 1862, the President had just about made up his mind that some sort of emancipation program was essential as a war measure. (It was less than a week after this talk with McClellan that he first told Secretary Seward and Secretary Welles that he had come to this conclusion.) In a sense, Lincoln had gone down to Harrison's Landing with a draft of the Emancipation Proclamation in his pocket. Yet here was the general of his most important army saying that the one thing which he, the President, had decided must be done to win the war could not and must not be done; telling him, in so many words, that if the slavery issue were raised the army would not fight—McClellan's army, made in his own image, bound to him by battle-tested ties of devotion.

And in the second place, McClellan's letter forced Lincoln to ask just who was running the country, anyway—the civil administration or a general? Obviously, if he accepted McClellan's advice, the general was running it. At that early date Lincoln was bumping into the ominous fact that when democracy makes all-out war the way is always open for military persons to take control on the plea that the military problem can't be solved unless all related political problems are adjusted, Procrustes-fashion, to fit. There had been plenty of talk for a year and more about the need for a dictator, whether in shoulder straps or frock coat. Some of it had been pumped into McClellan's own ears by none other than his present bitter enemy, Mr. Stanton. McClellan was by no means the only general who had been beguiled by such talk, nor was Stanton the only beguiler, and Lincoln knew it. Indeed, Lincoln's administration had not been a month old before Secretary Seward had given the President a letter, blandly offering to take over the job of running the government himself; did this letter of McClellan's, closing with the courteous disclaimer of any personal ambition, remind the President of that earlier letter of Seward's? The parallel is striking.

Whatever Lincoln might have thought as he read the general's remarkable letter, he gave nothing away. He thanked McClellan politely for it, put it in his pocket, and went back to Washington. Three days later he plucked General Halleck out of the lines along the Mississippi, brought him to Washington, and made him general-in-chief of the nation's armies.

And McClellan wrote to his wife that he had given the President the letter and that "if he acts upon it the country will be saved." He sent her a copy, asking her to preserve it as a document important to the record—a document proving, McClellan felt, "that I was true to my country, that I understood the state of affairs long ago, and that had my advice been followed we should not have been in our present difficulties."

Which is as it may be. It is doubtful if McClellan ever realized exactly what effect his letter had, or why such an effect might have been expected. He was acting, those days, with an incredible innocence. Understanding politics not at all, he put himself inextricably into politics; having given Lincoln a letter which was enough to destroy his own position, he now had to make certain that his enemies in Washington would be able to put the worst possible interpretation on it. He entertained in his camp Fernando Wood, recently mayor of New York, and one of the leaders in what was just beginning to be called the Copperhead movement.

Wood was a character any administration man might well look upon with suspicion. When the Southern states began to secede at the end of 1860 and the beginning of 1861, Wood had proposed that New York City itself secede and become some sort of free city on the coast, friendly to the new Confederacy, bringing from Lincoln the dry comment that the time hardly seemed ripe for the front door to detach itself and set up housekeeping for itself. Wood was by now the complete exemplar of those Northern Democrats who let their old sympathy for the South, their dislike of anti-slavery agitation, and their basic political opposition to the Republicans carry them over to the very edge of being pro-Confederate rather than pro-Union. Like many another Northern general—U. S. Grant, for a random example—McClellan was a Democrat and always had been; but he could not see now that under all the circumstances it was not quite politic for him to confer with Fernando Wood while his army recuperated from defeat within gunshot of Lee's outposts.

He talked politics with Wood, who felt and said that McClellan would be a good presidential candidate. He seems to have prepared for Wood a letter outlining his political views; a letter apparently embodying much the same points as were expressed in his letter to Lincoln, but dangerously susceptible to misinterpretation when given by the commanding general to a reckless conniver like Wood. McClellan showed the letter to one of his closest friends, General William F. Smith—"Baldy" Smith to the army, a good soldier and a stoutly loyal citizen. Smith, according to the surviving reports, read it and found the remnants of his hair standing on end; handed it back with the startled remark that "it looks like treason" and would be the ruin of McClellan and all who were close to him. On Smith's urging, McClellan destroyed the letter. His enemies in Washington, of course, never saw the letter and never knew just what had passed between Wood and McClellan; but they knew that Wood had visited McClellan, they knew that talk of McClellan as the next President was beginning to circulate, and they did know Wood.

After Wood left, Halleck came down for a conference. McClellan was stiffly polite; he considered Halleck an inferior person, in which he was quite correct, and he wrote to his wife that his self-respect would permit him to remain in command of the army "only so long as the welfare of the Army of the Potomac demands—no longer." That tie with the army had become by now the only thing that counted: "I owe a great duty to this noble set of men, and that is the only feeling that retains me. . . . I owe no gratitude to any but my own soldiers here; none to the government or to the country." The conversation with Halleck was inconclusive. McClellan was left with the feeling that his army would be reinforced and would be ordered to resume its advance on Richmond, and Halleck also seems to have promised that McClellan would ultimately be put in command of Pope's army as well as his own. This McClellan took with a grain of salt. He wrote home that as far as he could see the authorities "intend and hope that my army may melt away under the hot sun."

Then the blow fell. At the end of July, Halleck telegraphed that reports from Pope indicated a lessening of Rebel strength around Richmond and suggested a reconnoissance in force by McClellan. Hooker's division, accordingly, was sent forward to the old battlefield of Malvern Hill, and McClellan prayed that the Rebels would incautiously attack—then, with a counterattack, he might create an opening for a real advance on Richmond. But the Rebel attack did not develop, a sputtering of small-arms fire along the picket lines died away in the thickets, and Hooker was withdrawn, furious, like Kearny earlier, swearing that a determined push would have taken the Confederate capital. McClellan himself was hopeful and wired Halleck that if he were properly reinforced he believed he could march his army to Richmond in five days; but Halleck replied that there were no reinforcements to send and bluntly told him that it had been decided to withdraw the entire army from the James to the upper Potomac— McClellan must get busy, send his sick north at once, and put his army on the transports as fast as he could.

McClellan argued, and Halleck, an expert at conducting disputation by telegraph, argued back, and the old business of Pinkerton's overestimate of Confederate strength arose once more to cripple the army. If Lee, said Halleck, actually had two hundred thousand men, as McClellan was insisting, then it was potentially disastrous to leave Lee posted between the armies of Pope and McClellan: with that strength he could easily hold off one army and crush the other. In the face of such numbers the only possible course was to reunite the armies in front of Washington and make the best fight possible. This was unanswerable, and the withdrawal began—as promptly as possible, McClellan felt; slowly and with unpardonable delay, Stanton and Halleck believed.

It was almost a question, by now, whether McClellan was fighting the Confederates or the authorities at Washington. He still saw himself as the man who would finally save the country, but he believed that he would have to do it over the objections of the government, as he was fully convinced that the men in Washington were determined to get rid of him at any cost. "Their game," he wrote to his wife, "is to force me to resign; mine will be to force them to place me on leave of absence, so that when they begin to reap the whirlwind that they have sown I may still be in a position to do something to save my country." Reflectively, and as if there might be doubts about the matter, he added: "With all their faults, I *do* love my countrymen, and if I *can* save them I will yet do so."

So the retreat began, down the peninsula to the wharves around Fortress Monroe. Along the way McClellan found time to be the fond husband thinking of the wife and baby girl at home—he did hope the child wouldn't make too much progress in the way of learning to walk and to talk before he could get home to see her. He sent his wife a pressed flower, picked in an old cemetery at Jamestown, and he tried to imagine what things were like centuries earlier when John Smith first came up this river. He mused about the stateliness and comfort with which the colonial planters managed to surround their lives: "It would delight me beyond measure to have you here to see the scenery and some of the fine old residences which stud its banks."

And the army marched along the narrow roads, leaving much behind it: youthful innocence, many comrades, and the bright hope that the war might yet be won before it settled down into hatred and blind destruction and the deaths of half a million boys.

On the march the men found that less care was being exercised now to prevent the destruction of Rebel property. One division came to a fine old plantation whose owner, somewhat rashly, had defiantly posted a sign forbidding the burial of any dead Yankees on the grounds. The men surged in over the lawn, set fire to the house, and resumed the march, a black pillar of smoke rising behind them in the windless air.

FOUR

An Army on the March

1. INDIAN SUMMER

To THE PEOPLE of the North it seemed that September was bringing the outriders of doom up across the Potomac. Lee's army, so unbelievably thin and ragged in actual appearance, so greatly magnified and transfigured by rumor and by fear, came splashing through the shallows of the fording places like a legendary host, and the sound of its bands playing "Maryland, My Maryland" was like the first far-off notes of the last trumpet. The rebellion had not been put down, after all; it was here, over the border, ready with fire and sword to conquer and lay waste. The great war to save the Union, entered into with so many waving flags, so many cries and cheers for departing trainloads of young men in bright new uniforms, might be coming to sudden catastrophe before the autumn leaves had turned. Here was something government could not handle, after all. The war was coming to the people.

All across the North the people reacted, as if the country itself were beleaguered. When the news came that Pope's army had been crushed and driven, Boston bestirred itself. At the urging of Governor Andrew churches were made ready to receive wounded men, and freight-car loads of bandages and medical supplies were hastily prepared and sent to Washington. Martial law was declared in the Ohio River cities of Cincinnati and Covington—for in the West Rebel armies under Braxton Bragg and Kirby Smith had slipped the leash and were driving north in pace with Lee. A self-organized "national war committee" met in New York, proposed that Pathfinder Frémont be reinstated in army command, urged the enlistment of a special corps of fifty thousand men for his special use, appointed a delegation to meet next day at Providence with such governors of the New England states as could be on hand, and then dropped out of sight and was heard of no more. In Pennsylvania, Governor Curtin called for the formation of volunteer militia companies. At least fifty thousand men would be needed, he said, "for immediate service to repel the now imminent invasion by the enemies of the country." The mayor of Philadelphia called on "all able-bodied men" to assemble at election-district precinct houses to be organized for service, and places of business throughout the state were ordered closed at 3 P.M. daily so that the new units might drill.

Governor Morton of Indiana told counties bordering the Ohio River to form military companies as speedily as might be. In the Susquehanna Valley people prepared to evacuate their towns, if need be; in Lancaster the citizens formed a committee of public safety and a home-guard company, and advised sister cities and boroughs to do likewise and "to arrest every man who uttered a traitorous sentiment against the government." Several hundred women met in Boston's Park Street Church and resolved that women throughout the country should form "circles of prayer" to pray for "the outpouring of the Holy Spirit on the entire nation." Cincinnati reported that "over 1,000 squirrel hunters from the neighboring counties" had come in to offer their services. From the Army of the

Potomac, Major General John F. Reynolds was detached and sent to Harrisburg, to give professional direction to Pennsylvania's home-guard levies.[1]

The Army of the Potomac was pulling itself together in Washington, getting its second wind for a sprint after Lee. The people of the North might arouse themselves with any number of public meetings, emergency volunteer companies, massed squirrel hunters, and committees of public safety on guard against treason: Lee was not going to wait for that frothy, fluid outpouring to harden into tangible military strength. If he was to be stopped, it was the army that would have to stop him, and the army knew it perfectly well.

Even before the army had fully reassembled in the Washington lines, the men in the ranks could see that there had been a great change. The Popes and the McDowells were gone, and the organization was running smoothly once more; scattered brigades were pulled together without fuss, the frantic running around and feverish activity at army headquarters had given way to quiet competence, regular rations were being issued again, new uniforms and equipment were being passed out, and in general it began to look as if there was a man at the top who knew what he was doing. Once again the lounging stragglers were swept up off the streets. Stray detachments of men, posted at odd spots in and around the capital, not knowing why they were posted there and strongly suspecting that no one else knew either, were called in and given regular assignments. There is record of one cavalry command that had been camped in a suburban field for weeks, "waiting for orders," completely forgotten by the authorities; it was found and put to work after someone thought to make a check on the rations issued by the commissary department. In Alexandria a huge camp suddenly came into existence for returning convalescents, wandering soldiers who had lost their papers, detailed men whose regiments had moved off without them, paroled prisoners awaiting exchange, and the like, and there were arrangements for getting these men back where they belonged with a minimum of fuss and delay.

Squadrons of regular cavalry patrolled the streets; they straightened out the endless traffic jams caused by the great wagon trains and put a stop to the ceaseless, useless galloping of couriers, mounted orderlies, and other overenthusiastic horsemen. The encircling lines of forts, which had never been quite finished, were put into final shape and were strongly garrisoned as new troops came in from the North. Watching it all, seemingly fascinated and heartened at the way order was swiftly replacing disorder, was President Lincoln; almost daily he would saunter into the offices which had been set up for the defenses of Washington, to inquire gently, "Well, how does it look today?" He remarked that now, for a change, he was not bothered all day and could sleep all night if he chose.

While all of this was going on the army began to move north and west out of Washington, in pursuit of Lee. It was the same army that had gone up the river just a year earlier to picket the fords and season itself in the open country, the same that had embarked from the river wharves that spring with banners flying and hearts high; but it knew a great deal more than it had known then, and many things had happened since the halcyon autumn when the war seemed more than half for fun. Gallic Colonel Regis de Trobriand, leading the Frenchmen of his 55th New York past their old camp at Tennallytown, mused sadly on the changes:

"What a contrast between the departure and the return! We had started out in the spring gay, smart, well provided with everything. The drums beat, the bugles sounded, the flag with its folds of immaculate silk glistened in the sunshine. And we were returning before the autumn, sad, weary, covered with mud, with uniforms in rags. Now the drummers carried their cracked drums on their backs, the buglers were bent over and silent; the flag, riddled by the balls, torn by shrapnel, discolored by the rain, hung sadly upon the staff without cover.

"Where are the red pantaloons? Where were the Zouave jackets? And, above all, those who had worn them, and whom we looked in vain along the ranks to find, what had become of them? Killed at Williamsburg, killed at Fair Oaks, killed at Glendale, killed at Malvern Hill; wounded or sick in the hospitals; prisoners at Richmond; deserters, we knew not where. And, to make the story short, scarce 300 revisited Tennallytown and Fort Gaines on their way to fight in upper Maryland."[2]

But if the colonel fell into a *neiges d'antan* melancholy when he looked back on the past, the army as a whole marched out of Washington in the highest of spirits. It had its old commander back, and it devoutly believed that he would make right all that had gone wrong. It had the pride of men who had fought hard and well, and it was sure that it would win the war the next time it went into battle. Getting into Maryland, too, was like coming home. No longer did the Westerners and the New Englanders feel that this slave state was foreign soil. The farms and the countryside might not be like Massachusetts and Indiana, but they were even less like the flat, dank, wooded country of the Virginia peninsula, and they had not been scorched by the usage of war.

Best of all, the people themselves were friendly. In western Maryland, at least, public sentiment had settled on the side of the Union by the fall of 1862, and the inhabitants welcomed the army joyfully. Young Captain Noyes, on Doubleday's staff, remarked that girls with buckets of cold spring water waited at almost every gate to give tired soldiers a drink. "If my hat was off once, it was off thirty times," he wrote, adding ecstatically: "Fine marching weather; a land flowing with milk and honey; a general tone of Union sentiment among the people, who, being little cursed by slavery [Captain Noyes was the staunchest of abolitionists], had not lost their loyalty; scenery, not grand but picturesque, all contributed to make the march delightful."[3]

Nearly all of the soldiers who made that march and left a record of their thoughts made the same sort of comment. A diarist in the 22nd Massachusetts felt that the combination of beautiful country and friendly people did wonders for the army; around the campfires, he said, there was universal agreement that they would beat Lee decisively next time they met him. In the 27th Indiana it was agreed that getting back into Maryland made all the difference; the men felt better, and it wasn't because of McClellan—this regiment had never served under him before and had no ingrained hero worship to respond to. General Abram Duryée's brigade—97th, 104th, and 105th New York, plus 107th Pennsylvania—straggled badly coming out of Washington; too many men had loitered, as one writer confessed, to enjoy "the comforts of civilization," and the first day's march was hard. But the stragglers all caught up after a while, and the brigade stepped out gaily; in the town of Frederick, the brigade historian recalled, "hundreds of Union banners floated from the roofs and windows, and in many a threshold stood the ladies and children of the family, offering food and water to the passing troops, or with tiny flags waving a welcome to their deliverers." The 3rd Wisconsin found it hardly needed its army rations in Frederick, "so sumptuous was the fare of cakes, pies, fruits, milk, dainty biscuit and loaves" which the citizens were passing out. A regimental diarist added fondly: "Of all the memories of the war, none are more plesant than those of our sojourn in the goodly city of Frederick."

Men in the Black Hat Brigade noted that children stood in almost every doorway, offering pies, cakes, drinking water, and the like, and flags were hanging from almost every window. A soldier in the 9th New York found the streets "filled with women dressed in their best, walking bareheaded, singing, and testifying in every way the general joy." Captain Noyes spoke of the passage through Frederick as "one continuous waving of flags, fluttering of handkerchiefs, tossing of bouquets," and said the soldiers grew hoarse cheering in response. A veteran of the 7th Maine extended his grateful benediction to all of Maryland; the regiment found camp sites "conveniently situated as to chickens, and corn and honey and apple butter, and like the Israelites of old, we looked upon the land and it was good." Remembering the hostile people on the peninsula, he added: "The girls no longer made faces at us from the windows, and the people were down at their front gates with cold water, at least, if they had nothing better. It seemed like Paradise, this Maryland, and many were the blessed damosels we saw therein." As French's division passed through one town a private looked at the flags, the smiling girls, and the general air of wholehearted welcome and called out joyously: "Colonel! We're in God's country again!"[4]

All in all, it was as if a clean wind from the blue mountains had blown through this army, sweeping away weariness and doubt and restoring the spirit with which the men had first started out; restoring, for the last time in this war—perhaps for the last time anywhere—that strange, magical light which rested once upon the landscape of a young and totally unsophisticated country, whose perfect embodiment the army was. In a way, this army was fighting against reality, just as was Lee's army. The dream which possessed the land before 1861 was passing away in blood and fire. One age was ending and another was being born, with agony of dissolution and agony of birth terribly mingled; and in the Army of the Potomac—in its background, its coming together, its memories of the American life which it imagined it was fighting to preserve—there was the final expression of an era which is still part of our heritage but which is no longer a part of any living memories.

And there was for the soldiers, just then, a brief pause in the war, a quiet, unexpected breathing space between battles, a little Indian summer of the Army of the Potomac. The country was tense and anxious, and in Washington the President and Cabinet and general-in-chief lived through almost unbearable suspense, and beyond the mountains Lee was somewhere out of sight, his ominous designs cloaked by silence. But the Union Army itself was, for the moment, almost peaceful. It moved ahead very slowly, while far in front the mountain outriders cantered with smoking carbines up against Lee's shifting patrols, groping to touch the hard solidity of his massed infantry. By night the army rested in green fields that were like the fields of home; by day, if it moved at all, it moved in leisurely style, cheered by the greetings from farmhouse and village. The men were old soldiers by now, able to live entirely in the present moment. As they moved northwest along the old National Road, the white tops of the wagon trains bobbing in the slow columns like the covered wagons of some unimaginable new folk migration, it was as if they passed in unhurried review, fixing in one suspended moment of time the image of the country that had borne them.

There was in the army a regiment called the Bucktails: 13th Pennsylvania Reserves, actually, owning a nickname because a private, in training-camp days, had ornamented his hat with a snippet of fur cut from the carcass of a deer hanging in front of a town meat market, and all the other men in the regiment had seen it and had gone and done likewise. The Bucktails had been enlisted in the spring of 1861 in the mountain country of northern Pennsylvania, where leading citizen Thomas Kane had put up placards in all the towns and hamlets stating the he was authorized to accept for service "any man who will bring in with him to my headquarters a Rifle which he knows how to use," and urging: "Come forward, Americans, who are not degenerate from the spirit of '76!" The men came swarming in to the recruiting places and formed scattered companies; and when it was time to assemble at Harrisburg three of the companies bought lumber and built rafts, with a platform on one raft so that the colonel's horse could ride, too, and rafted it down the West Branch of the Susquehanna, camping out nights along the banks and pausing to sing "The Star-Spangled Banner" jubilantly after they had shot the rapids above Rattlesnake Falls. Another company, the "Raftsman Guards," coming from farther west, likewise went by raft, down the Allegheny to Pittsburgh, and took the cars thence to Harrisburg.

The men had thought they were enlisting for three months, under the first call for troops, but when they got to the capital they found the state's three months' quota was filled, so they signed up for three years instead. Company K, lumbermen from Clearfield County, who were recruited at a mountain inn called "Good Intent and People's Line," was a bachelor company; started out with 123 men, found that only 100 could be accepted, and sent home all the married men. When the regiment was finally assembled for mustering in, good Colonel Kane resigned, stating that he lacked military experience—he used to carry an umbrella for sunshade while drilling the troops—and asking the men to elect Charles Biddle, a Mexican War veteran, in his place. The men did so, but insisted on making Kane lieutenant colonel, and when Biddle resigned a few months later to enter Congress, Kane got the regiment after all. He became an excellent soldier, later winning command of a brigade.

The regiment marched overland from Harrisburg into Maryland in the summer of 1861, and as it drew near to Maryland the men were tense: crossing the Mason and Dixon line would mean stepping into slave territory, into the war itself. So they halted, while a lieutenant seized the colors, ran across the state line, and boldly planted the flag on Maryland soil, whereat the regiment fired a salute, ragged but noisy. They were officially designated a rifle regiment—hangover from the day when a soldier who had and could use a rifle was very much a specialist—and they were equipped with breech-loading single-shot Sharp's rifles.[5]

Then there was the 27th Indiana, which came from what was already beginning to be called Copperhead country—the region west and south of Indianapolis, where Lincoln Republicans were not popular and there were strong ties linking the countryfolk with the Southland. The atrocity stories that were spread after the first battle of Bull Run seem to have had a part in pulling these boys into the army; wild tales of Rebels bayoneting prisoners and mutilating corpses "were as a fire in the bones," the regimental historian recalled. The 27th came into the army without any physical examinations whatever; the mustering officer, an overworked major of regulars, simply looked each company over, man by man, before accepting them, and many physical defects were carefully concealed. Men with gray beards shaved clean in order to look younger, or dyed their hair; hollow-chested men stuffed clothing inside their shirts; recruits with crooked arms held them tightly against their sides so the defect would not be noticed; others who lacked fingers held their fists clenched. Underage boys would write "18" on the slip of paper and put it inside a shoe; then, when asked if they weren't pretty young, they could truthfully say, "I'm over 18." Many of the boys came from homes where there was no sympathy with the Union cause, and regimental officers helped them with these dodges to get by the mustering officer before angry parents could come and haul them back home. Sometimes a company was advised to muster in at twilight, when physical defects were less likely to be noticed.

It was a boast of the 27th that it had the tallest man in the army, Captain David Buskirk, who stood six feet eleven inches in his socks. They tried to give him a solid company of six-footers; couldn't quite make it, but did give him eighty of them. The whole regiment averaged large in size, for all the potential 4-F's who had slipped in; when the regimental quartermaster drew shoes he had to go around the other regiments, swapping fives and sixes for nines and tens. His favorite regiments for this purpose were the 9th New York and the 29th Pennsylvania, regiments of city chaps who were somewhat undersized. For all that it was from a rural area, the 27th boasted that it was a jack-of-all-trades group. It had bakers, who manned regimental ovens; printers, who could set type and run captured printing presses—they had actually done it while the regiment served under Banks in the valley; engineers, firemen, and brakemen, if they had to operate any railroad trains. The regiment used to wish that it might, in the freakish chance of war, sometime capture a steamboat: it had plenty of steamboat hands, plus a pilot licensed for all Western rivers. As the army marched up into Maryland the 27th's brigade got two new regiments, 13th New Jersey and 107th New York, which came in full strength. The Indiana boys, their own ranks much depleted by hard service, gaped at them. "We had not realized before how large a regiment really was." They noticed, too, that the faces and hands of the new soliders were white, their uniforms looked uncreased and new, and that they still had an inexpert way of bundling up and carrying their equipment.[6]

New York City had contributed the famous Irish Brigade—63rd, 69th, and 88th New York, Irish to a man, carrying regimental flags of pure emerald green embroidered in gold with an Irish harp, a shamrock, and a sunburst. Brigadier General Thomas F. Meagher led these soldiers. Famous as an Irish patriot who had had a part in the unsuccessful uprising of 1848 and had been sent to Australia on an English prison ship, he had escaped and come to America and in 1861 saw the Union cause as the cause of freedom. He had raised this brigade with the backing of Archbishop Hughes of New York, and the regimental flags had been presented at a fine ceremony in front of the archbishop's residence on Madison Avenue. Deep-chested, muscular, gay, witty, sporting a trim mustache and imperial, and entirely looking the part of the dashing Irish soldier, Meagher had made the brigade a valiant fighting force. It was in Bull Sumner's corps, and they said that on the peninsula, whenever he had to go into action, Sumner first inquired: "Where are my green flags?" To the brigade had recently been added the 29th Massachusetts, which was Irish enough to keep the average up and fit in all right. As a general rule the brigade did not like New England troops, considering them scheming Yankee bargain drivers and narrow anti-Romanists to boot.[7]

The 40th New York was called the "Mozart Regiment," not because the men were devoted to music, but because the regiment had been organized with the special blessing of Mayor Wood of New York City, whose personal faction in the New York Democratic party was known as the Mozart Hall group, in opposition to Tammany. Six of the Mozart's ten companies came from outside the state, four from Massachusetts and two from Pennsylvania. These companies were filled with men who had simply insisted on getting into the war: independent companies, organized in 1861 after their states' quotas had been filled, which had refused to disband and had gone shoopping around looking for some regiment that would take them. Mayor Wood had been having much trouble recruiting the 40th New York, his reputation as a devout patriot not being of the best, so by special dispensation the out-of-state companies were taken in. The regiment stayed up all night when it got word that it was to leave for Washington and the front; played tag and leapfrog and fired blank cartridges from the two brass cannon which were at that time part of the regiment's regular equipment. When they started out they needed ten wagons to carry the regimental baggage; now, in the fall of 1862, they carried their baggage on their backs.[8]

The 1st Minnesota bragged that it was really the first volunteer regiment to be offered for Federal service in the war. Governor Alexander Ramsey of Minnesota happened to be in Washington when Fort Sumter fell, and he hot-footed it over to the War Department early next morning to offer his men for service, thus making Minnesota the first state to respond to Lincoln's call for troops. The regiment had been built around a St. Paul militia company known as the "Pioneer Guards." Mustered in at picturesque Fort Snelling, it found to its disgust that it was to be assigned to duty on frontier posts watching the Sioux Indians, and didn't get away from Minnesota until mid-June. Lacking uniforms, the state had clothed the men in black felt hats, black pants, and lumberjacks' shirts of checkered red; the boys didn't get regular uniforms until after the first battle of Bull Run. Like the Mozart Regiment, the men stayed up all night to celebrate when orders finally came to start east. They left Fort Snelling by steamboat (no railroad in Minnesota at that time) and took a train east from a port downriver; paraded through Chicago, the mayor riding beside the colonel, and were hailed by the Chicago *Tribune* as "unquestionably the finest body of troops that has yet appeared on our streets."[9]

The country was proud of those early regiments, and it knew how to show it. Traveling cross-country, en route to Washington, was for most of them a long succession of cheering crowds, brass bands, spread-eagle speeches, and banquets. The 3rd Wisconsin, which started east in July 1861, recorded that it was cheered on every farm along the track in southern Michigan, was visited at Adrian by a committee with buckets of iced lemonade, was given a grand banquet at Toledo, and was met at Erie by a committee of women bringing baskets of food. At Buffalo there was a parade through the city and a speech of welcome by the mayor, after which there was a banquet at the railroad depot. Next morning "the ladies of Elmira gave us a sumptuous breakfast"; at Williamsport the ladies gave them dinner and also stuffed their haversacks with cakes and cold meats. It was this regiment, incidentally, which treasured one memory of the battle of Winchester, where Stonewall Jackson routed Banks's corps. The rout having taken place, the men had lost formation and were legging it for the rear, and General Banks rode among them to rally them, calling out earnestly: "Men, don't you love your country?" To which a realist in the 3rd Wisconsin yelled back: "Yes—and I'm trying to get back to it as fast as I can."[10]

If they took the enthusiasm and cheers as part of the natural order of things, the men in those early regiments were also suspicious, fancying that treason might be found almost anywhere. Riding the cars from New York to Baltimore, the 12th Massachusetts felt that the train's slow progress could only be due to secessionist leanings on the part of the engineer—who, presumably, wanted the war to end before the regiment got to the front; so at a convenient stop they put the engineer off the train, while a private in Company G who had been an engineer before the war went to the cab and ran the train the rest of the way. The 3rd Michigan had a somewhat similar experience, riding the train down from Harrisburg to Baltimore. The men were told (they were never quite clear about who told them) that the engineer, a Rebel at heart, meant to wreck the train, so they put an armed guard in the cab, notifying the engineer that he would be shot at once if there was any funny business. They had an engineer in their own ranks and could handle the train themselves if they had to.[11]

Like nearly all the other Northern regiments in 1861, this 3rd Michigan was nervous when it came time to march through Baltimore—Baltimore, strongly secessionist in sympathy, where the 6th Massachusetts had been mobbed during the first weeks of the war. The 3rd Michigan marched through town with loaded muskets, its band playing "Dixie"—not yet fully identified as a Rebel tune: many Union bands played it in those early days—and the colonel sternly warned the mayor that "if a man in my regiment is hurt the streets of Baltimore will run with blood." The progress through Baltimore of the 6th Wisconsin was somewhat ignominious. No arms had yet been issued, and the regiment tramped across the city escorted by a detachment of two hundred cops, while city roughs stood on the street corners and hooted. The Frenchmen in the 55th New York met jeers but no violence in Baltimore; the colonel wrote that the men "recompensed themselves by mocking airs and gestures more expressive than polite."

But if going through Baltimore in 1861 was a trying experience for nervous recruits, the army to a man enjoyed going through Philadelphia. At the start of the war a citizens' committee there had organized what was called "The Philadelphia Union Refreshment Saloon" and saw to it that every regiment that went by got proper treatment—airy, roomy washrooms with plenty of soap, hot water and towels, a lobby where the men could rest and write letters, a big dining hall with an abundance of good food. Furthermore, this wasn't just part of the enthusiasm of the first few months of the war; the Philadelphians kept it up right through to Appomattox, and even opened a second "refreshment saloon" when the first became overcrowded. A member of the 37th Massachusetts recorded that his regiment visited Philadelphia six times during the war and got the same friendly treatment each time. A veteran of the 10th Massachusetts Battery, looking back fondly long afterward, wrote: "When supper ended we began our march across the city with such a handshaking with young and old of both sexes, and such a Godspeed from all the population, as came from no other city or town through which we passed, and this was continued until our arrival at the Baltimore depot. Could the wives and sweethearts left behind have seen the affectionate leave-takings at this place it might have aroused other than patriotic emotions in their breasts."[12]

This was a deeply sentimental army, and it sang a great deal; not stirring patriotic songs, full of rally-round-the-flag heroism—they were for stay-at-home civilians—but slow, sad tunes that could express the loneliness and homesickness of boys who had been uprooted and sent out to face hardship and danger and death. Their favorite was a song called "When This Cruel War Is Over," by Charles Carroll Sawyer: a song which might well have been, momentarily, the most popular song ever written in America. It sold more than a million copies during the war, which would be equivalent to a sale of seven or eight million today—and that was before the era of canned music and artful song pluggers, before the day when there was a piano or other musical instrument, plus some sort of musical training, in every home. The song went like this:

> Dearest love, do you remember,
>   When we last did meet,
> How you told me that you loved me,
>   Kneeling at my feet?
> Oh, how proud you stood before me
>   In your suit of blue,
> When you vowed to me and country
>   Ever to be true.

And the chorus:

> Weeping, sad and lonely,
>   Hopes and fears how vain!
> Yet praying, when this cruel war is over,
>   Praying that we meet again.

Men would sing that song and cry. More than any other possession of the army, it expressed the deep inner feeling of the boys who had gone to war so blithely in an age when no one would speak the truth about the reality of war: war is tragedy, it is better to live than to die, young men who go down to dusty death in battle have been horribly tricked. The higher brass didn't admire the song at all; some fathead in shoulder straps at one time actually issued an order forbidding the singing of it in the Army of the Potomac, on the ground that it encouraged desertion—being quite unable to see that it really worked the other way by giving the boys a chance to express their war-weariness simply by opening their mouths and singing rather than by dropping their muskets and running away. As might be supposed, the order was totally ineffective and was soon rescinded.

Next in popularity, probably, was "Tenting Tonight on the Old Camp

Ground"; a song more familiar nowadays because it hung on after the war, being adapted to express the emotions of old soldiers at reunions, whereas "Weeping, Sad and Lonely" wasn't, exactly. There was, of course, not a trace in either song of the jingle and stir of what is commonly thought of as patriotic music. "Tenting Tonight" frankly states the soldier's dejection:

> We're tenting to night on the old camp ground,
>   Give us a song to cheer
> Our weary hearts, a song of home,
>   And friends we love so dear.

The chorus complains:

> Many are the hearts that are weary tonight,
>   Wishing for the war to cease;
> Many are the hearts that are looking for the right,
>   To see the dawn of peace.

And the conclusion, very soft and long-drawn out:

> Dying tonight . . . dying tonight,
> Dying on the old . . . camp . . . ground.

They were sentimentalists, all right, the boys who sang those songs around their campfires, with the regimental bands lifting the slow melodies up to the dark sky like drifting plumes of wood smoke from the embers; but they weren't milk-and-water sentimentalists. If they chose to make a song about "dying tonight," they were the men who had to go out and do the dying, and they knew it. (In the thrice-valiant 2nd Wisconsin the figures showed that by the end of the war nearly nine out of ten men in combat assignments had been shot. If noncombatants like company cooks, officers' servants, ambulance details, and so on, are included, the proportion is closer to nine out of twelve.)

They liked "Lorena," too, although that was perhaps more popular in the Southern armies—"Lorena" with its sugary, paper-lace-valentine romantics:

> The years creep slowly by, Lorena,
>   The snow is on the grass again:
> The sun's low down the sky, Lorena,
>   The frost gleams where the flowers have been.

North and South, the armies sang Stephen Foster—"My Old Kentucky Home," "Old Folks at Home," "Old Black Joe," and "Nellie Gray," especially the latter. Ranking close to "Tenting Tonight" was "The Vacant Chair"—

> We shall meet, but we shall miss him;
>   There will be one vacant chair—

and they liked old favorites such as "Drink to Me Only with Thine Eyes" and "Auld Lang Syne" and—deeply, tearfully—"Home, Sweet Home." It is recorded that during the long winter after the battle of Fredericksburg, when the two rival armies were camped on opposite sides of the Rappahannock, with the boys on the opposing picket posts daily swapping coffee for tobacco and comparing notes on their generals, their rations, and other matters, and with each camp in full sight and hearing of the other, one evening massed Union bands came down to the riverbank to play all of those songs, plus the more rousing tunes like "John Brown's Body," "The Battle Cry of Freedom," and "Tramp,

Tramp, Tramp the Boys are Marching." Northerners and Southerners, the soldiers sang those songs or sat and listened to them, massed in their thousands on the hillsides, while the darkness came down to fill the river valley and the light of the campfires glinted off the black water. Finally the Southerners called across, "Now play some of ours," so without pause the Yankee bands swung into "Dixie," and "The Bonnie Blue Flag" and "Maryland, My Maryland." And then at last the massed bands played "Home, Sweet Home," and 150,000 fighting men tried to sing it and choked up and just sat there, silent, staring off into the darkness; and at last the music died away and the bandsmen put up their instruments and both armies went to bed. A few weeks later they were tearing each other apart in the lonely thickets around Chancellorsville.[13]

Singing on the march was not very common except among recruits. After the first half-hour an army march settled down to a dull question of endurance; there was mud to contend with, or if there was no mud there were choking clouds of dust, and nobody had any breath or enthusiasm to waste on songs. On special occasions, though, the troops might fall into step and strike up a song: one of the German regiments (all especially noted for their singing) came tramping into Frederick with flags uncased, singing the John Brown song lustily. It was noted, too, that when troops were marched through Charles Town, where old Brown had been tried and hanged, they had a way of singing that song. Once in a while, when the day was cool and the road was good, a regiment might sing a bit on the march out of sheer good spirits; but when it did the song was apt to be a homemade ditty, neither sentimental nor patriotic, like the little song of the Zouave regiments:

> Oh we belong to the Zoo-Zoo-Zoos—
> Don't you think we oughter?
> We're going down to Washing-town
> To fight for Abraham's daughter.

When the soldiers used music to complain about their lot, it was not so much the fighting they were protesting against—although, being very human, they would have been glad to be shut of it. Boredom, dirt, disease, bad food, and the general air of doing everything the hard way which is inseparable from army life (it began, no doubt, in Julius Ceasar's legions) seemed to cause most of the grousing. A veteran of the 2nd Massachusetts found military martinets the soldier's chief cross. He wrote that his colonel once put a company commander under arrest for talking to a sergeant (during a halt while the army was on the march) without requiring the sergeant to stand at attention—a touch which sounds quite modern, somehow. A man in the 37th Massachusetts thought the worst thing about army life was the long delay, with everyone standing in ranks under full pack, which occurred on every march. In the 21st New York a private wrote that the shoddy uniform was the worst trial; it absorbed the rain and held it next to the skin, keeping the soldier wetter and colder than if he were naked. To the historian of the 3rd Wisconsin, by far the worst feature of the entire war was the camp diarrhea, which hit almost everyone sooner or later and which in many cases became chronic, weakening men and causing them to lose weight, often resulting in death or in a medical discharge. A soldier in the 17th Michigan found war's worst trial "the terrible, nauseating stench that envelopes a military camp." To a young officer in the 57th New York the worst thing was the old army officer from the regular service; such men, he said, "suffered from red-tape-ism, slowness, desire for a comfortable berth, and above and beyond all, jealousy." By contrast, among the enlisted men the regular officers often seemed to be better liked than the volunteers; a private in the 128th New York noted that the one officer in his regiment who tried to look out for the enlisted men was the lieutenant colonel, the regiment's lone regular. The historian of the 4th

Rhode Island was bitter about the food given sick and wounded men in hospital; the mainstay, he said, was "shadow soup." He gave the recipe: put a large kettle of water on to boil, then hang a chicken so that its shadow falls in the water, and boil the shadow for half an hour; add salt and pepper and serve.

These were the particularized complaints. But the whole was greater than the sum of its parts. War itself was the real evil, and the charge was never fully formulated. Those soldiers lacked the easy articulateness of the modern youth, and they could never quite say what it was that they hated so much—and so, being unable to say it, they took it out by singing the sad, mournful little songs that come down the years so inexpressibly moving.

Chaplains the army had in plenty—one for each regiment—to give the boys spiritual consolation. Yet as one reads the memoirs and diaries there is a distinct impression that as a group, and with honorable exceptions, the chaplains somehow did not quite measure up. There were too many misfits; in that free-and-easy age, too many unqualified men, perhaps, had taken holy orders. A Massachusetts regiment had a first lieutenant who was a minister in private life; he pulled wires to get himself made regimental chaplain, failed, and wound up by absconding with ninety dollars in company funds. A diarist in another Eastern regiment mentioned a chaplain who was court-martialed for stealing a horse, and added that as a general thing the chaplains were not too highly thought of. For a time the 48th New York enjoyed a special odor of sanctity because so many of its officers had been ministers. It fell from grace, however, when it was put to work opening a channel for gunboats through some tidal swamp during the expedition to Port Royal and the Savannah delta. The work was extremely hard and the weather was very hot and steamy, and all hands became excessively profane, ex-ministers and all. A brigadier, watching them at work one day, asked the lieutenant colonel if he really was a preacher. The officer replied apologetically: "Well, no, General, I can't say I'm a regularly ordained minister. I'm just one of those —— —— local preachers."[14]

With the shepherds backsliding in that way, the 48th as a flock quickly got a reputation for unbridled wickedness. Famous throughout the army was the story told about the 48th in connection with this same coastal expedition. An attack by a new ironclad Rebel gunboat was anticipated, and elaborate plans were made to entrap the monster with submarine obstructions that would cause it to run aground on a mud bank. But then the question arose: how to board the vessel, once it was trapped? It was sheathed in iron and its ports would be closed flush with its sloping slides, and it would be impossible to get into it and subdue the crew. The colonel of the 48th (according to the legend) had the answer. Parading his regiment, he said, "Now, men, you've been in this cursed swamp for two weeks, up to your ears in mud—no fun, no glory and blessed poor pay. Here's a chance. Let every man who has had experience as a cracksman or a safe-blower step to the front." To the last man, the regiment rolled forward four paces and came expectantly to attention.[15]

Which calls to mind the evil repute of yet another New York regiment, the 6th, which had a large enrollment of Bowery toughs—one officer spoke of it as "the very flower of the Dead Rabbits, the crème de la crème of Bowery society." Army rumor had it that before a man could enlist in this regiment he had to show that he had done time in a prison: a libel, beyond question, but the army liked to believe it. And it was alleged that when this regiment was about to take off for the South the colonel harangued the men; thinking to inspire them, he drew out his gold watch and held it up for all to see. They were going, he said, to the Deep South, where every plantation owner, living luxuriously among his slaves, was waiting to be despoiled of a watch quite as good as this one. If they were brave soldiers each might get one for himself. Five minutes later, looking to see what time it was, he found that his watch was gone. (Writing long afterward, the regiment's historian complained bitterly about the "vicious nonsense" which was circulated about the regiment. He blamed the regiment's colonel, who liked the stories, having "that essentially American cynic humor which often finds amusement in wild exaggeration.")

Those New York regiments seemed to breed odd stories. A devout chaplain, it was said, went to the colonel of a Manhattan regiment which had no chaplain and asked permission to hold services. The colonel was dubious; his men were a godless lot, he said, and he doubted that the chaplain would accomplish much. But the chaplain, who believed in saving sinners where he found them, was insistent. He had just held services, he said, in the neighboring Brooklyn regiment, and—but that was enough. Between the Brooklyn and Manhattan regiments there was a great rivalry, and the colonel instantly ordered the regiment paraded for divine worship, announcing that if a man smiled, coughed, or even moved he would be thrown in the guardhouse. The chaplain held his services, and at the end asked if any men would come up and make profession of faith; thirteen men had done so, he said, in the Brooklyn regiment. The colonel sprang to his feet.

"Adjutant!" he bellowed. "Detail twenty men and have them baptized at once. This regiment is not going to let that damned Brooklyn regiment beat it at anything!"[16]

For a few days there in Maryland the army came about as close to contentment as an army on active service ever gets. The future did not exist, and the past would somehow be made up for; there was only the present, with easy marches, friendly country, clear weather, and good roads. A veteran in George H. Gordon's brigade has left a picture of a noonday halt: each man building a tiny campfire, putting his own personal, makeshift kettle (an empty fruit can with a bit of haywire for a bail) on to boil water from his canteen, shaking in coffee from a little cloth bag carried in the haversack. "At the same time a bit of bacon or pork was broiling on a stick, and in a few minutes the warm meal was cooked and dispatched. Then, washing his knife by stabbing it in the ground, and eating up his plate, which was a hardtack biscuit, the contented soldier lit his laurel-root pipe, took a few puffs, lay down with his knapsack for a pillow, and dozed until the sharp command, 'Fall in!' put an end to his nap."[17]

2. CRACKERS AND BULLETS

The best thing about being in Maryland, the soldiers agreed, was that the people had plenty of fresh provisions to sell and were quite willing to sell them. The army was in funds; most of the men had put in four months on the peninsula, a war-ravaged country where the people had no food to spare and in any case scorned to deal with Yankees, and there had been little chance to spend anything. It had been but little different along the Rappahannock, although in the larger towns a man could usually make a deal; the 14th New York was alleged to have passed some three thousand dollars in counterfeit Confederate notes—obtained heaven knows how—among the luckless shopkeepers of Fredericksburg. But now, with money in his pocket and things to spend it on, the soldier enjoyed a few days of better eating than the regulations called for.

The Civil War soldier would have stared in amazement if he could have looked ahead eighty years to see the War Department, in World War II, thoughtfully retaining female experts on cookery to devise tasty menus for the troops and setting up elaborate schools to train cooks and bakers. No such frills were dreamed of in his day; the theory then seems to have been that if the raw materials of dinner were provided in quantity the army would make out all right. In a sense, the government might have been right. The army did survive, although, looking back at the provisioning and cooking arrangements, one sometimes wonders why it didn't die, to the last man, of acute indigestion. For while the government provided plenty of food of a sort, the business of getting it cooked and served was left entirely up to the soldiers.

One regimental historian—whose experience was quite typical—recalled that when his outfit was first assembled in camp the authorities simply issued quantities of flour, pork, beans, rice, sugar, coffee, molasses, and bread, made kettles and skillets available, and then suggested that the men had better form messes of from six to ten members and get busy on the cooking. The men did as instructed, and in each mess the men took their turns acting as cooks. (The phrase, "acting as," seems expressive, somehow.) A few of the fancypants Eastern militia regiments which turned out in response to the first call for ninety-day service had no trouble; they hired their own civilian cooks and got along fine as long as they stayed close to town in established camps where ranges, bake ovens, and civilian markets were handy. But these were the regiments where private soldiers wore tailor-made uniforms (bought at the individual's expense, as carefully fitted and frequently as gaudy as a Coldstream Guard colonel's) and they were never characteristic, nor did they last very long.

Neither, for that matter, did the extreme sketchiness of the informal regimental messes. Sooner or later the institution of the regular company cook was established: two to a company, detailed to the job by order and excused from drill and combat duty. Naturally, their quality varied greatly. Here and there a regiment was lucky enough to find that it actually had some professional cooks in the ranks, although that didn't happen often; nobody, from first to last, was ever enlisted as a cook. Mostly, the company cooks learned their trade on the job, and the soldiers had to eat what they prepared while they were learning. A soldier in the 19th Massachusetts, considering the matter with an indignation which a quarter century of peace had not diminished, summed it up in words which most soldiers would have endorsed: "A company cook is a peculiar being: he generally know less about cooking than any man in the company. Not being able to learn the drill, and too dirty to appear on inspection, he is sent to the cook house to get him out of the ranks."[1] A notable exception to all of this was, as might be expected, the 55th New York, full of transplanted Frenchmen. They knew something about cooking, and their officers' mess, at least, was famous. President Lincoln dined with them once while they were in camp on the edge of Washington, and told the officers afterward that if their men could fight as well as they could cook the regiment would do very well indeed. They had given him, he added, the best meal he had had in Washington.

A good deal depended on the higher officers. If they insisted that their men be well fed, the men usually fared pretty well. Phil Kearny used to have a habit of sticking his head into the company mess kitchens just before mealtime to sample the food. If the cooking was bad or if the shack was dirty, the company cooks—plus the company and regimental officers—were sure to have a bad time of it before the general left.

In many cases that strange Civil War figure, the contraband, came to the rescue. Now and then, among the escaped slaves who attached themselves to the army as the campaigns in Virginia progressed, were house servants who could cook, and when a detachment got hold of one it never let him go. One company in the 21st Massachusetts acquired somewhere along the Rappahannock a contraband named (apparently by themselves) Jeff Davis. He was a first-rate cook, and he served also as a sort of unofficial commissary agent and general factotum for the entire company. They picked up a mule for him from some secessionist farmer's stock, and he loaded the beast with his kitchen equipment and supplies. Every pay day he would pass the hat and each man would chip in a quarter or half a dollar which Jeff Davis used as a mess fund, so that the company often enjoyed extras like fresh eggs, butter, and garden truck, most of them lawfully bought and paid for. This priceless contraband served with the regiment to the end of the war and went north with the men after Appomattox; he settled near Worcester, married, raised a family, and, wrote the regiment's historian, lived happily ever after—one case where emancipation worked out nicely.

But even after the kitchen arrangements were formalized there were many, many occasions when cooking was strictly a matter of each man for himself. On any march where speed was essential, or where there were frequent brushes with the enemy, regiments would be separated from their wagon trains for days at a time. Then the men were given "marching rations"—three days' supply of hardtack, coffee, and salt pork per man, plus sugar and salt, all carried in the haversack—and, as far as the army authorities were concerned, that was what the men lived on until the wagons joined them again. As a result, the experienced soldier always carried kitchen equipment with him: a little tin pan or empty can for a kettle, and a tin plate or half a canteen with an improvised wooden handle for frying pan. With these, and a few splinters to make a fire, he could get by, although what the results must have done to his stomach is enough to make a dietitian wince.

The hardtack was the great staple. It was a solid cracker, some three inches square and nearly half an inch thick: solid, hard, nourishing, and—by surviving testimony—good enough to eat when it was fresh, which wasn't always the case. Nine or ten of these slabs constituted a day's ration, and a soldier who wanted more could generally get them, since many of the men couldn't eat that many and would give some away. For breakfast and supper, when on the march, the soldier was apt to crumble the hardtack in his coffee and eat it with a spoon. Now and then a whole hardtack was soaked in water, drained, and fried in pork fat, when it went under the name of "skillygalee" and was, said a veteran, "certainly indigestible enough to satisfy the cravings of the most ambitious dyspeptic." At times the hardtack was toasted on the end of a stick; if it charred, as it generally did, it was believed good for weak bowels. Boxes of hardtack, piled high, often stood in all weathers on open platforms at railway supply depots. If the hardtack got moldy it was usually thrown away as inedible, but if it just got weevily it was issued anyway. Heating it at the fire would drive the weevils out; more impatient soldiers simply ate it in the dark and tried not to think about it.

The issue of salt pork was frequently eaten raw, on hardtack, when the men were on the march, since it was hard to cook without regular kettles and tasted about as good one way as the other, anyhow. Occasionally the salt pork was rancid when the men got it. When salt beef was issued instead of salt pork the men objected loudly—except, it was noticed, the men who had been deep-sea sailors before the war; no army salt beef could phase men who had eaten it out of the harness cask after six months at sea. The beef was so deeply impregnated with salt that it had to be soaked overnight in running water to be edible, and for that reason it was seldom issued as part of the marching ration. When cooked, it generally stank to high heaven, for it was often very aged. Now and then, when an especially bad hunk of it was served out, the men would organize a mock funeral, parading through camp with the offending beef on a bier and burying it—where the colonel could see, if possible—with fancy ceremonies. Bacon was enjoyed, but on the march the men preferred salt pork: carried in the haversack in hot weather, bacon had a way of giving off liquid grease, staining a man's clothing and quickly becoming unfit to eat.

Herds of cattle usually were driven along with the army, to be butchered nightly to provide fresh meat; the beef thus obtained, one veteran recalled, was "not particularly juicy." The company cooks (naturally) were always accused of keeping the best portions for themselves, and one officer remembered, with a noticeable shudder of distaste, the "odious beef served quivering from an animal heated by the long day's march and killed as soon as the day's march was ended." It was nice, now and then, to get a piece of fresh beef from which steaks could be cut. The company cooks would hand the steaks out raw, and each man would broil his own on a stick.

The coffee ration was what kept the army going. The government bought good coffee and issued it in the whole bean to prevent unscrupulous dealers from adulterating it, and the men ground it for themselves by pounding the beans on a rock with a stone or musket butt. The veteran learned to carry a little canvas bag in which he mixed his ground coffee and his sugar ration, spooning them out together when he made his coffee. The ration was ample to make three or four pints of strong black coffee daily, and on the march any halt of more than five minutes was sure to see men making little fires and boiling coffee. Stragglers would often fall out, build a fire, boil coffee, drink it, and then plod on to overtake their regiments at nightfall. Cavalry and artillery referred to infantry, somewhat contemptuously, as "the coffee boilers."

The favorite ration of all was the army bean. It was no go, of course, on the march, but in settled camps it was one food the men never tired of. Even the most inexpert cook knew how to dig a pit, build a wood fire, rake out the coals, lower a covered kettle full of salt pork and soaked beans, heap the coals back on and around it, cover the whole with earth, and leave it to cook overnight. The mess kettle, incidentally, was simply a heavy sheet-iron cylinder, flat-bottomed, some fifteen inches tall by a foot wide, with a heavy iron cover. When potatoes were at hand they were invariably boiled in such a kettle, and beef was often added to make a kind of stew. A real cook could make such a stew quite tasty by adding vegetables (if he had any), doing an intelligent job of seasoning, and thickening the broth with flour.[2]

As a general thing, even though the coffee was good and the baked beans were palatable, the food the Civil War soldier lived on ranged from mediocre to downright awful. Looking at the combination of unbalanced rations, incompetent cooks, and crackers fried in pork fat, one wonders how the men kept their health. The answer, of course, is that many of them didn't. There were many reasons for the terrible prevalence of sickness in that army—the incomplete state of even the best medical knowledge of the day is certainly one of them: no one then knew how typhoid fever was transmitted, for instance, and typhoid killed tens of thousands of soldiers—but faulty diet must have been one of the most important. (One private who lived through it all left it as his opinion that the great amount of sickness was due to "insufficient supplies and brutal, needless exposure of the men by officers of high rank.")

Surprisingly enough, the health of the soldiers was better when they were actively campaigning than when they stayed in camp. The constant exercise and fresh air seem to have counterbalanced the destructive effects of salt pork and hardtack; or perhaps, bad as that diet was, it nevertheless was better than the stuff the company cooks turned out when they had unlimited supplies to draw on. At any rate, the regiments which suffered the heaviest combat losses were almost invariably the ones with the lowest losses from disease. From first to last, some 220,000 Union soldiers died of disease during the war, and a good fifth of them came from regiments which never got into combat at all. Half of the deaths from disease were caused by intestinal ailments, mainly typhoid, diarrhea, and dysentery. Half of the remainder came from pneumonia—"inflammation of the lungs," as it was called then—and from tuberculosis.

This prevalence of sickness meant that in every regiment there was a slow, steady process of attrition, which began the moment the men got into training camp and never ended. And it almost seems as if the authorities went out of their way to make sure that this attrition would take place. By modern standards the arrangements for keeping a regiment's strength up were appallingly bad. Very little was done to keep physical misfits out of the army in the first place, and there were practically no provisions for replacing such men when the hardships of army life remorselessly weeded them out. The 27th Indiana was by no means unique in getting into Federal service without physical examinations. The same thing happened in many other cases. A member of the 5th Massachusetts wrote that physical examinations for his regiment were informal and were not given by a physician—"zeal and patriotism were recognized as potent factors, and their outward manifestations were given full credence." The recruiting, of course, was not uniformly that carefree, but the physical examinations were never really rigid; the men were expected to be "sound of wind and limb," but that was about all.

Yet if the entrance standards were excessively lax, the standards by which a man could be given a medical discharge—a "surgeon's certificate of disability," in the army jargon of the 1860s—were fairly high. The regimental surgeons were for the most part able and conscientious men, and when they found that a man was unfit for active service they said so, and he was paid off. In the spring of 1861 the 2nd New York discharged 118 men for disability. Most of the men promptly re-enlisted in other regiments, the war spirit running high at the time.

Thus, in actual practice, the rigors of life in camp in the 1860s did what the original entrance examination is expected to do now—eliminate the men who, for one reason or another, just weren't rugged enough to stand the gaff. The result was that no regiment in the army, at any time after the first few weeks of its existence, was ever anywhere near its full paper strength. On paper a regiment was supposed to consist of approximately a thousand men. Actually, very few regiments got to the battlefield with anything like that number. The 20th Massachusetts was mustered in, full strength, on July 2, 1861, getting its first medical exams, incidentally, after the mustering in. By mid-August, when it left Massachusetts, it was down to 500 men. Recruits and returned convalescents later brought in 250 more, but that was high-water mark: from then on its strength went steadily downward. Within a year of its enlistment the 128th New York was down to 350 men, although it had had few battle casualties. The 125th Ohio, which enlisted in the summer of 1862, numbered 751 men when it left Ohio for the South. Six weeks later it was down to 572. A typical entry in the regimental history, made at a time when the regiment was not in action, shows seven deaths and eight medical discharges for one month. The 12th Connecticut took a thousand men from home and had 600 "present for duty" when it lined up to go into its first fight.

Yet with all these losses there were few replacements. Throughout the war men were recruited by the states, not by the Federal government. The governors liked to form new regiments—each one offered a chance for patronage, with a colonel's commission to be awarded to some distinguished, well-heeled citizen, who had exerted himself to round up recruits. (There is a record of one New York merchant who spent $20,000 to raise a cavalry regiment. He became its colonel but was never seen in camp, finding the avenues and hotel bars of Washington much pleasanter. The regiment finally went off to fight without him, while he, having good political connections, became a brigadier and wound up in command of some empty barracks safely inside the Union lines.) The states simply had no arrangements whatever for recruiting replacement troops, since it was politically more profitable to form new regiments. Each regiment had to do its own recruiting when and if it could. Now and then an officer, sometimes a whole company, would be sent home on furlough to drum up men, but this was seldom very effective. Only Wisconsin, of all the states, officially recruited replacements for regiments already in the field, which was one of the reasons why every general liked to have a few Wisconsin regiments around if he could manage it.

The result of all this, naturally, was that the war was fought with what would now be considered skeleton regiments. A colonel who could take 500 men into action considered himself very lucky indeed. By the fall of 1862, when the army was drifting up through Maryland after Lee, a regiment which mustered as many as 350 men was fully up to the average, and many regiments were far under that strength. Technically, a brigade was supposed to consist of four regiments; later in the war we find brigades with six, eight, or even ten, jumbled together in a desperate effort to give the organization the man power a brigade ought to have.

Battle attrition, of course, was deadly. Hardly anybody realized it at the time, but the Civil War soldier was going into action just when technical improvements in the design of weapons had created a great increase in fire power and had given the defense a heavy advantage over the attack. The weapons those men used do look very crude nowadays, but by comparison with earlier weapons—the weapons on which all tactical theories and training of the day were based—they were very modern indeed. It is not much of an exaggeration to say that the armies of 1861 were up against exactly the same thing that the armies of 1914 were up against—the fact that defensive fire power had made obsolete all of the established methods for getting an offensive action under way. As in 1914, the enlisted man paid with his life for the high command's education on this matter.

The basic, all-important weapon, of course, was the infantry musket, and the standard of the war was the rifled Springfield. This was a muzzle-loader, with an involved procedure for loading. Drill on the target range began with the command, "Load in nine times: load!" (The "nine times" meant that nine separate and distinct operations were involved in loading a piece; recruits were trained to do it "by the numbers.") The cartridge was a paper cylinder encasing a soft-lead bullet and a charge of powder. The soldier bit off one end of the paper, poured the powder down the barrel, rammed the bullet down with his ramrod, cocked the heavy hammer with his thumb, and had a percussion cap on the nipple to ignite the charge when he pulled the trigger. For most rifles, these caps came in long rolls which were inserted in a spring-and-cogwheel device in the breech, exactly like the rolls for a child's cap pistol today.

This weapon has long since been a museum piece, but the big point about it then was that it was rifled and had a bullet which took the rifling properly. The bullet was the Minié, named for the French captain who had invented it—the bullets were "minnies" to all soldiers—a conical slug of lead slightly more than half an inch in diameter and about an inch long, with a hollow base which expanded when the rifle was fired and prevented leakage of the powder gases. It would kill at half a mile or more, although it was not very accurate at anything like that distance. Its effective range was from 200 to 250 yards—"effective range" meaning the distance at which a defensive line of battle could count on hitting often enough to break up an attack by relatively equal numbers. A good man could get off two shots a minute.

Compared with a modern Garand, the rifle was laughable; but compared with the smoothbore which had been the standard weapon in all previous wars, it was terrific. Early in the Civil War, before the government got the rifled muskets into mass production, many regiments were equipped with the old smoothbores, which fired a round ball or, sometimes, a cartridge containing one round ball and three buckshot: the "buck and ball" of army legend. Regiments which had to use such muskets were disgusted with them. Extreme range was about 250 yards, and accuracy was almost nil at any range. As one of the backwoodsmen from Wisconsin remarked, it took a fairly steady hand to hit a barn door at fifty paces. At very close range, of course, they were quite effective, especially when firing "buck and ball," which gave a scatter-gun effect. These primitive smoothbores were discarded as fast as new weapons were produced, and by the fall of 1862 few regiments on either side carried them.

Yet it was these ineffective old smoothbores on which all established combat tactics and theories were based. That is why the virtues of the bayonet figured so largely in the talk of professional soldiers of that era. Up until then the foot soldier was actually a spear carrier in disguise, the bayonet was the decisive weapon, and an infantry charge was just the old Macedonian phalanx in modern dress—a compact mass of men projecting steel points ahead of them, striving to get to close quarters where they could either impale their opponents or force them to run away. All offensive infantry tactics were designed to enable a commander to throw that compact, steel-tipped mass against an enemy line of battle.

But with the rifled musket it just didn't work that way any more. The compact mass could be torn to shreds before it got in close. The advancing line came under killing fire four or five times as far off as used to be the case. As one student of Civil War casualties remarked: "There was a limit of punishment beyond which endurance would not go, and the old Springfield rifle was capable of inflicting it."[3] Like the machine gun in 1914, here was a weapon which upset all the old theories. The natural result was that actual hand-to-hand work with the bayonet was a great rarity in the Civil War, for all the fine talk of grand bayonet charges to be found in the generals' memoirs. The bayonet was still carried and it was still a threat, but very few men ever used it. Of some 245,000 wounds treated by surgeons in Union hospitals, fewer than a thousand had been made by bayonets. One reason, of course, may be that when a man did get bayoneted he usually died on the spot; nevertheless, the figure is significant.

The Confederate General John B. Gordon, who got into about as much truly desperate fighting as any other man on either side, wrote after the war: "I may say that very few bayonets of any kind were actually used in battle, as far as my observation extended. The one line or the other usually gave way under the galling fire of small arms, grape and canister, before the bayonet could be brought into requisition. The bristling points and the glitter of the bayonets were fearful to look upon, as they were levelled in front of a charging line: but they were rarely reddened with blood."[4] In several private soldier's memoirs one finds the remark that the bayonet was really most useful as a candlestick: its point could be jabbed into the ground easily and its socket was just the right size to hold a candle.

The rifled musket not only had a greater range and accuracy than anything soldiers had ever used before; it made an uncommonly nasty wound—actually, a good deal worse, in most cases, than the one inflicted by today's rifle, and infinitely worse than that of the round ball fired by the old smoothbore. Its muzzle velocity was high enough to give the bullet considerable shocking power, and the bullet itself was relatively huge; furthermore, it usually mushroomed when it hit bone or cartilage, with dreadful effect. The ghastly number of amputations performed at all field hospitals—veterans repeatedly told of vast, hideous piles of severed arms and legs lying by the hospital tents in battle—did not take place because the surgeons were unskillful, or because they knew less than modern surgeons know about the way to treat gunshot wounds. They took place because when one of those soft-lead rifle bullets hit a bone it usually splintered the bone so horribly that no medical magic could save the limb.

As one army surgeon wrote long afterward, when comparative experience with the effect of modern rifles was available: "The shattering, splintering or splitting of a long bone by the impact of the Minié or Enfield ball were, in many instances, both remarkable and frightful, and early experience taught surgeons that amputation was the only means of saving life." The same surgeon added that a wound in the abdomen inflicted by one of these rifles was almost invariably fatal; the Minié bullet tore the intestines as the old smoothbore ball seldom did.[5] The one advantage that the Civil War soldier enjoyed over today's soldier, in respect to bullet wounds, was that at a moderately long range the old Springfield lacked penetrating power. There were repeated instances of soldiers being knocked down by bullets which failed to break the skin because they were stopped by some unimportant obstruction in the pocket—a deck of cards, a bundle of letters, or a pocket Testament. (How many solemn homilies were delivered, in succeeding years, by devout churchmen on that one subject: the pocket Testament that saved a life!)

All of this meant that the soldier who got hit was likely to be hurt pretty badly. The official casualty figures don't quite tell the story. They show, usually, that from six to eight men were wounded for each man killed outright, which is apt to make a modern reader (to whom a muzzle-loader is more or less a joke, anyway) assume that the weapon was ineffective. What the casualty figures don't show is that a substantial number of the wounded died in hospital; usually, according to one authority, about two thirds as many as were killed instantly. Altogether, about half of the men wounded in any engagement were lost to the army for good: mortally wounded, or permanently disabled. In addition, a fair number of the men reported "missing" were dead—men who fell in dense underbrush or isolated ravines, or men who crawled off into thickets after they were hit and were missed by the ambulance parties and the burial details.

For example, a battle is fought and an army reports a hundred men killed and nine hundred wounded. Of the nine hundred, between sixty and seventy will die, while nearly four hundred will be too badly crippled ever to return to duty. The army, therefore, has not merely suffered a temporary loss of nine hundred men; it has lost, permanently, rather more than five hundred men. The casualty figures for every Civil War battle, ghastly as they are even on the surface, need to be adjusted upward if they are to tell the true story.

If the power of the infantry rifle had been stepped up, so had the power of the artillery. The rifled gun was just coming in, like the rifled musket, and most generals did not quite understand what could be done with it. Standard fieldpiece when the war began was the twelve-pounder brass smoothbore; the famous "Napoleon" one reads so much about in the Civil War stories. When McClellan's chief of artillery set things up for the peninsular campaign he specified that two thirds of the army's guns should be Napoleons. This proportion was greatly reduced later, but the brass smoothbore remained popular right to the end. The gun fired a round ball some four and one half inches in diameter, had an extreme range of about one mile, but was woefully inaccurate at anything over half that distance; was liked chiefly for close-range work, when it fired case shot—thin-walled shell filled with a bursting charge and a hatful of lead slugs—or, by preference, canister. The canister cartridge was a sheet-metal cylinder with a charge of powder in an attached container at one end and a thin wooden plug at the other, and it was filled with two or three hundred round bullets. Firing this, the Napoleon was really a sawed-off shotgun of enormous size, and at close ranges—say up to 250 yards—the effect was murderous beyond belief. The only trouble was that the range of the infantryman's rifle had increased so; troops could often pick off the gunners before they got within canister range, unless the battery could be rushed into action after a charge got under way. In addition, the Napoleon was heavy and hard to move across broken country.

The new rifles were much better for everything except the infighting. They had twice the Napoleon's range, and for that day were exceedingly accurate. The commonest types were the three-inch iron rifle and the ten- and twenty-pounder Parrotts. These were fairly light and easy to handle, and all were muzzle-loaders. Breech-loading cannon did not appear on Civil War battlefields, except for a few English guns the Confederates imported, which fired queer-looking projectiles that were twisted to fit the spiraled hexagonal tubes and raised a horrifying screech as they sped through the air. The muzzle-loaders could be served with fair rapidity, and generals who knew how to use them could often break up an attack before it got well started because of their great range and power. (General Henry J. Hunt, in charge of Union artillery at Gettysburg, insisted to the end of his days that Pickett's historic charge would never have reached the Union line if Hunt had been allowed to do what he proposed—keep the Federal guns out of action during most of the preliminary bombardment in order to save their ammunition and their gunners, and plaster the Rebel infantry with everything he had from the moment it lined up for the charge. He was probably entirely correct.)

The artillerist's big problem throughout the war was with his fuses. They weren't too precise, and the gunner was never quite sure just where a shell would burst or, for that matter, whether it would burst at all. Federals had a big advantage over Confederates in artillery. They had more rifled guns, which meant they could often outrange the Rebel gunners, hitting without being hit; even more important, their fuses and powder were of better quality, so that the Northern gunner had a much better chance of seeing his shells strike and explode where he wanted them to.

What all of this meant—rifled muskets for the infantry, rifled cannon for the artillery—was that the defense had a huge advantage. Field tactics were still built around the idea of sending massed troops smack into and over the enemy line, and all military thinking ran in that direction. But a battle line whose flanks were anchored and which had any kind of protection in front was, in fact, just about invulnerable to that kind of attack. At Gaines's Mill, Fitz-John Porter, with one army corps (plus very moderate reinforcements late in the day), stood off most of Lee's army for six hours and came close to holding his ground for keeps. At Malvern Hill, where the artillery had a clear field, the Rebel assaults just didn't have a chance. Likewise, at Second Bull Run, Jackson's men behind their railway embankment were in shape to hold their ground for the rest of the summer. The fight Gibbon's and Doubleday's men had with Jackson's corps there earlier, with both battle lines standing elbow to elbow and blazing away, might have been in the grand tradition of the earlier wars, but for the 1860s it was utterly useless; murderous enough to satisfy the most bloodthirsty, but almost as out of date as it would be today.

The armies had begun to adjust themselves to the new state of affairs. The skirmish line—which originally had been merely a thin cordon of scouts going ahead to make sure the enemy didn't have any unpleasant surprises concealed in advance of his main line—was being built up, bit by bit, into an attacking line. An assault on a hostile position was ceasing to imply a steady, unbroken advance by men whose one aim was to reach a hand-to-hand encounter; the old lithographs of Civil War battles, drawn by men who weren't present, have left a false impression. The most spirited "assault" on a hostile position was apt to be delivered by troops who were completely motionless, hiding behind any obstruction the ground afforded, moving forward—when they did move forward—by short rushes, advancing small parties here and there under a cover of protective fire, seeking to build up within effective range a firing line heavy enough to beat down the opposing fire and persuade the enemy that it was time for him to go. A battle line which was getting the worst of it often gave way almost imperceptibly, the men firing and then stepping back a couple of paces while they reloaded, the attackers moving forward in the same manner. While this happened the line that was being beaten would leak men to the rear, as individual soldiers here and there decided they had had enough and turned to run.

Small inequalities in the ground—an outcropping of rock, a sunken road, an old fence whose rails could be pulled loose and piled along the ground to provide protection—were apt to become of decisive importance. The great defect of the Civil War musket was that only a contortionist could load it when he was lying down; if he fought in a prone position, as he very often did, he needed some sort of protection so that he could load his piece safely. The soldiers early noticed that a surprisingly high percentage of crippling wounds occured in the right hand and arm, exposed when a man rammed a new charge down his muzzle-loader. When regular entrenchments were dug, so that men were fully protected while they loaded and fired, direct assault became practically impossible—as Grant finally realized at Cold Harbor.

It was because a frontal attack was so easily repulsed that the flanking movement was so important. In front, a brigade might have the direct fire power of fifteen hundred rifles; caught end-on, at either extremity of its line, it had a fire power of exactly two, and so was utterly helpless unless it could shift its position fast. Where a whole army could be flanked, the way incautious Pope let Longstreet flank him at Bull Run, the inevitable result was complete defeat; in any battle line, a gap between regiments or brigades was a sure invitation to disaster. Impregnable as his position was at Fredericksburg, Jackson had a few bad moments when Meade found an open place between two brigades; if Meade could have been supported, old Stonewall might have had serious trouble. Pickett's great complaint after Gettysburg was that he had to make his assault with no protection for his flanks: the Federals curled around the ends of his line and tore the heart out of him.

To get from marching formation into fighting formation, the soldier had to learn, and become letter-perfect in, a long series of intricate maneuvers, as formalized as a ballet dance. If he had to march any distance at all he did it in column—column of twos, of fours, of platoons, of companies, or what not. To fight, the column had to be spread out into a long line two ranks deep, and the complexities of infantry drill in those days, designed to bring this about, were something today's soldier is happily spared. Furthermore, those complexities weren't just parade-ground maneuvers; they had to be learned if the men were to be able to fight. There were a dozen different ways for shaking a marching column out into line, and the men and their officers had to know all of them—had to know them well enough so that the maneuvers could be performed under fire, for if an organization formed its battle line too soon it was all but impossible to get it forward into action. The wild rout at the first battle of Bull Run is perfectly comprehensible: most of the soldiers just did not know how to perform those maneuvers. Once they got into line, they fought well; the trouble was that neither officers nor men had ever had any experience at swinging a marching brigade into a formation from which it could fight, or vice versa, and they got hopelessly snarled up when they tried it. One participant recalled that a Massachuetts regiment was ordered to open fire while it was still formed in column of companies. Naturally, men in the leading ranks were killed and wounded by the fire of their own inexpert comrades in the rear. The wonder is that either army, in that first battle, was able to do any fighting at all.[6]

Unless troops were expected to capture a remote position and stay there overnight, in which case they would want food and blankets, the usual routine was to leave knapsacks and other surplus equipment in bivouac before moving up to fight. That order was always complied with gladly; no soldier ever enjoyed carrying his knapsack, but the one the Civil War soldier carried seems to have been especially irksome—it was poorly designed, so that its straps cut the shoulders and strained the back even more than its weight and bulk made necessary. Unless the regimental or brigade commander was a stickler for doing everything regular-army style, seasoned troops soon discarded the knapsack altogether and substituted the blanket roll. This was formed by spreading out the half of a pup tent which each soldier carried, laying the opened blanket on top of it, arranging such spare cothing as the soldier might have on top of that, and then rolling the whole business up as tightly as possible, tying it with straps from the discarded knapsack, looping the two ends together to form what the soldier called a horse collar, and then slipping it over one shoulder. The army was mildly amused when the spanking-new 118th Pennsylvania joined up on the way through Maryland. This regiment, known as the "Corn Exchange regiment" (it had been raised and equipped by elderly patriots of the Phildelphia Corn Exchange), carried oversized knapsacks, well filled with spare pants, boots, coats, and other oddments. When it came into camp the veterans urged the men to throw all that truck away and switch to blanket rolls, but the Pennsylvanians refused—they wanted to do things right, and the regulations said knapsacks and extra clothing, and they'd stick with 'em. A man in the 22nd Massachusetts, clucking at them noted: "I don't suppose there was a spare shirt in my company," and added that his mates traveled so light one man would carry a towel and another man a cake of soap—no sense in each man loading himself down with both.

Other new regiments besides this one from Pennsylvania came in while the army was in Maryland. They came in gaily enough, looking enormous by contrast with the war-thinned veteran regiments, and their uniforms and equipment were new and unstained. The veterans were glad to see them, and remarked that all the newness would get worn off soon enough. One officer, watching them march into camp, wrote: "Some were singing the John Brown song, and others found occasion for merriment in commenting upon the picturesque appearance of our weathered and sunburnt soldiers. They all seemed cheerful, and as their long columns and full ranks marched by, their polished arms glistening in the sun, one could scarcely repress a sigh at the thought that, with a certainty, hundreds of these men would fall in the battle which all knew was now closely impending."[7]

3. GENERALS ON TRIAL

Back in Washington there was General Halleck, and the general was worried. Worrying, he called for incompatibles, demanding in one breath a dashing pursuit and an extreme of caution. Lee must be overtaken, brought to battle, and crushed, no matter what; but the army must remember that its primary function was defensive. If it did not hurry, Lee might get away; if it went too fast, Washington might be exposed. McClellan should keep his left firmly anchored on the Potomac as he advanced, lest Lee slide past him to the south and dash into the capital. On the other hand, it was dangerous to stick too close to the river: Lee might angle off in the other direction, making (so to speak) a sweep around right end, seizing Baltimore and coming down on the capital from the north. All of these points glowed and sparkled by turns, like shifting specks before the eyes of a troubled strategist. Halleck's telegrams to McClellan at this time, although they were numerous, were nagging rather than helpful.

In the beginning McClellan had asked that the garrison at Harper's Ferry, some twelve thousand good men, be ordered back to join the main army. He argued that the place itself was of no great importance, that it could quickly be reoccupied once Lee had been driven south, and that it was wholly indefensible and could not be held in any case if Lee wanted to make a snatch at it. Halleck pooh-poohed at him: the twelve thousand men were safe enough, nothing to worry about there. Later, when Lee had his army squarely interposed between Harper's Ferry and the Army of the Potomac, Halleck notified McClellan that the garrison was his to command as soon as he could go pick it up. It couldn't get out unaided, so it would just have to hold on until McClellan could go and relieve it, which he had better do at his early convenience. And so on.

Old Brains was in the top command and he was not being particularly impressive. He was strictly a headquarters operator. General Pope (whom one could nearly feel sorry for, if he weren't Pope) had called on him, almost prayerfully, to come and take command in the field around the time of the second Bull Run fight, but Halleck felt insecure anywhere except at the Washington end of the telegraph line. He refused to budge then and he was not budging now, and he surveyed the war from his office in the War Department, at 17th Street and the avenue, and looked portentous as the papers piled higher and higher on his desk. As he studied these papers—or, for that matter, when he indulged in thought of any kind—he had a way of rubbing his elbows, slowly and methodically: a mannerism which drove Secretary of the Navy Welles almost frantic.

Welles had a number of dealings with him, there being divers matters on which army-navy co-operation was essential, and he came away from all of them feeling rather baffled. When he put a problem up to Halleck, he wrote, "he rubbed his elbow first, as if that was the seat of thought, and then his eyes," and then made noncommittal remarks; and Welles recorded in his diary the impression that Halleck "has a scholarly intellect and, I suppose, some military acquirements, but his mind is heavy and irresolute." Unvarnished old Andrew Foote, the diligent flag officer who commanded the navy's gunboats in the Mississippi early in the war, when Halleck commanded out there for the army, told Welles bluntly that Halleck was a military imbecile who might just possibly make a good clerk. And James Harrison Wilson, then a young officer of topographical engineers, later to become one of the Union's best major generals and an advocate of making war modern-style with magazine rifles, wrote long afterward of the impression he received when he called on Halleck in his office at the War Department:

"He had already received the sobriquet of 'Old Brains,' but when I beheld his bulging eyes, his flabby cheeks, his slack-twisted figure, and his slow and deliberate movements, and noted his sluggish speech, lacking in point and magnetism, I experienced a distinct feeling of disappointment which from that day never grew less. I could not reconcile myself to the idea that an officer of such negative appearance could ever be a great leader of men.... Long before the war ended he came to be recognized by close observers, and especially by the Secretary of War, as a negligible quantity."[1]

The record of Halleck's dispatches during the days just before and after Pope's disaster makes curious reading. At a time when the big problem on which the fate of the Union might depend was to get Pope's and McClellan's armies united before Lee could force a battle, Halleck was sounding partly like a dollar-a-year man worried because the newspapers were impertinently printing confidential memoranda, and partly like a tired bureaucrat fussily absorbed by trifles. He wired Pope to clean all the newspaper reporters out of his army and to let no telegrams go out except those signed by himself—there had been too many news leaks recently. Pope protested; Halleck replied that "your staff is decidedly leaky" and complained that the very order calling for a news black-out had been printed in the papers as soon as it was issued. Virtuously Halleck added that "there has been much laxity about all official business in this army."

Office details engrossed him. Three days before the great collision at Bull Run, Pope protested that he was not being kept up to date about the movements of McClellan's forces. Halleck wired back petulantly: "Just think of the immense amount of telegraphing I have to do and then say whether I can be expected to give you any details as to the movements of others, even when I know them." After the fighting began, when Pope implored Halleck to come out and take charge of things himself, Halleck wired tersely: "It is impossible for me to leave Washington." When the commander of the defenses of Washington complained that he could not man the fortifications owing to lack of artillerymen, Halleck replied: "If you are deficient in anything for the defense of the forts, make your requisitions on the proper office.... I have no time for these details and don't come to me until you exhaust other resources."

To anyone who has ever worked in Washington, Halleck is quickly recognizable for what he actually was: a typical old-line government-service hack, to whom the tidy operation of an office is an end in itself, infinitely more important than anything the office can conceivably *do*. If the papers progress smoothly from "incoming" to "outgoing," all is well, even though the Republic fall, and it is much less important to prevent the fall than to make certain that no wreckage lands on one's own desk. The Republic is strong and it has amazing resilience, and it can support people like that ordinarily without much trouble, but it can hardly endure having such a one in command of its armies at the height of a furious war.

In the midst of all the Bull Run confusion Secretary Stanton sent in a demand for the full record regarding McClellan's withdrawal from the peninsula: when was he ordered to leave, when did he leave, was the whole operation handled with such slackness as to endanger the country? Recognizing this as Stanton's search for ammunition to destroy McClellan, but bearing in mind also that McClellan might yet ride out the storm and be the hero of the nation, Halleck sent a facing-both-ways reply. He gave all the dates, stated that the withdrawal was not made with the speed the national safety required, but added that once McClellan did begin to move he moved fast and that McClellan at the time reported the delay as unavoidable. No matter who won, Halleck was safe. His reply could be read as condemnation or as vindication, as circumstances might require.

And so one more attempt by the President to solve the problem of army high command was flickering out in windy futility. Lincoln had demoted McClellan because, with McClellan in the number-one spot, nothing much ever seemed to happen. There had been no way to convey to the young general the terrible urgency of the moment, the need to bring the war to a close before it blew up into a raging flame that might consume more than it saved. For a time the President himself, aided by the Secretary of War, had been running things, which had brought nothing but disaster. Military affairs could not be handled by amateurs, even though the President, with a persistence both ludicrous and pathetic, drew military textbooks from the archives and boned up on strategy in his spare time. So Halleck, the genius recommended by General Scott, had been called in, and for a space Lincoln thought he had what he finally got when he called in Grant; but now Halleck was proving that Lincoln had just made another mistake.

Which was tragic, from any viewpoint. Almost anything—including a change in the American form of government—might happen if the command problem were not solved. McClellan's implied proposal for veto power by a soldier over political decisions by the civil authorities had been pigeonholed neatly enough, but some equally astounding suggestions were coming in from other quarters. Chase and Stanton were leading a drive for government by Cabinet: choice of the top generals, and with it control of the war, should be lodged with a junta of cabinet ministers. This drive was failing, partly because Lincoln would have none of it and partly because of the good sense and Yankee stubbornness of Gideon Welles, who flatly refused to be a party to it. Dimly allied with it was a move by Republican leaders to give executive control to Congress: Congress should pick the generals, pass on strategy, and set all war policies, and the Committee on the Conduct of the War—busily spreading fear and distrust and working with clumsy ruthlessness and undying energy—would be its instrument. Nobody who doubted the need for ending slavery overnight would be allowed to have any hand in army affairs—although private soldiers who were not abolitionists would still, presumably, be allowed to die in battle, if perchance they were hit by Southern bullets.

This pressure by the leaders of his own party was something Lincoln could by no means ignore. He had taken his political life in his hands by reinstating McClellan in command of the Army of the Potomac, and the party leaders were sounding off about it. Senator Zachariah Chandler of Michigan, almost incoherent with fury, underlining words with spluttering pen point, was writing that recent disasters to the army had been caused by "treason, rank treason, call it by what name you will," and could see no hope save in "a demand of the loyal governors <u>backed</u> by a <u>threat</u>" to bring about an immediate change in policy; the President was "unstable as water" and was letting himself be "bullied by those traitor Generals" who would yet create a military dictatorship.[2]

To the Republican leaders, everything was simple. The Army of the Potomac was not aggressively used and was shamefully pushed around by muscular Rebels. The reason, as they saw it, could only be that it was led by men whose hearts were not in the cause; by casehardened Democrats; by men who sympathized with slavery and who therefore did not really want the rebellion suppressed; by men disloyal, in plain English. The remedy was, of course, obvious: entrust the army only to generals whose abolitionist convictions were strong beyond all question and there would be no more of this pampering and cosseting of treason.

This led them into manifest absurdities. They considered John Charles Frémont ideal material for high command: he was sound on the slavery question, and that was enough. The mere fact that he was totally devoid of military ability was beside the point. They also felt that the ineffable Ben Butler would make a good army commander; he was fully as incompetent as Frémont in the military field, but he was "loyal" on the only issue which mattered—even now he was rubbing slaveholders' noses in it, in New Orleans. Franz Sigel, the transplanted German revolutionary, and David Hunter, who had rashly proclaimed emancipation along the Georgia coast, would be equally acceptable. No one ever accused those men of being especially qualified soldiers, but no one ever accused them of sympathy with slavery, either, and that was all that counted. Lincoln flared up once when burly Ben Wade was insisting on the removal of McClellan; if he removed him, asked the President irritably, with whom should he replace him? "Anybody!" cried Wade. Lincoln shook his head; "anybody" might do for Wade, he said, but he must have *somebody*.

Yet these men had a point. One could almost say that they were right for the wrong reasons—or partly right, at any rate, for reasons that were mostly wrong. There *was* a crippling deficiency in the army command, from the brigades and divisions on up, and it was the kind of deficiency from which the Confederate army of Northern Virginia did not suffer: a lack of the hard, grim, remorseless, driving spirit that must be on tap if wars are to be won.

Stonewall Jackson in the Shenandoah Valley offers an example: driving his men in pursuit of Banks with remorseless fury, sending them on far past the point of physical exhaustion, continuing to pursue even though most of his army had fallen out from sheer inability to take another step, keeping it up long after a more sober general would have realized that pursuit was impossible—but winning, in the end, because he forced Banks to fight at Winchester before Banks could rally his men and get set for the blow, which meant that Banks got licked disastrously.

Jackson was an undefiled genius, to be sure, and it is hardly fair to expect all corps and division commanders to measure up to his standard. But there was a touch of the same sort of thing in the other Confederate commanders. General A. P. Hill was too heedless and impetuous by far, rushing into the attack without proper caution—but, in the end, providing the killing punch, against the odds, that helped to knock McClellan's right wing back behind the Chickahominy. Longstreet was sullen and balky, ignoring Lee's expressed wish, waiting for his foe to make one more ill-advised maneuver. Yet finally, when the opening appeared, he came down on the enemy's exposed flank like an avalanche, every man in action, no reserves held back for use in case something went wrong; and he turned the second battle of Bull Run into a rout. The Confederacy's other General Hill, D. H. Hill, was a carping dyspeptic who observed that Lee's tactics at Malvern Hill were all wrong and that it was hopeless to assault the massed Yankee guns; but when finally ordered he went in with such a cold fury that he almost turned certain defeat into dazzling victory. The least common denominator of those men was that they fought all-out. If they hit at all they hit with everything there was. They had an exultant acceptance for the chances of war. They fought as if they enjoyed it, and they probably did. The Army of the Potomac just was not getting that kind of leadership. Kearny had had it, but he was dead. Most of the other generals seemed uninspired.

What the radicals really meant when they complained that the Federal generals were too easy with their opponents was that the generals kept missing their chances for lack of that extra ounce of deep combativeness. They were quite wrong in believing that this would be remedied by promoting stanch abolitionists, but they were quite right in insisting that more forceful leaders were needed; and they anticipated Clemenceau in believing that war was far too important to be left to the generals, anyway. The North had not yet found the men who had the flaming spirit of war. McClellan's army was not handled the way Lee's army was: neither as a whole nor in its divisions and brigades. The key perhaps lies in the fact that any attempt to show how a Northern general at this period failed to measure up usually makes its point by showing, for contrast, what his opposite number on the Confederate side was doing.

Canny old Secretary Welles in the Navy Department really had the answer. He was ceaselessly shuffling naval officers, looking for that hard-fighting, driving quality without which all other assets are vain. Over and over in his diary one finds him speaking of some distinguished officer who didn't quite measure up: "He had wordy pretensions, some capacity, but no hard courage . . . scholarly pretensions, some literary acquirements, but not of much vigor of mind. . . . Is an intelligent but not an energetic, driving, fighting officer, such as is wanted for rough work." He summed up the army's problem neatly enough: "Some of our best-educated officers have no faculty to govern, control and direct an army in offensive warfare. We have many talented and capable engineers, good officers in some respects, but without audacity, desire for fierce encounter, and in that respect almost utterly deficient as commanders."

A considerable part of the radicals' suspicion was directed at West Point. Had not that school been under Southern control for a generation or more? Had not some of its most distinguished graduates gone South when the war began? Did it not seem to produce, for the North, bookish and doctrinaire generals who made war by rote and neglected to hit the enemy when he should be hit? And was not war itself, for that matter, really quite a simple matter if a man had his heart in the right place? To the radicals, lack of professional training for army command was a positive asset, not a deficiency. A man whose heart was in the war was infinitely better than a professional who did not care.

Since most of the really successful generals in that war, Northern and Southern alike, finally turned out to be West Pointers, this attitude seems almost willfully obtuse today; yet here again the politicians had a point. The government's experience with the older regular-army officers in the early part of the war had not been too happy. Very few of the regulars had shown enthusiasm for the Northern cause. Many limited themselves to a strict performance of the letter of their duty, were utterly lacking in zeal, openly predicted defeat, and admittedly served the North only because the honor of a soldier required it. The stuffiness that had grown up in a small officer corps limited to routine duties in the long years of peace had not gone unnoticed. Jacob Cox of Ohio, a civilian who rose to become a better than average major general, has recorded that one general to whom he reported early in the war admonished him severely on the importance of obeying orders literally but not going one step beyond: "If you had been in the army as long as I have, you would be content to do the things that are ordered without hunting up others." Cox was quite as caustic as anyone in criticizing the incompetent officers who came in from civilian life, for political reasons, under the volunteer system, but he remarked: "It seems to me an entirely fair conclusion that with us in 1861, as with the first French republic, the infusion of the patriotic enthusiasm of a volunteer organization was a necessity, and that this fully made up for the lack of instruction at the start."[3]

And if the volunteer system elevated many a nincompoop to high command, it also brought up some good men with solid talents for war: more of them than one is likely to realize, reading the blanket denunciations of political generals. The North got men like John Logan and Frank Blair, for instance—untutored civilians who became such good soldiers that each was able to command an army corps under as grim a fighting man as William T. Sherman. Blair and Logan were political generals pure and simple, one the brother of a cabinet minister, the other a prominent Democrat whom it was important to placate, but they were first-rate soldiers as well. It may be that Sherman, with his rough informality and his utterly unregimented mind, had more of a knack for developing fighting men than anyone in the East had; it may be noted that in the Army of the Potomac O. O. Howard never showed a sign of anything but diligent mediocrity, but that when he was transferred west and went under Sherman he presently became an army commander. On his march to the sea Sherman had more ex-civilians than West Pointers among his generals, and they were men of his own choosing. Sherman's favorite corps commander was believed to be Joseph A. Mowrer, who never saw West Point.

In the East, too, some of the volunteer officers were measuring up. One of the best men in the Army of the Potomac was the amazingly warlike Manhattan lawyer, Colonel Francis Barlow, now commanding the 61st New York but ultimately to be an inspired, savagely fighting division commander. Barlow had the quality the Republicans were looking for, if they only knew it—the indefinable something which can best be summed up as a positive taste for fighting. Instead of wearing a regulation officer's sword he carried the heaviest cavalry saber he could find; said that when he whacked a laggard or a straggler with the flat of it he wanted to hit with something that would hurt. He had an obsession about preventing straggling, and he let it gnaw at him until he found the answer, which wasn't until after he came to division command. Then, when on the march, he used to detail a company to form a skirmish line, with fixed bayonets, at the rear of the division column, with orders to sweep up and drive forward all stragglers. It wasn't a pleasant assignment. Most of the men in the skirmish line had to scramble over ditches and fences and fallen logs and work their way through brambles and underbrush while the rest of the army was tramping the smooth highway, and they got all the dust the division kicked up. The natural result was that after an hour of it they were mad enough to bayonet their own parents, and a straggler who fell into their hands was due to get very rough treatment. As a consequence: no stragglers from Barlow's division.

Barlow was no stickler for the niceties of military dress. He wore his single-breasted uniform coat unbuttoned, and under it he wore a checked flannel shirt, lumberjack-style. He looked, one of Meade's staff officers wrote, "like a highly independent mounted newsboy," and a Brady photograph shows him as a slouchy, rangy, limber young man, black felt hat crumpled in one hand, heavy boots on his feet, clean-shaven, rather handsome, with quiet, deadly-cold eyes. After he got his division he took it where the fighting was. Somebody totted up figures after the war and found that in all the Federal armies there were nineteen regiments which had done so much hard fighting that each had lost at least sixteen officers killed in action; five of the nineteen belonged to Barlow's division. He had entered the army as a private in the spring of 1861; became a colonel a year later, and when the Maryland campaign began was commanding what might be called half a brigade—his own regiment, plus the 64th New York, which was attached to it.

There weren't many Barlows. But the army did contain the kind of generals the radicals were really looking for, and they were beginning to make their presence felt. One of them was General Israel B. Richardson, who—for all that he was a West Pointer—carried informality of dress and behavior to a point that made Barlow look like a fency-thet Briton in the Horse Guards. Richardson might have been modeling himself subconsciously after old Zachary Taylor, or maybe he just didn't care; at any rate, he went around camp with a battered straw hat on his head and his hands in his pockets, looking like a seedy old farmer—uniform coat discarded half the time, so that no insignia of rank were visible. A dapper young shavetail galloped up to his division headquarters one time with a dispatch; saw Richardson, took him for an orderly, and tossed him his bridle reins as he dismounted with a curt "Here—hold my horse." A few moments later the shavetail was admitted to the headquarters tent, to find the supposed orderly sitting behind a camp desk, eying him with grim amusement and asking, "And what do you want, sir?" Another time some privates of the 57th New York were washing in a little brook. A man whom they took to be a wagon driver came up and asked if he could borrow some soap. One soldier told him to go to hell and find his own soap, but some of the others were more generous; and the shabby wagon driver, after a wash, sat on the bank and told them stories about the Mexican War—pleasant enough old coot, the boys thought, in whose remarks there was a little old-timer lecture about how soldiers should always share things with their comrades. A day or so later it happened that three of these privates were detailed to take some contrabands to division headquarters. In front of the tent they found this same old-timer, and they asked him if he could tell them where to find General Richardson. "Well," he said, "I guess I can tell you. Sometimes they call *me* General Richardson—and other times they call me Greasy Dick."[4]

He was not pure eccentricity, however, and all that slouchiness was strictly confined to camp. In the field he was a first-rate fighter who had commanded a brigade to the eminent satisfaction of Phil Kearny and was now pleasing Bull Sumner, in whose corps he was. His men liked him immensely; called him "Fighting Dick" and bragged that he was the plainest general in the army. One private wrote that "he has good common sense, a rare commodity apparently." The men recorded that when they went into battle he would tell them to come on—"I won't ask you to go anywhere I won't go myself." It was his division, incidentally, which contained the irrepressible Barlow. Like so many of the successful generals in that war, Richardson had resigned from the army in the 1850s; was a Detroit businessman when war came, raised the 2nd Michigan Regiment, and won his general's stars shortly thereafter.

There were others. Among them there was a rising cavalry officer, Brigadier General John Buford, who had made first-rate use of Pope's cavalry until Pope's incessant, jumpy countermarching wore out horses and men alike. Buford was another of the plain-as-an-old-shoe soldiers; wore corduroys tucked into cowhide boots, always had a big pipe and tobacco pouch bulging his blouse pockets, and was beginning to show an ability to persuade the clumsy horsemen of the Federal cavalry that they might yet face Jeb Stuart's troopers on even terms. He had that streak of grimness the radicals were unconsciously looking for. He once hanged a guerrilla, in a neighborhood seething with secessionist sympathy, and left the body dangling from the limb of a tree under a big sign: "This man to hang three days; he who cuts him down before shall hang the remaining time." Also worth a passing glance was the 5th New Hampshire's Colonel Cross: a tall, lean, rangy man with reddish whiskers and a balding pate who had fought in the Mexican War and, later, had held a commission in the Mexican Army; a man of rough and jocose energy who had made his regiment one of the best combat units in the army and was obviously in line for promotion.

And there were better-known men, like Meade, with his flaming temper, his sardonic smile, and his constant attention to detail—woe to the regimental officer in his command who frittered away strength by the unnecessary assignment of men to non-combat jobs; like Hancock, who swore at his officers but always remembered their names and made them feel somehow that they were intimate with him, and who had a fine fury in the hour of action; like solid John Sedgwick, always cool and unruffled, who commanded a division under Sumner, was known as "Uncle John" to his men, and would one day command the army's most famous corps. They were there if one looked for them, the kind of men who could use this army as it was meant to be used.

But the trouble was that the radicals had the wrong touchstone. Neither West Point nor civilian life had failed: from both sources the driving, slashing, fighting type of general was coming up, and in the end the war would be grim enough to satisfy Ben Wade and his whole committee. But the men who were going to make it grim—to drive for the enemy relentlessly, grinding up his strength in pitiless combat and forcing victory no matter who got hurt—were not going to be the kind of men whose political beliefs would please the Conduct-of-the-War inquisitors. Take the list of Union officers who were in the key positions when the war was finally won—Grant, Sherman, Sheridan, Thomas, Meade: not an abolitionist in the lot, not a man who began the war with any particular animus against slavery.

And it was not just by accident that these men were so long in being called to the top spots. The radical bloc, demanding the kind of warfare which only such men could provide, was actually making it harder for the administration to find these men and use them: for it was providing an ideological qualification for purely professional jobs, and instead of inquiring about men's competence it was asking about their loyalty. The Army of Northern Virginia was able to find its best men quickly and it was able to use them once it found them; with all his problems, Jefferson Davis did not have to fight his war and run his country in the midst of a witch hunt. If the dominant leaders in the Confederate Congress—the men who had created and shaped the war party in the South—had worked night and day to keep the army out of the hands of General Lee, on the ground that Lee had not supported secession before Fort Sumter was fired on and hence must be a disloyal person, the story of the war in the Virginia theater would have been considerably different.

One thing must be said for the radicals. They believed their own gospel, down to the last inspired word. And during the weeks after Pope's inglorious defeat they suffered an agonizing extreme of suspense and gloom. They had had their way and nothing had worked out right. Pope was a hard-war man and he was also thoroughly "loyal" by their standards; but he was used up now, no pressure of politics could save him, and he was under orders to go back into obscurity in the Northwest, far from the Rebel generals whose minds he could not read. He was complaining enough about it, those days, bombarding Halleck with angry letters, reminding Halleck that he was under certain obligations to him, making veiled, ugly threats of political reprisal. There was some secret between the two men, and Pope was trying to let Halleck know that he would not be above telling it, if he had to, to re-establish himself. Whatever hold he might have thought he held over the general-in-chief, he at last let it go loose. But before departing he created one last, festering sore to plague the army. He filed formal charges against several generals, including chiefly Fitz-John Porter, alleging disobedience of orders at Bull Run and angrily claiming that a conspiracy of generals had foully done the North out of an overwhelming victory. With McClellan back in command, Porter had protection, and the charges were held in abeyance; if McClellan should ever leave the army, Porter would be at the mercy of every force in Washington that was hunting for a scapegoat.

The record of that first fortnight in September makes fantastic reading, showing as it does, enough ill will and all-round distrust afloat in Washington to lose any war. The Union cause had reached low-water mark for the war, and the infection in its central nervous system had all but induced complete paralysis. Lee was invading Maryland with an army so exhausted, ragged, and ill-equipped that by any ordinary standard it ought to have gone back to some rest camp for a couple of months' refit. But Lee knew what he was fighting against just then, and if his daring in beginning an invasion with a worn-out army can be explained only by the assumption that he held his opponents in supreme contempt, there were ample grounds to justify such a feeling.

The Federal mainspring had run down. That will o' the wisp of the Confederacy, foreign intervention, was on the verge of coming true. The Prime Minister of Great Britain, having compared notes with the Foreign Secretary, was getting ready to propose to the British Cabinet that England take the lead in inducing a concert of powers to step in and bring the Civil War to an end—which, of course, could only mean independence for the Confederacy. The Foreign Minister, agreeing, added that if such a concert of powers could not be arranged, England ought to go ahead on its own hook, granting full recognition to the South. The two men were waiting now to see how the invasion of Maryland turned out before taking final action.

At home the belief in victory had faded. As fine a soldier as General John Sedgwick had given up hope and had accepted the idea of two separate nations, North and South. On September 4 he was writing to his sister: "I am in despair of our seeing a termination of the war until some great change is made. On our part it has been a war of politicians; on theirs [the Confederacy's] it has been one conducted by a despot and carried out by able generals. I look upon a division as certain; the only question is where the line is to run. No one would have dared to think of this a few weeks since, but it is in the mouths of many now."[5]

In the White House, Lincoln had finally come to see that the war could not be carried on any longer as a simple fight to re-establish the Union. There had to be a broader base: the fight had to be pinned to a *cause,* something that would change the entire emotional climate, both at home and abroad, turning the deep vitality of the radical group into an asset rather than a liability, making foreign intervention impossible no matter what military setback might take place on the hills of Maryland or Pennsylvania. There was but one step possible: the war had to become a war for human freedom, a war to end slavery. Otherwise it was lost. So he had in his desk the draft of the Emancipation Proclamation—that amazing document which is at once the weakest and the strongest of all America's state papers.

But as things stood just then he could not issue it. Seward had warned him: Put that out now, when we have been defeated and our armies are in retreat, and it will look like a shriek of despair—not an attempt by us to help the black race, but an appeal to the black race to help us. We must have a victory first.

And Seward was right. The paper lay folded in a pigeonhole. The war could not be won without it, but it could not be issued until a victory had been won. And the rival armies now were drifting up through Maryland, eying each other like two boxers circling in the ring, jabbing tentatively with cavalry, looking for the opening.

It was all up to the army, then. Leadership had failed and chances had been missed, and the climax was here; the bewildered, homesick boys with muskets on their shoulders would finally have to say which way American history henceforth would go. They knew none of these things. They were quite "unindoctrinated," for none of the oratory and the lofty war talk had prepared them for this. All they knew was that there was going to be a big fight pretty soon, and most of the time they tried not to think about it. They had the general they wanted, and they seemed to be back among their own kind of folks, and maybe this time it would work out all right.

FIVE

Opportunity Knocks Three Times

1. AT DAYBREAK IN THE MORNING

THE 27TH INDIANA never forgot that day at Frederick. The day didn't especially stand out at the time, except for the welcome the townspeople gave, with the fruit and the ice water and the pretty girls waving flags; but afterward the soldiers built it up and made many stories about it, and almost everybody claimed to have been in on it, or to have seen it, or at least to have known about it. It was a Big Thing, as army talk had it, and it all began right in the middle of this Hoosier regiment.

The army got to Frederick on the twelfth of September, the mounted patrols going into town from the east just as the last of Wade Hampton's cavalry went out of it to the west, with a fine rackety-spat of flying hoofs on the turnpike and stray shots from carbines nipping through the orchards and the front-yard flower gardens. The 27th Indiana was pushed through in a long skirmish line next morning, and when it got to an empty field a courier rode up from the rear with orders from corps headquarters: stack arms in the field, put pickets out, and stand by for a while. The men broke ranks, and most of them sauntered about to find bits of wood to boil coffee.

It was a nice morning, and it wasn't too warm, and the men took it easy. The field had been a Rebel camping ground a few days before, and the boys didn't especially like that. It was never too pleasant to occupy a spot where the enemy had just camped, as departing armies weren't too tidy about picking up the litter they had made, and the ground was apt to be messy. Still, this was a big field, and the rest was good, and the men drank their coffee and lit their pipes and talked about nothing much; and two lounging non-coms suddenly became very important men. Corporal Barton W. Mitchell of Company E lay at full length chinning with his pal, First Sergeant John McKnight Bloss. A few feet away, half hidden in the tall, trampled grass, was a long, bulky-looking envelope. The two men stared at it idly for a while, lazily wondering who dropped it there and what might be in it, until at last Mitchell's curiosity got the better of him and he rolled over, stretched out one arm, and picked it up. It was unsealed, and it contained a long paper, covered with writing, wrapped around three cigars.

Three cigars were a find, any day. They appeared to be fresh, and the two soldiers began to feel in their pockets for matches. As they did so, Mitchell's curiosity—which, by one of the stupendous oddities of war, was that day the Republic's greatest asset—gave him another dig, and he uncrinkled the paper that had been folded around the cigars and took a lazy look at it. As he looked he forgot about the matches and nudged the sergeant: hey, would you take a look at this?

The paper was headed, "Headquarters, Army of Northern Virginia," and was dated September 9. It was labeled "Special Orders No. 191." and it was studded with names like General Jackson, General Longstreet, General McLaws, and so

126

on—names known to every enlisted man in the Union Army. It was signed "R. H. Chilton, Assist. Adj.-Gen.," and at the bottom was the name of the addressee; "Maj. Gen. D. H. Hill, Commanding Division."

Whatever this might amount to, it seemed altogether too hot for any two enlisted men to hang onto, so the soldiers got to their feet and hurried off to show it to Captain Kopp, skipper of Company E. The captain took one look and sent them to regimental headquarters, where they handed it to Colonel Silas Colgrove, who was having a chat just then with Brigadier General Nathan Kimball, brigade commander from Sumner's corps. These two read it and exchanged glances; Kimball went away and Colgrove got on his horse and went galloping off to his division commander, Brigadier General A. S. Williams. Williams took his turn reading it and beckoned to his assistant adjutant general, Colonel Pittman, who stuck the paper in his pocket, yelled for his horse, and set out for army headquarters as fast as the beast could carry him. And so the paper got to McClellan, while Bloss and Mitchell went back to the field and stretched out on the grass again.

It is irritating, in a mild sort of way, that none of the accounts of this affair mention what finally happened to the cigars. Bloss wrote later that he and Mitchell simply forgot about them; Colonel Colgrove had the impression that the boys had rewrapped the cigars in the paper and put them back in the envelope before they gave it to him. There the trail dies out. Did anybody ever smoke them, in the end—those cigars that were so important to the history of the war?[1]

Fate had not been too kind to McClellan up to now. After that first dazzling, too-lucky stroke that had lifted him from the western Virginia mountains to the top command at Washington he had had nothing but bad fortune. But as he studied the paper the Hoosier corporal had picked up he could see that the opportunity of a lifetime had come to him. For what he had in front of him was nothing less than Lee's official orders, telling where every last division of the Confederate Army was and what it was up to—the plans of Confederate GHQ in complete detail. It was just too good to be true, and McClellan was cautious: could the paper possibly be genuine? His staff examined it. One officer, it developed, had known Colonel Chilton, Lee's assistant adjutant general, quite intimately in the old army and was familiar with his handwriting. He studied the paper and gave his verdict: genuine, beyond a doubt—that was unquestionably written in Chilton's hand.

With that verdict the fog of war which always limits the vision of an army commander suddenly dissolved and everything became clear. McClellan knew as much about Lee's plans as if he had personally attended Lee's last staff conference. The game was being handed to him on a silver platter.

The town of Frederick, where McClellan then was, is some forty miles northwest of Washington. The National Road, as it was called in those days, comes up from Washington, passes through Frederick, and continues west and north until it reaches Hagerstown, about twenty-five miles farther on, where it swings west to reach Wheeling and the Ohio country. From Hagerstown, good roads drop southward to the Potomac and the Shenandoah Valley; other roads lead north into Pennsylvania. Just about halfway between Frederick and Hagerstown the National Road climbs over the long, wooded height of South Mountain—not an isolated peak, as one usually pictures a mountain, but a great, slowly curving ridge that begins on the Potomac nearly opposite Harper's Ferry and runs far up into Pennsylvania, where it passes a few miles west of Gettysburg. Just now it lay on McClellan's western horizon like an ominous thundercloud fifty miles long, full of veiled lightnings: for behind that blue curtain lay the striking power of the Confederacy, embodied in the dusty gray divisions of the Army of Northern Virginia, securely hidden from inquisitive Federal eyes.

Innumerable rumors had been coming in, but they were next to useless.

Peaceful civilians who saw a scouting detachment were apt to magnify it into an army corps when they reported it, and the nervous alarms they sent back were sure to be garbled in transmission. The news McClellan had been getting from beyond the mountain proved nothing except that there were a lot of Rebels over there somewhere and that the Union folk in the area were almighty worried. He had his cavalry forward trying to locate the army, but every road they took led them straight up against Jeb Stuart's patrols. Rebel cavalry had the gaps in the mountain well covered, and it would take more than Yankee cavalry to open those gaps. A forward lunge by the army itself would of course send Stuart's cavalry flying, but in the absence of any knowledge about Lee's position and intentions it seemed to McClellan that it would be dangerous to make such a lunge. The blow might take the army into the wrong place and enable Lee to go rampaging off unopposed, doing fatal damage among the rich and nearly defenseless cities of the North. Up to this moment Lee had all the advantage.

Now, in a twinkling, this advantage had passed from Lee to McClellan. Lee's Special Orders No. 191, which had been issued just four days ago, told precisely what the Confederate Army was doing and where it was situated. Right now it was in the act of gobbling up that isolated garrison at Harper's Ferry. Stonewall Jackson and his command had been detached from the army and sent back into Virginia, roundabout, to come up on Harper's Ferry from the south. The division of General A. P. Hill was with him. General John G. Walker, commanding another Rebel division, had also gone below the Potomac to approach the town from the east—he was to make for Loudoun Heights, a little mountain that rises on the eastern bank of the Shenandoah, where it joins the Potomac, and overlooks the little town where John Brown once raised the flag of slave revolt. Two more Confederate divisions under General Lafayette McLaws were descending on Harper's Ferry from the north and were to occupy the lofty ridge of Maryland Heights, on the north side of the Potomac, whence they could look right down the throats of the Union garrison. The rest of the Confederate Army— Longstreet's command, plus the division of D. H. Hill, together with the reserve artillery and the supply trains—was to wait at Boonsboro, a little town on the National Road just beyond South Mountain. When Harper's Ferry had been duly captured everybody was to head north and join up with Lee and Longstreet, either at Boonsboro or at Hagerstown, a dozen miles up the road.

There it was, all spelled out, and McClellan had it right on his desk. He was the beneficiary of the greatest security leak in American military history—the only one that ever finally affected the outcome of a great war.

Harper's Ferry, of course, was doomed. It was in the bottom of a soup bowl, and once the Rebels got up on the rim, there would be no stopping them. The place had always been indefensible, and Halleck's refusal to order the garrison out when there was time looked sillier than ever now. But quite unintentionally Halleck had baited a trap, and Lee was stepping right into it. His pause to capture this outpost (he banked heavily on McClellan's extreme caution) was giving McClellan the most dazzling opportunity any Northern general was to have throughout the whole length of the war.

For Lee's army was at this moment completely scattered, and McClellan, his own army united, was closer to the scattered pieces than those pieces were to each other. Lee was entirely at his mercy. There was nothing to keep the Army of the Potomac from breaking through the mountain wall and stamping out those separated segments of Lee's army one at a time. The Army of Northern Virginia could be destroyed, which would win the war overnight, and it could be done by a man whom the radicals in Washington were proclaiming a disloyalist who did not want to win!

There was just one catch in it. McClellan would have to move fast. Those orders would be out of date before long. They were four days old already, and the Rebel army could do a power of marching in four days, as sundry Northern generals had found out. The door was wide open, but it was likely to swing shut quickly. If McClellan was to take advantage of his opportunity he had no time to spare. Every minute might count.

And yet, actually, the situation was even better than McClellan supposed. Having given him this break, the fates were providing him with a little extra bulge to allow for contingencies. Lee's logistics were a trifle off, and the snatch at Harper's Ferry was taking longer than expected. Special Orders No. 191 did not give the time schedule, but Lee had anticipated that the job would be finished by now. The various elements had begun their march on September 10; by the twelfth, it had been believed, Jackson would be taking possession of Bolivar Heights, the long ridge that dominates Harper's Ferry from the south, Walker would be in position across the Shenandoah, and McLaws would be on top of Maryland Heights. On September 13, therefore, according to Lee's plan the garrison would be held by the throat and would have to surrender, prisoners and captured supplies could be started north, and the victors could be on their way north again.

But nobody had moved as fast as that. Only now, while McClellan was reading the order, was the head of Jackson's column coming within sight of the Federal troops on Bolivar Heights, and it would take another day for Jackson to get fully into position. Only now was McLaws fighting his way up the steep ridge to take possession of the peak north of the Potomac; only now was Walker getting his men in place on the crest of Loudoun Heights. McClellan was getting from one to two full days more than he had any reason to hope for. In addition, the rest of Lee's army was no longer concentrated at Boonsboro, close to the gap through which the National Road crossed South Mountain. Since writing the order Lee had heard a rumor (later proved false) that Federal troops were coming down from Pennsylvania in some strength, and he and Longstreet had moved up to Hagerstown to head them off. Nobody but D. H. Hill was anywhere near the all-important gateway, and Hill's division was so worn by hard fighting and straggling that it numbered barely more than five thousand muskets. Lee's army was even more scattered than the order showed, in other words, and it would take it longer to get reassembled. When the fates finally gave McClellan this break they went out of their way to make it a good one.

General John Gibbon happened to visit army headquarters early that afternoon. His Black Hat Brigade was getting thin and he wanted to have it strengthened if he could. He and McClellan were on friendly terms, having known each other back in the old army days, and he was admitted to McClellan's tent without delay. When he got in he could see that a good deal seemed to be happening. McClellan asked him to sit tight for a minute and went on dictating orders, receiving reports, sending staff officers hurrying off here and there, everybody energetic and active. Finally there came a lull. McClellan turned to him, taking a folded paper out of his pocket and displaying it jubilantly, his eyes sparkling.

"Here is a paper with which, if I cannot whip Bobbie Lee, I will be willing to go home," McClellan said. "I will not show you the document now, but"—he turned down one fold to show the writing—"here is the signature, and it gives the movement of every division of Lee's army. Tomorrow we will pitch into his center, and if you people will only do two good, hard days' marching I will put Lee in a position he will find it hard to get out of."

Gibbon, of course, was delighted; also, this gave him his opening, and he took it without delay as a good soldier should. He had a brigade, he said, that would do all the marching and fighting the general could ask for—four crack Western regiments that were as good as any in the army, if not a little bit better. But they had been worn down by hard service and the brigade was a little skimpy; when new troops came in could the general assign a good Western regiment to Gibbon's brigade? McClellan listened attentively. He always liked to hear his troops praised, and he glowed as Gibbon talked. When Gibbon finished McClellan promised that he would have the first Western regiment that came to camp. Gibbon left, feeling highly encouraged, and McClellan returned to the task of getting the ponderous army in motion.[2]

Basically his problem was fairly simple—to get across Southern Mountain while Lee's army was still in pieces, to overwhelm the separate fragments, and, if possible, to rescue the Harper's Ferry garrison so that those twelve thousand soldiers could be added to the Army of the Potomac.

Of the many roads that crossed South Mountain in various places there were ony two that mattered now: the National Road, leading through Turner's Gap to Boonsboro and thence to Hagerstown, and a road that forked off in a more southerly direction west of Frederick, crossed the mountain at Crampton's Gap, six miles south of Turner's Gap, and came out on the far side just five miles north and east of Harper's Ferry. A quick drive through Turner's Gap would bring the army down on what looked like Lee's main body—Longstreet's and D. H. Hill's commands. A simultaneous smash through Crampton's Gap would crush the two divisons led by McLaws, would open the door so that the men at Harper's Ferry could come out, and would leave Jackson and the others completely isolated on the south side of the Potomac. When all of that had been done, Jackson and A. P. Hill and Walker could be hunted down at leisure and there would be nobody of any consequence left in the entire state of Virginia to oppose an irresistible descent on the Confederate capital.

As McClellan faced the mountain range he would be striking at Turner's Gap with his right hand and at Crampton's Gap with his left. Conveniently placed to act as his left hand were some eighteen thousand good men under General William B. Franklin, a solid, highly respected soldier who commanded the VI Corps and who had with him his own two divisions and a third one temporarily attached. They would be a force ample to open the gap, crush Lafayette McLaws, and rescue the Harper's Ferry people. Franklin was ordered to get going—to do a lot of banging away with his artillery, even if he didn't have anything to shoot at, so that the commander at the Ferry would hear and know that help was on the way. Meanwhile the rest of the army, some seventy thousand men, would be the right hand and would go straight through Turner's Gap.

While all of this was going on, McClellan reflected, it would be helpful if somebody could come down on Lee from the north. Governor Curtin was frantically assembling Pennsylvania state troops, and General Reynolds had been detached from the army to help him; and while they probably had nothing that could stand up to Lee's veterans in an open fight, Lee might be bothered and delayed a good deal if a sufficient swarm of these home guards and militia could come edging in on him. So McClellan, having inspected the map, sent off a wire to "the commander of U.S. forces at Chambersburg" to concentrate all available troops and obstruct Lee's march until the Army of the Potomac could come up and make a real fight out of it. He didn't know who was commanding at Chambersburg, but it seemed likely that somebody was there, and the card looked like a good, inexpensive one to play.

As it turned out, this had no effect on the campaign, but it did give a bad forty-eight hours to that eminent Pennsylvania editor-politician, Alexander K. McClure. McClure had been in Washington when Lee marched north, and when Governor Curtin began building up the home guards it seemed wise to have a few of the state's leading citizens on hand to help, so McClure had been hastily given a major's commission and sent north to lend a hand. When McClellan's wire came in, McClure, uncomfortable but game in his new role as army officer, and accompanied by no troops whatever, was posted at Chambersburg. He gulped when he got the wire; combed the town and managed to round up about twenty home-guard cavalry, which were all the "U.S. forces" within reach. With these McClure began patrolling the roads valiantly, preparing to ward off the Army of Northern Virginia if by chance it came his way. Tough old Thad Stevens happened to be in Governor Curtin's office at Harrisburg when the wire came through. The thought of the unmilitary McClure and his twenty men standing between Pennsylvania and invasion tickled the grim abolitonist, and he chuckled. "Well, McClure will do something. If he can't do better he'll instruct the toll-gate keeper not to permit Lee's army to pass through." Then, reflectively: "But as to McClellan, God only knows what he'll do."[3]

McClellan rode through Frederick to make sure that the advance guard of the army was put in motion properly. A little outside of town he overtook the head of General Jesse Reno's IX Corps, which had the advance. Reno's leading division, two brigades of Ohio troops, under General Cox, was moving along, and McClellan stopped to talk a moment with Cox, who had been one of his assistants back in the springtime of the war, when McClellan was out in Columbus trying to get Ohio's first troops housed, uniformed, and drilled. Cox's men had done practically all of their fighting in western Virginia, having come east just within the last month, and they were happy to be with the Army of the Potomac. They had heard that it was far ahead of all other Union armies in drill, discipline, and marching ability, and its record seemed to make their own service in the mountains look commonplace, and they were anxious to make a good impression. There was a subtle difference between them and the rest of the army. They were more informal in bearing and discipline, and it was noticed that they marched with a longer, freer stride; the Army of the Potomac had been rigorously drilled to the regulation pace of twenty-eight inches, while the Westerners had been allowed to set their own gait. Incidentally, the Ohioans were already remarking that the men in these crack Eastern regiments straggled much more than did the mountain brigades. . . . McClellan gave Cox some last-minute instructions and went back to headquarters.

Pretty soon Reno himself came along. He was feeling good just now; had gone south on the Roanoke Island expedition as a brigadier under Burnside, had done well, and now held a corps command, and things seemed to be opening up for him in fine style. While the army was in Frederick, Reno had heard the Barbara Frietchie story, which seems to have been circulating freely among the Federals long before Whittier made a propaganda poem out of it, and he had gone around to the old lady's house to see her. As nearly as can be learned, at this distance, Barbara Frietchie had indeed waved a flag from her window, but she had waved it in welcome to the Union troops, not in defiance of Jackson's "Rebel horde." Some other woman in Frederick did wave a United States flag at Jackson, but he never saw it or her, and there was no blast of rifle fire to rip that or any other Union banner. The stories got all mixed up and added to, and old Barbara became the center and heroine of a garbled blend. Anyway, Reno had gone to her house that morning and offered to buy the famous flag. She wouldn't sell it to him—couldn't, very well, since the flag he wanted to buy didn't really exist—but she did give him a flag she had around the house, and the general had ridden off, well content.[4]

By dark Reno had pushed Cox's division across the Catoctin range, a low ridge that runs north and south halfway between Frederick and South Mountain; and the Ohioans went into bivouac near the tiny village of Middletown, while Rebel outposts of South Mountain saw the ridge to the east blossom out with campfires as darkness came down, and sent word back to D. H. Hill in Boonsboro that quite a lot of Yankees seemed to be coming up to Turner's Gap. Yankee cavalry skirmished with Confederate patrols in the valley and on the lower slopes of South Mountain and sent back their own reports: as far as they could find out, there was nothing in front of Turner's Gap except cavalry.

McClellan, meanwhile, was working on the orders for the rest of the army. The most important was the order for Franklin, and McClellan got it off a little after six that evening. Franklin was down at a place called Buckeystown, six miles south of Frederick and about twelve miles due east of the summit at Crampton's Gap, and McClellan gave him the picture in detail, telling him about the finding of Special Orders No. 191 and explaining the positions of Lee's troops. Cox was at Middletown, he said, and would be off first thing next morning, followed by the rest of the army, to get through Turner's Gap and land on Lee at Boonsboro. Franklin was to move "at daybreak in the morning" for Crampton's Gap. Once through the gap, his first duty was "to cut off, destroy or capture McLaws' command" and relieve the Union troops at Harper's Ferry, after which, depending on events, he would either rejoin the main army at Boonsboro or move west to Sharpsburg to cut off Lee's retreat. In order that it might be perfectly clear to him, McClellan added: "My general idea is to cut the enemy in two and beat him in detail."

All fine, so far. But as the courier galloped south with that order the first thin mist of what would soon be a serious cloud was beginning to rise across the gleaming face of McClellan's good fortune. McClellan's order was clear and precise, and it gave Franklin a perfect picture of the situation, but it was defective in just one respect: nowhere in it was there any hint of the extreme urgency of the moment.

For it was no ordinary strategic advantage McClellan was reaching for; he had it within his power to destroy Lee's army and end the war within the next few days, and every minute might count. South Mountain was still a screen, and there was no way to know how far or how fast Lee's troops might be moving, off on the other side. Franklin's troops were rested, they had not fought since the battles on the peninsula back in June, and presumably they were quite capable of a little extra exertion now, with the outcome of the whole war hanging in the balance.

Reflecting on this order, which lays out a job of work and breathes the very spirit of unhurried calm, one is conscious of that queer feeling of exasperation which, even at this distance, McClellan's acts occasionally inspire. With everything in the world at stake, both for the country and for McClellan personally, why couldn't the man have taken fire just once? To have Franklin march "at daybreak in the morning" was good—but to have him march that same evening, driving for that door through the mountains without giving the enemy an extra minute to repair his faulty dispositions, would have been infinitely better. The roads were good and the weather was clear, and a night march was perfectly feasible; making it, Franklin would be able to go through the gap first thing in the morning. In a great many ways the history of the country (to say nothing of McClellan's own place in it) could have been a good deal different if Franklin's eighteen thousand men had been put on the road that night under the stars.

But Franklin didn't move. McClellan didn't tell him to, and Franklin was no man to exceed the letter of his instructions. To be sure, McClellan had closed his letter by saying that he now asked of Franklin "all your intellect and the utmost activity that a general can exercise," which might have given him the hint; but McClellan was a courtly man who used that kind of language as the small change of polite correspondence, and Franklin was one more of those Union generals who were loyal and capable and conscientious but who utterly lacked that priceless little extra spark. He could drive his men just as hard as he himself was driven, but no harder: a first-rate soldier, in the ordinary way, but lacking the power to be first-rate in an extraordinary way.

So McClellan and Franklin and Franklin's eighteen thousand men got (one supposes) a good sleep that night, and any clock that headquarters might have possessed ticked on, unhurried but inexorable. On the morning of September 14 Franklin's corps broke camp and got off to a good early start, precisely as ordered, and set out on the twelve-mile hike to Crampton's Gap, with the cavalry trotting on ahead and stirring up hedge-hopping fights with Stuart's outposts.

Beyond South Mountain, where Crampton's Gap cuts through, there is an open space two or three miles wide bearing the neatly descriptive name of Pleasant Valley; and on the far side of Pleasant Valley is the humpbacked ridge of Elk Mountain, whose southern end is named Maryland Heights and looks down on the town of Harper's Ferry. Lafayette McLaws, a Confederate general who was almost exactly like the Union's General Franklin—solid, capable, unimaginative—had been dutifully industrious. He had chased the last Yankees off Maryland Heights, and he was putting in the morning getting his artillery up on top so that he could bombard the Yankee garrison on Harper's Ferry. It wasn't easy, the sides of Elk Mountain being very steep and the roads being sketchy, and in the end he had to put two hundred men on each gun and wrestle the ponderous weapons up by sheer muscle. Stuart warned him sometime during the morning that the Federals were coming up to Crampton's Gap, in his rear, and McLaws eventually sent a few regiments back to hold the pass. They didn't get there until midday had gone, and until then the little road over the mountain was guarded by nothing but Stuart's cavalry; but they arrived well ahead of Franklin and they found a good position at the eastern base of the ridge, behind a long stone fence. There they lined up, with dismounted cavalry on either flank.

Those Southerners were good men, but there were not nearly enough of them to keep the Federals out of the pass, and Franklin did not have to put half of his men into action. He planted a row of guns on the left, sent the 27th New York and the 96th Pennsylvania ahead as a heavy skirmish line, and backed them up with the 5th Maine and the 16th New York. The Rebels were well protected behind their stone wall, and there was a brisk fight for a while. McLaws was warned that a real push was on, but Franklin sent a brigade of New Jersey troops in on a charge, and the Confederates were driven away from the stone wall and went scrambling back up the mountainside, firing as they went. For a couple of hours after that it was an Indian fight, the Rebels too few to make a stand but giving ground slowly, Rebels and Yankees shooting at each other from behind tress, and Northerners coming on doggedly.

A private from a Vermont regiment, scrambling up the mountainside, slipped and fell, and went sliding off downhill to land, all in a heap, in a little hollow among the rocks, face to face with a Confederate private who somehow hadn't retreated when the others had. The two soldiers glared at each other for a moment, gripping their rifles; then they agreed that it would be foolish for them to carry on a personal, two-man extension of the war there in the hollow. They would wait where they were, suspending hostilities while everybody else fought, and at the end of the day they would see how the battle had gone. If the Federals got licked and retreated, then the Vermonter was a prisoner, but if the Confederates retreated, then the Reb was a prisoner. So they laid their rifles down and shared tobacco, leaning back among the rocks, and waited for the two armies to settle their fate for them.

Their comrades were having hot work for a while there on the wooded slopes. Firing down from above, the Confederates were shooting just a little high—not high enough to miss, the Northern boys complained afterward, but just high enough to inflict a dreadful number of head wounds, nearly all of which were fatal. Mindful of his orders, Franklin kept banging away with his artillery and made a prodigious racket, and down in Harper's Ferry the Union garrison—which knew perfectly well by this time that it was thoroughly trapped—heard the noise and began to feel hopeful again.

Late in the afternoon the last Confederate resistance dissolved, and the Federal assault waves cleared the crest of the ridge and halted, while the main body of Franklin's troops went marching through the gap and swarmed down into Pleasant Valley. McLaws awoke at last to the realization that he was in desperate trouble as the broken remnants of his rear guard came streaming back down the

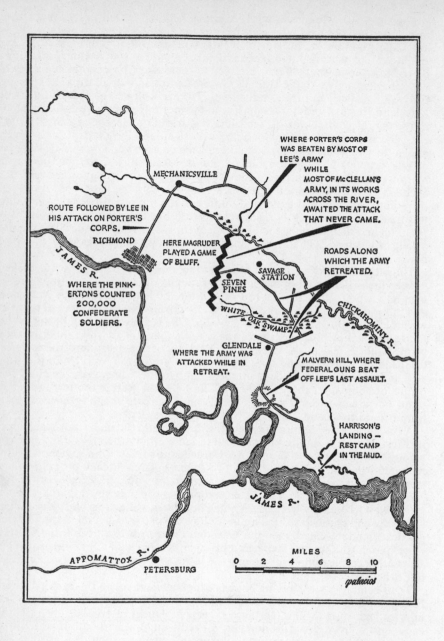

WHERE PORTER'S CORPS
WAS BEATEN BY MOST OF
LEE'S ARMY

WHILE
MOST OF McCLELLAN'S
ARMY, IN ITS WORKS
ACROSS THE RIVER,
AWAITED THE ATTACK
THAT NEVER CAME.

ROUTE FOLLOWED BY LEE IN
HIS ATTACK ON PORTER'S
CORPS.

MECHANICSVILLE

RICHMOND

HERE MAGRUDER
PLAYED A GAME
OF BLUFF.

ROADS ALONG
WHICH THE ARMY
RETREATED.

JAMES R.

WHERE THE PINK-
ERTONS COUNTED
200,000
CONFEDERATE
SOLDIERS.

SAVAGE
STATION

SEVEN
PINES

WHITE
OAK SWAMP

CHICKAHOMINY R.

GLENDALE
WHERE THE ARMY WAS
ATTACKED WHILE IN
RETREAT.

MALVERN HILL, WHERE
FEDERAL GUNS BEAT
OFF LEE'S LAST ASSAULT.

HARRISON'S
LANDING —
REST CAMP
IN THE MUD.

JAMES R.

APPOMATTOX R.

PETERSBURG

MILES

0 2 4 6 8 10

galacios

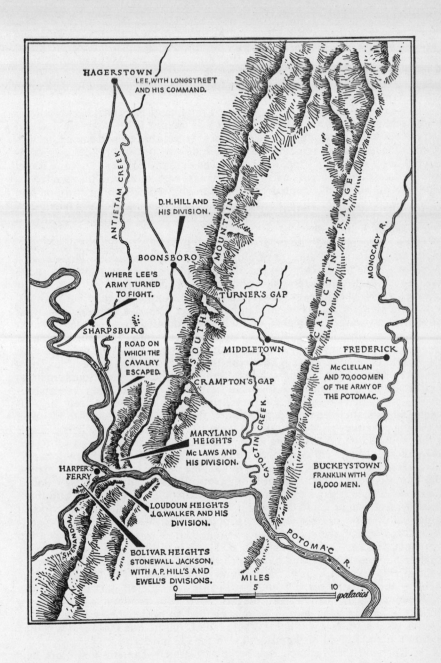

HAGERSTOWN — LEE, WITH LONGSTREET AND HIS COMMAND.

ANTIETAM CREEK

D.H. HILL AND HIS DIVISION.

BOONSBORO

WHERE LEE'S ARMY TURNED TO FIGHT.

TURNER'S GAP

SHARPSBURG

ROAD ON WHICH THE CAVALRY ESCAPED.

MIDDLETOWN

FREDERICK

McCLELLAN AND 70,000 MEN OF THE ARMY OF THE POTOMAC.

CRAMPTON'S GAP

SOUTH MOUNTAIN

CATOCTIN RANGE

MONOCACY R.

CATOCTIN CREEK

MARYLAND HEIGHTS — McLAWS AND HIS DIVISION.

BUCKEYSTOWN — FRANKLIN WITH 18,000 MEN.

HARPER'S FERRY

LOUDOUN HEIGHTS — J.G. WALKER AND HIS DIVISION.

SHENANDOAH R.

POTOMAC R.

BOLIVAR HEIGHTS — STONEWALL JACKSON, WITH A.P. HILL'S AND EWELL'S DIVISIONS.

MILES

0   5   10

palacios

valley, and he and Stuart took fresh troops and hastened up to repair the dike, while the long shadow of Elk Mountain filled the valley with evening dusk and began to creep up the side of South Mountain to the east. A Confederate briga- dier came pelting up to them, crying that all was lost, but McLaws and Stuart didn't think so. They formed a line of battle across the valley and got ready to make the best fight they could, while the fugitives were rallied and formed up to help the fresh troops.

Franklin rode through the gap, surveyed the line of Rebel soldiers a mile or more to the south, and considered that this was no time to be hasty. He had car- ried out the letter of his instructions, which is to say that he had forced his way through the gap. It still remained to "cut off, destroy or capture McLaws' com- mand," but it seemed to Franklin that he was outnumbered and that the Rebel line was too strong to break, what with darkness coming on and his own troops winded. Also, additional Confederate forces might well be coming down on him from Turner's Gap, for all he knew, and if he was fighting McLaws when they came he would be taken in the rear. So, in the end, he did nothing, deferring his next move to the morrow.

On top of the mountain that night the Federals who had carried the crest slept on the field of battle, gleaning it carefully for discarded valuables. The 4th New Jersey, which had been carrying the old smoothbore muskets, claimed to have re-equipped itself completely with rifled Springfields dropped by wounded or fugitive Rebels. The slopes were covered with the wounded men of both armies, and late at night the soldiers went clambering over the rocks, bringing casualties to the field hospital. They picked up their own wounded first and then brought in Confederates, until at midnight the exhausted surgeons, their linen coveralls streaked and smeared with blood, told them not to bring in any more because no more could be handled that night. So the 16th New York laid out a little camp- ing place on the mountaintop, built fires, and made the wounded Southerners as comfortable as they could, with food and water at hand. They had taken a num- ber of unwounded prisoners, and they detailed two of these to keep the fires going and look after the wounded men, and then they made their own bivouac. In the morning they found that the unwounded men had fled and half a dozen of the wounded had died during the night, and they carried the rest off to the hospital. Then they went down into Pleasant Valley and joined the main body.

Now it happened that night that there was one officer, in all the Union Army, who didn't believe in waiting until tomorrow. He was only a cavalry colonel, and he was inside Harper's Ferry, completely surrounded by Rebels, and there wasn't a great deal he could do about it, but what little he could do he proposed doing. Oddly enough, he was a Mississippian by birth—one of two Mississip- pians in the regular army, it was said, who had stuck with the Union when the war came. He was Colonel Benjamin F. Davis, called Grimes Davis at West Point and in the old army, and he was roosting in Harper's Ferry as commander of the 8th New York Cavalry. On the night of September 14 he knew as well as anybody else that the place would have to be surrendered next morning: the Confederates finally had all the heights lined with artillery, and the town couldn't be held an hour once those guns opened up, which they would unques- tionably do as soon as it was light. What made Davis unique that night was that he didn't intend to fold his hands and wait for the inevitable.

Like its colonel, his regiment was feeling frustrated. The 8th New York had been raised in the country around Rochester in the summer of 1861, and the government had been slow about the matter of providing horses: for a solid year the 8th had worn sabers and talked cavalry lingo but had gone about on foot, not having a horse to its name. The regiment had footed it up and down the Shenandoah Valley with Banks in the spring of 1862, sharing in the humilia- tions which befell that officer's command and feeling them more keenly because of its utter inability to ride as cavalry should. Finally, about the time Pope was getting licked at Bull Run, the 8th New York got its horses, and it had ridden brightly up the Potomac just in time to get penned up here at Harper's Ferry, where there was nothing whatever for cavalry to do and, currently, no prospect of anything better than a ride off to Libby Prison in Richmond. So when Colonel Davis finished a stormy conference that evening with the post commander and then came outside and whistled up his cavalry, the boys were ready for action—any kind of action, just so it got them out of that hole in the mountains to some place where they could ride.

What Davis proposed was that, since the post was going to be captured, anybody who could get out ahead of time should do so. He had finally won permission to take the cavalry and try it, the cavalry on hand consisting of his own 8th New York, and 12th Illinois, and a mixed handful from the 1st Maryland and 7th Rhode Island. A Unionist who lived in the region and knew all the mountain roads was going to act as his guide; in addition, Davis had one of his own scouts who had just slipped in through the Confederate screen and had a pretty good idea where all the Rebel commands were posted. As soon as the town got dark, then, Davis lined up his troopers, some thirteen hundred in all. The regimental sutler, knowing that he couldn't get his goods out and that he would inevitably be looted of all he owned next day by needy Rebels, passed down the ranks, giving away tobacco: an act of generosity that almost floored the soldiers, sutlers being men who never gave anything away.

Davis took his post at the head of the column, with his guide and his scout and a picked patrol of twenty-five troopers. The 12th Illinois and the Marylanders and Rhode Islanders came next, and the 8th New York was formed at the rear. In single file, moving at a walk, the little band crossed the Potomac on a pontoon bridge and headed off to the northwest on a narrow, winding road through the mountains—an obscure little road that ran right under the overhanging cliffs of Maryland Heights, the one road out that McLaws had failed to block. (It was the same road, if anybody had stopped to think about it, down which John Brown had moved, with death in his eyes and a monstrous vision of flame and bloodshed in his heart, when he made his descent on the Harper's Ferry enginehouse in 1859.)

The boys had quite a night for themselves. As soon as the head of the column got across the river it moved at a trot, so that the line kept getting longer and longer; Colonel Davis was ten miles up in Maryland by the time the last man left the bridge. The road took them within a few rods of McLaws's camp, but the jingling and the clattering seem to have escaped the notice of McLaws's pickets, and the cavalry got away clean. (Jeb Stuart had warned McLaws earlier to guard that lonely little road, but McLaws had other things on his mind and had paid no attention.) It was pitch-dark there under the trees, and except when they were going uphill—which was a good part of the time—the men rode at a trot. One trooper recalls that "the only way we could tell how far we were from our file leaders was by the horses' shoes striking fire against the stones in the road."

Two miles from the river Davis's advance patrol surprised and scattered a Confederate picket post. Two miles farther the Rebels had erected a road block of fence rails and overturned wagons, the routed pickets having broadcast a warning. Davis anticipated this, however, and led his command cross-lots by some winding woods path his guide knew about, and they left the road block behind. As they got out of the tangled mountain region they moved through cornfields and pastures as much as by road. Altogether it was a tough, grinding ride, and some of the horses gave out. When that happened, the dismounted men were taken up by their comrades; Davis was determined not to leave a man behind.

They swung out to by-pass the town of Sharpsburg, under the starlight, driving off a squad of Confederate cavalry that was patrolling the roads there. A few miles north of town they hit the Hagerstown turnpike and went clattering north in fine style. Then, up ahead in the dark, Davis heard the rumble of wagons. He spurred on past a fork in the road and ran into a big Rebel wagon train, escorted by a small detachment of cavalry, bound for Sharpsburg. It was too dark for anybody to see the color his uniform, and Davis had a fine Mississippi accent, so he simply posed as a Confederate officer and notified the driver of the leading wagon that he was to turn sharply to the right when he got the the fork in the road; and he told the commander of the Rebel cavalry escort to wait by the roadside and fall in at the rear of the train. Then he galloped back to his own command, formed the 8th New York alongside the fork to take care of the wagons, and got the rest of the men lined up to handle the Confederate troopers.

All unsuspecting, the sleepy wagon drivers took the right-hand fork, starting off on a road that led to Pennsylvania, while the 8th New York, riding single file, fell in beside the train. As the last wagon made the turn and the Rebel cavalry escort came up, Davis sent his Illinois troopers in on the charge with drawn sabers, and the surprised Rebels were broken up and sent scattering down the countryroads in the dark. When it began to grow light the wagoners came to a little, noticed the blue unforms, and asked the troopers what outfit they belonged to. Proudly the soldiers answered: 8th New York Cavalry. The teamsters pulled up in a hurry, swearing and fuming, and some of them jumped down to unhitch their horses, but the New Yorkers drew revolvers and persuaded them to climb back in their seats, and the train went jolting along, drivers very glum, cavalry bubbling over with delight.

At about nine in the morning the whole cavalcade got to Greencastle, Pennsylvania, where Davis called a halt and examined his capture. There he found that he had seized nothing less than General Longstreet's reserve ammunition train—forty-odd wagons, each drawn by six mules, with some two hundred prisoners. He had turned the train and prisoners over to the authorities and led his tired command into a field to get a little sleep. News of the capture got through the town, so that by the time the boys had their horses unsaddled and watered and picketed the townsfolk were coming out on foot and in buggies, carrying all sorts of things to eat—fresh bread, hams, baskets of eggs, and so on. The cavalry ate a tremendous breakfast and felt like heroes and stretched out for a good sleep in the shade, and one of their number wrote: "The boys thought that soldiering wasn't so bad, after all."[5]

It was a bright little exploit, all in all, and looking back on it, in its setting, one feels a twinge of regret that Grimes Davis was only a colonel. A little touch of his spirit, just then, in army headquarters or in the various corps headquarters, would have made the story of the rest of the war very different indeed. For by the time he got to Greencastle with his captured train, the garrison at Harper's Ferry had surrendered; and Franklin, with eighteen thousand men, was sitting by the roadside five miles from the scene of the surrender, reflecting on the perils of his situation and warily doing nothing at all. And Lafayette McLaws was in close touch with Stonewall Jackson and A. P. Hill and was no longer in any danger whatever.

2. DESTROY THE REBEL ARMY

From his perch on top of South Mountain, Confederate General Daniel Harvey Hill could look down and see the war coming up to meet him like a tremendous pageant, unspeakably grand. Five miles to the east lay the Catoctin ridge, with three roads coming over to the approach to Turner's Gap. Down each of these roads rolled an endless blue column, pouring down the slope and into the open valley as if the weight of unlimited numbers lay behind it, growing longer and longer and spraying out at last, at the foot of South Mountain, into long fighting lines, rank upon rank, starred with battle flags. The general looked, and reflected that the old Hebrew poet who used the phrase, "terrible as an army with banners," must have looked down from a mountain on just such a scene as this. Hill was one of the least timid men in the army, but he confessed afterward that he never in his life felt so lonely as he had that day: all of the soldiers in the world seemed to be marching up against him, and he had only five thousand men to stop them, some of which were still back in Boonsboro.

Over on the Union side there were men who saw the picturesque quality too. It was not very often, even in that day of close-order fighting, that an entire army was massed in the open where everybody could see it. This was one of the times when it happened, and it was enough to take the breath away to look at it. A private in the 9th New York, his regiment pausing for a breather on the Catoctin slope, wrote that it was a "beautiful, impressive picture—each column a monstrous, crawling, blue-black snake, miles long, quilled with the silver slant of muskets at a 'shoulder,' its sluggish tail writhing slowly up over the distant eastern ridge, its bruised head weltering in the roar and smoke upon the crest above." General Abner Doubleday, turning in his saddle to inspect his brigade, cried involuntarily: "What a magnificent view." And McClellan himself, one of the first to come over the ridge, reined up near the village of Middletown to watch his men marching past. As the men came up to him they took fire—the great open amphitheater of war, their own proud strength all on display, and the hero whom they trusted to the death sitting his horse, proud and martial-looking, the one man who could make war seem grand to men who had been in many battles: they broke into wild cheers, yelling until they were too hoarse to yell any more. A Massachusetts veteran described the scene:

"It seemed as if an intermission had been declared in order that a reception might be tendered to the general-in-chief. A great crowd continually surrounded him, and the most extravagant demonstrations were indulged in. Hundreds even hugged the horse's legs and caressed his head and mane. While the troops were thus surging by, the general continually pointed with his finger to the gap in the mountain through which our path lay. It was like a great scene in a play, with the roar of the guns for an accompaniment."[1]

It had taken time to build up this impressive scene, however. McClellan mounted amid the troops, pointing dramatically to the rising slope where the battle smoke was drifting up through the mountain laurel, is the center of an unforgettable picture, but the picture had been some hours taking shape. There had been nothing dramatic about the first two thirds of this day—which, since the stage was all set for drama, simply means that the army had been very leisurely about coming up for the assault. Indeed, during the entire morning a few regiments of cavalry plus General Cox's division of Ohio infantry had had the place pretty much to themselves, except for the Rebels on South Mountain.

Even so, this day—the fourteenth of September, the same day Franklin's men were coming up to Crampton's Gap, off to the south—began bravely enough. Union cavalry went across the valley at dawn, and as the foot soldiers became visible behind them the Confederate cavalry trotted back and went up the winding mountain roads. The sun had not been up very long before Cox started his men after them. The Ohio soldiers left the National Road a mile or two before it began to climb the irregular valley which constitutes Turner's Gap, and followed a country road which goes through another depression a mile or more to the south; two brigades of Western infantry, six regiments in all, perhaps a total of three thousand men. There was a brief delay after the troops took the side road. Cox and General Pleasonton, who had the cavalry, trotted on half a mile along the main highway to arrange a couple of batteries on a little knoll—a dozen twenty-pounder rifled Parrotts, long-ranged guns for those days. The guns began to shell the top of the mountain, and Confederate gunners on top answered them, while the infantry stacked arms and waited in a little field. As they waited a sergeant on horseback, with a big bundle back of the saddle, came

rocketing up to the 11th Ohio—mail from home, just arrived. The boys clustered round, and while the guns searched the wood with shell to prepare the way
for them they sat on the ground and read their letters—each letter, no doubt,
expressing the pathetic hope that the man who received it would survive whatever lay ahead of him, would "take care of himself" and, in the fullness of time,
would get back home safe and sound.

Just about the time the letters were finished the orders came, and the men
took up their rifles, formed a line of battle, and started up the mountainside. The
slope was not too steep, but in most places it was abominably tangled with laurel
and other scrubby growth, and the going was tough. At times the men found
themselves struggling ahead single file, and regimental formations were badly
mixed. As they got near the summit the growth became less dense and the
ground was more nearly level, and they came out at last in a more open region
of small farm clearings and pastures and found Rebels behind a stone fence.
Long volleys of musketry rolled back and forth along the mountain ridge, while
a Rebel battery near the gap to the north threw case shot into the Ohioans'
ranks. D. H. Hill had sent in one of his best men, Brigadier General Samuel
Garland, Jr., to hold this place, with a brigade of North Carolina troops and a
few squadrons of dismounted cavalry. Garland stayed up where the fire was
hottest, to encourage his men—they were outnumbered and they knew it, and
they were a little nervous—and presently a Yankee bullet found him and killed
him, and one of the Carolina regiments gave way. The 30th Ohio got through
the wall and hung on, and in a couple of places there the Carolina and Ohio
boys slugged one another with musket butts and jabbed with bayonets. Cox decided that if he could get some men up on a little rise of ground to the left all of
the Rebels would have to go away, so he sent the 11th Ohio off to tend to it.

Accompanied by its regimental dog, Curly—a frisky pooch who enjoyed
going out on the skirmish lines—the 11th went forward cautiously, the exact
Confederate position along the knoll not being known, and pretty soon the 11th
found itself in a nasty pocket, with Confederates shooting at them from three directions, so they got back out in a hurry.[2] Then the 23rd Ohio came up to help,
and the two regiments went storming up the hill, firing as they went. The lieutenant colonel of the 23rd, a promising chap named Rutherford B. Hayes, was
shot down, wounded; William McKinley, sergeant in the same regiment, was
unhurt. The regiments kept on going, struggling through dense thickets that
seemed to be alive and humming with bullets, and the Carolina brigade gave
way at last and drew off down the western slope of the mountain, most of the
men out of action for the rest of the day. This part of the mountaintop now belonged to the Army of the Potomac.

Actually, the whole mountaintop did, had the Army of the Potomac just been
on hand to take possession. Of the five brigades in his command, Hill had had
only two on South Mountain when the day began: one posted at the center at
Turner's Gap, where the National Road came through, and the other one off
here a mile to the south, where Cox and his Ohioans made their attack. The
other three were hot-footing it up from Boonsboro, but they wouldn't be on hand
for quite a while, and until they got there Hill had nothing left but the thin brigade on the National Road, some artillery, a few game remnants of the North
Carolina brigade, and such dismounted cavalry as Stuart had been able to leave
with him. It was at this time, when he reflected that he was standing there with
something like a thousand muskets to stave off the greater part of McClellan's
army, that General Hill experienced that great feeling of loneliness.

But the wind is tempered sometimes to the shorn lamb, and so it was here.
Thus far the Army of the Potomac was represented only by the division of General Cox—some three thousand men when the battle began. These men did their
best, and Cox had the right idea: he turned their faces toward the north, once the

Carolinians had been driven off, and prepared to advance along the crest to Turner's Gap. The ground was broken and uneven, and it took time to get the men formed up. The Confederates had a number of guns at the gap, with a good line on the little clearings where the Ohioans were. Somehow they got the guns far enough forward to fire canister, the charges ripping up the sod, as Cox wrote later, "with a noise like the cutting of a melon rind." Cox sent back to his corps commander, Reno, for help, and Reno sent more men forward. By the time they got there and found their way up the difficult slopes it was a couple of hours past noon, and by this time some of Hill's other brigades were coming up. Hill had made a good showing, meanwhile, with the men he did have, and although the heads of McClellan's long columns were coming over the Catoctin ridge, Hill had not yet had to fight anything very much worse than equal numbers. He was in an extremely bad spot, but he had already been given eight hours' leeway.

As more of Reno's men came up the mountain, with Reno himself spurring up after them, Cox made ready to renew the attack. General Orlando Willcox got his division into line somewhere off to the right of Cox's Ohioans, and pretty soon the men went struggling forward. In Willcox's outfit there were two untried regiments going in side by side—the 17th Michigan and the 45th Pennsylvania. The Michigan boys were so painfully new that they could hardly get from marching column into fighting formation. They had been mustered in only a month ago, had been rushed down to Washington in feverish haste when Stanton got panicky over Pope's defeat, and barely a week before this day on the mountaintop one member of the regiment had written sadly that they did not know even "the rudiments of military maneuvering," adding that "there is not a company officer who can put his men through company drill without making one or more ludicrous blunders." For some reason this regiment was made up largely of men nearing middle age—except for Company E, which had been enlisted from students at the State Normal School in Ypsilanti—and they were desperately self-conscious and anxious to do the right thing in this first engagement. They had their best clothes on—dress coats buttoned nearly up to the throat, high-crowned black hats, each with a feather stuck jauntily in the band. One veteran remembered that they even had their dress-parade white gloves carefully folded and stuffed in their pockets; looking back with a rueful smile, he wrote that it was "a wonder we did not put them on, so little know we of the etiquette of war." Anyway, here they were, clumsily forming line of battle in the underbrush, the sweating officers irritably horsing the men into place by hand. They went stumbling forward, their dress uniforms getting sadly torn by thorns and broken branches; and D. H. Hill's veteran artillerists were getting the exact range of the ground they would have to traverse.[3]

The Pennsylvanians who went in with them were not nearly so new, but they were equally ignorant of what battle was like. They had been in service nearly a year and had been sent down to South Carolina on the Port Royal expedition. That had been mere "Sunday soldiering," one of their number wrote afterward; they had occasionally seen isolated Rebels on other islands several miles distant, but their only fighting had been against gnats and mosquitoes, and they had lived high, eating oranges and sweet potatoes, green corn and watermelon, with fresh fish out of the ocean. Now they were in line beside the Michigan boys, forcing their way through a wood where their major, to his shame, found his horse suddenly turned balky, so that he had to dismount and proceed on foot, leaving the faithless beast behind. The regiments came out at last behind a rail fence all grown up with long grass and briars, with a pasture beyond and another of those ominous stone walls eighty yards off on the far side. As usual, the stone wall was held by Rebels, who squatted on their heels, rested their rifles atop the wall, and blazed away with deadly aim.[4]

The Pennsylvania and Michigan men knelt behind their own fence and fired back, discovering immediately that an open rail fence is not nearly as good protection as a solid stone wall. Somewhere beyond the Confederate firing line there were Rebel batteries, which opened with shell and solid shot, sending the fence rails flying. The greenhorns looked around nervously, saw General Willcox calmly sitting his horse right up by the fence, took heart, and kept peppering away at what they could see of the enemy across the field. Reno got some more troops up, and at last the outnumbered Confederates backed away, firing as they went, and disappeared in the forest. Reno sent fresher troops on after them while the two new regiments caught their breath and took stock of the situation. The Michigan men found that they had lost thirty men killed and about a hundred wounded—fairly heavy losses, considering that they took some five hundred men into action (they had been a thousand strong a month earlier, but nearly half the regiment was sick and had been left behind). The Pennsylvania regiment had had almost exactly equal losses. They had had their baptism of fire, and the Michigan men proudly recorded that the veterans who saw them in action told it around that they "fought like tigers." Also, they noticed that there were a good many dead Rebels behind that stone wall.

It was getting late in the afternoon by now, and General Reno—who was up on the mountaintop taking personal charge of the fighting—began to believe that the Confederates had retreated. Riding up to the front, he took as good a look as he could at the checkerboard pattern of clearings, woods, and laurel patches. There was nobody in sight on this side of Turner's Gap, as far as he could make out, and he got ready to march straight north along the crest to cinch matters.

Beside him was the 51st Pennsylvania, which had been fighting hard. He directed it into an open field and told the colonel to have the men stack arms and to let them boil coffee if they wanted to: it would be a few minutes before he had his marching column formed. He turned his horse, to ride back along the line—and just then a body of Confederates, darkly concealed in the woodland ahead, let fly with an unexpected volley that splintered the Pennsylvanians' stacked muskets, broke up the coffee-fire groups, and knocked General Reno out of his saddle, dead. The 51st hurried to grab its muskets and got into a horrible cross fire. There was still another of those green regiments, the 35th Massachusetts, lined up behind the 51st, and the 35th began wildly returning the Rebel fire without waiting to let the Pennsylvania boys get out of the way. There was an infernal mix-up for a while in that tree-fringed clearing, with a prodigious racket of small-arms fire, reeking smoke clouds hanging in the air, bullets zipping by from all directions, men getting hit, and a great shouting and cursing going up; but it finally got straightened out, and the Federals drove in hard on the Confederates in the wood and scattered them.[5]

It was now close to four in the afternoon, and all of the fighting so far had been done here south of the National Road by Reno's men. The Confederates were in the immediate, visible presence of seventy thousand Yankee soldiers, but they had not had to fight more than a tenth of that number. In a sense, McClellan's finding of Special Orders No. 191 was working to his disadvantage this afternoon. According to that document, Boonsboro—which was only a couple of miles or so beyond the summit of the mountain—was held by both Longstreet and Hill, and as a result McClellan, still clinging to the old, old idea of Lee's overpowering numbers, believed that South Mountain was occupied by at least thirty thousand men. Therefore, he played his cards cautiously, refusing to make a direct stab at the gap until he had plenty of men in line.[6]

Joe Hooker had been elevated to the command of the I Corps—McDowell had been relieved, a man unlucky beyond all other generals, taking his demotion in manful silence, without recrimination—and Hooker brought the I Corps down from the Catoctin ridge. McClellan had him spread it out for an advance up South Mountain to the north of the slopes where Reno's men had been fighting so long. Hooker had three divisions in his corps, Meade's, Ricketts's, and Hatch's —and he sent Meade's, Ricketts's, and most of Hatch's around on a big swing a mile or more to the right of the National Road, to go swarming up the heights that overlook Turner's Gap from the north. It took a long time to move an entire army corps into position in those wooded hollows, and it was getting along toward evening before they were ready to advance. Hooker kept Gibbon's brigade back, and he had it form right on the highway, with orders to start for the top as soon as the lines on the right began to move.

Gibbon had his Black Hat boys all keyed up, which was a good thing, since they had the toughest assignment of the lot. Turner's Gap is a long, curving valley in the mountain, the road following the narrow floor as it climbs to the summit; the soldiers who went up here would have no chance for any fancy maneuvering but would have to go straight ahead in the teeth of whatever direct fire the Confederates might arrange for them. Since Hill was now being reinforced by Longstreet—whom Lee had started back from Hagerstown in a hurry, first thing that morning, when he learned that McClellan was moving—his frontal fire was apt to be heavy. But Gibbon had told his boys, before they left Frederick, how McClellan wanted two days of good marching and how he had assured the general that this brigade could outmarch and outfight anything in the army, and the men were on their toes. McClellan himself was not far behind; on top of a little hill from which he could see the highway all the way to the summit; whatever they did would be done right under his eye.

Gibbon got his boys astride the road, 7th Wisconsin on one side and 19th Indiana on the other, formed "by the right of companies"—which meant that each regiment was made up of ten parallel columns, each column representing one company marching two men abreast. They couldn't fight in that formation, but they could get over rough ground easily and could be brought up into line of battle without delay. The 2nd and 6th Wisconsin fell in behind. The brigade was thin, with hardly more than eleven hundred men altogether, the four regiments averaging a little under three hundred men apiece. Two twelve-pounder smoothbores from reliable old Battery B were moved up into the roadway, and the command set out.

They came under rifle fire before long, and when they reached the Rebel skirmish line the two guns were wheeled around to blast the Rebels with canister. The skirmishers withdrew, and Gibbon swung his men into line of battle, bringing the two rear regiments up abreast of the two in front—pridefully noting that the men did it as smoothly as if they were on the parade ground, while McClellan watched through his field glasses from the hilltop far below. Confederate artillery was posted at the summit and it had the range: it put a shell into the middle of the 2nd Wisconsin just as those ten company columns were wheeling into regimental front, dropping a dozen men with that one burst. The two guns of Battery B did what they could to quiet the Rebel guns, and the battle line went scrambling up the mountainside.

Up near the summit they found the Rebel line—a formidable affair behind another of those stone walls, with the enemy tucked snugly away where he could shoot downhill. The Rebels were in high spirits, and when the Westerners came within handy range they yelled taunts in the dusk: "Oh, you damn Yanks! We gave you hell again at Bull Run!" Some of the Wisconsin boys called back: "Watch out, Johnny, this isn't McDowell after you now—this is McClellan!" Then both sides gave up the catcalling and began using their rifles, and the fight became hot and heavy, with the Black Hat Brigade unable to advance an inch, and with Gibbon wondering, presently, whether they could even stay where they were. Ammunition ran low, and details were formed to collect cartridges from the dead and wounded. The sun went down and it was pitch-dark, and back on his little hilltop McClellan could follow the fight by watching the pin points of stabbing flame from the muzzles of the muskets. Along toward nine o'clock the fighting died out from sheer exhaustion, and the Black Hat Brigade prepared to spend the night on the firing line. Since it started uphill it had lost some 280 men, about a quarter of its total number.[7]

Off to the north Hooker's corps had been making progress, although the progress had been slow. Meade had his division of Pennsylvanians in front, and they went clambering up a high, steep-sided spur of the mountain ridge on top of which Confederate Robert Rodes had his fine brigade of Alabama troops. The Alabamians were badly outnumbered, but they had all the advantage of position and were rated as shock troops, under a general who was one of the best brigadiers in the Confederate Army, and before night came down they gave the Pennsylvanians a bad time of it. Coming up through the wood, the Bucktails caught it from a slim Confederate skirmish line hidden behind trees. The Rebels here were expert marksmen, and woods fighting was their specialty. They went dodging back from tree to tree, reloading under cover and drawing a good bead before they fired. But the Bucktails came from mountain country and were pretty good riflemen themselves. They got the wood clear at last, and then Meade's men had nothing but open fields in front of them and the Rebels had to give ground.

There was a delay along toward twilight, when Meade thought he was about to be outflanked, but Hooker sent more troops in and the supposed danger evaporated. The Rebels just did not have enough men on the mountain to make a serious counterattack, and once McClellan got his available strength into action, there could be only one outcome to the battle. By the time it was dark the Pennsylvanians had got to the top and Rodes's brigade took some very rough treatment, with a couple of hundred men shot down and an equal number captured. The firing flickered out in the darkness finally all along the crest, and the exhausted Federals prepared for a cheerless bivouac on the mountaintop. During the night there was a good deal of firing by nervous pickets, and some of the Union commanders feared a counterattack, but actually the field had been won: Union troops were on the heights, where they had full command of the pass, and the Rebels were grateful for the dark and a chance to get away.

The Black Hat Brigade had a little tale to tell around the campfires. Late in the evening the brigade found that it had some prisoners to send back to army headquarters. A corporal and squad were detailed, and the corporal led the way back to a country house which McClellan had taken over. He was misdirected, somehow, when he went inside, and when he opened what he thought was the door of the provost marshal's office he unexpectedly found himself facing McClellan. McClellan, busy with some papers, looked up, frowning at the intrusion, and said somewhat curtly: "What do you want?"

The corporal gulped and explained: he had some prisoners to turn in and he had opened the wrong door by mistake. Softening a bit McClellan asked the boy for his name and regiment. When he was told his eyes brightened.

"Oh, you belong to Gibbon's brigade. You had some heavy fighting up there tonight."

"Yes, sir," said the boy. "But I think we gave them as good as they sent."

"Indeed you did. You made a splendid fight."

The corporal hesitated. Then, greatly daring, he said.

"Well, General, that's the way we boys calculate to fight under a general like you."

McClellan got up, came around the table, and gripped the corporal by the hand.

"If I can get that kind of feeling amongst the men of this army," said McClellan, "I can whip Lee without any trouble at all."

So the corporal went back to his regiment, and the Black Hat Brigade had a story which went through the whole army: General McClellan had shaken hands with an enlisted man and complimented him on his brigade's fighting qualities.[8]

At dawn there was a heavy mist on the mountaintop, as if the battle smoke of the previous day's fighting had lingered under the leaves. The commands there cautiously sent out patrols, which presently brought back word: no Rebels in sight. Pleasonton's cavalry came up the National Road and went down the western slope into Boonsboro as the mist evaporated, driving out Fitz Lee's Confederate troopers and provoking a series of running fights across the fields and down the country roads. A double handful of Rebel stragglers were combed out of the town, and McClellan ordered Sumner to push his corps through and take up the pursuit. Sumner put Richardson in front, and the 5th New Hampshire had the advance, sweeping along the road past dead cavalry horses, occasional wrecked caissons, and various other signs of a hasty retreat. The New Hampshire boys legged it so fast that they later remembered with pride that other commands had dubbed them "Richardson's cavalry." In French's division, which followed Richardson's, was the brand-new 130th Pennsylvania, whose untried soldiers gaped, wide-eyed, as they saw their first live Rebels—a band of prisoners being escorted to the rear. In this band was a dapper young Confederate officer, trim in a new gray uniform; one of the Pennsylvania rookies called out to him: "Are there any more Rebels left?" The officer replied grimly that they would see lots of Rebels very shortly—a prophecy, said the 130th's historian, which was amply fulfilled.[9]

Back on the mountaintop the brigades that had done the fighting the day before pulled themselves together, took stock of their losses—altogether, eighteen hundred Union soldiers had fallen—and sent out parties to bury the dead and pick up discarded equipment. Young Captain Noyes grew thoughtful as he watched one party laying dead Confederates in a trench, and noted in his diary: "How all feeling of enmity disappears in presence of these white faces, these eyes gazing upward so fixedly in the gray of the morning hour." And a soldier of the 9th New York, viewing a similar scene, remarked that "there was no 'secession' in those rigid forms, nor in those fixed eyes staring blankly at the sky." Less melancholy, a private in the 51st Pennsylvania recorded that he and his buddies looted the haversacks of dead Rebels and found them full of good food—better rations, he remarked, than the Union men were carrying. On the way down the mountain the 12th Massachusetts saw Joe Hooker, well pleased with the work of his new corps, "in the saddle taking his brandy and water, looking as clean and trim as though he had just made his morning toilet at Willard's."[10]

Piece by piece the army reassembled and took to the road, following Sumner. Without ceremony the XII Corps, which had been under the luckless Nathaniel P. Banks, found that it had a new commander—a white-haired, wintry-faced old regular named Joseph K. F. Mansfield, who had been graduated from West Point away back in 1822, before most of the soldiers in this corps had been born, and who showed up this morning in a fine new blue uniform, an improvised staff trotting at his heels. He took hold strong, while his corps was in the act of getting on the road, and one of the soldiers noted with approval that while he appeared to be "a calm and dignified old gentleman" he quickly showed that he "was the personification of vigor, dash and enthusiasm." Another recorded that he rode "with a proud, martial air and was full of military ardor."[11] Several new regiments, fresh from training camps at home, came plowing up through Frederick and joined the army—or tried to, anyway. There was a great traffic jam on the road between Frederick and Boonsboro, with ambulances and details of prisoners going back against the tide and with long wagon trains clogging the road as they tried to slip in between the marching divisions, and the recruits had to stand by in the cornfields and wait their turn.

The army was feeling good. It was enjoying an experience which, from one end of the war to the other, the Army of the Potomac did not have very often—chasing a Confederate army which was in full retreat, after a battle which had been a clear-cut Union victory—and it was like a tonic. The men had been told a day or so earlier that they were going to relieve Harper's Ferry and had not yet been informed that that place had already surrendered; and as the long miles passed underfoot the men in the ranks made good-natured gibes about it, asking one another: "Who in hell is this Harper, and where's his ferry?" Early in the afternoon the 5th New Hampshire passed through a little hamlet and came out on a chain of low heights overlooking a pleasant, winding little creek, with rising ground beyond and the steeples and housetops of a town showing over the hills. They were halted there, since the Confederates had guns posted on the opposite hills and seemed disposed to contest any further advance, and the rest of the army slowly came up and poured off into fields and farmyards on either side of the road. Pretty soon McClellan and his staff cantered up amid a long wave of cheers, and the general rode to a hilltop and spent a long time examining the lovely, rolling countryside with his field glasses, while a Confederate battery tossed so many shells at him that he sent his staff back into a hollow for protection.

The little town that he could just see beyond the hills was the town of Sharpsburg. The stream that wound through the open valley was Antietam Creek, gleaming brown in the afternoon sun and looking like a promising place to fish in the cool of a summer evening. A couple of miles away, in front and to the general's right, there was a little white church with a wood behind it: a church of the Dunker sect, whose members believed church steeples a vanity and held that war was sinful. Flags and guns and moving men were to be seen on the slopes between the church and the town. Lee and his army had stopped retreating and had turned to fight.

The sporadic cannonading died away and the afternoon became peaceful again. McClellan was in no mood to hurry things. Most of his army was still spraddled back over a long stretch of road, and it would take a good many hours to assemble all of it. Franklin was some miles away, near Crampton's Gap, and it might not be wise to call him in until it was certain that the Rebels who had seized Harper's Ferry were up to no more mischief in that area. So McClellan established headquarters on the lawn of a pleasant house on a hill overlooking the valley. That morning he had sent his wife a hasty telegram, saying that the army had "gained a glorious victory"; this he had followed with a note saying that he was pursuing the enemy "with the greatest rapidity, and expect to gain great results." The air had been full of jubilant talk that morning, and McClellan had written: "If I can believe one-tenth of what is reported, God has seldom given an army a greater victory than this." He had also reported the victory to the President, incautiously telling him that "General Lee admits they are badly whipped"—a statement which caused Secretary Welles to wonder tartly to whom Lee made this statement that it should be so promptly brought to McClellan's ears. In another message home McClellan proudly asserted that the victory had "no doubt delivered Pennsylvania and Maryland."

No doubt. And yet the sky was slowly but steadily darkening. The finding of Lee's lost order had put the game in McClellan's hands; forty-eight hours had passed since then, and two chances had been missed. The Harper's Ferry garrison had not been relieved, and the separate pieces of Lee's army had not been destroyed before they could unite. Two states might well have been "delivered," but the war had not been won—and it was final, shattering victory which McClellan had originally been thinking about. D. H. Hill had had some terribly lonely hours on top of South Mountain, but not until late afternoon had he been compelled to meet more of an attack than his slim numbers could handle, and it was dark before the Federals had brought up men enough to seize the crest by sheer force. The fight had been a Union victory beyond question, and yet, as

Hill himself remarked, "if it was fought to save Lee's trains and artillery, and to reunite his scattered forces, it was a Confederate success." And it was precisely that kind of success which McClellan could not afford to let the Confederates win just then.

If this point was obvious to the Confederate soldier, it was also dimly visible to Lincoln back in Washington, watching and waiting in almost unbearable suspense as the war came to its greatest moment of climax. Receiving McClellan's triumphant announcement that the mountain passes had been forced, Lincoln sent him this reply:

"God bless you and all with you. Destroy the Rebel army if possible."

3. TENTING TONIGHT

The country around Sharpsburg is surpassingly lovely, with low hills rolling lazily down to the Potomac on the west, and little patches of trees breaking up the green-and-brown pattern of the farmers' fields. The river comes down unhurried, going to the south in wide loops and then swinging to the east; and just before it turns again to go south the copper-colored Antietam comes down and joins it—another unhurried stream that makes little loops and bends of its own as it follows a north-and-south line to enter the river. Between the creek and the river is the town of Sharpsburg, lying on the western slope of a gentle ridge that slants off, east and west, to the two streams.

This ridge is not sharply defined; just a stretch of higher ground, tapering off to the south in the blunt angle where the creek meets the river, and merging imperceptibly with the hills of the Maryland countryside a mile or two north of town. It is full of minor heights and hollows, with easy spurs and valleys running east toward the creek, dotted here and there with little open groves. The main road from Sharpsburg to Hagerstown runs north from the town along the broad crest of this ridge. The other principal road goes east from the town, gets over the height, and goes down a long slope to cross Antietam Creek on an arched stone bridge, after which it runs off northeast to Boonsboro. Half a dozen miles to the east the blue mass of South Mountain lies upon the land.

All of this is good farming country, with a look of quiet and uneventful prosperity. There are many cornfields and pastures, orchards and gardens surround the farmhouses, and there are huge barns. Little country roads zigzag in between the fields, worn down by many generations of use until, in some places, they are below the level of the ground they cross. They are bordered by fences—mostly barbed wire, nowadays; weathered rail, two generations ago. Here and there the ground is broken by an outcropping of rock.

Now this country town, together with the streams and the principal roads, had names before the armies came together there, because men have to have names for such places in the daily routine of living. But most of the landscape lay nameless, except for purely local, informal titles like Piper's cornfield, or Poffenberger's wood, and it serenely and happily lacked history and tradition. Nothing had ever happened there except the quiet, undramatic, unrecorded round of births and deaths, christenings and weddings, cornhuskings and barn-raisings, the plowing of the ground in the spring and the harvesting of fat crops in the fall. Life moved like the great tide of the Potomac a mile or so to the west—slowly, steadily, without making a fuss, patiently molding the land to its own liking.

As one comes up the hill on the road from Boonsboro, after crossing the creek and just before entering the town, there is the National Cemetery, green and well kept, white headstones marking the places where many dead men lie in orderly military formations, with pleasant trees casting broken shadows on the lawn. It is a large cemetery, and it was not there at all on the morning of September 16, 1862; there was nothing there then but the broad crest and the peaceful grove, with the spires and roofs of Sharpsburg half hidden beyond. If a man stood in this grove and looked to the north he could see the white block of the little Dunker church, a mile away, beside the Hagerstown pike. And on that September morning in 1862, anyone who looked at the church would have seen two bits of woodland lying near it—one west of the Hagerstown road, surrounding the church on three sides and stretching northward for half a mile or more, and the other east of the road, separated from it by open fields several hundred yards wide. Two quieter bits of woodland could not have been found in North America, and no one outside the immediate neighborhood had ever heard of them; no one had ever taken human life in either of them. But ever since then, because of what was about to take place there, those two wood lots have had a grim, specialized fame and have been known in innumerable books and official records as the West Wood and the East Wood—as if, in all that countryside, there were no other bits of wood that lay just east and west of a country road. In the same way, there was a forty-acre cornfield lying on the east side of the road, between the two plots of trees, which ever since has simply been *the* cornfield, as if there had never been any other.

The woods have been cut down since then, and where the cornfield used to be there is a macadamized roadway flanked by gleaming, archaic-looking monuments and statues, with little markers here and there unobtrusively beckoning for attention. But in the fall of 1862 no one was dreaming of statues, and because they had had good growing weather the corn was in fine shape—more than head-high, strong, richly green, the tall stalks waving slowly in the last winds of summer.

And over and above all of this perfection of peace and quiet, on the sixteenth of September, there was a silent running out of time and a gathering together of the fates, as issues that reached to the ends of the earth and the farthest borders of national history drew in here for decision. The peace and quiet had already been destroyed. In the grove where it would soon be necessary to lay out a cemetery (grass waving in the summer breeze beside the tiny faded flags; it's all right now, it's all right) men in trim gray uniforms sat on their horses and looked to the east through field glasses. Many other men, much less neatly dressed in gray and tattered brown and every imaginable shade between, were filling the zigzag country lanes and trampling down the grain in the farmers' fields all along the ridge. Dust hung in the air as long columns of six-horse teams labored up the roads, swung off into the fields at higher places on the ridge, and sent polished guns into battery to the tune of crackling bugle calls. Now and then a set of these guns would shoot out quick jets of bright flame and rolling clouds of soiled smoke, the guns jarring backward with each discharge, scarring the ground beneath their trails and breaking the air with heavy sound.

On the eastern side of the Antietam, a mile away, the scene was much the same, except that here the men wore blue—very dusty, worn, and dirty, much of it—and there were many more of them. They brought guns up to the low heights bordering the east side of the creek: iron rifles, mostly, many of them bearing at the breech the heavy band that marked the long-range Parrott. From time to time they fired at the Confederate guns to the west, battery and section commanders standing a little apart, peering under the smoke to spot the shots. Behind the guns, safely under cover in valleys and hollows, were dense masses of infantry, the men glacing incuriously up at the guns as they moved into their places, each youthful face a tanned, expressionless mask. Now and then the crash of the rival batteries rose to a great tumult that sent long echoes rolling cross-country to the mountains off to the east; then the noise died down and the country seemed quiet, and the unending thump-shuffle of feet and the creaking of wagon wheels could be heard. When the guns were being fired it seemed as if a great battle were being waged, yet this was not really a battle at all; this was merely the preliminary feinting and sparring, most of it due to nothing but the overeagerness of the battery commanders and none of it doing very much harm.

On the right-hand side of the road from Boonsboro, nearly a mile before the road crosses Antietam Creek, there is a little rise of ground running out in a low spur overlooking the valley, and here a man named Pry had built a fine big two-story house of brick, with broad lawns and tidy outbuildings, and a grand view opening off to the west and south. In his yard, on the crest of the western slope, General McClellan had pitched his headquarters tents. Orderlies had driven tall stakes into the ground in front of the tents, and telescopes were strapped to the tops of these stakes, ready for use by any military eye that cared to search the Rebels' side of the Antietam. Camp chairs from the headquarters wagons had been set up, and a few regular armchairs had been brought out from Mr. Pry's house, and the commanding general had taken his post here, surrounded by his staff, their orderlies, the headquarters guard, and all the rest, with the headquarters flag flying from a tall pole in the center. The morning wore away and McClellan studied the long ridge to the west, and the generals came in to report and to receive their orders. What was going to be the battle of the Antietam was beginning to take shape, piece by piece, in the general's mind.

It was hot, that morning, with a blazing sun, and no air was stirring in the protected hollows where the troops took shelter. All through the morning the army kept coming up, the men filing into place to right and left of the Boonsboro road, headquarters officers cantering up and down the dusty road with papers in their hands to see that each unit got to the proper location. Now and then groups of soldiers would leave their places and walk to the top of some hill to see what the prospect might be. They never stayed long because the Confederate gunners were watchful and sprayed shell at any hillock where one of these groups appeared. When that happened the Union batteries would strike at the guns that had fired the shells, and the roar of the cannonade would rise to a brief crescendo, only to die away again as the men took cover. Toward noon the sky became overcast and a little breeze sprang up, and it was a bit cooler. McClellan stayed close to headquarters, conferring with his officers and studying the Rebel position through telescopes. Except for the guns and an occasional glimpse of moving men, there was not a great deal to see. Undulations in the ground kept most of the Confederate Army out of sight.

But the general felt that he was getting a tolerably good idea of its position, and as the day lengthened, his battle plan was formed. As far as McClellan could make out, the Confederate line ran north and south along the ridge, its southern end anchored among the hills south of the Boonsboro road, the other end going into the woods somewhere beyond the white Dunker church. The position was strong, and it was not going to be too easy for the Federals to reach it, because before they could get at it they would have to cross the Antietam, and good crossings seemed to be few. The bridge by which the Boonsboro road crossed the creek offered nothing but a direct frontal assault on the center of the Confederate line, where many batteries were clustered. A mile downstream there was another bridge, built of stone and arched like the first, from which a road followed a little ravine to cross the ridge and get into Sharpsburg from the southeast. This gave an approach to the southern end of the Confederate line, but the ground was bad. Steep hills looked down on the bridge from the Confederate side of the creek, and those hills appeared to be full of armed Rebels, and the guns in front of Sharpsburg commanded both the bridge and the road that led from it up the ravine. Forcing a passage over that bridge and up onto those hills would be just plain murder, unless Lee's attention could first be directed elsewhere.

North of the Boonsboro road the situation was more promising. In front of the Pry house, a mile upstream from the place where the Boonsboro road crossed the stream, there was a third bridge, sheltered in the valley so that the

Rebel guns could not reach it, with a winding road that went off through the farmlands to the north and west; and still farther upstream there were a couple of shallow places where men could wade the creek well out of sight of the enemy's artillery.

It looked, therefore, as if the sensible course was to cross the Antietam at these protected upstream crossings, get troops over to the Hagerstown road well north of the Confederate position, and send them sweeping down on top of the ridge, rolling up the Rebel line as they went. At the same time, in spite of the obstacles, it would be well to make a secondary attack at the bridge farthest downstream. That might be costly, but it would keep Lee busy at both ends of his line and prevent him from sending troops from his right, below the town, to support his left, up by the Dunker church. Then, as a final touch: when these two attacks were under way, watch the situation closely, and if all seemed to be going well make a third smash right through the middle—Lee would probably have weakened his center to support his two ends, and this third attack ought to break his line and finish him off.

Thus McClellan figured it out, while the troops waited in the valleys and the guns boomed heavily, fell silent, and broke into action again, and the hot day slowly passed. The whole Union Army was on hand except for Franklin, who was still watching the Rebel detachments over near Harper's Ferry. Franklin must be called in. Presumably he would be able to get his men up to the Antietam sometime next day. McClellan studied the landscape again, talked with corps commanders, and waited, while the sweating gunners brought more and more guns up to the low bluffs that overlook the Antietam from the east. He was going to have everything ready before he opened the fight, and nothing was going to be lost through overhasty action.

Or gained, either. He still had all the advantage, but time was continuing to run out on him, and the bright opportunity that had been handed to him by grace of the Indiana non-coms three days ago was getting dimmer and dimmer. Crampton's Gap: one chance missed. South Mountain: a second chance missed. His luck was still in, a third chance was offering, but there might be such a thing as stretching good luck too far. For it was not by any means the whole of Lee's army that faced him, this sweltering sixteenth of September. The afternoon before, when the weary Confederates planted themselves on the Sharpsburg heights and turned at bay, only the commands of Longstreet and D. H. Hill had been present. This morning Jackson and Walker had brought their men in— very tired and footsore men who had made an exhausting seventeen-mile night march from Harper's Ferry. (Night marches were feasible, after all, if the man who wore general's stars demanded them.) Three full Confederate divisions were still at Harper's Ferry and could not reach Sharpsburg until the next day. Lee had barely twenty-five thousand men on the field, while McClellan pondered his battle plan and weighed his chances and decided not to attack until everything was ready. The higher officers of the Army of Northern Virginia were frankly amazed as they saw Lee serenely awaiting attack with this slender force, while the blue columns were visibly building up overpowering strength on the far side of the creek. General Longstreet, who was a hard man to impress, wrote later that this day-long, ostentatious assembling of Federal legions was "an awe-inspiring spectacle." Yet it remained a spectacle and nothing more, all through the day, while the slow minutes ticked away.

For McClellan was facing an imaginary army rather than the real one which was spread so thin on the Sharpsburg ridge: an army that drew upon fabulous numbers and transcended all of the limitations which poor transportation and insufficient supplies always imposed on Confederate commanders. Whether the fault lay with the Pinkerton reports, with McClellan himself, or somewhere else, the incredible fact remains that McClellan was preparing to fight an army that simply did not exist. He believed Lee to have a hundred thousand men at his command that day. The Federal army was outnumbered; that offensive thrust which he must presently make, to drive the invader back below the Potomac, was an enormously risky venture which could not be undertaken at all except for the great valor of the troops and the undying love which they had for their commander.

Between this imaginary Rebel army and the flesh-and-blood army that was awaiting his attack there was an enormous difference. In his invasion of the North, Lee had taken a gamble even more desperately daring than the one he had taken on the Chickahominy, when he divided his army and wagered the Confederacy's independence that McClellan would never find out how thin was the screen that stood between him and Richmond. Lee crossed the Potomoc with an army that was on the verge of complete exhaustion. Shoeless men who could tramp the dirt roads of Virginia without too much discomfort just could not march on the hard roads of Maryland; they had fallen out by the thousands, along with other thousands who felt that they had enlisted to defend Virginia's soil, not to invade the North, and who in their unsophisticated way had turned back when they got to the Potomac, planning to join up again once the army returned to Virginia where it belonged. Altogether, from ten to twenty thousand Southerners had left the ranks between Pope's defeat at Bull Run and the arrival at Sharpsburg. Even when the troops at Harper's Ferry came up, Lee would have barely forty thousand men to throw into action.

In a way this was almost an advantage. Every faintheart, every weakling, every man whose spirit and body were not of the stoutest, had been winnowed out. The ones who were left were the hard-rock men who would be a long time dying. But even so, the odds were fantastic. It is hard to find in all of Lee's career any act more completely bold than his calm decision to stand and fight on the Antietam.

When Franklin came up McClellan would have, by his own estimate, eighty-seven thousand men—with abundant reinforcements not far off. His advantage, actually was not as great as the figures seem to show, because Confederates and Federals reckoned their numbers differently. The Rebels counted only the men who would actually be carrying muskets, and the Federals counted all who were "present for duty"—which meant that they included all the cooks, orderlies, train guards, ambulance details, and others who had non-combat assignments. Such details were particularly wasteful just then; a Northern general who fought at Antietam said that it was necessary to knock fully 20 per cent off the "present for duty" total to get the actual combat strength. But even with that reduction, McClellan had every advantage. Never before and never afterward, until the last gray days between Petersburg and Appomattox, were the two armies to collide with Rebel strength so greatly reduced. In addition, Lee must fight with his back to the Potomac, so that any blow which really crumpled his line would mean nothing less than absolute disaster. Retreat would be out of the question if the Yankees ever broke through.[1]

But McClellan saw the imaginary situation, not the real one. And he had, by any reckoning, abundant reason for caution. He might have been the man who could win the war in an afternoon; what he could not for a moment forget was that he was also the man who could lose it in an afternoon. Defeat north of the Potomac would mean the end of everything. The army had just been reorganized, and it had many raw troops; from a military point of view it was hardly an army so much as a collection of soldiers, fit to be taken into battle only in a great emergency.

And on top of everything else the old poison of distrust and hatred was still working. McClellan's own position was unstable, not to say downright irregular. He had been restored to command by President Lincoln personally, over the violent objection of the War Department, and Republican majority in Congress, and most of the Cabinet. Nobody had actually ordered him to take the army up here and fight the Confederates. All that showed on paper was that he had been put in command of troops "for the defense of Washington," and if anything went wrong here on the Antietam it was quite likely that Secretary Stanton would proceed against him for lawlessly exceeding his authority. McClellan wrote later that he fought the battles of South Mountain and the Antietam with a noose around his neck—which is to say that he fought, believing he would be executed for treason if he were beaten—a consideration hardly designed to make a bold, dashing fighter out of a man of McClellan's temperament.

So he bided his time: studying, calculating, attending to details. Noon came and went. Clouds formed in the sky and there was a little breeze to make the day cooler, and the guns on the hills fell silent. One of McClellan's staff officers wrote that "nobody seemed to be in a hurry. . . . Corps and divsons moved as languidly to the places assigned them as if they were getting ready for a grand review instead of a decisive battle."[2] McClellan rode from end to end of his lines, moving a detachment here and there into better position, endlessly watching the opposing heights. Once he detected a change in the position of a couple of Rebel batteries and conceived that Lee was regrouping his forces; that called for further delay, while additional surveys were made. Ammunition trains were coming up, and McClellan, always the good administrator, personally supervised the arrangements for supplying the troops and batteries.

As he perfected his plans he let himself create a mix-up in the chain of army command—unimportant enough, on the surface, but due to have far-reaching effects on the way the battle was fought.

Somewhat informally, McClellan had recently grouped his army into three principal sub-commands, or wings. General Sumner, commander of the II Corps, had been given command over General Mansfield's XII Corps as well. Franklin had his own VI Corps and Porter's V Corps; and General Ambrose E. Burnside, who had joined on the march up from Washington, had the direction of Reno's old IX Corps and of Hooker's I Corps. In planning his attack, however, McClellan scrambled this grouping—partly, his staff whispered, at the urging of Joe Hooker, who considered that he could make a better fight and win more glory if he were out from under Burnside's control. At any rate, the attack on the extreme right had been entrusted to Hooker, who was to have Mansfield's corps in immediate support, with Sumner standing by to lend a hand if necessary. In Franklin's absence Porter was to hold the center and act as army reserve, and when Franklin came up he would be put in wherever he seemed to be needed most. Burnside was on the extreme left, facing the downstream bridge, where he would attack as soon as Hooker's drive was rolling well.

Thus the new wing commands had completely fallen apart, and nobody in particular had general charge of anything. Hooker, theoretically under Burnside, was off on his own at the other end of the line. Mansfield, technically under Sumner, seemed to be temporarily attached to Hooker. Sumner, supposedly commanding a third of the army, had only his own corps and was to help Hooker, although Hooker was not empowered to give him any orders. And Burnside, who was new to the Army of the Potomac, was left to play a lone hand on the hardest front of all, attacking the bridge that crossed the Antietam under the overhanging hills to the south. All of the lines of responsibility had been cut, and if the next day's fighting was going to be co-ordinated in any way, the co-ordination would have to be provided by McClellan himself—and McClellan was a general who, like Lee, much preferred to leave the actual conduct of the fighting to his subordinates once the battle was begun.

The arrangement promised to make Hooker the hero of the next day's fight, and so that general, always eager for distinction, was very happy about it. It didn't sit at all well with Burnside, however, and it unquestionably had a grave effect on the fighting his men were to do.

There was to be a time when the Army of the Potomac would dislike and distrust Burnside intensely—not because he was personally objectionable, but because he presently developed an almost unfailing knack for bringing on defeat whenever he went into action. That time had not yet come, however, and in September 1862 he was immensely popular with the IX Corps, which knew him, and was generally respected by the rest of the army. Neither he nor the corps had been with the army very long, but both the general and the men brought a first-rate record in with them. Judging strictly by past performance, Burnside was a good man with the habit of success.

In 1861 he had been a Rhode Island businessman of some prominence, a West Pointer who had resigned from the army because garrison life in peacetime seemed unbearably dull. He got back in quickly enough when Fort Sumter was fired on, and raised the first of Rhode Island's troops. Late in that first summer of the war he proposed that an amphibious expedition be fitted out to descend on the North Carolina sounds, taking possession of seacoast cities and forts, giving Jefferson Davis a new front to defend, and closing the ports of entry for blockade runners. The suggestion was a good one and the administration accepted it, appointing Burnside to organize and lead the expedition. He got it under way early in January 1862, sailing from Hampton Roads with a heterogeneous fleet of transports and strong navy support.

Everything worked out fine, and the expedition was a brilliant success. Burnside made a good impression even before the fleet sailed. In the job lot of transports that had been collected so hurriedly there were some remarkably unseaworthy old tubs, and the soldiers protested strongly about having to go to sea in them: they had signed up to face Rebel bullets, but they didn't want to be drowned. Burnside promptly ended all grumbling by moving himself and his headquarters staff off the fine new steamer that had been set aside for him and embarking the smallest and most rickety little vessel of the lot—and almost paid for it with his life when the fleet ran into a gale off Cape Hatteras and the little steamer came within an inch of foundering.[3]

He seems to have been a very likable person, this Burnside. McClellan was very fond of him (until after the Antietam had been fought, anyhow) and used to write informal, chatty letters to him beginning "Dear Burn." Lincoln appears always to have retained a good deal of faith in him, even after Burnside had repeatedly demonstrated that it had been a military tragedy to give him a rank higher than colonel. One reason might have been that, with all his deficiencies, Burnside never had any angles of his own to play; he was a simple, honest, loyal soldier, doing his best even if that best was not very good, never scheming or conniving or backbiting. Also, he was modest; in an army many of whose generals were insufferable prima donnas, Burnside never mistook himself for Napoleon. Physically, he was impressive: tall, just a little stout, wearing what was probably the most artistic and awe-inspiring set of whiskers in all that bewhiskered army. He customarily wore a high, bell-crowned felt hat with the brim turned down and a double-breasted, knee-length frock coat, belted at the waist—a costume which, unfortunately, is apt to strike the modern eye as being very much like that of a beefy city cop of the 1880s.

At any rate, McClellan's order of battle for September 17 seems to have touched off all of Burnside's troubles. In a sense it left him all dressed up with no place to go. He was supposed to command two army corps, but one corps had been taken away from him. The one that remained had been commanded by Reno, and Reno had been killed on South Mountain; and Burnside, getting a bit stuffy for once in his career, refused to resume direct command of it because he felt that to do so would be to consent to a demotion. So he told General Cox, the ranking division commander, to assume command of the IX Corps; he, Burnside, would remain a wing commander even though the wing had been cut in half.

The result was that the IX Corps in this battle had two commanders—and no commander at all. McClellan gave his orders to Burnside, and Burnside majestically passed them on to Cox, and neither man was quite responsible for operations. Once the action began, there was likely to be a mix-up of the first magnitude.

On the afternoon of September 16, however, nobody foresaw any of that trouble. Along about four o'clock Hooker's corps pulled itself out of the fields along the Boonsboro road, followed a country lane back of the Pry house, and went splashing through the upper fords of the Antietam, with Hooker in the lead riding a magnificent white horse and looking every inch and quite consciously the gallant general. A soldier of the 6th Wisconsin remembered afterward that the way led through apple orchards and that the boys ducked out of ranks to fill their pockets and haversacks with the ripe fruit. Signal stations had been set up on the hills far ahead, and as they marched the men could see the flags wigwagging furiously. The corps began to climb through the rising farmland on its way to strike the Hagerstown road, and from the ridge to the west the move became visible, and Confederate guns banged away, groping ineffectually for the range.

The line of march led near the East Wood—that parklike open grove that lay half a mile northeast of the Dunker church—and the wood was occupied that afternoon by the Confederate division of John B. Hood: two brigades of Texas and Mississippi troops who were generally considered the hardest fighters in all of Lee's army, which is about all the compliment any troops need. They had their pickets well out in front, and before long the Yankee skirmishers brushed into them and there was a brisk interchange of small-arms fire. General Meade came riding up, brusque and impatient, to look the situation over. He sent couriers dashing off, and in a few minutes he had his Pennsylvania division deployed in line of battle facing the wood, and the Bucktails went forward in a long skirmish line. The rifle fire became heavy, and the colonel of the Bucktails was killed, and smoke and early twilight filled the fringes of the wood. Both sides rolled guns forward to take a hand in the fight, and as these opened, the guns farther back reached out at long range to make their own contribution, and for an hour or more there was a really vicious little battle there under the trees. Far off to the Federal left, soldiers of the 8th Ohio crept up on a hill to watch in the gathering dusk, and one of them—filled with all of a soldier's enthusiasm for a fight in which he himself does not have to take part—wrote: "Nothing could have been more grand. The red glare of flame along the Rebel line for more than a mile, the bright streams of light along the track of the shell, and the livid clouds of smoke as the shell burst in the air, constituted a spectacle brilliant beyond comparison."[4]

The firing was heavy and sustained enough to make Longstreet believe that a major attack had been made and repulsed. But the Federals didn't want the East Wood just then—Hooker was simply trying to protect the flank of his corps as it marched into position farther north and west—and the firing died out at dusk. Meade drew his division off, and only the rival picket lines were left to snipe at each other, sullenly, in the evening dark. On the Confederate side Hood's division was drawn back out of the wood, and replacement troops were sent up to bivouac where they had fought.

Hooker took his men well to the north before halting for the night. Doubleday's division, in the lead (Hatch had been wounded at South Mountain, and Doubleday had the division now), got to the Hagerstown road and formed up facing directly to the south, with Meade's Pennsylvanians on its left and a little more to the south, and the third division, that of Ricketts, to the left of the Pennsylvanians. Having thus reached what looked like a good jumping-off place for the next day's battle, Hooker established his headquarters in a farmer's yard a little east of the turnpike, and his men spread their blankets where they had halted and turned in for a little sleep.

It wasn't a very good night for sleeping. It began to rain after the sun went down, and there were intermittent spells of what one veteran recalled as "dismal, drizzling rain" all through the night; and out in front the pickets were nervous, opening up now and then with a blaze of firing that occasionally stirred some of the batteries and caused them to join in, although it was too dark for the gunners to hit much of anything. The gunfire rose to such a pitch, once, that an aide roused Hooker and called him out of his tent, fearing that the Rebels might be beginning a night attack. Hooker stood in the farmyard and listened, the raindrops glistening on his florid, handsome face, and looked at the spurts of flame off in the dark, estimating the direction of the fire. Then he shook his head. "The Rebels must be firing into their own men—we haven't any troops off that way," he said. Then he went back to bed.

There was a tension in the atmosphere for the whole army that night. Survivors wrote long afterward that there seemed to be something mysteriously ominous in the very air—stealthy, muffled tramp of marching men who could not be seen but were sensed dimly as moving shadows in the dark; outbursts of rifle fire up and down the invisible picket lines, with flames lighting the sky now and then when gunners in the advanced batteries opened fire; taut and nervous anxiety of those alert sentinels communicating itself through all the bivouacs, where men tried to sleep away the knowledge that the morrow would bring the biggest battle the army had ever had; a ceaseless, restless sense of movement, as if the army stirred blindly in its sleep, with the clop-clop of belated couriers riding down the inky-dark lanes heard at intervals, sounding very lonely and far off. The 16th Connecticut, a new and almost completely untrained regiment, which was lying along the Antietam near the downstream bridge, fell into a panic and sprang wildly to arms once when some clumsy rookie accidentally discharged his musket. Veteran regiments nearby cursed them wearily, cursed the high command for banning all campfires—the Rebels had had all day to spot the Union positions, but the top brass had ruled out fires that night for security reasons—and glumly munched the handfuls of ground coffee they couldn't boil. In Richardson's division the men were marched to the ammunition wagons in the darkness to draw eighty rounds per man, twice the usual allotment; they accepted the grim omen in expressionless silence.

Not far from the Pry house Mansfield's corps had turned in for the night. The men had been there since the afternoon of the day before, and they had their pup tents up and were feeling snug; but along toward midnight Mansfield came riding up from the Pry house to corps headquarters and the outfit was summoned to move—no drums and no bugles, just officers going down the regimental streets from tent to tent, quietly rousing the men and telling them to pack up. The sleepy soldiers made up their blanket rolls, took their muskets, and went off in the darkness, crossing the Antietam where Hooker had crossed in the afternoon, and following the guides he had sent back, old Mansfield riding at the head. They stumbled along, blind as moles in the drizzling night, holding their canteens and bayonets as they went, to keep them from jingling, following the obscure roads while the sky to the left was periodically lit by the mock lightning of the fitful cannonade.

They tramped for several miles and finally were halted on somebody's farm to the north and east of where Hooker's men were posted. General Mansfield spread a blanket for himself on the grass in a fence corner next to a field where the 10th Maine had turned in. The Maine boys were wakeful and did a lot of chattering—the march in the rain had roused them, and the thought of what was coming in the morning made it hard to go back to sleep—and the old general got up once and went over to shush them. They recalled that he was nice about it and not at all like a major general: just told them that if they had to talk they might as well do it in a whisper so that their comrades could get a little rest. And at last, long after midnight, there was quiet and the army slept a little.

How far they had marched, those soldiers—down the lanes and cross-lots over the cornfields to get into position, and from the distant corners of the country before that; they were marching, really, out of one era and into another, leaving much behind them, going ahead to much that they did not know about. For some of them there were just a few steps left: from the rumpled grass of a bed in a pasture down to a fence or a thicket where there would be an appointment with a flying bullet or shell fragment, the miraculous and infinitely complicated trajectory of the man meeting the flat, whining trajectory of the bullet without fail. And while they slept the lazy, rainy breeze drifted through the East Wood and the West Wood and the cornfield, and riffled over the copings of the stone bridge to the south, touching them for the last time before dead men made them famous. The flags were all furled and the bugles stilled, and the hot metal of the guns on the ridges had cooled, and the army was asleep—tenting tonight on the old camp ground, with never a song to cheer because the voices that might sing it were all stilled on this most crowded and most lonely of fields. And whatever it may be that nerves men to die for a flag or a phrase or a man or an inexpressible dream was drowsing with them, ready to wake with the dawn.

SIX

Never Call Retreat

1. TOWARD THE DUNKER CHURCH

THE MORNING CAME in like the beginning of the Last Day, gray and dark and tensely expectant. Mist lay on the ground, heavy as a fog in the hollow places, and the groves and valleys were drenched in immense shadows. For a brief time there was an ominous hush on the rolling fields, where the rival pickets crouched behind bushes and fence corners, peering watchfully forward under damp hatbrims. Little by little things began to be visible. The outlines of trees and farm buildings slowly came into focus against blurred backgrounds; the pickets grew more wary and alert, and when one of them saw movement in the half-light he raised his musket and fired. The two armies, lying so close in the rainy night, had been no more than half asleep; once aroused, they began to fight instinctively, as if knowing that the very moment of waking must lead to the fatal embrace of battle.

The random picket-firing increased as the light grew, and the advanced batteries were drawn into it. On the high ground around the Dunker church Stonewall Jackson had massed his artillery, and the gunners were astir early. As soon as they could see any details on the ridges to the north they sprang to their places and fired, and the men who were still in bivouac could feel the earth beneath them tremble faintly with the jar of the firing. Farther west, half a mile from the dusty line of the Hagerstown road, Jeb Stuart's horse artillery was drawn up on a wooded hill. When Jackson's guns opened, these guns began firing, too, and to the north and east the Yankee gunners returned the fire. Long before six o'clock the air shook with the rolling, rocking crash of gunfire.

Joe Hooker was up promptly, riding to the front before the light came. The men of his army corps had slept in a sheltered valley which ran eastward from the Hagerstown road, a mile or more north of the Dunker church, and Hooker went south through the bivouac, coming out on a wooded ridge and studying the landscape in the misty twilight. In front of him there was a broad field, sloping gently down to a hollow where there were an orchard, a patchwork of kitchen gardens and fences, and a big stone house, the home of a prosperous farmer named Miller. On the far side of the hollow, where the ground began to rise again, Mr. Miller had built a stout post-and-rail fence, going due east from the Hagerstown road to the edge of that pleasant grove which the generals were noting on their maps as the East Wood; and south of the fence, filling all of the ground between the road and the wood, was Mr. Miller's thriving cornfield—*the* cornfield, forever, after that morning. Beyond the cornfield and a little less than a mile from his present position Hooker could just see the white block of the Dunker church, framed by the dark growth of the West Wood. The high ground marked by that church was his objective; if it could be seized and held, Lee's whole army would have to retreat.

Hooker was an army politician and a devious man, approaching his ultimate goal—command of the Army of the Potomac—by roundabout ways which he discussed with nobody; but as a fighter he was direct and straightforward, and it was direct, straightforward fighting that was called for this morning. His army corps was camped due north of the Dunker church plateau; it would get there in the obvious way—by marching straight south, with Doubleday's division going along the Hagerstown road, Ricketts's division going through the East Wood, and Meade's Pennsylvanians going in between them. Each division would be massed so that reinforcements from the rear ranks could be hurried up to the front line quickly. Mansfield's corps was not far away and could be called on if Hooker's men needed help. Neither Hooker nor anyone else knew how many Rebels might be waiting in the cornfield and the wood. This was one of the things the advancing battle lines would have to find out for themselves. Meanwhile, it was time to get moving.

It was still early, and the gray light of the dawn was still dim. The army was awake, the men coming reluctantly out of sleep to the sound of the guns, knowing that this fight was going to be worse than anything they had ever been in before. Aroused by the cannon, the men reacted in their different ways. The 1st Minnesota, still safely behind the lines near McClellan's headquarters, noted the mist and the cloudy sky and profanely gave thanks that they would at least be fighting in the shade this day. (They were wrong, as it turned out; in another hour or two the mist would vanish and there would be a scorching sun all day.) Abner Doubleday found the men of his division hard to rouse; they took up their muskets and fell into ranks sluggishly, and they did not even grumble when they were marched off without time to boil coffee. Over in Mansfield's corps there was less of a rush and the men cooked sketchy breakfasts. There were many new regiments in this corps, and the veterans—quietly handing valuables and trinkets to members of the ambulance corps and other non-combat details for safekeeping—noticed with grim amusement that most of the straw-feet were too nervous to eat. In the 27th Indiana men stood up by their campfire to jeer and curse at one desperate soldier whose nerves had given way, out on the picket line, and who was running madly for the rear, oblivious to the taunts and laughter—a man whose legs had simply taken control of him. From one end of the army to the other, bivouacs were littered with discarded decks of cards. Card games were held sinful in that generation, and most men who were about to fight preferred not to have these tangible evidences of evil on their persons when they went out to face death.[1]

The men of Hooker's army corps left their bivouac and in heavy columns made their way through the timber to the ridge which was to be their jumping-

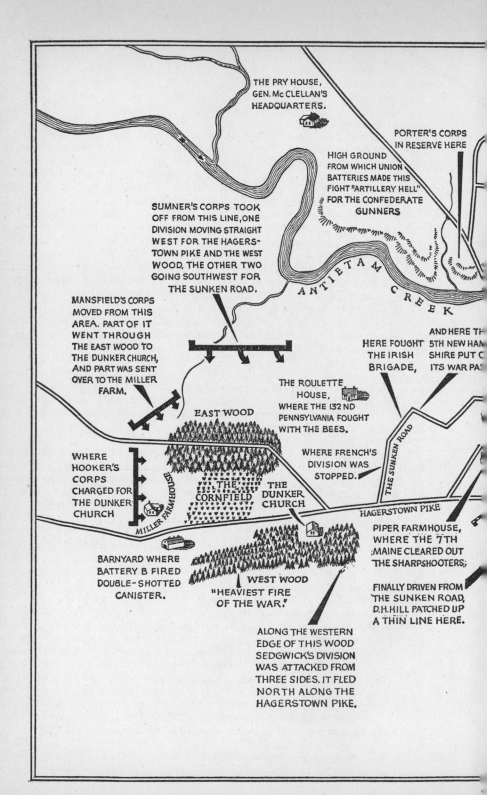

THE PRY HOUSE, GEN. McCLELLAN'S HEADQUARTERS.

PORTER'S CORPS IN RESERVE HERE

HIGH GROUND FROM WHICH UNION BATTERIES MADE THIS FIGHT "ARTILLERY HELL" FOR THE CONFEDERATE GUNNERS

SUMNER'S CORPS TOOK OFF FROM THIS LINE, ONE DIVISION MOVING STRAIGHT WEST FOR THE HAGERSTOWN PIKE AND THE WEST WOOD, THE OTHER TWO GOING SOUTHWEST FOR THE SUNKEN ROAD.

MANSFIELD'S CORPS MOVED FROM THIS AREA. PART OF IT WENT THROUGH THE EAST WOOD TO THE DUNKER CHURCH, AND PART WAS SENT OVER TO THE MILLER FARM.

ANTIETAM CREEK

AND HERE TH 5TH NEW HAM SHIRE PUT C ITS WAR PA

HERE FOUGHT THE IRISH BRIGADE,

EAST WOOD

THE ROULETTE HOUSE, WHERE THE 132 ND PENNSYLVANIA FOUGHT WITH THE BEES.

WHERE FRENCH'S DIVISION WAS STOPPED.

THE SUNKEN ROAD

WHERE HOOKER'S CORPS CHARGED FOR THE DUNKER CHURCH

MILLER FARMHOUSE

THE CORNFIELD

THE DUNKER CHURCH

HAGERSTOWN PIKE

PIPER FARMHOUSE, WHERE THE 7TH MAINE CLEARED OUT THE SHARPSHOOTERS;

BARNYARD WHERE BATTERY B FIRED DOUBLE-SHOTTED CANISTER.

WEST WOOD "HEAVIEST FIRE OF THE WAR."

FINALLY DRIVEN FROM THE SUNKEN ROAD, D.H.HILL PATCHED UP A THIN LINE HERE.

ALONG THE WESTERN EDGE OF THIS WOOD SEDGWICK'S DIVISION WAS ATTACKED FROM THREE SIDES. IT FLED NORTH ALONG THE HAGERSTOWN PIKE.

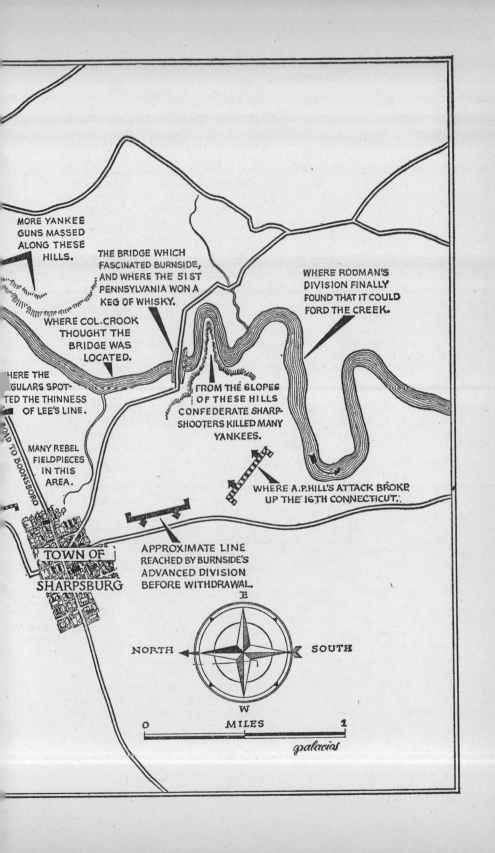

MORE YANKEE
GUNS MASSED
ALONG THESE
HILLS.

THE BRIDGE WHICH
FASCINATED BURNSIDE,
AND WHERE THE 51ST
PENNSYLVANIA WON A
KEG OF WHISKY.

WHERE RODMAN'S
DIVISION FINALLY
FOUND THAT IT COULD
FORD THE CREEK.

WHERE COL.CROOK
THOUGHT THE
BRIDGE WAS
LOCATED.

HERE THE
GULARS SPOT-
TED THE THINNESS
OF LEE'S LINE.

FROM THE SLOPES
OF THESE HILLS
CONFEDERATE SHARP-
SHOOTERS KILLED MANY
YANKEES.

MANY REBEL
FIELDPIECES
IN THIS
AREA.

WHERE A.P.HILL'S ATTACK BROKE
UP THE 16TH CONNECTICUT.

AD TO BOONSBORO

TOWN OF
SHARPSBURG

APPROXIMATE LINE
REACHED BY BURNSIDE'S
ADVANCED DIVISION
BEFORE WITHDRAWAL.

E

NORTH

SOUTH

W

0   MILES   1

palacios

off point. Some of the columns could be seen by the distant Confederate gunners, and the shells came over faster—the men had hardly started when one of Stuart's guns put a shell right in the middle of the 6th Wisconsin, knocking out thirteen men and bringing the column to a halt while stretcher-bearers ran in to carry off the wounded. The 90th and 107th Pennsylvania, moving up toward the outer fringe of the East Wood, also came within Stuart's range and had losses; and men were maimed for life who saw no more of the battle than a peaceful field and a sandy lane in the wood in the early light of dawn. As they reached the ridge the leading elements of the divisional columns sent out skirmish lines, and in the broad hollow of the Miller farm the sporadic pop-pop of picket firing became much heavier while the skirmish lines went down the slope—each man in the line separated from his fellows by half a dozen paces, holding his musket as if he were a quail hunter with a shotgun, moving ahead step by step, dropping to one knee to shoot when he found a target, pausing to reload, and then moving on again, feeling the army's way into the danger zone.

Rebel skirmishers held the Miller farm in some strength, and there were many more along the fence by the cornfield. The sound of the musket fire suddenly rose to a long, echoing crash that ran from the highway to the East Wood and back again. The Confederate batteries to the south and off to the right stepped up the pace, and the shells came over faster. Beyond the hollow ground the green cornfield swayed and moved, although there was no wind. The glint of bayonets could be seen here and there amid the leafage, and long, tearing volleys came out of the corn, while wreaths of yellowish-white smoke drifted up above it as if the whole field were steaming. More men were hurt, and the Yankee skirmishers halted and took cover.

There was a pause, while the battle lines waited under fire. Then there was a great rush and a pounding of hoofs as Hooker's corps artillery dashed up into line—six batteries coming up at a mad gallop, gun carriages bouncing wildly with spinning wheels, drivers lashing the six-horse teams, officers riding on ahead and turning to signal with flashing swords when they reached the chosen firing line. In some of these batteries orders for field maneuvers were given by bugle, and the high thin notes could be heard above all the racket, the teams wheeling in a spatter of rising dust—veteran artillery horses knew what the bugle calls meant as well as the men did, and would obey without waiting to be told. In a few minutes three dozen guns were lined up on the slope, limbers a dozen yards to the rear, teamsters taking the horses back into the wood, gun crews busy with ramrod and handspike. The guns began to plaster the cornfield unmercifully, and the air above the field was filled with clods of dirt and flying cornstalks and knapsacks and broken muskets as the canister ripped the standing grain.

Far off to the left, beyond the Antietam, McClellan's long-range rifles came into action, hammering hard at the Rebel guns by the Dunker church and reaching out to plow the cornfield with a terrible cross fire of shell and solid shot; and the waiting Federal infantry hugged the ground, half dazed by the tremendous waves of noise. Hooker exaggerated a little, but only a little, when he wrote afterward that "every stalk in the northern and greater part of the field was cut as closely as could have been done with a knife"; and he exaggerated not at all when he wrote that in all the war he never looked upon "a more bloody, dismal battlefield." The Confederates in the northern part of the cornfield went down in rows, scores at a time. Then after a while the great thunder of the guns died down a little and the Yankee infantry went forward.

It all looks very simple and orderly on the map, where the advance of the I Corps is represented by a straight line following neat little arrows, three divisions moving snugly abreast and everyone present presumably knowing at all times just what was going on and what the score was. But in reality there was nothing simple or orderly about any part of it. Instead there was an appalling confusion of shattering sound, an unending chaos of violence and heat and intense combat, with fields and thickets wrapped in shifting layers of blinding smoke so that no man could know and understand any more of what was happening than the part he could see immediately around him. There was no solid connected battle line neatly ranked in clear light; there was a whole series of battle lines swaying haphazardly in an infernal choking fog, with brigades and regiments standing by themselves and fighting their enemies where they found them, attack and counterattack taking place in every conceivable direction and in no recognizable time sequence, Northerners and Southerners wrestling back and forth in the cornfield in one tremendous free-for-all. The black powder used in those days left heavy masses of smoke which stayed on the ground or hung at waist level in long tattered sheets until the wind blew it away, and this smoke deposited a black, greasy film on sweaty skins, so that men who had been fighting hard looked grotesque, as if they had been ineptly made up for a minstrel show.

The fighting surged back and forth from the East Wood to the highway and beyond, and the most any general could do was push new troops in from the rear where they seemed to be needed—or, at times, rally soldiers who were coming disorganized out of action and send them back in again: what was happening up front was beyond anyone's control and depended entirely on the men themselves. And a wild, primitive madness seemed to descend on the men who fought in the cornfield: they went beyond the limits of sanity and endurance at times, Northerners and Southerners alike, until it seems that they tore at each other for the sheer sake of fighting. The men who fought there are all dead now, and it may be that we misinterpret the sketchy accounts which they left of the combat; yet from the diaries and the reports and the histories we get glimpses of what might well have been the most savage and consuming fighting American soldiers ever engaged in.

General Ricketts sent his men in through the East Wood—New York regiments, mostly, with a few from Pennsylvania and Massachusetts—and they fought step by step through the thickets and over the rocky ledges and fallen trees in the misty light of early morning, slowly driving the tenacious Confederates out and swinging around unconsciously until they faced toward the west, so that as they came out of the wood they went into the cornfield, with Stuart's cannon hitting them hard from the western hills. They pulled themselves together on the edge of the cornfield, getting an enfilade fire on a Confederate brigade there and sending it flying; then they advanced again, and as they moved the regiments were separated, each one automatically adjusting its lines to face whatever formation of Rebels might be in front of it. When they got deeper into the field the opposition became heavier, until at last whole brigades were shaken by the deadly, racking volleys—the most terrible fire, one veteran wrote, that they ever had to endure. Rifles were splintered and broken in men's hands, canteens and haversacks were riddled, platoons and companies seemed to dissolve. They closed ranks as well as they could amid the cornstalks, sweating officers gesturing with swords and yelling orders no one could hear in the overpowering racket, and they kept pushing on. They attacked and they were counterattacked; they drove certain Rebels and were themselves driven in turn; at times they exchanged stand-up volleys at incredibly close ranges, wrecking their enemies and seeing their own lines wrecked, while the smoke settled thicker and thicker and they fought in utter blindness.

At last they went back, straggling through the East Wood to reform in the rear—a full third of the division shot down and half of the survivors hopelessly scattered. The 12th Massachusetts—the kid-glove boys from Boston who had brought a great song to the war and carried a noble flag of white and blue and gold presented by the ladies of Beacon Hill—took 334 men into action and lost 220 of them, and when it tried to rally behind the wood fewer than three dozen

men were still with the colors. Duryée's brigade of four regiments found hardly
a hundred men to form a line when it finished its retreat. For the time being,
except for a few valiant fragments which hung on at the edge of the wood, the
entire division was out of the fight.

Meade's Pennsylvanians had gone into the cornfield at the center of the line,
and their story is just about the same: advance and retreat, charge and countercharge, victory and retreat all blended. Once the center brigade broke under a
driving Rebel charge and went streaming toward the rear. Meade came thundering up with the battle fury on him, yanked the 8th Reserve Regiment back
into line, hurried it off to a vantage point by Mr. Miller's fence. A Georgia regiment, lying unseen in the corn, let fly with a volley from a distance of thirty feet,
knocking out half the regiment at one sweep. The Pennsylvania color-bearer
went down with a foot shot off, struggled to his knees, jabbing his flagstaff into
the ground, and struck wildly at a comrade who tried to take the colors away
from him. A charging Georgian shot him dead and was himself killed by a
Pennsylvanian lieutenant; and there were wild tumult and heavy smoke and
crazy shouting all around, with the entire war narrowed to the focus of this single combat between Pennsylvanians and Georgians. Then the Pennsylvanians
broke and ran again—to be stopped, incomprehensibly, a few yards in the rear
by a boyish private who stood on a little hillock and kept swinging his hat,
shouting: "Rally, boys, rally! Die like men, don't run like dogs!"

Strangely, on that desperate field where men were madly heroic and full of
abject panic by turns, this lone private stopped the retreat. What was left of the
regiment fell in beside him. Fugitives from other regiments in the shattered brigade fell in with them, and Meade—who had gone galloping away to bring up a
battery to plug the gap—came back and got the uncertain line straightened out,
while canister from the new battery uprooted green cornstalks and tore the
bodies of Rebels who crouched low on the powdery ground. Then presently the
brigade went forward again.[2]

Over by the turnpike the Black Hat Brigade charged around the Miller farm
buildings, driving out the Confederate skirmishers but breaking apart somewhat
as the men surged past dwelling and outhouses under heavy fire. There is a
glimpse of a young Wisconsin officer standing by a gap in a fence, waving his
sword and crying: "Company E! On the right, by file, into line!" Then a bullet
hit him in his open mouth and he toppled over dead in mid-shout; and the brigade got by the obstruction and went into the cornfield near the highway. Here
it seemed to be every man for himself. There was Rebel infantry west of the
road, pouring in a tremendous fire; some of the men formed a new line facing
west, lying down behind the turnpike fence to fight back. Gibbon sent a couple
of regiments across the road to deal with this flank attack, and a moment later
Doubleday sent four New York regiments over there to help; part of his division
was going south through the cornfield and part of it was struggling desperately
in the fields and woods to the west, and shells and bullets were coming in from
all directions at once. Men said afterward that the bullets seemed to be as thick
as hail in a great storm. Formations were lost, regiments and brigades were
jumbled up together, and as the men advanced they bent their heads as if they
were walking into a driving rain. And under all the deafening tumult there was a
soft, unceasing clip-snip-clip of bullets shearing off the leaves and stalks of corn.
Near the highway some officer was yelling the obvious—"This fire is murderous!"—and then, at last, the sweating mob of soldiers came out by a fence at the
southern edge of the cornfield, and as they did so a long line of Confederates
arose from the plowed ground in front of them and the high sound of rifle fire
rose to a new intensity.

A terrible frenzy of battle descended on the fighting line. Men were possessed
by a hysterical excitement, shouting furiously, bursting out in shrill insane

laughter, crowding up to the fence to fire at the Rebel line. A survivor of this attack, recalling the merciless fire that greeted the men at the line of the fence, wrote: "Men, I cannot say fell—they were knocked out of ranks by the dozen." Cartridges were torn with nervous haste. Muskets became foul from much firing, so that men took stones to hammer their ramrods down. Wanting to fire faster than ever before, they found they could not—a nightmare slowness was upon them as the black powder caked in hot rifle barrels. Some soldiers threw their pieces away and took up the rifles of dead men.

All along the fence the men were jostling together, with soldiers in the rear ranks passing loaded rifles forward to the men in front: battle flags waved in sweeping, smoke-fringed arcs, color-bearers swinging the flag staffs frantically, as if the mere fluttering of the colors would help bring victory. Brigades and regiments were all helter-skelter—Pennsylvanians and New Yorkers were jammed in with men from Wisconsin and Massachusetts, everyone was cheering hoarsely, new elements were coming up from the rear to add to the crush along the fence, the noise of battle was one great unending roar louder than anything the men had ever heard before. And at last, as if by common impulse, the whole crowd swarmed forward over the fence and started up the open field toward the Dunker church—very near now, its whitewashed walls all splotched and patchy from flying bullets. The Confederate line, terribly thinned by rifle fire, broke in wild flight. Some of the Southerners tried to escape over the turnpike fences and were left spread-eagled on the rails as the Federals shot them; others fell back into the wood around the church. The Northerners raised a great new shout and went ahead on the run, with victory in sight.[3]

Then, dramatically, from the wood around the church a new Confederate battle line emerged, trotting forward with the shrill yip-yip-yip of the Rebel yell—John B. Hood's division, swinging into action with an irresistible counterattack.

Hood's men had been pulled out of the front lines late the night before, after their brush with the Pennsylvanians in the East Wood. They had been on short rations for days, and early this morning the commissary department finally caught up with them, delivering ample supplies of bread and meat. The division had been in the act of cooking the first solid meal in a week when word came back that they were needed up front without a moment's delay—the Yankees had broken the line and would have the battle won unless somebody did something about it. So the Texans and Mississippians left their half-cooked breakfasts, grabbed their rifles, and came storming out into the open, mad clean through: and here, within easy range, were the Yankees who were the cause of it all, the Yankees on whom the overmastering anger of hungry men could be vented.

Hood's men drew up and delivered a volley which, said a Federal survivor, "was like a scythe running through our line." It hit the Federals head-on and stopped them. There was a brief pause, and then the Northern soldiers turned and made for the rear on the run, back over the fence and into the raddled cornfield and down the long slope, Hood's men following them with triumphant, jeering shouts, while three brigades from D. H. Hill's command came in from below the East Wood and added their own weight to the pursuit.

Down in the open ground by the Miller house the flight was checked. General Gibbon had brought up old Battery B, and its six brass smoothbores were drawn up in a barnyard west of the road. The Rebels were advancing on both sides of the pike, converging on the barnyard—the Federals west of the road had had to retire when the cornfield was lost—and the guns became a strong point where the beaten soldiers could make a stand again. Some of the fugitives fell in behind the battery, kneeling and firing out between the guns. Gibbon got two of his regiments drawn up farther west, a little ahead of the guns and facing east;

General Patrick brought his four New York regiments up amid the crush; and the charging Confederates came out of the corn from the south and east, smashing straight at the battery, firing as they came.

Battery B was pounding away furiously, but Gibbon, looking with the eye of a gunner, noticed that in the mad excitement the gun crews had let the elevating screws run down so that the guns were pointing up for extreme long range, blasting their charges into the empty air. He shouted and gestured from the saddle, but no one could hear anything in that unearthly din, so he threw himself to the ground, ran to the nearest gun, shouldered the gun crew aside, and spun the little wheel under the breech so that the muzzle slowly sank until it seemed almost to be pointing at the ground. Gibbon stepped aside, the gunner jerked the lanyard, and the gun smashed a section of rail fence, sending the splintered pieces flying in the faces of Hood's men. The other gunners hastily corrected their elevation and fired double-shotted rounds of canister at the range of fifty feet, while the Northern infantry cracked in with volleys of musket fire. In all its history the battery never fired so fast; its haste was so feverish that a veteran regular-army sergeant forgot to step away from his gun when it was discharged, and as it bounded backward in recoil a wheel knocked him down and crushed him.

The front of the Confederate column was blown away, and the survivors withdrew sullenly into what was left of the cornfield. Some of the Federals west of the road raised a yell and went into the cornfield after them, were struck in the flank by unseen Confederates farther south, and came streaming back across the pike again to take shelter among the rocky ledges west of the guns. The Rebels re-formed behind a low ridge, then came on again. A soldier in the 80th New York, helping to defend the battery, called this assault "one of the finest exhibitions of pluck and manhood ever seen on any battlefield." But the heroism served only to swell the casualty lists. There were too many Yankees there and the guns were firing too fast; the charging Rebel line simply melted away under fire, the men who were not hit ran back into the cornfield again, and for a moment there was something like a breathing spell, while the rival armies lay as one soldier wrote, "like burnt-out slag" on the battlefield.[4]

Two hours of fighting in one forty-acre field, with the drumming guns never silent for a moment; Northerners and Southerners had fought themselves out, and the fields and woods for miles to the rear were filled with fugitives. A steady leakage had been taking place from each army as all but the stoutest found themselves carried beyond the limit of endurance. The skulkers and the unabashed cowards, who always ran in every battle at the first chance they could get—and there was hardly a regiment, North or South, which did not have a few of them—had drifted away at the first shock. Later others had gone: the men who could stand something but not everything, men who had stood fast in all previous fights but found this one too terrible to be borne; the men who helped wounded comrades to the rear and then either honestly got lost (which was easy to do, in the smoking madness) or found that they could not quite make themselves go back into it. All of these had faded out, leaving the fighting lines dreadfully thin, so that the loss of strength on each side was far greater, just then, than the casualty lists would show. Hooker's corps had lost nearly twenty-five hundred men killed and wounded—a fearful loss, considering that he had sent hardly more than nine thousand into action—but for the moment the story was much worse than that. The number of uninjured men who left the ranks was probably fully as great as the number of casualties. The proud I Corps of the Army of the Potomac was wrecked.[5]

On the Confederate side the story was about the same. The troops who had held the cornfield and East Wood when the fight began had been splintered and smashed and driven to the rear. Their dazed remnants were painfully trying to regroup themselves far behind the Dunker church, fugitives were trailed out all the way back to the Potomac, and field and wood were held now by the reinforcements, Hood's men and D. H. Hill's. There was still fight left in these men, but they had been ground down unmercifully. At the height of his counterattack Hood had sent back word that unless he could be reinforced he would have to withdraw, but that meanwhile he would go on as far as he could. He had gone to the northern limit of the cornfield, had seen the striking spearhead of his division broken by the Yankee guns and rifles around Miller's barnyard, and he was holding on now in a grim expectancy of a new Federal attack. The cornfield itself was a hideous spectacle—broken stalks lying every which way, green leaves spattered with blood, ground all torn and broken, littered everywhere with discarded weapons. Inconceivable numbers of dead and wounded lay in all parts of the field, whole ranks of them at the northern border where Hooker's first blasts of cannon fire had caught them—after the battle Massachusetts soldiers said they had found 146 bodies from one Rebel brigade lying in a neat, soldierly line. Hood wrote afterward that on no other field in the whole war was he so constantly troubled by the fear that his horse would step on some helpless wounded man. The Rebel brigades that were in the field when the fighting began had lost about 50 per cent of their numbers.

But there could be no lull. Hooker had Mansfield's corps at his disposal, and when the Rebels drove his men back through the cornfield he sent for it. Old General Mansfield went galloping up to his troops, his hat in his hand, long white hair and beard streaming in the wind. The men in Gordon's brigade jumped up and ran for their rifles as soon as they saw him coming, falling in without waiting for orders, cheering loudly. Something about the old soldier, with his air of competence and his unexpected mixture of stiff military dignity and youthful fire and vigor, had aroused their enthusiasm during the two days he had been with them. Mansfield reined up in front of them, calling: "That's right, boys, cheer—we're going to whip them today!" He rode down the line from regiment to regiment, waving his hat and repeating: "Boys, we're going to lick them today!"

They were a mile and more from the battlefield, and the uproar beat upon their ears as they moved forward. The noise seemed to be coming in great swinging pulsations, as if whole brigades or divisions were firing successive volleys. The booming of the cannon was continuous, so steady that no individual shots could be heard; and before the field could be seen the men could make out the great billowing clouds of smoke drifting up in the windless air. As they got nearer they met wounded men going to the rear—chipper enough, most of them, all things considered, calling out that they "had the Johnnies on the run." Gordon's brigade came out on the ridge near the Miller farm, with the northern border of the cornfield in view. Federal regiments were withdrawing across the hollow, stepping backward, loading and firing as they retreated. One pitiful skeleton of a beaten regiment saw the fresh 27th Indiana coming up behind it. Heedless that they were still under fire, the men shouted with joy, threw caps, knapsacks, and canteens in the air, waving jubilant welcome to the reinforcements; and when the Indiana soldiers came abreast of them the retreating soldiers halted, re-formed ranks, and started back into battle again without orders.

Mansfield went in at the head of his first brigade, heading straight for the northern part of the East Wood. The situation was not at all clear to him, and he halted the column briefly while he tried to make out what was in front of him. Hooker came cantering up, crying: "The enemy are breaking through my lines—you must hold this wood!" Then Hooker rode away and Mansfield started putting his leading regiments, 10th Maine and 128th Pennsylvania, into line of battle. The East Wood presented almost as ghastly a sight as the cornfield, by now—dead and living bodies everywhere, little groups of men trying to help wounded comrades to the rear, shattered limbs of trees lying on the ground in a tangle, wreckage of artillery equipment strewn about, with unseen Rebels keeping the air alive with bullets, and streaky sheets of acrid smoke lying in the air. Nobody knew whether there were Union troops in front or not. The ground was uneven, crossed with rocky ledges and ridges. Organized bodies of troops could be seen in the distance now and then, but the light was bad and the skirmishers, shooting at everything that moved, did not know whether they were firing at friends or enemies.

Brigadier General Samuel Crawford made his way through the wood, trying to get his brigade into line: an unusual man, doctor turned soldier, who had taken an unusual route to his general's commission. He had been a regular-army surgeon before the war and was in the Fort Sumter garrison. Back at the beginning of 1861, when Major Anderson moved the garrison from Moultrie to Sumter, all the line officers being busy, the doctor was posted at a loaded columbiad to sink the Confederate guard boat if it tried to interfere. He didn't have to shoot just then, but either that experience or the later bombardment itself apparently inspired him to give up medicine for line command, and when the garrison came north he got a brigadier's star. His brigade had been badly cut to pieces at Cedar Mountain early this summer, when Pope's advance guard had its first meeting with Stonewall Jackson. Since then Crawford had been vainly writing applications to have the brigade withdrawn for reorganization and recruitment, pointing out that his four regiments numbered only 629 men altogether, with so many officers gone that three of the regiments were in command of inexperienced captains. His 28th New York had been consolidated into four companies and was going into action today with sixty-five men. Crawford had got nowhere with his applications, but a couple of days before this battle the high command had given him three brand-new regiments of Pennsylvania recruits, and with this lopsided command—four understrength regiments of veterans and three big, half-trained regiments of rookies—he was now going into action against Hood and D. H. Hill. Understandably, he was nervous about it.

Most of the enemy fire seemed to be coming from the cornfield at the western edge of the wood, so Crawford wheeled his regiments in that direction. The Rebel skirmishers were playing Indian again, dodging back from tree to tree and ledge to ledge and firing from behind the piles of cordwood that some thrifty farmer had stacked here and there; but the Maine regiment, the veteran 46th Pennsylvania, and the tiny 28th New York finally got to the edge of the wood, and two of the greenhorn regiments struggling up on their right, and began to fire at moving figures among the shattered cornstalks. Mansfield rode up, worried; he still didn't know where the enemy was, and Hooker had given him the impression that Meade's Pennsylvanians were still in the field. He made the Maine regiment cease firing—"You are firing into our own men"—and put his horse over the fence and rode on ahead to get a better look. Some soldier called out, "Those are Rebels, General!" Mansfield took a last look, said: "Yes—you're right"—and then a volley came out of the cornfield. Mansfield's horse was hit, and when the old man dismounted to clamber over the fence he himself got a bullet in the stomach.

Some of the rookies from the 125th Pennsylvania picked him up, made a crude litter of muskets, and got him back into the wood, where they laid him down, uncertain what to do next. They had been soldiers for only a month, this was their first battle, and what did one do with a badly wounded major general, anyhow? Three boys from the 10th Maine took over—as veterans, one gathers, they knew a good excuse to get away from the firing line when they saw it—the Pennsylvanians went back to the fence, and the down-Easters tried to lug the general back to the rear. And they found, in the wood, a bewildered contraband who was company cook in one of Hooker's regiments and who, with a clumsy incompetence rare even among company cooks, had chosen this time and place to lose, and then to hunt for, a prized frying pan. The Maine boys seized him that he might make a fourth at carrying the general, who was heavy and helpless. The contraband demurred—he had to find the captain's frying pan, and nothing else mattered—but the soldiers pounded him with their fists, the whine of ricocheting bullets cutting the air all around, shells crashing through the branches overhead, and he gave in at last and poor General Mansfield somehow was got back to a dressing station. There a flurried surgeon pressed a flask of whisky to his mouth, almost strangling him; and, what with the wound and the clumsy handling, the old man presently died. He had had the corps only two days, but he had already made the soldiers like and respect him; it seems likely that he might have made quite a name if he had been spared.[6]

But there was no holding up the fight because a general had been killed. Crawford went down, too, with a bad wound, and a colonel took over the brigade, and the veterans and the rookies got into a tremendous fire fight with some of D. H. Hill's men along the east side of the cornfield. Farther west General Gordon drove his brigade in past the Miller farm buildings and over the pitiful human wreckage that littered the ground in front of Battery B. The Rebels in the corner of the cornfield and along the fence on the northern side were not disposed to go away, and the 3rd Wisconsin took a beating when it got up to the fence; but Gordon worked the 2nd Massachusetts around on the right and got an enfilade on the Texans, and the 27th Indiana came up on the other side, and the Confederate line gave way.

So once more there was a bitter fight in the cornfield, with the Federals coming in from the north and east; and Hood, as he had foreseen, was compelled to withdraw, with half of his men shot down. As Gordon's lines went in Hooker got a bullet in the foot and rode to the rear, dripping blood, and command of this part of the battle passed temporarily to Mansfield's senior division commander, General Alpheus S. Williams, who rode about the field with the unlighted stub of a cigar gripped in his teeth and who was called "Pop" by his troops—sure sign that they liked him. The retreating Rebels made a desperate fight of it. One of Crawford's men asserted that "on all other fields from the beginning to the end of our long service, we never had to face their equals," and the 27th Indiana came to a halt in the middle of the smoky field, standing erect in close order and firing as fast as it could handle its muskets, which finally became too hot to be used. One Hoosier, badly wounded, laid down his rifle and went a few yards to the rear, where he sat down, opened his clothing, and examined his wound. After studying it, he mused aloud: "Well, I guess I'm hurt about as bad as I can be. I believe I'll go back and give 'em some more." So he picked up a discarded musket and returned to the firing line.

The regiment shot up all its ammunition, a hundred rounds per man, and sent details around the field to loot the cartridge boxes of the dead and wounded. In this fight the 27th lost a good non-com—Corporal Barton W. Mitchell, who had caused the battle in the first place by finding Lee's lost order; he went down with a wound that kept him out of action for months. His company commander, Captain Kopp, to whom he had first taken the lost order, was killed.

At last the 2nd Massachusetts came in on the right, its colonel jubilantly waving a captured Texas battle flag, and the Confederate defense began to crumble. Crawford's men came out of the East Wood at last, rookies and veterans all yelling and firing as they came, and the Rebels gave way and went back, running south and west across the turnpike and into the West Wood. Once more the cornfield, for whatever it was worth, belonged to the Union. Gordon's and Crawford's men tried to get across the turnpike and pursue, but nobody had ever yet cleaned up on the Rebel strength to the west of this highway—Mansfield had sent a brigade over there when he first took his corps into action, but the regiments had been put in clumsily and had been driven off—and the Federal advance was halted along the rail fence, and that dusty country highway once more became a lane of death.

Half a mile farther east things were going better. General George Sears Greene, a relative of Revolutionary War hero Nathanael Greene, had the rest of

Mansfield's troops—a battle-worn division of some seventeen hundred men—and these had cut through the eastern fringe of the East Wood and had gone driving straight for the Dunker church. Some of the Confederates who had been driven out of the cornfield rallied and hit them in the flank as they got past the timber, some of Hill's men gouged at their other flank, and Lee brought reinforcements over from the right of his line to make a stand in front of the church. The Northerners had a hard time of it for a while, coming under fire from three directions, and when the Confederates came in with a counterattack the outlook was bad; but just in time a Rhode Island battery came galloping up, the infantry broke ranks to let the guns through, and the counterattack was smashed with canister and rifle fire. Then one of Crawford's rookie regiments—125th Pennsylvania, seven hundred strong, a giant of a regiment for that field—came up, separated from its brigade and slightly lost but anxious to get into the nearest fight; and Greene's division ran on past the guns and got into the West Wood around the Dunker church, forming a solid line on the far side of that battle-scarred building. Here was victory, if someone could just bring up reinforcements.

But the reinforcements didn't show up. This spearhead had got clear through the Confederate line. The high ground around the church, objective of all the morning's fighting, had been seized at last. But Greene had lost a third of his men, more than two hundred of the Pennsylvania straw-feet were down, and the survivors could do no more than hang on where they were, the Rebels keeping them under a steady fire. Completely wrecked, Hooker's army corps was trying to round up its stragglers and reassemble on the hills a mile to the north. The rest of Mansfield's corps was in position around the Miller barnyard and along the western edge of the cornfield, solidly posted but too busy to send any help. Greene's boys had reached the goal, but they couldn't do anything with it now that they had it. The fire that was being played upon their lines was not strong enough to drive them out, but it was too strong to advance against; and off to the southeast they could make out the movement of marching bodies of men, as if heavy Confederate reinforcements were coming up. The right wing of McClellan's army was beaten out, with this one advanced detachment huddling under the trees to mark high tide.

2. THE HEAVIEST FIRE OF THE WAR

It may be that life is not man's most precious possession, after all. Certainly men can be induced to give it away very freely at times, and the terms hardly seem to make sense unless there is something about the whole business that we don't understand. Lives are spent for very insignificant things which benefit the dead not at all—a few rods of ground in a cornfield, for instance, or temporary ownership of a little hill or a piece of windy pasture; and now and then they are simply wasted outright, with nobody gaining anything at all. And we talk glibly about the accidents of battle and the mistakes of generalship without figuring out just which end of the stick the man who died was holding. As, for instance:

By seven-thirty in the morning a dim sense that something had gone wrong had reached McClellan's headquarters. The signal flags had been wigwagging ever since it was light enough to see them, and at one time McClellan came out of his tent, smiling and saying, "All goes well—Hooker is driving them." But all had not gone well thereafter, and presently white-haired old General Sumner was ordered to take his corps across the creek and get into action. Sumner moved promptly, and before long, from Mr. Pry's yard, McClellan could see the three parallel lines of John Sedgwick's division threading their way up the farther hillsides, heading for the East Wood.

Sumner rode with Sedgwick, letting the two remaining divisions of his corps follow as best they could. He was strictly the Indian fighter of the Western plains this morning, putting himself in the front rank of the column of attack, ready for a straight cut-and-thrust onslaught on the Rebel lines. He knew almost nothing about what had happened so far—had the inpression, even, that the right wing of the army had gained a victory and that he was being sent in to make it complete. But when he got to the East Wood the omens under the shattered trees were sinister. The place was packed with wounded men, and there were far too many able-bodied soldiers wandering around trying to help them. (One of Sedgwick's colonels wrote sagely: "When good Samaritans so abound it is a strong indication that the discipline of the troops in front is not good and that the battle is not going so as to encourage the half-hearted.")[1] And when the division came out on the far side of the wood, facing west, the picture looked even worse. Sumner could see smoke and hear gunfire off to the right, where tenacious Rebels and Northerners still disputed possession of the Miller barnyard and adjacent pastures, and some firing seemed to be going on to the south by the Dunker church; but in front, as far as Sumner could see, there was nothing at all except for the ghastly debris that filled the cornfield. From the sketchy evidence he had, Sumner concluded that two whole army corps had ceased to exist: the right wing of the army was gone, except for scattered fragments, and he had this end of the battle all to himself.

The plan of attack which he decided on was very simple. If he was now beyond the Federal flank, then he must be beyond the Rebel flank as well: so he would move straight west, at right angles to the earlier lines of attack, advancing until he was in rear of Lee's left. Then he would wheel to his own left and sweep down the ridge behind Lee's line, crumpling the Army of Northern Virginia into McClellan's net. He had Sedgwick form his division in three lines, a brigade to each line, five thousand men altogether, and he started out across the cornfield full of confidence: if Sedgwick's men got into any trouble they could cut their way out, and besides, two other divisions were following.

Sumner supposed they were following, at any rate. They had been told to do so. But he was the cavalry colonel, riding in the front line as he led his men to the charge, not the corps commander staying back to make sure that everybody understood what he was to do and did it; and his second division was even now going astray, swinging about for an attack on the high ground southeast of the Dunker church, half a mile or more away from Sumner's target. The third division had not even started, staff work having been fouled up. Worst of all, Sedgwick's division was formed for a head-on attack and nothing else. The three brigade lines were so close together that maneuvering would be almost impossible, and if the division should be hit in the flanks there would be great trouble.

The five thousand enlisted men who would have to foot the bill if anything went wrong were not thinking of possible errors in tactics as they moved forward. They were veterans and they were rated with the best troops in the army, but the march so far had been rather unnerving. They had come up through all the backwash of battle, seeing many wounded, hearing many discouraging remarks by demoralized stragglers; they had seen ambulances jolting to the rear from advanced operating stations, carrying men who held the stumps of their amputated limbs erect in a desperate effort to ease the pain of the rough ride. When they formed line at the edge of the wood, even the veteran 19th Massachusetts had been so visibly nervous that its colonel had put the men through the manual of arms for a few minutes to steady their nerves. (This was another of the old fancy-Dan regiments; in the beginning it had elected not merely its officers but its enlisted men as well, just like a club, and when it left Boston in 1861 it had two complete baggage wagons for each company, four for regimental headquarters and four for the commissary—enough, as one member said, for an army corps, by later standards. It had learned much since those days.)

The division went west across the cornfield, the lines wavering as the men stepped carefully to avoid the dead and wounded, and it came under artillery fire. Stuart's horse artillery had moved south to a hill behind the West Wood, firing over the treetops, and the division was so wide and solid that the gunners could not miss—a shot that carried over the first battle line was sure to hit the second or the third. (One veteran wrote disgustedly afterward: "We were as easy to hit as the town of Sharpsburg.")[2] The men could see the shells coming, but they had learned by now that it was useless to duck and dodge, and they went straight ahead, bending their heads a little as if they were walking into a high wind. From the rear they made a handsome sight—long lines carefully aligned, battle flags fluttering, little white smoke clouds breaking out overhead here and there as shells exploded, green wood ahead of them: very nice to look at, so long as you could look from a distance. Far away, near McClellan's headquarters, staff officers swung their telescopes on the moving lines and remarked to one another that this was going to do it—that divison could not be stopped.

Out of the cornfield and over the turnpike they went, past narrow fields and into the West Wood, that long belt of trees which ran north and south from below the Dunker church to a spot opposite Mr. Miller's barnyard. The trees gave protection from the shells, and the only Rebels in sight were skirmishers who faded back and disappeared as the division came on. The wood was open enough so that the brigade lines were maintained without much difficulty, and in a few minutes the leading brigade came out on the far side, facing open fields that rose slowly to an irregular ridge several hundred yards off. Stuart's guns were up there, and a few thin lines of infantry, but nothing very solid. The division was halted, with nobody able to see anything much except the men in the leading brigade. Sumner's idea might be right: he was on the flank and all he had to do now was get his cumbersome battle lines out into the open, chase the last Rebels off that ridge, perform a left wheel, and march down toward Sharpsburg.

But it wasn't going to be that way. The left of Lee's line had been mangled quite as badly as the right of McClellan's, but in the precise nick of time Lee had sent up strong reinforcements—McLaws's division and Walker's, with Jackson's indomitable lieutenant, Jubal Early, bringing in his own brigade and such other stray elements as he could collect. And all of these, totaling more men than Sumner had with him, were now poised to attack just where it would hurt most—from the left.

The blow came with demoralizing suddenness, and for most of the men it was completely invisible, and there was nothing whatever they could do about it. One minute Sumner was sitting his horse amid the leading brigade, watching the firing that was coming from the Rebels on the ridge, sizing up the situation; the next minute there was a great uproar of musketry and screaming men in the wood to the left, the air was full of bullets, an unexpected host of new Rebels was going into line on the ridge in front, guns were appearing from nowhere and going into battery there, and there was complete and unmerciful hell to pay.

It hit the rear ranks first. One-armed General Howard had four Pennsylvania regiments in the third brigade—all the men came from Philadelphia, and the outfit was known as the "Philadelphia Brigade"—and these men, who had been standing at ease in the wood, abruptly found themselves under a deadly fire from behind. Regiments broke, men scrambled for cover, officers shouted frantically; the enemy was out of sight, dense smoke was seeping in through the trees, the air was alive with bullets, fugitives were running every which way. Howard—never an inspirational leader, but a solid citizen who was never scared, either—went riding along the line trying to get the men realigned, which was hard because nobody knew which way the men ought to be faced in order to fight effectively. Sumner galloped up, shouted something, and galloped off again. In the unceasing racket Howard could not hear a word he said: an aide yelled in his ear that Sumner had been shouting: "My God, Howard! You must get out of here!"—an idea which by now had seized every man in the brigade.

The 72nd Pennsylvania, at the far left, gave way completely, its frantic stragglers adding to the confusion. Some detachments were faced by the rear rank and started off, but that didn't seem to work—more often than not the men found themselves marching straight into a consuming fire; and presently the whole brigade simply dissolved and the men ran back out of the wood and into an open field, a disordered mob rather than a brigade of troops. In the field they were caught by artillery, the Rebels having wheeled up guns to sweep the open ground, and the rout of the brigade became complete. In something less than ten minutes the brigade had lost more than five hundred men and had hardly been able to fire a shot in reply.

Up front it was a little better, but not much. A savage Rebel charge came in from the open field, and the 15th Massachusetts took it head-on, exchanging volleys at a scant fifteen yards. One soldier in this regiment later wrote that "the loss of life was fearful; we had never seen anything like it." The 34th New York, which was at the left end of the front line, tried to move over to help and somehow got squarely in between two Confederate lines and took a horrible fire from front and rear at the same time, losing half of its men in a few minutes. General Sedgwick hurried back to his second brigade, trying to get a regiment or two wheeled around for flank protection, but it was simply impossible—there just was no room to maneuver in all that crush even if the Rebel fire had permitted it, which it didn't. Sedgwick got a wound in the arm and an aide urged him to go to the rear. He refused, saying that the wound was a nuisance and nothing more; then another bullet lifted him out of the saddle with a wound that kept him in hospital for five months. (He made a bad patient, it seems. Impatient with hospital routine, he jokingly said that if he ever got hit again he hoped the bullet would finish him off—anything was better than a hospital. Cracks like that are bad luck for soldiers: Uncle John got his wish at Spotsylvania Courthouse in 1864, when a Rebel sharpshooter hit him under the eye and killed him.)

Minutes seemed like hours in the uproar under the smoky trees. The sound of rifle fire rose higher and higher as more Rebel brigades got into action. Over and over, in official reports and in regimental histories, one finds Federals giving the same account of it—the heaviest, deadliest fire they ever saw in the entire war.[3] The rear brigade was gone and the second brigade was gone. General Dana, commanding the second brigade, managed to get parts of the 42nd New York and the 7th Michigan swung around to meet the fire from the left, but they couldn't hold on. When Howard's brigade went to pieces the Rebels came in from the rear and the two regiments were overwhelmed, with a few platoons managing to keep some sort of formation as they backed off to the north.

The colonel of the 59th New York rode back and forth with a flag, bawling: "Rally on the colors!" His men grouped themselves around him and tried to return a heavy fire that came out of the wood in front; and in the smoke and the confusion they volleyed into the backs of the 15th Massachusetts, and there was a terrible shouting and cursing amid all the din. Then a Confederate regiment worked its way around and fired into the 59th from the rear, and the New Yorkers lost nearly two thirds of their numbers. Young Captain Oliver Wendell Holmes of the 20th Massachusetts went down with his second wound of the war; and somehow, amazingly, that wandering rookie regiment from General Samuel Crawford's brigade, the greenhorn 125th Pennsylvania, showed up and fell into line beside the battered 34th New York, where it fought manfully. (Nobody ever knew quite how it got there; it had been fighting with Greene's boys south of the Dunker church, and in some incomprehensible manner it had got detached and in all the fury of this infighting had managed to get into the middle of Sedgwick's front line. Those rookies seemed to have a genius for wandering into fights, and they were packing a whole year's experience into one desperate morning.)

If the time seemed endless, it was really very short. Just fifteen minutes after the first shot had been fired, the last of the division retreated. From first to last, the division had not had a chance; it was attacked from three sides at once— front, left, and rear—and the collapse ran from rear rank to front rank. It left more than twenty-one hundred men dead or wounded in the West Wood, and a good half of its units had never been able to fire a shot; some of those that did fought facing by the rear rank. Confederate losses in this fight had been negligible; the sacrifice of Sedgwick's division had accomplished nothing whatever.

A few regiments got out in good order. The 20th Massachusetts proudly recorded that it left the West Wood at a walk, in column of fours, muskets at right shoulder; and the 1st Minnesota, which had been lucky—it had lost only a fourth of its men—went out beside it, similarly formed. These and a few other unbroken units were lined up perpendicular to the Hagerstown pike, a few hundred yards north of the spot where the division had crossed the road on its way in, and they laid down a strong fire when the triumphant Rebels came out of the wood to finish the rout. The Rebel lines swept into the cornfield—one more charge across that cornfield!—where wounded men cursed wearily and pressed their faces against the dirt, hoping that pounding feet and bursting shells and low-flying bullets would not hurt them further as they lay there helpless—and for a few minutes it looked as if this counterattack might destroy the whole right wing of McClellan's army and end the battle then and there. But the remnant of Sedgwick's division gave ground stubbornly and at a price, Gordon's tired brigade from Mansfield's corps came in to help, a good deal of rifle fire was still coming out of the East Wood, and an enormous line of fieldpieces was waiting on the slope north of the cornfield. For the last time that day the cornfield was swept by murderous fire, and the Confederates slowed down, halted, and went back to the shelter of the West Wood, while the beaten Federals withdrew to the ridge in rear of the guns, leaving a fringe of pickets and skirmishers behind.

And while this area north of the Dunker church was smoldering and fitfully exploding all the rest of the day with long-range rifle and artillery fire, there was no more real fighting here. There had been enough, in all conscience. In a square of ground measuring very little more than one thousand yards on a side—cornfield, barnyard, orchard, East and West Woods, and the fields by the turnpike—nearly twelve thousand men were lying on the ground, dead or wounded. It had not taken long to put them there, either. The fighting began with daylight—around five-thirty or six o'clock. It was now nine-thirty; four hours, at the most, from the time Hooker's batteries began to rake the cornfield to the end of the last Rebel countercharge. They fought with muzzle-loaders in those days, the men who got off two shots a minute were doing well, and it took, as one might say, a real effort to kill a man then. But considering their handicaps, they did pretty well.

When the beaten elements of Sedgwick's division crept north to safety, Sumner rode east to see about the rest of his army corps. The old man had done his best, and after that first desperate "My God, Howard! You must get out of here!" he had been as cool in all that fire as if he had been on parade, riding his horse at a walk amid the broken ranks of panicky soldiers, doing the little that could be done to pull fighting lines together, calming men by his stout refusal to recognize personal danger. But his best had been tragically inadequate: good enough to serve in the moment of disaster, but not good enough to keep the disaster from happening. He had been given an entire army corps, the biggest one in the army, eighteen thousand men in all; and he had left two thirds of it behind when he made his big attack. The one division which went astray and the other which was late in starting—these two, banked up beside Sedgwick's men, might well have broken Lee's flank beyond all hope of repair and the war would have been won by noon. The old man thought about them and went back to see about them after his attack had failed.

(Back by the Pry house sat McClellan, getting the messages of triumph and disaster from the wigwagging signal flags, studying the far-off slopes through his telescope, sending his aides here and there, watching the battle that he had planned, but not laying his own hand upon it; climax of the war taking place before his eyes, climax of his own personal fate, life or death for many thousands of young men depending on this day's battle. McClellan, quiet, composed, thoughtful, almost detached, listening with an inner ear for the still voice of caution and doubt, letting the battle go on without him.)

Yet the thing could still be done, and perhaps Old Winkey was the man to do it. Brigadier General William H. French, who had the second of Sumner's divisions, was red-faced and bluff, with a fantastic habit of bringing both eyes tightly shut spasmodically as he talked—thus "Old Winkey" or "Old Blinky" to his men. (One buck private, in the early days of the war, accosted by French about something or another while the division was on the march, had given way to laughter at all of this blinking. Since French was a hot-tempered man, the private had been hung by the thumbs from the nearest tree and left there to reflect on the sober respect that is due a general, until the following division cut him down.) French took his division across the Antietam in the wake of Sedgwick, under the impression that he was to strike for the Rebel line to the south of the Dunker church. As he brought his men up the hills west of the creek he had on his right hand a pillar of flame—the farmhouse of one Mumma, a solid citizen who had given the land where the Dunker church was built, his dwelling set ablaze that morning by D. H. Hill's outposts, who feared it might become a strong point for Yankee sharpshooters.

The division halted briefly to perfect its alignment, and about the time the last of Sedgwick's fugitives got back to the northern hills French had everything ready and the men started up out of the creek valley. The sun came out and the light was bright; ahead was the Roulette farm, a pleasant cluster of buildings on a broad knoll, surrounded by an orchard, shade trees, and a well-kept lawn. As the line reached this high place the officers back at headquarters got another look at the deceitful pageantry of war: broad, orderly lines of infantry going on in the sunlight, tiny puff balls of smoke appearing around the house as the Rebel skirmishers went into action, battle flags making high lights of gay color, officers posturing on their horses with glinting swords, a battery of artillery riding up fast and unlimbering dramatically; all very fine and bloodless-looking, just like the colored lithographs. Then the battle line divided as the men went by the Roulette house, the Federals combing belated Southern skirmishers out of stables and springhouse at bayonet point. Regimental surgeons, following close behind, moved into the big barn under the brow of a hill and prepared their operating tables, while orderlies spread out straw for wounded men to lie on. They would have plenty of work to do presently.

As the lines closed up beyond the farmhouse, with sharper rifle fire coming down from the crest of a rise in front, some of the men went through a yard where there was a long row of beehives; and just then a round shot from some Southern gun smashed through the length of these hives, and the air, which was already full of bullets, was now abuzz and humming with angry bees. The rookie 132nd Pennsylvania got the worst of it, and for a moment the bees almost broke up the battle. The green soldiers were marching into the rifle fire bravely enough, but the bees were more than they could take and the regiment went all to pieces as the men leaped and ran and slapped and swore. It took the united efforts of General Kimball, the brigade commander, his staff and the regimental officers to get the boys out of the yard and back in ranks again. To the end of their days the soldiers of the 132nd remembered the fight with the bees in the Roulette farmyard.

The Confederates who were defending the line in here belonged to D. H. Hill, and he had them cunningly posted at the crest of a hill, lying down almost invisible, firing steadily. As the Northerners came nearer these Rebels found themselves outnumbered and backed off; and when the advancing Yankee line got to the crest it looked down the reverse slope a hundred yards or more to a sunken road packed full of Rebels who yelled furious defiance. The Northerners' faces were already blackened by powder smoke, and a couple of regiments wore brand-new uniforms of blue darker than ordinary, which looked black in the morning sun, and the Southerners shouted: "Go away, you black devils—go home!" along with much else.

It was a bad layout. An eighth of a mile south of the Dunker church a country lane runs zigzag east and south from the Hagerstown road, going for a quarter of a mile under the lee of a long hill, climbing to a plateau for another quarter mile, and then making a sharp elbow as it turns south. By years of usage and erosion this land had been worn down several feet below the surface of the ground, and it was bordered on both sides by snake-rail fences. On the northern side the Rebels had taken these rails down and piled them in a low breastwork, and they were lined up strongly in the low road behind this obstruction, as securely entrenched as if they had been digging all night. Lying below the brow of the hill, the lane could not be reached by Federal artillery. The men who defended it were almost wholly protected; the men who tried to take it would have to advance in the open, exposed to a crippling fire. It was as nasty a strong point as the army ever ran up against: the famous sunken road, known forever after (for sufficient reason) as Bloody Lane.

The Yankee line halted on top of the hill, dressing its ranks. In the road below the Rebels held their fire, waiting for them. For a moment this part of the field was almost silent, and the waiting Confederates could hear the shouted commands of the Northern officers as the assaulting lines started forward. Down the slope they came, four ranks deep. A colonel in the sunken road paid his tribute to the brilliance of the spectacle: "Their gleaming bayonets flashed like burnished silver in the sunlight. With the precision of step and perfect alignment of a holiday parade this magnificent array moved to the charge, every step keeping time to the tap of the deep-sounding drum."[4]

Down the slope they came, nearer and nearer, the Confederates crouching low in their trench, officers standing just behind them, the whole field seeming breathless with suspense. Then, at a shouted command, the Rebels leveled their muskets and fired, and a long sheet of flame ran from end to end of the sunken road, a wave of smoke drifted up the hillside, and the Yankee charge ceased to look like a holiday parade. The first line of the assaulting wave was almost torn to pieces. The men halted, tried to re-form, and the Southerners, reloading with desperate haste, stood up and whacked in another volley. Back up the hill went the Northerners, to pull their broken lines together and come down again; but the Rebel fire was too heavy. The lines swayed to a halt halfway down the slope, and the men sprawled on the ground to return the fire from the sunken road, both sides volleying away at the closest range, while the terrible tumult of battle rose to a higher pitch than ever. The leading Federal brigade finally faded away, and French sent another one in to take its place.

Beyond the sunken lane were more Rebels in a cornfield (not *the* cornfield: this one belonged to a man named Piper), and they fired over the heads of the men in the lane, tearing the Yankee lines. Rebel guns came up on the high ground back by the Hagerstown road, and the great uproar of the battle was deepened and increased as Federal guns beyond the Antietam marked these Rebel batteries for destruction. The Southern gunners were in a hard spot. They were under orders to forget about the Yankee guns and attend to the infantry—this was the last line of defense, and if the Yankees broke through here it would be the end; and whole batteries of long-range rifles beyond the creek concentrated their fire on the Confederate guns, hammering the line from end to end, smashing gun wheels and limber chests, dismembering gunners, sending shells through whole ranks of waiting battery horses. Once a shell found a Confederate caisson and blew it up with a crash that resounded above all the din, while an immense cloud of black smoke shot upward. Never had the Southern batteries taken such a fearful pounding; throughout the rest of the war they remembered this battle as "artillery hell."

It was hell for the infantry too. The strange, frenzied, illogical exaltation of spirit that descended on the fighting men at times in this battle visited the troops who assaulted the sunken road and the troops who defended it. Once a group of Rebels scrambled out of the road and charged straight up the hill in a mad, doomed counterattack, shook the Yankee line briefly, and then went all to bits in the fire; one Federal who helped to repulse this attack said none of the Confederates got back to the lane. Farther north, some courageous Southern artillery officer rolled two guns out into an open field, and a mass of yelling Rebel infantry came out to beat in the right flank of the Yankee line. Red-faced French, storming and swearing with excitement, pulled the 8th Ohio and 14th Indiana out of line and sent them over to meet the threat, and the Westerners fired until their muskets were hot and foul, their ammunition gone, and half their men down. From somewhere in the rear a section of Yankee guns came clattering up, and the Rebel advance was driven back.

An immense sheet of smoke covered the battlefield, like a low thundercloud that was forever pulsing and glowing with lightning. The ground underfoot shook and trembled with the everlasting jar of the guns. The barn by the Roulette house was jammed with wounded men. Screams, prayers, and curses made it a horrible place, with hundreds of anguished men packed together on the straw begging the surgeons to attend to them—surgeons bare-armed and fearsomely streaked and spattered with blood, piles of severed arms and legs lying by the slippery operating tables, the uproar of the battle beating in through the thin walls. Stragglers from the fighting line crept into house and outbuildings and drifted downhill toward the creek, where the valley gave shelter.

French's division was fought to a standstill, but new troops were coming up. Franklin arrived on the field with his army corps from the valley north of Harper's Ferry, and he put a brigade in line on French's right to prevent any further flanking maneuvers by the Rebels there. What was left of Greene's division was pulled back from its lines around the Dunker church, to join this brigade of Franklin's; and to the south Sumner's third division, Richardson's, got across the creek at last and prepared to go into action. Richardson rode along the line—strictly business this morning, with the eccentricities of camp all shelved—and he shook out the Irish Brigade with the golden harps on its emerald flags to spearhead the attack.

Between the general and the Irishmen there was a warm friendship, and it all started because of a sly dodge worked by a member of Richardson's staff. Early in the war, when the Irish Brigade was first assigned to Richardson's division, this staff member—Captain Jack Gosson, himself as Irish as Dublin—felt that it would be fine if the general got a good first impression of the new brigade. So when Richardson started over to make his first inspection Gosson rode on ahead of him. He found the three regiments all drawn up, waiting, and he spurred up and addressed them eloquently about the merits of their new commander.

"And what do you think of the brave old fellow?" he cried at last, inspired to a great and beautiful lie. "He has sent to our camp three barrels of whisky, a barrel for each regiment, to treat the boys of the brigade; and we ought to give him a thundering cheer when he comes along."

This made sense to the Irishmen, and when Richardson came up they threw their caps in the air and gave him one of the most spirited ovations of the war. Naturally this pleased Richardson very much, he being ignorant of Captain Gosson's stratagem, and ever afterward he was especially devoted to the Irish Brigade. The complete non-appearance of the whisky was not held against him, somehow; probably the boys could recognize an artful Irish trick when they saw it. At any rate, this was Richardson's pet brigade and he was the brigade's pet general, and when he came up they yelled loudly and went swinging up the hill with their green flags snapping.[5]

They came up just in time, for French's men were in serious trouble. One brigade had been broken and the other two had been taking a deadly pounding, and the Rebels had mustered some new men and sent them forward beyond the lane, on the higher ground, to crush the Union left flank. The Irishmen went charging into this flank attack with savage power, the oncoming Confederate line halted to meet them, and on the open field there was a terrible shock of point-blank fire too hot for any troops to endure for long. General Meagher, who led the Irishmen, decided that the only way out of it was straight ahead—his men could charge or they could retreat; the one thing they could not do much longer was stand there and take it. He edged a few squads forward to tear down a fence that rose in their way, and then he stood up in his stirrups, raised his sword high, and shouted over all the battle thunder: "Boys! Raise the colors and follow me!" The green flags went tossing up and onward, the Irishmen cheered again, and the Rebels slowly fell back into the sunken road, where they rallied and poured out a fire which the Irish Brigade remembered afterward the way Sedgwick's men remembered the fire in the West Wood—the heaviest they had to face in all the war. Half of the 63rd New York fell in that first volley, all of the brigade color-bearers went down, and the men who snatched up the fallen flags went down likewise—carrying the colors was a mean job in that war, for hostile fire was always directed at the flags. A bullet killed Meagher's horse in full gallop, and the beast fell heavily, knocking Meagher out so that he had to be carried to the rear. The advance came to a halt a hundred yards from the sunken road, the Irishmen hugged the ground, and the last of their ammuniton gave out.

Richardson was close behind, and he sent a fresh brigade through them while the Irish soldiers went to the rear to get more cartridges. Still under fire, they marched to the rear in columns as orderly as if they were on the drill field, with no straggling, although the four regiments in the brigade were down to five hundred men now. Richardson met them as they came out, rode up to Lieutenant Colonel Kelly of the 88th New York, and cried: "Bravo, 88th—I shall never forget you!" and the exhausted soldiers gave him three cheers. Then Richardson rode back to the front, and his fresh troops pushed forward until they were within thirty yards of the sunken lane. All up and down the half-mile length of that little country lane in front of French and Richardson the air was ablaze beneath the smoke, and all the fury of the battle was coming to a new climax.

Everything seemed to happen at once. D. H. Hill found a gap between French and Richardson and sent troops forward, while other Confederates went prowling around to the south and east, trying still another flank attack around Richardson's new line. The first counterattack was broken up easily, and Richardson spotted the second one just in time and sent the 5th New Hampshire off to meet it. This regiment's Colonel Cross had a scalp wound, and had bound a red bandanna around his head. He took his men in with the grim warning: "If any man runs I want the file closers to shoot him. If they don't, I shall myself." The New Hampshire boys set off on a run through a ragged cornfield, collided with a North Carolina regiment on a little knoll, and halted for a vicious fire fight amid the tattered cornstalks. Richardson came up on foot—hatless, bare sword in hand, his face like a storm cloud. He had just pricked some skulking major out of a hiding place, and the men heard him shouting: "God damn the field officers!" He got into the front line, the men surged forward with him, the North Carolinians gave way, and the flank attack was beaten off.

There was a pause. The sunken lane and the main Confederate line lay just ahead, the heated air was full of drifting smoke and flying bullets, winded men snatched breath in convulsive gulps as they nerved themselves for a new advance. Colonel Cross, the old Indian fighter, got in front and turned to face them, face black with smoke, eyes flaming.

"Put on the war paint!" he yelled. The soldiers grabbed grimy cartridge papers and smeared their sweaty faces with soot.

"Now give 'em the war whoop!" shouted Cross.

Cheers went up in a wild falsetto chorus. The colonel swung his arm, and the line moved on. To the right the 81st Pennsylvania began to advance at the same moment. Still farther to the right, Colonel Barlow got the 61st and 64th New York regiments up to high ground where they could enfilade part of the sunken lane. For the first time the Southerners there came under a fire that was too hot to take, and they began to back away. Then at last the whole line caved in, the sunken lane was abandoned, and yelling Federals ran down the slope, clambered over the fence rails, and fired at the backs of the retreating enemy.

French's men were too dead-beat to do more than form a new line in the captured roadway, but Richardson's men were fresher, and anyway, Richardson was a driver. He lost little time sorting out the scrambled commands but took them on as they were, into the rolling fields south of the lane, so that they swarmed over the Confederates' second line, broke it, and went plunging down into hollow ground in the angle between the sunken road and the Hagerstown pike.

Once more the battle had come to a moment of supreme crisis, and final victory was within reach. The Confederate General Hill, imperturbable in the midst of disaster, somehow scraped the ultimate bottom of the barrel and got together a handful of men from his beaten command and led them forward in a new countercharge—taking a musket himself, it is said, to lead them in person. Barlow saw it coming and broke it up, and Richardson went off to get some artillery. His infantry got down into the hollow and drove the Confederates out of Mr. Piper's farm buildings, but there the disorganized attack lost its impetus, and by a supreme, despairing effort the Rebels kept them from going any farther. Richardson reappeared with Battery K, 1st U.S., and planted it on a hill south of the sunken road; it silenced a couple of Rebel smoothbores near the Hagerstown road, then came under a heavy fire and began to lose men. Richardson had the battery commander move back, cautioning him to save his guns and men: there would be a big advance just as soon as Richardson could get his division realigned, and the general wanted the battery in shape to accompany it.

The battery withdrew readily enough, as ordered, getting into a more sheltered spot where the Rebel fire wasn't quite so bad; and, apparently from nowhere and by magic, there appeared a well-dressed civilian with a two-horse carriage, who drove up without paying any attention to all the bullets, pulled up his horses, alighted, and began to hand baskets of ham and biscuits to the dumfounded gun crews. This done, he invited the wounded men to get into the carriage so that he could carry them back to a dressing station. As they got in he walked forward to inspect his team, a shell fragment having slightly wounded one of his horses. Satisfying himself that the animal was not badly hurt, he saw that the wounded men were comfortable, waved his hat cheerily to the astounded battery commander, and drove off—an unnamed man of good will who shows up briefly in the official reports and then vanished as mysteriously as he came.[6]

At this moment Lee's battle line was a frayed thread, held by scraps and leftovers of tattered commands who clung to the ridges by the Hagerstown road and fought like automatons. Batteries had been hammered all to pieces: a mile to the rear, officers and men were working feverishly with wrecked gun carriages and limbers, trying to make patchwork repairs so that at least some could be put back in service. Longstreet, who held top command along this part of the line,

had sent his own staff officers in to work the guns of one ravaged battery and
was standing nearby holding their horses and helping to correct the ranges. The
only infantry in his immediate vicinity was a lone regiment which was completely out of ammunition, waving its flags vigorously to create an illusion of
strength. He had called for reinforcements, but there were none to be had, except for a few worn-out skeletons of regiments and some stragglers rounded up
and sent back into the fight. The Confederates were still keeping up a brave fire,
but there was no weight back of it—no possibility that it might suddenly flare up
into a great, obliterating wave of destruction in case of need. Many years later
Longstreet confessed that at that moment ten thousand fresh Federals could
have come through and taken Lee's army and all it possessed.

The ten thousand fresh Federals were at hand, and to spare. Franklin's army
corps was on the field, and Franklin believed that he had brought it there to
fight. Richardson's division was still in good shape despite its terrible losses.
Franklin was preparing to advance and Richardson was moving guns up, getting his ranks reassembled, making ready to attack beside him; and at this distance it is very hard to see how that attack could ever have been stopped.[7]

The only trouble is that it never was made. Bringing some guns up to a new
location, Richardson was hit by a rifle bullet and was carried off the field—only
slightly wounded, it seemed, but in a few days an infection set in and the wound
killed him. Barlow went down, desperately wounded. McClellan detached Hancock from his own brigade and sent him in to take Richardson's place, so there
was still a fighting commander up front; but white-haired old Sumner, senior
office on this part of the field, shaken by the disaster in the West Wood and by
the killing he had seen since, countermanded the order for an offensive and forbade Franklin and Hancock to attack. Franklin argued hotly, but Sumner was
unyielding; he had seen nothing but catastrophe that day and he firmly believed
half of the army had been scattered, and he told Franklin that if his attack
should fail the day would be lost beyond saving.

One of McClellan's staff officers rode up, bearing from the commanding general a suggestion that the army attack if possible, and Sumner cried out at him:
"Go back, young man, and tell General McClellan I have no command! Tell
him my command, Banks' command and Hooker's command are all cut up and
demoralized. Tell him General Franklin has the only organized command on
this part of the field!"[8]

Back to headquarters went this gloomy message. McClellan reflected on it
briefly, considered once more the danger of being overbold—and upheld
Sumner. The ten thousand fresh Federals Longstreet was talking about stayed
where they were, and Lee's frayed line held.

Late that afternoon there was one final flare-up. The 7th Maine was detached
from the front line and sent forward to drive Rebel sharpshooters out of the
Piper farm buildings, down where Richardson's drive had reached high-water
mark a few hours earlier. The little regiment got to the farmyard, chased the
sharpshooters, found itself surrounded in an orchard, cut its way out, and came
staggering back to the lines with sixty-eight men around the colors—it had set
out with 240. A Vermont brigade which had watched the whole performance
stood up in the lines and cheered as the exhausted soldiers came back. The
skipper of the Maine regiment remarked afterward that if only that Vermont
brigade had been sent forward in support they could have broken the Rebel line
even then; up at close quarters he had seen for himself how weak the Confederate defenses really were.

But that was just one more of the might-have-beens. North of the town of
Sharpsburg the fighting was over. The Federals drew their line partly in front of
and partly behind the sunken road—the road itself was so full of dead men, so
horrible with its torn fragments of flesh, its congealing pools of blood in ruts and
hollows, that it could no longer be used as a trench.

3. ALL THE LANDSCAPE WAS RED

In the four years of its existence the Army of the Potomac had to atone for the errors of its generals on many a bitter field. This happened so many times—it was so normal, so much the regular order of things for this unlucky army—that it is hardly possible to take the blunders which marred its various battles and rank them in the order of magnitude of their calamitous stupidity. But if some such ranking could be made, this battle of the Antietam would surely be represented. Here, if anywhere, the soldiers were thrown into action and left to fight their way out. There would have been unqualified disaster if the generals had not been commanding men better than themselves.

The battle was fought in three separate parts. The first part was the fight around the cornfield, and the second was the fight in the West Wood and along the sunken road; and the third part—tardy, disjointed, and almost totally unco-ordinated, as if it had no relation to the rest of the battle—took place along the banks of the creek and on the hills and high ground beyond those banks, to the southeast of the town of Sharpsburg.

McClellan had planned to have the Union attack down here made at the same time as the attacks at the other end of his line, along the Hagerstown road, and if it had happened that way there can be very little doubt that Lee's army would have been crushed by the middle of the day. But somehow McClellan had very little control over this battle, and it did not work out at all as he had planned. The great assault on his left was hopelessly flubbed: a knockout punch, aimed at an enemy almost helpless on the ropes, which somehow turned into a mere shove. The private soldier fought as well here as he fought elsewhere, but he got no help whatever from the top.

When the day began the IX Corps was lying on the east side of Antietam Creek, south of the Boonsboro road, sprawled out among the low hills and sloping meadows which border that part of the stream. The Antietam runs in slow loops here, with steep high hills on its western bank, and these hills were held that morning by Rebel soldiers who opened fire as soon as they could see anything to shoot at; and as the light grew the Confederate batteries on the high ground in front of Sharpsburg joined in, to be answered promptly by the Federal guns east of the creek. So when the great uproar of the engagement north of the Dunker church filled the morning air there was an answering wave of sound from these hills on the left. For a while this was sound and nothing more (quite a number of men died under the shelling and the sharpshooting, to be sure, but their deaths were incidental, contributing nothing to victory or defeat); but somewhere around nine o'clock McClellan sent word to Burnside to attack the Rebel lines in his front immediately—Hooker and Sumner were hard pressed and a blow over here would greatly relieve them.

The two armies lay close together here with nothing between them but the valley of the Antietam. The valley itself is fairly broad, but the creek is insignificant—fifty feet wide, or thereabouts, and so shallow that a man could wade it in most places without wetting his belt buckle. For some unaccountable reason, however, this modest creek was treated that day as if it were quite impassable: a veritable Rhine River, not to be crossed except dry-shod on a bridge.[1] A little country road comes down over the hills on the eastern side, meanders close to the creek through the low meadows for a few hundred yards, and then makes a ninety-degree turn to the left, crossing the stream on a narrow bridge and following a winding ravine up to the high ground near Sharpsburg; and this road and this bridge, fatally, were the only features of this part of the landscape which the high command could think about that morning. When the order came to attack the enemy it was interpreted in terms of the bridge, as if the placid little creek could be passed in no other way. Corps and army command had had more than twenty-four hours to examine the terrain, but it seems to have occurred to no one in all that time to test the depth of this water the way young Lieutenant Custer had tested the Chickahominy—by going out in it and measuring it personally. There was rumored to be a ford half a mile or more downstream from the bridge, but the search for this ford consisted chiefly in an unavailing hunt for some farmer who knew where it was and could lead the way to it. Meanwhile, orders were to attack; to attack meant to cross the creek; and to cross the creek, in the foggy light that pervaded corps headquarters, meant to cross the bridge— that and nothing else. And the bridge was the worst of all possible places to make an attack: an ideal defensive spot where a few regiments could hold off a whole division.

Orders went bumping down the echelons of command, from corps to division to brigade, and presently Colonel George Crook, who had three regiments of Ohio troops, got the nod. Crook was a good man and made a fine record later in the war—and afterward in the Indian wars out West—but that morning he seems to have been infected by the mental paralysis which beset his superiors. He had his brigade in a little valley an eighth of a mile northeast of the bridge; formed line of battle, went boldly forward over the low hill, and lost his way completely, missing the bridge altogether and coming out on a low plateau in a bend of the creek upstream, with enough Rebel guns trained on him to make the place highly uncomfortable. He got his Ohioans forward to the bank and they lay down behind fences and underbrush and fired away at some Confederates across the stream, who promptly began to fire back. This brought about the killing of some dozens of boys but contributed nothing whatever to the capture of the bridge. Burnside's first assault was hardly even a fizzle.

Try again: and this time the order sent to General Sturgis, he who had sat in Colonel Haupt's office less than a month ago and explained patiently his intense dislike for General Pope. Sturgis had one asset—he at least knew where the bridge was—and he got the 2nd Maryland and the 6th New Hampshire lined up and sent them down the country road and along the riverbank toward the bridge. This was playing into the Rebels' hands. They had the hills on the western side covered with sharpshooters, with a couple of regiments drawn up under good cover in an old quarry overlooking the bridge itself, and they also had a substantial number of fieldpieces trained on the bridge and on the road that led to the bridge. All of these laid down a killing fire, and it was just too much for any troops to stand. The boys from Maryland and New Hampshire tried, but their lines were broken up before they reached the bridge, and presently the survivors went scampering back to the woods for shelter. General Cox got some infantry up to keep the Rebel defenders under rifle fire, and a tremendous bombardment was opened by the Federal artillery; and General Isaac Rodman was ordered to march his division downstream to hunt for that missing ford, which was the last anybody heard of that for some little time. Meanwhile, the morning had gone and the hour was past noon, and the right wing of Lee's army had hardly been annoyed.

About this time McClellan began to realize that although a great deal of noise was being made on Burnside's front nothing very much in the way of an assault was going on. He had already sent several messages urging haste, and now he sent a staff colonel with peremptory orders: get across the stream immediately and open an attack on the high ground. Burnside was sitting his horse beside a battery on a hilltop, surveying the battlefield with impressive calm, and the sharp tone of this latest order jarred him. He told the colonel: "McClellan appears to think I am not trying my best to carry this bridge; you are the third or fourth one who has been sent to me this morning with similar orders." The colonel agreed that McClellan was getting anxious, and Burnside rode off to see Sturgis about it.

Presently Colonel Edward Ferrero, commanding Sturgis's second brigade, came trotting up to his two pet regiments—51st New York and 51st Pennsylvania, waiting side by side in a protected valley a couple of hundred yards back from the bridge.

"It is General Burnside's especial request that the two 51st's take that bridge," called Ferrero. "Will you do it?"

There was a brief pause while the regiments presumably reflected on the consuming sheet of fire that lay upon the bridge and its approaches and nerved themselves for a desperate deed. Then some corporal in the Pennsylvania regiment sang out:

"Will you give us our whisky, Colonel, if we make it?"

Between the Pennsylvanians and the colonel, whisky was a sore point. Somehow the regiment had earned a reputation as a heavy-drinking crowd: its colonel once remarked that if the regiment were put ashore on some completely uninhabited desert island, the foragers would come back in the evening loaded down with demijohns of the stuff; and for this reason and that Ferrero had recently ordered their whisky ration suspended. (It should be explained that there was no regular issue of whisky to the troops in the Civil War. Regimental commanders were authorized to issue it, however, whenever they thought fit—in bad weather, after a hard march, after a battle, and so on—and many of them were fairly liberal about it.)

Ferrero—a trim, dapper, black-haired little man, something of a dandy in his dress—blinked for a moment, then laughed.

"Yes, by God!" he cried.

The regiments cheered, and Ferrero got them lined up side by side, each regiment in column of twos. They would dash straight downhill for the bridge instead of going along the road parallel to the Confederate line of fire, and when they got across, one regimental column would turn to the left and the other to the right. When the tail of the column was across, both outfits would face to the west, and they would have a two-regiment battle line ready to charge up the hill. Cox got the 11th Connecticut down to a stone wall by the creek to put a covering fire on the defenders, the 11th losing its colonel and suffering heavily but sticking to it manfully. Upstream a bit, Crook worked a battery down to the bank to blast the Rebels away from the western approaches. The fieldpieces on the bluffs stepped up their fire, throwing shells at every Confederate gun that could bear on the bridge, and the tumult of battle became a great, unbroken roar. Battle flags waving at the head of the column, the two regiments came up over their little hill and ran full-tilt for the bridge, shouting madly, men falling at every step as muskets and cannon slashed the column; and there was a wild chaos of smoke, flame, thunderous noise, and yelling men.

The Rebels across the creek were only twenty-five yards away and they could make every shot count, but they were under a furious fire now and it hurt, and there were not really so very many of them there, anyway, and they began to drift back up the hillsides. The colonel of the Pennsylvania regiment got to the near end of the bridge and stood there, one hand on the stone coping, waving his hat in great circles and yelling words of encouragement. The fighting men surged past him; his voice gave out, and the men could hear him rasping: "Come on, boys, I can't holler any more"—and then suddenly the column was across, fanning out into a line of battle, the handful of Confederates who remained were running, and the bridge had been won. The two regiments made their way to the crest of the hill, saw nothing in front of them but skirmishers—and, far away, Rebel batteries, which were keeping up a heavy fire but which had lost the range: shells were passing just overhead to explode harmlessly over the valley, and a man was safe enough if he stayed close to the ground—and they hugged the crest, waiting for reinforcements and further orders.[2]

· They had been hit hard, those two regiments, and they were winded, and presently they left a chain of pickets up front, slipped back down the hillside where there was shelter, lit little fires, and began to boil coffee. . . . A few days later there was a fancy ceremony in front of the brigade, with Colonel Ferrero getting a brigadier's commission as reward for the valor of the New Yorkers and Pennsylvanians. Just as he was given the commission—everything very formal, field all aglitter with high brass, Ferrero sitting his horse in front of regiments stiff with military reverence—some irrepressible in the Pennsylvania regiment called out, side-of-mouth fashion: "How about that whisky?" Ferrero heard it, grinned, and turned his head long enough to say: "You'll get it"—and next morning, according to the regimental historian, a keg of the stuff came over from brigade headquarters and the long dry spell was over. . . .

Meanwhile, the army was losing time. Sturgis got the rest of his division across and sent the 21st Massachusetts up front—a battlewise regiment which had educated its officers under fire and was proud of it. They had gone into action for the first time some months ealier at New Bern, North Carolina, where they had had to cross a shallow stream in a swamp with Rebel bullets whacking in all around them, men getting hit and everybody pretty tense. One of the officers had been a noted fiddler back home, much given to playing for country dances at which, in the custom of the day, he would call out the movements for the dancers while he fiddled; and at this river crossing he became greatly excited, so that pretty soon he was skipping about shouting all sorts of useless orders as fast as he could think of them, jittery himself and making everybody else the same way. So after a while one boy piped up: "All promenade!" and then another called: "Ladies—grand change!" and the regiment crossed the stream, shouting with laughter. The officer became quiet and, said a veteran, "behaved like a little man" for the rest of the war.[3]

Anyway, the 21st was out in front, and after a while the rest of the division was massed close behind it, and Sturgis got ready to advance—only to discover that in the wild fusillading of the morning the boys had used up all of their ammunition. No one, somehow, had thought to check on their supply and see that they got more before they crossed. So he sent back word that somebody else would have to make the attack, adding that his boys were all exhausted, anyhow; and finally his troops were ordered aside into reserve while a new division came across the narrow bottleneck of the bridge, and more minutes slipped by. There was a bad traffic jam there, with marching men, ammunition wagons, field guns, and caissons all trying to make the bridge at once. The Confederate gunners up near Sharpsburg were still shelling the place, and altogether two hours passed before everything was in order and the advance could begin.

General Willcox was in charge of the new division and he started his men off astride the little road in the ravine, getting them up to the higher ground with the 79th New York leading—the old Highlanders who had mutinied against Tecumseh Sherman back in the army's gawky adolescence and had made up for it since by hard fighting. They passed the crest and came out on open ground: fields full of haystacks, cut up by stone walls, Confederates shooting at them from under cover, batteries in front and to the left, a scorching fire coming in. The Highlanders came to a halt, the 17th Michigan moved up and charged one of the batteries, sending it flying in hasty retreat, and the fighting line went on and found more Rebels in an orchard and halted to drive them out with musket fire.

Confederate man power here was fastastically thin, even though it didn't seem that way to the Federals in the front line. All morning Lee had pulled men away from this part of the line (Burnside's attack not developing) to reinforce the defense up by the Dunker church and the sunken lane, and when the Federals finally got up on the plateau, about three in the afternoon, there were not more than twenty-five hundred Rebel infantrymen left to stand them off, with no help in sight. Confederate batteries and used-up parts of batteries were clattering up from wherever they could be found, and they had to play the same role here they had played along the Hagerstown road—ignore the Yankee guns and concentrate on the advancing infantry, getting hit without being able to hit back: artillery hell all over again, the Federal gunners having worked out a system of concentrating all their fire on one Rebel battery at a time, wrecking it and then moving on to the next. Some of Fitz-John Porter's regular infantry and some dismounted cavalry had got across the stream by the Boonsboro bridge and were sending sharpshooters forward to pick off the Rebel gunners—and, all in all, the Army of Northern Virginia, hammered almost into a daze, was staggering on the very edge of final defeat.

But the Federal commanders did not know it. McClellan, back at headquarters, was meditating on the fearful slaughter of the morning and wondering if his right wing could hold its ground. Sumner had already forbidden the assault which Franklin and Richardson had prepared and was thinking only of the reserves which must be kept in hand to repulse a possible Rebel counterattack. (Lee had no reserves whatever just then; every unit which could stand up and hold muskets was in there shooting, and parts of the line were being held by pure bluff.) And Burnside—well, it is impossible to figure out just what Burnside was thinking. He was across the creek at last and he had something like twelve thousand fighting men in his command, with barely a fifth of that number opposing them; but he had one of his four divisions completely out of action, resting and replenishing its ammunition, he had another in reserve behind the front, and a third was floundering around looking for that ford half a mile below the bridge. The upshot was that instead of driving into Sharpsburg with twelve thousand men he was making his big attack with three thousand.

The three thousand were making progress, but it was slow going. The tired Rebels who held this part of the line were few in number, but they kept laying down a heavy fire, and by now there were plenty of Confederate fieldpieces in action to help them despite the counter-battery work from across the stream. These stout Southern gunners were covering the open ground with a nasty cross fire, and the Yankees who were actually up in front doing the fighting were getting no benefit whatever from the fact that the defense in here would be completely swamped if Burnside could just get all of his men into action. The roar of battle grew louder and louder, choking smoke blanketed the hilltops and went rolling through the streets of Sharpsburg, and although the Rebels were giving ground they were being very stubborn about it. A sergeant in an advanced Pennsylvania battery, coming up to his guns after delivering a message to some other outfit, was walking across a field of dry standing timothy which seemed to be alive with wriggling, whistling rifle bullets; and he found himself ludicrously stepping high and walking on tiptoe to keep from treading on these venomous creatures whose trails he could see in the waving grass.

Rod by rod, going in little rushes from fence to fence, the Federal battle line got nearer and nearer to Sharpsburg. They had the high ground now, and the men who were farthest forward could see, down the western slope, the Rebels' behind-the-lines tangle of baggage wagons, stragglers, ambulances, and broken batteries. A stone mill on the edge of town was a strong point briefly, but the 45th Pennsylvania finally drove the Southern sharpshooters out of it. The Pennsylvanians insisted that the miller himself was there in his straw hat and overalls, taking pot shots at them from an upper window, and next day they wanted to find him and hang him but were dissuaded, at last, by the argument that the Rebels were a tattered lot and that the man they thought a civilian was probably a soldier who just didn't have a uniform.

Slowly the Rebel line of defense faded away—brigades up front all cracked, Sharpsburg filled with demoralized stragglers looking for shelter, the last desperate hour of the Confederate Army visibly at hand. On the northern side General Willcox found his men out of ammunition and called a brief halt so that he could dress his lines and get more cartridges; then he would go on, take Sharpsburg, and get squarely across Lee's only line of retreat.

    While all of this had been happening General Rodman had been having his
troubles downstream. His orders were to find that ford, get his men across, and
flank the Rebels who were defending the bridge, and he had started out just as
Sturgis got his first orders from Burnside. He had a guide picked up on some
farm thereabouts, but the guide couldn't seem to find the ford—one suspects
that he had "sesesch" sympathies and was laughing up his sleeve at the misguided Yankees—and the division did a power of more or less haphazard
marching around and the whole morning was wasted. Finally, about the time
Ferrero was sending in his valiant 51st's to storm the bridge, one of Rodman's
brigadiers had the 8th Connecticut deploy two companies of skirmishers and
moved them down to the stream to look for the ford. Quickly enough they found
it—or at least found that they could wade the creek, which came to the same
thing—and with this climactic revelation Rodman got his men over and prepared to join in the final assault on Lee's right.
    Rodman's division was not too strong. He had seven regiments in all, and one
of these had been detached earlier to support a battery on the east bank; altogether he might have taken close to three thousand men across the little creek.
The ground he had to fight on was a bit perplexing. The hills came down to the
creek steeply, where he was, all cut up by ravines and gullies and long hollows,
with the upper slopes planted in corn. It took a little time to get the two brigades
lined up abreast on the western side, with the right wing of the right brigade extended in order to get in touch with Willcox's men upstream. The Rebels were
waiting in the various cornfields and they put a stinging rifle fire down on the
slopes. Rodman's regiments drifted apart a little while they were forming. When
the advance began the left wing somehow didn't get the order; it got off to a late
start, and there was a gap between it and the other brigade.
    There were three New York regiments in the brigade on the right, and they
went plodding up a long hill, with Rebels behind a stone wall at the top and a
Rebel battery off at one side plowing the slope with accurate shell fire. All of this
fire seemed too much to buck, and the brigade commander had the men lie
down halfway up the hill; but the Confederate gunners in here were marksmen
and they shaved the ground with solid shot that mashed prostrate men and
kicked up great clods of earth. Lying there was worse than charging; one veteran
recalled that the Federal line broke out with "the most vehement, terrible
swearing I have ever heard"; it became quite unendurable, and at last the men
scrambled to their feet and made for their tormentors. Muskets blazed all along
the stone wall, the artillerists fired double-shotted charges of canister, and the
New Yorkers bent low and ran hard in the loose dirt, struggling for the hilltop.
One well-read member of the 9th New York wrote long aferward: "The mental
strain was so great that I saw at that moment the singular effect mentioned, I
think, in the life of Goethe on a similar occasion—the whole landscape for an
instant turned slightly red." And finally they got to the fence and drove the Confederates away, one regiment overran and captured a battery, and the brigade
dressed its ranks for a new advance.[4]
    The other brigade had gone off at a divergent angle, and the two were now out
of touch. Much to his surprise, Rodman was finding Rebel infantry on his left,
far south of Sharpsburg, and the brigade swung over to face it. It was hard to
make things out very clearly, with the smoke and the irregular hills and the tall
corn, and the brigade came to a halt, strung out on a long hillside, plenty of
bullets coming in but most of the men unable to see just where they were coming
from. The extreme left of Rodman's line—extreme left of the whole army—was
held by the 16th Connecticut, most pathetically unlucky of all the Federal units
in the battle. This was a brand-new regiment which had been mustered in just
three weeks ago. It was nine hundred strong, but it was totally unready for battle: had loaded its muskets for the very first time only the evening before, and
today it was maneuvering as a regiment for the first time, and doing it under fire.

The boys were willing enough, but they were completely bewildered; they were lying down in a cornfield now, very frightened, trying hard not to show it, well aware that they had no business being on the firing line, discovering that battle was not at all as they had imagined it. The grand and picturesque business of charging a Rebel line, which had sounded so impressive and inspiring back home, had come down to this—hiding in a cornfield and being shot by people who were completely out of sight.

Rodman came up, a quiet, conscientious man with a little pointed beard, worried now because the Rebels were still overreaching his left. He peered off over the corn tops, and from what he could see he gathered that a strong flank attack was about to hit him, and he told the Connecticut colonel to swing his regiment around so that it faced to the south. The colonel barked out the order—"Change front forward on the tenth company!" and the three-week soldiers got to their feet and tried it. This was one of those maneuvers that made long weeks on the drill ground essential in the Civil War solider's battle training: company at the left end of the regimental line does a ninety-degree wheel to the left, each succeeding company tramps through a forty-five degree turn and then marches straight ahead until its left reaches the new line, whereupon it does another forty-five-degree turn and then comes to a halt. Simple enough, in a way, but the sort of thing that called for a lot of practice, which the Connecticut boys had not had. Even on the parade ground they would have had trouble with it; here they were trying it from a bent line, with the corn and smoke making it impossible to see anything, and with a brisk Rebel fire knocking men out at every step. Inevitably they fell into a confused, trampling huddle, with different companies getting in each other's way and everybody tangled up; and while they tried to sort themselves out a tremendous volley swept the field, breaking what formation they had all to pieces.

Then, while the rookies were still trying to get collected, a hostile battle line came shouldering through the cornstalks, firing as it came, and it was too much—the 16th just fell apart and the men turned to run. Rodman was bringing up the 4th Rhode Island to help, and for a moment that made things even worse. The Confederates on this part of the field were wearing blue uniforms (part of the loot from captured Harper's Ferry, the Rebels being necessitous men) and between an advancing blue line in front and another advancing blue line in the rear, the confusion became absolute. The Connecticut boys could not make head or tail out of any of it, and the Rhode Islanders were all mixed up too— saw men in blue running away from other men in blue, held their fire just too long, and became involved in the rout, the oncoming Confederates being the only men on the field who knew just what was going on. Rodman was killed, and the two regiments together went streaking for the rear. A couple of Cox's Ohio regiments were brought over, but the advancing Rebels suddenly seemed to have become very numerous, and their charging line overlapped the reinforcements. Some of the Ohioans were puzzled by those blue uniforms and waited too long before they opened fire, and in the end the whole line gave way and the Federals all the way up to Sharpsburg had to withdraw. At the last possible minute Lee's army had been saved from defeat.[5]

What had saved it was the arrival from Harper's Ferry of A. P. Hill and the leading brigades of his division, which was one of the most famous organizations in the whole Confederate Army. These soldiers came upon the field at precisely the right time and place, after a terrible seventeen-mile forced march from Harper's Ferry, in which exhausted men fell out of ranks by the score and Hill himself urged laggards on with the point of his sword. A more careful and methodical general (any one of the Federal corps commanders, for instance) would have set a slower pace, keeping his men together, mindful of the certainty of excessive straggling on too strenuous a march—and would have arrived, with all his men present or accounted for, a couple of hours too late to do any good. Hill

drove his men so cruelly that he left fully half of his division panting along the
roadside—but he got up those who were left in time to stave off disaster and
keep the war going for two and one half more years.

This A. P. Hill was probaby as well known and deeply respected in the Union
army as any general in the Confederacy, just then. He was always a driver and
his men were valiant fighters, and the Federals had the impression that whenever they were prodded especially hard the prod was being applied by A. P. Hill.
They were so convinced of this that they had evolved a legend to account for it.
Back before the war, they said, Hill and McClellan had been rivals for the hand
of beautiful Ellen Marcy, daughter of an army officer. She chose McClellan at
last, and (so the soldiers believed) Hill carried a great anger against the successful suitor, which accounted for the violence of his attacks. And one morning,
when a rattle of firing aroused the army and told it that Hill's men were attacking again, one veteran raised his hand and growled disgustedly: "God's sake,
Nelly—why didn't you marry him?"[6]

It was late in the afternoon now, and Burnside had been beaten—Burnside
and his generals, strictly speaking, rather than Burnside's army corps. The rout
of his left had been disastrous, but after all it had involved only about a fourth
of the men under his command. Even after Hill's men came in there were still
twice as many Federals as Confederates in this part of the field. Willcox's division, waiting on the outskirts of Sharpsburg, was hardly under fire at all now
and was about ready to walk in and take possession, and Sturgis's division was
still under shelter in the Antietam Valley, resting and refilling its cartridge
boxes, the men so far out of the fight that they were wandering about examining
the haversacks and knapsacks of dead Rebels. The Ohio division was closer to
the front—some of its regiments had gone over to help when Rodman's line
collapsed—but as a division it was not in serious action. There were more than
enough men present to check Hill's charging ranks, hold the ground around
Sharpsburg, and stage a new attack. The trouble was that it did not occur to
anyone to try it. The Union commanders just took it for granted that they were
beaten, and they were quite right: they had been whipped, even if their men had
not been.[7]

So Willcox was told to bring his troops back, a new line was formed on the
brow of the hills overlooking the creek, and Burnside sent word to headquarters
that he thought he could hold his ground all right, although it would help if he
could be strongly reinforced. Altogether he had lost twenty-three hundred men,
nearly half of them from Rodman's luckless division—the 16th Connecticut
alone had lost more than four hundred, and when it called the roll that evening
only three hundred men were present, although a couple of hundred more came
wandering in during the night. For the rest, Burnside's worst losses had been incurred in the attacks on the bridge.

McClellan had stayed at the Pry house all day except for one brief excursion
to the right to talk with Sumner, after Franklin's attack had been called off. The
battle swung and surged back and forth in front of him, and he was like a bemused spectator; he accepted the decisions made by his subordinates but went
no farther. Once or twice, it seems, something struck a spark in his mind, and
he was on the verge of demanding a new offensive all along the line. But that
old, crippling belief in Lee's overwhelming numbers was still working. Every
time the fighting reached the stage where one more hard drive would finish
matters McClellan thought of the terrible fix he would be in if the Rebels should
make a counterattack and find him without reserves, and so one more hard drive
was never ordered.

There is a story—probably garbled, but nevertheless perfectly in character—
of McClellan at the end of the afternoon, sitting his horse beside Porter and
Sykes near where the Boonsboro road crosses the creek. Up ahead, near
Sharpsburg, some of Sykes's regulars had been sharpshooting on the outskirts of

the town, their skirmish line a link connecting the troops who had assaulted Bloody Lane with the advanced elements of Burnside's command. An infantry captain in the skirmish line had seen for himself how thin the Rebel defenses in front of him really were, and he sent back word of it, begging that an attack might be made—the attack was bound to win, he said, and it would break Lee's army in half. Sykes liked the idea, it is said, and urged that his division be sent in, followed by the rest of Porter's corps and everybody else who was available. (Here, for the last time, were those ten thousand fresh Federals of Longstreet's.) For a moment McClellan seemed ready to approve. And then Porter said: "Remember, General—I command the last reserve of the last army of the Republic"—and the attack was not made.[8]

It is only fair to point out that Porter, a perfectly reliable witness on other matters, said that no such conversation ever took place, and the story undoubtedly was much embellished in the telling. Nevertheless, it is the tip-off. Lee's army could have been broken then and there, and it was not broken because the men who might have done it had to be saved as the vital last reserve. The Northern fighting men had done their best, but they had not been able to shake their general's belief that his real responsibility was defensive. Whatever might have been the relative merits of the two armies, there is not a shadow of doubt that the Southern commanders that day had an unbeatable moral ascendency over the commanders of the North.

Another story: In midmorning, young Lieutenant Wilson of McClellan's staff finished a ride through the battered brigades of Hooker's and Mansfield's corps. He had seen the tired men forming new ranks behind the massed artillery which was anchoring McClellan's right, and he reflected that although these boys were deeply dejected—they had given their best and it hadn't been quite good enough—there were still enough of them to go sweeping in over the Rebel flank if proper inspiration were given them. He remembered, too, that next to McClellan Joe Hooker was the most popular general in the army, and while Hooker had been wounded he knew that Hooker's wound was comparatively slight. Lieutenants, of course, do not tell major generals what to do, but sometimes there are ways to work things. At headquarters just then was George Smalley, war correspondent for the New York *Tribune*, who was a good friend of Hooker; and Smalley told Wilson that Hooker, his injured foot bandaged, was lying in a farmhouse a mile or so from the place where his troops were.

"Smalley!" cried Wilson, excited. "Ride rapidly to Hooker and tell him to rally his corps and lead it back to the field, for by doing so he may not only save the day but save the Union also!"

Smalley's horse had been wounded, and he himself was weary and covered with dust from riding about the field, but he was game; he pointed out, however, that Hooker's wound would probably make it impossible for him to mount a horse.

"That makes no difference," said Wilson. "Let him get into an ambulance and drive back to the field. Or, what is still better, put him on a stretcher and with his bugles blowing and his corps flag flying over him let his men carry him back to the fighting line while his staff take the news to the division and brigade commanders."

Smalley took fire. "Hooker will go back—I'll answer for it!" he said, and he galloped away—to return crestfallen half an hour later with the report that Hooker said his wound was too painful to let him make the attempt. Wilson, always a caustic critic of Federal generals, wrote of Hooker: "From that day forth I regarded him as possessing but little real merit."[9]

Just what, if anything, would have been accomplished if this flamboyant project had gone through is, of course, an open question; but the young lieutenant's suggestion does stand out as the one proposal made at any time during the day to make use of the great reserve of enthusiasm and ardor which was possessed by that youthful army. Here were soldiers not yet grown battle-weary and army-cynical: young men still romantic enough to respond to the waving flag and the blaring bugle, foolish enough to try the impossible, and to do it, too, if the right man asked them to. McClellan had that force at his disposal as no other commander of this army ever had it—and he could never quite bring himself to the point of using it. As one of his veterans wrote long after the war: "It always seemed to me that McClellan, though no commander ever had the love of his soldiers more, or tried more to spare their lives, never realized the metal that was in his grand Army of the Potomac. . . . He never appreciated until too late what manner of people he had with him."[10]

And it seems that McClellan's great love for his soldiers actually worked to prevent him from making full use of them. He knew that his men had fought harder that day than they had ever fought before; believed, in fact, that they were completely fought out, that they had done all that any man could ask them to do. He dreaded to see their bloodshed and suffering, and he had been seeing nothing else all day. From one end of the war to the other the Army of the Potomac never lost so many men in one day's fighting as it lost here on the Antietam: not at Gettysburg, not in the Wilderness, not anywhere. McClellan's capacity for sending his men in to be hurt had simply been exhausted. So they were hurt no more that day—and were to go on fighting until 1865.

And the long day ended at last, and the long battle ended, and both sides were about where they had been at dawn. The sun went down over the western hills, blood-red in the smoky air: an observer at headquarters saw it, just as it was setting, with the gunners of one isolated battery silhouetted black against its enormous disk as they loaded for a final shot, seeming to stand in the sun. As the land grew dark, fires were visible; shells had ignited innumerable haystacks on the fields, and these glowed in the twilight. On Burnside's front, boys from the 21st Massachusetts carried their wounded into a farmhouse where an energetic young woman named Clara Barton had set up a dressing station. The sound of the guns died down, and a more dreadful noise rose from the battle lines—the steady, unceasing, unanswerable crying and moaning of thousands upon thousands of wounded boys who lay in the open where the stretcher-bearers could not reach them; a crying that continued throughout the night. A survivor of the mangled 16th Connecticut wrote afterward: "Of all gloomy nights, this was the saddest we ever experienced."

4. THE ROMANCE OF WAR WAS OVER

It all happened a long time ago, and that part of the reality which is represented by smoke and flame and bloodshed casts a thin shadow now, its original darkness bleached out by the years. Yet something endures, even if it is not more than the quiet truth that nothing is ever wasted, and the story of what happened along the Antietam is not just the story of young men who passed needlessly through the fire to Moloch. For in the end the young men who passed along that path were triumphant, and the incapacity which cost them so much has ceased to matter.

Their triumph was not the winning of a battle, for this battle seemingly was not won by anybody; to all appearances it was simply a stalemate that wrecked two armies. Yet victory was in it. After it had been fought—because it had been fought—history came to a turning point. Indecisive tactically, the battle shaped all the rest of the war: meant, at the very least, that the war now must be fought to a finish. There could no longer be a hope for a peace without victory. The great issues that created the war were going to be settled, at no matter what terrible cost. This fight was decisive.

Yet at the moment it did not look decisive. It looked like a stand-off, and the morning after the battle the two exhausted armies lay on the field staring blankly over the silent guns, as if they were appalled by what they had done to each other. Here and there men on the rival lines made an informal truce so that the wounded could be carried in, but the pickets were alert and scattered shots rang out now and then, warning the ranging stretcher-bearers not to go too far. All day long the soldiers awaited a new outburst of fighting. Heavy reinforcements came into McClellan's lines, and generals went out to study new angles of attack; McClellan listened to them, nodded sagely, and decided to delay the offensive until next day. On the opposite side Lee considered an attack north of the Dunker church, regretfully gave it up when Jackson reported the Federal position there too strong to be carried, and waited for the day to end; and the hot sun came down on fields and copses where lay thousands of unburied bodies. And at last it was night again, and after dark the Federals heard in their front a steady, unbroken sound like the flowing of a great river, hour after hour—the tramping of the brigades of Lee's army moving back to cross the Potomac on the return to Virginia. When morning came the noise had ceased and the Union Army had the field to itself, with none but dead men in front of it.

The cavalry and Fitz-John Porter's infantry were sent to the river to make sure the last Rebels had gone. They rounded up a few belated stragglers, and they did a good deal of sniping across the water at Lee's rear guard. Porter ran some artillery down to the bank, and that night some of his regiments crossed, captured a few guns, and went forward to see what further damage they could do. The Confederates struck back savagely in the gray of the next morning: A. P. Hill's division again, lashing out at McClellan for the last time. A new Pennsylvania regiment, which, having been armed with condemned muskets, somehow found itself on the front line, discovered that its weapons could not be fired, and took a brutal beating before it could get back to the northern shore. There was no more fighting. The Army of Northern Virginia withdrew slowly up the Shenandoah Valley, and the Army of the Potomac stayed where it was, too worn to pursue, and wearily went to work to tidy up the battlefield.

This battlefield was unspeakably awful by now. Swollen corpses darkened by the sun lay everywhere, giving off a frightful stench, and burial parties were put to work. (Any regiment which had got into the bad graces of its brigadier, a veteran wrote later, was sure to be given this assignment.) Great fires were built to consume the innumerable carcasses of dead horses, and nauseating greasy smoke went drifting down-wind and compounded the evil. The men dug long trenches for mass burials of dead Confederates—McClellan said they buried twenty-seven hundred of them, but the count seems to have been too high—and they tried to make individual graves for their own comrades, putting up little wooden markers with names and regimental numbers wherever they could.

Even men who had been in the thickest of the fighting were astounded when they went about the field and saw how terrible the killing had really been. One officer counted more than two hundred dead Southerners in a five-hundred-foot stretch of the Bloody Lane. An Ohio soldier wrote that the lane was "literally filled with dead." Stupefied Pennsylvania rookies gossiped fatuously that the Confederate bodies they were burying had turned black because the Rebels ate gunpowder for breakfast. One Northern soldier, moved by a somewhat ghoulish curiosity, carefully examined a body which hung doubled over a fence in rear of the Bloody Lane and found that it had been hit by fifty-seven bullets. Under the ashes of burned haystacks, in front of Burnside's corps, soldiers found the charred bodies of wounded men who had feebly crawled under the hay for shelter and had been too weak to crawl out when the stacks took fire.

Worst of all, perhaps, was the Hagerstown turnpike between the West Wood and the cornfield, where charge and countercharge had swept back and forth repeatedly, and where the post-and-rail fences on each side of the road were grotesquely festooned with corpses. The colonel of the 6th Wisconsin called this place "indescribably horrible" and said that when he rode through his horse "trembled in every limb with fright and was wet with perspiration." This officer served throughout the war, and when he wrote his reminiscences, in 1890, he said that what he saw along the Hagerstown road that morning was worse than anything he saw later at Spotsylvania's Bloody Angle, at Cold Harbor, or in front of the stone wall at Fredericksburg: "The Antietam turnpike surpassed all in manifest evidence of slaughter." Yet General Gibbon felt that the cornfield itself was even worse; the dead were actually piled on top of each other in places, and it seemed as if whole regiments had gone down in regular ranks. One soldier wrote that it would have been possible to walk from one side of the cornfield to the other without once stepping on the ground. There were two dozen dead horses and scores of human corpses in Mr. Miller's barnyard.[1]

There had been a great deal of killing, in other words. McClellan's official casualty list, which was made up a few days later, showed more than two thousand Federals killed in action and about ten thousand wounded. Rebel casualties were apparently slightly lower, although exact figures are lacking. Altogether, bearing in mind the number of wounded men who were to die, it is probable that five thousand young men lost their lives here; and whatever the correct figure may be, there seems no reason to doubt the accuracy of the contemporary writers who called the Antietam the worst single day of the entire war. Some regiments were down to pathetic remnants. Captain Noyes recorded that he met a company officer the morning after the battle who was carrying a huge piece of salt pork and was wondering what on earth to do with it—it was the day's meat ration for his company, just issued, and he was the company's sole survivor. Noyes added that he checked on this officer's amazing statement and found that it was true. Company G of the 12th Massachusetts had been reduced from 32 men to five; the whole regiment, even after it called in all convalescents and detailed men, numbered only 119 when it was formed for a review two weeks after the battle. The 80th New York had only 86 men to answer roll call the day after the battle, and the 28th New York—which had been a skeleton to begin with—was down to 53. The Irish Brigade had received 120 recruits just before the battle; it reported that 75 of the new men had been shot. Regimental losses of 50 per cent were common; had been suffered, for instance, by three of the four regiments in Sedgwick's front line during the fifteen-minute ambush in the West Wood.

The stragglers were at least coming back to the fold. General Meade, who was temporarily in command of Hooker's corps, wrote to his wife that the corps' "present for duty" total rose by five thousand in the three days after the battle, explaining that the increase was made up of "the cowards, skulkers, men who leave the ground with the wounded and do not return for days, the stragglers on the march, and all such characters." He added bitterly that this sort of thing was entirely due to the inefficiency of regimental and company officers.[2] Like a good brigadier, Gibbon made a careful check of his own returns and discovered that the Black Hat Brigade's strength had increased by eighty in those three days; and he wrote proudly that "*everyone* of these were men who had returned from detached service and hospitals so that I had *no* stragglers." To add to his pride, he was learning that his brigade now had a new nickname, used by the whole army—the Iron Brigade, a name it carried for the rest of the war. Nobody was quite sure where it came from. The accepted story was that McClellan, watching its progress up the gap at South Mountain, had exclaimed in admiration: "That brigade must be made of iron!" Whatever its origin, the name stuck, and the brigade lived up to it valiantly the next summer at Gettysburg.[3]

The soldiers themselves were slow to realize just what they had achieved. All through the eighteenth of September, when the two armies waited in each other's presence for a renewal of the fighting, the battle had seemed unfinished. The Federals held part of the Rebel position, but only part of it; every offensive had been stopped just short of the goal, and the soldiers who had been driven back from the Dunker church, the Piper farm, and the edge of Sharpsburg knew perfectly well that their enemies had not been routed. It was only after Lee's army went back to Virginia that the Army of the Potomac began to see that it had gained more than it had lost. Meade probably expressed the general feeling when he wrote, three days after the battle, that the retreat of the Confederates proved that "we had hit them much harder than they had us, and that in reality our battle was a victory."[4]

A victory, indisputably, even if a negative one. Lee had invaded the North with high hopes; he had been compelled to fight along the Antietam, and after the fight he had had to go back into Virginia. At enormous cost the Army of the Potomac had won a strategic victory. The invader had been thrown back; or, if not precisely thrown back, he had been fought to a standstill and then had been allowed to *go* back, his late hosts very glad to see the last of him. However qualified this triumph might be, at least the invasion was over. There would be a new campaign now, and it would take place south of the Potomac.

McClellan was looking ahead to it. A week after the battle, when the last of the dead had been buried, he was making his plans: possess Harper's Ferry with a strong force, then reorganize the army thoroughly, get an abundance of new equipment and supplies, make proper replacements for the fallen generals, get the rookie regiments into better shape, and—all of this done—start south afresh. Privately he was jubilant. He had been cautious at first, writing his wife only that "the general result was in our favor"; but as the days passed his very need for inner reassurance made him see it in brighter colors. He wrote about the stacks of captured battle flags that had been brought to him and told his wife gaily: "You should see my soldiers *now!* You never saw anything like their enthusiasm. It surpassed anything you ever imagined." He had no doubt that his enemies in Washington would keep trying to get rid of him, and they might succeed, but that hardly mattered: "I feel now that this last short campaign is a sufficient legacy for our child, so far as honor is concerned." It seems that at last, as he thought it all over, he could see himself measuring up to some private, invisible yardstick. He wrote rather pathetically—for this was the commander of a great army, not a schoolboy mulling over his part in last week's football game—"Those in whose judgment I rely tell me that I fought the battle splendidly and that it was a masterpiece of art."

Masterpiece of art it assuredly was not: rather, a dreary succession of missed opportunities. Not once had the commanding general put out his hand to pull his battle plan together and to undo the mistakes of his subordinates. The battle had been left to fight itself, and the general was a spectator; and in the end it had been a victory by the narrowest of margins—tactically, a victory only in the sense that the army had fought hard and then had not retreated afterward. Meade had said the most that could be said: we hurt them a little more than they hurt us.

Yet it was finally, and irrevocably, *the* decisive battle of the war, affecting the whole course of American history ever since.

For this stalemated battle—this great whirlwind of flame and torn earth and shaking sound, which seemed to consume everything and to create nothing—brought about the Emancipation Proclamation and put the country on a new course from which there could be no turning back. Here at last was the sounding forth of the bugle that would never call retreat.

All summer Lincoln had been waiting for a victory. Here it was, now: an uncertain victory, looking very much like no victory at all, but for all that, and with all of its imperfections, a victory, the all-important victory which he had to have if the war was to be won. One week later he issued the preliminary Emancipation Proclamation, and the war was transformed.

Like the battle itself, the Proclamation at first seemed an achievement of doubtful value. It was just words, promising much but doing nothing. They were not even bold, straightforward words, it seemed. Perversely, they ordained freedom in precisely those places where the Union armies could not make freedom a fact and left slavery untouched elsewhere. They infuriated all sympathizers with secession—Gideon Welles noted glumly that "this step will band the south together"—and they left the abolitionists unsatisfied. They seemed to be neither hot nor cold, a futile attempt to find a middle course in a struggle which had no middle course—and in the end they had more power than a great army with banners.

Their real effect was first seen afar off, in London, where they gave this war in America a new aspect, so that statesmen found to their surprise that it was something with which they could not interfere.

In October the Emperor of France formally proposed that England, France, and Russia step in and bring about a six months' armistice—which, in its practical effect, would mean (and was meant to mean) independence for the Confederacy. Britain's Foreign Minister recommended acceptance of the proposal. But the British Cabinet rejected it, for a pro-Confederate in England now was an apologist for slavery, whether he liked it or not. By mid-January, American Minister Adams was writing in his diary: "It is quite clear that the current is now setting very strongly with us among the body of the people," and a little later Jefferson Davis himself recognized that the chance for intervention was dead and withdrew those famous emissaries, Mason and Slidell. By June, when it seemed in Britain most certain that the Confederacy must win—Hooker had been beaten at Chancellorsville, Lee was north of the border again, the Northern cause had never looked worse—public opinion had completely hardened and recognition was impossible.

In substance, then, the Proclamation meant that Europe was not going to decide how the American Civil War came out. It would be fought out at home.

And it would be fought to the bitter end. The chance for compromise was killed.

Until now there had always been the prospect that sooner or later the war might simply end, with neither side victorious. Reunion, continuation of slavery, some adjustment, perhaps, on the thorny issue of states' rights: the whole body of Northern sentiment on which the Copperhead movement was based had exactly that in mind, and there was plenty of feeling along the same line in the South. But the Proclamation made that impossible. The war had been given a deeper meaning and had become something that would not be adjusted. The deep, tangled issues underneath the war—slavery, the permanence of the Union, the dawning concept that a powerful central government might protect the people's freedom rather than endanger it—all of these, now, must be settled, not evaded; and settled by violence, violence having been unleashed.

It might still be argued that they could far better be settled in some other way, but the argument was no longer relevant. The war now was a war to preserve the Union *and* to end slavery—two causes in one, the combination carrying its own consequences. It could not stop until one side or the other was made incapable of fighting any longer; hence, by the standards of that day, it was going to be an all-out war—hard, ruthless, vicious, with Sheridan carrying devastation across the Shenandoah and Sherman swinging a torch across Georgia and Grant pitilessly grinding two armies to powder so that the Confederacy, if it would not die in any other way, might die of sheer exhaustion. (Exhaustion of spirit, of people, of resources, of culture: a bleeding-white from which the country would be generations recovering.) The war must ultimately go that way henceforward. It had come through its period of uncertainty, the period in which it might lead to anything. Now it could lead only to this. It could no longer be fought on simple enthusiasm like a swords-and-roses romance of knightly legend. From now on it would be all grim.

Which meant, finally, that McClellan's part in it was finished. The men who wanted to be rid of him at all costs—who would even have been glad to see him beaten, because that would give grounds for dismissal—could act against him now, not because he had been beaten but precisely because he had won. His victory meant the last thing on earth he would have wished it to mean: sweeping triumph, not merely for the abolitionists whom he hated and considered traitors, but for the implacable spirit of force that was to take control of the nation's destiny. He had let himself be made a political symbol: symbol of the belief in a limited war for limited objectives, a war consciously aimed at something less than destruction of the Southland's way of life, a war that would not bring about profound alteration in the national government. The battle he won meant that the cause he symbolized was not to prevail, and so the symbol itself would have to vanish.

By one of the great ironies of history, this cause and McClellan himself might have been triumphant if the victory along the Antietam had been complete instead of partial. And a complete victory had been within his grasp, over and over again. Run down the might-have-beens for a moment:

He might have had it if there had been more drive and determination in the forty-eight hours immediately after the finding of the lost order. Later, he might have had it by attacking one day earlier at the Antietam. Still later, he might have had it by co-ordinating his blows so that they came together instead of in succession, by using instead of husbanding the ten thousand fresh troops Longstreet was brooding about, by driving Porter's column into Sharpsburg at the close of the action, or by renewing the battle vigorously the next day. Lastly, all else failing, he might have used his own unique magnetism to evoke in his soldiers a sustained enthusiasm to sweep Lee's army off the smoking ridges and drive it into the river. If, just once, he could have transcended his own limitations, he might have won the kind of victory which would have ended the war in the fall of 1862. A peace made then would not have been an abolitionist's peace. It would have been the kind of peace McClellan wanted.

But those are might-have-beens. McClellan did what he did, not what he can be imagined having done. And because his victory was exactly the kind of victory it was—no bigger and no smaller—his own military career had to end. The battle and what it brought with it left him no room to stand.

McClellan himself seems to have had some dim inkling of this when the Proclamation first came out. The day after it was published he told his wife that it was doubtful if he would remain in service much longer—"the President's late proclamation, the continuation of Stanton and Halleck in office, render it almost impossible for me to retain my commission and self-respect at the same time." A fortnight later he told her how a friend had been urging him that "it is my duty to submit to the President's proclamation and quietly continue doing my duty as a soldier"; he was not sure that this advice was sound, but he would at least think it over very fully. What held him in the service seems to have been a deep, mystic feeling that he and the army had become part of each other. To a member of his staff, about this time, he said: "The Army of the Potomac is my army as much as any army ever belonged to the man that created it. We have grown together and fought together. We are wedded and should not be separated."[5]

Lincoln came up early in October to talk to McClellan and to review the troops. The dead men were all underground by now, and the review seems to have been successful, as such things go, although the troops were somewhat subdued: President and general together did not quite draw the spate of cheers and applause that had come on former occasions. One veteran wrote that Lincoln was melancholy: "He rode around every battalion and seemed much worn and distressed and to be looking for those who were gone"—who were, heaven knows, numerous enough to distress a much less sensitive person.[6] McClellan, who was subtle enough in most ways although never subtle enough to understand Lincoln, found the President in good spirits. Their conversation would seem to have had a vaguely unreal quality. McClellan recorded that "I urged him to follow a conservative course, and supposed from the tenor of his conversation that he would do so"—a conservative course, in the jargon of that day, meaning one which would go directly counter to everything said or implied by the Emancipation Proclamation—and this two weeks after the paper had been signed and published.

The melancholy which a soldier thought he saw in the President was genuine enough. Lincoln was at grips with the problem of just whose army it was that he had been reviewing. Every general always says "my army" in ordinary speech. It is no more than easy shorthand for "the army which I am now commanding." Yet when McClellan said it, it seemed to mean more than that. Lincoln dispiritedly told a friend just after this review that it was not the Army of the Potomac he had been looking at—it was "General McClellan's bodyguard." From the record it looked as if that might be the case. The amazing, hysterical transformation that had taken place on the Virginia hillsides after the second battle of Bull Run meant that the men had for this general a devotion which they gave no other man; it might easily mean that he was literally irreplaceable. That devotion had compelled the administration to reinstate McClellan, much against its will; at that point he had been the only man alive who could turn the mob of disorganized soldiers into an army again. That he had done it, with his own peculiar magic, events proved. The men had instantaneously pulled themselves up from the depths of complete demoralization when he came back to them, and they had come up here to Sharpsburg to fight as they had never fought before. He had made this army, he spoke of it as "my army," and the men themselves seemed to feel exactly the same way about it. They were boys who had gone out blithely to fight a picture-book war, victims of a nationwide innocence, filled with a boyish yearning for impossible romance and adventure; nothing was left of that early spirit now except their love for McClellan. He remained as the justification of their early hopes, their last defense against complete disillusionment. Could the war go on if he were taken away? And yet could it be fought, in the only way now remaining, if he stayed?

For a time the wheel remained at dead center, and if Lincoln came to any final conclusion during his visit he kept it to himself. He went back to Washington, and McClellan busied himself with the job of reorganization. He needed much new equipment and he was not getting it fast enough; he argued endlessly with Halleck and the supply people in Washington, refusing to move until he felt the army was fully ready, insisting again that he must be heavily reinforced because Lee still outnumbered him. Lincoln prodded him ineffectually to get him to advance; lost his patience once, and when McClellan reported his cavalry horses worn out asked sarcastically just what his cavalry had been doing lately that would tire anybody's horses. Once Halleck sent peremptory orders, in Lincoln's name, to cross the river. McClellan ignored them; and while he was continuing to re-equip and reorganize, Jeb Stuart got north of the river with his cavalry and rode gaily clear around the army, getting back unhurt, while Federal detachments ran all over western Maryland looking for him. The bickering became sharper, much of it due to the old two-way misunderstanding—Washington's inability to see the need for proper organization and supply, and McClellan's own inability to realize that the enemy was in worse shape than himself and needed to be crowded a bit. But at last, seven weeks after the battle, the great army slipped down the river, crossed to the Virginia side, and started south.

McClellan seems to have planned this campaign intelligently. He took his army down on the eastern side of the Blue Ridge, evidently aiming to box Lee up in such a way that Lee would have to come out and fight at a disadvantage, and there is some reason to believe that he might have had the Rebel army in a bad spot had he been allowed to continue. But his number was up. It was a different war now, and he was due to go out of it, and it was really only a question of time. Lincoln appears to have made up his mind that he would remove him if he let Lee get east of the Blue Ridge and stand in his path to Richmond; and when Lee got his army—or part of it, at any rate—to Culpeper Courthouse ahead of McClellan, that pulled the trigger. But that was only the immediate excuse. If it had not been that it would have been something else. Whenever the actual decision was made, it had been in the cards for weeks. So . . .

November 7, near midnight; a snowy night, with a cold wind out of the mountains, and everybody huddled under shelter; McClellan in his headquarters tent, writing a letter to his wife. A special train had come down from Washington that afternoon, and a War Department functionary had left it and ridden several miles in a snowstorm, not to see the commanding general, but to call on General Burnside. This much McClellan knew, and he had a fair idea what it meant, but he said nothing and stayed in his tent, his staff all asleep. Finally there came a knock on his tent pole, and on his invitation two men came in—Burnside, looking very troubled and embarrassed, and the War Department's General Buckingham, powdered snow lying in the folds of his neat, unweathered uniform. McClellan was cordial and seemed unworried; sat them down and chatted pleasantly about this and that, quite as if a midnight call like this were an everyday occurrence. Buckingham at last remarked that maybe the general had better know what they were there for, and handed over the papers. Letter to McClellan from Halleck—"you will immediately turn over your command to Maj.-Gen. Burnside and repair to Trenton, N.J. [McClellan's home], for further orders"; and an order from the adjutant general setting forth that "by direction of the President of the United States" the command of the army was passing from McClellan to Burnside.

McClellan read them, seeming quite unruffled—apparently the man could take it when he had to—and looked up at Burnside with a little smile. "Well, Burnside, I turn the command over to you." Almost tearfully, painfully conscious that he was not qualified to command the army, Burnside begged him to delay the transfer for at least a day or two so that Burnside might be brought up to date on troop movements, intelligence reports, campaign plans, and the like. McClellan agreed and the visitors left, and McClellan went back to the letter he was writing. He gave his wife the news and added: "Alas for my poor country! I know in my inmost heart she never had a truer servant."

True servant or false, it was all one now; and his part was finished. There were a couple of days of earnest activity at headquarters while Burnside was fitting his own staff into place—something of a scramble for assignments going on, with many jobs open for new men and with the men who were being displaced trying to find suitable billets, every officer who had a wire to pull yanking on it for all he was worth. Burnside conscientiously went to work to study the intricate web of facts, pending orders, and strategic plans which he was inheriting. Evidently they were just too much for him; he hesitated for a time, and all army movements were halted, while off to the south Lee's officers wondered briefly why the Yankees had stopped moving just when they seemed to be maneuvering effectively. Then Burnside canceled everything and decreed that the army should move east. It is hard to tell just what he had in mind, the sure professional touch at GHQ having departed with his arrival, but he seems to have had some notion of slipping unobserved around the Confederates' right flank—the one maneuver which no Federal general ever succeeded in accomplishing against Robert E. Lee. So the army pulled itself together and made ready to move.

Meanwhile, one little ceremony remained: to say good-by to General McClellan. On November 10, the order of removal having been published, McClellan rode through the camps around Warrenton, and for the last time the fighting men raised their shouts to the wintry sky as the jaunty little man on the great black horse came riding down the lines.

There they were, brigade after brigade, desperately yelling their farewell: the men who had been a loose militia muster until he made them an army, the men who had found pride and strength in being soldiers because it was he who taught them soldiering, the men who, for all their hard knowledge of battle, could still see a shine and a color in war as long as he led them. They had struggled in the Chickahominy swamps and sweltered in the noisome camp at Harrison's Landing, they had gone laughing under the flags at Frederick and had stormed through the smoke to the Dunker church, and he was part of it all; he had lived through those things with them and somehow had given them meaning, so that endurance and hope had been easier because of him. And now he was going away and they would never see him again, and if they were to have endurance and hope they would have to find them for themselves because no one at the top was going to provide them any more.

McClellan passed by the long ranks, and the cheers went up as long as his figure was in sight; and in his wake there rang out yells of "Send him back! Send him back!" Here and there a regiment threw down its arms, swearing angrily, saying it would fight no more. One general was heard (or was reported to have heard) to call out: "Lead us to Washington, General—we'll follow you!" He came down the Centreville pike at last—that already historic road of battle, the road that had led Pope and McDowell to Bull Run, the road along which the Iron Brigade had found its first experience of combat—and Sumner's corps was lined up on one side of the road, Porter's corps on the other. (Porter himself was doomed now, a sure sacrifice to the vindictive charges filed by Pope; only with McClellan in command could he be protected, and the same officer who brought down the orders relieving McClellan had brought other orders relieving Porter. He was to be court-martialed and cashiered before the winter ended.) These two corps, where affection for McClellan ran higher than anywhere else in the army, stood in long ranks facing the roadway, batteries of field artillery drawn up here and there in the intervals between brigades. They snapped to present arms as the general came up, and then the rigid rows of muskets jerked all askew as the men began to yell, and there was a great cry all along the road.

He passed by and went out of sight, and came finally to the railroad station, where a guard of two thousand men had been drawn up for a final salute. McClellan got on the special train, the guns boomed out—and then the men broke ranks, swarmed about the car, uncoupled it, swore that he should not leave them. McClellan came out on the rear platform and raised his hand, and they fell silent.

"Stand by General Burnside as you have stood by me, and all will be well," he said. The demonstration stopped. Silently the men recoupled the car, the conductor waved a signal to the engineer, and the train clanked out of the station. A veteran recorded: "When the chief passed out of sight, the romance of war was over for the Army of the Potomac."[7]

Washington seems to have breathed a collective sigh of relief when he went. There had been fears that the army would mutiny—fears that seemed well grounded, if the loose talk that had been flying around army headquarters was listened to. Young Lieutenant Wilson noted that staff officers had been drinking heavily and had been "talking both loudly and disloyally," and there was a good deal of campfire chatter to the effect that the army ought to "change front on Washington," oust the government, and put McClellan in control of civil and military affairs alike. But this was just staff talk, after all, and it reflected the hysteria of individuals rather than the temper of the soldiers. The men who yelled and wept and threw down muskets were expressing grief and anger, but it does not appear to have entered their heads that the order from Washington might actually be disobeyed by one hundred thousand trained men who had weapons in their hands. Washington need not have worried; they just were not that kind of army.

Indeed, there were mixed feelings among the men here and there. In Burnside's IX Corps the change was actually welcomed: those men had not served under McClellan very long, they did not yet realize how Burnside had misused and wasted them on the hills southeast of Sharpsburg, and they felt that their likable corps commander should do very well indeed at the head of the army. In the New England regiments, where abolitionists were numerous, there was very little grumbling. Some soldiers comforted themselves with a tale that McClellan was really being called back to Washington to replace Halleck. And there were a few men who had seen enough of the final thinness of the Rebel lines at the Antietam to feel that McClellan had failed them there: men who recorded that after the battle the army's cheers for the general had not quite had the warmth they had had before.[8]

It was left for a campfire group in the 17th Michigan to provide the characteristic soldier's comment. These men discussed pros and cons that evening. They were profoundly depressed—the regiment had fewer than three hundred men now, and it had left Detroit in August a thousand strong; the boys had learned a lot these last three months. They suspected that the worst would come of this change in generals, and now that they thought about it they concluded that none of their generals really amounted to very much. So, said their historian, they finally agreed that Lincoln ought to retire all of the generals "and select men from the ranks who will serve without pay, lead the army against Lee, strike him hard, and follow him until he fails to come to time." Having expressed this crude front-line wisdom, they grinned ruefully, wagged their heads, and went off through the sleety rain to their pup tents.[9]

And presently the army began to move again; not down the line of the railroad, where McClellan's plan would have taken it, but southeast along the Rappahannock toward Fredericksburg, where Burnside wanted to go. The bugle calls spattered through the camps, wagons were loaded, and regiment after regiment swung into column and marched out into the muddy road. The veteran who put it down on paper was right: the romance was gone from the war now. They had left it behind them, with the lemonade and fried chicken of the ladies' committees at the railway stations, with the brightness of the uniforms that had never known mud or smoke, with the lighthearted inconsequence of those early days when it seemed as if the war might be more than half a lark, when the sky was bright with wonder and the chance of death was only a challenge to set vibrant nerves tingling.

The romance had gone—inevitably, because the war itself was not romantic. The young soldiers were veterans at last. They were not McClellan's army any longer, and they never could be again; they were Lincoln's army now, or the country's, or the army of some inscrutable tide that was flowing down the century to change everything they were used to and break the way for something unimaginable. They had been that army all along, as a matter of fact, and now the war was something that could not be fought on tag ends of youthful hero worship. Now it was going to be ugliness and dirt and pain and death, with the good men getting all the worst of it while the shirkers went straggling off to safety; and the men knew it, and put their feet on the Virginia road to go where it might lead them.

The road ahead was long, and it was to lead them to worse than they had had: to Fredericksburg and Chancellorsville, to Gettysburg and the Wilderness, to the sickening meadows at Cold Harbor and the squalid trenches around Petersburg; to the ultimate misery and bleak wisdom that lie at the end of all the roads of war. They were on their own now, fighting for something they had not been asked about; they had made the victory through which the war had been given its lasting meaning, and now they would have to go on to the end of it, marching doggedly to the dark fields where they would be called on to give the last full measure of a devotion which they themselves could never understand or define.

One after another, flags cased under a gray sky, the regiments moved out of the camp grounds and took to the road for Fredericksburg. The 24th New Jersey kept the cadence a little while after it got on the road, instead of lapsing at once into route step, and struck up a little ditty which it had composed to the tune of the John Brown song:

> *"We'll soon light our fires on the Rappahannock shore;*
> *We'll soon light our fires on the Rappahannock shore;*
> *And tell Father Abraham he needn't call for more—*
> *While we go marching on."*

Down the road they went, and the song died away, and the army trudged off to the east.

Bibliography

The principal source regarding troop movements, battle orders, etc., is of course that voluminous and invaluable set of volumes, *The War of the Rebellion: A Compilation of the Official Records of the Union and Confederate Armies* (Washington: Government Printing Office, 1902). In addition, the following works were consulted:

BOOKS DEALING WITH THE WAR AS A WHOLE, AND WITH ITS POLITICAL AND MILITARY BACKGROUND

Abraham Lincoln: The War Years, by Carl Sandburg. 4 vols. New York, 1939.

Abraham Lincoln and Men of War Times, by Alexander K. McClure. Philadelphia, 1892.

Battles and Leaders of the Civil War. Grant-Lee edition, 4 vols. New York, 1884–87.

Campaigns of the Army of the Potomac, by William Swinton. New York, 1866.

The Diary of Gideon Welles. 3 vols. Boston & New York, 1911.

The Diary of a Public Man, with Prefatory Notes by F. Lauriston Bullard. Rutgers, 1946.

The Hidden Civil War: The Story of the Copperheads, by Wood Gray. New York, 1942.

History of the Civil War, by James Ford Rhodes, 1-vol. edition. New York, 1917.

Lincoln's War Cabinet, by Burton J. Hendrick. Boston, 1946.

The Movement for Peace without Victory during the Civil War, by Elbert J. Benton. Publication No. 99 of the Western Reserve Historical Society, Cleveland, 1918.

Pictorial History of the Civil War, by Benton J. Lossing. 3 vols. Philadelphia, 1886.

Photographic History of the Civil War, edited by Francis Trevelyan Miller, 10 vols. New York, 1911.

The Rebellion Record, edited by Frank Moore. 12 vols. New York, 1862–71.

AUTOBIOGRAPHIES, BIOGRAPHICAL STUDIES, ETC.

Advance and Retreat, by John B. Hood. New Orleans, 1880.

Autobiography of Oliver Otis Howard. 2 vols. New York, 1907.

Correspondence of John Sedgwick, Major General. 2 vols. Privately printed, De-Vinne Press, 1902.

Days and Events: 1860–1866, by Colonel Thomas L. Livermore. Boston, 1920.

Four Years with the Army of the Potomac, by Brevet Major General Regis de Trobriand. Translated by George K. Dauchy, Boston, 1889.

From Bull Run to Chancellorsville, by Brevet Major General Newton Martin Curtis. New York, 1906.

General Hancock, by Brevet Brigadier General Francis A. Walker. New York, 1894.

General Philip Kearny, Battle Soldier of Five Wars, by Thomas Kearny. New York, 1937.

Grant and Lee: A Study in Personality and Generalship, by Major General J. F. C. Fuller. New York, 1933.

Jeb Stuart, by John W. Thomason, Jr. New York, 1930.

The Life and Letters of George Gordon Meade, by Colonel George Meade. 2 vols. New York, 1913.

Life and Letters of Wilder Dwight, Lieutenant Colonel, 2nd Massachusetts Infantry. Boston, 1868.

Life of General George Gordon Meade, by Richard Meade Bache. Philadelphia, 1897.

Lee's Lieutenants, by Douglas Southall Freeman. 3 vols. New York, 1942.

Major General Hiram G. Berry, by Edward K. Gould. Portland, Me., 1899.

McClellan's Own Story, by Major General George B. McClellan. New York, 1887.

Meade's Headquarters, 1863-65, by Colonel Theodore Lyman. Boston, 1922.

Military Reminiscences of the Civil War, by Jacob Dolson Cox. 2 vols. New York, 1900.

Personal Recollections of the Civil War, by Brigadier General John Gibbon. New York, 1928.

The Pinkertons: A Detective Dynasty, by Richard Wilmer Rowan. Boston, 1931.

Reminiscences of General Herman Haupt. Milwaukee, 1901.

Reminiscences of the Civil War, by General John B. Gordon. New York, 1905.

R. E. Lee: A Biography, by Douglas Southall Freeman. 4 vols. New York, 1934.

Robert E. Lee, the Soldier, by Major General Sir Frederick Maurice. Boston, 1925.

Selections from the Letters and Diaries of Brevet Brigadier General Willoughby Babcock, by Willoughby Babcock, Jr. New York, 1922.

The Spy of the Rebellion: Being a True History of the Spy System of the United States Army during the Late Rebellion, by Allan Pinkerton. New York, 1883.

Stonewall Jackson, by Colonel G. F. R. Henderson. London & New York, 1936.

Under the Old Flag, by Major General James Harrison Wilson. 2 vols. New York, 1912.

SOLDIERS' REMINISCENCES, REGIMENTAL HISTORIES, ETC.

Awhile with the Blue, by Benjamin Borton. Passaic, N.J., 1898.

The Bivouac and the Battlefield: or, Campaign Sketches in Virginia and Maryland, by Captain George Freeman Noyes. New York, 1863.

A Brief History of the 28th Regiment New York State Volunteers, by C. W. Boyce. Buffalo, 1896.

The Diary of an Enlisted Man, by Lawrence Van Alstyne. New Haven, 1910.

The Diary of a Line Officer, by Captain Augustus C. Brown. New York, 1906.

The Diary of a Young Officer, by Brevet Major Joseph Marshall Favill, 57th New York. Chicago, 1909.

A Duryée Zouave, by Thomas P. Southwick. Privately printed. New York, 1930.

Following the Greek Cross: or, Memories of the 6th Army Corps, by Brevet Brigadier General Thomas W. Hyde. Boston, 1894.

Four Years Campaigning in the Army of the Potomac, by Daniel G. Crotty. Grand Rapids, 1874.

Forty-six Months with the 4th Rhode Island Volunteers, by Corporal George H. Allen. Providence, 1887.

Hardtack and Coffee, by John D. Billings. Boston, 1887.

A History of the "Bucktails," by O. R. Howard Thomson and William H. Rauch. Philadelphia, 1906.

History of Duryée's Brigade, by Franklin B. Hough. Albany, 1864.

A History of the 11th Regiment Ohio Volunteer Infantry, compiled from the Official Records by Horton and Teverbaugh, Members of the Regiment. Dayton, 1866.

A History of the 5th Regiment New Hampshire Volunteers, by William Child. Bristol, N.H., 1893.

History of the 51st Regiment of Pennsylvania Volunteers, by Thomas H. Parker. Philadelphia, 1869.

History of the First Brigade New Jersey Volunteers, by Camille Baquet. Trenton, 1910.

History of the First Regiment Minnesota Volunteer Infantry, by R. I. Holcombe, Stillwater, Minn., 1916.

History of the 40th (Mozart) Regiment, by Fred C. Floyd. Boston, 1909.

History of the 45th Regiment Pennsylvania Veteran Volunteer Infantry, by Allen D. Albert. Williamsport, Pa., 1912.

History of the 100th Regiment of New York State Volunteers, by George H. Stowits. Buffalo, 1870.

History of the Second Army Corps, by Brevet Brigadier General Francis A. Walker. New York, 1886.

History of the 16th Connecticut Volunteers, by B. F. Blakeslee. Hartford, 1875.

History of the 10th Massachusetts Battery, by John D. Billings. Boston, 1881.

History of the 3rd Indiana Cavalry, by W. N. Pickerell. Indianapolis, 1906.

History of the 3rd Regiment of Wisconsin Veteran Volunteer Infantry, by Edwin E. Bryant. Madison, Wis., 1891.

History of the 12th Massachusetts Volunteers, by Lieutenant Colonel Benjamin F. Cook. Boston, 1882.

The History of a Volunteer Regiment, by Gouverneur Morris. New York, 1891.

I Rode with Stonewall, by Henry Kyd Douglas. Chapel Hill, 1940.

The Irish Brigade and Its Campaigns, by Captain D. P. Conyngham. New York, 1867.

Letters of a War Correspondent, by Charles A. Page. Boston, 1899.

A Military History of the 8th Ohio Volunteer Infantry, by Franklin Sawyer. Cleveland, 1881.

Music on the March, by Frank Rauscher. Philadelphia, 1892.

Musket and Sword, by Edwin C. Bennett. Boston, 1900.

Notes of a Staff Officer of Our First New Jersey Brigade on the Seven Days Battle on the Peninsula, 1862, by E. Burd Grubb. Moorestown, N.J., 1910.

Opdyke Tigers: 125th Ohio Volunteer Infantry, by Charles T. Clark. Columbus, 1895.

Personal Recollections of the Civil War, by James Madison Stone. Boston, 1918.

Recollections of a Boy Member of Co. I, 14th Maine Volunteers, by Ira B. Gardner. Lewiston, Me., 1902.

Recollections of the Civil War, by Mason Whiting Tyler. New York, 1912.

Recollections of a Private, by Warren Lee Goss. New York, 1890.

Reminiscences of the Civil War, by Theodore M. Nagle, Erie, Pa., 1903.

Reminiscences of the 19th Massachusetts Regiment, by Captain John G. B. Adams. Boston, 1899.

The Road to Richmond: Civil War Memoirs of Major Abner R. Small, edited by Harold Adams Small. Berkeley, Calif., 1939.

Service with the 6th Wisconsin Volunteers, by Brevet Brigadier General Rufus R. Dawes. Marietta, O., 1890.

The Seventh Regiment: A Record, by Major George L. Wood. New York, 1865.

A Sketch of the 8th New York Cavalry, by Henry Norton. Norwich, N.Y., 1888.

A Soldier's Diary: The Story of a Volunteer, by David Lane. Privately printed, 1905.

The Story of the 15th Regiment Massachusetts Volunteer Infantry in the Civil War, by Andrew E. Ford. Clinton, Mass., 1898.

Three Years in the Army of the Potomac, by Henry N. Blake. Boston, 1865.

The 20th Regiment of Massachusetts Volunteer Infantry, by Lieutenant Colonel George A. Bruce. Boston, 1906.

The 27th Indiana Volunteer Infantry in the War of the Rebellion, by a Member of Company C. Indianapolis, 1899.

The "Ulster Guard" and the War of the Rebellion, by Theodore B. Gates. New York, 1879.

Under Five Commanders, by Jacob H. Cole. Paterson, N.J., 1907.

"War Music and War Psychology in the Civil War," by James Stone. *Journal of Abnormal and Social Psychology,* Vol. 36, No. 4, October 1941.

War Years with Jeb Stuart, by Lieutenant Colonel W. W. Blackford. New York, 1945.

BOOKS RELATING TO SPECIFIC BATTLES AND CAMPAIGNS,
MILITARY TACTICS AND WEAPONS, ETC.

The Antietam and Fredericksburg, by Brevet Brigadier General Francis Winthrop Palfrey. New York, 1882.

The Army of Northern Virginia in 1862, by Lieutenant Colonel William Allan. Boston, 1892.

The Army under Pope, by John C. Ropes. New York, 1881.

Atlas of the Battlefield of Antietam. Prepared by the Antietam Battlefield Board. Published by the War Department, 1904.

Camp and Outpost Duty for Infantry, by Brigadier General Daniel Butterfield. New York, 1862.

The Campaign in Maryland and Virginia, by Lieutenant E. W. Sheppard of the 10th Battalion, Manchester Regiment. New York & London, 1911.

Campaigns in Virginia. Vols. I and XIV, *Papers of the Military Historical Society of Massachusetts,* edited by Theodore Dwight. Boston, 1895.

General John Sedgwick: An Address, by Adjutant General Martin T. McMahon, VI Army Corps, before the Vermont Officers Reunion Society at Montpelier, Vt., Nov. 11, 1880.

The Generalship of Ulysses S. Grant, by Colonel J. F. C. Fuller, New York, 1929.

A History of the United States Navy, by Edgar Stanton Maclay. 3 vols. New York, 1898.

History of the Campaign of the Army of Virginia, by Brevet Brigadier General George H. Gordon. Boston, 1880.

In Memoriam: George Sears Greene. Published by authority of the State of New York under supervision of the New York Monuments Commission, 1909.

Indiana at Antietam. Report of the Indiana Antietam Monument Commission. Indianapolis, 1912.

Joseph K. F. Mansfield: A Narrative of Events Connected with His Mortal Wounding, by John Mead Gould. Portland, Me., 1895.

The Long Arm of Lee, by Jennings C. Wise. 2 vols. Lynchburg, Va., 1915.

Manual of Instruction for the Volunteers and Militia of the United States, by Major William Gilham. Philadelphia, 1861.

New York at Antietam. Published by the New York Monuments Commission. Albany, 1923.

Papers of the Kansas Commandery, Military Order of the Loyal Legion of the United States. 1894.

Papers Read before the Missouri Commandery, Military Order of the Loyal Legion of the United States. St. Louis, 1887.

The Peninsula: McClellan's Campaigns of 1862, by Major General Alex S. Webb. New York, 1885.

Pennsylvania at Antietam. Report of the Antietam Battlefield Memorial Commission of Pennsylvania. Harrisburg, 1906.

Record of Dedicatory Ceremonies held on the Battlefield of Manassas, or Second Bull Run . . . under Auspices of the Veterans Association of the 5th Regiment New York Volunteer Infantry.

Regimental Losses in the American Civil War, by Lieutenant Colonel William F. Fox. Albany, 1889.

Report of Major General George B. McClellan, from July 26, 1861, to Nov. 7, 1862. Washington: Government Printing Office, 1864.

Rifle and Light Infantry Tactics, by Brevet Lieutenant Colonel William J. Hardee. Philadelphia, 1855.

The Second Admiral: A Life of David Dixon Porter, by Richard S. West. New York, 1937.

The War of Secession, 1861-62, by Major G. W. Redway. London & New York, 1910.

Notes

The general bibliography lists all of the works which were consulted in the preparation of this text. No attempt has been made to cite the authority for every statement of fact. It has seemed advisable, however, to list the sources for direct quotations and to give at least a general indication of the works which have been principally drawn on for each chapter. This material is as follows:

CHAPTER ONE

1. THERE WAS TALK OF TREASON

A full account of the railroad man's meeting with McClellan, his dealings with Hooker, Sturgis, and Stanton, and the problems which were visited on him in connection with the second battle of Bull Run is to be found in General Herman Haupt's *Reminiscences.* Use has also been made of material in the *Official Records,* Series I, Volume XII, Part 3, and of McClellan's autobiography. In his *Military Reminiscences,* General Jacob Cox shows what the second defeat at Bull Run looked like from the fortified lines near Alexandria. Good sketches of Hancock appear in the works cited under Footnote 3.

Specific references are:

1. *Reminiscences of General Herman Haupt.*
2. Ibid.
3. *History of the Second Army Corps,* by Brevet Brigadier General Francis A. Walker. See also the same author's *General Hancock; Following the Greek Cross,* by Brevet Brigadier General Thomas W. Hyde; *Meade's Headquarters,* by Colonel Theodore Lyman, and Brevet Major Joseph M. Favill's *Diary of a Young Officer.*
4. Haupt's *Reminiscences.*
5. *Military Reminiscences of the Civil War,* by Jacob D. Cox.

2. WE WERE NEVER AGAIN EAGER

The innocent, romantic spirit in which young men went off to war in 1861 (and which they shed quite as rapidly as need be) is reflected in any number of the accounts written by participants. Sometimes the account expresses the writer's individual point of view, as in the case of *The Bivouac and the Battlefield,* by Captain George Freeman Noyes, who wrote his book while the war was still going on—and who, being a staff officer, seems to have retained his innocence a trifle longer than most. Sometimes it is revealed in the accounts of the things green officers and men did as they struggled to turn themselves into soldiers. Two appealing pictures of the formation of the famous Black Hat Brigade are available—one in the memoirs of its first commander, General John Gibbon, and one in the regimental history of one of its components, the 6th Wisconsin Infantry.

Specific references are:

1. *Three Years in the Army of the Potomac,* by Henry N. Blake; *Following the Greek Cross,* and *The Diary of an Enlisted Man,* by Lawrence Van Alstyne.

2. *The Bivouac and the Battlefield.*

3. *Personal Recollections of the Civil War,* by Brigadier General John Gibbon. (A book well worth reading; a likable and admirable soldier unconsciously reveals himself in it.)

4. For the foregoing incidents, see *Service with the 6th Wisconsin Volunteers,* by Brevet Brigadier General Rufus R. Dawes.

5. *War Years with Jeb Stuart,* by Lieutenant Colonel W. W. Blackford.

This amazing fight which introduced the Black Hat Brigade to actual combat is of course described briefly in all standard accounts of the second battle of Bull Run. Most of the details in the text are from General Gibbon and General Dawes.

3. YOU MUST NEVER BE FRIGHTENED

Federal reports of the second battle of Bull Run are to be found in the *Official Records,* Series I, Volume XII, Part 2. Running accounts of the battle from the Federal viewpoint are contained in General George H. Gordon's *History of the Campaign of the Army of Virginia* and in *The Army under Pope,* by John C. Ropes. For the Confederate side, see Douglas Southall Freeman's exhaustive accounts in his *R. E. Lee* and *Lee's Lieutenants,* and Colonel G. F. R. Henderson's *Stonewall Jackson.* General Pope's curious special pleading about the battle is in Volume II, Part 2, of *Battles and Leaders of the Civil War.*

Specific references are:

1. *The Bivouac and the Battlefield.*

2. *Under the Old Flag,* by Major General James Harrison Wilson.

3. A good study of that extremely fascinating character, Kearny, is contained in *General Philip Kearny: Battle Soldier of Five Wars,* by Thomas Kearny, from which the quotations in this paragraph are taken.

4. *Four Years Campaigning in the Army of the Potomac,* by Daniel G. Crotty.

5. *Service with the 6th Wisconsin Volunteers.*

6. Ibid.

7. *A Duryée Zouave,* by Thomas P. Southwick.

8. *History of the 12th Massachusetts Volunteers,* by Lieutenant Colonel Benjamin F. Cook.

9. *Personal Recollections of the Civil War,* by General Gibbon.

10. *General Philip Kearny.*

4. MAN ON A BLACK HORSE

There are innumerable accounts of the disorder and despair attending the retreat from the field of Second Bull Run. One of the most detailed is in General Regis de Trobriand's fascinating *Four Years with the Army of the Potomac.* See also Charles A. Page's *Letters of a War Correspondent,* General Oliver Otis Howard's autobiography, the second volume of *Battles and Leaders,* and any number of regimental histories. The soldiers' odd distrust of General McDowell also crops out in many of the regimental histories.

Specific references are:

1. "Personal Experience under Gen. McClellan," by Brigadier General Henry Seymour Hall, from *Papers of the Kansas Commandery, Military Order of the Loyal Legion of the United States.*

2. For the preceding quotations, see *Three Years in the Army of the Potomac,* by Henry N. Blake; *History of the 3rd Regiment of Wisconsin Veteran Volunteer Infantry,* by Edwin E. Bryant; *History of the 12th Massachusetts Volunteers,* and *Ser-*

vice with the 6th Wisconsin Volunteers. There is a good discussion of the soldiers' antagonism toward McDowell and Pope in General Cox's *Military Reminiscences.*

3. This quotation, and the ones in the immediately preceding paragraphs, are from General de Trobriand's book mentioned above.

4. *Autobiography of Oliver Otis Howard.*

5. *Military Reminiscences* of General Cox.

6. *Personal Recollections* of General Gibbon.

7. Articles by Captain William H. Powell and George Kimball in *Battles and Leaders,* Vol. II, Part 2.

8. *Following the Greek Cross.*

CHAPTER TWO

1. A GREAT WORK IN MY HANDS

No bit of Civil War literature is much more interesting than *McClellan's Own Story*—that oddly organized autobiography which tells so much more about its author than the author can possibly have dreamed. The quotations from McClellan in this chapter are taken from that work, and it has hardly seemed necessary to clutter up the text with footnotes identifying each quotation.

Specific references are:

1. For a good account of McClellan's Ohio experience, see General Cox in Vol. I, Part 1, of *Battles and Leaders.*

2. Ibid.

3. *Under the Old Flag.*

4. *Selections from the Letters and Diaries of Brevet Brigadier General Willoughby Babcock.*

5. *Three Years in the Army of the Potomac.*

6. *Reminiscences of the 19th Massachusetts Regiment,* by Captain John G. B. Adams.

7. *Military Reminiscences* of General Cox.

2. AYE, DEEM US PROUD

Since it was an unimportant engagement in a military sense, Ball's Bluff gets little space in most histories of the war. There is a good account in Volume II, Part 2, of *Battles and Leaders,* and the histories of the 15th and 20th Massachusetts regiments give interesting details. Colonel Baker is described in Volume I of Carl Sandburg's *Abraham Lincoln: The War Years.*

Specific references are:

1. *The Story of the 15th Regiment Massachusetts Volunteer Infantry in the Civil War,* by Andrew E. Ford.

2. *Personal Recollections of the Civil War,* by James Madison Stone.

3. *Four Years with the Army of the Potomac.*

4. *History of the First Regiment Minnesota Volunteer Infantry,* by R. I. Holcombe.

5. *The 20th Regiment of Massachusetts Volunteer Infantry,* by Lieutenant Colonel George A. Bruce.

6. *The Story of the 15th Regiment Massachusetts Volunteer Infantry.*

7. For a summary of this strange case, see "Ball's Bluff and the Arrest of General Stone," by Richard B. Irwin, in *Battles and Leaders,* Volume II, Part 1.

3. I DO NOT INTEND TO BE SACRIFICED

It is one of the oddities of Civil War history that General McClellan's handling of his purely military problems cannot be understood unless the purely political problems of President, Cabinet, and Congress are understood also. Along with the military histories, it is necessary to consult such books as Sandburg's *Abraham Lincoln*, whose rambling, discursive, all-inclusive account of the currents that swirled about Lincoln makes clear so much that McClellan never understood at all. *Lincoln's War Cabinet*, by Burton J. Hendrick, sheds a good oblique light on the situation, while books by such contemporaries as Gideon Welles and Alexander K. McClure are invaluable. Again, the McClellan quotations in this chapter are from *McClellan's Own Story*.

Specific references are:

1. *The Diary of a Public Man*, with Prefatory Notes by F. Lauriston Bullard.

2. Scott's letters are found in *Battles and Leaders*, Volume II, Part 1.

3. See Volume II of *A History of the United States Navy*, by Edgar Stanton Maclay, and *The Second Admiral: A Life of David Dixon Porter*, by Richard S. West.

4. Nothing in Douglas Southall Freeman's monumental biography of Lee is much more significant than its picture of Lee's great tact and depth of understanding in his handling of a political problem which was, potentially, quite as explosive as the one which confronted McClellan. It was a problem which was altogether too much for as able a soldier as General Joseph E. Johnston.

5. *Following the Greek Cross.*

CHAPTER THREE

1. BUT YOU MUST ACT

The argument over the rights and wrongs of the administration's interference with McClellan's peninsular campaign will not end, probably, until the Civil War itself drops out of discussion. Where certainty is impossible, about the most that can be done is to try to see *why* the administration did the things McClellan complained of so bitterly. A very good detailed analysis of the way in which McClellan laid himself open to the charge of failing to protect Washington adequately is found in *Campaigns in Virginia*, Volume I, *Papers of the Military Historical Society of Massachusetts*. The growth of the misunderstanding is traced in two nearly contemporaneous works—William Swinton's *Campaigns of the Army of the Potomac*, and Benton J. Lossing's *Pictorial History of the Civil War*. See also *The Peninsula: McClellan's Campaigns of 1862*, by Major General Alexander S. Webb.

Specific references are:

1. *The Rebellion Record*, edited by Frank Moore.

2. For an interesting examination of this point, see Alexander K. McClure, *Abraham Lincoln and Men of War Times*, pp. 221–22.

3. Two good discussions of this savage little fight and its far-reaching effects are in Freeman's *Lee's Lieutenants*, Vol. I, and Henderson's *Stonewall Jackson*.

4. *Following the Greek Cross.*

2. THE VOICE OF CAUTION

The reader who cares to see a complete account of McClellan's espionage and intelligence system in operation can do no better than read *The Spy of the Rebellion: Being a True History of the Spy System of the United States Army during the Late Rebellion*, by Allan Pinkerton. A good analysis of the troubles his faulty reports got McClellan into is to be found in General Cox's *Military Reminiscences*. Pinkerton's reports appear in the *Official Records*, Series I, Vol. XI, Part 1, pp. 268–70.

Specific references are:

1. *General Philip Kearny.*

2. *A Duryée Zouave.*

3. *History of the First Brigade New Jersey Volunteers,* by Camille Baquet.
4. *Following the Greek Cross.*
5. *The Diary of a Young Officer.*
6. *Autobiography of Oliver Otis Howard.*
7. For Meade, see *Letters of a War Correspondent* and *Meade's Headquarters.*
8. *Under the Old Flag.*
9. De Trobriand: *Four Years with the Army of the Potomac.*
10. For McClellan's remarks to the soldiers, see *The Rebellion Record.*

3. TOMORROW NEVER COMES

An odd and frequently overlooked fact about the fighting on the peninsula is that in no single battle was anything like the whole strength of the Army of the Potomac put into action. The climactic struggle of Gaines's Mill was, for most of the soldiers, simply off-stage noises. In many ways McClellan himself was not much better off than the man in the ranks. A study of his letters and telegrams in *McClellan's Own Story*—from which, in this as in previous chapters, quotations have been drawn liberally—unmistakably depicts a man who never quite knew what was going on.
Specific references are:
1. Howard's autobiography.
2. For a good view of Cross—an uncommonly talented regimental commander, and an interesting person—see *Days and Events,* by Colonel Thomas L. Livermore, and *A History of the 5th Regiment New Hampshire Volunteers,* by William Child.
3. *The Diary of a Young Officer.*
4. Moore's *Rebellion Record,* Vol. V.
5. *Recollections of a Private,* by Warren Lee Goss.
6. *General Philip Kearny.* See also *Major General Hiram G. Berry,* by Edward K. Gould, for an extended description of this incident by Major H. L. Thayer.
7. *Battles and Leaders,* Vol. II, Part 1, p. 375.
8. Ibid., Part 2, p. 431.
9. *Recollections of a Private.*
10. *Battles and Leaders,* Vol. II, Part 2, p. 432.

4. PILLAR OF SMOKE

One of the things McClellan seems never to have understood, in his dealings with the Lincoln administration, was the weight which the Copperhead movement in the North threw into the scales against him. There is a wealth of literature on this move for a negotiated peace. Two studies which were found especially helpful are *The Hidden Civil War,* by Wood Gray, and *The Movement for Peace without Victory during the Civil War,* by Elbert J. Benton.
Specific references are:
1. *Pictorial History of the Civil War,* Vol. II.
2. See *A Military History of the 8th Ohio Volunteer Infantry,* by Franklin Sawyer, and *Recollections of a Private.*
3. *Under Five Commanders,* by Jacob H. Cole.
4. *A History of the 5th Regiment New Hampshire Volunteers.*
5. *General Philip Kearny.*
6. *Four Years Campaigning in the Army of the Potomac.*
7. *Notes of a Staff Officer of Our First New Jersey Brigade,* by E. Burd Grubb.
8. *Diary of Gideon Welles,* Vol. I, p. 107.
9. *Abraham Lincoln and Men of War Times.*

CHAPTER FOUR

1. INDIAN SUMMER

The innumerable regimental histories now gathering dust on the shelves of libraries and secondhand bookshops are a rich mine of material on the kind of men who enlisted in 1861, the spirit with which they came forward, and the strangely innocent way in which the process of turning them into soldiers was undertaken. In many ways, most of these histories are very dull—poorly written, uncritical, full of an inexpert rehash of military history culled from standard texts. But despite these faults they provide the flavor of the young army as nothing else could do, giving the homely and often almost incredible little touches which make those far-off soldiers suddenly come alive. They have been a principal reliance in the preparation of this book and were used extensively in the preparation of this chapter.

Specific references are:

1. For a newspaper roundup of these rather effervescent activities, see Vol. V of *Rebellion Record.*

2. *Four Years with the Army of the Potomac.*

3. *The Bivouac and the Battlefield.*

4. References to the friendly reception in Maryland have been taken from *Musket and Sword,* by Edwin C. Bennett; *Following the Greek Cross; The 27th Indiana Volunteer Infantry in the War of the Rebellion,* by a Member of Company C; *History of the 3rd Regiment of Wisconsin Veteran Volunteer Infantry; History of Duryée's Brigade,* by Franklin B. Hough; *Service with the 6th Wisconsin Volunteers,* and *Battles and Leaders,* Vol. II, Part 2, p. 556.

5. For the story of this regiment, see the delightfully artless little book, *A History of the "Bucktails,"* by O. R. Howard Thomson and William H. Rauch. Incidentally, while the name "Bucktails" belonged to this regiment alone, the rest of the army often applied it indiscriminately to the entire division of Pennsylvania Reserves.

6. Another charmingly unsophisticated history is *The 27th Indiana Volunteer Infantry in the War of the Rebellion.*

7. *The Irish Brigade and Its Campaigns,* by Captain D. P. Conyngham.

8. For a good side light on the way in which a regiment was sometimes recruited, see *History of the 40th (Mozart) Regiment,* by Fred C. Floyd.

9. *History of the First Regiment Minnesota Volunteer Infantry.*

10. *History of the 3rd Regiment of Wisconsin Veteran Volunteer Infantry.*

11. For these incidents, see *History of the 12th Massachusetts Volunteers* and *Four Years Campaigning in the Army of the Potomac.*

12. *History of the 10th Massachusetts Battery,* by John D. Billings. See also *Recollections of the Civil War,* by Mason Whiting Tyler.

13. For a fine study of the Civil War soldier and his songs, see "War Music and War Psychology in the Civil War," by James Stone, in the *Journal of Abnormal and Social Psychology,* October 1941.

14. *Under the Old Flag.*

15. *Battles and Leaders,* Vol. II, Part 1, p. 6.

16. *Recollections of a Private.*

17. *History of the 3rd Regiment of Wisconsin Veteran Volunteer Infantry.*

2. CRACKERS AND BULLETS

The fact that the Civil War soldier was compelled to solve, under fire and without much help, a set of quite modern-looking tactical problems raised by the improvement in his weapons is a point that deserves more emphasis than it usually gets in Civil War histories. Two interesting discussions of this matter, written by professional British soldiers shortly before World War I, are *The Campaign in Maryland and Virginia,* by Lieutenant E. W. Sheppard, and *The War of Secession,* by Major G. W. Redway. See also *The Generalship of Ulysses S. Grant,* by Colonel J. F. C. Fuller.

Specific references are:

1. *Reminiscences of the 19th Massachusetts Regiment.*

2. For a good review of Civil War rations, cookery, and camp life in general, see John D. Billings's entertaining *Hardtack and Coffee.* Good details are also to be found in *The Diary of an Enlisted Man.*

3. *Regimental Losses in the American Civil War,* by Lieutenant Colonel William F. Fox.

4. *Reminiscences of the Civil War,* by General John B. Gordon.

5. From "Field and Temporary Hospitals," by Deering J. Roberts, M.D., in Vol. VII, *Photographic History of the Civil War.*

6. The reader who is interested can study these tactical details in such standard Civil War texts as *Rifle and Light Infantry Tactics,* by Brevet Lieutenant Colonel William J. Hardee; *Manual of Instruction for the Volunteers and Militia of the United States,* by Major William Gilham, and *Camp and Outpost Duty for Infantry,* by Brigadier General Daniel Butterfield.

7. *History of Duryée's Brigade.*

3. GENERALS ON TRIAL

A considerable volume of correspondence between Halleck and Pope, covering the period of the second Bull Run campaign and ending with Pope's exile to the Indian wars on the Western frontier, is available in the *Official Records,* Series I, Vol. XII, Part 3; and while nothing of very great importance is contained in it, it is worth reading for the picture it gives of the queer deficiencies of the army's high command. Studying it, one senses that the army's chief command problem just then was at the very top, embodied in the person of the general-in-chief. If McClellan was overcautious, Halleck was just a plain fussbudget; and if the need of the day was for someone to infuse drive and energy into army commanders, Halleck's own dispatches make it clear that he was the last man for the job. Gideon Welles seems to have been almost alone in his realization that it was the iron-hard spirit of war that was needed, and Vol. I of his *Diary* has been drawn on for quotations. For a consideration of the danger of foreign intervention in the fall of 1862, see James Ford Rhodes's *History of the Civil War.*

Specific references are:

1. *Under the Old Flag.*

2. Quoted in *The Hidden Civil War.*

3. *Military Reminiscences* of General Cox.

4. *Under Five Commanders.*

5. *Correspondence of John Sedgwick, Major General.*

CHAPTER FIVE

1. AT DAYBREAK IN THE MORNING

Extensive use has been made in this work of Major General James H. Wilson's spirited memoirs, *Under the Old Flag.* Wilson was a young engineer lieutenant who served on McClellan's staff for a time and who later became a very distinguished cavalry leader. As a young aide he appears to have been brash and cocky, with a knack for confusing his own functions with those of the major general commanding—altogether, it would seem, an uncomfortable young man to have around headquarters. Opinionated as his book is, however, it casts a most revealing light on the shortcomings of the high command at this period. The staff of the commanding general of the Army of the Potomac was no place for an ardent young perfectionist—not until Grant came along, which is another story.

Specific references are:

1. For details about the finding of the lost order, see "Antietam and the Lost Dispatch," by John McKnight Bloss, in *Papers of the Kansas Commandery, Military Order of the Loyal Legion of the United States.* Brigadier General Silas Colgrove tells the story in *Battles and Leaders*, Vol. II, Part 2.

2. Gibbon's *Personal Recollections.*

3. *Abraham Lincoln and Men of War Times.*

4. For Reno and Barbara Frietchie, see *Personal Recollections of the Civil War*, by James Madison Stone.

5. An enthusiastic account of this surprising little exploit occurs in a quaint pamphlet, *A Sketch of the 8th New York Cavalry*, by Henry Norton.

2. DESTROY THE REBEL ARMY

Regimental histories usually give a very faulty picture of a battle as a whole, since each author is responsible only for what he himself saw and relies on other authority—camp gossip, as often as not—for events which took place out of his sight. But when they are used to supplement the more formal reports and narratives, these histories are invaluable. They bring life and color; with their help these battles of the long ago cease to be bloodless set pieces out of military textbooks and become as real and as moving as something out of today's newspaper.

Specific references are:

1. For these quotations, see *Battles and Leaders*, Vol. II, Part 2, pp. 551 and 558.

2. Details from *A History of the 11th Regiment Ohio Volunteer Infantry.*

3. See *A Soldier's Diary: The Story of a Volunteer*, by David Lane.

4. *History of the 45th Regiment Pennsylvania Veteran Volunteer Infantry*, by Allen D. Albert.

5. See the sprightly *History of the 51st Regiment of Pennsylvania Volunteers*, by Thomas H. Parker.

6. Writing some years after the war, General Hill made this argument himself, but indignant Southerners—who were inclined to blame him for losing Special Orders No. 191 in the first place—howled him down. It does seem, however, as if he almost had a point.

7. For the experiences of the Black Hat Brigade, see Gibbon's *Personal Recollections* and Dawes's *Service with the 6th Wisconsin Volunteers.*

8. Gibbon's *Personal Recollections.*

9. See *History of the 5th Regiment New Hampshire Volunteers* and *Pennsylvania at Antietam.*

10. *Battles and Leaders*, Vol. II, Part 2, p. 558; *The Bivouac and the Battlefield;* *History of the 51st Regiment of Pennsylvania Volunteers*, and *History of the 12th Massachusetts Volunteers.*

11. *History of the 3rd Regiment of Wisconsin Veteran Volunteer Infantry* and *Joseph K. F. Mansfield: A Narrative of Events Connected with His Mortal Wounding*, by John Mead Gould.

3. TENTING TONIGHT

The literature on Antietam is, of course, extensive, but most of it pays little attention to the wasted day of September 16, when McClellan was flexing his army's muscles. The various articles in *Battles and Leaders*, Vol. II, Part 2, are helpful, particularly the one by General Cox. Palfrey's *The Antietam and Fred-*

ericksburg is excellent and draws attention to the strange mix-up which occurred in connection with the command of the three "wings" of the army. Henderson's *Stonewall Jackson* makes clear the opportunity which McClellan lost by his inactivity on this day. It should go without saying, probably, that anyone who writes about the Army of the Potomac will get an invaluable indirect light on that army from Douglas Southall Freeman's books about its great opponents—*R. E. Lee* and *Lee's Lieutenants.*

Specific references are:

1. For an analysis of the discrepancy between the numbers on McClellan's rosters and the numbers that could actually be put on the firing line, see Francis Winthrop Palfrey's *The Antietam and Fredericksburg.*

2. *Under the Old Flag.*

3. For Burnside's account of this, see his article in *Battles and Leaders,* Vol. I, Part 2, pp. 660–63. One would give a good deal for a stenographic report of his staff's remarks about the transfer.

4. *A Military History of the 8th Ohio Volunteer Infantry.*

CHAPTER SIX

1. TOWARD THE DUNKER CHURCH

Considering the fact that Antietam was a head-on, slam-bang fight with no involved tactical maneuvering, it is a battle whose details are uncommonly hard to trace. Principal reliance, of course, is placed on the innumerable reports in the *Official Records,* Series I, Vol. XIX, Part 2; but one is hampered by the fact that each commander, from corps down to regiment, seems to have assumed that his own outfit had the hardest assignment and gave and received the deadliest blows. In addition, there are great discrepancies from report to report in the descriptions of the ground, statements of numbers involved, and accounts of time sequences. And if the reports of the Federal commanders are hard to reconcile, it is even harder to dovetail them with the Confederate reports; one sometimes has the feeling that the Federals and Confederates are describing two different battles.

Palfrey's *The Antietam and Fredericksburg* is perhaps the best account of the battle. General Cox wrote of it extensively, both in *Battles and Leaders* and in his own *Military Reminiscences.* An excellent narrative is contained in Lieutenant Colonel William Allan's *The Army of Northern Virginia in 1862,* and the descriptions in Freeman and Colonel Henderson are extremely detailed and vivid.

Specific references are:

1. For details, see *History of the First Regiment Minnesota Volunteer Infantry; The 27th Indiana Volunteer Infantry in the War of the Rebellion; Life and Letters of Wilder Dwight, Lieutenant Colonel, 2nd Massachusetts Infantry,* and *Service with the 6th Wisconsin Volunteers.*

2. "How Does One Feel under Fire?" by Captain Frank Holsinger, in the *Kansas Loyal Legion Papers.*

3. There is a good picture of this fighting in *Service with the 6th Wisconsin Volunteers.*

4. General Gibbon described the fighting of Battery B in his *Personal Recollections.* See also *The "Ulster Guard" and the War of the Rebellion,* by Theodore B. Gates, and Theodore M. Nagle's *Reminiscences of the Civil War.*

5. This may be a good place to indicate the vast difference between the numbers listed as "present for duty" and the numbers actually engaged. On the books, Hooker had 14,856 men in his I Corps, and it is usually assumed that he sent approximately that number into the fight. Actually, it is very hard to see how he could have had more than 9,000 men in action. He had three divisions—those of Meade, Ricketts, and Doubleday. In the official reports Meade stated that his divi-

sion went into action "under 3,000 strong," and Ricketts said that he took 3,158 men into the fight. Doubleday did not give the strength of his division, but it seems quite certain that it was no stronger on the firing line that morning than the other two. It contained four brigades. One—Hoffman's—was detached as flank guard and did not get into the fighting at all. Of the other three, at least two were far under strength. Gibbon's four regiments were probably under 1,000 strong, all told: he says he had fewer than 1,200 men at South Mountain, where he had 280 casualties. Phelps's brigade, according to the report of its commander, took only 425 men into action at Antietam. The remaining brigade, Patrick's, consisted of four New York regiments which had seen much service, and 1,500 would be a liberal estimate of the brigade's strength.

6.   For Mansfield in action, see *Joseph K. F. Mansfield: A Narrative of Events Connected with His Mortal Wounding; A Brief History of the 28th Regiment New York State Volunteers,* by C. W. Boyce; *Pennsylvania at Antietam; The 27th Indiana Volunteer Infantry in the War of the Rebellion,* and *History of the 3rd Regiment of Wisconsin Veteran Volunteer Infantry.*

2. THE HEAVIEST FIRE OF THE WAR

A detailed description of the way in which Sumner put his corps into action, with especial reference to the unwieldy formation adopted for Sedgwick's division, is contained in Walker's *History of the Second Army Corps.* The same points are also considered at some length in Palfrey's *The Antietam and Fredericksburg.* Sumner did not survive the war and so is not represented in the polemics which cluster around all Civil War battles; his own ideas about the action, however, are presented in an article by his son, Major General Samuel S. Sumner, in Vol. XIV of the *papers of the Military Historical Society of Massachusetts.*

Specific references are:

1.   *The Antietam and Fredericksburg.*

2.   *History of the First Regiment Minnesota Volunteer Infantry,* by R. I. Holcombe. This author remarked that his entire brigade had been drilled to fight in close order, in the obsolete elbow-to-elbow manner. The Confederates, he added, never made that mistake; "a hundred of them would string out for more than a quarter of a mile, or cover an acre." It may actually be true that the Confederate private's refusal to concern himself overmuch about the niceties of drill was a positive asset on the battlefield.

3.   Two of Sedgwick's three brigade commanders, Generals Gorman and Dana, in their official reports characterized the Confederate fire here as the deadliest they ever saw. One of the most striking things about this whole battle, indeed, is the frequency with which Federal survivors described the Southern fire as the worst in their experience. That testimony comes from men who fought in the cornfield and along Bloody Lane, as well as from the men in Sedgwick's division.

4.   *Reminiscences of the Civil War,* by General John B. Gordon. The good general's memory may have betrayed him in regard to the use of the drum during this charge.

5.   For a gay account of this incident, see *The Irish Brigade and Its Campaigns.* In his *Days and Events,* Colonel Livermore records that General Sumner once exploded at Gosson: "Mr. Gosson, if you were not such an incorrigible rascal I would cashier you." A graduate of Dublin University, Gosson had seen service in a European hussar regiment.

6.   This amazing anecdote appears, not (as one would suppose) in some imaginative regimental history, but in the official report of Captain William M. Graham of Battery K, 1st U.S. Artillery. It can be found in the *Official Records,* Series I, Vol. XIX, Part 2, pp. 343–44.

7.   Another misconception of the number of Federals engaged at Antietam arises from the common assumption that Franklin's corps was thrown into offen-

sive action. Actually, only one of Franklin's brigades saw any serious fighting—a total of five men were killed in all the rest of the army corps—and most of the loss of the one brigade which did fight was incurred by one regiment, the 7th Maine.

8. *Under the Old Flag.*

3. ALL THE LANDSCAPE WAS RED

One of the things which helped to make the Antietam a badly fought battle appears to have been a misunderstanding as to the nature of the attack which Burnside's IX Corps was supposed to make. Burnside and Cox evidently understood that the attack was simply to be a diversion, to relieve the pressure on the right of the Federal battle line, while McClellan seems to have wanted an attack that would more or less go hand in hand with Hooker's. An argument on this point—which, happily, we need not go into here—became quite heated, during and after the war, and led to coolness between the once firm friends, McClellan and Burnside. Anyone who is interested may study the pros and cons in *McClellan's Own Story* and in Cox's account of Antietam in Vol. II of *Battles and Leaders.*

Specific references are:

1. Major Henry Kyd Douglas of Stonewall Jackson's staff lived in the immediate vicinity of Sharpsburg and had an intimate personal acquaintance with Antietam Creek. In his book, *I Rode with Stonewall,* he is extremely sarcastic about Burnside's difficulty in crossing the stream. ("Go and look at it," he writes, "and tell me if you don't think Burnside and his corps might have executed a hop, skip and jump and landed on the other side."

2. For the story of the whisky, the attack on the bridge, and Ferrero's subsequent promotion, see the engaging *History of the 51st Regiment of Pennsylvania Volunteers.*

3. *Personal Recollections of the Civil War,* by Stone.

4. *Battles and Leaders,* Vol. II, Part 2, pp. 661–62.

5. For a rather pathetic picture of the plight of the rookie soldiers, see *History of the 16th Connecticut Volunteers,* by B. F. Blakeslee. Additional interesting details are to be found in *Forty-six Months with the 4th Rhode Island Volunteers,* by Corporal George H. Allen, and in the official reports of Colonel Edward Harland, commanding Rodman's second brigade, and Colonel Joseph Curtis of the 4th Rhode Island.

6. Interestingly enough, in a letter to his wife from in front of Richmond, just after the battle of Seven Pines, McClellan told of receiving a flag-of-truce message from a Confederate commander in his front, and said: "Well, whom do you think the letter came from? From no one else than A. P. Hill, major-general commanding the Light Division."

7. An examination of that grim barometer of military pressures, the list of killed and wounded, shows what happened in Burnside's corps. Rodman's division was almost torn to pieces by Hill's counterattack, and Sturgis's division lost heavily during the assaults on the bridge, but the divisions of Cox and Willcox had losses which— by the standards of that terrible day—were comparatively light. It is to be noted that no two of these four divisions were at any time under heavy fire simultaneously.

8. *Battles and Leaders,* Vol. II, Part 2, p. 656.

9. *Under the Old Flag.*

10. *Following the Greek Cross.*

4. THE ROMANCE OF WAR WAS OVER

Military critics are still discussing Lincoln's removal of McClellan, and the majority seems to feel that the removal was a profound mistake. Considered strictly from a military point of view, this is possibly correct. The basic problem with McClellan, however, was always more political than military, and to understand and appraise Lincoln's action it is necessary to study the political history of the times rather than the reports of military action. After September 1862 the dominant fact was the Emancipation Proclamation. Nothing in the *Official Records* sheds any real light on the change in commanders. Actually, the explanation is in McClellan's letters, if you read them carefully, and the thing to study now is the fascinating self-portrait which is so unconsciously and revealingly painted in *McClellan's Own Story.* The McClellan quotations in this chapter are, with one exception, drawn from that book. The verse at the end of the chapter is from *Awhile with the Blue,* by Benjamin Borton.

Specific references are:

1. Gibbon's *Personal Recollections; Service with the 6th Wisconsin Volunteers.*
2. *The Life and Letters of George Gordon Meade.*
3. Gibbon's *Personal Recollections.*
4. *The Life and Letters of George Gordon Meade.*
5. *Under the Old Flag.*
6. *Musket and Sword.*
7. *History of the Second Army Corps.* Be it noted that this talk about the romance of war comes from an officer, and a general at that. The private soldier who had fought at Antietam had no more illusions about war's romance than the veteran of Okinawa.
8. See *History of the 3rd Indiana Cavalry,* by W. N. Pickerell, and *Forty-six Months with the 4th Rhode Island Volunteers.* The theory that McClellan was to replace Halleck is recorded in *A Duryée Zouave.*
9. *A Soldier's Diary.*

GLORY ROAD

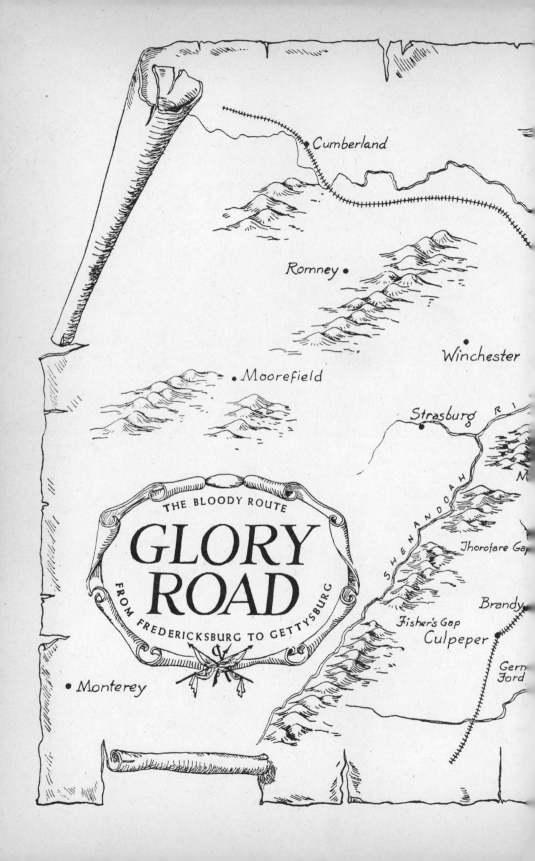

Sue Ramsey

To My Mother

ONE

Deep River

1. FOR WHAT THERE WAS IN IT

RETURNING to his regiment in the fall of 1862 after a furlough in his home city of York, the chaplain of the 102nd Pennsylvania Infantry looked at the ravaged Virginia countryside and noted in his diary that war was very mysterious. It destroyed and wasted, and wherever the armies had gone "the desolation has become almost complete," but back home it was not like that at all. Pennsylvania had put 150,000 men into uniform, and by now a good many of them had gone under the sod, whether with or without appropriate graveside ceremonies. Yet what one actually saw in that state was the hustle and excitement of boom times. Never (to all appearances) had the country been so well off.

"What a marvel is here!" wrote the chaplain. "Something new under the sun! A nation, from internal resources alone, carrying on for over eighteen months the most gigantic war of modern times, ever increasing in its magnitude, yet all this while growing richer and more prosperous!"[1]

As a summary of the effects of war on the national well-being this was neither complete nor wholly accurate, and it might have been bitterly disputed by some of the chaplain's own fellow Pennsylvanians. In the town of Berkeley, in Luzerne County, little more than one hundred miles from boom-town York, insurgent citizens recently had rioted in protest against the military draft and had subsided only after the militia had fired upon them, with four or five insurgents left dead in the streets. Nor was this spirit of dissent confined entirely to Pennsylvania, where it was noted that the anthracite fields were filled with unrest. Similar riots had taken place in the West, notably in the picturesque lakeside town of Port Washington, Wisconsin, and if the country was in fact benefiting by the war, the benefits seemed to be highly uneven and the distribution of them most inequitable.[2]

Yet in a sense the good chaplain was quite correct. He had put his finger on something which contained the germ of much history. Whether he was in fact commenting on an effect of the war or on a strange, elusive symptom of something which had actually helped to cause the war may be another matter. At the very least he had spotted something important, and he was justified in using exclamation points. He had seen one side of the war very clearly.

The trouble in that autumn of 1862 was that there were so many sides to see. Lord Lyons, British Minister to the United States, was being given a glimpse of quite a different side, and in mid-November he was reporting on it to Her Majesty's Foreign Secretary, Lord Russell. The Federal government had finally nerved itself, once and for all, to remove General McClellan from command of the Army of the Potomac, and the deep significance of this act had not been lost on various Northern leaders of the Democracy. They had seen it clearly enough as an indication that the administration was now determined to crush the rebellion completely. The last chance for compromise had ridden out of the war on the special train that carried McClellan out of the Virginia theater to his home

221

at Trenton, New Jersey; and these Northern Democrats were dismayed, since a ruthless war to the bitter end might not be a war which they could enthusiastically support.

In his dispatch to Lord Russell, Lord Lyons tried to analyze the attitude of the leaders of the Democratic party, North.

"At bottom," he wrote, "I thought I perceived a desire to put an end to the war, even at the risk of losing the Southern states altogether; but it was plain that it was not thought prudent to avow this desire."

Nothing would come of this immediately, his lordship believed; but the Democrats who quietly confided in him—cautious men who talked obliquely, stopping short of flat commitments, letting inferences and gestures speak for them—had implied that if their party came into power in the North "they would be disposed to accept an offer of mediation, if it appeared to be the only means of putting a stop to hostilities."[3]

Thus a great deal depended on the point of view, for war's different sides had different meanings. To one point of view war meant boom times, intense activities, and good money in the pocket; to another it meant slow death for sacred American ideals. And to still another it meant personal opportunity, with sure advantage coming to him who was canny enough to play the angles correctly. For it was becoming clearer and clearer that the profound changes which were being wrought by this war were in effect creating a new country here, with all of the opportunities that are usually to be found in a new country. There was a folk saying which followed the expanding frontier: "It's good to be shifty in a new country." In 1862 there were any number of openings for the shifty.

As witness the case of Major General Joseph Hooker.

General Hooker that fall had been enjoying a slow recuperation from a light wound received at Antietam. He spent his convalescence in Washington, where he found comfortable quarters in the national insane asylum—a fact of which, luckily, nobody bothered to make anything in particular—and as a wounded hero and a man undeniably gifted with charm he had been lionized to a degree; most especially by certain people who could do an ambitious general a great deal of good.

There had been, for instance, the Secretary of the Treasury, Mr. Salmon Portland Chase, who came to see the general bearing a large basket of fruit and accompanied by his daughter, the beautiful Katherine Chase. Pictorially, the meeting was indubitably a success—handsome general, pink and clean-shaven, bandaged foot resting elegantly on a cushioned stool; stalwart cabinet minister looking almost unutterably dignified and distinguished, inclining his head and saying: "General, if my advice had been followed, you would have commanded after the retreat to James River, if not before"; and Katherine, young and tall and altogether lovely, devoted to her father, the most talked-about and ultimately the most tragically unfortunate young woman in wartime Washington. . . . The American album would be richer if a cameraman had been present.

General and Secretary sparred gently, each one devoting his not inconsiderable talents to the job of finding out where the other stood and just how he could be useful. It seems that they came finally, in this and in later meetings, to an unspoken understanding. Each one was inordinately ambitious, but their ambitions did not conflict—one wanted to lead the country's armies, the other wanted to live in the White House, and it might be that they could rise together. Chase confided to his diary that Hooker struck him as "a frank, manly, brave and energetic soldier, of somewhat less breadth of intellect than I had expected, however, though not of less quickness, clearness and activity"—which was not too bad an appraisal. Hooker, being no diarist, did not record his impression of Mr. Chase. He did, however, shortly after the meeting, issue a public statement strongly supporting the Emancipation Proclamation.[4]

For if Hooker had no great breadth of intellect, he was at least shrewd; shrewd enough, in any event, to perceive the trend of the tide that was setting in just then and to place himself in proper relationship to it. Beginning with the fall of 1862, it was obvious that the great war for reunion was also to be a war against slavery, and the implications of that fact were there for any man to read. What Lord Lyons's confidants had made out, Joe Hooker had made out also. Final control of things was very likely to rest in the hands of men who could forgive any sin to him whose heart was right on the matter of the Negro. If a belief in emancipation were essential to salvation, henceforward General Hooker would have such a belief.

Sign and symbol of his conversation could be seen in his new friendship for the Vice-President, Mr. Hannibal Hamlin of Maine. Mr. Hamlin had no more actual authority than any other vice-president of the United States, and yet he was a man worth cultivating. He was a stalwart among the abolitionists, and if he lacked power he did not lack influence. The group in Congress which was visibly and with apparent success moving to make this war its own personal possession was close to him; it would hear a word spoken in his ear, it would probably show gratitude for any favors which he might receive. So when Vice-President Hamlin visited Hooker's sickroom accompanied by Brigadier General Hiram Berry, seeking a favor, he got an excellent reception.

Hooker and Berry were well acquainted already, of course. Berry had led a brigade in Phil Kearny's division on the peninsula and was by that fact alone marked as a good soldier: in the brief time he had before a Confederate bullet found him, Kearny had made his Red Diamond Division famous, and one of his brigadiers was bound to carry some of that fame with him. Furthermore, Berry reflected some of the glory that had been glimpsed and lost that gloomy June night in front of Richmond, when Kearny and Hooker had gone to McClellan to demand that orders for retreat be canceled. They themselves would lead their troops in a wild assault on the Rebel lines, swords flashing in the smoky dusk along the pine flats, triumph snatched from defeat by a victory-or-death charge at the desperate eleventh hour, destruction for all traitors and everlasting fame for the soldiers who had dared so nobly. Berry had been present when the demand was made, had heard McClellan's icy refusal and Kearny's furious reply that risked a court-martial, and—as a citizen of Maine and a good friend of Mr. Hamlin—had written to the Vice-President some highly informative letters about the whole business, helping thereby to improve Hooker's standing with what was now the dominant group in Washington.[5]

Hooker greeted his callers with warmth. Stretched out on a lounge with his wounded foot on a cushion (the foot now was just about healed), he swung into a breezy discussion of the battle of Antietam. The Vice-President was known to be no admirer of McClellan, and Hooker rose to the occasion, explaining just where and how McClellan's generalship fell short on that bloody field. The subject was a congenial one—Hooker seldom was in better voice than when he was pointing out the defects of his superior officer—and a good deal of time passed. Then at last there was a pause and the inevitable question: Well, gentlemen, what can I do for you?

What he could do, it developed, was to recommend General Berry for promotion. Berry was now a brigadier and wanted to be a major general, and Hooker's recommendation would help. Hooker replied with enthusiasm. The promotion was richly deserved, he declared, and he would do everything in his power to help bring it about. He added that he would even like to see Berry given command of the division which he, Hooker, once had led—a solid testimonial, this last, going beyond mere politics, for it was a crack outfit and still called itself Hooker's division, and a soldier like Hooker was certain to be proud and touchy about such things. It was perfectly characteristic of Hooker to embed one flash of genuine feeling in the middle of a calculated political stroke.

True to his word, when the guests left Hooker at once wrote to Henry Wager Halleck, general-in-chief of the nation's armies. He was quite aware that as far as Halleck was concerned the word of Joe Hooker might not carry too much weight. Halleck had seen a good deal of Hooker in his pre-war California phase, when the dashing army officer had descended almost to the level of beachcomber, and Halleck definitely did not admire him. Indeed, the best surviving evidence that Halleck really did have some of the acumen he was then supposed to have may consist in the fact that from the very beginning he was firmly convinced that sooner or later the flawed character which he had observed along the Sacramento would get General Hooker into serious trouble. Hooker assumed, possibly with some justification, that it was principally Halleck who had kept him from getting command of the Army of the Potomac when McClellan was relieved.

Yet if Halleck was distrustful, he was not opposing Hooker in all things. If the battle of Antietam had had an individual hero, that hero was probably Hooker; and McClellan, either not knowing or not caring that Hooker was one of his bitterest critics, had recommended, before his own removal from command, that Major General Hooker, U.S. Volunteers, be commissioned also as Brigadier General Hooker, U.S. Army—a recommendation which the War Department had accepted and acted upon, so that by the time he returned to active duty Hooker had the new commission in his possession. This was the best possible evidence that Hooker stood well with the administration, for promotion in the regular ranks was the greatest reward the War Department could offer to a professional soldier. Every regular-army officer was at all times conscious that this war, be it nobly won or miserably lost, was in any event going to *end* someday; and when it ended all of the fine volunteer commissions, with the various perquisites and the increased pay and allowances that went with them, would at once evaporate. Upon that day a regular who had gone to bed a major general might wake up to find himself a mere captain once more, responsible only for one flea-bitten battery of artillery and possessing no more than a captain's pay and prospects. Promotion in the regular ranks represented security. No matter what happened, Hooker would be a general the rest of his life; he could retire as a general and he would infallibly be buried as a general, with a starred flag to mark his gravestone.[6]

From a cold and calculating viewpoint, therefore, Joe Hooker had already made a success out of the war. Yet even though the army contained very few officers who were more completely capable of taking a cold and calculating view of things, Hooker was no man to be satisfied with a partial achievement. As Secretary Chase had seen, his ambition was great. Also, a good part of Joe Hooker was perfectly genuine, and a great deal of the criticism which he so freely bestowed on his superiors came simply because his professional competence was outraged by the blunders he had had to witness. He felt that he could handle things better himself, and he had reason for thinking so. If such blunders continued—and it seemed very likely that they would—it was as certain as anything could be that the high command would someday be groping desperately for a man with military abilities like those owned by General Hooker. When that day came, Hooker proposed to be standing where the high command could not help reaching him.

It was good to be shifty in a new country. The Secretary of War, Edwin M. Stanton, with his hot little eyes, and the fire-breathing abolitionist from Michigan, Senator Zachariah Chandler, followed Secretary Chase's lead, dropping in to sound the general out and to size him up. At the same time obscurer men came in to do what General Berry had done: to seek favors and simultaneously to exhibit political backing. One of these was an Indiana colonel named Solomon J. Meredith, who very much wished to be a brigadier general. He was not especially noteworthy in his own right, but he had political connections as good as the very best.

Meredith was a breezy giant of a man in his early fifties. A North Carolinian by birth, he had moved to Indiana as a young man, settling in Wayne County, near the Ohio line, and getting a firm foothold in county politics. He had a gift for it. During the next two decades, while he developed a prosperous farm, he was twice elected sheriff of his county, was sent to the state legislature for several terms, and finally won appointment as United States marshal for the district of Indiana—the kind of political plum that goes only to a man with first-rate credentials. In addition to a record of loyal service with the new Republican party, Meredith's assets included a firm personal and political friendship with one of the Midwest's most remarkable men, Oliver P. Morton, the famous war governor of Indiana.

No general who was properly mindful of his own chances for advancement was going to overlook any claims that might be supported by Governor Morton. As far as the Midwest was concerned, Morton *was* the Union cause incarnate—a man without whom (to the certain knowledge of Abraham Lincoln and others) war west of the Alleghenies could not successfully be carried on. He was a man of savage driving force, and in his code the only binding rule in war was that you had to win. He struck with equal fury at those disloyal to the sacred cause and those who got across the political path of Oliver P. Morton. In sum, he was a man of influence, and if General Hooker had had any doubts about it the recent experience of Major General Don Carlos Buell might have enlightened him.

General Buell had had the command in eastern Kentucky and Tennessee, charged with quieting the troubled border region while Grant, farther west and south, groped down the Mississippi Valley toward Vicksburg. Buell was a West Pointer, a close friend of McClellan, a grave and serious man of considerable ability. He had had many difficulties in recent months, one of the worst of them being a complete inability to get along with Governor Morton. Buell had many Indiana regiments in his command, and Morton, as the governor who had raised and equipped those troops, always tried to retain some control over them even after they had gone on active service far outside Indiana. General and governor had bickered about this off and on for some time.

The matter had come to a head, apparently, at the end of September, when Confederate armies led by Braxton Bragg and Kirby Smith slipped through the loose Federal cordons and came driving up through Kentucky toward the Ohio River, raising Middle Western temperatures to a high pitch, especially Governor Morton's. Morton rushed a number of green Indiana regiments to Kentucky to help meet the invasion, and they had bad luck. One Confederate invading wing caught a column of these men near the town of Richmond, southeast of Lexington, and broke it to pieces, inflicting a thousand casualties and capturing upward of four thousand men. The other invading wing seized a Union fort at Munfordville a fortnight later, capturing four Indiana regiments entire. The Confederates seemed on the verge of making a complete conquest of Kentucky, and Morton hurried there in person, bitterly blaming Buell for the disasters. At the end of September, accompanied by a Union brigadier general bearing the unlikely name of Jefferson Davis, Morton stalked into the Galt Hotel at Louisville looking for trouble.

It seemed likely that he would find it. Davis was Indiana-born and -bred, a regular-army officer who had been in the Fort Sumter garrison in the spring of 1861 and who, coming north after the fort fell, had taken leave of absence and had gone to Indiana to raise and become first colonel of the 22nd Indiana Infantry. Just now he was under a cloud. He had quarreled bitterly with Major General William Nelson, one of Buell's corps commanders, and had been sent north of the Ohio with an official rebuke spattered across his service record. As a good

Hoosier, he had gone at once to Indianapolis to see Governor Morton. Morton was already denouncing Nelson, whom he held largely responsible for the defeat at Richmond, so when he went to Louisville he had Davis come along, and if an Indiana general who was rebuked could stay rebuked they would find out about it. In the hotel lobby they encountered Nelson himself.

Nelson was a huge ox of a man—three hundred muscular pounds on a frame six feet four, a man who alternately glowed with hail-fellow geniality and stormed with titanic rage. A former navy lieutenant turned soldier, he had raised and trained many Union troops in Kentucky. He had a breezy way in battle; in one fight he comforted green troops by telling them: "If they don't hit me you needn't be a bit afraid, for if they can't hit me they can't hit the side of a barn." Buell considered him one of the Union's most valuable officers.

Now he and Davis immediately began to bristle at each other. From bristling they went to snarling, passing profanities hotly, and presently it was the back of Nelson's great hand across Davis's face. Then Nelson stalked majestically away. Davis hesitated, borrowed a revolver from an aide, strode after Nelson, called to him, and when he turned around shot him dead. He then surrendered his revolver and submitted quietly enough to military arrest.

So here was a sensation and a clear case for the sternest military discipline: Buell's most trusted lieutenant shot dead (before a hotel full of witnesses) by a subordinate, in Buell's own headquarters city, on the eve of a fateful battle. And yet somehow nothing whatever came of it.

The fateful battle was fought and the Confederates retreated—not so much because of anything Buell's troops had done to them as because of the strange caution of the Rebel commander, General Bragg. Shortly thereafter Buell was relieved of his command, and the Civil War knew him no more. And Brigadier General Jefferson C. Davis received not so much as a slap on the wrist for killing a major general. Instead he presently returned to duty, ultimately to advancement.[7]

Before he was relieved from duty Buell requested General Halleck to appoint a military court to try Davis for murder. The subject was considered at Washington, and late in October Secretary of the Navy Welles noted that the case was discussed by the Cabinet. But in the end Davis was released to the civil authorities, a grand jury refused to vote an indictment, and any Union general who meditated upon the matter was bound to conclude that this Governor Morton was a man of very solid and far-reaching influence.

So when Colonel Meredith of the 19th Indiana came asking for preferment and displayed himself as an intimate friend of Governor Morton, Joe Hooker was going to listen very attentively and he was going to be obliging if he could. Meredith did want quite a lot, to be sure—a brigadier's commission, to begin with, plus command of the most famous fighting brigade in the army, General John Gibbon's magnificent Iron Brigade, of which the colonel's 19th Indiana was a part.

Command of the brigade was vacant just then, Gibbon having been promoted to divisional command. The only trouble was that Meredith was by no means the logical person to take the brigade. He had been in the brigade's first battle—at Groveton, on August 28, when the four green regiments had stood off Stonewall Jackson's entire corps and had lost 33 per cent of the numbers engaged—and had conducted himself well enough there, suffering a minor injury and rejoining his regiment on the march up through Maryland. But at Antietam, where the brigade had spearheaded Hooker's furious attack on Lee's left, Meredith had not even been present. He had reported himself unfit for duty a day or so earlier because of the hurt received at Groveton and the fatigue of the marching since and had gone off to Washington to recuperate and to angle for promotion. In the stern code of John Gibbon this was about enough to write him off the army roster, especially since the lieutenant colonel who led the regiment in Meredith's absence was killed in action. It was Gibbon's feeling that either Colonel Fairchild of the 2nd Wisconsin or Colonel Cutler of the 6th Wisconsin fully deserved promotion to brigade command and that Meredith did not deserve it at all.

General Gibbon's advice was not asked, however. Hooker took counsel, one supposes, with his own ambition and meditated on the strong long arm of the governor of Indiana, then wrote out the requested recommendation. And so Meredith, early in December, with a brigadier's star on either shoulder, took command of the Iron Brigade, while Gibbon stormed fruitlessly and wrote Hooker down as a man who "sacrificed his soldierly principles whenever such sacrifice could gain him political influence to further his own ends."[8]

Which is as it may be; bearing in mind that everything, or nearly everything, depends on the point of view, and that the reality of the Civil War was different for different people. The war meant boom times for canny civilians, as a chaplain had noted, and it meant high danger for sacred ideals, as leading Democrats had confided to the British minister; and to a General Hooker it meant infinite alluring possibilities, with personal advancement coming surely to the man who was shifty enough to play his cards skillfully. Yet these points of view were not the only ones valid in that fall of 1862. There was also the point of view of the private soldier, whose outlook upon the war was necessarily narrow but who at least stood, as he made his own personal survey of things, a little closer to the ultimate realities of life and death.

There was the point of view, to be more specific, of this same Iron Brigade, to whose command the swanky new brigadier from Indiana was just now ascending.

The brigade had been whittled thin these last few months. In mid-August it had mustered in its four regiments close to twenty-four hundred men. Three battles and five weeks later it stood at less than a thousand, and just before Antietam, General Gibbon had appealed to the high command to give him a new regiment—a Western regiment, if possible, since the Iron Brigade men came from Wisconsin and Indiana and would get on better with men from their own part of the country. A few weeks after Antietam his request was granted, and on October 9 the brigade was drawn up on the parade ground to give formal welcome to its new comrades, the brand-new soldiers of the 24th Michigan Volunteer Infantry.

The welcome was of the coldest, and the ceremony seems to have pleased no one. On one side of the parade stood the four regiments of veterans—19th Indiana and 2nd, 6th, and 7th Wisconsin: rangy, sun-tanned men in worn and dusty uniforms, who lounged in the ranks with that indefinable easy looseness which only veterns possess and who wore the black slouch hats which were the distinguishing headgear of this brigade as if they were badges of great honor—which, as a matter of fact, they were. The veterans looked across the open ground at the newcomers with complete and unconcealed skepticism and hostility. In every line of their bearing—in the set of their jaws, the tilt of their heads, the look about their eyes peering out from under those valued hatbrims—they expressed for all to see the age-old, impersonal, unformulated feeling of the veteran for the recruit: We have had it and you have not, and until you have been where we have been and have done what we have done we do not admit you to any kind of fellowship.

The boys from Michigan got the message perfectly. They came up to line nervously that morning, thoroughly aware that the newness and neatness of their uniforms proclaimed them rookies with the test of manhood still ahead of them. Their very numbers were a count against them. Here they were, one regiment, with nearly as many men present for duty, armed and equipped, as were present in all four of the regiments across the parade. With their arrival the brigade had nearly doubled in size. And with the inexorable illogic of the soldier, it was somehow just then the fault of these boys from Michigan, and a just ground for shame to them, that they brought 900 to the field instead of the veterans' 250.

In addition to which they wore the regulation forage caps instead of the black hats which the brigade had made famous.

Yet this mere matter of being new and green and clumsy would not, of itself, have caused real estrangement between the four veteran regiments and the one new one. The veterans would have been wary, of course, reserving judgment until they had seen these newcomers under fire, treating them with a lofty but not really malicious contempt until after their first battle, and then either outlawing them entirely or receiving them to full brotherhood without reservation. But they would not have given them a cold and savage hostility, which was what even the least sensitive mental antennae were picking up on this field today. For a damning word had come to camp ahead of this new regiment. Here, said camp rumor—unsubstantiated, but accepted as gospel—here were *bounty men.*[9]

The bounty man was comparatively a new addition to the Army of the Potomac. For the most part, the army was still made up of what even then were beginning to be called "the old 1861 regiments": volunteers in the purest sense of the word, men who had enlisted for no earthly reason except that they wanted to go to war, moved by that strange and deceiving light which can lie upon the world very briefly when one is young and innocent. That light was leaving the landscape rapidly in 1862, and volunteering was much slower. To stimulate it, various states, cities, and counties were offering cash bounties to recruits: solid rolls of greenbacks, adding up, in some cases, to as much as a thousand dollars, and in all cases to several hundreds.

Now this business of the bounty somehow summed up all of the contrasting truths about the war—boom times, noble ideals becoming sullied, great opportunities for the calculating; plus the fact, beginning to be visible to private soldiers, that the man who was moved by pure patriotism and by nothing else was quite likely to get the worst of it. For while the bounties were enabling local units of government to fill their quotas, they were also bringing into the army a great many men whose primary concern in enlisting had been neither the saving of the Union nor the satisfaction of some sacred and indefinable inner instinct, but solely the acquisition of sudden wealth. Some of these men, having taken the money, might earn their wages by becoming good and faithful soldiers. Others would slack and skulk and beyond any question would desert the first time occasion offered—going off to some other state to enlist for another bounty, as likely as not. All of the confusion and contradiction of war were mixed up in this bounty system, in the way it worked and in the fact that it had been adopted at all.

The old volunteer regiments of the army were, conceivably, the last reservoir of the original hope, enthusiasm, and incredible lightness of spirit with which the war had begun. Beyond the scheming and the driving and the solid achieving of the governors and the generals and all the others, the war finally would come down to this spirit that lived in the breasts of the enlisted men. It was what the war was ultimately about, and if the war was finally going to be won it was what would win it, the men who had carried the spirit being killed, the spirit somehow surviving. The veteran inevitably drew a sharp distinction between the man who volunteered because this spirit moved him and the bounty boy who joined up for what there was in it; and here, in the Iron Brigade itself, proudest and hardest of the army's warriors, there was a bounty regiment!

Actually, there was nothing of the kind. Camp rumor once again had outrun the truth. Like every one of the thousands of regiments in the Civil War armies, this 24th Michigan had its own history, different from all of the others, just as each soldier had his individual biography, unwritten but unique. In plain fact, instead of being one of the first of the bounty regiments, this outfit was one of the last of the old rally-round-the-flag groups of simon-pure volunteers.

In July 1862 the mayor of Detroit had called an open-air mass meeting of patriotic citizens to consider how Detroit would provide recruits under the most recent call for 300,000 volunteers. The meeting had been a failure—had, indeed, broken up in an actual row. There had been hissings, catcalls, fisticuffs, until finally the speechmaking dissolved in a free-for-all fight, with Southern sympathizers tearing down the speakers' rostrum and manhandling the speakers, and the sheriff and his deputies coming on the scene with drawn revolvers to restore order and send everybody home. Good citizens felt this as a shame and a disgrace. The rowdies who broke up the meeting, they declared, were not native Copperheads but secessionists-in-exile from Canadian Windsor, across the river. Detroit must redeem its good name; it did so, finally, by holding a new, better policed citizens' meeting at which it was agreed that Wayne County should raise an extra regiment in addition to the six called for by the new quota.

A rousing campaign for recruits was put on. Judge Henry A. Morrow, who had seen some service in the war with Mexico, was made colonel of this extra regiment, and Sheriff Mark Flanigan—he who had led the flying wedge of deputies to subdue secession at the lamentable first mass meeting—was announced as lieutenant colonel; and by the end of August the regiment had been fully recruited. Many of the recruits were wage earners with families, and it would be some time before the army paymaster would make his rounds. To avert hardships, Detroit businessmen raised a relief fund and some of the men drew money from it   whence came the report that the 24th was a bounty regiment.

The 24th took off for the East just before the Army of the Potomac fought at Antietam, and it left Detroit in a fine glow of patriotic sentiment. Nearly all of its officers carried presentation swords—Colonel Morrow's the gift of the Detroit bar, Lieutenant Colonel Flanigan's the gift of the deputy sheriffs of Wayne County, while one of the company officers carried one given by the printers of the Detroit *Free Press,* of whose composing room he had been foreman. The regiment was feted along the road en route east: there is mention of an elaborate banquet at Pittsburgh, where every man was presented with a bouquet by a pretty girl and where, as a veteran wrote later, "a portion of the regiment was in a fair way of being captured." The regiment got to Maryland just in time to see the dusty files of the Army of the Potomac marching up to the shattering fight at Antietam. After that battle was over the 24th was moved up to join the army, and it camped on the battlefield in dismaying closeness to a huge pile of amputated arms and legs.

Then came the ceremony by which the 24th joined the Iron Brigade. Colonel Morrow unfortunately felt that the occasion called for a speech and made one, pulling out all the stops to let the brigade know how glad the 24th was to be here. He drew for his pains a dead silence, not a cheer or a ripple to show that anybody had heard him. A diarist in the 24th wrote glumly: "A pretty cool reception, we thought. We had come out to reinforce them, and supposed they would be glad to see us."[10]

The camp comradeship which these recruits had heard so much about would apparently have to be earned. It could be earned only in battle. Meanwhile, the regiment might as well get ready. It was drilled prodigiously; Colonel Morrow gave the boys battalion drill for six hours every day, with an additional four and one half hours of "other evolutions of the school of the soldier." When General Gibbon left the brigade for divisional command early in November, he told Morrow and the other field officers they had the best-drilled regiment he had ever seen for a rookie regiment.

This was heartening as word trickled down through the ranks. But it was not enough. There were those four veteran regiments which refused to warm up. The brigade broke camp and began a long march from the upper Potomac to the Rappahannock as the Army of the Potomac moved glacially southeast in a well-meant effort to get around Robert E. Lee's flank. As it moved it out-marched the wagon trains and the men went hungry. The 24th, which was living those days under an almost unendurable tension anyway, waiting for the chance to fight its way into the brigade's fellowship, set up a chant one rationless morning of "Bread! Bread! Bread!" The veteran regiments, equally unfed and for that matter equally capable of kicking up a noisy row over it, looked at them coldly and refused to join in the clamor. Once more the 24th had been put in its place.[11]

December came, and the Iron Brigade, along with most of the rest of the army, went into camp near a little town called Falmouth, a mile or so upstream from the charming colonial city of Fredericksburg. There were flurries of snow and there was a good deal of cold rain, with abominable mud underfoot, and for the 24th Michigan there began that endless process of attrition which, for some regiments, was even more deadly than battle itself. Boys began to get sick, and many of the sick ones died. Like all new regiments, the 24th held formal military funerals in such cases, until one day a rookie soldier on the firing squad mistakenly loaded his musket with ball cartridge and shot a comrade through the body.[12] This might have caused the veterans to jeer—clumsy soldiers who shot each other at a military funeral!—but it did not happen. The veterans were not even admitting the 24th to the implied comradeship of derision. They were simply cold and aloof.

This new regiment would have only one chance at salvation. Before long, by signs which even the private soldiers could read, the army would go across the Rappahannock to fight. When that day came, the 24th would have to prove itself. Its salvation, like so many other values in this strange and terrible war, would in the end have to be bought by the stand-up valor of the private soldier.

2. JORDAN WATER, RISE OVER ME

A desolate wasteland of war, as bleak and comfortless as what the last man will see when he takes his last look around, lay between Fredericksburg and the Po-tomac River landings. It had been pleasant enough in that other geological epoch before the war: nice rolling country marked off into plantations and small farms, well timbered between the pastures and the tilled fields, with great houses on the hilltops and small cabins placed at intervals along the meandering roads. Men had lived here for two centuries and they had given the region a look of order and prosperity. But the armies had come, and everything had been swept away.

The railroad line that ran from Fredericksburg to the riverside terminus at Aquia Creek, where travelers from the south in the old days had left the cars to go aboard the waddling river steamers for the last leg of the leisurely trip to Washington—this line with its bridges, culverts, and docks had been destroyed, rebuilt, destroyed again, and rebuilt anew. All of the timber had been cut down to make trestles and crossties, to corduroy the unpaved roads, to build wharves and piers and stockades and sheds and huts, to provide fuel for locomotives and steamboats and firewood for the stoves and campfires of the soldiers. Colonel Herman Haupt, superintendent of military railroads, complained that the loco-motives of his construction trains now had to haul all their own fuel up from the landing, to which place it came down-river in barges. Along the road from the landing up to Fredericksburg there remained now not so much as a stick.

Most of the houses had fared as the wood lots had fared. Some had been torn down for building material, some had been burned by accident, and some had simply been destroyed. A newspaper correspondent saw "tall chimneys standing, monuments of departed peace, in the midst of wastes that had been farms." Nothing else remained. The livestock was all gone, the fences had vanished, every bit of household furniture or farm equipment that could be carried away had disappeared. The desolation was complete.[1]

Much of this was just the inevitable wastage of war. The Army of the Potomac sprawled over a wide strip of land to the north and east of Fredericksburg, close to the Rappahannock River, and its main lines of supply ran back to the Potomac River landings, Aquia Creek and Belle Plain. Over the fifteen or twenty miles of atrocious roads which crossed this country, all of the food, clothing, ammunition, and other supplies for 130,000 men had to be carried—of grain and hay alone the quartermasters had to move 800 tons a day—and the endless wagon trains that lumbered back and forth over the cramped roadways, drivers shouting and swearing and fighting one another for the right of way, were a destroying force that rolled over the landscape and mashed it flat. If a culvert collapsed on a road near somebody's house, the house was torn down to provide timber for a new culvert, and that was that. Moving or standing still, the army could not help creating its own wasteland.

But there was beginning to be more to it than that. The army had grown lawless, although it had not been lawless earlier. It had marched the length of the Virginia peninsula the preceding spring, it had spent many weeks in front of Richmond, it had maneuvered for a time near this same Fredericksburg, and there had been a long hike up to western Maryland. In all of it the foraging, pillaging, and wrecking which took place had been of minor consequence. But during the last few weeks the soldiers seemed to be turning into unabashed thieves. What had been done before had been furtive, a matter of individual soldiers sneaking away from their commands, grabbing what they wanted, and then running for cover. Now it was being done quite openly, with soldiers sweeping up chickens, hogs, cattle, sheep, and everything else that they could carry off. Some of the men, it is recorded, had learned how to steal beehives without being hurt. Houses were invaded and ransacked, fruit cellars and corncribs were despoiled, and the disorderly skein of stragglers that raveled out around the army knew very few restraints when desirable rebel property was encountered.

Indeed, the job could not be blamed entirely on stragglers. If much foraging was done in defiance of officers, much of it also was done with their hearty encouragement. Some men of the 6th Wisconsin complained to their colonel that they were short of rations. The colonel pointed to a clump of farmhouses on a hill and said: "I'm going to take a short nap. Don't let me see or hear of your foraging on this march. I think I see a smokehouse near that white residence." The 5th New Hampshire raided a well-stocked hen house and its Colonel Cross scolded the men sharply—because they let one hen escape. Later, after a sheepfold had been raided, when General Hancock wanted to search the camp of the 5th for traces of stolen sheep, Cross stalled him off until his men were able to plant the bloody pelts in the adjacent camp of the 7th New York. That evening Cross enjoyed roast mutton with the rest of the regiment.[2]

A Pennsylvania recruit in General Andrew Humphreys's division recalled that as many as two hundred men from one regiment in his division were arrested on the march with stolen goods in their possession. Yet they were not punished, aside from begin confined overnight, and the stolen property was not confiscated. This soldier wrote that the men were convinced that "it was their bounden duty to forage upon all inhabitants of the enemy's country."[3]

Other explanation there was none. And yet this was a curious business. These outbreaks were not coming from rookies or from third-rate troops. There were no better regiments in the army than the 6th Wisconsin and the 5th New Hampshire, and there were no better colonels than theirs. Humphreys's division, commanded by one of the best men in the army, belonged to the V Corps, where regular-army discipline prevailed. If these men were suddenly getting the notion that it was right to spoil the Egyptians, the army was changing and the change deserved study.

But the high command had more pressing things to think about.

The high command just then was Major General Ambrose E. Burnside, to whom the administration seemed to have given the Army of the Potomac in a mood of sheer desperation. In some ways Burnside was about as imcompetent a general as Abraham Lincoln ever commissioned, and he comes down in history looking stiff and stuffy with frock coat and incredible whiskers, a man who moved from disaster to disaster with an uncomprehending and wholly unimaginative dignity. Yet there must once have been a warm, rather lively human being somewhere back of the major general's trappings. Burnside was gay and frisky as a West Point cadet, and when he was commissioned a second Lieutenant in 1847 and was sent off to Mexico he gambled away his passage money on an Ohio River steamer and had to borrow from a Louisville merchant in order to make the trip. Later, in Mexico City, he played cards so enthusiastically and unskillfully that his pay was in hock for six months in advance, and he would have had to resign in disgrace if a senior officer had not loaned him enough to pay up. He fought Apaches in New Mexico after the war, acquiring a wound and some modest distinction. Transferred east, he wooed a Kentucky belle and took her to the altar, only to be flabbergasted when she returned a firm "No!" to the officiating minister's climactic question. (The same girl later became engaged to an Ohio lawyer, who apparently had heard about Burnside's experience. When the wedding date arrived this man displayed to her a revolver and a marriage license, telling her that it had to be one or the other and she could take her pick. This time she went through with the ceremony.)[4]

In 1852 Burnside invented a breech-loading rifle, resigned from the army to build a factory and manufacture it, and went broke when he lost a War Department contract which had seemed to be certain. George B. McClellan, then vice-president of the Illinois Central Railroad, bailed him out by giving him a job in the railroad's land office, and when the outbreak of the war called him back into military service Burnside had become treasurer of the road.

It must be admitted that the tradition of failure thus seems to have been fairly well established before he ever became a general; yet it also seems that the man who put that record together was at least not a stodgy person. Something essential in his make-up must have got bleached out in the long years since he got into the history books. He was never anything resembling a great general, yet he apparently was an interesting sort of human being.

The soldiers themselves, in this fall of 1862, were beginning to warm up to him. For the most part they were taking their cue from the IX Corps, which had invaded the Carolina islands with him earlier that year and which felt that "Old Burny" was as good as the best. The IX Corps recalled that under Burnside in Carolina the rations had always been good. The general had forever been poking his nose into the mess shacks, sampling the food, checking on the supplies issued by the commissary. A veteran in the 48th Pennsylvania, applauding him for that remembered care, wrote sententiously that "the nearest way to a soldier's heart lays right through his haversack," and a V Corps private agreed that the men were always willing to cheer when they saw Burnside's "manly countenance, bald head, and unmistakable whiskers."[5]

With his new duties as army commander, Burnside was spending no time looking into company kitchens or harassing the commissaries. This was a little oversight for which he was to pay a high price a bit later, and in its small way it illustrated his whole problem. He needed to be a good strategist and an able tactician, to be sure—after all, he had to lead his troops into action against Robert E. Lee and yet in some ways it was almost more important for the commander of the Army of the Potomac at that time to be a good housekeeper. This army lived and moved under the weight of a peculiar curse. So many incompetents wore shoulder straps, and there was so much lost motion between orders and their execution, that unless the commanding general did spend part of his time looking into the matter of his soldiers' rations, those rations were going to deteriorate very swiftly.[6]

As with rations, so with weightier things. As a sample, there was the relationship between pontoon boats and high strategy.

The high strategy by which Burnside was moving in mid-November of 1862 was not too bad. Burnside had inherited the army in the general vicinity of Warrenton, with an advance in progress down the line of the Orange and Alexandria Railway. To continue that advance as McClellan had begun it struck Burnside as unwise. The farther the army got, the more it would expose its communications. To General John Pope, some three months earlier, Lee and Stonewall Jackson had demonstrated the evil things that could befall Yankee supply lines that were rashly exposed in that part of the country, and the lesson had not been forgotten.

So Burnside had decided to swing the whole army over to tidewater. There would be wide rivers to cross that way, but the lines of supply would be short and pestilent Rebel raiders could not easily get at them. He would have his advance guard wade the Rappahannock at the fords a little way upstream from Fredericksburg to drive off the Confederate outposts. Then he would lay pontoon bridges at Fredericksburg and cross the rest of the army and the supply trains before Lee's army could reach the vicinity to contest the crossing. He must have, he calculated, twelve days' rations in the wagons, together with a big drove of beef cattle, and Colonel Haupt was assembling workers and material to rebuild the railroad bridge once the town had been secured. All of this done, the army would move southward, and somewhere below the Rappahannock it would meet and fight the Army of Northern Virginia.

On November 12, a few days after he had taken command, Burnside submitted this plan to higher authority. General Halleck was not in favor of it. He was rarely in favor of any plan devised by a subordinate, and he knew perfectly how to qualify any approval he did express so that if disaster came his own record would contain no stain. President Lincoln, who was beginning to catch onto this trait of the general-in-chief, examined Burnside's proposal for himself and on November 14 he telegraphed his approval, remarking that the plan would succeed if Burnside moved fast—otherwise not. On the next day Burnside put the army in motion.

By the morning of November 17 Burnside's advance reached the Rappahannock River fords, and Yankee patrols went prowling down to the bank to exchange gibes with the Confederate sentries across the river. The advance was styled the Right Grand Division and constituted a third of the army, the II Corps under Darius N. Couch and the IX Corps under Orlando Willcox. Commander of the whole was Major General Edwin V. Sumner—Bull Sumner of the white whiskers and the tremendous parade-ground voice, the ramrod-backed old regular who had been commissioned a second lieutenant away back in 1819 and who, in more than forty years of service, had become the very embodiment of the code by which the old-time professional soldier lived. The code was simple. One automatically gave complete loyalty to all persons in superior authority, one obeyed all lawful orders without question, and one never, under any circumstances, was afraid of anything. Made incarnate in the person of an aging major general, the code had its limitations. It did not necessarily produce a man fitted to command a third of an invading army. It did, however, produce a man you could count on, and if the old man's virtues were limited, they were solid. Worse men have worn a major general's stars.

Sumner got his two corps up to the river, and the rest of the army went into bivouac not far behind him, within easy marching distance of the Fredericksburg crossing where the pontoon bridges were to be made. So far the movement had been remarkably deft and speedy—a point that is often overlooked when the dreary mistakes of the Fredericksburg campaign are recounted. Across the river Lee had hardly more than a corporal's guard—a couple of batteries of field artillery, a skimpy regiment of cavalry, and a few hundred infantrymen. Far upstream Jeb Stuart was scouting to learn whether the Yankees had in fact left Warrenton. A division from James Longstreet's corps, plus the army artillery reserve, was under orders to march from Culpeper to Fredericksburg, but it would not show up for several days. Jackson and his half of the army had not yet left the Shenandoah Valley. The way was open. Sumner's men could wade the river, the rest of the army could cross the river on the pontoon bridges at Fredericksburg, ample supplies could be carried across in the wagons, and Lee's army would find itself neatly outflanked.

Thus it was not at all a bad program which Burnside had mapped out. Its execution, however, depended on the immediate appearance, on the Yankee side of the river opposite Fredericksburg, of several dozens of the clumsy wooden scows with which the army built its pontoon bridges. And these scows were not there, nor did it appear that they were anywhere else where a harassed army commander could quickly get hold of them. In the entire military hierarchy, from general-in-chief down to humblest private, nobody seemed to know exactly where these scows were, except for a weary regiment of volunteer engineer troops, and these lads—wrestling personally with the ungainly things scores of miles from the spot where Burnside's army was waiting—had no idea that anybody in particular wanted them or that there was any especial hurry about anything.

No pontoons, no bridges; no bridges, no crossing of the river. The equation, to Burnside, seemed complete. A gambler might have felt otherwise, might have sent Sumner and his advance guard across at once, trusting that the old man could hold his position and feed his men until the missing pontoons did show up. But it would have taken a gambler to order it. It was beginning to rain. A late November rain is apt to be a long one, and the Rappahannock is quite capable of rising six feet in twenty-four hours when the rain comes down. If Sumner's forty thousand crossed and the Rappahannock did rise, the fords would cease to be fords, Sumner could neither be supplied, reinforced, nor withdrawn, and Lee might well find himself in position to destroy a solid third of the Union Army. It seemed to Burnside that, having moved his army here in lawful expectation of pontoons, he could do nothing now but sit down by the waters as hopefully as might be and wait for them.[7]

In which posture, then, he paused by the river, not looking his best but definitely more sinned against than sinning. He waited because other men had failed and because he himself, decent, amiable man, could not conjure up the storm that would blow slackness and incompetence out of the channels of command. The general waited and the army waited, and on the opposite shore the Army of Northern Virginia began to assemble in all of its strength, and it waited likewise. What could once have been done with ease became presently a matter of great danger and difficulty. The overdue pontoon train which was the cause of all of this delay moved down from the upper Potomac like a bewildered snail, the men who were directly responsible for it doing their best but making little progress.

These bridge tenders belonged to the 50th New York Engineers, one of the few volunteer sapper regiments in the army. The 50th New York had had the boats, balks, planks, wagons, and other equipment some fifty miles northwest of Washington, and just now it was this regiment's singular fate to epitomize the way in which things went wrong in this army.

The engineers had had a bridge across the Potomac at Berlin, Maryland, ever since early October, and when McClellan moved his army down from western Maryland to the Warrenton area this had been the principal crossing. There was another pontoon bridge six miles upstream at Harper's Ferry, with a subsidiary bridge there over the Shenandoah as well. At Berlin, in addition to the bridge, there were fifty-six additional boats in the Chesapeake and Ohio Canal, plus a land train of twenty boats stacked up, ready to go, on ponderous wagons, together with other wagons full of supplementary equipment. The army had gone on south and the engineers sat idly and happily by their unused bridges and spare boats and waited for orders.

When orders finally came they were six days late: first in the series of blunders which the army was eventually to pay for at Fredericksburg. GHQ had decided on November 6 to move the pontoon train down to Washington so that it could quickly be brought down into Virginia in case of need, but some functionary at GHQ forgot that there was such a thing as a military telegraph line and simply put the orders in the mail. As a result, it was November 12 before orders got to Berlin and were opened by Major Ira Spaulding, commander of the 50th New York Engineers. Six days behind schedule, then, Major Spaulding learned what he was supposed to do.

GHQ wanted to keep the bridges at Harper's Ferry, so Spaulding was to detail a company to take charge up there, sending with that company certain additional boats and planking for maintenance. The Berlin bridge was to be dismantled and its component parts were to be taken to Washington, along with all of the spare boats, wagons, and odds and ends of surplus equipment which were at Berlin. When Major Spaulding had got his regiment and all of this equipment to the Volunteer Engineer Brigade depot in Washington, his instructions said that he was to make up a pontoon train on wheels as rapidly as possible and stand by ready to move on a moment's notice.

The major went to work promptly. By evening he had his bridge disassembled and a train of thirty-six boats was in the canal moving down toward Washington. Next morning another train of forty boats and matériel got off and the wagons were made ready to begin the journey overland. The company which had been detailed to stay at Harper's Ferry was made responsible for getting the last odds and ends rounded up and shipped; the rest of the regiment was on the way, either floating down the canal with the water-borne scows or slogging along overland with the great wagons. After making a final checkup Spaulding himself went to Washington by railroad, and late that night he reported to his boss, Brigadier General Daniel P. Woodbury. Woodbury looked at Spaulding's orders, and thus himself learned for the first time that a pontoon train was to be prepared for possible service with the army. The hour being late, he told Spaulding to come back next morning and they would see what new orders there might be.

Next morning was November 14: the same day President Lincoln was telling Burnside that his plan of action was approved but that if he moved he had better move fast. While Spaulding waited at Woodbury's headquarters, Woodbury went off to see Halleck, who by now knew that Burnside had permission to move via Fredericksburg and who had previously been warned that if this move were made Burnside would have to have the pontoons immediately. Just what Halleck had on his mind that morning nobody ever quite made out, but in any case, Woodbury finally returned to his own office and told Spaulding to put his boats and wagons in depot as fast as they reached town and to put his men into camp. This, of course, countermanded the original orders to make up a new train and stand by.

The first lot of boats came in that evening and more arrived next morning, November 15, as did a telegram from an engineer officer on Burnside's staff asking how about those pontoons. By night all of the men and matériel which had been at Berlin were in Washington. The matériel was stowed away in the engineer depot on the Anacostia River just above the navy yard, and the 50th Engineers were in camp nearby. That evening General Woodbury gave Spaulding a new set of orders: make up two pontoon trains of twenty-four boats each to go down to Belle Plain by water, the boats being made up in rafts, each boat to be loaded with its own allotment of planking, timbers, ropes, and other gear. As far as General Woodbury knew, the boats were wanted at Belle Plain, not elsewhere. Consequently, no wagons were sent with them, which meant that when they did reach Belle Plain there would be no way to carry them over to the Rappahannock.

Getting these boat-rafts together was a chore, but the engineers kept at it smartly and next morning the steamer *Hero* showed up, took the rafts in tow, and went off downstream. This done, Spaulding was ordered to make up a train of twenty more boats, with transportation for forty, to go down to the Fredericksburg area by land. It took much longer to get this ready. First the major had to go to the quartermaster depot and draw two hundred horses. Then he had to indent for two hundred sets of harness, which were delivered at the engineer depot in their original boxes and so had to be unboxed and fitted together before they could be put on the horses—many of which, it then developed, had never been in any kind of harness before and had strong objections to being harnessed now. While this was going on, the major had to get teamsters detailed from the casuals' camp at Alexandria, had to draw rations and forage, and had to keep his own men busy loading the cumbersome boats and their equipment on wagons. All in all, it was the afternoon of November 19 before the train finally went creaking down from the engineer depot, rumbled across Long Bridge, crept on through Alexandria, and at last camped for the night in a pelting rain half a dozen miles from its starting point.

Now Major Spaulding and his men had been working very hard, and they had even harder work ahead of them, but they were men who toiled in a gray nightmare and all that they did was vanity and a mockery. For while they were making up their train, and while the paddle-boat *Hero* with its ungainly rafts was chugging down the Potomac—to go hard aground, at last, and wait some hours for release—while all of this was happening, General Burnside and General Sumner were waiting by the Rappahannock fords with forty thousand good soldiers who could either cross the river free now or cross it at a dreadful price a little later on, and who were barred from doing it now because Major Spaulding, his engineers, and the pontoons were still many miles away.

The nightmare was to get worse. The next day was November 20, and Sumner still waited at Falmouth with his forty thousand men, while Joe Hooker moved in close behind him with forty thousand more. Across the river the leading elements of Longstreet's corps were beginning to dig themselves in on the range of low hills that runs north and south behind the town of Fredericksburg. The time left to the Army of the Potomac was beginning to be very short indeed. And on the Telegraph Road south from Alexandria the rain was continuous and the road was turning to clinging, bottomless mud. The wagons mired down—there were few heavier, unhandier things on wheels in those days than an army wagon carrying a pontoon boat—and in places the soldiers had to lift them along by sheer muscle. The steamer *Hero* docked her pontoons at Belle Plain, but there was no good way to get them to Falmouth; the men in charge of them did not know that anyone over at Falmouth wanted them, and anyway, no one seems to have notified Burnside that they had reached Belle Plain.

The rain continued to fall. Major Spaulding wrote plaintively that "the roads are in such a shocking condition that I find I cannot make over five miles a day with my bridge train, and to do even this much I am obliged to haul many of my wagons for miles by hand and work my men half the night."[8] The engineers were struggling knee-deep in mud in a perpetual cold rain, and the worst part of the whole route—the notoriously boggy bottom lands along Chopawamsic Creek—lay ahead of them. Major Spaulding decided that something would have to be done.

It must be remembered that, as far as the major knew, time was no particular object. General Woodbury wrote later that "no one ever informed me that the success of any important movement depended in the slightest degree upon a pontoon train to leave Washington by land." Both he and Major Spaulding supposed that this was simply a routine movement involving no especial reason for hurry.[9] Even so, a conscientious engineer officer was apt to balk at a routine movement which took all winter, which was what his trip down the Telegraph Road was beginning to look like. So Spaulding at last gave in and sent an officer back to Washington to get a steamboat and bring it down to the mouth of Occoquan Creek. At that point they would make their boats up into rafts, load the dismantled wagons and the rest of the matériel aboard, have the steamboat tow them down to Belle Plain, and send the horses along by land.

They did it that way in the end, having a prodigious amount of trouble rafting their boats through the shallows at the mouth of the Occoquan. By November 24 they had everything afloat and were on their way, and late that night they reached the sprawling wharves at Belle Plain. The horses had not arrived yet—even without any wagons to pull, it was weary plugging down that muddy highway—but Spaulding was able to draw other horses from the base quartermaster, and he kept his men working most of the night. The following afternoon he was able to report at Burnside's headquarters with the long-lost pontoons close behind him.[10]

Apparently he got meager thanks for his effort. He had obeyed orders and he and his men had worked very hard to do it, but by now the situation had developed in such a way that everybody concerned would have been much better off if the engineers and their boats had remained stuck in the mud all winter. All of Longstreet's corps was in position across the river now, and Lee was there with it. Jackson had begun to pull his troops out of the Shenandoah Valley, where he had been hoping against hope that the misguided Yankees would try to attack him, and was en route to Fredericksburg.

So Burnside's plan, which had been good enough a week ago, was no good at all any more. He had never had any idea of fighting his way across the river here. He just wanted to get across and then do his fighting somewhere farther to the south, and this had seemed like a good place to do the crossing. Yet now, when a crossing right here was looking more and more inadvisable, Burnside and his army waited stolidly on the riverbanks, and the charming little colonial town began, in spite of logic, to take on more and more military importance, as if something in its atmosphere had from the beginning been fated to draw the charge of lightning from the gathering storm clouds.

The railroad from Aquia Creek to Richmond crossed the river at Fredericksburg—or at least it had done so in the old days, before war smashed the bridge—and it was much on Burnside's mind. He was suggesting now to Colonel Haupt that a supply of railroad iron had better be floated up the Rappahannock under navy convoy for use in relaying the track south once Lee had been driven away. Haupt was objecting to this, pointing out that they could not rebuild the line south until they had first rebuilt the bridge, and that once the bridge had been rebuilt they could bring the new rails in by train and save a laborious transshipment at the riverside. Still, Burnside was boss, and "it shall be done if you desire it."[11]

Haupt had found Burnside a good man to deal with. To a subordinate about this time he wrote that "General Burnside is one of the most reasonable and practical men I have ever met." Haupt was a man of many expedients, and he had invented a species of car ferry which was saving much time and labor in the supply of this army. At Alexandria, Haupt had assembled a number of Schuylkill River coal barges. These had been lined up in pairs, side by side, each pair bound firmly together with long timbers bolted transversely, railroad tracks laid lengthwise on top. Each pair of barges thus treated made one serviceable car float capable of carrying the sixteen loaded freight cars which made up a military supply train. The trains, then, as they came down from the north to Alexandria, were simply run on the floats there and were towed down to the railroad docks at Aquia Creek. It took about an hour to transfer a train to the float, six hours for towage, and another hour to get the train back on the tracks again. Without breaking carloadings, a freight train of supplies for the army could get from Washington to Falmouth between dawn and dusk.[12]

A capable operator, this Haupt. The Northland may have had trouble finding competent generals just then, but when it sent up an industrial technician it invariably sent up a good one. Just now Haupt rather doubted that there would be much new track to lay once the army got possession of Fredericksburg. The line south from Fredericksburg was still intact, and if a battle were fought and the Rebels were driven off, it seemed improbable that in their retreat they would have time to destroy much track. However, to play safe he agreed that he would order an extra ten miles of rails, just in case.

Haupt's letter was significant on a couple of points. The casual reference to the purchase of ten miles of railroad rails as a form of insurance demonstrated that the United States was an industrialized nation waging industrial warfare, even though that fact was not yet understood. A great deal of industrial muscle was available if ten miles of railroad iron were the small change of the latest military offensive. (In the South the progressive deterioration of the railroads was already a serious problem, and there were not ten miles of spare rails in all the Confederacy.)[13] More immediately, Haupt's unemotional calculation that Lee would probably be driven out of Fredericksburg too abruptly to leave time for railroad destruction was an indication that the high command was already accepting as inevitable what it had not even dreamed of a fortnight earlier: a bloody battle for mere possession of the opposite bank of the Rappahannock.

The high command, of course, was of several minds. Burnside was toying with ideas of feints downstream to draw off the bulk of Lee's strength, feints upstream to draw it in the opposite direction, feints right here to make possible an unopposed crossing elsewhere. Exactly what all of this would amount to was never clear, but the ideas were at least stirring in his mind. Sumner, who had the great virtue of loyalty, stoutly supported Burnside's plan even though he did not quite understand it. Joe Hooker had more than enough military intelligence to perceive the folly of an attempt to force a crossing here, and he left none of the army's ranking commanders in doubt about his feelings. Nor, for that matter, did he leave Washington in doubt. As early as November 19 he had sent a private letter to Secretary Stanton, putting on record his own criticism of his commanding officer. When Hooker wrote he had just come up behind Sumner, and he had his two army corps camped close to United States Ford on the Rappahannock. He told Stanton that, boats or no boats, he ought to be allowed to take his men across the river and go driving south without worrying about pontoon bridges or anything else. He could live off the country; he would be entering, he said, a rich agricultural district unspoiled by war, and the foraging would be good. In general, he could smash things up so thoroughly that the enemy would have to hurry back to protect Richmond and would not be able to defend the Rappahannock crossings here or anywhere else.[14]

In many ways Hooker's idea was perfectly sound. But Hooker—was Hooker; strange mixture of the conniver and the sincere patriot. In sending to the Secretary of War a pointed criticism of his own commander, he was violating both military law and military etiquette, not to mention the canons of ordinary civilized behavior. And since there was obviously no chance whatever that the Secretary of War, getting Hooker's letter, would promptly reverse Burnside and order the movement which Hooker suggested, what Hooker was really trying to do with all of this irregularity was to get his own rightness and Burnside's wrongness on record in advance of the catastrophe which Hooker scented on the wind. Burnside, Hooker felt, was not going to last long. After Burnside?

Yet the important thing about this army was never the rivalry of its generals, nor, for that matter, the generals themselves. For this was an army that had to operate strictly on its own. From beginning to end, at one level or another, its command was either erratic or beset with slackness and incompetence. Something like this business of the pontoons was always happening, something was always going irretrievably wrong, owing less to any single shortcoming than to a general failure on the part of someone in shoulder straps. It is impossible to disagree with the historian who remarked that the army was cursed "by a line of brave and patriotic officers whom some good fairy ought to have knocked on the head."[15] What the army finally was to do, if indeed it was to do anything, would at last depend almost entirely on the men in the ranks. Individual leaders who were worthy of them, these men did indeed have here and there, at varying levels of command from company to army corps. But leadership which, as a whole, came even close to being good enough for them—that, from the day the war began to the day it ended, these men never got.

In addition, they had suffered lately a psychic wound, having lost McClellan, the one commander for whom they felt affection and with whom they felt at ease. They had no light to follow now but the light they might find in their own spirits, and that light was guttering very low as they waited by the riverbank with the weather growing colder and the muddy bivouac becoming more and more cheerless. It seems that they began to get a premonition of disaster, a premonition that was less the result of a conscious appraisal of their chances than the product of many small failures and minor irritants, aggravated by the fact that the indecision at general headquarters was too obvious for the most heedless private to miss. They had cheers for Old Burny when they saw him by the roadside, but the cheers were growing perfunctory. The soldiers were a glum crowd now and they rarely felt like cheering anyone.

For one thing, they had not been paid for months. For another, in this movement down from Warrenton a great many units had somehow been marched away from their equipment and were now enduring the sleet and snow without tents or blankets. For still another, the quality and quantity of the rations were visibly deteriorating. Fights broke out as regiments which the commissaries had missed tried to raid the supplies of better-nourished outfits. A diarist in the 9th Massachusetts recalled later: "Never were we any worse off for supplies." A veteran in the 22nd Massachusetts wrote feelingly of their bivouac, from which 588 men of the regiment were absent because of sickness: "This plain became a wallow-hole; the clay surface freezing at night and thawing by day, trampled by thousands of men, made a vast sea of mud. . . .It had to be scraped and washed off to prevent our tents from becoming hog pens." The rookie 146th New York, which had just joined up, learned that army life was not quite as it had been imagined, and its historian recalled: "Many of the older regiments around us were tired of the service and anxious to return home, and the infection spread among the new regiments."[16]

Often enough, spirits went up or down with the quality of the food. For six mortal weeks the 79th New York had had nothing to eat but hardtack and salt meat. One day, by great good luck, a captain in this regiment got some potatoes. He sliced them and fried a huge panful and sat down with his tent mate, the regimental chaplain, to eat them. In blissful silence the two men ate fried potatoes, emptying the pan to the last crinkly slice, carefully dividing and eating that, and then leaning back to light their pipes, feeling that life might be joyous after all. The chaplain had said grace over their meal, and after that the two had spoken not a word; but at last the captain took his pipe from his mouth and said gravely: "Chaplain, those potatoes needed *salt.*" The chaplain thought it over, then nodded judicially, and the two men resumed their contented silent smoking.[17]

However, it is quite clear that, taking the army as a whole, something more was wrong than a mere shortage of rations. What was going on was not just the normal grousing of soldiers who have begun to see that war is not quite as much fun as they had expected it to be. This army was beginning to understand its own handicaps, and it was beginning to lose confidence. Most of the rank and file knew no more about what the high command had in mind than the rank and file usually knows, but the rank and file was not in the least stupid and it could read the omens as well as anybody. What lay back of these myriad complaints about mud, bad food, and poor leadership comes out in a letter written just at this time by one soldier who happened to be completely articulate—Captain Oliver Wendell Holmes, Jr., of the 20th Massachusetts, a twice-wounded man of proven valor from a stout, battle-tried regiment. On November 19 Holmes wrote:

"I've pretty much made up my mind that the South have achieved their independence & I am almost ready to hope spring will see an end. . . .The army is tired with its hard and its terrible experience & still more with its mismanagement & I think before long the majority will say that we are vainly working to effect what never happens—the subjugation (for that is it) of a great civilized nation. We shan't do it—at least the army can't."[18]

What Holmes could put into words in a letter to his own kin, other soldiers could only think—or, more likely, feel, leaving the thought unformulated and being conscious only of a deep depression. Yet the depression and what lay back of it were hidden if possible. Like the two officers who found uplift in a pan of fried potatoes, the soldiers kept their spirits up with such devices as were available, which included, for the men on picket duty along the river, the exchange of not wholly ill-natured insults with the Confederate pickets across the river. As, for instance:

"Oh, Yank! How did you like Bull Run?"

"Better bury your dead on South Mountain."

"What do you think of the New York election?" (Democrats had just made Horatio Seymour, suspected of strong Copperhead tendencies, governor of New York, roundly defeating the Unionist candidate, General James Wadsworth, and the Confederates were inclined to make much of it.)

"What do *you* think of Ben Butler?"

"Oh, the Louisiana Tigers will bring him to Richmond."

"The Louisiana Tigers? There's none of them left—the last died running."[19]

And so on, very like the catcalling of schoolboy gangs on the playground, except that these gangs unaccountably carried rifles and might at any moment quit yelling and start shooting at each other. The exchange had a sharp edge now and then. The whole army chuckled over the answer one brash Federal got when, observing that the Confederate on the opposite bank was exceedingly ragged, he called across to know if Rebels did not have any decent clothes. The Reb looked him over for a minute, then called back: "We-uns don't put on our good clothes to butcher hogs."

But whether it approached the event with grousing, with despairing letters home, or with jeers at the enemy's pickets, the army knew that it was drifting steadily toward a battle. It drifted with fatalism. In fact, so contradictory is the spirit of man that the soldiers even displayed a febrile enthusiasm, for although all the signs were bad, yet action was action, the battle might possibly be won, and a great battle won would bring the war near an end. A newspaper correspondent in early December wrote that "the Army of the Potomac never felt better" than it did when the long blue columns at last began to draw out of the scattered camps and head toward the banks of the deep unbridged river.[20]

For Burnside, after sitting there bemused for three weeks, had finally come to a decision. It seemed to him now that the enemy would be more surprised by a crossing right at Fredericksburg than by a crossing at any other place, and in a way he was right. Probably nothing in all the war surprised Lee quite as much as the discovery that his enemy would move up for a frontal assault at Fredericksburg, although this was not a surprise that gave the Federals any military advantage. In any case, on December 9 Burnside called the Grand Division commanders to headquarters and instructed them to have their commands ready to move at daylight of December 11, each man carrying three days' rations and sixty rounds of ammunition, battery and ammunition wagons to carry three days' forage for their horses. To Major Spaulding, Burnside sent word to stand by: the army was at last ready to use those pontoons.

There is record of a party given by officers of a New England regiment in a riverside hut the night the orders came out. Some twenty men who had no illusions about the kind of reception they were going to get when they crossed the river met to sing songs and to drink whisky punch. At the end, just before the party broke up, someone lifted his glass and cried: "To the health of Little Mac!"

The hut rocked with cheers and the glasses went bottoms up, and a man who was present wrote that the soldiers were sustained that night by a positive faith that McClellan would yet return and lead the army to victory.[21]

With that faith, or such other faith as they could muster, the men marched up to the river. As the 16th Maine marched through deserted camps the men could hear the high soft voice of a contraband camp servant lifted in the song, "Jordon Water, Rise over Me."[22]

3. BIG STARS ARE BUSTING

IT WAS THREE o'clock on a cold December morning, and there was a heavy wet fog along the river and many strange noises in the night: a creaking and a thumping and a scrabbling, the sound of wagons and horses and men getting great hollow weights down a steep bumpy road where no one could see three feet beyond the end of his nose. There was this river, and beyond it there was a silent lifeless town, and beyond the town there was an open plain bordered by low hills, and in this bleak three-in-the-morning chill all of these lay invisible, and the shadow of death rested upon them and could be felt there in the dark by the riverside. The 50th New York Engineers were going to throw pontoon bridges across the Rappahannock to Fredericksburg.

Major Spaulding had his orders, and he was building three bridges: one of them opposite the dock at the lower end of town, where steamboats used to receive passengers and freight in the days when Fredericksburg had a normal life to live, and the other two a bit farther upstream, opposite the center of town. He had chosen his spots by daylight, and now the men were extending the bridges into a void, building for a farther shore which they had to take on faith, anchoring their scows in the chuckling black water and binding them together with long timbers and fastening planking on top of the timbers, trying to do it silently, but knowing perfectly well that whatever faith might say about the farther shore there were alert enemies over there somewhere, hearing these sounds and cannily interpreting them and preparing to act as soon as the light should come. For a few hours the darkness was a protecting cloak.

The darkness did not last nearly long enough. By six o'clock it had thinned, and although the fog remained there was a dim gray light along the river. From the Confederate side there came a measured boom-boom of two fieldpieces, the signal by which the Rebel commander on the water front notified his army that the Yankees were coming across. Presently the engineers could see the water-front buildings of Fredericksburg in the mist not far off. There were many Confederates hidden in and about those buildings, and as the slow light grew these looked at the bridgebuilders over the sights of their rifles. There was a crackling snap-snap of infantry fire all along the water front, and the engineers ran back off their half-finished bridges to take cover, leaving dead and wounded men along the wet planking.

The Yankee water front along here belonged to General Couch, who commanded the II Corps, and as soon as the firing began he spread a line of infantry along the bank to return the fire. This did no good. It was so dark and misty that the Federals could not see any targets across the river, and although they did a good deal of shooting they killed no Rebels. The firing died down after a while and the engineers ran out on the bridges again, thus getting close enough to the Fredericksburg shore to be perfectly visible to the waiting Confederates, who zestfully reopened fire and again drove the men to cover.

When it got lighter things were not much better. The Confederates in the town were Mississippians, and they hid in basements and behind low barricades and in rifle pits dug in the lee of brick buildings, and the Federals across the river had very little chance to hit any of them. The men who tried to complete the bridges had to do their work less than a hundred feet from the Confederate shore, and they were sitting ducks to be shot. Time and again the engineers ran out to finish the job; each time, with very little delay, the waiting Confederates drove them back; each time the supporting Federal infantry fired completely ineffective volleys.[1]

General Burnside had certain plans, and they called for the building of two sets of bridges: this group of three, opposite the town itself, where he proposed to cross the right wing of his army, and another set a mile or more downstream, where the left wing was to cross. The downstream-bridge gang had it easy. The Confederate shore there was open and could quickly be swept clear, and by midmorning the downstream bridges were finished and ready for use. But upstream it was obvious that no bridges could be completed until the Rebels had been driven out of Fredericksburg, and they were never going to be dislodged by any long-range infantry fire.

The Federal army that morning contained 120,000 men, and most of them were lined up on the high ground overlooking Fredericksburg, waiting for a chance to get across, and here they were, stopped cold by a solitary Confederate brigade, 1,500 men at the most—an unwelcome modern version of Horatius at the bridge. It was intolerable, and Burnside at last called in his chief artillerist, Brigadier General Henry J. Hunt, and told him to blast Fredericksburg off the face of the earth if he had to—anything, just so he pulverized that Mississippi brigade and made it possible for the New York engineers to finish their job.

This Hunt was a notable gunner, one of the most useful officers the Union Army possessed, a good organizer and solid fighting man, keen student of the new science of gunnery, a man who believed in great massed sheaves of gunfire but who also insisted that each individual gun crew must take the time to get on the target before it fired. He had lately taken the Federal gunners over the coals about this latter point, decreeing that except when they were firing canister at close range they must not, even in red-hot action, fire at a rate faster than one round per gun in two minutes. To fire faster, he remarked, was to fire wildly, which did no good. Furthermore, an officer who shot up all his battery's ammunition in a hurry was probably an officer who wanted a good excuse to take his guns back out of action. He would be treated as such henceforth, in any case, and no battery hereafter would be allowed to withdraw from action just because it was out of ammunition. It would send for more ammunition, and while it waited it would remain under fire, officers and men at their posts, unless higher authority ordered it to withdraw.[2]

Hunt had been spending a week or more getting his batteries posted on Stafford Heights, as the high ground above the river was called. He had more than 140 guns in line—Rodman three-inch rifles, ten and twenty-pounder Parrotts, and a handful of four-and-one-half-inch siege guns, long monsters too cumbersome for field maneuver but useful in a spot like this. Rather more than one hundred of these guns would bear on the water front opposite the frustrated bridgebuilders, and he gave the gunners their orders—fifty rounds per gun, pick your targets, and remember what the regulations say about firing deliberately.

So the guns opened, and a tremendous cloud of smoke came rolling down from Stafford Heights to cover the river and the open plain and the tormented town, and presently tall columns of blacker smoke from burning buildings went up to the blue sky, and the waiting Federals saw walls and roofs collapse and bricks and timbers fly through the air, while men who had lived through Malvern Hill and Antietam said this was the most thunderous cannonade they had ever heard. Most of the inhabitants of Fredericksburg had left town, so that to an extent Hunt was shelling a deserted town; even so, soldiers recorded that it was not pleasant to see the whole might of their artillery turned upon human habitations.[3]

The bombardment ended at last, and there were many wrecked buildings along the water front. The engineers trotted out on the bridges again, but the ominous pin points of flame sputtered around basement windows and low barricades, and more engineers were shot down, and once again it was too hot to build bridges. General Hunt had wrecked Fredericksburg, but he had not driven out the Mississippians. Huddling under cover, they had had a hard time of it, but they had not had more than they could take, and as soon as the gunfire ceased they were ready to fight again. They were teaching Hunt the lesson which artillerists have to learn anew in each generation—that a bombardment which will destroy buildings will not necessarily keep brave defenders from fighting on amid the wreckage.

The solution to the problem was at last accomplished by the infantry under Colonel Norman J. Hall, who had one of General Oliver Otis Howard's brigades in the II Corps and to whom General Hunt suggested that the way to get the Rebels out of Fredericksburg was to go over and push them out personally. Colonel Hall took his 7th Michigan down to the water front, borrowed some of Major Spaulding's pontoons to use as assault boats, got some of the engineers detailed as oarsmen, and sent landing parties across the river despite losses. The Michigan men got a foothold along the far bank, the 19th and 20th Massachusetts were sent over as support waves, and the three regiments finally combed the last Confederates out of the waterside gun pits and went driving on to secure the town.[4]

This fight was rough while it lasted. There was a swirl of door-to-door fighting, and the 20th Massachusetts lost ninety-seven officers and men in a street-fighting advance of fifty yards. Colonel Hall, a regular-army officer who admired nonchalance in action, recalled later how very Bostonian and unemotional the New England soldiers were during this fight. There was the 20th's colonel quietly telling a company commander: "Mr. Abbott, you will take your first platoon forward." Platoon advances and is almost instantly knocked out by rifle fire. "You'll have to put in the second," says the colonel; and the captain, acting slightly bored by the whole affair, goes forward with the second platoon in the best old-world style. In his official report Colonel Hall said he could not presume to say all that ought to be said about "the unflinching bravery and splendid discipline" of these Yankees. Privately, in conversation with one of the regimental officers, he remarked that the 20th, like the regulars, did its fighting without bothering to strike heroic attitudes. Groping for the expression he wanted, he hit upon an odd one: "The 20th has no poetry in a fight."[5]

In the end, the soldiers got the town secured and went on to skirmish with Rebels on the outskirts. The bridges were finished, the rest of Colonel Hall's brigade came across, and from Stafford Heights the Federal gunners looked for targets beyond the town, firing furiously whenever they found one.

So the long day ended, and men remembered afterward that a strange golden dusk lay upon the plain and the surrounding hills, as if a belated Indian-summer evening had come bewildered out of peacetime autumn into wintry wartime. There was a haze on the horizon, and the western sky was scarlet and purple as the sun went down, and most of Fredericksburg seemed to be burning. A chaplain in the 33rd New York wrote that the smoke "rolled gently upward in dark columns, or, whirling aloft, chased itself in graceful rings like a thing of beauty." As it grew darker, these smoke clouds glowed red when the shell exploded, and the gun pits on Stafford Heights were picked out by stabbing flames as the guns were fired. A newspaper correspondent wrote: "Towering between us and the western sky, which was still showing its faded scarlet lining, was the huge somber pillar of grimy smoke that marked the burning of Fredericksburg. Ascending to a vast height, it bore away northward, shaped like a plume bowed in the wind."[6]

Attended by whatever beauties of nature and burning homes, the Federals now had a foothold on the southern bank of the Rappahannock—which at Fredericksburg is actually the western bank, the river running nearly north to south just there—and Burnside could put his troops across as he pleased. There may have been some reason for haste. Lee was still unable to believe that Burnside planned to make his main assault here, for the hills behind Fredericksburg, where Lee's army had been entrenching for weeks, made an ideal defensive line, and to the last moment the Confederates thought this crossing at Fredericksburg must be a ponderous feint. As a result, Jackson's corps was still watching possible crossings a dozen miles downsteam. When Colonel Hall's men secured the town Lee had only half of his army on hand. But Burnside frittered away the next day with a deal of marching and countermarching, and Lee had plenty of time to call in Jackson and assemble the seventy-eight thousand men of the Army of Northern Virginia on the high ground west of the Fredericksburg plain.

That ground actually is not so very high, the hills for the most part rising only forty or fifty feet above the plain. For Lee's purposes, however, the ground was exactly right—high enough to offer an impregnable defensive line, but not high enough to scare the Federals and keep them from attacking at all. Directly west of the town, and a little less than half a mile away, rose the modest ridge known as Marye's Heights, with a white-pillared Virginia mansion picturesquely sited on the crest. To the north, slightly higher hills slanted off to the river, offering Lee's left flank a position that could not be taken. (It could be turned, to be sure, if the Yankees cared to march eight or ten miles upstream, but the field of Burnside's vision had narrowed so that he could see nothing but what was immediately in front of him.) To the south, the high ground pulled farther and farther away from the river, ending, nearly four air-line miles from Marye's Heights, in a wooded knoll that overlooked a weedy grade crossing on the Richmond railroad, a spot known locally as Hamilton's Crossing. From the protected left-flank position to the hill by Hamilton's Crossing, the Confederates were well dug in, all set to kill as many Yankees as might come at them.

Burnside was a trained soldier who presumably knew the folly of smashing head-on into a perfect defensive position, and he had evolved a plan which might just possibly have worked if everything had gone exactly right. The left wing of his army, styled the Left Grand Division, was commanded by Major General William B. Franklin, who had demonstrated in the Antietam campaign that he would not drive ahead any faster than his commander forced him to do, but who, that limitation aside, was a solid and capable soldier. Franklin had under him two excellent army corps, the I Corps under John F. Reynolds and the VI Corps of William F. Smith—"Baldy" Smith, that staunch friend of the departed McClellan who seems to have had the stamina once to tell McClellan to his face that his dealings with Copperhead leaders looked like treason.

Franklin was to take his men across by the downstream bridges, and Sumner was to cross his Grand Division by the upper bridges. Hooker, with the remaining third of the army, was to stand by ready to support either or both. Burnside's general idea appears to have been for Franklin to drive through past Hamilton's Crossing, outflanking Lee's right and rolling his line up to the northward. Once this had begun, Sumner was to break through at Marye's Heights, Lee would then have to retreat in great haste, the jubilant Federals could despoil and slay in his wake, and the war would come to a close.

That, at any rate, is what Burnside later said that he had planned and directed before the battle began. His written orders appear to have called for something rather different: a simple reconnaissance in force by Franklin, an advance by Sumner to a providentially unoccupied hill, the intervention of a fortunate army between two separated retreating bodies of Confederate troops. One of Burnside's notions, apparently, was that the Rebels would withdraw as soon as they were pushed a little, and he was careful to warn Franklin and Sumner not to let their men fire into each other when they got up on top of the line of hills.

Burnside's planning, in brief, was very foggy; and as a crowning misfortune it developed that one of the worst of his failings was a simple inability to use the English language clearly. None of his subordinates understood just what he wanted them to do, and under the circumstances the battle could become nothing but a simple exercise in the killing of Union soldiers. Some of the soldiers appear to have been aware of this. A newspaper correspondent going about the camps that day asked various officers what the Confederate Army was up to. There it was, with scores of guns on commanding hills and with more and more of the Union Army parading into town under the very muzzles of those silent guns; why didn't the Rebels open fire? He got a variety of explanations: the Rebels were low on ammunition, Lee did not wish to bombard a Virginia town, the Southern army was in retreat, and so on. Finally the reporter tagged an enlisted man, who looked over toward the silent, ominous hills and remarked: "They want us to get in. Getting out won't be quite so smart and easy. You'll see."[7]

Whatever the Rebels may have wanted, the twelfth of December was a mild sunny day, and during the whole of it the Army of the Potomac assembled its hosts on the heights east of the river and sent them slanting down to the water in endless blue columns bright with flags and polished muskets, their crossing announced by the unceasing route-step tramp of tens of thousands of men on the hollow swaying bridges. Some of the Rebel guns on the western hills might have reached these bridges and the approaches. Mostly they did not try, except for one of Jackson's batteries which possessed an English-made Whitworth rifle, a breechloader with a range longer than the artillerists of that day quite knew how to use. These gunners fired a few rounds at Franklin's downstream crossing, putting one bolt through a paymaster's tent on the Yankee side of the river just as the paymaster had spread his greenbacks out on a barrel-and-plank table. The bills went whirling and dancing up about the wrecked tent like a green blizzard, and the ensuing scramble by stragglers and orderlies was something the army long remembered.[8] Otherwise the crossing was peaceful enough. If the deluded Yankees were indeed going to make their fight here, no Confederate commander wanted to keep them from trying it.

Yet the Federal strength was great, and this unending muster of the troops was so impressive that even stolid, impassive Longstreet began to worry at last, and he asked his chief of artillery if he had not better get some more guns to defend Marye's Heights. The gunner laughed at him; once he opened fire, he said, not even a chicken could live on the plain between the hills and the town. Longstreet looked again and was reassured. Later, when Lee asked him if the overpowering weight of Federals might not be too heavy for him, Longstreet promised to kill every man in the Union Army, provided his ammunition held out.[9] The Yankees were with power, but in all the war the Southerners never had to worry as little about a battle as about this one.

Sumner sent his entire command into Fredericksburg, but he did not go with it. Burnside kept him on the home side of the river, feeling that if the old man once got over the bridges he would be unable to keep from getting up into the front line of attack, which was no place for a Grand Division commander. There was a day-long sputter of rifle fire on the skirmish lines outside of town as Federals and Confederates bickered over the approaches; and inside the town there was a prodigious amount of looting of the empty houses, so that Couch finally put a provost guard at the bridges to keep the looters from getting their plunder across the river. By nightfall, he wrote, the guards had collected "an enormous pile of booty."

Franklin put in the day getting his divisions across by the lower bridges, and by evening he had them posted on a north-and-south line facing the Confederate hills, with Abner Doubleday's division acting as flank guard on the left. As the men took their places the Iron Brigade, by chance, found itself quartered on the Bernard plantation, some three miles below Fredericksburg, and the Company C of the 6th Wisconsin had a contraband cook who until comparatively recently had been held in servitude on this very estate. This one was highly pleased to be back, a free man protected by Lincoln's soldiers, on the plantation where he was born and bred. Yet when he saw some of his soldiers chopping down a fine shade tree to get firewood he ran up to them, pointing toward the manor house and pleading earnestly: "You break dat ol' man's heart if you cut down dat tree! His grandfather planted dat tree!"[10]

Night came at last and army movements ceased, and this great host of Federal soldiers, put down here so deliberately and so ostentatiously, waited for the action which the morning was sure to bring. The generals at the downstream end of the line were nervous. Franklin and his two corps commanders, Reynolds and Smith, interpreted Burnside's orders as calling simply for an armed observation of enemy strength. In a chat with Smith, Burnside had agreed that a good deal more than that was needed, and he had promised to send over supplementary orders. The generals sat up until three in the morning waiting for them, but they never came, either then or thereafter. Franklin, who was prepared to go by the script though the heavens fell, told Reynolds his original instructions stood: send out one division when day came, to seize the hill at Hamilton's Crossing, hold another division ready to support it, and if all goes well, which is not likely, someone will doubtless order something additional.

Dawn came in cold and foggy, with a slow wind in the leafless trees. As the brigades moved out to take their places they could hear the innumerable army noises, but they could see neither their own ranks nor the enemy's, and George Meade spread out his Pennsylvania division in a gray watery light facing west along the edge of a muddy road that led south. Doubleday took his men in on Meade's left, and Gibbon, going into action as a division commander for the first time, lined his men up on the other side. Everybody lounged in the ranks and waited for the fog to lift.

It lifted at about eleven o'clock, and when it went up it went up dramatically, like the curtain of a theater. The Federals were spread out all across the plain south of Fredericksburg, rank upon long rank, with national and regimental banners bright in the morning breeze, guns drawn up at intervals between the brigades, everything looking very martial and splendid, as if war were some sort of pageant. The Rebels were hardly visible. The hills which sheltered them were heavily wooded, and a low railway embankment that ran across the plain in front of the hills was fringed with a stubbly second growth where some advanced lines were concealed. They had a mass of guns planted on the knoll by Hamilton's Crossing, and a mile farther north they had another big bank of guns half hidden in a rising grove. Stonewall Jackson was an old artillerist himself, and he always made good use of his guns. As the last wisps of fog blew away, the Southern gunners stared at the limitless target that lay in front of them, trotted up to their pieces, pulled at trail handspikes and spun elevating screws, and opened fire. Gibbon's and Meade's men, drawn up along the highway, had to stay there and take it, while the Federal batteries rolled forward to make reply and a great turbulence of boiling smoke and heavy sound went tumbling up the sky.

Holding still to be shelled is about as unpleasant a job as infantry gets, and the Yankees in the open plain found it especially hard because they could very easily see the cannoneers who were firing at them. Naturally, they hated them; one soldier wrote that the Rebel gunners, visibly busy around their pieces, looked "like fiends who stirred infernal fires." An indignant general routed one straggler out of a ditch and ordered him to rejoin his command. The straggler saluted and said: "General, I will, jest as soon as them fellers quit throwin' railroad iron at us." And back on the far side of the Rappahannock the chaplain of a Pennsylvania regiment, returning to camp with some wounded men, told the contraband cook of the regimental officers' mess to take some hot coffee over to the embattled regiment. The contraband, looking wide-eyed at the flashing shells that were exploding all over the plain, shook his head emphatically. "I'se not gwine up dar whar so many big stars are busting!"[11]

It was at times like this that the Civil War officer was supposed to display a dramatic disregard of danger. To keep his troops steady he had to expose his own person; he had to do it with an air, as if to show that he simply was not aware that there was any danger. The boys of the 16th Maine, growing restive under the cannonade, presently found themselves gaping at Captain James Hall, who had his 2nd Maine battery drawn up in action beside them and who was blithely sitting his horse, carrying on a conversation with the 16th's commander, Lieutenant Colonel Charles W. Tilden, and the brigadier, Colonel Adrian Root, who were on their horses a dozen yards away from him. Since the air was full of truly deafening noise, the three officers had to shout at the top of their lungs to make themselves heard, but aside from that they might have been three civilian horsemen who had met on a bridle path in a park on a pleasant May morning and were stopping to pass the time of day.

While the soldiers hugged the ground and watched admiringly, a Rebel shell came whistling in between Captain Hall and the two colonels, narrowly missing the colonels and going on to crash into a caisson in the rear, exploding it with an earth-rocking crash. Captain Hall looked faintly annoyed. Very deliberately he dismounted, walked over to one of his guns, and painstakingly sighted it at the Rebel battery which had fired the shot. Satisfied, he stepped back and waved his hand to the gun crew. The gun was fired and landed a direct hit, dismounting a Rebel gun amid a cloud of torn earth and flying splinters. The battery commander walked back to his horse, mounted, and resumed the interrupted conversation as if nothing had happened.[12]

Such dramatics might help to make shell fire endurable, but in the end the battle would be decided by what the infantry did. By noon or thereabouts the Federal gunners had beaten the Confederate gunfire down just enough so that the infantry could go forward. Meade took his division into a ragged patch of woodland along the edge of the railroad track, Gibbon went into the fringe of the same woodland a little later and a little farther north, and the artillerists let their guns cool while the foot soldiers fought in the swampy underbrush. Meade's division by good fortune stumbled into a gap in Jackson's lines and for a short time made great headway, crumpling up a couple of A. P. Hill's brigades, killing one of his brigadiers, taking prisoners, and just for a moment making it look as if Burnside's battle plan might make sense after all. But although there were more than sixty thousand armed Federals on this plain south of Fredericksburg (one of Hooker's two corps had been sent down here as insurance), these two divisions seemed to be all that Franklin could get into action. The Army of the Potomac was up against its old, old difficulty: visibly outnumbering its enemy, it nevertheless was put into action in such a way that where the actual fighting was going on there were more Rebels present than Yankees. Stonewall Jackson sent in fresh troops, and the Federal assault columns were smashed and came running back into the open, hotly pursued. Across the open plain, shaken by the blast of many guns, there rose the high unearthly keen of the Rebel yell.

That yell—"that hellish yell," a Michigan soldier called it—appears to have been an actual power in battle, worth many regiments to the Confederacy. A Federal surgeon wrote after the war: "I have never, since I was born, heard so fearful a noise as a Rebel yell. It is nothing like a hurrah, but rather a regular wildcat screech." And lest that be thought the nervous reaction of a timid noncombatant, here is the verdict of a front-line veteran from the 6th Wisconsin: "There is nothing like it this side of the infernal region, and the peculiar corkscrew sensation that it sends down your backbone under these circumstances can never be told. You have to feel it, and if you say you did not feel it, and heard the yell, you have *never* been there."[13]

A spine-chilling thing, the Rebel yell. Not for nothing did old Stonewall himself, grimmest of all America's soldiers, call it "the sweetest music I ever heard."

Yelling like fiends, then, and inspired equally by hatred of the Yankee invader and the desire to plunder the invader's camp and person of good boots, blankets, and coffee, the Rebels came storming across the railroad and down into the plain as if they would shove the last Federals into the river. But Franklin's supply of support troops was practically limitless, and the Federal artillery was ready and waiting. The battery commanders held their men in until the Confederates were within point-blank range, and then hit them hard with canister and slammed in additional salvos as fast as they could load their pieces, this being one occasion when General Hunt's one-round-in-two-minutes rule did not apply. The Confederate fighting lines were cut and broken and the men withdrew to their trenches on the wooded hillsides, and all of the important fighting on this part of the battlefield was over.

It remained, however, for the Iron Brigade to carry out a little assignment which had no effect on the battle itself but which at least restored internal harmony to the brigade.

This brigade was down at the extreme left of the army, and while the serious fighting was going on elsewhere, Jeb Stuart's horse artillery and dismounted cavalry had been making pests of themselves in some broken country near the river. The Iron Brigade was ordered to go out and put a stop to it. So Solomon Meredith, wearing his general's stars in action for the first time, sent the rookie 24th Michigan into a tangled bit of woodland where Rebel snipers lurked, with the 7th Wisconsin in immediate support and the rest of the brigade following after.

Despite all the fine things the generals and the war correspondents wrote about troops being eager to get into battle, Civil War soldiers were as sensible as any others and went into action usually because they had to and not because they liked it. But this was one of the times when some men really wanted to fight. This 24th Michigan had been ostracized for two solid months and it had had all it could take. If it did not soon redeem itself under fire its life simply was not going to be worth living any longer, and nothing the Rebels could do to it was half as bad as the cold contempt it was getting from the rest of the brigade. So when orders came through the men went forward with a grim determination that might have taken them straight through the middle of Jackson's main line if anyone had thought to point them that way. The brigade rolled forward, the four veteran regiments happy enough to let someone else go in the front line, watching the straw-feet with the half-amused, critical eyes of old-timers.

Into the wood went the 24th, and Stuart's gunners fired at them with cold accuracy. One man was beheaded by the first shot, and then a shell tore an arm off a file closer, and another man was mashed and still another was beheaded—all dreadfully unnerving for green soldiers. But Colonel Morrow halted them, and while unseen snipers fired at them and shell came crashing through the trees to inflict more casualties, he dressed the regiment's lines with elaborate care and coolly put the men through the manual of arms. The soldiers had been drilled within an inch of their lives that dreary fall, and now they went through all of this with regular-army precision. They were not killing any Rebels just then, but they were demonstrating to one and all that they could take it, and the veterans, some distance in the rear, looked on with dawning approval. Then the 24th went ahead again, taking great pains with its alignment, marching through that woodland like the West Point corps of cadets. General Doubleday admired them hugely but disliked the way Meredith was handling the brigade and deposed him and gave the command to Lysander Cutler, colonel of the 6th Wisconsin. The wood was cleared at last and Cutler flung a skirmish line out on the far side, and the shooting ended.

That evening the 2nd Wisconsin had the picket line, and as battlewise veterans they quickly made a deal with the Rebels in their front by which neither side would do any shooting without giving due warning in advance, so that nobody had to stay under cover. But in the morning the Michigan regiment relieved the 2nd Wisconsin. Being very ardent and trigger-happy, they opened fire at once without waiting to be told about the agreement, and although the Wisconsin boys yelled a frantic last-minute warning, a good many Rebels were shot and a furious little fire fight raged up and down the picket lines, almost bringing on a general engagement. Toward the end of the day there came one of those odd incidents which were perfectly characteristic of that strange war, although it is hard to imagine them happening in any other war known to history. In all of this firing and sniping, a certain Confederate private and one of the Wisconsin soldiers began to develop a personal enmity toward each other, so that between shots they yelled bitter insults, and finally they got so angry that just shooting at one another would not answer. The thing went too deep for killing, and it had to be settled with fists. So the other soldiers called an informal truce, and the two men laid down their weapons and went out into the clearing and had a furious, emotion-releasing fist fight—these two boys who had been perfectly satisfied to try to kill each other up to the moment when their enmity became personal.

The rest of the soldiers cheered them on, agreed in the end that the fight was a draw, and worked it out so that there was no more firing on the picket line. Rebels and Yanks got together and traded coffee for tobacco and agreed not to fight any more unless the higher-ups actually ordered an advance. The two pugilists, presumably, washed the blood off their faces, and the 24th Michigan sat down by its campfires to count its losses.

These had not actually been very heavy—a total of thirty-six, as the regiment's historian remembered it, of whom only seven were dead; the fighting in the wood and along the picket line had not been very severe after all. But somehow the way the regiment had handled itself under fire thawed out the veterans. From enlisted men up to commanding officers they agreed that these Michigan boys would do, and there was no more talk about "bounty boys" after Fredericksburg. An officer in the 6th Wisconsin wrote grandiloquently: "They showed themselves of a fibre worthy to be woven into the woof of the Iron Brigade." The enlisted men used no fancy language, but they did begin dropping into the 24th's camp at the close of day to borrow tobacco and swap yarns, just as members of friendly regiments always did, and the historian of the 24th noted that "the greatest cordiality ever after prevailed."[14]

So the great battle of Fredericksburg accomplished this much, if nothing more; it enabled a new regiment to come out of Coventry and join the brotherhood of proven fighters. In that brotherhood it would appear that the boys had plenty of company.

4. BURNISHED ROWS OF STEEL

THE MEN OF the II Army Corps were veterans and they knew a bad spot when they saw it. From the moment they crossed the river they disliked the looks of this Fredericksburg setup. They had had one laugh, coming over, when the Rebels began to shell the road right where the band of a nine-month regiment had posted itself. The musicians all ran for cover except the bass drummer, who simply cowered in the dust behind his big bass drum and fancied himself secure.[1] Other laughs were few. The heights west of town looked dangerous, and those heights were obviously where the high command intended the II Corps to go.

There was something eerie about the morning of the battle. Stragglers were on the prowl in alleys and back yards between the ruined looted houses, some of the men capering grotesquely in women's chemises stolen from ransacked bedroom closets. Sidewalks and gutters were littered with smashed furniture, crockery, wearing apparel, and other odds and ends carried out of homes by aimless marauders. Generals and generals' aides went cantering up and down the crowded streets, very busy, while the regiments dressed their ranks on the side streets to a thin spatter of bugle calls and shouted commands. Heavy cold mist filled the air, so that every down-street vista was like an open window into nothingness. In the air, too, palpable as the December fog itself, was the chill suspicion that cruel disaster lay just out of town to the west.

By midmorning the ranks were lined up in the proper order, and the sun burned away the fog. From the south the men could hear the crash of gunfire as Franklin's men made their unavailing assault on Jackson's lines. (On the Stafford Heights a green company cook asked what that noise was. Rebel guns, they told him. He listened and shook his head and said: "You fellers needn't think you can fool me. I've heard that noise too often in Philadelphia; they're unloading boards somewhere.")[2] There was a final flurry of galloping aides with orders, and then burly General William H. French sent his skirmish line trotting across the yards and around the outbuildings on the fringe of town and out into the open plain. The Rebel outposts fired a few shots and leisurely fell back toward the chain of hills to the west. General Darius N. Couch, commanding the II Corps, climbed to the cupola of the courthouse to look things over. The main body of French's division began to march out of town, and all the cannon in the

Rebel army seemed to come to life at once, flashing along the hilltops from left to right as far as the men could see.

If the army had tried, it could not have found a worse place to make an attack. Between Fredericksburg and Marye's Heights there was a hollow plain perhaps half a mile wide. The town itself was on a little plateau; leaving it and advancing toward the heights, one went down a little slope and came presently to a wide ditch carrying the spillway of a canal from a paper mill a mile to the north. There was not much water in this canal, but the ditch itself was deep and its banks were steep. A spry individual could cross it anywhere, but a formal column of attack could cross only where it was bridged, and it was bridged in just two places.

To make an attack, therefore, the troops had to come out in solid columns of fours—of all formations, the one most vulnerable to enemy fire, with the men all bunched together in a cohesive target and nobody able to use his own weapon in reply. Reaching the open, these dense helpless columns must march straight ahead for two hundred yards within easy range of the Confederate artillery, which could smite them from in front and on both flanks. (Rebel sharpshooters on the heights also had them within range.) Then the columns must cross the ditch by the two bottleneck bridges, one of which had been partly destroyed, so that the men had to walk on the stringers; and after they were across, the columns had to turn right and left and spread out into the long lines of battle, two ranks deep, by which the actual assault would be made. Fortunately the ground rose sharply just beyond the ditch, so that the men would be under cover while they deployed. But as soon as the lines were formed they must climb the little slope and come out in the open and tramp forward for four hundred yards to reach Marye's Heights, at the foot of which there was a wide sunken road with a four-foot stone wall on the Fredericksburg side, as invulnerable a trench as the Rebels could have found in the whole state of Virginia.

In this sunken road and behind this wall Longstreet had put four ranks of riflemen, with abundant reinforcements nearby. Above them, on the hill slopes, were more infantry. Still higher, and extending far to the right and left so that they could lay down a horrible crisscross of fire, were the guns. The artillerist had not exaggerated very much: once all of these people commenced to fire, a chicken would have had a hard time getting across that plain.

French's men started off bravely enough. Nathan Kimball's brigade was in the lead, and he had a couple of new regiments which had never before been under fire. Kimball sat his horse by the roadside as these green regiments came by, noticed the white-lipped tension in the ranks, and cried out: "Cheer up, my hearties, cheer up! This is something we must all get used to! Remember, this brigade has never been whipped—don't let it get whipped today!" The rookies felt that this helped a little, but not much, and when the veteran regiments raised a cheer the two new regiments could not quite find their voices.[3]

Kimball brought his two parallel columns out of town in fine order, flags gay in the breeze, weapons at the right shoulder, field officers tramping along with drawn swords and turning as they tramped to shout commands. Longstreet's gunners began hitting the marching columns before they were fairly outside the town, but they kept coming on. They got across the canal at last and swung into line and then came up over the bank, four regiments abreast, rookies and veterans together. One hundred yards behind them there was another brigade, with a third brigade coming up behind that one. The Rebel guns fired faster and faster, and the files shifted to right and left as the men closed up the gaps that were made by the shell. It was more comforting to march elbow to elbow, and as long as a man could feel his comrades immediately beside him he was willing to keep going.

From the far side of the Rappahannock, General Hunt's massed artillery

opened fire furiously, striking at Longstreet's guns, trying to beat down the
Rebel fire and give the infantry a chance. The earth seemed to rock and a choking mist lay on the plain. Hunt's gunners found that they could not silence the
Confederate batteries. The range was long, the Southern guns were protected by
earthworks, and the fuses for the long-range shell were worthless. Sometimes
the missiles exploded over Federal troops instead of over Rebels; more often
they simply did not explode at all. One exasperated gunner reported afterward
that "as solid shot, the ordnance shrapnel was serviceable."[4]

About one hundred yards short of the sunken road there was an almost imperceptible rise in the open ground, a little swell which would not be noticed ordinarily but which today was like a high mountain ridge swept by great storms.
If they lay flat on the ground just before they got to this rise, attacking troops
might be protected from the fire of the Confederate infantry; but once they got
on this insignificant crest, the fight had to be to a finish. There could be no more
hiding—a man lying down could be shot as easily as a man standing erect—and
it was precisely here, where they made a perfect target at shotgun range, that the
assaulting troops must halt to deliver their own fire. An infantry attack in that
war rarely implied an uninterrupted advance with the bayonet. It usually meant
getting the attackers to close quarters so that they could break the defensive line
with their own fire. This little rise was where the Federals must stand to deliver
the fire that would break the Rebel line—unless, indeed, it should develop that
this particular Rebel line could not be broken by any weight of fire whatsoever,
in which case this was where the boys would stand while they found out.

Kimball's men had lost heavily crossing the plain, but they were still in formation, and as the long brigade lines wavered to a halt on this low crest the men
set up a cheer. Nobody could hear it in the tremendous tumult. The stone wall
seemed to blaze from end to end with one crackling sheet of flame, the guns on
the heights crashed and thundered, and if Kimball's brigade had not been
whipped before, it was whipped now. The men had never run into anything like
this. Standing four ranks deep behind perfect protection, the Southern riflemen
could keep up an almost continuous fire. The attacking brigade got off an un-
steady volley or two, a few men irresolutely stumbled forward a few steps, and
then the brigade fell completely apart. Some of the men ran for the rear, some
huddled behind a square brick house which stood in the middle of this last rise
in the ground, and others found shelter amid a few shacks by the main highway,
a couple of hundred yards to the right. Most of the men simply dropped back a
few yards, lay on the ground amid the dead and wounded, kept their tattered
flags flying, and maintained as much of a fire as they could.

Up came the second brigade, a double line of blue more than a quarter of a
mile from end to end, swinging up over the bank by the canal and rolling
forward into the battle smoke. It reached the last fiery crest and halted there to
open fire, and the Rebel musketry overwhelmed it. When it broke, the third brigade came marching up to take its place, and the third brigade, too, was
smashed and French's entire division had been put out of action. The survivors
clung desperately to the bare ground and to moderately protected spots behind
the scattered buildings, firing pluckily but without much effect. To General
Couch, aloft in his cupola, peering down through the blanketing smoke, it
looked as if the division had simply vanished. One of the men who cowered behind the brick house wrote afterward that although the Southern artillery was
firing as fast as ever, the musketry was so continuous and so intense that he
could not recall hearing the reports of any cannon.[5]

Winfield Scott Hancock had been ordered to follow French into action, and
he had his men moving out of town as soon as the last of French's brigades
crossed the canal. Hancock formed his division as French had done, in three
successive brigade lines, he himself riding personally back and forth along the

outskirts of the city to gouge the stragglers out of alleys and fence corners, driving his men in. His leading brigade dressed its ranks carefully when it mounted the high ground beyond the canal, and then it went ahead bravely, the battle-tested veterans crouching low as they walked forward.

From the open field where no man stood erect there rose a wan, scattered cheer, prostrate men shouting their greeting. Hancock's men made a fine sight coming up, and a wounded man was seen to prop himself on one elbow and wing his cap in welcome. Some of the men who had been lying down scrambled to their feet to go forward with this new charge. The Confederate gunners knocked great holes in the wide blue lines, and the stone wall blazed out as wickedly as ever. When the leading regiments tried to tear down a fence just beyond the final rise in the ground, the fire from the sunken road broke them all to bits. The men who were not shot ran back through the swirling smoke, or stumbled over to the lee of the brick house, or lay on the ground amid the dead and wounded. To the Confederates on the heights, when the smoke drifted away, it looked as if all the plain had turned blue.

Second wave now—General Thomas F. Meagher's Irish Brigade, Meagher himself magnificent in a tailored uniform coat of darkest green, silver stars embroidered on black shoulder knots, a yellow silk scarf across his breast—"a picture of unusual grace and majesty," a Pennsylvania soldier wrote. The Irishmen had only one of their green flags this day, the others having grown too tattered for use and the replacement flags not having arrived, and this one green flag was borne by the 28th Massachusetts, a regiment of Bay State Irish specially recruited for this brigade. Every man in the brigade wore in his cap a sprig of evergreen, and Meagher sent them down Hanover Street and out toward the canal, 69th New York in the lead.[6]

Like the others, the brigade formed beyond the canal and went swinging ahead, and the men who lay on the ground raised their heads and cheered as they saw them coming. The men tramped on, past the dead and the wounded and the beaten-out men of the other commands, and got up to that deadly, insignificant little high place in the flat plain, and the smoke rolled down on them like a killing cloud. The men could see very little and they could hear nothing at all but the unending racket of the firing. It was all but impossible for officers to pass an order in the choking, confused tumult. Now and then men got a glimpse of a few officers farther forward trying to tear down an obstructing fence. The 88th New York knelt behind another fence and opened its own fire, and the whole field was a pandemonium of smoke and flame and shouting men. Captain Condon of the 63rd New York learned that he was in command of the regiment, and when he tried to get the men together he could find only nine of them. As he was lining up this remnant of a command he saw a slightly larger fragment drifting up out of the smoke, a green flag at its head: the colonel of the 28th Massachusetts, who had a dozen men with him. The two officers shook hands and agreed that the brigade had been cut to pieces,[7] and in the end they got their men back to the riverbank and found General Meagher rallying other survivors. By evening he was able to assemble 250 men out of the 1,400 the brigade had taken into action.

The plain was covered with smoke, and men on each side saw the fighting only in glimpses, and what they saw was always the same. Up in front, in that last deadly zone between fifty and one hundred yards from the stone wall, one firing line would be crumbling and going to pieces under the fearful Confederate fire; farther back, while this was happening, the broad blue lines of a new brigade would be coming up into view on the high ground near the canal; and back by the town, compact columns would be marching down the parallel highways, making their way toward the canal. There never seemed to be any end to it, and the Confederates lost all track of the number of separate assaults they had repelled. While the Irish officers were plucking their men out of the smoke fog, Hancock's third brigade was coming over the plain—Brigadier General John Caldwell's men, who had broken the Rebel line at Bloody Lane above the Antietam, going in now as then on the heels of the Irish.

What had been done by the Antietam could not be done here. Caldwell got part of his brigade up to the high-water mark—his valiant 5th New Hampshire, Colonel Cross and three successors all down with wounds, the regiment under its fifth commander in ten minutes; part of his 81st Pennsylvania, with the combined 61st and 64th New York beside them. They could advance no farther. The very endurance and determination of the survivors of the earlier attacks were a handicap. These men lay by the hundreds all across the front in a ragged belt two hundred yards deep, keeping up such fire as they could manage, and in the blanketing smoke they shot wildly, hitting their own comrades in the front lines.[8] Meanwhile, the fire from the sunken road and from the heights came without a moment's letup. No man who stood upright in the open plain could hope to live long.

Yet there were men who wanted to try. Up to Caldwell came the slim, handsome young colonel who commanded the two New York regiments, a dandy of a man with pointed mustaches, the name of him Nelson Miles. He wanted permission to take his two regiments and make a bayonet charge straight up the road for the stone wall. It needed just one spirited dash to clear that wall, he argued, and if two regiments started, men all over the plain would jump up and follow them. But Caldwell refused. There were no supports; if the men did breach the Rebel line they could not stay there, the thing was just impossible. . . . And then Caldwell was wounded and was carried off the field, and Miles took a bullet in the throat and went to the rear with blood dripping through the fingers which he held pressed against the wound. There was nothing for the survivors to do but hug the ground and hope for the best.[9]

From his perch in the cupola General Couch had seen some of this—not much, for the smoke was very heavy, and from the rear one could make out little but the dim forms of blue-clad men swaying uncertainly in a terrible haze that glowed and sparked with deadly fire. (One man who watched the attackers from the heights beyond the river found himself amazed that the heavy fire "did not absolutely sweep them from the face of the earth.") General Howard, who stood beside Couch for a time, heard him gasp as the smoke lifted briefly: "Oh, great God! See how our men, our poor fellows, are falling!"[10]

Couch decided that enough of them had fallen in front of the stone wall, so he told Howard to lead his division farther to the right, where the Rebel line looked a bit softer. If this impregnable line could not be stormed, perhaps it might be flanked, and Howard must try. There were plenty of troops available to follow him in if his men won any success, and Howard rode off to put his division into action.

Couch's idea was a good one, but the shape of the ground was against it. Although no one seems to have realized it at the time, it simply was not possible for an attack issuing from Fredericksburg to hit the Rebel line anywhere except along that impassable sunken road. It looked as if Howard could cross the ditch where the others had crossed and could then shift to his right until he was half a mile or more north of Marye's Heights; but when his men tried it they found that they could edge to the right only a little way before striking impassable ground. A long slough, known locally as Gordon's Marsh, ran to the north on the western side of the ditch: an unobtrusive dike which forced every Federal assault on this part of the field to drift to the left and go crashing up against the one front that could not be broken.[11]

Howard's men drifted and instead of flanking the stone wall they came in, at last, over the wreckage of the other two divisions, fared as they had fared, and reached the outer boundaries of human endurance on that same little rise of ground in front of the wall. Survivors hid out behind houses or face-down on the earth as the others had done, and it seemed that no one could live out in the open. Howard wrote that he had "a feeling akin to terror" whenever he had to send an aide or a mounted orderly foward with a dispatch.[12]

The men who lay in the open used what poor cover they could get. One officer saw three men sheltering behind a dead horse. Here and there a man would be able to get two or three rocks which he would pile up in a pitiful little barricade. Many a soldier lay behind the corpse of a comrade while he loaded and fired. In the brick house and in other houses back on the edge of town sharpshooters found vantage points from which they could fight effectively. They and the men in the field kept up a fire which now and then stung the Southerners painfully. The Confederate brigadier who commanded the troops back of the stone wall was killed, various guns in the upper pits were put out of action from time to time, and it was made risky for any Confederate to pass from one level to another of the defenses on the smoking hillside. But there was nothing in this fire that could possibly drive the defenders away. One Federal who remembered how effectively the Rebels were hidden behind the wall remarked that "no doubt for every Johnny hit a ton of lead was expended," and the men could hear their bullets spattering harmlessly on the stones and knew they were killing very few of the enemy.[13]

Somewhere far to the rear, beyond the deep river, insulated from reality by distance, by the trappings of command, and by sheer mental confusion, there was a guiding intelligence for this army, and to it there came dimly the news of this great fight. It sluggishly sent back repeated and unvarying orders to attack and to keep on attacking. Divisions from the III, V, and IX Corps came over to join in the fight, and always the story was the same. The men who went into action were mostly veterans, and as they marched out into the range of the Confederate gunners they were able to assay with complete accuracy the exact measure of their chances on this smoking plain; yet it is not recorded that any of them turned away or refused to go forward, and each brigade went in with a cheer, however it might be fated to come out.

A brigade from the V Corps tried to come in through an unfinished railway cut at the left. The Rebel gunners, vigilant above the battle smoke, saw the brigade coming and swung their guns over and waited for it, and when it came out on the level ground they racked it. The men who were not hit were blinded by the dirt and gravel kicked up by the flying canister, and the brigade drifted back and took refuge in a stretch of low ground near the railway and found to its horror that it was huddling in a spot which had been a sink for a Rebel camp. In the 22nd Massachusetts it was recalled that while the men cowered in this unpleasant spot the quavering voice of a very proper ex-schoolteacher in the ranks was lifted in inquiry: "Who is in command of Company H?" A sergeant growled a reply: who wanted to know, and why? And the ex-schoolteacher—primly, as if the village debating society had convened here in front of the stone wall—made his answer: "I move that we be taken out of here by some responsible officer." The regiment's historian wrote that this drew an unfeeling reply from the sergeant.[14]

Most of the soldiers on the plain would have seconded the motion if they could have heard it. But the high command kept putting more people in instead of taking them out, and the Rebels methodically shot them down as fast as they came in, and the rifle fire rose to an unheard-of intensity. General Caldwell, up by the brick house, wrote that it was "the hottest I have ever seen," and a private soldier said the men in an attack "stood as though they were breasting a storm of rain and sleet, their faces and bodies being only half turned to the storm, with their shoulders shrugged."[15] Finally, in desperation, Couch ordered field artillery out into the open. His chief of staff protested that no battery could live in that field, and Couch agreed that that was probably true but said the gunners

would have to go out there anyway: something had to be done to cut down the
Confederate fire, and anyway, it was better to lose guns than men.

So the artillery went in at a gallop, clattering across the ditch and swinging
into battery on the higher ground just beyond—a Rhode Island and a New York
battery from the II Corps and a battery of regulars from the IX Corps. They
were in trouble from the very start. Sharpshooters were hitting the regulars before they even had their guns unlimbered, and the Rebel artillerists quickly
found the exact range and began exploding their shells right over the battery.
Within twenty minutes the battery commander and a dozen men had been
knocked out, most of the horses had been killed, and the survivors had been
driven away from the guns three times. Never had they been in so hot a spot.

It was the same with the others. The Rhode Island battery lost men so fast
that its skipper, Captain John G. Hazard, went back to the ditch, rounded up
infantry stragglers, and brought them up to help work his guns. General
Howard, who saw it all, wrote that his conduct was "equal to anything I ever
saw on a field of battle." And presently young Lieutenant Adams, commanding
the right section of this battery, limbered up one of his guns and went galloping
madly forward with it until he was less than 150 yards away from the stone wall,
where he unlimbered in the open road. This looked like nothing in the world but
a spectacular way to commit suicide, and three cannoneers in succession were
killed at the gun's muzzle before the first charge could be rammed home. But the
gun and its crew stayed there, pounding at close range at the stone wall, firing, as
one of Hancock's staff reported, as coolly as if they had been firing blank cartridges on a review.[16]

The winter twilight came, and Couch rode forward to the brick house and
found the smoke and dusk so heavy that he could not see the enemy and supposed that the enemy could not see him, although, as he wrote later, he was
"aware of the fact that somebody in our front was doing a great deal of shooting." It seems that he rode from one end of his prostrate battle line to the other,
chatting with Lieutenant Adams and his gunners for a while and then riding
slowly to the other flank. Except for the gunners and the men who were sheltering behind the brick house, he was the only man in the field who was not
lying down taking cover. At length, cool and unhurried, he rode back to town,
and if there was anything about the plight of his troops which he did not know it
was not because he had failed to go out and see for himself.[17]

And still the high command had not had enough. It kept sending fresh troops
in as resolutely as a butcher pushing raw material into a mincing machine. General Andrew Humphreys from the V Corps brought forward his two untried
brigades of Pennsylvanians—nine-month troops enlisted the previous summer,
hurried down to Antietam just too late to get into the fighting there, somewhat
looked down upon by the long-term troops, but drilled and disciplined by one of
the sharpest taskmasters in the army. Humphreys was tall and slim; he had been
born without nerves and was decidedly a martinet, and as he took his regiments
in he left no one behind. The colonel of one outfit had detailed half a dozen of
the youngest, frailest soldiers to guard the regiment's knapsacks which had been
piled in a side street, but Humphreys made harsh remarks about stragglers and
relentlessly drove the boys on with the rest.

He got his soldiers across the canal and formed them into two lines in the
murk of the fading day, and it seemed to him that the only possible chance was
to keep going without a halt. If the men ever stopped to fire they were lost, best
make a straight bayonet charge out of it. He issued his orders accordingly, his
rookies fixed bayonets, and forward they went. As they came up through the
human debris of all the previous charges, the unwounded men on the ground
reached up and tried to hold them back, telling them that it was no use to go on.
It was nearly dark, the field was very muddy, and the men stumbled on through

the dead and wounded and the clutching hands of the unwounded, and their lines grew disordered. A staff officer galloped up, sword swinging in the dim light, yelling to the men to close and dress their ranks; and just then a great sweep of fire lit up the entire length of the stone wall, and farther up the hill and far off to right and left there were incessant quick flashings from the Rebel cannon, and the staff officer was shot down and so was nearly half of the division. The men staggered to a halt—as close to the wall, Humphreys noted proudly, as anyone got that day, and it simply was not in them or in any men to get any closer—and they fired a ragged volley or two. Then they gave way as all the others had done and went streaming back toward the town.

The 9th Massachusetts, coming up to this inferno of a field on the heels of this repulse, saw Humphreys sitting his horse all alone, looking out across the plain, bullets cutting the air all around him, and the men spontaneously set up a cheer. They were standing in the same fire themselves, but something about the way the general was taking it pleased them, and they cheered. Humphreys looked over, surprised, waved his cap to them with a grim smile, and then went cantering forward into the deadly twilight.[18]

It was almost entirely dark when Rush Hawkins's brigade from the IX Corps made one final assault, coming up from the railway cut and swinging out into the open ground comparatively undamaged, and then getting the worst of it in one tremendous blast that seemed to shake whole regiments apart. The colonel of the 13th New Hampshire wrote that "with one startling crash, with one simultaneous sheet of fire and flame, they hurled on our advancing lines the whole terrible force of their infantry and artillery." Others who saw that charge said that the whole field was lit up as if by sheet lightning when the Rebels opened fire. For a few moments there was a wild melee as the broken lines swayed back and forth; some of the men, unhurt by the Rebel fire, were injured simply by being knocked down and tramped on in the unendurable confusion, and Colonel Hawkins noted that "everybody, from the smallest drummer boy on up, seemed to be shouting to the full extent of his capacity." Part of the brigade overlapped the left of the II Corps line and was shot by Federal bullets, and finally what was left of it sagged back into the shelter of the railway cut, and it was too dark to fight any more that day.[19]

Around midnight Joe Hooker had the V Corps move up to relieve the exhausted survivors of the afternoon's assaults, and a couple of brigades of regulars were sent out into the plain to form a strange belly-to-earth line of battle in the pitch-darkness in front of the stone wall. When light came the regulars found their situation extremely uncomfortable. In the darkness they had stretched out just before reaching the flat summit of that final, invisible little ridge. The ground sloped just enough so that they could not be hit by the Rebels marksmen if they lay absolutely flat. The man who sat up or even lifted his head was almost certain to get hit, for the Confederates, standing at ease behind their stone wall or being equally easy in the rifle pits and gun emplacements farther up the hill, had nothing to do and were very much on the alert. As one soldier wrote, "The Confederate gunners seemed to follow the rule of Donnybrook Fair and whenever they saw a Yankee head they tried to hit it with a solid shot or shell." A regular officer recalled that from dawn to dusk the men were "unable to eat, drink, or attend to the calls of nature, for so relentless were the enemy that not even a wounded man or our own stretcher-bearers were exempted from their fire." Not until night could the men be withdrawn. One brigade, which had accomplished nothing whatever during its all-day vigil and had not fired a shot, reported that it had suffered 140 casualties.[20]

The 24th New Jersey, one of the greenhorn regiments in Kimball's brigade, could find only thirty-six men when it called the roll after the fighting stopped. During the night several scores of lost men and bewildered stragglers rejoined, but the regiment was still skimpy and the men were very blue next day when word came to fall in: there was going to be another attack on that stone wall. Obediently, but without a trace of enthusiasm, the 24th fell in—under a captain, all of the field officers having fallen. The captain stood before the regiment, noted that the color-bearers had not survived the action, and called out: "Who will carry the flags?" There was a dead silence. Then two non-coms quietly stepped forward and took up the state and national colors. The captain quietly shook hands with them, and the regiment dressed its ranks. And after a bit news came that orders had been changed, the attack was off, and the men relaxed.[21]

The story of Fredericksburg comes down at last to a simple account of the bravery which men can display and the price that can be exacted of them because they do display it; and if the men gain anything at all by any part of it, there is a transcendental scale of values in operation somewhere which it would be nice to know about. One of Humphrey's colonels remarked that the battle had been a great defeat "owing to the heavy fire in front and an excess of enthusiasm in the rear." The correspondent of the Cincinnati *Commercial* disgustedly wired his paper: "It can hardly be in human nature for men to show more valor, or generals to manifest less judgment, than were perceptible on our side that day."[22]

And yet this disastrous fight, as barren of concrete results as any battle the Army of the Potomac every fought, was nevertheless in its own tragic way a dim beacon light for the future—a dull smoky flame burning reddish-black deep in the night, a flow rather than a blaze, shedding a very patchy and imperfect light, yet nevertheless keeping the winter dark from becoming absolute.

For the significant thing about that endless succession of doomed assaults across the plain was not, after all, the fact that a stupid general ordered them, but the fact that the army which had to make them had never once faltered.

Over and over, hour after agonizing hour, the story had been the same: up front a column of attack being hammered to a bloody wreck, in the rear a new column forming, going in with a cheer even though everyone from file closers to brigadier knew just what was going to happen. Each new column moved up and was broken and another one formed in its rear and came on without any hesitation, long ranks of polished rifle barrels gleaming in the December sunlight. Here they were, moving forward endlessly, those burnished rows of steel in which the poet of the battle hymn had seen the unanswerable writ of a fiery gospel. They were borne by an army that was uninspired and badly led, an army which by its own account of things had lost all its morale but which somehow kept coming on.

TWO

All Played Out

1. A LONG TALK WITH ROBERT

THE SECRETARY of the Navy was familiar with the omens, and on December 14 they were very bad. It was generally known in Washington that a great battle had been fought at Fredericksburg, and while the War Department had nothing whatever to say about it, Mr. Welles felt that it was giving the show away by the very manner in which it kept silent. He had found, Mr. Welles noted in his diary, that whenever the War Department had unwelcome news which it would greatly prefer not to publish, it managed to perform the purely negative act of not publishing "with a great deal of fuss and mystery, a shuffling over of papers and maps, and a far-reaching vacant gaze at something undefined and indescribable."[1]

This entry reflects in part the extreme irritation which Secretary Stanton and General Halleck always seemed able to arouse in Mr. Welles, who was very articulate when irritated. But it also reflects the fact that the department had very good reason for shuffling its papers and looking off into space. The country was not believed in condition to absorb any more really bad news—as hardy a patriot as Governor Morton of Indiana had recently warned Lincoln that "nothing but success, speedy and decided, will save our cause from utter destruction"[2]—and the department had the worst of news for it. What was likely to happen next was more than the Secretary of War or the general-in-chief had any idea.

General Burnside at least had his army back on his own side of the river. For a time he had nourished the wild notion of making one more great assault on the stone wall. He would lead his own IX Corps, which still loved him, in a wild charge that might puncture and destroy that defensive line which the rest of the army had been unable even to reach. This idea he had settled upon in the desolate night hours following the disastrous attacks on December 13, and his subordinate generals, after some argument about who should bell the cat, had finally been able to make him see that no one in the entire army, aside from himself, had the faintest notion that such a charge could possibly succeed. Indeed, it may be that Burnside himself felt the same way about it. General Couch, talking to him in the ruined town that evening, "could see that he wished his body was also lying in front of Marye's Heights," and the whole project may have been an unreasoned groping on Burnside's part for a dramatic and honorable exit from the mess into which he had blundered.[3]

Dissuaded from this insane venture, Burnside ordered a retreat. Here again his subordinates disagreed with him, and Hooker and Couch argued strongly that the town at least should be held as a bridgehead to make possible a new offensive thrust later on. Their advice may have been sound, but Burnside had had all the Fredericksburg he wanted and he would not listen. On a wild, windy night two days after the battle the army went back to the eastern bank, pulling its bridges behind it, and the men assumed that they were going to go into winter quarters and began to build canvas-roofed huts for warmth and comfort.

259

Yet Burnside was not through. The streak of obstinacy which had kept him ordering his brigades up to Marye's Heights long after everyone else had seen that it was hopeless was still in him. He had no intention of giving up his plans for an offensive—believing, apparently correctly, that an offensive before midwinter was what the administration wanted—and he quietly began to formulate new plans while the army licked its wounds and counted up the costs of the great battle.

Put down on paper, those costs were just as dreadful as they had seemed likely to be in the heat of action. In killed, wounded, and missing the army had lost more than 12,600 men, of whom almost exactly 10 per cent had been killed in action. The great bulk of the casualties had been incurred in front of the stone wall, where more than 900 Federal corpses had been counted, and there had been nothing whatever to show for them. Confederate losses on that part of the field had been very light, and there had not been at any time the slightest chance that the Federals could break through there. In the fight made by Franklin's men near Hamilton's Crossing the terms had been more nearly equal. Confederate losses there had been at least comparable to the Union losses, and the Confederate grip on the line of higher ground had been shaken briefly, even if not seriously threatened.[4] Yet if that was the most that could be said—and it was— the battle as a whole had to be written down as a dismal failure. Lee's army had lost only 5,300 men, and much the greater part of it had not been in action at all.

If Lee's army had not suffered much, the town of Fredericksburg had suffered dreadfully. In plain English, the town had been sacked, and the destruction which General Hunt's guns had caused had been the least of its woes. Both before, during, and after the actual fighting, the Army of the Potomac had unleashed upon this historic town the spirit of unrestrained rowdyism. The very divisions which had mustered the incredible heroism to make the repeated attacks on the stone wall had also put on display the very essence of jackbooted vandalism. A veteran of the 118th Pennsylvania left a description:

"The city had been rudely sacked; household furniture lined the streets. Books and battered pictures, bureaus, lounges, feather beds, clocks, and every conceivable article of goods, chattels, and apparel had been savagely torn from the houses and lay about in wanton confusion in all directions. Fires were made, both for warmth and cooking, with fragments of broken furniture. Pianos, their harmonious strings displaced, were utilized as horse troughs, and amid all the dangers animals quietly ate from them." A soldier in another Pennsylvania regiment noted "great scenes of vandalism and useless destruction of books, furniture, carpets, pianos, pictures, etc.," and reported a grotesque carnival aspect in streets still swept by Confederate shell as Union soldiers cavorted about in women's dresses and underwear. "Some of these characters," he added, "might be seen with musical instruments, with big horns, violins, accordions, and banjos"; and he noted that his own regiment took several hundred bottles of wine out of someone's cellar, a part of this wine appearing later on the colonel's own mess table. One illiterate private rifled an express office and carried off a huge bundle of receipts and canceled checks under the impression that he was robbing a bank and getting money.[5]

Brigadier General Alfred Sully, from Howard's division, took over a handsome house for his headquarters and told members of the 1st Minnesota, of which he had previously been colonel, to go through it and take anything they wanted. It belonged to his brother-in-law, who, he said, was a damned Rebel. Perversely, the Minnesota boys took nothing whatever from it and even established a guard there so that nobody else could loot it either. The regimental historian, maintaining that the sack of Fredericksburg was justified by the laws of war, added regretfully that "It would be pleasanter to remember Fredericksburg had there been no looting."[6]

Some of the higher officers, indeed, looking back on it, did argue that by the ancient rules of warfare Fredericksburg was properly open to pillage. An inhabited town, it had been called on to surrender before the battle and it had refused, and the troops had then taken it by storm. Since time immemorial, a town taken under such conditions was fair prey for the men who had captured it. But the men who looted Fredericksburg were not going by the books. The Army of the Potomac behaved there as it had never behaved before, and none of the explanations commonly advanced for lawless behavior by Union troops in this war holds good in this case.

Looting, pillaging, and illegal foraging by Federal soldiers are usually blamed on loosely disciplined Western troops, or on the riffraff bounty men, or on the German regiments brought up in the European tradition, or on the excesses natural to an army which is supplying itself from the enemy's country, or on the studied policy of commanders like Sherman and Sheridan who were frankly out to make Southern civilians tired of the war. But not one of these reasons is any good here. Fredericksburg was ransacked, not by free-and-easy Westerners but chiefly by Easterners of the II Corps and the V Corps, crack outfits with excellent discipline. The army contained no bounty men to speak of, and the German regiments were not in Fredericksburg. The army was not living off the enemy's country but was solidly planted on its own supply lines, and it was under the direction of a general who, however breath-taking some of his deficiencies may have been, was at least a good, amiable man who tried not to make war on civilians. If the usual explanations are good, Fredericksburg should have survived the occupation with minor damage. Actually, the army all but took it apart.

It seems that a new spirit was taking possession of this army. It had been visible before the battle; there had been that wild epidemic of sheep stealing and general lawlessness on the march down from Maryland, which was obviously the prelude to the spoiling of a taken town. A soldier in the 24th New Jersey had written that his conscience bothered him when he saw his fellow soldiers "robbing the poor families of all the little they possessed." At breakfast-time campfires, he said, it was common to hear men tell how "helpless women cried to see their small stock of poultry carried away."[7] A man from the 8th Ohio was heard arguing with a man from the 19th Indiana as to which regiment had managed to collect and send home the greater amount of plunder, and an officer in the 79th New York noted sadly that "wanton destruction of property and all the probable results of a successful siege develop only the most devilish propensities of humanity."[8]

This officer considered that misbehavior by Northern troops simply strengthened Southerners in their desire for independence. He argued, logically enough: "I think, were low ignorant ruffians to visit my home while I was away fighting, burn my house, lay waste my property, insult mother and sisters, beggar the little children I might love, taunt the gray hairs I might respect, leave starvation in the place of plenty, I should feel singularly strengthened in my early delusion." He blamed the whole trouble on "the accursed conduct of the press with its clamor for a vigorous prosecution of the war," and he spoke bitterly of "the effect of the savage appeals of our journals at home."

The New York soldier was beginning to see it. The war was changing, and it was no longer being looked upon as a species of tournament between unstained chivalrous knights. It had reached a point now where the fighting of it was turning loose some unpleasant emotional drives. It had become a war *against*— against slavery, perhaps against the men who owned slaves, by inevitable extension against that man and his family and his goods and chattels who by living with the hated institution seemed to have made war necessary and who in any case were standing in the road when the avengers came. The people here in Virginia had become aliens, and their land was strange and foreign, and therefore subject to hate. The 14th Vermont came down from the North and went into camp in Alexandria, the very first Southern city the regiment had ever seen, and a member of the regiment promptly commented that "the dirty, filthy condition of the streets in Alexandria is not only discoverable in all Southern cities but exhibits very plainly the blighting effects of slavery." A soldier in the equally green 33rd Massachusetts took his first look at Virginia, found its sleepy hamlets unlike New England's trim villages, and wrote caustically: "Let me say here that the towns of Virginia are composed of a barn, one outhouse, and a haystack."[9] Behind such sentences, obviously, lay a feeling of being among the infidels. If the war must be carried on with greater vigor, as all the spokesmen of government were saying, then these infidels were not to be treated too gently, and if bad things happened to them it did not matter very much.

It was not a genteel, restrained, orderly country that was feeling this changed emotional current. It was a nation with the infinite raw strength of graceless youth, moving with gigantic careless energy into a future that was not known to have any bounds whatever. It was feeling its oats and it was flexing muscles bigger than anybody else ever had, and if people got hurt along the way it was not even going to notice. It had been like that from the beginning and it had not yet grown mellow and thoughtful, and it was not for nothing that its national air was a little tune called "Yankee Doodle," which has no words to speak of and expresses no sentiment on earth but sheer perky impudence.

This was the country of the boisterous forty-niner, the hell-roaring lumberjack, and the riverman who was half horse and half alligator. Without rancor (and also without the slightest hesitation) it annihilated Indian tribes so that it could people a wilderness, asserting that the only good Indian was a dead Indian and remarking casually of its own pioneers that the cowards never started and the weak died along the road. As it faced the cathedral aisles of endless virgin forests it shouted for immediate daylight in the swamp, even if whole generations must be brutalized for it. It was the country that invented the bucko mate and the Shanghai passage, and if the skysails of its incredible clippers gleamed on the farthest magic horizon they were taken there by men under the daily rule of clubs and brass knuckles. This nation accepted boiler explosions as the price of steamboat travel and it would boast presently of a dead gandy-dancer for every crosstie on the transcontinental railroad. It wore seven-league boots and scorned to look where it planted them, and each of its immense strides was made at immense human cost. And the army of this country, buckling down to it at last in a fight which had to go to a finish, was going to be very rough on enemy civilians, not because it had anything against them but simply because they were there.

Of genuine hatred this army had practically none. The wild young men who ruined ancestral portraits and pranced in the smoky streets wearing the embroidered undergarments of gentlewomen were expressing nothing but plain hooliganism, which somehow was the obverse side of the medal that had laid nine hundred corpses in front of the stone wall west of town. Both sides of the medal bespoke raw youth which cheered and guffawed by turns, whose noble best forever went arm in arm with its ugly worst.

Before Burnside pulled his men back across the river there was a truce, and details from both armies went out to relieve such wounded as still lived and to bury the dead. In front of that stone wall, where all the dead men were Yankees, the lifeless bodies were nearly all naked. During the cold night needy Rebels had come out to help themselves to the warm coats and pants and the good Yankee shoes which the dead men would no longer need. An officer from the 48th Pennsylvania, supervising the work of one detail, fell into conversation with a Confederate officer, and the Confederate told him: "You Yankees don't know how to hate—you don't hate us near as much as we hate you." The Confederate gestured toward the pitiful naked rows of despoiled corpses and asked in effect: Do you think we could ever treat your dead that way if we didn't hate you?[10]

Whether that Confederate hatred was real or whether the casual stripping of Yankee corpses was simply one more manifestation of the brutally realistic American spirit may be a story in itself. The point is that others besides that one Rebel officer felt the Federals to be lacking in hatred: among them, none other than Burnside himself. Congressman George W. Julian of Indiana, one of the sternest of the abolitionist leaders, had a chat with Burnside not long after the battle and wrote:

"General Burnside told me our men did not feel toward the Rebels as they felt toward us, and he assured me that this was the grand obstacle to our success. Our soldiers, he said, were not sufficiently fired by resentment, and he exhorted me, if I could, to breathe into our people at home the same spirit toward our enemies which inspired them toward us."

Burnside's soldiers might have explained things a little differently if anyone had asked them about the grand obstacle to success. As a matter of fact, they did put it differently—quite differently—and without being asked. A soldier in the 5th Wisconsin wrote after this battle: "Was there ever an army so cruelly handicapped as the Army of the Potomac? Is there, in military annals, any record of men preserving their discipline, patriotism, courage, in spite of such adverse circumstances as beset these men of the North?"[11]

However, Congressman Julian had been talking to the commanding general, not to the enlisted man, and no leader of the abolitionists ever needed to be told twice to go out and stir up more hatred. Julian later recounted that in the political campaign of the following summer "I fully entered into the spirit of General Burnside's advice . . . to breathe into the hearts of the people a feeling of animosity against the Rebels."[12] The wind was being sown and the whirlwind would soon be ready for reaping.

Yet it seems that the soldiers who would have to be around when the reaping took place had small part in the sowing. This army was doubly deficient—in leadership and in vindictiveness—and the men do not appear even to have tried to hate their enemies. On the contrary, they exercised a good deal of ingenuity in order to open a highly illegal but quite friendly trade with them, with the wide Rappahannock as the bearer of their peaceful cargoes. The classical essentials for a thriving peacetime trade were present; that is, each side had a surplus of goods greatly in demand by the other side, the Federals having plenty of coffee and the Confederates having an excess of tobacco. And as the pickets walked their posts by the river it soon occurred to Northerners and Southerners alike that the war would get on just as well and would be a good deal less onerous to the individual if some of that coffee could be swapped for some of that tobacco.

It is probable that every regiment which was stationed on the river took part in this trade at one time or another, and the routine was always much the same. The following appears to have been typical:

Sunny winter day: 17th Mississippi on picket on the Rebel side of the stream, 24th New Jersey guarding the shore just opposite. Shouted conversation over the water reveals a mutual desire to trade. Jersey men presently get a small board, whittle it into something resembling the shape of a boat, put in a mast, use an old letter for a sail, put a load of coffee aboard, point it for the Confederate shore, and let it go. The intention is good, but the performance is poor: the homemade craft capsizes in a mid-river gust of wind and floats off downstream, bottom up, its cargo a total loss.

Among the Mississippians there seem to have been men who knew a bit more about the design and construction of sailing vessels, and they presently brought a much more practical craft down to the water—a little boat two feet long or thereabouts and five or six inches wide, carefully hollowed out to provide cargo space and equipped with rudder and sails that would actually work. This boat made a successful passage. The Jersey soldiers who received it took from its hold a note reading:

"Gents U.S. Army: We send you some tobacco by our packet. Send us some coffee in return. Also a deck of cards, if you have them, and we will send you more tobacco. Send us any late papers if you have them." The letter was signed by "Jas. O. Parker, Co. H., 17th Mississippi Vols."

The vessel's lading was as stated in the manifest, and in addition there was a small book, *Questions on the Gospels,* by the Reverend R. Bethell Claxton, D.D., which one of the Federals kept with him through the rest of the war. And the Jersey men sent coffee and hardtack over on the little boat's return trip, with a note promising that there would be a deck of cards the next time the outfit came on picket. The boat made a number of round trips and became quite famous—so much so that the better part of each regiment would come down to the shore to greet it.[13]

This tendency on the part of the soldiers to forget that there was a war on worried the high command, and stern orders were issued, to which the soldiers paid no more attention than they had to. Now and then the thing went farther than toy boats loaded with coffee and playing cards. Men crossed the river at times to get together personally with their enemies, and a Confederate general left a half-scandalized, half-amused account of how he nabbed a few Yankee soldiers visiting his own men and prepared to send them off to Richmond as prisoners of war, only to have his men plead almost tearfully that he just couldn't do it—they had given the Yankees their word of honor that if they came over to visit they would be allowed to go back again. In the end the general relented on a stern don't-let-it-happen-again basis.[14] The elements in this war were mixed and contradictory. If one side robbed corpses and the other side robbed housewives, there was on both sides, deep in the bones and the spirit, this strange absence of rancor, which may, in the end, explain why it was that the two sections were finally able to reunite after a war which would seem to have left scars too deep for any healing.

It does not appear that this willingness to fraternize ever appreciably dulled the fighting edge of either army, but it undoubtedly led to a good many security leaks. Armies whose outposts spend much of their time exchanging gossip are not likely to keep their secrets very well. This probably hampered Burnside more than it hampered Lee, for the Confederates just then did not need to make many plans and hence had few secrets to keep. Their job was just to stand by and keep the Yankees from doing whatever they proposed to do next. Burnside was supposed to be aggressive, and he did his best to live up to the role. But to the end of his career as commander of the army he seems to have kept very few secrets from his opponents.

Since nothing came of the plans which he laid after Fredericksburg, the fact that Lee quickly found out about them did no particular harm. What really made trouble for Burnside was the fact that he could not keep his plans hidden from his own subordinates, who learned about them long before they were supposed to and, learning, made much trouble for him.

Burnside bestirred himself on the day after Christmas, nearly a fortnight after the battle. All of the wounded had been removed from the field hospitals to the general hospitals farther to the rear, many of them having been transferred by steamer all the way back to Washington. The unwounded survivors of the battle were making themselves tolerably comfortable in the camps near Falmouth—camps which, as a historian of Hancock's division wrote, now had "room enough to spare," a full two thousand of Hancock's five thousand men having been shot.[15]

As before, Burnside's first problem was to get across the river. This time he would leave the Fredericksburg crossing strictly alone. He would make an elaborate feint at crossing by the fords upstream, and then he would throw the bulk of his army across at Muddy Creek, some seven miles below Fredericksburg. Artillery positions to protect the crossings were selected, and access roads were corduroyed. In addition, Burnside decided to try to make some sort of effective use of his cavalry.

Army of the Potomac cavalry had been very poorly handled thus far in the war. It operated under many handicaps, the initial one being that it was almost uniformly recruited from among ardent young men who thought that it would be fine to be dashing troopers but who had never in their lives been on horseback before enlisting. As a result, a Yankee cavalry regiment needed a lot of training. Before it could even begin to amount to anything as cavalry, everybody from the company officers on down had first to learn how to get on a horse and how to stay on once the brute began to move. Since practically all of the Confederate cavalrymen were superb horsemen to begin with, their squadrons started with an enormous advantage. Worse yet, the Yankee high command in the first part of the war does not appear to have understood exactly what cavalry was for. All too often the cavalry commands were split up and attached to separate infantry units, and there was a common tendency to employ them largely for routine picket and courier duty. Hardly anyone ever tried to use them the way Stuart used his mounted brigades. One result of this was that cavalry's standing in the army was not high. A cavalry officer recalled ruefully that "it was a byword in our army that a reward would be paid for a *dead* cavalryman."[16] A disgruntled foot soldier remembered:

"Our cavalry had lost caste altogether with the infantry. Their reported skirmishes with the enemy, and 'driving in the Rebel pickets,' were received with incredulous smiles and jeers until they became mum as oysters. When hailed for information . . . they would gaze at the infantry in stupid wonder at such questions, then would laugh among themselves at some remark of one of theirs about 'doughboys'; the laugh would then change to sullen anger as some shrill-voiced infantry veteran would inquire, loud enough to be heard a mile away, 'Did you see any dead cavalrymen out there?' This pertinent question had the effect of making every rider drive spurs into his horse and briskly move forward, while the sounds of laughter and jeers long and loud of their tormentors the 'doughboys' followed them."[17]

Cavalry's status was not going to improve until somebody made effective use of the mounted arm, and this Burnside set out to do. He detailed fifteen hundred mounted troops to ride upstream in connection with the army's projected move. Five hundred of these, to deceive the Rebels, were to make a feint toward Warrenton and Culpeper, as if the army planned a sally in that direction, and then were to return to Falmouth as ostentatiously as possible. The remainder—picked men, chosen from eight of the army's best cavalry regiments—were to cross the Rappahannock at Kelly's Ford, speed over to the Rapidan and cross it at Raccoon Ford, and then strike boldly south, breaking both the Virginia Central and the Fredericksburg railroads, swinging clear west of Richmond, and then plunging south all the way to the coastal point of Suffolk, where the Federals had a small garrison under General John Peck. At Suffolk transports would be waiting to bring the troopers back to Aquia Creek.

Whether even a picked body of Federal cavalry could at that time have performed a risky maneuver like that under the noses of Stuart's sharp-eyed, hard-riding patrols is probably open to serious question. The mere fact that the venture was to be tried, however, indicated that Burnside was prepared to use the mounted arm with boldness and imagination, and it raised cavalry morale immensely. Major Henry Lee Higginson of the 1st Massachusetts Cavalry called the project "a risky expedition but a buster," and felt that it was "a brilliant plan," and when the squadrons trotted upstream it looked as if a new day was about to dawn.[18]

But these moments of bright hope never seemed to last very long in this army. The cavalry made a brisk thirty-mile march and went into bivouac just inshore from Kelly's Ford, full of enthusiasm, and never got any farther. For just as they were making their camp Burnside got a cryptic telegram from Abraham Lincoln saying, "I have good reason for saying you must not make a general movement without letting me know of it," and the cavalry had to be told to stop and await further orders. Major Higginson wrote angrily that "we could and would have done anything," adding that "such checks destroy the enthusiasm of any army."

Lincoln's telegram was a stunner. As far as Burnside was aware, no one in the army aside from a couple of his most trusted staff officers knew that a general movement was in the cards. He concluded hopefully that something special, to which the movements of his own army had to conform, must be going on in some other military theater, so he went up to Washington to see the President and find out what was up.

What was up was the kind of intrigue which had become standard operating procedure for the officer corps of the Army of the Potomac.

Just before New Year's Day two brigadiers in Baldy Smith's VI Corps had taken leaves of absence. These officers were John Newton, commanding Smith's 3rd Division and John Cochrane, who had the 1st Brigade of that division. Having taken Smith and the Grand Division commander, Franklin, into their confidence, these generals quickly left for Washington to indulge the perennial recourse of the unhappy army officer; viz., to See Their Congressmen. Specifically, they intended to see Senator Henry Wilson of Massachusetts, chairman of the Senate Military Committee, and Congressman Moses F. Odell of New York, a member of the powerful Joint Committee on the Conduct of the War. As so often happened in the Army of the Potomac, however, their militarty planning was deficient because of a failure of intelligence; that is, they had neglected to note that Congress was in recess over the holidays, which meant that both of these statemen were out of the city. Cochrane, however, had been an important Republican congressman himself back in 1861, and he had connections, so presently the two generals were talking with Secretary of State Seward, and before the day was over Seward took them to the White House and got them in to Lincoln's study.

Newton was senior officer and he spoke up first, doing a good deal of clumsy beating around the bush and almost defeating his own purpose. He tried to tell Lincoln that the army was in a bad way and would come to pieces if Burnside tried to maneuver it again, but he said it poorly. Later Newton explained that "I could not say directly to the President that the whole trouble was that the privates had no confidence in General Burnside," although it is hard to see why he could not. That was what he and Cochrane had come to Washington for, and somewhere along the line a little frankness might have helped. As it was, he gave Lincoln the idea that here were two self-promoting officers who simply wanted to get their commander's job, and Lincoln spoke up with a good deal of heat— no doubt, in one way and another, having had about all of that sort of thing he cared to take in his twenty-one months as President. Cochrane, who was a little more outspoken, assured Lincoln that they were moved solely by patriotism and were just trying to give the President information which he needed to have. This got Newton back on the rails, and he went on to say that in his opinion the condition of the army was such that if it were again led into defeat along the Rappahannock it would be utterly destroyed. The two generals wagged their heads to corroborate themselves, suggested that the President might want to look into things for himself, and at last took their leave.

And this was what lay back of Lincoln's telegram, as Burnside learned when he reached the White House. Halleck and Stanton sat in with him, while Lincoln gave the gist of the complaint, withholding the names of the two talebearers. Burnside angrily demanded that the two men be cashiered, and for once Halleck supported him, but after all, that was a side issue. The big question was the intricate relationships existing among Burnside, his generals, the enlisted men in his army, the War Department, and the President, and nobody quite seemed to know what the next step ought to be.[19]

A bit later Burnside had a private talk with Lincoln in which he had some remarks of his own to make about lack of confidence. Secretary Stanton, he said bluntly, "has not the confidence of the officers and soldiers" and probably lacked the confidence of the country also, and the same went for Halleck. There was likewise a gulf between Burnside and his own generals; Burnside was convinced that the army ought to drive forward for another river crossing, "but I am not sustained in this by a single Grand Division commander in my command." It was his belief, he added, that he himself ought to resign, not merely from the command of the army, but from his commission as a general, becoming a civilian once more. Meanwhile, since it was vital for the President to have about him officials whom the country and the army believed in and would support, the President might want to give some thought to the idea of replacing Stanton and Halleck too.[20]

After Burnside left the White House the President tried desperately to get a little help out of Halleck. Brushing aside the question of resignations, Lincoln put it up to Halleck bluntly: Burnside wanted to renew the offensive, but his top commanders disagreed, and wasn't this a spot where the general-in-chief ought to go into action? Lincoln wanted Halleck to go down to Fredericksburg, look the ground over, talk with the various generals, and then either tell Burnside to go ahead or have him call the whole thing off. With that tartness that he could use when he had to, Lincoln told Halleck: "If in such a difficulty as this you do not help, you fail me precisely in the point for which I sought your assistance."

This hurt Halleck's feelings. He wrote to Stanton, offering his resignation, and the sounds of his grief reached the White House. In the files Lincoln's letter to him acquired the notation in Lincoln's handwriting, "Withdrawn, because considered harsh by General Halleck." More than this Halleck did not do, until a few days later he got a letter from Burnside stating that officer's belief that he was entitled at least to some general directions as to the advisability of crossing the Rappahannock. This finally roused Halleck a little, and on January 7 he wrote to Burnside saying in effect that he had always been in favor of a forward movement, that the object was to defeat Lee's army rather than to capture Richmond, and that since Lee's army lay beyond the river it would be necessary for Burnside to cross the river if he proposed to fight. The big idea, Halleck went on solemnly, was "to injure him all you can with the least injury to yourself." But Halleck made it clear that it was entirely up to Burnside to decide when, where, and how to get across the river.

Beyond this Halleck would not go. With the whole machinery of government thrown into action, he had a last been put on record as believing that the commander of the army ought to do something. If between the army commander and the generals who would have to make his strategy effective there was such paralyzing doubt and distrust that any campaign was foredoomed to failure, Halleck was going to keep his hands out of the whole mess. Lincoln had brought him to Washington to handle just such tangles as this, but when Halleck had told the army commander that in any fight it was advisable to inflict more injury than he received, he had reached his limit. Lincoln dropped Burnside a line saying that he had seen Halleck's letter and he endorsed the idea of a forward movement, although Burnside must understand that the government was not trying to drive him. Meanwhile, Lincoln did not see how it would help any just now to accept Burnside's resignation. Burnside would have to take it from there and do the best he could with it.[21]

This Burnside would do. His soldiers and the country might have been better off if Burnside had been more of a quitter, but that was one defect which he lacked. He had a responsibility which he knew was too big for him, but as long as he had it he would go ahead with it. The man seems to have felt the lonely isolation of his position very keenly. General Baldy Smith dropped in on him one evening, and Burnside was very frank about it. Everybody he ever talked to, said Burnside, had some personal interest to serve. The commander of the army could never be sure that what was said to him was motivated by either loyalty or friendship. Therefore, Burnside continued, it was his custom every night, after everything had quieted down, to send for Robert and have a long talk with him.

Robert was an aged and devoted colored servant who had been with Burnside for many years and who had charge of the cooking at army headquarters. Every night in the big Virginia mansion which had been taken over for army head-quarters, with the trim patrols from the crack cavalry squadron which acted as headquarters guard standing on the alert outside, and the dapper staff officers in sashes and epaulets ornamenting the anterooms within, Robert and the general sat down by the fire for a long talk. Only then, said Burnside, could he feel that he was talking with someone who really had his interests at heart. And Baldy Smith wondered irreverently if that was how the Fredericksburg battle plan had been drawn up.[22]

2. THE FOOLS THAT BRING DISASTER

THE AUTHORITIES had not said anything about going into winter quarters, be-cause there was this plan of Burnside's for a winter campaign, and sooner or later something was likely to come of it. But the soldiers figured that nothing more was going to happen until spring, which was quite reasonable of them, and in the five weeks that followed the battle of Fredericksburg they went to work to provide themselves with all-weather houses in place of the pup tents that were government issue for times like these.

This army carried thousands of axes in its wagons, and the soldiers took them and swarmed over the hills and ravines that bordered the Rappahannock, fell-ing trees and trimming them into logs, until the land for miles around was bleak and naked under the January sky.[1] It would appear that some of the men were handy with axes and that some of them were not. There is a reminiscence in one of the old books about a regiment of backwoodsmen from Wisconsin which watched one day while a detail of city-bred New Yorkers labored mightily to cut up a pile of logs into ties for Colonel Haupt's railroad. The Wisconsin men stood it as long as they could, and finally they sent over a delegation: Give us those axes before somebody kills himself, and we'll cut the ties![2]

Every regiment took its turn with the axes, and not long after the first of the year the great sprawling camp of the army began to look like a crude but perma-nent city. The log-and-canvas huts which covered hills and plains were ranged in orderly fashion along company and regimental streets, with broad main-traf-fic arteries going past division and corps headquarters. The city even had its own barren parks—open fields, the earth packed down like concrete, where brigade and battalion drills were held. A few genuine civilian houses survived here and there, serving as quarters for high-ranking officers and their staff. Most of the houses were simply torn down for their lumber.

The huts in which the army lived were much of a pattern. The usual course was for four men to club together to make and occupy one hut. They would lay up pine logs to a height of three or four feet, in a rectangle twelve feet long by a little more than six feet wide, and there would be a ridgepole running from end to end of the enclosure six feet off the ground. Four shelter-tent halves (each of which measured approximately six feet by four) were then buttoned together, thrown over the ridgepole, and brought down to the logs at the sides and made secure. The logs were carefully chinked with mud, and the gable ends were filled with whatever was available—with woodwork if the men could shape it easily, with extra shelter tents if such could be stolen, sometimes with rubber blankets if the men happened to own them. A door was cut in one end and a fireplace was built beside it with a mud-and-stick chimney which usually was somewhat defective. (A favorite trick at night, one soldier remembered, was to lay a flat board across the top of the nearest smoking chimney and then run before the resulting smudge sent the occupants out looking for a fight.) At the far end of the hut there generally would be two double bunks running from wall to wall. The theory was that two men sleeping together and sharing their blankets could keep warmer than if each man had to bunk to himself.

Styles in bunks varied, however. A New York soldier wrote that in his outfit the men took planks and made oblong frames on the ground inside their hut, "like onion beds in a garden," filling the frames with dead leaves or pine boughs. If the planks were wide enough to make the bed-place fairly deep, and if enough leaves or boughs were gathered, he said, the bed was as snug as anyone could wish. A Massachusetts soldier remarked that on cold nights the rookie would put on all of his clothing, overcoat included, before he went to bed, but that the old-timer would undress and then use his discarded clothing as extra covers on top of his blankets. It was much warmer that way, the veteran said.[3]

But even though its camp was snug enough, this army was very dispirited as the new year began. It was not well, for one thing. There was much sickness and there were many deaths, and never a day passed without the sound of firing squads discharging their farewell volleys over new graves in the cheerless hills. The rookie regiments in particular lost men from disease, but there were deaths among the veteran regiments too, and it seemed that these losses somehow were much more depressing that the deaths that occurred in battle. One soldier wrote that death in a military camp was just as moving, and caused just as much grief to be felt and shown, as death in time of peace in one's own home town.[4] These young men were far from their families, and if they had the rude strength of youth, they also had youth's terrible capacity for loneliness, and when a man fell ill that loneliness took hold of him very hard. Then his comrades did their best to take a little of his loneliness away by visiting his sickbed, bringing him camp gossip and any dainties which they might have, writing letters for him and showing other little attentions. If he died, they inherited his loneliness (it would be quite unendurable to suppose that he took it with him) and the mourners who went about the streets of this military city were desperately unhappy.

Yet death and loneliness visit the camp of a victorious army of high morale also. Men fell ill and died that winter, and were sincerely mourned, among the high-spirited Confederates across the river, and yet no Southerner remembered the winter afterward as a time of unrelieved gloom. The trouble on the Yankee side of the river was that there did not appear to be any sensible reason for anything. There had been many deaths and it looked as if they had all been wasted. It was as certain as anything could be that there would be more deaths in future, and it seemed likely that they would be wasted too. The soldiers were left with nothing to believe in. A thoughtful chaplain recorded:

"The phrensy of soldiers rushing during an engagement to glory or death has, as our boys amusingly affirm, *been played out*. Our battle-worn veterans go into danger, when ordered, remain as a stern duty so long as directed, and leave as soon as honor and duty allow. Camp followers, and one third of our armies may now be classed in that category, keep out of the range of shell and minnie." When illustrated magazines came to camp, the padre continued, the soldiers would look at the pictures showing mounted officers with drawn swords nobly leading their heroic troops into action and would jeer loudly and repeat: "All played out!"[5]

The eminent Bostonian cavalryman, Major Higginson, wrote that "stupidity and wickedness" ruled the army, and concluded: "We are getting on to perdition. If the people at home do not take the mismanagement of this war and this government to heart, we shall have a disgraceful peace before summer." A less distinguished Bay Stater in the 33rd Massachusetts wrote that "our poppycorn generals kill men as Herod killed the innocents," and even stouthearted Major Rufus Dawes of the 6th Wisconsin wrote home that "this army seems to be overburdened with second-rate men in high positions, from General Burnside down. . . . This winter is, indeed, the Valley Forge of the war."[6] William Thompson Lusk, a former medical student who was gloomily serving in the 79th New York, gave way to despairing anger in a letter which indicates that President Lincoln himself was not out of the reach of a soldier's resentment just then:

"Alas my poor country! It has strong limbs to march and meet the foe, stout arms to strike heavy blows, brave hearts to dare—but the brains, the brains— have we no brains to use the arms and limbs and eager hearts with cunning? Perhaps Old Abe has some funny story to tell, appropriate to the occasion." A week later this same soldier wrote, in another letter: "Mother, do not wonder that my loyalty is growing weak. . . . I am sick and tired of disaster and the fools that bring disaster upon us."[7]

Thus the army, apparently. And yet there are few ventures which offer as many chances for error as this business of trying to determine exactly how an army feels and what it proposes to do about it. Private soldiers have hidden emotional reserves which neither they nor anyone else can bring out for inspection and analysis, and the very men who declare that loyalty is for fools and courage a delusion may be precisely the ones, who, when ordered, will lift a cheer and tramp across a fire-blasted meadow to attack a stone wall which they know full well is death to approach. They can sometimes take a good deal more than one thinks, and when they finally approach the point at which they will flatly refuse to take any more they are not likely to do very much talking about it. The thing to watch then is what they do and what they fail to do, and not what they say.

In this, oddly enough, the private soldier most closely resembles the private civilian, which indeed he is in another incarnation. Those who fancy that he would not go anywhere if they themselves were not there, heaven-sent, to lead and inspire him, can do a great deal of fruitless worrying about him, and early in this winter of 1863 this worrying was reaching its high point for the whole war.

Among those who worried was the Union quartermaster general, Montgomery C. Meigs, a grave and estimable man who deserves just a little better of posterity than he seems likely ever to get. Meigs had a hard job to do and he did it extremely well, and yet he is remembered today principally because an impish Confederate cavalryman hung the barb of a practical joke upon him. Confederate cavalry raided deep behind the Yankee lines that winter and seized a telegraph office, from which there presently came a dispatch to General Meigs in his office at Washington protesting bitterly about the poor quality of the mules which the Confederacy was getting via its captures of Yankee wagon trains. The wire was signed with the mighty name of Jeb Stuart, which has kept it from being forgotten, and it tends to be the only thing one thinks about when Meigs's name comes up.

As 1862 ended and 1863 began, Meigs sat down to send a friendly unofficial letter to General Burnside, and the general tenor of it was that if the army did not soon win a victory the country would be too discouraged to go on with the war any longer. The army was very expensive (said Meigs, who had to purchase much of its matériel and equipment) and it was consuming the country's resources:

"I begin to apprehend a catastrophe. . . . Exhaustion steals over the country. Confidence and hope are dying. . . . I begin to doubt the possibility of maintaining the contest beyond this winter, unless the popular heart is encouraged by victory on the Rappahannock."

In broad and somewhat hasty strokes Meigs then sketched a plan of campaign, which seemed chiefly to call on Burnside to get his army in between the Confederate Army and Richmond—sound advice, unquestionably, if there were just a way to carry it out. Meigs mentioned rapid marches of the kind made by Napoleon at Jena and Robert E. Lee at Second Bull Run, and then ascended to high rhetoric with a demand for speedy action: "Rest at Falmouth is death to our nation—is defeat, border warfare, hollow truce, barbarism, ruin for ages, chaos!"[8]

Which might possibly be so. Yet the whole case is a bit curious, and the anxiety of General Meigs comes down from the long ago as the deathless symbol of the reluctance of important folk to trust the courage and endurance of their less distinguished fellow citizens. This army had fought for different reasons at different times—to capture Richmond, to repel invasion, to save itself from destruction, and so on. Now, apparently, it must fight to encourage the civilians; or, more accurately, to encourage government officials who believed that the civilian needed to be encouraged. Never before had the army been asked to fight for a reason so inadequate.

Nor was the moment propitious. The weather had been clear and mild ever since the battle of Fredericksburg, which meant that the roads were dry and consequently passable. But the calendar said that midwinter was arriving, and sooner or later midwinter would bring a good deal of rain and snow. To begin a campaign now would be to gamble that more than 100,000 men, plus many thousands of very heavy wheeled vehicles, would be able to move swiftly over a network of totally unpaved roads which would become literally impassable once normal winter weather set in. The dismayed populace which was looking anxiously for victory along the Rappahannock might very easily, instead, see its principal army stuck hopelessly in the mud. The soldiers who had built winter quarters without waiting to be told had things sized up: warfare was just impossible at this time of year, and no sensible man would try it.

Sensible men, however, really had very little to do with it. The war itself did not make very much sense, which may have affected the way it was directed. It was being fought because emotion had been evoked to deal with a crisis that called for intelligence. There had been the great argument between men and sections, with many old values endangered, and on each side there had arisen men with blazing eyes and hot hearts to arouse their fellows to imminent peril. Fear had been called forth (because it is thought that men are most surely to be aroused by fear), and then came the anger that goes with fear, and finally the great unreason that goes with both had come out to take control of things—a situation deeply lamented by all who had created it.

So it might be quite true that a sensible man would not try to begin a campaign in roadless Virginia in mid-January, and yet a mid-January campaign could be ordered for all of that. The young men who were on the march had to walk in the glare cast by all of those frightened yesterdays, which could light both the wise and the foolish in but one direction. Just now the army was being asked to outmarch and outfight Robert E. Lee for the sake of the emotional uplift which such a victory would provide for the people back home: people who themselves neither marched nor fought but simply paid the bills and endured and were therefore believed to be in dire need of emotional uplift, and who, since emotional ties could not easily be dissolved, would be obliged to mourn such men as were destroyed by the marching and the fighting. None of this made any sense. The winter campaign was a complete triumph of unreason, and it would be useless to judge it by the standards of sensible men.

After his fashion Burnside had learned something by experience. He was not going to try to cross the river at Fredericksburg, and instead of going headlong over those deadly entrenchments on the low hills he would attempt to go bloodlessly around them. The plans that he now laid called for a swift march upriver with pontoon bridges put across the Rappahannock at United States Ford. The army would cross there, Lee would be outflanked, and the Fredericksburg line would be evacuated; and while General Meigs's rosy dream of actual interposition between Lee and Richmond might fail, it should at least be possible to force a battle in the open country, where superior Federal muscle could make itself felt. It would be tried, in any case, and the orders went out.

They were no sooner out than they had to be changed slightly. Lee was just as much aware as was Burnside that the crossing at United States Ford led straight to his rear, and it developed presently that he had a force dug in there to contest the crossing. So Burnside made Banks Ford, near Falmouth, the objective, and directed that pontoons and other equipment for five bridges be on the bank there by dawn of Wednesday, January 21. General Hunt was to line the hills with guns to deal with any Confederates who tried again to obstruct Yankee bridgebuilders. Hooker and Franklin were to set their grand divisions in motion on Tuesday morning, January 20. Sumner was to wait at Falmouth and put his men over the river after these two had crossed. All in all, here was a new campaign, and maybe it would have an outside chance to work if the weather would just hold.

The weather had been very good so far. January was more than half gone and the ground was dry and firm and the air was balmy—the men had played baseball in the open drill fields, and there had been a big match between a team from the 19th Massachusetts and one from the 7th Michigan for a sixty-dollar side bet, with Howard's entire division looking on. (It was won by the 19th Massachusetts; irritatingly enough, the scribe who recorded the event forgot to say what the score was.)[9] Burnside issued a general order announcing that "the auspicious moment seems to have arrived to strike a great and mortal blow to the rebellion," and the rookie 33rd Massachusetts was drawn up and harangued by its colonel, who announced that no Massachusetts regiment had yet lost a flag and added that they would be in action with the enemy "tomorrow morning at 6 o'clock." The regiment cheered and the band struck up "Yankee Doodle" and the army got under way.[10]

It took bugles and drums and flags—these last held aloft by men who bought the privilege of carrying them by taking extra risks in all battles—to get an army started in those days. On this twentieth of January the Army of the Potomac moved out of its unhappy camps near Falmouth under the thin January sunlight with hope and doubt riding invisible, of equal status, at the head of the column. After breakfast, by way of starting things off, the buglers in each brigade sounded a call known as "the general," which alerted everyone. (All bugle calls had names: breakfast call was "peas on a trencher," dinner was "roast beef," and the call which summoned men to advance against the enemy was known for some reason as "Tommy Totten.") The men struck their tents and packed their knapsacks and loaded the regimental wagons, and then they fell into their places by squads. Half an hour later the bugles blew "assembly" and the squads formed into companies—tall men at the right, short men at the left, everybody jostling elbows and passing wisecracks as the lines stiffened across the field, company officers out in front barking little orders and being important. Then, with all the companies formed, the colonels and the brigadiers came out and the bugles sounded "colors," the national and regimental flags were unfurled, and the companies moved in to right and left of them to form regimental front, each regimental adjutant carefully noting which company was last to come into line and assigning that company to the rear of the regimental column during the march.[11]

One after another the regiments swung and wheeled into column and went down through the emptying camps—bands playing, drums rolling and crashing, feet hitting the ground all together, nobody lapsing into the informal route step until camp had been left behind. Maybe the road ahead was going to be smooth and dry and easy to walk on, with a pleasant campground at the end of it in the cool of a clear twilight, and maybe it was going to lead through mud to some soggy cold swamp, and indeed, for all anyone knew, it would perhaps for some of the men be the last of all the roads on earth, curling over a far-off horizon from which nobody could take a backward glance. There were always those possibilities every time the army broke camp and took to the road; and this day the army set out glad for the winter sunlight and doubtless hoping for the little favors which a soldier is permitted to expect—dry ground, pleasant sun, clear skies at night.

If the army hoped for these things it did not get them. The sky clouded over during the afternoon, even though the air remained warm for a while, and by evening it was raining; a slow drizzle first that soon became a steady downpour, with a howling wind whipping the rain down the country roads, setting in like a winter storm that has no intention of stopping. Up in Washington, fifty miles to the north, Secretary of the Navy Welles looked out of his snug office into a "furious storm" and worried over the safety of two of Navy's most prized ships, monitors *Weehawken* and *Nahant*, cruising coastwise down the Atlantic in the trough of this nor'easter. Their skippers, he hoped, would have the caution to take shelter behind Delaware breakwater. (*Nahant* did put in, Welles found out later; *Weehawken* rode out the storm, being more seaworthy than the secretary dared hope.)[12] And the army, launched on a campagin which involved using unpaved roads to get at an unwhipped enemy who lay beyond an unbridged river, took what shelter it could in the tangled second growth back from the river crossings and wondered what was in the cards for tomorrow.

What was going to happen tomorrow was more of the same, only a great deal worse, and there was a very uncomfortable night to endure first. The men pitched their pup tents for covering from the icy rain, and they tried to build fires under the dripping branches. The air seemed too heavy to carry the smoke away and the wood was too wet to burn decently anyway, and the smoldering useless campfires made a monstrous smudge miles across and indescribably thick, and the men blinked smarting eyes and lay flat on the soaked ground to get a little air. All wagon trains were lost somewhere in the waterlogged rear, and if a man had food in his haversack he ate.[13] He did not eat a hot meal, in most cases, because it was very hard to kindle the wet wood into enough of a blaze to boil coffee or frizzle salt pork.

Morning came and the rain grew worse. The New York *Times* correspondent, surveying the situation with the dispassionate reserve proper to his station, wrote to his paper that "the nature of the upper geologic deposits of this region affords unequaled elements for bad roads." Virginia soil, he explained, was a mixture of clay and sand which, when wet, became very soft, practically bottomless, and exceedingly sticky.[14]

This was putting it mildly. The rainy dawn lightened reluctantly to a dripping daylight, and the troops floundered out into the roads and tried to resume the march. Someone got the orders mixed, and two army corps presently met at a muddy crossroad, committed by unalterable military decree to march squarely across each other. They moved sluggishly but inexorably, the men plodding on with bowed heads, big gobs of mud clinging to each heavy foot. In some fantastic manner the two blind columns did manage to get partly across each other, and everybody was cursing his neighbor, the Virginia mud, the cold rain, and the whole idea of having a war at all. In the end the two corps came to a helpless standstill, having got into a tangle which half a day of dry weather on an unimpeded drill ground would not have straightened out.[15]

But that was a minor problem, the way things were going. The ponderous pontoon trains which were supposed to lead the way to the river had got off to a very late start. Once again headquarters had forgotten to tell the engineers that their boats were going to be needed. When word finally got through the roads were bad, and the tardy trains moved more and more slowly and at last ceased to move at all, axles and wagon beds flat against the tenacious mud. Mixed in with them, and coming down parallel roads and plantation lanes, were the guns and caissons which were also wanted at the riverbank. There were also many quartermaster wagons and ambulances and battery wagons and all of the other wheeled vehicles proper to a moving army, and by ten in the morning every last one of them was utterly mired, animals belly-deep in mud.[16]

The high command made convulsive efforts to hitch along. Infantry was ordered out into the fields on either side of the road so that it might march past these stalled trains—*somebody* ought to be moving somewhere—and the columns quickly churned the fields into sloughs in which a man went to his knees at every step. A soldier in the 37th Massachusetts told what came next:

"Finally, after we had advanced only two or three miles, we filed into a woods and details were made of men to help pull the wheeled conveyances of the army out of the mire. At this we made very little progress. They seemed to be sinking deeper and deeper, and the rain showed little inclination to cease. Sixteen horses could not move one pontoon with men to help."[17]

The man from the *Times* noted that double and triple teams of horses and mules were harnessed to each pontoon, and wrote: "It was in vain. Long powerful ropes were then attached to the teams, and 150 men were put to the task on each boat. The effort was but little more successful. They would flounder through the mire for a few feet—the gang of Lilliputians with their huge-ribbed Gulliver—and then give up breathlessly."[18]

A New York soldier noted that guns normally pulled by six-horse teams would remain motionless with twelve horses in harness. In some cases the teams were unhitched and long ropes were fastened to the gun carriages, and a whole regiment would be put to work to yank one gun along. When a horse or a mule collapsed in the mud, this soldier added, it was simply cut out of its harness and trodden underfoot and out of sight in the bottomless mud.[19] Another veteran recorded:

"The army was accustomed to mud in its varied forms, knee-deep, hub-deep; but to have it so despairingly deep as to check the discordant, unmusical braying of the mules, as if they feared their mouths would fill, to have it so deep that their ears, wafted above the waste of mud, were the only symbol of animal life, were depths to which the army had now descended for the first time."[20]

The day wore on and the rain came down harder and colder than ever. A cannon might be inched along for a few yards with triple teams or three hundred men on the draglines; when there was a breather and it came to a halt, it would sink out of sight unless men quickly thrust logs and fence rails under it. Some guns sank so deeply that only their muzzles were visible, and no conceivable amount of mere pulling would get them out—they would have to be dug out with shovels. All around this helpless army there was a swarm of stragglers, more of them than the army had ever had before, men who had got lost or displaced in the insane traffic jams, men who had simply given up and were wandering aimlessly along, completely bewildered. A private in the 63rd Pennsylvania wrote that "the whole country was an ocean of mud, the roads were rivers of deep mire and the heavy rain had made the ground a vast mortar bed."[21]

The situation grew so bad that the men finally began to laugh—at themselves, at the army, at the incredible folly which had brought them out into this mess. One soldier remembered: "Over all the sounds might be heard the dauntless laughter of brave men who summon humor as a reinforcement to their aid and as a brace to their energies," which doubtless was one way to put it. The impression gathered from most of the accounts is that it was the thoroughly daunted laughter of men who had simply got punch-drunk. Men working with the pontoons offered to get in the boats and row to their destination. One sweating soldier remarked that the army was a funeral procession stuck in the mud, and a buddy replied that if they were indeed a funeral procession they would never get out in time for the resurrection. Luckless Burnside came spattering along once, and the teamster of a mired wagon, recalling the general's pronunciamento which had begun this march, called out with blithe impudence: "General, the auspicious moment has arrived."[22]

Most of this was taking place close to the river, and the Rebels on the far side saw what was going on and got into the spirit of things, enjoying themselves hugely at the sight of so many Yankees in such a mess. They shouted all sorts of helpful advice across the stream, offered to come over and help, asked if the Yankees wanted to borrow any mules, and put up hastily lettered signs pointing out the proper road to Richmond and announcing that the Yankee army was stuck in the mud.

Night came and brought no improvement, except that the pretense of making a movement could be abandoned for a while. Many of the soldiers found the ground too soggy to permit any attempt at sleep and huddled all night about inadequate campfires. The supply wagons were heaven knew where, and the rain soaked the men's haversacks, ruining hardtack and sugar and leaving cold salt pork as the only food. Once again a vast smudge drifted across the country. An engineer officer on duty at Banks Ford wrote that the army's campfires presented "the appearance of a large sea of fire" and added that the smoke covered the entire countryside and even blanketed the Rebs on their side of the Rappahannock.

The smoke was the only Yankee creation that did cross the river. This engineer officer wrote to Burnside, earnestly urging that the enterprise be abandoned. The Confederates were waiting for them, he said; they had a plank road on their side of the river by which they could easily wheel up all the guns they needed. The Army of the Potomac, which had planned to build five bridges, would do very well to get up enough pontoons for two, "but if we could build a dozen I think it would be better to abandon the enterprise."[23]

Burnside was a hard man to convince, and next morning the old orders stood: get down to the river, make bridges, go across, and lick the Rebels. The *Times* man wrote that the dawn came "struggling through an opaque envelope of mist," and recorded that the rain showed no signs of stopping. Looking out at the sodden countryside, he continued: "One might fancy that some new geologic cataclysm had overtaken the world, and that he saw around him the elemental wrecks left by another Deluge. An indescribable chaos of pontoons, wagons, and artillery encumbered the road down to the river—supply wagons upset by the roadside—artillery 'stalled' in the mud—ammunition trains mired by the way." In a brief morning's ride, he said, he had counted 150 dead horses and mules. The chaplain of the 24th Michigan wrote: "The scenes on the march defy description. Here a wagon mired and abandoned; there a team of six mules and horses on either hand; ten, twelve, and even twenty-six horses vainly trying to drag a twelve-pounder through the mire."[24]

Somehow, that morning, the high command did get a few wagons forward, and some commands received a whisky ration. In Barnes's brigade of the V Corps the officers who had charge of the issue seem to have been overgenerous, and since the whisky went down into empty stomachs—for the men had had no breakfast—there was presently a great deal of trouble, with the whole brigade roaring drunk. There were in this brigade two regiments which did not get along too well, the 118th Pennsylvania, known as the Corn Exchange Regiment, and the 22nd Massachusetts. Just after the battle of the Antietam the brigade had been thrust across the Potomac in an ineffectual stab at Lee's retreating army and it had been rather badly mauled. Most of the mauling had been suffered by the Pennsylvanians (it was their first fight and they carried defective muskets), and somehow they had got the notion that the Massachusetts regiment had failed to support them as it should. This morning, in the dismal rain by the river, with all the woes of the world coming down to encompass them round about, the Pennsylvanians recalled this ancient grudge and decided to make complaint about it. In no time the two regiments were tangling, and when some of the 2nd Maine came over and tried to make peace, the argument became three-sided. Before long there was a tremendous free-for-all going on, the men dropping their rifles and going at one another with their fists, Maine and Massachusetts and Pennsylvania tangling indiscriminately, inspired by whisky and an all-inclusive, slow-burning anger which made hitting someone an absolute necessity. The thing nearly took an ugly turn when a Pennsylvania major drew a revolver and made ready to use it, but somebody knocked him down before he could shoot, and in the end the fighters drifted apart with no great damage done.[25]

By noon even Burnside could see that the army was helpless, and all thought of getting across the river was abandoned. One private wrote afterward that "it was no longer a question of how to go forward, but how to get back," and that sized it up. Slowly, and with infinite difficulty, the army managed to reverse its direction and began to drag itself wearily back to the camps around Falmouth.

The home-coming was cheerless enough. Before the march began the men had been ordered to dispose of all surplus baggage and camp equipment, which meant that they had to destroy all of the improvised chairs, tables, desks, and other bits of furniture which they had made for their comfort, since there was no way to ship these things to the rear. They returned, therefore, to camps which had been systematically made bleaker and more barren than they had been before. (Here and there the regimental officers had evaded these orders. The colonel of the 9th Massachusetts had told his men to destroy nothing, as they would probably be back soon enough—he apparently had little faith that any march of Burnside's was going to lead to anything—and when they set out on the march he left the regimental quartermaster and a detail to look out for things. As a result, the 9th still had all of its little extras.) There were occasional mix-ups and quarrels. The 6th Wisconsin found the 55th Ohio in what it considered its own camp and prepared to fight. The Ohio colonel made peace by explaining that his men had been ordered there by corps command, by inviting the Wisconsin men to share the supper which his Ohioans had just cooked, and by pointing out that the ground was roomy enough for both regiments anyhow.[26]

Very few of the regiments came back as compact, well-organized bodies. They came trailing and straggling in, many of the men at the point of complete exhaustion, and it took days to get everyone reassembled. A good many soldiers, in fact, never did get back. Some of them just quietly wandered away, disgustedly leaving an army which could do no better than wade up to its thighs in winter mud, and these elusive waifs were hard to catch. The 24th Michigan found it had thirty absentees when it returned, and its lieutenant colonel was Mark Flanigan, who used to be sheriff of Wayne County, owned a sword presented by the county's deputy sheriffs, and had had much experience at catching defaulters and fugitives. Sheriff Flanigan took a military posse and backtracked up the river looking for his wandering soldiers. He returned after some days with a baker's dozen of them, plus a few civilians whom he had arrested for helping deserters to escape. He reported that the trail of the other soldiers was too dim to follow.[27]

Some of the men indeed had gone beyond the reach of any sheriff. Spending forty-eight hours in the cold rain and mud without warm food or dry clothing was just as hard on the ordinary human constitution of 1863 as it would be now, and there was a dreadful toll of sickness and deaths as a result of this march. In some cases men who became too exhausted to walk back to camp simply lay down in the swampy fields and died, their bodies remaining by the roadside for days afterward. Many more managed to get back to camp but went off to the hospital tents with pneumonia or other maladies. Altogether, it is probable that this mud march killed and disabled as many soldiers as were lost in some of the army's regular battles. The men settled back into camp with gloom thick and heavy. A diarist in the 3rd Michigan wrote: "I never knew so much discontent in the army before. A great many say that they 'don't care whether school keeps or not,' for they think there is a destructive fate hovering over our army."[28]

There exists an informal history of one of the New York regiments in this army, a book in which the military career of every member of the regiment is briefly summarized. The regiment had an eventful career and suffered numerous losses, and after many of the names in its roster are entries like "Killed in the Wilderness," "Died in Andersonville Prison," and so on. But the commonest one of the lot is the simple "Died at Falmouth."[29] The Wisconsin officer who said that this winter was the army's Valley Forge was hardly exaggerating.

Yet there was a hard indestructible core in the army somewhere, a grimly humorous acceptance of the worst that could happen. A staff officer in the II Corps, which did not make the mud march, wrote that during the week following this disaster the roads around Falmouth were covered with disorderly wandering parties of returning soldiers, bedraggled, unhappy-looking, weapons and uniforms encased in mud, faces lean and glum and unshaven, the men looking like the tattered ends of some Falstaff's army that had come completely unraveled. The staff officer encountered such a group one day: twenty men, or thereabouts, plodding through the mud. The sight offended him, and he barked out the starchy demand of the staff officers: "Who *are* these men?"

He got his answer from a non-com, who spoke up as promptly and as proudly as if he were announcing the arrival for inspection of the most polished and pipeclayed regiment in the army's dandiest corps:

"Stragglers of the 17th Maine, sir!"[30]

3. THE THIRD THAT REMAINED

SOMEONE HAD SENT to army headquarters a boned turkey as a gift for the commanding general, and Robert, the faithful retainer, who alternately cooked for the general and soothed his tired spirit with a rare and complete selflessness, was serving it up for lunch. General Burnside seemed to have regained his poise. During the mud march, as he confessed to a friend, the strain had driven him almost frantic. Now the mud march was over, and that part of the army which maintained its organization had extricated itself from the villainous roads and was back in its camps. The general was more easy, and today he had guests at the luncheon table.

They may have been oddly chosen, all things considered. They came out of the past, when it had been possible for General Burnside to have friends in the army. It did not seem possible now. The weight of command made him suspect the motives of all around him. It would appear, too, that his strange, unmilitary humility did have its limits. It had been broad enough immediately after Fredericksburg to make him write to Halleck, "For the failure of the attack I am responsible"; broad enough to make him declare both before and after that battle that he knew he was not competent to command an army.[1] But a good deal of time had passed. The battle was fought on December 13 and it was now January 23, and Burnside was no longer able to accept the responsibility for all of the terrible things that had happened. He had had black nights after Fredericksburg, when he repeated over and over, "Oh, those men! Those men over there!" as if the frozen, blue-carpeted field in front of the stone wall remained constantly before his eyes.[2] One gathers that he had to prove to himself that it was not entirely his fault that all of those bodies had been flung there. Someone else must be at fault too.

He had with him as his luncheon guests General Franklin and General Smith, and the two found him somewhat moody. Understandably so: for although they did not know it, he was just then convincing himself that these two friends, among others, had helped to bring about defeat in battle. He did not seem able to tell them about it at this lunch where they ate delicate boned turkey, but blame was taking shape in his mind. He was talkative and morose by turns. Once, after a spell of silence, he burst out: "You will presently hear of something that will astonish you all!"[3]

More than that he would not say, and his visitors at length took their leave, well fed but somewhat puzzled. After they left, Burnside wrote a document which was to be the vehicle of the promised astonishment. It bore the heading, "General Order Number 8," and it contained the substance of his confused analysis of the disaster at Fredericksburg, together with an expression of his dim feeling that he who had not deserved high command had at least deserved better subordinates than he had been given. Brooding upon these things, he had distilled a bitter fury, the exquisite rage of pure impotence, and he gave full vent to it.

When fury and rage are turned loose they have to have a target, and Burnside's target was principally Joe Hooker.

General Order Number 8 had a great deal to say about Hooker, most of it quite true. It alleged that he habitually uttered "unjust and unnecessary criticisms of the actions of his superior officers," that he tried "to create distrust" in the minds of fellow officers, that he said and wrote things designed to create false impressions, and that he was much given to "speaking in disparaging terms of other officers." It climaxed these variously phrased allegations by asserting that, as a man unfit to hold an important commission, Hooker "is hereby dismissed the service of the United States."

Almost by afterthought, as if he had suddenly realized that it took authority higher than that of an army commander to cashier a general, Burnside added that this order was issued "subject to the approval of the President of the United States."

Having unburdened himself about Hooker, Burnside then went on, apparently, to take in everybody else whose habits or actions had bothered him.

A second paragraph announced that Brigadier General W. T. H. Brooks, a division commander in the VI Corps, had been complaining of the policy of the government and had been using language tending to demoralize his command. Brooks, like Hooker, was dismissed from the service—subject, again, to the approval of the President.

A third paragraph took care of General Newton and General Cochrane, who had made that hurried end-of-the-year trip to Washington with a tale to tell, and whose identities had at last become known to Burnside. "For going to the President of the United States with criticisms of the plans of their commanding officer," these two were to meet the fate of Hooker and Brooks.

A final paragraph wrapped up the odds and ends. It undertook to relieve certain officers from duty, "it being evident that they can be of no further service to this army." Among them were the recent luncheon guests, Franklin and Smith. Franklin, Burnside felt, had done less than he might have done in the attack at Hamilton's Crossing, and Smith—blameless enough so far as Fredericksburg went—lacked faith in the success of an overland move toward Richmond; they must go, along with Franklin's assistant adjutant general, a Lieutenant Colonel Taylor. Burnside was swinging blindly by now. Into this proscription list he put one of his own favorites, Brigadier General Ferrero of the IX Corps; someone had told him that Ferrero had recently overstayed a leave of absence. He also got Cochrane into this list of those who were to suffer the lesser punishment of losing their commands but not their commissions—apparently forgetting that a few sentences earlier he had ordered him cashiered outright.[4]

With all of this committed to writing, Burnside took off for Washington to show it to the President and, if possible, to get his approval. There was no way to undo defeat. The Angel of the Resurrection could not be summoned down to the ghastly field below Marye's Heights to restore the fallen to life, but it might at least be possible to revive the modest self-esteem of the commanding general. If this army's great handicap had been a clogging of the channels of command by enmity and distrust toward the commander, here was a purge to set everything straight. If nothing else could be said for it, the paper would at least make interesting reading for all ranks. As Burnside had promised his guests at luncheon, it was a stunner.

It was not, in the end, anything more than that. Like most presidents, Lincoln was forever being given dramatic compositions by men in high positions with the assurance that his signature at the foot of the paper, his nod of approval to the man who had written it, would solve everything and enable him to sleep quietly of nights. Seward had offered to run the White House for him back in the early days when the war was hardly begun, presenting him with a cunning letter which survives as a historical curio. A year later General McClellan had written down his own solution for the nation's ills and had handed it to the President in order that the country might be saved. Now Burnside, and this; while the army sickened in a dirty camp by the cold river and by every sign an army can give indicated that it had made up its mind about things.

Lincoln presumably could read the signs. They had rarely been any worse.

General Hooker himself, focusing the sharpest of eyes upon the opportunities which defeat and disaster were opening for an energetic man at the top of the heap, was contemptuously telling a New York *Times* correspondent that President and Administration were "played out" and that there ought to be a dictator. General Howard, pious soldier and unyielding anti-slavery man, was noting that he had just been obliged to bring to trial two officers "for disloyal language directed against the President and the general commanding." He stopped their mouths, but he wrote that "discontent had taken deep root" and he himself felt "a want of confidence in the army itself."[5] And just when Burnside was writing his screed, German-born Carl Schurz, a devoted but slightly inexpert major general in the XI Corps, was saying in a letter to Lincoln:

"I am convinced that the spirit of the men is systematically demoralized and the confidence in their chief systematically broken by several of the commanding generals. I have heard generals, subordinate officers, and men say that they expect to be whipped anyhow, that 'all these fatigues and hardships are for nothing, and that they might as well go home.' Add to this that the immense army is closely packed together in the mud, that sickness is spreading at a frightful rate, that in consequence of all these causes of discouragement desertion increases every day—and you will not be surprised if you see the army melt away with distressing rapidity."[6]

But those, after all, were the comments of the generals—three generals as completely dissimilar, by the way, as could be found in all the army—and generals are often mistaken about what their men are thinking. The really ominous signs in those days were coming from the enlisted men themselves, and it was what the men were doing, not what they were saying, that was ominous.

They were not, as a matter of fact, saying anything at all, which in some ways was the worst sign of the lot.

There had been a big review of the II Corps not long since, and Burnside and Sumner had ridden down the lines together, gold-braided staff officers clanking at their heels. Ordinarily this would have brought cheers, regardless of the identity or personal popularity of the generals; the men liked to cheer at such times and were quite ready to accept any decent excuse to start. But this time a sullen, unnatural silence lay across the field. White-haired old Sumner was outraged. Some sort of cheer at a review was as much the commanding general's due as a salute, and this was shameful flouting of military etiquette. He told General Couch, commander of the corps, to make the men do their duty.

So, on order, corps and division and brigade commanders and their aides rode up and down the lines, swinging their hats and swords and earnestly calling for three cheers. Not a cheer did they get. The silence lay unbroken upon the wintry field save for their own piping exhortations and, here and there, a single derisive cry in response: as embarrassing a moment, one would suppose, as a commanding general could well experience.[7]

They had made up their minds about things, those soldiers, and they were expressing themselves unmistakably. They were saying nothing where normally they would have been noisy. Also, in steadily increasing numbers, they were simply laying down their weapons and going home, quietly piling up the enlisted man's ultimate vote of no confidence in the war and in the men who were running it.

A veteran in the Iron Brigade wrote that desertions from the Army of the Potomac after the mud march were averaging two hundred a day, stimulated to some extent, no doubt, by a flood of letters from anti-war people in the North, who seemed to be engaged in an organized letter-writing campaign to encourage desertion. If a soldier yielded to such pleas, things were usually made as easy for him as possible. His best course was simply to write to his family or to his friends, saying that he wanted to come home. They would send to him by express a box containing civilian clothing. (Such boxes were coming in that winter almost literally in carload lots.) The soldier would put on the civilian clothing, slip quietly out of camp, and, usually, that would be that.[8]

In Washington the provost marshal had his patrols watching every road and every bridge, for the tide of deserters was flowing north in full spate. Detachments of troops held all three of the bridges over the Potomac—Chain Bridge, well upstream, Aqueduct Bridge at Georgetown, and Long Bridge at the foot of Seventh Street. A string of pickets guarded every road leading from the city to the open country, and there was an especially heavy guard over the Anacostia Bridge near the navy yard. This bridge led to roads for Baltimore and Annapolis, gave access to other roads leading to the shore of Chesapeake Bay, and communicated also with the road south via Port Tobacco, which was the principal route for contraband trade with the South. Cavalry patrolled all of the country roads near Washington, and there was a navy patrol along the water front. Provost guards were stationed at every dock and pier and rode the ferries to Alexandria. A chain of pickets surrounded Baltimore.[9]

Every train that left Washington bound north was examined by the provost guard as it pulled out of the station. In addition, other guards came aboard to search the cars afresh when the train reached Annapolis Junction, twenty-five miles out. Enlisted men legitimately traveling north on furlough were infuriated by all of this, especially since part of the function of the provost guards seemed to be to keep private soldiers out of the first-class carriages. "This is what makes a soldier hate himself and all others, for he thinks a dog is thought more of than he is," wrote a Michigan veteran savagely. Not until one passed Harrisburg, said this soldier, did he escape from the interfering vigilance of the guards.[10]

Yet all of this did very little good. There were many ways by which a soldier who wanted to desert could be helped on his way. The Confederates circulated handbills through the Federal camps, offering free transportation to practically any spot on earth to all who would come through the Rebel lines and give themselves up. Many men accepted these offers. A few—foreign-born mechanics and artisans, for the most part—tried to remain in the South and earn a living, their skills being in much demand. More often, the men who surrendered simply gave their paroles as prisoners of war and presently were shipped back through the lines to Annapolis, where the Federals maintained a camp for paroled men who were awaiting formal exchange.

In theory a soldier at this camp stayed there until he had been exchanged (on paper) for some paroled Confederate, whereupon he went back to duty with his regiment. In actual practice, however, paroled men tended to consider themselves more or less out of the war for keeps, and at times it was almost impossible even to keep them in camp, to say nothing of getting them back to their outfits. In mid-January 1863 the commander of the Annapolis camp estimated that fully three fourths of his men were arrant shirkers, and said that they were not five hundred men in his camp who either knew or cared what army corps they belonged to. He added: "If the men in my camp were a sample of our army we would having nothing but a mob of stragglers and cowards."[11]

Permitting oneself to be captured in order to get a parole, and thus a chance to slide out of the war sideways, had by this time become a widespread evil fully recognized by army authorities. Many men got to the parole camps without bothering to go through the formality of first being captured by the Rebels. There was a thriving trade in forged parole certificates. A man who got one would straggle off, present himself at the parole camp, and either old-soldier it there or take the first chance to set out for home. Or if he preferred he would simply wander north at once, counting on his parole paper to serve for a pass whenever the provost guard might halt him.[12]

Extensive as this practice was, however, most of the men who deserted used other means. There was an "underground railway" operating between Alexandria and Baltimore, its object being to get soldiers past the guards and pickets around Washington. It appears to have been operated by Confederate sympathizers, motivated either by Southern patriotism or by a desire to earn an honest dollar. Its agents would take a deserter at Alexandria, smuggle him across the Potomac, and get him over to the Leonardtown road, where he would be hidden until a little group of fugitives had been collected. The men were then taken across country by way of Upper Marlboro to Fair Haven on the Chesapeake shore, where a steamer would put in to take them to Baltimore. On the boat the men would be given civilian clothing, if they did not already possess it, and would be told how to make their way north out of Baltimore.[13]

Alexandria, to be sure, was a good many miles upsteam from the army's camps. But Burnside's administration was never able to keep the men in camp, not even though Burnside's provost marshal, annoyed by "the alarming frequency of desertion from this army," had ordered corps and division commanders to redouble their vigilance, to patrol the immediate vicinity of their camps with infantry, and to maintain cavalry on the roads farther out, arresting everybody who lacked a pass. This was of slight effect. Deserters usually followed the roads that led via Aquia Creek through Dumfries and Occoquan, riding in the wagons of sutlers, army traders, farmers, or others, which were allowed to travel the muddy roads without much examination. Sometimes the men passed themselves off as details sent out to repair the telegraph lines, which was fairly easy to do since most patrols knew nothing whatever about the electric telegraph and could easily be made to believe that it took huge gangs to keep the lines in order.[14]

But even this represented more trouble than was really necessary. The principal thing was to get across the Potomac into Maryland, for the contraband trade between North and South had such well-established routes through places like Leonardtown and Port Tobacco and passed through an area so strongly Southern in its sympathies that a deserter could usually count on getting north safely once he was over the river. Crossing was not too hard. Navy patrolled the river, but it was easy to hide rowboats along the shore and easy to slide across in them on dark nights. One naval officer frankly told the army people that the only way to stop the transriver traffic in deserters would be to break up all the rowboats between Aquia Creek and Washington, which clearly would be impractical.[15]

Now and then the army would load a regiment or so on a steamboat and, under navy convoy, cruise down to the "northern neck," the long peninsula between the Potomac and the Rappahannock southeast of Fredericksburg, in an attempt to break up the bases for the contraband trade. These attempts never amounted to very much, except, as one officer noted, that the pillage and freebooting indulged in by the troops probably confirmed the inhabitants in their disunionist leanings. The creeks and inlets which were the centers for this traffic were very shallow, and the steamers usually ran aground.

Both army and navy kept details on the Maryland side of the Potomac, and each service insisted that the other was muffing its opportunities. According to the navy, the army details there were rowdy, undisciplined, drunken, and insubordinate; army replied that the navy folk showed altogether too much friendship for local secessionists. Both services agreed that there was an immense traffic in contraband goods and spies back and forth between Virginia and Maryland. There was a regular mail and express route north from Richmond via Warsaw Courthouse and Leonardtown to Washington, with two scheduled deliveries a week and an established ferry service, and boss traders were growing rich by it. Cavalry went downstream and raided a ferry point on the Virginia shore, seizing coffee and sugar and tobacco and "nearly fifty barrels of villainous whisky" but causing the smugglers only momentary inconvenience. One Federal officer who had tried in vain to tighten the controls reported that "blockade running and dealing in contraband articles have become professions."[16]

So here was a veritable Yukon Trail running wide open not twenty-five miles away from the chief supply line of the nation's principal army, crossing deep rivers which were under steady navy patrol, and using highways which were fully controlled by Yankee cavalry and infantry. There are probably several explanations, including the fact that Americans of every generation seem to have a positive genius for smuggling, but the principal one appears to be that Burnside's army was just naturally the kind of army to which things like this were bound to happen. Operating deep in hostile territory, it was going to be run dizzy by enemy agents stealing its secrets and sending them south and stealing its soldiers and sending them north, and its high command simply was not going to know how to stop it.

By the end of January 1863, desertions from the Army of the Potomac totaled 85,123.[17]

A startling figure, which does not quite mean what it appears to mean.

It does not, for instance, mean that 85,000 men had willfully laid down their weapons and gone home. Heavy as desertions had been, they had not been that heavy. Most of the men who were on the army's rolls but not with the army had not so much run away as drifted away. They had been sloughed off by the army's own inefficiency. With many of them there probably had never been a conscious decision to desert, a moment when the soldier in his own mind ceased to be a soldier temporarily absent and became instead a civilian who was never going to go back unless somebody came and got him.

The hospital system, for instance, was practically guaranteed to leak men back into civil life, and to do it in such a way that the leaks could not easily be plugged. By a freak of chance this was so because the army had been making an honest and generally successful effort to give its men better medical care than any soldiers on earth had ever had before.

For uncounted generations—ever since military life was invented, as a matter of fact—all of the world's armies had apparently operated on the theory that the soldier was always going to be healthy. If he fell ill or got wounded he was a poor dog. Provided he did not die too quickly, he would eventually be put in a hospital and allowed to get well if he could, but getting well was pretty much his own responsibility and no concern of the army. From the military viewpoint, the ailing soldier was just a nuisance and the big idea was to get him out of the way.

But in this war it had to be different. Here the army was of the people and the people kept in close touch with their soldiers. If the soldiers had troubles the people quickly became concerned, and the people had devised a number of most effective ways to make their concern felt in high places. The war had not been going on very long before the War Department had to overhaul its hospital system from top to bottom so that the soldier could have better care.

In fact, before the War Department quite knew what was happening its hospital system was being overhauled for it, the instrument of overhaul being the United States Sanitary Commission. In its essentials, the Sanitary Commission was the women of America, brought together through thousands of spontaneously organized Ladies' Aid Societies and grimly determined that their menfolk in this war were going to be looked after properly. It also included doctors, bankers, merchants, and men vaguely but justly known as "civic leaders." It had almost unlimited financial backing, and it enjoyed enough sheer political influence to move mountains. By the middle of 1861 the commission had won quasi-governmental status, plus War Department permission to inquire into the sanitary condition of the troops, the provision of nurses and hospitals, and similar matters.

It appears that the War Department, which knows nothing about women, originally supposed that the commission would be quite happy with this permission to investigate and that the things investigated might go on as they had gone on before, but the War Department was quite mistaken. The commission was presently getting Congress to vote a thorough reorganization of the army's medical department, and in the peninsular campagin the commission was running hospital ships, providing nurses and medical supplies, getting sick and wounded men brought back to where their lives might be saved, and in general turning the army way of doing things upside down. By the end of 1862 the entire system of collecting, housing, and treating sick and wounded soldiers had been transformed.[18]

This, of course, was all to the good, and the soldiers had reason to bless every last member, officer, and paid employee of the Sanitary Commission. But in the process of providing medical care for soldiers in a manner to satisfy the women of America, the War Department also tried to make the state governors happy, and the result was a system by which a man who went to hospital could very easily slip out from under army control altogether.

What the department did for the governors was to establish general hospitals in the Northern states and to provide that sick or wounded men might be transferred to these from the front, either singly or in organized bodies, if it seemed likely that the change would help them to recover. This pleased the soldiers, who were glad enough to get back home, and it simply delighted the governors, who could gain much political advantage from getting them back. (For one thing, they could *vote,* and for whom would a soldier vote if not for an ardently patriotic war governor?) Before long most of the states had agents who visited army hospitals in the forward areas, looked up home-state patients, and pulled wires to get them sent to the home-state hospital. Thus there developed a steady flow of men moving from the areas of active operations to the Northern states. By the middle of the war it was estimated that between one and two hundred thousand men had been transferred to the various Northern hospitals.[19]

Which would have been all right, except that when a man was sent to a general hospital in his home state the odds were quite good that the army would never see him again.

The hospitals were practically independent. Each was run by a medical officer who was answerable to the surgeon general of the army, not to any line officer. The soldier who got into the hospital was completely out from under the control of his own outfit. Neither his company commander, his colonel, or his army commander had any authority to order him back to duty. That could be done only by the medical officer who ran the hospital, who did not need to take anything from army brass. He had generally got his job through political patronage, and his patron would be the governor of the state, who, as a result, had effective control of the situation.

Thus all kinds of openings were offered to the soldier who was not eager to get back to the front. It was often possible to induce the hospital director to carry him on the rolls as sick long after he had recovered. If he had any useful little skills, if he could cut hair or mend cupboards or tend chickens or do any of the other little things that need to be done at behind-the-lines army posts, he was likely to be kept forever.

Medical directors were authorized to detail convalescents as nurses, orderlies, cooks, and so on, and an army officer familiar with such arrangements reported that in most cases the men so detailed "ceased to be soldiers in fact and spirit" and became "mere hangers-on of hospitals." Not long before his own dismissal McClellan was pleading for a strict investigation of each Northern army hospital "to ferret out the old soldiers hidden away therein." Such an inspection, he said, would produce more fruit in one week than the entire recruiting service would yield in three months. He added that not more than a tenth of the soldiers who went to the home-state hospitals ever rejoined the army, and cited the case of one regiment which had sent five hundred men to hospitals in the rear and had got back only fifteen or twenty of them.[20]

The general theory was that a man's own home was the best place for his convalescence. Normally, a soldier recovering at a Northern hospital had no trouble getting leave to go home, and if he could not get leave there was little or nothing to keep him from going home anyway. Once he got home, whether he was there legally or otherwise, no one in authority had any especial incentive to get him back. His own regiment could not touch him because he was absent from the hospital rather than from the regiment. The hospital was supposed to call him in and return him to his proper command as soon as he was strong enough, but it was more likely than not simply to forget about him. If the hospital authorities happened to be unduly conscientious about such things there were various dodges that could be tried. Away from his own regiment where people knew him, a man could pretend that he was a victim of some wasting disease brought on by overexposure. Naturally, a malingerer usually picked some malady whose symptons were rather vague and nonspectacular; rheumatism was the favorite, and before the war was half over the army had been compelled to prohibit the granting of medical discharges for rheumatism under any circumstances whatever.

For one of the biggest loopholes of all was the fact that doctors in these Northern hospitals were authorized to issue medical discharges. In the forward areas a regimental surgeon naturally would try to make sure that such a release was given only to a man who genuinely deserved it, but a doctor at a Northern hospital was not likely to care very much, and the soldier who was unable to persuade the hospital authorities to give him a discharge was apt to be either tragically devoid of any kind of political pull or flagrantly and incurably healthy. Even if he tried to get a discharge, failed, and then went off home on his own hook, he still had a good chance to make everything legal. For when the War Department began trying to round up these hospital absentees, it ruled in its wisdom that any of them might get a lawful discharge if he could present a certificate of disability signed by any civilian "physician of good standing." The man who, safely perched in his own home town, was unable to come up with such a paper was a poor stick indeed.[21]

Yet most absentees seem not to have bothered to make the effort. It simply was not necessary.

When the war began there was a standard reward of thirty dollars payable to any peace officer or private citizen who caught and returned to custody a deserter from the army. For some incomprehensible reason, once the war began and desertion became a serious problem, this reward was cut to five dollars and expenses. A tangled web of red tape was then thrown over the business of collecting it. The applicant had to get a voucher from the local provost marshal stating that a genuine deserter, properly identified by name, company, and regiment, had in fact been turned in. The voucher also had to identify, by description or otherwise, the citizen who had brought the deserter in, and expenses incurred had to be specified in detail, with supporting documents to prove that they had actually been incurred and with other documents proving that it had really been necessary to incur them. Any government paymaster, natually, could keep an applicant for five dollars and expenses at bay for a year with a setup like that. As an inevitable result, no city cop or county sheriff in his senses would bother to arrest deserters unless they became unmitigated disturbers of the peace.[22]

Before very long it was obvious to everybody that a man who deserted from the army ran very little risk of arrest or punishment. Everything about the situation encouraged the fainthearted and the chronic slackers to desert the first time they got the chance. If such a one, having returned to his home town, felt guilty or insecure, he could make things easier for himself by telling his fellow townspeople tall tales about the fearful treatment a man got in the army. A principal obstacle to enlistments, after the first year of the war, was the presence in every town and hamlet of these deserters "and the false stories they spread abroad of the cruelty and unnecessary hardships to which the men were subjected by their officers."[23]

Such stories of course were usually much exaggerated. Every generation knows the self-pitying ne'er-do-well who finds himself brutally mistreated when he is required to get up promptly in the morning, keep his clothing and his person clean, and turn in an honest day's work in return for his pay, food, and lodging, and such characters were quite as common and as vocal in the 1860s as at any other time. Although army discipline then lacked the impersonal tautness to which a later generation is accustomed, it apparently had a good deal more of the brutality which comes from sheer thoughtlessness and incompetence; and if the imperfect soldiers who drifted north told tales of hardships, those stories were not without a solid base in unpleasant fact.

At the end of 1862 a brigadier general controlling a camp for paroled prisoners in Illinois sent to the War Department an indignant protest about the treatment soldiers got when they had to travel long distances by railroad.

"If the railroad companies," he wrote, "will put a barrel of water in each car and will make coarse but decent arrangements, as they do in emigrant trains, for the men to get drink and answer the calls of nature in the cars, which is never done, officers could be responsible for their men. Now the instant the train stops the men rush out for these necessary purposes, as they claim, and any man wishing to desert 'gets left' and the conductor assists the deserter by refusing to stop the train, as he must 'make his schedule.' "[24]

Another officer was even more specific:

"Brave men, including many sick and wounded, have been crowded into common boxcars in the dead of winter without fires, or fuel, or lights, or any other conveniences that had been enjoyed by the cattle that occupied the cars before them, and in this condition the poor fellows were compelled to make journeys of hundreds of miles. In other instances the same class of cars were used in the hottest weather, and without having been cleansed of the filth left by the cattle, hogs, and other stock. Many deaths have occurred from diseases caused by the cold, suffocation, and stench endured in these trains, while a few were not able to hold out to the end of the route and were taken out dead."[25]

In other words, having shown the soldier that if he ran away he probably would not be bothered, the government was losing very few opportunities to make him feel that running away might be a fine idea. If the stupidity which could produce a Fredericksburg and a mud march failed to teach this lesson, the way in which hospitals in the combat area were directed might suffice. At about the time when Burnside was going through his final *Sturm und Drang* period, in January 1863, the surgeon general of the army had a doctor make a close inspection of the army's camps and hospitals at Falmouth. This officer reported that the regimental hospitals needed almost everything, from ordinary bed sacks on up. Hospital tents were cold. There were plenty of stoves, but they were of no use, some simpleton having ordered huge coal stoves which could not be used in tents. There were on the market plenty of little sheet-iron wood-burning jobs that would do nicely, but this kind the army had not bought. There was a lack of hospital clothing, and the nursing was of the worst: typhoid fever patients had been frostbitten because of lack of care.

"I do not believe," wrote the wrathy inspector, losing a bit of his professional poise, "that I have every seen greater misery from sickness than exists now in the Army of the Potomac."[26]

Veteran regiments, he said, which numbered no more than two or three hundred men because all the weak had been weeded out by casualties and disease, and in which the line officers and surgeons had learned by experience how to care for sick men in the field—such regiments usually had hospitals which were "tolerably comfortable in their appointments." (The only catch was that such regiments had few or no sick men.) In the entire army there were perhaps three or four brigade or divisional hospitals which the inspector found fairly satisfactory. All of the rest, especially the hospitals of the new regiments, in which there was the most sickness, lacked almost everything.

The worst single problem was food, and men died because of it. Much of the army's sickness was the direct result of bad diet. The diarrhea, dysentery, constipation, and malnutrition which made men easy victims to other ailments were the natural end products of a steady diet of fried meat, hardtack, and black coffee. (Considering the matter after the war, Charles Francis Adams wrote: "My intestines were actually corroded with concentrated nourishment. I needed to live on bread, vegetables, and tea; I did live on pork, coffee, spirits, and tainted water.")[27] The army was even seriously troubled that winter with scurvy— scurvy, the deep-sea malady which even then was recognized as a deficiency disease, to be cured by a diet of fresh fruits and vegetables. The men in the hospitals at Falmouth that winter got exactly the same food that was issued to the healthy men in camp: salt pork, hardtack, and coffee.

This was not happening because the army could not get the right kind of food for sick men. It had bought lavish quantities of the very foods these invalids needed, and these foods filled whole warehouses at Aquia Creek. The whole trouble (as this medical inspector found and reported) was simply this: the army command was so abysmally incompetent that it was quite unable to move the good food from the warehouses to the hospitals.

For there was nobody who was empowered to make out the proper requisitions.

Unable to live by anything more inspiring, the army was living by its paper work, and when the paper work was done wrong, which naturally happened every day, military life being what it is, men died.

The warehouses full of good food lay only a few hours from the most remote of the regimental hospitals. Unfortunately, however, there did not exist any man or set of men whose job it was to see that the food got up to the hospitals where the men for whom it had been bought might actually eat some of it. Nobody made out the required papers, and without the papers the food could not move. In the quartermasters' offices there were the blank forms and in the warehouses there was the food, and in between there were open roads and empty wagons and teams of strong horses; but there was not a regular commissary of subsistence for the hospitals, and so the sick men ate salt meat and hard bread, and the vegetables and fruit and chicken and jellied broth stayed in the warehouses and spoiled, or vanished mysteriously down the channels of petty thievery and corruption. The sick men, often enough, went into new graves on the Rappahannock hillsides. And the men who were not sick faded out of the army as fast as the express trains could bring new boxes of civilian clothing, and it was necessary to picket all the roads around Baltimore and Washington, and President Lincoln had General Burnside's little paper setting forth the conditions upon which the present commander of the Army of the Potomac might consent to remain in office.

These conditions the President decided not to meet. Burnside went to the White House, and his last hour of command had visibly arrived. There issued presently an official document which, instead of cashiering anyone, simply announced that General Burnside was relieved of his command. Then Lincoln wrote a strange and canny letter to Joe Hooker, letting that soldier know that his remarks about the need for a dictator and his bitter criticisms of all of his superior officers had been heard and would be remembered in the White House, but nevertheless placing in his hands, as the prize of much hard striving, the command of this luckless army. General Franklin penned his own verdict on Burnside: "I can only account for his numerous mistakes upon the hypothesis that he is crazy."[28] Hooker remarked that he rather doubted if the army could be saved to the country.

It might be that that would largely be up to Hooker. The army would stick around, if he could give it reason to feel that there was any point in it. For the army was still there: the hard core of it, which had come up through great tribulation and which might be indestructible. A veteran in the 12th New Jersey commented that many men had been lost, but said that was only to be expected: "In a company of one hundred enlisted men, only about one third of the number prove themselves physically able and possessing sufficient courage to endure the hardships and face the dangers of active campaigning; the rest, soon after going into the field, drift back to the hospitals and finally out of the service."[29] The most drifted out, and a good many died, but about a third remained, and the men who made up that third would stand a great deal of beating. It might even be that the right man could win a war with them.

THREE

Revival

1. MEN WHO ARE GREATLY IN EARNEST

THE WAR was the sum of all the things all the people in the country were doing. It was the weary private plodding through the mud or dying unattended in a cold hospital tent or defying his officers in order to trade coffee for tobacco with men whom he would try to kill as soon as the weather improved. It was also all of the people who were not in the army, whose lives touched this private's life at any point, and the truths about the war were various. At times the truth was what any of these people believed about the struggle that was going on, and at other times it was the contrast between what they believed and what was really so. By turns the truth was greed, and coarseness, and pain, and shining incredible heroism; and somehow, because the war was made up of people and of what people thought and felt and did, the whole of it was mysteriously greater than the sum of its parts. There was an ultimate truth lying half hidden behind what men were saying and doing, and it is rarely possible to single out any one happening and say, "This is what the war really meant." The war meant a great many things, and in the end it may have meant all of them together, with a saving intangible strangely added. But now and then the infinite complexity of this war seemed to be expressing itself briefly through one man or one event, where the currents that moved below the surface broke open with a foaming of great waters and showed how events were trending.

Specifically, in this winter of 1863 there was the barrel-chested governor of the Hoosier state, Oliver Perry Morton, a great bull of a man who fought for the sacred union of the states and also for the greater glory of O. P. Morton, and who did much which he had not set out to do.

Morton was the son of a country innkeeper, and he was born in rural Indiana one decade after Oliver Hazard Perry won his schoolbook victory over the detested British on Lake Erie. Morton's parents gave him the Commodore's name, which carried magic in the youthful Middle West, and by and by the "Hazard" was dropped. Morton, orphaned before he reached his teens, was reared through adolescence by two maiden aunts in Springfield, Ohio, worked for a time as apothecary's clerk, was bound out to a hatter, and wound up finally as an indifferent student in Miami University, where he managed to complete two years as "an irregular." He left college, married, read law in a country law office, moved to Centerville, Indiana, became county prosecutor and later county judge before he was out of his twenties, and then decided that he could do with more schooling. He went to Cincinnati and attended law school, and in the early 1850's returned to Centerville to become one of Indiana's most spectacular lawyers.

He was not its most profound lawyer, nor, from the professional viewpoint, one of its most distinguished. It was noted that in pleadings before the State Supreme Court, where cases were presented upon written briefs and oral arguments were almost unknown, Morton never amounted to much. The practice of law, for him, had to be personal combat, with a visible enemy present whom one could engage with all but physical violence. It is recorded that he did little office work, but that "before a jury he was irresistible." He was a bulldozer, a fighter; he was remembered as a great massive man having "a fine leg and a large soft hand," with strangely pale skin, a great deal of coarse black hair, and a voice like the crier in the tower of darkness. In court he was savage. An associate recalled that "he literally annihilated everyone connected with the Bar of Wayne County, and walked roughshod over all the other lawyers of his circuit."[1]

In that time and place the law courts had the limelight, and a gifted thunderer was known by the people and could hardly avoid a political career. Morton would not have tried to avoid it. He prospered financially, handling much railroad litigation, and he moved into Indiana politics—always, from the early nineteenth century, a rough-and-tumble affair—as inevitably as water flows downhill. Like most practical politicians, he knew the pitfalls that lurk in humor, and he carefully avoided them. Many a young man, he said, had wrecked himself by being witty. "A politician who goes into wit must expect to sacrifice everything else to it. He will gain no reputation as a sound man. His judgment will be suspected."[2] Morton sacrificed nothing to wit, and he early established repute as a sound man.

He was, in fact, a most orthodox Democrat to begin with, a sharp foe of the abolitionists, a man who voted in 1851 for the New Indiana constitution which ordered free Negroes not to come into the state and provided penalties for white folk who dared to hire them. In 1852 he voted for the Northern Bourbon, Franklin Pierce, and he was shaken out of soundness and orthodoxy only in 1854 by the Kansas-Nebraska Bill, which shook so many and so much. When the new Republican party came in he joined up as a moderate, riding along with but never espousing the anti-foreign Know-Nothing groups. In 1856 he ran unsuccessfully for governor and was accounted so much a moderate that his associate, the George W. Julian who presently became an implacable anti-slavery congressman, did not regret his defeat. At the party's state convention in 1860 Morton was anti-Seward, considering him too inflexible on the slavery issue, and pro-Lincoln. (It was at this convention that Morton was placed in nomination for lieutenant governor by "Mr. Meredith, of Wayne County";[3] the same Mr. Meredith who later, as colonel of volunteer infantry, was to carry Morton's blessing to Joe Hooker in successful quest for promotion.)

No one on the outside ever knows exactly what jars a man loose, and just what happened to Morton next is a bit obscure. But by the fall of 1860 the former moderate had become a fire-eater, and before November was out he was demanding that secession be beaten down by force: "If South Carolina gets out of the Union I trust it will be at the point of the bayonet after our best efforts have failed to compel her submission to the laws." In all the North he was one of the first public men to declare for the use of force against the new Confederacy. Early in 1861 he showed up, unscheduled, at a statehouse flag-raising in Indianapolis, injecting himself into a program of pleaders for compromise, state equality, and erring-sisters-go-in-peace, to declare sharply: "I am not here to argue questions of state equality but to denounce treason."[4]

He was presently put into a key position. Governor Lane resigned to enter the Senate, and Morton became governor by peaceful accession, moving up from the lieutenant governorship to which Solomon Meredith, to his own subsequent glory, had nominated him. A week earlier a convention of Indiana Democrats had voted opposition to "the coercion of sister states," and over in Ohio a leading Democrat warned Jacob Cox that if it came to fighting, 100,000 Ohio Democrats would take up arms to prevent any coercive force from getting even as far south as the Ohio River.[5] But Morton saw war coming and welcomed it, and by the end of April he was driving Indiana deeply into it, getting votes for men and supplies from the legislature, working hand in glove with a semi-secret "vigilance committee" of patriotic citizens which needled lukewarm legislators, worked to break up contraband trade with the South, and in general did its best to cultivate a warlike spirit along the Wabash.

Indeed, it seems that Morton had more energy and patriotic fervor than any one state could hold. He was war governor of Indiana, and working at it, but he quickly took Kentucky under his wing also and made it a Hoosier sphere of influence. Kentucky wobbled and swayed, trying to be neutral in a fight where a state could no more achieve neutrality than it could square the circle. Morton moved in, invited the Kentucky Unionist recruiter, Lovell H. Rousseau, to organize and train his troops in Indiana,[6] and all in all became known as the man who kept Kentucky in the Union. This was a slight exaggeration, for a good many men kept Kentucky in the Union, but Morton was active enough to deserve a good part of the credit.

A characteristic story was told of this period. Morton made one of his frequent visits to Louisville at the height of the neutrality argument, and as always he put up at the Galt House. A member of his party, sitting in the hotel lobby looking out of the window, saw a local secessionist leader walking along the street, laughing at some joke a friend had just told. The Morton man hurried outside, walked up to the Southerner, and promptly knocked him flat. When he was asked why he did this—for the Southerner had committed no offense—he replied stoutly that no damned secessionist was going to laugh while Oliver P. Morton was in town.[7]

A humorless man, this Morton, with humorless followers, operating in a time and a place which had little room for laughter. He was the embodiment of the Union cause, perhaps in a way its personal proprietor, in a state where almost more than any other in the North people were feeling the tearing, agonizing cross-strains set up by the war. The Ohio River flowed through a rich valley where the folkways and habits of thought ran back to planter-land tidewater quite as much as to town-meeting New England, and where the hateful stiff-necked particularism that had brought fire and sleet and candlelight to a young and happy people could be traced to Boston quite as easily as to Charleston. More people of Southern ancestry or Southern sympathies lived in Indiana than in any other free state. Not even in Kentucky, which yearned in vain for an unattainable virginal neutrality, had the war set people against themselves more poignantly.[8] If at times the war threatened to destroy more than it could possibly save, nowhere did the danger seem as real or as desperate as in Indiana. The man who proposed to take this tragically divided state and make it the keystone of the Union arch needed to be a man of uncommon force and daring.

Which, to be sure, was the least that could be said about Governor Morton. He was making himself one of the leading figures of a war which, among other things, clearly aimed to reduce the power of state governors, and he acted as if the governor of Indiana were an independent potentate with whom the government at Washington might negotiate but to whom it could issue no orders. Washington found out about this in what should have been a routine matter, the business of supplying overcoats to Indiana's soldiers.

Early in the war there were Indiana troops in the West Virginia mountains, where nights were cold, and these men lacked overcoats. Morton heard of it—he always heard of everything that happened to Indiana troops—and he made the life of the United States quartermaster at Indianapolis quite miserable, finding time also to spray letters and telegrams at Quartermaster General Meigs in Washington. Government sent him four thousand overcoats in response, but these went astray somewhere. Morton sent his private secretary out as a detective to trace the missing coats, took the matter up vigorously with General Rosecrans, the Union commander in West Virginia, and after six weeks of bickering announced that he personally would see about Indiana's overcoats thereafter. He accordingly bought some twenty-nine thousand of them and had them distributed to Indiana troops. Then, his natural force quite undimmed, he got the Federal government to assume his contracts.

The luckless quartermaster of Indianapolis found all of this most irregular, especially since Morton in his haste had agreed to pay prices far above the Federal maximum, but when the quartermaster (who was only a major) protested, he was transferred away from there and the business was settled Morton's way. Morton then established the Indiana Sanitary Commission, with agents and depots in Washington, Louisville, Nashville, and elsewhere, to look after Indiana soldiers, and was denounced for it by officials of the United States Sanitary Commission, who saw in this "another development of that obnoxious heresy of state sovereignty," but Morton stuck to it and was proud of his accomplishment. He also, without any authority in law, established an arsenal in Indianapolis for the manufacture of ammunition. Later he boasted that this was done "by me, on my own responsibility."[9]

Between times Morton raised troops. When Braxton Bragg came into Kentucky in the fall of 1862 Morton put on a big recruiting drive. There was a bounty law, but the legislature had forgotten to vote money to pay the bounties, and recruits hung back. Morton personally borrowed $100,000 from a Cincinnati merchant, borrowed $30,000 more from an Indianapolis bank, saw that the bounties were paid, and eventually got the state to pick up his notes. When the Confederate invasion reached its height he rushed green Hoosier regiments across the river to meet the Rebels, went over himself to witness Bragg's retreat, played his own strange role in the murder of General Nelson, and pulled such wires as were handy to get Buell removed from command. To Lincoln he wrote that the war would never be won by "the cold professional leader, whose heart is not in the cause." Victory would come, he said, only when leadership was given to "the hands of men who are greatly in earnest, and who are profoundly convinced of the justice of our cause."[10]

And Morton was greatly in earnest, which was the lump that leavened the loaf. A passionate man, he stood among high-minded Laodiceans who tried without success to command troops against passionate, earnest men from the South, and he spent the strength that was in him to get those who had no passion taken out of the places of command. He tried for a time, vainly, to get himself commissioned a major general. Then, in the dead winter of the Union cause after Fredericksburg, the whole issue of success or failure in Indiana was placed in his hands, and the times quietly challenged him to show whether he was elemental force or windy bluff.

In the fall of 1862 the Democrats had won the elections in many Northern states—among them, most notably, Indiana. As 1863 began a solid majority of the legislators convening at Indianapolis were Democrats who seemed ready to unite in the belief that there must be a better way to settle this family quarrel than one which came home so painfully to the private pocketbook and the village cemetery. These men cocked their eyes at Governor Morton, who wired Stanton that his legislature was likely to adopt a joint resolution recognizing the Confederacy and urging states of the Northwest to sever all relations with a national government dominated by New England. Morton was perhaps a bit too nervous about this, as the legislators apparently did not plan to go quite that far. They did have certain definite ideas, however, chief of which was that peace-loving Democrats rather than fire-breathing Oliver P. Morton would hereafter control Indiana's part in the war.

Morton met this legislature head-on, sending it on January 8 a governor's message full of stirring patriotic sentiments. The legislature contemptuously refused to accept this. Instead, it voted thanks to Governor Horatio Seymour of New York for the message he had just sent to his legislature, a message which denounced emancipation (recently made national policy by Abraham Lincoln) and upheld the ancient theory of states' rights, for which the Confederates were shedding much blood in Virginia and elsewhere. Having done this, the legislature voted to investigate Morton's involved financial dealings, filed and endlessly debated a whole sheaf of resolutions denouncing practically everything the Republican administration had done, and then got down to the main course: a carefully drawn bill which would take all military power away from Morton and give it to a "military board" of hand-picked Democrats, most of them strongly anti-war and every man Jack of them vehemently anti-Morton.[11]

To good Union men this looked like taking Indiana out of the war and ultimately losing the whole of the Middle West, and to any eye it was clear that war-weariness had reached a climax. Many things were responsible for this, including the fact that this war was most damnably complicated by plain old-fashioned politics, played with venom and without much restraint even in the piping times of peace, and played in wartime with all of its ordinary qualities at double or triple strength. It could appear, in Indiana and elsewhere, that the war was being fought for unadorned Republican supremacy at all levels, from the county courthouse on up. It could also appear that the Democratic party proposed to regain those courthouses even at the price of stopping the war and conceding Southern independence. Beneath these appearances was the possibility that the whole war was no more than a party fight, involving nothing much holier than the proper division of the loaves and the fishes. These unhappy appearances were at least partly true, although the whole truth lay beyond them; and if the people were growing heartsick and confused because of it all, they were getting the terrible casualty lists from Fredericksburg and Stone's River for their daily reading matter, and the incompetence in army command was cutting deeper and deeper into their consciousness. So Indiana might possibly, this winter, fall completely out of the war.

Morton himself had tried to warn the national administration. He had forecast the Democratic victory in the fall election, giving Lincoln a précis of the opposition arguments—that selfish moneygrubbers from New England were exploiting the Northwest and growing rich by the war, that geographically and economically Indiana and her sister states were forever tied to the Southland with the Mississippi as the destined artery and outlet for their commerce, that the war had been forced upon the South by the anti-slavery fanatics, and that the Southerners had offered reasonable compromises which, if accepted, could have led to a just peace. "In some of these arguments," Morton had written, "there is much truth."[12]

Much truth, seen also by New York's Governor Seymour, who feared that the war was concentrating economic power in New England, to the lasting harm of his own New York. Much truth, and also much error and much failure to see what was going on in the world. For the railroads had bitten clear through the fated Mississippi artery and had tied the hinterland firmly to the markets and the banks of the East, so that the Lost Cause with its bronze garlands and its swords sheathed forever had perhaps been lost before the war even began. Yet the strange, tantalizing fact that lies beneath that entire war did remain as something for Lincoln, Morton, and all the others to grapple with: doomed to defeat, with the very stars in the sky marching against it, the Lost Cause might nevertheless triumph simply because the men who had to fight about it could conceivably overthrow destiny itself.

History does not have to go logically, and its inevitables are never really inevitable until after they have happened. One of the things that are real about any situation is what the people involved in that situation think about it. What the people in 1863 thought was that the war in the end would go as they made it go, and if anybody had told them that circumstances were going to be controlling, they would have retorted that they would fix all of that by changing the circumstances. In this belief, as Governor Morton might have said, there was much truth.

Among the possible victims of circumstances in this winter of 1863 were the Democrats who made up a majority of the Indiana legislature. Without realizing it, these men were struggling against the fact that the American political system, wide enough for many things, had not by the founding fathers been made wide enough to contain a civil war. They were Democrats taking normal advantage of the fact that they had won an election, and what they were running into was the fact that there was no way, in this moment of all-out war, by which they could do that and nothing more. They wanted to oppose the party that was running the war, and in spite of themselves they could do no less than oppose the war itself. There could be no delicate shadings of action or belief. The administration was fighting for complete victory; to stand against the administration in the ordinary way, using the grips, feints, and arm locks of normal political struggling, meant in actual practice to stand for something less than victory—something a good deal less, perhaps, if the wrestling got really strenuous, so that the struggle might finally appear to be a struggle against the war itself rather than simply against the people who were conducting the war.[13]

So the air was full of rumors, and Indiana that winter was a place where reality blended with the outrageous shapes of Cloud-Cuckoo-Land itself. The victorious Democrats were luxuriating in their new legislative majority, whose precise use they had not yet determined, and were camped comfortably in the center of the stage. (Too comfortably, in fact, for they went sound asleep and were taken.) From the wings, to complicate their job and to precipitate crisis before they were ready for it, came strange far-off noises of wondrous gabbled conspiracies, with oath-bound armies swearing a fantastic fealty. Not for the last time, this prairie state was nurturing an invisible empire complete with weird ceremonials, and what mattered about it was not whether any of it was especially real, but simply that a great many people believed in it devoutly, some with springing hope and some with fear and hatred, but in any event believed.

The name of this invisible empire varied. It was known as the Order of American Knights, and as the Mutual Protection Society, as the Circle of Honor, the Knights of the Golden Circle, and the Order of the Sons of Liberty. It may have stemmed originally from some obscure pre-war fraternity in the South, and its members came together with the belief that the Lincoln government had somehow usurped authority and should be overthrown. The original declaration of principles simply restated a strong states' rights doctrine, upheld chattel slavery, and called piously for a restoration of the old Union.

It was perfectly legal for any Northern citizen to believe in these things, but it was very hard for him to do anything concrete about his belief without appearing to give aid and comfort to the enemy. So this Copperhead order went underground, proliferated its cells from city to city and from town to town, and took on a darker coloration. It came to favor a Northwest confederacy, then it undertook to encourage desertion from the Federal armies, and it prepared at last to give active help to the Southern cause. It bought arms, drilled members in military tactics, commissioned its own "major generals," prepared for active field operations, and called for the assassination of Abraham Lincoln.

Possibly a great deal of this was sheer unconscious make-believe. There was an uncommon amount of froth to the whole affair, and even now it is hard to say what was real and what just seemed to be real. This is not for any lack of facts. There are whole volumes of facts. This Copperhead order must have been one of the most thoroughly spied-upon organizations in human history. Reading the reports and the records, one at times feels that the secret-service men and the counterespionage agents must have been stumbling over one another's heels as they moved through its inner councils. All of these agents abundantly proved that the order had a huge membership—125,000 in Indiana alone, it was said—and they could cite chapter and verse to show that it was a malign revolutionary conspiracy which seriously tried to overthrow the government and lose the war.[14]

The only trouble is that one can never be sure how far the conspirators really meant it, and even the conspirators themselves do not seem to have been entirely certain. The great order never actually did much of anything. On the few occasions when Jefferson Davis tried to make use of it and sent operatives north to promote a little action, the soggy conspiracy came apart at the seams. The handful of hard-eyed Confederate veterans who came north to bring on some overt acts were a different breed from the well-intentioned, well-fed civilians who conspired in village lodge hall and in prairie grove. These Southern veterans were out for blood and they proposed to transform all of this mummery into irrevocable violence in which large numbers of the mummers would unquestionably get killed. It appears that they scared the conspirators almost out of their senses.

Yet in the winter and spring of 1863 this strange unreal plot was a genuine factor. It was believed in, North and South. In Richmond the war clerk-diarist, J. B. Jones, wrote confidently at the end of January that he had no doubt the year would bring "the spectacle of more Northern men fighting against the United States Government than slaves fighting against the South." On February 1 Jones noted:

"It is said and believed that several citizens from Illinois and Indiana, now in this city, have been sent hither by influential parties to consult our government on the best means of terminating the war; or, failing that, to propose some mode of adjustment between the Northern states and the Confederacy, and new combination against the Yankee states and the Federal administration." A fortnight later he was gravely remarking that when the Northwestern states did withdraw from the Union, Virginia probably would take them under her wing "if they earnestly desired to return to her parental protection." He added that if Indiana and Illinois joined the South, victory would be assured.[15]

If the business was taken as seriously as that in the capital of the Confederacy, one can hardly be surprised to find it treated as a matter of life or death in the capital of Indiana. Here men had it in their back yards, and to say that treason stalked the streets by daylight was to do more than indulge in a mere figure of speech. There was a war on, and Indiana regiments in the field were sending home resolutions denouncing all Copperheads—and here was where the Copperheads lived and moved and acted; here they uttered hair-raising threats in public; here their conspiracy was a matter of common street-corner knowledge.

In addition to all of which, the thing was a natural. It was dressed to command attention from skeptic and believer alike. It had an elaborate ritual of oaths and ceremonials which was intended to impress new converts but which probably had the ultimate effect of making a great many sober citizens feel that all Copperheads should be hanged. For this multifariously named order with its degrees and its grips and its ritualized impotent hatred created the atmosphere in which men who supported the Union could be ruthless. It made compromise impossible, and it drove both the war party and the peace party to extremes.

The new member of the order was taught a handclasp for recognition of other members: shake in such a way that the tip of the forefinger touches the pulse of the other man's wrist. He was given a sign of recognition to be used in public places when it was vital to know if other of the faithful were present: shade the eyes with the right hand, put the other hand on the left breast, and never mind if the pose looks odd to the uninitiate. There were verbal signals with which a beset Knight could call for help in a crowd: the word "Aokhoan!" uttered loudly (provided the beset Knight could just pronounce it), or at times the word "Nu-oh-lac," which was "Calhoun" spelled backward. The ritual set forth that a member who violated his obligations was to meet "a shameful death"; specifically, his body was to be divided into four parts, which were to be cast out at the four gates of the temple, the temple being the local Odd Fellows' hall, the room over the corner hardware store, or such other mundane spot as had been chosen for secret meeting place. Becoming slightly more practical, the order also warned its members that if one were brought into court or haled before a grand jury he should refuse to answer questions on the constitutional ground that he could not be made to incriminate himself.[16]

Clearly enough, all of this adds up to a great deal of mumbo-jumboism and nothing much more. But it was a cloak for men who felt deeply, even though they did not really feel deeply enough to risk their lives if they could help it. Until the moment of final risk came they might easily believe that they were going to risk everything, and if they felt that way they would talk—and, up to a point, act—accordingly. And this was going on in a gossipy, chatty, neighborly Middle West where there were really no secrets and mumbo-jumbo would become a matter of universal knowledge in no time. If the participants themselves could believe that this was real and no sham, those on the outside would believe the same.

So when the Democratic majority in the Indiana legislature prepared to whittle down Indiana's part in the war, Morton had his cue. The immediate issue was the bill which would take control of all military matters—troops recruitment, purchase of overcoats, all else—out of the hands of the governor and vest it in a board of hand-picked Democrats. There were in both houses of the legislature the votes to pass this bill, and Morton knew it. He could of course veto the bill, but the Indiana constitution contained an oddity, a provision that the legislature could re-enact a vetoed measure by a simple majority. The Democrats would infallibly pass this law over any veto which Morton might lay down.

If that happened, Morton said bluntly, there would be unshirted hell to pay; "it would involve the state in civil war in twenty-four hours," and "our people would be cutting each other's throats in every county." For Morton was not on any account going to give up his power, no matter what was voted and no matter what the law said. There was as he saw it but one way out, and "that was to break up the legislature."[17]

Indiana's constitution contained a second oddity: not less than two thirds of each house of the legislature constituted a quorum. Without a quorum, of course, no business could be done. So that winter the Republican members quietly bought tickets home and disappeared. The legislature could not act because it lacked a quorum, and so the Democrats went home, too, and Indiana's government consisted solely of Governor Morton and the rest of the executive branch.

The Democrats were unworried. Since it convened early in January the legislature had done nothing but orate, caucus, and investigate. No appropriation bills had been passed, there was no enabling legislation making appropriations legal, and the state treasury had no money and no way to get any. Morton might in effect prorogue the legislature, but sooner or later he would have to have money. To get money he would have to call in the legislature, because only the legislature could raise money. Once the legislature reconvened, the Democrats would have him over a barrel. It was an open-and-shut case, and all the Democrats had to do was wait a little while and be patient.

Except that there was a revolution in progress, and Morton was a perfectly genuine revolutionist. He was, in fact, one of the few men in all history who have understood how a dictatorship can be set up and operated in America. In the winter of 1863 he put that knowledge to work.

The muddle-headed conspirators who devised ancient-mariner recognition signals and who talked solemnly about casting the divided bodies of traitors out of the gates of mystical temples had been carrying on as if someday they would do a fearsome thing, but they were in fact legalists. They professed bloody revolution, and they were to go on doing so for another eighteen months, but in action they relied on a legislative majority. They knew that the majority would eventually make the decisions because the books said so. But when the showdown came the other side was ready to play by different rules, and all of the books went out of the window.

Morton proposed to rule Indiana so that it would stand in the front line of the war against secession. He could not do it legally without the money which he could get only from the legislature, and he had sent the legislature home. Therefore, unable to rule legally, he would rule illegally. He would get the money where he could and he would keep Indiana in the war, and Northern Democrats who did not like it might come around after the war was over and speak their minds fully. Until that time Indiana would have a one-man government named Morton, in whose presence no damned secessionist was going to laugh.

The money problem being at the heart of things, Morton organized a Bureau of Finance, which appealed to bankers, to heads of town and county governments, to the people themselves. Some of the towns and counties responded promptly, appropriating sums ranging from $2,000 to $20,000 and placing the money at the disposal of the governor. Additional money came from citizens and from business firms, and there was a loan of $15,000 from a railroad. There was also that state arsenal, which had acquired illegality ahead of time and which was now showing a fairly substantial profit.[18]

Most important of all, there was the Federal government, which was what really kept Morton in business.

The Secretary of War was Edwin M. Stanton, who had a knack for devious operations, and Stanton had at his disposal certain funds which could be used somewhat loosely. Morton went to Stanton asking for help, and Stanton dipped into these funds and got money for him. (Technically, it appears that the money was "advanced" to Morton as a disbursing officer dimly representing the War Department. The device was probably legal enough as long as the all-out-war crowd could make its own definitions of legality.) So Morton got a Treasury warrant for $250,000, and as he got it he reflected on the way they were stretching the law.

"If the cause fails," he said, "you and I will be covered with prosecutions, imprisoned, driven from the country."

"If the cause fails," said Stanton, who now and then could emit a very highsounding sentence, "I do not wish to live."[19]

So Indiana got money and paid its bills, and Indiana troops remained in the field, and it continued a hard war for Hoosiers. Morton continued to be a dictator for two years, during which time he was considered a great man by ardent Union folk and an unspeakable tyrant by peace-minded Democrats. What few people noticed was that he and his opponents, between them, had helped to accomplish something which they had no faintest desire to accomplish. They had made a prairie revolution, and their handiwork lived after them.

Indiana had a dictator, and he was a man of force and power in his own right, but he really existed by grace of the Federal government, which was paying most of the bills and providing all of the law. Separatism was dying, and beneath the old concept of the sovereignty of the states there was opening a gulf filled with great darkness and echoing quiet. The Democratic legislators and the stage-struck conspirators had succeeded only in forcing the Republicans to go farther than they had consciously meant to go. If the Lincoln administration was demonstrating in South Carolina and in other Southern states that the real power was to be found henceforth in Washington, it was demonstrating exactly the same thing in Indiana.

2. THE IMPERATIVES OF WAR

IT WAS REALLY the army's doing. The old tables were being broken up and far-reaching change was riding down the winds of war, and even such a man as Morton himself, with his heavy hands and his pale hairy flesh and his booming, be-damned-to-you-sir voice, was more a symbol than a prime mover. In this winter of discontent American institutions could be recast, not to fit the ideas of anyone in particular, but simply to make it possible for the army to do the things which it had been created to do. A process had been set in motion which was beyond stopping, and the fact that these hundreds of thousands of young men had been turned into soldiers had become dominant for the whole country.

The changes, of course, did not begin in the camps. In the camps there was the old routine, with snow in the woods and mud on the roads and unending drills on the hard-packed parade grounds, and the immense restlessness of uprooted youth was reaching constantly for an outlet.

When occasion offered there were mild sprees. March brought St. Patrick's Day. There were many Irishmen in camp, and they saw to it that the day was observed notably. The 9th Massachusetts held open house for the 62nd Pennsylvania, broaching barrels of beer and erecting a greased pole on the parade, with a fifteen-day furlough pinned to the top. (The pole had been greased too well, and nobody was able to get to the top.) A half-mile race track was laid out and there were horse races, which wound up with an accident that killed two horses and the regimental quartermaster, who had fancied himself as a gentleman rider.[1]

The Irish Brigade, naturally, put on the biggest party of all on this day, and General Hooker and his staff and all of the officers of the II Corps were guests. General Meagher turned out garbed as a crimson-coated master of hounds, and at the close of the day he had a huge banquet, with more guests than places at table. Addressing the throng, he begged the unseated guests to remember that "Thomas Francis Meagher's hospitality is not so large as his heart." Nobody really minded very much because there was an enormous punch bowl filled with what one officer remembered as "the strongest punch I ever tasted," and the evening ended with a grand row between Meagher and his brigade surgeon, who furiously challenged each other to a duel that was never fought.[2]

Meagher was famous for his parties. The whole II Corps remembered a fabulous banquet the Irish Brigade had thrown in ruined Fredericksburg on the fifteenth of December, while the dead men lay still unburied on the frozen fields in front of the stone wall, and the echoing town itself presented bleak roofless walls to the wintry sky, with rival gunners on Marye's Heights and Stafford Heights blessing the place now and then with casual rounds of high explosive. Meagher's brigade had just received three new regimental flags, purest green silk made up by the ladies of New York, and nothing would do but a jollification. So they had taken over some half-wrecked hall and had invited in everybody who was anybody in the II Corps. Long tables had been set up amid the wreckage, loaded with chicken and cold turkey and ham, and good things to drink had been circulating liberally, and when the flags were presented to the Irish regiments there had been a great deal of oratory. In the end everybody had such a good time and cheered so loudly that even Burnside's moribund headquarters on the far side of the river had caught on and had sent staff officers over with frantic orders: stop the party and send everybody home, or the Rebels will take notice of all this noise and open a new bombardment.[3]

It was a hard-drinking army as far as its officer corps was concerned. Any officer could legally buy all the whisky he thought he could handle from the commissary stores, and the commissary whisky was originally famous as "a cheap and reliable article." Later on, as the original supply became exhausted, it was raw and harsh, although it continued to be cheap enough. Some officers would simmer it over a fire in order to reduce the harshness; others believed in setting fire to it and letting it burn awhile, arguing that this destroyed the fusel oil and other harmful substances. However they treated it, they used a good deal of it, and the soldiers' sleep was occasionally disturbed by singing and yelling from the officers' quarters. Colonel Cross of the 5th New Hampshire broke up one such party in his own regiment by stalking in with his drawn saber in one hand and a pair of handcuffs in the other.[4]

But the parties and the whiskey were not for the enlisted men, except very rarely and by good luck. The VI Corps had a tale about one of its most distinguished brigadiers, who attended one of these festive occasions and came out full of a rich, sympathetic fellow feeling for his orderly, who presumably had been standing in the cold all evening, holding the brigadier's horse. The brigadier took his bridle reins and teetered gently on his heels and remarked to the orderly: "Do you know, I'd like to take a drink with you." Then sadly he added that this just would not do because there was a great gulf fixed between them. "You're an orderly, sir, and I'm a general, sir; recollect that, sir." The orderly swayed in the dim light, exhaling an aroma fully as fruity as that of the brigadier's and replied: "By George, General, hadn't you better wait till you're asked?"[5]

For the most part, the private soldier found his life unexciting, not to say dull. A Pennsylvanian that winter wrote in his diary that military glory consisted in "getting shot and having your name spelled wrong in the newspapers," and a man in the 12th New Hampshire recorded that he and his fellows had enlisted too early. Bounties were running as high as fifteen hundred dollars per man up in the White Mountain country, and the average citizen was cheerfully voting for higher taxes to pay for them because "every such enlistment made his chances one less of having to go himself."[6]

It was a confusing sort of war, and if the enlisted man sometimes wondered what it was all about it is not surprising. Up the Rappahannock, Federal pickets continued to make friends with the Rebels across the water, to the horror of security-minded officers. A major in the 2nd Rhode Island wrote that he had 340 of his men on riverside picket duty, under strictest orders to have no truck with the men on the far side of the stream. Yet one day he heard the Confederates calling across to let the Rhode Island boys know that the Yankee paymaster had just got to camp and that the Rhode Islanders, accordingly, would get their pay very shortly. This, the major remarked glumly, happened barely fifteen minutes after the paymaster had arrived. Next day the Rebels told the Rhode Island pickets that the Yankee cavalry had moved up upstream, and one Rebel called across to ask what had been done with a Rebel who had deserted into the Federal lines the night before: would he be conscripted into the Yankee army? The Rhode Islanders called back that that would not happen, whereupon the inquiring Confederate asked them to look out for him—he would be over himself as soon as it got dark.[7]

Scandalized by such laxity, the provost marshal of the army, Brigadier General Mason R. Patrick, a gruff old party with flowing white hair and whiskers, who held little prayer meetings in his tent every morning and then went forth (as the men supposed) to bite the heads off tenpenny nails, reported that when the 62nd New York was on duty by the river its officers took charge of rigging and sending out the toy boats which carried on the illicit trade with the Rebel army. One of Patrick's officers seized such a boat, laden with coffee and sugar, in an effort to break up the trade, and was immediately denounced angrily by a regimental officer as a spoilsport.

Worse yet, said Patrick, he had detected pickets of the 169th Pennsylvania in flagrant verbal communication with the Rebels. A Rebel had called across: "Any signs of a move?" and a Pennsylvanian had replied: "Yes, we've got eight days' rations and we expect to move in a few days." When the Rebel asked which direction the move would take, the Pennsylvanian obligingly told him that it would be upstream, to the right. Quite gratuitously the Yankee outpost added that they were going to use pack mules for transportation and hence obviously would not be following the line of the railroad.[8] What chance, asked General Patrick wrathfully, did an army have to deceive the enemy with that sort of talk going on?

From Ohio the governor was writing the War Department that for the past sixty days he had been trying to recruit men but that "success had been trifling," and the governor of Iowa was asking for five thousand stands of arms to use on dissidents who opposed recruitment and a vigorous prosecution of the war. Also from Iowa, a United States marshal was reporting that there had recently been a public meeting in Madison County at which armed men hurrahed for Jefferson Davis and declared that they would like to see Iowa join the Southern Confederacy. Simultaneously the governor of Illinois was wiring the War Department that "an extensive and dangerous traffic in arms" was going on between Illinois exporters and ultimate consumers in the Southland, and a draft-enrolling officer at Chambersburg, Pennsylvania, was quitting his job because indignant citizens had gone around and burned his sawmill.[9]

All of these things were happening, and it was hard for any man to say which incidents were really important and which were frothy bubbles on the surface. One significant occurrence could have been the publication of a formal document which was issued from the White House about the time General Burnside had his day and ceased to be as commander of the army.

This paper recited the findings of a recent court-martial and closed by asserting that "the foregoing proceedings, finding and sentence. . .are approved and confirmed"—as a result of which Major General Fitz-John Porter was cashiered and dismissed from the service and was barred from ever again holding any office of trust or profit under the United States Government.[10]

Fitz-John Porter's was a name which had once carried weight. Brave, talented, and handsome, Porter had been McClellan's right-hand man all through the peninsular campaign; he had, in fact, done most of the actual fighting which kept McClellan's army from destruction when Robert E. Lee cast a net for it in the Chickahominy bottom lands. He had been trusted to fight Gaines's Mill and Malvern Hill by himself, and at Second Bull Run he had led a final forlorn-hope assault on Stonewall Jackson's invulnerable lines, and he had been respected and honored among men. Now he was being ruined, his career as a professional soldier closing in black disgrace. The signature at the end of the paper which condemned him was that of Abraham Lincoln.

This paper was rather surprising, for a conviction had not generally been looked for. Porter himself had been so confident of acquittal that he had recently gone to the White House to discuss with Lincoln himself his next assignment in the army. Since his day the verdict has come to seem cruel and unjust, the passasge of time having indicated that the military court was hasty and biased, its principal function having in fact been to make somebody sweat for the loss of the second battle of Bull Run. John Pope, who commanded the army that lost that battle, had pointed the finger at Porter in a frantic effort at self-exculpation, and so Porter had come to trial.

Porter found himself accused, specifically, of violation of the ninth and fifty-second articles of war, the general idea being that he had refused to attack the Rebel flank as ordered by Pope and that the battle therefore had been lost. Porter had tried to show that his orders could not be executed, since the Rebel flank was nowhere near where Pope thought it was, but it had done him no good. He was a close friend of McClellan, and McClellan had been uprooted so that there could be an all-out war. The wind and the sun had bleached white the bones of Bull Run's unburied dead, Pope was in exile in Minnesota fighting the Sioux Indians, and not for another generation could there be a full understanding of the ins and outs of the tragic lost battle. Meanwhile, Porter had been broken, and there was in the action a meaning which did not appear on the surface.

While it was valuable to punish a scapegoat for Bull Run, a more important motive seems to have been operating in the background. One interpretation can be found in the carefully worded memoirs of Alexander K. McClure, who as a Republican politician and editor had a fair understanding of what was happening in Washington then. McClure wrote that the military court, as set up by Secretary Stanton, was "studiously organized to convict." Lincoln, he added, approved the verdict even though he was by no means convinced that Porter was in fact a faithless officer. Said Editor McClure: "New conditions and grave military necessities confronted Lincoln; and while he did not approve of the judgment against Porter, he felt that Porter and others of his type merited admonition to assure some measure of harmony in military affairs, and he finally decided that to approve the judgment would be the least of the evils presented to him."[11]

The administration was groping through a red fog toward a shore dimly seen, and if McClure might not be qualified to say what was in Lincoln's mind, he could at least identify the angle from which the administration's action made good political sense. Porter was blameless, but he was being crushed because, in an excessively slippery situation, the civil authorities were finding it necessary above all things to get a solid grip on the army and on the war. Porter might not in fact be an obstacle in their way, but they thought that he was, which was what mattered. At the very least he had come to symbolize the obstacles which, being intangible, could not be dealt with directly.

Ordinarily the government would not need to ruin a general in order to establish its control, but these things were far from ordinary. Fear and hate and suspicion had been created in order that these incomprehensible soldiers who failed to hate their enemies might at least be inspired and directed by men who did hate. (Grim old Thad Stevens had recently offered in Congress a resolution denouncing, as guilty of "a high crime," anyone in the executive branch of the government who should so much as propose a negotiated peace with the South.)[12] Everybody in Washington was being victimized, and the bloodcurdling fol-de-rol of the Indiana conspirators was part of the emotional background. Porter was one victim. Another victim, looking with unutterable melancholy to a day beyond death and hatred, brooding darkly about what the people might buy with this sacrifice of their blood if they could be enabled to make their purchase with charity and without malice, was Abraham Lincoln. In between the two, the immediate victim and the tragic humorist who was appointed to sit in judgment upon him, there were many others. Among them was the coarse, savagely cruel, everlastingly vital little man with the straggly whiskers and the furious eyes, Secretary of War Edwin M. Stanton.

Stanton represented driving force. He was a terror to all traitors, to most Democrats, and to a good many officers of the United States Army. There were those who said that if one who came before him for a scolding barked back at him sharply the Secretry would change his tack and become ingratiating, and it appears that old-fashioned fortitude in personal combat may not have been one of his basic virtues.[13] McClellan had considered him a double-dealer who could talk falsely of friendship while he dug a pitfall before one's feet. Others spoke of his intolerable insolence, and it was a byword that his favorite cry to officers brought before him was a passionate "I'll dismiss you from the service!"

Stanton looked at the army and found its officer corps full of cliques—the friends of McClellan, the pals from West Point, the tent mates from the old Indian-fighting army from the Western plains. He saw, also, that this army somehow was not quite responsive to the will of the government. On the horizon lay the fleeting shape of a vision which was noble beyond utterance, but in the immediate foreground there were the blood and the mud and the inexpressible ignobility which doomed sick men to a diet of salt pork and hardtack, or squandered men's lives through sheer incompetence, or schemed and plotted for rank and promotion. The contrast was beyond endurance. So as a first step, and beginning with the destruction of the luckless Porter, Stanton would break up the cliques.

The technique was brutal, but the idea was sound enough. A rather obscure brigadier of cavalry, who served for a time in the provost guard in the capital and hence got a good look at the seamy side of things, applauded vigorously as he watched what the Secretary was doing.

"When Stanton was appointed," this officer wrote, "a military aristocracy of the regular army and of immense power had arisen in the bosom of the army of the volunteers. This aristocracy had at its head the commander-in-chief and stretched its roots into every corps, regiment, and bureau, defying the government at home with only a little less disdain than Davis manifested at Richmond. Our own army was first to be made subordinate to the President, and then the Southern army made subordinate to it. To relieve McClellan, court-martial Porter, and eliminate all traces of West Point class traditions, uniting by nicknames, I consider victories as important as Appomattox, and these nothing but the wooden and numb audacity of Stanton dared to achieve."[14]

The crack about West Point nicknames, to be sure, indicates a general of volunteers whose feelings were hurt one day when he found that he did not belong to the club, and this doubtless colored what he had to say. Yet he did have a point. There was ever so much more to the Porter business than Porter himself. Porter was an innocent who stood in the line of fire, and he got hit. From this winter onward the army might have many defects, but one thing at least was certain: its higher officers would realize that a hard war was called for.

Others besides the offended cavalry general got the point. Major Dawes of the 6th Wisconsin, who never suffered from his own lack of a West Point nickname, wrote in March that army morale had been restored, and he set down the verdict of a front-line fighting man:

"By the prompt dismissal of disaffected and disloyal officers, the army is being purged of the damnable heresy that a man can be a friend to the government and yet throw every clog in the way of the administration and prosecution of the war."[15]

Fuzzier, yet speaking an honest emotion springing from the upswing that followed Stanton's purge, was the outburst written down by the eminent Bostonian, Major Henry Lee Higginson of the 1st Massachusetts Cavalry:

"We'll beat these men, fighting for slavery and for wickedness, out of house and home, beat them to death, this summer, too. . . . We are right, and are trying hard; we have at last real soldiers, not recruits, in the field, and we shall reap our harvest. . . . My whole religion (that is, my whole belief and hope in everything, in man, in woman, in music, in good, in the beautiful, in the real truth) rests on the questions now really before us."[16]

Neither Major Dawes nor Major Higginson quite said it. Yet there was something unexpressed, perhaps something finally inexpressible, lying beneath the change which they saw coming over the army and the war that winter and spring. America was changing, changing by violence, with much blood to be shed and many lives to be wrecked. Nobody was ready for it, and nobody could quite understand it now that it was happening. But somehow it was being determined that democracy henceforth, perhaps for some centuries to come, would operate through a new instrument. Sovereignty of the states was dying, North as well as South, and going with it was the ancient belief that the government which governs least is the government which governs best.

Between that fact and the mangling of General Porter the connection might seem to be remote, but it was there. Neither Porter nor the men who broke him could have told quite what was happening, nor could they have said why it was happening. All men were victims and agents of the irresistible current of change. It was necessary for some of them to die of dysentery, eating bad food in unheated hospital tents beside the Rappahannock, and it was necessary for others to hammer a desk and threaten army officers with ignominy, and in the end something bigger than any man knew would come of it all.

In this desperate war which America was waging—with itself and with its own past, and with all of the habits of thought which had grown up out of that past—the nation was unexpectedly finding that it possessed enormous strength. The possession of that strength was a fact of incalculable significance. None of the old means for wielding and controlling it seemed to be any good. Yet the power existed, and the one certainty was that someone would eventually control it no matter what happened to the war, to the country, or to the country's traditional method of governing itself. So the necessity of taking control of this immense power was going to dominate everything for a time, and it was going to work through many instruments.

One of these instruments—least likely of the lot, perhaps, but extremely effective—was Joe Hooker, exercising the functions of the profane hard-drinking soldier to bring the army back to fighting pitch, and inspiring Boston's Major Higginson to a confused rhapsody about the higher values. Another was Secretary Stanton, smashing blindly at officer cliques to extend the power of the central government. Still another was the great anonymous private soldier himself.

He was the central fact in the whole situation. For the time being, government existed for him. He fought without poetry, as the regular said of the New Englanders, and he died by platoons when the time came for him to die, and all of the raw power which the country was beginning to assert had meaning only through him. Without in the least intending to, he was now driving the government on to a fuller assertion of its own powers.

He fought and he died without any particular complaint (except for remarks about bad food and incompetent leadership), but someone had to keep sending him up to the firing line. This job originally fell to the several states, and they had done nobly as long as individual Americans would respond to the call. But the unhappy fact was that volunteering had just about ceased. The states had tried coercion—that is, they had gingerly tried drafting their own people—but that was not working well either. The war had begun as an effort by one coalition of states to impose its will on another coalition of states, and it could not be fought that way any longer.

Hooker's army contained something like 120,000 men. Nearly 30,000 of these were men who had signed up for short terms—many of them were nine-month men, enlisted the summer before when Lee drove north into Maryland and made Northern pulses flutter—and their enlistments would expire in mid-May. There was no way to hold these men in service, since they had enlisted with the states and not with the Federal government. (Hooker was remarking that even the men who were willing to re-enlist would insist on being sent home and paid off first, so that they could join new regiments and collect fat bounties.)

The states were not what they had been. The corn belt had its troubles, with every governor sending plaintive cries to Washington asking for help. New York, which had refused to elect a fighting man, had a Copperhead for governor, a high-minded eloquent man who would stop now to reason and argue in a situation that was past reasoned argument. Horatio Seymour was an old-school Democrat, a man with a plausible smooth face fringed by under-the-chin whiskers, who dreaded the coercion of the states about as much as he dreaded disunion. He believed that hard-minded Republicans were shamefully making political capital out of a war which they had taken over for their own purposes—which, as a matter of fact, was perfectly true—and he was protesting that the only way to prevent the establishment of a despotic central government was to preserve the powers of the several states. The war, he declared, must not be turned into "a bloody, barbarous, revolutionary, and unconstitutional scheme" to destroy state sovereignty.[17]

Seymour stood at one of the extremes. He was an honorable extremist, driven by the cruel logic of events into speaking for forces which he would not ordinarily uphold, and behind him were men whom he himself would not endorse. Yet even loyal, all-out-war governors were complaining this winter that the government's policies were destructive. Andrew of Massachusetts, a fire-eating abolitionist who got into the war almost before Washington itself, had recently begged Lincoln to rely on nine-month militia regiments rather than on draftees, arguing that the draft would "disturb everything."[18]

The unhappy fact was that many governors had either lost control over their own states or had become men who did not believe in the kind of war that was now being fought. They were no longer supplying the army with adequate numbers of recruits, and since the war had become grim and unlimited, that seemed to be their principal reason for existence. The men who would come into the army willingly had just about been used up, and the men who would come in only if somebody made them come could not be brought forward in adequate numbers by mere governors. But to get on with the war now it was necessary above all else to keep the stream of recruits flowing into the army. The unsung private on the firing line might be voiceless, but unless he remained on the firing line the war was lost forever, and he was not going to remain there indefinitely unless he had company.

To keep him there and to provide him with the replacements he needed, the government had to use force. It was already using force on the states, and now it must use force on individual citizens as well. State sovereignty was dying in the smoke and dust of a dozen battles; dying with it was the old idea that the government of the United States could not reach out and tap the shoulder of the ordinary man. From now on the government must do exactly that or cease to be a government.

That was what government had come to, and that was what government now did. This same winter and spring of 1863 which saw the administration warning all army officers, via the ruined career of General Porter, that the civil government was in charge of things also saw the passage of a national conscription law.

The emphasis was on the word *national*. There was conscription already, with the states enrolling their citizens, appointing agents to harry them into camp, and making such deals as they could—at the price of fabulous bounty acts by cities, counties, and townships—to get a sufficiency of men under arms. But from now on Washington was not going to get its men from the states. It was going to reach out with its own lengthened arm and take them direct. The lists of men subject to conscription would be made up by representatives of the government at Washington and not by men named by the governors. If penalties were inflicted for non-compliance, they would be inflicted by Washington, for a drafted man who evaded the call was no longer merely a citizen who had thumbed his nose at the state authorities: he was a deserter from the United State Army, and the Federal government might shoot him if it could catch him.

In the month of March, accordingly, the country went over to this new system of recruitment, which embodied, all in all, one of the most revolutionary changes ever made in the American form of government, since it permanently reduced the role of the states in the American political picture. State sovereignty, South, had fired cannon at Fort Sumter, leading to a great deal of this and that along the border. Now it was state sovereignty, North, which was coming under the guns.

Among those who immediately detected the sweeping nature of the change that was being made was New York's Governor Seymour. He protested heatedly that national conscription was unconstitutional, and he argued that the government should depend solely on the states even though the dome of heaven fell in. Ironically, there arose to his voice a splenetic echo from the heart of the deepest South, where Governor Joseph E. Brown of Georgia was making exactly the same kind of fight against Jefferson Davis. Brown was hotly telling Davis that "your doctrine carried out not only makes Congress supreme over the states at any time when it chooses to exercise the full measure of its power to raise armies, but it places the very existence of the state governments subject to the will of Congress."[19]

If the central government, cried Brown, can draft men, and if it is the central government which can specify who is to be exempt from the draft, then the central government could, if it chose, utterly destroy the state governments simply by drafting all state officials into the army. Congress, complained the governor of Georgia, was supposed to be the agent of the states. How now, if it could reach into the states and make its writ good within state territory? Were not the people thereby reduced to "a state of provincial dependence upon the central power?"

Indubitably. Yet it is recorded that while the angry plaints of Governor Brown caused Jefferson Davis to sigh wearily (and, the sighing over, to explode into icy polemics) they had no effect on Davis's program to raise the Confederate armies by conscription. Governor Seymour had no better luck in the North. The imperatives of war were at work, and there was a chill wind blowing in on theories and theorists. The New Yorkers and the Georgians who killed each other across the stone wall at Fredericksburg would have found cold comfort in the idea, but the fact was that they had left their respective governors high and dry.[20]

Thus while the administration moved to take the army away from the generals, it was also taking it away from the governors. The army would never again be an assemblage of troops contributed by the several states. (In 1861 Secretary Chase had protested that "he would rather have no regiments raised in Ohio than that they should not be known as Ohio regiments." He still felt that way, yet now he was one of the principal instruments of change.)[21] From now on it would be a national army.

One step led to another. Decreeing that the United States Government would be responsible for its own armies henceforth, the administration also gave thought to the question of making soldiers out of Negroes. The colored man seemed in some distracting way to be what this war was, at bottom, chiefly about. By presidential declaration the war now must go on until the colored man had been given his freedom. Might the colored man not fight as a soldier in the ranks, then?

So the decree went forth for the enlistment of regiments of colored troops, the tide of events having carried everyone some distance beyond Ben Butler's tentside pronouncement that fugitive slaves were mere contraband of war. This was at first balm and a delight to the harassed Northern governors. If colored men could be enrolled, perhaps a state's quotas could be met that way, white men being loath to come forward. Andrew of Massachusetts thought this should be tried, and he hastened to enlist a solid colored regiment, the 54th Massachusetts. Simultaneously he sent agents all across the North to enlist other colored folk for Massachusetts regiments.

This might have been a good trick for stay-at-home Yankees, busy with the prosperity of a wartime boom that went beyond anything in anybody's earlier imagination, if it had just worked. In the very nature of things, however, it could be carried only so far before it collapsed of its own weight. There were not any prodigious numbers of able-bodied colored men in all the Northern states together. When all was said and done, the North had been inhospitable to the Negro. Some of the states which stood strongest for the war had laws forbidding settlement by Negroes, and as fantastically underprivileged folk the free Negroes tended to live under bad health conditions and so produced many young men who could not pass army physical examinations. It became clear, at last, that even if the Northern colored population furnished recruits in the same proportion as Northern whites had furnished them the army would gain only eighteen thousand new soldiers.[22]

What this meant was that if any appreciable number of Negroes were to come into the army they would have to come from the South. Obviously, the national government was the only agency which could recruit them. (The irrepressible Governor Andrew did try to recruit some Massachusetts soldiers from among the colored contraband in the occupied areas, but the effort fizzled.) The colored recruit, therefore, rounded up by semi-literate, hard-handed agents who moved in the train of the armies, was, above all, a recruit to a national army.[23] His very presence in uniform testified to the existence of a new power in Washington.

All of these things happened, not at once and dramatically, but over a period of weeks. Their significance might or might not have been seen at the time. The atmosphere in Washington in the long winter that followed Fredericksburg seemed to be one of disintegration and despair, and it was none other than Governor Andrew who was writing that in Washington just then he found few men "of practical sagacity and victorious faith." Yet the sagacity and the faith were at work, and something was being done. The war was a long way from being won, but at last the things were being done which would make it possible for it to be won. Uncertainly and without a clear plan, Washington was removing obstacles from the army's path.

3. SOLDIERS' BARGAIN

BEYOND ANY question, Joe Hooker was the handsomest commander the Army of the Potomac ever had. Crusty Publisher Alexander K. McClure grew fairly dreamy-eyed when he tried to describe him: "A man of unusually handsome face and elegant proportions, with a complexion as delicate and silken as a woman's." Major Dawes of the 6th Wisconsin spoke of Hooker's "Apollo-like presence," and a newspaper correspondent noted that the general had large gray-blue eyes, a rosy skin, and an abundance of blond hair, and said that he looked like an ideal soldier with his erect carriage and his square shoulders. To another correspondent Hooker looked "as rosy as the most healthy woman alive." Hooker had more than a little of the old McClellan touch, and the soldiers were always ready to cheer when they saw him, as if the tattered clouds of war's forgotten glory still trailed after him even for regiments which had gone through Antietam and Fredericksburg.[1]

He had won command at a bad time. The army was in disorder. A veteran in the 24th New Jersey said afterward that "at no period in its history were the troops more disheartened or less hopeful of achieving success," and a soldier in the 3rd Michigan wrote that winter that there had been many desertions and that "unless something is done to prevent it our ranks will grow pretty thin in a short while."[2] This man was an admirer of Hooker, but he was not sure whether the general could do much now that supreme command had been given him, and he wrote dubiously:

"We all feel that General Hooker will be like the poor man that won the elephant at the raffle. After he got the animal he did not know what to do with him. So with fighting Joseph. He is now in command of a mighty large elephant, and it will remain to be seen if he knows what to do with him."

Hooker himself was under no illusions. He was to show, in the end, a great capacity for deceiving himself, but at the start he knew exactly where he was. As he took over the command he examined the troubles of Burnside with brutal clarity, remarking that although the army was actually on the verge of dissolution Burnside had not even suspected it, the reason being that Burnside "has no other idea of the organization and government of an army than that of arranging it in such a way that the commanding general will have nothing to do. The nearer the army reaches that point, the greater the excellence in his estimation."[3]

That mistake Hooker himself would not make. The peculiar flaws in his make-up were not of the kind that would handicap him at the beginning. Editor McClure remembered being told by an officer who knew Hooker in the old California days that "Hooker could play the best game of poker I ever saw until it came to the point where he should go a thousand better, and then he would flunk."[4] The time for going a thousand better had not yet arrived. The game was still young, and at this point the general held it firmly in his own hands and played it with great skill.

If he shared with McClellan the ability to draw cheers from tired men who had seen much of war, he also shared with that departed officer an extreme distaste for letting army administration take care of itself. Quite unexpectedly Hooker turned out to be a first-rate organizer and military housekeeper. He looked upon himself, and caused others to look upon him, as the dashing leader of troops in battle; actually, in this winter of despair, his great service to his country lay in this prosaic matter of making certain that the men got enough to eat and stayed well.

Just now he needed to display none of his more flamboyant qualities, the qualities which seemed to be most characteristic of him, the dash and the rough soldiers'-campfire good-fellowship, and the "sublime courage at the battle front." (That last testimonial comes from an officer in the Iron Brigade, where they tended to be connoisseurs of courage.) The troops, indeed, might make up and gaily sing a little ditty[5] which stated:

> Joe Hooker is our leader,
> He takes his whisky strong—

But what they got from Joe Hooker first of all, what they got that made the rough places straight and convinced them that it was going to be a great day in the morning—what, in fine, was genuinely important to them and to the national cause—was the sober, unimaginative, routine work of eternally checking up on rations, clothing, hospitals, living quarters, and other little details which in the long run make all the difference.

The first trouble was food. The government had bought much very good food, including the fresh vegetables for want of which men sickened and died, in addition to the hardtack, salt pork, and coffee which were the iron rations of this army. The only problem lay in the fact that none of this good food got to the ultimate blue-uniformed consumer. With the canny eye of one who himself lacked innate virtue sufficiently to understand the inner motivations of sinful unwatched man, and who hence knew all of the angles, General Hooker looked into this with a very cold gaze. What he found was that the officers designated as commissaries of subsistence—the officers whose job it was to get this food from the warehouses to the mess kitchens—had discovered in Uncle Sam's bounty a good way to get rich.

The fresh vegetables, the onions and cabbages and potatoes and the patented desiccated vegetables—known to all ranks, inevitably, as "desecrated vegetables," since soldiers will always mispronounce a word if they can manage it— were being sold for cash money to outsiders, including a number of the unredeemed residents of rebellious Virginia. The money thus received went into the commissary officer's private purse, and the monthly returns were falsified in order to show that the soldiers themselves had been the recipients. Nobody had ever set up a system by which there would be a stream of monthly vouchers showing that all of this stuff had gone to the men for whom it had been bought. It was, as a soldier remarked later, "a system of single (not to say singular) entry that enriched many a captain and assistant commissary of subsistence for the rest of his life."[6]

On this singular system Joe Hooker landed with a heavy foot. There came from army headquarters presently an order announcing that flour or soft bread would be issued to the troops at least four times a week, with fresh potatoes and vegetables coming out twice a week and desiccated mixed vegetables at least once a week. Commanders of corps, divisions, brigades, and detached commands would require any commissary officer who failed to make such issues to file a written statement from the officer in charge of the depot warehouse proving that the warehouse did not have any of the foods in question.[7] That took care of the commissary officers.

Next came the matter of cooking. On the march each man cooked for himself, and since the average soldier could do little more than boil coffee and frizzle a strip of bacon or salt pork, the marching ration consisted of fried pork, hardtack, and coffee. In camp things were supposed to be better. And yet, administration having been lax, and foods other than pork and hardtack and coffee having vanished en route to the regiments, in most outfits here in the camps near Falmouth marching rations were the regular diet for troops which were not marching at all. Regimental commanders now were required to see to it that the regular company cooks went to work, and if there were no company cooks they were instructed to create some, so that the soldier could get decent meals in place of the intestine-destroying stuff he cooked for himself.

It was true that most of these company cooks lacked skill. Some noticeably lacked even the desire to be skillful, since most of them were simply enlisted men detailed from the ranks to do a two-month stretch in the mess kitchen. Nevertheless, bad as they might be, it was at least possible for them to cook and serve fresh vegetables. They could use the desiccated foods to make soups and stews, and when fresh meat was issued they could do something besides fry it in pork fat. The soldier cooking for himself, blessed with no kitchen utensils except a little frying pan and a tin can in which coffee might be boiled, could do none of those things no matter what raw materials he might have.

One veteran, reminiscing years later, recalled the new order of things: "From the commissary came less whisky for the officers and better rations, including vegetables, for the men. Hospitals were renovated, new ones built, drunken surgeons discharged, sanitary supplies furnished, and the sick no longer left to suffer and die without proper care and attention. Officers and men who from incompetence or disability could be of no further use to the service were allowed to resign or were discharged, and those who were playing sick in the hospitals were sent to their regiments for duty."[8]

And so between the fresh foods and the better cooking, army surgeons presently noticed the disappearance of the cases of scurvy which had been extending the regimental sick lists. At the same time there was a sharp drop in the perennial scourge of diarrhea, together with a general decline in "all the more serious diseases to which troops in camp are liable, and especially those which depend upon neglect of sanitary precautions." In addition, the surgeon general reported to Hooker that there had been "an improvement in the health, tone, and vigor of those who are not reported sick; an improvement which figures will not exhibit but which is apparent to officers whose attention is directed to the health of the men."[9]

Part of this was due to better food, and another part because somebody at last made it his business to see that elementary rules of sanitation were observed in the camps. The log-and-canvas hutments in which the men lived had become little better than pigsties, especially those in which the men had raised their shelters over shallow pits dug in the earth. It appears that young men living without women have no especial desire to be clean. Under Hooker's prodding the army's surgeons caught onto that fact and took corrective action. The canvas roofs of all huts were ripped off periodically so that the sun and the clean wind could strike the interior; wherever possible, the entire hut had to be moved to new ground at the end of each week. The worst of the camps were abandoned outright and the troops moved to new camp sites. It was required that blankets and other bedding be aired daily, that hut floors be carpeted with pine boughs or other material so that men would not bed down on the bare earth, and regimental commanders were ordered to require the digging of eighteen-inch drainage ditches around each habitation. Kitchen refuse had to be buried each day, proper sinks were dug for every camp, and "the men should be required to wear their hair cut short, to bathe twice a week, and put on clean underclothing at least once a week."[10]

Elementary as most of the rules seem to be, the mere fact that they were now embodied in official orders indicates the extent to which they had not been observed previously. The change that took place in this army, once decent food and decent living conditions became the rule, was remarkable. The soldiers themselves testified to the great improvement by setting up wild cheers whenever they saw their handsome general sitting proudly on his big white horse as they passed by. One wrote that "General Hooker proved a veritable Santa Claus to the army under his command." Another said that "the whole army was impressed with the feeling that strength, energy, and intelligence were all working together at headquarters," and a third remarked simply that "under Hooker, we began to *live.*"[11] Writing long after the war, a Massachusetts soldier looked back ecstatically:

"Ah! the furloughs and vegetables he gave! How he did understand the road to the soldier's heart! How he made out of defeated, discouraged, and demoralized men a cheerful, plucky, and defiant army, ready to follow him everywhere!" Most of the accounts agree with another regimental scribe, who recorded that "cheerfulness, good order, and military discipline at once took the place of grumbling, depression, and want of confidence."[12]

There were furloughs. Thinking along non-military lines, Hooker concluded that if the men wanted more than anything else to see the folks back home the thing to do was to let them go, and there was presently a system by which one man in each company, in turn, could get a ten-day furlough. This could not take care of everybody, of course, but it took care of a good many, and the effect was good. At the same time, it was made harder to desert. The mails down from Washington were put under control of the army provost marshal, and stern orders were issued governing express packages. No package would be received for transmission to anyone in the army unless it bore an invoice stating that it did not contain civilian clothing, the invoice to be certified by the agent who had accepted the package for shipment. From President Lincoln there came an order granting amnesty to all absentees who returned to the ranks before April. At the same time, the kindhearted President was persuaded to relinquish his right to review all court-martial sentences, and it now became possible to shoot deserters. Picket lines around the army were tightened, parties representing themselves as telegraph-repair details had to exhibit written proof that they were telling the truth, and no wagons of any kind could go north without proper passes, while the pickets were ordered to shoot any wandering persons who failed to halt and account for themselves when challenged. Drinking in the camp was squelched (except among the officers, including especially the commanding general), and the guards on the bridges at Washington were presently confiscating five hundred dollars' worth of liquor a day. One result of this was that regimental sutlers, until the authorities caught on, did a land-office business in such canned goods as brandied peaches.[13]

There were also many drills—"constant and severe," as one soldier remembered them. If the men were down in the dumps, Hooker did not propose to give them leisure to sit around and brood about it, and from morning to night the drill fields rumbled with the tramp of many feet. Officers went to school evenings and next day went out to maneuver companies, regiments, brigades, and divisions in the tactics thus studied. There were reviews with the old McClellan touch, with everybody in dress uniform, brass bands blaring under the wintry sky, and Hooker looking on with visible pride. A man in the 16th Maine recalled "the evident satisfaction of Hooker and the conscious power shown on this handsome but rather too rosy face."[14]

It seemed that many men added that sort of qualification when they wrote an enthusiastic verdict on Hooker. He was too handsome, too roseate with good health and vigor, too confident that this army which was beginning to fit into his hand so nicely would prove an irresistible weapon. (He dismayed Abraham Lincoln once this spring by remarking jauntily that the question was not *if* he got to Richmond, but simply *when*.) The tide was visibly turning. Hooker himself had caused it to turn, perhaps he would ride the flood to fortune, yet it could hardly be quite that simple. There would always be a catch in it for this army—finest army on the planet, Hooker was calling it; he could march it clear to New Orleans if he had to, and the word would soon be "God help the Rebels."[15] It had labored under glamorous McClellan, braggart Pope, and plodding Burnside, coming uniformly to ill fortune under each. Now it had a general who seemed to blend the traits of all three of these predecessors, and it might be that it would do better under him. Yet even while he aroused confidence he created a small grain of doubt. The man whose beautiful skin was a bit too rosy might also, in the end, himself be a little too good to be true.

Yet the army did revive. The rank and file took Hooker at face value, and showed it by their actions. Hooker was proudly writing after a fortnight in command that desertion had practically ceased.[16] These soldiers, who were prepared to give everything, could drive no hard bargain for themselves. They wanted to be decently fed and clothed, and they wanted now and then to see some sign that the man at the top knew what he was doing. Beyond that they asked for nothing. They lived that winter in a strange vacant place in the middle of time. Behind them there were terrible names like Antietam and Fredericksburg, proudly written now on the regimental banners which sparkled like marsh-fire flames up and down the long blue columns. Ahead of them, as yet unknown, were other names equally great and terrible, and no one thought about them. The men were veterans and they would live in the immediate present, looking neither before nor after, coming once again to believe in themselves, proudly wearing the new corps badges which Hooker had cannily devised for them, parading when the President and the commanding general passed them in review—a great army with banners, marching through the mud and the dirt toward the battle smoke which veiled the stars.

There were changes at the upper level. Amid rumblings, General Franklin had departed, muttering sotto voce that he would not serve under Hooker. Gone too, was Baldy Smith, to whom Burnside had confided the first hint of a great and amazing thing which was to happen. With Smith went Burnside's own troops, the faithful IX Corps, sent away to serve once more down the coast, or inland, or anywhere save with this luckless Army of the Potomac. Gone, too, finally, was the stout old Bull of the Woods, Major General Edwin V. Sumner, with his simple code and his unimaginative bravery and his rigid old-army loyalties. He had taken no part in all the backbiting which followed Fredericksburg, telling the congressional committee simply, "There is too much croaking in the army." In midwinter he was relieved, gone forever from the army which for better or for worse he had helped to stamp with his own imprint. He rested in the North awhile, then was ordered west to take command in Missouri and fell ill, an old man worn down by the war, his life coming to its close in a Syracuse sickroom. He lay in a stupor, and as he came out of it he seems to have thought of old battles—perhaps of Seven Pines and its reeking swamps, of the ambush by the Dunker church in the Maryland hills, or of the doomed advance toward the stone wall below Marye's Heights. He cried out suddenly: "The II Corps never lost a flag or a cannon!" His attendant came over to him, and Sumner repeated more feebly: "That is true—never lost one." He was raised in his bed, and the attendant gave him a glass of wine. He took one sip, intoned, "God save my country, the United States of America," dropped the glass, and died, an old soldier gone to join the great God of Battles.[17]

Hooker found new men for the vacant places, and in the process he did a strange and seemingly an uncharacteristic thing. For the all-important job of his chief of staff he asked the War Department to assign to him Brigadier General Charles P. Stone.[18]

Stone was a man out of the past, deeply buried in disgrace. A brigadier without a command, a soldier without a visible future, he was a ruined living symbol of the fact that the hatred which General Burnside had failed to find among the fighting men had sprouted and flourished mightily among the stout civilians who controlled the destinies of the fighting men. This hatred, mixed with fear and grown old and gray and venomous, Abraham Lincoln greatly lacked, but it seemed that nearly everyone else in Washington had a share in it, most notably the very men to whom General Hooker had made his gestures and his overtures as he scrambled toward the top of the heap. General Stone had been its first sacrificial victim.

In the fall of 1861 General Stone had commanded troops along the upper Potomac. In a misguided moment he had thrust a brigade across the river to reconnoiter near Leesburg, and the brigade had blundered into trouble at Ball's Bluff and had been butchered. Butchered among many less notable had been its commander, Colonel Edward D. Baker, the Illinois-born Californian who had helped save Oregon for anti-slavery Republicanism and who was intimate with the leading men of the party which stood for all-out war. The war party wanted to punish someone for this disaster, and to do that job it had organized the Joint Committee on the Conduct of the War.

Looking into things, the committee had decided that General Stone was at fault and must be punished. It made no formal accusations and it took no direct action against him; it simply received and published accusations against his loyalty, turning him presently into an untouchable, a man who could not be defended, so that he was removed from his command and was even imprisoned for a time, although he had never been charged with any crime. The radical Republicans who had done this had nothing in particular against General Stone. They were simply using him to perfect the new technique which they had accidentally stumbled on. As an object lesson Stone had been extremely effective.

And it was this man whom Joe Hooker was now asking the War Department to send to him to become chief of staff of the Army of the Potomac.

Nothing came of it, to be sure. Stone had to remain on the shelf until Grant came along with a prestige that could overawe even the radical Republicans, and in the end Hooker took for his chief of staff Brigadier General Dan Butterfield, a stocky little ex-militia officer from New York. And yet Hooker's act in asking for General Stone is one of the most interesting things he ever did.

It was completely out of character, or perhaps it proved that Hooker's character was not the open-and-shut case which on the surface it appears to have been. Hooker had schemed and calculated until it had seemed that there was no conceivable thing that he would not do to make political capital with the radicals. Yet now, untested in his perilous new job, he laid schemes and calculations aside and for one brief moment stood up as a straightforward soldier who would defy politics and politicians. He never bothered to explain what made him do it, and it seems that a passion for self-analysis may have been one of the few passions he lacked. He simply did it, leaving the fact that he had done it as a testimonial to something real in his strange, complex soul. It is a point to remember, because to speak up for General Stone took moral courage, a quality which Joe Hooker is rarely accused of possessing.

One like that was enough, and Hooker was not the man to go on sailing too close to the wind. Denied General Stone, he made do with General Butterfield, a strange but politically safe little man who had an unsuspected streak of poetry under his breezy bluster and who in an unexpected way left a permanent mark on the United States Army.

Butterfield was a New York businessman when the war began, and he raised New York troops and commanded a brigade on the peninsula under McClellan. He early noticed that when his brigade bugler sounded a call (which would be picked up and repeated at once by all regimental buglers in the brigade) there was apt to be confusion, since other brigades were usually within earshot. So he invented a little recognition call—three whole notes, followed by a couple of triplets—which would precede all brigade calls, and the boys quickly fitted a chant to it: "Dan—Dan-Butterfield!" It appears that one day in the camp at Harrison's Landing, shortly after Malvern Hill, Butterfield called his bugler into his tent, whistled a little tune for him, and asked him to sound it on his bugle. Somewhat struck, for generals did not ordinarily behave so, the bugler obeyed. The result did not quite suit Butterfield, and he did a little more experimental whistling, until finally he had it the way he wanted it. The bugler wrote the call down on the back of an old envelope, and Butterfield instructed him to use the tune thereafter in place of the call prescribed by regulations for "lights out." The regulation call, said Butterfield, was not musical; he wanted one which would somehow express the idea of a darkening campground with tired men snugging down to a peaceful sleep, and he hoped his new call would do it.

So the bugler used the new call after that, and other buglers heard it and liked it and came over to copy the tune, until before long it was used all through the Army of the Potomac. Later on, when some of the troops were transferred west, the bugle call was taken up in the Western armies, and at last it became regulation and has remained regulation to his day, the drawn-out haunting call that puts the lights out for soldiers and that hangs in the still air over their graves at military funerals—"Taps."[19]

In addition to having an ear for music, Butterfield appears to have had a personality that fitted Hooker's. Hooker could relax when the day's work was over, and Butterfield could help him. There were army officers who felt that the atmosphere at headquarters in those days was not wholesome. Greatly admired by his troops, Hooker was at no time a favorite among his generals. His military capacity they often admitted, but they were inclined to be dubious about the man underneath the soldier, and they did not like the tales about revelry at headquarters. Looking down a lengthy Adams nose through cold Bostonian eyes, Charles Francis Adams wrote (it may be with some exaggeration) that Hooker's tent was a place to which no gentleman cared to go and to which no lady could go.[20]

George Gordon Meade, irascible but fair-minded, wrote that he himself liked Hooker better than most and thought him a good soldier, but he added: "I do not like his entourage." In this entourage Meade specifically mentioned Butterfield and the new commander of the III Corps, Major General Dan Sickles. He wrote that they were cleverer than Hooker and that because they had political pull Hooker was likely to put himself under their influence. Meade would say nothing in particular against Butterfield and Sickles, but he primly told his wife that "they are not the persons I should select as my intimates."[21] Lumping Hooker, Butterfield, and Sickles together, Adams declared that "all three were men of blemished character."

Of the three, Sickles was the most obvious target. He wore notoriety like a cloak, so that if it never quite seemed becoming it at least looked natural on him. In any army so many of whose general officers have come to seem stuffed and posed, undistinguishable from one another in the shadowy portrait gallery of the half forgotten, Sickles remains a recognizable individual. Whether he was drinking, fighting, wenching or plotting, he was always operating with the throttle wide open. He might have had more faults than virtues, but everything about him was perfectly genuine.

Sickles came out of Tammany Hall. He was in his middle thirties when the war started, and even at that age he had already first conceived and then been obliged to discard a planned career of extraordinarily lofty proportions, for in the beginning he had told himself that he would become nothing less than President of the United States. He had lived too hard for that, had lived, loved, killed, and been cast into outer darkness by his fellow men, and the war offered him a chance to come back up the ladder a bit. He saw himself now as a military hero, and as a corps commander he could be on the way toward making his vision real. It would depend partly on the throw of the dice and partly on the valor of the men whom he was leading. Luck was with him on this second point, for his corps was made up chiefly of the divisions formerly led by Phil Kearny and Joe Hooker, and they were as good as the best.

Sickles had served in the New York State Assembly, had been corporation counsel in Manhattan, and when James Buchanan went to London as United States Minister, in the high and far-off times when the conflict between North and South looked like something that would wither and die of its own accord, Sickles went along as first secretary of legation. In London he had been somewhat gay, and he appears to have been one of the juniors who cooked up the once-famous Ostend Manifesto, which sought to commit the United States to the threat to seize Cuba by force if Spain, "actuated by stubborn pride and a false sense of honor," should refuse to get rid of the island by forced sale. Returning to America, Sickles had been a state senator and then member of Congress, a valiant states'-rights Democrat, a prosperous lawyer on the side, a militia officer and a student of the military arts, a fixer who knew all of the tricks of Tammany at its crookedest but who seems not to have taken graft himself. He had his sights fixed on the presidency, and he was making about as much progress in that direction as a Tammany man can.

And then he killed Philip Barton Key.

Son of the man who wrote "The Star-Spangled Banner," Key was a dabbler in politics, captain of a crack militia company, a drifter and a man about town, known for a time as "the handsomest man in all Washington society." He handled certain legal business for Sickles, and Sickles in turn helped to persuade President Buchanan to reappoint Key as United States attorney when his term expired. Key became friendly with Mrs. Sickles, had assignations with her in a shabby flat on Vermont Avenue in Washington, and one day was shot dead by Sickles on the sidewalk bordering Lafayette Square, across from the White House. Having killed him, Sickles walked down the street and surrendered his revolver and his person to Attorney General Black.

His trial was a circus. It belonged in the 1920s, in the era of sob sisters and flashlight bulbs. Edwin M. Stanton was one of defense counsel, and he and the other lawyers pulled out all of the stops. They raised—it appears to have been for the first time—the plea that Sickles was not guilty because of temporary insanity brought on by the shock of discovering that his wife had been untrue to him with his best friend. Like the plea, the verdict set an immutable precedent. Sickles was triumphantly acquitted.

So far, so good. The unwritten law ran strongly in predominantly Southern-chivalry Washington of the 1850s, and it was hard to think the worse of a man who killed by it. But Sickles then put himself beyond the pale by the simple act of forgiving his wife and restoring her to his bosom. It may be that after his own fashion he loved her.[22]

This was a shocker. Washington was scandalized to the eyebrows and re-

marked that Sickles's career was ruined. Mary Boykin Chesnut, the South
Carolina diarist, sat in the House gallery one day and saw Sickles deliberately
and totally ostracized. He was sitting all alone, like Catiline, every other member careful not to come near him—"left to himself as if he had the smallpox."
His offense, Mrs. Chesnut conceded (demonstrating that the aristocracy of
Charleston could be quite as censorious as that of Boston), was not that he had
killed his friend but that he had condoned his wife's profligacy. Sickles wrote a
defiant open letter to the press, remarking: "I am not aware of any statute or
code of morals which makes it infamous to forgive a woman," but it did no
good. Mrs. Sickles lived for eight years, an infinitely lonely little woman in a
huge house that no one would enter. When she died after the war four major
generals were among her pallbearers.[23]

When the war started Sickles resigned from Congress and went back to New
York to raise troops. He got a commission from the governor to raise eight
companies of volunteers and succeeded in getting this expanded into authorization to raise an entire brigade of five regiments. He raised it, saw it dubbed the
Excelsior Brigade—New York regiments numbered 70 to 74, inclusive—and financed its camp for some time out of his own purse, while state and Federal authorities argued over the validity of his commission. At one time he rented a
circus tent from P. T. Barnum to house several hundred of his recruits. At another, with a dozen companies or more quartered in a bare hall on lower
Broadway, he contracted with a cheap bathhouse to give fourteen hundred men
a shave and a shower bath at ten cents apiece. He got his brigade regularized at
last, served with it under Hooker on the peninsula, and was promoted to divisional command just before Fredericksburg.

Now he was one of the intimates of the commanding general, and there were
those who felt that no good would come of it. Yet if Hooker's tent that winter
was not a place in which an Adams could feel at ease, a great deal of very hard
work was done there and the army benefited by it.

Among other problems, Hooker tackled the cavalry. He began by consolidating all of the cavalry with the army into one corps, in place of leaving it split up
by regiments among the different infantry divisions, and for its commander he
selected a solid regular-army officer, Major General George Stoneman—not the
ideal choice, perhaps, for what Hooker really wanted was a Sheridan, and
Stoneman was neither fiery nor lucky. However, unification meant that the cavalry would at least have a chance to do cavalry's real job, and Stoneman was
conscientious and did his best.

Cavalry's job that winter was practically impossible anyway. It was supposed
to form a screen around the entire army, which meant that it had to patrol an
outpost line one hundred miles long. This line for the most part ran through a
broken country of dense second-growth timber which was crisscrossed by innumerable winding lanes and pathways, most of them so obscure that nobody but
a regular inhabitant of the region could even find them, let alone tell where they
led. The inhabitants of this country had the strongest of secessionist sympathies
and formed an unofficial but highly effective Confederate intelligence network
from which it was impossible to keep secrets. One Federal officer reported ruefully that even the women and children "vied with each other in schemes and
ruses by which to discover and convey to the enemy facts which we strove to
conceal."[24]

This meant bad times for Yankee cavalry. Little bodies of Rebel horsemen
could always slip across the Rappahannock and concentrate on some remote
forest-hidden farm. Knowing exactly where the Yankee vedettes and picket stations were, and guided through the timber by men or boys who could find their
way blindfolded, they could descend on the isolated groups of Federals, smash
things up, take prisoners, and get clean away before cavalry headquarters had a
chance to know what was happening. Stoneman found that his cavalry was

wearing itself out simply by doing outpost duty, which, under the circumstances, could not be done effectively anyway. He had twelve thousand men, of whom on any given day one third would be on duty, with another third either going or coming.[25] Nobody was happy, the army's secrets were open to inquiring Rebel eyes, and all of the horses were foundering. In addition, the outposts were getting so jittery that nobody could depend on the reports they sent back. Army headquarters had to warn cavalry that "those whose fears magnify trifling squads into large bodies of the enemy as richly deserve death as the base wretch who deserts his country's flag or his comrades in battle."[26]

That was all very well, but in the long run the only way to keep Jeb Stuart out of the Yankee lines was to go across the river in a body and attack him on his own home ground. This idea occurred to various people; among others, to youthful Brigadier General William W. Averell, who commanded one of Stoneman's cavalry divisions and who at West Point had been a classmate of Fitz Lee, now one of Stuart's brigadiers. This Fitz Lee had elevated the technique of annoying Yankee cavalry to a fine art, and he used to send taunting messages to his old pal Averell asking when the Yankee cavalry was going to begin to amount to something, and so on. His most recent message had been an invitation to Averell to come across the river and pay a little visit, bringing some coffee with him if possible. So Averell, who had won a reputation as a bold fighter against the Western Indians just before the war, at last came to Hooker and asked if he might not take his division across the river and look for a fight.

This was right in line with Hooker's ideas and he agreed, saying that there had not been many dead cavalrymen lying around lately but that if Averell went over and fought Fitz Lee there would be.[27] Averell hurried back to his division and made his men sharpen their sabers, promising them a chance to use them in action. In mid-March he led some three thousand troopers down to the Rappahannock at Kelly's Ford, pushed aside the Confederate river guards after a sharp little skirmish, and went barreling across country looking for Fitz Lee and trouble.

He found both quickly enough, but Lee came on the scene with only about half as many men as Averell had, and the Northern troopers were at last beginning to believe that they could face up to Stuart's men in an open fight. The Confederate columns were driven back half a mile or more, charging columns colliding head-on at full gallop in the dust and smoke, horse artillery banging away, everybody yelling and sabers clanging and the fields and roads and woods full of wild uproar. Lee's men counterattacked and were driven off, and opportunity quietly opened a door for young General Averell. He had the bulge on his old classmate now. He could move on and completely rout Lee's birgade and destroy its camp, and it was at a time like this that a good general had to have the instinct of a killer.

That instinct Averell did not have. He straightened his lines for a new attack, but then he began to get cautious. Prisoners told him that Stuart himself had come on the scene. This was true enough, although the prisoners forgot to add that Stuart had come all by himself, with no reinforcements. But the mere weight of Stuart's name was equal to a brigade or two in those days, and besides, Averell heard that Rebel infantry was near. So after a time he had his buglers blow the recall and the Yankee cavalry trotted back to its own side of the river.

The boys were proud of themselves—among other achievements, they had killed the fabulous Major John Pelham, commander of Stuart's artillery—and Averell was happy too. Before recrossing he had left a sack of coffee and a note for Fitz Lee: "Dear Fitz, here's your coffee. Here's your visit. How do you like it?"

But Hooker was angry. Cavalry morale might have been given a lift, but Hooker wanted more than that. In his own way he was a perfectionist—for a while, at least—and he wrote sharply that Averell had had a sweeping victory in his grasp and had lost it because of "imaginary apprehensions."[28] Many a victory this army had missed because commanding generals became nervous and saw things moving in the shadows. Under Joe Hooker this was not to happen. At XII Corps headquarters, about this time, Hooker voiced his confidence.

"If the enemy does not run, God help them!" he cried.[29]

4. MAY DAY IN THE WILDERNESS

The Confederacy's fortified lines ran for twenty-five unbroken miles, from Port Royal all the way to Banks Ford. Trenches zigzagged along the lower slopes of the hills, with gun emplacements above them sited so that the gunners could cover all possible approaches. Where the line came out in the open and ran across level plains it was anchored at proper intervals with built-up redoubts. Lee's army could take position anywhere along the immense shallow crescent which faced Fredericksburg and the nearby river crossings, and no imaginable frontal assault could dislodge it. Professional soldiers of that era were brought up on Napoleonic lore, and it was only natural for a young Confederate officer who was trying to explain how invulnerable these lines were to exclaim: "The famous lines at Torres Vedras could not compare with them."[1]

In December, when these field fortifications were not half so strong, Burnside had broken his army's back on them. Now Hooker had the army, and he was chock-full of bubbling confidence. Over and over he repeated that this was the finest army on the planet. He told one caller that he would take the army across the river before long and seize the Rebels where the hair was short, and in a moment of extreme expansiveness he said that he hoped God Almighty would have mercy on the Confederates because he, Joe Hooker, would have none. This led Senator Sumner, at the capital, to mark him down disgustedly as a blasphemous wretch,[2] but it also indicated that Hooker felt that he knew how to get at the Rebel army without going smack over the middle of those impregnable trenches.

Thanks to his own energy and good military sense, Hooker had one asset which his predecessors had lacked—a corps of excellent cavalry whose morale was beginning to be high. The boys had learned how to ride. It was no longer necessary for a cavalry colonel to look hawk-eyed at his ranks to make sure that his gawky troopers were not hanging onto the reins with both hands, letting their elbows flap like crows' wings, or seeking to control their horses by clucking or saying "Whoa," "Git-up," and "Go-along" instead of using bit and spur the way honest cavalrymen should. They had also learned how to fight, and they had lately been outfitted with new-model carbines, Sharps single-shot breech-loaders, which lacked the range and penetrating power of the infantry rifle but which could be fired much faster and hence enabled cavalrymen fighting on foot to give a good account of themselves.

The army now had nearly twelve thousand of these troopers, and Stoneman was supposed to be a first-rate soldier. He was just over forty, a West Pointer who, as a young second lieutenant of dragoons, had served as quartermaster of the famous "Mormon Battalion" during General Stephen Kearny's march across the plains to California in the Mexican War. He was at Fort Brown in Texas when the Civil War broke out, and when the departmental commander, old General Twiggs, went over to the Confederacy and advised his subordinates to do likewise Stoneman defied him and succeeded in getting north with part of his command. At Fredericksburg he had commanded an infantry corps, and he was Hooker's own choice for cavalry commander.[3] The plan of attack which Hooker was shaping now would depend in large part on Stoneman's initiative and determination.

Hooker's basic idea was to pry Lee's army out of its fortified lines and make it fight in the open. By the first of April he had concluded that Stoneman's cavalry would be the instrument with which he would do the prying. Stoneman would take the cavalry far up the Rappahannock, cross over, and go swinging south until he hit the line of the Virginia Central Railroad, when he was to turn east and head for Hanover Junction, which was believed to be Lee's principal supply depot. If he could get there with ten thousand cavalry, Lee would have to retreat, Hooker would cross the river and pursue, and with Stoneman in front of him Lee would not be able to retreat with speed. There would be a big fight, and since Hooker's army had a solid two-to-one advantage just now—Lee's force was somewhat scattered, Longstreet having taken a good part of his corps down below Richmond to foil Yankee raiders in the Suffolk area—the Rebels would be shoved back into the Richmond lines. There would eventually be a siege which could have but one outcome.

So went the plan, and on paper it worked out very well. By April 1 Hooker was stripping his army for action, ordering all surplus baggage and equipment sent to the rear and warning the War Department to have siege equipment ready for delivery. Among other things, he wanted ten thousand shovels, five thousand picks, five thousand axes, and thirty thousand sandbags shipped to him in front of Richmond for the making of saps and parallels. He also asked Army Secret Service to prepare authentic maps of Richmond defenses, and the commissary department was told to have one and one half million rations on boats, ready to be floated up the Pamunkey River to meet the army when it got that far.[4]

Hooker was a canny man, and Lee was not going to learn about this plan through any security leaks if Hooker could help it. Lincoln got a hint of it by letter around the first of the month, and a bit later when he came down to Falmouth to review the troops, Hooker told him some more. Things looked good, and Hooker took the large view, and in his chats with the President he kept beginning sentences with "After we have taken Richmond—" Lincoln listened soberly and found this excessive confidence depressing and warned Hooker and Couch, who was second-in-command: "In your next fight, gentlemen, put in all of your men." He may have been thinking of the fifty thousand soldiers whom Franklin had had on the field but had not used in the Fredericksburg fight. Whatever he was thinking about, Couch reflected, he was giving perfectly sound advice.[5]

A bit later Hooker sent Dan Butterfield up to Washington to give the President all of the details. Washington was full of leaks, then as now, and Butterfield was sternly ordered to tell the President everything but to say nothing at all to anyone else. This made it a bit embarrassing, for he was shown in to Lincoln's office just at the end of a cabinet meeting and found the President surrounded by expectant cabinet ministers, including the fearsome Secretary Stanton, who enjoyed being kept out of no secrets. Butterfield kept mum, stalled while the ministers got out, and stood mute while a New England senator, ears wide open, hung around making small talk with Mr. Lincoln. In the end the general saw the President alone, told him all, and returned to army headquarters with his mission accomplished.[6]

It was time to get going at last, and on April 13 the long columns of Federal horsemen went trotting along the dirt roads to the upstream crossings. Stoneman had picked a good man to go over first: Grimes Davis, the Mississippi-born brigadier who had snaked his regiments out of Harper's Ferry the previous September when Stonewall Jackson surrounded and captured the place in the Antietam campaign. Davis took his brigade over the stream several miles above the railroad bridge and came down fast on the southern side, while Stuart's pickets galloped desperately on ahead with the warning: Yankees over the river! Stoneman's main body was to cross at Rappahannock Bridge and at Beverly Ford, which was close to it. It got down to the banks and found the opposite shore strongly held, and Stoneman paused to consider whether he ought to be rash.

He had with him enough men to force a crossing—Sheridan or Bedford Forrest would have got over while Stoneman was counting noses—and in any case Davis was coming down from above to take the Rebels in flank, so that the resistance could not have been prolonged. But they were thirty miles or more from the rest of the army, and Stuart occasionally had unpleasant surprises for rash Yankee cavalrymen. Stoneman decided to wait so that he could have everything ready, and then it began to rain. It rained harder and harder, so that it was difficult for Stoneman to move his artillery, and while the cavalry waited the river began to rise prodigiously. Before long the water at the ford was deep and foaming and the rebuilt railroad bridge was wobbly, and Stoneman began to feel that the whole project was pretty risky. Messages were got to the other side, round about, and Davis angrily brought his brigade back and returned to the northern shore.[7]

Back in Falmouth, Hooker waited for news. On April 15 he wired Mr. Lincoln that the rain was a bad break, but added: "I am rejoiced that Stoneman had two good days to go up the river, and was enabled to cross it before it had become too much swollen. If he can reach his position the storm and mud will not damage our prospects." A few hours later Hooker messaged Lincoln that Stoneman's guns were stuck in the mud but that he had been ordered to go ahead without them. Lincoln, who was beginning to have his doubts, replied that as far as he could see "Stoneman is not moving rapidly enough to make the expedition come to anything." The President tallied up times and miles on his fingers. "He has now been out three days, two of which were unusually fair weather, and all three without hindrance from the enemy, and yet he is not twenty-five miles from where he started. To reach his point he still has sixty to go, another river (the Rapidan) to cross, and will be hindered by the enemy. By arithmetic, how many days will it take him to do it?" All of which, Lincoln concluded, was beginning to smell like another failure.

Lincoln was quite right. Hooker got the bad news from Stoneman next day—every creek and brook swimming-deep, roads impassable for guns and wagons and nearly so for horses, Rappahannock out of its banks and still rising. All the cavalry was north of the river, said Stoneman, and he thought this was a very good thing, for if it had crossed it would have an impassable river in its rear and the doubtless equally impassable Rapidan in front of it, with malevolent Rebels all about. All in all, the omens were bad. They were being cursed, he added, with "one of the most violent rainstorms I have ever been caught in."[8]

For the time being, that was that. Hooker fumed and entered a debit against Stoneman's name in his little black book, and the army huddled in its camps and waited for the rain to end, having missed a chance once again because a general lacked a driving spirit. And yet it may be that the army had not really lost much. Hooker's plan looked good on paper, but there may have been something too hopeful about the idea that Lee's whole army would meekly retreat just because some cavalry was threshing about in its rear. When Hooker set to work to make a new plan he adopted a different line.

This time he would not rely so much on cavalry. He would move by his right with infantry, flanking Lee out of his lines. Cavalry, as before, would cross far upstream and maneuver around to get on Lee's supply route, but the rest of the army would not wait for it. It would go upstream also, and if it moved fast and with proper secrecy it should be able to get across before Lee knew that it was doing anything, and when the infantry was south of the river it would move east. Instead of putting ten thousand cavalry in Lee's rear, Hooker would put seventy thousand infantry there, accompanied by artillery, and the cavalry would frolic about farther south and destroy railroads and supply depots.

Hooker had raised his sights. Originally he had been looking for a good way to make Lee pull back to the defenses of Richmond. Now he was thinking about annihilating the Rebel army outright. "I not only expected victory," he said later, "but I expected to get the whole army." Butterfield recalled that the real purpose of the campaign was "to destroy the army of General Lee where it then was."[9]

In general terms, Hooker's idea was that he would move so many men in behind Lee's left that Lee would have to retreat in a great hurry. The retreat would in effect be a flank march across Hooker's front, Hooker would attack, and that would be the end of the Army of Northern Virginia. Duly inspired, staff went to work to translate this plan into orders.

Staff had problems, because in making these plans one point was clear. If the infantry was going to outflank the enemy and take a position close in rear of the Rebel left it would have to go on a very long hike.

It could not move downstream for a flanking maneuver because the river below Fredericksburg was too wide and deep to ford and would have to be bridged. Also, moving in that direction would leave Washington uncovered, a point on which Mr. Lincoln was notoriously sensitive. Upstream there were two handy crossings—Banks Ford, not far from Falmouth, and United States Ford, half a dozen miles farther on. The Rebels held these in some strength and had dug trenches and gun pits, and anyway, these fords were so close to Fredericksburg that Lee could get his entire army to them on short notice. If it crossed the river at all, the Union Army would have to go some distance upstream.

There the problem began to get complicated. Just above United States Ford there was a fork in the river, with the Rappahannock coming down from the northwest and the Rapidan slanting in from the west to meet it in a looping, irregular angle. Operating in this angle was tricky business. John Pope had nearly come to total disaster there a fortnight before he fell into trouble at Bull Run, and from one end of the war to the other this area represented a puzzle which the Federals could never quite solve. To cross above United States Ford meant crossing two rivers instead of one. In addition, on the southern bank of the Rapidan lay the scrambled, brambly maze of the Wilderness, a long stretch of second-growth forest with narrow winding roads and infrequent clearings, where a soldier might walk into ambush at any moment and where the magnificent Federal artillery would have little room to operate.

Cutting across this Wilderness was one decent road, the Orange turnpike, which ran west from Fredericksburg to hit the Orange and Alexandria Railroad at Orange Courthouse. If Hooker proposed to cross the Rappahannock upstream, what he was up against was the job of getting over both rivers, striking the Orange turnpike, and moving east on it until he had emerged from the Wilderness—and all before the Confederates found out what he was up to and came out to waylay him.

His immediate strategic goal would be a tiny crossroads with the overgrown name of Chancellorsville, a dozen miles behind Lee's extreme left. If he could put his army there undetected, he might be able to make some of his boasts good. A simple march of four or five miles from Chancellorsville would get Hooker clear out of the Wilderness onto open ground southwest of Fredericksburg, and there, if he could just get there intact, he would have a fine chance to destroy the enemy.

This was a glittering vision for a general who had announced—perhaps just a shade ahead of time—that he would soon have the Rebels by the short hairs, and Hooker undertook at once to turn it into a reality. He was known as a slam-bang head-down fighter, but now he became the cool executive, concerned with matters of organization and logistics. Wagons would delay the march, so except for irreplaceable ammunition wagons and a few ambulances he would take no wagons. The soldiers could carry extra loads on their backs, and what they could not carry would be borne by some thousands of pack mules especially bought for the occasion. The foot soldier would have more than sixty pounds to carry, exclusive of his rifle, but he would just have to make the best of it.[10] It would not be for long, and victory would make up for everything. Pontoons would be sent up to the fords just in case the river began to rise again, and details would be appointed to strengthen that railroad bridge which had given Stoneman the jitters.

Stoneman still led the cavalry, and his function would be to cross where he had been supposed to cross before, to strike south, smashing up all Rebel cavalry outfits which crossed his path, and in general terms to create as much trouble as possible. His orders specified that he was to get in close to the enemy: "If you cannot cut off from his column large slices, the general desires that you will not fail to take small ones. Let your watchword be fight, fight, fight."

The rains stopped at last and the roads dried, the sun came out, and the Virginia spring was at its warmest and balmiest, and the Army of the Potomac pulled itself out of its camps and took to the highways.

The men were feeling good. As they started northwest on back roads, well out of sight of prying Rebels, the soldiers felt that this time they were headed for a victory, and their spirits went sky-high. As they left camp the bands played "The Girl I Left Behind Me," for leaving Falmouth seemed almost like leaving home, and along the roads the anemones and violets were growing, with dogwood in blossom in the groves and the peach trees glowing pink around deserted farmhouses. All along the river, cavalry patrols were rounding up local residents and making them stay inside their houses. There were going to be no secessionist civilians slipping across the river with news of this march if Joe Hooker could help it.[11]

The weather was hot and there was a long way to march, and the loads the men carried were heavy. The inevitable happened, and the roads soon began to be littered with discarded coats, shirts, blankets, and other things. The army found that it was being followed by people whom the soldiers dubbed "ready-finders"—civilians eager to collect the riches which the soldiers were dropping. A slightly scornful man in the 12th New Hampshire described them:

"An old horse or mule, sometimes, but oftener an old ox, a steer or a cow, strangely tackled by means of an old harness or yoke, spliced together and tied up by ropes, strings, and pieces of twisted bark to a primitive kind of a two-wheeled, nondescript kind of cart that no Yankee would care to make or imitate if he could, with an old man or woman or a young boy, and sometimes a girl, for a driver, and a cord or string of some kind tied to the bits or horns—as the animal motive power might belong to the equine or bovine order—for reins, and the pen picture is by no means complete, but only a scratch-sketch of some of the picking-up teams of the stay-at-home natives that used to follow our armies."[12]

By the evening of April 28 the first part of the job had been done, and there was a general feeling, as one man put it, that the Army of the Potomac at last "had got a leader who knew what to do and was going to do it."[13] In the woods and fields just back from Kelly's Ford—a few miles below Rappahannock Bridge, thirty-odd miles from Falmouth—were three army corps, V, XI, and XII, forty thousand men in all, with the skipper of the XII Corps, Major General Henry Slocum, in general command of the lot. These troops were there secretly, with Stoneman's cavalry screening all the crossings. Back at Banks and United States fords, close to Falmouth, was the II Corps, showing itself on the riverbank in order to make Lee think that the major effort was going to be there. In and below Fredericksburg, likewise keeping in plain sight and being busy with pontoons and the like preparatory to making a crossing, were the I Corps and the VI Corps under John Sedgwick, recovered now from the three wounds he had received at Antietam. Behind these two corps was Dan Sickles with the III Corps, awaiting orders. So far the troops were exactly where the plan said they ought to be, and the Rebels had caught onto nothing except that the Yan-

kees seemed at last to be on the move. Stuart's patrols were suggesting that
Stoneman and his cavalry might be preparing to move up into the Shenandoah
Valley.

Slocum got his three corps over the Rappahannock without much trouble.
Stuart's patrols were alert, and as the Yankee infantry formed up on the southern side the Confederate squadrons stabbed at them with galloping detachments, seeking to take prisoners for purposes of identification. A few men on
each side were killed in these little forays—killed just as dead as if they had
fallen dramatically in some great battle, although none but the next of kin ever
knew anything about it—and Stuart found out what he was looking for and sent
word back to Lee: three army corps coming over the river, looks like something
big. Stoneman's cavalry went trotting down the line of the railway, and Slocum
led the infantry off southeasterly toward the two fords over the Rapidan, Ely's
and Germanna.

The boys crossed the Rapidan the next night, April 29. April had brought too
much rain, and the river was deep and swirling, black under the moonlight with
flecks of bubbling white foam. As the endless columns came down to the crossings huge fires were lit on each bank to help the men see where they were going,
and the flames put a ruddy tinge on the dark water. Foot soldiers went slogging
across, waist-deep and more, and a few were swept away and drowned in the
strong current, and cavalry patrols took station in the crossings to pick up the
casualties. On the northern bank soldiers unloaded the pack mules so that the
animals could swim across, infantrymen carrying the mules' packs and not liking it much. In some outfits the officers forbade the men to take their pants off at
the ford—Rebels might attack as soon as they got across, and a line of battle
couldn't be formed without pants—but in others the commanders were more
sensible, so the men did not have to spend the rest of the night in wet clothing.
Men who were there remembered that the river was extremely cold, and not
everybody had a chance to get around the big bonfires and dry out. The men
and animals came out of the river dripping, of course, so the climb to higher
ground on the south side was soon very slippery and muddy for men carrying
heavy loads.

All in all, however, it seems that there were more gay shouts and whoops of
laughter than curses that night. Some pictorial quality in the scene, with the
firelight dancing on the water and the white clouds drifting across the face of the
moon and the limitless lines of men coming down over the northern hills,
splashing through the water and shaking themselves out on the southern side,
seems to have caught the soldiers' fancy. They remembered it long afterward,
this crossing of the Rapidan in the April moonlight, and all of these precocious
amateur strategists realized that Hooker was getting them safely around the
dreaded entrenchments back of Fredericksburg, and everybody was ready to
believe in his general, his army's chances, and his own lusty, irrepressible youth.
The thickets and dim clearings and shallow ravines back of the Chancellorsville
crossroads were still innocent that night. Men remembered that the whippoorwills sang.[14]

Next day was April 30. Slocum pushed his men forward. He was a good man,
this Slocum, and from one end of the war to the other the Federals developed
few better corps commanders. By noon George Meade had his V Corps at the
Chancellorsville clearing, where a ponderous white manor house with tall pillars
looked down on the country crossroads. The advance guard chased away a
small Rebel outpost, and a bit later the head of Slocum's corps came up, Slocum
himself riding in front. Meade rode to meet him, fairly bubbling over with enthusiasm—a rare state for Meade, a saturnine man who was sometimes lifted
out of himself by hot fury at human error but rarely by any lighter emotion.

"Hurrah for old Joe!" cried Meade. "We're on Lee's flank and he doesn't
know it."[15]

This was only a slight exaggeration. John Sedgwick had pushed his VI Corps across the river just below Fredericksburg, laying his pontoon bridges where Franklin had crossed in December, and he had his soldiers drawn up on the open plain south of the town, looking warlike and menacing, the idea being to make Lee think that a full-dress attack was about to develop. This was nothing but a bluff, and Lee was beginning to see through it. Stuart had warned him that a good many Yankees were crossing the Rapidan, and by nightfall Lee would conclude that Sedgwick was merely trying to annoy him and that the real attack was coming from his left rear.

Nevertheless, there was reason for Meade to feel exultant. This advance to Chancellorsville had already forced the Confederates to withdraw the troops which had been defending United States Ford, and two divisions of the Yankee II Corps were crossing there unopposed. By dusk Hooker would have fully fifty thousand men at Chancellorsville, together with the artillery reserve and a handful of cavalry. The open rear of Lee's field fortress on Marye's Heights lay barely a dozen miles to the east, with only one Rebel division—eighty-five hundred men or thereabouts—standing in the way. Almost equally close, and even less protected, were the main highway and the railway which led from Fredericksburg to Richmond, the life lines of Lee's army. Hooker had done precisely what he had planned to do, and he had done it with remarkable skill.

Meade's effervescence did not last long, however. What he wanted to do, he told Slocum, was to keep moving, take what troops were present and start down the road for Fredericksburg with them, "and we'll get out of this wilderness." But Slocum had a late message from army headquarters at Falmouth. Dan Sickles and his corps had been ordered to Chancellorsville, and Slocum was to make no move until they arrived, which would not be until next day. The army went into bivouac, with Meade slightly crestfallen.

Meade had touched on one cause for unease: they were still in the Wilderness. There was a little open plain about Chancellorsville itself and there were a few stunted farms scattered here and there, but in the main the army was surrounded by a forest which looked literally impenetrable—a mean sort of woodland, its second-growth timber clotted by vines and thorns and tangled underbrush, with boggy little streams leading from nowhere to nowhere, crossed by a few very narrow, inadequate roads. Advantages of numbers and guns could be canceled out if it should come to fighting here. If Hooker proposed to destroy the Rebel army, he had not quite reached the right place for it.

One other reason for doubt was cropping up that night, if anybody had bothered to notice it. Out on the byroads to the south and the west Yankee cavalry detachments were being driven in by hard-riding Confederates, Stuart himself riding at the head of one furious charge down a moonlit lane. These Yankee detachments were being driven in partly because they got confused in the patternless forest roads, but mostly because they were badly outnumbered. In view of the fact that Yankee cavalry was much stronger than Confederate cavalry that spring, this was odd.[16]

Stoneman had crossed the river and had gone riding south as ordered, heading for the remote, unguarded Rebel rear. Stuart had assigned one skimpy brigade to follow him—a detachment so weak it could hardly do more than keep him under observation—and with the bulk of his men had come pelting cross-country to join up with Lee. As a result he was now in shape to ride rings around Hooker's army. Having built up his cavalry so that it could dominate the field, Hooker had sent all of it away except for four regiments, and these were groping blindly against the cordon that Stuart was pulling in around the army.

However, all of that might not mean much. For once in history the Army of the Potomac tonight had the jump on its rival, and spirits were running high: Hooker's spirits, and the spirits of the men, who were laughing and shouting as they chopped firewood and pitched their pup tents in the little clearings and along the margins of the turnpike. Hooker reached the crossroads that evening and promptly issued General Order Number 47, which was read to all the troops at evening parade:

"It is with heart-felt satisfaction that the commanding general announces to the army that the operations of the past three days have determined that our enemy must either ingloriously fly, or come out from behind his defenses and give us battle on our own ground, where certain destruction awaits him."[17]

The soldiers were feeling good, and that was just what they wanted to hear. They believed in themselves again and Joe Hooker was responsible, and if now he said that the enemy was about to be whipped, everybody was ready to take him at his word. Parade lines broke up with men cheering and tossing their caps and knapsacks in the air, the brigade bands began to play, and the army sat around its campfires feeling jubilant, which it had not felt since the early days of the war.[18]

Next day was May Day. It came in with a slow misty rain, dank and chilly under the trees, a thin fog hanging in the narrow roads and the scattered fields. Dan Sickles rode in at the head of his troops, the day turned fair and the sun dried things up, and a little before noon the army wheeled into thick columns and started out for Fredericksburg.

Three roads led there: river road meandering to the left to follow the curves of the Rappahannock, turnpike in the center, old plank road curving around to the right and joining the turnpike halfway to Fredericksburg. Meade had his three divisions up in front and he sent two of them along the river road and had George Sykes and his regulars go along the turnpike. On the right, Slocum started down the plank road with the XII Corps. The other outfits present were ordered to stand by.

As the corps commanders understood it, they were to push ahead until they were out of the Wilderness on open ground. There they would join hands, with Meade's extreme left touching the river and uncovering Banks Ford—a matter of some importance, this last, since it would cut in half the distance from Chancellorsville to Sedgwick's men. With all of this done, the army would be ready for the big fight.

The divisions on the river road had an uneventful time, but Sykes's regulars ran into trouble. From Chancellorsville, going east along the turnpike, the ground rose in a long slope heavily covered with jack pines and scrub oaks and spiky bushes and cut up by little streams. It was very bad walking, as the skirmishers who went on ahead soon dicovered. A couple of miles from Chancellorsville this gentle slope reached a broad crest, where the Wilderness thinned out and the country began to look more prosperous. Along this crest Sykes's advance guard ran into Rebel skirmishers.

There was a little intermittent firing, and then as the enemy skirmishers faded back they disclosed solid lines of Confederate infantry, supported here and there by artillery. The guns began to plaster the road and the wood with shells, and as the regulars struggled through the underbrush to deploy, the opposition became heavier. Men were hit, and the firing rolled out in long, echoing volleys, and Sykes realized that because the roads diverged he was in touch neither with the rest of Meade's corps on his left nor with Slocum's men on his right. From Slocum's front, as a matter of fact, more firing could be heard, with a dirty-looking cloud of smoke going up toward the sky. The Rebels began to assail the flanks of Sykes's line, and he sent word back to Hooker that he needed help.

Back at Chancellorsville, Hooker had heard the firing and he sent Couch down the road with Hancock's division to help. When Couch came up he found Sykes pulling his men back into a better defensive position, the Rebel attack having become quite strong. Couch prepared to bring Hancock's men up, restore contact with Slocum and Meade, and resume the advance. Before he could do much about it, however, new orders came in from Hooker: call everything off and bring everybody back to Chancellorsville.[19]

Couch sent an aide back to protest that Sykes was in no real trouble and that they could soon butt their way through the Rebel line to the open ground where Hooker wanted to go, but it did no good. The aide returned with orders for retreat reiterated. Off to the right and left, Slocum and Meade were bringing back the rest of the troops, Meade storming and demanding, "If he thinks he can't hold the top of the hill, how does he expect to hold the bottom of it?"[20] Glumly Couch swung Hancock's men into line to act as rear guard, and the regulars marched back to Chancellorsville.

He was a cool customer, Couch. Slight, rather frail, a professional soldier who had won much reputation and lost nearly all of his health in the Mexican War, he was a man who had great personal courage. After Hancock's deployment the gunners in a distant Rebel battery saw massed troops on the turnpike and began to throw shells, trying to find the range. Couch turned to his staff and said, "Let us draw their fire," and led his officers up to an open knoll where the gunners could not fail to see them. The trick worked—gunners could seldom resist a chance to shoot at a cluster of mounted officers—and the infantry on the road escaped punishment. As it happened, nobody was hit, although it is written that the staff was not especially enthusiastic about any part of the deal.[21]

By evening the troops were back in the lines they had left that morning, the higher officers very dubious, enlisted men puzzled but not especially disturbed. Couch found Hooker full of reassurance: "It's all right, Couch, I've got Lee just where I want him." Couch said nothing, but made a mental note to the effect that the major general commanding was a beaten man.[22]

Couch may have been right. Hooker was talking too much, too loudly, too confidently—and, as Senator Sumner would have said, too blasphemously. To officers at headquarters he proudly announced: "The Rebel army is now the legitimate property of the Army of the Potomac." A little later he declared: "The enemy is in my power, and God Almighty cannot deprive me of them."[23] Then, descending to business, he dictated a circular order to corps commanders, instructing them to put their lines in a condition of defense, with wagon trains parked in the rear, and he closed with the statement:

"The major general commanding trusts that a suspension in the attack today will embolden the enemy to attack him."

Of all the hopes Joe Hooker ever had, that was the one destined to be the most completely realized.

FOUR

On the Other Side of the River

1. SOME OF US WILL NOT SEE ANOTHER SUNRISE

PERHAPS JOE HOOKER had lost his nerve. He could be debonair under fire, riding unconcerned into the middle of the fighting line, and the soldiers considered him very courageous. But here in the gloomy forest, with responsibility settling down over headquarters like the shades of blackest night, it was a little different. The showdown had come before he was quite ready. He had planned to be out in the open, and the Rebels had hit him ahead of time. There was a soft spot in the man, and the cruel test of war had found it. Now it was Robert E. Lee who was going to say what happened next.

Where do those soft spots come from? Somewhere between West Point and Chancellorsville—a few hundred miles in an air line, an incalculable distance as a man's life goes—there had developed in this man's character a little place that would collapse under pressure. No one had known it was there, Hooker least of all, but it was giving way right now as the moon came up over the forest and the campfires glowed under the trees, while the shooting died away on the picket lines and a misty light lay on the narrow roads.

Tragically enough, the army itself had its own soft spot, a place that might collapse if touched sternly, a soft spot that was part of the army's character just as Hooker's was part of his character. It was different in that its growth and development could be traced exactly. One can see where it began, and extensive casualty lists show what it led to, and the steps in between are quite visible. The army's soft spot was the XI Army Corps, Major General Oliver Otis Howard commanding.

The XI Corps was the Cinderella of the army, the unwanted orphaned child, and it was deeply aware of its own status. It seems to have felt, collectively, like a poor ignored wallflower at a high school dance. The corps contained many German soldiers, known to one and all as Dutchmen, a contemptuous title by which the soldiers expressed the national feeling—that men who talked with a foreign accent just did not need to be taken seriously. It is hardly going too far to say that what happened at Chancellorsville was the price the country paid for its indulgence in that feeling.

The nation had inherited something rich and strange when the German revolutionary movement of 1848 broke up in blood and proscription lists, with the best men of a dozen German states hastening to America. The nation had received these men, but it had never quite known what to make of them. These Germans were deadly serious about words which Americans took blithely for granted, words like liberty and freedom and democracy. They made up a substantial part of the ground which the free-soil men had cultivated in the 1850s, and when war came they had seen the Union cause as their own cause, with freedom for the black man as one of the sure ultimate goals. Their leaders were men who had lost their fortunes and risked their necks, taking up arms for liberty in a land of kings and who resisted change, and these leaders called the

Germans to the colors as soon as Fort Sumter was bombarded. Even more than the New England troops, these German regiments had welcomed and supported the Emancipation Proclamation. If the anti-slavery cause had an old guard, they perhaps were it.[1]

This old guard was the kernel of the XI Corps. About half of the men in the corps, as it happened, were native Americans; only fifteen of the twenty-six regiments were listed as German, and several of these contained a number of non-Germans.[2] But it was the German regiments which set the tone for the corps. They had brought to it officers with names like Von Steinwehr and Von Gilsa and Buschbeck and Schimmelfennig and Kryzanowski, they had come in with a number of incomparable bands and singing clubs, they had brought in both solid professional soldiers from Europe and a set of fortune hunters combed out of petty ducal courts, and in the end it appears that they had also brought their own tradition of incredible bad luck.

Louis Blenker originally had commanded most of these German regiments. He was out of the army now, dying of an accidental hurt received in a fall of his horse, but early in 1862 he had had a great name. He was a revolutionist in exile, a man who had led the men of Hesse-Darmstadt against Prussian troops and who had had to fly for his life when the revolution of 1848 was suppressed. A resident of New York when the Civil War came, he had raised the 8th New York, one of the first of the German regiments, and he and it had fought well at First Bull Run. Early in 1862 McClellan had given him a division composed of three brigades of Germans from the East and Midwest.[3] The Germans' woes had begun shortly afterward.

In the spring of 1862 this division was posted in Virginia, spraddled out from near Manassas to the edge of Alexandria. Just at that time the administration was giving John Charles Frémont an army command in western Virginia. Frémont was the unspotted hero of the abolitionists, and it seemed advisable to give him abolitionist troops whenever possible, so when he needed reinforcements McClellan was ordered to detach Blenker's Germans and send them to him.

It was a long hike up over the Bull Run Mountains and the Blue Ridge, across the Shenandoah Valley and on to Frémont's headquarters at Petersburg, deep in the Alleghenies, and American soldiers have rarely had a more miserable time than these troops of Blenker's had on what was supposed to be a perfectly routine cross-country move.

The first trouble was that through some lapse in paper work the division was sent out lacking the most elementary kind of equipment, from shelter tents (of which they had none at all) to overcoats, blankets, shoes, and rations. The next trouble was that the division got lost. The War Department forgot all about it. The division had moved out from under McClellan's control, but it had not yet come under Frémont's, and apparently no one gave Blenker a decent map. So the Germans went floundering cross-country through cold spring rains, losing sick men and stragglers wholesale, and leaving the country smoldering with angry complaints from the citizenry, who alleged that homes and barns and corncribs were being looted by ragged Germans who seemed not to have been fed for generations. On top of all other troubles, the division quartermasters had no money to use when they went out to buy provisions, so they simply requisitioned what they needed. They spoke poor English and they acted hastily, and anyway, the inhabitants were secessionists and objected to the whole process on principle. The Germans got the name of being the worst thieves and looters unhung. Crossing the Shenandoah, it seemed characteristic that some inexpert subaltern managed to swamp a ferryboat, and forty men were drowned.

Eventually the authorities realized that they had lost a division of troops, and Major General William S. Rosecrans was sent out to find the Germans and bring them in. He did so (after hunting around for several days), his eyes popping out of his knobby red face as he took a look at this lost command. Blenker's men, he reported to Stanton, "were short of provisions, forage, horseshoes and horseshoe nails, clothing, shoes, stockings, picket ropes and ammunition, without tents or shelters, and without ambulances or medicines for any important work." They were also practically out of horses, and the men had not been paid since December. All thing considered, said Rosecrans, it was "not much wonder they stole and robbed."[4]

All in all, it took the division six weeks to get up from Alexandria and join Frémont's troops. The union was not happy. Frémont's native American regiments were discontented. Yankee soldiers were sniffing the air and reporting, "The air around here was found to be rather Dutchy," and Ohio soldiers objected to the presence of so many foreigners on Frémont's staff. It seems that these foreign officers rode their horses with the English rising seat, whereas the Middle Western boys believed that a man ought to get on his horse and go jogging along without any fancy tricks of equitation. Sentries coming to salute when these bedizened aides rode by were presently discovered to be saying something as they saluted. Upon investigation it was found that they were repeating: "Don't rise for me, sir," a gag which pleased everyone but the aides.[5]

Frémont's mountain campaign was less than a success. It almost duplicated, as a matter of fact, the experience Blenker's division had already had, with rations running out and soldiers collapsing from hunger, fatigue, and sickness. By the end of May fewer than six thousand of Blenker's original ten thousand were present for duty, Frémont's medical director was demanding "in the name of humanity" that something be done to restore the soldiers' health, and Carl Schurz was warning Lincoln that the whole outfit was half starved "and literally unable to fight."[6]

Things improved after Frémont left. His place was taken by Franz Sigel, another revolutionist in exile—little more of a soldier, unfortunately, than Frémont himself, but a good deal more of a man. When he took over the command the Germans were proud, and "I fights mit Sigel" became a catch phrase all across the North. When Sigel's command was finally denominated the XI Corps of the Army of the Potomac, the fact that Sigel led it helped to fix it, in the army's eyes, as a German command.

The rest of the army did not welcome this XI Corps. The corps had never licked anybody under Frémont and it had done little better under Sigel; it got to Falmouth too late to fight at Fredericksburg, and its camp there happened to be isolated from the camps of the other corps. Anyway, the soldiers were Dutchmen, or at least a good many of them were, and their broken-English dialect struck the other soldiers as comic.

When the spring of 1863 came, Sigel left. After Hooker he was the ranking general in the army. His corps was the smallest of the lot, and Sigel thought that in simple justice to himself it ought to be enlarged. Halleck had an anti-foreign bias and would do no favors for Sigel, who then asked to be relieved and saw that one request granted immediately. General Howard was also a man with a lot of seniority, and he had been complaining because Sickles, his junior, had been given a corps while he, Howard, still led a mere division. Sigel's departure offered a chance to pacify Howard, and he got the XI Corps,[7] which decided quite soon that it did not like him very much.

Howard was not the type to make soldiers warm up to him quickly. He addressed them as "my men," which did not go over any better in the 1860s than it would today, and he was a little too widely known as the Christian soldier, a major general who went to hospitals on Sundays to distribute baskets of fruit, which were welcomed, and religious tracts, which regrettably were not. This did not add to his popularity. His Germans were mostly freethinkers with a strong anti-clerical tradition, and his native Americans were inclined to be jocose about excessive piety. There were contradictions in the America of that generation, with deep religious feeling going hand in hand with rough skepticism, and these two warring traits had to be embodied in this one unhappy army corps. In addition, Howard brought in a pair of new generals, Charles Devens and Francis Barlow, who were ferocious disciplinarians and who displaced generals the soldiers liked. Howard wrote later that "I was not at first getting the earnest and loyal support of the entire command."[8]

So it was the soft spot, this army corps. It had a tradition of bad luck and defeat, it was unhappy with itself and with its leadership, and, worst and most dangerous of all, it was an outcast from the spirit and affection of the army.[9]

In this reaction the army simply reflected national sentiment. The Civil War had come to a nation which was suspicious of its immigrants. Its traditions and habits of thought still deified the simple, uncrowded, slow-moving society of an earlier day. In its adolescence the country was beginning to look back fondly to a lost golden age when there had been no problems that hard work and plain living would not solve. Fantastic growth and development were taking place, the old traditions were outdated, the new arrivals were part of this growth, and somehow the incomprehensible, unwelcome changes seemed to be their fault.

So men of foreign birth were, in plain fact, second-class citizens, and the men of the XI Corps wore the uniform of a country which did not like them. Hardly half a dozen years had passed since the Know-Nothings had been a powerful political party, and a country which hated foreigners almost as much as Negroes was now using the one to enforce freedom for the other and was suffering from emotional indigestion as a result. It might yet find that a fight to end slavery would also, in the end, be a fight to improve the lot of the immigrant, and that was something it had not counted on.

The way Hooker had his army lined up on the morning of May 2, it seemed unlikely that the XI Corps would have much to do, which was perhaps a measure of the general feeling that the men were something less than the first-class troops.

The left end of Hooker's line ran along a wooded ridge from the Rappahannock to a clearing a few hundred yards north of Chancellorsville and was held by Meade and his V Corps. Next to Meade, covering the turnpike from Fredericksburg and the ground on either side of it, stood Hancock's division of the II Corps. On Hancock's right, bulging out in a big horseshoe curve to cover the plateau of Fairview Cemetery, a lonely country burying ground a few rods southwest of the Chancellorsville mansion, Slocum's XII Corps was dug in, with guns massed in the rear. Just west of this, holding a line that also bulged out to the south to take advantage of the elevated fields of Hazel Grove farm, were two divisions of Sickles's III Corps. On Sickles's right, running straight west along the turnpike for more than a mile, was the line of the XI Corps.

Hooker apparently was waiting for the Rebels to attack him. If they did they would be coming along the turnpike from Fredericksburg and they would hit either Hancock's men or Slocum's, shock troops, well entrenched, men who could be counted on. If they swung off to the north they would strike Meade's corps, equally reliable and occupying a practically impregnable position. Howard's men held the sector farthest removed from any possible point of attack, and to get at them Lee would have to march squarely across Hooker's front—a fatal maneuver, as any student of Austerlitz could testify. Anyway, the woods and underbrush around Howard's front were so thick and tangled that a regular line of battle could not get through. The Dutchmen might stack their arms and butcher their cattle and let their excellent bands play, while the real army of the Potomac took care of the fighting.

The day came in warm and sunny, and the army held its lines and waited. It was hard to know just what was going on. The Wilderness was bewilderingly dense, and Jeb Stuart's men were knocking Hooker's inadequate cavalry patrols back into camp every time they stuck their horses' noses out. In front of Hancock and Slocum there was a good deal of firing. Rebel patrols kept prowling forward, batteries sprang to life here and there, and there was a lot of skirmishing and sniping going on. Hancock's advanced skirmish line, commanded by youthful Nelson Miles who had just recovered from the throat wound received at Fredericksburg, took a good deal of punishment. The skirmish line held and there was no attack, but from headquarters it seemed that the Rebels were tapping for soft spots, looking for a good place to strike.

Hooker toured his lines that morning, looking at trenches and rifle pits and murmuring: "How strong! How strong!" The soldiers sprang to their feet when they saw him, the handsome general with his handsome mounted staff riding at his heels, headquarters flag fluttering in the May sunlight, and a tremendous cheer rolled up from the lanes and clearings. Here was Hooker, and he had saved these men from the head-on assault on the evil Fredericksburg lines, he had given them health and self-confidence again, he had promised that Lee's army would be destroyed, and the very look of him was the look of hope. So this morning, for the last time in its history, the Army of the Potomac sent up a wild cheer of genuine affection and enthusiasm for its commanding officer.[10]

Back to headquarters went Hooker, to wait for destiny on the pillared veranda of the Chancellorsville house; and out in front Dan Sickles saw what he believed to be a dazzling opportunity beckoning from beyond the cedars.

Looking off to the south, Sickle's men had been getting glimpses of Rebels in motion—a big column, with guns and wagons and infantry trudging through the woods, apparently heading south.[11] The forest was thick and open vistas were few, but by noon it was clear that something big was under way and the high command took thought. It was just possible that Lee did have some notion of circling around and hitting the army's right, and Hooker sent a note to Howard suggesting that he consider the possibility of being flanked.

But this idea soon evaporated. There were many wagons in the line of march—Stonewall Jackson's ammunition train and ambulances, infinitely ominous if anyone had known—and it looked as if what Sickles's men saw might be Lee's army in full retreat. To be sure, intermittent firing was still taking place in front of Slocum and Hancock, but that was probably just rear-guard stuff. Lee was flying lest destruction overtake him, just as Hooker had predicted. Why should not Hooker's good friend Dan Sickles take a couple of divisions, lunge forward through the Wilderness, and smite this retreating column to make victory complete?

Hooker struggled against this idea only briefly. It was what he wanted to believe. Jubilantly he gave Sickles his orders. (Couch, still glum, permitted himself to wonder: If the enemy really is in retreat, why do we pursue with only a small part of our force?)[12]

Sickles's soldiers had been having a quiet day of it so far. They had lounged under the trees, smoked, joked, and speculated about what was going to happen next. If a man put his ear to the ground he could hear the rumble of wheels and the tramp of many feet, and this seemed to jibe with the rumor that the Rebels were running away. Rookies, it was noticed, swallowed the rumor whole and rejoiced. Old-timers were more skeptical and said they could not quite see Lee and Jackson retreating without a fight. But while they speculated orders arrived, and Birney's and Whipple's divisions formed column and went south across the Hazel Grove plateau.[13]

Going in front as an advanced skirmish line was Colonel Hiram Berdan's brigade, the 1st and 2nd regiments of U. S. Sharpshooters, one of the most unusual outfits in the army. In the summer of 1861 Colonel Berdan had got permission to enlist these two regiments, with eligibility restricted to men who, at two hundred yards range, could put ten consecutive bullets inside a ten-inch circle. Solid companies had been enlisted from the different states—four from New York, four from Michigan, three from Vermont, and so on—and the men had been given special physical training not unlike that given commando or ranger battalions in more recent time. After a struggle Berdan got them equipped with breech-loading Sharps rifles. The army chief of ordnance had wanted to give them smoothbores, old Winfield Scott had warned Berdan that "breechloaders would spoil his command," and standard army equipment for a sharpshooter was a huge muzzle-loader with ponderous telescope attached, the whole business weighing around thirty pounds and fit to be fired only from a fixed rest. It seems that Lincoln himself finally decided matters in Berdan's favor, and with their breechloaders and their skill as marksmen the two regiments had won fame in both armies. Usually the different companies were detailed for temporary duty with different divisions, but today the brigade was fighting as a unit, a very snappy-looking unit, the men wearing dark green uniforms instead of the regular blue, with plumed hats and leather leggings and fancy calfskin knapsacks, a *corps d'élite* and fully aware of it.[14]

The sharpshooters went forward through dense thickets and over a soggy little creek, up the side of a ravine and through more thickets, until at last they reached open ground by an old iron foundry, where they got into a hot fight with Rebel infantry. Before long the Rebels wheeled up some guns and held the sharpshooters off, but Berdan took his men around a little hollow and captured two or three hundred of the Confederate infantrymen, neatly uniformed, husky-looking men from the 23rd Georgia, who remarked to their captors that they had come over to "help eat them eight-day rations."[15] The advance came to a halt. Sickles threw his divisions into line of battle and sent back word that he was among the enemy's trains and could do wonders if he were just reinforced.

This was what Hooker wanted to hear. Sickles was applauded and told to keep it up, Slocum was ordered to put some of his men in on Sickles's left, and from the right Howard was told to send Sickles a brigade. Such cavalry as Hooker had with him trotted forward to the Hazel Grove clearing so that it could ride out and slash fugitive Rebels as soon as the infantry broke through.

Cavalry got to the clearing, dismounted, and waited for orders. Past them came the Georgia prisoners, heading for the rear under escort, and the troopers jeered: "We'll have every mother's son of you before we go away." One stooped, elderly Confederate looked up sourly and replied: "You'll catch hell before night." Another was more specific: "You think you've done a big thing just now, but you wait until Jackson gets around on your right."[16]

Major generals do not often pay much attention to what angry prisoners say when they are kidded, and these warnings were ignored. It was more pleasant to listen to Sickles, who was among the enemy's trains. Headquarters was happy, the whole army was happy—except for the despised Dutchmen of the XI Corps, who held the right in lonely isolation and who as the day wore on began to be very nervous indeed.

The corps had had a quiet morning and stacked arms at noon to eat a leisurely dinner. Then a feeling of unease developed, sifting up from the lower ranks. Pickets went forward, south of the turnpike which formed the line of the corps, and they sent back disturbing reports: Rebel cavalry was active, parties of Rebel infanty were moving behind it, lots and lots of Rebels were moving over toward the right. West Pointers at corps headquarters wagged their heads and spoke of a rolling reconnaissance. Lower ranks knew nothing of such fancy terms but did know that something was developing and that it did not in the least look like a retreat.

The Dutchmen that afternoon discovered several things overlooked by higher authority. One was that a large part of the Rebel army was coming in closer and closer, giving every indication that it was looking for a fight rather than running away from one. Another was that the advance of Sickles had left the XI Corps completely isolated, with a gap of more than a mile separating it from the rest of the army. A third was that when Howard sent Barlow's brigade off to help Sickles pursue the fleeing Rebels he took away the corps' only reserve. These facts were very likely to add up to a full-fledged military disaster, and some of the soldiers were well aware of it.

Their situation invited a catastrophe. The corps was spread out in a thin line that was more than a mile long but for the most part was only two ranks deep. It faced south, and if the attack came from that direction everything would be fine, but if the attack should come from the west or from northwest there would be no way on earth to keep the corps from being completely wrecked. As the afternoon passed and evening approached it became more and more obvious that the Confederates were going to attack from west and northwest in overwhelming strength, but the soldiers who detected this could not make anybody hear them when they tried to tell about it. Of all the tragic experiences which blunders in high places inflicted on the Army of the Potomac, the one which took place on this evening of May 2 was the most nightmarish.

Eastern end of the corps line, the end that had meshed with Sickles's line before that ardent man went forward to pursue distinction in the bogs south of Hazel Grove, lay in fairly open ground, with Dowdall's Tavern and its yard south of the turnpike and the cleared space around the Wilderness Church and the Hawkins farm extending for half a mile or so on the north side. There was a low ridge crossing the road just here, and corps artillery had been stacked up north of the highway. The tavern had been designated a strong point and was set off by gun emplacements and rifle pits, most of which faced due south.

About the rest of the corps line there was nothing remarkable. It ran west along the road through dense woods, and after a while it simply came to an end. At the place where it ended two guns had been planted in the middle of the road. North of them, at right angles to the rest of the line, two regiments had been posted, facing west. They had been formed in one rank, the men three feet apart—a heavy skirmish line rather than a line of battle—and in front of them was a flimsy slashing of brush and saplings. Neither Hooker, Howard, nor anyone else could possibly have supposed that that skirmish line would be a real defense against a flank attack, but nobody supposed that there would be a flank attack—nobody, that is, except a considerable number of men of no especial rank or distinction, who as evening approached were quite certain that there was going to be hell to pay before the sun went down.

By ill chance many of these belonged to the brigade commanded by Brigadier General Nathaniel C. McLean, a good soldier recently demoted from divisional command to make room for Brigadier General Charles Devens. Devens came from Boston, and he seems to have felt that he had been brought into this second-rate Dutch corps to bring the men up to snuff. As a result he tended to be very stiff and military with his subordinates—the more so, perhaps, when those dealings took place via General McLean, between whom and Devens the situation was slightly delicate.

At any rate, Devens commanded the western end of the corps line, and it was McLean's men who first discovered that the Rebels were about to attack. Colonel Lee of the 55th Ohio had got so many reports of Confederate masses moving off to the right that he went to see McLean, who promptly took him to Devens. Devens pooh-poohed at him, but Lee stuck to his story, insisting that big trouble was coming down the wind, whereupon Devens loftily remarked that Western colonels were more scared than hurt. McLean and Lee went away, and presently Colonel Richardson of the 25th Ohio appeared, saying that his scouts had seen huge masses of Rebel infantry deploying not half a mile from the right and rear of the corps. McLean took him to Devens, who said icily: "I guess Colonel Richardson is somewhat scared; you had better order him in to his regiment." McLean obeyed orders and Richardson returned to his regiment, called in his company officers, and told them to have the men eat supper early. While he was doing that, McLean took Lieutenant Colonel Friend of the 75th Ohio to Devens with a duplicate of Richardson's story. Devens unbent just a trifle and explained that corps headquarters, which would surely know if a flank attack were in the making, had sent him no alert. As a result, Friend hurried off to corps headquarters, where Howard's aides laughed at him and begged him not to bring on a panic.[17]

The brigade at the western knuckle of the line was commanded by Colonel Leopold von Gilsa, sometime major in the Prussian Army and a veteran of the Schleswig-Holstein war. Von Gilsa knew what was up, and when he received a note from his picket line saying that the enemy was massing, begging, "For God's sake, make dispositions to receive him!" he went to Howard with it. Howard explained that the forest west of Von Gilsa was so thick that no line of battle could ever get through it. Von Gilsa unhappily returned to his lines just as Leatherbreeches came riding over from Carl Schurz's division.

Leatherbreeches was a character. He was Captain Hubert Dilger, former officer in the Baden Mounted Artillery, who had taken leave and come to America when the Civil War broke out and who was now skipper of Battery 1, 1st Ohio Artillery, in Schurz's division. He was a scientific gunner and a man of fantastic daring, and he was known as Leatherbreeches because of a pair of doeskin pants he liked to wear. At this moment he was out to do a bit of scouting. Schurz, the one non-professional soldier among all the higher brass in the XI Corps, had taken the alarm along with Von Gilsa and McLean and was quietly rearranging some of his men in the clearing around Wilderness Church so that they could fight facing west if they had to. He had told Dilger to be ready to meet an attack from the rear, and Dilger had got his horse and gone out to look things over for himself.

Von Gilsa warned him not to go west on the turnpike beyond the picket lines or he would be captured. But Dilger was not going to take anybody's word for anything, and he rode on out of sight—rode for nearly a mile, ran smack into a battle line of Rebel infantry, and very nearly met the fate Von Gilsa had predicted. He galloped madly north, being cut off from the XI Corps lines, and after a long detour that took him nearly over to the Rapidan he got up to the Chancellorsville crossroads, where he went at once to Hooker's headquarters to tell what he had seen. He was received there by a long-legged cavalry major, a very superior person who did not see why the commanding general's people should bother with mere artillery captains, especially those who spoke with a strong German accent. The major told Dilger to trot along and peddle his yarn in his own corps, where doubtless there would be someone who could find time to listen.

So Dilger went next to Howard's headquarters. There it was made clear to him that corps command did not approve of artillery captains going off on unauthorized scouting trips, and it was explained that since the Rebel army was in full retreat, with Howard leading Barlow's brigade off to join in the pursuit, Dilger must have things all mixed up. Dilger went back to his battery, where he told his men not to take the horses to water but to keep them handy—they might have to move the guns fast at any moment.[18]

On the picket line the men were more and more uneasy. They could see but a few yards in the bushes and vines and thick saplings, but the Confederate skirmishers were very close now and there was a good deal of shooting. Some oddity in the acoustics kept these shots from being heard by any generals, but the lower echelons were not fooled. Three of McLean's colonels rode out to compare notes with Von Gilsa, and when they came back Colonel Reily called his 75th Ohio together and said: "Some of us will not see another sunrise. If there is a man in the ranks who is not ready to die for his country, let him come to me and I will give him a pass to go to the rear, for I want no half-hearted, unwilling soldiers or cowards in the ranks tonight."[19]

The sun was getting low. Far away beyond the woods to the south there was a muffled sound of musketry as Sickles's and Slocum's men fought a Confederate rear guard. Most of the private soldiers in the XI Corps, knowing that all alarms had been passed on to headquarters, assumed that the generals must know what they were doing, and tried to relax. Some regiments stacked arms and began to eat supper, sitting on their knapsacks in rear of the rifle pits. Behind the lines a few details were butchering cattle. One of the German bands was playing "The Girl I Left Behind Me," and a tune called "Come Out of the Wilderness." A private in Reily's 75th Ohio sauntered off to a spring in the wood and dipped his tin cup in the water for a drink. An officer in the 25th Ohio lay on his side in a farmyard just back of the front line, holding the end of his reins while his horse cropped the grass.

There was a ripple of laughter and cheering from the soldiers in the shallow trench along the road, and the officer sat up to see what was going on. Into a little clearing in front of the trench innumerable deer had suddenly emerged from the wood to the west and were galloping madly toward the east, while the soldiers waved their hats and whooped. Then as the deer scampered off into the underbrush the quiet of the spring evening caved in with a tremendous crash.[20]

Out of the forest in the west there came a handful of rifleshots, then the wild weird falsetto of the Rebel yell, followed by great rolling volleys of musketry. A shell exploded against a tree beside the spring where the Ohio private was getting his drink, and he dropped his cup and ran for his regiment. Down the road two Confederate cannon suddenly wheeled into view and fired, and a solid shot crashed through the branches over the head of the officer who had sat up to look at the deer. Another shot slammed into a farmhouse beside which General Devens was lying on the grass taking his ease—he had bruised his leg the day before and it hurt him to stand—and the general belatedly realized that his subordinates had known what they were talking about. And Von Gilsa's skirmish line of two German regiments looked up to see all of the Rebels in the world shouldering their way through the tangle, firing their rifles and yelling like fiends, their line extending far beyond vision to right and left. The Germans got off a few hasty shots and then the flood rolled over them.

The men on the road were completely helpless. They spun about, trying to change position so they could at least face this onslaught, and were knocked out of the way before they could get started. The two guns at the knuckle were captured, and jubilant Confederates swung them around and began to fire down the packed roadway. Colonel Lee galloped to General Devens and begged him to order a change of front to the west. Devens, still trying to figure out what was happening, and perhaps also hoping that he would get some sort of word from corps headquarters, told him: "Not yet." Then the tide swept in, and the road was full of running men. Colonel Reily got his 75th Ohio swung around in the underbrush without waiting for orders and managed to hold out for ten minutes, fighting furiously. He was killed, the light of tomorrow's sunrise guttering out quickly, and 150 of his men were shot down, and then the 75th folded up and ran like all the others.[21]

In a matter of minutes Deven's entire division had collapsed. There was nothing else it could have done, for Stonewall Jackson had hit it with the full power of twenty-eight thousand men, attacking in a line more than a mile wide and four divisions deep, his men crashing through the woodland that was supposed to be impassable by any line of battle, getting their uniforms ripped completely off at times by thorns and broken branches, but coming on regardless. Devens's men had not a chance in the world. The fighting came in from their right and rear. McLean had to put his men on the opposite side of their breastworks, and Colonel Lee wrote dryly after the battle that "a rifle pit is useless when the enemy is on the same side and in rear of your line."[22] There was nothing the men could do but run.

So a confused, yelling, stumbling, running horde of men and horses was jammed in the turnpike, dense woods on either side, Rebel canon slashing through the mass with shrapnel and canister. Here and there, in the forest, regiments and parts of regiments tried to make a stand, but it was hopeless. Jackson's men beat them down and swept over them, their battle line so wide that any strong point could be surrounded and taken in no time. Brigade and regimental organizations were utterly lost. Fragments of McLean's Ohio regiments were mixed together, trying in vain to put up a fight, but fugitives from the broken line to the west plowed through them, and then a great gust of Confederate rifle fire blew them back toward Chancellorsville. Some of the fugitives drew knives and cut their knapsack straps as they ran, not taking time to stop and unbuckle them. It was noticed, though, that most of the men hung onto their rifles, and many individuals paused in the rout now and then to fire at their pursuers.[23]

The disorganized mass rolled east and came presently to the open ground around the Hawkins farm and the Wilderness Church. Here Schurz had posted a few German regiments facing west, and for twenty minutes they put up a good fight, while Leatherbreeches wheeled his guns into line and swept the Rebels off the turnpike. But the odds were too great. The line was outflanked at both ends and attacked with overpowering numbers from the front, and Schurz's Dutchmen finally had to go back like everybody else. Dilger found himself fighting alone, his infantry supports gone, and the Rebels were creeping in on him through ravines and thickets. He stayed there, firing double-shotted canister, until the enemy were almost among his guns, then limbered up to leave. As the guns began to move, three of the six horses attached to one piece were shot. Dilger tried furiously to drive the gun away with three dead horses dragging in the harness, found that it was impossible, and at last withdrew without it.[24]

Last stand of the corps was made by the brigade of Adolph Bushbeck, another Prussian-trained soldier, who took over some inadequate rifle pits dug earlier in the day by the departed Barlow. Dilger paused here to help, elements of the retreating regiments tried to rally, and once more the Confederate tide was checked for a time. The sun went down, a vast cloud of smoke thickened the twilight, and there was an unceasing uproar. The Rebels paused to rearrange their lines slightly—they had got nearly as mixed up by all this Wilderness fighting as the Federals themselves—and at last they came on again, Bushbeck's line broke, and the rear guard withdrew toward Chancellorsville.

There was little disorder to this part of the retreat. Most of Buschbeck's men went back in regular columns, and Dilger stayed in the road as rear guard. The road was narrow and he could use but one gun, so he sent the others back, telling the men to report to the first artillery officer they found. Dilger himself stayed with his one gun, firing it like a pocket pistol—a couple of shots down the road, limber up and go back a hundred yards, unlimber again and fire some more: one man and one gun, standing off the advance of Stonewall Jackson. A nucleus of infantry gathered around him with some higher officers. Howard had come galloping madly back from the excursion south of Hazel Grove, the staff of a flag tucked under the stump of his amputated right arm. If there was anything that plain personal bravery could do to stem the rout, Howard was going to do it.[25]

Now they were going back across the big gap that had been created by the advance of Sickles's men, and there was no help in sight. For some odd reason the racket created by Jackson's assault had not penetrated far. Back at headquarters, Hooker had been standing on the veranda, surrounded by his staff, while his right wing was folding up, and nobody had known anything about it. Finally some echo of the firing reached the Chancellorsville house and an aide stepped out into the road to see what he could see. He got out there just in time to meet a tumult of horses without riders, men without officers, wildly bouncing wagons and guns, coming directly at him. He had time to yell, "My God—here they come!" and then the fugitives went streaming past headquarters, and Hooker vaulted into the saddle and went tearing forward to see what could be done.

Frantically Hooker ordered forward Hiram Berry's division—his own division in the old days, left in reserve when Sickles made his advance—and he rode forward with it, telling the men: "Receive 'em on your bayonets! Receive 'em on your bayonets!"[26] Someone was collecting cannon and posting them in a long line by Fairview Cemetery, facing west. Full night came down, and the moon came out, and the smoke and the noise rolled up over the thickets and the white narrow roadways.

The open clearing by Hazel Grove was another place which the first noise of battle failed to reach. Cavalry lounged at ease there, waiting for the order to go down and cut up Rebel wagon trains. With them were three or four batteries of artillery, likewise at ease, and a collection of ambulances, ordnance wagons, battery forges, and odds and ends of the rear echelon. Up to the 8th Pennsylvania Cavalry rode a courier, and to its skipper, Major Pennock Huey, he gave a message: General Howard was over by the Wilderness Church somewhere and he wanted some cavalry. There was no urgency to the message, no inkling that catastrophe had descended. Major Huey broke up his poker game, got his men on their horses, and took his regiment down a narrow woods lane in column of twos, sabers all in scabbards, the men talking casually of this and that.

A dozen yards from the turnpike the major suddenly realized that something had gone very wrong. He had barely time to order his men to draw their sabers and move at a gallop. Out into the turnpike came the cavalry, crashing squarely into the middle of Confederate General Robert Rodes's division of infantry. There was a wild confused melee, with nobody knowing what was happening, Rebels as surprised as Federals, troopers slashing with the sabers and taking bullets in return. A good many saddles were emptied, and Huey's survivors finally came drifting back to the Chancellorsville clearing, their mission unaccomplished.[27]

This was in some ways the least significant incident of a night filled with blunders and things gone wrong, and yet it may have been the most important thing done by Union troops that evening. For the Confederates, pausing to straighten out their lines before resuming the advance, got the impression that Yankee cavalry was on the alert and could be expected to make sporadic assaults, and the advance guard grew extremely wary whenever unidentified horsemen loomed up in the uncertain moonlight. And just a little bit later, when Stonewall Jackson and his staff came riding in from a scouting mission ahead of the lines, an overeager North Carolina infantry regiment fired a volley that knocked Jackson out of the saddle with a wound that was to take his life.

2. HELL ISN'T HALF A MILE OFF

The explosion that wrecked the Dutchmen left Sickles's men isolated. They had heard little or nothing of all the firing in their rear, and when darkness came down in the dense thickets around the ironworks they had supposed that everything was going as it should. Sickles himself was skeptical when he first got the news about what had happened to Howard. Convinced at last, he pulled his men back to Hazel Grove, with Berdan's sharpshooters forming the rear guard, sniping at Rebel patrols which moved forward to maintain contact. The sharpshooters were interested mostly in the exploits of one of their chaplains, the Reverend Lorenzo Barber of the second regiment, who had taken one of the old-fashioned telescopic-sight rifles and had gone out on the skirmish line, where legend magnified his exploits prodigiously, leading to the assertion that he had shot Rebels out of trees a mile away. From that time on, it is recorded, Chaplain Barber always had a crowd when he held services. "The chaplain practices what he preaches," said one soldier. "He tells us what we should do, and goes with us to the very front to help us in battle"[1]

Back in Hazel Grove, the fifteen thousand men Sickles had with him began to realize that their situation was potentially serious. Between them and the rest of the army there seemed to be a large number of Confederates. The moon was high, the sky was cloudless, and there was a ghostly light in the roads and clearings, with acrid layers of smoke drifting about like an evil fog, but under the trees the night was black as ink, and nobody's sense of direction seemed to mean anything in this tangled woods country. Most of the men had got wet wading creeks and swamps, and the night had turned chilly. Near Chancellorsville and the turnpike the night pulsed and glowed with intermittent gunfire. Hooker had put thirty-six guns in line by the little cemetery, and the gunners looked out over a land of hazy moonlight and deceptive shadows and fired whenever they believed that they saw movement.[2]

Sickles felt that he was in a desperate position, and he prepared to have his men fight their way back inside the Union lines. In the queer twilight about the Hazel Grove clearing he tried to form an assaulting column, with confused officers getting the men headed in the general direction of Chancellorsville, and he sent couriers flying down the dark woods roads to notify Hooker and Slocum. While he was getting his men lined up, an advancing Rebel patrol came into the clearing from the south, and the darkness all around twinkled and sparkled with rifle fire, stampeding all of the wagons and camp followers into wild flight back toward the Rappahannock and safety. The batteries which had been parked in the clearing swung into position and knocked the Confederates back into their own lines—a little exploit which the imaginative cavalryman, General Alfred Pleasonton, later magnified into a great save-the-Union repulse of Stonewall Jackson's entire corps.[3]

Back by Fairview Cemetery the gunners were alert. A few hundred yards west of them Berry's division and four or five thousand unpanicked survivors of the XI Corps had formed a line across the turnpike, and when the gunners fired at the Rebels their shell passed low over this line. That unnerved the infantry and now and then killed a few of them, since the shell fuses and propellants of that era were slightly erratic, but there was no help for it. The gunners fired at anything that looked like a target and opened a tremendous cannonade once when they saw a shadowy mass of Rebel infantry on the moonlit highway. The gunfire almost destroyed the party which was carrying the wounded Stonewall Jackson to the rear, did wound General A. P. Hill, and disrupted the formation of a division which he was preparing for a new assault.[4]

The Confederates had not yet lost sight of the fact that their big hope that night was to keep moving. Their lines were nearly as disorganized by victory as the Federal lines were by defeat, there were more Yankees than Rebels around Chancellorsville, and if the Yankees ever got properly reorganized the situation could easily be reversed. Jackson had one great virtue of an aggressive soldier: he believed that no victory was complete as long as a single enemy was on his feet and breathing. When he was shot down he was trying to find a way to slide his troops to the northward, past the Chancellorsville clearing, and cut the Yankees off from their line of supply and retreat over the Rappahannock. On paper it is hard to see how he could have done it, since Hooker had an unused army corps in the vicinity, but in all that Wilderness nobody but Jackson really knew what the chances were that night, and if the man had not been shot he might possibly have done what he wanted to do. In any case, the Rebels had not yet given up for the night.

Around the Chancellorsville house there was the utmost confusion. The clearing was a wild jamboree of stragglers, riderless horses, advancing troops, and galloping couriers, fragments of regiments trying to rally, wagons and pack mules going at the dead run down the roads and across the fields. Huge fires were burning in the woods, stretcher parties were coming and going, and here and there brass bands were industriously making music to restore the spirits of defeated men. Shells exploded overhead, the blast of the massed guns by the cemetery lit the sky like recurrent sheet lightning, and the fringes of the woods broke out with little pin points of flame as skirmishers and pickets fired into the darkness. There was an unending racket, and most of the time the low-hanging smoke blotted out the moonlight.[5]

In all of this seething confusion Sickles's couriers went astray, and his intention to fight his way back into the lines was known to no one. In addition, Sickles did not know that there was a solid Federal battle line drawn up across the turnpike and angling off through the woods to the south.[6] Men could see very little in that intermittent smoking moonlight, and what they could see was not reliable. Everybody was nervous, and nobody knew where anybody else was or what was apt to happen next.

In spite of everything, Sickles got his men moving at last and they went forward into the blind second-growth jungle, moving north to get to the turnpike. Sickles had three regiments in front—1st New York, 3rd Michigan, and 37th New York—and these advanced "by the right of companies," each company going in its own column of twos, a dozen yards or more separating each column from its neighbors. From the rear, divisional officers sent forward warnings to incline to the right—the columns were drifting to the left; they'd get into Howard's old lines if they weren't careful—and the attack became a blind, aimless drift, pressed forward by sheer weight of numbers.[7]

In the darkness the men heard voices, sentries challenged, the shadowy outline of earthworks came into view. There were a few shots from skirmishers, then a great sheet of flame lit up the jammed woodland and dropped a choking cloud of smoke, and the company columns ran and stumbled and collided with trees and with each other, trying to get up into line. A Michigan soldier recalled: "Some commence to fire, others follow suit, and all blaze away, not knowing what at, and all seems to be one vast square of fire. All begin to yell and cheer, some go forward, some to the right and others to the left." On the left the men ran into a Confederate entrenchment behind which alert Rebels were waiting, and there was blind hand-to-hand fighting in the darkness. A Pennsylvania private remembered the "awful grandeur" of this attack, and recalled "the demoniac yells of the Rebel forces—the flash of invisible guns marking the line of the enemy's defenses through the darkness—the gleaming of glittering bayonets in the pale moonlight."[8]

On the right the advancing Federals bumped into a line of Slocum's soldiers who thought the Rebels were charging them, and there was a desperate fight between opposing groups of Union troops. In the midst of all of this the Yankee gunners by the cemetery sprang to their pieces and began to hammer the contestants indiscriminately with canister and shell, and Rebel artillery off to the west began firing in reply. In the road and under the trees there was perhaps the most complete infernal mix-up of the army's entire experience, Rebel yell and Federal cheer mixed in together, officers swearing and beating ineffectively with their swords, men screaming, "Don't fire—we're friends!" and nobody able to straighten anything out.[9]

Looking back on it afterward, General Alpheus Williams of the XII Corps remembered "such an infernal and yet sublime combination of sound and flame and smoke, and dreadful yells of rage, of pain, of triumph, or of defiance." Less emotionally, General Slocum reported: "I have no information as to the damage suffered by our troops from our own fire, but fear that our losses must have been severe." A Massachusetts infantryman who watched from a vantage point near the cemetery wondered how anyone at all survived the assault and the cannonade, especially the latter. The Federal gunners were filling their pieces with all kinds of old iron, he said, including such things as trace chains.[10]

Far back to the rear, by Ely's Ford over the Rapidan, Yankee cavalrymen on a hilltop looked off through the night, and one of them described what they saw:

"A scene like a picture of hell lies below us. As far as the horizon is visible are innumerable fires from burning woods, volumes of black smoke covering the sky, cannon belching in continuous and monotonous roar; and the harsh, quick rattling of infantry firing is heard nearer at hand. It is the Army of the Potomac, on the south of the Rappahannock, engaged at night in a burning forest. At our feet"—for the flying debris of the army had got that far by now—"artillery and cavalry are mixed up, jammed, officers swearing, men straggling, horses expiring."[11]

Somehow, at last, the fighting lines were disentangled. Somehow, at last, part of Sickles's men got back inside the lines. The rest stayed in the Hazel Grove clearing and made the best bivouac they could. It was not a very good one. From a barn near the clearing, where wounded men had been taken, came a steady chorus of agonized cries, and off in the woods the men could hear the dreadful screaming of wounded horses. Sporadic outbursts of firing lit the sky, sometimes bringing nervous soldiers to their feet in expectation of attack. Men remembered oddly that when the racket of this fearful night subsided the whippoorwills were singing. Far to the rear, men of the I Corps, hastily summoned as reinforcements, came marching up the hollow roads from United States Ford singing the John Brown song.[12]

It was probably the gunners by the cemetery who stabilized the situation, if anything about that chaotic mess could be called stable. After Jackson and Hill were wounded, the Confederates found that the gunfire had so broken up their attempted regrouping that nothing more could be done until morning, and some while after midnight the effort to continue the advance was officially suspended. The moon went down and the firing stopped, and both armies got what sleep they could.

Morning brought better visibility and a great deal more fighting. Hooker was worried about Sickles's men in Hazel Grove, and as soon as it began to get light he ordered them to come on back into the lines—a fatal decision, for it gave to the Confederates what turned out to be an invaluable artillery position, and the Confederates began moving guns into the clearing as soon as the Federals left.

Jackson had broken Hooker's right wing into fragments, but the Union Army still had a perfectly good position, and if Hooker had only realized it he was standing squarely between the two disconnected pieces of Lee's army, with a tremendous advantage of numbers on his side. But Hooker just was not realizing things at Chancellorsville.[13] Some paralysis of spirit was on him. The idea of a counterattack seems not to have entered his head. Instead he sent hasty word to Sedgwick, who was supposed to be keeping the Rebel rear guard amused in front of Fredericksburg, ordering him to march to the rescue at once. For the rest, he had the men dig in around the Chancellorsville clearing and prepare to hang on.

The digging was not easy, shovels and spades not being at hand. The men loosened the earth with bayonets or sharpened sticks and then scooped it out with tin plates, pieces of board, or their bare hands. Axmen went forward fifty yards in front of the line and felled trees to form an abatis, or entanglement—a highly effective obstacle when the trees were big enough and were felled so that their branches became intertwined. With some of the branches slashed off and others tied together, the fallen trees could be an almost impassable barrier for advancing infantry. The artillerists by the cemetery had been kept busy all night digging gun pits, and by morning the guns and gun crews were well protected.[14]

Confederate Jeb Stuart, meanwhile, had taken command of the infantry Stonewall Jackson had led. Old Stonewall himself was awakening from an amputation in a field hospital far behind the lines, beginning to drift slowly but surely toward the invisible riverbank which he was to speak of in his last moment on earth. Stuart had Jackson's own ideas about the virtues of an unceasing offensive. Dawn had hardly come before Stuart had his men swinging forward.

They swung first into the Hazel Grove plateau, getting there just as the last of Sickles's men were preparing to leave, and what had begun as an orderly withdrawal turned suddenly into a rout. (An XI Corps soldier who witnessed this noted with satisfaction that these III Corps cocks-o'-the-walk were "apparently as much panicstricken, and as much stampeded, as any of Howard's men had been. The writer saw these demoralized and disorganized men with his own eyes.")[15] One of Slocum's brigadiers wrote bitterly that he saw an entire red-pants regiment of Zouaves legging it desperately for the Union lines, pursued by about half of its number of jeering Southerners. He tried to stop these Zouaves, he said, so that they could stand beside his men and fight, but the Zouaves kept on going and the 20th Connecticut came out and drove the pursuers back.[16]

This was the 20th's first fight, and there was in the regiment one man who had said openly, back in bivouac, that he was such a great coward that he believed he would certainly run away the first time he came under fire. His captain made a mental note to keep an eye on him, but when the fighting began he had other things on his mind and forgot the man. Suddenly he came upon him, down on one knee behind a log barricade, loading and firing as coolly as a veteran. The private looked up at him, bit a paper cartridge open, and grinned a leathery Yankee grin. "Hello, Cap'n," he said. "I believe the powder goes in fust, don't it?"[17]

The Rebels were beaten back and they rallied and came on again, along with thousands more. The attacking line may have extended two miles from end to end, but the ground was so broken and the wood so thick that nobody could see more than a fraction of it. Brigadier General John W. Geary, former mayor of San Francisco, commanded a division here, and his men disputed possession of a sketchy trench line with some possessive Southerners and got into a bitter fight at the closest range. Geary brought some guns forward, the Rebels hit him with their own artillery from in front and from the flank, and finally he had to retire after a fire "of the most terrific character I ever remember to have witnessed."[18]

Confederate General Archer came up with his brigade, striking at a part of the line held chiefly by the 27th Indiana. During the night that regiment's Colonel Colgrove, a red-cheeked, white-whiskered old chap who was a great deal sprier than he looked, had rounded up fragments of two broken regiments and added them to his command, and early that morning he had pounced on a couple of abandoned cannon and rolled them into his works, commandeering a stray artillery lieutenant and detailing a couple of dozen infantrymen to serve the guns. With this impromptu brigade the colonel was fighting briskly—in his shirt sleeves, as usual—and when the Rebel line came close he took personal charge of one of the guns, calling out to his major: "Here, boy, you run the regiment while I run this here gun."

Archer's men got up within seventy yards and then broke and went to the rear, and a new Confederate brigade charged forward. Colgrove led his men out in a counterattack, and the 2nd Massachusetts and 3rd Wisconsin went forward with them, and the Northern and Southern boys got into a blind, vicious fight in the midst of the abatis, where the low branches held the smoke close to the ground and men trying to fight were trapped and could not get free and so were shot or bayoneted. In the end the Rebels withdrew and Colgrove reported exultantly that these Indiana, Massachusetts, and Wisconsin outfits were "the three best regiments I have ever seen in action." At one stage the 2nd Massachusetts was fighting hand to hand with the 1st South Carolina, the two extremist fire-eating states fighting their fight out personally. Afterward a Massachusetts soldier wrote meditatively that although his regiment had been in a great deal of very hot fighting, this was one of the few times they had actually seen their enemies.[19]

Slocum's regiments had hard fighting that morning. Sickles's men and French's division of the II Corps, put in on their right, had it even harder. They were in line for the most part north of the turnpike, and the Confederates came surging in through the timber in three successive lines of battle, which in the confusion of the fighting eventually merged into one dense mass. General Hiram Berry, proudly leading Hooker's old division into action in the post he had coveted so long, scorned to send couriers with orders to his brigade commanders but rode back and forth delivering his orders in person. He got too far up front at last and a Rebel sharpshooter in a tree shot him off his horse and killed him. A confused brigadier, noting his fall and thinking all was lost, led his brigade out of action (thereby leading himself entirely out of the war), but Sickles slammed in a New Jersey brigade to plug the gap. It made a hot counterattack, taking prisoners and capturing Rebel colors, but it got into position too far forward, hung on there for a time, and then had to retreat after heavy losses.

Another gap developed, and the 12th New Hampshire was thrown in—a rookie regiment, taking 550 men into their first fight. These took post on a little knoll and stayed there for more than an hour, most of the officers shot down and the men fighting Indian-style behind trees and logs. Nearly surrounded, the New Hampshire boys finally withdrew, fewer than 100 men around the colors, a lieutenant the ranking officer. They came out through a little ravine, and Sickles saw them and galloped up to check the fire of waiting Federal artillery with a frantic shout: "Hold on there—hold your fire—these are my men in front!" He rode up to the lieutenant who was leading the men in and demanded: "What regiment, and where's the rest of it?" Proudly the lieutenant answered: "Twelfth New Hampshire, and *here's* what's left of it."[20]

Stuart had abandoned Jackson's plan for a continual movement around to the north, to cut the Yankees off from United States Ford, and instead was shifting steadily to his right, to regain contact with the rest of Lee's army. What Jackson had tried to do the night before almost certainly could not have been done this morning, for Hooker had Meade and his V Corps planted right where they could foil such a move, although they were too far in the rear to take part in the immediate action. In any case, Stuart continued pressing toward the right, and the Federals considered that his left flank offered a chance for a counterblow, and French's brigades were moved forward. They made some progress, took prisoners, then came to a halt in the eternal woodland twilight while the Rebels rallied for a new push.

It was beginning to be clear that the Yankee line could not be broken by infantry alone. The Confederates tried over and over, but the Federals were well dug in, it was hard to keep an attacking line in order in the thick woods, and the artillery back by Fairview Cemetery was a mighty power. But the high clearing at Hazel Grove had passed under Confederate control and Stuart had a smart gunner working for him that morning, Colonel E. P. Alexander, and Alexander had been running battery after battery up onto this plateau ever since the Yankees left. By midmorning these guns were taking charge. They enfiladed a good part of the Union infantry line, they hit the Federal gunners at Fairview paralyzing blows, and they blew shot and shell all over the Chancellorsville clearing, disrupting supply lines and leaving the advanced units and some of the artillery with no way to replenish ammunition. They were aided in this by some thirty Rebel guns which had been drawn up near Dowdall's Tavern and by other guns over to the east of Fairview inside of Lee's lines, and presently all of these guns were taking Chancellorsville and everything near it under an overwhelming converging fire.[21]

The 8th Ohio, which had been left behind as artillery support when French's brigades went forward, was posted in a thick oak swamp toward the right of the line, and it reported that shell seemed to be coming in from all directions at once. The lines began to dissolve under this fire, the woods were full of fugitives looking desperately for the rear, and all of the narrow roads were choked with wagons, artillery, ambulances, stray detachments of cavalry, and frantic droves of beef cattle. The woods were on fire in a dozen places, underbrush blazing furiously, flames creeping up to the crown of the taller trees. The air grew unendurably hot, and the heavy wood smoke mixed with the battle smoke under the trees, almost suffocating the fighting men. From the south and east Lee's men kept edging in closer, rolling their guns forward and putting the crossroads under the additional fire. The smoke went billowing upward, and the day was muggy and close and a monstrous clamor of exploding powder and clanging metal and shouting men went up the sky, while the starred Confederate battle flags came tossing closer and closer through the broken timber.[22]

Out in the open men fought in a blinding fog, and as they fought, in a clearing by the turnpike there appeared in the front lines a young woman, one of the characters of the III Corps, gentle, respected Annie Etheridge, who wore a black riding habit with a sergeant's chevrons and who had been part of the army since the early days of the war.

Annie had gone to war with the 3rd Michigan as a laundress. When the regiment first left Washington to go to the front, the other laundresses went home, but she stuck with the regiment, sharing its marches and its bivouacs. It is recorded that she was "a young and remarkably attractive girl," that she was "modest, quiet, and industrious," and that any soldier who dared to utter a disrespectful word to or about her had to fight the entire 3rd Michigan. Gallant Phil Kearny saw her, after a battle on the peninsula, caring for wounded men at a front-line dressing station, and he more or less adopted her into the division, providing her with a horse and saddle and a sergeant's pay and detailing her officially as cook for the officers' mess.

This morning, in the hottest of the fighting, Annie came riding forward with a sack of hardtack and a dozen canteens of hot coffee, and she trotted brightly up to a busy general and his staff and offered refreshments. The officers tried to shoo her back to safety, she refused to budge until each one had had something to eat and drink. The Rebel bombardment was at it worst, and three horses in this mounted group were smashed by solid shot while she was about this business, but an admiring Pennsylvania soldier who watched it all wrote that "she never flinched or betrayed the slightest emotion of fear." A bit later she appeared from nowhere beside an all but disabled Union battery which had lost all of its horses, several caissons, and a good many men. The gunners were about to abandon their pieces, but Annie talked them out of it. She smiled at them and cried, "That's right, boys—now you've got a good range, keep it up and you'll soon silence those guns." The men raised a little cheer, made her go to the rear, and returned to the service of their guns. One sweaty cannoneer remarked that all the officers in the army could not have had as much influence with them just then as "that brave little sergeant in petticoats."[23]

The Confederate fire grew heavier and heavier, scourging the length and breadth of the Chancellorsville clearing, breaking up battery after battery in the line by the cemetery. One shot split a wooden pillar on the veranda of the Chancellorsville mansion. Hooker was leaning against it at the time, and the shock threw him to the ground heavily, stunning him. His favorite specific, brandy, was brought to him as he lay on a blanket his staff had spread out for him, and he revived and got to his feet—just in time, because a cannon ball came along and ripped through the blanket where he had been lying. Other shells went through the mansion itself, where surgeons had taken doors off their hinges and set them up on top of chairs for operating tables. One shell killed a man while a doctor was operating on him, others set the building on fire, and Hancock detailed the 2nd Delaware to get the wounded out. All around the building the ground was plowed up by the vicious missiles, and wounded men who had been carried from the burning building were killed as they lay helpless on the ground.[24]

Hooker was taken to a tent half a mile behind the crossroads, and he sent for General Couch. Other officers took heart when this happened. Couch was a desperate fighter, and if Hooker turned the command over to him he would unquestionably call some of the unemployed troops into action and turn the tables. But Hooker did not do that. He instructed Couch to take temporary command, but only for the purpose of withdrawing the men to a new defensive line back behind the crossroads, covering the road to United States Ford. Couch came out of the tent, disappointment visible on his face. Meade, who had been standing by hopeful that Couch would tell him to lead his corps forward, turned away dejected.[25]

The withdrawal began, and it fell to the lot of Hancock to cover the retreat. Hancock had his division in line facing east, covering the turnpike from the direction of Fredericksburg. Lee's men had been pressing him all morning, but as the troops behind him caved in, Hancock's division began to get all of it, and the right wing had to be pulled far back. Before long the division was formed in two separate lines, back to back, only a few hundred yards apart. The last of the guns went away from Fairview, Stuart's and Lee's troops made contact with each other, and an enormous horseshoe of fire encircled Hancock's division, with shell coming in from every point of the compass except the sector between northeast and northwest.

Hancock was born for moments like this. He had a thundering voice and an unrivaled command of profane army idiom. The II Corps treasured for the rest of the war the way he had exploded the evening before when a panicked soldier from Howard's corps, still fresh after a two-mile run from the Rebels, dashed up to him in confusion and asked to be directed to the road leading to the river pontoon bridges and ultimate safety. (The corps historian noted primly of his answer that "it is best not to put it into cold and unsympathetic type.")[26]

To the east, Nelson Miles held an advanced skirmish line, and he boldly rode his horse up and down the line immediately behind the men, holding them to their work. It was an effective stunt—the men liked to know that a ranking officer was up front with them, taking what they had to take—but it took an uncommon amount of nerve, because the infantry on both sides usually fired just a little high and the man on horseback was right where he could get the worst of it. Miles seemed to glory in it, and once Hancock sent an aide spurring forward to tell him that he was worth his weight in gold. A Rebel marksman finally got him with a bullet through the abdomen and Miles was carried off the field, supposedly dying—belly wounds were almost invariably fatal in that war.

Colonel Cross of the 5th New Hampshire, bald-headed and red-bearded, an old-time Indian fighter and soldier of fortune, had been given command that morning of two other regiments besides his own—he was a top-notch soldier, already marked for brigade command—and he had with him a number of stragglers from the XI Corps whom he had rounded up and pressed into service the night before. He was up and down his line this morning, right in his element in this hot fight. He came upon a soldier once cowering behind the useless protection of a flimsy cracker box. He kicked the box out of the way, kicked the soldier and yanked him to his feet, crying that he would disgrace the whole division. When a gun fell silent for lack of cannoneers, Cross ran to it and helped some of his infantry load and fire it.[27]

Rebel guns now were firing from a distance of hardly more than five hundred yards. This was canister range, and the Rebel gunners were choking their guns to the muzzle with anything they could lay their hands on, including some twelve-inch pieces of old railway iron which they happened to have with them. Amid the whirring fragments that filled the air there was a file which struck in a tree beside General Caldwell. The general looked at it coolly and was quite unable to resist the temptation to remark to his staff that this was real file firing.[28] The parallel lines of Hancock's eleven regiments were being hit from in front, from the rear, and from the flank.

Into an orchard in the open between the lines came Lieutenant Stevens with the 5th Maine battery, unlimbering and going into action in desperate haste. Confederate guns from all around the arc opened on the battery with fury, getting the exact range at once, exploding shells overhead, firing canister and solid shot to hit just short and go ricocheting in off the hard ground at waist height. Horses were killed, caissons blew up, limber chests were smashed, men were slain, and Stevens made his gun crews fire slowly so that every shot would count, with half the guns detailed to fire at Rebel artillery and the other half under orders to shoot only at infantry. Ammunition ran low and the battery was a wreck. Stevens was down, all the officers were down, and Couch detailed an officer of regulars, Lieutenant Kirby of the 1st U.S. Artillery, to come in and take charge. Kirby went down with a mortal wound and was carried to the rear. (He survived in hospital for a fortnight and did not die before he received a lieutenant colonel's commission from Abraham Lincoln in recognition of his valor.)[29]

The dusty plain around the crossroads was covered with smoke from the guns and the exploding shell and the burning woods. The old mansion was all aflame, and a dense blanket of fumy, stifling smoke from the pine thickets was rolling across the open space, where the men and equipment for whom Hancock's men were buying time moved to the rear. In the thickets, wounded men were burned to death, and corpses were consumed, and all the debris left behind by retreating troops took fire. A fearsome stench came down with the smoke, and a Confederate brigadier leading troops up to the clearing wrote: "The dead and dying of the enemy could be seen on all sides enveloped in flames, and the ground on which we formed was so hot as at first to be disagreeable to our feet." A Federal officer noted soberly: "Fortunate were those that had to die, that they did so before the holocaust began," and cavalry far in the rear could see great plumes of soiled white smoke rising from the reeking woodland.[30]

It was getting on toward noon now, and Confederate troops were sweeping out into the open around Fairview Cemetery, setting up an enormous cheer, Lee himself visible in their midst. Hancock's guns were out of ammunition and almost out of men, and word came up from headquarters that he could leave now—the army was established in its new lines closer to the river. The advanced skirmish line where Miles had taken his wound came back first, withdrawing in good order except for a few companies which missed their direction and marched smack into the middle of the Confederate advance and were captured.

It was time to get the guns out, but most of the horses were gone and hardly any gunners were left. Hancock sent to the rear for a detail of infantry, and men from the Irish Brigade came up to the wrecked battery. The Irishmen found just one gun left in action, directed by a corporal who was firing his last shot. All of the battery's limber chests had either been exploded by enemy action or were now empty. If the guns got out they would have to be taken out by hand, and so prolonges were attached—long ropes fastened to the trails of the gun carriages, the men tailing onto the ropes three dozen at a time—and the lumbering, ungainly weapons were hauled slowly to the rear. Rebel skirmishers were barely 150 yards away when the guns began to move.

Now the infantry could leave—and high time, too, with the Rebel fire heavier than ever and enemy skirmishers coming in for pot shots at point-blank range. When the word to retire came through, the outfit nearest the enemy about-faced and started off at a trot. Hancock, who always saw everything, spotted them and came storming over at a gallop to demand: "Why are these men running?" Immediately the regiment slowed down to a walk, and at a walk the men left the field. One man who made this march admitted afterward that although they went out at a walk it was a good *brisk* walk.[31]

The new lines covered a wide angle of ground enclosing the Rappahannock bridgehead, and the flanks were firmly anchored, left flank running down to the Rappahannock and right flank running clear to the Rapidan. Hooker had more than enough troops, seventy thousand altogether, a good half of whom had not been in action, and his trench line was substantial. On the right and left the Confederates followed with inquisitive patrols, probing forward through the Wilderness to find out just where the new Yankee line might be.

In the center, coming from the Chancellorsville crossroads, a solid mass of Rebels was advancing as if Lee planned to break through the angle by sheer weight and drive the whole Union Army into the river. This part of the line was held by Meade, and he rode up to his divisional commander, General Charles Griffin, pointed to the approaching enemy column, and told him to drive it back.

Griffin was an old artillerist, one of the numerous excellent generals contributed to the Union Army by the regular artillery, and he still liked his guns. (One of his men once remarked that Griffin would have run his guns out on the skirmish line if he had been allowed to.) He now asked Meade if he might use artillery instead of infantry to check the Rebels. Meade told him that would be all right if he thought gunfire alone would do the job.

To an old gunner there could be just one answer to that.

"I'll make 'em think hell isn't half a mile off!" cried Griffin. He wheeled a dozen guns up into line. Dismounting, he told the gunners to load with double charges of canister, to wait until the assaulting column was within fifty yards, "and then roll 'em along the ground like this," stooping and swinging his arm forward like a bowler. The gunners did as directed. The head of the Confederate column was smashed in, and the rest drew back. For the time being, at least, the army was safe.[32]

Indeed, the high command that afternoon seems to have nourished some final shred of hope that perhaps a victory was being won. Half an hour after noon, with the army snugged down at last in this purely defensive position, Quartermaster General Rufus Ingalls wired an encouraging progress report to Dan Butterfield, who was back at the old headquarters at Falmouth:

"I think we have had the most terrible battle ever witnessed on earth. I think our victory will be certain, but the general told me he would say nothing just yet to Washington, except that he is doing well. In an hour or two the matter will be a fixed fact. I believe the enemy is in flight now, but we are not sure."[33]

3. GO BOIL YOUR SHIRT

Out in front the Wilderness smoldered, and a drizzling rain dampened the thickets and caused the smoke to drift in heavy spiritless clouds that hung low over the woodlands. Hooker's men held a line in the shape of a vast horseshoe, five miles or more from end to end, cleverly posted on high ground with ravines and bogs in front. Throughout the night the men were kept busy digging dirt and felling trees, and by the morning of May 4 the entire line was fortified.

There were trenches four feet deep, with a solid breastwork of logs and earth facing the Rebels, heavy slashing of fallen timber out in front, a "head log" lying atop the breastworks with a four-inch slot under it for the riflemen. Brigadier General Thomas Kane, who as a patriotic amateur had helped organize the famed Bucktails in the first summer of the war and who now capably led a brigade in Slocum's corps, noted that "any force that the nature of the ground would allow the enemy to bring against us would meet with a certain and disastrous repulse," and said that his men were confident of success and were looking forward to a renewal of the fighting. In a letter to his wife Hancock wrote that "the battle is not through yet by a long ways."

Yet the fighting was not renewed. The Confederates pushed skirmishers forward, and there was a bit of long-range artillery fire, but for the most part the army sat in its trenches, peered out at a dull inactive landscape of charred brush and smoking flatlands, and waited to see what would happen next. Far away to the east there was a sound of gunfire, but nothing much seemed to come of it. Rain came down harder, and in places the trenches were flooded so badly that details were put to work cutting gaps in the breastworks so that the water might drain away.[1]

Hooker had left General John Sedgwick and his overstrength VI Corps at Fredericksburg to beguile the foe, and when disaster took place around the Chancellorsville crossroads Hooker sent word that Sedgwick must advance, brushing aside any Rebels who opposed him, and come over to join the rest of the army. Sedgwick had close to twenty-five thousand men, and on paper his job looked easy: one quick lunge up over the heights back of Fredericksburg and then a straight hike of ten or twelve miles to Hooker's lines, and the job would be done. In actual practice, as Sedgwick realized perhaps too well, it was far from simple.

Lee had left Jubal Early, the army's reserve artillery, and some ten thousand infantry to oppose Sedgwick's passage, and Early was a stubborn character who never retreated unless he had to. He had his men dug in along the line which had proved so impregnable when Burnside assaulted it the previous December, and although this line now was held by a skeleton force, the memory of the December tragedy was strong and Sedgwick was very cautious. He got his men up through town, sparred at long range during most of the morning, and at last sent ten regiments out across the Fredericksburg plain, over the ground where so many men had died in the last great battle.

Early's men were posted on Marye's Heights and in the sunken road, and they proposed to stay there. The Federals charged twice and were driven back with losses, and for a time it looked as if this particular nut would be just as hard to crack as it had been when all of Lee's army was on hand. The 5th Wisconsin was finally shaken out as a skirmish line, and its Colonel Allen, who commanded the advanced column of assault, addressed the men briefly: "When the signal *forward* is given you will advance at double-quick. You will not fire a gun, and you will not stop until you get the order to halt. You will never get that order."[2] The men raised a cheer and went in on the run, the rest of the assaulting column at their heels. The charge wavered when it got close to the wall. Rebel defenders here were few, compared with last December, but they were firing fast and the position was all but invulnerable. Then the Federals at the right of the line swept in through a complex of kitchen gardens and board fences, vaulted over the wall, bayoneted the men who barred the way, and got a killing enfilade fire on the rest.[3] The surviving Confederates fled, guns were abandoned, and five months after Burnside had first imagined it the United States flag waved on top of the heights and this part of the battle had been won.

Sedgwick paused and took thought: plain, unassuming, weathered John Sedgwick, greatly liked by his troops, broad-shouldered and heavy-framed, an unmilitary-looking character with muddy boots, red shirt under his blue coat, old slouched black hat on his head, and a tangled brown beard, one of the best of the Yankee generals but not the man for daring decisions and rapid movement.[4] If he pursued Early's beaten detachment he might be able to wipe it out, but his orders said that he was to move straight on to Chancellorsville, and anyway, he had no cavalry to beat the bushes for fleeing enemies, so he reorganized his command and put it on the turnpike. He was methodical about it, and today he was being very cautious, and the afternoon was well along when he finally got the column moving.

If Hooker had been wide awake now Lee's army might have been crushed, but all of this was happening only a few hours after Hooker had been stunned by the cannon ball which fractured the pillar on the Chancellorsville mansion, and while Sedgwick's corps was tramping forward along the turnpike Hooker was meekly pulling his seventy thousand men back into the bridgehead entrenchments and was leaving Sedgwick to look out for himself. As a natural result, Lee posted a detachment to watch Hooker's trenches and took most of his army back to deal with this new threat to his rear.

Sedgwick's leading division ran into the Rebel battle line at Salem Church, half a dozen miles east of Hooker's inactive army. The division attacked gallantly and for a few moments had things all its own way. But Sedgwick had opened the fight without waiting for the rest of his corps to come up. The attacking division found itself outnumbered, and before long it was splintered and broken and forced to retreat, with the balance of Sedgwick's command reaching the field just in time to round up stragglers and form a new defensive line. When night came down the men found themselves drawn up in a ragged quadrangle near Banks Ford with Rebels on three sides of them and the river on the fourth, and the big question was not whether they could get to Chancellorsville to help Hooker but whether they themselves could get out of this fix without being captured in a body.

They put in a gloomy night. Losses had been heavy, the lanterns of the stretcher-bearers were bobbing through the woods and across the fields for hours, and Sedgwick stayed awake almost all night, trying to get word of his plight to Hooker and to get some sort of intelligent instructions in return. One soldier remembered that the "night was inexpressibly gloomy," and the 95th Pennsylvania recalled an episode of eerie horror. One of their number had been killed while climbing over a rail fence and by some appalling freak remained balanced upright astride the top rail all night, rocking slowly to and fro in the breeze, his comrades in bivouac a few hundred feet away able to see his white face distinctly in the light of the full moon. Rebel pickets held the line of the fence, and when they fired, the flash of their pieces put a lurid light on the ghostly figure.[5]

The next day was May 4, and Hooker's main body stayed in its lines while Lee tried to destroy Sedgwick's corps. Lee might have succeeded if he had been able to mount his attack in time, but one of his division commanders was sluggish and the ground was difficult, and in the end Sedgwick was able to stand the Confederates off until after dark, when he finally managed to get his men back to the north side of the Rappahannock. From first to last his venture had cost forty-seven hundred casualties and had done no good whatever, except that for some thirty-six hours it had diverted Lee's attention from Joe Hooker.

May 5 came in rainy, with Hooker's men huddled in trenches or in dripping woods behind the lines. The Rappahannock was rising rapidly, and the pontoon bridges at United States Ford, only remaining avenue of communication between the Army of the Potomac and the North, were swaying insecurely on the flood. The eight days' rations had all been eaten or lost, supply trains were back around Falmouth, and it seemed to Hooker that he and his army were in a desperately bad spot. Army intelligence said that Longstreet had brought his corps up from below Richmond to take a hand in the game, and after Sedgwick's defeat there was obviously nothing to keep Lee from assaulting Hooker's lines with everything he had.

Army intelligence was wrong about Longstreet, who was still far away. Its information came from Rebel deserters, who seem to have been planted for purposes of deception. However, Hooker was having a stiff case of McClellan caution, and that evening he called his corps commanders into council to see whether it might not be time to retreat.

The meeting was neither happy nor harmonious. Slocum was late and did not get to headquarters until after the meeting had adjourned. Meade was angry, full of fight and eager to resume the battle. Howard was somewhat subdued, feeling that his corps had been responsible for the army's troubles, but he too was all in favor of fighting it out. Reynolds was sullen and weary. He told Meade to vote his proxy for an offensive, and then lay down in a corner and went to sleep. Couch, slight and pale, looking more like a clergyman than a corps commander, was quietly bitter, making it clear that he would vote for an offensive if someone besides Hooker were to be in command but not otherwise. Sickles confessed himself an amateur soldier among professionals and was frankly ready to vote for a retreat. Hooker let his generals talk by themselves for a while and then came back in to say that his mind was made up and that the army would go back to Falmouth. As the meeting broke up Reynolds inquired savagely (quite loud enough for Hooker to hear him, one said): "What was the sense of calling us all together if he had decided to retreat anyway?"[6]

So here was the end to all the bright prospects and the fine talk, and Hooker's boasts would dance about in the newspaper columns to torment him for many a fine day. Meade's V Corps took station in the wet wood to act as rear guard, with a long picket line strung out in the darkness, and in the black night over atrocious roads the brigades and divisions of the rest of the army climbed out of their trenches and headed back for the river. There were the usual delays and mix-ups, and some regiments stood in line for hours, men falling asleep where they stood, so that orders had to be relaxed to permit the men to lie down in place and sleep in the mud and pelting rain if they could. Wind and rain grew worse, and somewhere after midnight the rising river broke the bridges. Hooker had already gone back to Falmouth, and here was the army on one side of the river and its commanding general on the other, all communication cut off and nobody able to say when or whether it would be restored. Somebody told General Couch about it, remarking that under these circumstances he, Couch, was now in effective command of the army. Couch replied that if that was so the army would turn around next morning and fight, but that meanwhile he was going to go to his tent and try to get a little sleep. Later the bridges were rebuilt and stern orders came from Hooker to resume the retreat, and by the middle of the morning the last of the rear guard was north of the river and the engineers were dismantling the bridges.[7]

The march from United States Ford back to Falmouth was slow and dreary. Tired and dejected, the soldiers fell out by platoons, some of them exhausted by fighting and marching, others fed up with the war and ready to quit. For the rest of the week all the countryside within a twenty-mile radius was swarming with stragglers, some of them in a lawless, ugly mood. They were pillaging houses for food, robbing citizens of their clothing and then putting it on in place of their own uniforms, and striking out for Alexandria and the road home. The provost marshal had squads of cavalry combing the woods and fields, but before long he was notifying the high command that he was outnumbered and asking for help.[8]

The rain did not let up—one diarist spoke of "a tremendous cold storm"— and the infantry came slopping in, soaking wet and covered with mud, in an atmosphere as glum as a funeral. Somewhat bewildered, a private in the 83rd Pennsylvania wrote that "no one seems to understand this move, but I have no doubt it is all right." He added that his outfit got back to camp completely exhausted, saying: "Most of the way the mud was over shoe, in some places knee deep, and the rain made our loads terrible to tired shoulders."[9] General headquarters was getting a count on the losses and was discovering that this Chancellorsville battle had cost more than seventeen thousand casualties, of which six thousand came under the heading "missing." A good many of these latter entries stood for men who had quietly died in the dark forest without being noticed by surviving comrades, but the list also represented many men captured by the Rebels, which indicated that things might not have been too good in some of the combat outfits. Desertions were heavy from the XI Corps, as might have been expected. Surprisingly enough, they seemed to be equally heavy from Slocum's XII Corps, which had fought magnificently on May 3, and from Reynolds's I Corps, which had not had to fight at all.[10]

Back in Falmouth, Hooker began to find out what his cavalry had been doing, and the story did not please him. Stoneman had started down from the river full of enthusiasm, apparently minded to carry out his orders to the letter. He was supposed to get as rapidly as possible to Hanover Junction, which was where the Virginia Central Railroad crossed the line of the Fredericksburg Railroad, for if that junction and its adjacent tracks and bridges were properly smashed, Lee's supply problem would have been impossible. Once he got under way, however, Stoneman had second thoughts. He sent half of his command off under Averell to keep Rebel cavalry at a distance, and Averell wandered over to Rapidan Station and went into bivouac there, confused and inert, as much out of the war as if he had been in Cuba. With the rest, Stoneman rode down to the line of the Virginia Central and then got entangled in his own eloquence.

Calling his regimental commanders together, he explained that "we had dropped in that region of country like a shell, and I intended to burst it in every direction, expecting each piece or fragment would do as much harm and create nearly as much terror as would result from sending the whole shell, and thus magnify our small force into overwhelming numbers."[11] This was putting it very nicely, and it showed that General Stoneman could thrash about in the rank second growth of the English language as valiantly as the next man, but it did not describe the part which Hooker had expected his cavalry to play. There had been nothing whatever to prevent Stoneman from marching his men into Lee's immediate rear. Practically all of Lee's transportation was collected at Guiney's Station, some eighteen miles south of Chancellorsville, and the guard there was of the sketchiest. Stoneman's division could have destroyed the lot, together with all of the supplies collected there, and Hooker's dream of the Rebel army in desperate retreat might have become a reality.

Instead of doing that, however, Stoneman broke his troops up into raiding parties (the "bursting shell" motif), which did spread a good deal of alarm in Richmond but which Lee simply ignored. A contributory factor may have been that Stoneman suffered extensively from piles at this time, so that riding was torture to him and the driving, twenty-hours-in-the-saddle kind of advance which Hooker had expected was just too much for him.[12] But whatever the cause, the result was that the cavalry had been wasted. One disgusted trooper wrote that "our only accomplishments were the burning of a few canal boats on the upper James River, some bridges, hen roosts, and tobacco houses." Hooker furiously relieved Averell of his command—a soldier remembered passing cavalry headquarters the day that order came out and seeing Averell seated in his tent, his head in his hands, the very picture of dejection—and a bit later he relieved Stoneman as well, putting Pleasonton in his place.[13] That would not undo what had been done, however, and the unhappy fact remained that the Hooker who had turned the Yankee cavalry into an effective instrument had not been able to get any service out of it when the big test came.

But if Hooker's cavalry had let him down, the worst let down had come from Hooker himself. He had planned his campaign like a master and had carried out the first half of it with great skill, and then, when the pinch came, he had simply folded up. There had been no courage in him, no life, no spark; during most of the battle the army to all intents and purposes had had no commander at all. With a two-to-one advantage in numbers, Hooker had let his men fight at a numerical disadvantage at every important point on the battlefield. Howard's XI Corps had been mashed by an irresistible flank attack, but the real reason for that disaster was the fact that neither Hooker nor anyone else in authority would listen to the specific warnings which the unhappy Dutchmen had repeatedly sent in. Thereafter, while Lee and Stuart crushed his lines around Fairview and Chancellorsville, Hooker had held thirty thousand good troops out of action; he had cowered in his trenches while Lee broke up Sedgwick's corps; and then, to cap it all, he had hastily retreated across the river just as he was about to be given a chance to redeem the whole situation.

For on the morning the army recrossed the river Lee had actually been planning a full-scale assault on Hooker's lines. Those lines were strong; Hooker still had a two-to-one advantage in numbers, he had 106 guns in emplacements with 140 more in reserve, and by all military logic that assault should have resulted in a Confederate defeat as bad as the one at Malvern Hill.[14]

Yet it may be that military logic would have had nothing to do with it. Lee had not been contending with the Yankee army at Chancellorsville. He had been contending with Joe Hooker; he was more of a man than Hooker was, and Hooker knew it. Couch may have been right: if Hooker was to remain in command the thing to do was to get back across the river as fast as possible, because victory just was not in the man. Years later, when someone asked Hooker what went wrong at Chancellorsville, the general knew a rare moment of humility and remarked, "Well, to tell the truth, I just lost confidence in Joe Hooker."

In Washington there was deep dejection because of the battle—in Washington, which is always convinced that the soul-tearing doubts which come from looking at operations from the under side will immediately overwhelm every American citizen. Senator Sumner, tall and handsome, bearing on his face the indescribable shadow of the brain injuries left by Bully Brooks's cane, stalked into Secretary Welles's office, threw out his arms dramatically, and cried: "Lost—lost—all is lost!" Welles was hardly surprised. He had already noted that the War Department was shuffling papers, staring at the ceiling, and talking the vaguest of double talk, and by these infallible signs he knew the army had been beaten again. Horace Greeley cringed in print at the thought that the finest army on the planet had been defeated by "an army of ragamuffins." Lincoln had been hopeful as long as there was any room for hope, but he finally got the bad news in the form of a laconic telegram from Dan Butterfield. He read it, and his sallow face turned ashen-gray, and to a caller he said, as if dazed: "My God! What will the country say?"[15]

The President's anguished question went across the capital in muffled echoes, and government waited in deepest suspense for the answer. And at last, slowly, imperceptibly, it became evident that the country was not going to say anything at all.

There were sensitive weather vanes in Washington, and in the days following Chancellorsville they caught no breeze whatever. The profound depression which had settled down on the nation after Fredericksburg did not reappear. The editors and orators who could make political capital out of disaster flailed the air as usual and seemed to get no particular response. Most significant of all, perhaps—like the inactivity of the dog in the nighttime in the Sherlock Holmes story— was the great quietude of Secretary Chase. Secretary Chase never wavered in the faith that it would be his deserved good fortune to displace Abraham Lincoln, once Lincoln's inability to fight a winning war became manifest. Here was Chancellorsville, the most inexcusable and costly of all the military defeats the Lincoln government had suffered, and yet in the reaction to it Chase saw no opening. He continued to believe that Joe Hooker should be in command of the army, and he made his attitude known, to the discomfort, said gossip, of Secretary Stanton and General Halleck, who were anxious to remove Hooker but who lacked the nerve to try it as long as the Secretary of the Treasury continued to back him.

There was a turning point in this war, and the country had passed it. It had done so undramatically and without realizing it, and the turning point itself can hardly be identified precisely even at this distance in time. It may have been the adoption of a national draft act, or the decision to recruit Negro troops, or even—so strange are the ways by which a people shows how its spirit is moving—the decision in the middle of a desperate war to build a railroad to the Pacific Coast and to create a million small farms in the Western wilderness by means of a national homestead act. Whatever it was, it had been there somewhere, invisible beneath the oratory and the headlines, the bloodshed and the suffering. Nobody had consciously made a decision about anything, yet here suddenly everybody was taking something for granted: that the war would be fought out no matter how many ups and downs it might have, that there would never be any turning back, that out of the horror of this lost battle in a forest fire there would come a renewed determination and an unutterable grimness. The high-water mark of the rebellion had been left behind, even though men would still have to die under a clump of trees on a heat-blistered ridge in Pennsylvania to make the fact manifest. From now on the road wound upward.

Nobody could see it at the time, least of all in the Southland. In the Army of Northern Virginia men's spirits had never been higher. Lee was reorganizing and was preparing to invade the North, mourning that Jackson was irreplaceable but sure that the superb fighting quality of his soldiers could overcome any handicap. Longstreet and his corps had returned, Longstreet confident that Lee's plan of invasion would succeed if he could just place his army on Northern soil in such a way that the Yankees would have to attack it; strange reminder of Hooker's lost faith that his position at the Chancellorsville crossroads would force the Rebels to march forth to certain destruction.

The Army of the Potomac settled back in its camps at Falmouth again. It was as if an evil fate condemned this army to be forever marching out of camp gaily and forever returning a bit later, its banners in the dust. (A solid year after this, when Grant took off for the Wilderness, veterans warned rookies not to burn the winter quarters—chances were they'd be back in them in a week or so.) The soldiers were utterly bewildered, knowing that they had lost a battle in which half of them had not fought at all, and the only thing clear was that topside had somehow got all of its arrangements most completely fouled up. As a symbol of this there was the experience of the Philadelphia Brigade, which had put in a dreary week guarding fords, hearing the sound of battle from a distance. Returning to camp with the dull realization that it had been beaten even though it had seen no enemies, the brigade found itself with a week's accumulation of orders, announcements, and what not, all of which were read off to the troops by regimental adjutants at evening parade. The first one—brigade staff had been too groggy to weed it out—was Hooker's jubilant May 1 announcement: ". . . the enemy must either ingloriously fly or come out from behind his defenses and give us battle on our own ground. . . ."[16]

There were recriminations, especially in the XI Corps, which discovered that the rest of the army and most of the country believed that the battle had been lost because of the cowardice of Dutchmen. Howard remarked in general orders to the corps that he could not "fail to notice a feeling of depression on the part of a portion of this corps." He added, perhaps unnecessarily: "Some obloquy has been cast upon us." Carl Schurz reported that the men had had about all they could take, and he appealed vainly to the War Department for justice: "We have been overwhelmed by the army and the press with abuse and insult beyond measure. We have borne as much as human nature can endure."[17]

The corps believed that a great deal of this was directly inspired from army headquarters, and General Schimmelfennig angrily complained that "the most infamous falsehoods" had been given to newspaper correspondents by members of Hooker's own staff. There was so much of this that German-Americans in New York City held a mass meeting to try to clear the corps' name. Among the speakers was General Meagher, who testified that his Irish Brigade had been guarding roads to the rear during the battle and that of the many stragglers he intercepted only a very few spoke with a German accent.[18]

The complaints made by Howard's corps, however, were as nothing compared with the backbiting that went on at the top levels of army command. Most of the corps commanders had had their doubts about Hooker from the beginning, and as they looked back on fumbled battle their doubts became nagging certainties. Couch tried to get the others to join him in asking the President to remove Hooker from his command. Slocum sided with him and went to see Meade about it, and Meade, who was no part of a plotter, replied that he would join in no round robin, although if the President asked him for his opinion he would cheerfully give it. Members of the heavy-handed Committee on the Conduct of the War came down to ask questions and express opinions, and the administration did not help matters much by taking clumsy soundings to see if there was a general present who would care to take Hooker's place. Nobody seemed to want the spot, but word of the overtures got around.

Sedgwick and Hooker had an angry argument about the way Sedgwick had handled his part of the battle, and Hooker and Meade quarreled over whether Meade had voted in favor of retreating. General Gibbon wrote that Hooker was looking for a scapegoat. Hooker's own opinion may have been reflected in the comment of his chief engineer, Brigadier General G. K. Warren, who wrote home that "our great weakness, in my opinion, is the incompetency of many of our corps commanders." Couch finally notified the President that he would not serve under Hooker any longer and asked to be relieved of his command. His request was granted and he went north to command home-guard levies in Pennsylvania, and command of the II Corps went to Hancock. Hancock himself, famous throughout the army for his vigorous cursing, had found himself shocked at Hooker's boast that God Almighty could not keep him from beating the Rebels, and he piously wrote to his wife that "success cannot come to us through such profanity."[19]

One would suppose that the army was in a bad way. It had had a humiliating defeat which seemed all the worse because of the high hopes that had preceded it. The men had thought they were really going to win this one, and one soldier asserted that "in no other battle of the East did the Union troops have so much confidence in their leader or so strong a hope of winning a complete and decisive victory."[20] The letdown had been sharp, casualties had been heavy, more than twenty thousand of the short-term troop had been paid off and had gone home, one full army corps was suffering from a slow burn because everybody considered it a set of cowards, and the principal generals were visible and violently at odds with their commander. It seemed likely that all of the old cliques and officer-corps antagonisms would begin making mischief once again, and army morale might have been thought ruined beyond repair.

Yet actually the army was not in a bad way at all. It was not in the least demoralized, and if it was downhearted, the mood did not persist for long. A brigade historian wrote that the men were "puzzled to know how they had been defeated without fighting a decisive battle," but there was nothing remotely like the sullen discouragement that had followed Fredericksburg. Old-timers might have longed for a return of McClellan, in the mood of a middle-aged man yearning for the golden time of his early youth—a surgeon in the 20th Massachusetts noted that "the whole army cries for 'Little Mac' "—yet there was no particular loss of regard for Joe Hooker. It is possible that some of the blame for defeat which the men might have directed at Hooker was diverted in such a way that it came down on the ill-starred members of the XI Corps instead. General Schimmelfennig probably knew what he was talking about when he accused Hooker's staff of planting stories with the press. But the point is that the self-confidence which the army had reacquired during the winter was not diminished.[21]

Indeed, in a remarkably short time the army settled back into its old routine. There were drills and inspections and reviews—the weather was getting hot now, and by special dispensation drills and fatigues were held to a minimum around the middle of the day—and one morning Birney's division of the III Corps was paraded to witness a fancy ceremony. Birney had devised a new decoration called the Kearny Medal, a bronze Maltese cross to be given to enlisted men for valor, and this day the division stood at attention while the medal was pinned on the blouse of little Annie Etheridge, who had served hot coffee and cheered gunners under fire at Chancellorsville. On this same day the Iron Brigade also was paraded, and its 24th Michigan proudly came up to the line wearing for the first time the distinctive black hats which the brigade had made so famous, black hats turned up at one side, with a jaunty feather sticking out above the curled brim.[22]

Along the banks of the Rappahannock the Yankee pickets were carrying on trade and exchanging half-amiable insults with the Confederates across the water. The 46th New York, sending a little sailboat across, freighted it with a letter inviting the Rebels to come over for a visit in the evening. The letter closed with the words: "In the hope that Jeff Davis and Abe Lincoln will give us peace, we send our respects." One day a Confederate picket yelled across to a group of Federals: "Say, you Yanks, why didn't you shoot General Hill? He stood right here half an hour ago." The Federals replied that they were sorry to have missed a chance; they had seen him but supposed he was simply an officer of the guard and not worth shooting. One Confederate, asking loudly, "Where's Joe Hooker now?" was tartly informed: "He's gone to Stonewall Jackson's funeral."[23]

It was noticed that where New England troops had camped any stream or brook was sure to be improved by little dams and sluices, with water wheels made out of shingles and old fruit cans spinning merrily in the sunlight. A Maine regiment which was sent off on picket duty left little signs by its camp asking people not to disturb these grownups' toys because the owners would be back before long, and a colonel of regulars looked wonderingly at the display by a brook in a New Hampshire camp and meditated aloud that only mechanically minded Yankees would behave so.[24]

Four days after the battle the colonel of the 7th Wisconsin sent a note to his adjutant:

"There is a large crowd of soldiers in the grove below, engaged in the interesting game called chuck-a-luck. My chaplain is running his church on the other side of me, but chuck-a-luck has the largest crowd. I think this unfair, as the church runs only once a week but the game goes on daily. I suggest that one or the other of the parties be dispersed."[25]

Clearly enough, this was the climate of March and April all over again, and except for the new graves and the charred bodies in the Wilderness, and the thousands of maimed men in the hospitals, it was nearly as though Chancellorsville had not been fought. The battle had been almost totally devoid of results. The army had been defeated once more, but now, for the first time, the defeat did not seem to count.

A good deal has been said and written about the army's retreat to Falmouth in the rain after Hooker brought it back to the north side of the river. That retreat had in truth been a dreary affair, and the occasion is not referred to fondly in any memoirs or regimental histories. Yet there had been a different tone to it from that of the bleak marches that had followed earlier defeats. This time, as the tired men came back into camp, the early arrivals turned to line the roads and watch the rest come in, and the watchers and the marchers called out derisive greetings to each other: "Here's another played-out set". . . "Go lay down in the mud". . . "Turn out the provost guard and pick up those stragglers". . . "There comes the home guard". . . "Go boil your shirt."[26] That kind of interchange can mask practically any emotional state imaginable except a state of dejection and despair. It was as a staff officer remarked: "The Army of the Potomac was no band of schoolgirls. . . . With the elation of victory or the depression of defeat, amidst the hardest toils of the campaign, under unwelcome leadership, at all times and under all circumstances, they were a reliable army still."[27]

The army had come of age. It was a professional army now in all but name. It was built around the volunteers of 1861, who had come in singing songs and dreaming dreams, and the songs had come down to camp doggerel and the dreams had been knocked out and the men were old soldiers now, proud with the pride of soldiers, able to do their jobs no matter who led them or how he did it. It was observed that now and then the waiting ranks would set up a cheer for some particular regiment or brigade. The cheers might simply be in welcome to old friends who had not been seen for some time, but more often they were the soldiers' spontaneous tribute to troops which they recognized as good fighting men. On this return from Chancellorsville Berdan's sharpshooters, who tended to be a rather hard-bitten lot, set up a mighty shout when the Iron Brigade came marching in. As it happened, the Iron Brigade had not been in action at Chancellorsville, while Berdan's men had been pretty thoroughly shot up, but something about the bearing of the Western soldiers made the sharpshooters toss their caps and yell—the Army of the Potomac, giving and receiving the only accolade it would ever know or care for. Long after the war one of Berdan's officers wistfully remembered the sight of "that famed body of troops marching up that long muddy hill, unmindful of the pouring rain but full of life and spirit, with steady step, filling the entire roadway, their big black hats and feathers conspicuous." To remember it, he said, filled him with "the pride of looking upon a model American volunteer."[28]

FIVE

Lincoln Comin' Wid His Chariot

1. THE GRAPES OF WRATH

OUT IN front there were the eternal lines of weary men in dusty blue plodding through the sunlight into heavy mist and curling smoke, and it seemed that the only reality was the hard reality of combat and death. Yet in the background there was a great force adrift, and the future was beginning to take shape. No man could say what the future would be like, yet now and then strange hints of it seemed to come down the tainted winds. The gunfire and the shouts of men in battle and the unimaginable cruelties and agonies of war seemed to lift at times to permit a glimpse of something new and incalculable, bought with the lives of men who would never see it. A young soldier who was commissioned an officer in one of the new Negro regiments this spring heard his men singing one of the hackneyed war songs:

> Yes, we'll rally round the flag, boys, we'll rally once again,
> Shouting the battle cry of freedom!

and he wrote that he had never before heard such singing.[1] These colored men were not just repeating the empty words of a good marching tune. They were putting everything they had into a song that had suddenly taken on enormous meaning, and words like "the flag" and "freedom" had become revolutionary, the keys to a great future.

It might be, indeed, that this idea of freedom was something that had no limits whatever. It might begin as a limited thing, simple legal freedom from purchase and sale for the poor black man, and in the end it would become freedom for white men too, freedom also for all of the unguessed potentialities of an amazing country that had hardly begun to dream of its own destiny.

Thoughtful men occasionally talked as if they saw a gulf opening beneath their feet. Gideon Welles was as sober a conservative as party politics could bring to a president's cabinet, yet he saw something that spring as he meditated that privateering and support for blockade-runners might yet bring England into a war with America. Such a war, he wrote, could have unlooked-for consequences. Instead of being a conventional war it could bring about "an uprising of the nations." He talked with Lincoln about it, and in his diary he stated his belief: "If war is to come it looks to me as of a magnitude greater than the world has ever experienced—as it would eventuate in the upheaval of nations, the overthrow of governments and dynasties. The sympathies of the mass of mankind would be with us rather than with the decaying dynasties and the old effete governments."[2]

Wendell Phillips, the gadfly of abolition, was on the rostrum that spring crying out that the power which dwelt in this idea must be used as a telling weapon. He saw the war between North and South as something infinitely portentous, not confined to one continent:

"Wherever caste lives, wherever class power exists, whether it be on the Thames or on the Seine, whether on the Ganges or on the Danube, there the South has an ally. . . . Never until we welcome the Negro, the foreigner, all races as equals, and melted together in a common nationality, hurl them all at despotism, will the North deserve triumph or earn it at the hands of a just God."[5]

These were brave words, and they went farther than Phillips himself imagined. His catalogue of the rivers where caste existed was impressive but incomplete. He might have extended it: the Thames and the Seine, the Ganges and the Danube—and, very much closer home, the rolling Susquehanna as well.

Caste and despotism existed along the Susquehanna, and in 1863 some of the people most affected were rising to demand that something be done about them. They were not putting their demand in very intelligible words, for they were ignorant Irish immigrants and they had no better idea than anyone else of the ultimate meaning of a war for freedom. So confused were the times, and so mixed were the values which men believed they were serving, that these men actually seemed to be allies of the Confederacy, and patriotic Northerners tended to look upon them as traitors. But if their intent was not especially clear, either to themselves or to anyone else, they were at least speaking in a language that could not be ignored—the language of riot and gunfire and murder done in hot blood, so that the anthracite field of eastern Pennsylvania seemed to be aflame in that spring of 1863.

On the surface, all that was happening was that the men who worked in the anthracite mines did not like either the war or the military draft and were going to extremes of violence to make their dislike known. Yet it is clear enough that the discontent went deeper than that. It went all the way down, as a matter of fact, to the injustices which the growing industrialization of a lusty, heedless country was inflicting on men who, if they did not look out, would soon be ground down into a submerged caste as unfortunate as any submerged caste along Mr. Phillips's rivers overseas. The Pennsylvania anthracite region, in short, was having a bad case of labor trouble, and since labor trouble was something relatively new in a nation which still believed itself to be a land of small farmers, it went more or less unrecognized and the authorities considered that they were dealing with a set of malignant Copperheads.

The anthracite area included principally Lackawanna, Luzerne, and Schuylkill counties. Population had mushroomed in the years just before the war, and production of anthracite had gone up from a scant million tons a year in 1840 to eight and one half million tons in 1860. Of protective legislation, mine safety regulations and the like there was not a vestige, and the clerk of the Schuylkill mining district was presently to write of "the danger to be encountered working in deep mines" in which "standing gas, decay of timber, the absence of ventilation, and standing water" made working conditions perilous. Within recent memories, mines had been small and each mine owner knew personally his handful of workers and was on friendly terms with them. The small holdings had coalesced into large ones, mutual acquaintance and understanding had vanished, and the average miner knew the owner of his mine only through the "ticket boss," who checked the cars of mined coal and so determined, impersonally, how much each man's earnings would be. Competition for labor had disappeared, and large numbers of penniless Irish were imported to work in the diggings. The era of company housing had arrived—very bad housing, most of it, with one room downstairs and two above, furnished with bedsteads made of square timbers by company carpenters, a rough table, and a few benches, with an open grate built into one wall for cooking and heating. Along with company housing came the company store, run in such a way that many miners received no pay whatever for their work. (A full decade after the war a Pennsylvania legislator felt it necessary to introduce a bill to require coal companies to pay their workers in cash.)[4]

On top of all of this there were acute racial and religious difficulties. The miners were Irish and the mine bosses, to a man, were English, Welsh, or Scotch. The grip of the Know-Nothing movement was upon the land, and "No Irish Need Apply" signs were common in city employment offices. Native Americans looked upon the Irish miners as an uncouth lawless group given to fighting and drunkenness, the squalor of their existence somehow a national characteristic rather than the end product of bad pay and worse housing. The miners had never been received into the community. They were outsiders and they were made to feel that way, an oppressed class, exploited in every conceivable way by a country which seemed determined to convince them that they did not belong. As a recent student of the case has remarked: "The situation in the Pennsylvania anthracite coal fields in the middle of the nineteenth century was such, in short, that industrial strife and disorder were to be anticipated. If one sought to improvise a combination of factors calculated to produce trouble, he could hardly hope to improve on the example offered by eastern Pennsylvania."[5]

So here, although he never dreamed of it, was what Wendell Phillips had been talking about. The war had brought all of these pressures to a head and had laid on top of them the exciting idea that freedom was a thing which men in this land would fight and die for. As an inevitable result there was an uprising going on.

It was the draft which touched off the trouble. Plenty of recruits had been obtained from the anthracite area. The 48th Pennsylvania, which was a first-class outfit, was famous as a regiment of Schuylkill County coal miners, and in 1864 in front of Petersburg its miners were to dig the long tunnel which resulted in the famous battle of the crater.[6] It does not appear that the miners' objection to the draft reflected any especial reluctance to fight. Rather, it grew out of deep dissatisfaction with intolerable conditions of life, which made the draft look like one injustice too many. Men were compelled to enroll for the draft. Any man who had three hundred dollars (which no miner had) could buy exemption if his name was called. There was a suspicion that men considered "undesirable" in any mining community by the mine bosses were sure to be called up first, and tales were told of drafted miners being tied to cavalrymen's stirrups and marched off to war willy-nilly. All of the resentment which these Irish immigrants felt because of their second-class status boiled over, and there was bloodshed.[7]

It had begun the previous fall in a little mining town where a crowd of men beat a mine boss to death after an argument about the war. Not long after, in a neighboring town, two hundred miners raided a colliery, beat up the office staff, took possession of the company store, fired shots in the air, and announced that they would really make trouble if the hated store were ever reopened. Mobs visited homes of men supposed to be in sympathy with the draft, hauled them out of bed, and killed them. Organized bands appeared to have complete control over many parts of the anthracite region. A Pennsylvania newspaper asserted that the disturbances were the work of a mysterious secret organization known as the Molly Maguires.

It is very comforting in time of war or other national emergency to be able to see all colors as straight blacks or whites. Secretary Stanton saw things that way, and to him this whole affair was a Copperhead plot in which the emissaries of Jefferson Davis had doubtless been active. But the real difficulty would seem to have been that the miners were trying, somewhat ineptly perhaps, to put on some sort of labor-union organizing drive. There was a slightly vague Workingmen's Benevolent Association somewhere back of that Molly Maguire label; the miners for years had been making fitful efforts to get an effective labor organization started, and in the conditions then prevailing in the coal fields a union had to be both conspiratorial and militant if it hoped to survive. Under all of the talk about Copperheads and traitors, a bitter clash of economic interests is easily discernible. The retail price of coal in the cities had gone sky-high, and there was talk that this was all due to the greed and the violent behavior of the miners. A citizen of Mauch Chunk wrote in outrage that the rioters "dictate the price for their work, and if their employers don't accede they destroy and burn coal breakers, houses, and prevent those disposed from working." As remedies, he demanded that a large military force be sent to the coal fields, that martial law be declared, and that "summary justice be dealt out to these traitors." He also proposed that "protection be afforded to those willing to work."[8]

The civil authorities often appeared to be powerless, or at least in many cases very reluctant to use what powers they did have. General Couch, who was now commanding the military in Pennsylvania, wrote that "the ignorant miners have no fear of God, the state authorities or the Devil," and added that "the Democratic leaders have not the power of burnt flax over them for good." It seemed, indeed, that there was a good deal of sympathy for the miners. Governor Curtin flatly refused to use the state militia to enforce the draft in the coal fields, and in Schuylkill County, where the trouble was worst, it was alleged that the Molly Maguires dominated county politics and had judges and jurors under their thumbs. Couch reported that nothing but a vigorous use of Federal troops would answer.[9] Stanton agreed with him, and various detachments were sent into Pennsylvania. In at least one of these regiments, the 10th New Jersey, the soldiers themselves became sympathetic with the miners, and in the end the regiment's colonel begged the War Department to send his outfit back to the Army of the Potomac before it got entirely out of hand.[10]

The Pennsylvania politician in charge of conscription was A. K. McClure, the editor-politician who had a knack for getting oil onto troubled waters. His draft commissioner for Schuylkill County was another editor named Benjamin Bannan, and when Bannan drew a list of conscripts and notified the men that they must take a train for Harrisburg, where blue uniforms awaited them, the waters became troubled enough to demand McClure's attention. A few of the draftees were farmers, who seemed ready enough to go. Most of them were miners, who announced that they would go under no circumstances whatever. When departure day came a huge mob of miners surrounded the train, turned all of the draftees loose, and completely nullified the whole procedure.

Stanton took fire and sent word that the draft must be enforced "at the point of the bayonet" if necessary. McClure and Curtin begged him to go slow, but Stanton would not cool off, and the regiments showed up next day, ready for business. Then McClure did what hard-pressed public officials so often did in those days: he dumped the whole problem in Lincoln's lap via a carefully worded telegram in cipher.

To him, a day or so later, came a puzzled War Department officer bearing a verbal message from the President. Mr. Lincoln, this officer told McClure, was of course anxious to see the law executed, or—Mr. Lincoln had emphasized this point—at least appear to have been executed. What the President was talking about this officer did not know, but he said that Mr. Lincoln had added: "I think McClure will understand."

McClure did—the ways of Pennsylvania politics bring to a man a breadth of understanding at an early age, and McClure had been at it for a long time—and he went into a huddle with Governor Curtin and Bannan. McClure remembered that there had been enrollment districts which had been able to prove that their quotas were already filled by showing that numbers of their people had enlisted in other cities and hence had not been counted properly. Bannan, who was warning that the draft could not be executed in his region without a bloody fight, slipped away quietly. He returned next day with a big stack of affidavits showing that any number of Schuylkill residents had in fact joined the army in places like Philadelphia, Harrisburg, and where not. McClure solemnly inspected them, agreed that the draft quota had indeed been filled, and revoked the call for conscripts. There was a truce, and the law at least appeard to have been executed.[11]

A bit later the same dodge was worked in reverse. Philadelphia was the great Republican stronghold, and Washington's figures showed that Philadelphia that spring was shy of its quota by three thousand men. McClure got busy again. (He commented long afterward that "there were experienced lightning calculators in those days.") Many persons from other parts of the state had enlisted in Philadelphia and had been properly credited to their own districts. A magic hand passed over the figures, and it immediately became evident that at least three thousand of these men were in fact Philadelphians. This brought no more troops to the Army of the Potomac, but it at least kept the Republicans from losing Philadelphia, which had seemed to be imminent, and all was well.[12]

Philadelphia was symptomatic. There was infinite bewilderment in the land. The beloved Union for which men were dying was, after all, an abstraction, and the Negro, for whom deaths were also being recorded, was an utter social outcast, looked upon in the North with very little more friendship than in the South. From New York to the Mississippi River the average Northern worker had an uneasy fear that emancipation would bring a great horde of low-wage Negroes into the North, to take away the jobs and livelihood of honest white men. Times were not easy. An inflationary boom was on, and prices were going up faster than incomes. This came on top of older troubles which had been building up in America for years.

Here was a land of freedom and plenty, and somehow it had been changing so that many people felt that the freedom was a trifle hollow and the plenty was a myth. Far down below the foundations of society there had for years been a deep potential of unrest, of which the senseless Know-Nothing agitation had had been only a symbol. Long before anyone fired a cannon at Fort Sumter, such dissimilar men as Thaddeus Stevens and John C. Calhoun had warned of the danger of "social convulsion." Stevens himself, a "radical" in the jargon of that day, was in fact a typical Pennsylvania Republican (in the modern sense of the term) on most issues aside from slavery. He was as much a conservative, in his own way, as Calhoun himself, a spokesman for solid established interests. It was precisely men of that kind who had brought this war about, and the war had taken the lid off things. In one sense, the great fight over slavery and the Union had channeled off the resentments which might have produced the convulsion which Stevens and Calhoun had both feared.[13] In another sense, it was giving those resentments an opening. In the incredible last analysis, victory might yet mean that to destroy one kind of slavery was to weaken all other kinds.

Meanwhile men were confused and bewildered, and there were strange eddies and backwashes in the tide of history in 1863. If there was trouble in Pennsylvania there were other troubles all across the Middle West, following a familiar pattern: opposition to the draft, sporadic riots, occasional murders, with the Copperhead leaders tossed about on waves which they supposed they were controlling. What was coming up seems to have been less a will to end the war than a blind, angry determination to make it mean something, even though no one could say just what that something might be. As one perplexed Republican reported, "the people are desirous of some change, they scarcely know what."[14]

In southern Illinois most of the people were recent immigrants from the Southland, and although they were stoutly loyal to the Union they disliked the Negro and refused to fight to end slavery. The 128th Illinois, recruited from that territory, lost nearly all of its members by desertion, the men declaring that "they would lie in the woods until the moss grew on their backs rather than help free the slaves."

So that spring Federal troops went into Illinois, and the 16th Illinois Cavalry, not sharing the anti-Negro sentiments of the 128th, found itself clumping and clanking across Williamson County to quell disturbances and lay the fear upon all Copperheads. They hit the countryfolk with a hard heavy hand. The Union League, newly organized by loyalists as a counterweight to the Knights of the Golden Circle, had been busy sniffing out treason, and it provided the cavalry with long lists of places where deserters were hidden. The regiment split up into platoons which went about the countryside, each with its little list, and the alarm was spread and people took to the woods. A young officer in charge of one of these squads found himself deeply puzzled by the whole business. He had enlisted to fight the Southern Confederacy and here he was, harrying the people of his own state in their own homes, and he wrote, bewildered:

"What were we there for? It is true that they had been harboring and secreting deserters from the Union Army, but for this was their property to be consumed by fire and were they to be marched off to some fort, there to be guarded as prisoners of war?"

It was a poor day, he recorded, when they brought fewer than twenty-five prisoners into camp, but he acknowledged that "such jumping fences, such riding through fields and woods, such searching smokehouses, garrets, barns, and cellars, such hanging men to trees for the purpose of extorting secrets, such breaking up and dispersing courts and grand juries, such foraging"—in plain violation of all law, as he felt—"I never before heard of at any time, in Illinois or any other state."[15]

Thus in Illinois, with barns and hayricks ablaze, and farm folk hiding out in the timber while troopers rode through the cornfields with drawn sabers glinting in the sun. There was also Ohio, and in Ohio there was a man named Clement Laird Vallandigham, until recently a Democratic congressman, who was minded now to become governor of Ohio and to make some use of the discontent and weariness and perplexity born of the war. Vallandigham was a tall handsome man with a politician's too-easy smile, a talent for using words, and a long record of unwavering opposition to the coercion of the South. Barely a month after Lincoln's election Vallandigham had warned a caucus of Ohio's congressional delegation that he would under no circumstances agree to the use of force against the South. Some of those present understood him to threaten war in the North if force should be tried. He was cold, calculating, profoundly ambitious, with a way of expressing himself that sounded self-righteous at times, a man not above appealing to prejudice when it would serve his turn. Early that winter of 1863, as a lame-duck congressman (his district had been gerrymandered to prevent his re-election) he had taunted the Republicans in the House:

"The war for the Union is, in your hands, a most bloody and costly failure. . . . War for the Union was abandoned; war for the Negro openly begun, and with stronger battalions than before. With what success? Let the dead at Fredericksburg and Vicksburg answer." He wanted peace, and peace at once, and he cried: "Ought this war to continue? I answer no—not a day, not an hour. What then? Shall we separate? Again I answer no, no, no!" His program was simple, based upon faith: "Stop fighting. Make an armistice. Accept at once friendly foreign mediation."

Under the surface Vallandigham saw, or at least professed to see, the same specter that had haunted Calhoun and Stevens, and the belief that desperate forces might be let loose by continued war ran under his impassioned sentences like a somber leitmotif: "I see nothing before us but universal political and social revolution, anarchy and bloodshed, compared with which the Reign of Terror in France was a merciful visitation."[16]

So here was Vallandigham, stumping Ohio for the governorship, seeking to capitalize on the people's deep belief that a word should be spoken that would explain this war and give it meaning. Also in Ohio, by the oddest chance, was Major General Ambrose E. Burnside, and his path was about to cross Vallandigham's.

After his ineffectual effort to purge the high command of the Army of the Potomac, Burnside had been quietly shelved. His offer to resign his commission had not been accepted, and he had been assigned to command the Department of the Ohio, which included the states of Ohio, Kentucky, Indiana, and Illinois. There was no great number of troops in his department and not much fighting was going on there, and the assumption seems to have been that even this well-meaning author of misfortune could hardly bumble his way into any very serious trouble now.

But Burnside was an intensely loyal man, and the wave of unrest that was going across the land troubled him. Like Stanton, he saw things in unshaded blacks and whites, and it seemed to him that a great many things which were being said and done in his department smacked strongly of outright treason. He began to issue restrictive orders, prohibiting the citizens from keeping or bearing arms, and placing limits on the right to criticize the military policy of the administration. He climaxed these at last by promulgating General Order Number 38, which stated flatly, if somewhat clumsily, that "the habit of declaring sympathy for the enemy will not be allowed in this department. Persons committing such offenses will be at once arrested, with a view to being tried . . . or sent beyond our lines into the lines of their friends." To make it perfectly clear, the order added that "it must be distinctly understood that treason, expressed or implied, will not be tolerated in this department."

Having said this, Burnside appointed a military commission to try any persons who might offend against General Order Number 38 and waited to see what would happen next.[17]

What would happen next would be a speech by Vallandigham, who was opening his political campaign with a big meeting in the town of Mount Vernon on May 1, the same day the Army of the Potomac was gathering around the Chancellorsville crossroads, with Hooker feeling the first chill wind of doubt and with Meade wondering how the bottom of a hill could be held if the top was untenable. It appears that Vallandigham accepted Burnside's order as a challenge, and a huge crowd was on hand to hear him respond to it. American flags floated from the tops of hickory poles (emblems of the Democracy ever since Andrew Jackson's day), and there was a great horse-drawn float carrying thirty-four pretty girls, who represented the thirty-four states of the whole Union. It was noticed that many men in the crowd wore in their lapels the emblems which had given the anti-war Democrats their name of Copperhead—copper heads cut from pennies and mounted on pins or clasps. In the crowd, lounging close to the platform with pencils and notebooks, were two officers of Burnside's command prepared to take down Vallandigham's words.

These officers did not give Burnside a very coherent account of the speech, contenting themselves with taking down stray phrases and sentences, but with the huge crowd cheering him on, Vallandigham spread himself. He talked sarcastically of "King Lincoln," specifically denounced General Order Number 38, and repeated all of his familiar arguments, seeing the war as a step toward despotism and demanding an immediate peace. It was a wild, fire-eating speech, coming tolerably close to an outright declaration of sympathy for the Confederacy, and when Burnside's officers got back to Cincinnati they gave the general notes which ruffled his whiskers. Reading them, Burnside concluded that he had an open-and-shut case. Without bothering to discuss the ins and outs of the matter with anybody, Burnside issued an order for Vallandigham's arrest.[18]

A night later an officer on Burnside's staff collected a company of infantry and took a special train from Cincinnati to Dayton, which was where Vallandigham lived. A little after two in the morning—graveyard watch, town silent as the tomb soldiers' footsteps echoing off the cobbles of quiet streets—heavy hands beat loudly on the door of Vallandigham's house. From an upstairs window the orator asked what was wanted and was told to open up, men had come to arrest him. A revolver was fired into the air, and Vallandigham lifted his voice to yell, "Asa! Asa! Asa!" into the night, this call being the alarm signal for anti-war Democrats. Musket butts smashed in the door, and the officer and a squad of soldiers went to Vallandigham's bedroom and told him he had just time to get dressed and catch a train. Protesting bitterly, and dressing the while, Vallandigham went with them, and that morning he was lodged in a military prison in Cincinnati. In Dayton an angry mob sacked the office of a Republican newspaper, starting a fire that burned out several non-partisan business establishments, and from his prison cell Vallandigham issued statements denouncing the author and the manner of his arrest and asserting: "I am here in a military bastille for no other offense than my political opinions."

This was true enough as far as it went, but the military were in control, and on May 6 Vallandigham went on trial before Burnside's military commission, accused of violating General Order Number 38. The two officers who had taken notes testified for the prosecution: Vallandigham had denounced the war as "wicked, cruel, and unnecessary" and had said in so many words that it was not being waged to preserve the Union but "for the purpose of crushing out liberty and erecting a despotism." He had unquestionably violated Burnside's order, if that order had any validity.

Vallandigham did not think it had any, and he refused to recognize the commission or to plead his own cause, contenting himself with summoning one witness, another Democratic congressman, the widely known anti-war man S. S. Cox, who had been among the speakers at Mount Vernon but whose remarks had been somewhat less inflammatory. Vallandigham was returned to his prison cell, and a lawyer went to the United States Circuit Court to demand a writ of habeas corpus.[19]

Rightly or wrongly, writs of habeas corpus did not run in this case, and the court refused to intervene. So on May 16 the military commission announced that it had found Vallandigham guilty of violating General Order Number 38 by publicly expressing "sympathy for those in arms against the government of the United States, and declaring disloyal sentiments and opinions with the object and purpose of weakening the power of the government in its efforts to suppress an unlawful rebellion." It sentenced him to be imprisoned for the duration of the war. Burnside promptly confirmed the sentence, ordering the man confined in Fort Warren at Boston.

Up to now Vallandigham had been just another candidate for the Democratic nomination for governor of Ohio. By act of Burnside he immediately became a martyr, nationally famous, and the land erupted with mass meetings of furious Democrats denouncing military despotism. Vallandigham's nomination for the Ohio governorship was a foregone conclusion. Worse yet, it was equally certain that the Democratic party in Ohio—and possibly everywhere else in the North—would now pass firmly into the hands of the faction that wanted to make immediate peace with the Confederacy. And this mess was dropped on Lincoln's desk while Lincoln was still trying to digest the bad news from Chancellorsville.

Unfortunately Burnside was not yet out of ammunition. Having struck a blow at treason in Ohio, he looked over into Illinois, where in addition to Southern-born residents who hid deserters and supported the Knights of the Golden Circle there was a pestiferous newspaper, the Chicago *Times,* which had long been saying in print exactly the sort of thing Vallandigham had said on the Mount Vernon platform. Burnside never had been able to tell a good strategic move from a bad one, and he was always fated to make a defect rather than a virtue out of the fact that he never knew when he had bitten off more than he could chew. Early on the morning of June 3, by his express order, cavalrymen rode up a Chicago street and mounted guard at the door of the *Times* office, and an hour or so later two companies of infantry from Camp Douglas came marching into the place. They took the building over, stopped the presses, and prevented further publication of the paper.

Thus after suppressing freedom of speech Burnside had suppressed freedom of the press, and it was up to Lincoln to say whether it was going to be that kind of war from now on.

Lincoln moved warily. Both actions had been taken without his knowledge, and the Vallandigham case was by far the hotter potato of the two. It may be that as he cast about for an expedient the President remembered Burnside's earlier statement that offenders against General Order Number 38 might be sent "beyond our lines into the lines of their friends." In any case, that finally seemed to strike him as a solid idea, and he canceled that part of the military commission's verdict which ordered Vallandigham imprisoned. Instead he had him sent down under guard to General Rosecrans, who was holding the line in front of Murfreesboro, Tennessee, and one morning not long after that a squad of soldiers escorted the orator out into the desolate no man's land between Union and Confederate lines and turned him over to the Confederacy, to do with as the Confederacy might choose. Suppression of the Chicago *Times* was revoked outright, the troops were removed, and Burnside was warned to arrest no more civilians and shut down no more newspapers without prior authorization from Washington.

The Confederacy hardly knew what to do with its new guest. He flitted crosscountry to Charleston, South Carolina, his position sufficiently embarrassing both to himself and to his hosts, and eventually he took a ship for Canada. Before he sailed he found time to hold a quiet conversation with a representative of Jefferson Davis's government, in which he is alleged to have betrayed an inner fear—that the Confederacy might yet fold up, leaving Vallandigham without a cause. The Northern peace party, he insisted, was on the climb, and if the South could just hold out for another year everything would be fine, as the Democrats would then "sweep the Lincoln dynasty out of political existence." He offered one curious piece of advice which was totally ignored but which might profitably have been listened to: Whatever happens, do not again invade the North, because if you do all parties there will unite to throw you out and Lincoln's hand will be so strengthened that he will be able to go on with the war with new vigor.[20] (Lee was perfecting his plans for a march into Pennsylvania, and farther west John Hunt Morgan was marshaling his troopers for a dash across the Ohio, and it was as if this leader of the Copperheads was crying, Don't take our Copperhead uprisings so seriously. We won't stick if it comes to real fighting; we are men of politics and fine words and that is all we can ever be.)

In Canada, a martyr-in-absentia, Vallandigham issued statements and exhortations to the faithful in Ohio, and when the Ohio Democrats held their state convention in Columbus in June they drew an enthusiastic crowd of forty thousand people. For the balance of the summer Lincoln was painstakingly explaining his course in regard to Vallandigham's arrest, sounding at times, perhaps, rather more like a clever lawyer than a statesman but at least explaining, and leaving one difficult question for the opposition to answer as best it could: "Must I shoot a simple-minded soldier boy who deserts and not touch a hair of the wily agitator who induces him to desert?"[21]

For Lincoln was shooting soldier boys that spring, and desertion was no longer being treated as a minor fault. The V Army Corps was drawn up in an open field one day, solid masses of bronzed veterans grouped around three sides of an open square, tattered flags motionless above them. One of the soldiers remembered afterward:

"The impressive silence was not broken by a single sound. Each line of soldiers looked more like the section of a vast machine than a line composed of living men. The silence was suddenly and sadly broken by the sounds of approaching music—not the quick, inspiring strains with which we were so familiar, but a measured, slow and solemn dirge, whose weird, sorrowful notes were poured forth like the moanings of lost spirits. Not a soldier spoke, but every eye was turned in the direction from which came the sad and mournful cadences, and we saw the procession."

First came a band playing the "Funeral March." Then came sixty men from the provost guard, spick-and-span in dress uniforms, rifles at the shoulder. After them were four soldiers carrying a black coffin, followed by a condemned deserter in blue pants and white shirt, a guard on either side of him; then four more men with another coffin, followed by another prisoner, and another detachment with another coffin, and so on—five condemned deserters in all, each preceded by his coffin, with a final detachment from the provost guard bringing up the rear. The procession came to the open side of the square, where five graves had been dug. A coffin was put on the ground before each grave, and each prisoner sat on the end of his coffin. Black blindfolds were put on the prisoners, thousands of men looking on in utter silence, and then the chaplains came up beside the condemned men for a final word and a prayer. The chaplains retired, and a firing squad of twelve men took post facing each prisoner, one blank charge in every twelve rifles, so that any member of a firing squad might later, if it comforted him, think that perhaps he himself had not actually killed anyone. An officer stepped out, brisk and businesslike, sword hooked up at his side, and the great silence was broken by his thin cry: "Ready—aim—*fire!*" And the thing was done, five bleeding bodies lay across the coffins, and the band piped up a quickstep while the soldiers marched off the field.[22]

That was the spring when words were no good in America. The war had given the country problems for which the past offered no guide—problems, indeed, which grew out of the total explosion of the shell which the past had built around human institutions—and men were not going to talk their way out of them. It was what they did that was going to count. A musket butt could smash in a man's door in the dead of night, troopers with drawn sabers might drag farmers off to a prison camp under a prairie moon, veterans of great battles might have to stand in formal ranks to see deserters executed, and what it all added up to could be told only after men had acted.

Yet there was an immense vitality at work. In their reaction to war-weariness and defeat both the people and the government were showing signs of a new temper. Here was no inert resignation to despair. Trouble was being met head-on now—stupidly, in some cases, brutally in others, but at least squarely. The country was no longer numb. Slowly and with infinite pain, strength was being gathered, and the danger soon would be that the ultimate answer might be sought in strength alone. The Republican stalwart, War Governor Buckingham of Connecticut, was exultantly telling his legislature to get on with the war: "Let the retribution be so terrible that future generations shall not dare to repeat the crime." The final tragedy would occur if retribution alone should become the answer.

The word could not be spoken yet. The grapes of wrath were being tramped out, and there was a great clamor of many voices. There would have to be, finally, an hour of decision, with the uproar coming to its own terrible climax. After that, if anyone could understand and speak for the myriad people who were crying their complaints, a voice might be heard.

2. GLORY! GLORY! HALLELUJAH!

Things were looking up, and it seemed that the crisis had been passed, and the newspaper editor took up his pen and wrote his jubilation for all the world to read.

"Aladdin with his wonderful lamp could scarcely have worked a more magical change," he announced. "All honor, we say, to the men who have battled long and bravely to secure this consummation—who have stood up in the dark days of the enterprise and pressed onward, through the most discouraging difficulties, until their efforts have been finally crowned with glorious success!"

The editor was a loyal Pennsylvanian, editor of the Crawford County *Democrat,* writing in the very middle of the Civil War, but he was not talking about the progress of the national arms, the suppression of Copperheads, or the state of the war for union and freedom. Instead he was being inspired by the fact that a new railroad line had pushed its way into the heart of the Pennsylvania oil fields, and what he was growing most lyrical about was the sight of half a dozen locomotives all puffing at once, long trains of cars laden with oil barrels waiting in the yards, a brand-new brick refinery, a handsome hotel, many new dwelling houses, the ensemble now visible "where, but a few months since, stood the primeval forest." This was in the town of Corry, which in a short time had mushroomed from nothing at all to 10,000 inhabitants and a $12,000,000 annual business. At Meadville, the editor saw further marvels, including a new depot with a 327-foot train shed, and a fine hotel "which has brought to this little city of the west the luxury and magnificence of New York living." He paid his respects to "the old fogies who have imagined that our town was finished and should be fenced in," and he announced unhesitatingly that "a new era of prosperity is about to dawn upon us."[1]

The editor was quite right. Prosperity was at hand, for Meadville or Corry and for all the rest of the North, and it might seem that the great news of the day was not so much the progress of the armies as the miracle that was taking place behind the lines. Pennsylvania was having an oil boom, with a new product and a new technology coming up to provide wealth and employment that had not previously existed. (In 1859 oil production was a scant 84,000 gallons; three years later it had gone up to 128,000,000, the cheap kerosene lamp was beginning to displace candles and whale oil, and a pious young businessman named John D. Rockefeller was watching attentively.) Yet this new industry was only one of many, and possibly the year of jubilee was at hand. All across the North a tremendous transformation was taking place, and if an editor babbled about magic and Aladdin's lamp, it was hardly surprising. The country was on its way with a rush and a roar, gaining new strength almost by geometrical progression, and perhaps the war was a spare-time venture, with most of the country's attention fixed on more important matters.

(General Robert E. Lee was beginning skillfully to move toward the upper Rappahannock, concealing the shift behind a show of strength along the hills back of Fredericksburg, and Jeb Stuart was assembling the largest cavalry corps the Confederacy ever saw on the open hills and fields near Brandy Station, preparing for a hard thrust into the North. His equilibrium regained, Hooker watched closely and prepared countermoves, and men began to see the prospect of a great climactic battle on Northern soil.)

In the West the wagon trains rolled across the frontier without a halt. The same Eastern newspapers that printed news from the fighting fronts announced that interested parties could obtain maps of the Western regions at the front office, and much was printed about the best routes to the new mining fields of Nevada and Colorado, of Idaho and Montana—great names now, as important in their way as names like Fredericksburg and Chancellorsville. Every day from twenty-five to one hundred wagons were ferried across the Missouri at Council Bluffs, and on the Iowa side the road was usually packed for half a mile or more with wagons waiting their turn. One man noted a solid string of twelve hundred wagons on the road leading west from Omaha, and a traveler in Kansas reported that he met five hundred wagons every day bound for Colorado and California. Some of the men who made this westward migration were frankly anxious to get beyond the reach of the army draft, yet the army lost little. The country had men and riches to spare; it could fight a great war and at the same time open a wilderness to settlement, and the government was actually encouraging the move by giving away, free, 160-acre farms to anyone who would take the trouble to occupy and improve the land. (It gave away two and one half million acres to homesteaders during the war years.)[2]

The farm belt had been drained of men of military age. In one Wisconsin village which contained 250 men of voting age, 111 had gone into the army, and in an Illinois rural township 117 of 147 men liable to the draft had volunteered. Yet the farm states were far more populous than when the war began, and farm production had increased beyond imagination. In the cities there were new factories building reapers, mowers, revolving horse rakes, two-horse cultivators, rotary spaders, grain drillers, and other appliances, and between the immigrants and the new machinery the lost labor of the volunteers simply did not matter. Like the Pennsylvania editor, men who took time to look about them were impressed with the sense that a prodigious change was taking place. The president of the Illinois Agricultural Society wrote ecstatically:

"Look over these prairies and observe everywhere the life and activity prevailing. See the railroads pressed beyond their capacity with the freights of our people; the metropolis of the state rearing its stately blocks with a rapidity almost fabulous, and whitening the northern lakes with the sails of its commerce; every smaller city, town, village, and hamlet within our borders all astir with improvement; every factory, mill, and machine shop running with its full complement of hands; the hum of industry in every household; more acres of fertile land under culture, fuller granaries and more prolific crops than ever before; in short, observe that this state and this people of Illinois are making more rapid progress in population, development, wealth, education, and in all the arts of peace than in any former period, and then realize, if you can, that all this has occurred and is occurring in the midst of a war the most stupendous ever prosecuted among men."[3]

Traffic on the Great Lakes was booming. Passenger travel had declined, and many of the passenger boats had been dismantled so that their engines could be installed in freighters, but these freighters were carrying a huge trade. The same Civil War which saw naval warfare revolutionized by the introduction of ironclads saw also a revolution in Great Lakes traffic. Iron steamers were coming in, the canal at the Soo had been opened, and the iron mines of upper Michigan were sending more and more ore down to the lower lakes. The first year's shipment of ore, shortly before the war, had amounted to a mere 132 tons; by the middle of the war ore was coming down to Cleveland at 235,000 tons a year, to be smelted there or to be sent on by rail to Pittsburgh, which was creating its characteristic pillar of smoke against the sky.[4]

For the transportation industry, 1863 was the most prosperous year in history. Hundreds of locomotives and thousands of freight cars had been built since the war began. The Pittsburgh foundries that turned out guns and armor and mortars for the military were also busy with castings for the locomotive manufacturers, with machinery for iron mines and gold mines, with equipment for the oil refineries, with the production of railroad rails, with countless other items needed by an industrialized nation.

At Washington the Patent Office was active. Americans were inventing things in these war years at a greater rate than ever before, and while some of these had to do with war goods, most of them had nothing to do with the war but were aimed strictly at civilian wants. There were new patents for passenger elevators, steam fans for restaurants, milk-condensing machinery, steam printing presses, flypaper, fountain pens, roller skates, dredges, washing machines, and heaven knew what else.[5] With so many men gone in the army, there was naturally an emphasis on labor-saving equipment, but a heavy flood of immigration from Europe was coming in without ceasing, so that the population increased steadily month by month despite the loss in camps and on battlefields. No fewer than 800,000 immigrants arrived during the war years, bringing with them something like $400,000,000 in cash, and if the war was costing the unheard-of sum of two millions a day, there would be no trouble about paying for it.

The export trade was thriving. New York merchants had been panicky when the war began, remembering that two thirds of the export trade normally was in cotton and wondering how this deficit would ever be met. With the war in full stride they forgot their worries. Manufactured goods went overseas. One New York exporter, in the first three years of the war, sent $800,000 worth of sewing machines to Liverpool, and a New York merchant exulted that Yankee clocks "are ticking all over England." Most important of all, there was wheat. England and Europe had had drought, and crops were down. Civil War America was raising wheat, corn, and hogs as never before, and England's purchases of American wheat and flour increased prodigiously over the pre-war level. English factory hands were idle because Southern cotton could not be imported, and in Richmond men still believed that eventually this pressure would bring England in on the side of the Confederacy. What they overlooked was that while England could get along somehow without American cotton, it could not under any circumstances get along now without American wheat. Back of the export figures lay that solid fact which in the end was to make British intervention impossible—a fact which the South could not even see but which was a force as mighty for the Union as an army with banners.[6]

(In Richmond, Vice-President Stephens was starting off under a flag of truce, hoping to get to Washington to present proposals for peace. It was believed that he would reach Washington while Lee reached Pennsylvania, and that the irresistible pressure of the Army of Northern Virginia on a North undermined by Copperheads would compel the Lincoln government to talk to him and to offer acceptable terms. One-legged Dick Ewell, perkily riding his horse with a peg leg sticking out at an angle, was leading Confederate troops on the road of invasion, and the only man in his outfit who had ever heard of a rocky Pennsylvania knoll named Culp's Hill was a young fellow who used to live there.)[7]

Railroads and shipping, iron ore and wheat, patents and immigrants—the North was exploding with new strength and energy. A sober man of business in New York reviewed the war boom a few months later and found it unlike anything that had ever happened before.

"There is a mania abroad," he wrote. "There are thousands of new schemes, and new companies, forming almost every day; and although many of them prove failures, yet there is one remarkable fact connected with them, differing entirely from those speculations in years gone by. . . . Men are not now going to banks and getting notes discounted that have been endorsed by neighbors. The fact is the people have got the money and they are looking about to see what to do with it. These companies are organizing for the very purpose, and most of them are honestly intending to develop the material interests in the country, and to this end hundreds of millions of dollars in the last four years have been devoted."[8]

There was money to be made, and a young officer in the Army of the Potomac was writing in wonder about "my country, hardly feeling this draft upon its resources, and growing richer every day."[9] It was noteworthy that the richest fields for money-making were no longer, as in the past, merchandising, shipping, and real estate speculation. The big money now was in manufacturing, in mining, and—as an inescapable by-product—in the manipulation of stocks. The factory system had arrived full blast. The sewing machine, coming in just in time to make it possible to meet enormous army orders for uniforms, had created a vast new ready-made-clothing business, and 100,000 people were employed by this trade in New York alone. Textile factories were consuming, among other things, 200,000,000 pounds of wool annually and were making fabulous profits. One manufacturer reported that he was making $2,000 a day. A new stitching machine for joining soles to uppers had revolutionized the boot-and-shoe industry, and big factories were going up in New York and Philadelphia, in Lynn and Danvers and Haverhill. The distilling trade enjoyed a delirious boom, and profits for one fat war year were estimated at $50,000,000. St. Louis (which as a distilling center got a generous slice of that profit) boasted of its new Lindell Hotel, built at a cost of a million and a half, with twenty-seven acres of plastering and thirty-two miles of bell wire. Chicago built eight large packing houses and sixteen smaller ones in a single year. In 1863 alone, Philadelphia put up fifty-seven new factories. A party of 230 Western businessmen was taken on a promotional junket to Portland, Maine, by aggressive city boosters. War-torn America displayed a great new fondness for horse racing, the new tracks in Boston, Chicago, and Washington drawing enormous crowds. Twenty-seven cities built street railways, there was an unprecedented rise in the sale of school textbooks, and fifteen colleges and universities were founded, including such institutions as Vassar, Swarthmore, and Cornell.[10]

In Richmond the Confederacy's chief of ordnance was dolefully noting that the North had thirty-eight arms factories able to turn out nearly 5,000 infantry rifles every day. This, he said, "exhibits a most marked contrast to our own condition," as the South was making only 100 a day. Theoretically, he added, Southern capacity was nearly 300, but skilled workmen were lacking.[11] What nobody was able to see at the moment was that this volume production of weapons with interchangeable parts was teaching Northern industrialists one of the great secrets of mass production.

The New York merchant who had exulted in the prosperity born of the war declared that "the mind staggers as we begin to contemplate the future," and concluded that there was coming to the nation a greatness "which no other country in the world has ever seen." He had reason to talk that way. There had never been anything like this before. Whole generations of growth and development seemed to be crammed into a few years. Here was eternal Yankeeism triumphant, grinning because it was possible to grow rich out of a ruinous war, but here also was ever so much more than that—a dazzling expansion of strength, a welling up of vitality and energy that could create faster than any possible destruction, a tapping of powers so profound that the whole get-rich-quick tribe could not quite reduce them to a mere matter of dollars and cents.

Perhaps it is time to ask what was really going on here, anyway. Had the war already been won, with a doom from beyond the stars pronounced in advance on a rash Confederacy which never really had a chance?

William Tecumseh Sherman saw it so. That grim soldier with the ultra-modern viewpoint had called the turn before the war even began when he warned a Southern friend: "In all history no nation of mere agriculturists ever made successful war against a nation of mechanics. . . . You are bound to fail." Apparently his prophecy was being borne out. This war which was bleeding the Confederacy to absolute exhaustion was making the North stronger than ever before, stronger than men had dreamed possible, stimulating a growth which in a few generations would create the mightiest power in history. A Northern victory, it might seem, was inevitable.

But the war was not over and the war had not yet been won. The war, on the contrary, could very easily be lost, and Robert E. Lee had with him seventy thousand lean and hungry men who would quickly arrange it that way if something were not done about them. If destiny had arrived at a verdict, it was a verdict which could still be reversed. All of the weight of power might lie on one side, yet in actual contemporary fact Northern victory was not in the least certain. The spreading factories and the burdened busy trains and the limitless fields of wheat were not going to appear on the firing line, and it was on the firing line that this affair must finally be settled. Up there, under the muzzles of the guns, there would be living men, as self-centered and as shortsighted and as careless of historical imperatives as any men that ever lived, and in the end it was all going to be up to them. If a general lost his nerve or a brigade lost its head, or if the thousands of obscure young men in dirty, sweat-stained uniforms failed by whatever justifiable margin to come up to the mark, then the riches and the power and the might were phantoms to drift away with the battle smoke as the flags came tumbling down.

It was not going to be easy, either. Lee's men were at their peak. Chancellorsville may have been a delusive victory, yet it had seemed to confirm their jubilant feeling (and Lee's feeling, too, that strong gray man who never once let emotion run away with him) that there was no enemy anywhere whom they could not lick. Jackson was gone, but Longstreet was back, and a division commanded by one George Pickett was beginning the long hike northward to keep a certain engagement that was written, perhaps, in the Doomsday Book. Lee's army was beginning to move northward, and its men stepped off the miles as if they had heard the bell of destiny ringing for them.

In the Army of the Potomac there was no such jubilation. The army had little room for either elation or despondency any more. It had mostly a grim antic humor and a deep hard-bought toughness, and although it would unfurl the colors, strike up the band, and march in step when it passed through a town, it slouched along most of the time without parade or display, hiding whatever it most relied upon under an irreverent and derisive spirit. While it still kept to its camps around Falmouth there was an exchange of prisoners, and there were returned to the army men who had spent months in Southern prison camps, skinny, tattered men who were dirty beyond anything anyone had ever heard of. One of these rejoined his outfit, drew a neat new pile of clothing, and invited his squad to go down to the river with him and scrub the dirt off him—there was so much of it, and it had been there so long, that he was sure he could never do much with it himself. So his friends went down to the river, and everybody stripped and got into the water. The men went to work on him with soap and scrubbing brushes, while his miserable discarded rags went floating off downstream. At last one of the scrubbers wiped away a mound of lather with a sweep of his brush, peered closely at the ex-prisoner's torso, and announced flatly that something was wrong with his skin. The other men looked more closely, agreed, scrubbed some more, and discovered suddenly that the man still wore his undershirt.

The ex-prisoner expressed great pleasure and surprise at this discovery. He had thought, he said, that that undershirt had been lost six months ago, and it was a comfort to him to know that he still had it. As they peeled it off and cast it adrift he asked to be allowed to keep it for a souvenir, but the men hooted loudly and refused to hear of it. . . .[12]

Rumors of the Confederate movement reached camp, and Hooker sent his cavalry up the Rappahannock under orders to cross over and, if possible, see what the Rebels thought they were up to.

Pleasonton had the cavalry now—a stylish little soldier with a pert straw hat and kid gloves and a shifty eye—and he was more of a cavalryman than Stoneman had been, though he was a long way from being Phil Sheridan. His reports were better than his battles, and he gained fame that way. There were those who noticed that he was a good deal of a headquarters operator, but he had close to ten thousand mounted men at his command, and they had learned how to ride and shoot, and in spite of Chancellorsville their morale was high. Pleasonton had some good subordinates, too, most notably a brigadier named John Buford, a solid man who was hard to frighten and who was greatly admired by the men of his division. There were others: harum-scarum Judson Kilpatrick, for instance, a lanky little man with stringy side whiskers; a fantastic mustachioed soldier of fortune, Sir Percy Wyndham from England and the Continent; and a flamboyant hell-for-leather horseman named Goerge Armstrong Custer, who possessed the great basic virtue of liking to fight. All in all, the cavalry corps now was a different outfit from the clumsy, lumbering conglomeration which had been wearing out good horses on Virginia roads earlier in the war.[13]

Pleasonton got his men down to the upper fords of the Rappahannock all unnoticed, and in the mist of an early dawn on June 9 he sent them down to the river to cross with a whoop and a wild splashing gallop. They promptly crumpled up the Confederate outpost line and went careening up from the riverside toward the open fields and knolls around Brandy Station, where Stuart had just been reviewing his own cavalry.

What followed was the biggest cavalry fight of the war—a wild, confused action in which cavalry charged cavalry with sabers swinging, dust clouds rising so thickly that it was hard to tell friend from enemy, and the rule was to cut hard at the nearest face and ride on fast. For once in his life Stuart was taken by surprise. A vicious fire fight developed in the meadows near a little country church, where dismounted troopers of the 8th Illinois Cavalry fired their carbines so fast that some of the weapons burst, and a flanking column went thundering up a side road and came within an inch of capturing Fleetwood Hill, where Stuart had his headquarters tents. In the final nick of time Stuart got his squadrons back, and there were charge and countercharge all up and down the Fleetwood slopes, Confederate troopers riding through a battery of Yankee horse artillery and cutting down the gunners, and the air was full of dust and the thunder of pounding hoofs and the clang of steel and the sickening sound of head-long columns crashing bodily into one another.

By the narrowest margin Stuart's men held the hill. One of Pleasonton's columns went astray somehow and did not get into action, and scouts notified Pleasonton that gray infantry was showing itself around Brandy Station, which made him feel that there might be such a thing as going too far. In the end, the Yankee cavalry rode back to the river and went back where it came from, the corps as a whole having left approximately ten per cent of its members behind as casualties. Among these, shot dead from his saddle in the first yelling charge up from the riverbank, was Mississippi-born Grimes Davis, who had shown a great knack for making rowdy volunteers take regular-army discipline and like it, and who had begun to look like one of the army's most promising cavalry officers.

This fight was not without effect. The Federal cavalry had finally been beaten and had had to withdraw, but it had at last stood up to the Rebel cavalry in open combat, and the men were immensely pleased with themselves. A Confederate critic remarked ruefully of this battle that "it *made* the Federal cavalry," and a New York private said gleefully that "the Rebels were going to have a review of their cavalry on that day, but our boys reviewed them." This soldier could not understand why the Yankee troopers had been withdrawn after what he considered a winning fight, but he concluded hopefully that "the head officers knew all about it." A Massachusetts major, after admitting that "there was more fighting than generalship," added that the Rebels here "lost their prestige and never recovered it."[14]

That may have been overstating the case a bit, but the cavalry had reason to feel proud. By and large, the Yankee troopers were men who had come up the hard way. They had learned a good deal on the way up, much of it at the hands of their enemies. Gone were the fancy uniforms and the cumbersome equipment provided for by old-army regulations—light blue trousers, dark blue waist-length jacket with brass scales on the shoulder, the whole topped with what one man recalled as "a predacious-looking hat with yellow cord." This struck the men as overfancy, and anyhow, after an hour on the road in dry weather everybody got so dusty that nobody could tell what they were wearing, and by now most of the men had provided themselves with plain infantry pants and tunic and forage cap. They generally managed to buy or steal great piratical boots, into which they stuffed their pants legs, with a revolver tucked into the right-leg boot along with the pants.[15]

They were beginning to discover that the revolver was a better weapon than the traditional saber. The handgun furnished cavalry at the start of the war was just about useless—a cumbersome museum piece known as a dragoon pistol, a muzzle-loader a foot long with a ramrod swiveled on the under side of the barrel. It kicked so hard that the man using it was in nearly as much danger as the man he was shooting at, and it had such a hard trigger pull that one cavalryman insisted that if a man shot at an enemy in battle, "by the time his pistol was discharged he was liable to be shooting at the men in his own regiment." This man added that "it was never wise to choose for a mark anything smaller than a good-sized barn."[16]

In the course of time the army replaced these miserable weapons with up-to-date revolvers, with which the men felt much more at home than they felt with sabers. These latter were supposed to be carried at all times in scabbards which dangled from a man's waist belt, but the metal scabbard and its rings jingled and made a lot of noise, and the weapon was just a nuisance to a man on foot. So the average trooper simply lashed his scabbard firmly to the near side of the saddle, nearly parallel to the horse's body, so that his left leg was over it when he was on his horse. That way he did not have to bother with it when on foot, it stayed put and did no flopping or jangling when he was riding, and if he needed it he could draw it quickly enough. Left to himself, though, he usually preferred to use his revolver.

Most cavalrymen were notorious foragers, not to say thieves, if only because the possession of a horse enabled them to carry more booty and make a quicker getaway than were possible for a foot soldier. As a general thing they found an easy rationalization for their marauding. A slightly prejudiced Illinois trooper wrote of the luckless Virginia farmers: "These simple people seemed to think that they could send their sons into the Rebel army to destroy our country and murder our soldiers, and that we would not only protect them but spend our time in guarding their chicken roosts, pigpens, and beehives. But they soon learned that Western soldiers came for other purposes." The cavalry tradition stipulated that a good trooper was a good provider, having forage for his horse even when government issue failed and, for the matter of that, having occasionally a new horse as well. When a cavalry regiment camped in a hitherto untrodden part of the country, it invariably happened that certain of the men would show up with new horses, and if an officer made inquiries it is recorded that he generally got "an irrelevant answer." A farmer would come in, as likely as not, to make complaint and would be invited to look over the picket rope and claim his horse if he could see it. That rarely did much good. As one veteran put it: "It was odd how a little art would change a horse's appearance so that his own dam would not know him, let alone owner or breeder. . . . With a pair of scissors, a very nice imitation of a brand would be made to appear on shoulder or hip. A little hair dye would remove all white marks, and the same scissors would so change mane and tail as to make the animal unrecognizable. . . . Almost any change in appearance or gait could be produced at short notice by the cunning trooper."[17]

Once in a blue moon a lucky cavalry outfit could loot by official order rather than in defiance of the rules. After the Brandy Station fight the army prepared to move, and as a security measure headquarters ordered all sutlers to leave the army. Here and there a sutler would evade the order, trusting to luck that he could move along by unused side roads and keep within shopping distance of the bivouacs without drawing the attention of the provost marshal. On the move up from the river one sutler miscalculated disastrously and met a whole column of cavalry while he was plodding along a narrow lane which he had thought the army would not use. Cavalry jangled to a halt because the sutler's wagon blocked the entire lane, and in a few moments an officer of the provost guard came trotting up to see what the trouble was. He took the situation in at a glance and wasted no words on the sutler. Instead he raised his voice and called to the head of the column: "What regiment is that?" First Massachusetts Cavalry, he was told. "Well, 1st Massachusetts Cavalry," he cried, pointing to the wagon, "go through that sutler!" The troopers came on with a whoop, and one of them asserted that in less than fifteen minutes "the contents of that wagon were distributed through the whole length of the regiment."[18]

Aside from lifting cavalry morale, the fight at Brandy Station had one other effect. The glimpse which had been obtained of Confederate infantry so far upstream persuaded Hooker that Lee was beginning to move around the Federal right flank, presumably by way of the Shenandoah Valley but possibly on a narrower arc, and he alerted his army for a countermove. It struck him that if Lee was moving north and west the thing for the Army of the Potomac to do was either to pitch into the Confederate rear or to march straight for Richmond, but Washington overruled him: Lee's army was his objective and the protection of Washington was his responsibility, and he had better go where Lee went and stay between him and the capital.

This made Hooker grumpy. Herman Haupt went to him a few days after Brandy Station to ask what the next move was to be, and he found Hooker in a very bad humor. Hooker said that he had no plans: he had made various suggestions and they had been turned down; from now on he would do nothing except what he was ordered to do, and if trouble came of it, it would not be his fault. Haupt did not care a great deal for this attitude and eventually he told Halleck about it. Meanwhile Hooker unbent a bit and by mid-June orders went out to evacuate the great supply bases at Aquia Creek and Belle Plain and start the army north.[19] (Haupt noted that the order to evacuate a base, with the consequent destruction of many supplies, was always welcomed by quartermaster and commissary officers, because such a move automatically settled the deficiencies in everybody's accounts.)

By June 15 the army was on the roads again. The Virginia coastal plain can get hot in June, and the Army of the Potomac remembered the first few days of this march up from Falmouth as the worst march of the entire war. The sun came out blistering hot, roadside springs and brooks were scarce, and unfriendly Rebels had filled many of the wells with stones. The roads were ankle-deep in dust, and each regiment moved in a choking opaque cloud. When a column did reach a small spring the rush of men to fill canteens quickly turned it into a mud puddle, and in any case the water in canteens reached blood heat in no time. Any number of men were prostrated by the heat—a Sanitary Commission nurse wrote that there were 120 cases of sunstroke in one division—and a good many deaths occurred.[20]

To add to the discomfort, GHQ was in a hurry, and long marches were ordered. The XII Corps did thirty-three miles to Fairfax Courthouse in one day, and Humphreys's division of the III Corps was kept marching all night, following the railroad to Manassas Junction. When morning came with no break for breakfast the men began to chant "Coffee! Coffee!" until they were finally turned into a field and allowed to take a nap until noon. The Philadelphia Brigade remembered doing twenty-eight miles on the dustiest of roads, and as the army moved on at this killing pace it littered the whole countryside with stragglers. John Gibbon, commanding a division in the II Corps, sternly announced in general orders that "in the vast majority of cases the straggler is a skulking cowardly wretch who strives to shift his duties upon the shoulders of more honest men and better soldiers." He told his men that the 15th, 19th, and 20th Massachusetts regiments customarily reached camp at night with few or no absentees, and said that showed that "straggling, even in the worst weather, is inexcusable," The historian of the 15th proudly recorded this tribute to his regiment's steadfastness but admitted that on the very evening the order was issued the 15th came into camp with only fifty-three men to stack arms. The remaining three hundred men in the outfit came stumbling in at all hours.[21]

Cavalry horses, like foot soldiers, often gave out on this march. Many of these were simply abandoned by the troopers, and it often happened that after a rest they would revive and go sauntering along, following the army. This was a boon to many footsore infantry stragglers, who would capture the beasts, rig makeshift reins and bridles out of strips of tent cloth or other material, and go riding along bareback—until, no doubt, the provost guard got them. It was noticed that stragglers who were congenital shirks would hide out in barns or sheds when sundown came in order to escape the guard, but that good men who had honestly been trying to keep up would tramp along until late at night to overtake their regiments.

A few days of this intensive marching pulled the army far away from the Rappahannock, and its bivouacs presently ran from the Bull Run Mountains all the way up to the Potomac. It was generally believed by the men in the ranks that if Lee had not already gone north of the river he would do so shortly, and some of the old-timers were wagging their heads and telling each other that they were going to have Antietam all over again. Nobody in his right mind wanted to repeat that fight, but the men who had marched through Maryland remembered it as a green and pleasant land where the citizens were glad to see Union soldiers, and there was a general feeling that this army could not fail to win once it got north of the Potomac.[22] After a few days of forced marches the high command let the men take it a little more easily as they got nearer the river, and the army caught its breath and found its spirits reviving.

Late one afternoon the I Corps was hiking along the road toward Leesburg. The column went past an old plantation, and on a rail fence by the roadside there was an unexpected audience—some dozens of the plantation's colored folk, perching on the fence and rolling their eyes hugely as the Lincoln soldiers went by. The mounted officers at the head of the column passed along, and the color guard with the cased dusty flags, and then came the infantry, rank upon endless rank, tramping the miles off with the stolid silence of veterans. The colored folk were simple people who knew very little about many things, but they were familiar with the apocalyptic visions and the wild sharp poetry of Scripture, and as they looked at these tired soldiers they saw what the reviewing officers would never see—Freedom stepping lightly along the hills, the King of the Earth striding by with a ram's horn in his hand, the walls of Jericho itself collapsing to the sound of far-off trumpets—and before long they began to rock and sway on their perch, and they shouted "Hallelujah!" and "Bless de Lord!" and some of them cried out that Lincoln was a mighty warrior.

In front of the fence, close to the road, stood a gray-haired bent old patriarch, and he finally spoke up to ask where Lincoln was personally. Soldier-like, the men answered that he wouldn't be along for a while yet—he was back behind the mule train, and maybe it would be tomorrow before he showed up. The slaves on the fence took this in, and they continued to shout, and before long the old man by the roadside began to sway and chant, and the first thing anyone knew he was leading the colored people in a song, all of the bodies rocking back and forth with the music, while the tanned soldiers with their gleaming rifles marched by:

> "Don't you see 'em, comin', comin', comin',
> Millions from de odder shore?
> Glory! Glory! Hallelujah!
> Bless de Lord forever more!

> "Don't you see 'em, goin', goin', goin',
> Past ol' massa's mansion door?
> Glory! Glory! Hallelujah!
> Bless de Lord forever more!

> "Jordan's stream is runnin', runnin', runnin'—
> Million soldiers passin' o'er:
> Lincoln comin' wid his chariot—
> Bless de Lord forever more!"

One of the soldiers who marched past them wrote that it seemed to him as if he could see the rocking figures and hear the singing far into the night, while the army kept on its way to the river.[23]

Yet this army rarely heard the echoes of a glory-hallelujah chorus as it tramped the long roads of war, and it was much more likely to punctuate its endless rambling narrative with a ribald jeer than with a chant about Jordan's flowing stream.

Part of the army came up to the North by a road that took it straight across the old Bull Run battlefield. It was ten months since the great battle there, but many dead had never been buried. The day was as sultry here as everywhere else in Virginia, and the men tramped along the historic turnpike, with bleached skulls and ribs and shinbones lying in the meadows amid heaps of rotted clothing. The men glanced casually aside from time to time, but they kept walking along and they said nothing, except to curse wearily when galloping staff officers or couriers crowded them. Finally they passed a too-shallow grave by the roadside. From it there extended a dead hand, withered to parchment, reaching bleakly toward the sky as if in some despairing, unanswered supplication. A New Jersey soldier saw it, reflected upon it, and was moved to mirth.

"Look, boys!" he called, pointing to the lifeless hand. "See the soldier putting out his hand for back pay!"[24]

The men guffawed briefly and tramped on without another glance.

3. WHITE ROAD IN THE MOONLIGHT

Off beyond the Blue Ridge Lee's army was moving, and Federal outposts in the Shenandoah Valley collapsed before a tidal wave of Rebel soldiers who struck as suddenly and as hard as if Stonewall Jackson himself still led them. Stragglers from the routed Union detachments scrambled back through Harper's Ferry, and a long rabble of civilian refugees went rocketing clear up into Pennsylvania, blocking the roads, picking up strength as they went, taking horses and cattle and household goods with them, as if the destroying angel and the original flood were hard upon their heels. Among these refugees, bewildered and lost, were hundreds of free colored folk, headed for no discernible goal short of the north star. Word had gone forth that the Confederates were rounding up all colored people and sending them south into slavery, and no Negro cared to wait to see if the rumor were true or false.[1]

Clearly enough, this was invasion again and not a mere cavalry foray, and the North took the alarm. At Washington's request, Northern governors called out the militia, and as far away as New York the natty home-guard regiments fell in at their armories, counted themselves and their equipment, and took the trains for Pennsylvania. At Harrisburg, where national guardsmen felled trees and dug up wheat fields to build fortifications, there was infinite excitement. The toll bridge over the Susquehanna did the biggest business in its history as people cleared out from before Lee's advance guard. There was the greatest demand for railroad tickets the city had ever known; the state capitol was stripped of its valuables—including the expressionless oil paintings of bygone governors—which were crated for shipment to some safer place, and around the railroad depot the pavement was blocked with trunks and boxes piled up six deep.[2]

To President Lincoln, from disturbed opposition party governors, town councils, and frightened pro bono publicos, there came an old familiar plea: Put McClellan back in command of the army, put him at least in command of our brave but untrained militia; if this is done the people will rise en masse and we may yet get out of our scrape. Lincoln filed most of these pleas with his miscellaneous papers. To one of the complainants, Governor Joel Parker of New Jersey, he coolly replied that Lee's march north represented opportunity, not disaster, for the Union cause, and he reminded the governor that no one outside of the White House could quite understand "the difficulties and involvements of replacing General McClellan in command."[3]

Between Joe Hooker and General Halleck there passed many telegrams, a running debate by wire, Hooker trying to get some sort of firm instructions, Halleck vetoing Hooker's suggestions but offering few of his own. The Army of the Potomac moved closer to the Potomac, and Pleasonton and the cavalry galloped west to go knifing at Stuart's protective cordon in front of the Blue Ridge gaps in an effort to get authentic news of Lee's movements. Stuart was on the job and his squadrons struck back, and for four days in mid-June there was a series of desperate little fights around Middleburg and Aldie.

Yankee cavalry lived up to its new reputation in these fights. On one occasion the 1st Rhode Island, led by dapper French Colonel Duffié, went swirling through Middleburg and made Stuart himself take to his heels, paying for it a few hours later when Stuart came storming back with reinforcements in a countercharge that tore the little regiment to pieces. The fields in this part of the country were cut up with stone fences, and the Federals displayed a talent for fighting dismounted, the troopers lining up behind the walls and using their carbines like infantry, and the Confederates were pressed back to the mountain wall so that in the end Longstreet had to send infantry forward to help bar the way.

After one of these running fights a Federal cavalry officer rode across the stony upland field and studied the dead Confederates, lean men in homespun, their saddles and harness and other equipment mostly homemade and makeshift, many of their carbines made by cutting down the barrels of infantry rifles. He compared this with the abundant equipment that was available to the Yankee cavalry, and he mused: "How desperately in earnest must such a people be, who, after foreign supplies are exhausted, depend on their own fabrics rather than submit."[4]

Desperately in earnest they were, and in the end they finally held the gaps, so that no Yankee saw what was happening beyond the Blue Ridge. But what went almost unnoticed at the time was that this succession of fights screened the Army of the Potomac as well. With June two-thirds gone and Lee beginning to slip his infantry over the Potomac and up across Maryland toward Hagerstown and the Pennsylvania line, Stuart was somewhat in the dark as to the location and intent of the Federal infantry. This fact was to have important consequences.

As Lee got the bulk of his infantry north of the Potomac, the need for Stuart's screening operation ended, and it became important to get the cavalryman up into Pennsylvania with the advance echelons of the army. The obvious way would be to have Stuart pull his troops back through the Blue Ridge gaps, follow the rear of the army across the Potomac, and then go spurring northward on Lee's right flank. The route was roundabout, however, considering that Stuart was expected to pick the advance guard up around York, and going up the valley to the fords behind infantry and wagon trains would mean delay. Stuart accordingly proposed that he repeat his famous old stunt of riding clear around the sluggish Yankee army, crossing the Potomac somewhere east of the Blue Ridge, and striking north cross-country to meet Ewell. The way would be shorter, and there probably would be a chance to annoy the Yankees by molesting supply lines. For this plan Stuart got Lee's approval.

It appears that Stuart believed that Hooker's army was lying behind the Bull Run Mountains, facing west, in a formation that had no very great depth. Also, he considered that the Federals were being pretty static just then. That conception had been given him by John S. Mosby, the famous Rebel ranger, who had just been riding through Hooker's camps and found them all quiet. It seemed to Stuart, therefore, that by making only a short march to his right he could get around Hooker's flank and that he could then march north, west of Centreville, and hit the Potomac at Dranesville or thereabouts. The Federal "rear" which he felt ought to be disturbed was, under this conception, the territory between Bull Run and Washington.

In accordance with his orders, then, Stuart began his march at 1 A.M. on June 25. He immediately ran into trouble. The Federal army was sprawled out over more territory than had been supposed. The VI Corps was at Centreville, well to the east of the spot that was thought to mark the army's rear, and the III Corps was at Gum Springs, which was on Stuart's projected route to the Potomac. And although Mosby had been correct when he reported that the army was quiet, his information had gone out of date and the whole army was on the move, filling all the roads and making Stuart's move impossible. Stuart had to make a disastrous long detour south and east, and the upshot was that he rode his cavalry right out of the campaign.[5]

Meanwhile, Hooker had not been entirely in the dark. As early as June 18 he got his pontoons into the Potomac opposite the mouth of the Monocacy, ready to lay bridges if a crossing became necessary. By June 23 he had definitely located the advance Confederate corps north of Hagerstown, Maryland. On that date one division of Rebels led by Jubal Early was up in the Pennsylvania mountains, laying irreverent hands on the Caledonia Ironworks owned by Thaddeus Stevens. Stevens's resident manager gave Early a moving argument about this property, saying that to destroy it would simply put several hundred people out of work; it would not hurt Stevens, because the place had been operating at a loss for a decade. Early was as skeptical as the next man, and he remarked dryly: "That's not the way Yankees do business," after which he ordered the whole place destroyed, with provisions and livestock confiscated for the benefit of the Confederacy. Visiting the place later, Stevens figured that he was out $75,000, and said the destruction was total—"They could not have done the job much cleaner."[6]

Hooker waited no longer but ordered three army corps to move over the river at once, and by June 27—while Stuart was still floundering north toward the Potomac, and his brigadier, Fitz Lee, was sending him a hot bulletin to the effect that the Federal army was converging on Leesburg, doubtless planning to cross the Potomac—the entire Army of the Potomac was in Maryland, and one wing of the army was moving west to the passes in South Mountain.

This was tolerably fast action, all things considered. Hooker's army had completed its crossing only twenty-four hours after the last of Lee's infantry had crossed, and the whole of it was in Maryland before either Stuart or Lee knew that the crossing had even begun.

But if Hooker was handling the army skillfully, the fact was not impressing his immediate superiors, Secretary Stanton and General Halleck. They were still refusing him the reinforcements he was demanding.

The Army of the Potomac was lean just now. The Chancellorsville losses had not yet been made good, twenty thousand short-term troops had taken their discharges and gone home, and the forced marches in the sweltering heat had greatly extended the sick list, so that Hooker had fewer than seventy-five thousand effectives with him, not counting cavalry.[7] To be sure, there were plenty of other Federal troops within reach—the eternal Washington garrison, the brigades and regiments that were scattered about in Maryland, whole divisions down on the Virginia peninsula—but these were not for Joe Hooker. Halleck and Stanton would not let him have them, and when he asked for them he got pin-prickings and naggings in return.

Halleck and Stanton obviously did not want to see Hooker in command of the army in another battle. Yet with the greatest battle of all drawing nearer every day they could not quite nerve themselves to remove him. They had in mind, possibly, what Meade was calling "the ridiculous appearance we present of changing our generals after each battle." They also had in mind Hooker's chief cabinet sponsor, Secretary Chase, who was still a power in the land and still firmly committed to Hooker, which meant that to fire Hooker was to invite a shattering political upheaval. So these two set out to make things unpleasant for Hooker in the hope that he would take the hint and resign, and the Hooker who had criticized McClellan so bitterly in the old days began to find out what McClellan had been up against.

It is never safe to come to any firm conclusions about what Stanton really had in mind, but the probability is that he simply mistrusted Hooker's nerve. The blue funk that had suddenly materialized at Chancellorsville might appear again, and Stanton was taking no chances. For the time being, however, Hooker was a first-rate general. Considering the fact that the War Department had not given him a free hand but had limited him to the role of following Lee and trying to parry his blows, Hooker handled the army very well that June. But he felt himself a man on the end of a tether, with Washington restraining his every move, and he was a hot-tempered man, never famous for his patience. There was bound to be a blowup sooner or later, and if one thing did not touch it off some other thing would.

It came to a head at last over the same sore spot that had bothered McClellan during the Antietam campaign—control of the garrison at Harper's Ferry. Hooker could see no point in trying to hold this indefensible spot and he demanded permission to withdraw the troops and use them elsewhere. Halleck refused, and Hooker gave way to petulance and, just conceivably, to an inner reluctance to face once more the searching test of battle in supreme command. Whatever may have been his real reason, he hotly sent off a telegram of resignation, and the War Department accepted it with bland promptness. That night a War Department official took a special train west, and in the early morning hours of June 28 he entered Meade's tent, aroused that sleeping soldier, and informed him that he was now the commander of the Army of the Potomac.

Meade was genuinely surprised, so much so that when he first woke up and saw the War Department man standing by his cot he believed foggily that he was being placed under arrest, and he hastily searched his conscience to consider what he could have done to deserve it. He tried to decline the promotion and was told that that was impossible, he had been put in command whether he liked it or not. Dressing hastily, Meade made his way to Hooker's headquarters to give that officer the news.[8]

Meade was a good, decent man, and nothing in all his story is much more creditable than the attitude he had taken toward his own promotion. Ever since Chancellorsville he and other ranking officers had expected that the army would get a new commander, and Meade had heard some gossip that he himself would be named. Considering the matter dispassionately, he concluded that the appointment just was not coming to him, and on June 25 he wrote a long letter to his wife explaining why he felt that way. For one thing, he told her, there would be great opposition from the innumerable cliques and factions of the officer corps itself, and Meade soberly analyzed these:

"They could not say that I was an unprincipled intriguer who had risen by criticizing and defaming my predecessors and superiors. They could not say I was incompetent, because I have not been tried, and so far as I have been tried I have been singularly successful. They could not say I had never been under fire because it is notorious no general officer, not even Fighting Joe himself, has been in more battles, or more exposed, than my record evidences. The only thing they can say, and I am willing to admit the justice of the argument, is that it remains to be seen whether I have the capacity to handle successfully a large army. I do not, however, stand any chance, because I have no friends, political or others, who press or advance my claims or pretensions, and there are so many others who are pressed by influential politicians that it is folly to think I stand any chance upon mere merit alone. Besides, I have not the vanity to think my capacity so pre-eminent, and I know there are plenty of others equally competent with myself, though their names may not have been so much mentioned."

Having explained all of this, Meade went on to twit his wife gently: "Do you know, I think *your* ambition is being roused and that you are beginning to be bitten with the dazzling prospect of having for a husband a commanding general of the army. How is this?"[9]

He was genuinely but uneffusively fond of his wife, and in the early days of army life he wrote to her about the "terrible agony" of parting from her when the army sent him off to a distant post. On their twenty-first wedding anniversary he wrote her that he doubted if any other couple alive "have had more happiness with each other than you and I." If he was irritable and touchy in camp, possessed of a famous temper and imperfect means for controlling it, it never cropped out in his letters home. He was deeply and quietly religious, content to do his duty in the sphere where God had placed him, expressing his gratitude to God whenever his health (about which he worried a good deal) improved enough to let him feel robust. A professional soldier, he was inclined to distrust volunteers, and he had no use whatever for abolitionists.[10]

This latter trait, as a matter of fact, had got him into the bad books of one of the most influential of all abolitionists, Senator Zach Chandler of Michigan, which was doubtless one reason why Meade felt that he would never be given Hooker's place. Meade had been stationed in Detroit when Fort Sumter was fired on, and while he was a staunch Unionist he was dismayed by the arrogance of the fire-eaters, to whom Southern secession looked like a simple riot which would be suppressed by the mere appearance of Federal troops. Detroit civic leaders called a huge mass meeting to whip up patriotic fervor and pass resolutions, and they invited all army officers stationed in Detroit to appear on the platform and publicly take the oath of allegiance to the Union. Meade and his fellow officers flatly refused to do this, notifying the War Department that they would freely take all the oaths the department asked them to take but that they would not take any in the circus surroundings of a mass meeting. For this stand Meade was publicly denounced at the meeting, and Senator Chandler had distrusted him ever since.[11]

With the War Department man, Meade went to Hooker's tent. Hooker took the news as gracefully as a man could under the circumstances, and he called in Dan Butterfield, his chief of staff, and sat down with Meade to explain where the army was and what current plans were. (Meade had long since expressed his dislike for Butterfield, and he had tried this morning to bring in G. K. Warren, the army's chief engineer, as his chief of staff. He was talked out of it by Warren himself, who explained that it would simply be impossible to break in a new chief of staff when a collision with the enemy might take place at any moment.) Butterfield and Hooker flared up once when Meade, after looking at their map, remarked unguardedly that it seemed to him the army was rather scattered, but that was smoothed over and the men got down to business.[12]

Hooker told Meade that Lee had no pontoons with him and therefore could not be planning to cross the Susquehanna River, to whose bank Ewell's corps had progressed. If the rest of Lee's army followed Ewell, Hooker continued, Lee must be planning to move down the western bank of that river in order to cut off Baltimore and Washington, which meant that the line of march of Lee's invasion would follow a huge semicircle, curving northeast, east, and southeast. The Army of the Potomac, Hooker explained, had been placed so that it could move by a shorter arc inside of this semicircle, covering Baltimore and Washington and falling on Lee's flank if there was an opening. The explanations completed, Hooker withdrew and the army was Meade's.[13]

He got it at a bad time—bad for him, and bad for the army. In the whole career of this body of troops, no greater test was ever put upon it than this business of getting a new commander on the very eve of the war's most crucial battle. It had had bad commanders and it had had fairly good ones, and all of them had been heckled and second-guessed by Washington, by the press, and by their own subordinates, but never before had there been anything like this. Meade's appointment on the eve of battle was an act of sheer desperation, done solely to get rid of a man whose heart and nerve were distrusted. What happened now would be largely up to the men themselves. In effect they had no leader. They were almost within rifleshot of a supremely aggressive enemy, and there was no time for a shakedown, no time for high strategy and careful planning, no time for reorganization and regrouping. Whatever happened during the next week, the one certainty now was that the soldiers themselves would run this next battle. The most that could be expected of Meade was that he would make no ruinous mistakes. For the rest . . .

For the rest there were the men in the ranks, the hard brown survivors of the old 1861 regiments, the new levies that had come in to pick up the tone and the casual, unemotional spirit of the old-timers, the men who occasionally cheered one another in tribute to bravery and stoutness of heart which they themselves had seen, but who looked for no cheers or tributes from any other source. These men now were coming up from the river, and the weather was hot again, and the order was out for forced marches—Meade disagreed with Hooker's strategy, feeling that his cue was to follow Lee north and force him to turn and fight— and for a day or so the fate of the Union was going to rest on the sinewy legs of the men who had to do the marching.

The army came up from the Potomac, and some of the men were taken up a narrow strip of land between the river and the Chesapeake and Ohio Canal, the march continuing long after dark, rain coming down and mud underfoot and Cimmerian darkness all around. Humphreys was in command—Humphreys, grandson of the naval constructor who had designed the U.S.S. *Constitution,* a slim dapper driver who had taken over Berry's old division in the III Corps. Humphreys was a grim courtly man who just before he took his troops up to the stone wall at Fredericksburg had bowed to his staff and had said pleasantly: "Gentlemen, I shall lead this charge; I presume, of course, you will wish to ride with me?" Since it was put like that, staff had so wished, and five of the seven officers got knocked off their horses. He was a stickler for the regulations, and the United States Army has possessed few better soldiers, and he was driving his men north now without regard for human frailty.

The march went on and on, and men fell out and lay down in the mud and went to sleep. When the rain stopped, men who kept going lighted candles and stuck them in the muzzles of their rifles, and the straggling column lurched on, will-o'-the wisp fires flickering in the night, and the riverbank was lined for ten or fifteen miles with officers and men who could not keep up. One survivor wrote that "it was impossible to say whether colonels and brigadier generals had lost their commands, or regiments and brigades had lost their commanders." When day came, after a sketchy bivouac, the column pulled itself together— Humphreys was the man to see to that—and by noon all hands were accounted for and the march was going on compactly again.[14]

Up past Frederick they went, pulling for the Pennsylvania line, and the men's spirits rose with the green fields and blue mountains about them, citizens cheering them on when they passed through towns, girls standing by farmhouse doors to wave flags and offer drinks of cold water. The army had its own method of greeting these girls. The wolf-call whistle was unknown to soldiers at that era, but they had an equivalent—an abrupt, significant clearing of the throat, or cough, which burst out spontaneously whenever a line of march went by a nice-looking young woman, so that at such a time, as one veteran said, "The men seemed terribly and suddenly afflicted with some bronchial affection."[15] Coughing and grunting, and vastly pleased with themselves, the men followed the dusty roads, and while they had no idea where they were going, it seemed to them that at last they were marching to victory. As one man put it: "We felt some doubt whether it was ever going to be our fortune to win a victory in Virginia, but no one admitted the possibility of a defeat north of the Potomac."[16]

The advance crossed the line into Pennsylvania, and the veteran 2nd Massachusetts went into a little town at the head of one column and found that word of their coming had gone on ahead. The citizens were out in force, and on each side of the main street there were long tables spread with all sorts of good things to eat, pretty girls standing behind the tables, wanting nothing so much as to serve good Union soldiers. There was much coughing and grinning and waving of hands, and the men fixed their mouths for apple butter and pie and soft bread, when bang-bang-bang! from the northern edge of town there came the sound of rifleshots, and couriers came galloping back, and the regiment swung its rifles to the right shoulder and went doublequicking on through the village to help the cavalry drive off Rebel skirmishers. But when they got to the open country there were no Rebels, and nobody seemed to know what the scare had been about, and the 2nd Massachusetts awoke at last to the knowledge that the regiment had been had. They could not retrace their steps back into town, regiments farther back in the line got all of the lunch, and to the end of their days the Massachusetts boys were convinced that the whole thing had been a put-up job devised by scheming characters envious of the regiment which marched at the head of the column.[17]

On every road the long column went north. To the 3rd Michigan, the march seemed pleasant, what with pretty girls and cheering villagers, and one veteran wrote that "the roads around here are beautiful and macadamized and we enjoy marching over them very much. Every man in the ranks feels jubilant." To an Irishman in the 9th Massachusetts there was poetry in the very landscape: "The picturesque farmhouses and granaries appeared under the bright sunlight as white as driven snow. The undulating farming lands were covered with their rich nodding plumes of yellow grain which rose and fell in the breeze, before the approaching eye, on plateaus, valleys, and hills with pleasing effect. The scenery of it all, in its greatness, when viewed from a vantage ground, was a magnificent spectacle." Not all of the notes were quite so enthusiastic. Some soldiers found that when they tried to buy fruit or food they were badly overcharged, and when this happened the men sometimes helped themselves to contents of store or roadside stall and, departing, airily told the proprietor to "charge it to Uncle Sam." On such occasions the inhabitants would try to shame the men by saying that Lee's soldiers had been much more gentlemanly, but this rarely seemed to have an effect.[18]

Then came the news that Meade had replaced Hooker. It was unwelcome news, for the enlisted man still liked Hooker, and outside the V Corps Meade was hardly more than a name. In the ranks men asked angrily: "What has Meade ever done?" and bleakly answered: "Nothing!" But if most of the soldiers felt that the government had made a mistake in this change of commanders, they kicked up no fuss over it. The ardent hero worship of the old volunteer days was gone now, and it would never come back again, partly because the heroes were departed but mostly because the men themselves had lost their old need to make and worship heroes. The soldiers were sorry to see Hooker go, but they did not bother to carry on about it.[19] The man at the top might be anybody. It no longer seemed to matter very much. In the ranks there seems to have come slowly and painfully the realization that the man who would finally get the army through its trials was a profane, weary man with no stars on his shoulders and scant hope of any in his crown, the everlasting high private who was being challenged now, once and for all, to show what kind of man he really was.

Meade announced his accession by a circular to corps commanders, calling on officers to explain to their men the immense issues involved in Lee's invasion of Pennsylvania. Meade said that "the army has fought well heretofore," and he believed that it would fight "more desperately and bravely than ever if it is addressed in fitting terms." He added, somewhat maladroitly—the capacity to sound an inspirational note simply was not in this gnarled gray-bearded man—that corps and other commanders "are authorized to order the instant death of any soldier who fails to do his duty at this hour."[20]

The army moved on, some of its segments doing thirty miles and more in a day, and in rear of the moving troops there was pandemonium. A newspaper correspondent who got to Frederick just after the army marched out noted that the place was full of stragglers, with all the liquor shops running full tilt and drunken soldiers wandering all over town, trying to steal horses or sneak into private dwellings, "inflamed with whisky and drunk as well with their freedom from accustomed restraint." On the road north from Frederick he found more of the same, and he wrote bitterly:

"Take a worthless vagabond who has enlisted for thirteen dollars a month instead of patriotism, who falls out of ranks because he is a coward and wants to avoid the battle, or because he is lazy and wants to steal a horse to ride on instead of marching, or because he is rapacious and wants to sneak about farmhouses and frighten or wheedle timid country women into giving him better food and lodging than camp life affords—make this armed coward or sneak thief drunk on bad whisky, give him scores and hundreds of armed companions as desperate and drunken as himself—turn loose this motley crew, muskets and revolvers in hand, into a rich country, with quiet, peaceful inhabitants, all unfamiliar with armies and army ways—let them swagger and bully as cowards and vagabonds always do, steal or openly plunder as such thieves always will—and then, if you can imagine the state of things this would produce, you have the condition of the country in the rear of our own army, on our own soil, today."[21]

The debris that was set afloat by this backwash of the moving army littered towns and hamlets all along the Maryland-Pennsylvania border, underlining the regrettable fact that not all soldiers are shining sons of light; emphasizing, too, the queer gaps in this army's discipline, which meant that a hard march usually cost the army about as many men as a hard battle. How could it have been otherwise? Here was an army in which the whole problem of command had gone unsolved. In the past ten months the army had fought four great battles—Bull Run, Antietam, Fredericksburg, and Chancellorsville. It had had a different commander for each one, and now with a fifth battle approaching it had its fifth commander. Of the seven army corps, not one was being led now by the man who had led it at the time of Antietam. All but three of the nineteen infantry divisions had changed command since then. Fewer than half of its fifty-one infantry brigades were led by men who had the proper rank for the job, the rank of brigadier general, and only ten of the fifty-one had led their brigades for as long as ten months.

In the regiments the condition was apt to be even worse. Army regulations rewarded regimental officers who kept their men out of the hottest action and penalized those who took them into the thick of the fighting. When regimental strength declined, as it invariably did, since there was no adequate system for providing replacements, a regiment sooner or later was apt to fall below the minimum strength at which it was permissible to muster in a full colonel or to maintain a regular regimental staff—quartermaster, surgeon, commissary officer, adjutant, and so on. Most of the veteran regiments were commanded by majors or captains, and promotion for these men was impossible no matter how much they might deserve it, simply because their regiments were too small to carry higher ranks. (The three New York regiments in the famous Irish Brigade had been consolidated to two companies apiece now, and these battalions were led by company officers.) If a brigade made up of such regiments was reinforced with a brand-new rookie regiment and the brigadier then got shot or fell ill or resigned, command of the whole brigade would go by seniority to the untested rookie colonel even though the junior officers who led the veteran battalions knew ten times as much as he knew about leading troops.[22]

The leadership which men got under this system was apt to be haphazard and unpredictable, and when the army moved it was bound to dribble men to the rear, unraveling a loose fringe of ne'er-do-wells and fainthearts and out-and-out skulkers to ravage the countryside and to scandalize right-thinking war correspondents. Yet it was noticed that in those outfits which did have good leadership there was very little straggling, and indeed it was more or less an axiom in the Army of the Potomac that a regiment, brigade, or division which fought well also marched well. A commander who "looked after his men," as the expression went, and who insisted on soldierly behavior, would always get a response.

The II Corps had gone under Hancock after Couch departed, and Hancock was driving it along the highways unmercifully in the end-of-June heat and dust, but very few of his men were leaving the ranks. They remembered afterward being driven so hard that when they had to ford any creek or river they were not allowed to fall out to remove their shoes and socks, which meant that they had to march with wet feet and so got very footsore by the end of the day. It was on this march that the skipper of one of Hancock's best regiments, Colonel Colville of the 1st Minnesota, was sternly placed under arrest because he had let his outfit make a little detour in order to cross a certain stream by a footbridge instead of sending the men splashing straight ahead through the shallows.[23]

As it reached Pennsylvania the army began to encounter militia regiments— regiments dressed in fancy uniforms, carrying the full complement of equipment, with muskets polished until the barrels shone like mirrors. The veterans looked at these militiamen with dour curiosity and uttered wisecracks designed to put the holiday soldiers in their places. North of Frederick the XII Corps encountered the New York 7th, a dandy regiment wearing, among other things, nice white gloves. There was a rain coming down and the roadside was muddy, and the militiamen were not looking their best as Slocum's veterans cast critical eyes on them. The XII Corps advised the militiamen to come in out of the rain before the dress-parade uniforms got spoiled, asked them where their umbrellas were, and suggested that the boys join the army someday and see what soldiering was like. On another road the VI Corps met a Brooklyn home-guard regiment dressed in uniforms of natty gray, and the veterans coldly advised the militia to dye those uniforms blue: if they ever got into a fight the Army of the Potomac was apt to shoot anybody it saw who came to the field in a gray uniform. Now and then a veteran would ask the home guards where they buried their dead.[24]

As it moved the army covered a very wide front, thirty-five or forty miles from tip to tip. Orders were vague because plans were vague. Lee's army was somewhere between York, on the east, and Chambersburg, on the west, and as June ended it became apparent that the Confederates were beginning to pull their far-flung detachments together, heading toward some sort of concentration east of the long barrier of South Mountain. Meade considered that when it came to a fight the line of Pipe Creek, a meandering little stream along the Pennsylvania border, would be a good place for the Army of the Potomac to make its stand. He was uneasy about it—Halleck was warning him that he was pretty far west and that Lee might be able to make a dash around his right and strike at Baltimore or Washington—and he kept his men pushing on, tentacles of cavalry reaching forward, looking for a contact. In York an agent of the Sanitary Commission got inside the Rebel lines and took a look at one of Ewell's camps, finding the Rebels "well stripped for action and capable of fast movement."

"Physically, the men looked about equal to the generality of our own troops, and there were fewer boys among them," this man wrote. "Their dress was a wretched mixture of all cuts and colors. There was not the slightest attempt at uniformity in this respect. Every man seemed to have put on whatever he could get hold of, without regard to shape or color. . . . Their shoes, as a general thing, were poor; some of the men were entirely barefooted. Their equipments were light as compared with those of our men. They consisted of a thin woolen blanket, coiled up and slung from the shoulder in the form of a sash, a haversack swung from the opposite shoulder, and a cartridge box. The whole cannot weigh more than twelve or fourteen pounds." He asked one of these lanky Rebels if they had no shelter tents, and the soldiers was scornful of such comforts, saying, "I just wouldn't tote one."[25]

John Buford was leading his cavalry division north from Frederick and Emmitsburg, prowling close to the slope of South Mountain, trying to find the enemy. On the last day of June, after narrowly missing a collision at the little town of Fairfield, he drew a bit farther to the east and late in the afternoon brought his men into the town of Gettysburg, a pleasant place in the open hilly country where many roads converged, with the long blue mass of the mountain chain lying on the horizon off to the west. Confederate patrols had been in the town, and they went west on the Cashtown pike as Buford's troopers came in. Somewhere not far beyond them, clearly, there must be a solid body of Rebel infantry. Buford strung a heavy picket line along a north-and-south ridge west of town, threw more pickets out to cover the roads to the north (army intelligence warned that Ewell's corps was apt to be coming down those roads from Carlisle before long), and snugged down for the night with headquarters in a theological seminary.

The brigade which was responsible for picketing the roads north of town was commanded by Colonel Tom Devin, and as Buford and Devin talked that night Devin doubted that there was any substantial number of Rebels anywhere near him. He would keep a good watch, he said, but he could handle anything that could come up during the next twenty-four hours. But Buford was convinced that most of Lee's army was within striking distance, and he warned Devin sharply.

"No, you won't," he said bluntly. "They will attack you in the mornning and they will come booming—skirmishers three-deep. You will have to fight like the devil until supports arrive."[26]

Buford was more anxious that night than his staff had ever seen him, and he kept his scouts moving all night, west and north of town. He impressed on his subordinates that they must be alert—"Look out for campfires during the night and for dust in the morning"—and he messaged Meade that there might be trouble next day. He was told to hang on, Reynolds and the I Corps would be up sometime in the morning, and Howard with the XI Corps would not be far behind.

There was a bright moon that night, and most of the army kept to the road long after the sun had gone down. Nothing had actually happened yet, but there was a stir in the air, and the first faint tug had been felt from the line that had been thrown into Gettysburg, a quiet hint that something was apt to pull the

whole army together on those long ridges and wooded hills. The soldiers kept on
marching, and a strange thing happened, significant because it showed how little
the men who led this army understood the spirit of the men they were leading.
Somewhere in the officer corps a little plot was hatched: the men would be told
that McClellan was back in command, and they would be so inspired and heartened that they would fight and win this battle before they found out that the
rumor was false.[27]

In various moving columns that evening staff officers galloped up in mock
frenzy and shouted out the news: "McClellan is in command again!" The boys
cheered and tossed their hats, and for half an hour the business was a sensation,
yet it appears that something about the news failed to ring true, and most of the
soldiers were not greatly deceived. Here and there veterans wagged their heads
and agreed that maybe if they lost this next battle and were forced back into the
lines around Washington, McClellan would indeed be called in to save the
day—otherwise, not a chance.

Inspired or otherwise, the men kept moving. Colonel Strong Vincent, leading
a brigade in the V Corps, took his men through a little town, where the moonlight lay bright on the street, and in every doorway there were girls waving flags
and cheering. The battle flags were broken out of their casings and the men went
through the town in step with music playing, and Gettysburg lay a few miles
ahead. Vincent reined in his horse and let the head of the column pass him, and
as the colors went by he took off his hat, and he sat there quietly, watching the
flags moving on in the silver light, the white dresses of the girls bright in the
doorways, shimmering faintly in the cloudy luminous dusk under the shade
trees on the lawns. To an aide who sat beside him the colonel mused aloud:
"There could be worse fates than to die fighting here in Pennsylvania, with that
flag waving overhead. . . ."[28]

There was the long white road in the moonlight, with the smalltown girls
laughing and crying in the shadows, and the swaying ranks of young men waving to them and moving on past them. To these girls who had been nowhere and
who had all of their lives before them this was the first of all the roads of the
earth, and to many of the young men who marched off under the moon it was
the last of all the roads. For all of them, boys and girls alike, it led to unutterable
mystery. The column passed on through the town and the music stopped and
the flags were put back in their casings, and the men went marching on and on.

In the Gettysburg cemetery, quiet on a hilltop just south of the town, there
was a wooden sign by the gatepost—just legible, no doubt, in the last of the June
moonlight, if anyone had bothered to go up there and read it—announcing that
the town would impose a five-dollar fine on anyone who discharged a firearm
within the cemetery limits.

SIX

End and Beginning

1. THE ECONOMICS OF EIGHTY PER CENT

WEST OF GETTYSBURG the land rolls to the mountains in a long easy ground swell, without whitecaps or breakers. The ridges run north and south and they are broad and rounded, with wide shallow valleys between. It is good farming country, and by July most of the land is bright with growing crops. Here and there are open groves, with farmhouses and big stone-and-timber barns close by.

On the morning of July 1, 1863, Yankee cavalry held one of these ridges a mile west of town. The troopers were a mixed group, New York and Illinois men mostly, with a couple of squadrons of Hoosiers, and their pickets looked down a gentle slope toward a little brook, Willoughby Run, which came lazily south and crossed the graveled pike that ran toward Cashtown, a little village half a dozen miles to the west, close to the mountain wall. The pickets looked west, and the dawn came up behind them, throwing long gray shadows across the hollows and lighting the blue crest of South Mountain. Men who glanced back noted an ominous red sky in the east, with a promise of heat.

The light grew, and a dun-colored column of troops came snaking eastward. John Buford had had it pegged: the column was preceded by a triple line of skirmishers who overflowed the wheat fields and pastures beside the Cashtown road and came along jauntily, their muskets ready. The Confederates belonged to the division of Harry Heth in A. P. Hill's corps. Hill was sick that morning, and it seems he did not believe there would be many Yankees around Gettysburg. Heth thought the Gettysburg stores might contain shoes, and he wanted to get them, or so it is stated, at any rate, although Jubal Early's men had gone through the place a week earlier, and it was most unlikely that they would have overlooked anything useful. It may be that these Confederates simply were looking for a fight. They had seen nothing in Pennsylvania so far but militia, and as far as they knew there was nothing but militia in front of them. And so as Buford had predicted, they came booming over the western ridge, skirmishers three-deep, striding forward into the rising sun.

The first Federals to get a good look at them were a corporal and three men of the 9th New York Cavalry near Willoughby Run. The corporal sent his men back to spread the alarm while he trotted across the stream and up the hill for a closer look. Rebel skirmishers loosed a few long-range shots at him, and he rode back to the little bridge, and as the skirmishers came over the ridge he fired a few times with his carbine and then turned and galloped back to the main line. With that harmless exchange of shots the battle of Gettysburg had begun.[1]

If the Confederates were looking for a fight, Buford was just the man for them. Unsupported cavalry was not expected to stand off infantry, and for a couple of hours or more Buford's two brigades would be entirely unsupported, but Buford liked to fight and he did not propose to leave until somebody made him leave. He dismounted his regiments and spread them out along the ridge, one man in every four standing fifty yards in the rear holding horses, the rest squatting behind fences, bushes, trees, or what not and peering at the Rebel skirmishers over their stubby carbines.

Buford had to keep part of his men patrolling the roads that came down from the north, because the word was that Ewell's troops would be approaching from that direction before long, so his fighting line was a bit skinny. He had six guns with him—Battery A, 2nd U.S. Artillery, under Lieutenant John Calef—and he sent them out the Cashtown road to take position in the center of the line of dismounted cavalrymen. Calef swung his guns into battery, trained a piece on a knot of mounted Confederate officers three quarters of a mile off, and nodded to the gunner, who jerked the lanyard. The flash and the echoing report and the bursting shell notified the Confederates that they were expected, and the ridge to the west blossomed out with rolling spurts of dust as the Rebel guns went in at a gallop to unlimber and return the fire. Rebel skirmishers began working their way up from Willoughby Run, and there was an intermittent clatter of rifle and carbine fire.

Two or three hundred yards east of the ridge where the cavalry and the guns were posted there was another rise of ground, slightly higher and much longer, and a little way south of the Cashtown pike on this high ground there was a Lutheran theological seminary, its white bell tower rising above walls of ivied brick. Buford went back to this building and climbed up in the tower to survey the situation. It did not take him long to see that if Yankee infantry did not come up soon the cavalry would be in a bad spot. Rebel infantry was present in strength and more was coming up all the time, and Heth was putting additional guns into battery on the far side of Willoughby Run. Buford sent gallopers hurrying away to give the news to General John Reynolds, who was to bring the I Corps up toward Gettysburg from the south. The Confederate skirmish line pushed in more closely, the racket of the firing was getting louder, and men were being hit. Confederate artillery was blasting the crest of the ridge, and Calef was firing fast in reply, and the weight of metal was all in the Confederates' favor.

South of Gettysburg, Reynolds's infantry could hear the firing, and they quickened their pace. Reynolds galloped on ahead of them and rode into town, got a quick size-up of the situation from a scout, and turned west and rode fast to the seminary. Buford saw him from the belfry, called out, "There's the devil to pay!" and came clattering down in a rush. He told Reynolds what he knew, and Reynolds got off a hasty note to Meade: the enemy was coming on, but "I will fight him inch by inch, and if driven into the town I will barricade the streets and hold him back as long as possible."[2] A courier went pounding back with the note, and the head of the infantry column swung west as it neared the town, crossing the fields to get over to Seminary Ridge.

The column was led by Major General James Wadsworth, a vigorous white-haired old man who had been a well-to-do gentleman farmer in New York State before the war and who was turning into a good general. His men liked him immensely. He was a stickler about things like adequate rations and decent housing, and in winter quarters the men found it not at all unusual to wake up before dawn on cold mornings and see the old chap poking his nose inside to find out for himself whether the huts were warm and decently ventilated. He had run unsuccessfully for governor of New York against Copperhead Seymour the previous fall, scorning to go home and campaign on the ground that it did not befit a soldier.[3] Now he was leading his division into action, an old Revolutionary War saber in his hands, Reynolds galloping back to meet him to tell him where to put his troops.

Wadsworth's division contained just two brigades, but they were good ones. One of them was composed of four New York regiments and one regiment from Pennsylvania, led by Brigadier General Lysander Cutler, and the other was the Iron Brigade, Influential Citizen Meredith riding at the head of it. As this brigade approached Gettysburg, Meredith or someone else ordered the flags uncased and set the fife-and-drum corps playing at the head of the column, and the Westerners fell into step and came swinging up the road, their black hats tilted down over their eyes, rifle barrels sparkling in the morning sun. There were eighteen hundred fighting men in this brigade, and the men were cocky. Officially they were the 1st Brigade of the 1st Division of the I Army Corps, and they figured that if the army were ever drawn up in one long line for inspection they would stand at the extreme right of it, which somehow was cause for pride. On the ridge to the west there was a crackle of small-arms fire and a steady crashing of cannon, with a long soiled cloud of smoke drifting up in the still morning air, and at the head of the column the drums and the fifes were loud— playing "The Girl I Left Behind Me," probably, that perennial theme song of the Army of the Potomac, playing the Iron Brigade into its last great fight.[4]

On Seminary Ridge, Reynolds divided the column, telling Cutler to form line north of the Cashtown pike and calling the Iron Brigade into action on the south side. The veteran regiments wheeled into line and the dismounted cavalrymen came sifting back through the intervals to take their horses again. They had done well enough, holding A. P. Hill's men off for two hours, and now they could go to the rear while the infantry took over. Back with them went Calef and his battery, one gun limping along with but two horses left to pull it. Into the place Calef had vacated came the 2nd Marine battery, Captain James Hall, the same who had so impressed the rookies on the line at Fredericksburg by his extreme coolness under fire, sitting his horse and making chit-chat with a brigadier while the Southern gunners used him for a target.

There was no time now for Captain Hall to put on a show for nervous infantry. The Rebels had a good deal of artillery in action, and twelve guns promptly opened on this Maine battery, getting it in a deadly cross fire. Confederate infantry was getting in close, too, and skirmishers were shooting down the gunners. Cutler's boys relieved this situation slightly when they opened fire, but the Confederates were coming on with a rush, their line extending farther to the north than Cutler's line, and before long the Federals found themselves flanked, with a couple of Southern regiments advancing on their right and crumpling them up. The infantry was ordered to retire, the 147th New York did not get the order and was left isolated, in danger of being captured en masse, and Hall suddenly found that he was all alone on the ridge, with a Rebel column on his right barely sixty yards off. Coolly he ordered his right and center sections to swing over and blast the charging column with canister, while the two guns of his left section continued to duel with the twelve guns on the ridge to the west. The enemy charge was broken, but it realigned itself and came on again, skirmishers creeping forward to pick off the gunners. Hall's men did their best, but as a Federal infantry officer who saw the fight remarked, "Artillery against skirmishers is like shooting mosquitoes with a rifle."[5]

Clearly it was time for the guns to go. Hall wrote later that he ordered the battery to retire by sections, "feeling that if the position was too advanced for infantry it was equally so for artillery." His right section went back seventy-five yards, unlimbered again, and opened fire to protect the retirement of the other pieces. The Rebels got in close and killed all of the horses of one of the guns in this right section, so that the men finally had to remove the piece by hand. As Hall's last gun was being removed all of its horses went down, and Hall was about to ride back and bring it off personally when Wadsworth came up and told him not to waste time worrying over one gun—the thing to do was to get the rest of the guns into position back nearer the town to cover the retreat. Hall obeyed, but he did detail a sergeant and five men to go out and see if they could not yet save the gun. They tried but none of them came back, and the gun stayed there, a bleak silhouette on the smoldering sky line.[6]

As Hall's guns retired, Calef's regulars came up again to take their place, accompanied by Battery L, 1st New York Light Artillery. Those guns went into line and the Rebel guns stormed at them, killing horses and men and smashing gun limbers. Cutler reassembled his infantry, and the brigade formed line at right angles to its original position, drawn up in the roadway facing north. A hundred yards in front there was the cutting of an unfinished railway line running parallel to the road, and somewhere beyond it the isolated 147th New York was still hanging on, invisible in the smoke. Two regiments of Southerners took shelter in the cut and swept the road with a steady fire.

South of the highway things had gone better. General Abner Doubleday, stiff and formal and just a shade pompous, still wearing his laurels as an "old Sumter hero," had come up ahead of his divisions, and Reynolds told him to take charge south of the road while Wadsworth looked after affairs to the north. Doubleday led the Iron Brigade forward to the crest of the rise overlooking Willoughby Run, where there were a plot of trees and a little farm, and Archer's Confederate brigade was coming up the slope in a long line, skirmishers out in front.

Like so many other generals of that era, Doubleday felt that troops going into action needed a word of encouragement, and he called out to the men that this spot was the key to the whole battlefield and must be held "to the last extremity." The men yelled back: "If we can't hold it, where will you find men who can?" or so Doubleday reported later: he had a weakness for touching up the things soldiers said in action. He got the 2nd and 7th Wisconsin into line, and they ran into Archer's men head-on, while the 24th Michigan and the 19th Indiana worked around toward the south and took the Confederate brigade in the flank. Rifles blazed all along the slope and in the grove, and the Confederates suddenly realized that they were up against the first team. The Iron Brigade could hear the Southerners telling each other: "Here are those damned black-hat fellers again. . . . 'Tain't no militia—that's the Army of the Potomac!"[7]

Reynolds rode forward with the battle line. He was a handsome man and a first-rate soldier, who had come up originally with the Pennsylvania Reserves and who had once declined command of the army because he did not think he would be given a free hand. The morning Meade replaced Hooker, Reynolds had carefully put on his dress uniform and sash and had gone formally to call on him; and when Meade, who looked like a wagon master that morning, with an old uniform and muddy boots and a general air of unmilitary slouchiness, had tried to express his embarrassment at being promoted over the man who until recently had been his superior, Reynolds had decently stopped him, assuring him that the post had gone to the man who most deserved it. Now Reynolds was studying the battle, trying to make out just how much weight lay back of the Rebel attack, and a Southern sharpshooter in an old stone barn got him in the sights of his rifle and shot him dead.

Reynolds went down, and his aides took his body to the rear and put it in an ambulance, and the Iron Brigade closed in savagely on Archer's men, getting them off balance, pushing them down into the valley, and driving them back in wild rout. A muscular Irish private in the 2nd Wisconsin ran forward and seized General Archer bodily and made a prisoner of him, hundreds of lesser Confederates surrendered, and the rest of the brigade went staggering back to the high ground to the west.

North of the road, too, there was a success. The 6th Wisconsin had been sent over to help Cutler's men, and it suddenly charged forward to the railway cut, the 84th and 95th New York following it. The Wisconsin men were running in an uneven V-shaped line, the colors at the peak of the V, Colonel Dawes riding along, yelling: "Align on the colors! Close up on that color!" The men swept into the railway cut at the end of the Rebel line, getting a deadly enfilade fire down the length of the Rebel regiments packed between the steel banks, the southern rim of the cut flamed with musket fire, and there was a vicious flurry of hand-to-hand fighting. A Wisconsin private grabbed for a Confederate flag, a Confederate shot him down, a comrade leaped forward swinging his musket like a ball bat and brained the man who had shot him, a corporal ran in and got the flag— and then, all along the line, the Federals were shouting: "Throw down your muskets! Throw down your muskets!"

Hundreds of Southerners obeyed. Dawes shouted for the colonel of the nearest Southern regiment, and the dazed colonel came forward and handed over his sword. Six of his subordinate officers came up and did the same, and Dawes had an awkward moment, standing there with his arms full of swords, until his adjutant relieved him of them. Some of the Rebels escaped by running out at the western end of the cut, but hundreds surrendered, and the beleaguered New York regiment north of the cut was rescued. It had lost two thirds of its men in half an hour's fight.[8]

So for the moment the Federals had won a decided victory, with two Southern brigades beaten back and a good bag of prisoners going to the rear. (General Archer, understandably, was not in good spirits. En route to the rear he met Doubleday, whom he had known before the war, and Doubleday somewhat tactlessly came forward, crying: "Archer! I'm glad to see you!" Archer refused to shake hands, muttering, "Well, I'm not glad to see you by a damn sight." The Irish private who captured him had manhandled him, and his feelings were all out of joint.)[9] Doubleday reflected that Howard and the XI Corps would be up shortly, and it seemed to him that the day was off to a fine start.

It was a start, but no more. A new infantry line appeared on the western ridge, and more and more Confederate guns came up to blast at the Union line. It was not yet noon, and although there was a brief lull there was trouble in the air. The Confederate battle line kept reaching farther and farther to the north—A. P. Hill's corps was twice the size of Reynolds's—and as Doubleday's own division came up it was hurried into position north of the turnpike to match the extension of Confederate strength. All available Federal guns were in action. Hall's half-wrecked battery was called back from its position on the edge of Gettysburg, and it came galloping up the grade of the unfinished railway. A couple of Rebel guns had an exact line on that cutting and they slammed in solid shot and shell, and because the banks were high Hall's men could neither turn around nor go back but had to keep on for half a mile, taking cruel punishment all the way. They got out of the horrible little ravine at last, turned to the left, and went into battery over near the seminary, where Doubleday had men building a half-moon embankment of fence rails and earth as a strong point.[10]

From the north Buford's pickets were frantically reporting that a heavy new Rebel column was coming in, and these enemies appeared presently on Oak Hill, a rounded tree-clad knoll at the northern end of Seminary Ridge, taking the Yankee line in flank. Doubleday sent the last of his reserves up to meet this threat—a division led by General John C. Robinson, a salty old regular of whom a soldier said that "in a much-bearded army, he was the hairiest general I ever saw."[11] Robinson got his men in behind some stone walls and beat off the first Rebel attack, but there were dust clouds all along the northern horizon marking the impending arrival of still more Confederate troops.

Up from the south came the head of the XI Corps, the Dutchmen who still carried Chancellorsville on their shoulders. The men were tired, and on the long hike up from Falmouth their shoes had given out and some of them were barefooted, and they did the final half mile or so into town on the double under the hot July sun.[12] Howard galloped west to the seminary, taking command by virtue of his seniority, and he told Doubleday to stand firm—the Dutchmen would protect his right flank. Two of Howard's divisions he sent straight north through town, planning to seize Oak Hill, but before the men got there a new Confederate battle line was tramping south through the open country east of the hill, and there was nothing for it but to form a hasty line and try to beat them off.

Just south of Gettysburg there was a high hill with a cemetery on top, and

Howard put his headquarters there, holding with him General von Steinwehr with some artillery and two thin brigades of infantry. Steinwehr had been a Prussian professional, and he immediately put his men to work digging pits for the guns and banking earth up against the stone walls about the cemetery. A soldier remembered how strange it was to see batteries galloping helter-skelter into the burying ground, knocking over tombstones and setting up their guns, as often as not, on top of graves.[13]

The right end of the Yankee line north of Gettysburg was in charge of Brigadier General Francis Barlow, the slim, clean-shaven young New York lawyer who had gone into the war as a militia private and now commanded a division, and he tried to anchor it on a little knoll near a stream known as Rock Creek. He planted guns there, a stout regular battery under Lieutenant Bayard Wilkeson, whose father, a correspondent for the New York *Times,* was at that moment coming up toward Gettysburg to see what the news might be. Barlow put the 17th Connecticut in to protect Wilkeson's guns and made note that still another Southern column was materializing on the far side of Rock Creek, away to his right and rear.

The XI Corps line measured perhaps a mile, from Barlow's knoll to its western end. It lay in flat open country, and between its left flank and General Robinson's position below Oak Hill there was a quarter-of-a-mile gap. Up into this gap came Leatherbreeches Dilger and his six brass smoothbores of Battery I, 1st Ohio, and these guns immediately got into a spirited duel with the Rebel guns on Oak Hill. Dilger believed that the place for smoothbores was as close to the enemy as they could get—they were splendid for close-range work but were not of much account for the longer distances—and when a battery of rifled guns came up beside him he asked its commander, Lieutenant William Wheeler, to lay down a covering fire while he went forward. Wheeler did so, and Dilger's battery trotted straight ahead for several hundred yards, halting once under fire while Dilger had the men collect fence rails and other debris to fill a ditch that blocked the way. Dilger at last got into position at the range he liked, and while he fired Wheeler brought his own guns up to join him, and in a short time the two batteries had dismounted five Rebel cannon.[14]

It was early afternoon by now, and the Rebel line formed a long semicircle from southwest clear around to northeast. From end to end this semicircle flamed and crashed, and Howard sent couriers off, breakneck, to the nearest Federal troops, Slocum's and Sickles's corps, begging them to come on to Gettysburg as fast as they could. West of Willoughby Run (although the Federals did not know it) was Lee himself. He had not at first planned to bring on a general battle, but he was finding that the setup was practically ideal, with the Yankees badly outnumbered and outflanked, and he ordered an advance of all the line. The wild uproar of battle rose to a crescendo and the great blazing semicircle began to roll forward.

Something had to give, and the break came first on the knoll where Barlow had his guns. Rebel infantry charged in close and laid down a killing fire, and two Confederate batteries hit the knoll with everything they had, and Barlow went down critically wounded. Young Lieutenant Wilkeson was coolly picturesque on his white horse amid his guns, but a sharpshooter killed him, the supporting infantry gave way, and then the guns limbered up hastily and went to the rear. At the other end of the line Confederate infantry drove for the gap between the two corps formations. The left-flank element of the XI Corps, 75th Pennsylvania, changed front to the left to meet this threat, lost 111 men in fifteen minutes' fighting across a snake-rail fence and then had to run for it. All along the line regiments caved in, and the position was lost.[15]

For the rest of the life of the Army of the Potomac there would be arguments about this, and other troops were to complain that the miserable Dutchmen had let them down again, but the line simply could not be held, and when the men rallied a few hundred yards in the rear the Confederates who had been advancing beyond Rock Creek got in behind the right flank and shook them loose once more. Before long the whole corps was in retreat again, and from the cemetery Steinwehr saw the rout and sent one of his two brigades out through town to form a rear guard.

Dilger's and Wheeler's batteries had to limber up quickly, with four Southern batteries lashing at them and yelling Southern infantry only a hundred yards away. As the guns moved off a solid shot smashed the axle of one of Wheeler's pieces. He halted and put his sweating gunners to work arranging a rope lashing to sling the dismounted gun beneath one of the limbers—hot enough work it was, too, under the blistering sun, with Rebel bullets whipping in all around and the plain draining itself of men in blue. They got the gun fixed at last and went off again, but a gun is one of the most perverse of all inanimate objects, and before the battery had gone far this one broke loose from its lashing and thumped down on the ground. Wheeler left it there and went off without it. (After the battle he came back and found it, remounted it, and put it back in service.)[16] From time to time Dilger halted a section and fired a few rounds of canister at the pursuers.

From Oak Hill all the way to the south of the seminary there were boiling smoke clouds and a tremendous racket of guns and rifles and yelling men. On the extreme right of this line General Robinson had planted the 16th Maine, with instructions to stay there no matter what, and these men were fighting against enemies who had come in so close that the Federals could hear the Rebel officers shouting orders to their men. The 16th's colonel protested that he had only two hundred men and could not stay where he was, but Robinson repeated that orders were to hold on at any cost. The regiment edged back a trifle and found itself isolated on a narrow, wedgeshaped ridge, Southern infantry firing fast from behind a rail fence on one side, a new battle line charging in on the other. This could end in just one way, and everyone present knew what that way was going to be. The color-bearer went dodging along the line at last, and each man tore off a piece of the regimental flag and tucked it in his pocket, and then it was every man for himself, and those who were still on their feet struck out for Cemetery Hill south of town. That evening thirty-five of them reassembled there.[17]

Farther south the line was in no better shape. The whole of Robinson's division was cut to pieces, more than sixteen hundred of its twenty-five hundred men being shot, among them Brigadier General Gabriel R. Paul, a white-haired regular who got a bullet through both eyes. A Pennsylvania infantry brigade led by Colonel Roy Stone got into a tremendous series of fights around the unfinished railroad cut, captured it, lost it, recaptured it and lost it again, seized it for a third time, and then was blasted out for good by two Rebel batteries posted to shoot lengthwise down the cut. The brigade retired with a loss of two thirds of its numbers, and Colonel Stone wrote proudly that his men fought "as if each man felt that upon his own arm hung the fate of the day and the nation."[18]

They all fought that way, but there were just too many Confederates present, and after the XI Corps line collapsed the line west of town was bound to go. Cutler's brigade retreated at last, leaving a thousand men dead and wounded on the ground, and when he came to write his report Cutler remarked sadly: "I can only hope that the country may not again require that these brave men shall go through so severe an ordeal."[19]

Off to the left, near the rail-and-dirt barricade which Doubleday had had the men build near the seminary, the Iron Brigade grimly hung on in the grove which the general had told them to hold to the last extremity. The last extremity had visibly arrived. The Rebels were attacking from three sides, and the brigade was dissolving in fire and smoke and ear-shattering noise. General Meredith was knocked out when his horse was killed and fell on him, the 19th Indiana lost eight color-bearers, Colonel Fairchild of the 2nd Wisconsin went down with a wound that was to cost him an arm, and Private Patrick Maloney, who had captured General Archer, was killed.

And here in the middle of it all was the 24th Michigan, with a county judge for a colonel and a county sheriff for lieutenant colonel and all the line officers carrying presentation swords; the regiment that had once been ostracized because its valor was unproven. Since Fredericksburg the regiment had been accepted, but in the unfathomable economics of army life the men seem to have felt that they still owed the rest of the brigade something, and here on Seminary Ridge the bill had come up for payment. Three times Colonel Morrow sent back word that the position was untenable, and each time General Wadsworth grimly ordered him to hold on anyway. Some of the survivors remembered forming line of battle six times that hot afternoon, with the rank battle fog lying low under the trees and unappeasable enemies coming in from all directions at once. Four color-bearers were killed, and the regiment sagged toward the rear, and Colonel Morrow ordered the fifth color-bearer to jab the flagstaff in the ground and stand beside it for a rally. The man was killed before he could obey, Morrow himself took up the flag and waved it, a private ran up and took it away from him, muttering that it wasn't up to the colonel to carry the colors and then this private was killed and another man took the staff. Then he too was shot, and Morrow got the flag after all, after which a bullet creased his skull and he himself went down.[20]

Back went the Iron Brigade to the barricade by the seminary, held by a tough handful of the troops who had been fighting north of the turnpike. The Rebels paused for breath and realignment, then sent a strong column straight in on the low breastworks, and the colonel of the 7th Wisconsin complained that he had trouble making his men hold their fire until the Rebels got to close quarters. The range suited him finally, and the Westerners put in a smashing volley. The whole front rank of the Rebel line seemed to go down in smoke and dust, but there were other ranks behind that kept on coming, and the artillery flailed those ranks without mercy.[21]

Howard had sent word that the guns were to make a last-ditch stand on Cemetery Hill, but Doubleday's chief of artillery had understood him to say Seminary Hill and so he had plugged in a dozen guns, hub to hub, beside the half-moon barricade and they were firing canister as fast as the men could load. Over in the turnpike was one of the veteran artillery outfits, Battery B of the 4th Regulars, the battery General Gibbon used to command when he was a captain fighting Indians out West. It was led now by Lieutenant James Stewart, and he was on his horse amid his guns, facing always toward the enemy—partly because he was a brave man and partly because his horse was a veteran with certain fixed ideas about battle. In some previous action a shell fragment had cut off most of the horse's tail, and ever since then this beast steadfastly refused to expose his rear to the foe when the shooting started. Stewart swung his guns around now and hit the charging Confederates in flank, and for the moment the assault was beaten back.[22]

It was only for the moment. A. P. Hill was piling his men in remorselessly and they were great fighters. Their line outflanked the Union line both north and south, and there was no possibility of stopping them. The line by the seminary crumbled and finally collapsed, and when the retreating Federals left the ridge they had to run the gantlet with Rebel battle lines closing in on them from north and south while still other Rebels fired at them from the west. The 7th Wisconsin lost more men on this retreat from the seminary than in all the rest of the day's fighting, and Buford's cavalry came back in to fight dismounted in valiant protection of the left flank. Some of the horse holders turned their animals over to retreating infantrymen so that they themselves could get into the scrap.

From Cemetery Hill the men in reserve looked down on a wild panorama of retreat. Thick battle fog lay on the ridge and the late afternoon's sun shone down through it, and out of it came the swaying lines of beaten men, turning now and then to fire a defiant volley, batteries lunging down roads and lanes with men clinging to gun limbers and caissons, shreds and patches of smoke lying in the hollows and on the plain, with flags making bright spots of color here and there as the breeze caught them. One man recalled seeing a color-bearer plant his flag and turn to face his pursuers, part of his regiment clustering about him. The smoke from their rifles floated up, the charging Confederates fired heavily in reply, and the knot of soldiers around the colors broke up in flight. The man with the flag remained by the staff, shaking his fist at his foes as they came nearer, then someone drew a bead on him and he went down and the flag went down and the retreat was unbroken again.[23]

Going through the town was worst of all. All of the lines of retreat converged here, and a considerable number of Confederates had got into town, and there was a maddening chaos in the streets and between the houses—thoroughfares all clogged with guns, wagons, and ambulances, retreating regiments colliding with each other and getting hopelessly intermingled, Rebel gunners hitting the place at long range so steadily that a number of soldiers were wounded by bricks and other debris knocked down from buildings, Rebel infantry regiments firing unexpectedly down the streets, dense smoke clouds settling down so that nobody could see which way he was going. One of the High Dutch regiments, the 45th New York, went double-quicking down a side street to avoid a traffic jam and ran into Confederate infantry fire. It turned and ducked down an alley and found itself in a cul-de-sac. There was no way out but the way by which it had come in, which was blanketed by rifle fire. Barely a third of the men got out of it and went back to Cemetery Hill. Steinwehr's rear-guard brigade helped, and Dilger ran a gun section out in a street near the public square and held the pursuit back for a time, but before the day ended several thousand Federals were taken prisoner in Gettysburg.[24]

The rest of the army pulled itself together on Cemetery Hill in the smoke-stained evening. Losses had been appalling. The I Corps had taken between 9,500 and 10,000 men into action and had approximately 2,400 left. Its divisions and brigades were mere remnants. The Iron Brigade, which had had the worst of it, had lost almost exactly two thirds of its 1,800 effectives, and for the rest of the war it existed as a shadow, always a great name but never again a mighty force in battle. The 2nd Wisconsin had brought only 69 men back to the hill. As the 7th Wisconsin came up the slope a shell wounded Sergeant Daniel McDermott, who had carried the regimental flag in every battle of the war, and splintered the flagstaff. They laid McDermott on a caisson which lumbered along just ahead of the regiment, and he rode up onto the hill, still feebly waving the tattered flag on the broken staff. The 24th Michigan, largest regiment in the brigade, had had the most fearful loss: 399 of its 496 men had been shot, for a loss of 80 per cent, and whatever it was which the men had felt they owed the rest of the brigade, it would seem to have been paid by now. In a house in Gettysburg the Confederates had laid a number of the 24th's wounded, and later that evening Colonel Morrow was carried in to share the quarters with them. As he was brought in the wounded men raised their heads and asked him if he was finally satisfied with his regiment.[25]

Howard's corps had suffered heavily too. There had been fewer outright casualties, but nearly 4,000 men had been captured in the wild mix-up attending the retreat through town, and 1,500 more had fled to the rear, to be rounded up later that evening by the provost guard of the oncoming XII Corps.[26] All in all, as evening came down there were no more than 5,000 fighting men left of the two corps which had fought that day. These were grouped in a semicircle on and around Cemetery Hill, and between the height of the ground and the trenches and gun pits Steinwehr had dug they put up a bold front, but if the Confederates had followed up their victory they probably could have taken the hill and everybody on it. The expected attack did not come, however. Lee's orders were vague and seem not to have been well understood, and the Confederates themselves had been badly mauled in the day's fighting and were ready for a rest.

As the exhausted Federals took position on the hill they met Howard, still defiant, riding back and forth with a battle flag tucked under the stump of his right arm. Better yet, they met Hancock, who had been sent up by Meade to look things over and see whether the whole army should go to Gettysburg and make a finish fight of it. Hancock got there just as the retreat was ending, and he had a brief passage at arms with Howard. Howard outranked him and did not see how Meade could send a junior to take charge, and he was slightly stuffy about it for a time. But in the end the two men straightened things out without too much of an argument and saw to it that an orderly line of battle was formed. Hancock decided that Gettysburg was a good place for a fight, sent Meade a note saying so, and continued to look about him.

Straight east from Cemetery Hill there was a saddle of high ground running for half a mile to another high point, Culp's Hill, all rocky and overgrown with trees. A ravine cut into this saddle from the north, halfway between the hills, and Rebel patrols were edging forward into it, and it occurred to Hancock that if the Rebels got up on Culp's Hill the whole Union position would be ruined. He spurred over to the west side of Cemetery Hill, where Doubleday was collecting the remnants of the I Corps, and told him to send a division over to occupy Culp's Hill.

Doubleday demurred: his men were disorganized, they were almost out of ammunition, many of their officers were dead, they had had a hard day, someone else would have to go to Culp's Hill. Hancock was not the man to take excuses, and in his pocket he had Meade's letter giving him control for that evening over everybody around Gettysburg. He stood up in his stirrups and he raised one hand and he thundered largely, and a soldier who watched noted that despite the heat and dirt of the day Hancock then, as always, wore spotless white linen, gleaming cuffs visible at the ends of his sleeves.

"Sir!" concluded Hancock. "*I* am in command on this field. Send every man you have got!"[27]

So Wadsworth and his division went over to Culp's Hill, and the day's fighting was over. The sun went down, and the air was all tainted with smoke and death. Slocum's men came up, and some of Sickles's, and Hancock galloped back to Taneytown to see Meade. Sometime after midnight he and Meade reached the battlefield, and Meade went around to see what he could see, in the warm July moonlight, of the field where his army had begun its greatest fight. From southwest all the way around to northeast, Confederate campfires glowed in the night.

2. ALL THE TRUMPETS SOUNDED

Philippe Regis de Trobriand, French-born colonel commanding the 3rd Brigade of the 1st Division of the III Corps, climbed to the bell tower of St. Joseph's Convent in Emmitsburg, eight miles south of Gettysburg, to see what he could see. On the lawn in front of the convent his five regiments had stacked arms, and wisps of smoke from the fires of innumerable coffee boilers were floating up through the trees in the still evening air. Some guns were in park across the road, and there was a great coming and going of couriers, staff officers, and other mounted persons. Off to the north there was an uneven jerky rumble coming down the wind, faint but unmistakable. Colonel de Trobriand looked around, found that he could learn nothing in this belfry that he did not already know, and came down, his jack boots clumping incongruously in the quiet halls. At a window he came upon a group of nuns peering shyly out at this invasion of soldiers. Being a Frenchman, he stopped for a word with them, and he chided them lightly for giving way to the venial sin of curiosity.

"Permit me," he said, "to make one request of you. Ask St. Joseph to keep the Rebel army away from here; for if they come before I get away I do not know what will become of your beautiful convent."

The nuns vanished and the colonel went on down and came out on the lawn, and the brigade quieted down for the night. Early next morning—July 2, clear and warm after a rainy night—orders arrived, and the brigade fell into line and took the dusty road north toward Gettysburg, and a Michigan man in the ranks knew a moment of homesickness, reflecting that the bells chiming for morning mass sounded just like the church bells in his home town. As they went on up the road the colonel thought about the way war had broken the peaceful isolation of the convent, and years later he wrote: "I have never returned to Emmitsburg, but it would astonish me very little to hear that the two armies had gone to Gettysburg to fight on account of the miracle performed by St. Joseph, interceding in favor of these pious damsels." Meditating thus, the colonel got his brigades up to the hills south of Gettysburg and joined the rest of the army.[1]

The morning was hot and the army was tired. Most of the men who had not fought the day before had been on the roads far into the night. An air of foreboding lay upon the battlefield, heavy as the muggy weight of the July heat. There was an occasional spat-spat of picket firing, and now and then a battery loosed a few rounds at some temporary target, but these outbursts only emphasized the expectant quiet. The Army of the Potomac waited grimly, and in rear of Cemetery Ridge the 120 ambulances of the II Corps were ranked on a slope, the chief of ambulances making the rounds to see that each wagon was properly equipped—keg of water under the end of each of the two leather-covered benches, supply of beef stock and bandages under the front seat, a stretcher properly hung on each side. Tough Colonel Cross of the 5th New Hampshire, promoted recently to brigade command, rode past and grinned, and called out: "We shan't want any of your dead carts today."[2] Farther up the slope, Meade had set up headquarters in a two-room cottage.

Meade had put his men where the ground was high. His line curled around Culp's Hill on the east, ran west across the saddle to Cemetery Hill, made a ninety-degree turn to the left in a little wood called Ziegler's Grove on the western slope of this hill, and then went straight south for a mile or more along Cemetery Ridge. This ridge lost altitude, trailing off at last to lower ground covered with small trees and broken by tiny watercourses, and rising finally to two dominant hills—Little Round Top, very craggy and full of boulders, and a quarter of a mile south of it a higher hill, Big Round Top, sometimes known locally as Sugar Loaf.

From Culp's Hill through Cemetery Hill the line was held by Howard's men and Slocum's men and the remnants of the I Corps. Hancock's II Corps held Ziegler's Grove and the open ridge immediately south of it, and Dan Sickles had been told to put his III Corps in beside Hancock. It was Meade's idea that Sickles could hold whatever part of the ridge Hancock's men could not cover, and that in addition he would be able to occupy the Round Tops. George Sykes had brought his V Corps up during the night and was held in reserve behind Cemetery Hill.

The position was strong, and some of the officers remarked that if the Rebs attacked here it would be Fredericksburg in reverse, and they frankly liked the idea. But Sickles was not happy. He had the low part of the ridge—it was so low where he was that it practically ceased to be a ridge at all—and he believed that the ground would be very hard to defend. The Round Tops would be a good anchor, but Sickles did not think he could stretch his two divisions to reach them. Meade's orders did not seem clear, and Sickles had some of his men posted farther west than Meade had intended, down in flat land bordering a little brook known as Plum Run. As the morning wore on Sickles grew very uneasy, and he kept looking out at the Emmitsburg road in front of his position.

This road ran southwest from Gettysburg, skirting Ziegler's Grove and going down over rolling country, getting farther and farther away from Cemetery Ridge. Half a mile due west of the low ground which Sickles was occupying the road passed over a broad flat hill on top of which there was a peach orchard, and this hill was somewhat higher than the ground where Sickles's men were. Sickles believed that if the enemy put men and guns in the peach orchard they could drive him out. He noticed, too, that an uneven fold of high land ran off southeast from the peach orchard in the direction of the Round Tops. This ground was rugged, with little hills and ravines and woods and rocky ledges, and if the Rebels got in there they would be squarely on the Federal left flank and it might be extremely hard to dislodge them.

Sickles finally grew so worried that he rode over to headquarters and asked Meade to come down and have a look. Meade refused. Ordinarily he was a front-line operator, but now that he was army commander he was a little immersed in details at headquarters. He believed that morning that the real fighting was apt to break out near Culp's Hill, and anyway, he did not care much for Sickles, and at last he bluntly told Sickles to put his men where the original orders told him to put them, and be done with it. When Sickles still protested, Meade unbent enough to send Artillerist Henry Hunt over to survey the ground and make a recommendation. Sickles and Hunt went away, and Meade went back to his other concerns.

To make Sickles feel still worse, when he got back to his troops he found that the cavalry was gone. Buford's troopers had been convering the left flank, but through some misunderstanding Pleasonton had taken them away from there without sending anyone in to replace them. Sickles felt naked. He put a skirmish line out on the Emmitsburg road, and the skirmishers kept having little brushes with Rebel patrols, and around noon Hunt suggested that Sickles make a reconnaissance to find out just what the enemy was doing off to the west. So Sickles called in Colonel Berdan and told him to take four companies of his sharpshooters, with the 3rd Maine Infantry for support, and go out to investigate.[3]

Noon came, and everything was quiet except for a vicious little fight on the skirmish line in front of Ziegler's Grove, where General Alexander Hays was posted with the third division of Hancock's corps. In the empty land halfway between his line and the enemy's there was a big barn, and Federal and Confederate skirmishers were bickering over it, each side wanting to possess it as an advanced post for sharpshooters. The firing grew rather heavy, and General Hays decided he would ride out and look into it. He would go alone, he said, except for one mounted orderly.

A little Irish private on a big white horse was detailed for this job, and Hays looked him over and asked him brusquely if he were a brave man. The private grinned and said nothing, but Hays was a brigadier general, and when he spoke to an enlisted man he liked to get an answer, so he barked angrily: "Will you follow me, sir?" The Irishman saluted and said: "Gineral, if ye's are killed and go to hell it will not be long before I am tapping on the window." So the general and the private made the trip, Hays carrying his divisional flag and the orderly riding close at his elbow. Neither of them was hit, and Hays got the skirmishers straightened out.[4]

Meanwhile, Berdan was leading his men west. They crossed the highway and passed through a belt of woods, coming out on the southern part of Seminary Ridge, and before long they passed a farmhouse. A small boy, who must have been having a big day for himself, came out from behind the barn, big-eyed and excited, and pointed to another wood ahead of them, crying: "There are lots of Rebels in there—in rows!" The men laughed at him and doubtless told him to go down in the cellar and be safe, and they kept on going. They found out shortly that the small boy knew exactly what he was talking about.

They found a line of Rebel skirmishers, got into a fight with them, and when the skirmishers withdrew and Berdan's men pursued they ran into any number of Rebels all in rows, just as the boy had said. For twenty minutes the opposing lines blazed away at each other under the trees, the 3rd Maine coming up beside the sharpshooters. Berdan realized at last that he had found what he was looking for, and he took his men back to Sickles's line east of the road and told Sickles that a solid body of Rebel infantry was moving around to the left.[5]

That was enough for Sickles. Here was Chancellorsville all over again, with the Confederates marching through the wood past Sickles's front, and hot-blooded impetuous Sickles was unable to contain himself. This time he did not jump to the conclusion that the Rebels were in retreat. On the contrary, he knew perfectly well what they were up to—a smash at the Federal left flank—and the only trouble was that Sickles decided to answer the threat himself without waiting to consult headquarters, and in his haste he came up with the wrong answer. He did ask Hunt if he could move forward to the Emmitsburg road, but Hunt warned him that this was a question for Meade to answer, and then Hunt rode away. So Sickles issued his orders anyway. He took his whole corps forward, a mile-long line of battle with waving flags and rumbling batteries rolling west in the afternoon sunlight. John Gibbon, commanding Hancock's 2nd Division on Cemetery Ridge, looked out in amazement and wondered if a general order to advance upon the enemy had somehow missed him.

What Sickles got out of his advance was a longer line than he had had before. He wanted to hold the road and the peach-orchard hill and to bend the rest of his line back to the Round Tops, and he did not have enough men for it. Humphrey's division took position in the road, and Birney's division crammed the little orchard with men and guns and extended its line back toward the southeast, down a little slope from the orchard, across a rolling wheat field, and up through a maze of thickets and boulders and rocky crevices to a little hill which went by the descriptive name of Devil's Den. At Devil's Den, Birney ran out of troops. He got some guns up there beside his infantry—uncommonly rough work it was, too, manhandling the clumsy weapons up the little hill through rocks and trees and gullies—and he managed to plant one regiment and two guns down in a valley that separated Devil's Den from the Round Tops, but he could do no more than that. His line was thin, and he had no reserves.

Just as the men were getting into their places Meade decided to call a conference of his corps commanders. Sedgwick was coming up with his VI Corps, his men winded after an all-night hike of thirty-five miles, and the army was complete at last. Meade issued the conference call, but before the generals assembled Meade heard about what Sickles had done and he rode over, at last, to see about it personally.

When he joined Sickles and looked out at the new line he became wrathy. Sickles's corps was half a mile out in front of the rest of the army. Its left had no support, on the right all connection with Hancock had been broken, and the peach orchard looked to Meade like a vulnerable spot which the enemy could assail from three sides at once. He spoke of these matters with some heat, and Sickles asked him if he should take his men back to the original line. Meade said that he should, and then what the army had been waiting for all day began to happen, starting with an earsplitting crash of artillery. Confederate James Longstreet had put forty-six guns in line where they would bear on the orchard and the rest of Birney's line and they all began firing at once. A long cloud of smoke went rolling up above the distant trees, and Birney's line was laced with exploding shell.[6]

Meade immediately reversed himself. He barked at Sickles that it was too late to withdraw now—Sickles would have to stay where he was and the rest of the army would try to support him. Then Meade went galloping back to headquarters, where he told Sykes to get his corps down to the left end of the line as fast as he could. He had no sooner given this order than another cannonade opened on the right of the Federal line, and the hills to the northeast and northwest became alive with a long semicircle of flashing guns. Enormous echoes went rocking back and forth from the ridges, Gettysburg was ringed in fire and smoke and shaking sound, and the Federal gun positions on Cemetery Hill were caught in a cross fire that smashed tombstones, splintered gun carriages, tore men's bodies apart, and sent the horrible mixed fragments flying through the blinding smoke. So confusing was this fire that a Massachusetts regiment which had been crouching behind a stone wall facing north finally crawled over on the enemy's side of the wall, figuring that it was on the whole somewhat safer.

One shell exploded directly beneath a Federal gun, putting the entire gun crew out of action, and an artillery officer remarked with approval that men ran in and put the gun back in action before the wounded were removed. Another shellburst put twenty-seven men out of action—a fantastic toll for one shell, in those days—and an Ohio private noted later that the ground around one battery was hit by 115 separate projectiles. The Federal gunners fired furiously in reply. Northeast of Culp's Hill they pulverized a Rebel artillery battalion, smashing guns and killing men and, in the end, knocking the props out from under the murderous bombardment of Cemetery Hill.[7]

On Sickles's front General Hunt kept piling battery after battery in from the artillery reserve, and the guns took position just behind the peach orchard along a little country lane and got into a tremendous fight with Longstreet's gunners. For a time they followed the old tactics that had been worked out at Antietam, twenty or thirty guns concentrating at a time on one Rebel battery, shifting to another when they had put the first out of action. One gunner reported that they silenced five batteries in succession. But they were not having things all their own way, and the Confederate fire was heavy, especially in the peach orchard, where shell and solid shot took a frightful toll. A New York battery there found itself fighting two enemy batteries at once, one section dueling with one while the other two fought the other. The Rebels had the exact range. Supporting Yankee infantry hugged the ground behind fences and mounds of earth, trees were stripped and broken, men and horses were mangled, and the battery commander wrote that he was in "as sharp an artillery fight as I ever witnessed."[8]

Then the high quaver of the Rebel yell went up from field and wood and the infantry came out—John B. Hood's famous division, charging in from the southwest, driving straight for the Devil's Den, forcing its way through ravines and thickets and sweeping over the rocky little hill and around into the valley between Devil's Den and the Round Tops.

The two guns and one regiment which Birney had put in this valley put up a prodigious fight, but they had to give ground, and the defenders of Devil's Den itself were swamped. This was miserable ground for a fight, the rocks and gullies breaking up formations so that there seemed to be no connected lines of any kind. Men fought by regiments and by companies and squads, a choking haze of smoke lying close to the ground. The Rebels got in among the guns and captured three of them, and Birney sent off desperate appeals for help. Colonel de Trobriand, who was in the wheat field and the wood beside it, had to send two of his regiments over to help, and he was left holding part of his line with the 5th Michigan deployed as skirmishers, volleying away against a host of Rebels who found shelter in a muddy little ravine that ran across his front. He said later that if the Confederates had jumped up and charged then his whole brigade would have been demolished. Even as it was, his line was visibly melting away, and it seemed to him that each of his men was fighting as if "the destiny of the Republic was attached to the desperate vigor of his efforts." He wedged the 17th Maine in behind a little stone wall, and to the left the terrible uproar of firing and shouting men came closer and closer and he knew that Devil's Den was being lost.[9]

Sickles took a brigade away from Humphreys and sent it pounding over double-quick, but the line had been stretched too thin. The brigade came in just as fragments of the battle line were breaking to the rear. De Trobriand's Maine regiment was flanked out from behind its wall, his Michigan skirmish line collapsed, and at last the whole left of Birney's line gave way in wild confusion. The men who had been defending the valley below the Round Tops were driven back, yelling Confederates came charging through, and a solid Rebel brigade swung off and went plunging straight ahead for Little Round Top, upon which at that moment there was no one in Union blue except a few men in a signal detachment.

Here was unrelieved and final disaster, coming on fast and yelling like fiends, for if the Rebels ever got Little Round Top the whole of Cemetery Ridge would have to be abandoned and the battle would be lost once and for all. Up on the hill with the signal men was General Warren, and he spotted the danger just in time and hurried off for help. Just north of the hill he met George Sykes bringing his corps down to reinforce the left as Meade had ordered—George Sykes, stiff and crusty and very much old-army, looking always a little tired and out of sorts, uninspired and uninspiring, but all soldier for all of that. Sykes was sending two brigades down into the flat land along Plum Run to reinforce Birney, and at Warren's request he shot another brigade straight south to defend Little Round Top.

This was the brigade of Colonel Strong Vincent, who had sat in the moonlight a couple of nights earlier to reflect that a man could do worse than die on Pennsylvania soil under the old flag. Vincent got to the southern slope of the hill and swung his four regiments into line just as the Confederates came lunging up the valley. The Confederates clambered up over the boulders to finish things, the Federals squatted behind the boulders and met them with fire, the valley was filled with smoke and flame and a great deafening clamor, and the Rebels shifted their strength to break in the flanks of this new Yankee line.[10]

At the extreme left of Vincent's line was the 20th Maine led by Colonel Joshua Chamberlain, who had been college professor and minister of the gospel before the war and who was becoming a good deal of a soldier. Vincent went to the southern end of the hill with him, pointed down the slope, and told him to take his 350 men down there and hold the ground at all hazards, and the 20th ran down the hill and collided with a powerful flanking column that bent the left half of the regiment back at a ninety-degree angle and threatened to overwhelm the whole outfit by sheer weight. Chamberlain had to space his men several paces apart to keep the Rebels from getting around his left, and when the first wild rush was beaten back the Rebels settled down among the logs and trees and rocks for the sharpest fire fight this Maine regiment was ever in. The reeking smoke filled the air, the Yankee line swayed and staggered as if the weight of the attack were a tangible force that shoved men off balance, and the valley rang with rifle fire, with the clang of metal ramrods in hot musket barrels, with the yells and cries of Northerners and Southerners caught up in a great fury of combat.

Far behind him Chamberlain heard a new burst of shooting and yelling, which for all he knew might mean that the other end of Vincent's line had caved in. Nearly half of the 20th was down, ammunition was almost gone, here and there the colonel could see men preparing to swing their muskets as clubs when the next Rebel assault was driven home. In sheer desperation—for that next assault would inevitably crush the entire line—Chamberlain ordered his men to fix bayonets and charge.

No one could hear a shouted order in that terrible racket, but somehow the word was passed along the line, by gesture and by example, and the men glanced right and left, nerving themselves for the shock. A young lieutenant suddenly waved his sword, yelled: "Come on! Come on, boys!" and ran toward the Confederate line, which was barely thirty yards away. The color guard followed him, streamers of smoke eddying about the shaken flags. There was a moment of hesitation, and then with a wild cry the whole regiment charged in a long, ragged line.

Perhaps it worked because it was so unexpected. The Confederates fell into confusion as the charge hit them—Chamberlain remembered one Rebel officer firing a pistol with one hand while he held out his sword in token of surrender with the other—and the whole first line broke and ran. The second line collapsed a moment later, the Maine regiment swung up over the slope of Big Round Top, and Chamberlain at last had trouble getting his men to halt and adjust their line, the men crying that they were "on the road to Richmond." They sent upward of four hundred prisoners to the rear.[11]

Yet if that wildly improbable counterattack had saved the army's flank, it had saved it only for the moment. This was a day on which crisis followed crisis. While they were hitting the 20th Maine the Confederates were also working around the right of Vincent's line. They made better progress here, and the right-flank regiment, 16th Michigan, was broken and driven back. Vincent ran down into the melee to rally his men and the Rebels shot him dead, and once more the way was open for Confederate conquest of Little Round Top.

General Warren was still on hand, watching, and he saw this new disaster and once again rode madly off for help. The first regiment he met was the 140th New York, part of General Stephen Weed's brigade in Sykes's corps, and while he was still fifty yards away Warren began shouting to Colonel Patrick O'Rourke to bring his men up the hill as fast as they could run. O'Rourke protested that he was under orders to follow the rest of the brigade somewhere else, but Warren replied: "Never mind that, Paddy! Bring them up on the double-quick—don't stop for aligning! I'll take the responsibility!" And because Warren was known to be intimate with Meade, O'Rourke assumed that he could square things, so he took the 140th up on Little Round Top at a dead run.

He had no time whatever to spare. The Rebels who had broken the Michigan regiment were coming up the hill. O'Rourke jumped off his horse, tossed the reins to his orderly, called out: "This way, boys!" and ran down the slope toward the enemy, his men at his heels. It was as strange a counterattack as the army ever saw. The men went in with unloaded weapons. They did not stop to fix bayonets, they did not even club their empty muskets: they simply ran straight at their foes, and the only weight their charge had was the weight of their running bodies. Perhaps the mere appearance of fresh troops was enough for the moment. The Confederates wavered and drew back, and the 140th went into line beside Vincent's brigade, and in a few minutes the rest of Weed's brigade was on the hill with them.[12]

So was a battery of six three-inch rifles, whose sweating gunners had practically carried their guns to the hilltop piece by piece since there was nothing resembling a road up this rocky height. This battery began to fire on Rebel reinforcements in the valley—the gun muzzles could not be depressed enough to hit the men on the sides of Little Round Top itself—and from the Rebel line in front and from a host of sharpshooters in Devil's Den a new fury of rifle fire hit the Federals. General Weed was killed as he gave some order to the battery commander, and when that officer bent over him to examine his wound, a sharpshooter got him too, and he fell dead on top of the general, and all of the hill with its steep slopes and its rocks and its tangled underbrush was smoking and crackling like a volcano.

In front of the Round Tops everything was coming loose. The Devil's Den line had long since dissolved, the wheat field was gone, and all of the uneven half mile between Round Top Valley and the peach orchard was smoke and flying bullets and wild shouting. Two of Sykes's brigades came in to hold the ground between the peach orchard and the wheat field, and their division commander, General Barnes, lined them up and made a few patriotic and inspirational remarks, while the men cheered bravely (So says the record, at any rate. One of the private soldiers involved wrote that the general told them: "Boys, I want you to put in a few licks for Pennsylvania. The Bucktails will go in on your left. Forward!")[13]

For a time these brigades made progress, and Hancock sent a whole division in to retake the wheat field and drive the Rebel line back on its supports—the ghost of the old Irish Brigade storming along beside red-bearded Colonel Cross and his soldiers, the men who had broken the Rebel line at Antietam and swarmed nearly to the stone wall at Fredericksburg and held on in the great last-ditch fight at Chancellorsville. These men got into woods and hollows south of the wheat field, and Sykes's division of regulars came in on their left, and it seemed briefly that the whole position had been stabilized.

Then Longstreet sent in a fresh division, and the Rebels caught the peach-orchard angle from three sides at once, just as Meade had foreseen. In from the west came General Barksdale and his Mississippians—the same general and the same troops who had held the Fredericksburg water front against the bridge-builders—and they charged straight through a picket fence, knocking it down by sheer impact, and they shot and stabbed at a Pennsylvania regiment that was dug in behind it, and after a flurry of hand-to-hand fighting under the shattered peach trees the Union defenders turned and ran and the peach orchard was gone.

With this position lost, there was no way on earth to save Birney's line. (It was "Birney's" line only by courtesy now, the reinforcements far outnumbering the original defenders, all the units so mixed up that nobody quite knew where anybody else was.) The Rebels who had broken in the angle drove straight on toward Little Round Top, and they took the entire line in flank, destroying one segment after another. The artillery which General Hunt had lined up behind the peach orchard enfiladed the charging Rebels and killed them by platoons, but these Southerners were tough and they kept on going, and one after another the brigades which had restored Birney's line found that the Rebels were coming in on their right rear.

The volunteer brigades Sykes had sent in discovered it first. They faced south, and a color-bearer rode up to his brigade commander and said: "Colonel, I'll be damned if I don't think we are faced the wrong way. The Rebs are up there in the woods behind us, on the right." The Colonel investigated and found that the man was right, and sent an aide back to tell the division commander. The aide ran into a host of armed Rebels right where division headquarters was supposed to be, and the whole Union line seemed to have vanished in smoke and confusion. Rebel units were intermingled with Federals, some regiments were surrounded without knowing it, the 4th Michigan saw its colonel killed with a bayonet while he was still in the saddle, and the only order or pattern in any of it was the fact that defeat and collapse progressed steadily from right to left, from the peach orchard toward Devil's Den.[14]

The division Hancock had sent over was forced to retreat, more than a third of its men killed or wounded, three of its four brigade commanders shot down. (Among them was Colonel Cross, carried to the rear in one of the ambulances which he had gaily said would not be needed this day, wounded mortally.) When this division fled the regulars were flanked, and as they went back toward Plum Run they crossed open marshy ground and came under a storm of musket fire, losing nine hundred of their two thousand men. The skipper of the 11th U.S. Infantry reported grimly that he had lost half of his men "without inflicting the slightest damage upon the enemy."[15] Of Birney's entire line, reinforcements and all, nothing whatever was left except a dense carpet of dead and wounded men lying on the ground, and broken waves of fugitives going back toward Cemetery Ridge, some in good order and under control, some altogether out of control and in no order whatever. And there was a huge gap in the line of the Army of the Potomac.

This gap immediately got bigger. After the peach orchard fell, Humphreys's line along the Emmitsburg road was doomed, particularly so since a division of A. P. Hill's men assaulted it in front while Longstreet's men were flanking it from the south. As the left end of this line began to crumble the artillery had to leave. Humphreys tried desperately to swing his line back so that he could maintain contact with the troops that had been driven out of Birney's line, but he found that there was nothing left to maintain contact with and the Rebels were getting his own line under what he later described as one of the hottest rifle and artillery fires he ever saw.

Near the orchard some Massachusetts gunners were removing their guns by hand, all horses having been killed, and a man who watched them wrote that "it is a mystery to me that they were not all hit by the enemy's fire, as they were surrounded and fired upon from almost every direction." Humphreys was riding amid the thickest of the fighting. A captain on his staff threw up his hands and cried, "I'm shot!" Humphreys rode up beside him to hold him in his saddle, when a cannon ball went through the wounded officer's horse and tore the head off an orderly who was starting to lead it to the rear, and Humphreys's own horse, already six times wounded, got another bullet and sprang into the air, throwing the general to the earth. Humphreys got up, took an aide's horse, and went on trying to patch up his collapsing line.[16]

Things had gone past the point where a general could help much. The 7th New Jersey was coming forward on the run up a narrow lane, and it collided with a Federal battery going to the rear, frantic drivers lashing frantic horses, battery and infantry hopelessly tangled in the cramped dirt road, guns overlapping guns and locking wheels. The 2nd New Hampshire, running back from the peach orchard, got involved in the mess, and Rebel skirmishers trotted forward and took the whole mad turmoil of yelling men and plunging horses under fire, and a few companies of the New Jersey regiment tried a bayonet charge just in time to be routed by a new Rebel line. Barksdale was pushing his Mississippians on relentlessly, riding back and forth behind the infantry lines, driving his men on. One of Humphreys's brigadiers detailed an entire company to concentrate its fire on the man, and at last Barksdale went down mortally wounded, with five bullets in his body.

On the Emmitsburg road, regiments were going to pieces in smoke and fire, trying to cope with a flank attack and at the same time beat back a heavy assault from in front. The colonel of the 11th New Jersey was shot as he began to put his regiment through a confused left wheel. The major took over and spun round like a top when a bullet caught him in the knee. Someone notified the senior captain that he was in command, but he was killed just as he got the news, and the captain who took over from him was immediately wounded. Four men picked him up to take him to the rear, all four were shot down, and the captain was hit again and killed. One more captain tried to take charge and was killed, and a corporal finally rallied what was left of the regiment behind a little hedge.[17]

At the right of Humphreys's line, Gibbon had sent forward two regiments from his division to try to fill the gap between the two army corps. A whole Rebel brigade hit them and tore them apart, and their commander, Colonel George Ward of the 15th Massachusetts, who had lost a leg at Ball's Bluff and was now going around on an ill-fitting peg, went stumping along the line with a cane in one hand and a sword in the other, until a Confederate rifleman killed him, and what was left of the two regiments went to the rear. The 12th New Hampshire hung on for a while by a log house beside the Emmitsburg road, and a Rebel battle line suddenly appeared over a rise in ground just in front, yelling and firing like mad, and the two battle lines volleyed at point-blank range in blinding smoke.

For a few minutes the Union line there held as the sun went low and the smoke brought the dusk in ahead of time, and back on Cemetery Ridge an officer saw unreal drama in the parallel battle lines: "The smoke of their rifles encircled them, the flashes lighted up the field upon which the shadows of evening were advancing, and the scene resembled one of those battles which are seen in pictures, where the lines of battle are formed with mathematical exactness." The Confederate guns around the peach orchard came into action and the Yankee line broke, and the Rebel columns advanced with wild cheers.[18]

Between the Round Tops and Hancock's position there was nothing now except a vast, disordered retreat. The III Corps was altogether out of the fight, and its survivors were going east for the reverse slope of the ridge, to reorganize there if possible, but in any case to get there, out of the danger zone. The brigades that had gone in as reinforcements had suffered heavy losses and, like Sickles's men, were at least temporarily out of action. Most of Slocum's corps had been ordered down from the right of the line, but it had not arrived yet, and great masses of Rebel soldiers were coming up the slope almost unopposed.

Sickles had been carried to the rear, one leg gone—he went back jauntily, smoking a cigar, game enough for a regiment—and Meade told Hancock to take charge and stop the rout. It was a good choice, for Hancock was probably the best combat general on the Federal side that day. Yet neither Meade, Hancock, nor anyone else could do anything unless somewhere, on that long slanting plain, some of the fighting men dug their heels in and bought a little time. There was not much any general could do about this. If out of what it originally was and what it had learned the army had developed the swift instinctive reflexes which are all that will serve in the moment of disaster, then the situation might be saved—by Meade, by Hancock, or by sheer good luck. If not, then the war was about over.

For ten minutes or so it would be entirely up to the gunners. Lieutenant Colonel Freeman McGilvery of the artillery reserve had been pulling batteries and parts of batteries out of the retreat, and he was building up a line of two dozen guns just behind Plum Run. It was an army axiom that guns unsupported by infantry could not hope to beat off a charge, but the gunners averaged pretty tough in this army and McGilvery proposed to see what they could do on their own. While he was organizing the line he sent word out to Captain John Bigelow, who had the 9th Massachusetts battery posted in the barnyard of a farmer named Trostle, a few rods west of Plum Run, informing Bigelow that no matter what happened the Rebels must be held off until this new rank of guns could be installed.

The Massachusetts boys had never been in action before this day but they were making up for it very fast. Several Confederate batteries had their range and were firing fast and accurately, but Rebel infantry was coming in so close that Bigelow told his men to forget about counter-battery fire and knock off the foot soldiers. For a time the gunners loaded their guns with canister all the way to the muzzles, firing at pistol range, and then they switched to shell with the fuses cut entirely off so that the projectiles would explode the instant they left the muzzles of the guns. Fighting thus, they gained just the time McGilvery needed, and when he finally called them in the battery had lost half of its men, sixty of its horses, four of its six guns, and all of its officers.[19]

McGilvery's guns no sooner opened fire than the Rebel infantry charged home. A Mississippi regiment which had overrun Bigelow's guns followed the survivors in, broke in among McGilvery's guns, and got into a desperate hand-to-hand fight with the cannoneers, who hit them with rammers and handspikes and even grappled with them like rowdies rioting back of the grandstand at the county fair, everybody yelling and cursing, officers firing pistols, dense smoke settling down over everything. One entire regular battery was put out of action, and for a moment it seemed that this Mississippi regiment might break all the way through and get into the Union rear. But the fire of the other pieces never stopped, and the rest of the Confederate line was compelled to halt, and the Mississippians at last sullenly withdrew.[20]

It was getting dark and the air was streaky and blurred with smoke, and the advancing Confederate masses were almost indistinguishable in the twilight. Reinforcements were coming up from the Union right and rear at last, and officers were casting forward looking for the spots where these new troops were needed the most.

Among these officers was Hancock, and he saw a Confederate brigade advancing toward him, its uneven line coming up out of a little hollow a hundred yards off. He trotted back, saw a Union regiment coming up in column of fours, and galloped over to it. It was the 1st Minnesota out of his own corps. Hancock pointed to the Rebel line, whose flags were just visible in the murk.

"Do you see those colors?" he demanded. The regiment's Colonel Colville had just been released from arrest, which he had incurred by refusing to make his men wade a creek on the march north. He looked forward and nodded laconically.

"Well, capture them!" barked Hancock.

Down the ridge came the 1st Minnesota, still in column of fours, and it hit the slightly disordered Rebel column and knocked it back. The Rebels quickly rallied from the shock—they greatly outnumbered this lone Minnesota regiment— and they formed a firing line in the underbrush and woods on the edge of the ravine, and the Minnesota men swung into a line of their own, and the fire lit the dusk like great flashes of irregular sheet lightning. The Confederates worked their way around on each flank and got the 1st Minnesota into a pocket, sending their fire in from three sides, and the whole war had suddenly come to a focus in this smoky hollow, with a few score Westerners trading their lives for the time the army needed. Off to the left McGilvery saw what was up, and while the Confederate batteries by the Emmitsburg road concentrated their fire on him he swung his guns around and pounded the underbrush with canister, and on the other side Hancock found some more troops and sent them in. After a time the Confederates began to draw back, and when they came out into the open the guns hit them hard, and finally they went into full retreat.

What was left of the Minnesota regiment came back to reorganize. It had taken 262 men into action and it had 47 men left, and the survivors boasted that while the casualties amounted to 82 per cent (which seems to have been a record for the Union Army for the entire war) there was not a straggler or a prisoner of war on the entire list.[21] They had not captured the flag that Hancock had asked them to capture, but they still had their own flag and a great name, plus those 47 exhausted survivors, and as they came back it might have been as John Bunyan wrote: "So he passed over, and all the trumpets sounded for him on the other side."

North of there Meade himself was on the firing line, and he and his staff saw another advancing Confederate line which had got clear up on top of the ridge and was possessing itself of some Union cannon. For a moment it seemed that no one but the commanding general was there to meet this assault, but an officer cried, "There they come, General!" and looking back, Meade saw a Federal battle line coming in on the run. He spurred back, waved his hat toward the Rebels, and started riding forward again in the middle of the firing line, hat still in his hand, calling to his staff: "Come on, gentlemen!" His aides finally got him out of the front line, the line charged, the Confederates ran back out of the guns and down the slope, and Cemetery Ridge was clear.[22]

Behind the ridge there was a great tangle of men and animals and equipment, jammed together like the debris of a hopelessly defeated army. On the hillsides, beaten regiments and brigades tried to reassemble. Walking wounded were limping toward the rear, ambulances were clattering down the bumpy roads, broken batteries were jolting back for a refit, and dazed stragglers and non-combatants were wandering about in a daze, drifting back and forth like the shreds of smoke that came seeping in through the trees from the west. Over all there rolled a great pall of sound: many guns firing, an unending crackle and sputter of small arms, and above all the yelling and screaming of many men. Slocum's corps was being moved up, and one column was coming along a country lane in the twilight, marching toward a firing line which it could not yet see; and it seemed to these men that the high screech of the Rebel yell coming out of the darkness ahead "was more devilish than anything which *could* come from human throats." These men were veterans, but there was something about this twilight march, with those unearthly cries just ahead, which put them on the edge of panic.

They passed a little cabin, and by the roadside in front of it there was a bent old woman—an "old crone," as one soldier ungallantly called her—and she caught the feel of their unease, and as the ranks passed her she kept repeating soothingly: "Never mind, boys—they're nothing but *men.*" A soldier who heard her wrote that these commonplace words "seemed almost sublime as she uttered them, standing unmoved by all the uproar of battle," and he said that they calmed the men so that they shook off their panic and were brave soldiers once more.[23]

Cemetery Ridge was secure at last, and yet still the day would not die. Far to the right a great crescent of fire and smoke was climbing the sides of Culp's Hill, encircling the lone Union brigade which held that point, and it seemed to observers in the rear that all of the wooded hill was ablaze with jagged bolts of chain lightning. Among Slocum's men who had been holding this hill were many New England lumbermen, and these men had spent the day with their axes making stout breastworks of solid logs. When Slocum took his men away to reinforce the line on Cemetery Ridge he had left General George Greene's brigade behind, and these men in their good breastworks were putting up a desperate fight. Four times the Rebels surged up the slope through the trees, a solid division of first-rate troops, and each time the fire over the logs drove them back. Yet part of the Union line, which ran through low ground southeast of the hill, was overrun, and as the darkness came down the Union position here was still insecure. It was as certain as anything could be that the Confederate attack would be renewed at dawn.

On the saddle between Culp's Hill and Cemetery Hill there was one final brush with disaster. While the fight raged on Culp's Hill the Union troops along this saddle saw a long Rebel line forming in the plain to the north, just east of Gettysburg, and the ranked batteries came to life and fired at it long-range in the fading light. The line moved closer, dipping down into lower ground, wheeling a little toward the west, and then striking straight up the ravine where Hancock had spotted danger the evening before. On a little knoll at the head of this ravine stood the 5th Maine Battery, six brass smoothbores, and it fired so fast at the advancing line that gunners dropped exhausted in the hot dusk and had to be relieved by volunteers hastily called from the nearest infantry regiment. On up the ravine came the Rebels, and the rising ground shielded them from the waiting batteries on the east side of the Cemetery Hill. It was dark now, and the Union line on the rim of the ravine was traced in fire as the infantry went into action.

Along part of the rim the sparkling lights suddenly went out. The Rebels were in the Yankee line, fighting hand to hand with Von Gilsa's brigade, and they shattered it and sent it flying. The Maine battery kept on firing until it had shot away the last of its ammunition, and beside it the 33rd Massachusetts and what was left of the Iron Brigade got the Rebels in flank at close range, and most of the charging line went to pieces and slid back downhill in the dark. But some of the Confederates—very tough men, these, from Louisiana—kept coming on, and they ran in among the guns on the eastern slope of Cemetery Hill, and once again there was savage fighting between gunners and infantry, cannoneers clubbing Rebels with anything they could lay their hands on, including fence rails. The Louisiana boys spiked a gun in Ricketts's battery, overran a New York battery beside it, and tried to drag some gunners off bodily as prisoners, and here once more the Federal grip on a key position was being broken.

Then over the top of Cemetery Hill a shadowy mass came rolling forward—Carroll's brigade from Hancock's corps, sent over on the run when Howard called for help. The daylight was entirely gone now, and in the darkness Carroll's men could see nothing except the points and splashes of flame in the over-run batteries, and they came running blindly down the slope, shouting breathlessly as they ran. There was a confused sound of pounding feet and colliding human bodies, grunts and yells and curses and a crackle of rifle fire—and the last of the Confederates were driven out, Carroll's brigade drew up along the lip of the ravine, and the line was secure once again.[24]

The day's fighting was over at last. The noise died down, and the smoke drifted away, and a huge brilliant moon came up, flooding all of the ghastly battlefield with a rich mellow light.

3. AND IT MAY BE FOREVER

Around the foot of Culp's Hill the men had an uneasy night. There was a hollow meadow where the ground was low and spongy, dark as a pit under the trees and streaky with thin smoky moonlight in the open, and where there should have been alert skirmish lines there were listless exhausted men who had lost their sense of direction and had no idea where their enemies might be. Near the foot of the hill there was a spring, and shadowy figures from both armies came up in the dark to fill canteens, lounging nearby for low-voiced casual conversation. Some of Slocum's men who had just returned from Cemetery Ridge came wandering in to get some of the water. One of them remarked that "the Rebs had caught Hail Columbia" over on the left that evening.

A Confederate heard and sprang up, yelling: "Hell—those are Yankees!" and it was as if his shout reminded the men that they were in the midst of a battle. Someone fired his musket, other shots were fired, and men struck blindly at each other in the dark, swinging clubbed muskets and firing with their fists. The uproar aroused the authorities, and after casualties had been given and taken, including on each side a moderate haul of disgusted prisoners, officers came in and pulled the rival forces apart and established orderly military lines across the swale with sentries in front.

Behind the sentries men tried to sleep, but they did not do very well at it. The sentries kept peering forward into the gloom, and when one of them heard footsteps or thought he saw movement he fired. Men on the other side would fire at the flash of the rifle, still other men would fire at them, and a fusillade would break out all along the line, with no one able to see what he was shooting at. The sleeping men would stumble to their feet, grab their weapons, and get ready to beat off an attack. Then quiet would slowly return, the men would go back to sleep, and fifteen minutes later it would happen all over again.[1]

Nobody in the army got much sleep that night. It was hot, and the fighting had gone on until after the last of the long summer twilight faded, and there was so much rearranging of battle lines that one soldier wrote: "The entire army seemed to be in motion the greater part of the night." There was a great scarcity of drinking water. (One man remembered kneeling by a hoofprint in a muddy cowpath and laboriously spooning into his tin cup enough dirty water to make some coffee.)[2] Ambulances and stretcher parties were busy all along the western slope of Cemetery Ridge, where there was more than enough work for them. Searching the hillside with them were many private soldiers who had been assigned to no stretcher details but who were simply looking for missing comrades. One of the things that held those thin regiments together was the strong sense of personal attachment the men had for each other. Most of the men in any given company came from the same town or county and knew each other from before the war, and a man who was left wounded on the field knew that his friends would come out to help him if they could. So men went across the torn thickets and meadows in the late moonlight without orders, hunting for comrades who had not come back.

Behind the lines there were the field hospitals, and every house and barn within reach had been filled with wounded men. Brigadier General Zook of the II Corps, shot through the belly with one of those wounds which medical knowledge of that day could not cure, was carried back to a small house on the Baltimore Pike. The house was full of wounded men, most of them screaming—the overworked doctors had not got to the place yet—and the floors were hideous and slippery with blood. An aide asked Zook if he should bring the chaplain to him, but Zook shook his head and said quietly that it was too late, and after a while he died.[3] Colonel Cross had died before midnight, gasping: "I did hope I would live to see peace and our country restored. . . . I think the boys will miss me." The boys would, those who were left—his old 5th New Hampshire had lost 100 out of 150 men that day, and its surviving fragment was detached from the army and sent home to recruit as soon as the battle was over. One of the soldiers paid his tribute to the redheaded colonel in words which any troop commander in that war might have been proud of: "He taught us to aim in battle, and above all things he ignored and made us ignore the idea of retreating. [Cross used to boast that his regiment simply did not dare to retreat without orders.] Besides this he clothed us and fed us well, taught us to build good quarters, and camped us on good ground."[4] Cross was camping on far ground tonight, and many good men had gone to keep him company there.

Late at night Meade called a meeting of his corps commanders. They met in a stuffy little box of a room at headquarters, the principal generals of this army, and they quietly talked over the fighting they had had that day. The army's losses had been fearful—probably twenty thousand men in two days—and the immediate, temporary loss made it a good deal worse than that, since, as always, a good many thousand additional men had got blown loose from their regiments, had wandered off heaven knew where, and would not be back in line for days to come. Nobody seemed to think that the army ought to retreat, but nobody thought that it ought to attack, either. The moral dominance of Robert E. Lee over the Federal commanders was all but complete. In a crisis like this they were bound to come up with the one idea: hold on if we can, wait and see what Lee is going to do, and then try to stop him.

For some reason—perhaps because he was new in command and did not know many of his generals very well—Meade turned the meeting into a formal council of war, with specific propositions put up for a vote and with Dan Butterfield writing down the answers. The verdict was unanimous: the army should stay where it was and await attack. Meade nodded and said, "Such, then, is the decision," and the meeting broke up. As the generals left, Meade stopped John Gibbon, who commanded Hancock's 2nd Division along the crest of Cemetery Ridge near Ziegler's Grove.

"If Lee attacks tomorrow, it will be in your front," said Meade. Gibbon asked him why he thought so, adding something to the effect that if Lee did attack there he would be repulsed. Meade replied that Lee had attacked both flanks the day before and had failed, and if he attacked once more he would hit the center.

Gibbon went off to an improvised bed in an ambulance, reflecting that this was an odd application of the law of probabilities.[5]

When the first streaks of daylight came it was apparent that Lee was not yet through with the Federal right flank. His men had seized nearly half of the Culp's Hill line the evening before, and they held a half-open door leading directly to the army's unprotected rear. Slocum had all of his corps reassembled, and during the night he and General Hunt had been planting guns on some high ground by the Baltimore Pike. At dawn these guns opened a rapid bombardment at no more than eight hundred yards' range—Ewell's men were that close to the Federal rear—and after fifteen minutes the gunfire was stopped and Slocum's men prepared to charge. But the Rebels were ready first and they made their own attack before the Federals could take off, and there was bitter fighting all up and down the wooded hillside and across the hollow ground where the men had blundered into each other in the darkness. Try as they might—and they tried with uncommon desperation—the Confederates could not get to the top of the hill. The Federals here had the unusual experience of standing in good trenches where they could inflict much more loss than they received, and they laid a blistering fire on the slopes while the guns in the rear fired as fast as the men could load. Some of the fire fell short, and a few of the advanced Federal regiments were hit. Doughty Colonel Wooster of the 20th Connecticut saw one of his men lose both arms from the explosion of a Federal shell, and he angrily sent back word to the battery commander that if it happened again he would pull his men out of line, face them about, and charge his own guns. (Long afterward, at a veterans' reunion, a member of this regiment told his comrades: "He was just the man to keep his word, and you were just the boys to execute his threat.")[6]

The lines on top of the hill were unshaken, but there was still a good deal of Rebel strength down in the lower ground to the southeast, and the high command wanted a counterattack. No one was sure how many Rebels were in there, and a division commander ordered skirmishers thrown forward to feel the line and get a little information. Somehow this order reached the front as a straight order for attack by the two leading regiments, 2nd Massachusetts and 27th Indiana. Colonel Charles R. Mudge, commanding the 2nd Massachusetts, blinked when the aide gave him the order, for he knew there were many more Rebels just ahead than any two regiments could handle.

"Are you sure that is the order?" he demanded.

The aide assured him that it was.

"Well," said Mudge, "it is murder, but that's the order." He raised his voice to a great parade-ground shout. "Up, men—over the works! Forward, double-quick!"

The two regiments put up a cheer and charged out into the little meadow. There were three Rebel brigades within range, concealed among trees and rocks, and they cut loose with what wintry-faced old Colonel Colgrove of the Indiana regiment later described as "one of the most destructive fires I have ever witnessed." The charge collapsed before it reached the trees and the survivors came back to a little stone wall, where they beat off a countercharge. Colonel Mudge was killed, his regiment lost four color-bearers, nearly 250 men were shot, and the only advantage was that the division commander now knew that the enemy held the far side of the swale in great strength.[7]

One more valiant Confederate attack was made. Slocum had plenty of men now—two brigades from the fresh VI Corps had come in to help—and the charging Confederates never had a chance. Their left-flank elements came under a killing fire from Federals down in the flat, and the hilltop trenches were still invulnerable. In front of the 7th Ohio some seventy Confederates raised the white flag of surrender, and when the Federals ceased fire a doughty Rebel staff officer rode up, indignant, and tried to stop the surrender. The Federals killed him and took their beaten enemies into their lines. By ten-thirty the attack had been beaten off for good, and the Confederates had sullenly withdrawn to the lines they had occupied the day before, leaving thousands of dead and wounded behind them.[8]

As the fighting around Culp's Hill ended, an uneasy quiet came down on the great battlefield. It ceased briefly when the old row over that barn in front of Hays's division broke out again, with Hancock's and A. P. Hill's gunners suddenly running to their pieces and exchanging salvos in an immense meaningless cannonade. The barn took fire at last, its flames burning thin and insubstantial in the hot midday sunlight. The quarreling skirmishers fell back, and the cannonade died down as quickly as it had begun. It had happened almost by reflex action, as if the armies were so edgy that anything could touch off a fight, and the silence that followed was uneasy and insecure. Somehow, invisible but sensed by everyone, a slow fuse was burning toward one final, supreme explosion. The battle was following its own course now, and perhaps nobody controlled it. These two armies had come together, a gigantic thunderhead was stacked up higher than anything the war had known before, and it was full of a terrible, shattering tension that sooner or later would have to discharge itself. The soldiers held their places and waited for it in silence.

Whatever was coming, it was going to hit Cemetery Ridge when it came. From private to commanding general, everyone took that for granted. The soldiers cowered behind low stone walls and insubstantial earth-and-rail breastworks, the heat of the sun heavy on their shoulders. In front of Ziegler's Grove one regiment which still carried the old-style smoothbore muskets emptied its cartridge boxes on the stone wall in front, for easier access in reloading, and most of the men tore apart their buck-and-ball cartridges and made up new ones containing a dozen or more buckshot apiece.[9] General Hunt went along the ridge, making sure that the guns were ready and that caisson and lumber chests were full. Off to the left, where the ridge sagged, McGilvery had thirty-nine guns in line, and he had his men building a little earthen embankment in front of the guns for protection.

Not far away, up in the front line, was a brigade of nine-month men from Vermont. They had enlisted in the preceding fall and had gone down to Washington green as grass. A diarist in one regiment wrote of their train ride across New Jersey that "such a night of suffering and misery is far beyond the power of any pen to portray," because they had to ride in unheated cars. In Washington they had manned the fortifications all winter and spring, and they had not been any too happy about it. Such veterans as they met showed lack of respect for their status as soldiers, and their historian noted moodily that "we have been called, by some, nine-monthlings, hatched on two-hundred-dollar bounty eggs." Being Vermonters, they did not care very much what other people said about them, but they did want to fight, and they were pleased when, near the end of June, they had been pulled out of the forts and sent up to join the Army of the Potomac.[10] Now for the first time they were in the presence of the enemy, even though the enemy's infantry was invisible under the trees on Seminary Ridge, and they showed a certain nervousness as they waited.

The enemy's artillery was far from invisible. It was very much in evidence, as a matter of fact. All morning there had been a ceaseless, ominous activity, with more and more Confederate batteries coming up into one prodigious line that began at the peach orchard and ran north along the Emmitsburg road and just west of it—scores and scores of guns, more of them than the Federals had ever seen in one row, bleak and silent in the bright light, their muzzles staring blankly toward the center of Cemetery Ridge. Farther north the Confederates had still more guns glinting out of the shade on Seminary Ridge, and off to the northwest on Oak Hill a few long-range pieces were placed in order to bear on Ziegler's Grove and the cemetery.

Meade was busy in his little headquarters house on the far slope of Cemetery Ridge. There were many things to see to, and there was much coming and going of the staff. There were occasional interruptions too. Somehow a civilian got in to see Meade that morning, a man who lived on the outskirts of town, coming in angrily to protest that the Federal troops were using his house for a hospital, were burying dead soldiers in his garden, and were strewing amputated arms and legs all over his lawn. He wanted damages, and he demanded that Meade give him a paper which he could use as a claim on the government. Short-tempered Meade blew up at him, told him that if this battle were lost he would have no government to apply to and no property that was worth anything, and hustled him out of there with the warning that if he heard any more from him he would give him a musket and put him in the ranks to fight.[11]

Twelve o'clock and after, and John Gibbon thought about Meade and went to see him. He found the general looking haggard and asked him to come over to division headquarters and have some lunch—Gibbon's mess staff had picked up an old rooster somewhere and the bird had just been cooked. Meade demurred, saying that he was needed where he was, but Gibbon told him that he must keep up his strength and that the paper work could wait, and Meade finally gave in. With Hancock and some staff officers the generals sat down by an ambulance near the crest of the ridge and ate the chicken. (Rather a tough old bird, as Gibbon remembered it.) Meade finished early and went back to headquarters, and the rest of the group sat there and idled. Hancock called an aide and began dictating an order regarding the supply of beef for his corps.

One o'clock, and the day was hotter than ever, and there was still that great fragile quiet upon the broad shallow valley between the opposing ridges, with the endless row of Confederate cannon ranked there in the open, not a sound or a sign of movement. Then at last there was a quick bright flash of light, and a white puffball of smoke floated up from a gun down near the peach orchard and hung, slowly turning and expanding, in the windless air, and the dull clang of the discharge echoed over the hollow. Silence for a few seconds, then another flash and smoke puff and echoing report from the same battery. There was a quick ripple of movement all along the line of Confederate guns as hundreds of gunners sprang to their feet and ran to their places. Then every gun in the line was fired in one titanic, rolling crash—the loudest noise, probably, that had ever been heard on the American continent up to that moment—and a hurricane of exploding shell came sweeping over Cemetery Ridge and the air was all smoke and stabbing flame and unendurable noise and deadly flying iron.

For just a moment Hancock tried to finish his dictation. The gesture was impossible, and it was not solely because nobody could hear what he was saying. The surrounding circle of couriers, orderlies, horse holders, and aides swirled away in what Hancock's chief of staff described as "a scene of confusion such a is seldom seen even on a field of battle." Men and horses were blown to bits where they stood. Some of the horses broke away and galloped off riderless in a frenzy of terror. The ambulance which held the luncheon equipment bounded wildly over the rocks when the team took to its heels after the driver fell from his seat, killed by a shell fragment. Officers were running for their horses, shouting at the top of their voices, and Gibbon, who could see neither his horse nor his orderly, ran up the ridge toward the battle line.[12] From end to end of the ridge Federal gunners were scrambling to their feet to open fire in reply.

One hundred and thirty Rebel guns were smiting the Yankee line, and it was like nothing the oldest soldier had ever imagined before. Men who thought that at Antietam and Fredericksburg they had seen and heard the worst that a massed cannonade could do confessed that this went beyond the bounds of their experience. Dazed Federal gunners, firing the eighty-odd guns on the ridge in feverish haste, found that exploding Rebel shell overhead and all around them made such a stupendous racket that the sound of their own guns was muffled, as if the guns were being fired a great way off.

One of General Hays's soldiers, whose brigade had to shift its position slightly just then, wrote afterward: "How that short march was made I don't know. The air was all murderous iron; it seemed as if there couldn't be room for any soldier upright and in motion." Farther to the left, a veteran in the 1st Minnesota got the same impression, declaring that "it seemed that nothing four feet from the ground could live." Infantry lying flat behind walls and barricades was nearly suffocated by the choking clouds of smoke. One man recalled that the men were very quiet. Usually, in a cannonade, the infantry would make wisecracks, and when shell flew overhead the men would offer derisive advice to the Rebel gunners: "Shorten your fuses" . . . "Depress your guns." But this was like no previous bombardment, and the men were silent, hugging the ground and saying nothing.[13]

The artillery was taking a frightful pounding. Caissons and limber chests were exploding, sending huge fountains of black smoke high in the air. Gun wheels were broken; men and horses were killed, and the dead and wounded were torn apart afresh by shell that skimmed low over the earth. Vicious fragments of broken rock, as dangerous as actual shell fragments, whirred through the air when the projectiles hit the ground. Ziegler's Grove seemed to be filled with flying fence rails, limbs of trees, and splinters from broken gun carriages and limbers. Through it all Colonel Richard Coulter, commanding blinded General Paul's brigade, was walking along holding his limp left arm in his right hand and asking, bewildered: "Who in hell would suppose a sharpshooter could hit a crazy bone at that distance?"

General Hunt somehow made his way along the line, ordering the gunners to save their ammunition even if they had to cease firing altogether. An infantry attack, he was sure, would follow this bombardment, and he wanted to have shell enough to break it up before it reached the line. Off to the left, in McGilvery's line of guns, his order was obeyed, but on the II Corps front Hancock countermanded it, feeling that his infantry would stand the punishment better if its own artillery kept on firing. So the cannoneers kept to their work, firing smoothly and without fuss, battery commanders standing amid the turmoil calling: "Number One, fire! . . . Number Two, fire!" as methodically as if they were firing parade-ground salutes.

All along the line there was what General Gibbon called "the most infernal pandemonium it has ever been my fortune to look upon." In the entire valley there was nothing to be seen but a dense coiling smoke bank, glowing and sparkling wickedly with the unceasing flashing of the Rebel guns. On Cemetery Ridge the smoke hung a couple of feet off the ground, so that only the legs of the busy gunners were visible. The cannonade was taking a horrible toll of the horses, and as he watched the poor beasts Gibbon was struck by the stolid, almost apathetic way in which they endured their ordeal, standing motionless in their places even while those beside them were kicking in their death agonies. Going over to a certain little clump of trees near the center of his line, Gibbon met the officer who commanded there, Brigadier General Alexander Webb, who was sitting on the ground smoking his pipe, as if the whole battle were no concern of his, and it occurred to Gibbon suddenly that men behaved under fire very much as horses did.[14]

Oddly enough, the extreme front line was the safest place on Cemetery Ridge. The Confederates were making just one mistake in this shattering bombardment: uniformly, they were firing just a little too high. Along the II Corps front the infantry suffered comparatively little from the shelling. Gibbon went far out in front of his firing line, trying in vain to see what the Confederates might be doing behind their flaming line of guns, and he found that he could walk erect there in almost complete safety. The farther back one went, the greater was the danger, and beyond the crest, over on the eastern slope of the ridge, it was worst of all. Most of the shell just cleared the crest and curved down to strike or explode in the rear, out of sight of the gunners who had done the firing.

As a result the whole rear-guard population—orderlies, clerks, cooks, servants, musicians, ambulance drivers, and just plain stragglers—went streaming back along the Baltimore Pike as fast as they could run, scourged out of what had seemed like a safely protected hillside by the worst shelling they ever saw. A soldier who saw them go wrote with satisfaction that "it seemed as if half of the army was running away, but it was only the noncombatants," and a regiment acting as training guard a mile or so down the road speedily rounded up five hundred fugitives to turn over to the provost guard.[15] It was impossible to take wounded men back from the ridge through this zone of fire, and caisson drivers who had to take fresh ammunition forward needed to be fantastically brave or reckless.

Most dangerous spot on the whole slope may have been the field immediately around Meade's headquarters. A newspaper correspondent there wrote that from two to six shells were exploding around the little cottage every second, and he counted sixteen dead horses lying mangled by the fence, grotesque in death with their halters still tied to the top rail. An ambulance went careening by, one horse galloping madly on three legs, a solid shot having removed the fourth. One shell knocked away the front steps of the cottage, another broke one of the two pillars by the door, another went through the low garret, still another smashed the second pillar. Meade came to the doorway to look things over, and a shot smashed through the doorjamb, missing him by inches. He got his staff out in the yard, figuring that flying splinters made the inside of the little house more dangerous than the outside.

Unconsciously the men huddled in the lee of the building, which was far too flimsy to stop any shell. Noticing this, Meade chuckled grimly—extreme coolness under fire was always his long suit—and he leisurely recounted an anecdote of the Mexican War. At Palo Alto, he recalled, old Zachary Taylor had come upon a wagon driver crouched behind his two-wheeled cart in the midst of a cannonade and had called out: "You damned fool, don't you know you are no safer there than anywhere else?" The driver had replied: "I don't suppose I am, General, but it kinda feels so." Staff no doubt laughed dutifully and rather hollowly, and Meade then decided that there was no sense trying to carry on headquarters business here and moved everybody over to Slocum's headquarters, out of range.[16]

How long all of this went on no one ever quite seemed sure, and the estimates ranged all the way from thirty minutes to two hours; but eventually, almost imperceptibly, the weight of the bombardment grew less. Hunt had pulled some wrecked batteries out of the II Corps line and was persuading others to cease firing, and along the right of the line many guns had exhausted all of their shell and solid shot. As the Federal firing died down, firing from the Confederate guns slackened also. The smoke still lay heavy between the armies, and Gibbon was trying in vain to peer through it from his post out in front, when the signal station on Little Round top wigwagged a message to army headquarters: Here come the Rebels!

The smoke lifted like a rising curtain, and all of the great amphitheater lay open at last, and the Yankee soldiers could look west all the way to the belt of trees on Seminary Ridge. They were old soldiers and had been in many battles, but what they saw then took their breath away, and whether they had ten minutes or seventy-five years yet to live, they remembered it until they died. There it was, for the last time in this war, perhaps for the last time anywhere, the grand pageantry and color of war in the old style, beautiful and majestic and terrible: fighting men lined up for a mile and a half from flank to flank, slashed red flags overhead, soldiers marching forward elbow to elbow, officers with drawn swords, sunlight gleaming from thousands of musket barrels, lines dressed as if for parade. Up and down the Federal firing line ran a low murmur: "There they are. . . . There comes the infantry!"

Lee was putting fifteen thousand men into this column—George Pickett riding into storybook immortality with his division of Virginians, Heth's division led today by General Pettigrew, two brigades of Pender's division under General Trimble, coming out of the woods to march across a mile-wide valley to the heights where the Yankees were waiting with shotted guns. Rank after rank came out of the shadows, and the Rebel cannon were all silent now, gunners standing aside to let the infantry come through, and for the moment the Federal guns were silent too, as if both armies were briefly dazzled by the war's most dramatic moment. In the Confederate line there were officers on horseback, and if the Federals looked closely they might have seen one who held his sword high over his head, his black felt hat on the point of it as a guide for his brigade—General Lewis Armistead, who was coming over the valley to meet death and an old friend.

Back in the spring of 1861, when the country was just breaking apart and officers of the regular army were choosing their sides, there was a farewell party one evening in the officers' quarters of the army post at the little California town of Los Angeles. The host was Captain Winfield Scott Hancock, and he was giving the party to say good-by to certain Southern officers who were going east to Richmond, where they would take commissions with the new Confederacy. The departing guests were sad—it was not easy for those regulars to cut loose from the army they had given their lives to—and a tragic shadow lay across the little gathering, and just before the party broke up Mrs. Albert Sidney Johnston sat at the piano and sang "Kathleen Mavourneen." Good-by and good-by, the grand dawn will be breaking soon and our old comradeship in this intimate little army world is fading, it may be for years and it may be forever. When the song was ended Major Armistead came over and put his hands on Hancock's shoulders, tears streaming down his cheeks, and said: "Hancock, good-by—you can never know what this has cost me."[17] Then the guests left, and next morning Armistead and the others started east, and a little later Hancock himself came east to fight on the Northern side, and he and Armistead had not seen each other since. Now Hancock was on his horse on Cemetery Ridge, waiting with the guns all around him, and Armistead was coming up the slope with his black felt hat on the end of his sword, and the strange roads of war the two old friends had followed were coming together at last. . . .

Long and bright and perfectly aligned, the lines came down the far slope and began crossing the valley, and the open space in front was dotted by little bursts of smoke as the rival skirmishers began to shoot at each other. This was the moment General Hunt had been waiting for, and all along the left of the Union line the guns opened fire and began to hit those neat ranks, tearing ragged holes in them. On Little Round Top the rifled guns that had been lugged up over the rocks the afternoon before were finding the range, and McGilvery's long line was flaming and crashing, and the Rebels were closing the gaps as they moved forward—no Rebel yell now, the men were coming on silently, they were still out of musket range. The yelling and the firing and the stabbing would come later.

Pickett's division was at the southern end of the advancing line, and Pickett's objective was the clump of trees under which General Webb had been smoking his pipe. Pickett wanted to mass his troops for greater impact, and he had his brigades do a half left wheel to bring them closer to the center. The maneuver was done smartly, and the waiting Yankee infantry praised it, but as the brigades swung around they offered their flanks to McGilvery, and his gunners took cruel advantage. Pickett's men were in the open and the range now was hardly half a mile, and shell ripped down the ranks from end to end, one shell sometimes striking down ten men before it burst. Along Hancock's line the guns were silent, for they had nothing left but canister and they would have to wait for point-blank range. Gibbon was riding along the line—an aide had found a horse for him at last—cautioning his men to take it easy and not to fire until the enemy got in close, and the gray lines came swinging up the rise, nearer and nearer.

Webb's brigade would get it first, and the Confederates continued to crowd in toward the center, building up the strength that would overwhelm the little rectangle of torn, littered ground which the brigade was holding. Webb had two Pennsylvania regiments in line behind a low stone wall that ran just in front of the little clump of trees and extended a few rods toward the north, and the rest of his brigade was on the crest of the ridge, perhaps a hundred yards in the rear. Hancock had put three batteries in here, and they had been almost completely destroyed. Beside the trees and down close to the wall were the two guns that remained of Battery A, 4th U. S., commanded by a girlish-looking young lieutenant named Alonzo Cushing. The ground around these guns was hell's half acre. Four guns had been dismounted, caissons and limbers had been exploded, nearly all of the horses had been killed, and there were just enough men left to work the two guns that remained. It had been impossible to remove the wounded, and they lay there amid smashed wheels, fragments of wood and indescribable mutilated remains of men and animals. One gunner, dreadfully cut by a shell fragment, had been seen to draw a revolver and put himself out of his pain by shooting himself through the head.

Cushing had been wounded three times, and he was there by his two guns, a sergeant standing beside him to hold him erect and to pass his orders on to the gunners. (He was calling for triple charges of canister.) The Rebel artillery had renewed its fire, and this part of the line was being hit again, and the advancing Rebel infantry was up to the post-and-rail fences by the Emmitsburg road now, barely two hundred yards away. One of Cushing's two guns was knocked out, and he was almost entirely out of ammunition. The Federal infantry opened fire and the smoke cloud settled down again, thick and stifling. Dimly the men behind the wall could see the Confederates coming in over the fences, brigade lines disordered, the spearhead of the charge a great mass of men sweeping over the fences and up the last of the slope like an irresistible stream flowing uphill.[18]

Farther south the nine-month Vermonters got their chance at last. Hancock was down there with them, pointing to the exposed flank of Pickett's line, and the Vermont regiments swung out, wheeled toward the right, and opened up a blistering flanking fire at close range. Some Pennsylvanians and a New York regiment went in with them, and the Confederate lines here gave way and began to fall back, and as the men wavered McGilvery's cannoneers pounded them afresh, three dozen guns hitting them all at once.

Just south of the clump of trees the stone wall ended and the men had raised a little breastwork of earth. Behind this barrier were the regiments commanded by Colonel Norman J. Hall—the same officer and men who had floated across the Rappahannock in pontoon boats to drive Rebel sharpshooters out of Fredericksburg so many months ago. The advancing Confederates here went down into a little hollow, seeming to vanish from sight. Then they came up out of it, appearing suddenly, as if they had popped up out of the earth, so close that Hall's men could see the expressions on their faces. The breastwork blazed from end to end as the men from Massachusetts and New York and Michigan opened fire. The Rebel line staggered visibly, came to a halt, and opened its own fire in reply, and then it began to drift slowly to its left, toward the dense crowd by the clump of trees.[19]

In front of Ziegler's Grove, to the north, Pettigrew's division was coming up to the Emmitsburg road. It had lagged slightly behind the rest of the Confederate attack, but it still kept its formation, and Hays's men looked in admiration at the trimness of its lines and, as they admired those lines, made ready to destroy them. The 8th Ohio had been posted west of the road in skirmish formation, and this regiment drew back and got into a little country lane on the Rebel flank and opened fire. Along the ridge and in the grove the Federals waited, and the foremost Federal brigade stood up to level its muskets, and the Rebel line came very near. Then at last every musket and every cannon in this part of the Yankee line opened at once, and the whole Confederate division disappeared in an immense cloud of smoke and dust. Above this boiling cloud the Union men could see a ghastly debris of guns, knapsacks, blanket rolls, severed human heads, and arms and legs and parts of bodies, tossed into the air by the impact of the shot. One observer wrote: "A moan went up from the field, distinctly to be heard amid the roar of battle, but on they went, too much enveloped in smoke and dust now to permit us to distinguish their lines of movement, for the mass appeared more like a cloud of moving smoke and dust than a column of troops."[20]

The mass rolled in closer, the Federals firing into the center of the storm cloud. The men with the improvised buckshot cartridges in smoothbore guns had a target they could not miss, and the XI Corps artillery on Cemetery Hill was sending shell in through the gaps in the Yankee line. Suddenly Pettigrew's men passed the limit of human endurance and the lines broke apart and the hillside was covered with men running for cover, and the Federal gunners burned the ground with shell and canister. On the littered field, amid all the dead and wounded, prostrate men could be seen holding up handkerchiefs in sign of surrender.

But if the right and left of the charging Confederate line had been smashed, the center was still coming on. Cushing fired his last remaining charge, and a bullet hit him in the mouth and killed him. Most of the Pennsylvanians behind the wall sprang up and ran back to the crest, and the few who remained were overwhelmed as the Rebel line rolled in and beat the life out of them. Most of the Rebels stayed behind the wall or crowded in amid the clump of trees and opened fire on the Yankees on the crest, their red battle flags clustering thick, men in front lying prone or kneeling, men in the rear standing and firing over their heads. A handful leaped over the wall, Armistead in the lead, and ran in among the wreckage of Cushing's battery. Armistead's horse had been killed and his hat was down on the hilt of his sword now, but the sword was still held high, and through the curling smoke the Union soldiers got a final glimpse of him, one triumphant hand resting on a silent cannon.[21]

This was the climax and the bloody indisputable pay-off; the next few minutes would tell the story, and what that story would be would all depend on whether these blue-coated soldiers really meant it. There were more Federals than Confederates on the field, but right here where the fighting was going on there were more Confederates than Federals, and every man was firing in a wild, feverish haste, with the smoke settling down thicker and thicker. From the peach orchard Confederate guns were shooting straight into the Union line, disregarding the danger that some of their own men would be hit, and the winging missiles tore ugly lanes through the disorganized mass of Yankees.

A fresh Union regiment was moving up through Ziegler's Grove, and as the men came out into the open they heard the uproar of battle different from any they had ever heard before—"strange and terrible, a sound that came from thousands of human throats, yet was not a commingling of shouts and yells but rather like a vast mournful roar." There was no cheering, but thousands of men were growling and cursing without realizing it as they fought to the utmost limit of primal savagery. The 19th Massachusetts was squarely before the clump of trees, and the Confederate mass kept crowding forward, and for a time the file closers in the rear of the Massachusetts regiment joined hands and held the thin line in place by sheer strength.[22]

Gibbon was down with a bullet through his shoulder, Webb had been wounded, and Hancock was knocked off his horse by a bullet that went through his saddle and drove a tenpenny nail and bits of wood deep into his thigh. Except for one valiant staff officer, there was not a mounted man to be seen. Hunt was in the middle of the infantry, firing his revolver. On the open crest of the ridge men were volleying at the Confederates behind the wall and among the trees. From the left, regiments were running over to help, coming in through the smoke like a mob gone out of control.

These were Hall's men, and men from Harrow's brigade on the left—famous old regiments, 20th Massachusetts and 7th Michigan and "that shattered thunderbolt" (as an officer on Gibbon's staff called it), the remnant of the 1st Minnesota. They were not "moving by the right flank" or "changing front forward" or executing any other recognized tactical maneuver, and they were not obeying the commands of any officers, although their officers were in their midst, yelling hoarsely and gesturing madly with their swords. No formal tactical move was possible in that jammed smoky confusion, and no shouted command could be heard in the everlasting din. One soldier wrote afterward that the only order he remembered hearing, from first to last, was "Up, boys—they're coming!" right at the start.[23] This was not a controlled movement at all. It was simply a crowd of armed men running over spontaneously to get into the middle of an enormous fight, Yankee soldiers swarming in to get at their enemies, all regimental formations lost, every man going in on his own.

Some of the men stopped and fired over the low earthen barricade toward the front where there were still Rebels in the open. Others jammed in toward the clump of trees, firing through gaps in the crowd ahead, sometimes hitting their own comrades. Off to the left the Vermonters were still out in front, facing north, tearing the Confederate flank to tatters, and from the right Hays's men and the guns in the grove were firing in obliquely. The heavy smoke went up toward the sky, so heavy that Lee over on Seminary Ridge could get nothing but an occasional glimpse of red battle flags adrift in the murk.

Back on the crest, facing the clump of trees, the line swayed as men worked up their nerve. The mounted staff officer was shouting, men were yelling to each other, and a color-bearer jumped up and ran forward, waving his flag. The staff was broken by a shot, and he grabbed the stump and held the ragged colors above his head, and by ones and twos and then all along the crest men sprang to their feet and followed him, firing as they ran. Armistead was stretched out on the ground now with a bullet in him, and the other graycoats who had got in among the guns were down too, and the Federals came in on the Rebel mass among the little trees, and the smoke hid the hot afternoon sun.

Pickett's men were in a box now. On their left Pettigrew's division had evaporated, on the right they were dissolving under an unceasing flank fire, in front they were getting a head-on assault that was too heavy to take, and there was no support in sight. Longstreet had sent a brigade up to cover their right, but in the blinding fog the brigade had lost its direction and was heading straight for McGilvery's ranked cannon, which blasted it with deadly aim, and the Vermont regiments wheeled completely around and got the brigade in flank. It fell apart and its bits and pieces went tumbling back to Seminary Ridge. And suddenly the tension was gone and the firing was dying down, and the Confederates by the clump of trees were going back to their own lines or dropping their muskets and raising their hands in surrender. Meade came riding up to the crest just now, and an officer met him and told him that Lee's charge had been crushed, and Meade raised his hand and cried "Thank God!" The last of the fugitives went back toward their starting point, Federal gunners following them with shell, and Gibbon's weary soldiers were sending a great mass of Rebel prisoners back to the rear. The fighting was over.

Hancock was on a stretcher, dictating a note to Meade. He believed that a quick counterattack now would take the Rebel army off balance and finish it, and he urged that the men be sent forward without delay. He added proudly: "I did not leave the field so long as a Rebel was to be seen upright." An aide came up to him and handed him a watch, a pair of spurs, and other trinkets. They came from Lewis Armistead, whom the aide had found dying there beside Cushing's last gun. Armistead had asked that these mementos of an old friendship be sent to Hancock, and he had gasped out some sort of farewell message.[24] "Tell Hancock I have done him and my country a great injustice which I shall never cease to regret" was the way the aide had it; he may have dressed it up a good deal or, for that matter, he may have dreamed it all, and it does not matter much either way. Armistead had died, going beyond regrets forever, and as if he had been waiting for this last message, Hancock had the stretcher-bearers carry him off to the field hospital.

The smoke drifted away and the noise died down, and a soldier who looked out over the ground where the men had fought said that he looked upon "a square mile of Tophet."[25]

4. VALLEY OF DRY BONES

One day they would make a park there, with neat lawns and smooth black roadways, and there would be marble statues and bronze plaques to tell the story in bloodless prose. Silent cannon would rest behind grassy embankments, their wheels bolted down to concrete foundations, their malevolence wholly gone, and here and there birds would nest in the muzzles. In the museums and tourist-bait trinket shops old bullets and broken buckles and twisted bayonets would repose under glass, with a rusty musket or so on the wall and little illustrated booklets lying on top of the counter. There would be neat brick and timber cabins on the hillsides, and people would sleep soundly in houses built where the armies had stormed and cried at each other, as if to prove that men killed in battle send forth no restless ghosts to plague comfortable civilians at night. The town and the woods and the ridges and hills would become a national shrine, filled with romantic memories which are in themselves a kind of forgetting, and visitors would stand by the clump of trees and look off to the west and see nothing but the rolling fields and the quiet groves and the great blue bank of the mountains.

But first there would have to be a great deal of tidying up.

The day after the battle began muggy and cloudy, and there was a tremendous rainstorm. (There always seemed to be a great rain after a hard battle in that war, and men believed that something in the firing of many guns brought rain clouds and jarred the moisture out of them.) The long line of Rebel cannon along the Emmitsburg road had been pulled back, and when Slocum and Howard sent scouting parties out to the north and east of town they found no Rebels except wounded men and a few stragglers. On Seminary Ridge the Confederates were still in evidence, and for a time Meade appears to have been uncertain whether the battle was really over.

But the Confederate Army had had enough. It had lost 25,000 men, artillery ammunition was nearly exhausted, supplies were low, and Lee was holding his line on Seminary Ridge merely to let his trains and his advance guard get a decent start on the long roads back to Virginia. A wagon train seventeen miles long, loaded with wounded men, crawled over the mountain road toward Chambersburg. It was a nightmarish procession of pain. A great many of the wounded men had received no medical attention whatever, the almost springless wagons rolled and jolted over the uneven road, and no halts were permitted for any reason. The cavalry officer in charge of the train said that he learned more on that trip about the horrors of war than he had learned in all of his battles.[1]

As the signs of a Confederate retreat multiplied, Meade worked the VI Corps forward to take up the pursuit, but he was in no hurry about it. If the Rebels wanted to go back to Virginia, it seemed like a good idea to wish them Godspeed and let them go.

Meade was able to see some things very clearly. He knew that the victory had been brutally hard on his army, and above all things he was determined not to do anything that might create any risks. A quick checkup after the battle showed him that he had no more than 51,000 men armed and equipped and present for duty. This total was approximately 38,000 below the number he had had just before the battle. Casualties had been about 23,000, so it was evident that the impact of battle had jarred fully 15,000 uninjured men loose from the ranks. They would be back later, but for the moment they were lost, and the army was not half as large as it had been when Hooker took it down to the Rappahannock fords two months earlier.[2] The I Corps was hardly as big as an ordinary division, and the III Corps was not a great deal better off. (Both of these famous corps were mortally hurt, as it turned out; in the army reorganization of the following winter they were broken up and their survivors were transferred to other units.) The II Corps had lost more than a third of its men, and its best generals, Hancock and Gibbon, would be out for months. The XI Corps had suffered nearly as much and in additon had had another blow to its reputation and morale, with the rest of the army making caustic remarks about its wild flight through town, the astounding number of prisoners it had lost, and its inability to keep the Rebels out of the guns on Cemetery Hill on the evening of July 2. Some of the army's finest combat units had been all but destroyed—the Iron Brigade, the 5th New Hampshire, the 1st Minnesota, the 2nd Massachusetts, and the 16th Maine, among others—and artillery losses had been so severe that Hunt had to consolidate some of his best batteries. Three of the seven army corps were under temporary commanders.

Of all these things Meade was acutely aware. The old habit of caution was strong at army headquarters, and another heritage from the McClellan era was cropping out just now: Meade somehow had been persuaded that the Rebel army in this campaign was larger than his own. So he waited where he was, ignoring the clear signs that he was in the presence of a badly beaten enemy, and he moved his patrols forward very carefully.

The soldiers themselves had no doubt about how the battle had come out. On the afternoon of July 3 they had seen something they had never seen before— the principal attacking column of the Army of Northern Virginia running in desperate disordered fragments back to its lines after a smashing repulse—and some of the men on Cemetery Ridge had stood up exultantly and cried "Fredericksburg!" as they watched. As they went forward through the town and down to the Emmitsburg road they were dazed by the human wreckage they saw. Toward the left, where for a time nothing but artillery had beaten back the Rebel attack, they found bodies dreadfully broken and dismembered. An officer who went over that part of the ground wrote that on no other field had he seen such appalling numbers of dead. In places where the infantry fire had been especially intense the dead men lay in great rows, and in the twilight it seemed as if whole brigades had made their bivouac there and had gone to sleep. On the ground covered by Pickett's charge one officer wrote that "I saw men, horses, and material in some places piled up together, which is something seldom seen unless in pictures of battles, and the appearance of the field with these mounds of dead men and horses, and very many bodies lying in every position singly, was terrible, especially as the night lent a somber hue to everything the eye rested on."[3]

A fearful odor of decay lay over the field. A cavalry patrol went through Gettysburg to scout the Cashtown road to the west, and as it came out by the fields where dead bodies had been lying in the heat for four days the cavalrymen sickened and vomited as they rode. The country here was the ultimate abomination of desolation: "As far as the eye could reach on both sides of the Cashtown road you see blue-coated boys, swollen up to look as giants, quite black in the face, but nearly all on their backs, looking into the clear blue with open eyes, with their clothes torn open. It is strange that dying men tear their clothes in this manner. You see them lying in platoons of infantry with officers and arms exactly as they stood or ran—artillery men with caisson blown up and four horses, each in position, dead. You meet also limbs and fragments of men. The road is strewn with dead, who the Rebels have half buried and whom the heavy rain has uncovered."[4]

Here and there by the road the cavalrymen met oddly embattled farmers, armed with pitchforks and flails, who had rounded up small batches of Rebel stragglers and wanted to turn them over to the authorities. These farmers, it appeared, were moved not so much by patriotic fervor as by old-fashioned rage. In their retreat the Confederates had left the roads and had marched across the fields, trampling down the ripening wheat and rye in great swaths, and if the farmers could not have justice, they at least wanted to see the destroyers locked up.

The town of Gettysburg looked as if some universal moving day had been interrupted by catastrophe. Streets were barricaded up to window levels with everything that would serve—wagons, rocking chairs, bureaus, stoves, fence rails, old lumber, and piles of rocks—and there were scars from cannon balls and bullets. In row houses facing Cemetery Hill the Rebel sharpshooters had found vantage points in second-floor rooms, and they had knocked out walls between houses to provide communication along their line. One civilian had been killed—a girl named Jennie Wade, shot down by a stray bullet while she baked bread in her kitchen. When she died she had in her pocket a picture of her fiancé, Corporal Johnson Skelley of the 87th Pennsylvania, and she never knew that two weeks earlier Corporal Skelley had been mortally wounded in the fighting around Winchester, Virginia.[5]

Details were at work all over the field, collecting the last of the helpless wounded and burying the dead. This last was an almost impossible job, since more than five thousand men had been killed in action. Federals who were buried by men of their own regiments were given little wooden markers, with the name and regimental identification carved with a jackknife or scrawled with pencil, but in hundreds and hundreds of cases no identification was possible and the men went into the ground as "unknown." Long wide trenches were dug and the men were laid in them side by side, and sometimes there was nothing more in the way of a gravestone than a little headboard at one end of the trench stating the number of bodies that were buried in it. In places the burial details just gave up and did not try to make graves, but simply shoveled earth over the bodies as they lay on the ground.[6]

There was an immense harvest of discarded weapons to be picked up. As a first step the men attached bayonets to the rifles which lay on the field and stuck them in the ground for collection later, and along Cemetery Ridge there were whole acres of these, "standing as thick as trees in the nursery." Ordnance officers who took charge of these weapons noted an oddity. Out of more than thirty-seven thousand muskets which had been left on the field, nearly a third were loaded with more than one cartridge. In the excitement of battle men forgot to fix percussion caps, sometimes even forgot to pull the trigger, and reloaded automatically without realizing that they had not fired. One man remarked briefly that "not all the forces attacking or attacked are fully conscious of what they are doing," and veterans were free to admit that in this as in all other battles there had been a great deal of wild, ineffective shooting. Whole regiments at times fired volleys with the line of musket pointing vaguely toward the sky at an angle from the vertical of no more than forty-five degrees, and men were often seen to fire with both eyes tightly shut. An Ohio soldier in the XII

Corps reflected that in the Culp's Hill fighting on the morning of July 3 every man in the corps had fired 250 rounds, and he mused that "the mystery exists how any Rebels escaped."[7]

It was a rough war for wounded men. Immense field hospitals had been established in the low ground east of the Baltimore Pike, by Rock Creek, and the heavy rains of July 4 flooded this ground, and some of the helpless wounded men were drowned. An attempt was made to get some of the less seriously wounded over to the railroad, where they could be sent back to established hospitals in Baltimore, York, and Harrisburg, but Stuart's cavalry had broken the railroad and for a few days no trains were running. The wounded lay where they had been dropped, unsheltered on the bare ground, and the best that the army's medical inspector was able to report was that within a few days they were "made as comfortable as circumstances would permit," although it was admitted that things would have been better if the Medical Corps had been able to get straw for the men to lie on.[8]

The wounded men were not much given to complaining. A man in the Corn Exchange Regiment saw an amputee sitting outside a hospital tent, perky enough, considering that he had but one leg, playing cards with a wounded comrade. An orderly passed by hauling a hideous load of amputated arms and legs from the operating tent, and the one-legged man looked up with interest, laid down his cards, and asked the orderly to stop and let him inspect the haul. He wanted to take one more look at his lost leg, he said, and he would be able to recognize it because of a certain bunion. The orderly had no intention whatever of shuffling through his ghastly cargo, and \e rebuked the soldier and told him that if he believed in the resurrection of the body as a good Christian should, he could wait for the Last Day and take a good look at his missing limb then. The cardplayer agreed that that made sense and went on with his game.[9]

Slowly, and with immense effort, this shot-to-pieces army pulled itself together and took to the road. The VI Corps was out in front, and it had suffered little in the battle and had rested from its prodigious twenty-four-hour hike, but Meade was still cautious and John Sedgwick was equally so, and the pursuit was not pressed. Pulling the army out of Gettysburg was like pulling a shod foot out of deep mud—something to be done slowly and carefully, with infinite pains— and the air of urgency was gone. Colonel Chamberlain of the battle-bruised 20th Maine looked back at his regiment's final bivouac and reported:[10] "We returned to Little Round Top, where we buried our dead in the place where we had laid them during the fight, marking each grave by a headboard made of ammunition boxes, with each soldier's name cut upon it. We also buried fifty of the enemy's dead in front of our position of July 2. We then looked after our wounded, whom I had taken the responsibility of putting into the houses of citizens in the vicinity of Little Round Top, and on the morning of the fifth took up our march on the Emmitsburg road."

The Emmitsburg road had been the last long mile for many men—for handsome John Reynolds riding to meet an unknown Southern sharpshooter in a farmer's barn, for the black-hatted Western regiments with their fife-and-drum corps playing them into battle, for many unheard-of men who stepped off it into unmarked graves on slanting rocky fields—and for a few days it had been a famous military highway, pumping a stream of troops off to the unfathomable chances of war. Now it would be a quiet country road again, with a farmer's load of hay or drove of cattle as its most exciting wayfarers, the mountain wall to the west dropping long shadows across it in the blue summer evenings, the dust and the clamor and the rumbling guns gone forever. It was over at last, this enormous battle with its smoke and its grimness and its unheard-of violence, and here again was a simple road leading from one country town to another, with a commonplace little name that would ring and shine in the books forever.

Meade was on the road with his troops, an infinitely weary man with dust on his uniform and his gray beard, feeling responsibility as a paralyzing weight. He had been one of the few men who could have lost the war irretrievably in one day, and he had managed to avoid the mistakes that would have lost it. He would continue to avoid mistakes, even if he had to miss opportunity. Lee's army was at bay on the northern bank of the Potomac, the river too high for fording and all bridges gone, and there might still be a chance to sweep down on him, to force him to battle again and to destroy him and his army and the star-crossed, legendary cause which they represented in one last, blazing, triumphant assault. But it was a chance and no more than that. Meade could see all of the things that might go wrong with it: could see the Potomac, moreover, as a border between two countries, so that the important thing just now might be to get the Southern army across that border back into the land where it belonged. Meade brought his army up to the river very slowly. Nevertheless, when he found that the Rebels were still there, well dug in on a great crescent of rising ground not many miles from the old Antietam battlefield, he put his own men into line of battle and took them carefully forward.

It was more than a week after Gettysburg by now, and some of the army's temporary losses had been made good. The army rolled forward on a front six miles wide, battle flags snapping in the wind, sunlight glittering from thousands of bright muskets, guns clanking along ready to go into battery on command. A soldier who marched with it was struck with the picture: "Throughout the miles of deep lines it presented a beautiful sight as with the swinging cadenced step of veterans they moved over cultivated fields of grain, over roads, orchards, and vineyards, on plain, valley, and hill. Obstructions were leveled by the pioneers in advance, and regardless of damage the army of blue swept over the ground with heavy tread, leaving in their rear destruction and desolation."[11]

The long blue lines halted and skirmishers were sent out in front to guard against Rebel surprises, and that night there was a heavy rain and the army entrenched, while Meade summoned his corps commanders to determine whether the army should attack or not. The corps commanders were decidedly against it, and the army waited for a day. On July 14 Meade put it in motion again, having quietly concluded that he would try to do what his lieutenants had advised him not to do. But now it was too late. The Army of Northern Virginia had gone south of the river at last, leaving a small rear guard for a delaying action. Meade's cavalry and infantry picked up some Rebel wounded and stragglers, killed the General Pettigrew who had commanded the left wing of Pickett's great assault, and captured a gun or two. That was all. If the war was ever to be won, it would have to be won later—and somewhere else.

All of which was to the infinite displeasure of Abraham Lincoln.

The President had learned a great deal about the military art since those early amateurish days when he had decreed that all Union armies should advance willy-nilly on Washington's birthday and had juggled troops frantically back and forth from McClellan's army to the Shenandoah Valley in a vain effort to catch Stonewall Jackson by telegraphic order. It could even be argued now that he was as canny a strategist as the North possessed, and he had followed the army's slow progress down from Gettysburg in an agony of impatience. He still saw things as he had seen them three weeks earlier, when the governor of New Jersey had asked him to reinstate McClellan: Lee's advance into Pennsylvania had been an opportunity for the Federals, not for the Confederates; if the affair were handled right neither Lee nor his army should ever get back to Virginia; and all of this talk about "driving the enemy from our soil" struck him as deplorable blindness. Vicksburg had fallen and the back door to the Confederacy lay open; one more blow and it would all be over. This war could be won, once and forever, between Pennsylvania and the Potomac River, in this month of July 1863, if someone really set out to win it.

The flaming driving spirit of war, which could find no congenial home anywhere among the top commanders of the Army of the Potomac, had actually found its place at last in the mysterious heart of that melancholy, quizzical civilian, the President of the United States, the man who had confessed that he could not so much as kill a chicken for Sunday dinner without wincing at the sight of bloodshed. Lincoln wrote a harsh letter to Meade, crying in effect: *Why* couldn't you, just this once, go in and smash things and let me worry about picking up the pieces? He wrote it, and then characteristically he did not send it, letting it gather dust in a White House pigeonhole.

Halleck warned Meade that the President was dissatisfied, and Meade, worn almost to a frazzle, with a temper that was never stable, flared back that in that case, since he had done his level best, he would like to be relieved of his command. Halleck soothed him with a friendly, appreciative letter, and Lincoln in turn swallowed his vexation and decided to be grateful for what had been won.[12] And the army crossed the river, marched south, and made a stab at trying to pen Lee's army up in the Shenandoah Valley. The III Corps had the advance, and the corps was now commanded by bumbling, red-faced General W. H. French, who mishandled his troops so flagrantly that Hooker's and Kearny's veterans sardonically referred to their outfit as "the III Corps as we understand it."[13] The chance was missed and the Confederates got away, and the Army of the Potomac went down to the Rapidan country and went into camp, to rest and refit before taking up the fight again.

So there would be a new campaign, with other campaigns to follow, and in due time the great gloomy Wilderness around Chancellorsville would know gunfire again, and the wild tumult of battle, and the screams of wounded men trapped in burning thickets. It would be the hard fate of this army to fight dreadful battles without glory and without triumph, using itself up so that the victory might be won by other armies on other fields. The army would be ready for it, but it would be a different army henceforth. The ranks were thinner and there was a new name on the regimental flags, and the men were wiser than they had been before. They were beginning to realize that while a great thing had been done they had really done it themselves.[14] Meade was "old Four-Eyes," a general who had won his battle chiefly because his men were incomparably good soldiers. They had fought at Gettysburg with the highest pitch of inspiration, but the inspiration had come from within themselves and had not been fired by anyone at the top, and the staff officers who had felt obliged to hearten the men by spreading the McClellan rumor had simply shown that they themselves did not know what the men were really like. This army was a military instrument at last, and it could be used to the last full measure of its own inexpressible devotion, but from now on it would display enthusiasm for no generals.

A few days after Gettysburg, Meade issued a general order congratulating his troops on their victory, and the order was read in all the regiments at evening parade. The men were very matter-of-fact as they listened. In one regiment the colonel waved his hat and called for three cheers for General Meade, but the cheers were not forthcoming—not, as one of the men explained, because the men disliked Meade, but simply because they did not feel like cheering any more. These soldiers, he pointed out, "with their lights and experiences, could not see the wisdom or the occasion for any such manifestation of enthusiasm"; the army had matured, "its business sense increased with age," and hereafter it would wait and see before it tossed its caps in the air.[15]

It would wait and see, and there would still be a great deal to look at, for half of the price had not yet been paid. Yet the biggest test had been passed. Meade might draw no cheers, but in his own way he had not done too badly. At Gettysburg, for the first time, the Army of the Potomac had not been crippled by the mistakes of its commanding general. It had been given a chance, and the chance had been enough. At the crisis of the war everything had come down to the naked fury of the fighting men, and the fighting men had stood up under it— along Willoughby Run and Seminary Ridge, amid the rocks and bushes by Little Round Top, on the slopes back of the peach orchard and the wheat field, in the smoky twilight around Culp's Hill and the cemetery, and in the dust of the terrible pounding near the little clump of trees. They had won a victory. It might be less of a victory than Mr. Lincoln had hoped for, but it was nevertheless a victory—and, because of it, it was no longer possible for the Confederacy to win the war. The North might still lose it, to be sure, if the soldiers or the people should lose heart, but outright defeat was no longer in the cards. Both the army and the country were in shape to win at last, and from now on it would be a question of courage and endurance.

If the army was not especially enthusiastic, no more was Meade. He was crabbed and dyspeptic, a regular-army officer who had never cared very much for the volunteer system, and less than a year ago he had remarked that most of the men in the army had not the faintest idea of what soldiering really meant. But he paid his tribute, just the same, in one sentence of a letter which he wrote to Mrs. Meade two days after the battle: "The men behaved splendidly; I really think they are becoming soldiers."[16]

If anyone had doubted it, there was still plenty of proof around Gettysburg. An army medical officer was telling no more than the plain truth when he wrote that the ten days immediately after the battle were "the occasion of the greatest amount of human suffering known to this nation since its birth." This country market town of two thousand inhabitants had been presented with some twenty-two thousand wounded men, and the place was swamped with them. They lay on the fields and in ditches, in the woods under trees, in barns and haystacks and homes and churches for miles around.[17] The very fact that the battle had been a victory made the men's lot worse, for instead of remaining on the field where it could care for them the army had marched south in expectation of a new battle and had been able to leave behind it only a fraction of the required number of doctors and hospital attendants.

So appalling was the number of men awaiting attention that the overworked doctors had begun with a grim job of sorting out, separating the men who were bound to die from those whose lives might be saved. In one wood there was a long, pathetic row of semi-conscious men who lay on the ground, moaning and twitching fitfully, completely unattended—men who had been shot through the head and whose wounds, upon hasty inspection, had been pronounced mortal and who had simply been put aside to die as quickly as they might. Not far away there was a long table where for an entire week doctors worked from dawn to twilight cutting off arms and legs, with an army wagon standing by to carry off the wreckage and hurry back for a new load. A young woman who came to Gettysburg to help nurse the wounded entered a church which had been hastily converted into a hospital and found that planks had been laid across the tops of the pews so that the entire auditorium was one vast hard bed, jammed with wounded men lying elbow to elbow: "I seemed to stand breast-high in a sea of anguish." Permeating everything in and near the town was the foul, overpowering stench of the unburied dead—an atmosphere which, as this woman said, "robbed the battlefield of its glory, the survivors of their victory, and the wounded of what little chance of life was left to them."[18]

Little by little order was restored, the army working hand in hand with the Sanitary Commission and the Christian Commission. The one railroad leading into Gettysburg had been broken, but Herman Haupt was on the job almost before the battle ended, and as always he made things happen. He found the railroad totally inadequate, even after its breaks had been made good—a country railroad without experienced officers, with no more sidings, water tanks, turntables, or fuel than were needed for its normal traffic of three or four trains a day. It was necessary now to operate thirty trains a day, and he had locomotives and cars sent up from Alexandria. He improvised water tanks, brought in loads of fuel, got repair crews on the job with prefabricated bridges and culverts, and before long he had the railway in shape to move fifteen hundred tons of freight each way every day. The army medical service was telegraphing frantically to Baltimore for immediate shipments of alcohol, creosote, nitric acid, permanganate of potassium, tin cups, buckets, stretchers, bed sacks, and other equipment, and the Sanitary Commission made up a special train of food, tents, clothing, stoves, and bandages which reached the town three days after the battle.[19]

All across the northeast, in the pulpits of hundreds of churches, ministers read appeals for help. Money was needed, and food, and medicines, and the little delicacies sick men need—and, above all, "all females qualified for usefulness in this emergency." Nurses were brought in; regular-army nurses recruited by Miss Dorothea Dix, who sternly refused to accept women who were either young or pretty, considering such persons quite unsuited for work in army hospitals, and women enlisted by the Sanitary Commission, which had agents at railroad stations in the big Eastern cities to interview applicants and organize them into working units. Pennsylvania militia regiments were brought in to guard the place, and as the hospital tents were set up in the groves near the town those soldiers marched all visitors away at four every afternoon so that the nurses might not be exposed to nameless perils. The nurses found themselves far too busy to be in any danger, however. Five days after the battle ambulances were still going about the fields collecting hundreds of men whose wounds had not yet been dressed and who had had nothing to eat except such hardtack as they happened to have in their haversacks.[20]

As these women worked, an ancient tradition quietly died. It had always been supposed that army nursing was strictly a job either for enlisted men or for superannuated trollops who were beyond contamination. But here they were, women precisely like the wives and sisters and mothers the soldiers had left behind, up to their elbows in it and taking no harm whatever. One of them quietly wrote: "I have been for weeks the only lady in a camp of seven hundred men, and have never been treated with more deference, respect, and kindness." Uniformly, these women testified that the men they cared for were nothing less than magnificent, and in a letter to her sister a little New Jersey Quaker wrote: "More Christian fortitude was never witnessed than they exhibit, always say—'Help my neighbor first, he is worse.' " After some weeks, when the emergency had passed and one group of women prepared to leave, two army bands turned out to escort them to the railroad station.[21]

As rapidly as the men became well enough to be moved they were sent off to permanent hospitals in Baltimore, Washington, York, and Harrisburg, and before long six hospital trains were leaving town every day. Until the army got hold of this business the trips were pretty grim. A medical inspector who looked into matters protested with fury that "the railroad companies, who got the only profit of the battle, and who had the greatest opportunities of ameliorating the sufferings of the wounded, alone stood aloof and rendered no aid." He specified: trains were fearfully unclean, there were no attendants for the wounded, there was no water, there was not even straw for the men to lie upon—"absolutely nothing but the bare cars, filthy from the business of transporting cattle and freight." He cracked down hard, and a medical officer was detailed to accompany each train, water coolers and bedpans and medicines and bandages were provided, and at the first junction point agents of the Christian Commission were alerted to meet the trains and provide any help that might be needed. In the end, things were fairly well organized, and in three weeks sixteen thousand men were sent away.[22] The Gettysburg hospitals still contained four thousand more who were too sick to be moved, but the worst of it was over.

So the wounded were taken care of. There were still the dead. Many bodies had never been buried—the gullies and rocky crannies around Devil's Den contained some horrible relics—and the rains had washed the earth away from bodies imperfectly covered, and there were many unmarked graves. Governor Andrew Curtin visited the place and appointed a local businessman as his agent to see to it that the state of Pennsylvania did what was necessary, and toward the end of July, at Curtin's request, this agent got in touch with the governors of all of the Northern states whose men had fought at Gettysburg and proposed that they got together to provide a proper cemetery. There were meetings and an exchange of letters, and by mid-August money had been raised and Pennsylvania had bought seventeen acres of land on Cemetery Hill, and the work of establishing a cemetery was under way.[23]

It would be a project for the states, naturally. They had thought of it first, they were putting up the money, their governors were making the arrangements, and anyway, the national government was busy with other matters. As the lifeless bodies were moved up to Cemetery Hill it was agreed that they should be grouped there by states—one plot for New Yorkers, another for Pennsylvanians, and so on down the list—and if from these honored dead each governor could take increased prestige, with visible proof that his state had done its full share, that would be so much the better, because possibly this battle had really been an affair of the separate states from the beginning.[24] As host, Governor Curtin was the man of the hour, and he invited the famous orator, Edward Everett, to do the talking when the cemetery was formally dedicated. He also asked General Meade to attend if he could.

Everett could come, but he would need more time. A speech commemorating the Gettysburg dead could not be put together overnight, and Everett had certain engagements. The date originally selected was October 23, and it would not be possible for him to complete his preparations by that time: could not there be a postponement? Governor Curtin and the others agreed that there could, and the ceremonies were put off until November 19. General Meade sent his regrets, pointing out that military affairs in the state of Virginia would be taking all of his time.[25]

Settled, then, for the nineteenth of November, and the battlefield could be fairly well policed up by that time. There were still a few wounded men around, but by late November it should be possible to get all of them shipped off, and the air was becoming fit to breathe again. The summer wore away, the burial squads were busy, the hilltop was being nicely landscaped, and down below the Potomac the army was maneuvering back and forth, getting into small fights occasionally, losing a few men here and killing a few Rebels there, sparring the time away until a new campaign could be begun. The drafted men were coming in to fill the ranks—coming in under guard, with a roll call every two hours, because most of them had very little intention of remaining with the army if they could help it—and the veterans looked forward to their arrival with a certain unholy pleasure. Their attitude was pretty well expressed by a diarist in the 15th Massachusetts, which had been consolidated to four companies because of heavy battle losses, who wrote: "I wish the conscripts were out here now. I want to see them. I want to put some of them through the drill. I want to see them live on salt pork and hard bread. I want to see them carry their knapsacks."[26] Admittedly, the draftees were not very good material, but there were men in the army who would see that they became soldiers once they got to camp.

The great day came at last, and there were troops in Gettysburg again, and bands, and special trains bringing distinguished guests, and there was a big parade through the town and up to the hill with parade marshals in their sashes, horses shying and curvetting affectedly, much pomp and circumstance, and a famous orator with an hour-long speech in his hand. There was also Abraham Lincoln, who had been invited more or less as an afterthought—the invitation went to him on November 2, suggesting that he might honor the occasion by his presence—and Mr. Lincoln was to say a few words after Mr. Everett had made the speech. After the usual fuss and confusion the procession climbed the hill and the honored guests got up on the flag-draped speakers' stand, and eventually a certain degree of quiet was restored. A chaplain offered a prayer, and a glee club sang an ode composed especially for the occasion, and at last the orator got up to make his speech.

An oration was an oration in those days, and it had to have a certain style to it—classical allusions, a leisurely approach to the subject matter, a carefully phrased recital of the background and history of the occasion, the whole working up to a peroration which would sum everything up in memorable sentences. Mr. Everett was a master of this art form and had been hard at work for many weeks, and he stood up now in the center of the field where five thousand men had died and began his polished cadenced sentences. He recalled how the ancient Greeks commemorated their heroic dead in the days of Pericles. . . .

There were many thousands of people at this ceremony, and among them were certain wounded veterans who had come back to see all of this, and a knot of these wandered away from the crowd around the speakers' stand and strolled down along Cemetery Ridge, pausing when they reached a little clump of trees, and there they looked off toward the west and talked quietly about what they had seen and done there.[27]

In front of them was the wide gentle valley of the shadow of death, brimming now with soft autumn sunlight, and behind them the flags waved lazily about the speakers' stand and the voice droned on, building up toward a literary climax. The valley was a mile wide, and there was the rolling ground where the Rebel guns had been ranked, and on the crest of this ridge was the space where a girlish artillery lieutenant had had a sergeant hold him up while he called for the last round of canister, the ground where file closers had gripped hands and dug in their heels to hold a wavering line together, the place where the noise of men desperately fighting had been heard as a great mournful roar; and the voice went on, and the governors looked dignified, and the veterans by the trees looked about them and saw again the fury and the smoke and the killing.

This was the valley of dry bones, waiting for the word, which might or might not come in rhythmic prose that began by describing the customs of ancient Athens. The bones had lain there in the sun and the rain, and now they were carefully arranged state by state under the new sod. They were the bones of men who had exulted in their youth, and some of them had been unstained heroes while others had been scamps who pillaged and robbed and ran away when they could, and they had died here, and that was the end of them. They had come here because of angry words and hot passions in which they had not shared. They had come, too, because the drums had rolled and the band had blared the swinging deceitful tunes that piped men off to battle . . . three cheers for the red white and blue, here's a long look back at the girl I left behind me, John Brown's body lies a-moldering in the grave but we go marching on, and Yankee Doodle on his spotted pony rides off into the eternal smoky mist of war.

Back of these men were innumerable long dusty roads reaching to the main streets of a thousand youthful towns and villages where there had been bright flags overhead and people on the board sidewalks cheering and crying and waving a last good-by. It had seemed once that there was some compelling reason to bring these men here—something so broad that it would encompass all of the terrible contradictory manifestations of the country's pain and bewilderment, the riots and the lynchings, the hysterical conspiracies with their oaths written in blood, the hard hand that had been laid upon the countryside, the scramble for riches and the scheming for high place, and the burdens carried by quiet folk who wanted only to live at peace by the faith they used to have.

Perhaps there was a meaning to all of it somewhere. Perhaps everything that the nation was and meant to be had come to a focus here, beyond the graves and the remembered echoes of the guns and the wreckage of lives that were gone forever. Perhaps the whole of it somehow was greater than the sum of its tragic parts, and perhaps here on this wind-swept hill the thing could be said at last, so that the dry bones of the country's dreams could take on flesh.

The orator finished, and after the applause had died away the tall man in the black frock coat got to his feet, with two little sheets of paper in his hand, and he looked out over the valley and began to speak.

The writer of any book which is concerned with a war that is no longer a part of any living memories incurs many obligations to the helpful people who run libraries. For their kindness in finding and making available needed material, and for their interest and patience, I am indebted to various persons, including Mr. David C. Mearns, chief of the Manuscript Division of the Library of Congress; Colonel Willard Webb, distinguished combat soldier and chief of the Stack and Reader Division of that library; Mr. League Obear, chief of the Library's Loan Division; Miss Georgia Cowan and Mr. Walter D. Campbell of the History Division of the District of Columbia Public Library, and Mr. Paul Howard, Librarian of the U.S. Department of the Interior.

Bibliography

A principal reliance in the preparation of this book has of course been the voluminous *War of the Rebellion: A Compilation of the Official Records of the Union and Confederate Armies,* published by the War Department in 1902. Unless otherwise noted, volumes cited in the notes are from Series I of this compilation. Use has also been made of Appleton's *Cyclopedia of American Biography,* published in 1888, and of the more modern *Dictionary of American Biography.* In addition, the following works were consulted:

GENERAL HISTORICAL WORKS AND BOOKS DEALING WITH THE POLITICAL AND ECONOMIC BACKGROUND OF THE WAR

Abraham Lincoln and the Fifth Column, by George Fort Milton. New York, 1942.
Abraham Lincoln and Men of War Times, by Alexander K. McClure. Philadelphia, 1892.
Adventures of America, 1857–1900, by John A. Kouwenhoven. New York, 1938.
Annual Report of the Commissioner of Patents for 1864. 2 vols. Washington, 1866.
Centennial History of the City of Washington, D.C., by H. W. Crew. Dayton, 1892.
Discontent in New York City, 1861–65. A dissertation submitted to the Faculty of the Graduate School of Arts and Sciences of the Catholic University of America, by Brother Basil Leo Lee, F.S.C Washington, 1943.
Experiment in Rebellion, by Clifford Dowdey. New York, 1950.
In French Creek Valley, by John Earle Reynolds. Meadville, Pa., 1938.
The German Soldier in the Wars of the United States, by J. G. Rosengarten. Philadelphia, 1886.
The Growth of the American Republic, by Samuel Eliot Morison and Henry Steele Commager. 2 vols. New York, 1942.
The Hidden Civil War, the Story of the Copperheads, by Wood Gray. New York, 1942.
History of the Administration of President Lincoln, by Henry J. Raymond. New York, 1864.
History of the National Capital, by Wilhelmus Bogart Bryan, 1916.
History of the United States from the Compromise of 1850, by James Ford Rhodes. 9 vols. New York, 1899.
Influence of the War on Our National Prosperity, by William E. Dodge. New York, 1865.
Labor Disturbances in Pennsylvania, 1850–1880. A dissertation submitted to the Faculty of the Graduate School of Arts and Sciences of the Catholic University of America, by J. Walter Coleman. Washington, 1936.
Lincoln and the War Governors, by William B. Hesseltine. New York, 1948.

Lincoln's Daughters of Mercy, by Marjorie Barstow Greenbie. New York, 1944.
Lincoln's War Cabinet, by Burton J. Hendrick. Boston, 1946.
The Long Ships Passing, by Walter Havighurst. New York, 1942.
The Molly Maguires, by Anthony Bimba. New York, 1932.
The Movement for Peace without Victory during the Civil War, by Elbert J. Benton. Cleveland, 1918.
Old-Time Notes of Pennsylvania, by Alexander K. McClure. 2 vols. Philadelphia, 1905.
Photographic History of the Civil War, edited by Francis Trevelyan Miller. 10 vols. New York, 1911.
Pictorial History of the Civil War, by Benson J. Lossing. 3 vols. Philadelphia, 1866.
Political and Social Growth of the American People, by Arthur M. Schlesinger. New York, 1941.
The Rebellion Record: A Diary of American Events, edited by Frank Moore. 12 vols. New York, 1864.
Recollections of War Times, by Albert Gallatin Riddle. New York, 1895.
Social and Industrial Conditions in the North during the Civil War, by Emerson David Fite. New York, 1910.
South after Gettysburg: Letters of Cornelia Hancock from the Army of the Potomac, 1863–65, edited by Henrietta Stratton Jaquette. Philadelphia, 1937.
Speeches, Correspondence and Political Papers of Carl Schurz, selected and edited by Frederic Bancroft. 6 vols. New York, 1913.
A True History of the Reign of Terror in Southern Illinois, by James D. Fox. Aurora, Ill., 1884.
War Government, Federal and State, 1861–1865, by William B. Weeden. Boston, 1906.

AUTOBIOGRAPHIES, BIOGRAPHICAL STUDIES, MEMOIRS, ETC.

Abraham Lincoln: The War Years, by Carl Sandburg. 4 vols. New York, 1939.
Autobiography of Oliver Otis Howard. 2 vols. New York, 1907.
Charles Francis Adams: An Autobiography. Boston, 1906.
Dan Sickles, Hero of Gettysburg and "Yankee King of Spain," by Edgcumb Pinchon. New York, 1945.
Days and Events: 1860–1866, by Colonel Thomas L. Livermore. Boston, 1920.
A Diary from Dixie, by Mary Boykin Chesnut, edited by Ben Ames Williams. Cambridge, 1949.
Diary of Gideon Welles, with an introduction by John T. Morse, Jr. 3 vols. Boston, 1911.
Fighting Joe Hooker, by Walter H. Hebert. Indianapolis, 1944.
General Hancock, by General Francis A. Walker. New York, 1894.
Gouverneur Kemble Warren: The Life and Letters of an American Soldier, by Emerson Gifford Taylor. Boston, 1932.
Jeb Stuart, by John W. Thomason, Jr. New York, 1930.
Jefferson Davis: The Unreal and the Real, by Robert McElroy. 2 vols. New York, 1937.
Lee's Lieutenants, by Douglas Southall Freeman. 3 vols. New York, 1942.
The Life and Letters of George Gordon Meade, by Colonel George Meade. 2 vols. New York, 1913.
Life and Letters of Henry Lee Higginson, by Bliss Perry. Boston, 1921.
The Life and Public Services of Salmon Portland Chase, by J. W. Schuckers. New York, 1874.
The Life and Services of Ambrose E. Burnside: Soldier—Citizen—Statesman, by Ben Perley Poore. Providence, 1882.

Life of Oliver P. Morton, by William Dudley Foulke. 2 vols. Indianapolis, 1899.

Lincoln and the Episodes of the Civil War, by Brevet Brigadier General William E. Doster. New York, 1915.

Major General Hiram G. Berry, by Edward K. Gould. Rockland, Me., 1899.

The Military Services of Gen. Ambrose E. Burnside in the Civil War, by Daniel R. Ballou. Providence, 1914.

Old Thad Stevens: A Story of Ambition, by Richard Nelson Current. Madison, 1942.

Personal Recollections of the Civil War, by Brigadier General John Gibbon. New York, 1928.

Personal Recollections of Distinguished Generals, by William F. G. Shanks. New York, 1866.

Political Recollections, by George W. Julian. Chicago, 1884.

Ranger Mosby, by Virgil Carrington Jones. Chapel Hill, 1944.

A Rebel War Clerk's Diary, by J. B. Jones, edited by Howard Swiggett. 2 vols. New York, 1935.

Recollections of Half a Century, by Alexander K. McClure. Salem, Mass., 1902.

R. E. Lee: A Biography, by Douglas Southall Freeman. 4 vols. New York, 1934.

Reminiscences of the Civil War, by General John B. Gordon. New York, 1903.

Reminiscences of Winfield Scott Hancock, by His Wife. New York, 1887.

Robert E. Lee, the Soldier, by Major General Sir Frederick Maurice. Boston, 1925.

Sketch of the Life, Character and Public Services of Oliver P. Morton, prepared for the Indianapolis *Journal* by Charles M. Walker. Indianapolis, 1878.

Stonewall Jackson and the American Civil War, by Colonel G. F. R. Henderson. London and New York, 1936.

The Tall Sycamore of the Wabash: Daniel Wolsey Voorhees, by Leonard S. Kenworthy. Boston, 1936.

Three Wisconsin Cushings, by Theron Wilber Haight. Madison, 1910.

Touched with Fire: Civil War Letters and Diary of Oliver Wendell Holmes, Jr., edited by Mark De Wolfe Howe, Cambridge, 1946.

MILITARY HISTORIES AND BOOKS DEALING WITH SPECIFIC BATTLES OR CAMPAIGNS

The Antietam and Fredericksburg, by Francis Winthrop Palfrey. New York, 1882.

The Army of Tennessee, by Stanley F. Horn. Indianapolis, 1941.

The Battle of Chancellorsville, by Augustus Choate Hamlin. Bangor, Me., 1896.

The Battle of Chancellorsville and the Eleventh Army Corps. Reprints of speeches at a mass meeting in the Cooper Institute, New York, June 2, 1863.

The Battle of Gettysburg, by Colonel Frank Aretas Haskell. Madison, 1908.

The Battle of Gettysburg, by the Comte de Paris. Philadelphia, 1886.

Battles and Leaders of the Civil War. Grant-Lee edition. 4 vols. New York, 1884.

"From Burnside to Hooker" and "The Army of the Potomac under Hooker": articles by William Howard Mills in the *Magazine of American History,* Vol. XV.

Camp and Outpost Duty for Infantry, by Brigadier General Daniel Butterfield. New York, 1862.

The Campaign of Chancellorsville, by John Bigelow, Jr. New Haven, 1910.

Campaigns of the Army of the Potomac, by William Swinton. New York, 1866.

The Celebrated Case of Fitz-John Porter, by Otto Eisenschiml. Indianapolis, 1950.

Chancellorsville and Gettysburg, by Major General Abner Doubleday. New York, 1882.

The Charge of the 8th Pennsylvania Cavalry at Chancellorsville, by Pennock Huey. Philadelphia, 1884.

The Crisis of the Confederacy, by Cecil Battine. London and New York, 1905.

Fredericksburg: A Study in War, by Major G. W. Redway. New York, 1906.

General Halleck and General Burnside: a reprint, with additions, of two articles originally communicated to the Providence *Journal* by "W." Boston, 1864.

Gettysburg and Lincoln: The Battle, the Cemetery and the National Park, by Henry Sweetser Burrage. New York, 1906.

History of the Army of the Potomac, by J. H. Stine. Philadelphia, 1892.

History of the Second Massachusetts Regiment of Infantry: Gettysburg, by Colonel Charles F. Morse. Boston, 1882.

The Iron Brigade at Gettysburg, anonymous. Cincinnati, 1879.

Lincoln Finds a General, by Kenneth P. Williams. 2 vols. New York, 1950.

The Long Arm of Lee, by Jennings Wise. 2 vols. Lynchburg, Va., 1915.

Maine in the War for the Union, by William E. S. Whitman and Charles H. True. Lewiston, Me., 1865.

The Military Genius of Abraham Lincoln, by Brigadier General Colin R. Ballard. London, 1926.

The Military Policy of the United States, by Brevet Major General Emory Upton. Washington, 1916.

New Jersey and the Rebellion, by John Y. Foster. Newark, 1868.

New Jersey Troops in the Gettysburg Campaign, by Samuel Toombs. Orange, N.J., 1888.

Our Campaign around Gettysburg, by John Lockwood. Brooklyn, 1864.

Papers of the Military Historical Society of Massachusetts, edited by Theodore Dwight. 10 vols. Boston, 1895.

The Second Massachusetts Infantry and the Campaign of Chancellorsville, by George A. Thayer. Boston, 1882.

The 17th Connecticut Volunteers at Gettysburg. Pamphlet. Bridgeport, 1884.

Strong Vincent and His Brigade at Gettysburg, by Oliver W. Norton. Chicago, 1909.

REGIMENTAL HISTORIES, SOLDIERS' REMINISCENCES, ETC.

Army Letters, 1861–1865, by Oliver Willcox Norton. Chicago, 1903.

Army Life: A Private's Reminiscences of the Civil War, by the Rev. Theodore Gerrish. Portland, Me., 1882.

Berdan's United States Sharpshooters in the Army of the Potomac, by Captain C. A. Stevens, St. Paul, 1892.

The Bivouac and the Battlefield, by Captain George F. Noyes. New York, 1863.

Camp, March and Battlefield; or, Three Years and a Half with the Army of the Potomac, by the Rev. A. M. Stewart, chaplain of the 102nd Pennsylvania. Philadelphia, 1865.

Campaigning with the 6th Maine, by Brevet Lieutenant Colonel Charles A. Clark. Des Moines, 1897.

Campaigns of the 146th Regiment New York State Volunteers, compiled by Mary Genevie Green Brainard. New York, 1915.

Civil War Diary of James T. Ayres, edited by John Hope Franklin. Springfield, Ill., 1947.

Deeds of Daring; or, History of the 8th New York Volunteer Cavalry, by Henry Norton. Norwich, N.Y., 1889.

The Diary of a Young Officer, by Josiah M. Favill. Chicago, 1909.

The Dutchess County Regiment, edited by S. G. Cook and Charles E. Benton. Danbury, Conn., 1907.

A Famous Battery and Its Campaigns, 1861–64, by Captain James E. Smith. Washington, 1892.

The Fifth Regiment Connecticut Volunteers: A History, by Edwin E. Marvin. Hartford, 1889.

The 48th in the War: being a Narrative of the Campaigns of the 48th Regiment, Infantry, Pennsylvania Veteran Volunteers, during the War of the Rebellion, by Oliver Christian Bosbyshell. Philadelphia, 1895.

Four Years Campaigning in the Army of the Potomac, by D. G. Crotty. Grand Rapids, 1874.

Four Years in the Army of the Potomac: A Soldier's Recollections, by Major Evan Rowland Jones. London, 1881.

Four Years with the Army of the Potomac, by Regis de Trobriand, translated by George K. Dauchy. Boston, 1889.

Henry Wilson's Regiment: History of the 22nd Massachusetts Infantry, by John L. Parker. Boston, 1887.

History and Honorary Roll of the 12th Regiment, Infantry, N.G.S.N.Y., by M. Francis Dowley. New York, 1869.

History of a Cavalry Company: A Complete Record of Company A, 4th Pennsylvania Cavalry, by Captain William Hyndman. Philadelphia, 1870.

History of the Corn Exchange Regiment, 118th Pennsylvania Volunteers, by the Survivors Association. Philadelphia, 1888.

History of the 8th Cavalry Regiment, Illinois Volunteers, by Abner Hard. Aurora, Ill., 1868.

History of the 87th Pennsylvania Volunteers, by George R. Prowell. York, Pa., 1903.

A History of the First Regiment of Massachusetts Cavalry Volunteers, by Major Benjamin W. Crowninshield. Boston, 1891.

History of the First Regiment Minnesota Volunteer Infantry, by R. I. Holcombe. Stillwater, Minn., 1916.

The History of the 9th Regiment Massachusetts Volunteer Infantry, by Daniel George MacNamara. Boston, 1899.

History of the Philadelphia Brigade, by Charles H. Banes. Philadelphia, 1876.

History of the Sauk County Riflemen, by Philip Cheek and Mair Pointon. Privately printed, 1909.

History of the Second Army Corps in the Army of the Potomac, by Brevet Brigadier General Francis A. Walker. New York, 1886.

History of the Tenth Massachusetts Battery, by John D. Billings. Boston, 1881.

History of the Third Indiana Cavalry, by W. N. Pickerill. Indianapolis, 1906.

History of the 12th Regiment New Hampshire Volunteers in the War of the Rebellion, by Captain A. W. Bartlett. Concord, N.H., 1897.

History of the 21st Regiment Ohio Volunteer Infantry in the War of the Rebellion, by Captain S. S. Canfield. Toledo, 1893.

History of the 24th Michigan of the Iron Brigade, by O. B. Curtis. Detroit, 1891.

I Rode with Stonewall, by Henry Kyd Douglas. Chapel Hill, 1940.

Journal History of the 29th Ohio Veteran Volunteers, by J. Hamp Se Cheverell. Cleveland, 1883.

Letters from a Surgeon of the Civil War, compiled by Martha Derby Perry. Boston, 1906.

Life in Camp: A History of the Nine Months' Service of the 14th Vermont Regiment, by J. C. Williams. Claremont, N.H., 1864.

A Military History of the 8th Regiment Ohio Volunteer Infantry, by Lieutenant Colonel Franklin Sawyer. Cleveland, 1881.

A Narrative of the Formation and Services of the Eleventh Massachusetts Volunteers, by Gustavus B. Hutchinson. Boston, 1893.

Nineteenth Indiana Volunteer Infantry: taken from *Indiana at Antietam.* Report of the Indiana Antietam Monument Commission. Indianapolis, 1911.

The 95th Pennsylvania Volunteers, by G. Norton Galloway. Philadelphia, 1884.

The Ninth Ohio Volunteers, by Carl Wittke. Columbus, 1926.

The Old Fourth Michigan Infantry, by O. S. Barrett. Detroit, 1888.

On the Parallels; or, Chapters of Inner History, by Benjamin Borton. Woodstown, N.J., 1903.

Recollections of a Confederate Staff Officer, by General G. Moxley Sorrel. New York, 1905.

Recollections of a Private, by Warren Lee Goss. New York, 1890.

Recollections of a Private Soldier in the Army of the Potomac, by Frank Wilkeson. New York, 1887.

Recollections of the Civil War, by Mason Whiting Tyler. New York, 1912.

Record of the 33rd Massachusetts Volunteer Infantry, by Andrew J. Boies. Fitchburg, Mass., 1880.

Red-Tape and Pigeon-Hole Generals; as Seen from the Ranks during a Campaign in the Army of the Potomac, by a Citizen-Soldier. New York, 1864.

Regimental History of the First New York Dragoons, by the Rev. J. R. Bowen. Lyons, Mich., 1900.

Reminiscences and Record of the 6th New York Veteran Volunteer Cavalry, by Alonzo Foster. Privately printed, 1892.

Reminiscences of General Herman Haupt. Milwaukee, 1901.

Reminiscences of the 19th Massachusetts Regiment, by Captain John G. B. Adams. Boston, 1899.

The Road to Richmond: The Civil War Memoirs of Major Abner Small, of the 16th Maine Volunteers, edited by Harold Adams Small. Berkeley, Calif. 1939.

Service with the Sixth Wisconsin Volunteers, by Rufus R. Dawes. Marietta, O., 1890.

The 61st Ohio Volunteers, 1861-1865, by Frederick Stephen Wallace. Marysville, O., 1902.

A Soldier's Diary: The Story of a Volunteer, by David Lane. Privately printed, 1905.

Some Personal Reminiscences of Service in the Cavalry of the Army of the Potomac, by Colonel Hampton S. Thomas. Philadelphia, 1889.

The Story of a Thousand: Being a History of the Service of the 105th Ohio Volunteer Infantry, by Albion W. Tourgee. Buffalo, 1896.

The Story of the 15th Regiment Massachusetts Volunteer Infantry, by Andrew E. Ford. Clinton, Mass., 1898

The Story of the 48th, by Joseph Gould. Philadelphia 1908.

Three Years Campaign of the 9th N.Y.S.M. during the Southern Rebellion, by John W. Jaques. New York, 1865.

Three Years in the Army of the Potomac, by Henry N. Blake. Boston, 1865.

Three Years in the Field Hospitals of the Army of the Potomac, by Mrs. William H. Holstein. Philadelphia, 1867.

The Three Years Service of the 33rd Massachusetts Infantry Regiment, 1862-65, by Adin B. Underwood. Boston, 1881.

Trials and Triumphs: The Record of the 55th Ohio Volunteer Infantry, by Captain Hartwell Osborn and Others. Chicago, 1904.

The Twentieth Connecticut: A Regimental History, by John W. Storrs. Ansonia, Conn., 1886.

The 25th Ohio Veteran Volunteer Infantry in the War for the Union, by Edward C. Culp. Topeka, Kans., 1885.

The Ulster Guard and the War of the Rebellion, by Colonel Theodore B. Gates. New York, 1879.

Under the Maltese Cross: Antietam to Appomattox: Campaigns of the 155th Pennsylvania Regiment, narrated by the Rank and File. Pittsburgh, 1910.

Under the Red Patch: The Story of the 63rd Regiment Pennsylvania Volunteers, compiled by Gilbert Adams Hays. Pittsburgh, 1908.

War Letters of William Thompson Lusk. Privately printed, New York, 1911.

War Years with Jeb Stuart, by Lieutenant Colonel W. W. Blackford. New York, 1945

NOTES

CHAPTER ONE: DEEP RIVER

FOR WHAT THERE WAS IN IT

1. *Camp, March and Battlefield,* by the Rev. A. M. Stewart, p. 248.
2. *The Rebellion Record,* edited by Frank Moore, Vol. VI, Part 2, p. 4; *The Hidden Civil War,* by Wood Gray, p. 111.
3. For the Democrats' conversations with the British Minister, see Lord Lyons's dispatch, quoted in *Pictorial History of the Civil War,* by Benson J. Lossing, Vol. III, p. 47.
4. Chase's visits with Hooker and what came of them are related in *Fighting Joe Hooker,* by Walter H. Hebert, p. 147. The National Insane Asylum, now St. Elizabeth's Hospital, was built in the mid-1850s on what was then a rural estate not far from the Anacostia River, and was designed to care for mental patients from the District of Columbia, and the armed services. (*Centennial History of the City of Washington, D.C.,* by H. W. Crew; *History of the National Capital,* by Wilhelmus Bogart Bryan.) During the Civil War the hospital offered a pleasant place in which a high-ranking general might recuperate from a light wound.
5. The visit of Hamlin, Berry, and Hooker is described by General Charles Hamlin, son of the Vice-President, in E. K. Gould's *Major General Hiram G. Berry,* p. 229. It might be noted that at this time Hooker's sardonic brother officer, George Gordon Meade, was writing to his wife: "Hooker is a Democrat and anti-abolitionist—that is to say, he was. What he will be, when the command of the army is held out to him, is more than anyone can tell, because I fear he is open to temptation and liable to be seduced by flattery." (*Life and Letters of George Gordon Meade,* Vol. I, p. 319.)
6. As distinguished a soldier as John Gibbon, who closed the war as a major general commanding an army corps, became a captain again in 1866. This cataclysmic descent is recalled in Gibbon's *Personal Recollections of the Civil War,* pp. 370–71.
7. Buell's account of his difficulties with Morton, the killing of Nelson, and the failure of all efforts to bring Davis to trial appears in *Battles and Leaders of the Civil War,* Vol. III, pp. 42–44. From a very different point of view, the same topics are also discussed extensively in William Dudley Foulke's *Life of Oliver P. Morton,* Vol. I, pp. 187–95, and in *Sketch of the Life, Character and Public Services of Oliver P. Morton,* by Charles M. Walker, pp. 70, 73, 79. An interesting picture of the breezy Nelson as his troops saw him in battle appears in *History of the 21st Regiment Ohio Volunteer Infantry in the War of the Rebellion,* by Captain S. S. Canfield, pp. 32–33. Colonel R. M. Kelly describes Nelson vividly in *Battles and Leaders,* Vol. I, p. 375 ff., and another picture of the man is found in *The Story of a Thousand,* by Albion W. Tourgee, p. 70 ff. There is a brief sketch of the slightly satanic General Davis in Vol. 2 of Appleton's *Cyclopedia of American Biography.* Union defeats during the

Bragg invasion are well described in Stanley F. Horn's *The Army of Tennessee,* pp. 164, 168–69.

8. General Gibbon's indignant account of the Meredith-Hooker deal and his caustic verdict on both men, in all of which Meredith is never mentioned by name, appear in his *Personal Recollections,* pp. 107–9. Unfortunately there is no full-length history of the 19th Indiana. A sketch of the regiment's career is printed in *Indiana at Antietam,* pp. 107–23; it remarks that the 19th was "a pet regiment" of Governor Morton's, emphasizes the close tie between Meredith and Morton, and is notably reserved about Meredith's promotion. Meredith is briefly described in Appleton's *Cyclopedia.* Foulke's *Oliver P. Morton* (pp. 152–53, Vol. I) reveals that Morton incurred a good deal of criticism in Indiana by giving Meredith his colonelcy in the first place. In the early spring of 1861 Morton was employing Meredith as a special emissary to the War Department (*Official Records,* Series III, Vol. I, p. 243.)

9. The allegation is discussed by two enlisted veterans of the Iron Brigade in *Battles and Leaders,* Vol. III, p. 142.

10. *History of the 24th Michigan,* by O. B. Curtis, p. 65. The early portion of Curtis's book has been drawn on extensively for material on the regiment's organization, background, and general personality. For glimpses of the ceremony at which the 24th was received (if not welcomed) into the Iron Brigade, see Gibbon's *Personal Recollections,* p. 92, and *Service with the 6th Wisconsin Volunteers,* by Rufus R. Dawes, p. 101.

11. *History of the 24th Michigan,* p. 69; *Service with the 6th Wisconsin Volunteers,* p. 105.

12. *History of the 24th Michigan,* p. 84.

JORDAN WATER, RISE OVER ME

1. Haupt to Burnside, *Official Records,* Vol. XXI, p. 850; *Rebellion Record,* Vol. VI, Part 2, pp. 94–100; *Camp, March and Battlefield,* p. 250.

2. *History of the Sauk County Riflemen,* by Philip Cheek and Mair Pointon, p. 215; *Days and Events,* by Colonel Thomas L. Livermore, p. 156. The technique of beehive stealing is described by Frederick Stephen Wallace in *The 61st Ohio Volunteers,* pp. 10–11.

3. *Under the Maltese Cross … Campaigns of the 155th Pennsylvania Regiment,* narrated by the Rank and File, pp. 87–88.

4. *The Life and Public Services of Ambrose E. Burnside,* by Ben Perley Poore, pp. 26–34, 50–52, 57, 73–74.

5. For these tributes, see *The 48th in the War,* by Oliver Christian Bosbyshell, p. 47, and *Red-Tape and Pigeon-Hole Generals,* by a Citizen-Soldier, p. 226. Bosbyshell, recalling the Carolina junket, rhapsodized: "Constant were the visits of General Burnside through the camps of the various regiments, and frequent his interviews with the company cooks."

6. A British soldier who wrote a study of Fredericksburg several years before World war I remarked: "The general in command of the Army of the Potomac at this period, whoever he might be, had need of tremendous force of character, of an indomitable will, and of absolute authority, to accomplish the task he had been set." (*Fredericksburg: A Study in War,* by Major G. W. Redway, p. 22.)

7. Burnside's explanation of all of this is found in his report on Fredericksburg, *Official Records,* Vol. XXI, pp. 82–97. Major Redway remarks that Burnside's original plan was not bad, but that the man seems to have underestimated the time that would be required to set up a new base of supplies and get his army properly established on the Rappahannock. There is a good, if highly partisan, discussion of Burnside's plan and the effect upon it of the non-arrival of the pontoons in *General Halleck and General Burnside,* by "W."

8. *Official Records,* Vol. XXI, pp. 790–91.

9. Ibid., p. 794.

10. A detailed account of this fantastic operation, written by Brigadier General Rufus Ingalls, chief quartermaster of the Army of the Potomac, can be found in the *Official Records,* Vol. XXI, pp. 148–51. Interestingly enough, though probably inaccurately, General Howard suggests that Halleck purposely delayed the arrival of the pontoons in order that Burnside would have to go into winter quarters, thus postponing a battle until spring. (*Autobiography of Oliver Otis Howard,* Vol. I, p. 318.)

11. *Official Records,* Vol. XXI, p. 832.

12. For the invention and operation of the car floats, see *Reminiscences of General Herman Haupt,* pp. 165–66, 179–80. His tribute to Burnside appears on p. 179.

13. In February 1865, Lieutenant Colonel F. W. Sims, C.S.A., reported to the Superintendent of Railway Transportation, Confederate States Quartermaster Department, that railroad lines could be maintained only by taking rails from sidings and branch lines: "Not a single bar of railroad iron has been rolled in the Confederacy since the war, nor can we hope to do any better during the continuance." (*Official Records,* Series IV, Vol. III, p. 1092.) Haupt's promise to buy an extra ten miles of rail appears in *Official Records,* Vol. XXI, p. 832.

14. *Official Records,* Vol. XXI, pp. 773–74.

15. William B. Weeden in *War Government, Federal and State, 1861–1865,* p. 95.

16. *History of the 9th Regiment Massachusetts Volunteer Infantry,* by David George MacNamara, p. 241; *Henry Wilson's Regiment: History of the 22nd Massachusetts Infantry,* by John L. Parker, p. 219; *Campaigns of the 146th Regiment New York State Volunteers,* compiled by Mary Genevie Green Brainard, p. 22; *Under the Maltese Cross,* p. 85.

17. *War Letters of William Thompson Lusk,* p. 241.

18. *Touched with Fire: Civil War Letters and Diary of Oliver Wendell Holmes, Jr.,* edited by Mark De Wolfe Howe, p. 73.

19. *The 48th in the War,* p. 93.

20. Correspondence of the Cincinnati *Commercial,* reprinted in Moore's *Rebellion Record,* Vol. VI, Part 2, p. 94 ff.

21. Ibid., p. 96.

22. *The Road to Richmond,* by Major Abner R. Small, p. 59.

BIG STARS ARE BUSTING

1. A detailed account of the attempt to lay the bridges appears in Major Spaulding's report, *Official Records,* Vol. XXI, pp. 175–77.

2. Ibid., pp. 827–28.

3. *Rebellion Record,* Vol. VI, Part 2, pp. 94–100; *Days and Events,* pp. 167–68.

4. Graphic accounts of the bombardment of the town and the fight over the bridges appear in *Battles and Leaders,* Vol. III, pp. 75, 86–89, 108, 121–22. General Hunt's remarks on the artillery's inability to silence the river-front riflemen are in *Official Records,* Vol. XXI, p. 183. See also, in that same volume, General Couch's report, p. 221, and Colonel Hall's, pp. 282–85.

5. *Touched with Fire,* p. 90; *History of the Second Army Corps,* by Brevet Brigadier General Francis A. Walker, p. 150.

6. *Rebellion Record,* Vol. VI, Part 2, p. 92.

7. Ibid., p. 98.

8. *Battles and Leaders,* Vol. III, p. 142.

9. Ibid., pp. 79, 81.

10. *Service with the 6th Wisconsin Volunteers,* p. 110.

11. Ibid., p. 111; *Major General Hiram G. Berry,* p. 219; *Camp, March and Battlefield,* p. 281.

12. *The Road to Richmond,* p. 65.

13. *Letters from a Surgeon of the Civil War,* compiled by Martha Derby Perry, p.

38; *History of the Sauk County Riflemen,* p. 39. See also *Four Years Campaigning in the Army of the Potomac,* by D. G. Crotty, p. 74.

14. *History of the 24th Michigan,* pp. 100–2, 203; *Battles and Leaders,* Vol. III, p. 142; *Service with the 6th Wisconsin Volunteers,* p. 112. General Doubleday's report, which praises the 24th conduct, is in Vol. XXI, of the *Official Records,* pp. 461–65. Note that Meredith's suspension was temporary; he was reinstated in brigade command after the battle.

BURNISHED ROWS OF STEEL

1. *History of the Second Army Corps,* p. 152.
2. *History of the Corn Exchange Regiment,* by the Survivors Association, p. 114.
3. *On the Parallels; or, Chapters of Inner History,* by Benjamin Borton, p. 65. Good accounts of the ground to be covered and of the difficulties of the approach are in *History of the Second Army Corps,* pp. 159–64, and in General Walker's *General Hancock,* pp. 64–68. See also General Orlando Willcox's report, *Official Records,* Vol. XXI, p. 310 ff.; *History of the Philadelphia Brigade,* by Charles H. Banes, p. 141, and Palfrey's *The Antietam and Fredericksburg,* pp. 161–62, 167.
4. Complaints about defective shell may be found in General Hunt's report, *Official Records,* Vol. XXI, p. 189, and in the reports of various subordinate gunners, pp. 192, 195, and 200 of the same volume.
5. *On the Parallels,* pp. 68–69; *Autobiography of Oliver Otis Howard,* Vol. I, p. 341.
6. *The 48th in the War,* p. 96; Meagher's report, *Official Records,* Vol. XXI, pp. 240–46.
7. Ibid., pp. 249–50.
8. Ibid., pp. 277–80.
9. Ibid., pp. 233, 236–38.
10. *Battles and Leaders,* Vol. III, p. 113.
11. I am indebted to Francis Wilshin, historian of the Fredericksburg and Spotsylvania Courthouse National Military Park, for calling my attention to the existence and importance of this generally neglected feature of the terrain, and for producing a map of Fredericksburg, dated 1867, which shows where the slough was. It is also referred to by Captain John Bigelow, Jr., in the *Papers of the Military Historical Society of Massachusetts,* Vol. III, pp. 244–45. Couch's official report, describing the canal and the open ground beyond and telling of his orders to Howard to try to turn the Confederate left, is in the *Official Records,* Vol. XXI, pp. 221–25.
12. *Autobiography of Oliver Otis Howard,* Vol. I, p. 344.
13. *History of the 9th Massachusetts,* p. 257; *Under the Maltese Cross,* p. 102.
14. *Henry Wilson's Regiment,* p. 228.
15. *History of the 9th Massachusetts,* p. 256; *Official Records,* Vol. XXI, p. 233.
16. Ibid., pp. 262–65, 267–68; *History of the Second Army Corps,* pp. 177–78.
17. *Battles and Leaders,* Vol. III, pp. 115–16; *History of the Second Army Corps,* p. 180.
18. *History of the 9th Massachusetts,* p. 256; *Official Records,* Vol. XXI, pp. 430–34; *The Antietam and Fredericksburg,* p. 172; *Red-Tape and Pigeon-Hole Generals,* p. 241. For Humphreys's roundup of the young soldiers who had been detailed to stay in the rear, see *Under the Maltese Cross,* p. 97.
19. *Rebellion Record,* Vol. VI. Part 2, p. 84; *Official Records,* Vol. XXI, pp. 335–36, 338–43; *War Letters of William Thompson Lusk,* p. 246.
20. *History of the First Regiment Minnesota Volunteer Infantry,* by R. I. Holcombe, p. 269; *Official Records,* Vol. XXI, pp. 425–26. For a particularly vivid account of the trials of these helpless regiments, see *Battles and Leaders,* Vol. III, pp. 122–25.
21. *On the Parallels,* p. 90.
22. *Under the Maltese Cross,* p. 99; *Rebellion Record,* Vol. VI, Part 2, p. 100.

CHAPTER TWO: ALL PLAYED OUT

A LONG TALK WITH ROBERT

1. *Diary of Gideon Welles*, with an Introduction by John T. Morse, Vol. I, p. 192.

2. *Life of Oliver P. Morton*, Vol. I, p. 198.

3. *Battles and Leaders*, Vol. III, pp. 117, 127.

4. Major Redway, the British critic suggests in his *Fredericksburg: A Study in War*, that the attack on the Union left need not have been as hopeless as it now appears to have been. General Meade, who was well qualified to judge, wrote shortly after the battle that he believed the attack there would have succeeded if Franklin had put in all of his men. He added, however, that Burnside's orders were far from clear. (*Life and Letters of George Gordon Meade*, Vol. I, pp. 359–60, 361–62, 365–66, 367.)

5. *History of the Corn Exchange Regiment*, p. 122; *Under the Maltese Cross*, p. 105.

6. *History of the First Regiment Minnesota Volunteer Infantry*, pp. 266–68. This writer appears to have borrowed his combined justification and expression of regret verbatim from Walker's *History of the Second Army Corps*, p. 153.

7. *On the Parallels*, pp. 39–40.

8. *War Letters of William Thompson Lusk*, pp. 231–32.

9. *Life in Camp: A History of the Nine Months' Service of the 14th Vermont Regiment*, by J. C. Williams, p. 7; *Record of the 33rd Massachusetts Volunteer Infantry*, by Andrew J. Boies, p. 17.

10. *The 48th in the War*, p. 100.

11. *Political Recollections*, by George W. Julian, p. 225; *Four Years in the Army of the Potomac: A Soldier's Recollections*, by Major Evan Rowland Jones, p. 104.

12. Julian's *Political Recollections*, p. 235.

13. *On the Parallels*, pp. 122–25. The regimental history of the 1st Minnesota also describes the making and sailing of miniature cargo carriers.

14. *Reminiscences of the Civil War*, by General John B. Gordon, pp. 111–12.

15. Report of Dr. J. H. Douglas, of the Sanitary Commission, in *Rebellion Record*, Vol. VI, Part 2, pp. 90–92; Walker's *General Hancock*, p. 69.

16. *History of a Cavalry Company: A Complete Record of Company A, 4th Pennsylvania Cavalry*, by Captain William Hyndman, p. 74. There is an excellent account of the training, organization, equipment, and use of Federal cavalry, and a comparison with the same features of the Confederate service, in Major Benjamin W. Crowninshield's *History of the 1st Regiment of Massachusetts Cavalry Volunteers*, pp. 3–39. There is also a good description of the training undergone by green cavalrymen in *Regimental History of the First New York Dragoons*, by the Rev. J. R. Bowen, pp. 96–98.

17. *History of the 9th Massachusetts*, p. 227.

18. Major Higginson's remarks on the expedition can be found in *Life and Letters of Henry Lee Higginson*, by Bliss Perry, p. 176. For a formal statement of the projected venture, see *Official Records*, Vol. XXI, pp. 895–96.

19. An exhaustive treatment of this whole affair is William Howard Mills's "From Burnside to Hooker," *Magazine of American History*, Vol. XV, pp. 44–56. There is also a good account in Sandburg's *Abraham Lincoln: The War Years*, Vol. I, pp. 632–37.

20. Burnside wrote to Lincoln on January 1, 1863, saying that he was putting on paper a résumé of the remarks which he had just made to the President in person, so that Lincoln could have a formal record if he wished one. See *Official Records*, Vol. XXI, pp. 941–42.

21. This series of letters—Lincoln to Halleck, Halleck to Stanton, Burnside to Lincoln, Halleck to Burnside, and so on—is in Vol. XXI of the *Official Records*, pp. 940, 944–45, 953–54.

22. Letter of General W. F. Smith in *Magazine of American History,* Vol. XV, pp. 197–201. According to Poore's *Life and Services of Ambrose E. Burnside,* pp. 136–37, Robert was captured by the Confederates at the first battle of Bull Run; months later Burnside got him back by arranging an exchange for a Confederate captured on Roanoke Island.

THE FOOLS THAT BRING DISASTER

1. *A Soldier's Diary: The Story of a Volunteer,* by David Lane, p. 29.

2. *History of the Sauk County Riflemen,* p. 28.

3. There is a graphic picture of the sprawling log-and-canvas military city and a detailed description of the construction and furnishing of a typical hut in Colonel Livermore's *Days and Events,* p. 160. Other details are from *Under the Maltese Cross,* p. 119, and *Campaigns of the 146th Regiment New York State Volunteers,* pp. 51–52.

4. *Four Years Campaigning in the Army of the Potomac,* p. 75.

5. *Camp, March and Battlefield,* p. 280.

6. *Life and Letters of Henry Lee Higginson,* pp. 176–77; *The Three Years Service of the 33rd Massachusetts Infantry Regiment,* by Adin B. Underwood, p. 15; *Service with the 6th Wisconsin Volunteers,* p. 115.

7. *War Letters of William Thompson Lusk,* pp. 244–45, 256.

8. *Official Records,* Vol. XXI, pp. 916–18.

9. *Reminiscences of the 19th Massachuetts Regiment,* by Captain John G. B. Adams, 60–61.

10. *Official Records,* Vol. XXI, p. 127; *Record of the 33rd Massachusetts Volunteer Infantry,* p. 20.

11. The normal routine for breaking camp and taking to the road, as prescribed in General Daniel Butterfield's *Camp and Outpost Duty for Infantry.*

12. *Diary of Gideon Welles,* Vol. I, p. 225.

13. *Four Years Campaigning in the Army of the Potomac,* p. 80.

14. The New York *Times* article from which this quotation comes is the best description of the mud march which this writer has encountered. It has been drawn on liberally in the preparation of this chapter and is printed in full in Moore's *Rebellion Record,* Vol. VI, Part 2, pp. 396–400.

15. Ibid., p. 398.

16. *Official Records,* Vol. XXI, pp. 1000–1; *The Bivouac and the Battlefield,* by Captain George F. Noyes, pp. 325–28; *History of a Cavalry Company,* p. 85; *History of the Corn Exchange Regiment,* pp. 160–64; *Recollections of a Private,* by Warren Lee Goss, pp. 136–39; *Four Years with the Army of the Potomac,* by Regis de Trobriand, pp. 407–9.

17. *Recollections of the Civil War,* by Mason Whiting Tyler, p. 71.

18. *Rebellion Record,* Vol. VI, Part 2, p. 398.

19. *Campaigns of the 146th Regiment New York State Volunteers,* p. 58.

20. *Recollections of a Private,* p. 136.

21. *Under the Red Patch: The Story of the 63rd Regiment Pennsylvania Volunteers,* compiled by Gilbert Adams Hays, p. 169. It was at this time that an engineer officer, making out a requisition for a detail to work on some of the stalled equipment, wrote an order calling for "50 men, 25 feet high, to work in mud 18 feet deep." (*Berdan's United States Sharpshooters in the Army of the Potomac,* by Captain C. A. Stevens, p. 231.)

22. *Recollections of a Private,* p. 138; *Service with the 6th Wisconsin Volunteers,* p. 116.

23. *Official Records,* Vol. XXI, pp. 989–90.

24. *Rebellion Record,* Vol. VI, Part 2, p. 399; *History of the 24th Michigan,* p. 112.

25. *Henry Wilson's Regiment,* pp. 244–45. Memories appear to have been hazy regarding this fight; the historian of the 118th Pennsylvania recalls the whisky ration

and the ensuing fisticuffs but remembers a different origin. (*History of the Corn Exchange Regiment*, p. 162.)

26. *History of the 9th Massachusetts*, p. 271; *Service with the 6th Wisconsin Volunteers*, p. 117; *The Road to Richmond*, p. 77.

27. *History of the 24th Michigan*, p. 113.

28. *Four Years Campaigning in the Army of the Potomac*, p. 80.

29. The book referred to is *Campaigns of the 146th Regiment New York State Volunteers*, pp. 311–418.

30. *History of the Second Army Corps*, p. 200.

THE THIRD THAT REMAINED

1. *Official Records*, Vol. XXI, p. 67; *Recollections of Half a Century*, by A. K. McClure, p. 346.

2. *Battles and Leaders*, Vol. III, p. 138.

3. This luncheon party and Burnside's bewildering outburst are presented in detail by General Smith in *Magazine of American History*, Vol. XV, pp. 197–201.

4. General Orders No. 8 is found in *Official Records*, Vol. XXI, pp. 998–99. Burnside's explanation of the mistake regarding General Ferrero appears in the same volume, p. 1123. A little later, when Burnside had been assigned to duty in Ohio, he specifically asked that Ferrero be assigned to serve there with him. (*Official Records*, Vol. XXV, Part 2, p. 503.)

5. *Fighting Joe Hooker*, p. 164; *Autobiography of Oliver Otis Howard*, Vol. I, p. 348.

6. *Speeches, Correspondence and Political Papers of Carl Schurz*, selected and edited by Federic Bancroft, Vol. I, p. 221.

7. *History of the Second Army Corps*, p. 198.

8. *History of the 24th Michigan*, p. 113; "The Army of the Potomac under Hooker," by William Howard Mills, *Magazine of American History*, Vol. XV, p. 185; *Official Records*, Vol. XXV, Part 2, p. 73.

9. Details about the measures taken to catch deserters around Washington and Baltimore are in *Lincoln and the Episodes of the Civil War*, by General W. E. Doster, pp. 68–73, 99. See also *Official Records*, Vol. XXV, Part 2, p. 123.

10. *Four Years Campaigning in the Army of the Potomac*, pp. 77–78.

11. Ibid., p. 81; *Official Records*, Series II, Vol. V, p. 194.

12. Ibid., p. 169. For other abuses of the parole systems, see *Official Records*, Series II, Vol. IV, pp. 449, 546, 562.

13. *Lincoln and the Episodes of the Civil War*, pp. 99–101.

14. *Official Records*, Vol. XXI, p. 985; Vol. XXV, Part 2, p. 86.

15. Ibid., pp. 36–37, 43.

16. Ibid., pp. 1112–15, report of Colonel Henry A. Morrow, 24th Michigan. For other reports on attempts to break up the transit of contraband goods and persons, see that same volume, pp. 13–17. A good account of cavalry's part in these forays is in *History of the 8th Cavalry Regiment, Illinois Volunteers*, by Abner Hard, pp. 238–41. For the argument between army and navy regarding their mutual sins and responsibilities, see *Official Records*, Vol. XXV, Part 2, pp. 124–27.

17. Hooker's report to J. C. Kelton, assistant adjutant general, dated February 15, 1863.

18. An extremely readable account of the way the women of America, aided and financed by a few men, forced a revolution in the War Department's method of caring for wounded men is contained in Marjorie Barstow Greenbie's excellent book, *Lincoln's Daughters of Mercy*. There is also an interesting picture of the way women worked with the Sanitary Commission, through Ladies Aid Societies and otherwise, in *Three Years in Field Hospitals of the Army of the Potomac*, by Mrs. William H. Holstein, pp. 12, 26–27, 41–57.

19. *The Military Policy of the United States,* by Brevet Major General Emory Upton, pp. 402–4, 406, 409.

20. Ibid., p. 409; *Official Records,* Series III, Vol. V, p. 543 ff.

21. *Military Policy of the United States,* pp. 407, 412.

22. *Official Records,* Series III, Vol. V, p. 752.

23. Ibid., p. 678.

24. Ibid., Series II, Vol. IV, pp. 594–95.

25. Ibid., Series III, Vol. V, p. 840.

26. Report of Thomas F. Perley, medical inspector general, dated January 8, 1863: *Official Records,* Vol. XXI, pp. 957–59.

27. *Charles Francis Adams: An Autobiography, p. 163.*

28. *Official Records,* Vol. XXI, p. 1008.

29. *On the Parallels,* p. 134.

CHAPTER THREE: REVIVAL

MEN WHO ARE GREATLY IN EARNEST

1. *Life of Oliver P. Morton,* by William Dudley Foulke, Vol. I, pp. 23–25, 51. The early pages of this book have been followed by this sketch of Morton's boyhood and youth.

2. Ibid., p. 28.

3. Ibid., p. 67.

4. Ibid., pp. 92, 102.

5. *Battles and Leaders,* Vol. I, p. 86.

6. *Sketch of the Life, Character and Public Services of Oliver P. Morton,* by Charles M. Walker, p. 70.

7. Foulke's *Life of Oliver P. Morton,* Vol. I, p. 148.

8. *The Tall Sycamore of the Wabash: Daniel Wolsey Voorhees,* by Leonard S. Kenworthy, pp. 55–56; *War Government, Federal and State, 1861–1865,* p. 143.

9. Foulke's *Life of Oliver P. Morton,* Vol. I, pp. 163–67, 179.

10. Ibid., pp. 187–88, 196–97.

11. Ibid., p. 213 ff.

12. Ibid., p. 209; *The Hidden Civil War,* pp. 63–70.

13. For a good discussion of this point, see the introduction to *War Government, Federal and State, 1861–1865,* p. xiv ff. An excellent analysis of the development of the "peace Democrats" during the war years is also to be found in Elbert J. Benton's *The Movement for Peace without Victory during the Civil War.*

14. Judge Advocate General Holt's extensive and somewhat wide-eyed report on this order is printed in *Official Records,* Series II, Vol. VII, pp. 930–53.

15. *A Rebel War Clerk's Diary,* by J. B. Jones, edited by Howard Swiggett, Vol. I, pp. 253, 259.

16. Most of these details as to countersigns, shameful deaths, and what not are drawn from Holt's report. See also *Official Records,* Series II, Vol. VII, pp. 629–31, 643–44, 657.

17. Foulke's *Life of Oliver P. Morton,* Vol. I, pp. 238–39.

18. *Sketch of the Life, Character and Public Services of Oliver P. Morton,* pp. 100–1; *Lincoln and the War Governors,* by William B. Hesseltine, pp. 311–15.

19. *Recollections of War Times,* by Albert Gallatin Riddle, p. 321.

THE IMPERATIVES OF WAR

1. *History of the 9th Massachusetts,* p. 280.

2. *History of the Philadelphia Brigade,* p. 155; *The Diary of a Young Officer,* by Josiah M. Favill, p. 225.

3. *History of the 9th Massachusetts,* p. 259.

4. *A History of the 1st Regiment of Massachusetts Cavalry Volunteers*, p. 298; *Four Years with the Army of the Potomac*, by Regis de Trobriand, p. 399; *Days and Events*, p. 183.

5. *History of the Corn Exchange Regiment*, p. 215.

6. *History of the Philadelphia Brigade*, p. 157; *History of the 12th Regiment New Hampshire Volunteers in the War of the Rebellion*, by Captain A. W. Bartlett, p. 19.

7. *Official Records*, Vol. XXV, Part 2, pp. 217–19.

8. Ibid., p. 219. For a good sketch of General Patrick, see *The Ulster Guard and the War of the Rebellion*, by Colonel Theodore B. Gates, pp. 191, 192, 198, 199.

9. *Official Records*, Series III, Vol. III, pp. 35–36, 62–63, 69–71, 116, 324.

10. *The Celebrated Case of Fitz-John Porter*, by Otto Eisenschiml, p. 17.

11. *Recollections of Half a Century*, by A. K. McClure, pp. 435–36.

12. *Old Thad Stevens: A Story of Ambition*, by Richard Nelson Current, p. 174.

13. Gideon Welles did not care greatly for Stanton and referred to him acidly a number of times; he gives a caustic opinion on the War Secretary's stamina, or lack of it, in Vol. I of his famous *Diary*, pp. 67–68.

14. *Lincoln and the Episodes of the Civil War*, pp. 124–25.

15. *Service with the 6th Wisconsin Volunteers*, p. 125.

16. *Life and Letters of Henry Lee Higginson*, pp. 179–80.

17. *Lincoln and the War Governors*, p. 281. For the decline in recruiting in 1863, see *Official Records*, Series III, Vol. V, pp. 599, 601, 612, 618–19. Hooker's belief that few of his short-term men would re-enlist is in Vol. XXV, Part 2, p. 243.

18. *War Government, Federal and State, 1861-1865*, p. 219.

19. *Official Records*, Series IV, Vol. I, p. 1162.

20. For the Davis-Brown exchange, see Ibid., pp. 1133–38, 1156–69. There is a first-rate dissection of Brown and his unrealistic opposition to conscription in Clifford Dowdey's *Experiment in Rebellion*, pp. 165–67.

21. *The Military Policy of the United States*, p. 234.

22. *Lincoln and the War Governors*, p. 289.

23. A glimpse of the men and methods employed in recruiting ex-slaves is provided in *Civil War Diary of James T. Ayres*, edited by John Hope Franklin. Ayres, who referred to his work as *Gathering Up Sambo*, could write reflections such as "No niggers enlisted yet. . . . Pore ignorant devils, they would Rather Stay behind and geather up Boxes, oald shoes and oald shirts and Pants our Boys have left than be Soldiers." He also wrote that he had told a colored woman: "I want your man. You ought to be a slave as long as you live and him too if he is so mean as not to help get his liberty but sneak around our camps to live on the rags we throw away when he might do better."

SOLDIERS' BARGAIN

1. *Recollections of Half a Century*, p. 347; *Service with the 6th Wisconsin*, p. 132; *Fighting Joe Hooker*, p. 154; *Personal Recollections of Distinguished Generals*, by William F. G. Shanks, pp. 190–91.

2. *On the Parallels*, p. 132; *Four Years Campaigning in the Army of the Potomac*, pp. 80–81.

3. *Official Records*, Vol. XXV, Part 2, pp. 855–56.

4. *Recollections of Half a Century*, p. 348.

5. The little song about Joe Hooker, which touches on many other matters as well, is printed in *History of the Corn Exchange Regiment*, pp. 166–67.

6. *History of the 9th Massachusetts*, p. 276.

7. *Official Records*, Vol. XXV, Part 2, p. 57.

8. *History of the 12th Regiment New Hampshire Volunteers*, p. 58.

9. Report to Hooker from Jonathan Letterman: *Official Records*, Vol. XXV, Part 2, p. 239.

10. Ibid., pp. 491–92; *Berdan's United States Sharpshooters,* p. 235.

11. *History of the 9th Massachusetts,* p. 276; *Recollections of the Civil War,* p. 76; *Henry Wilson's Regiment,* p. 248.

12. *The Three Years Service of the 33rd Massachusetts Infantry Regiment,* p. 18; *Henry Wilson's Regiment,* p. 248. For a good general discussion of the improvement brought about under Hooker, see De Trobriand's *Four Years with the Army of the Potomac,* pp. 413–17.

13. *History of the Corn Exchange Regiment,* p. 165; *Official Records,* Vol. XXV, Part 2, pp. 73, 74, 84, 86; *Lincoln and the Episodes of the Civil War,* pp. 141–42.

14. *Recollections of the Civil War,* p. 76; *The Campaign of Chancellorsville,* by John Bigelow, Jr., pp. 50–52; *History of the 9th Massachusetts,* pp, 283–84; *Road to Richmond,* p. 81; "The Army of the Potomac under Hooker," by William Howard Mills, pp. 185–95 of the *Magazine of American History,* Vol. XV.

15. *Fighting Joe Hooker,* p. 182. For Lincoln's dismay at Hooker's boasts, see *Abraham Lincoln: The War Years,* Vol. II, p. 80.

16. *Official Records,* Vol. XXV, Part 2, p. 52. The remark would seem to have been something of an overstatement.

17. *History of the First Regiment Minnesota Volunteer Infantry,* p. 227. For Sumner's criticism of army "croaking," see *The Military Services of Major General Ambrose Everett Burnside in the Civil War,* by Daniel R. Ballou, Part 2, p. 44.

18. *Battles and Leaders,* Vol. III, p. 154.

19. *Army Letters, 1861–65,* by O. W. Norton, pp. 327–28. There is a sketch of Butterfield in the *Dictionary of American Biography,* Vol. III, pp. 372–74, and he appears sporadically in M. Francis Dowley's *History and Honorary Roll of the 12th Regiment, Infantry, N.G.S.N.Y.,* of which he used to be colonel.

20. *Charles Francis Adams: An Autobiography,* p. 161.

21. *Life and Letters of George Gordon Meade,* Vol. I, pp. 351, 354.

22. This material on Sickles follows the account of *Dan Sickles, Hero of Gettysburg and "Yankee King of Spain,"* by Edgcumb Pinchon.

23. *A Diary from Dixie,* by Mary Boykin Chesnut, edited by Ben Ames Williams, p. 247; Pinchon's *Dan Sickles,* pp. 136–37.

24. *Fighting Joe Hooker,* p. 173 ff.

25. For the difficulties of outpost duty that winter, see *History of the First Regiment of Massachusetts Cavalry Volunteers,* p. 33; *Deeds of Daring; or, History of the 8th New York Volunteer Cavalry,* by Henry Norton, pp. 56–58; *The Campaign of Chancellorsville,* pp. 60, 72.

26. *Official Records,* Vol. XXV, Part 2, p. 197.

27. *The Campaign of Chancellorsville,* pp. 73–74. This apparently is the origin of the belief—widely held during the war—that it was Hooker who originated the common wisecrack, "Whoever saw a dead cavalryman?" (In the Confederacy, the remark was generally attributed to acid-tongued D. H. Hill.)

28. This cavalry fight and Hooker's reaction to it are detailed in *The Campaign of Chancellorsville,* pp. 89, 98–102, 105. Good descriptions of the fight occur in J. H. Stine's *History of the Army of the Potomac,* pp. 319–22, and in John W. Thomason's *Jeb Stuart,* pp. 355–61.

29. *Fighting Joe Hooker,* p. 182.

MAY DAY IN THE WILDERNESS

1. *R. E. Lee,* by Douglas Southall Freeman, Vol. II, p. 480.

2. *Diary of Gideon Welles,* Vol. I, p. 336; *Recollections of Half a Century,* p. 348; *The Campaign of Chancellorsville,* p.108.

3. Stoneman is sketched briefly in the *Dictionary of American Biography,* Vol. XVIII, p. 92.

4. *The Campaign of Chancellorsville,* p. 110 ff; *Official Records,* Vol. XXV, Part 2, pp. 199–200.

5. Ibid., pp. 199–200; *Battles and Leaders,* Vol. III, p. 155.

6. Stine's *History of the Army of the Potomac,* footnote, pp. 324–35.

7. Stoneman's abortive attempt to cross the river is discussed in *Jeb Stuart,* pp. 364–66, and in *The Campaign of Chancellorsville,* pp. 148–58.

8. For the exchange of letters between Hooker and Lincoln, and between Hooker and Stoneman, see *Official Records,* Vol. XXV, Part 2, pp. 213–14, 220–21.

9. Testimony before the Committee on the Conduct of the War, cited in *The Campaign of Chancellorsville,* p. 166.

10. *The 95th Pennsylvania Volunteers,* by G. Norton Galloway, p. 48; *Official Records,* Vol. XXV, Part 2, p. 488.

11. *History of the 12th Regiment New Hampshire Volunteers,* p. 65; *The Second Massachusetts Infantry and the Campaign of Chancellorsville,* by George A. Thayer, p. 10; Life and Letters of Henry Lee Higginson, p. 182.

12. *History of the 12th Regiment New Hampshire Volunteers,* p. 68.

13. Ibid., p. 68.

14. *History of the 9th Massachusetts,* pp. 296–97; *History of the Corn Exchange Regiment,* p. 169; *The Campaign of Chancellorsville,* pp. 197–200.

15. Ibid., p. 221.

16. *Battles and Leaders,* Vol. III, pp. 175–77; *Jeb Stuart,* pp. 368–71.

17. *Battles and Leaders,* Vol. III, p. 224.

18. *History of the Corn Exchange Regiment,* pp. 169–70; *Battles and Leaders,* Vol. III, p. 157; *Days and Events,* p. 190; *The Fifth Regiment Connecticut Volunteers: A History,* by Edwin E. Marvin, p. 251.

19. The best account of this fruitless operation is in *The Campaign of Chancellorsville,* pp. 243–54.

20. *History of the Second Army Corps,* p. 224.

21. Ibid., p. 223.

22. *Battles and Leaders,* Vol. III, p. 161.

23. *The Campaign of Chancellorsville,* pp. 236–37. For the circular which expresses the confidence that the Rebels will be bold enough to attack, see *Official Records,* Vol. XXV, Part 2, p. 328.

CHAPTER FOUR: ON THE OTHER SIDE OF THE RIVER

SOME OF US WILL NOT SEE ANOTHER SUNRISE

1. An exceptionally good discussion of this point is contained in *The Ninth Ohio Volunteers,* by Carl Wittke, a booklet which is not so much a history of the regiment as a study of its background. See also *The German Soldier in the Wars of the United States,* by J. G. Rosengarten, pp. 92–93, 95.

2. *Official Records,* Vol. XXV, Part 1, pp. 660–61.

3. Blenker is sketched in Appleton's *Cyclopedia of American Biography.* References to his work as a recruiter are in *Official Records,* Series III, Vol. I, pp. 534, 623.

4. *Official Records,* Vol. XII, Part 3, pp. 81, 82, 86, 92, 96, 99, 186–87; also Vol. XII, Part 1, pp. 27–28. There is an account of some of the trials of Blenker's men in *Trials and Triumphs: The Record of the 55th Ohio Infantry,* by Captain Hartwell Osborn and Others, pp. 25–26.

5. *The Three Years Service of the 33rd Massachusetts Infantry Regiment,* p. 11; *Trials and Triumphs,* p. 29.

6. Frémont's report is in the *Official Records,* Vol. XII, Part 1, pp. 3–13. See also p. 30 for his medical director's report, and p. 647 for Frémont's account of the straggling. Carl Schurz to Lincoln is in Vol. XII, Part 3, pp. 397–401.

7. *The Campaign of Chancellorsville,* pp. 39–42.

8. *The Road to Richmond*, p. 9; *Three Years Service of the 33rd Massachusetts*, p. 96; *The Battle of Chancellorsville*, by Augustus Choate Hamlin, p. 34; *Trials and Triumphs*, p. 61; *The 25th Ohio Veteran Volunteer Infantry in the War for the Union*, by Howard C. Culp, p. 59; *Autobiography of Oliver Otis Howard*, Vol. 1, p. 349.

9. For references to the XI Corps' status as a pariah, see *History of the Second Army Corps*, pp. 229–30; *The Battle of Chancellorsville*, pp. 23–24; Walker's *General Hancock*, p. 84.

10. *Battles and Leaders*, Vol. III, p. 195.

11. *Four Years Campaigning in the Army of the Potomac*, p. 82.

12. *Battles and Leaders*, Vol. III, p. 163.

13. *History of the 12th Regiment New Hampshire Volunteers*, pp. 71–72.

14. *Berdan's United States Sharpshooters*, pp. 2–7, 16, 20–21, 235–37, 244–45.

15. Ibid., p. 251.

16. *History of the 12th Regiment New Hampshire Volunteers*, p. 448; *Battles and Leaders*, Vol. III, p. 183. There is a detailed examination of the XI Corps' arrangements in Bigelow's *The Campaign of Chancellorsville*, pp. 284–86. Even more exhaustive is the account in Hamlin's *The Battle of Chancellorsville*, pp. 34–47, 55–58—a book which devotes itself with a good deal of success to the thesis that this corps was much more sinned against than sinning.

17. *Trials and Triumphs*, pp. 68–69; *The 25th Ohio Veteran Volunteer Infantry*, pp. 61–64; *The Campaign of Chancellorsville*, p. 287.

18. Ibid., pp. 288–89; *Trials and Triumphs*, pp. 69–70; *Official Records*, Vol. XXV, Part 1, pp. 652–53.

19. *The Battle of Chancellorsville*, p. 62.

20. *Trials and Triumphs*, p. 80; *The Three Years Service of the 33rd Massachusetts Infantry Regiment*, pp. 41, 97; *The 25th Ohio Veteran Volunteer Infantry*, pp. 64–65.

21. *Official Records*, Vol. XXV, Part 1, pp. 632–37, 640–46; *The Campaign of Chancellorsville*, pp. 296–97.

22. *Official Records*, Vol. XXV, Part 1, p. 643.

23. *The 25th Ohio Veteran Volunteer Infantry*, pp. 65–66; *The 61st Ohio Volunteers, 1861–1865*, by Frederick Stephen Wallace, pp. 13–14.

24. *Official Records*, Vol. XXV, Part 1, pp. 655–56.

25. Ibid., p. 657; *The Campaign of Chancellorsville*, p. 297; *The Battle of Chancellorsville*, p. 76; *Battles and Leaders*, Vol. III, pp. 200–1.

26. *The Campaign of Chancellorsville*, p. 306.

27. *The Charge of the 8th Pennsylvania Cavalry at Chancellorsville*, by Pennock Huey, a little booklet which is an excellent corrective to General Pleasonton's imaginative and dramatic story in *Battles and Leaders*, Vol. III, pp. 179–81.

HELL ISN'T HALF A MILE OFF

1. *Berdan's United States Sharpshooters*, pp. 275–76.

2. *Four Years Campaigning in the Army of the Potomac*, p. 82; *History of the 12th Regiment New Hampshire Volunteers*, p. 72 ff.; *Official Records*, Vol. XXV, Part 1, p. 487.

3. *The Battle of Chancellorsville*, pp. 93–100; *Battles and Leaders*, Vol. III, pp. 179–82, 188. See also "The Romances of Chancellorsville," by Lieutenant Colonel Theodore Dodge, *Papers of the Military Historical Society of Massachusetts*, Vol. III, pp. 202–17.

4. *Official Records*, Vol. XXV, Part 1, pp. 483–84, 657, 885.

5. *Campaigns of the 146th Regiment New York State Volunteers*, p. 84; *History of the Corn Exchange Regiment*, pp. 182–83; *Days and Events*, p. 203; *The Campaign of Chancellorsville*, p. 303.

6. Ibid., pp. 324–25.

7. *Official Records*, Vol. XXV, Part 1, p. 437.

8. *Four Years Campaigning in the Army of the Potomac*, p. 84; *Under the Red Patch*, p. 181.

9. *The Fifth Regiment Connecticut Volunteers: A History*, by Edwin E. Marvin, p. 253; *Four Years with the Army of the Potomac*, pp. 447–55.

10. *The Campaign of Chancellorsville*, p. 327 *Official Records*, Vol. XXV, Part 1, p. 670; *The Three Years Service of the 33rd Massachusetts Infantry Regiment*, p. 67.

11. *Lincoln and the Episodes of the Civil War*, p. 195.

12. *Berdan's United States Sharpshooters*, p. 259; *History of the 12th Regiment New Hampshire Volunteers*, p. 76; *The Road to Richmond*, p. 86; *Journal History of the 29th Ohio Veteran Volunteers*, by J. Hamp Se Cheverell, pp. 64–65.

13. For an appreciation of the tactical opportunities open to Hooker that morning, see *The Military Genius of Abraham Lincoln*, by Brigadier General Colin R. Ballard, pp. 157–58.

14. *Official Records*, Vol. XXV, Part 1, pp. 724, 726, 729, 754–56, 764. For a standard method of making an abatis of felled trees, see *The Diary of a Young Officer*, p. 127.

15. *The Three Years Service of the 33rd Massachusetts Infantry Regiment*, p. 69.

16. *Official Records*, Vol. XXV, Part 1, pp. 684–89.

17. *The 20th Connecticut: A Regimental History*, by John W. Storrs, p. 57.

18. *Official Records*, Vol. XXV, Part 1, p. 731.

19. Ibid., p. 711; *The Three Years Service of the 33rd Massachusetts Infantry Regiment*, pp. 73–74; *The Second Massachusetts Infantry and the Campaign of Chancellorsville*.

20. *History of the 12th Regiment New Hampshire Volunteers*, pp. 81–86.

21. *The Long Arm of Lee*, by Jennings Cropper Wise, Vol. II, pp. 507–11; *The Crisis of the Confederacy*, by Cecil Battine, p. 80.

22. *A Military History of the 8th Regiment Ohio Volunteer Infantry*, by Lieutenant Colonel Franklin Sawyer, p. 114; *History of a Cavalry Company*, p. 93.

23. *Under the Red Patch*, pp. 185–86. There is a glimpse of Annie ministering to wounded men on the firing line in *Henry Wilson's Regiment*, p. 294. For an appealing sketch of this remarkable young woman, see *Lincoln's Daughters of Mercy*, p. 135.

24. *Battles and Leaders*, Vol. III, p. 221; *Official Records*, Vol. XXV, Part 1, pp. 314, 399–403, 714; *The 20th Connecticut*, p. 53.

25. *Battles and Leaders*, Vol. III, pp. 169–70.

26. Walker's *General Hancock*, p. 83.

27. *Days and Events*, pp. 202, 205–6.

28. Ibid., p. 196.

29. *Official Records*, Vol. XXV, Part 1, pp. 284–85, 307, 314; *History of the Second Army Corps*, pp. 245–46; Walker's *General Hancock*, pp. 90–91.

30. *Official Records*, Vol. XXV, Part 1, p. 917; *Berdan's United States Sharpshooters*, pp. 264–65.

31. *Days and Events*, p. 206. For the removal of the guns, see *History of the Second Army Corps*, p. 247; *Official Records*, Vol. XXV, Part 1, pp. 328–29.

32. *History of the Corn Exchange Regiment*, p. 187.

33. *The Campaign of Chancellorsville*, p. 381.

GO BOIL YOUR SHIRT

1. *Official Records*, Vol. XXV, Part 1, pp. 749, 751; *Reminiscences of Winfield Scott Hancock*, by His Wife, pp. 93–94; *Three Years Campaign of the 9th N.Y.S.M. during*

the Southern Rebellion, by John W. Jaques, p. 141; *History of the Corn Exchange Regiment,* p. 201.

2. "The Battle of Marye's Heights and Salem Church," by Captain John W. Bigelow, Jr., *Papers of the Military Historical Society of Massachusetts,* Vol. III, p. 255.

3. One of the Federals who stormed the wall wrote: "It is not true that bayonets were never crossed during the war. They were used at the stone wall by our men, and after the battle it was found, by actual count, that 40 of the enemy had been bayoneted there." (*Campaigning with the 6th Maine,* by Lieutenant Colonel Charles A. Clark, p. 33.)

4. *Army Life: A Private's Reminiscences of the Civil War,* by the Rev. Theodore Gerrish, pp. 340–41.

5. *The 95th Pennsylvania Volunteers,* p. 74.

6. General Couch's account of this meeting is in *Battles and Leaders,* Vol. III, p. 171. See also *Gouverneur Kemble Warren: The Life and Letters of an American Soldier,* by Emerson Gifford Taylor, p. 110; *History of the Second Army Corps,* pp. 250–51.

7. *History of the 12th Regiment New Hampshire Volunteers,* p. 92; *Battles and Leaders,* Vol. III, p. 171. For a good picture of the miseries of the rear-guard details on that rainy night, see *History of the Corn Exchange Regiment,* pp. 203–5.

8. Report of Provost Marshal General Patrick, *Official Records,* Vol. XXV, Part 2, pp. 476–77.

9. *History of the 12th Regiment New Hampshire Volunteers,* p. 93; *Army Letters, 1861–65,* pp. 150–51.

10. General Patrick's report, cited in Note 8.

11. *The Campaign of Chancellorsville,* p. 444.

12. Ibid., p. 458.

13. *Some Personal Reminiscences of Service in the Cavalry of the Army of the Potomac,* by Colonel Hampton S. Thomas, p. 9; *Lincoln and the Episodes of the Civil War,* p. 202; *The Campaign of Chancellorsville,* pp. 458–59.

14. Ibid., pp. 378, 482.

15. *Diary of Gideon Welles,* Vol. I, pp. 291, 293; *Abraham Lincoln: The War Years,* Vol. II, p. 97.

16. *History of the Philadelphia Brigade,* pp. 164–65.

17. *Official Records,* Vol. XXV, Part 1, pp. 631, 658.

18. Ibid., p. 622; *The Battle of Chancellorsville and the Eleventh Army Corps,* p. 48.

19. *Life and Letters of George Gordon Meade,* Vol. 1, pp. 373, 377, 379; *Personal Recollections of the Civil War,* p. 120; *Gouverneur Kemble Warren,* p. 111; *History of the Second Army Corps,* pp. 155–56; *Reminiscences of Winfield Scott Hancock,* pp. 94–95.

20. *History of the 12th Regiment New Hampshire Volunteers,* p. 90.

21. *History of the Philadelphia Brigade,* p. 166; *Letters from a Surgeon of the Civil War,* p. 41. A Massachusetts soldier asserted: "The morale of the Army of the Potomac was better in June than it had been in January. . . . The diaries and letters of the members of the 15th show nothing of that spirit of insubordination and despondency . . . which had prevailed in the middle of the winter." (*The Story of the 15th Regiment Massachusetts Volunteer Infantry,* by Andrew E. Ford, p. 253.)

22. *Under the Red Patch,* p. 186; *History of the 24th Michigan,* p. 142.

23. *The 95th Pennsylvania Volunteers,* p. 56; *Army Letters, 1861–65,* p. 156; *The Campaign of Chancellorsville,* p. 488.

24. *History of the Corn Exchange Regiment,* p. 147; *History of the 12th Regiment New Hampshire Volunteers,* p. 94.

25. *History of the 24th Michigan,* p. 138.

26. *Berdan's United States Sharpshooters,* p. 277.

27. *The Battle of Gettysburg,* by Colonel Frank Aretas Haskell, pp. 3–4.

28. *Berdan's United States Sharpshooters,* pp. 277–78.

CHAPTER FIVE: LINCOLN COMIN' WID HIS CHARIOT

THE GRAPES OF WRATH

1. *Army Letters, 1861-65*, p. 281.
2. *Diary of Gideon Welles*, Vol. 1, pp. 251, 259.
3. *Abraham Lincoln: The War Years*, Vol. II, pp. 172–74.
4. *The Molly Maguires*, by Anthony Bimba, pp. 11–28; *Labor Disturbances in Pennsylvania, 1850-1880*, by J. Walter Coleman, pp. 3, 10, 17.
5. Ibid., p. 23.
6. In the spring of 1864, when the 48th Pennsylvania "veteranized"—i.e., re-enlisted as a regiment for three more years—and returned to Schuylkill County to recruit, it had no trouble getting men, and its historian noted that it quickly got more recruits than the regulations required. (*The Story of the 48th*, by Joseph Gould, p. 160.)
7. *Labor Disturbances in Pennsylvania*, p. 42.
8. Ibid., pp. 40–69; *The Molly Maguires*, p. 11; *Discontent in New York City, 1861-65*, by Brother Basil Leo Lee, F.S.C., pp. 175–76; *Official Records*, Series III, Vol. III, pp. 1008–9.
9. Ibid., p. 629.
10. See the chapter on the 10th New Jersey in *New Jersey and the Rebellion* by John W. Foster.
11. McClure's account of all of this is in his *Old-Time Notes of Pennsylvania*, Vol. I, pp. 542–49.
12. Ibid., p. 550.
13. *Old Thad Stevens: A Story of Ambition*, pp. 53–54.
14. *The Hidden Civil War*, p. 110.
15. *A True History of the Reign of Terror in Southern Illinois*, by James D. Fox, pp. 13–14.
16. *History of the United States from the Compromise of 1850*, by James Ford Rhodes, Vol. IV, pp. 226–27.
17. *The Life and Public Services of Ambrose E. Burnside*, pp. 206–7.
18. Rhodes's *History of the United States*, Vol. IV, p. 247.
19. Ibid., p. 248; *Abraham Lincoln: The War Years*, Vol. II, p. 162.
20. *A Rebel War Clerk's Diary*, Vol. 1, p. 357.
21. *History of the Administration of President Lincoln*, by Henry J. Raymond, p. 359.
22. *Army Life: A Private's Reminiscences of the Civil War*, pp. 124–28.

GLORY! GLORY! HALLELUJAH!

1. *In French Creek Valley*, by John Earle Reynolds, p. 304 ff.
2. *Social and Industrial Conditions in the North during the Civil War*, by Emerson David Fite, pp. 11, 32–41.
3. Ibid., p. 23.
4. Ibid., p. 32 ff.; *The Long Ships Passing*, by Walter Havighurst, pp. 140–41, 184 ff.
5. Among the bewildering list of patents in the *Annual Report of the Commissioner of Patents, 1864*, is one for a device (pictured in Vol. II, p. 306) which appears to be a fair approximation of the modern strapless bra.
6. *Influence of the War on Our National Prosperity*, by William E. Dodge, pp. 9, 11, 13; *The Growth of the American Republic*, by Samuel Eliot Morison and Henry Steele Commager, Vol. I, p. 703.
7. *I Rode with Stonewall*, by Henry Kyd Douglas, p. 251. Wesley Culp moved to Virginia before the war and enlisted in 1861 in the 2nd Virginia, of the famous

Stonewall Brigade. He was killed in the assault on Culp's Hill within sight of the house where he had been born.

8. *Influence of the War on Our National Prosperity,* pp. 15–16.

9. *The Bivouac and the Battlefield,* p. 338.

10. *Social and Industrial Conditions in the North,* pp. 85–91; *Adventures of America, 1857-1900,* by John A. Kouwenhoven, Section 90; *Political and Social Growth of the American People,* by Arthur M. Schlesinger, pp. 40–41; *The Growth of the American Republic,* Vol. I, p. 704 ff.

11. *Official Records,* Series IV, Vol. III, p. 677.

12. *Berdan's United States Sharpshooters,* p. 237.

13. For Pleasonton, see Haskell's *The Battle of Gettysburg,* p. 70, and *Lincoln and the Episodes of the Civil War,* p. 232. Wyndham was a fabulous character who had served in the British, French, Austrian, and Italian armies and in the French Navy as well. He survived the Civil War, edited a comic magazine in Calcutta, undertook cotton and timber speculations in Mandalay and Burma, and finally lost his life in the explosion of a balloon in which he was giving aeronautical exhibitions in India. He is sketched in *New Jersey Troops in the Gettysburg Campaign,* by Samuel Coombs, pp. 402–6.

14. *Deeds of Daring; or, History of the 8th New York Cavalry,* pp. 66–67. This delightfully unsophisticated little book, one of the pleasantest of the regimental histories, contains fascinating glimpses of the way Grimes Davis turned a collection of rookies into a crack cavalry outfit. See also *Some Personal Reminiscences of Service in the Cavalry of the Army of the Potomac,* pp. 9–10; *History of the 8th Cavalry Regiment, Illinois Volunteers,* pp. 243–47; *A History of the First Regiment of Massachusetts Cavalry Volunteers,* pp. 18, 140.

15. Ibid., p. 296; *Reminiscences and Record of the 6th New York Veteran Volunteer Cavalry,* p. 67.

16. *History of the Third Indiana Cavalry,* by W. N. Pickerill, p. 12.

17. *History of the 8th Cavalry Regiment, Illinois Volunteers,* pp. 202–3; *History of the First Regiment of Massachusetts Cavalry Volunteers,* pp. 291, 294–95.

18. Ibid., p. 159.

19. *Reminiscences of General Herman Haupt,* p. 205.

20. *Three Years in the Field Hospitals of the Army of the Potomac,* pp. 34–35; *Military History of the 8th Regiment Ohio Volunteer Infantry,* p. 119; *Three Years Campaign of the 9th N.Y.S.M.,* p. 149; *History of the 12th Regiment New Hampshire Volunteers,* p. 114.

21. *The Story of the 15th Regiment Massachusetts Volunteer Infantry,* by Andrew E. Ford, p. 256. See also *The 20th Connecticut: A Regimental History,* p. 70; *History of the Philadelphia Brigade,* p. 172; *New Jersey Troops in the Gettysburg Campaign,* pp. 104–5.

22. *Military History of the 8th Regiment Ohio Volunteer Infantry,* p. 122.

23. *The Road to Richmond,* pp. 95–96, with the spelling very slightly modernized.

24. *New Jersey Troops in the Gettysburg Campaign,* pp. 92–93.

WHITE ROAD IN THE MOONLIGHT

1. *Rebellion Record,* Vol. VII, Part 2, pp. 194–95, 197.

2. *Our Campaign around Gettysburg,* by John Lockwood, pp. 35–58; *Rebellion Record,* Vol. VII, Part 2, p. 10.

3. *New Jersey Troops in the Gettysburg Campaign,* pp. 126–27.

4. *Lincoln and the Episodes in the Civil War,* p. 213. Duffié's report on the fight is in *Official Records,* Vol. XXVII, Part 1, pp. 963–64. There are some good glimpses of this cavalry fighting in *History of the 8th Cavalry Regiment, Illinois Volunteers,* pp. 251–54, and there is Confederate testimony to the improvement in Federal cavalry

in *War Years with Jeb Stuart,* by Lieutenant Colonel W. W. Blackford, p. 221.

5. The most detailed recent study of Stuart's moves in Freeman's, in *Lee's Lieutenants,* Vol. III, pp. 51–72. See also Thomason's account in *Jeb Stuart,* pp. 420–29, and *Ranger Mosby,* by Virgil Carrington Jones, pp. 145–50.

6. This anecdote is from Current's *Old Thad Stevens.*

7. *Official Records,* Vol. XXVII, Part 1, p. 151; abstract from returns of the Army of the Potomac, June 20, 1863.

8. The most generally accepted account of the reasons for Hooker's removal is Charles F. Benjamin's in *Battles and Leaders,* Vol. III, pp. 239–43. The British critic, General Ballard, remarks that Hooker simply quit in a fit of petulance. (*The Military Genius of Abraham Lincoln,* pp. 163–64.) Writing in 1879, Colonel Theodore Gates of the 80th New York suggested that Hooker quit because he was afraid to command the army against Lee in another battle. (*The Ulster Guard and the War of the Rebellion,* p. 404.)

9. *Life and Letters of George Gordon Meade,* Vol. I, pp. 388–89.

10. Ibid., pp. 19, 30–32, 34–35, 37–38, 161 ff., 241, 243.

11. Ibid., pp. 214–15.

12. *Battles and Leaders,* Vol. III, p. 243; *Gouverneur Kemble Warren,* p. 119.

13. *The Battle of Gettysburg,* by the Comte de Paris.

14. *New Jersey Troops in the Gettysburg Campaign,* p. 134; *History of the 12th Regiment New Hampshire Volunteers,* pp. 116–17. There is a good sketch of Humphreys by Major General James H. Wilson in *Papers of the Military Historical Society of Massachusetts,* Vol. X, pp. 71–96.

15. *The 48th in the War,* p. 88.

16. *History of the 2nd Massachusetts Regiment of Infantry: Gettysburg,* by Colonel Charles F. Morse, p. 4.

17. Ibid., p. 5.

18. *Four Years Campaigning in the Army of the Potomac,* p. 88; *History of the 9th Regiment Massachusetts Volunteer Infantry,* p. 312; *Army Life: A Private's Reminiscences of the Civil War,* p. 99.

19. References to the soldiers' deep disappointment at Hooker's removal are innumerable, and it is clear that if the higher officers had lost confidence in him the enlisted man had not. See *Four Years in the Army of the Potomac,* p. 106; *New Jersey Troops in the Gettysburg Campaign,* pp. 128–29; *The Story of the 15th Regiment Massachusetts Volunteer Infantry,* p. 260; *History of the 12th Regiment New Hampshire Volunteers,* pp. 118, 130; *Army Life: A Private's Reminiscences,* p. 100; *Military History of the 8th Regiment Ohio Volunteer Infantry,* p. 123; *The 20th Connecticut: A Regimental History,* p. 73; *The Three Years Service of the 33rd Massachusetts Infantry Regiment,* p. 110.

20. *Rebellion Record,* Vol. VII, Part 2, pp. 20–21.

21. Ibid., pp. 86–87.

22. See Josiah M. Favil's *Diary of a Young Officer,* p. 218: "The aim of the government would seem to be to encourage officers to keep their commands out of dangerous places, for their chances of promotion are lessened in exact proportion as they lose their men by fighting." For a similar complaint by Rufus Dawes, see *Service with the 6th Wisconsin Volunteers,* p. 188.

23. *Days and Events,* p. 234; *History of the First Regiment Minnesota Volunteer Infantry,* p. 347.

24. *The 20th Connecticut: A Regimental History,* p. 75; *Our Campaign around Gettysburg,* pp. 121–22.

25. *Rebellion Record,* Vol. VII, Part 2, p. 122.

26. *The Ulster Guard and the War of the Rebellion,* p. 422.

27. *Henry Wilson's Regiment,* p. 331; *Army Life: A Private's Reminiscences,* p. 101; *The Old Fourth Michigan Infantry,* pp. 21–22; *History of the 9th Regiment Massachusetts Volunteer Infantry,* p. 312; *History of the Sauk County Riflemen,* p. 70; *Battles*

and Leaders, Vol. III, p. 301. In most cases the report seems to have been formally announced to the troops by mounted staff officers, which is not the way the spontaneous army rumor circulates.

28. *Army Letters, 1861-65,* p. 322.

CHAPTER SIX: END AND BEGINNING

THE ECONOMICS OF EIGHTY PER CENT

1. *Battles and Leaders,* Vol. III, pp. 274-75; *History of the 8th Cavalry Regiment, Illinois Volunteers,* pp. 256-57.

2. Stine's *History of the Army of the Potomac,* pp. 453-54.

3. Wadsworth is affectionately sketched in *The Ulster Guard and the War of the Rebellion,* pp. 153-54, and in *Lincoln and the Episodes of the Civil War,* pp. 49-54.

4. *History of the Sauk County Riflemen,* p. 71; *History of the 24th Michigan,* p. 142.

5. *History of the Army of the Potomac,* p. 462-63.

6. *Official Records,*Vol. XXVII, Part 1, pp. 359-60.

7. *History of the Sauk County Riflemen,* p. 73; *History of the 24th Michigan,* p. 160; Doubleday's report, *Official Records,* Vol. XXVII, Part 1, p. 244.

8. *History of the Army of the Potomac,* pp. 466-67; *Service with the 6th Wisconsin Volunteers,* pp. 168-69; *Official Records,* Vol. XXVII, Part 1, p. 281 ff.

9. *Battles and Leaders,* Vol. III, p. 285.

10. *Official Records,* Vol. XXVII, Part 1, p. 360.

11. *The Road to Richmond,* p. 80.

12. *Official Records,* Vol. XXVII, Part 1, p. 723.

13. *Trials and Triumphs,* p. 96.

14. *Official Records,* Vol. XXVII, Part 1, pp. 229, 752, 754.

15. Ibid., pp. 727-28, 756; *Battles and Leaders,* Vol. III, p. 281. Battine's *Crisis of the Confederacy,* pp. 195-99, has an excellent account of the XI Corps' fight and its relation to the fighting west of town. There is a very detailed story of the first day at Gettysburg in Stine's *History of the Army of the Potomac,* pp. 452-93.

16. *Official Records,* Vol. XXVII, Part 1, p. 753.

17. *The Road to Richmond,* pp. 99-102—an exceptionally good description of this part of the battle.

18. *Official Records,* Vol. XXVII, Part 1, pp. 291, 330-31.

19. Ibid., p. 284.

20. Colonel Morrow's report. Ibid., pp. 267-73; *History of the 24th Michigan,* p. 165.

21. *Official Records,* Vol. XXVII, Part 1, p. 280.

22. Ibid., pp. 356-57, 260; *History of the 24th Michigan,* p. 121.

23. *The Three Years of the 33rd Massachusetts Infantry Regiment,* p. 118.

24. *Official Records,* Vol. XXVII, Part 1, pp. 286, 716, 729, 735, 742, 755; *Service with the 6th Wisconsin Volunteers,* pp. 176-78.

25. Captain Edward N. Whittier in Vol. III, *Papers of the Military Historical Society of Massachusetts,* p. 315; *Official Records,* Vol. XXVII, Part 1, p. 281; *The Iron Brigade at Gettysburg,* p. 15; *History of the 24th Michigan,* p. 184.

26. *Reminiscences of Winfield Scott Hancock,* p. 189.

27. Ibid., p. 190. For the encounter between Hancock and Howard, see *Battles and Leaders,* Vol. III, pp. 285-86.

ALL THE TRUMPETS SOUNDED

1. De Trobriand's engaging account of the stay at Emmitsburg is in his *Four Years with the Army of the Potomac,* pp. 486-87. See also Crotty's *Four Years Campaigning in the Army of the Potomac,* p. 89.

2. *Days and Events,* pp. 240, 247.

3. *Battles and Leaders,* Vol. III, pp. 295–96, 301–3; *Life and Letters of George Gordon Meade,* Vol. II, pp. 66, 71, 74; *Four Years with the Army of the Potomac,* p. 494.

4. *Reminiscences of Winfield Scott Hancock,* p. 193.

5. *Berdan's United States Sharpshooters,* pp. 303–11.

6. *Battles and Leaders,* Vol. III, p. 303; Gibbon's *Personal Recollections of the Civil War,* pp. 135–36; *Life and Letters of George Gordon Meade,* Vol. II, pp. 72–73; *The Long Arm of Lee,* Vol. II, p. 644.

7. *Trials and Triumphs,* pp. 101, 249; *Official Records,* Vol. XXVII, Part 1, p. 358; *The Three Years Service of the 33rd Massachusetts Infantry Regiment,* p. 123; *The Long Arm of Lee,* Vol. II, p. 652; *Papers of the Military Historical Society of Massachusetts,* Vol. III, p. 320.

8. *Official Records,* Vol. XXVII, Part 1, pp. 881, 900.

9. *Four Years with the Army of the Potomac,* pp. 497–500. For a good account of the artillery in Devil's Den, see *A Famous Battery and Its Campaigns,* by Captain James E. Smith, pp. 101–12.

10. *Strong Vincent and His Brigade at Gettysburg,* by Oliver W. Norton, p. 8. Sykes is sketched from Haskel's *Battle of Gettysburg,* p. 69.

11. An uncommonly vivid description of this fighting is in *Army Life: A Private's Reminiscences of the Civil War,* pp. 107–11. Almost equally good is Colonel Chamberlain's report, *Official Records,* Vol. XXVII, Part 1, pp. 623–25.

12. *Strong Vincent and His Brigade at Gettysburg,* pp. 8–17; *Official Records,* Vol. XXVII, Part 1, pp. 616–17; *Campaigns of the 146th Regiment New York State Volunteers,* pp. 116–19; *Gouverneur Kemble Warren,* p. 128.

13. *Official Records,* Vol. XXVII, Part 1, p. 611; *The Old Fourth Michigan Infantry,* p. 23.

14. *Official Records,* Vol. XXVII, Part 1, p. 612.

15. Ibid., pp. 623, 640–41, 646, 650.

16. Ibid., p. 882; *Papers of the Military Historical Society of Massachusetts,* Vol. X, pp. 84–85.

17. *New Jersey Troops in the Gettysburg Campaign,* pp. 223–24, 239–40.

18. *The Story of the 15th Regiment Massachusetts Volunteer Infantry,* pp. 267–69, 280; *History of the 12th Regiment New Hampshire Volunteers,* pp. 123–25; *Days and Events,* pp. 251–52.

19. *Three Years Service of the 33rd Massachusetts,* p. 126; *Official Records,* Vol. XXVII, Part 1, p. 886; *History of the Corn Exchange Regiment,* p. 267. According to this latter book (pp. 287–88) Bigelow's 9th Massachusetts battery would not have been at Gettysburg at all except for a freak chance. With other new batteries, it put in at Centreville, Va., in the spring of 1863. When the Army of the Potomac marched north, the Keystone Battery of Philadelphia was ordered to leave the reserve at Centreville and join up with the army. It delayed in order to accommodate a general of the II Corps in the matter of transporting some of his personal effects in a battery wagon. The delay irked General Hunt, the army's chief of artillery, and he canceled the Keystone's orders and called up the Massachusetts battery in its place.

20. *Official Records,* Vol. XXVII, Part 1, pp. 882–83, 897–98.

21. *Reminiscences of Winfield Scott Hancock,* p. 199; *History of the First Regiment Minnesota Volunteer Infantry,* p. 344 ff. Hancock gave the 1st Minnesota credit for capturing the flag, but the regimental historian insisted that this was not so; the flag the regiment got, he said, was taken in the repulse of Pickett's charge next day.

22. *Life and Letters of George Gordon Meade,* Vol. II, p. 89.

23. *History of the Second Massachusetts Regiment of Infantry. Gettysburg,* pp. 8–9.

24. Probably the best description of this attack and its repulse is Captain Whittier's in Vol. III, *Papers of the Military Historical Society of Massachusetts,* pp.

326–31. Another good narrative is in *The Three Years Service of the 33rd Massachusetts Infantry Regiment,* pp. 129–30. See also *Official Records,* Vol. XXVII, Part 1, pp. 360–61, 894.

AND IT MAY BE FOREVER

1. *The 20th Connecticut: A Regimental History,* pp. 88–91.
2. *Journal History of the 29th Ohio Veteran Volunteers,* p. 70; *Four Years Campaigning in the Army of the Potomac,* p. 91.
3. *The Diary of a Young Officer,* pp. 246–47.
4. *Pictorial History of the Civil War,* Vol. III, p. 67; *Days and Events,* pp. 255–56.
5. *Personal Recollections of the Civil War,* pp. 141–45.
6. *The 20th Connecticut: A Regimental History,* p. 194.
7. *Papers of the Military Historical Society of Massachusetts,* Vol. III, pp. 346–47; *Official Records,* Vol. XXVII, Part 1, pp. 781, 813–15.
8. Ibid., p. 841; *The Dutchess County Regiment in the Civil War,* p. 36.
9. *New Jersey Troops in the Gettysburg Campaign,* p. 290.
10. *Life in Camp: A History of the Nine Months' Service of the 14th Vermont Regiment,* an unassuming little record which is pure Vermont.
11. *The 20th Connecticut: A Regimental History,* pp. 104–5.
12. The story of the lunch party and the way the bombardment scattered it is from Gibbon's *Personal Recollections,* pp. 146–47; *Reminiscences of Winfield Scott Hancock,* p. 207; Haskell's *Battle of Gettysburg,* pp. 95–96.
13. *Papers of the Military Historical Society of Massachusetts,* Vol. III, p. 353; *The Road to Richmond,* p. 105; *History of the First Regiment Minnesota Volunteer Infantry,* p. 366; *History of the Corn Exchange Regiment,* p. 259.
14. *Personal Recollections of the Civil War,* pp. 147–48.
15. *The 20th Connecticut: A Regimental History,* pp. 95–96; *Official Records,* Vol. XXVII, Part 1, p. 902.
16. *Rebellion Record,* Vol. VII, Part 2, p. 101; *Life and Letters of George Gordon Meade,* Vol. II, pp. 106–7.
17. Mrs. Hancock tells about this farewell party in *Reminiscences of Winfield Scott Hancock,* pp. 69–70.
18. An unforgettable picture of Cushing and his battery on Cemetery Ridge is given in *Three Wisconsin Cushings,* by Theron Wilber Haight, pp. 47–50, 53, 57.
19. Haskell's *Battle of Gettysburg,* pp. 124–25; *Battles and Leaders,* Vol. III, pp. 388–89.
20. *Military History of the 8th Regiment Ohio Volunteer Infantry,* p. 131.
21. *Three Wisconsin Cushings,* p. 54.
22. *The Road to Richmond,* p. 106; *Days and Events,* p. 262.
23. *The Story of the 15th Regiment Massachusetts Volunteer Infantry,* pp. 275–76. See also *Days and Events,* p. 262, and Haskell's *Battle of Gettysburg,* p. 127.
24. *Reminiscences of Winfield Scott Hancock,* pp. 215–16.
25. *The Road to Richmond,* p. 107.

VALLEY OF DRY BONES

1. *Battles and Leaders,* Vol. III, p. 424.
2. The Comte de Paris's *Battle of Gettysburg; Official Records,* Vol. XXVII, Part 1, pp. 153, 187, 193; *Battles and Leaders,* Vol. III, p. 440.
3. *Four Years with the Army of the Potomac,* pp. 512, 514; *Days and Events,* p. 266.
4. *Lincoln and the Episodes of the Civil War,* p. 221.
5. Ibid., p. 222; *War Years with Jeb Stuart,* p. 231; *History of the 87th Regiment Pennsylvania Volunteers,* p. 84.

6. *New Jersey Troops in the Gettysburg Campaign,* p. 320; *Henry Wilson's Regiment,* p. 345.

7. *The Story of the 15th Regiment Massachusetts Volunteer Infantry,* p. 286; *Three Wisconsin Cushings,* pp. 50–51; *Journal History of the 29th Ohio Veteran Volunteers,* p. 72.

8. *Official Records,* Vol. XXVII, Part 1, p. 25; *New Jersey Troops in the Gettysburg Campaign,* p. 327; *Reminiscences of the 19th Massachusetts Regiment,* p. 71.

9. *History of the Corn Exchange Regiment,* pp. 274–75.

10. *Official Records,* Vol. XXVII, Part 1, p. 626.

11. *History of the 9th Regiment Massachusetts Volunteer Infantry,* p. 333.

12. The Meade-Halleck interchange can be found in *Battles and Leaders,* Vol. III, pp. 383–84. For the letter Lincoln wrote but did not send, see *Abraham Lincoln: The War Years,* Vol. II, pp. 353–54.

13. *Four Years with the Army of the Potomac,* p. 517.

14. For the enlisted man's point of view on this, see *Henry Wilson's Regiment,* p. 339: "If there ever was a battle won through the indomitable courage and intelligence of the rank and file of the Army of the Potomac, without planning strategical movement, or audible commands from their superior officers, it was Gettysburg."

15. *History of the Corn Exchange Regiment,* p. 269.

16. *Life and Letters of George Gordon Meade,* Vol. II, p. 125.

17. *Official Records,* Vol. XXVII, Part 1, p. 28; *Lincoln's Daughters of Mercy,* p. 169.

18. *South after Gettysburg: Letters of Cornelia Hancock,* edited by Henrietta Stratton Jaquette, pp. 4–5.

19. *Official Records,* Vol. XXVII, Part 1, pp. 22–23.

20. *Lincoln's Daughters of Mercy,* pp. 169–72.

21. *Three Years in the Field Hospitals of the Army of the Potomac,* p. 55; *South after Gettysburg,* p. 9; *Lincoln's Daughters of Mercy,* p. 173.

22. *Official Records,* Vol. XXVII, Part 1, pp. 26–28.

23. *Gettysburg and Lincoln: The Battle, the Cemetery and the National Park,* by Henry Sweetser Burrage, pp. 81–86.

24. For the indignation which this burial-by-states aroused in a fighting man, see Haskell's *Battle of Gettysburg,* p. 183: "If it be not one of the lessons that the war teaches, that we have a country paramount over faction, and party, and state, then was the blood of 50,000 citizens shed upon this field in vain." It might be noted that Colonel Haskell wrote his invaluable account of the battle while the war was still on. He was killed at Cold Harbor.

25. *Gettysburg and Lincoln,* pp. 87–90.

26. *The Story of the 15th Regiment Massachusetts Volunteer Infantry,* pp. 288, 290.

27. Gibbon's *Personal Recollections,* p. 184.

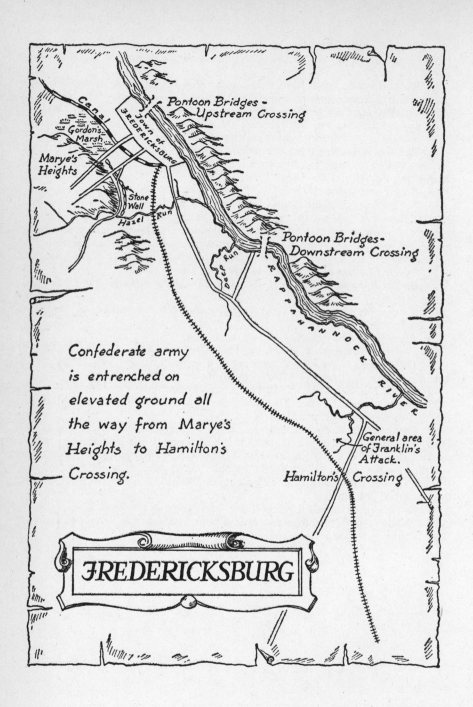

Pontoon Bridges – Upstream Crossing

Canal

Gordon's Marsh

Town of Fredericksburg

Marye's Heights

Stone Wall

Hazel Run

Deep Run

Pontoon Bridges – Downstream Crossing

RAPPAHANNOCK RIVER

Confederate army is entrenched on elevated ground all the way from Marye's Heights to Hamilton's Crossing.

General area of Franklin's Attack.

Hamilton's Crossing

FREDERICKSBURG

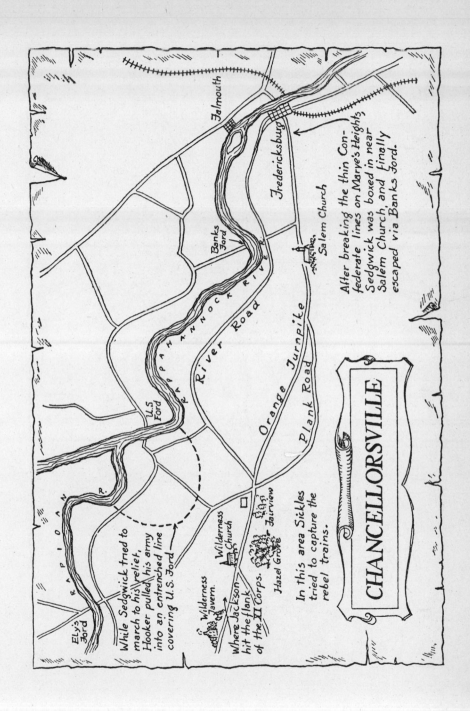

CHANCELLORSVILLE

Falmouth

Fredericksburg

Salem Church

After breaking the thin Confederate lines on Marye's Heights Sedgwick was boxed in near Salem Church, and finally escaped via Banks Ford.

Banks Ford

RAPPAHANNOCK RIVER

River Road

Orange Turnpike

Plank Road

U.S. Ford

RAPIDAN R.

Ely's Ford

While Sedgwick tried to march to his relief, Hooker pulled his army into an entrenched line covering U.S. Ford.

Wilderness Tavern

Where Jackson hit the flank of the XI Corps.

Wilderness Church

Hazel Grove

Fairview

In this area Sickles tried to capture the rebel trains.

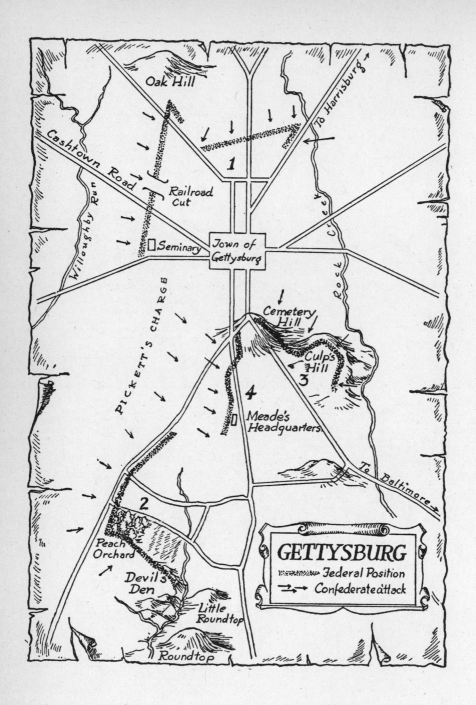

Oak Hill

To Harrisburg

Cashtown Road

Willoughby Run

Railroad Cut

1

Seminary

Town of Gettysburg

Rock Creek

PICKETT'S CHARGE

Cemetery Hill

Culp's Hill

3

4

Meade's Headquarters

To Baltimore

2

Peach Orchard

Devil's Den

Little Roundtop

Roundtop

GETTYSBURG

〰〰〰 Federal Position

⇒→ Confederate attack

A STILLNESS
AT
APPOMATTOX

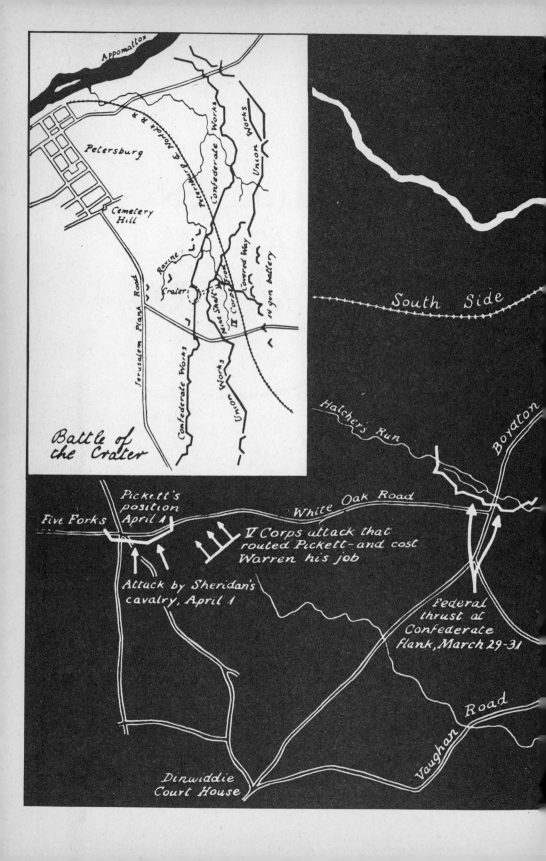

Battle of
the Crater

Appomattox

Petersburg

Cemetery
Hill

Petersburg & Norfolk R.R.

Confederate Works

Union Works

Union Works

Jerusalem Plank Road

Ravine

Crater

Mine Shaft

IX Corps Front

Covered Way

14 gun battery

Confederate Works

Union Works

South Side

Hatcher's Run

Boydton

Five Forks

Pickett's
position
April 1

White Oak Road

V Corps attack that
routed Pickett — and cost
Warren his job

Attack by Sheridan's
cavalry, April 1

Federal
thrust at
Confederate
flank, March 29-31

Road

Vaughan Road

Dinwiddie
Court House

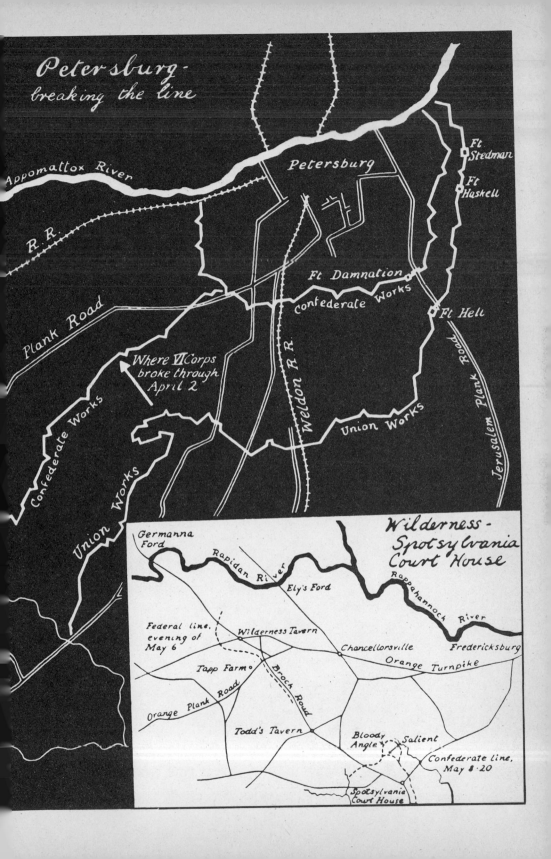

Petersburg -
breaking the line

Appomattox River

R. R.

Petersburg

Ft. Stedman

Ft. Haskell

Ft. Damnation

Confederate Works

Ft. Hell

Plank Road

Where VI Corps
broke through
April 2

Confederate Works

Union Works

Weldon R. R.

Union Works

Jerusalem Plank Road

Wilderness -
Spotsylvania
Court House

Germanna
Ford

Rapidan River

Ely's Ford

Rappahannock River

Federal line,
evening of
May 6

Wilderness Tavern

Chancellorsville

Fredericksburg

Tapp Farm

Brock Road

Orange Turnpike

Orange Plank Road

Todd's Tavern

Bloody
Angle

Salient

Confederate line,
May 8-20

Spotsylvania
Court House

To my sister Barbara

ONE

Glory Is Out of Date

1. A BOY NAMED MARTIN

EVERYBODY AGREED that the Washington's Birthday ball was the most brilliant event of the winter. Unlike most social functions in this army camp by the Rapidan, it was not held in a tent. There was a special, weatherproof ballroom—a big box of a building more than a hundred feet long, whose construction had kept scores of enlisted men busy. Some of these had been sent into the woods to fell trees. Others had taken over and operated an abandoned sawmill, to reduce the trees to boards. Still others, carpenters in some former incarnation, had taken these boards and built the building itself, and it was pleasantly odorous of new-cut pine, decorated with all of the headquarters and regimental flags which the II Army Corps possessed. The flags may have been worth seeing. It was the boast of this corps that although it had suffered nearly 19,000 battle casualties it had never yet lost a flag to the enemy.

At one end of the ballroom there was a raised platform on which, to dazzle the guests, there was an idyllic representation of what the ladies from Washington might imagine to be a typical army bivouac—spotless shelter tents pulled tight to eliminate wrinkles, piles of drums and bugles, tripods of stacked muskets, mimic campfire with cooking kettles hung over it, and as a final touch two brass Napoleons, polished and shining until their own gun crews would hardly know them, reflecting the light of Chinese lanterns, as brightly festive as any instruments of pain and death one could hope to see.

Some of the guests—the wives of officers who had enough rank or influence to be attended by their womenfolk while in winter quarters—were more or less permanent residents of this highly impermanent camp. Others, who had come down from the capital by train just for this occasion, were quartered in wall tents, and since a woman in a hoop-skirted party gown could neither ride horseback nor walk on the muddy footways of an army camp, their escorts called for them in white-topped army ambulances.

The escorts were of course officers, both of staff and of line. They wore their dress uniforms, and they had their swords neatly hooked up at their belts, and even though they were to spend the evening dancing many of them wore spurs. It was remarked that both escorts and guests seemed to make a particular effort to be gay, as if perhaps the music and the laughter and the stylized embrace of the dance might help everybody to put out of mind the knowledge that in the campaign which would begin in the spring a considerable percentage of these officers would unquestionably be killed.

That knowledge was not easy to avoid. The war was just finishing its third year, the end of it was nowhere in sight, and what lay ahead was almost certain to be worse than what had gone before. Neither the officers who wore spurs and swords to the dance floor, nor the women who swirled their voluminous skirts to the music without regard for these encumbrances, retained any romantic illusions about this war. Yet they still had the ability—perhaps there was a necessity

461

about it—to create illusions for the moment; and this evening there seems to have been a conscious effort to enter into the Byronic mood, an eagerness to see a parallel between this ball and the fabulous ball given in Brussels by the Duchess of Richmond on the eve of Waterloo. The dancers tried to act the parts which the romantic tradition called for, and while the music lasted—the brave music of a military band, playing the swinging little tunes that would keep reality at bay—they could maintain their chosen attitudes, changing tragedy into a dreamy unobtrusive melancholy that would do no more than highlight the evening's gaiety. It was at one of these dances that a young woman found herself chatting with a general officer whose only son had recently been killed in some outpost skirmish up the river. She offered her sympathy. The general bowed: "Yes, madame, very sad! Very sad! He was the last of his race. Do you waltz?"[1]

The dance lasted until the small hours, and at last the ambulances went off through the sleeping camp, and there was a final tinkle of chatter and laughter and so-glad-you-could-come under the frosty stars as the guests went to their tents. And the next afternoon everybody reassembled in and around a reviewing stand in an open field for a grand review of the II Corps, with the commanding general of the Army of the Potamac taking the salute as the long ranks of veterans went past.

Like the dance, the review was an occasion: a quiet reminder, if anybody needed one, that dances and bright officers and everything else rested finally on the men in the ranks, who went to no parties and who could be turned out to parade their strength for the admiration of the officers' ladies. It was noted that the major general commanding, George Gordon Meade, was in rare good humor. He was lean and grizzled, with a great hawk nose and a furious temper, and his staff had learned to read omens in his behavior. When the army was about to do something he gave off sparks, and those around him did well to step quietly and rapidly, but today the omens were good. He was lighthearted, making small jokes and telling stories, enjoying the review and the company of the guests, and acting the part of a major general who had nothing in particular on his mind. Staff observed and took heart; some weeks of quiet must lie ahead of the army.[2]

In this judgment the staff officers were wrong. There was a movement afoot, and General Meade did not wholly approve of it. He was at ease, perhaps, merely because the imminent movement would involve only a fragment of the army, and because it did not seem likely to have any great importance one way or the other. Visible sign that something was in the wind was the presence at this infantry review of the 3rd Cavalry Division of the Army of the Potomac, led by Brigadier General Judson Kilpatrick.

Kilpatrick was in his mid-twenties, young for a brigadier, a wiry, restless, undersized man with blank eyes, a lantern jaw, and an imposing growth of sand-colored sideburns; a man about whom there were two opinions. A member of Meade's staff wrote in his diary that it was hard to look at Kilpatrick without laughing, and the common nickname for him around army headquarters was "Kill Cavalry." His division fought well and paraded well—at this review it put on a noble mock charge, a thundering yelling gallop across the dead grass of the plain, troopers rising in their stirrups with gleaming sabers extended, all very stimulating for the visiting ladies—but its camp was usually poorly policed and in bad order, its horses were overworked and badly groomed, the clothing and equipments of the men had a used-up look, and its carbines were mostly rather dirty.

Yet the man had a quality, somehow. In combat he was valiant, and he was afraid of nothing—except, possibly, of the final ounce of the weight of personal responsibility—and he was slightly unusual among the officers of this army in that he neither drank nor played cards. At West Point he had been noted as a gamecock, anxious to use his spurs. Born in New Jersey, he was ardent for the Union and against slavery, and he had had many fist fights with other gamecock cadets from the South. William Tecumseh Sherman, with his genius for brutal overstatement, may have summed him up when, a bit later in the war, he asked to have Kilpatrick assigned to him for the march to the sea, explaining: "I know that Kilpatrick is a hell of a damned fool, but I want just that sort of man to command my cavalry on this expedition."

Kilpatrick had ambitions. It was his belief that if he survived the war he would become, first, governor of New Jersey, and then President of the United States. At the moment, however, he was more concerned with the thought that he would presently become a major general, and various events hung upon this conviction. [3]

While the officers of the II Corps were having their ball, Kilpatrick had been having a party of his own—a lavish affair, held in a big frame house near Brandy Station, where Kilpatrick had his headquarters. The guests included a number of important senators—the Senate had to confirm the promotions of all general officers—and if the general did not drink he saw to it that any guests who did were taken care of. The party appears to have been loud, merry, and successful. One guest recalled that Kilpatrick had been "as active as a flea, and almost as ubiquitous." When the review was held on the following day Kilpatrick, who had arranged to have his cavalry take part, saw to it that his guests had places in the reviewing stand. [4]

But the senators were only part of it. In his reflections on the road to promotion Kilpatrick that winter had thought of two other points. One was the anxiety of Abraham Lincoln to extend friendship and amnesty to any citizens of the Confederacy who would return to their old allegiance to the Federal government. Mr. Lincoln had recently issued a proclamation offering such amnesty, and he greatly wanted copies of it distributed in the South. The other point was the relatively defenseless condition of Richmond, capital of the Confederacy, where there were confined many thousands of Union prisoners of war.

Putting these two points together, Kilpatrick had evolved a plan. A well-appointed cavalry expedition, he believed, under the proper officer (who might well be Judson Kilpatrick) could slip through General Lee's defenses, get down to Richmond before the Army of Northern Virginia could send reinforcements, free all of the Union prisoners, and in its spare time distribute thousands of copies of the President's proclamation. Having thought of this plan Kilpatrick managed to get word of it to Washington, and in the middle of February he had been formally summoned to the White House to explain the scheme to Mr. Lincoln and to the Secretary of War, Edwin M. Stanton.

This summons Kilpatrick had obeyed gladly, amid mutterings on the part of his chief, Major General Alfred Pleasonton, who commanded the cavalry corps and who had a low opinion both of Kilpatrick's plan and of Kilpatrick's action in dealing direct with the White House. Pleasonton remarked tartly that the last big cavalry raid—Stoneman's luckless expedition, during the Chancellorsville campaign—had accomplished nothing of any consequence and had cost the army 7,000 horses. He added that if the President wanted his amnesty proclamation circulated in Richmond that could be done by regular espionage agents without taking a single cavalryman away from the army. [5]

But Pleasonton was not listened to and Kilpatrick was. He may have owed a good deal to Secretary Stanton, who had a weakness for fantastic schemes. He probably owed more to Mr. Lincoln himself, who was forever hoping that the seceding states could be brought back into the Union before they were beaten to death, and who, from long dealings with officers of the Army of the Potomac, had come to look with a kindly eye on those who were willing to display a little initiative. In any case the project had been approved at the very top, and orders came down from Washington to give Kilpatrick 4,000 troopers and let him see what he could do. Simultaneously, whole bales of pamphlets reprinting the amnesty proclamation arrived at Brandy Station.

The enthusiasm aroused by all of this at army headquarters was tepid. Army intelligence was well aware that Richmond was lightly held this winter. There were strong fortifications about the city, but hardly any troops occupied them, the chief reliance being on militia—and on the presence just below the Rapidan, far from Richmond but close to the Army of the Potomac, of the indomitable soldiers of the Army of Northern Virginia.

In theory, Richmond was open to a sudden grab. But headquarters could not help remembering that a plan not unlike Kilpatrick's had been cooked up a month earlier by the imaginative but incompetent Ben Butler, who commanded Federal troops around Fortress Monroe. Butler had proposed that the Army of the Potomac make a pretense of an offensive, to keep Lee busy, while Butler's own troops marched up the peninsula and seized Richmond, and after a good deal of correspondence back and forth the thing had been tried. The Army of the Potomac had done its part, getting into a smart little fight at Morton's Ford and suffering two or three hundred casualties, and with Confederate attention thus engaged the way had been open for Butler to do what he proposed to do. But somehow nothing much happened. Butler's troops advanced, encountered a broken bridge several miles below Richmond, paused to contemplate it for a while, and at last retreated, and everything was as it had been before except that Lee had been alerted and now held the Rapidan crossings in greater strength.

Major General John Sedgwick, unassuming and wholly capable, who commanded the army just then in the temporary absence of General Meade, commented indignantly on the business in his dispatches to Washington, but he succeeded only in ruining his own standing at the War Department.[6] The administration still believed that Richmond could be taken by a bold stroke, and an officer who disagreed was likely to be considered fainthearted and politically unsound. Also, there were all of those pamphlets to be distributed.

Orders were orders, in other words, and Meade dutifully set about obeying them. His part was to enable the cavalry to get through the Rebel lines along the Rapidan, and he devised a little stratagem: the army would make an ostentatious lunge toward the right, as if it meant mischief somewhere down the Orange and Alexandria Railroad, and while the Confederates were looking in that direction Kilpatrick's men could go slicing off to the left. If the trick worked, so that the expedition once got past Lee's army, the whole project might very well succeed.

It was all top secret, of course, for everything depended on taking Lee by surprise. As far as headquarters knew there had been no leaks. And then one day, just about the time the ladies were gathering for the Washington's Birthday ball, there came limping across the railway platform at Brandy Station a youthful colonel of cavalry whose mere presence here was proof that the story was all over Washington.

This officer was Ulric Dahlgren. In addition to a colonel's commission, he possessed, at twenty-one, much glamor, a wooden leg, and some extremely important connections. His father was Rear Admiral John A. D. Dahlgren, a world authority on ordnance and one of the Navy's hard-case shellbacks to boot. Inventor of the heavy bottle-shaped Dahlgren gun which the Navy favored so much, he was also a good friend of Abraham Lincoln. Currently, the admiral was in charge of the fleet which was vainly trying to batter its way into Charleston Harbor. A square-jawed, bony, tenacious Scandinavian, lean and sharp-cornered, he rode in the front line of action in a hot ill-ventilated monitor instead of taking his ease in his admiral's suite on the flagship, and he was deeply proud of the son who freakishly had forsaken the Navy and sought fame in the hard-riding, headline-happy squadrons of the cavalry corps.

Young Dahlgren was tall and slim and graceful, with a thin tawny beard and much charm of manner. He was alleged to be the youngest colonel in the Army, and an admiring Confederate wrote of him that he had "manners as soft as a cat's." Born in Pennsylvania, he had grown up in the Washington Navy Yard, and when the war began he was studying civil engineering. Early in 1862 he decided that it was time for him to fight—he had just passed his nineteenth birthday—and he was forthwith given an Army captaincy by Secretary Stanton himself. A bit later he found himself on the staff of General Joe Hooker.

He may have been commissioned by pure favoritism, but he turned out to be a good soldier. In the fall of 1862 he won distinction by leading a cavalry raid into Fredericksburg—a stroke that accomplished nothing much but showed boldness and leadership—and the next summer, during the Gettysburg campaign, Dahlgren made his reputation.[7]

While the fighting was beginning around Gettysburg, Dahlgren took a couple of troops of cavalry and went prowling far around in Lee's rear, and he captured a Confederate courier coming up from Richmond with dispatches. The capture was important, for the courier bore a letter from Jefferson Davis telling Lee that the government did not think it advisable to bring Beauregard and a new army up to the Rappahannock to add weight to Lee's invasion of the North. The letter was promptly sent to Meade, who was thus enabled to campaign in the secure knowledge that Lee was not to be reinforced.

A few days after this, Dahlgren's outfit got into a fight with Rebel cavalry at Boonsboro, Maryland, and Dahlgren was badly wounded. His right leg was amputated, and he spent the next few months convalescing at his father's home in Washington. Then, in November, a one-legged army officer on crutches, he went down to the fleet off Charleston and lived on his father's flagship, going ashore now and then with the Navy in small-boat expeditions of one kind and another. Early in the winter he returned to Washington to receive a colonel's commission and to have an artificial leg fitted, and just as this was done he heard about the Kilpatrick expedition. (The bar at Willard's was abuzz with it.) Dahlgren hurried down to see Kilpatrick about it, satisfied himself that he could ride a horse despite the handicap of a wooden leg, and shortly after the II Corps review he wrote to his father:

"I have not returned to the fleet, because there is a great raid to be made, and I am to have a very important command. If successful, it will be the grandest thing on record; and if it fails, many of us will 'go up.' I may be captured or I may be 'tumbled over' but it is an undertaking that if I were not in I should be ashamed to show my face again. With such an important command I am afraid to mention it, for fear this letter might fall into wrong hands before reaching you. I find I can stand the service perfectly well, without my leg. I think we will be successful, although a desperate undertaking. . . . If we do not return, there is no better place to 'give up the ghost.' "[8]

Kilpatrick gave Dahlgren a key assignment. When the expedition moved there would be an advance guard of 500 troopers which would swing west to strike the James River some miles above Richmond. While the main body approached the city from the north and east, this group would cross the river and come up to the city from the south. With the attention of the defense centered on Kilpatrick, it was believed that this party could enter Richmond almost unopposed. It would seize the principal prison camp at Belle Isle, free the 15,000 prisoners there, lead them out on the north side, rejoin Kilpatrick's column there, and all hands would go romping back to the Union lines. And this advance contingent, on which the success of the whole movement would very largely depend, was to be commanded by Colonel Dahlgren.

So it was all arranged, and Kilpatrick got his formal orders on February 27. He was to "move with the utmost expedition possible on the shortest route past the enemy's right flank," and next day various cavalry commands were ordered to report at his headquarters, where the men were issued five days' rations and officers were ordered to see to it that all the horses were well shod and that the men's arms and equipments were in order. The troopers obeyed gleefully, for this sounded like a raid, and as one man remarked, "It is easier to get a trooper or even a hundred for a raid than to get one to groom an extra horse."[9]

Ponderously but surely, the army machine began to move. John Sedgwick took his VI Corps upriver toward Madison Court House, and flamboyant young Brigadier General George Armstrong Custer, with his gaudy uniform, his anointed curls, and his hard, expressionless eyes, took his cavalry division off on a dash toward Charlottesville—wondering, as he rode, whether he might not be cut off entirely and so be compelled to ride all the way to Tennessee to join Sherman's army. The bait thus dangled was taken, and the Army of Northern Virginia took thought for its left flank; and on February 28, a fine starlit evening with a moon putting a shimmer on the waters of the Rapidan, Dahlgren and Kilpatrick took their men down to the river at Ely's Ford, rounded up the Rebel pickets there, and set off on their long ride.[10]

They were good men, and there was a chance that they might succeed. Yet they were pursuing a dream, because peace could not now be won by planting pamphlets about amnesty in the Confederate capital, and the thought that it might come so was essentially a romantic thought, however noble. This venture was a departure from reality, of a piece with the officers' dances at which men and women quoted Byron to themselves and borrowed, for their own beset lives, the tag ends of implausible poetry describing a bloodless bookish war. It was born of a romantic dream and it was aimed at glory, and glory was out of date, a gauzy wisp of rose-colored filament trailing from a lost world. Victory could no longer be imagined as a bright abstraction, lying like the sunrise at the end of a shining road. It was an ugly juggernaut that would crush and smash many values and many lives into the everlasting mud, and it was the only thing that counted nowadays. The longer the war lasted the more victory was going to cost, and a dazzling cavalry raid would not even be the small change of the final purchase price.

Still, for whatever it might be worth, the expedition rode on, and the men slipped safely past Lee's right flank, trotting at dawn through a sleepy crossroads town known as Spotsylvania Court House, where Kilpatrick reined in briefly to let Dahlgren's men go on ahead. The troopers were in high spirits, and they were in enemy country, and they reflected that the five days' rations issued to them did not include any meat, which indicated that they were expected to forage liberally on pasture and farmhouse. A Pennsylvania regiment came down a country road, and in a farmyard there was an old woman with a flock of geese, and it amused the soldiers to ride into the flock, sabers swinging, to see how they might decapitate the long-necked birds without dismounting or coming to a halt. The woman seized a broom and fought with them in frantic despair, and the men shouted and guffawed as they dodged her blows, and they advised her that "the Yanks are hell on poultry." At last all of the geese were killed, and the woman slammed the gate of her front-yard fence and screamed the protest of the defenseless civilian who lay in the path of war—"You 'uns are nothing but dirty nasty Yankees after all!"[11]

The column rode on, collecting foodstuffs as it rode, and a staff officer went through the regiments announcing that the Rebels had no troops in Richmond, no one but government clerks and bookkeepers to bar the way. It was a fine bright day and a pleasant war, and the march went on unbroken except for a very short breather now and then. But during the afternoon the sky grew cloudy, and when dusk came there was a cold, gusty wind driving icy rain into the men's faces. Twenty-four hours in the saddle, and no rest in sight, and the war began to look a little less like a rowdy picnic; and they came to Beaver Dam Station after dark, and while the rain turned to sleet, freezing on overcoats and scabbards and carbine barrels, the men set fire to station and freight house and box-cars and outbuildings, cavorting madly about their bonfire, pleased that they were laying a heavy hand on the republic's enemies, making strange prancing silhouettes against the red flames in the smoky night. Then they went on again, leaving their fires as a great meaningless beacon, and they followed narrow roads in Egyptian darkness, and men in the outside files lost their caps to the low branches of unseen overarching trees.

Dahlgren and his party were off to the west somewhere, presumably, making for the James River crossing, and from time to time a signal corps officer who was riding with Kilpatrick turned aside to send up a rocket as a signal to the detached party. The rockets sputtered and climbed the wet black sky and went out, futile signals from nowhere to nobody, and there was no way to tell where Dahlgren was or whether he ever saw them. The blind column went on and on, everbody cold and soaked and exhausted.

There were Rebel skirmishers adrift somewhere in the night, and at intervals these spattered the column with bursts of fire, carbine flashes winking ominously in the surrounding blackness. Up ahead there were parties cutting down trees to obstruct the road, and the progress of the column became a maddening succession of confused stops and blind gallops—sudden traffic jams as the regiments jangled to an unexpected halt, men swaying in their saddles with fatigue or clumping heavily to the ground to rest their horses, then going on again at top speed to catch up with the rest, and it began to be possible to see why the young general was known as Kill Cavalry. Horses foundered, and some of the troopers had to plod along on foot, carrying their saddles, getting help by clinging to a comrade's stirrup. The storm grew worse and no one could see anything, and whether a man collided with a tree or with his neighbor was entirely up to his horse.[12]

Sometime during the night there was a brief, unsatisfactory halt for rest. Then the column moved on, having more brushes with Confederate bushwhackers, and a gray cheerless dawn came in; and at last, around midmorning of Tuesday, March 1, the men came out on the Brook Pike within five miles of Richmond. Up ahead were the permanent fortifications of the capital, and by all information these could be held only by militia, and Kilpatrick flung out a dismounted skirmish line, brought up his six field guns, and prepared for his big moment.

Yet the war that morning seemed to be full of evil omens, and there was no way to tell where Dahlgren was. According to the plan, he should at this moment be in Richmond, followed by a multitude of released prisoners of war, and Kilpatrick opened with his guns to let Dahlgren know that the main body was where it was supposed to be. But there came no answering sign from Dahlgren. Instead there were Confederate guns which opened a brisk fire, and from somewhere Kilpatrick heard, vaguely, that veterans from Lee's army had entered the lines, and it began to seem to him that he was in trouble.

The skirmishers crept forward, peppering the Rebel lines and getting peppered in return. Kilpatrick rode to the front, and a soldier heard him complain: "They have too many of those damned guns; they keep opening new ones on us all the time." What had begun as the prelude to a smashing attack slipped imperceptibly into a sparring match, with everybody waiting hopefully for some indication that Dahlgren had got into Richmond and would presently get out again. But the gray skies and the bleak countryside gave no sign. The Confederate trenches lay half a mile away across a level plain, the fields heavy with cold mud, chilly mist, and smoke lying low over all. The Rebel fire grew stronger, and the day dragged on toward evening.

Kilpatrick had imagined this expedition, he had pulled wires to get it approved and to win command of it, and now he and his division were here at the gate of Richmond, and his advance guard was lost off beyond the smoky flats and someone a good deal tougher than government clerks seemed to be manning the Rebel guns. The quick victorious assault that had looked so possible back at Brandy Station seemed now an effort too great for worn-out unaided cavalrymen to make. At last the weight of responsibility was too much, and at dark—feeling that an attempt to enter the city at that point would but end in bloody failure"—Kilpatrick called in his skirmishers, wheeled his command about, and headed back to the north side of the Chickahominy River. There, beyond the Meadow Bridge, the command went into bivouac.[13]

The bivouac was not a success, although the expedition had been without sleep for sixty hours. The men had no shelter tents, and the weather grew much worse. One trooper recalled their woes, in a breathless expressive sentence: "A more dreary, dismal night it would be difficult to imagine, with rain, snow, sleet, mud, cold and wet to the skin, rain and snow falling rapidly, the roads a puddle of mud, and the night as dark as pitch." He added that it was impossible to build fires to cook food, and anyway all of the poultry that had been taken so blithely had long since been consumed.

Late in the evening Kilpatrick partially recovered his grip on himself and determined to make one more try. He ordered two columns formed for a dash up the Mechanicsville Pike, but it took time to get exhausted men and horses into line in the consuming storm, and before the columns were half ready a swarm of Confederate cavalry—no militia, now, Wade Hampton's veterans from Lee's army—came pelting in through the slush and opened a heavy fire. Hampton had brought two fieldpieces with him, and these slammed case shot in at destructive range, and befogged soldiers found the inky woods full of flashes of fire and angry yells of "Git, you damned Yankees!" and there was great confusion and much shouting and fruitless cursing.[14]

In the end the attack was beaten off, but this clearly was no place to make a camp, and the troopers got on their horses again and went squelching off through the mud, with scattered Confederates following to prick them along with rifle fire from the dark. Finally, long after daybreak, the outfit made another camp some miles away from Richmond, and while the men got what sleep they could Kilpatrick waited for news of the missing Dahlgren.

He got it, late that day, when some 300 of Dahlgren's men came stumbling into camp, without Dahlgren. Their story made Kilpatrick no happier.

Dahlgren's 500 had got down to the James River on schedule, burning sundry gristmills and canal boats on the way, and they stopped briefly at a plantation owned by James A. Seddon, the cadaverous-looking aristocrat who was Secretary of War in President Davis's cabinet. Dahlgren went up to the big house, full of boyish charm and abundantly living the part of the dashing romantic cavalryman, and he found that Secretary Seddon was not at home. Mrs. Seddon was, however, and Dahlgren charmed her, and they sat in her drawing room and chatted. When he identified himself she confided, prettily, that his father the admiral had been a beau of hers, back in the old days, and now she and the admiral's son sat there and pledged each other in blackberry wine out of silver goblets, and apparently for the young man and the older woman the war narrowed to the misty focus of something by Sir Walter Scott. Then Dahlgren took his leave, very knightly and courtly, and he rode down to the river to make his crossing.[15]

At the river bank the knightly pose vanished. Earlier in the day Dahlgren had picked up a young colored man, held in servitude on some looted plantation, and this man had said that he knew where and how the James River could be forded, and he had been the guide who led the party to this spot. But when the cavalcade came jingling down to the river bank at the place the guide had chosen, the water was deep and wicked-looking, swollen by rains and clearly not to be crossed save in boats, of which the cavalry had none. There was sudden wrath, a cry of treachery, and Dahlgren decided—apparently rather hastily, but a raider as deep in enemy territory as he was would hardly take a judicial view of things—that the guide had maliciously misled him. He immediately ordered the lad hanged to the nearest tree.

One can picture the business, after all these years: stern young colonel, coldly furious at this mischance breaking in on his bright dream of glory, befuddled guide, staring blankly at a river all black and foaming where normally a man could wade across; expectant staff, seeing death in the young colonel's eyes and whipping a picket rope from the nearest saddle; oak tree with convenient branch overhanging the bank, quick flurry of movement and smothered cry of protest, tanned hard faces looking on expressionless—and then the finished deed, inert body dangling at the end of a taut cord, and the law of war is hard and there is more to a cavalry raid than laughing troopers splashing through the shallows in winter moonlight, more to it even than a bright young colonel drinking a toast to his father's old-time sweetheart with purple wine reflecting candleshine in a silver cup. Some echo of the colonel's anger seems to have reached the lower echelons, because the troopers went back and burned Secretary Seddon's barns.[16]

Unable to cross the river, Dahlgren and his men went trotting toward Richmond on the north side, things vaguely going wrong and the shadow of disaster rising on the cold dark sky. Far ahead they heard Kilpatrick's guns, and toward evening they got up close to the city's defenses. But it was too late now; Kilpatrick had seen too many Rebel guns and had retreated, the Confederates in Richmond were waiting for them, and Dahlgren was in a desperately bad spot—cut off from the main body, men and horses ready to drop, the whole country roused against him, safety many miles away.

Dahlgren did his best to get his men out of it. He rode at the head of the column, and he got the command away from Richmond and north of the Chickahominy in a driving sleet storm, and it seemed as if all the soldiers in the Confederacy were buzzing around like hornets to sting the invaders to death. For a time the command had to fight its way along the road—miserable fighting in the dark, nothing to be seen but a ragged line of fire as unseen infantry assailed the outriders, quick spat-splash of flying hoofs as the troopers charged up the road, jeering taunts from the fields as the Rebels slipped away—with the whole business repeated, as likely as not, a quarter of a mile farther on.

Somehow, in the night and the storm and the weird intermittent firing, Dahlgren's column broke in half, the separated halves losing touch and stumbling on as best they could. The 300 who had just come in to Kilpatrick's camp constituted one of these halves. The other half, with which Dahlgren himself had been riding, had vanished, and these survivors had no notion where it was or what had happened to it.[17]

Only one thing was clear, to Kilpatrick and to everyone else: the whole expedition was a flat failure, and there was nothing for it but to ride down the Virginia peninsula and get within Ben Butler's lines before disaster became absolute. This, at length, Kilpatrick did, and in the course of the next few days he learned about what had happened with Dahlgren.

Followed by some 200 troopers, Dahlgren had struck off for the northeast. All handicaps considered, his party made good progress, achieving a spectacular crossing of the Mattapony River, with Dahlgren remaining on the southern shore in personal command of the rear guard, firing his revolver at Rebel pursuers, while men and horses ferried themselves across on some scows they had found. Dahlgren crossed last of all, moved up to the head of the column, and resumed the march. But the state was aroused, and the march was not unlike the British retreat from Lexington and Concord, with every bush, barn, and tree seemingly sheltering a Confederate sniper.

The final catastrophe came at night. A body of Virginia cavalry had got around in front of the Dahlgren party, and these men and some home guards and embattled-farmer types laid an ambush in a forest. Dahlgren came along with his men trailing out behind him, his revolver in his hand, and in the blackness beside the road he heard men moving. He raised his weapon and shouted his challenge: "Surrender, you damned Rebels, or I'll shoot you!" For answer there was a heavy volley from encircling foes. Dahlgren fell from his horse, dead, with four bullets in him, and his command dissolved in a bewildering sequence of shots, cries, confused riding, and hand-to-hand grapplings. Most of the men who were not killed outright were quickly run down and captured.[18]

So that was that, and the raid was over. For achievements, the men could count a number of barns, flour mills, railroad buildings, and freight cars burned, and some incidental waste and ravage on a good many farms—there had been, for instance, the demonstration that an agile mounted man could behead a goose with his saber. Also, thousands of copies of the amnesty proclamation had been thrust into the hands of dazed bystanders, left in homes and shops and churches, stowed away in books on the shelves of manor houses, and generally left lying about so that any Confederate who felt like coming back into the Union might learn the terms on which his return could be negotiated. All of this, whatever it might amount to, had been done at minor cost, as such things were figured: one promising young cavalry colonel, 340 of other ranks, and about a thousand horses, plus some damage to prestige.

A fizzle, in other words, worth no more than a passing glance—except that the war had changed, and something hard and cruel and vicious was coming to the surface, and this raid was a dark ominous symbol of it, with bitterness and hatred visible behind it and growing out of it.

The men who killed Colonel Dahlgren (he himself had thought there was no better place to give up the ghost) had not been kind to his body. Someone had cut off a finger to get a ring he was wearing. Another took his artificial leg as a souvenir. Others got his watch, additional valuables, and his clothing. His body itself was carted off to Richmond in a pine box without a lid, and it went on display in a railroad station there, a show for the curious. And someone also took from his pockets the papers on which he had written down the objects of the expedition, and these papers seem to have been tampered with, so that they finally appeared to prove that his principal aim had been to burn and sack the city of Richmond and to murder Jefferson Davis and all his Cabinet; and these papers were openly published, to put a ramrod in the spine of Secession.

Braxton Bragg, chief military adviser to President Davis, forwarded them with an endorsement denouncing "the fiendish and atrocious conduct of our enemies," and Secretary of War Seddon sent them on to Lee, suggesting that since arson and assassination had been on the agenda the Yankees taken prisoner from Dahlgren's command ought to be hanged. Lee himself, who had sanity enough for three or four cabinet officers, agreed the papers were atrocious, but he doubted that executing the prisoners would help much. After all, he remarked, the projected murder and rapine had not actually taken place, the validity of the papers was in some question, and anyway the Federals held certain Confederate raiders who had looted a train along the upper Potomac and were considering accusing these men of plain highway robbery—and altogether if the business of hanging prisoners were started no one could be sure just how it would end. Lee sent the papers on to Meade under a flag of truce, with a note asking, in effect: Is this the kind of war you are going to be fighting from now on, and if so how about it?[19]

A sensation, indubitably: possibly offsetting the effect of Mr. Lincoln's offer of amnesty and brotherhood. Kilpatrick reported bitterly that the Confederates had used bloodhounds to hunt down fugitives from Dahlgren's scattered command, Northern publicists fumed and foamed over the mutilation of Dahlgren's corpse, and the old admiral wrote to General Butler to say that he would appreciate it if, by any flag of truce negotiations, the body could be recovered and brought north for decent burial. Meade wrote to Lee that neither President Lincoln, he himself, nor General Kilpatrick had ordered any cities burned or civilians killed, and a Richmond newspaper acidly commented that the chief casualty of the expedition had actually been "a boy named Martin, the property of Mr. David Meems, of Goochland"—he whom Dahlgren had incontinently hanged for leading him to a ford that was not a ford.

The newspapers had a field day. The Richmond *Examiner* urged its readers to realize that "we are barbarians in the eyes of our enemies," and called for reprisals, saying that the war now was "a war of extermination, of indiscriminate slaughter and plunder on the part of our enemies." The editor dilated on the wickedness of the Yankee design of "turning loose some thousands of ruffian prisoners, brutalized to the deepest degree by acquaintance with every horror of war, who have been confined on an island for a year, far from all means of indulging their strong sensual appetites—inviting this pandemonium to work their will on the unarmed citizens, on the women, gentle and simple, of Richmond, and on all their property." The New York *Times,* in its turn, exulted that the expedition had at least destroyed millions of dollars in Rebel property, and spoke zestfully of what the raiders had seen in war-racked Virginia—"the large number of dilapidated and deserted dwellings, the ruined churches with windows out and doors ajar, the abandoned fields and work shops, the neglected plantations." It mentioned Martin, the luckless colored guide, as a man who "dared to trifle with the welfare of his country" and it approved his hanging as "a fate he so richly deserved."[20]

So in both North and South there was fury, and the propagandists righteously sowed the wind, and the war between the sections, which once seemed almost like a kind of tournament, had at last hardened into the pattern of total war.

Kilpatrick's cavalry got back to the Army of the Potomac, after a time, taking ship from Fortress Monroe and debarking at Alexandria. The men were supposed to have a few days of relaxation at the Alexandria rest camp, but there was an unfortunate incident. Alexandria was policed by colored troops just then, and the cavalry of this army had no use for Negroes in uniform, and one of the colored guards halted a Michigan trooper to enforce the rule that none but couriers, orderlies, and other persons on duty were permitted to ride through the town's streets. The Michigan soldier drew his saber and killed the man, on the spot, and punishment followed quickly: the whole command had to march back to its camp on the Rapidan at once, without a chance to rest or to draw new clothing.[21]

2.   TURKEY AT A SHOOTING MATCH

The army had always been impatient of restraint, and even in its early days a provost guard which tried to arrest dashing cavalrymen had to make a certain allowance for breakage. Yet provost guards had not hitherto been cut down with sabers; nor had they ever before been men with black skins, recently elevated from property to manhood, wearing the national uniform and empowered to enforce the national will. The army was dubious about it. (A colored sergent, about this time, given an argument by an unruly private, leaned forward and tapped the chevrons on the sleeve. "You know what dat mean?" he demanded sternly. "Dat mean *guv'-ment!*")[1]

The colored man had been part of the war from the beginning, to be sure, but in the old days nobody had to spend much time thinking about him. He was just Uncle Tom, or a blackface minstrel with a talent for slow humor, or a docile contraband who could be made to do chores for soldiers. If he was none of these things he was a mystery, and figuring him out might bring a headache.

A New York cavalryman remembered that back in 1862 he and a comrade made friends with a free colored man, an aged Negro called Uncle Jake, who had a log cabin not far from their Virginia camp, and one day the old man asked the two soldiers to come to dinner. They went, and found themselves in a neat little room with a dirt floor, dinner cooking at the fireplace, table set for two. They had never imagined a dinner at which host and hostess stood by and ate nothing while the guests sat and ate, so they insisted that Uncle Jake and his wife draw up chairs and dine with them. Uncle Jake flatly refused, and he appears to have been slightly scandalized. Never in his eighty years, he said, had he heard of a Negro sitting at table with a white man, and all of their entreaties would not move him. So the soldiers ate the dinner—a good dinner, the cavalryman recalled, with roast possum as the main course—and went away, puzzled and ill at ease about the queer line drawn between host and guest.[2]

But that had been in the early days. Nothing in all the world was the same now as it used to be—not the war, nor the army, nor for that matter the colored man himself. He was coming out of the shadows and a new part was being prepared for him, and although the army did not like the transformation it was nevertheless the army which had brought it to pass. For the army had created a myth and the myth held a kernel of truth, and no cruel misuse of sword or noose would quite kill it.

The myth rode with Custer's men, as they came sloping back from their stab at Charlottesville—rain frozen on weapons and uniforms, saddles creaking with ice, trees along the way all silver with frozen sleet, tinkling when the branches moved. They found themselves at the head of a strange procession. As they went along the Virginia roads their bugles sounded down the wind like the trumpets of jubilee, and the slaves laid down their burdens and came out by the scores to follow. Before long the cavalrymen were leading an outlandish tatterdemalion parade of refugees, men and women and helpless children, people jubilant and bewildered and wholly defenseless, their eyes on the north star.

Some of these had carts and wagons, some of them rode on mules or oxen, and some stumped along on foot, carrying their few possessions. They took their place just ahead of the rear guard, and in the struggle to keep up they endured great hardships. When the Confederates assailed the retreating Yankees, Custer's officers would ride through, shouting and pleading and threatening, and there was general bedlam—bullets in the air, crying children, livestock grown either panicky or balky, creating fearful knots and tangles in the traffic, troopers swearing and women screaming, weaklings here and there falling out by the roadside and watching in despair as the column moved on without them. When they were not storming with rage the troopers were braying with laughter. It struck them as very funny to see a desperately frightened Negro riding a runaway mule, holding onto one of its ears with one hand and its tail with the other. Despite all difficulties most of the refugees kept going, and as they plodded along in the cold rain and mud one of the soldiers felt that the Union Army was "the representative to them of the great idea of freedom."[3]

For that was the myth that this army had created, and it had vitality, and it went like a bent flame down plantation roads and country lanes. When Kilpatrick's division crossed from Richmond to Butler's lines the colored folk greeted it with ecstasy, and the raid that accomplished so little was a light across the sky to many hundreds of people. As the division passed one big plantation house, forty or fifty slaves crowded down to the road to watch. A young woman suddenly sprang up on the fence, waving her sunbonnet and crying: "Glory! Glory hallelujah! I'se gwine wid you! I'se gwine to be free!"

The whole crowd came surging out in a moment, and Old Marster was running down from his veranda shouting fruitless threats, a helpless Canute berating an unheeding tide.[4] The scene was repeated, with variations, over and over, until presently the cavalrymen were surrounded and followed by thousands of slaves whom no one any longer owned and for whom no one in particular was likely to be responsible: a devoted shuffling multitude, men and women carrying bundles, tiny children trudging along big-eyed, gray-haired old folk leaning on canes, scores and hundreds of people coming out of the past into the unknown.

All of this was stimulating to tired soldiers, for it was pleasant to be hosannahed and wept over as bringers of freedom. But finally the men got to New Kent Court House, and there for the first time the cavalry saw colored soldiers—some of Ben Butler's men, trim and neatly uniformed, lining the roadside to greet the cavalry, cheering wildly as the head of the column came up, white eyes a chalkline in a long row of black faces. Cavalry returned the cheers, and one trooper wrote that "a mountain of prejudice was removed in an instant." Yet somehow there was a catch in it, and prejudice had not been removed so far that it could not quickly return. Late that night it began to rain again, and Kilpatrick's men were making a sodden bivouac without shelter, and they suddenly realized that these colored soldiers occupied a warm dry camp with wall tents standing. So along toward midnight the cavalry attacked the camp, driving the colored soldiers out into the cold with blows and angry words and taking the tents for themselves, and there was no further exchange of cheers.[5]

The soldiers were not the same men they had been three years ago, and they dimly realized the fact. An Ohio soldier looked back wistfully to the time when they had all been recruits, with knowledge ahead of them—to "those happy, golden days of camp life," when each regiment eagerly awaited its marching orders and the only worry was the haunting fear that the war might end before a man got his fair chance to fight.[6] In those days there was a great difference between regiment and regiment, and between man and man. Western regiments derisively yelled, "Paper collars!" at Eastern regiments, which they considered dressed up and dudish, and the Easterners retorted that the Westerners were uncouth backwoodsmen. The city man looked and acted unlike the man from the country, and even a casual glance would show the difference between Hoosier and Ohioan, between Pennsylvanian and down-East Yankee. Now the distinctions were gone, and all of the volunteers looked very much alike. An officer in a Maine regiment mused that the army was a great leveler, and he wrote how "rich men and poor, Christians from pious back-country homes and heathen bounty-jumpers from the slums of New York . . . would bathe in and drink from the same stream, whether prior or subsequent to the watering of the brigade mules."[7]

The army had put its stamp on all of its infinitely various members. It had produced a type, at last, and the volunteer had become the old-timer—rusty in a worn uniform, wearing his forage cap with its broken visor tugged down over his eyes, tolerant of high authority but not especially respectful toward it (one fussy brigadier was greeted on all sides as "Old Bowels"), taking eventual triumph for granted, but fully aware that he himself was the man who was going to pay for it.

Yet to say all of that is merely to say that the army had done to its members what armies always do to recruits. The men had changed and that was that, and if the gates of Eden had swung shut nothing had happened that does not happen to everyone sooner or later. But along with all of this, something had happened to the army itself. Once it had reflected what was left of frontier democracy, loose-jointed and informal, bound together by a sharing of traditions and ideals. Now it was becoming professional, and the binder was beginning to look like cold force. Old relationships had shifted, and the typical army campfire was no longer a little glow in the dark lighting the bronzed faces of sentimentalists singing sad little songs. Army life had an edge to it now. The word "comrade" was ceasing to be all inclusive, and because that was so the gap between officer and man was ominously widening.

In the beginning this gap had not been very impressive. Most of the men had known their company and regimental commanders before the war. They had been neighbors then and they expected to be neighbors again, and although they were willing to obey any orders which seemed to be sensible they saw no reason for anyone to be stuffy about it. Government was mostly by consent of the governed and discipline was casual and haphazard, which sometimes led to odd happenings on the march and in battle. It was getting ever so much tighter and sterner now, partly because loose discipline irked the army command but chiefly because the situation in which the loose discipline of a volunteer army could be tolerated no longer existed.

Except for the old-timers, the Army of the Potomac was not really a volunteer army any more, and it could not be conducted as one. The men who were coming into the ranks now were for the most part either men who had been made to come or men who had been paid to come. The former—the out-and-out conscripts—sometimes made good soldiers, for their principal shortcoming (aside from a certain reluctance to volunteer) was poverty; a draftee with money could either hire a substitute and so gain permanent exemption, or pay a $300 commutation fee and at least win exemption until his name came up in some new draft call. Unfortunately, however, not many of the new recruits were conscripts. Most of them were men who had joined up only because they got a good deal of money for doing it, and in the great majority of cases these men were worse than useless.

The number of men to be drafted in any state, city, or county always depended on the number that had previously volunteered. If many had volunteered, few or none would be drafted. Since nobody liked the draft, it was to everbody's interest to promote volunteering, and this was done principally by the payment of cash bounties. By the winter of 1864 these were running very high. States, cities, and towns were bidding against each other—some were almost bankrupting themselves in the process—and the drafted man who wanted to hire a substitute was bidding against all three. The results were fantastic. The provision by which a drafted man could buy his way out of the service was a remarkably effective device for making young men cynical about appeals to their patriotism. When it went hand in hand with a system of bounties which often ran as high as a thousand dollars per enlistment, there was in operation an almost foolproof system for getting the wrong kind of men into uniform.[8]

This system had created the institution of the substitute broker—the man who for a fee would find potential soldiers and induce them to enlist. Some of these brokers may have been relatively honest, although there is nothing in any contemporary accounts to make one think so, but for the most part they seem to have inspired army authorities to some of the most glowing invective in Civil War annals. At times they operated precisely as waterfront crimps operated, making their victims drunk, getting them to sign away their bounty rights, and then rushing them through the enlistment process before they recovered. Now and then an authentic deep-sea sailor, congenitally disposed to being shanghaied, got caught in this net. Such men, when they came to, usually made the best of things and went on to become good soldiers.[9]

Most of the time the broker did not need to go to the trouble of drugging anybody. It was simpler to dredge in the backwaters of city slums and find human derelicts who, for a little cash in hand, would willingly assign their bounty rights and go and enlist. Hardly any of these men were physically fit to be soldiers, but the broker made such enormous profits that he could usually afford any bribery that might be necessary to get them past the examiners. Horrified medical officers in the Army of the Potomac were finding that new lots of recruits often included hopeless cripples, lunatics, and men far along in incurable disease. Of fifty-seven recruits received that winter by the 6th New York Heavy Artillery, seventeen were so completely disabled that even a layman could see it—some, for instance, had but one hand, and a few were out-and-out idiots. Of recruits received by the cavalry corps in March, 32 per cent were on the sick list when they reached camp.

A Federal enrollment officer in Illinois wrote that the substitute broker's business was conducted "with a degree of unprincipled recklessness and profligacy unparalleled in the annals of corruption and fraud." Rising to genuine eloquence in his indignation, he protested that it put the uniform "upon branded felons; upon blotched and bloated libertines and pimps; upon thieves, burglars and vagabonds; upon the riff-raff of corruption and scoundrelism of every shade and degree of infamy which can be swept into the insatiable clutches of the vampires who fatten upon the profits of the execrable business."

Helpless immigrants speaking no word of English, some still wearing their wooden shoes, were swept up from the docks at seaports and hustled off to the recruiting officers. A veteran in a Massachusetts regiment said scornfully that more than half of one draft of recruits his regiment got that winter came in under assumed names, and that most of these men forgot what names they had used and were unable to answer at roll call. He remembered that the last set of recruits in whom the regiment felt any pride was a detail that came to camp in the fall of 1862.[10]

Even worse than the gangs sent in by the brokers, however, were the professional bounty-jumpers. These often were out-and-out criminals, who had found that their familiar arts of burglary, highway robbery, and pocket-picking were much more laborious and less rewarding than the racket which was made possible by the high-bounty system. They made a business of enlisting, collecting a bounty, deserting at the first chance, enlisting somewhere else for another bounty, deserting again, and keeping it up as long as they could get away with it. Since the authorities never solved the problem of checking desertion, they were usually able to get away with it about as long as they wanted to keep on trying, and if a few of them were caught and executed now and then the hazards of the profession were, on the whole, no worse than the risks they normally ran with the police.

These men brought into the Army of the Potomac an element the army had never had before, and of which it could not possibly make the slightest use. In camp they were valueless, and early in 1864 the army command stipulated that no bounty men could be used on picket or outpost duty. "If those fellows are trusted on picket," remarked one veteran, "the army will soon be in hell."[11] The mere business of guarding them to see that they did not desert or plunder their honest comrades took time and effort that should have been used in other ways. In battle they were a positive handicap. Under no circumstances could they be induced to fight. If by tireless effort a regiment succeeded in getting any of them up to the firing line they would immediately desert to the enemy, and their utter unreliability made any regiment which had them in its ranks weaker than it would have been if it had received no recruits at all.

A New Hampshire soldier reported indignantly that "such another depraved, vice-hardened and desperate set of human beings never before disgraced an army," and he pointed out how the bounty-jumpers and substitutes, simply by their presence in camp, corrupted the relationship between officers and men in the veteran regiments:

"Before their advent, common toil, hardship and danger, for months and years, had made them a band of brothers. Between the officers and men there existed the most perfect confidence and friendship. Punishment was uncalled for, as disobedience, demanding it, was unknown; and camp guard had long been a thing of the past. The men came and went almost at their pleasure."

But as the new men came in this idyllic situation changed:

"No pleasure or privilege for the boys in camp any more, for the hard lines and severe discipline of military necessity apply with a rigidness never before applied."[12]

A Connecticut soldier called the 300 recruits his regiment got that winter "the most thorough-paced villians that the stews of New York and Baltimore could furnish—bounty jumpers, thieves and cut-throats, who had deserted from regiment after regiment in which they had enlisted under fictitious names, and who now proposed to repeat the operation. And they *did* repeat it." Two hundred and fifty of the 300, he said, ran away within a few weeks.[13]

In three years of war the soldiers of the Army of the Potomac had seen many things, but they had never seen anything like the habits and morals of these new comrades in arms. One veteran remembered listening, dumfounded, to the tales the new men told: "They never tired of relating the mysterious uses to which a 'jimmy' could be put by a man of nerve, and how easy it was to crack a bank or filch a purse. They robbed each other as freely as they did others. We noticed on their arrival that nearly every man had his pocket cut."

The bounty-jumpers had plenty of money, and when they were not picking one another's pockets they spent their spare time gambling. Poker had always been a favorite diversion of the private soldier, but the games that developed now were played for huge stakes, with professional cardsharps sitting in: "Thousands of dollars would change hands in one day's playing, and there were many ugly fights indulged in, caused by their cheating each other at cards." A man in the 13th Massachusetts wrote indignantly:

"We often talked over, among ourselves, this business of filling up a decent regiment with the outscourings of humanity; but the more we thought of it, the more discontented we became. We longed for a quiet night, and when day came we longed to be away from these ruffians."[14]

Some of the new men found army life pleasant—three meals a day, lodging taken care of, plenty of chance to loaf—and instead of deserting they became old soldiers, in the traditional army meaning of the term, pretending to be sick or disabled so that they could avoid drill and take their ease in the hospital tents. Some claimed to have rheumatism so badly that they could not bend their knees. The doctors would chloroform such men, and while they were unconscious would manipulate their legs. If this indicated that nothing was actually wrong, the men when they came out from under the anesthetic would be sent back to camp on foot, guards walking close behind ready to jab them with bayonets if they faltered. An Illinois soldier recalled a man who spent weeks in hospital, insisting that one of his hip joints was crippled by some obscure malady. In desperation the hospital stewards one day strapped him to his cot and applied red-hot pokers to the hip. After the third application the man cried out in pain and admitted that he had been shamming. He was allowed to stay in hospital until the burns healed and then was sent back to duty.[15]

An immense amount of work was required by the mere task of getting the new recruits from the enlistment centers to the army camps. Details of veterans were sent north to do guard duty at the recruit camps, and they quickly found that nothing but prison discipline would do.

In Boston Harbor there was an island on which new recruits were housed, uniformed, given some rudiments of drill, and assigned to different regiments. Men from the 22nd Massachusetts were sent up to guard this camp, and they found the work irksome. Day and night, every foot of the island's shore had to be patrolled to foil desertion. The shore was rocky and in winter the rocks were icy, and sentinels slipped and fell and wished fervently that they were back along the Rapidan. One man wrote fondly: "Large portions of Virginia are absolutely free from rocks." The veterans guarded the steamers which brought recruits to the island, and at the wharf they had to search all of the new men as they came ashore, seeing to it that no liquor or weapons were smuggled into camp. They took each recruit's money from him and deposited it with the provost marshal's clerk, for delivery when the man finally reached his regiment. It was held unwise to let the men have any money while they were on the island, for fear they would bribe their way to freedom.

One of the men who performed this guard duty wrote that "Some of the most noted, hardened and desperate villains in this country" were to be found among the recruits, and he said that to smuggle money past the guards these men would hide hundred-dollar bills in anything from hollow coat buttons to the inside of their ears.[16] A soldier who guarded a similar rendezvous at Riker's Island, New York, wrote: "As for the conscripts, they were unspeakable," and asserted that many of them had to wear the ball and chain while they were waiting for assignment to combat regiments. An artillerist from the IX Corps, guarding replacements at a camp in Kentucky, wrote that he and his fellows "preferred to go into an engagement with the enemy rather than guard such a rabble," and a New Hampshire veteran who guarded recruits at Point Lookout, Maryland, said that "there were many desperate and dangerous criminals among them who would not hesitate to commit any crime that passion avarice or revenge might incite them to." He remembered with glee one group of six which got hold of a rowboat and tried to escape in it. For punishment, four of the men were compelled to carry the rowboat around camp all day long, while their two fellows sat in it and industriously rowed in the empty air.[17]

A steamship transporting these recruits from New York or Boston to Virginia was usually a floating bedlam. The steamer's civilian crew, more often than not, would be in league with the bounty-jumpers, and sometimes the officers likewise had been bribed, and whisky would be hidden in coal bunkers, in staterooms, and in odd corners below decks. Winter storms being common, hatches were usually battened down as soon as the vessel sailed, and the hold was jammed with desperate unwashed men, most of them seasick and the rest of them drunk, high-stake card games going on in the smoking light of swaying lanterns, bitter fights taking place as the more defenseless recruits were openly robbed. Some fairly important money would be involved, on these trips; a draft of a few hundred men each carrying his bounty might easily have a quarter of a million dollars in cash in its collective possession. Sometimes a group of these replacements would try to mutiny, and then the veterans with loaded muskets and fixed bayonets would go into action. When the steamers came up Chesapeake Bay or the Potomac, and land was not far away, men would spring from the decks to swim ashore, and at such times the guards would coolly fire, reload, and fire again until the swimmer sank out of sight in a little swirl of bloody water.[18]

Early in this winter of 1864 a teen-ager in upstate New York enlisted in a battery of field artillery—a veteran battery on duty in Virginia which had sent back for a few replacements—and to his amazement as soon as he had signed the papers he was put in a penitentiary building at Albany, the army having chosen this place as the only suitable depot for its new recruits. He found approximately a thousand draftees and bounty-jumpers there, closely guarded by double lines of sentinels, and he appears to have been about the only man in the lot who had joined up for love of country.

"If there was a man in all that shameless crew who had enlisted from patriotic motives, I did not see him," he wrote afterward. "There was not a man of them who was not eager to run away, not a man who did not quake when he thought of the front. Almost to a man they were bullies and cowards, and almost to a man they belonged to the criminal classes."

In due time orders came to send 600 of these men down to the Army of the Potomac. After roll call there was a frantic scurrying for cover. Some men cut open their straw mattresses and crept inside to hide. Others hid under bunks, or in latrines. One man was fished out of a huge garbage can in the mess hall, where he had burrowed down under coffee grounds and other oddments. He was kicked down a flight of stairs and prodded out to the parade ground with bayonets. When the detail at last was formed, an officer stepped out and announced that any man who tried to run away during the trip would be shot.

The officer's word was good. Three men were shot dead as the crowd marched through Albany to the steamboat wharf. Two more, who jumped from the steamer as it went down the Hudson, were shot in midstream. Four more were shot in New York, as the men were marched from one pier to another. After the steamer finally unloaded its consignment at Alexandria and the men were put on freight cars to go to the front, five men tried to escape from the moving train and were shot dead. All in all, the young recruit said that his associates were "as arrant a gang of cowards, thieves, murderers and blacklegs as were ever gathered inside the walls of Newgate or Sing Sing."[19]

Recruits like these helped to spoil some men who were already in the army and who might otherwise have behaved fairly well. Every regiment had its quota of scapegraces who were always on hand at mess call but who worked or fought only under compulsion. They tended to follow the lead of the worst elements in camp, and the worst elements now were about as bad as they could be. A veteran in one of Phil Kearny's old regiments left his own classification of the different varieties of worthless soldier to be found in the army:

I will explain here and make a few remarks about shirks, bummers, sneaks and thieves, all called camp followers. The first is a man that when the army comes up, and is expecting that every man will do his duty, now that we are ready to meet the enemy, he looks around to see if any of his comrades are watching him and *drops* to the rear—deserts his comrades in time of danger. He then becomes a bummer, and prowls around, and will do anything to keep himself away from danger in the ranks. He then becomes a sneak and tries to get an ambulance to drive, or 'sich.' After that he becomes the thief, and will steal from friend and foe alike, and is devoid of all principle. Reader, look around you, and see if there is such men in your midst. Shun them as you would a viper, and show to them that they are despised in private life by their neighbors as they were in the army by their comrades."[20]

There undoubtedly is exaggeration in some of these accounts. The old-timers in the Army of the Potomac disliked conscripts and utterly despised high-bounty men, and in writing about such people they were not likely to remember anything good about them if they could help it. Certainly the army that winter did get some recruits who made good soldiers. One veteran, admitting that the army as a whole was not as good as it had been a year earlier, asserted that the old battalions were still superb even when they had absorbed fairly large numbers of replacements. Some states sent down whole new regiments, and while these "high-number" regiments were never accounted the equals of the ones with lower numbers, which had enlisted in 1861 or 1862, several of them made excellent records. The Irish Brigade brought its five regiments up to full strength early in 1864, and it got fighters. Most of the IX Corps regiments filled their ranks during the winter—the corps had been serving in Tennessee, and when it was brought East the regiments were given a chance to go home and do their own recruiting—and the corps does not seem to have lost its old fighting quality with the transfusions. It would undoubtedly be a strong overstatement to say that all of the men brought in by draft and bounty were useless.[21]

Yet if there is exaggeration in the complaints there is not very much exaggeration. The testimony about the evils which the high bounty system caused is unanimous, and it comes from high officers as well as from private soldiers. The provost marshal general of the army, in a report written at the end of the war, said flatly that "the bounty was meant to be an inducement to enlistment; it became, in fact, an inducement to desertion and fraudulent re-enlistment." He pointed out that the states paying the highest bounties were precisely the ones with the largest proportion of deserters, and emphasized that desertions all through 1864 reached the astounding average of 7,300 each month. Not only was this a prodigious rise over all former figures; it meant that in the long run the army lost nearly as many men through desertion as it lost in battle casualties.[22]

For a long time the Confederate authorities made a distinction between Federal deserters who voluntarily came into their lines and soldiers who were captured in battle, and to the former they offered jobs in war plants and freedom from restraint. In the spring of 1864, however, they concluded that it was no go. The deserters were pure riff-raff, of no more use in a Richmond factory than in the Union Army, and one day the Richmond papers announced that henceforth all such would be locked up in prison camps along with soldiers taken in action. The colonel of a Connecticut regiment got a copy of a paper containing that announcement, and waved it happily in front of his men, declaring:

"The colonel commanding hopes that all the scoundrels who desire to desert to the enemy after swindling the government out of heavy bounties have already left us"; but in case a few still remained he would read the Confederate announcement, which he did, adding that a prospective deserter ought to realize that "neither army considers him fit to be trusted anywhere, or able to earn his living." Since prisoners of war were subject to exchange, the colonel reminded his men that deserters might some day find themselves back with their regiment. If that happened, he said, they would be shot.[23]

What all of this meant was that the Army of the Potomac had to take on Regular Army discipline. The Regulars were used to hard cases and knew how to handle them. In ordinary times a Regular regiment would expect to lose perhaps a fourth of its men through desertion, but it could turn the rest into fighters. Now the volunteer regiments were following suit, caste lines were hardening, and discipline was enforced by brutality.

The artillerists led the way. The volunteer batteries had always had more of a Regular Army flavor than the infantry regiments, possibly because in the early days General McClellan had taken pains to brigade one regular battery with every three batteries of volunteers, and the force of example had been strong. In any case, the gunners this winter were pounding their recruits into shape, hurting them with cold ferocity when they needed correction. Their favorite punishment centered around the fact that every artillery caisson carried a spare wheel, mounted at the rear of the caisson a couple of feet off the ground at a slight angle from the vertical. An insubordinate artillerist was made to step on the lower rim of this wheel, and then he was spread-eagled, wrists and ankles firmly lashed to the rim. This done, the wheel was given a quarter turn so that the man was in effect suspended by one wrist and one ankle. He would be left in this position for several hours, and if he cried out in pain—as he usually did, before long—a rough stick was tied in his mouth for a gag.

Even worse was being tied on the rack. At the rear end of every battery wagon was a heavy rack for forage—a stout wooden box, running across the end of the wagon and protruding a couple of feet back of the rear wheels. The man who was up for punishment was made to stand with his chest against this rack while his wrists were tied to the upper rims of the wheels. Then his feet were lifted and tied to the lower rims, so that he was left hanging with all of his weight pressing against the sharp wooden edge of the rack. He was always gagged first, because not even the toughest customer could stand this punishment without screaming. The man generally fainted after a few minutes of it, and some men were permanently disabled. One gunner recalled that men sentenced to the rack sometimes begged to be shot instead.[24]

The infantry had no spare wheels or forage racks, but it had its little ways. Commonest punishment was the "buck and gag." The erring soldier was made to sit on the ground, his knees drawn up to his chin and his hands clasped over his shins. After his wrists were bound together a heavy stick was thrust under his knees and over his arms, and a gag was tied in his mouth. He was then left to sit there for some hours, suffering no extreme of pain but utterly helpless and voiceless, enduring cramps, thirst, and the jibes of unfeeling soldiers. It was also found effective to tie a man by his thumbs to the branch of a tree, pulling him just high enough so that he could keep his thumbs from being torn out of joint only by standing on tiptoe.

In a way there was nothing new about all of this. Brutal punishments had always been on tap, but hitherto they had hardly amounted to more than the army's backhanded way of cuffing the ne'er-do-wells and misfits who had found their way into the ranks. Now the harshness was becoming central. An important number of soldiers responded to that sort of language, and therefore it was being addressed to all of the soldiers. There was a new tone to the army. The old spirit had been diluted and the old ways had changed. The veterans drew closer together, seeming almost to be aliens in the army which they themselves had created.

And the great danger now was that the veterans might presently get out of the army altogether and leave everything to the newcomers. Under the law they might do this, and nobody could stop them, and if that happened the war was lost forever, because conscripts and bounty men could not make Robert E. Lee's incomparable soldiers even pause to take a deep breath.

Federal regiments in the Civil War enlisted, usually, for three years. There had been a number of nine-month regiments, earlier, and some had come in to do a two-year hitch, but the three-year enlistment was the rule. Now the time was running out. The old 1861 regiments had just about finished their terms. In May and June and July and August they would come to the end of their enlistments, and under the law there was no way to compel their members to remain in service if they did not choose to remain.

Fighting was expected to begin in April or May. The prospect, therefore, was that just as the campaign got well under way the army would begin to fall apart. The army authorities could see this coming but there was nothing on earth they could do to keep it from happening except go to the veterans—hat in hand, so to speak—and beg them to re-enlist.

The big thing was to get them to re-enlist as regiments, and inducements were offered. If three fourths of the men in any regiment would re-enlist, the regiment could go home as a unit for a thirty-day furlough, and when it got back to camp it would keep its organization, its regimental number, its flag, and so on. In addition, the veterans would be cut in on some of this bounty money. Adding state and Federal bounties together, the average soldier who signed on for a second enlistment would get about $700, on which he might have quite a time for himself during that month's furlough. So the authorities put on a big campaign, and the old regiments were called together and cajoled and orated to, and the men observed that on such occasions a good deal of whisky seemed to be available for the thirsty.

Now the high command was talking to men who had had it.

The record of these three-year regiments contained the whole story of the war in the East, down to date—Bull Run and the Seven Days, Antietam and Fredericksburg, Chancellorsville and Gettysburg, plus the mean little skirmishes and minor battles in between, the hard marches in dust or mud, the dreary months in unsavory camps. Whatever there could possibly be in war to make a man say, "Never again!" these soldiers knew about it. There were in the North thousands upon thousands of young men who had had no part in the war, and the veterans knew all about them and knew that if they themselves re-enlisted these men would remain civilians, with every night in bed and nobody shooting at them. They knew, too, that the thousands of recruits who were coming in now were corrupting the army and giving it little of value. When the fighting began again the load would have to be carried by the old-timers, the men who had survived many terrible battles and whose numbers, by the mere law of averages, must be about due to come up. The veteran who was asked to re-enlist had a good many things to think about. A man in the 3rd Michigan wrote:

"After serving three years for our country cannot we go home, satisfied that we have done our share toward putting down the rebellion, and let those who stayed at home come and give their time as long; the country is as dear to them as us."

A man in the 25th Massachusetts noted that few of his comrades were signing up, and he spelled out his own feeling:

"I shall not re-enlist, and my reasons are, first, I have no desire to monopolize all the patriotism there is, but am willing to give others a chance. My second reason is that after I have served three years my duty to my country has been performed and my next duty is at home with my family."

A member of the 13th Massachusetts noted that his regiment "listened with respectful attention" while officers urged re-enlistment and extolled the valor of old soldiers, but he added: "It was very sweet to hear all this, but the 13th was not easily moved by this kind of talk. The boys knew too well what sacrifices they had made, and longed to get home again and, if possible, resume the places they had left." In the end the 13th refused to re-enlist, except for a handful who signed up for places in another regiment.[25]

Altogether, there are few facts in American history more remarkable than the fact that so many of these veterans did finally re-enlist—probably slightly more than half of the total number whose terms were expiring. The proffered bounty seems to have had little influence on them. The furlough was much better bait. To men who had not seen their homes for more than two and one half years, a solid month of freedom seemed like an age. A member of the 5th Maine said that it actually seemed as if the war might somehow end before the furloughs would expire, and he wrote of the men who re-enlisted: "What tempted these men? Bounty? No. The opportunity to go home."[26]

It was not hardship that held men back. The 100th Pennsylvania had been marooned in eastern Tennessee for months, cut off from supplies and subsisting on two ears of corn per day per man, but when the question of re-enlistment came up only 27 out of the 393 present for duty refused to sign. In the 6th Wisconsin, which had done as much costly fighting as any regiment in the army, it was noted that the combat men were re-enlisting almost to a man; it was the cooks, hostlers, clerks, teamsters, and others on non-combat duty who were holding back. And the dominant motive, finally, seems to have been a simple desire to see the job through. The government in its wisdom might be doing everything possible to show the men that patriotism was for fools; in the end, the veterans simply refused to believe it. A solid nucleus did sign the papers, pledging that the army would go on, and by the end of March Meade was able to tell the War Department that 26,767 veterans had re-enlisted.[27]

The men signed up without illusions. A company in the 19th Massachusetts was called together to talk things over. The regiment had left most of its men on various battlefields, in hospitals, and in Southern prison camps, and this company now mustered just thirteen men and one wounded officer. These considered the matter, and one man finally said: "They use a man here just the same as they do a turkey at a shooting match, fire at it all day and if they don't kill it raffle it off in the evening; so with us, if they can't kill you in three years they want you for three more—but I will stay." And a comrade spoke up: "Well, if new men won't finish the job, old men must, and as long as Uncle Sam wants a man, here is Ben Falls."

The regiment's historian, recording this remark, pointed out that Ben Falls was killed two months later in battle at Spotsylvania Court House.[28]

3. FROM A MOUNTAIN TOP

On the tenth day of March, 1864, Lieutenant General Ulysses S. Grant came down to meet General Meade and to have a look at the Army of the Potomac.

They made an occasion of it, and when Grant reached headquarters they turned out the guard. The guard included a Zouave outfit, 114th Pennsylvania, which had seen much hard fighting before the luck of the draw pulled it out of combat ranks and assigned it to headquarters, and it was natty with baggy red pants, white leggings, short blue jackets, and oriental-looking turbans. With the guard came the headquarters band, also of the 114th Pennsylvania; a melodious group, distinguished from most of the other army bands by the fact that all of the players were always sober when time came to make music. It had learned to play the kind of music Meade liked—something soft and sweet, usually—and it tootled away vigorously today, quite unaware that the lieutenant general was completely tone-deaf, disliked all music rather intensely, and could not for the life of him tell one tune from another.[1]

The meeting between Grant and Meade was brief. Meade suggested that it might suit the new general in chief if the commander of the Army of the Potomac quietly retired, and Grant quickly rejected the offer—and wrote that he was favorably impressed by the way it was made. Mostly, the two men seem to have spent their time sizing each other up, and each man liked what he saw. They would appear to have made an odd picture, standing together. Grant was five feet eight, stooped, unmilitary in his gait, with creased horizontal wrinkles across his brow giving him a faintly harassed look, and for once he was togged out in dress uniform, black sugar-loaf hat set squarely on his head, sash about his waist, straight sword of a general officer belted at his side. Meade was taller, skinny, and bearing something of a patrician air, harsh lines cutting down from the corners of his nose. He spoke of the army as "My people," and he wore a felt hat with peaked crown and turned-down brim which gave him a Tyrolean appearance.[2] They had their talk, and then the Zouaves presented arms and the band played ruffles and flourishes, and Grant went away. He came back, a little more than a fortnight later, and from that moment on, in spite of fact and logic, the army was known as "Grant's army."

Grant made his headquarters in a plain brick house near Culpeper Court House, with tents for his staff pitched in the yard, and he got down to work. He was commander of all of the armies of the United States—counting everything, he had twenty-one army corps and eighteen military departments under him, for a total of 533,000 soldiers—and he had a diversity of jobs to do, from winning the war down to keeping the politicians from running the Army of the Potomac, and he had very little time for small talk.[3]

Ulysses S. Grant was a natural—an unmistakable rural Middle Westerner, bearing somehow the air of the little farm and the empty dusty road and the small-town harness shop, plunked down here in an army predominantly officered by polished Easterners. He was slouchy, round-shouldered, a red bristly beard cropped short on his weathered face, with a look about the eyes of a man who had come way up from very far down; his one visible talent seemingly the ability to ride any horse anywhere under any conditions. These days, mostly, he rode a big bay horse named Cincinnati, and when he went out to look at the troops he set a pace no staff officer could match, slanting easily forward as if he and the horse had been made in one piece, and his following was generally trailed out behind him for a hundred yards, scabbards banging against the sides of lathered horses, the less military officers frantically grabbing hats and saddle leather as they tried to keep up.

Somewhere within the general in chief there hid the proud, shy little West Point graduate who put on the best uniform a brevet second lieutenant of infantry could wear when he went home to Ohio on furlough after graduation, and who got laughed at for a dude by livery-stable toughs, and who forever after preferred to wear the plain uniform of a private soldier, with officer's insignia stitched to the shoulders. He had three stars to put there now—more than any American soldier had worn except George Washington and Winfield Scott—

and he had little eccentricities. He breakfasted frequently on a cup of coffee and a cucumber sliced in vinegar, and if he ate meat it had to be cooked black, almost to a crisp: this author of much bloodshed detested the sight of blood, and was made queasy by the sight of red meat. When he prepared for his day's rounds he accepted from his servant two dozen cigars, which were stowed away in various pockets, and he carried a flint and steel lighter with a long wick, modern style, so that he could get a light in a high wind.

He received many letters asking for his autograph, but, he admitted, "I don't get as many as I did when I answered them." He was not without a quiet sense of humor; writing his memoirs, he told about the backwoods schools he went to as a boy, saying that he was taught so many times that "a noun is the name of a thing" that he finally came to believe it. As a man he was talkative but as a general he was closemouthed. When the crack VI Corps was paraded for him and officers asked him if he ever saw anything to equal it (hoping that he might confess that the Army of the Potomac was better drilled than Western troops, which was indeed the case) he remarked only that General So-and-so rode a very fine horse; the general in question, a brigade commander, having recently invested $500 in a fancy new saddle of which he was very proud.[4]

Nobody knew quite what to make of him, and judgments were tentative. One of Meade's staff officers commented that Grant's habitual expression was that of a man who had made up his mind to drive his head through a stone wall, and Uncle John Sedgwick, canniest and most deeply loved of all the army's higher officers, wrote to his sister that he had been "most agreeably disappointed" both with the general's looks and with his obvious common sense. (As it happened, "common sense" was the expression most often used when men tried to say why they liked Sedgwick so much.) Sedgwick was a little bit skeptical. He said that even though Grant impressed him well, it was doubtful whether he could really do much more with the army than his predecessors had done, since "the truth is we are on the wrong road to take Richmond."[5] Having unburdened himself, Sedgwick retired to his tent to resume one of his everlasting games of solitaire, leaving further comment to other ranks.

Other ranks had their own ideas, which did not always approach reverence. A squadron of cavalry went trotting by one day while Grant sat his horse, smoking, and one trooper sniffed the breeze and said that he knew the general was a good man because he smoked such elegant cigars. Two privates in the 5th Wisconsin saw Grant ride past them, and studied him in silence. Presently one asked the inevitable question: "Well, what do you think?" The other took in the watchful eyes and the hard straight mouth under the stubble beard, and replied: "He looks as if he meant it." Then, reflecting on the problems which politics could create for a general, he added: "But I'm afraid he's too near Washington." The first soldier said that they would see for themselves before long, and remarked contemplatively: "He's a little 'un."

One man said that while the soldiers often saw Grant he was always riding so fast that they could not get a good look at him, and another commented: "After the debonair McClellan, the cocky Burnside, rosy Joe Hooker and the dyspeptic Meade, the calm and unpretentious Grant was not exciting anyway." He felt that the most anyone really saw was "a quiet solidity."[6]

If the general had solidity he would need it, because he was under great pressure. Hopes and fears centered on him, not to mention jealousies. The country at large believed that he was the man who at last was going to win the war, possibly very quickly. The day when men easily expected miracles and hoped to find another Napoleon under the newest general's black campaign hat had died out long ago, but if miracles were out of order ruthless determination perhaps would do, and that much seemed to be visible.

Over in the Army of Northern Virginia, James Longstreet was quietly warning people not to underestimate this new Yankee commander: "That man will fight us every day and every hour till the end of the war."[7] Nobody in the North heard the remark, but the quality which had called it forth had not gone unnoticed. Here was the man who looked as if he would ram his way through a brick wall, and since other tactics had not worked perhaps that was the thing to try. At Fort Donelson and at Vicksburg he had swallowed two Confederate armies whole, and at Chattanooga he had driven a third army in headlong retreat from what had been thought to be an impregnable stronghold, and all anyone could think of was the hard blow that ended matters. Men seemed ready to call Grant the hammerer before he even began to hammer.

Yet if there were many who uncritically expected much, there were some who had corrosive doubts. Congress had passed an act creating the rank of lieutenant general, knowing that if the act became law no one but Grant would be named, knowing that in passing the act it was doing only what the situation and the country demanded. Yet Congress had had one worry all the while it was acting—a worry expressed in the simple, vulgar question: If we turn the country's armies over to this man, will he stay sober?

The question was never debated publicly and never forgotten in private. Never before had there been anything quite like this uneasy concern that the nation's survival might hang on one man's willingness to refrain from drinking too much. Along with the legend of victory, there had arisen about Grant this legend of drunkenness—bad days in California, forced resignation from the army, hardscrabble period in Missouri and Illinois, surprise at Shiloh. All of these were items in the legend, and men who knew nothing whatever about it had at least heard of President Lincoln's offhand crack that he would like to buy for his other generals some of Grant's own brand of whisky. Men looked at Grant and saw what they had been led to see. Some saw quiet determination, and others, like Richard Henry Dana, saw "the look of a man who did, or once did, take a little too much to drink," and considered that there was an air of seediness and half pay about the fellow.

The question had finally been resolved in Grant's favor, of course, but not without much soul searching on the part of those who had to resolve it. And as a hedge against a chancy future, Congress had created for the lieutenant general the post of chief of staff, and into this post there had come the thin, impassioned, consumptive little lawyer from Illinois, John A. Rawlins.

Rawlins knew no more about military matters than any other lawyer, except for what had rubbed off on him through three years with Grant, but that did not matter. He ran Grant's staff capably enough, although high policy sometimes got away from him and he was hesitant about asserting himself where officers of the Regular Army were concerned, but what was really important about him was the fact that he had a mother hen complex. He was devoted to the Union with a passion that was burning the life out of him, but he was even more devoted to U. S. Grant, and his great, self-chosen mission in life was to guard the general's honor, well-being, and sobriety. In elevating Grant the government had in effect elevated Rawlins as well. Unformulated but taken for granted was the idea that he was the man who would save the man who would save the country.[8]

There was a good deal of needless worry in all of this. Grant was no drunkard. He was simply a man infinitely more complex than most people could realize. Under the hard, ruthless man of war—the remorseless soldier who hammered until men foolishly believed him raw strength incarnate—there was quite another person: the West Point cadet who hated military life and used to hope against unavailing hope that Congress would presently abolish the military academy and so release him from an army career; the young officer who longed to get away from camp and parade ground and live quietly as a teacher of mathematics; a man apparently beset by infinite loneliness, with a profound need for the warm, healing, understanding intimacy that can overleap shyness. Greatly fortunate, he found this intimacy with his wife, whom he still loved as a young man loves his first sweetheart, and when he was long away from her he seems to have been a little less than whole. On the eve of every great battle, after he became a famous general, with the orders all written and everything taped for the next day's violence, and the unquiet troops drifting off into a last sleep, he would go to his tent and unburden himself in a long, brooding letter to this woman who still spoke of him, quaintly, as "Mister Grant."

So it could happen badly with him, when he was alone and cut off and the evils of life came down about him. Marooned in California, far from his family, tormented by money problems, bored by the pointless routine of a stagnant army post under a dull and unimaginative colonel, he could turn to drink for escape. He could do the same thing back in Missouri as a civilian, working hard for a meager living, all the luck breaking badly, drifting into failure at forty, Sam Grant the ne'er-do-well. Deep in Tennessee, likewise, sidetracked by a jealous and petty-minded superior, the awful stain of Shiloh lying ineradicable on his mind, his career apparently ready to end just as it was being reborn, the story could be the same. There was a flame in him, and there were times when he could not keep the winds from the outer dark from blowing in on him and making it flicker. But it never did go out.

In any case, the Army of the Potomac was hardly in a position to look down its nose on officers who drank. It had an abundance of them, and they had been seen in every level from army commander down to junior lieutenant. There had been times when the sleep of enlisted men had been broken by the raucous noises coming from the tents of drunken officers. There had been one notable occasion this past winter when a famous corps commander got drunk, walked full-tilt into a tree in front of his tent, and was with difficulty restrained from court-martialing the officer of the guard on charges of felonious assault. A little Quaker nurse in a II Corps hospital, commenting on the fact that both a corps and a division commander had been drunk during a recent battle, wrote bitterly: "I don't care what anyone says, war is humbug. It is just put out to see how much suffering the privates can bear, I guess." Perfectly in character was the tale told of a major who commanded an artillery brigade, a heavy drinker despite the fact that he came from prohibitionist Maine. This man had a birthday coming up and he wanted to celebrate, and he called in his commissary officer and asked how much whisky they had in stock. The officer said there might be as much as two gallons, and the major was indignant.

"Two gallons!" he repeated. "What is two gallons of whisky among one man?"[9]

To do the army justice, it did not worry about Grant's drinking. A general who never got drunk was a rarity—so much so that his sobriety was always mentioned in his biography, as a sign that he stood above the common run. What troubled the officer corps—and to an extent, the enlisted man as well— was the fact that Grant came from the West. The West seemed to be a side show where a general could win a reputation without really amounting to much. (After all, there had been John Pope.) Federal troops in the West were thought to be an undisciplined rabble. Also—which was what really mattered—they had never been up against the first team. They had never had to face Robert E. Lee.

Lee was the one soldier in whom most of the higher officers of the Army of the Potomac had complete, undiluted confidence. Among the many achievements of that remarkable man, nothing is much more striking than his ability to dominate the minds of the men who were fighting against him. These men could look back on several years of warfare, and what they saw always seemed about the same—the Army of the Potomac marching south to begin an offensive, well-equipped and full of confidence, and, within days or weeks, fighting doggedly and without too much confidence to escape annihilation. Twice the army had won a defensive battle, letting its enemies go away unmolested afterward, but when it took the offensive it invariably lost the initiative. Its own plans never seemed to matter, because sooner or later both armies moved by Lee's plans. Grant was untried. His record probably meant nothing. Just wait until he tried tangling with Lee![10]

As it happened, this attitude worked both ways; if soldiers in the East had a low opinion of soldiers in the West, the Westerners returned the feeling with interest. A Federal general in one of the Western armies, reading the sad news from Chancellorsville the preceding spring, had remarked that "we do not build largely on the Eastern army," and continued: "When we hear, therefore, that the Eastern army is going to fight, we make our minds up that it is going to be defeated, and when the result is announced we feel sad enough but not disappointed." Westerners believed that the Army of the Potomac had never been made to fight all out and that when all was said and done there was something mysteriously wrong with it. The Westerners had had no Antietam or Gettysburg, but they had had a Shiloh and a Stone's River, and they felt that they had seen the Confederates at their toughest. When the IX Corps was sent to Tennessee in the fall of 1863, Western troops greeted the boys with the jeering question: "All quiet along the Potomac?" and announced caustically: "We'll show you how to fight."[11]

So there were mutual doubts, and the effect was unfortunate. The officers of this army not only viewed Grant's advent with strong skepticism; in many cases this skepticism verged on outright hostility, so that it was ready to burst out with a bitter, triumphant "I told you so!" if the new general should run into trouble. Grant's presence here was an implied criticism of the army's prior leadership and strategy. Through him, the administration was striking its final blow at the whole complex of emotions and relationships which had come down from McClellan—and McClellan remained, next to Lee, the man in whom most of the veteran officers still had implicit confidence.

Among the private soldiers there was mostly a great curiosity. It was noticed that all of a sudden the enlisted man had become a student of newspapers and magazines, reading everything he could find about the new general in chief. Men made themselves familiar with Grant's campaigns, and it was not uncommon to see campfire groups drawing maps in the dirt with sticks to demonstrate how Vicksburg and Chattanooga had gone. At the worst, there was resigned acquiescence. One man summed up his company's opinion by saying: "He cannot be weaker or more inefficient than the generals who have wasted the lives of our comrades during the past three years." He concluded that "if he is a fighter he can find all the fighting he wants."[12]

Ohio and Pennsylvania soldiers, huddling together on a picket post, talked it over:

"Who's this Grant that's made a lieutenant general?"

"He's the hero of Vicksburg."

"Well, Vicksburg wasn't much of a fight. The Rebels were out of rations and they had to surrender or starve. They had nothing but dead mules and dogs to eat, as I understand."

The men nodded, and one said that Grant could never have penned up any of Lee's generals that way. Longstreet or Jeb Stuart "would have broken out some way and foraged around for supplies."[13]

An impressionable newspaper correspondent might describe Grant as "all-absorbed, all-observant, silent, inscrutable," a man who "controls and moves armies as he does his horse," but the enlisted man wanted more evidence. He liked the fact that Grant went about without fuss and ceremony, and he was ready to admit that "a more hopeful spirit prevailed," but for the most part he went along with the company officer who said that only time would tell whether this new general's first name was really Ulysses or Useless.[14]

Yet there was a change, and before long the men felt it. There was a perceptible tightening up, as if someone who meant business had his hands on the reins now. Orders went forth to corps and division commanders to make a radical cut in the number of men who were borne on the returns as "on special, extra, or daily duty," and attention was called to the discrepancies between the numbers reported "present for duty" and those listed as "present for duty, equipped." In brigades and divisions the inspectors general became busy, and where equipment had been lacking it suddenly materialized. Long trains of freight cars came clanking in at Brandy Station, to unload food and forage, uniforms and blankets, and shelter tents and munitions. Men found that they were working harder now than in the past. Subtly but unmistakably, an air of competence and preparation was manifest.

Cavalry found that a new day had dawned. The Pleasontons and Kilpatricks were gone, and at the top there was another Westerner—a tough little man named Phil Sheridan, bandy-legged and wiry, with a black bullet head and a hard eye, wearing by custom a mud-spotted uniform, flourishing in one fist a flat black hat which, when he put it on, seemed to be at least two sizes too small for him. Like Grant, he rode a great black horse when he made his rounds and he rode it at a pounding gallop, and it was remarked that he "rolled and bounced upon the back of his steed much as an old salt does when walking up the aisle of a church after a four years' cruise at sea."

Cavalry's camps were better policed, the endless picket details were reduced, and it appeared that Sheridan was going to insist on using his corps as a compact fighting unit. When Sheridan was taken to the White House to meet the President, Lincoln quoted the familiar army jest—"Who ever saw a dead cavalryman?"—and it was obvious that Sheridan was not amused. Meeting a friend at Willard's a little bit later, Sheridan said: "I'm going to take the cavalry away from the bobtailed brigadier generals. They must do without their escorts. I intend to make the cavalry an arm of the service."

One trooper complained that people now were checking up on all routine jobs, so that a man grooming his horse had to put in a full sixty minutes at it: "There is an officer watching you all the time, and if you stop he yells out, 'Keep to work, there!' " With all of this came businesslike new weapons: seven-shot Spencer magazine carbines, made regulation equipment by a recently revived Cavalry Bureau.[15]

Artillerists were put through endless maneuvers, wheeling back and forth in the dust and mud to become letter-perfect in such intricacies as "changing front to the right on the first section," and banging away in constant target practice. Batteries were taught to come galloping up to a line, halt and unlimber, completely disassemble their pieces until wheels, guns, gun carriages, and limber chests lay separate on the ground, then at a word of command reassemble the whole business and go galloping away again. One gunner declared that a good gun crew could perform the whole maneuver in several seconds less than one minute, and another grumbled that all of this "was of as much practical use to us as if we had been assiduously drilled to walk on stilts"; and whether it was useful or otherwise the drill was repeated over and over and the gun crews got toughened up for the approaching campaign.[16]

None of this, naturally, missed the infantry. There were unending drills, and much target practice. The army command had caught on to the notorious fact that some soldiers simply did not know how to shoot. On every battlefield, ordinance officers had collected hundreds of discarded muskets containing anywhere from two to a dozen unexploded cartridges. In the heat of battle men failed to notice that they had not pulled trigger, and reloaded weapons which had not been fired; or, indeed, they were so untaught that they did not even know enough to cap their pieces and so pulled trigger to no effect, failing to realize in all the battle racket that they had not actually fired. A circular from headquarters decreed that every man in the army should be made to load and fire his weapon under supervision of an officer, since "it is believed there are men in this army who have been in numerous actions without ever firing their guns."[17]

The bark of the drill sargeant echoed across the hard-trodden parade grounds where new levies were being put into shape. (In the Irish Brigade, an irate non-com was heard shouting: "Kape your heels together, Tim Mullaney in the rear rank, and don't be standing wid wan fut in Bull Run and the other in the Sixth Ward!") Transportation was cut down—one wagon to a brigade was the rule now—and many wagon drivers came back to the ranks and shouldered muskets. One of these passed a wagon train one day and heard a mule braying. Fixing his eye on the beast, the man retorted: "You needn't laugh at me—you may be in the ranks yourself before Grant gets through with the army." All in all, it was as a New England soldier wrote: "We all felt at last that *the boss* had arrived."[18]

There were many reviews: no McClellan touch now, with pomp and flourish, but a businesslike marshaling of troops to be seen by the general in chief, who rode by always at a gallop, sometimes on Cincinnati, sometimes on a little black pacer named Jeff Davis, and who for all his speed always seemed able to look each man in the ranks squarely in the eye. The general did not appear to care whether anyone cheered or not. The Iron Brigade was drawn up one day in line of massed battalions, a cold drizzle coming down, and as Grant came along the line regiment after regiment gave him a cheer. Grant was preoccupied, studying the faces of the hard fighters in this famous brigade, and he neglected to give the customary wave of the hat in response, and so the colonel of the 6th Wisconsin at the far end of the line told his men not to cheer but simply to give the formal salute. They obeyed, and as Grant came along he noticed the omission and slowed to a walk. The colors were dipped, and Grant took off his hat and bowed. The Wisconsin boys were pleased, and after the parade broke up they said that "Grant wants soldiers, not yaupers."[19]

What the soldiers liked most of all was the far-reaching hand with which Grant hauled men out of the safe dugouts in Washington and brought them into the army.

The Washington fortifications had been manned for two years with what were known as heavy artillery regiments—oversized regiments mustering around 1,800 men apiece, trained both to act as infantry, with muskets, and to man heavy guns in the forts—and these regiments never had any trouble keeping their ranks filled, because men could enlist in them in full confidence that they would have to fight very little and march not at all. They led what the Army of the Potomac considered an excessively soft life, with permanent barracks, no trouble about rations, and every night in bed.

Their possessions were many, because infantry commands leaving Washington for the front always discarded (or could be quietly despoiled of) much property, and so the "heavies" had extra blankets, stoves, civilian-type bedsteads, and good table equipment. Their hospitals boasted white sheets and pillowcases, and some regiments even maintained regimental libraries. Certain regiments actually kept pigs, feeding them on swill from the company kitchens and dining frequently on fresh pork. One outfit of mechanically minded Yankees set up a little machine shop, and before inspection they would take their muskets in and have the barrels turned in lathes to take on a dazzling gleam and polish, with machine-driven buffers to put a glossy sheen on the stocks. These men had been enjoying a very comfortable war, and the combat troops had been resenting it (and envying them) for a long time.

Now, without warning, these huge regiments left their happy homes, marched down to the Rapidan, and began to pitch their shelter tents in the mud just like everybody else, and the infantry was jubilant. Veterans would line the roads, whooping with delight, calling out all manner of greetings—asking the new regiments why they had not brought their fortifications along, referring to them derisively as "heavy infantry," inquiring when their guns would arrive, and offering instruction about various aspects of the soldier's life. These heavy artillery regiments were many times as large as the veteran infantry outfits—the colonel of the 12th Massachusetts was protesting just now that his regiment could muster only 207 enlisted men for duty—and the veterans would make heavy-handed remarks on the fact; when a new regiment came in they would ask what division this was.[20]

Certain cavalry commands met a similar fate, and got just as much sympathy. Some of these had been in camp at Washington for a refit, waiting with perfect resignation for the slow processes of government to provide them with remounts. These abruptly found themselves deprived of sabers, of carbines, and of all hope of new horses, given infantry muskets instead, and sent down to the Rapidan on foot. A Connecticut heavy artillery regiment, meeting such a command of dismounted Maryland cavalry, asked incautiously: "Where are your horses?" A Marylander replied sourly: "Gone to fetch your heavy guns." The Official Records contain a plaintive and quite useless protest by an outraged colonel, who recited that he led a spanking new regiment of Pennsylvania cavalry into Washington that spring—1,200 men, well mounted, disciplined, drilled, and equipped—only to be ordered to turn in his horses and weapons, draw muskets, and consider his command infantry thenceforward.[21]

All of this pleased the infantry greatly, cavalry in general not being too popular with foot soldiers, and there was admiration for the general who had brought it all to pass. With this admiration came a dawning respect for his power. Pulling the heavy artillery and the dismounted cavalry down to the Rapidan meant that Washington was being left almost defenseless. In earlier times, White House and War Department had insisted on keeping 40,000 men or more within the Washington lines, even though no enemies ever came within miles of them. If this new general could override that insistence he must have prodigious strength. Apparently he could have things just about the way he wanted them, and the army would move with greater power. At the very least, it seemed that the country's strength was going to be *used*. When he rode the lines, a soldier wrote that the men would "look with awe at Grant's silent figure."[22]

Not all of the changes were popular. One which was bitterly resented by thousands of the best soldiers in the army was a shake-up which consolidated the five infantry corps into three. Actually, this was none of Grant's doing, Meade having put it in the works before Grant took over, but it was announced while all the other changes were taking place and it was generally accepted as part of Grant's program. Meade seems to have made the move partly because he felt that the army would work better with fewer and larger units, and partly because there were not as many as five qualified corps commanders in the army anyway. The consolidation enabled him to shelve several generals who had been withering on the vine—the best of them, probably, crusty and slow-moving George Sykes, famous because of the work his Regulars had done in the early days.

What made this shake-up unpopular with so many men was the fact that the I Corps and the III Corps ceased to exist, their brigades being distributed among the three corps which survived. These two corps had been famous and their men had been cocky, wearing their corps badges with vast pride, and they were brought almost to the verge of mutiny by the change. (One army historian, writing more than twenty years later, asserted that "the wound has never yet wholly healed in the heart of many a brave and patriotic soldier.")[23] The two organizations had been wrecked at Gettysburg and it had never been possible, somehow, to repair the damage and bring them up to proper strength. Yet the consolidation was unfortunate. Heretofore, each corps had had its own individuality and its own tradition, and these had done much for morale. Just as the three which remained were striving to digest the miscellaneous lot of new recruits which were coming in, they were given the unhappy brigades and divisions from the two corps which had been abolished. The result was that nobody quite felt that his old outfit was what it used to be. There was also the possibility that the great increase in the size of each corps would put a new strain on the corps commanders.

In the midst of all of this reshuffling the army almost lost John Sedgwick. Sedgwick had never felt it necessary to assure Washington that he hated Democrats and loved emancipation, nor had he ever concealed his admiration for McClellan, and these thing had made him suspect with Secretarty Stanton. Early this winter Sedgwick had bluntly told the War Department that Butler's poorly handled attempt to capture Richmond had done the Union cause more harm than good, and since Butler was a pet of the radical Republicans—a standing test of the other generals' allegiance to the cause, so to speak—this was remembered where it would hurt. In February Sedgwick wrote to his sister that the army grapevine was predicting a reorganization "to get rid of some obnoxious generals," and he admitted that he himself might be on this list. It would not bother him much, he said, if this turned out to be true: "I feel that I have done my part of field duty. . . . I could even leave altogether without many regrets."

So when Meade began to make changes Stanton told him that it would be well to find some other place for Sedgwick, and after some argument back and forth it had finally been agreed to put Sedgwick in command up in the Shenandoah Valley. It would have been an odd sort of demotion, for the valley command was destined to be very important, but it was all upset at the last minute when Mr. Lincoln unexpectedly gave the job to Franz Sigel, and in the end Sedgwick remained in command of the VI Corps.[24]

With the men of this corps he was very popular. One day in this winter of 1864 Wheaton's brigade of the VI Corps came in to camp after several months of detached service in western Virginia. The brigade detrained in a miserable cold rain, and since all of the good camp sites had been taken it appeared that they would have to pitch their tents in a muddy field, with no shelter from the elements and the nearest source of wood for campfires several miles away. There was a fine grove near by, to be sure, but some brigadier and his entourage had long since pre-empted it. While the men stood disconsolate in the wet, a burly horseman in a muddy cavalry overcoat came splashing up—Sedgwick. He took in the situation at once, rode over to the little grove, told the brigadier and his henchmen to pack up at once and move to some other place, and ordered Wheaton to have his brigade take over the vacated campsite.[25]

Winfield Scott Hancock led the II Corps. He had been badly wounded at Gettysburg and the wound still bothered him, but he came back at the end of the winter with all of his old gusto and the men were glad to see him. He was a vivid, hearty sort of man—his chief of staff, with strong understatement, remarked that he was "absolutely devoid of asceticism"—and it was believed that he could conduct a long march with less straggling and more professional competence than any other officer in the army. He differed from most Regular Army officers (including Meade himself) in that he liked volunteer soldiers and did his best to make them feel that they were as good as Regulars, and his army corps repaid him for that attitude.[26] The corps badge was a trefoil, and when the men went into action they had a way of yelling: "Clubs are trumps!"

To the V Corps, in place of the departed Sykes, came one of the most baffling figures in the army—Major General Gouverneur Kemble Warren.

Warren was thirty-four, with long jet-black hair and a mustache which he was fond of twirling; a slightly built man with sallow complexion, looking not unlike an Indian, well liked by the troops because he displayed great bravery under fire. (No officer could be popular in this army unless he could show a spectacular contempt for danger.) He was a queer mixture of the good and the ineffective—a fuss-budget with flashes of genius, a man engrossed in detail and given to blunting his cutting edge by worrying over trifles which a staff captain ought to have been handling. He had never heard of delegating authority, and he had a certain weakness for setting his own opinion above that of his superior officer's.

He had had two great days. One was at Gettysburg, when as an engineer officer on the commanding general's staff he had stood on Little Round Top, had seen the coming danger, and by a hair's thin margin had got Union troops there in time to save the day. The other was at Mine Run, in December, when half of the army had been given to him for a mighty assault that was to destroy the Rebel army and make General Warren a national hero. At the last minute General Warren had discovered that the Confederate line was far stronger than had been supposed: so strong, indeed, that the attack could not possibly succeed and would be no better than a second Fredericksburg. With no time to refer matters to the army commander he had had the moral stamina to call things off, let Meade's wrath descend entirely on himself, and take whatever rap might be coming.

He came from Putnam County, New York, and as a young man he was a sobersides, not to say a bit of a prig. He can be seen, at twenty-two, a very junior second lieutenant, writing home to his mother telling her how to rear the eleven other children she had borne: "You must dress them warmly and give them the best of shoes to keep their feet dry. . . . Put flannel underclothes on them all. Cold fingers and cold ears are not much account, but cold feet is the cause of a great deal of sickness. If Edgar is still troubled with that tickling in his throat, put woollen underclothes on him, place a plaster on his chest, keep his feet warm and dry, and I know it will disappear." Yet he would not merely give advice: "I have money to spare, if that is lacking."

An engineer officer, he had worked on Mississippi River flood-control projects, and under Harney he had fought the Sioux Indians. He had an unmilitary ability to be sensitive to human suffering. The worst thing about fighting Indians, he wrote, was that one shot a good many women and children, and when it came time to dress their wounds afterward one discovered that they were just like any other women and children and not at all like howling savages. He had filled in for Hancock in charge of the II Corps, this past winter, and now he had a corps of his own. It included many good fighters and contained some of the best of the troops from the departed I Corps, and what it might do would depend a good deal on General Warren.[27]

So the army had been made over, with familiar organizations broken up and familiar faces gone, and what nobody could miss was the fact that it was being made larger and at the same time harder and more compact. The three rebuilt army corps were grouped more closely together. The detached troops which had been spending dreary months guarding the line of the railroad back to Alexandria were all called back into camp. To replace them there appeared an old familiar figure from the unhappy past—Major General Ambrose E. Burnside, dignified and friendly and incurably addicted to fumbling, short jacket belted tightly around his tubby figure, bell-crowned hat shading his incomparable whiskers.

His IX Corps had been brought up to full strength again (it now contained a solid division of colored troops, who had gone wild with enthusiasm when they paraded past Abraham Lincoln in Washington) and it was coming down from its rendezvous at Annapolis to occupy the line of the railroad. The corps was not formally a part of the Army of the Potomac. It was to act with the army, receiving direct orders from the general in chief; meanwhile it was on the railroad, and its arrival meant that the army could operate as a unit, none of its manpower wasted guarding the line of supply.

Imperceptibly, a new spirit was appearing. Competence and confidence had arrived, neither one obtrusive, both unmistakable. Yet the soldier lived at the bottom of the pool, in a dim greenish light in which no outlines were very clear. He had seen army commanders come and he had seen them go, and he was going to take very little for granted. The only certainty was that the campaign ahead was going to be very rough, and the men frankly dreaded it—more on account of the marching, they said, than of the fighting. The viewpoint was aptly expressed in a letter which a Pennsylvania private wrote at the end of April: "If Congressmen at Washington, or the Rebel Congress at Richmond, were required to endure the hardships of a soldier's life during one campaign, the war would then end."[28]

Army life went on, despite shifts in command. There were baseball games, as spring dried the fields—the 13th Massachusetts beat the 104th New York one day by a score of 62 to 20—and there were the endless chores of army routine. An Illinois cavalry regiment came to camp after a spell of provost guard duty in Washington, reporting that it had been policing upwards of a hundred houses of prostitution, and a trooper confessed that "this work, although it amused the men for a time, and was arduous to perform, did not satisfy those who longed for more active service." There were the age-old attempts to wangle furloughs. An Irish private one day went to his regimental commander, explaining that his wife was ill and the children were not well and that it was necessary for him to make a short visit to his home. The colonel fixed him with a beady eye and said: "Pat, I had a letter from your wife this morning saying she doesn't want you at home; that you raise the devil whenever you are there, and that she hopes I won't grant you any more furloughs. What have you to say to that?"

Quite unabashed, the soldier replied that there were "two splendid liars in this room" and that he himself was only one of them: "I nivir was married in me life."[29]

Perhaps the abiding reality this spring was the unseen army across the river, the Army of Northern Virginia. A fantastic sort of kinship had grown up in regard to that army. There was no soft sentimentality about it, and the men would shoot to kill when the time for shooting came. Yet there was a familiarity and an understanding, at times something that verged almost on liking, based on solid respect. Whatever else might change, these armies at least understood one another.

Physically, they were not far apart, and the pickets often got acquainted. One Federal picket detail, which was ordered to hold certain advanced posts by day but to pull in closer to camp at night, discovered that a deserted log hut which it was using by day was being used by Rebel pickets at night, the Confederate arrangement here being just the reverse of the Federals'. Two groups of rival pickets met at this hut one morning, the Confederates being tardy in starting back to camp. There was a quick groping for weapons, a wary pause, then a conversation; and the Southerners said that if the Yanks would give them a few minutes to saddle up they would get out and the old schedule might go on. It was so arranged, with a proviso that each side thereafter would leave a good fire burning in the fireplace for its enemies.[30]

The enlisted men knew their enemies better than the officers did. Cedar Mountain was just inside the Union lines, and there was a signal station on top of it, and one day, with marching orders imminent, two officers from a Maine regiment climbed this mountain to take a glimpse of the Rebel country. Far below them, in rolling broken fields and woods, they saw the storied land of the Rapidan—"grinning," as one of them wrote, "with dreadful ghosts," for many men had died in the fighting along this river during the last three years. Today everything looked peaceful, and spring was on the land, and through telescopes they could see a Confederate camp. There were men lounging about in shirt sleeves, some of them smoking their pipes and washing their clothes, others playing ball. The two officers stared at them for a long time, getting their first look at Confederate soldiers off duty. At last they put down their telescopes, and one officer turned to the other.

"My God, Adjutant," he said. "They're human beings just like us!"[31]

TWO

Roads Leading South

1. WHERE THE DOGWOOD BLOSSOMED

IT WAS the fourth day of May, and beyond the dark river there was a forest with the shadow of death under its low branches, and the dogwood blossoms were floating in the air like lost flecks of sunlight, as if life was as important as death; and for the Army of the Potomac this was the last bright morning, with youth and strength and hope ranked under starred flags, bugle calls riding down the wind, and invisible doors swinging open on the other shore. The regiments fell into line, and great white-topped wagons creaked along the roads, and the spring sunlight glinted off the polished muskets and the brass of the guns, and the young men came down to the valley while the bands played. A German regiment was singing "John Brown's Body."

Beside the roads the violets were in bloom and the bush honeysuckle was out, and the day and the year had a fragile light that the endless columns would soon trample to fragments. The last campaign had begun, and a staff officer sat on a bank overlooking the Rapidan and had a curious thought: how odd it would be if every man who was to die in the days just ahead had to wear a big badge today, so that a man watching by the river could identify all of those who were never coming back!

The men of this army left books and letters behind them, and in these there is a remarkable testimony that the men who marched away from winter quarters that morning took a last look back and saw a golden haze which, even at the moment of looking, they knew they would never see again. They tell how the birds were singing, and how the warm scented air came rolling up the river valley, and how they noticed things like wildflowers and the young green leaves, and they speak of the moving pageant which they saw and of which they themselves were part. "Everything," wrote a youth from Maine, "was bright and blowing." It would never be like this again, and young men who were to live on to a great age, drowsing out the lives of old soldiers in a land that would honor them and then tolerate them and finally forget them, would look back on this one morning and see in it something that came from beyond the rim of the world.[1]

Cavalry took the lead, moving down through the busy camps to the historic Rapidan crossings, Germanna and Ely's fords. Foot soldiers watched them go, and called out, in what they conceived to be the idiom of their Southern foes: "Hey there! Where be you-all going?" Jauntily, the troopers called back they were on their way to Richmond. But although the army felt that this campaign was going to be better than previous ones it still was skeptical, and cavalry needed to be put in its place anyway, so the infantry cried out: "Bob Lee will drive you-all back just as he has done before."[2]

The troopers pushed on and crossed the river, and they left the sunlight behind and went up the winding woods roads that led into the Wilderness.

This was a mean gloomy woodland, a dozen miles wide by half as deep, lying silent and forbidding along the southern bank of the river. Its virgin timber had been cut down years ago, mostly to provide fuel for small iron-smelting furnaces in the neighborhood, and a tangled second growth had sprung up—stunted pines, innumerable small saplings, dense underbrush, here and there a larger tree, vines and creepers trailing every which way through dead scrub pines with interlaced spiky branches; there were very few places in which a man could see as far as twenty yards. The soil was poor, and there were hardly any farms or clearings, and the land under the trees was like a choppy sea, broken by ridges and hillocks and irregular knolls.

There were dark little streams that never saw the sun, and these had cut shallow ravines, some of which had very steep banks. These water courses wandered and twisted and turned on themselves, soaking the low ground into bush-covered swamps, and the thickets covered their banks. Once in a great while there would be a house—paintless, sometimes made of hewn logs, looking gaunt and forsaken like the forest itself, with a hopeless corn patch and weedy pasture around it—and there were a few aimless lanes, hardly more than tracks in the jungle, which did not seem to go anywhere in particular.

It was the last place on earth for armies to fight, and the entire Army of the Potomac was marching straight into it.

Actually, the high command had little intention of fighting here. The two armies had been facing each other, with the Rapidan between them, a number of miles upstream from the Wilderness, and when Grant made his plans he had two choices. He could move by his right flank, sliding along the line of the Orange and Alexandria Railroad in the general direction of Gordonsville, swinging past Lee to the west, and forcing him to fight in open country; or he could go by his left, slipping quickly through the Wilderness, heading for a position behind Lee's right—where, as in the other case, there could be fighting in the open.

He had taken the second choice, for reasons which seemed good to him. Chief reason was the matter of supply. Counting everybody, he would be taking some 116,000 men with him, and more than 50,000 horses, and it seemed improbable that the single-tracked railway line could supply all of them adequately. Furthermore, the railroad led through country infested with guerillas—John S. Mosby's famous irregulars, mostly, who attacked Yankee supply lines and outposts so viciously and effectively that the region between Brandy Station and Alexandria was commonly known as "Mosby's Confederacy." If the Federal army dangled at the end of a hundred miles of railroad, these men would have a field day, and so would Jeb Stuart's far-ranging cavalry, and half of the army would have to be left behind to cope with them. So the army was going to the left, where if it made progress there would be seacoast bases, with a short roadway for the enormous wagon train.

There might have been a third choice: McClellan's old route of 1862, putting the army on boats and going down by water to the tip of the Virginia peninsula, with a landing at Fortress Monroe and a quick march toward Richmond between York and James rivers. That way, the army could get up within shooting distance of Richmond without trouble, and the long overland hike with exposed supply lines and hard fighting at every crossroads would be avoided. Before he got to Brandy Station Grant felt that that was the way to go, and soldiers as good as John Sedgwick agreed. Why fight one's way to Richmond when the army could travel most of the way by water and come up to the doors of the Rebel capital fresh and unbloodied?

The trouble was that it was not that kind of war any more. Meade's soldiers had noticed many changes this spring, but what they had not seen was the fact that the role of the Army of the Potomac itself had changed. The goal now was not to capture Richmond but to fight the Army of Northern Virginia—to begin to fight it as soon as possible and to keep on fighting it until one side or the other could fight no more.

Whatever happened, Lee must never again be allowed to take the initiative. It might or it might not be possible to beat him, but it was all-important to keep him busy. It must be made impossible for him to detach troops to oppose Sherman, who was breaking his way into Georgia with the contemptuous remark that when you pierced the shell of the Confederacy you found hollowness within. Also, Ben Butler was advancing toward Richmond on the south side of the James, and if the Army of the Potomac spent the first month of the campaign getting on and off of steamboats Lee could concentrate against Butler, destroy him and his army, and thus win a dazzling victory at comparatively low cost.

For all of these reasons, then, the Army of the Potomac had one paramount responsibility: it must get close to the enemy as soon as possible and it must stay close until the war ended. If it did that, victory would come. It might not come in Virginia, and the price paid for it might be terribly high, but it would come in the end.[3]

So the army was heading down into the Wilderness, hoping to cross that unwholesome area quickly and to get the Army of Northern Virginia by the throat immediately thereafter. It was a good enough plan. The difficulty might lie in the fact that Lee was notoriously averse to fighting battles when and where his enemies wanted to fight them.

Some of the soldiers felt this, and as they crossed the river they were vaguely uneasy. A cavalry regiment got over in the middle of the night, drove off the Rebel pickets at the crossing, and went jogging up the sandy roads into the black forest. As they rode the men talked, and one man said that he never thought "the army went hunting around in the night for Johnnies in this way." A comrade explained: "We're stealing a march on old man Lee."

They thought that over briefly, and someone suggested: "Lee'll miss us in the morning."

"Yes," said another, "and then look out. He'll come tearing down this way ready for a fight."[4]

Lee was on Grant's mind, too, that day. At noon Grant crossed the Rapidan and made temporary headquarters in a deserted farmhouse overlooking the ford, and a newspaper correspondent brashly asked him how long it would take him to reach Richmond. About four days, said Grant soberly; then, as the newspaperman goggled at him, he went on—four days, provided General Lee was a party to the agreement. If not, it would probably take a good deal longer.

Grant had ridden past the troops in midmorning, his ornamented staff trotting at his heels. Riding beside him there was the lone civilian amid all those thousands of soldiers—Congressman Elihu B. Washburne of Illinois, Grant's personal friend and political sponsor, a headquarters visitor for the opening days of the campaign. Washburne wore civilian clothes of funereal black, and when the soldiers saw him they asked one another who this character might be. A staff officer heard one rear-rank wit telling his mates that it was simple: the Old Man had brought along his private undertaker.[5]

For the first twenty-four hours nothing happened. Warren and Sedgwick got their men over the river at Germanna Ford and headed south. The day was warm, and in the hollow roads no air was stirring, and before long the roadside was littered with packed knapsacks, overcoats, extra blankets, and other bits of gear which sweating soldiers found too heavy to carry. The veterans wagged their heads: all of that stuff was a sure sign that there were lots of recruits in the ranks—no old-timer would load himself down with excess baggage at the beginning of a march.

Artillerists gloated, and scampered about collecting loot; they had an advantage over infantry, in that gun carriages and caissons offered handy places to carry such extras. The more experienced gunners warned their mates not to be hasty. If they waited for heat and fatigue to become a little more oppressive, some of the straw-feet would begin discarding even their haversacks, and those must be collected at all costs. If this march was like most others, they would leave the supply trains far behind, and it was important to lay in surplus of food.[6]

The road wound and climbed slowly for several miles, and at last it came out into an open space by a crossroads. Off to the left there was a run-down, abandoned stage station, still known as Wilderness Tavern, a ruinous place with its yard full of weeds, half hidden by scraggly trees. Behind it was a meadow where, just a year ago, the Confederates had had a field hospital during the battle of Chancellorsville, and in that field the doctors had amputated the arm of Stonewall Jackson.

A general who came down from Germanna Ford and stood here by the deserted tavern facing south was practically in the middle of the northern fringe of the Wilderness. To get through the Wilderness he could turn right, turn left, or go straight ahead, and no matter which way he went he had about six miles of Wilderness to cross. Squarely across his path lay the region's principal east-west highway, the Orange Turnpike, which ran from Fredericksburg through Chancellorsville to Orange Court House. Two or three miles to the south there was a companion road roughly parallel to the Turnpike, the Orange Plank Road, a narrow track with a strip of planking running beside a strip of dirt. (The rule in the old days was that a loaded wagon was entitled to stay on the planking; unloaded wagons had to yield the right of way and turn off into the mud.)

The road south from Germanna Ford crossed the Turnpike, slanting off toward the east as it went south, crossed the Plank Road, and finally got to the southern border of the Wilderness and the open country beyond. About halfway between the Turnpike and Plank Road crossings it became known as the Brock Road. The names of these three highways were presently to be written in red on the annals of the Army of the Potomac.

Thus, of the three main highways here, two ran east and west and one went north and south. Interlaced across them were various minor roads and lanes, mapped imperfectly or not at all, giving the appearance of going nowhere and, often enough, actually doing it. Only on the three main roads was any sense of direction to be had. All of the minor roads just wandered.

Somewhere to the west lay the Army of Northern Virginia. Presumably it was moving south, in order to get below the Wilderness and head the Yankees off. If by any chance it proposed to make trouble here in the Wilderness, the Turnpike and the Plank Road were the avenues by which trouble would come. Hence before the army halted for the night it was important to picket those roads, and late in the afternoon of May 4 it was so arranged, with cavalry riding west on the Plank Road and infantry solidly planted on the Turnpike.

While Warren's and Sedgwick's troops were making their bivouac along the Germanna Road and around the Wilderness Tavern, Hancock and the II Corps were making camp half a dozen miles to the east. They had crossed the Rapidan at Ely's Ford, and their route had led them to the historic Chancellorsville crossroads, where the ruins of the old Chancellor house lay charred amid the vines and the creepers, and where the bones of many unburied dead men took on a pallid gleam in the dusk. According to the plan, Hancock's men were to move on in the morning, swinging south and west in a wide arc, getting far down on the lower edge of the Wilderness. They could have gone farther this day, and it might have been well if they had done so, but the belief was that the army had the jump on its enemies. So Hancock's men camped in a haunted gloaming, where Hooker's men had fought a year earlier, and eerie omens were afloat in the dusk.

The army was spraddled out over a wide expanse of country. Burnside's IX Corps was coming down to the Rapidan from the north, the great wagon trains were trundling up behind Hancock at Chancellorsville, and scores of silent guns were parked by the Turnpike. There was something uncanny and foreboding in the air, and when night came seeping up out of the blackness under the low trees the camps were invaded by memories and premonitions.

It was the last night for many young men—the last night, in a sense, for the old Army of the Potomac, which had tramped down many roads of war and which at last was coming up against something new. The men were bivouacked on the sharp edge of a dividing line in the war, and it appears that somehow they sensed it. After tonight, everything was going to be different. The marching and the fighting were going to be different, and the comradeship around the campfires was going to be thinned out and changed, and nothing they had learned was going to help very much in the experience that lay just beyond the invisible treetops, where a wind made a stir and rustle in the branches.

In a New York regiment, in Warren's corps, it was remembered that the ordinary songs and campfire chat were missing, and the men were uneasy. They felt that they were far down in the enemy's country, and this dank Wilderness did not seem a good place to be, and they carried "a sense of ominous dread which many of us found it almost impossible to shake off." In one of the cavalry regiments the chaplain brought a group together for divine service, and he read a text about buckling on the whole armor of God and urged the men to "be prepared to stand an inspection before the King of Kings," and the usually irreverent troopers listened in silence, standing with firelight flickering on brown young faces, and some of them wept.[7]

In Hancock's artillery park the gunners found many unburied skeletons from last year's fight, and the old-timers recalled the horror of that fight, where men with broken backs or shattered thighs lay in the underbrush and watched the flames that were going to burn them alive creep closer and closer. One man predicted that "these woods will surely be burned if we fight here," and others said that they did not fear being killed nearly as much as they feared being wounded and left helpless for the forest fires. A soldier stood by a campfire and abstractedly prodded a grinning whitened skull with his toe: moved by a gloomy impulse, he turned to his comrades and cried: "This is what you are all coming to, and some of you will start toward it tomorrow." Off in the woods the whippoorwills began their remote mournful whistling, and near Wilderness Tavern pickets in the dark wood could hear a dull featureless rumbling far away to the west and they knew that somewhere in the night the Rebels were moving in great strength.[8]

Morning came in clear, with a promise of warmth later in the day, and the army began to move before sunrise. Warren's corps was to go south, sidling toward the west as it went, with Sedgwick's men following close behind and Hancock's corps swinging around farther to the left, and the troops got under way promptly. As they moved, Warren sent one division west on the Turnpike, just to make certain the flank was protected, and the colonel who had the advanced skirmish line in this division rode to the top of a rise and looked westward. The roadway here was like an open glade pointing straight toward Lee's army, its dusty white floor lying empty in the dawn, shadowy woods on either side; and far down this avenue the colonel dimly saw a column of moving troops, with men filing off into the forest to right and left, and he sent a courier hustling back to his division commander with the message: Rebels coming this way![9]

His division commander was Brigadier General Charles Griffin, a lean man with a big walrus mustache and a knack of exuding parade-ground smartness even when he was unbuttoned and dirty: an old-time Regular Army artillerist and, like many such, a hard case. His troops liked him very much—once when he came back from sick leave the men pulled him off his horse and carried him to his tent on their shoulders, which did not often happen to generals—and he had very advanced notions about getting his guns well to the front in battle. It was said that in one fight a battery commander whom he was sending forward looked at the approaching enemy and protested: "My God, General, do you mean for me to put my guns out on the skirmish line?" To which Griffin answered impatiently: "Yes, rush them in there—artillery is no better than infantry; put them in the line and let them fight together."[10] So this morning, with Rebel skirmishers approaching, Griffin pulled a section of guns out of the nearest battery and sent it rolling west on the Turnpike to support his own skirmishers. He had the rest of his division form a line of battle astride the Turnpike, and when the line was formed he ordered it to advance. If the Confederates wanted to start something here he would find out about it soon enough.

This was mean country for a moving line of battle. One hundred feet from the Turnpike a man lost sight of the road entirely, and there seemed to be no other landmarks whatever. No regiment could see the troops on its right or left unless an almost literal elbow-to-elbow contact was maintained, and no general could see more than a small fraction of his troops, or control them except by sending aides and couriers stumbling off through the woods—amid which, in most stretches, it was quite impossible to ride a horse. The going was tough, with scrubby thickets and clumps of saplings breaking the lines apart and all manner of tangled dry stuff underfoot, but the men struggled along and by and by they heard scattering shots from the skirmishers in the woods ahead.

They overtook their skirmish line, at last, and there seemed to be a substantial number of Confederates in front of them.The firing grew heavier, and it turned into regular volley firing, and a rank fog came in as the battle smoke was trapped under the low branches. To right and left and in front the dark woodland began to glow fitfully with savage, pulsating spurts of reddish light.

Keeping their formation as well as they could, the men stumbled on. They could see nothing of what lay in front of them, but the firing grew heavier every minute. The Rebels obviously meant to make a regular fight of it; the firing line was a mile wide, and everyone was shooting desperately into a gloom where moving figures were glimpsed only at rare intervals. Griffin wheeled his two guns a little farther along the road—there was no way to get them off into the woods because nothing on wheels could possibly leave the highway—and they fired straight down the Turnpike, and what had begun as an affair of the skirmishers developed into a full-dress battle.

Griffin sent men back with the news. It was very hard for him to tell what was going on more than a few rods from where he stood, but it seemed obvious that he had had a head-on collision with a Rebel assaulting column fully as big as his own, and the high command had better know about it right away. Meade got the word in his headquarters in a field near Wilderness Tavern, and it seemed to him that Lee must have left a rear guard here to hold the road while he took his main army farther south. He prepared to get other troops up to help Griffin push the rear guard out of the way, and he sent an officer spurring back toward Germanna Ford to tell Grant about it.[11]

In a few minutes Grant came up. He talked with Meade and Warren, and listened to the firing, which kept getting heavier and heavier, and word was sent out to stop the movement south: if Lee really wanted to fight here the whole Army of the Potomac would accommodate him. Sedgwick had better bring his men up as fast as he could and Hancock must start back from his thrust below the Plank Road.

Grant's people pitched his headquarters tents in a little meadow in the southwest angle of the crossroads and Grant himself rode up on a knoll just south of this meadow. He dismounted, sat on a stump, lighted a cigar, drew out a pocket knife, picked up a twig, and began to whittle. A staff officer remembered that Grant was all dressed up this morning, wearing his best uniform with the frock coat unbuttoned, a sash about his waist, sword at his side; he was wearing tan cotton-thread gloves which he forgot to remove, and his work with the twigs and the pocketknife began to snag the fingertips of these gloves and before long they were ruined.[12] Grant was sitting here quietly, whittling like a Yankee, and as he smoked without ceasing he issued the orders that would feed more and more troops into this fight.

The fight kept growing bigger. Griffin's men were advancing but it was very slow going, and as the rising wind whipped wisps and streamers of powder smoke through the treetops the advance came to a halt. The Confederates were being reinforced, although hardly any of the Federals had seen any of them. They knew of their presence only as the firing grew stronger, and as bursts of rifle fire came from farther and farther to the right and left.

The smoke intensified the forest gloom and made it opaque. Splinters and tiny branches came down as the bullets clipped through the trees, and only in the rare clearings could any man get a glimpse of his enemies. A Maine regiment came up to a little field, and the bullets were hitting the dried soil and raising little spurts of dust as if the first big drops of a heavy rain were falling.[13] The dry underbrush and matted duff underfoot began to take fire, here and there, so that malicious little flames ran along the battleground.

It was like fighting blindfolded. Here they were, in a woodland so dense that even in peacetime maneuvers a division would have been unable to keep its alignment; now there did not seem to be any alignment at all, and what was supposed to be a battle line was nothing more than a sprawling, invisible series of groups and individuals, each one firing into the woods and the smoke as if it was the Wilderness itself that was the enemy and not the men in it. A company or a regiment would crouch in the underbrush and fire manfully, taking losses but holding firm; then a sudden swell of firing would be heard off to one side or toward the rear, and for all anyone knew the rest of the army had run away and the Rebels were taking over, and men would begin to retreat, firing as they went, looking for some place where they could feel that they were part of an ordered line.

The battalions of Regulars in Griffin's division were ordered forward, and they found the undergrowth all but literally impassable. One company commander reported afterward that in order to get forward at all he had to back through the vines, creepers, and bushes, breaking a trail so that his company could follow in single file. When a more open space was reached the men would form company front, but in a few moments they would have to return to single file. Inevitably, men lost touch with their comrades, whole regiments disintegrated, and scores of men blundered into the Confederate lines and were made prisoner. There were regiments which could not even learn the direction from which the musketry that was destroying them was coming. Nothing whatever could be seen but trees and brush and blinding smoke. As one man said, it was "a battle of invisibles with invisibles."[14]

So the line crumbled and came back, and the wild noise of battle was a high-pitched, nerve-racking tumult, and at last Griffin found his men back where they had started from, Rebels on both flanks and things getting worse instead of better. Griffin knew that some of Sedgwick's men had been ordered up on his right and some of Warren's men on his left, but they seemed to have gone astray somewhere and as far as he could learn his division was all alone. He got his line stabilized somehow, and put his men to work improvising breastworks, and then he went back to headquarters, an angry man all fuming. He galloped up to Meade on the knoll where Grant was whittling and he threw himself from his horse and bitterly denounced the generals who were supposed to be helping him but whose troops were not appearing.

Griffin swore and shouted and then hurried back to his troops. Grant had heard him, and he was not used to brigadiers who publicly and profanely denounced their superiors, and as Griffin stormed off Grant—who somehow had not quite caught his name—went over to Meade and asked: "Who is this General Gregg? You ought to put him under arrest."

For once in his life Meade was calm and not irascible. He stood facing Grant, towering head and shoulders over him, and he murmured gently: "His name's Griffin, not Gregg, and that's only his way of talking"; and as he spoke he leaned forward and buttoned up Grant's uniform coat for him, for all the world like a kindly father getting his son ready for school.[15] Then Grant went back to his stump and his twigs and his cigars, and couriers dashed off with orders, and in the trackless forest the support troops shouldered their muskets and tried to go forward through the midday twilight.

It was becoming increasingly obvious that this was no rear guard the Federals were fighting. (As a matter of fact, it was Confederate General Ewell's whole army corps: far from looking for a battleground to the south, Lee was making his fight right here, and if the Federals got one foot of Wilderness ground they were going to have to pay for it.) One of Sedgwick's divisions went stumbling up a cow track in the woods, and at what seemed to be a suitable place the men tried to form a proper battle line and go on to close quarters. But the trees and the undergrowth were too thick. A battle line could not advance, could not even be formed, and at last the separate regiments went blindly forward in column, giving up the formation in which they could fight for a formation in which they could at least move. They reached ground that had been fought over, and around them was the pungent smoke of a forest fire, and they plowed through burnt-over spaces where their feet kicked sparks and smoke puffs out of the matted ground. Dead men lay in these cinders, their bodies charred and partly consumed, and a fearful stench lay in the air.[16]

There was no enemy to be seen anywhere. A brigadier made his way to his division commander and asked where he should put his men. "Move," said the commander grandly, "to the sound of the heaviest firing." This was no help at all, because as far as the brigadier could tell the firing came from everywhere, and the only way to find the Rebel battle line was to blunder into it. The smoke became heavier and heavier as the men advanced, and the sound of rifle fire and shouting men and crackling flames grew louder, and the bullets came faster and more deadly. A Wisconsin soldier wrote that the men in his regiment, quite unable to see where they were going or whom they were shooting at, simply knelt in the twilight and "fired by earsight."

There was a high wind, and it whipped the little flames in the underbrush into big flames, and its roar in the treetops mingled with the roar of battle as if some unimaginable tempest were lashing this dark forest. Men who fought were aware that all about them wounded men were pathetically trying to drag themselves along the ground away from the fires.

In one place the soldiers came to a swampy ravine, all overgrown with scrub pines. The ravine was not a hundred yards wide, but the farther bank was completely invisible. There were Rebels there in plenty, as the men could easily tell; some of them were shooting, and others were using axes to cut trees for breastworks, and the wild racket told just what was going on, but from first to last there was no one to be seen. So the men of the VI Corps piled up logs and scooped up earth for breastworks of their own and hung on in the twilight, trading death with enemies they never saw, and at times the noise of musketry all about them swelled up to a clamor such as they had never heard before in any of their battles. There was no sound of artillery, because guns could not be advanced or fired in this jungle—Griffin had long since lost the two guns he had pushed along the open Turnpike—but thousands upon thousands of men were firing their muskets as fast as they could load, until the whole Wilderness seemed to throb with the endless concussion.[17]

These VI Corps men were coming up on the north side of the Turnpike. South of it, Warren was hurrying about through the woods, trying to get his other divisions up on Griffin's left. Grant was still sitting on his stump on the little knoll behind the lines, but his staff officers were ranging far and fast through the tangle, and the orders they carried were infusing something of the bearded little general's relentless drive all down the army's chain of command. Nobody had planned to fight here but here was where the fight was, and if in the past the Army of the Potomac had never quite managed to get all of its men into action that fault was not going to be repeated now.

There had never been a fight like this before. Things were clear enough on the map, and Grant had an uncanny way of studying a map once and then carrying it in his memory, but neither he nor anyone else had ever tried to fight a battle in a place where nobody could see anything at all. The armies were visible neither to their enemies nor to their own commanders. It would do no good for the commanding general to ride out along his lines, because there was quite literally no place where as many as a thousand men could be seen at one time, and in any case where the men were fighting the forest was so dense that riding was impossible. There were no adequate roads, and the Federal maps were very imperfect anyway, and the most careful directives could come down to a matter of saying—The enemy is over there somewhere; go and find him and fight him.

Warren cantered along a farm lane and came up to one of his trusted division commanders, Major General James Wadsworth—white-haired, crowding sixty, an old man as ages were reckoned in the army—and Warren told him to get his men into action just south of the Turnpike. Wadsworth was a stout fighter, much admired by his men; he was very wealthy and he was serving without pay, and they honored him for it, and they remembered how on the weary march to Gettysburg he had seized civilians who stood cheering by the roadside and had taken their shoes for his own men to wear. He was quite willing now to go in and fight beside Griffin's division, but he did not know where Griffin's division was and he asked Warren. Warren pulled out a pocket compass and studied it—tactics here were as much a matter of navigation as anything—and he told him to march straight west. Wadsworth's division fell into line, crossed an open field, and plunged into the wood.[18]

The division marched quickly into trouble. Either Wadsworth had no compass or it was defective, or perhaps in that incomprehensible undergrowth it was not humanly possible to move any body of troops in a straight line. In any case the men swung round toward the north, and instead of coming in beside Griffin's men they came in on an angle, presenting their left flank to the Confederates just at the moment when the Confederates were sending in reinforcements for a counterattack. The noise of the firing swelled to a terrible new pitch as enormous rolling volleys came out of the woods to break regiments and brigades to bits.

No one could remember anything very distinctly, afterward. Some regiments found that they had got in behind other regiments that were supposed to be far off to one side. Others knew they were near the Rebels only when they found themselves being shot at—shot at with deadly aim, they noticed: the Confederates were hugging the ground and firing low, and if they could not see much of their targets they were hitting it with murderous efficiency.

There seemed to be whole acres where the musketry had cut the saplings in two a few feet from the ground, so that the tops lopped over drunkenly to make progress even more impossible. Wadsworth tried hard to swing his division around to face the flanking fire, but it could not be done. Troops could not be maneuvered in this ground. Companies fought by themselves, lone squads by themselves sometimes, and the fact that no connected battle line could be seen seemed to give a new terror to the fighting. Some regiments broke and fled, not because they were being punished but because the crash of battle suddenly sounded beside or behind them and the panic cry: "We're flanked!" was raised.

Beyond Wadsworth, Warren had found his division of Pennsylvania Reserves. The Reserves were famous veterans—Meade's own division, once upon a time, the division whose command the governor of Pennsylvania once offered to George B. McClellan in the springtime of the war. It was led by a former army surgeon, Brigadier General Samuel W. Crawford, a member of the original Fort Sumter garrison: "a tall, chesty, glowering man, with heavy eyes, a big nose and bushy whiskers," as one of his men remembered him, who "wore habitually a turn-out-the-guard expression." Crawford tried to bring his men in beside Wadsworth's, but he had even more trouble than Wadsworth had had. One regiment blundered straight into the middle of a Confederate brigade and was captured almost entire, and the others stumbled around in the underbrush, lost all sense of direction and contact, and knew only that they were constantly being shot at from the most improbable directions by men they could not find. It seems that the Reserves were just a trifle lukewarm about things, anyway, this day. Most of them had refused to re-enlist, and the division was fully aware that it had only twenty-seven more days to serve before it would be sent home. Understandably, this tempered enthusiasm: who wanted to get shot, so near the end of his time as a soldier?[19]

The whole Wilderness seemed to be boiling and smoking, with dense clouds going up to blot out the sunlight. From the rear, Warren pushed the rest of his corps into the fight, and there is no coherent story to be told about any of it: it was all violent confusion, with occasional revealing glimpses to be had in the infernal clogged mist.

The Iron Brigade went forward and was routed, and for once in their history the men of this famous command ran for the rear, all organization lost— to be rallied, somehow, half a mile back, just in time to fix bayonets and check the rout of another brigade which came streaming back over them. A New York regiment crossed a weedy little field, got into more of a fight than it could handle, and ran back to the other side of the field, leaving many wounded men in the open space. The woods were on fire, and the flames were driven by the wind across the dried growth in the field where the wounded men lay, and the New Yorkers looked on in paralyzed horror as the flames reached these helpless men and ignited the paper cartridges in the boxes at their waists. (One man remembered how the noise of these exploding cartridges—which made dreadful wounds in the sides of the wounded men—made quite a cheerful-sounding pop-pop-pop which could be heard despite all of the surrounding din.) For a moment the fighting around this field ceased, and Northerners and Southerners alike went out into the open to try to drag the men to safety.

The smoke blew down across the field, and all around to right and left there was the unending sound of rifle fire, and the log breastworks the Confederates had built took fire and sent heavy yellowish white smoke billowing out in choking clouds, and the living and dead bodies that lay under it were burned beyond recognition.[20] And all of this was a part of the fight to see which side could hold its ground astride the Orange Turnpike.

This was one battle. Two miles to the south of it, along the Plank Road, there was a wholly separate battle, just as desperate, drawing men in as the first battle had done, a battle which for a time was a fight by the Army of the Potomac for simple survival.

Key point here was the place where the Plank and Brock roads crossed. A thin line of cavalry had been patrolling the Plank Road, and while Griffin's men were going into action along the Turnpike this cavalry found Confederate infantry pressing up the Plank Road. The infantry began to seem very numerous and determined, and it drove the Yankee cavalry away, and if the Confederates could seize the crossroads the Federal army would be cut in half, with Hancock's corps isolated off to the south, the rest of the army fighting west of Wilderness Tavern, and the Rebels planted squarely in between. So the cavalry sent couriers riding frantically off to headquarters, men who rode with crumpled envelopes held in their teeth, one hand for the reins and the other for the carbine.

Back on his knoll, Grant read these dispatches and he reached out for the nearest troops. These happened to be Brigadier General George W. Getty's division of the VI Corps—6,000 soldiers as cool and as tough as any, including in their number a Vermont brigade which is still remembered as one of the two or three best in the army. Getty was told to get his men over to the Plank Road at top speed and clear the Southerners out of there. At the same time gallopers were sent off to Hancock to tell him to double back on his tracks and get to that vital crossroads as fast as he could.

Getty made it with seconds to spare. He rode ahead of his troops, his staff and mounted orderlies trotting at his heels, and the last of the cavalry had gone and the advancing Confederates were clearly visible. It would be a few minutes before the Federal infantry could get up, so Getty coolly planted himself and his mounted people in the middle of the road, to make it look as if cavalry reinforcements or artillery or somebody of consequence was making a stand here. The bluff worked, briefly, the advancing Confederates slowed down and sent skirmishers creeping forward to find out what was going on, and in the minutes that were bought Getty was able to get his leading regiments into line of battle and start them moving west.[21]

There was enough to keep them busy. The Confederates here belonged to A. P. Hill, and he had a way of piling his men in fast and hard, and the rival battle lines ranged deeply into the woods and fired as fast as they could handle their muskets. Getty could see that he was outnumbered, and he wanted to fight at long range and wait for help. But Grant felt that the day was made for fighting, and he sent down word to wait for nothing—pitch in and attack, and if any reinforcements show up we'll send them to you.

So Getty's bugles sounded, high and thin over the noise of the firing, and the Federal battle line went crashing forward through the timber. It got to close quarters at once, and in the pathless tangle on both sides of the Plank Road there was an enormous shock and crash of battle, Federals and Confederates shooting at each other at fifty paces, artillery on both sides firing down the narrow road and making it a place where no man could live.

One officer noted that this was like no fight he had ever heard of. Usually, he said, when two rival lines of infantry met at close range the fight was quite brief, one line or the other quickly giving way. But here there was no giving way whatever. The men simply lay on the ground or knelt behind logs and stumps and kept on firing, and the very intensity of their fire pinned both sides in position—the only chance for safety was to crouch low or lie flat; if a man stood up either to advance or to run away he was almost certain to be shot.[22]

In a way, the fact that the men could rarely see what they were shooting at made it even worse. They simply pointed their rifles into the rolling smoke and the thick stunted trees and blazed away, shooting low by instinct, and a sheet of flame swept over the desolate intricate woodland, hitting anything that stood three feet off the ground. So this fight went on for no one knew how long—an hour, two hours, an eternity—and the battle zone grew wider and wider as Confederates came groping blindly forward on the flanks. The woods took fire, just as they had done farther north, and the crackle of flames mingled with the wild yelling and cursing of men and the swinging, whacking crash of rifle fire, and the dense forest seemed to trap the roar of battle and press it close to the ground so that the noise became unendurable, more terrible than anything that had ever been heard before. Getty had all of his men in action and there were not enough of them, not by half, and the Vermont Brigade hung on with a thousand of its men killed or wounded, and the terrible little flames came snaking forward through the dead leaves and dry pine thickets. Wounded men were seen to load and cap their muskets so that they could shoot themselves if the fire reached them.[23]

Somewhere to the north old Wadsworth was ordered to swing his battered division around and come down to help. He was in a good spot to land on the Rebel flank and he was only a mile away, but his regiments and brigades were trying to wheel around in the densest part of the Wilderness and he was taking a good deal of care because he did not want to drift into battle by the flank a second time—and, all in all, he might as well have been north of the Rapidan. By prodigious effort he got his men faced south and they started to move, but they could reach no one but isolated Confederate skirmishers. They stood squarely in front of a great gap in the Confederate line, but they could not come close to finding it, and they drifted down through the blinding forest like a hulk gone out of control, to run aground at last a few furlongs away from the place where they were needed.

In the rear, Hancock's men were at last coming up the Brock Road. Hancock was in the lead, shoving the winded men out of column and into line in the miserable second growth, prudently putting some of them to work building a log breastwork at the edge of the road for use in case anything went wrong.

There was a nightmare slowness about it all. The Brock Road was no better than a narrow lane, bordered closely by all but impenetrable woods—it had taken Stonewall Jackson two mortal hours to form a battle line in this area, just a year ago—and the road was clotted with artillery and confused moving troops and men felling trees and piling up log barricades. The day grew old and the sun was going down, the western light coming all red and tarnished through the blowing clouds of heavy smoke, and Getty's exhausted line was about ready to fall clear out of the war; and at last Hancock got a couple of brigades lined up and he sent them in to the attack.

When they hit they hit hard—they were veterans, and they believed that when Hancock told them to charge he meant for them to keep on going—and as Hancock slid new troops in behind them and on both sides they swept into the littered woods like a tornado. They overran Getty's tired men and bent the Confederates back, and now it was the enemy's turn to feel that they were outnumbered, outflanked, and forsaken. But if the Yankees had one of their crack combat outfits in here, so did the Confederates, and in these murky woods any little knot of determined men could cause much trouble, and there was a titanic wrestle in the darkening woods, and it is possible that in all the war the men of the North and the South did no more desperate fighting than they did right here, on the two sides of the Plank Road.

The Federals had had much close-order drill, and they were used to fighting in solid ranks, where each man could see his comrades at his side. This was not like that at all. It was Braddock and his British Regulars fighting the Indians all over again, and the scrub pines, the brush piles, and the massed saplings broke the advancing lines apart, leaving fragments that felt isolated and alone. As one veteran recalled it, "the troops were so scattered and disorganized by the straggling way they had got forward that there was no central discipline to bind the men together." So this advance was no triumphal march; it had wide gaps in it, and terrible routs and defeats, and desperate deeds of bravery and of cowardice which no one ever knew about. The veteran 1st Massachusetts, shock troops if there ever were any, was cut up into squads and platoons, and the fragments came up toward a little rise of ground and got a close-range volley from Rebels lying prone just beyond the ridge, and broke and ran for it in wild fright. Their panic spread to right and left, for cohesion and spirit were gone, and in a moment a whole division was running away—Gershom Mott's men, who had been Joe Hooker's division long ago, famous as one of the stanchest divisions in the army, shattered and useless now.[24]

But Hancock had more men than Hill had, and in the end they made their weight felt. The fugitives lost their panic when they got back to the log breastworks by the Brock Road, and the men who had not run kept on advancing, and the Confederates along the Plank Road were on the edge of final disaster when night and sheer breathlessness and muscle weariness at last came down and stopped the fighting. The armies did not draw apart. They simply stopped where they were, and regiments and brigades lay all over the Wilderness, facing in every direction, nobody knowing where he or his neighbors or his enemies might be. Northerners and Southerners were all intermingled in the dreadful night, so close together that men were constantly blundering into the wrong camp and being made prisoners. Skirmishers were awake, firing at any sound or movement, and afterward it seemed to some men that the battle really went on all night without much letup. Deep in the woods many fires sparked and smoldered.

There were horrors in the night. An officer from a New England regiment, out hunting stragglers, groped through the fathomless dark and somewhere far in the rear a wakeful battery sent over a casual, unaimed shell. It burst near him, and its sudden flare lit up a dogwood tree right before him, white blossoms waxen and mystically motionless in the quick red light. Half blinded, the officer moved on in the succeeding darkness, missed his path, stumbled, and kicked a heap of smoldering leaves into flame; and the flame caught in the hair and beard of a dead sergeant lying in the path, lighting up a ghastly face and wide-open sightless eyes.[25]

2. SHADOW IN THE NIGHT

Never before had there been a night like this one. A reek of wood smoke, powder smoke, and the dreadful odor of burned bodies hung in the air, soiling the night and dimming the stars. There was no silence. Pickets and skirmishers were nervous, firing at everything and at nothing, and from the rear there was a steady rumble and murmur as troops marched up to take new positions. From miles of scorched ground, up front, there was an unceasing crying of wounded men.

Usually wounded men on the battlefield did not make a great deal of noise. The bad pain generally came later on, and while men here and there might moan and cry out and call for water, most them took what they had to take in a stunned, half-dazed silence. But this night was different. The underbrush was aglow with stealthy fires, and the ground was matted with dead leaves and dry pine needles, and the terror of the flames lay upon the field so that men who could not move screamed for comrades to come and help them. On both sides, stretcher-bearers tried to do what they could; but it was very dark and the woodland was a creepy maze, and anyway a man who went out to help the wounded was very likely to be shot. A Federal wrote that "the Rebels were fidgety and quick to shoot," and a Confederate officer said the Yankee skirmishers made it impossible for his troops to help wounded men who lay only a dozen paces outside of their lines.[1]

Behind the front there was ceaseless movement: steady tramp of long columns getting into place for the next day's fighting, and a confused coming and going of stragglers and broken squads and companies hunting their proper commands. In all of this, too, there was a restless stirring by veteran soldiers who were operating a strange, unofficial, and highly effective little system by which the enlisted man kept himself informed about things.

After every battle, men by twos and threes would slip away from their bivouacs and wander up and down the lines, visiting other campfires to exchange information. They were always welcomed, and they were always watched quite closely, because they were notoriously light-fingered and would steal any haversacks that were within their reach. The army called these men "news walkers," and they were in fact amateur and self-appointed reporters, hunting the information by which they could judge how the battle was going, what army morale was like, and what the prospects were for the morrow. They were on the prowl tonight, and one of Hancock's gunners told how he and his mates would look up from their campfires to see "shadowy forms hurrying rapidly through the woods or along the roads." The gunner described their method of operation:

"Frequently these figures would halt, and then, seeing our fire with men around it, they would issue forth from the woods and join us. They would sit down, filling their pipes, light them with glowing coals, and then, with their rifles lying across their knees, ask for the Second Corps news, inquire as to our losses and whether we had gained or lost ground, and what Confederate command was opposed to us. They would anxiously inquire as to the truth of rumors of disaster which they might have heard during the day. They would listen attentively to what we said, and it was a point of honor not to give false information to these men. And they would briefly tell the Fifth or Sixth or Ninth Corps news, and quickly disappear in the darkness."

So it went tonight, with the smoky tainted air heavy under the trees, and men who had fought all day were hiking for miles to find out what had really been happening. Their system was effective. It was notorious that no headquarters announcement was believed unless it jibed with what the news walkers picked up. Often enough the soldiers had a better line on the situation than the generals had, and when they criticized strategy or tactics they usually knew what they were talking about. As the movement finally died out and the men turned in for such sleep as they could get, the army had a pretty fair notion of what had been happening and what was apt to come next.[2]

What would come next, indeed, was fairly obvious: a big attack along the Plank Road, where the disordered pieces of A. P. Hill's Confederate corps lay crisscross in the darkness. Lee had fought with part of his army missing, and the missing portion—Longstreet's corps—would not be up until midmorning or later. What was in the cards therefore was a hard smash at Lee's right, to overwhelm it before Longstreet's rough veterans could get on the scene, and the fighting was apt to begin as soon as the first faint light broke over the eastern sky.

Grant wanted the attack made at four o'clock, but the corps commanders were having much trouble getting their disordered divisions sorted out and Meade persuaded the general to allow a postponement. Burnside's IX Corps was south of the Rapidan now, and Burnside was under orders to get his men down to the Plank Road and join in the assault. Meanwhile, by a little after five in the morning, Hancock got his own troops and Getty's thinned division from the VI Corps lined up for action, and he immediately sent them west on both sides of the Plank Road.

They ran into action at once. Hill's Confederates had hardly so much as tried to straighten their lines during the night—all of the ordinary difficulties of moving troops in this jungle were infinitely intensified in the darkness—and they were not in the best shape to meet an attack. But they were very tough characters and they started firing as soon as the first Yankee skirmishers came crashing through the underbrush, and beneath the low branches the gray half-light of dawn became spectral with wispy layers of smoke. The skirmishers waited to let the main battle line catch up with them, and then everybody went plunging forward and the battle of the Wilderness was on again.

Hancock was a driver, and he sent his men on like a flood tide. From their dark bivouac north of the road, Wadsworth's division from the V Corps fell into line and came tramping down at an angle, flanking some of Hill's men and knocking them out of the way. The Federal battle line was more than a mile wide and it moved with enormous weight, overrunning the islands of stubborn resistance and shooting down the Rebels who were groping for new positions, and an unearthly racket of musketry went rolling up the sky.

Back by the crossroads Hancock was elated. The wound he had received at Gettysburg still hurt him, and he had official permission to go about in an ambulance if he chose, but he was astride his horse today and as reports came back he felt that everything was going as it should. To one of Meade's staff officers he called out gaily: "We are driving them, sir—tell General Meade we are driving them most beautifully!" He was robust and handsome and the joy of battle was on him, and to look at him as he sat his horse in this moment of triumph was to understand why the war correspondents liked to tag him "Hancock the superb."

Yet even as he exulted in his success he was beginning to fret. Burnside's men were coming down much more slowly than had been expected. They were supposed to take part in this big attack and they should be here now, but they were not showing up and Hancock began to worry. He told Meade's man that with their weight added to his own column of attack "we could smash A. P. Hill all to pieces!"[3]

Yet things were going well, regardless. Two miles west of the crossroads where Hancock was waiting, the cheering Federals were sweeping in on the edge of a meager little clearing around the Widow Tapp's farm, where Lee himself stood among his guns and tried to patch up a dissolving battle line. Just beyond him the white tops of the Confederate wagon trains were visible, and if Hancock's men could just go driving on across this clearing Hancock's goal would be won.

And there was a moment, just here by the Tapp farmstead, with dawn coming up through the smoke and the Northern advance breaking out of the trees, when the authentic end of the war could be glimpsed beyond the ragged clearing. If Hancock's men could go storming on for another half mile, Lee's army would be broken and it would all be over. It may be that the Army of the Potomac never came nearer to it than this—neither above the Antietam, nor at Gettysburg, nor anywhere else—and final victory was just half an hour away. But the magical half hour flickered and was lost forever, and if any Northern soldier saw victory here he saw no more than a moving shadow distorted by the battle smoke.

Confederate artillery was massed in the open ground, and the guns fired before the last fugitive Rebels had time to get out of the way, and for a moment the pursuing Federals were knocked back into the woods. Then west of the clearing there rose the high, quavering scream of the Rebel yell, and Longstreet's men— here at last!—came running in, gripping their rifles in their tanned fists. Lee was in their midst, swinging his hat and trying to lead them until they made him go back (for they knew that the Confederacy could live no longer than that man lived) and there was a staggering shock as the Northern and Southern assault waves dashed together. Above and below the Plank Road, far off into the dark murky wood, the fighting swelled and rolled as more and more of Lee's last-minute reserves came running into action, and the counterattack broke the force of the Federal charge.[4]

But the charge was still on. Back by the Brock Road Hancock was still driving reinforcements forward. Almost half of the army was under his command this morning, and he proposed to use every man who had been given him. Wadsworth's men struggled out of the jungle at last and the Plank Road lay across their way, and they surged forward in a great crowd, yelling mightily. They got into the path of Getty's division, which was driving west along the road, and there was a heavy traffic jam, two divisions all intermingled, men swearing, officers thwacking about with swords, and the disordered mob sagged off toward the south; and Lee's guns in the Tapp farm clearing caught the right flank of Wadsworth's uneven line and blasted it with fearful effect. Wadsworth was galloping desperately up and down the Plank Road, his old Revolutionary War saber in his hand, trying once again to get his line wheeled around so that it could face the firing instead of getting it all in the flank. Back to the right and rear the leading division of Burnside's corps was at last creeping down through the woods, and far to the north by the Orange Turnpike Warren's and Sedg-wick's soldiers opened a hot fire on Ewell's men, to keep the Confederates from sending help from their left to their right.

The focus of it all was the narrow Plank Road and the deadly woods on both sides of it. Never before had the Army of the Potomac thrown so many men into one assault as were thrown in here. Twenty-five thousand soldiers were moving up in one stupendous charge, and most of them were battle-trained veterans. Yet what they had learned in other battles seemed to be of little use here, and in the Wilderness numbers did not seem to count. They were fighting a strange, desperate fight, without color and without drama. The whole thing was invisi-ble. It was smothered down out of sight in five miles of smoking wilderness, and even men who were in the storm center of it saw no more than fragmentary pic-tures—little groups of men moving in and out of a spooky, reddish luminous haze, with rifles flashing indistinctly in the gloom, the everlasting trees and brush always in the way, the weight of the smoke tamping down everything ex-cept the evil flames that sprang up wherever men fought.

In other battles these soldiers had known the fearful pageantry of war. There was none of that here, for this was the battle no man saw. There was only the clanging twilight and the heavy second growth and the enemies who could rarely be seen but who were always firing. There was no more war in the grand style, with things in it to hearten a man even as they killed him. This was all cramped and close and ugly, like a duel fought with knives in a cellar far un-derground.

Up from the forest came a tumult such as none of the army's battles had made before. It had a higher pitch, because so little artillery was used, but more rifles were being fired than ever before and they were being fired more rapidly and continuously, and the noise was unbroken, maddening, beyond all description. A man in the VI Corps called it "the most terrific musketry firing ever heard on the American continent," and a New Yorker said that from the rear it sounded like "the wailing of a tempest or the roaring of the ocean in a storm." Groping for the right superlative, another soldier wrote that "the loudest and longest peals of thunder were no more to be compared to it in depth or volume than the rippling of a trout brook to the roaring of Niagara." Far back by Wilderness Tavern Meade's chief of staff tilted a professional ear and commented that the uproar "approached the sublime."[5]

Always the little flames sprang up, as the blast from rifle muzzles hit the dried leaves and the brittle pine twigs, and the fear of these flames haunted every sol-dier. Often, when they were hit, men cried at once for help—anything was better than to lie in a firetrap and wait for the flames. It may be that the heavy blanket of stifling smoke that drifted on ahead of these fires was a mercy, for there were men who believed that it often suffocated the wounded, quickly strangling the life out of them before the fire could torture them to death.[6]

Behind the lines, far to the rear where the smoke-fog and the noise came roll-ing down the wind, there was a constant movement of walking wounded looking for field hospitals. Some came alone, using muskets as canes or crutches. Others came in little groups, supporting each other, the halt leading the maimed and the blind. All of them were bloody. Cavalry patrols ranged all approaches to the rear areas and when a straggler appeared their curt demand was: "show blood!" The man who could not do it was arrested as a runaway.

The wounded came back with tight, bloodless lips, and in most cases their clothing was disarranged. Unless he was totally disabled, the wounded man's first act, usually, was to tear his clothing open and look at his wound, to see whether it was going to be mortal. The examination over, some men would look relieved, confident that they had little to worry about. Others would turn pale and stare blankly at nothing, convinced that they could not recover. These men had seen many gunshot wounds, and they were pretty fair diagnosticians.

On this day the wounded brought discouraging tales back to the dressing stations. They said the fighting was not going well, and one man remarked glumly that "the Confederates are shooting to kill, this time." Hospitals were alive with rumors of disaster: the right wing had crumbled, Lee had seized the Rapidan crossings, the army would soon find itself surrounded. The adolescent drummer boys had been pressed into service, along the firing lines, as stretcher-bearers. Properly, this was not drummer boys' work, but as one man said, "It was in the Wilderness, under Grant," where "even boys counted."[7]

Along the Plank Road there was complete pandemonium. The narrow lane was choked with moving men—regiments and bits of regiments trying to reform, hundreds of Confederate prisoners who had been disarmed and told to hike to the rear and who were trying hard to get back out of range, stretcher-bearers and walking wounded moving along with the same idea in mind, dazed stragglers and lost men hunting in vain for their regiments or for some quiet place to hide or for a safe road to the back country. There was such a tangle in every great battle, of course, and during every attack there were places just behind the front where it looked as if the army were coming apart. Yet the confusion in the Wilderness this morning was something special.[8] The commanders behind the lines—Grant, smoking and whittling and noting all the dispatches, Meade near him talking busily with staff officers, Hancock at the crossroads ordering men forward—they had no conception of what was really going on up in front. They could not have one. The battle was out of their control, fighting itself, a great curtain of distance and forest and choking smoke cutting them off from contact and knowledge. Things were going wrong, and they could not know about it—nor, if they did know, could they do anything about it.

In this forest it was almost as bad to win as to lose. Either way, a battle line was certain to get thrown into hopeless disorder. Along five miles of fighting front there was hardly one brigadier who could really control his own line, because there was hardly one brigadier who could put his hand on more than a fraction of his own command. The lines had been jumbled as they had never been jumbled before. Divisions and brigades were all divided. Along the zone of the heaviest firing there was not a single regiment which had on either flank a regiment which so much as belonged to its own army corps.[9]

Commands were broken into moving fragments which floated blindly about trying to reassemble without the faintest idea where their comrades might be. Reinforcements lost their way as they tried to go forward and made the trouble worse, so that instead of adding weight to the attack they crippled it. In one place, men would be standing ten ranks deep, and a few hundred yards to right or left there would be a complete gap in the line, with nobody at all to hold the ground and only the bushes and the blinding haze to keep the Confederates from seeing what an opening lay in front of them. Brigades got in behind one another and shot blindly into ranks of their own friends.[10]

One of Hancock's best brigadiers was ordered to move up the road and support Getty's division, but before he could get started Getty's division had been crowded over to some other part of the battlefield, so that the support troops moving in without skirmishers ran head on into a Southern battle line, which opened a deadly fire before the Federals realized that they were anywhere near the enemy. The brigadier did not know whether he was within half a mile of the place where he was supposed to be—nor did he know what he was supposed to do, now that he was wherever he was, except fight, which he could not help doing with Rebels all around him. Long after the war he wrote that he still did not know what had been expected of him. What he had actually done was to get several hundred of his men shot to no purpose at all, and it seemed improbable that that was quite what Hancock had wanted.[11]

Near the road, Wadsworth was still moving his regiments about so that they could renew the attack. The old man was tired and he felt unwell, and he told an aide that he really ought to turn command of the division over to someone else and go to the rear, but there was too much to do just now and he would wait for a lull. Somewhere behind him, men from the IX Corps were pushing forward; the men said afterward they made the final fifty yards of their advance crawling on hands and knees through a pine thicket, and when they got through the thicket they had a terrible hot fight with some Rebels behind a fence-rail breastwork. South of Wadsworth's division, soldiers said that all morning long they had seen neither a general officer nor a staff officer to tell them what to do. They were without commanders, and each regiment was fighting entirely on its own.[12]

This sort of thing could last just so long before something gave way. Nobody knew what was happening because nobody could see 100 feet in any direction, but suddenly, without any warning, the sprawling line across the Plank Road began to come to pieces. Out of the smoke came men who had stopped fighting and were unhurriedly going back out of action, and nothing that anyone said to them seemed to make the slightest difference. One of Wadsworth's soldiers said it was the strangest sight ever seen: the men pressing to the rear did not seem to be demoralized or scared, and yet they did not quite look like organized troops retreating under orders, either. They were just going back, looking like "a throng of armed men who were returning dissatisfied from a muster." One of Meade's staff officers noticed that the men were not running, and were neither pale nor frightened, nor had they thrown away their weapons: "They had fought all they meant to fight for the present and there was an end to it." A New Jersey soldier noted the same baffling traits and said the only explanation he could make was that "a large number of troops were about to leave the service."[13]

Whatever had happened, there it was—an unpanicked but irreversible retreat by the army's shock troops, thousands of men turning their backs and sauntering calmly toward the rear. Wadsworth's men caught the infection, and as they turned to go the Rebels hit them with hard volleys that turned the retreat into actual rout, and the whole division dissolved, thousands of men streaming off through woods. Wadsworth stormed along trying to rally them, but a Confederate bullet killed him and for the time being his division simply went out of existence; of 5,000 men who advanced with it in the morning, fewer than 500 could be rallied that evening, the rest all scattered over five square miles of unplumbed forest. (It might be noted that 1,100 of the 5,000 had been shot.)[14]

So the whole advance crumbled, and back by the Brock Road it looked as if this half of the army had broken up. Hundreds of men were pouring down the Plank Road, and other hundreds were breaking out of the woods, and the whole Wilderness seemed to be leaking beaten Yankees. Hancock's inner thoughts just then were not recorded, but he must have thanked the god of battles that the evening before he had had his men build a stout log breastwork all along the western side of the Brock Road, a heavy fence of piled-up saplings standing three feet high and running north and south for two miles or more.

It was just the dike that was needed to check this retreat. Disorganized men who reached it looked about them, fell in behind the barricade, loaded their muskets and peered into the blank woodland from which they had just emerged. Shattered regiments and brigades, crawling over this rude fence, managed to form new ranks on the east side of it, and stood there waiting for orders, their panic gone. Off to the north the roar of battle continued, for Burnside's men at last were making their presence felt, but they had come in too late and their attack was not heavy enough, and nothing that they could do could change the situation on the south side of the Plank Road.

What had happened was perfectly simple, and it had turned into catastrophe largely because nobody could see what was going on.

When Hancock made his advance that morning he had been plagued by a report (which happened to be false) that some or all of Longstreet's men were apt to come up into action from the south. On his extreme left, therefore, he held one division out of action as flank guard. All sorts of wild rumors about approaching Confederates had been circulating that morning, and the result was that some 8,000 of Hancock's best soldiers had been immobilized. Furthermore, as the rest of the corps advanced along the Plank Road, a gap two miles wide had opened between the assaulting column and this reserve division.

Eventually Hancock decided that all of the rumors were false, and he sent word to this idle division to advance so as to come up on the left flank of the men who were making the attack on the Tapp farm. If this had been done, Longstreet's counterattack would probably have been blunted. But all of Hancock's messages seem to have gone astray—couriers hit by stray bullets, or captured by Confederates, or just plain lost in the battle turmoil—and John Gibbon, the highly competent soldier who commanded the reserve division, never got the orders. So the division stayed out of action, and when the Federals began to fight with Longstreet's troops in the wild chaos two miles to the west their southern flank was unprotected.[15]

Longstreet discovered this, and mounted a cunning flank attack. This hit the left end of the Yankee firing line and broke it just at the moment when the confusion of the whole line was at its worst. The effect was like tipping over the first in a row of dominoes. The men who were driven in by the flank attack went north, toward the Plank Road, retreating across the immediate rear of all the troops that were in line. Blind and bewildered, and quite unable to see anything, the men in front knew only that the troops on the left were running away; and in the invisibility out of which they had emerged there sounded much musketry and the jeering, triumphant sound of the Rebel yell. The fight had not been making much sense for half an hour or more; now it was ceasing to make any sense at all, and one after another the men headed back for the Brock Road—not panicky, for the most part, but not doing any more fighting just now, either.

For a while there was a lull. The Confederates were as much disorganized by their victory as the Federals had been by their own a little earlier. In the confusion Longstreet was shot by his own men, and he was carried to the rear coughing blood, out of action for months to come, and it was going to take an hour or more to get his brigades unscrambled so that the advance could be resumed. So Hancock was given precious time to organize his defenses along the Brock Road, and when the Rebel attack was at last renewed the men were ready for it.

Not too ready, possibly: the men had fallen in behind the log barricade willingly enough, yet it was noticed that in some places they simply cowered close to the earth, pointed their muskets up toward the treetops, and maintained a fire that could hurt no one except birds. Yet by this time the forest fire was just about taking charge, anyway. The Rebel battle line that charged up to the Brock Road came splashing through little pools of fire, and here and there the log breastworks themselves caught fire and blazed up hotly, so that neither side could hold possession, and attackers and defenders stood a dozen yards apart and fought each other through a sheet of flame. In some places cannon had been put into line, their muzzles protruding out over the logs, and the gunners tried to work these in spite of the fire. Some of these men were horribly wounded when cartridges were exploded at the gun's muzzles.[16]

In a few places the Rebels came through the line. But there were reserves to deal with them—Samuel Carroll's brigade, which had driven Jubal Early's men out of the guns on Cemetery Hill at Gettysburg, on the night of the second day's battle there—and these men rammed the attackers back. The Southerners finally retreated out of sight through the burning woods, and all that had been accomplished—about all that was possible, under the circumstances—was to increase the casualty lists on both sides.

Grant had spent most of his time on the knoll over by the Turnpike, and there had not been much that he or anyone else could do to control this insane battle that slipped out of sight every time the fighting lines went into action. Yet somehow he had created a new atmosphere around headquarters, and around noon he sent word to Hancock to put on a new offensive, early in the evening, with the same men who had been driven back in the morning. The Rebel assault on the Brock Road had of course canceled this plan, but if anyone cared to make a note of it, there it was—the commanding general's only reaction to news of a reverse had been to call for another attack.[17]

It had been somewhat the same, once that day, when Ewell's men bent the Union line back near the Turnpike and got some guns far enough forward to shell the very knoll where Grant was sitting. An anxious staff officer came up and asked if it would not be prudent to move the whole headquarters setup back out of range until they knew whether this position was going to be held. Grant took a quiet drag on his cigar and said that it would be even better to wheel some guns of their own up on the knoll and make certain that the position was held; so the guns were brought up, and the general kept on whittling twigs— completing the ruination of his tan gloves, in the process—and the Confederate attack was beaten off.[18]

Now and then the grim news that came back from the firing lines had a personal touch. An aide came over from Hancock's front once to tell Grant that the Rebels had killed Brigadier General Alex Hays—red-haired, coarse-grained, hard-drinking, and hard-fighting, who had spent three years with Grant at West Point, had served in the old 4th Regulars with him after graduation, and had been with him in Mexico, where Hays had marveled at Grant's ability to get his supply train through in spite of all obstacles. Hays commanded a brigade in the II Corps, and he had helped to beat off Pickett's great charge at Gettysburg, and now a bullet had found him in the wild mix-up along the Plank Road. Grant took the news quietly, saying that he was not surprised to learn that Hays had been in the front line of action when he was killed: "It was just like him."[19]

Dusk came at last, with smoke and a muffled crying in the air, and still the battle was not over. Lee had a pugnacity to match Grant's and just a year ago on the edge of this Wilderness he had flanked a Federal army quite as large and as confident as this one and had sent it scurrying back across the Rapidan in utter defeat. Now, as the day ended, one of Lee's brigadiers pointed out that up north of the Turnpike the right flank of John Sedgwick's line was exposed, and in the gathering dark a Confederate striking column came whooping down on this naked flank and drove it headlong.

As so often happened, the Confederates had found a soft spot. The Union flank here was held by Sedgwick's 3rd Division, two brigades which had not been with the VI Corps very long. Their earlier experience had mostly been in the Shenandoah Valley under the command of a flamboyant and remarkably inefficient general named Milroy, who had led them to a number of defeats. The rest of the corps dubbed them "Milroy's weary boys," and considered them something less than full-fledged members of the club.

They had been posted in the woods facing west, with several miles of unoccupied country between the end of their line and the Rapidan River, and during the day Sedgwick had worried about them. He had sent a cavalry regiment over to keep an eye on the flank—a regiment of recruits, unfortunately, which failed to do its job—and a bit later he had a staff officer go on a long scout to make sure that the Rebels were not up to anything sinister. Everything had been quiet at the time, but now at dusk the Confederates broke these two luckless brigades into splinters, and throngs of disorganized excited men went rushing through the thickets past Sedgwick's headquarters.

Sedgwick was on his horse at once, galloping over to the scene of the disaster, and he sent his staff flying along the dark woods trails to bring up reinforcements. The men who had run away kept on running, and before long they were scudding back past army headquarters, bearing wild tales of ruin and collapse, while a mighty sound of musketry and cheering went up from the woods to the north.[20]

The news that came to Grant and Meade had an alarming sound. Sedgwick held the army's extreme right, and if the Confederates once broke his line and got well around it the whole army was cut off and utter disaster might be in the cards. A couple of Sedgwick's brigadiers who tried to rally the defeated troops were captured, as were several hundred of Milroy's weary boys, and at one time Grant and Meade were told that Sedgwick himself had been captured and that his whole corps had gone to pieces. Various officers from the beaten brigades, their nerve wholly gone, had wild tales to tell, but Grant and Meade seemed quite unshaken.

Meade was coldly furious with two staff officers who came rocketing in to tell him that all was lost. "Nonsense!" he shouted. "If they have broken our lines they can do nothing more tonight"; and he sent the Pennsylvania Reserves over to stem the tide. Another officer came up to Grant, crying that he had seen this sort of thing before and that he knew just what was happening: Lee was getting around to where he could cut the army's communications, and if something weren't done about it they were all in a terrible pickle. Grant heard him out, and then he blew up, ceasing for once to be the phlegmatic sphinx of legend. He was sick and tired, he declared with heat, of being told about what Lee was going to do: "Some of you always seem to think he is suddenly going to turn a double somersault and land in our rear and on both our flanks at the same time." As for the panicky officer himself, Grant had a curt order: "Go back to your command and try to think what we are going to do ourselves, instead of what Lee is going to do!"[21]

Sedgwick, meanwhile, was competently busy. He pulled unshaken troops out from the left of his line and without fuss or apparent haste got them faced north and sent them in to halt the triumphant Rebels. (One of these soldiers remembered how his own colonel, taking his cue from Sedgwick, went along the line telling the men: "Don't be in a hurry, boys—let them come well up before you let them have it!") The Confederate attack was checked, at last, at substantial cost, and once things were stabilized Sedgwick put in the rest of the night drawing a new line more to the right and rear and getting troops into it so that the army's flank could be more firmly anchored. Just at dawn, with the job finished, the Vermont Brigade came tramping up from the scene of its two-day fight along the Plank Road, and as the column came by Sedgwick the soldiers let out a wild cheer. Sedgwick waved his hat, and a staff officer noticed that he "blushed like a girl" with pleasure at the cheering.[22]

There had been some anxious moments at headquarters, for all of the outward calm. After the needful measures had been taken, and there was nothing to do but wait for an hour or so to see whether those measures would work, Grant went into his tent, lay down on his cot, and had a very bad ten or fifteen minutes of it. One of his staff wrote later that Grant went to sleep at once and slept as quietly as a baby, but that was just part of the legend. The army had rubbed elbows with sheer catastrophe that night and Grant knew it, and when he was alone he could be as much tormented by suspense as anyone else.[23]

Yet the catastrophe had never materialized, and on the morning of May 7— forty-eight hours after the battle began—the two armies were just about where they were at the start. It was a foggy morning, and there was heavy smoke from the brush fires, and officers on reconnaissance could see very little, even on the roads or in clearings. Along the Turnpike, rival skirmishers had little spats now and then, although nobody seemed ready to bring on a real fight.[24] On the Plank Road the Confederates had drawn back—the burnt-over acres where there had been so much fighting the day before were no place for a battle line—and the hot day wore away with little active contact between the armies.

From end to end of the Union line there were breastworks—stout affairs of piled logs, on the Brock Road; lighter constructions of heaped wood and earth, deeper in the forest—and the men made themselves as easy as they could behind these works and speculated about what was likely to happen next. They did a great deal of talking about it, and mostly it boiled down to the simple question: Had they just fought a second battle of Chancellorsville?

The two battles were very much alike. They had been fought in very nearly the same place. Each time, a Union army with a great advantage in numbers had plunged into a forest where numbers did not help much, had seen its flanks broken in, and had had very heavy losses. (The toll for the two days in the Wilderness was more than 15,000 casualties, about equal to Chancellorsville.) After Chancellorsville, the army had admitted defeat and had gone back across the river. Would it do the same thing now?

In the Philadelphia Brigade the men were cynical. They agreed that by all precedents the army would retreat, would grant furloughs lavishly to restore morale, would spend weeks reorganizing and ordering new equipment, and—after getting reinforcements—would probably think about making some new move. That afternoon the wagon trains got under way, creaking slowly off toward Fredericksburg. A Massachusetts soldier admitted that "most of us thought it was another Chancellorsville, and that next day we should recross the river," and a cavalryman said his comrades "supposed they were on another skedaddle."[25]

Night came at last, and couriers sped to corps and division headquarters, and the men in Warren's corps—unspeakably weary, after two days of fighting and practically no sleep—left their trenches, fell into column, and started marching. They found themselves on the Brock Road, and in the darkness they were filing south immediately in rear of Hancock's men, who still held their charred log barricades; and as they marched the men realized that they were not heading toward the river crossings at all but were going south toward the lower edge of the Wilderness. The road was crowded, and nobody could see much, but as the men trudged along it suddenly came to them that this march was different. Just then there was a crowding at the edge of the road, and mounted aides were ordering: "Give way to the right!" and a little cavalcade came riding by at an easy jingling trot—and there, just recognizable, was Grant riding in the lead, his staff following him, heading south.

This army had known dramatic moments of inspiration in the past—massed flags and many bugles and broad blue ranks spread out in the sunlight, with leadership bearing a drawn sword and riding a prancing horse, and it had been grand and stirring. Now there was nothing more than a bent shadow in the night, a stoop-shouldered man who was saying nothing to anyone, methodically making his way to the head of the column—and all of a moment the tired column came alive, and a wild cheer broke the night and men tossed their caps in the darkness.

They had had their fill of desperate fighting, and this pitiless little man was leading them into nothing except more fighting, and probably there would be no end to it, but at least he was not leading them back in sullen acceptance of defeat, and somewhere, many miles ahead, there would be victory for those who lived to see it. So there was tremendous cheering, and Grant's big horse Cincinnati caught the excitement and reared and pranced, and as he got him under control Grant told his staff to have the men stop cheering because the Rebels were not far away and they would hear and know that a movement was being made.[26]

It was the same on other roads. Sedgwick's men backtracked to Chancellorsville, and as the men reached that fatal crossroads the veterans knew how the land lay and knew that if they took the lefthand fork they would be retreating and if they turned to the right they would be going on for another fight. The column turned right, and men who made the march wrote that with that turn there was a quiet relaxing of the tension and a lifting of gloom, so that men who had been slogging along quietly began to chatter as they marched. Here and there a regiment sang a little.[27]

Back by the wagon trains one of Sedgwick's officers came upon Burnside's division of colored soldiers, so dust-colored the men looked white. They were heading south like everyone else, and the officer saw a big colored sergeant prodding his men on with the butt of his rifle and ordering, "Close up dere, lambs."[28]

3. ALL THEIR YESTERDAYS

This was the night when everybody was dog-tired. The whole army was on the march, the wood smoke hung in the still air on the windless roads, and the only noise was the endless shuffle and scuffle of feet in the dirt, and now and then the clank of bayonets rattling against canteens. The men were drunk with fatigue, and nerves were as frazzled as muscles. The dust rose in choking clouds, so that blue uniforms looked gray when the columns passed campfires, and the men in the ranks staggered against each other and tripped on one another's heels. Looking back on it afterward, a man in the VI Corps felt that the whole night was "a medley of phantasmagoria," and the one sustaining thought was that at the very least they were going to get out of the Wilderness.[1]

The main road south was the Brock Road, and Warren's men had the lead. They came around midnight to an obscure crossroads where Todd's Tavern was situated, and there they ran into an insane traffic tie-up. This had many causes, most of which could be blamed on an attempt to make a forced march, along inadequate forest roads, with an army that was almost out of its head with weariness; but it was one of the most expensive traffic tie-ups in American history, because in the long run it cost many lives.

It was a bad time for delay. Off to the southeast was the tiny hamlet of Spotsylvania Court House; a sleepy village where a few stores and houses stood grouped about a little park containing a brick box of a building with Greek-revival pillars across the front, the whole place as insignificant and as unknown to the world at large as Chickamauga and Antietam creeks had been a year or so earlier. Now the village was about to take on a sinister and enduring fame, because in this region of meandering unpaved highways it was an important road crossing. The outcome of the war might depend on which army got there first. If the Army of the Potomac could win the race, it would stand between Lee's army and Richmond, and the outnumbered Confederates might be forced to destroy themselves attacking Yankee breastworks. Thus there was need for haste, and the march was pressed.

But it was like moving in a nightmare. The road was narrow and the darkness was absolute, and the men dozed stupidly as they walked. Somewhere off to the right was the Confederate army, a moving presence which every man could feel and which made itself physically known, now and then, through a spat-spat of skirmish fire somewhere ahead. Rebel cavalry had been ranging these parts and it had cut down trees and left them lying across the road, and men with axes had to go forward and cut these logs apart before the army could pass.

Yankee cavalry was moving about in the night, too, and it was even more of a trial than the Confederates. It clogged the roads, and at Todd's Tavern it seemed to be all bunched up, overflowing the highway and making a murmur of talk and clumping hoofs and clanking gear, and the infantry came to a halt and waited for someone to clear the way.

Headquarters had gone on in front, as was proper, and headquarters included various detachments of enlisted men who had troubles of their own. Among the escort troops was the 3rd Pennsylvania Cavalry, a veteran regiment which despised all recruits and had learned to look out for itself; and it happened that in the thick midnight the escort troops took a wrong turn and went off down a lane which would have landed them inside the Confederate lines if someone had not discovered the mistake and called a halt. The Pennsylvanians pulled up presently and began marching back toward the main road, troopers all very irritable. Nothing would have come of it if the Pennsylvanians had not been followed by a brand-new regiment of cavalry which had just come down from the Giesboro Point depot in Washington, brave with unused equipment and neatly groomed, unwearied horses—a regiment which, simply because it was new, the Pennsylvanians held in deep contempt.

In the countermarch, then, the Pennsylvanians had to pass the long column of recruits, and as the two regiments overlapped it occurred to the veterans that a cavalryman, all in all, was no better than his horse, that their own horses were worn out and in bad order, and that the horses of the recruits were fresh and vigorous. Nobody said anything in particular, but just as the two regiments were stretched out side by side on a pitch-dark road the Pennsylvanians by a common impulse sprang to the ground, pushed the rookies off their horses, sprang into the vacant saddles, and thus obtained remounts in the twinkling of an eye.

The rookies had never been warned about this sort of thing, and for the vital seconds that really mattered they were too dazed to resist. They came to fast enough, once the exchange had been made, and a tremendous fist fight boiled up in the middle of the forest—men on foot trying to grapple with mounted men, nobody able to see so much as his clenched fist in front of his nose, the fight streaming out along the byway and spilling over into the main road and turning into a complete unregimented riot which nobody but the 3rd Pennsylvania understood and which nobody on earth could quell.

It went on for an hour or more, and the advance of the whole Army of the Potomac came to a halt, infantrymen falling asleep in the dust while Yankee cavalry fought Yankee cavalry and the noise of the combat went up to the unheeding sky. It ended at last, with the Pennsylvanians getting away on their new horses and the rookies doing their grumbling best on the beaten nags they had inherited. Next morning the officers of the 3rd Pennsylvania looked their men over and remarked, sagely: "The horses look remarkably well after the night's march," and the first sergeants innocently said, "Yes sir," and that was all there was to it. But the army had lost a couple of hours on the road to Spotsylvania Court House.[2]

The escort troops were got out of the way at last, and cavalry skirmishers were trotting on in front, and the the gray of earliest dawn the infantry saw puffs of smoke rising from fields and woodlots up ahead where Confederates disputed the right of way. The column halted, while officers went forward to see how the land lay, and the 12th Massachusetts had the advance, followed by the 9th New York. As they stood in the road a solitary horseman came back from the skirmish line and began ordering the regimental officers to deploy their men on the left of the road. The horseman was undersized and swarthy, and he wore a funny flat felt hat with a floppy brim, and he talked as one having authority, and the infantry colonels bluntly asked him: Who are you, giving us orders like this?

The horseman flipped up the brim of his hat so that his face could be seen—olive-dark face with heavy mustaches and hard eyes—and he barked out his name: "Sheridan!" He added that Rebel infantry was just ahead, strung out behind brush piles and cowsheds in the rolling farm land, and it was time for Yankee infantry to go in and chase them out. So the New Yorkers and New Englanders filed off the road, deploying into fighting formation, and Sheridan kept saying: "Quick! Quick!"[3]

Presently the lines were formed, and their officers told the infantry that nothing but dismounted cavalry lay in front, and the battle line went forward in the hazy dawn. It went for a mile or more, ground very rough, Rebels withdrawing very slowly, and a great many Federals fell out of ranks from sheer exhaustion. Those who kept on found the enemy resistance pretty stiff to be coming from any dismounted cavalry, and as the light grew and they could see better one man turned to his mates and grumbled: "Pretty dismounted cavalry—carrying knapsacks!" They pulled up at last on a wooded knoll, discarding their own knapsacks—they were at the last pitch of weariness, and the loads were heavy—and while the men caught their breath their division commander, bushy-bearded General John Robinson, rode forward and tried to make out what was in front of him.

From the foot of the knoll the ground ranged down into a little valley, with the road to Spotsylvania Court House cutting squarely across it. A quarter of a mile away, on the far side of the valley, there were woods on the rising ground. These woods were not as dense as those in the Wilderness, and in them the general could see a fairly long line of Rebel soldiers, working feverishly to throw up a low breastwork of fence rails and earth. Most of his own division was trailed out behind him over several miles of road and he had just one brigade in line, and it seemed to him that he should let the men rest, wait for the rest of the division to come up, and then if he had to fight go in with everybody together. But then Warren came up, all eager and impetuous, and Warren told him to keep going.

It was hardly seven o'clock but the morning was hot already, and Robinson did not think his beaten-out men could make it. He asked for more time, so that he could at least mass his division for the assault, but Warren was impatient and told him to go ahead without waiting. Orders were orders.

Robinson took a last look at the Rebel position—it looked pretty strong, with the trench line stretching along the crest of the opposite hill—and he consoled himself by thinking that if the attack were made now the Rebels at least would not have time to bring up artillery and make the job completely impossible. So he gave the word, and his men got to their feet and went down into the valley.

There was a chance that they might make it. The Confederates had marched all night, too, and were in no better shape than Robinson's men, and they were still busy trying to finish their trenches. A mile beyond them lay the courthouse and the vital road crossing, and a rattle of carbine fire came faintly over the treetops from a dispute the rival cavalry patrols were having there. If Robinson's men could push this one line of Confederates out of the way, the town and the crossing belonged to the Union and Lee was cut off, and the war would take a very different turn.

But the going was very hard, and there were mean little gullies cutting across the ground, and the Confederates began to lay down a scorching fire of musketry, so that the advancing brigade took heavy losses. The men forced their way through an entanglement of felled pines, started up the farther slope, found the Rebel fire too heavy, and hugged the ground in lee of a steep little bank that gave some protection, waiting for the support troops to come up.

Looking back, they could see Robinson's second brigade, Maryland troops, mostly, falling into line on the knoll and starting forward, and for a moment they took heart. But more Confederates had come up, and these fired over the advanced brigade's heads and hit the Marylanders hard, so that the support wave fell into confusion and began to break for the rear. Robinson himself came along the slope to rally them, but a bullet hit him in the knee and he went down with a wound that would cost him his leg and take him out of the war for keeps. The Maryland brigade ran away and the rest of the division had got into a fruitless fight off to the right somewhere, too far away to lend any help here.

The Federal attacking line hung on for a while, and then a new Confederate brigade appeared off to one side, driving in a fire that went lengthwise along the huddled line and killed men who crouched flat against the slope, and it was too much. The men made a final, desperate attempt to charge the Rebel line, and a few of them reached the breastworks and got into a leaden-armed bayonet fight with men as weary as themselves. Then at last they gave up and ran—a queer, slow, stumbling flight, because they were simply too tired to run fast, even when discipline was gone and they were running for their lives.

The brigadier commanding these troops wrote later that he himself very much wanted to run at top speed, but could do no more than hobble along using his unsheathed sword as a cane. He fell in a field before he got very far, and he was carried off, unconscious, and the Rebels kept on firing as the men retreated. The remnant of Robinson's division at last regrouped itself back of the knoll from which it had started. Its division commander and every brigade commander had been put out of action, more than 2,000 enlisted men had been shot, there were stragglers all over the place, and there was no more fight left in anybody. The division had fought its last fight. A day or so later army headquarters broke it up and assigned its remnants to other units.[4]

The rest of Warren's corps came up, followed by Sedgwick's and the fight that had begun as an advance-guard scrap for possession of an insignificant little ridge spread all across both sides of the little valley and began to pull two whole armies into it. The troops which had been racing for Spotsylvania Court House were running a dead heat to this rolling, half-wooded area a mile west and north of the hamlet, and as fast as the men came up they were strung out on the firing lines, each line unrolling to north and south as more troops arrived. Batteries were brought up, their gun crews glad to see open ground again in place of the impossible Wilderness tangle, and the guns took position on the high ground and began hammering.

It was a confused fight that grew by what it fed on, with separate regiments colliding briefly here and there as they struggled for favorable positions. There was a whole series of little assaults and counterassaults which cost lives and drained away reserves of strength and endurance but which were buried in the reports as incidental to the general process of getting the battle lines established. Toward evening, though, Grant felt that there were enough men on hand to make a real fight of it, and the Federals staggered forward for an attack.

Gruff General Crawford got his Pennsylvania Reserves ahead so that they overlapped the right end of the Confederate line and for a moment it looked as if they might break something loose, but the men were simply too exhausted to drive their attack home. Also, at the last minute they collided with Robert Rodes's division of Confederates, which had just come on the scene in a state of equal exhaustion. For a time the worn-out troops blazed away at each other at short range, and then the Pennsylvanians pulled back and the day ended with the rival armies spread out in a great crescent, the concave side to the east, with Spotsylvania Court House nestled on the Confederate side of the curve. Sedgwick's and Warren's men were in line side by side, and Hancock was coming up behind and Burnside was bringing his corps down through the night from somewhere off to the north.

The infantry lines were restless as the darkness came down, and patrols and skirmishers were forever prodding at one another and firing sharply at the sight or sound of movement, and now and then the chat-chatter of their firing provoked the artillery to add its own voice. Farther back, the immense column of Yankee cavalry was all astir. It was taking off on a ponderous move that might turn into a very big thing, and while there were certain military reasons for the move the controlling factor in all of it was the fact that two very hot-tempered men had just had a violent argument.

George Gordon Meade commanded the Army of the Potomac, and when he rebuked a man he did it with angry words that struck sparks. On this day he was furiously dissatisfied with the job of his cavalry. The tangle which his own escort troops had kicked up was the least of his worries. What bothered Meade was that the cavalry corps itself, Sheridan's command, had failed in the early morning hours to clear the road from Todd's Tavern down to Spotsylvania. Sheridan had issued certain orders for this movement, and Meade had canceled some of them without bothering to tell Sheridan, and it appears that neither man had planned the business very well anyway. The upshot had been that the army was delayed and missed a big chance. So when Sheridan came to Meade's headquarters, around noon, Meade greeted him with angry words that resounded all over the place, loudly denouncing him for letting his cavalry get in infantry's way.

Phil Sheridan was an uncomplicated man whose chief trait, for good or for evil, was a driving combativeness, and he replied in words just as hot. It was Meade's fault, he shouted, because Meade had countermanded his orders; he was fed up with it, and if he could just pull his cavalry together and use it the way cavalry ought to be used, he could go out and whip Jeb Stuart out of his boots. So it went, back and forth, with staff and orderlies pretending to be deaf and drinking it all in, and at last Meade stalked off to tell Grant about it.

Back of this row was something more than a mere clash of temperaments. Meade was correct in blaming most of the delay on Sheridan, but Sheridan did have a proper complaint. Army headquarters still held more than a trace of the crippling old theory that the cavalry corps after all was pretty much a staff outfit like the signalers, its commander in effect ranking as a member of the general's staff rather than as a leader of combat troops. McClellan had seen it so, and only the departed Hooker had disagreed with him. Sheridan wanted to use his men the way Stuart used his—as a hard, compact, striking force—and it was not possible. What the generals were really arguing about was whether cavalry was to be regarded as a fighting corps or as a collection of train guards, scouts, and couriers, and Grant saw the point as soon as Meade began to talk to him.

When Meade reported how Sheridan had said he could whip Stuart if he could take his men and go off on his own, Grant looked up.

"Did Sheridan say that?" he asked. "Well, he generally knows what he is talking about. Let him start right out and do it."[5]

So the cavalry corps had been collected in one imposing mass—13,000 mounted men, plus horse artillery, a sinewy column such as this army had never before mustered; and presently it set out on a wide swing that would carry it clear away from the camps and battle lines and take it down cross country on a beeline for Richmond. Stuart would not dare ignore it, the way he had ignored Stoneman's raid in the Chancellorsville campaign, for if he did it had weight enough to go straight into the capital, or to work ruinous damage in the army's nexus of transportation and supply. He would have to follow it and bring it to bay and get into a stand-up fight with it, and then it would be seen what came of it all.

When it set out the cavalry did not go jingling off at a trot, pressing for stray minutes and wearing out its horses. It moved at a walk, conscious of its power, as if it had all the time in the world. Once the advance guard brushed into a Rebel skirmish line, and sent a few squadrons forward to tap the line and see what it was made of. The firing grew brisk and the squadrons came tumbling back. Up came Sheridan, hotly asking what was the matter here. Too many Johnnies up ahead, the men told him.

"Cavalry or infantry?" he demanded. Cavalry, he was told.

"Keep moving, boys—we're going on through," he ordered. "There isn't cavalry enough in all the Southern Confederacy to stop us."

The men cheered, and Sheridan waved his hat, and they broke through the skirmish line and the column kept on going—slow, remorseless, powerful.[6]

On their swing away from the army the troopers went back across the Wilderness, and on the Plank Road they met a great wagon train of wounded men, heading east toward Fredericksburg. It was a dreary procession. There were not ambulances enough to carry all of the men who had been wounded in the Wilderness, and empty ammunition wagons, ration wagons, and similar vehicles had been put into service. These wagons had no springs, and the roads were very rough, and a steady, monotonous sound of moaning and screaming went up from the long train and could be heard far away, long before the wagons themselves came into sight. For miles the wagons filled the road, so that the cavalry had to get off to the side and go trampling through the underbrush.

Between and beside the wagons were the walking wounded, and these men begged for water as the cavalrymen went by, so that the column was slowed while troopers hastily offered their canteens. They were not supposed to do this, but as one trooper wrote, the calls of the wounded men were "an appeal that could not be denied. . . . We had water in our canteens and we took time to dismount and hold them to the lips of the thirsty comrades." The wagons jolted on, an enormous cloud of dust lying in the air above and all around, and now and then the train would halt while some wounded man who had died was taken out and laid in the woods.[7]

Never had the wounded men had it any worse. The fighting in the Wilderness had caused more casualties than Antietam itself had caused, and the medical corps was snowed under. First orders had been to send the trains northwest back across the Rapidan to a spot on the Orange and Alexandria Railroad, so thousands of men had been loaded in wagons and started in that direction. But when the army moved down toward Spotsylvania those orders had to be changed, because the old route by Germanna and Ely's fords was no longer being guarded and Mosby's raiders would unquestionably capture any hospital train that tried to use it. So it had been decided to send the wounded over to Fredericksburg, and the clumsy procession had countermarched (giving the men an extra twenty-four hours in the graceless wagons) and the new trains were made up to carry more of them, and thousands upon thousands of wounded were now making the agonizing trip to Fredericksburg.

The medical corps that was taking charge of all this was fearfully short-handed, because the army had marched off to fight new battles and most of its doctors, hospital attendants, and loads of medical supplies had to go along. A few could be spared for the men in the trains, but nobody knew what would happen when they finally reached Fredericksburg because that was a firmly secessionist town badly ravaged by war and it was not currently occupied by any Federal troops. An abundance of stretcher-bearers had been detailed, a party from each regiment, but most of them were quite useless. Human nature being what it is, the average colonel picked out for this detail the men who were least likely to be of any help if they remained with the regiment, the inevitable consequence being that the worst loafers and thieves in the army had been appointed to help care for the wounded. Doctors noticed that the pockets of nearly all of the dead men and most of the helpless wounded men had been slit open for the easier removal of purses and watches.

The surgeons had done what they could. They began by sorting the wounded men into three classes—those who could probably walk back, those who had to be carried, and those who could not be moved at all and so would have to remain in field hospitals in the Wilderness, which was still smoldering and which stank to the highest heavens, what with thousands of unburied bodies. A very few doctors could be spared to remain with these men—four of them, two regular hospital stewards, and twenty of the priceless detailed attendants, as it was finally worked out, for about a thousand totally disabled men.

When the wagons were loaded there had been a further sorting out. Some of the men could sit up, and empty ammunition boxes were supplied for them to sit on, so that sometimes six or ten could ride in one wagon. With the amputees there was a differant classification. It was quickly discovered that men took up less room if they lay on their sides than they required if they lay on their backs, so the leg cases were grouped accordingly: if each man in an ambulance had lost his right leg, each man could lie on his left side—for however many terrible hours the trip might last—and they could fit together nicely, like so many spoons, and it was so arranged.[8]

It was about one in the morning of May 9 when the head of this great caravan of misery came creaking down into sleeping Fredericksburg, a wrecked, half-lifeless town that lay across the path of war, which had seen much suffering and now was to see more.

It had been a drowsy pleasant place, once. In the old days the tubby English merchant ships drifted lazily up the river and moored here, and the grave men in knee breeches and silk stockings who traded in them had built formal homes of red brick on the quiet streets, and back of the town on the heights they had put up mansions with white pillars, so that an eighteenth-century air of order and certitude had given the place a special flavor. But the old days were long dead and now there was a bitter new flavor, and the very name of the town had taken on a hard ring, and in many homes North and South it was a name of death and deep shadows: a sinister word, carrying a shudder with it, one of the homely American place names made dreadful by war. The town had known violence and gunfire and screaming, and the meadows beyond had seen naked corpses turning blue under a frozen moon, with guns flashing from the hilltops and the wreckage of old houses littering the streets. All of that, earlier in the war, and now this: seven thousand wounded men coming in at one in the morning, with no one riding on ahead to announce their coming or to get things ready for them, and not one sullen resident owning the slightest desire to help the Army of the Potomac in any way whatever.

A regiment of dismounted cavalry had come along as train guard, and it sent men scurrying about to knock the town awake and find places to put the wounded. Churches were taken over, and warehouses, mills, public buildings, and the larger private homes, and all through the night the wagons were laboring up to these doorways and unloading. In some cases, wounded officers of rank were quartered with Fredericksburg families, and these men got along well enough. Nobody in town had any sympathy for Yankees, but the people were not brutal or callous, and so a very fortunate few of the wounded got into real beds.

Most of them were simply laid on the floor—any floor that was handy. Many buildings were still half-wrecked from Burnside's bombardment of December 1862 and contained puddles of stagnant rain water that had come in through gaping holes in the roof, and men were dumped down in this seepage so that the pools became bloody. One warehouse which had contained leaky barrels of molasses had a quarter inch or more of gummy treacle all over the floor. No straw was available for bedding. There was nothing for it but to put the men on the bare floor—in rain water, half-dried syrup, or whatever—and hope that they could make the best of it.

The best was not very good. Washington had had no warning that this move was coming, and so no supplies had been sent down. There were just thirty army doctors on hand to look after the 7,000 wounded, all of whom by now needed attention very badly; needed at the very least to be bathed and given fresh clothing and hot soup, and to have their bandages changed. Practically none of these things could be done, partly because of a woeful shortage of help and partly because the medicines, fresh dressings, and food that were on hand were strictly limited to the little that had been carried in the wagons. The man who got so much as a hardtack and a drink of water that day was in luck. It took more than twenty-four hours just to get the men out of the wagons. A good many of them died, which meant that some of the attendants had to ignore the living and serve on burial details.[9]

The doctors did their best, and some of the stretcher-bearers finally turned out to be fairly useful, and it might not have been so bad if they could once have got the situation stabilized. But the army kept pumping new streams of wounded men in on them faster than the ones they already had could be cared for, and although the men who were trying to cope with this in-gathering of misery worked until they were gray-faced and stupid with fatigue, they kept falling farther and farther behind. It was as if war, the great clumsy machine for maiming people, had at last been perfected. Instead of turning out its grist spasmodically, with long waits between each delivery, it was at last able to produce every day, without any gaps at all. Since the medical service had never been up against anything like this before—had never dreamed of anything like it, in its wildest hallucinations—there was bound to be trouble.

One doctor wrote that for four days in a row—including most of the intervening night hours—he did nothing whatever but amputate arms and legs, until it seemed to him that he could not possibly perform another operation. Yet hundreds of cases were waiting for him, and wounded men kept stumbling in, begging almost tearfully to have a mangled arm taken off before gangrene should set in. "It is a scene of horror such as I never saw," he cried. "God forbid that I should ever see another." A day or two later he had found no end to it: "Hundreds of ambulances are coming into town now, and it is almost midnight. So they come every night."[10]

For the fighting at Spotsylvania began before any of the men who had been wounded in the Wilderness had been got back to Fredericksburg. The job of cleaning up after one battle had barely been begun when a brand-new battle was opened. Robinson's men had their bloody fight for the approaches to the courthouse crossroads while the army's ambulances were still full of men who had been hurt two or three days earlier, and these ambulances were getting farther and farther away from the army right when the army was developing an urgent new need for them. Some 1,500 men were wounded in Robinson's fight, and they were collected at dressing stations not far behind the front. This collection was made easier by the fact that the army was having an unprecedented amount of straggling. Medical directors estimated that from two to four ablebodied men were leaving the ranks with each wounded soldier, and while that made it almost impossible for the army to fight successfully, it did solve momentarily the problem of getting wounded men back out of danger. The trouble was that very few of these volunteer helpers of the afflicted went back to their regiments afterward. They faded away, following wagon trains north or simply dematerializing in the general confusion, and most of them showed up sooner or later in Fredericksburg.

And so that tragic little city, already completely swamped with wounded men, became equally swamped with men who wandered about on foot, stole food, got in everybody's way, and in general succeeded in doubling the size and complexity of the problem which existed here at the Rappahannock crossing. The stragglers mingled with the walking wounded. A great many of them picked up bloodstained bandages and put them on so that they could pose as wounded men and, if their luck held out, get aboard the hospital steamers and ride back to Washington. Some of them carried realism even farther, and the harassed doctors eventually discovered about a hundred cases of self-inflicted wounds.

Up at the front, Meade was desperately trying to find more ambulances. Most general officers had commandeered one or more ambulances for personal use. They made comfortable living quarters, as a matter of fact, and generals were using them much the way auto-trailers were used in the 1940s, and now Meade ordered all of these turned over to the army's medical director at once. From general headquarters and from the three army corps upwards of fifty ambulances were thus acquired, and with these and with empty ammunition and forage wagons a regular shuttle service back to Fredericksburg was established.[11]

Just in time to avert complete chaos, the first steamers from Washington came down the Potomac. These could not come around to Fredericksburg yet—guerillas made the Rappahannock unsafe, and the Navy was sending a couple of light-draft gunboats to see about it—and they tied up at the old Potomac River landings, Aquia Creek and Belle Plain. These landings were twelve or fifteen miles from Fredericksburg, via villainous corduroy roads, which meant an extra spell in purgatory for any wounded man who made the trip. (A ride in a springless wagon over a corduroy road was about as bad as anything war had to offer.) Yet once a man was put aboard one of the steamers the worst was over, and in a few hours he would be in a regular hospital around Washington: a poor enough place, perhaps, by modern standards, but paradise itself compared with lying unfed and unattended in a springless wagon or on the wet gummy floor of a half-roofed warehouse.

There was a good deal of a jam at the river landings, for the piers were inadequate, and before the boats could take wounded men aboard they had to unload their own cargoes, and usually the narrow makeshift dock that was to receive the cargo was crammed with long lines of stretchers and a huddled mass of walking wounded. The stragglers and malingerers got in the way very badly, and the good civilian doctors who came down with the hospital ships could be imposed on by these men as regular army surgeons could not have been, so that transportation needed by suffering men was often pre-empted by men whose only trouble was a desire to get away from the zone of fighting. The army caught on to this, eventually, and in a few days no man could get aboard any of the steamboats until he had been examined by a hard-boiled army doctor who knew all of the dodges.[12]

The steamers brought down the things the impromptu Fredericksburg hospitals needed—foods, medicines, bandages, doctors, and hospital attendants—and they came just in time to keep the situation from becoming completely impossible. But mostly they brought down supplies for the army itself. The emphasis was on the job ahead, not on the wreckage that was being left behind, and it was obvious to everybody that the army was not going to stop to lick its wounds. If the lot of the wounded men could be made endurable, that would be fine, but the only thing that really mattered was the fighting.

The wounded men themselves realized this, and they took a sardonic pleasure in the sight of reinforcement troops moving south through Fredericksburg. One day a heavy artillery regiment, fresh from the Washington barracks, came marching through—muskets polished, uniforms neat and unfaded, band playing in front—and the wounded men on the sidewalks and in doorways set up a derisive cheer. One man called out: "Go it, Heavies—old Grant'll soon cut you down to fighting weight!" Another man sourly eyed the band and cried: "Blow—you're blowing your last blast!"[13]

Days after full steamboat connection with Washington had been established, a nurse in a II Corps hospital in Fredericksburg wrote that the wounded men were still getting nothing to eat but hardtack and coffee, and when she contemplated the lot of the average private she exploded: "O God! such suffering it never entered the mind of man or woman to think of!" What she saw in Fredericksburg, she added, was worse than what she had seen in the hospitals at Gettysburg, the sole improvement here being that most of the men were at least under cover.[14]

The men at the front were given no time to worry about what happened behind the lines. For a long time they had told one another that one thing they wanted (aside from an end to the war) was a fighting general in command. Now they had him, and they were learning that there were elements in the bargain on which they had not counted. The trench lines in the country around Spotsylvania Court House grew longer and longer, and as they did so the men began to see that the heavy fighting had hardly so much as started, and that what had begun in the Wilderness was to go on and on with no end to it. There was no more maneuvering for position, no more tapping a line cautiously to find a soft spot. Men were simply lined up and sent forward, and sometimes it was like the Wilderness fighting all over again, rival lines colliding drunkenly in the dusk of pine thickets, no order or plan to the battle, armies fighting like infuriated mobs.

There was an obscure bit of ground here called Laurel Hill, and both sides wanted it, and a man in the 20th Maine recalled how they fought for it:

"The air was filled with a medley of sounds, shouts, cheers, commands, oaths, the sharp report of rifles, the hissing shot, dull heavy thuds of clubbed muskets, the swish of swords and sabers, groans and prayers. . . . Many of our men could not afford the time necessary to load their guns . . . but they clubbed their muskets and fought. Occasionally, when too sorely pressed, they would drop their guns and clinch the enemy in single combat, until Federal and Confederate would roll upon the ground in the death struggle."[15]

John Sedgwick had brought his corps up into action, and after he got the men to the spot where Robinson's luckless men had made their attack his staff officers felt that the general was gloomy and depressed. One of them recorded a general impression "of things going wrong, and of the general exposing himself uselessly and keeping us back, of Grant's coming up and taking a look, of much bloodshed and futility."

Yet no mood of depression ever lasted very long with Sedgwick. He had had all the war he wanted, to be sure, and in his letters to his sister in Connecticut he was writing longingly of the day when he could get out of the army and come home to stay—"Can any spot on earth be as beautiful as Cornwall Hollow?" he asked her—but he never let gloom get the better of him for long. The morning after he got his corps to the front he was up early, and when he called briefly at Grant's headquarters, men there remembered that he seemed especially cheerful and hopeful. Grant had compliments for the way he had been handling his troops, and Sedgwick presently returned to his own tents, which were pitched on a little hill close to the place where Robinson's men had formed for their fight the day before. When he got there Sedgwick found that random shots from Rebel sharpshooters were causing trouble, so he sent his young Major Hyde to advance the pickets a little, to end this nuisance.

Major Hyde came back, after a while, and Sedgwick was seated on a cracker box under a tree; and Sedgwick had the major sit down by him, and pulled his ears for him, and joked with him while Hyde reported on his mission. Then Sedgwick walked over to an artillery emplacement to give the battery commander some directions, and the sharpshooters' bullets were pinging around and the gunners were ducking, and Sedgwick laughed at them and told them not to worry—the sharpshooters were so far away "they couldn't hit an elephant at this distance."

A minute after this there was a sharp cry from the gun pits—"The General!" The headquarters people ran over and there was Sedgwick on the ground, a bullet hole under the left eye, killed by one of the sharpshooters whose aim he had derided. They put his body in an ambulance and carried it back to army headquarters, where it was laid in an evergreen bower with the Stars and Stripes wrapped around it. When Grant was told, he seemed stunned. Twice he asked, "Is he really dead?" Later he told his staff that to lose Sedgwick was worse than to lose a whole division of troops.[16]

Washington was many miles away, and little was known there about how the fighting was going, except that the army was constantly calling for more men and more food and ammunition. But the real storm center was the White House. Here was Lincoln, sleepless and gaunt and haggard, his tough prairie strength tried now as never before. He had once characterized another man, who could see no wrong in human slavery, by musing that he supposed that man did not feel the lash if it were laid on another man's back instead of on his own. That kind of insensitivity he himself did not have, and the fact that he lacked it was his greatest asset and his heaviest cross.

He could feel what hit somebody else, and however remote the quiet rooms in the White House might be from the fearful jungles below the Rapidan, all of the lines led back here, because here was held the terrible power to still the tempest or make it go on to the very end. Lincoln could pardon condemned soldiers who fell asleep at their posts, or who broke and ran for it in the heat of action—he called these latter his "leg cases," saying that a brave man might be cursed by cowardly legs which he could not keep from bearing him back out of danger—and he was the man who with a word could have stopped all of the killing, and he had to will that the killing go on.

Now John Sedgwick was dead, and the great wagon trains were lumbering down to Fredericksburg, every day and every night, and the white ash and charred twigs of the Wilderness were dropping on disfigured bodies which no one would ever name, while long columns of weary men went blindly into new fights that would be worse than what they had just come away from; and Lincoln sat late at night with a volume of Shakespeare's tragedies, and to a friend he read the lines of Macbeth's despair:[17]

> Tomorrow, and tomorrow, and tomorrow
> Creeps in this petty pace from day to day
> To the last syllable of recorded time,
> And all our yesterdays have lighted fools
> The way to dusty death. . . .

This was in the White House. The young men of the Army of the Potomac had had many yesterdays to light their dusty way, but they did not talk about them. They simply lived by the remembered light those days had given them, and the days were various, and nobody can say just where all of the light came from or what it finally meant. (Take a morning in Ohio, for example. The land is flat, and when dawn begins there is a thin mist everywhere, and it glows with the first light so that the green trees begin to come out black in the distance, and the earth rolls gently off to meet them, and the truth about many things lies not quite veiled in the hollow places where the mist lies the longest; and a man who sees it know something, but what sort of light is that for a soldier?)

One of the things these men had got out of their long yesterdays was a toughness and a jaunty humor. On the morning after the Laurel Hill fight, Grant came riding past the littered slopes to a new place that had been picked for his headquarters. A fife and drum corps was somewhere about, and when the musicians saw the general they suddenly, on inspiration, struck up a rollicking little tune.

Many soldiers were near, and when they heard the tune they looked about them and saw Grant, and then they all began to cheer and laugh. Grant noticed it, and he was quite unable to tell one tune from another—he had a feeble jest, to the effect that he knew just two tunes: one was Yankee Doodle, and the other wasn't—and he asked an aide what the band was playing to cause all of this commotion. The aide explained that it was playing a popular camp-meeting ditty which the whole army was familiar with: a little number entitled, "Ain't I glad to get out of the wilderness!"[18]

4. SURPASSING ALL FORMER EXPERIENCES

There were many young men in the army and one of them was a colonel named Emory Upton. He was thin, wiry, freckled, with unruly hair and a trim goatee and mustache; an intense passionate man, a Regular Army officer who was impatient with the army's way of doing things and especially with the ways of its higher officers. None of these, he said contemptuously, knew how to lead men.

They commanded the best soldiers in the world but they did not know what to do with them.

Like John Sedgwick, in whose corps he served, Upton poured out his thoughts in long letters to his sister. To her he spoke his mind about generals: "I have never heard our generals utter a word of encouragement, either before or after entering a battle. I have never seen them ride along the lines and tell each regiment that it held an important position and that it was expected to hold it to the *last*. I have never heard them appeal to the love every soldier has for his colors, or to his patriotism. Neither have I ever seen a general thank his troops after the action for the gallantry they have displayed."

Having written this, young Colonel Upton added that when he meditated on all of the incompetence in starred shoulder straps, and then considered his own qualifications, "there is no grade in the army to which I do not aspire."

Upton was the son of a New York farmer. He had spent a couple of his teenage years at Oberlin, in Ohio, just in time to absorb the fervid religious and abolitionist sentiments that yeasty place was germinating then. He was a sober youngster, worrying about his soul, about the Union, about slavery, about his own health—at one stage he refused to sleep on a pillow for fear it would make him round-shouldered—and he entered West Point in 1856 and was graduated shortly before the war began, number eight in his class. He could have gone into the engineers, the army's *corps d'élite,* but for some reason he chose artillery instead. He had various staff and line appointments in the early days of the war, and then went over into the volunteer service and became colonel of the 121st New York, whose boys found him stiff on the matter of discipline but, on the whole, a man they could like.[1]

Because he was a good leader of men and also a thoughtful scientific soldier, he had risen to brigade command, although (and the fact irked him) he had not yet been made a brigadier general. In the fall of 1863, when Meade and Lee maneuvered fruitlessly back and forth across the Rapidan country, Upton had led a surprise attack on a Confederate fort at Rappahannock Station, winning a sparkling little victory and capturing more than a thousand prisoners. Now he was restlessly observing what happened when the army butted up against the solid trenches that appeared like magic whenever the Rebels drew their lines, and it seemed to him that there was a better way to do things.

Upton, in short, felt that he knew how to break through those Rebels entrenchments, and he spoke up about it, and on the afternoon of May 10 they gave him twelve picked infantry regiments, his own 121st New York among them, and told him to go ahead.

There was much fighting that day. The opposing lines lay in a great rambling curve, and off toward the Federal right some divisions from Hancock's and Warren's corps made a savage and costly assault on the Rebel trenches, coming up through a grove of spiky dead pines as tangled as anything in the Wilderness and being rebuffed with heavy loss. Half a mile or more north and east of the place where they fought, Upton massed his twelve regiments late in the afternoon.

The spot that had been picked for him was not promising. Upton's men faced east, looking toward a wood. There was a little road going off through the trees, and it came out into a field which sloped up for 200 yards to the enemy's works, which were formidable. Out in front there was a heavy abatis of felled trees, the sharpened branches pointing toward the Federals, and the main trench line was several dozen paces beyond. This trench was solidly built of logs and banked-up earth, and along the top there ran a head log, blocked up a few inches above the dirt so that Confederate riflemen could stand in the trench, aim and fire their pieces through the slit under the log, and enjoy almost complete protection. Heavy traverses—mounds of earth running back at right angles from the main embankment—had been built at frequent intervals as a protection against enfilade fire. This line was strongly manned with first-rate troops, and a hundred yards in the rear of it there was a second line, not yet wholly completed but also held by good troops. Here and there along the front line there were emplacements for artillery, so that all of the slope out in front could be swept both by rifle fire and by canister.

The obvious fact here—at least it was obvious to Upton—was that an assaulting column's only hope was to get a solid mass of riflemen right on the parapet as quickly as possible. If the men stopped on open ground to exchange volleys with those thoroughly protected Confederates they would be destroyed in no time. So Upton formed his men in four lines, three regiments side by side in each line, and he issued explicit orders: every man was to have his musket loaded and his bayonet fixed, but only the men in the three leading regiments were to cap their muskets. (To "cap" a Civil War musket was to put a copper percussion cap in the breech so that it could instantly be fired. With uncapped weapons, the men could not fire as they charged but would have to keep on advancing and so would reach the trench with loaded muskets which could then very quickly be capped for close-range firing.) When the first three regiments reached the trench they were to fan out to right and left and drive the defenders off down the line, while the second wave swarmed in behind them to open fire on any reinforcements that might try to come up from the Confederate second line. The remaining two lines were to lie down just short of the trench for use as they might be needed.

Officers were taken out to the edge of the open space and were shown the ground, everything was carefully explained, and then the twelve regiments moved forward. They got to the edge of the woods, Upton took them out into the open, and they set out up the slope on a dead run, yelling like maniacs.

A sharp fire greeted them, and getting through the abatis was tough, but the solid column kept on going and swept up to the trench without a halt. At the parapet there was brief, desperate, hand-to-hand fighting. As Upton remarked in his report, the Confederates "absolutely refused to yield the ground," and the first Yankees who got up on the parapet were shot down or bayoneted. Others pitched their bayoneted rifles over the parapet like deep-sea harpooners spearing whales, or held their pieces out at arm's length, pointing downward over the parapet, and fired. Then men began to jump over into the trench, clubbing and stabbing, the weight of numbers began to tell, the defenders were killed or driven away, and Upton's leading regiments swept down the line to right and left while the next wave dashed across the open ground and seized the second trench. All in all, the thing had worked, and the twelve regiments had broken the Confederate line wide open right where it was strongest, taking prisoners and waving flags and shouting with triumph.[2]

But to break the line was only half of it. Upton's men were three quarters of a mile away from the rest of the Union army, and the Rebels were bringing up strong reinforcements and opening a heavy fire from in front and from both flanks. Now the twelve regiments must hold on while their comrades in the rear came up to exploit the break-through.

This had been arranged for. On high ground off to the left and rear Mott's division from the II Corps was lined up ready for the word, and it was sent forward as soon as Upton's men got their grip on the Rebel position. But Mott's was an ill-fated division, and most of the fire was burnt out of it. Its morale had been ruined when it was transferred from the defunct III Corps, early that spring, and in the Wilderness fighting it had been shot up and driven in panic, and Mott seems not to have been the officer who could pull the men together. In addition, the division had to advance down a broad open glade, half a mile long and 400 yards wide, and at the end of the glade the Confederates had twenty-two cannon in line, waiting. These guns had a direct line of fire down the glade, and they could not miss, and they broke Mott's division before it got fairly started. Better troops might have got farther, but the artillery would probably have taken charge anyway, and this assault went entirely awry and never got within a quarter of a mile of the Rebel line.[3]

Down to the right were the troops which had made the unsuccessful attack earlier in the day, and it was resolved to send them in again. The men had just succeeded in re-forming their lines after their repulse when a staff officer came galloping up, riding from brigade to brigade with orders for a new attack. One of the men who had to make this charge wrote afterward that "there was an approach to the ridiculous" in the way in which these orders were given. He specified:

"No officer of higher rank than a brigade commander had examined the approaches to the enemy's works on our front, and the whole expression of the person who brought the message seemed to say, 'The general commanding is doubtful of your success.' The moment the order was given the messenger put spurs to his horse and rode off, lest by some misunderstanding the assault should begin before he was safe out of range of the enemy's responsive fire."[4]

That kind of spirit never broke any Confederate lines, and this charge was beaten before it was made. The men moved out sluggishly, convinced that their job was hopeless. After a brief advance they halted and opened fire, but before long they seem to have concluded that there was no sense in it, and everybody turned and ran for the rear. Rebel fire followed them, and the dead pines in the thicket took fire, and what began as a fairly orderly retreat ended as a rout. The soldier who wrote so bitterly about the way the charge was directed confessed that some of the best men in the army "not only retired without any real attempt to carry the enemy's works, but actually retreated in confusion to a point far in the rear of the original line and remained there until nearly night." Staff officers sent to recall them found the men quietly grouped around their regimental flags, making coffee.[5]

So Upton's regiments were left out on a limb, with a good part of the Rebel army gathering to destroy them and no help coming up; and the young colonel at last had to lead his men back to their lines, with a thousand of them left dead or wounded on the ground. They brought a thousand prisoners back with them, and they had made an authentic break in a formidable line, but in the end it had all been a failure.[6]

Yet when night came down the high command felt that the general picture was encouraging. These cruel trenches were not invulnerable, after all, and what twelve regiments had done could perhaps be repeated with a bigger force. An Ohio cavalryman who was serving as orderly at Grant's headquarters saw Grant talking with Meade about it, puffing his cigar as he talked, and he heard Grant say: "A brigade today—we'll try a corps tomorrow." A little later the new commander of the VI Corps, General Horatio Wright, came in. Wright was stocky and bearded, slow-moving, competent rather than brilliant, not beginning to fill the place in the soldiers' affections that Sedgwick had filled; but he was the man Sedgwick himself had once designated as his successor, and he felt that the whole trouble today had been failure of the supporting troops. He said earnestly to Meade: "General, I don't *want* Mott's troops on my left; they are not a support; I would rather have no troops there."[7]

In the end, the generals concluded that Lee's army might be utterly defeated if Upton's technique were used on a larger scale, properly supported, and Meade's staff immediately went to work to plan an enormous blow that would send Hancock's entire corps through the lines and would bring all of Wright's and Burnside's men up as supports.

It would take time to mount an attack of this size, and it could not be done overnight. So on May 11 the troops held their lines, and another great train of wounded was started back toward Fredericksburg. Yet although the front was comparatively inactive there was a steady firing all day long, and the toll of killed and wounded on both sides crept constantly higher. In midafternoon it began to rain—a sullen, persistent drizzle that looked as if it might go on for days—and when the sun went down the air turned chilly, and the battlefield was smoldering with little brush fires and wreathed in flat layers of smoke that hung low in the rain. When night came it was dull and starless, and long after dark there began a tramping of great columns of troops as the men followed obscure roads to their new positions.[8]

More than half of the army was on the move. Grant and Meade had chosen a new spot for their break-through—the very spot that Mott's men had so ingloriously aimed at, made inviting in spite of its banked-up cannon by an accident of geography.

The Confederate lines covering Spotsylvania Court House were uneven and they did not run in straight lines for more than a few rods at a time, but in general they formed two tangents—a long one, opposite the Federal right, facing roughly toward the north, and a shorter one somewhat to the east of this facing northeast and east. These two lines did not intersect. Instead, they were joined by a great loop of entrenchments that bulged out toward the north to cover some high ground: a huge salient nearly a mile deep and half a mile wide, dubbed by the Confederates, from its outline on the map, the Mule Shoe. It was the western side of this salient that Upton had attacked on May 10, and the guns that had broken up Mott's dispirited formation were placed at the northernmost tip of the salient where the lines of the Mule Shoe came to a blunt angle.

If this salient could be broken, Lee's army would be cut in half. By military teaching, the point of a salient was a hard place to defend, since the fire from the defenders on the two sides of the point tended to diverge. It was for that reason that the Confederates had stacked up so many guns at the broad tip, and since there was a clear field of fire in front of this place the guns were extremely effective. But it was believed that if a solid corps of infantry made a sudden rush at the very moment of daybreak—a rush patterned after Upton's, with no firing and no stopping until the parapet was reached—the men could overrun the tip of the salient before the guns could hurt them very badly. Then, with the end of the salient punched in, the support troops could come piling in on either side— and there, it might be, was the recipe for victory.

So Hancock's corps was to take position three quarters of a mile north of the tip of the salient, and at the first light of day it was to go into action. On Hancock's left Burnside's corps was in line, and Wright's corps was lined up on Hancock's right, and they were to come in the moment Hancock's men needed help. On the extreme right of the army was Warren's corps, and it was to be on the alert also, ready to smash the Confederate left down below the salient. Thus virtually all of the troops would be thrown into the offensive, which was a new note: never before had the army tried to put its entire weight into one co-ordinated smash.

There have been worse battle plans, and although neither Grant nor Meade realized it they were helped by a thumping piece of good luck. During that rainy afternoon of May 11, Rebel scouts had seen Federal trains moving off toward the northeast, and it seemed to Lee that Grant was beginning to shift around the Confederate right. It would be necessary to move fast to meet the shift, and during the evening Lee ordered that all artillery which was posted where it could not move quickly should be pulled out of the line and held in readiness for a quick start. This applied principally to the twenty-two guns in the nose of the salient, and sometime before midnight all of these guns were limbered up and taken back to the rear. General Ewell, who commanded the Confederates who held the salient, was left without his ace of trumps.[9]

A good plan, then, and unexpected good luck to go with it; and yet, as that black wet night unrolls its story, one gets the impression of a queer, uncertain fumbling, as if there mysteriously existed in the army a gap between conception

and execution which could never quite be bridged. Meade's chief of staff was
General Andrew A. Humphreys, and Humphreys was very capable; the column
of attack belonged to Hancock, who was by all odds the army's best corps commander; but with good men to plan and lead, and ample staffs to aid them, what
finally came out of it all was a blundering lunge which hit the right spot largely
by accident and which missed turning into an incredible disaster only because
those twenty-two guns had been taken away.

Never before had the soldiers and their leaders gone into action so completely
ignorant about where they were supposed to go and what they were going to
find when they got there. Hancock wrote that he had sent a couple of staff officers out the afternoon before, with an officer from Grant's staff, to look the
ground over, "but owing to the uncertainty as to the exact point to be attacked
no very definite information was obtained."[10] He tried to use Mott's dejected
soldiers to drive in the Rebel picket line so that he could get a better view of
things, but the attempt was a flat failure and when it came time to move the
corps up to the jump-off point the best corps headquarters could do was to lay a
map on a farmhouse table and study it. Here where the troops were forming
there was a house, clearly shown on the map; off to the south the map showed
another house, which seemed to be approximately in the middle of the Rebel
salient; draw a line, then, from house to house on the map, see what compass
point the line hits, and give that to the division commanders for a guide.

It was done so, by lamplight, while the rain came down in sheets outside, and
the division commanders got their instructions, which were vague—the attack
was supposed to hit the Rebel flank, it was a move of more than ordinary importance, and if it succeeded the country would owe a great debt to the officers responsible; that was about it, as men who were present recalled it. No one knew
anything about the strength of the enemy or even about the enemy's position,
except that it was off to the south. When it was time to move, staff and engineer
officers would be on hand to take the men to the spot where they were to begin
their charge.[11]

Hancock gave the lead to his first division, which was led by Brigadier General Francis Barlow. Barlow had been a New York lawyer before the war,
knowing nothing about military matters, and after Fort Sumter he had joined a
militia regiment as a private. He had a knack for leadership, and he liked to
fight, and in the reshuffle that followed Bull Run he became a colonel. He had
been badly wounded at Antietam and again at Gettysburg, and he was a slight,
frail-looking man with no color in his cheeks, a loose-jointed unsoldierly air
about him when he walked, with deadly emotionless eyes looking out of a
clean-shaven face, and when he spoke his voice seemed thin and lackluster.

To all appearances he was no soldier at all, but the man who went by Barlow's
appearance was badly deceived. He was hard and cold and very much in earnest,
a driving disciplinarian who began by making his men hate him and ended by
winning their respect because he always seemed to know what he was doing and
because the spirit of fear was not in him. When he wrote his reports he often
lapsed into legalistic jargon: his troops moved "on or about" a certain hour, and
after various experiences they took "the aforesaid hill" or wood lot or whatever,
and through it all there is the echo of a lawyer's clerk preparing a deposition; but
underneath everything there was a ferocious fighting man who drove himself
and his men as if the doorway to Hell were opening close behind them.[12]

Barlow got his men together in the dripping night. Upton's example had
struck home, and the division was put into a solid mass one regiment wide and
twenty or thirty ranks deep, everybody elbow to elbow and each line right on
the heels of the line ahead. Orders were to advance in complete silence, nobody
yelling or touching the trigger of his musket until they reached the Rebel
trenches. On Barlow's right, invisible in the inky wet, was the division led by
General David Bell Birney, a pale, ascetic-looking man with a wispy beard and

a Puritanical devotion to his duty, and somewhere back of these men were John Gibbon and his division, with Mott's unhappy warriors till farther to the rear waiting to be called on if needed. Altogether, there were more than 15,000 men grouped together here in the leaking dark, their clothing as wet as if they had all fallen in a river, nothing ahead of them but the silent night and the loom of indistinct hills and forests in the downpour. Barlow was the guide, to take them up to the tip of the Rebel salient.

After much blind galloping by couriers and staff officers, the immense mass of soldiers began to move, mud clinging to heavy feet at every step. Barlow had his compass points straight, and he set out confidently enough, with two staff officers beside him for guidance. But as they moved he learned that these officers knew no more than he did about what lay ahead of them. Indeed, they were complaining bitterly about being sent to conduct a move when they knew nothing whatever about it. They staggered and stumbled on—by Barlow's orders all horses were left behind, and division commander and all other officers were tramping along on foot—and nobody could see anything and nobody knew anything, and presently the whole situation began to strike General Barlow as very funny in a horrible sort of way.

At his side was Hancock's chief of staff, and this man, Barlow wrote, was "a profane swearer" who as they plodded on kept making pungent remarks about the conduct of the war. As this officer made the high command's utter ignorance about everything connected with this venture more and more obvious, Barlow asked him finally, and in straight-faced jest, if he could at least be sure that there was not an open canyon a thousand feet deep between the place where they then were and the place where the Confederates had built their trenches, and the officer frankly confessed that he had no such assurance; upon which firebrand Nelson Miles, one of Barlow's brigadiers, voiced his disgust so loudly and bitterly that Barlow had to tell him to shut up. The rain stopped, and the sky began to grow dull and pale, and a thick clammy fog floated up from the lower ground. The vast column oozed along down a slanting field, and Barlow at last told the staff people: "For Heaven's sake, at least face us in the right direction, so that we shall not march away from the enemy and have to go round the world and come up in the rear."[13]

This much the staff officers could do, and at some point or other in the predawn grayness they called a halt, and they gestured brightly toward the fog ahead and said that the enemy was off there somewhere, although they confessed freely that they did not know how the enemy's works were built or how many enemies were in them or what the ground in front of the enemy's position might be like. Barlow had a mental picture of a crude map which an officer in the 16th Massachusetts had scratched on a kitchen wall for him, an hour or two earlier, and he tried to keep that in mind. Then the staff officers went away, and Barlow was on his own, and he ordered his men forward and the big assault was on.

Not all of the men knew that they were actually beginning an attack. So hazy were the arrangements that some of them supposed they were simply making a routine change of position, and at the rear of the divisional column there were officers' servants, camp cooks, and so on, leading mules loaded down with spare tents, cooking equipment, and provisions. Out in front of the blind column the 66th New York had been deployed in a dense skirmish line, and presently this line rolled over the Rebel pickets, coming in out of the milky obscurity so suddenly that the pickets had no time to sound the alarm. The pickets were disarmed and sent to the rear and the division plodded on.[14]

It broke through a thicket and approached a little ridge, and the men thought this ridge was the Rebel line and they raised a sudden cheer and everybody broke into a run. As they ran, the troops lost all formation and became a dense, crowding mass. They passed over the ridge, finding no Confederates on it, and swept down across a broad hollow, the dim light slowly growing brighter, and in the hollow they ran into the heavy abatis their foes had prepared for them. They sprang on this entanglement and tore it apart hand by hand, working in frenzied haste, and the Confederate line was not a hundred yards beyond. The racket had roused the defenders, and the trenches began to spit flame as the men who stood in them opened fire.[15]

As the Federals ran forward there was a careening rush just behind the Confederate line, and the twenty-two missing guns came back over the muddy ground on a spattering gallop. The Confederate command in the salient had sniffed trouble during the night and had sent desperate appeals for the return of these guns, and now they were coming up to the rear of the trench line just as the Northerners were coming up to the front of it. If the guns had been in position, the piled-up division that was coming up the slope would have given them the kind of target gunners dream about, and Barlow's men would have been murdered, but the Yankees' luck was in and the guns did not quite make it.

Two or three guns did manage to swing into the gun pits and fire a round or two—one shell went sailing over the combat men and smashed into one of the misguided headquarters details that were stupidly coming along in the rear, dismembering a pack mule and filling the air with frying pans, sides of bacon, and other matters—but it was too late. The massed Federals went flooding over the trenches as if a dam had been broken, stabbing with their bayonets and cheering to split their throats, and the whole end of the salient was broken in. Twenty of the guns and three or four thousand Confederate infantrymen were captured en masse, and the yelling soldiers went streaming on into the foggy woods and ravines beyond the trenches.[16]

They were on their way—somewhere, no one knew where, impelled by a rush that was both powerful and fragile. The ground was rough and the trees and thickets were obscure in the wet hazy light, and no one knew a thing except that the Rebel line had been smashed and that the thing to do was probably to keep on running. The different regiments and brigades were as thoroughly scrambled as if the whole division had been tossed in a giant's blanket. What ran down the open space inside the Mule Shoe was not the hard spearhead of an army corps but simply an excited mob, wholly confused and without any vestige of organization or control. It would be an irresistible flood tide up to the moment when it ran into something solid. Then it would turn into foam and the wave would recede.

Midway down the Mule Shoe the something solid appeared—an ably led division of Confederate veterans bent on driving the Yankees back to where they came from. Lee himself was among them, getting them set for a counterattack, trying to lead it himself until the Southern Army's sure instinct for self-preservation forced him to the rear. These Southerners formed a battle line and tilted their muskets down and came charging up the salient, and they hit the disorganized Yankees and sent them running. There were wild moments of confused fighting in the misty woods and up across the little fields and hollows, and then the Federals came pelting back to the captured trenches. Here they stopped running and turned around and dug in to hold onto what they had gained, while the high command sent fresh troops up from the rear to exploit the break that had been made.

For half a mile or more, all along the toe of the salient, the men of the II Corps held the Confederate trenches. These were wide and deep, with so many traverses built back from them that they were like a series of adjoining cellars, and their walls were made of piled logs and banked-up earth, the ground at the bottom all muddy and covered with inches of filthy rain water. In this long jagged ditch the Federals suddenly went on the defensive, while the Rebels came storming out of the woods to wrest the line away from them.[17]

Practically all of Hancock's corps was up now, and there was not room for nearly all of the men to get on the firing line. In places they were jammed forty ranks deep, outside of the trenches, trying to crowd their way forward so that they could shoot Confederates. They had seized the captured guns and swung them around, but there were no gunners among them and few of the infantrymen knew much about handling cannon. One man remembered how they loaded these weapons with any bits of metal they could find, including broken muskets, and fired them helter-skelter, endangering themselves about as much as their enemies. An Irish private was gleefully fitting a primer into the breech of one of the guns, and a comrade tried to tell him that the weapon was elevated for extreme long range, so that it would shoot far above the oncoming Rebels. "Never fear!" yelled the Irishman, jerking the lanyard and firing the piece. "It's bound to come down on somebody's head!"[18]

The Federals were here in overwhelming numbers, and their very numbers were a handicap. Barlow tried desperately to get the men reformed, so that an organized attack could be resumed. There was no point in trying to go down the open ground in the middle of the salient. The recipe for victory now was to organize an advance that would sweep along the trench lines to right and left, flanking the Confederate defenders and widening the breach until it was past mending. But as fast as Barlow could get a few elements sorted out and put into line a new mass of reinforcements would come lopping in from the rear, and the line would vanish.

Things had happened too fast. What sketchy planning there had been was based on the theory that a great deal of sheer muscle would be needed to break the Rebel line. What actually happened, however, was that the line broke at the first touch, and what was needed immediately thereafter was quick footwork rather than brute strength. But the muscle was still coming in and there was no way to stop it and footwork was quite out of the question. There was nothing for it now but for everybody to get together and shove.

Both sides were shoving at once, and in the same place, and the result was the wildest, bitterest in-fighting of the entire war.

In effect each side was making a charge and repelling a charge at the same moment and with the same troops. The Confederates were fighting with a last-ditch fury. Far to their rear Lee was building a new trench line across the throat of the salient. It would be an all-day job and until the line was finished the men up front must at any cost whatever either drive the Yankees out or at least keep them from coming in any deeper. That meant close-range fighting carried out without any letup. The battle front was a mile wide by now, with Burnside's men fighting their way through the woods on the east and Wright sending his VI Corps in on the west, and in no place along this front were the rival firing lines more than a few yards apart.

It began to rain again, and the men in the trenches stood to their knees in bloodstained water, and the ground outside the trenches, trampled by massed thousands of men, turned into a stiff gumbo in which bodies of dead and wounded men were trodden out of sight. From the rear Barlow could see an immense mass of Federals lying flat in this muck, twenty or thirty ranks jammed together in a formless crowd, the men in the rear passing loaded muskets forward to the men in front. An orderly brought Barlow his horse and the general galloped back to Hancock to beg that no more men be sent forward.

Never before on earth had so many muskets been fired so fast on so narrow a front and at such close range. About all that kept the two armies from completely annihilating each other was the fact that most men were firing too rapidly to aim. A whole grove of trees behind the Rebel line was killed by shots that flew too high, and the logs of the breastworks were splintered and, a Confederate officer said expressively, "whipped into basket-stuff." Bodies of dead and wounded men were hit over and over again until they simply fell apart and became unrecognizable remnants of bloody flesh rather than corpses. There were big charges and little charges, with bayonet fighting when the men came to close quarters, and at times Union and Confederate flags waved side by side on the parapets, with bullets shredding them into tattered streamers.[19]

A few hundred yards to the east of the blunt tip of the salient there was a place where the Rebel trench line made a little bend to the south, and right at this bend a spirited Confederate counterattack regained part of the breastworks. On the Yankee side of the works there was a ditch, and as the Southerners retook their trench, men of the VI Corps came charging in and occupied the ditch, and for a distance here the rival battle lines were literally face to face with only the log breastwork between them.

Men fired at one another through chinks in the logs, or stabbed through the chinks with their bayonets, or reached over the top to swing clubbed muskets. Where the Vermont Brigade was fighting, men were seen to spring on top of the logs and fire down on their enemies as fast as their comrades could pass loaded muskets up to them. Each man would get off a few rounds before he was shot, and usually when one of these men fell someone else would clamber up to take his place. Dead men fell on top of wounded men, and unhurt men coming up to fight would step on the hideous writhing pile-up.[20]

Emory Upton had his thinned brigade in beside the Vermonters. He was riding his horse back and forth just behind the firing line, the only mounted man in sight, going unhurt by some miracle—every man on his staff was either killed or wounded. He was proud of the way his men were fighting, but he felt that they would do even better if they had the help of some artillery, and he sent back for a section of guns. In a few moments two brass fieldpieces from a regular battery came splashing madly up through the rain, wheeling about to unlimber within literal whites-of-their-eyes range—artillery charging entrenched infantry, as if all roles were reversed in this mad war.

The gunners sent double charges of canister plowing through the Confederate ranks, and at this close range the effect was fantastic. Inspired by it, the gunners laid hands on their pieces and ran them forward until they touched the very parapet, and then they resumed firing and kept it up as long as the guns could be manned, which was not very long. When the guns at last fell silent they could not be removed because all of the horses were dead, and of the twenty-four men who came on the field with them only two were on their feet unwounded.[21]

There had been hand-to-hand fighting before, but it invariably reached a quick climax and then ended, one side or the other breaking and running away. Here nobody broke and nobody ran. The fighting did not stop for a moment, and the unendurable moment of climax hung taut in the air and became fixed, a permanent part of some insane new order of things. Some regiments sent details a dozen paces to the rear to clean muskets; men were firing so continuously that their weapons became foul with burnt powder and could not be loaded. Amazingly enough, as the day wore on exhausted men from time to time would stagger a few feet away from the firing line, drop unhurt in the mud, and fall sound asleep. Now and then men had to stop fighting and lift the bodies of dead and wounded comrades out of the wet ditch and drop them in the mud outside. There were so many bodies they interfered with the fighting.[22]

This was the Bloody Angle, the place where a trench made a little bend, and where the two armies might have clasped hands as they fought; and it was precisely here that the war came down to its darkest cockpit. It could never be any worse than this because men could not possibly imagine or do anything worse. This fighting was not planned or ordered or directed. It was formless, monstrous, something no general could will. It grew out of what these men were and what the war had taught them—cruel knowledge of killing, wild brief contempt for death, furious unspeakable ferocity that could transcend every limitation of whipped nerves and beaten flesh. There was a frenzy on both armies, and as they grappled in the driving rain with the smoke and the wild shouting and the great shock of gunfire all about them this one muddy ditch with a log wall running down the middle became the center of the whole world. Nothing mattered except to possess it utterly or to clog it breast-high with corpses.

There were no victory in all of this and there was no defeat. There was just fighting, as if that had become an end in itself. A Massachusetts soldier wrote that the firing continued "just so long as we could see a man," and a Pennsylvanian agreed that "all day long it was one continuous assault." A man in the Iron Brigade probably spoke for every man in the army when he called this fight at the Bloody Angle "the most terrible twenty-four hours of our service in the war." An officer in the VI Corps, trying to describe the fight afterward, wrote that he had only confused memories of "bloodshed surpassing all former experiences, a desperation in the struggle never before witnessed." Trying to sum up, he concluded: "I never expect to be fully believed when I tell what I saw of the horrors of Spotsylvania, because I should be loath to believe it myself were the case reversed."[23]

The fighting went on all day long and it continued after dark—there were men on the firing line who said they fired more than four hundred cartridges apiece, from start to finish. Finally, somewhere around midnight, it died out. The Confederates had at last finished the cutoff line at the base of the salient, and they slipped quietly back to it, and in the darkness the entire salient disappeared. The exhausted Federals got a drugged sleep in the rain, and in the morning they went cautiously forward to take a look at the ground they had won.

There was nothing remarkable about it, except that the region around the Bloody Angle offered the most horrible sights of the war. In places, the trenches held corpses piled four and five deep, and sometimes at the bottom of such a pile a living wounded man would be found. The firing had been so intense that many bodies had been hit over and over again and were mutilated beyond any chance of identification. One of Wright's staff officers remembered that once during the previous day he had ordered some guns up to an advanced position, and he could not remember having heard anything from them thereafter, so he went out to look. The two guns, he found, had reached the designated position, and each piece and caisson was wheeled halfway around, but the guns had never got into battery. A burst of Rebel fire had caught them in mid-turn and every man and horse had been killed, "and they lay as if waiting the resurrection."[24]

Clearly, the ground that had been won was not worth what it cost, either from an esthetic or a military standpoint. The Rebel line had been broken but it had been mended again, and the armies were just about where they were before. The Federals had gained a square mile of quite useless territory at the price of nearly 7,000 casualties. Rebel losses, to be sure, had been heavier, but that was cold comfort. The big push had been made and it had not quite worked.

Yet perhaps all of that did not really matter. Something inexorable was moving, and old words like victory and defeat had lost their meaning. The slouchy little man with the stubbly red beard meant to keep going, and the entire war was one continuous battle now, and if one blow failed another one would immediately be struck. The day after the Bloody Angle fight new orders came down, and that night Warren drew his V Corps out of its place at the extreme right of the Federal line and marched it around in an enormous circle, behind the rest of the army, to a place on the extreme left. It was a cruel march, for the rain was still falling and the roads were knee-deep in mud, and the soldiers were as nearly dead with fatigue as living men can be, so that when Warren reached his destination in the morning he had only about 1,000 men with him. But the laggards came up later and there was a hard, wearing, inconclusive fight, and the next day there was another fight, and the army kept sidling around to its left, forcing Lee's army to shift to meet it.[25]

A week went by, with a battle of some sort fought every day, and the Union army which had been directly west of Spotsylvania Court House on May 8 was directly east of it on May 19, and every unit in the army had fought as it never had fought before. There had not been an hour, day or night, in all that time when there had not been firing somewhere along the front. Every day the wagons went back to Fredericksburg with wounded men, and every day other wagons came up to the front with supplies so that the endless fighting might continue.

On this nineteeth of May the Confederates made another of their patented blows at the Yankee flank. Ewell's corps went out beyond the Union right and came down through the woods heading straight for a road where the vast wagon trains were unloading, and all that stood in the way was an untested division made up of some of those heavy artillery regiments which had been uprooted from their comfortable berths in the Washington forts.

The veterans had not been kind to these men. As they were marched up to go into their first fight, the ex-artillerists passed a batch of wounded men who were awaiting medical attention. These men exhibited their wounds, some of which were pretty ghastly, and pointed out that the heavies would very soon be getting hurt as badly as this or even worse. Some called out, "Dearest, why did you leave your earthworks?" Others pulled a covering blanket from a dreadfully mangled corpse that lay by the road and invited the green soldiers to look at what happened to combat soldiers. There was nothing for the heavies to do but swallow hard and keep marching, and before long they formed line of battle and went off through the underbrush to fight with Lee's veterans.

The heavies knew nothing about fighting, but they were willing to learn. For an hour or more they had it out with Ewell's men, back and forth across a series of wooded hollows and little ravines, and at the end of that time the Confederates were in full retreat, with 900 dead and wounded left on the ground. About an equal number of the heavies had been shot, and when a newspaper correspondent asked how they had behaved, one of their officers explained: "Well, after a few minutes they got a little mixed and didn't fight very tactically, but they fought confounded plucky." It is recorded that ever after that the Army of the Potomac had no more jeers for heavy artillerists but admitted them to full comradeship.[26]

A day or so after this the army began to move again. It was not just edging a little farther around the Confederate flank, this time, but was really taking to the road, heading south. The soldiers' spirits rose with the move—the Spotsylvania area was one any soldier would be glad to leave—and although a light rain was falling, it merely served to lay the dust, and as they marched a number of the battle-thinned regiments did what veterans rarely did: they began to sing while they marched.

Yet moods could change fast, and the singing did not last long. A regiment would be trudging down the road, singing as if all of war's trials were far away. Then, inexplicably, the song would come to a sudden stop. There would be a brief silence, and then from one end of the regiment to the other, spurred by a common impulse, the men would yell: "I want to go home!"[27]

THREE

One More River to Cross

1. THE CRIPPLES WHO COULD NOT RUN

THE DRAMA no longer lay in the great events that took place down by the footlights. At the back of the stage there was a silent unbroken procession of young men who looked old and tired, wearing uniforms much the worse for weather and hard wear: a procession that moved eternally out of life and into death or mutilation, compelling the attention simply because there were so many men in it that it was hard to think about anything else. Lincoln had to see it, and he paced the halls of the White House without sleep, a grotesque lanky figure who could feel the lash on another man's back, and he considered the sound and fury which Macbeth had heard on his own stage and he listened for something beyond it. If that something was there it would come out someday, and if it was not there then the sooner the idiot's tale was told and finished the better for everyone. Always the silent procession kept moving, and there were off-stage sounds of hoarse cheers, and bursts of musketry and the thudding of the guns, and the maddening imperious command of the bugles.

In the old days there would have been a lull. There had been continuous fighting or marching for more than two weeks, and the soldiers had neither taken off their clothing nor had an unbroken night's rest since they crossed the Rapidan. Losses had been appalling. Many brigades were no bigger than regiments ought to be, and any number of regiments were down to normal company strength. Two whole divisions had been cut up so badly that they had to be discontinued, the remnants consolidated with other units. Behind the army there was a litter of broken human bodies extending all the way back from Fredericksburg to the crowded hospitals around Washington.

The casualty lists told a story. The army moved south from Spotsylvania Court House a little more than a fortnight after it had crossed the Rapidan. In that time more than 33,000 men had been lost. Averaged out, this meant that 2,000 men were being killed or wounded every twenty-four hours. Fredericksburg and Chancellorsville together had taken no such toll as this. Now, instead of pulling back for a breathing spell, the army was going to plunge even more deeply into action, with every prospect that the killing would go on and on without a respite.

Grant had had to change his plans, for this move south had not been on his program. In the heat of the fighting around the little courthouse town he had told Washington that he would fight it out along this line if it took all summer, and when he said it that promise made sense. Lee's army was smaller than the Army of the Potomac, and in the fighting thus far the two armies were losing just about the same percentages of the numbers engaged. If they were applied long enough these percentages meant certain doom for the weaker army. The mathematics were ugly but inexorable: sooner or later, Lee's army would be too thin to stand the hammering.

But the picture had suddenly changed, and instead of forcing a decision

537

where it was, the Army of the Potomac now had to march for the open country, trying to get into such a position that Lee would have to stop digging invulnerable trenches and come out to attack. Those deadly percentages would work for the Federals only as long as Lee was deprived of reinforcements. Grant had made certain arrangements to bring that deprivation about, and those arrangements had unexpectedly collapsed.

In the Shenandoah Valley there was a little Union army under Franz Sigel, moving south to close that granary and highway of war to the Confederacy, and south of the James River Ben Butler was leading two army corps up toward the Rebel capital. It did not really matter very much whether either of these generals actually reached his goal, so long as both of them kept diligently trying to reach it. But both men had failed.

Sigel met a scratch Confederate army at a town called Newmarket and was driven back in wild rout, a devoted and unskilled soldier failing in a task he should never have been given. (How differently John Sedgwick might have done it, if the demotion Stanton had planned had been accomplished!) Butler had done no better. With much ceremony and scheming he managed to let inferior numbers drive him into a broad peninsula jutting out into the James. The Confederates promptly dug in across the neck of the peninsula, leaving him locked up as securely as if he and all his soldiers had been in prison.

With these two disasters, everything came unstitched. Grant got the bad news while he was still hammering at the Spotsylvania lines, and the evil part of it was the certain knowledge that, because Sigel and Butler had been beaten, the Confederates who had been fighting them would immediately move up to reinforce Lee. That meant that to "fight it out along this line" was no longer a good move. The Confederates had had heavy losses in the past fortnight—in the first week of the action, 7,000 Rebel prisoners had been sent north, and more were coming in—and up to now the terrible percentages had been working for the North. But now the defeats along the James and the Shenandoah meant that Lee's losses would all be made good. In effect, the Army of Northern Virginia was going to be about as strong after three weeks of fighting as it had been before the fighting began. Plans which had been based on the assumption that it would be a great deal weaker would have to be changed.

So Grant sat down at his field desk and wrote orders for another move by the left flank: a move like the one which took the army out of the Wilderness, a shift east and south, maneuver in place of continued fighting. In a way this might be playing Lee's game, but there was no help for it. Reinforced, Lee could hold his Spotsylvania lines indefinitely. If there was such a thing as a road to victory, it led around those trenches, not over them.[1]

As the army began to move, Grant and Meade studied the casualty lists together. They were in contrast, those two soldiers. Men who had long since lost their enthusiasm for generals looked at them curiously when they appeared side by side. There was a gunner who remembered how his battery was brought forward one day to beat in some Rebel strong point which was holding up an infantry advance. Shortly after the guns opened Grant and Meade rode up and posted themselves under a nearby tree to watch the fight. Meade was nervous, moving about, constantly stroking his beard, fretting when the fight went badly. Grant stood quietly, a cigar in his teeth, his face utterly expressionless in its wreath of tobacco smoke, and he seemed like a man forced to watch something that did not interest him at all. The fight failed, and the open field in front was stained with blue bodies, and the two generals mounted and rode off, Grant still looking as if he had seen nothing in particular.

"The enlisted men looked curiously at Grant," wrote the gunner, "And after he had disappeared they talked of him, and of the dead and wounded men who lay in the pasture field; and all of them said just what they thought, as was the wont of American soldiers."[2]

Yet the contrast between the two generals was not quite what it seemed to be. Grant was the stolid, remorseless killer and Meade was the sensitive man who sparred and drew back and tried at all times to conserve the lives of his men; yet of the two it was Grant who winced in agony at the price men were paying for the fighting. It was he and not the other man who felt the compulsion to look at the unbroken column moving across the back of the stage, the men who marched from life to death and carried the war on their bowed shoulders. It seems that the thought of this wrung some kind of outcry from him—*must* there be all of this killing?

It was Meade who laconically gave him such comfort as could be given.

"Well, General," said Meade, "we can't do these little tricks without losses."[3]

The whole army had grasped this point, accepting it without enthusiasm but with a minimum of complaint. Yet the burden of the losses lay everywhere, and now and then it caused an outcry, unheard at the moment, echoing faintly down the years. In a Wisconsin regiment a devout chaplain somehow found a quiet hour and managed to hold divine services, and to the tanned veterans who were grouped about him in the firelight he preached a thumping sermon full of hell-fire and eternal punishment, predestination darkly illumined by grace abounding, and the regiment's colonel was rubbed where it hurt. He called the chaplain to his tent after the services and told him off.

"I don't want any more of that doctrine preached in this regiment," said the colonel sternly. "Every one of my boys who fall fighting this great battle of liberty is going to Heaven, and I won't allow any other principle to be promulgated to them while I command the regiment."[4]

A Michigan infantryman, looking back on the fighting, noted in his diary that General Lee must be a great strategist. No matter where the army went, the Rebels were always there in front of it, and the Rebel line always seemed to hold firmly no matter how hard it was hit. And the soldier mused: "Now what is the reason that we cannot walk right straight through them with our far superior numbers? We fight as good as they. They must understand the country better, or there is a screw loose somewhere in the machinery of our army."

Commenting on the Bloody Angle fight, the same soldier was moved to a protest:

"Surely, we cannot see much generalship in our campaign so far, and the soldiers are getting sick of such butchery in such a way. Half the time the men are fighting on their own responsibility, and if there is anything gained so far it is by brute force and not by generalship."[5]

Whatever the ins and outs of it might be, the soldier had touched on a basic point. The only value that seemed to amount to anything any more was the simple courage of the enlisted man. In different ways the various units of the army recognized the fact and reacted accordingly, and the soldiers found their own direct and brutal ways to punish the men who did not measure up.

In a Pennsylvania regiment which fought at the Bloody Angle there was one man who ran from the fighting and found safety in the rear. He was fished out of his transient security, and the next day the colonel devised a horrible punishment. He had the man bucked and gagged and deposited him, trussed up and helpless, in front of regimental headquarters. Then he had the man's own company march past him in single file, and as they did so the colonel ordered them to spit in the face of the man who had run away. The men obeyed without a quibble and felt that the punishment was simple justice.

A New York battery had a different system. This battery was in the IX Corps line during hard fighting to the east of the Bloody Angle, and a general who came by in the heat of the battle found one wriggling man tied up between two trees near the guns, a helpless target for all of the Confederate bullets. The general asked about it, and was told that the man was a notorious shirker, present for duty only when it was time to draw rations; the men had caught him this time and had spread-eagled him under fire, hoping that he would be hit. The general laughed and told the battery commander to keep the man tied up until sundown, and an infantry major who happened by burst out: "I'll bet he is a big-bounty man. Keep the --- ------ --- -- - ----- there and get him killed, if possible, for the good of the service!" In some miraculous way (for the Rebel fire was very heavy) the man escaped all harm. He was released at night and he vanished in the dark and the battery never saw him again.

A Massachusetts soldier wrote that a straggler in his regiment was taken to the colonel, given a drumhead court-martial, and immediately shot to death—an event, he said, which noticeably discouraged straggling in the regiment thereafter. A company of Regular sharpshooters was paraded one evening, between fights, to see a runaway comrade drummed out of service in the old manner. The man's head had been shaved and the buttons of his uniform had been cut off, and he was marched down between the facing rows of his fellows, each man standing with lowered musket and fixed bayonet; and a squad came along just behind the man with more bayonets to prod him on his way. As the scapegrace shaven figure shambled along, the fife and drum corps piped the "Rogue's March":

> *Poor old soldier—poor old soldier—*
> *Tarred and feathered*
> *And then drummed out*
> *Because he wouldn't soldier.*

At the end of the ceremony the man fled into the woods, and the men saw no more of him.[6]

Yet, if the soldiers would readily kill or humiliate cowards, they could also laugh at them. A standard army joke was the story of the notorious slacker who bragged that when the battle was at its worst he could always be found where the bullets were thickest—far to the rear, safely hidden under an ammunition wagon. The army also liked the story about the Irish private (a good story was always pinned on an Irishman in those days, if possible) who used as his own means of escape from action the shopworn excuse that he had to help a wounded comrade to the rear. In one battle, according to this story, the soldier undertook to help a comrade who cried that his leg had been shot off. Bending down, he got the wounded man over his shoulder and started out. As he stumbled along a cannon ball came out of nowhere and took off the head of the man he was carrying. After a time the Irishman got to a dressing station and offered his burden to the doctors, who asked him what he expected them to do for a man who had no head. Dumfounded, the soldier looked at the corpse and cried indignantly: "The deceiving creature—he told me it was his leg!"[7]

Sometimes the army's stories were told on Confederates. The Philadelphia brigade claimed that at Spotsylvania a ragged Rebel jumped out of the opposite trench and came running toward the Union lines. Just as he reached his goal a bullet hit him, and when the Federals came to pick him up he gasped: "I'm sorry you shot me—I was coming over to take the oath of allegiance." His captors confessed that they had no copy of that famous oath, but one of them remarked that they did have a canteen with a little whisky in it. Reviving, the Confederate sat up and said eagerly: "That will do just as well."[8]

The mail service caught up with the army just as it was leaving the Spotsylvania Court House area, and for the first time since they crossed the Rapidan the men got letters from home. They also got newspapers, which they read with eager curiosity, and as they read these papers they discovered anew that the war as it was described for people back home bore very little resemblance to the war which they themselves were actually fighting. In a Massachusetts battery the men hooted at newspaper accounts which proclaimed that Lee's army was "utterly routed and fleeing in confusion." One of the gunners remarked disgustedly that this, "like so much of the trash published by the papers during the war, would have been decidedly important if true."[9]

It did not really make much difference, for there was nothing the outside world could tell these soldiers anyway. The army's world was enclosed by cavalry patrols and moving skirmish lines, and in the obscurity beyond those boundaries there was the Rebel army, sometimes out of sight but never out of touch. The normal state of all previous armies—the state in which most of the soldier's time was spent—was neither marching nor fighting but quiet life in camp, barracks, or garrison. An army might march far and fight furiously, but when all of its days as an army were added up it would be found that most of them had been dull, monotonous days of inaction. But from the moment the Army of the Potomac crossed the Rapidan on May 5 to the end of the war, eleven months later, there was no inaction whatever. Instead there was marching or fighting every day, and very often both together, and physical contact with the enemy was never wholly broken.[10] The final grapple had begun, and the war had become a war of using up—using up men and emotions and the wild impossible dreams that had called the armies into being in the first place—and everything that Americans would ever do thereafter would be affected in one way or another by what remained after the using up was completed.

The armies were moving on parallel lines. They were never far apart, and they bumped and jostled each other as they moved, a fringe of fire running up and down the lines, with cavalry patrols fighting for the possession of lonely road crossings, artillery defending the fords and bridges at streams, infantry skirmishers colliding on plantation fields. By day and by night there was always the chance that any of these little tussles might develop into a full-scale battle.

There were many wearing night marches, and the men were very tired, and one soldier said long afterward that the very appearance of the army had changed, as if everything that had happened looked out of the faces of the marching men: "The men in the ranks did not look as they did when they entered the Wilderness: their uniforms were now torn, ragged and stained with mud; the men had grown thin and haggard; the experience of those twenty days seemed to have added twenty years to their age."

This soldier remembered that there was much straggling in these marches, and yet it was not the familiar business of sloughing off the fainthearts who always dropped out of ranks when the army moved. Now good men who wanted to keep up were dropping by the roadside because they could not take another step, and the nightly bivouacs had a strange appearance. An average company might have fifteen men present when it grounded arms for the night. Five of these would promptly be detailed for picket duty. Of the ten who remained, at least half would fall to the ground, too exhausted to collect wood or water or build campfires or do anything else. The men who remained on their feet would hunt fence rails or sticks to make a fire, and would collect canteens to get water, and in one way or another would provide a meal for the company. The sure sign that the men who lay inert and did nothing were not shirkers was the fact that these men would cook coffee and meat for them.

No night's rest was ever unbroken. There would always be picket firing, or some unexplained call to arms at midnight, and if nothing else happened there was a constant trickle of tired laggards going through the camp waking up those who slept to ask where their own regiments might be.[11]

If infantry and cavalry happened to bivouac together, dawn would reveal an oddity. Cavalry was always awakened by bugle calls, but the morning summons to infantry was the long roll beaten on the drums. The cavalrymen would sleep soundly through the beating of the drums but would rouse instantly when their own bugles sounded, while it was just the other way around with infantry—bugles would not awaken them, but they got up at once when the drums began to beat. Sometimes a wakeful battery would fire a few salvos in the night, and get answering salvos from an unseen Rebel battery, and the troops would remain asleep. But the same men would come out of their blankets at once, fumble for their muskets, and fall into line if a few musket shots were fired by their own pickets.[12]

Yet if everybody was tired, morale was good. The country the army was in now had never been touched by war and it looked clean and open and prosperous, with houses that had neither been pillaged nor abandoned and fields where good crops were growing. For all the toll taken by hard marching, a newspaper correspondent wrote that there were fewer stragglers and less grumbling than when the campaign first began, and a New York officer agreed that "the men never marched with so little complaining or so little straggling." If the white inhabitants were all stanchly secessionist, the plantation colored folk were strongly inclined in the other direction, and men's spirits rose when a teen-age colored girl stood by a fence corner waving her sunbonnet and calling out gaily: "I'se right glad to see you, gen'l'men, I'se right glad to see you."

There were abundant fence rails for campfires, and army authorities made no more than a pretense of enforcing the standing rule against destroying fences. In one regiment it was remembered that when the column halted for the night, with the men eagerly spotting the wealth of rails in the nearest field, the colonel, before they broke ranks, would sternly call out: "Now boys, I don't want to see one of you touch a rail." He would then face in the opposite direction, keeping his gaze fixed on the distant hills, resolutely seeing nothing while his men took the fences completely to pieces.[13]

Now and then the private soldier would encounter the aristocratic spirit of the Old Dominion in all of its pristine freshness. As the army got down to the North Anna River, a regiment was sent across at Jericho Ford, and hostile Confederates were believed to be very near, so the regiment formed line of battle in a well-tilled garden just behind a pleasant country house. As the men fell into place in this garden, examining muskets and cartridges to see if they had been dampened by the ford, an elderly woman came out of the house to lodge a dignified protest:

"Gentlemen, why have you come? Mr. Lee is not here. You are spoiling my garden."

The men chuckled and paid little attention until the colonel finally ordered: "Boys, keep between the rows."[14]

The inevitable foraging on defenseless civilians seems to have been kept to a minimum. There were dairy herds in this area, however, and the men did want fresh milk, and they occasionally tried to get it for themselves. (The average soldier in those days knew how to milk a cow.) This did not always work out very well. A Massachusetts soldier explained why: "To hold a dipper with one hand and milk with the other, particularly when three other hands were endeavoring to do the same thing on the same cow, and she unwilling to stand still, required a degree of skill that few of us possessed."[15]

The farmers' worst troubles probably came because both armies had by now acquired the habit of digging trenches the moment they halted. Any position where a brigade stopped might easily become the scene of a fight, and the great virtues of an entrenched position had by now become visible to everyone. It was rarely necessary for an officer to tell the men to entrench. Usually they began digging even before they started to boil their coffee.

Every division carried axes and spades in its ammunition wagons, but the men rarely waited for these to be brought forward. They would begin the work by themselves, using bayonets, sharpened pieces of wood, and any small tools they might carry with them. All of this digging did not improve the farmers' fields very much, and a Philadelphia veteran reflected on the loss that was involved. One day, he said, his division fell into line on a well-cultivated farm and put in several hours digging a long, deep trench, tearing down a barn and several outbuildings that stood in the way. No sooner was this finished than the presence of Rebel forces was reported off on the flank, so a new trench was dug at right angles to the first. By the time it was finished the enemy had changed front again, and so a third line was constructed—after which orders to move were brought in and the division marched away, leaving the luckless farmer with fields that were completely crisscrossed by deep ditches. What the farmer ever did about it the soldier was quite unable to imagine.[16]

The Confederates had learned about digging trenches, too—had in fact learned it before the Federals did. It was an axiom by now that if the Rebels had half a day in any given position they would build good fieldworks, and if they were given an extra twenty-four hours they would get dug in so completely that they could not possibly be pushed out. The private soldier was getting war-wise, and if he was called on to attack an entrenched position, he could usually tell at a glance whether the attack had any chance to succeed. It was commonly said in the army that the heavy artillerists had suffered heavy losses in the Spotsylvania fight largely because the men were so green: they had advanced to attack the enemy in solid ranks, worrying about keeping their alignment and fussing over parade-ground details, and thereby had presented a target the Southern marksmen could not miss. Veteran troops would have spread themselves out, going forward in short rushes, lying down between volleys and protecting themselves as they fought.[17]

For a number of days the army's existence consisted of a series of attempts to get around Lee's flank so that there could be fighting after the old manner, with nobody hidden in trenches and every Rebel out in the open where he could conveniently be shot. This never quite happened, since Lee could move just as fast as Grant could move, and the Confederates knew the country better; and there was a confused, meaningless series of little fights for river crossings and road centers—little only by comparison with what had gone before, big enough for the men directly involved, in their casualty lists and their drain on energies.

As always, the pickets made close contact, and one day across a stream some Confederates asked Wisconsin soldiers why they had come down to steal the slaves of men who had done them no harm. The Westerners replied that they did not care about slavery: all that concerned them was to save the Union.

"You-all aren't Yankees," cried a Confederate. "You 'uns and we 'uns ought to go together in this war and let the Yankees go by themselves!"[18]

Strange new names were entered on the army's annals—Ox Ford and Quarles Mill and Jericho Ford, and the other crossings of the North Anna River; roads down to the Pamunkey, places like Hawes's Shop and Bethesda Church, and the rambling network of highways that led to a desolate crossroads known as Cold Harbor. In all of these places there was fighting, and before and after each fight there was a forced march, and the army neither won nor lost as it moved on. It added to its knowledge and to its losses, and it got deeper and deeper into Virginia, but it never quite got around the end of the Rebel army and the big showdown was always somewhere ahead.

The army had conquered nothing and it possessed not a foot of Virginia soil except the ground on which it actually stood. All the way back to the Rapidan, Virginia was still Confederate territory, and the men who strayed past the army lines to the rear were quite as likely to be shot or captured as if they had strayed out to the front. Rebel cavalry roamed far and wide, and it was assisted by pestiferous bands of guerillas—informal groups of semiofficial mounted men, who were peace-loving farmers half of the time and blood-thirsty raiders the rest of the time. These bands covered all of the rear, and no wagon train could pass between the army and the river bases north of Fredericksburg without a strong escort.

Grant scorned to look behind him. To keep a safe supply line open all the

way back to Belle Plain and Aquia Creek on the Potomac would take too many
fighting men away from the front, so he simply refused to try. When the army
left Spotsylvania the bases on the Potomac were closed. For the time being a
new base was opened at Port Royal, downstream from Fredericksburg on the
Rappahannock. That was closer to the army, and as soon as the distance back to
Port Royal became too great a new base could be opened at White House, on
the Pamunkey. Later, if things went well, there could even be a base on the
James River itself. Whatever happened, the army would no longer be tied to the
Potomac by a long, cumbersome wagon train.

There was significance in this, for names can be important. At the beginning
of the war the army had been named the Army of the Potomac, and the over-
tones of that name had never been forgotten. Above everything else, the army
had been the shield of Washington, standing near the Potomac River to defend
the capital. Now the ties had been cut. The army had left the river from which it
took its name, and it was not going to see that river again while the war lasted. It
was going south—going glacially, destroying itself as it destroyed other things,
but moving with inevitability. Except in its name, which it wore proudly, like a
battle flag prized all the more because weather has stained it and bullets have
cut it, it was no longer the Army of the Potomac. The Potomac had become a
backwater. Hereafter the rear was going to have to take care of itself.

That meant problems for the rear echelon, and these problems were borne
largely by a strange little detachment of hopelessly crippled men who did not
seem to think that mere physical disability need keep a man out of the army.
These men, officially, were members of the 18th Regiment of the Veteran Reserve Corps, and they made up as unusual a fighting force as the United States
ever armed and equipped for action.

Sometime earlier the authorities had meditated on the great loss of manpower
involved in the discharge of wounded veterans who were still sound enough for
light duty behind the lines, and they had organized a body which they called the
Invalid Corps, which was recruited in army hospitals. Any wounded man who
was permanently unfit for field service but who could still be moderately active
might, if he chose, enlist in the Invalid Corps. Some thousands of wounded men
joined up, and they were scattered all over the North—guarding prison camps
and arsenals, acting as hospital guards, doing provost guard duty at draft offices,
and so on. It was a sound idea, but it got off to a bad start. The name "Invalid
Corps" grated on everybody, and the field troops poked a good deal of fun at it,
and members of the corps asked to be sent back to the front or discharged outright rather than bear the title "Invalid." Also, the authorities in their wisdom
had devised a uniform of delicate robin's-egg blue, which nobody liked. After a
time, therefore, the organization was renamed the Veteran Reserve Corps and
given regular army uniforms, and it settled down to do useful work.

There were different classifications within the corps. The most nearly fit men
were enlisted in what was called the First Battalion, which meant that they
could be used for noncombat garrison and guard duty. Below them came the
Second Battalion, whose men were too crippled or enfeebled to carry muskets or
move about freely on their feet and who accordingly were designated for the
lightest kind of duty. The 18th Regiment was composed of six companies of Second Battalion men—nearly 500 men, altogether—and ordinarily they would
have had no business within fifty miles of the Potomac River bases. But Grant
was running things these days and he had stern ideas about making use of army
manpower, and so in mid-May the 18th Regiment was put on a transport in
Washington and told to guard a batch of the priceless bounty men who were
being shipped down to the army.

The colonel in charge of the 18th Regiment was dubious. He pointed out that
his men were supposed to be too infirm to carry muskets at all, and that they
certainly could not march. However, he supposed they could fire at deserters, if

they had to, and so the men were lined up and equipped as regular infantry and they got on the boat and set sail. They were not very military-looking. Some of them were crippled in such a way that they could carry their muskets only on the right shoulder and some could carry them only on the left, and some could not wear cartridge boxes and had to stuff their ammunition in their pockets. Most of them were not hearty enough to carry the regulation forty rounds anyway, and could take only five or ten.

They disembarked, finally, at Belle Plain, where they were put on guard duty. They were badly needed. There were incoming drafts of recruits to look after, and there was a steady stream of Confederate prisoners to be guarded and sent north, and there was a vast accumulation of stores to watch over and keep safe from marauding guerilla bands. Ordinarily a few regiments of front-line troops would be detached for this work, but Grant had other uses for these and there was nobody to do the job but the cripples.

As long as they stayed at the base things were not too bad. To be sure, these disabled men had no pup tents or any other kind of shelter, and the weather was very rainy. Somebody had forgotten to supply them with any blankets, and they had no surgeon or medical stores. But they did their job, reporting proudly that they successfully guarded nearly 3,000 Rebel prisoners—two of these escaped, and one other tried it and got shot—and that all of the recruits and army stores were guarded without loss. Their real troubles began when the base was shifted to Port Royal.

By land, Port Royal was twenty-five miles away. The army liked to have its men go places under their own power if possible, and so when moving day came the regiment was lined up for inspection, to see how many men could make the march. Of the 474 men present, the doctors reported that 166 might possibly be able to do it, provided that they carried no knapsacks. (All of the officers reported themselves fit and refused to let the doctors examine them.) The rest were put on a transport to go down by water, and the shaky 166 set out on foot in a driving rainstorm.

Somehow, they made it. The column's best speed was one mile an hour. The road was infested with guerillas, and a general at Port Royal sent back an anxious message to the colonel of the 18th: Can your men fight, if the guerillas attack them? Back came the reply: "Tell the general that my men are cripples and so they can't run away." Fortunately, they did not have to fight. They plodded and staggered along, marching for fifteen minutes and then resting for ten, with officers going up and down the line pleading and coaxing all day long. After two days they finally got to Port Royal. The next morning, only 42 of the 166 were able to get on their feet and answer at roll call.

Later on, they actually did have a fight, one time when Wade Hampton took Confederate cavalry up for a wild swipe at the Federal base, and they made out very well, helping a handful of sound men to beat the raiders off. The rest of the time they did guard duty. By special dispensation, those who could not walk were allowed to sit down as they guarded their beats. After a month of it a medical board got a look at the regiments and reported in horror that four fifths of the men were not only unfit for any kind of duty but were actually unfit to be out of hospital beds. So the 18th Regiment of the Veteran Reserve Corps was finally sent back to Washington, leaving its brief record as testimony that it was a hard war that was being fought nowadays.[19]

A hard war, bringing changes, and there was no road back any more. The only roads that were left led on into more fighting, and the army that followed these roads looked less and less like the army that had crossed the Rapidan a few weeks earlier. Famous old organizations were vanishing and famous old names were disappearing. What had once been Joe Hooker's division no longer existed, and the Iron Brigade was no longer recognizable. The 3rd Michigan, Phil Kearny's pet in the early days of the war, was going off the army roster, and the 12th Massachusetts would do likewise in a few days—it had taught the army and the nation to sing "Glory, Glory Hallelujah!" and to date it had had 792 battle casualties. The great 2nd Wisconsin, being reduced to fewer than 100 rank and file and having lost all of its field officers, was recalled from combat duty and assigned to the provost guard.[20]

After the war was over someone asked crusty Brigadier General Romeyn Ayres if his famous old division of Regulars was still in service at this time. Ayres replied that the Regulars had mostly been killed.

"I had regulars—what were known as the regular division—before I went into the battle of Gettysburg," he said. "I left half of them there, and buried the rest in the Wilderness. There were no regulars left."[21]

2. JUDGMENT TRUMP OF THE ALMIGHTY

The rivers of eastern Virginia slant down toward the sea from the northwest. Some of them are wide and deep and some are quite insignificant except during time of heavy rains, but each one can be a barrier to a moving army. In the spring of 1864 the Army of the Potomac had to cross all of them, and the crossings could be made only where there were no defenders. These facts shaped the route of the army, and all through the month of May it moved in a series of wide zig-zags.

Wanting to go due south, the army was forever going southeast in order to find a good place to cross a river. Having crossed, it would turn southwest to get back on the route, and presently it would run into the Confederate army and there would be a fight. Since the Confederates could not be driven away from one of these spots where they elected to make a stand, the Federal army after a time would move southeast once more, sagging away from the direct road to Richmond but sooner or later crossing another river and cutting back to the southwest again. It moved like a ponderous ship tacking against a strong wind—a long slant to the left, a short leg to the right, another beat to the left and another slogging drive to the right; and if progress was slow it was steady.[1]

Many rivers had been crossed—the Rapidan and the Ny, the North Anna and the Pamunkey. If the Army of the Potomac was constantly being pushed toward the east, it was also gaining ground toward the south. The Confederate army always stood between it and Richmond, but the distance to Richmond was growing shorter and shorter. As May came to an end, the two armies were facing each other in a flat, featureless country of little streams and low ridges and small farms, spotted here and there with bogs and interlaced by narrow, winding roads. There was just one more river to cross—the Chickahominy, which ran across the Confederate rear just five miles away. Five miles beyond the Chickahominy was Richmond itself.

It was good to be this close to Richmond, and although they had packed more fighting and hard marching into the last month than they usually saw in half a year, the men were feeling hopeful. They seemed to be getting somewhere, at last, and a Massachusetts soldier reflected that "no backward steps were being taken," which, he remarked, was a brand new experience. He went on: "The Army of the Potomac having been unaccustomed to the sunshine of victory, rejoiced at the change and became buoyant with hope. The discouragement that hitherto attended us vanished as our confidence in Grant increased." He remembered that his regiment marched by a railroad siding one day and saw Grant, his uniform all dusty and worn, perched on a flatcar gnawing at a ham bone; the men cheered, and Grant casually waved the bone in acknowledgment and went on eating.

One officer insisted: "Never were the men more hopeful or in better spirits, more willing for marching, more ready to fight, than at this time," and he said they had "an idea that we were still advancing, that there was a plan that would be carried out successfully." Another officer wrote that "the men cannot help feeling that the worst is over, now that our great leader has pushed the enemy almost to the wall," and a new recruit who joined up just after Spotsylvania wrote home that the veterans with whom he talked "place unbounded faith in General Grant." A man in the IX Corps, recalling that his regiment lost its flag in the fighting east of the Bloody Angle, told how the men talked about the loss and agreed finally that it was the cause for pride rather than for shame, since it proved that they had been in a very hot place; and he added stoutly, "Be it considered a disgrace by whom it may, that does not make it one."[2]

Looking back on the campaign, men remembered a series of pictures which, as one soldier said, were "like the fragments of a half-forgotten dream, distinct in themselves but without any definite connection as to time or place." He sketched in a few of these fragments: "I see a long column of weary soldiers, winding along over hill and valley, in the night, gliding past a stately mansion, with beautiful grounds and shaded walks, and everywhere the freshness and fragrance of spring. Again I see a line of battle stretching out across an open field, the men resting lazily in the ranks. A little to the left, near some shade trees, stands a battery ready for action, the guns pointing toward some unseen enemy beyond. It is noon, and the sunlight is pouring down upon the scene, bright and clear."[3]

If they were close to Richmond at last, and feeling good about it, the Rebels were always in front of them, ready for business. Furthermore, the field of maneuver was growing very narrow. The army could no longer swing back and forth in wide arcs, going twenty miles to one side in order to get five miles forward. This was coffin corner, and there was little room to sidestep. Any road that was taken now had to lead to Richmond, and all of the roads to Richmond were blocked by pugnacious Southerners, who had trenches and gun pits wherever there was high ground.

Right now the Confederates were dug in behind the headwaters of Totopotomoy Creek, an insignificant watercourse whose turns and swampy banks offered good defensive ground. The chance of breaking this line looked no better than in the Wilderness or at Spotsylvania. It was better to go around the line than to try to go through it, and to go around it would be harder here than it had been before.

Down below the Federal left, within a mile or so of the Chickahominy, there was another of those seedy taverns that dotted the Virginia landscape—a quiet place at a sleepy crossroads, the name of it Cold Harbor, perched unobtrusively on a highway that wandered up from the Federal supply base, back at White House on the Pamunkey, and went on to cross the Chickahominy and go to Richmond.

This war went by a queer script of its own, and it had a way of putting all of its weight down on some utterly unimportant little spot that no one had ever heard of before—Shiloh Church, or Chancellorsville, or some such—and because armies contended for them, those place names became great and terrible. Now there was Cold Harbor, a wide spot on a lonely dusty road, set in a broad plain that was furrowed by tedious ravines and went rolling off to a chain of low hills on the south and west.

The weather was hot and the landscape looked barren, and a Federal officer who visited the place wondered how it had ever got its name. There was no harbor within miles, and the place was far from cold—was, in fact, as he reflected, very much like a bake oven—and the roads were ankle-deep in powdery dust that hung in low, choking clouds whenever a marching column went by, and it seemed that no man in his senses would ever want to come here. Years afterward, a veteran remarked that all of the battlefields of the war, Cold Harbor was the one spot he had never heard any soldier express a desire to revisit.[4]

Cold Harbor lay beyond the flanks of the armies. If the Federals were going to side-step once more they would have to come through here. Conversely, if the Confederates planned a countermove of their own this was a good spot for them to take, because if they held this crossroads they would be closer to the Yankee base at White House than the Yankees were themselves. So as May came to an end the storm clouds of the war drifted down to Cold Harbor, with a hurricane of fire to sweep the dreary plain, and the name of the run-down little tavern became a name to remember forever.

The cavalry got there first. Phil Sheridan had led his horsemen back to the Army of the Potomac a week earlier after a wild, eventful swing that took him to the very edge of Richmond. He had destroyed a good deal of Confederate property, he had released certain captured Yankees who had been on their way to the Richmond prisons, he had had a big fight with the Confederate cavalry—and he had done one of the grim things that had to be done if the Confederacy was to die: he had killed Jeb Stuart. Now the raid was over and cavalry was back on the job again, and on May 31 Sheridan brought two mounted divisions cross country, shook them out into a line of battle, and drove them yelling and clattering over the crossroads.

Confederate troops were already there. Lee and Grant had simultaneously realized the need to occupy this spot, and Rebel cavalry stiffened with infantry had come on the scene just in time to meet Sheridan's hard drive. Sheridan's men forced them out—they had at last turned from mere raiders into hard men of war, these cavalrymen, and their magazine carbines gave them prodigious fire power at close range, and they got off their horses and fought on foot and got a grip on the flat land around the crossroads, sending the Confederate advance guard back in defeat.

Lee was not going to take this meekly, and he sent in a fresh division of infantry to drive Sheridan's troopers out. The troopers hung on, working the levers of their carbines fast and kicking up the dust with low-flying bullets, and when evening came Sheridan sent back word that he did not think his men could stay where they were. He was told to stay anyway because Federal infantry would be up shortly, and while the dismounted cavalrymen dug in their heels and fought, couriers rode northeast to where General Wright had his VI Corps, on the right end of the Yankee line, and told him to get his men around to Cold Harbor as fast as they could travel.[5]

The Army of the Potomac had moved by its left many times in this campaign, but it always did it in reverse order; if the army had simply faced to its left and started marching it would have invited a ruinous flank attack. On a shift to the left, the first troops to move were always those on the extreme right. They would fade back, move around behind the army, and come up on the other end of the line.

So it was today. The VI Corps held the right; now it left its trenches and during the night and early morning it went slogging along through choking dust which raised a foul, strangling cloud over every regiment and made it impossible to see the length of a company. Intermittent messages kept coming from Sheridan—hurry up, hurry up, cavalry alone can't hold this position much longer—and one of Wright's staff officers who rode on ahead to Cold Harbor found Sheridan "the most nervy, wiry incarnation of business, and business only, I had yet met." The men remembered this march as about the worst they ever made, and when they got to Cold Harbor in midmorning of June 1, dirt-caked and completely worn out, they were happy to find that the firing had died down. They formed line of battle, an empty echoing plain before them, and most of the men dropped in their tracks and fell into a drugged sort of sleep.[6]

Reinforcements were coming. Down on the James River Butler's army was huddling ingloriously in its haven at Bermuda Hundred, and Grant had notified

Butler that if he could not fight there he could at least send some of his men up to help the Army of the Potomac. So General Baldy Smith put 16,000 men on transports and took them down the James, around Point Comfort, and up the Pamunkey to White House. He was under orders to get down to Cold Harbor as fast as he could, and he should have reached the place while Sheridan's fight was going on, but there had been a mixup in his orders and he made a wearing, useless march up the river before higher authority caught up with him and put him on the right track. Late in the afternoon of June 1, Smith's men came down to the crossroads by the tavern and began to file into line on the right of the VI Corps—very tired, short of ammunition and artillery, with a great many stragglers wandering about on the lost roads somewhere off to the rear.[7]

The plain was covered with dust raised by the marching men, and the dust hung in the air like a gritty cloud bank. The artillery began to hammer at the Confederate works, half a mile away, and the smoke mingled with the dust and the setting sun looked dull-red and enormous through the haze. As the reinforcements moved in, Wright's men roused themselves reluctantly. A Connecticut soldier tugged the arm of a sleeping comrade and told him: "Jim, there's a pile of troops coming. I guess there's going to be a fight." Jim blinked and declared: "I don't care a damn. I wish they'd shoot us and be done with it. I'd rather be shot than marched to death."[8]

It was remembered later that the men seemed stupid with weariness as they formed line of battle, and the feverish excitement that often ran through a body of men lining up for a charge was missing. The road from Cold Harbor toward Richmond led off between fields and little plots of woodland toward the rising ground where the Rebels were waiting, and the road served as the guide line for the attack, with Wright's troops on the left of it and Smith's on the right. The men got under way at last, and where the ground began to rise they came on the entanglement of felled trees and sharpened saplings which the Rebels had put thirty yards in front of their firing line. As the Federals began to tear this apart the Southern riflemen opened fire with one long, rolling volley—"a sheet of flame, sudden as lightning, red as blood, and so near that it seemed to singe the men's faces," one survivor described it. Up and down the front of the two army corps the attacking lines wavered, and here and there men turned and ran for the rear. Then the lines surged forward again, and on the slopes near the Richmond road Ricketts's division and some of Smith's men broke into the Rebel works, taking prisoners and sending the rest of the defenders flying.

Ricketts's men were out to redeem themselves. They were Milroy's weary boys from the valley, the ones who had broken and fled in panic in the Wilderness fight, and the rest of the VI Corps had let them know that they were accounted second-rate soldiers not worthy of belonging to a good fighting corps. Ricketts had been nursing them along ever since, and he seems to have pulled them together and made soldiers out of them, and on this evening their division was the only unit in the VI Corps that gained its objective. To right and left the Confederate line held firm, and as the evening deepened into a wild twilight there was a furious fire fight.

Emory Upton had his brigade up close to the enemy, as usual—he had just learned that he was being promoted brigadier general because of his feat at Spotsylvania—and in line with the gospel he had been preaching he was on the firing line personally, helping his men to beat off a sharp Rebel counterattack. One of his regiments, the 2nd Connecticut Heavy Artillery, began to waver, and Upton galloped into the middle of it, shouting: "Men of Connecticut, stand by me! We *must* hold this line!" The wavering stopped and the regiment held, and one soldier remembered seeing Upton, dismounted, standing in front rank firing an infantry musket. When one disheartened officer came up to report that he did not think his command could drive the Rebels back, Upton snarled at him: "If they come there, catch them on your bayonets and pitch them over your heads!"[9]

Darkness came at last and the fighting died away, and the Federals dug in where they were and counted their losses. These were fairly heavy—a total of some 2,200 for the two army corps—but the Confederates had had substantial losses, too, and 750 Southern prisoners were on their way back to the provost marshal's stockade. All in all, the day's action had been a success. The Confederates had been driven out of Cold Harbor and the Federal grip there was secure. Also, it appeared that this might be a good jumping-off point for a major attack.

Cold Harbor was not far from the Chickahominy, and there was no more room for shifting to the left. But the place was right on the Confederate flank, and while Lee had sent a good many troops down here they had been kept very busy and it did not seem probable that they could have built a strong defensive line. If there was any place along the line where an attack might succeed, it was right here, and success here would be dazzling because the Chickahominy ran across the Confederate rear and a beaten army trying to retreat fast across that river would be in dire trouble. Here, perhaps, was where the blow that would end the war could be struck. On top of these considerations there was the obvious fact that a blow could not very well be struck anywhere else. It was either fight here or develop a whole new campaign.[10]

These points had great weight, and Grant considered them and decided accordingly—which is to say that he ordered an all-out attack for daylight the next morning, with Wright's and Smith's corps to be reinforced by the twenty-odd thousand in Hancock's command, and with the rest of the army throwing its weight in where it was. Yet between a decision by the lieutenant general commanding and the ultimate appearance on the firing line of the soldiers who must make that decision effective there were many separate steps, and at Cold Harbor all of these were steps leading down into great darkness. There is a house-that-Jack-built quality to the tale: this went wrong because that went wrong, and that went wrong because of what happened just before, and that in turn.... Attitudes of mind and habits of thought formed when Cold Harbor was as remote as the mountains of the moon were still at work, each one affecting what was going to happen next, all of them put together forming a recipe for disaster.

Whatever was going to be done would have to be done very quickly. The whole idea was that at half-past four on the morning of June 2 the Confederates facing Cold Harbor would be off balance, unprepared to resist a solid blow. That assumption might well be correct; and yet it was as certain as anything could be certain that the Confederates would not stay off balance or unprepared very long, and that what was possible at dawn might be utterly impossible by midafternoon. The big attack that was set for dawn, in other words, had better take place at dawn and not at some other time.

But the reflexes of the chain of command in the Army of the Potomac had never yet been trained for speed. There was power here, and bravery, and simple determination—but the furious, implacable insistence on doing simple things quickly was not there at all. It had been bred out of the army in the leisurely days of 1862, when half a month one way or the other did not seem to make very much difference and the delay of a mere day or so did not make any difference at all, and nothing that the tough little man from the West had been able to do had changed things very much.

In all the history of this army, no general had yet been disciplined for being just a little bit late. Back of almost every defeat there was the story of chances lost because some commander had not done what he set out to do with the necessary vigor and speed. The assumption always seems to have been that the man on the firing line would somehow make up for all slackness and all delays.

In other ways, too, the generals had been brought up wrong. The tradition they had learned was that of close-order fighting in open country, where men with bayonets bravely charged a line of men firing smooth-bore muskets. That used to work well enough, because the range at which defenders could begin to kill their assailants was very short. Between the moment when charging men got into that range and the moment when they actually reached the enemy line, the defenders could fire no more than one or two shots apiece. Given a proper advantage in numbers, a charging line was bound to get to close quarters provided the men could just stand the gaff during the last hundred yards of their advance.

But the rifle came in and it changed all of that. The range at which charging men began to be killed was at least five times as great as it used to be, which meant that about five times as many of the assailants were likely to be hit. Furthermore, men on the defense had learned how to dig deep, solid trenches instead of standing up unprotected in the open; and the trench and the rifle put together meant that the old tradition was as dead as Hannibal. A few men, like young Colonel Upton, sensed that new tactics were called for, but most men could not quite get the idea. The way to beat the enemy was to pile into him head on, and if a great many men were killed that way it could not be helped because to get killed was the soldier's hard fate and it would never be any other way.[11]

The hard fact was that by 1864 good troops using rifles and standing in well-built trenches, and provided with suitable artillery support, simply could not be dislodged by any frontal assault whatever. This fact had been visible on many previous occasions, if anyone had thought about it. At Gettysburg, Slocum's brigades held solid log trenches on Culp's Hill, and in the reports their officers submitted after the battle there is evident a sort of dazed bewilderment that the men had been able to wreck a whole Rebel army corps at comparatively small cost. One Union general found 1,200 dead Southerners in front of his line, estimated that four times that many had been wounded, and noted that the trenches "rendered our casualties surprisingly incompatible with so terrible and prolonged an engagement." The same thing had been true, with the shoe on the other foot, at Spotsylvania. Meade's chief of staff assessed the fighting there and wrote that behind trenches "the strength of an army sustaining an attack was more than quadrupled"; then he revised his estimate upward and said that "there is scarcely any measure by which to gauge the increased strength" conferred by good earthworks.[12]

Yet although this lesson was obvious it was not being applied. A subtle weakness infected the system of command. Something was always going wrong, someone was forever leaving something undone, the loose ends were never quite tied up in time. The experience at Spotsylvania was the classic example. When the big attack on the salient was made no one really knew where the enemy was, how the land lay, or what the defenses were like. The man who had to lead the charge was at last forced to ask, in bitter jest, that someone at least point him in the right direction so that he might not miss the Rebel army entirely.

Taken as a group, the generals on whom the army's success depended so greatly seem to have slipped back during the campaign; or perhaps they simply stood still while the war moved on ahead of them. They were used to a war of successive broad panoramas, in which a corps commander could always find some spot from which he could get a fairly good general view of his whole line. Now there were no more panoramas and it was never possible for anyone to see more than a fraction of the field. If a general rode up front for a closer survey there was nothing for him to see but the backs of a few of his skirmishers. Trench warfare was new to everybody and it provided unheard-of complications for an army acting on the offensive. What used to be done visually had to be done nowadays with maps. (Just to make things worse, practically all of the maps owned by the Federal commanders contained very bad errors.)

In effect, the army was fighting blindfolded and most of the generals knew little more than the men in the ranks knew. A IX Corps soldier wrote that the whole campaign was confusing: "Of the previous movements we had been able to form some conception; but the operations since crossing the Pamunkey, conducted rapidly in jungles, swamps and labyrinths of forest; in storm and darkness; by marches and counter-marches, advances and withdrawals—all seemed to us to be conducted without consistent plan or purpose." The generals could have said the same thing. Indeed, Meade did say it, complaining that in this country he had to fight a regular battle just to conduct an ordinary reconnoissance.[13]

Meade's temper was getting worse than ever. At Cold Harbor on June 1 he was denouncing Warren and Wright—the one for moving without orders, the other for moving too slowly with orders—and he was complaining angrily that the corps commanders ought to act for themselves and not lean constantly on army headquarters. At this untimely moment, one of Baldy Smith's staff officers came in to report that Smith had arrived with his troops but had brought little ammunition and no transportation and considered his position precarious.

"Then why in hell," demanded Meade, "did he come at all?"[14]

The big job on the evening of June 1 was to get Hancock and his II Corps around to Cold Harbor in time for the dawn attack, and the orders breathed unusual urgency: "You must make every exertion to move promptly and reach Cold Harbor as soon as possible. . . . Every confidence is felt that your gallant corps of veterans will move with vigor and endure the necessary fatigue." An engineer officer was sent to lead the march, and just after sunset the movement began.

The II Corps had no better luck with its guide here than at Spotsylvania. Since the march would be long the engineer officer undertook to lead the corps on a short cut along an unmapped woods road, and this road was not good. There was profound darkness under the trees, and the dust rose in unbelievable clouds, and the road grew narrower and narrower until it was no more than a path and the corps artillery finally got jammed in between the trees and could go neither backward nor forward.

The long column piled up, and in the dusty darkness regiments and brigades intermingled, and the still air was very hot. Officers rode back and forth, colliding with trees and falling down invisible banks, and it was too dark for anyone to identify them or for them to see the troops they were trying to straighten out, and organization dissolved completely. Eventually, most of the troops had to countermarch by another road, and what was supposed to be a nine-mile hike turned out to be fifteen miles.[15]

The corps was to be in position to assault at daybreak, which at that time of the year meant around 4:30 in the morning, but by seven o'clock it was just beginning to come up to Cold Harbor, blue uniforms all Rebel gray with dust, stragglers strewn all over the line of march, everyone too blown to do more than put one heavy foot ahead of another. One of Meade's staff commented that a fifteen-mile march at night was more tiring than a twenty-five-mile march by daylight, and he added that these soldiers were all worn out before the march even began: "Our men no longer have the bodily strength they had a month before; indeed, why they are alive I don't see."[16] To make an immediate attack was plainly out of the question, and Meade ordered the fight postponed until four in the afternoon.

But in the afternoon things looked no better. The battered VI Corps was in place along the Richmond road, ready to go, but General Smith on the VI Corps' right was telling headquarters that what with battle losses and heavy straggling he had only 9,000 men in line of the 16,000 soldiers he had brought up from Bermuda Hundred, and if the Rebels should attack him he was not sure that he could hold his position. "An attack by me," he added, "would be simply preposterous." Beyond Smith's men, innumerable adjustments had to be made in the positions of Warren's and Burnside's corps, and they were doing a good deal of marching to and fro to get into new positions—being considerably pestered, the while, by intermittent Confederate stabs and thrusts—and it began to seem best to have those two corps act on the defensive and hold their positions while the fight was made at Cold Harbor.

At last, unable to get the unwieldy machine moving properly, headquarters ordered another postponement and fixed the hour of attack for daybreak on June 3. Darkness came, and there were bursts of rain, turning now and then into hail. All along the disordered lines the men dropped off to sleep, lying face down on the ground in the wet, glad that it was raining because it would lay the dust and cut the heat, dimly conscious that a good many thing had been going wrong.[17]

Much had gone wrong, and what mattered most was that the attack was going to be twenty-four hours late. An assault at dawn on June 2 might possibly have succeeded, since on that morning the Rebels in front of Cold Harbor had not had time to get set for it. An assault at dawn on June 3 would not have a chance in the world to succeed, and the felony was compounded by the fact that nobody in particular had thought to study the lay of the land and the position of the Confederate defenses.[18] The Union army had spent the twenty-four hours of delay chiefly in wearing itself out; the Confederates had used the time with enormous industry and clever engineering skill to build a network of trenches, gun emplacements, and skirmishers' pits like nothing the Army of the Potomac had ever encountered before.

It was no simple line of breastworks that the army was going to attack in the morning. From the Chickahominy swamps all the way to the Totopotomoy, the Confederate line on the morning of June 3 was cunningly and elaborately designed to take advantage of every ravine, knoll, and hillock, every bog and water course, every clump of trees and patch of brambles, so that unending cross fires could be laid on all possible avenues of approach. A newspaper correspondent wrote of these lines: "They are intricate, zig-zagged lines within lines, lines protecting flanks of lines, lines built to enfilade an opposing line, lines within which lies a battery . . . a maze and labyrinth of works within works and works without works, each laid out with some definite design either of defense or offense."[19]

The ground was deceptive. The Confederate works lay on an uneven chain of low hills and ridges, none of them high enough to look frightening, all of them just high enough to be ideal for defensive purposes. There was hardly a spot on the front which could not be hit by rifle fire and artillery fire from dead ahead and from both sides. The very pickets and skirmishers were dug in, and to make matters worse the Union front at Cold Harbor bowed out slightly, so that advancing units would follow diverging paths and would expose their flanks to heavy fire.[20]

Neither Grant nor Meade had ordered anybody to make a detailed survey of the ground. Apparently they assumed that the corps commanders would do that as a matter of routine. The assumption was wrong, since corps routine in the Army of the Potomac did not extend to such matters, and so nobody knew anything of any consequence about what lay ahead. All that was certain was that 40,000 men in three army corps were to begin marching toward Richmond at dawn. What they were going to run into along the way was something they would have to find out for themselves.

The rain stopped just before dawn, and as the sky grew lighter it was clear, with a promise of heat. Gunners in the Federal gun emplacements could just see and hear the infantry columns moving forward in the dim light. A moment later they saw orderlies come back, leading riderless horses, by which they knew that the regimental and brigade commanders were going in on foot. The light grew stronger, and half a mile ahead the men could see the main line of Confederate works—an uneven tracing of raw earth across the fields and through the groves, looking empty but somehow ominous. Then couriers came spurring up to battery commanders, and on the II Corps front one cannon was fired as a signal, and along three miles of gun pits the men ran to their places.

A gigantic crash of artillery broke the morning quiet just as the crackle of skirmishers' fire began. Suddenly the empty-looking Rebel trenches were dotted with black slouch hats and thousands of musket barrels, long sheets of flame ran from end to end of the trench lines, an immense cloud of smoke blotted out the sight of them, and the rocking volume of sound dazed men who had been in the war's worst battles. One of Hancock's gunners wrote, in awe: "It had the fury of the Wilderness musketry with the thunders of the Gettysburg artillery super-added. It was simply terrific."[21]

This was the army's major offensive, the culmination of a month's bloody campaigning, and it was not one fight but many fights: a conglomeration of charges by individual brigades rather than one massed assault. There was no one line of battle, wide and deep, each part supporting all the rest. Instead there were many separate assaults, all going forward at once, each one more or less isolated from the others, so that every unit felt that it was advancing unaided into the very center of the strongest enemy line it had ever seen.

Hancock had three divisions of infantry, and he sent two of them in with the third held back for support. The divisions promptly separated. Barlow took his men in with two brigades in front, and these swept across a sunken road, beating down the Southern skirmishers who held it, and charged on and broke into the main line of Confederate works, capturing several hundred prisoners and three guns and, for an incredible instant, making it look as if they were going to win an amazing success. Yet the ground just behind them was swept by a terrible cross fire from Confederates off to the right and left, and when the support troops tried to come forward they were broken and driven back, and Barlow's two leading brigades were isolated.

From both sides Rebel gunners were sending shell and solid shot plowing the length of the captured trench with murderous effect, and from the ground ahead of Barlow's men, massed infantry plastered them with an unbearable volume of musket fire. The men stayed there as long as they could, but it was not very long, and in a few minutes they ran back, crouched down behind a low swelling in the ground, and with bayonets and tin cups began frantically to dig in. They had done their best, and instead of retreating to their starting place they were val-iantly hanging on within a few rods of the Confederate line, but they had not opened the road to Richmond.

On their right, Gibbon's division had even worse luck. It set out bravely enough, the veterans knowing full well that they were going into a death trap but setting their teeth and going forward anyway. As the lines moved into range of the Confederate fire the color-bearer of the 19th Massachusetts was shot, and the regimental commander told Corporal Mike Scannell to pick up the flag and carry it. Mike promptly declined, explaining: "Too many corporals have already been killed carrying colors." The commander blinked at him, and then prom-ised: "I'll make you a sergeant on the spot." "That's business," said the corporal. "I'll carry the colors." So he picked up the flag and the regiment went on.[22]

Two hundred yards from the starting point Gibbon's division hit a deep swamp whose existence nobody had known about, and the swamp split the line in two, half of the men going to one side and half to the other. The swamp grew wider as the men advanced and the separated halves of the line could not rejoin, and in the swamp there were many snipers who took a heavy toll, and in the end two separated brigades went staggering up to the invulnerable trenches. One of these got onto the Rebel line very briefly—there is memory of a colonel standing on the parapet, swinging his sword and shouting to his men to come on. But the colonel went down, his lifeless body draped across the parapet, and he was hit thereafter by so many stray bullets that when a truce was declared a few days later he could be identified only by the buttons on his sleeve. The other men who got up to the line did not fare much better than he did, and the attack collapsed a few seconds after it had touched the breastworks. The other brigade never reached the line—partly, it was said, because it contained many new troops who went charging in with great dash and much cheering, anxious to prove themselves, and who made such excellent targets of themselves that they were destroyed before they got within fifty yards of their enemies.

Gibbon tried to bring his rear brigades up to help, but orders got mixed somehow and the men were sent in wrong, and in any case the Confederates had an artillery cross fire that made it impossible for them to advance, and one brigade retreated with no surviving officer of higher rank than captain. Inside of twenty minutes Gibbon's whole attack was a flat failure, with more than a thousand casualties. A staff officer noted with admiration that the beaten men did not run for the rear, as usually happened when an assault failed. Like Barlow's soldiers, they simply found places where the ground offered a little protection and began to scrape out foxholes for themselves, keeping up such fire as they could, while far to their rear the Federal artillery thundered and crashed in a vain effort to beat down the Confederate fire.[23]

On Wright's front the story was about the same, except that the lines of attack were repelled more quickly. The men found themselves advancing into what seemed to be a semicircle of Rebel trenches, with guns a mile away smiting their flanks with shell while the everlasting riflemen in front fired as if they all owned repeaters. The VI Corps by now was accounted the stoutest fighting corps in the army, but it could do nothing whatever. Along most of the corps front no more than ten minutes elapsed from the moment the men began their charge to the moment when those who had been hit started to burrow for shelter. Dense thickets and impassable briar patches, and little bogs which no man could cross, broke the lines into fragments, and the commands were all disconnected. "And all the time," one soldier remembered, "there was poured from the rebel lines, which we could not see, those volleys of hurtling death."[24]

If it was possible for anything to be worse than what was happening to Hancock's and Wright's men, it was what was happening to Smith's undermanned brigades. At the right and left of his line Smith had found the ground so bad that a major assault hardly seemed possible, but in the center a shallow ravine offered some protection and he put the weight of his attack there. The men ran out of the sheltering hollow in column of regiments, with the 12th New Hampshire in the front, its colonel waving a ramrod for baton in place of his sword, and like the other columns the men felt like they were charging into the center of a great flaming crescent, with guns and musketry hitting them from three sides at once.

A New Hampshire captain confessed afterward: "To give a description of this terrible charge is simply impossible, and few who were in the ranks of the 12th will ever feel like attempting it. To those exposed to the full force and fury of that dreadful storm of lead and iron that met the charging column, it seemed more like a volcanic blast than a battle, and was just about as destructive." A sergeant said that the men involuntarily bent forward as they advanced, as if they were walking into a driving hailstorm, and he related that they fell "like rows of blocks or bricks pushed over by striking against one another."

One man remembered that as he ran forward he suddenly saw all of his comrades drop to the ground, and he thought that someone had passed the order for everyone to lie down, so he did the same. His company commander came over, indignant, and began prodding the prostrate with his sword, trying to get them to rise and resume charge. He got nowhere, because they were all dead, and as another officer remarked, "nothing but the judgment trump of the Almighty would ever bring those men upon their feet again." Another man, marching forward at the right of his company, glanced to his left, saw no comrades, and assumed he had fallen a few paces behind. He hurried forward, only to find himself in another company; everybody else in his own line had been shot down.

In the dust and the smoke the men of this assaulting column never once saw their enemies, although they were charging across open ground. They saw nothing but a line of flashing fire and billowing smoke that seemed almost to close behind them as they advanced, and the musketry fire was so unbroken that it seemed "like one continual crash of thunder."

Altogether, it took the Confederates rather less than a quarter of an hour to break this attack and destroy the attacking column, and it is quite conceivable that in this particular fight the Rebels lost no men whatever. A few days later, when men met between the lines during a truce to bury the dead, a Confederate officer told one of the New Hampshire men: "It seemed almost like murder to fire upon you."[25]

And this, strangely and terribly enough, was the battle of Cold Harbor—a wild chain of doomed charges, most of which were smashed in five or ten minutes and none of which lasted more than half an hour. In all the war, no attack had ever been broken up as quickly or as easily as this, nor had men ever before been killed so rapidly. The half hour's work had cost the Union army 7,000 men.[26]

Yet if the attack was quickly over, the fighting did not end. For the most amazing thing of all in this fantastic battle is the fact that all along the front the beaten men did not pull back to the rear. They stayed where they were, anywhere from 40 to 200 yards from the Confederate line, gouged out such shallow trenches as they could, and kept on firing. Behind them the artillery continued to hammer away relentlessly, and all day long the terrible sound of battle continued. Only an experienced soldier could tell, by the sound alone, that the pitch of the combat in midafternoon was any lower than it had been in the murky dawn when the charges were being repulsed.

The fighting went on and on, only now it was carried on by men who had just taken the worst beating of the war, men who lay on their bellies in the dust, a sheet of Rebel bullets just overhead, piling little mounds of earth in front of them, rolling behind these to load, and firing as best they could. Now and then orders came up from the rear—brought by officers or couriers who crept across the open on their hands and knees—to renew the assault. When such orders came the men would fire a little faster than before, but no one would get up to charge. They were not being mutinous about it; getting up was simply impossible.

The long day wore away, and the heat and the flaming guns seared the great plain, and wounded men between the lines were hit and broken apart by the flying bullets and the exploding shell. One of Grant's staff officers rode up on a little hill and looked forward through his field glasses. An officer of a battery of field artillery posted on the hill asked him, sarcastically, if he could see Richmond. The staff man said that he could not, but that he expected to be able to do so very soon.

"Better get the barrels of that glass rifled, so they'll carry farther," said the gunner.

That night a private in the VI Corps wrote to his parents:

"If there is ever again any rejoicing in the world it will be when this war is over. One who has never been under fire has no idea of war."[27]

3. SECONDHAND CLOTHES

Life began with the darkness. All day long the men out in front huddled close to the ground, dust in their teeth, a glaring sun pressing on their shoulders. To peer over the rim of earth that lay between the firing line and the enemy was to ask for a bullet, and it was almost certain death to try to go to the rear for any reason

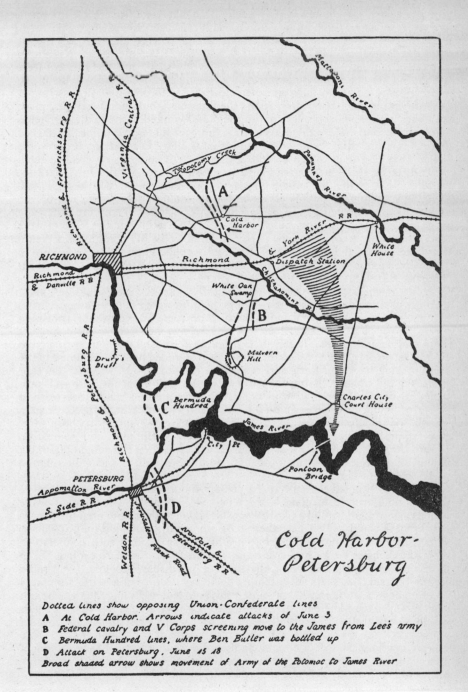

Cold Harbor-Petersburg

Dotted lines show opposing Union-Confederate lines
A At Cold Harbor. Arrows indicate attacks of June 3
B Federal cavalry and V Corps screening move to the James from Lee's army
C Bermuda Hundred lines, where Ben Butler was bottled up
D Attack on Petersburg, June 15-18
Broad shaded arrow shows movement of Army of the Potomac to James River

at all—to have a wound dressed, to get food, to fill a canteen with muddy warm water, or to attend to a call of nature. Death was everywhere, its unspeakable scent in every breath men drew, the ugly whine of it keening through the air over the flat whack of the sharpshooter's rifle. On distant elevations, obscure in the quivering haze, there were the guns, cleverly sited, and the gunners were prompt to fire at anything that moved. From one end of the army to the other, men endured heat and thirst and nameless discomforts and waited for night.

At night the front came alive. Along the lines men took the shovels and picks and axes which details brought out to them and worked to make their trenches deep and strong. Where there were trees, they cut them down, put the slashed branches out in front for an abatis, and used the logs to make the breastworks solid. They dug their trenches deep, so that a man could stand erect in them without being shot, and they cut zig-zag alleyways through the earth back toward the rear, so that they might go to and from the front without being killed.

Being very human, the soldiers on both sides often dug their trenches so deep that while they offered almost perfect protection against enemy fire they were quite useless for fighting purposes. In each army it was found that there were long stretches of trench in which a man could not possibly point his musket toward the enemy, and from both blue and gray headquarters orders went out to front-line commanders warning that there must alway be fire steps on which riflemen could stand to shoot their foes.[1]

Along much of the line trenches were so close that the men could hear their enemies chatting together. In many places the lines were not far enough apart to give the pickets proper room, and in these places there was constant skirmishing all the way around the clock. Even where there was a decent distance, the lines were seldom quiet. Half a dozen shots from the skirmish lines could bring great rolling salvos from the guns, so that at times it sounded as if an immense battle were rocking back and forth over the desolate bottomlands. Most of this cannonading did no great harm, for the men in the deep trenches were well protected against missiles fired with relatively flat trajectory, and fuses were so imperfect that even the best gunners could rarely explode a shell directly over a trench. To get around this difficulty the artillerists brought up coehorn mortars—squat little jugs of iron that rested on flat wooden bases and pointed up toward the sky, which could toss shells in a high arc so that they might fall into a distant slit in the earth. At night the fuses from these shells traced sputtering red patterns across the sky.[2]

The infantry hated the mortars, regarding them, as one veteran said, as "a contemptible scheme to make a soldier's life wretched." The weapons were usually out of sight behind a bank of earth, and when they were fired the men in the trenches could neither hear the report nor see the flash and puff of smoke. They had no warning: nothing but the hissing spark that rose deliberately, seemed to hang in the air high overhead, and then fell to earth to explode. Even more than the mortars, however, the soldiers hated sharpshooters. They had a feeling that sharpshooters never really affected the course of a battle: they were sheer malignant nuisances, taking unfair advantages and killing men who might just as well have remained alive. One artillerist wrote that the sharpshooters would "sneak around trees or lurk behind stumps" and from his shelter "murder a few men," and he burst out with the most indignant complaint of all: "There was an unwritten code of honor among the infantry that forbade the shooting of men while attending to the imperative calls of nature, and these sharpshooting brutes were constantly violating that rule. I hated sharpshooters, both Confederate and Union, and I was always glad to see them killed."[3]

So much of the killing these days seemed to be meaningless. In a great battle men died to take or defend some important point, and it could be seen that there was some reason for their deaths. But there were so many deaths that affected the outcome of the war not a particle—deaths that had nothing to do with the progress of the campaign or with the great struggle for union and freedom but that simply happened, doing no one any good. There was one day when a Federal battery took position in the yard of a farmhouse and began to duel with a Confederate battery a mile away. The firing grew hot, and the people who lived in the farmhouse huddled inside in desperate fear; and presently a poor colored servant in the house, driven beside herself with terror, sprang up in a lunatic frenzy, scooped up a shovelful of live coals from the hearth, ran to the doorway, and threw the glowing coals out in a wild swing. The coals landed in an open limber chest, which blew up with a mighty crash. Two or three gunners were killed outright, two or three more were blinded forever, the woman was quite unhurt—and there were more names for the casualty list, testifying to nothing except that war was a madman's business.[4]

Now and then higher authority considered making a new assault. One day a note from II Corps headquarters came up to General Barlow, asking if he thought that the works in his front could be carried. Barlow was one of the few general officers in the army who actively enjoyed a good fight, but this time he advised against an attack, explaining that "the men feel just at present a great horror and dread of attacking earthworks again. . . . I think the men are so wearied and worn out by the harassing labors of the past week that they are wanting in the spirit and dash necessary for successful assaults."[5]

The men had become very war-wise. They knew better than anyone else the impossibility of carrying the Rebel trenches, and as Hancock said, when they were ordered to attack "they went as far as the example of their officers could carry them"—no farther. Officers who could persuade them to do the impossible were becoming scarce. There had been more than a month of fighting, and the best company and regimental officers were getting killed off. The best officers were always going into the most dangerous places, and there had been dangerous places without number in the past month, and the law of averages was working. The famous II Corps had lost noticeably in efficiency, not merely because its best enlisted men had been shot, but also because it was no longer officered as it had been. A brigade which was commanded by a lieutenant colonel, its regiments led by captains, and its companies commanded by junior lieutenants and sergeants, just was not able to do the thing it had done before. The old leadership was gone.[6]

There were veteran outfits, of course, in which the men more or less led themselves. Yet the enlistments of many of these were about to expire, and the men were becoming very cautious. Every man in the army knew the exact date on which he would be released from service, and as that date drew near he resented being asked to run risks. Members of a Rhode Island battery complained that on their last day of service they were thrown into an exposed position and compelled to keep up an expensive artillery duel, and the battery's historian exploded in anger: "It was clear to everyone's mind that some mean, malignant villain, not worthy of wearing shoulder straps, had got the battery into this dreadful position purposely, for our term of service expired the next day, and we had long range guns, while short range guns were fired a quarter of a mile in our rear, the shells exploding over our heads instead of reaching the enemy's works."[7]

A week passed after the day of the disastrous assaults, and another week began, and as far as the men could see there was no change; perhaps they were to remain here at Cold Harbor forever, fixed in impregnable trenches that could never be captured and would never be abandoned. The trench system imposed its routine, which was not pleasant. These sandy ditches caught and held all of the sun's heat, so that the scanty supply of water in canteens became hot and distasteful, and the men tried to rig little awnings out of shelter-tent halves and cowered under them, hot and unwashed and eternally thirsty. A New Hampshire soldier predicted that trench life by itself "would soon become more dangerous to the Federal army than rebel bullets," and a Pennsylvanian remembered that what his outfit wanted most in those days was a complete issue of new clothing—what they wore had got beyond washing, and there was no water to wash it in anyway.[8]

When Cutler's division was briefly taken out of the line on June 8 for a short stay in the rear, its commander noted that this was the first day in more than a month in which no man in the division had been reported killed or wounded. One of his colonels wrote that he had had neither an unbroken night's sleep nor a change of clothing since May 5, and another remarked that he was so groggy with fatigue that it was impossible for him to write an intelligent letter to his family: "I can only tell my wife I am alive and well. I am too stupid for any use."

And General Warren, sensitive and high-strung, turned to another officer one day and burst out:

"For thirty days it has been one funeral procession past me, and it is too much!"[9]

Warren was showing the strain, and both Grant and Meade were noticing it. He had been a good friend of Meade for a long time, and Grant had been favorably impressed by him. When the army crossed the Rapidan, Grant even made a mental note that if anything should happen to Meade, Warren would be a good man to put in command of the army. But somehow he was not bearing up well. Details engrossed him, and he seemed to have a stiff pride which made it hard for him to accept direction and counsel. Worst of all, he was never quite able to get his corps moving promptly. It was felt that he was slow in bringing his men into action the first day at Spotsylvania, and when the attack was made at the Bloody Angle and Warren was supposed to hit the Confederate left there had been a three-hour delay—a costly thing, which led Grant to tell Meade to relieve Warren of his command if he delayed any longer. Meade replied that he was about to do it without orders, but Warren finally got his corps in motion just in time to save his job.[10]

As a matter of fact, corps leadership throughout the campaign had been a good deal less than distinguished. Even Hancock seemed uninspired; it may be that the wound he got at Gettysburg, which was still very far from healed, was slowing him up more than anyone realized. John Sedgwick was gone, and Wright was not yet fully tested. He was obviously brave and diligent, but there were signs that he might be stiff and slow. Burnside was no more expert than he had ever been, and his relations with Meade were delicate. His IX Corps had at last formally been made a part of the Army of the Potomac. He ranked Meade, and was touchy about taking orders from him, and Meade was not a tactful person who would try to smooth down his ruffled feathers. Smith had served with Grant at Chattanooga and had won his confidence there, but he was not fitting smoothly into the Army of the Potomac.

Looking back on the Cold Harbor assault, a staff man in the VI Corps wrote scornfully that "its management would have shamed a cadet in his first year at West Point."[11] Emory Upton went into more detail in a bitter letter to his sister:

"I am disgusted with the generalship displayed. Our men have, in many instances, been foolishly and wantonly sacrificed. Assault after assault has been ordered upon the enemy's entrenchments when they knew nothing about the strength or position of the enemy. Thousands of lives might have been spared by the exercise of a little skill; but, as it is, the courage of the poor men is expected to obviate all difficulties."

Reflecting further on the matter, he wrote a few days later:

"Some of our corps commanders are not fit to be corporals. Lazy and indolent, they will not even ride along their lines; yet, without hesitancy, they will order us to attack the enemy, no matter what their position or numbers. Twenty thousand of our killed and wounded should today be in our ranks."[12]

Grant was well aware that there were grave shortcomings in command, but they were not too easily identified by a man who was looking down from the top rather than up from underneath. To Grant's tent one day came young Brigadier General James H. Wilson, leader of one of Sheridan's cavalry divisions, earlier in the war a member of Grant's own staff and therefore a man with whom Grant might talk frankly. Wilson was one of the young, fire-eating, just-out-of-West Point officers, like Upton, who studied the older men with the eyes of impatient perfectionist youth. Also, he had served in the Western armies, where Grant had had lieutenants like Sherman and Thomas and McPherson.

In the privacy of his tent, Grant asked the young brigadier:
"Wilson, what is the matter with this army?"

Wilson replied that a good deal was the matter—so much that it would hardly do to go into detail—but he said that he could easily suggest a good remedy. One of Grant's staff officers was Colonel Ely Parker, swarthy and massive and black-haired, a full-blooded Indian of the Iroquois persuasion. Give Parker, said Wilson, a scalping knife and a tomahawk, fill him full of the worst commissary whisky available, and send him out to bring in the scalps of a number of major generals.

Grant chuckled mildly and asked which ones. That did not really matter much, said Wilson; just tell Parker to attack the first ones he came to and not to quit until he had scalped at least half a dozen. After that Grant would have a better army.[13]

The soldiers themselves were not complaining a great deal. They felt toward their officers about as private soldiers usually do, but there is little to show that Cold Harbor affected that feeling very much. Their complaints were usually like the one voiced by the Michigan private, who inquired grumpily: "Who is putting down this monster rebellion? Is it the officers?" These, he noted, had servants to wait on them, and good food in their baggage wagons, whereas "the poor wearied soldiers who do the fighting" got nothing but dry hardtack to eat and had to sleep in the mud.[14]

Clearly enough, the soldiers hated Cold Harbor and the trenches and the dust and the heat, and most of them would have agreed with the New York private who wrote: "A fellow sufferer very truly remarked that we are in a very bad state—the state of Virginia."[15] Yet there is nothing to show that they had had any especial loss in morale. What the men left in writing shows weariness and a longing to get away from the sound of gunfire for a while, but nothing more.[16] If the generals were clumsy, most of them had always been that way and there was no reason to expect them to be any different. The Army of the Potomac seems to have spent more time talking and thinking about its opposite number, the Army of Northern Virginia, than about its own high command.

Its relationship with the Confederate army was unusual, a queer blend of antagonism and understanding. At times the feeling between the two armies was downright savage. A man in Smith's corps complained bitterly that long after the June 3 attacks had ended, Confederate riflemen amused themselves by shooting at the wounded men between the lines. Sometimes, he said, they even fired at corpses. There was a wounded New Hampshire officer who lay, helpless, twenty yards in front of the Union trenches, and all day long the Confederate sharpshooters kept anyone from going out to help him. One man was killed in the attempt, and after that the Union soldiers tried throwing canteens of water and bags of hardtack out to the wounded man, but nothing effective could be done for him as long as the Rebels could see to shoot. After dark, men dug a shallow trench out to where the officer lay, and after three hours' work they managed to get him back to safety. All of the soldiers in the line set up a cheer when the officer was brought in, and the cheer promptly drew a volley from the Confederate rifle pits.[17]

That was one side of the coin. For the other side, there was the fact that the pickets constantly arranged informal truces, meeting between the lines to trade knives, tobacco, newspapers, and other small valuables, and as they traded they talked things over. One of these peaceful meetings, unhappily, broke up in a row. A Confederate asked a Yankee who was going to win the Northern presidential election, and the Yankee said that he reckoned he himself would vote for Old Abe.

"He," said the Southerner, "is a damned abolitionist."

This immediately brought on a fist fight, and officers had to come out to break it up. Still, men who felt enough at home with each other to argue about politics and fight with their fists over it were hardly, at bottom, sworn enemies estranged by hatred.

A Massachusetts soldier on the II Corps front told how his regiment made friends with a Confederate regiment opposite it and worked out a fairly extended cessation of hostilities, and he said that if the enlisted men of the two armies had the power to settle the war, "not another shot would have been fired." The friendly Confederate regiment was at length moved away from there, and just before it left a Rebel soldier stood up on the rampart and called out a warning: "Keep down, Yanks—we 'uns are going away." As soon as the replacements came in the firing was resumed. When the V Corps was shifted around to the left of the Union line, so that it faced the Confederates across the Chickahominy River, the 118th Pennsylvania and the 35th North Carolina put in the day sitting on opposite banks of the narrow stream, fishing and chatting.

A soldier in a New York heavy artillery regiment wrote that it seemed, now and then, as if an increasing number of Confederates were willing to slip over to the Union side after dark and surrender, yet he added wryly that "when it comes to fighting, one would not suppose that any of them had the faintest idea of surrendering." Between fights, he said, Northerners and Southerners talked things over, concluded that peace would be a very fine thing, and agreed that "if a few men on both sides who stayed at home were hung, matters could easily be arranged."[18]

Yet the soldiers were only a part of it, and what happened to them out along the rifle pits amid the choking dust was having a queer reverse effect on men back home who would never know what it was like to charge a line of riflemen in the smoky twilight, gun butt raised to crush a human being's skull. For this was the year when the shadow of death lay all across America, and grotesque shapes moved within the shadow and laid hold of men's hearts and minds. The soldiers at the front could look ahead to peace within seeing it through a veil of hatred, and if they talked lightly about the need to hang a few stay-at-homes, they spoke as men who had seen so many killings that a few more might not make much difference. Yet there were quiet civilians who were talking of hangings, too, these days. They were men of years and peace, who might inspire violence but who had never actually seen any of it, and the war had worked upon them until they could feel that death and heartbreak were positive goods.

Some were men who had always lived by the sword, and they were beginning to see in this war a chance to reach a monstrous goal, with an undying fire blazing across a wasteland which had once been peopled by men who disagreed with them. But others were moderates, not usually given to thoughts of vengeance and reprisal, carried away now by the fury of war.

There was Gideon Welles, for instance, Secretary of the Navy, a white-whiskered, brown-wigged man, God-fearing and humorless and gossipy, a good Connecticut editor and politician who lived austerely, fathered a large family, and worshiped at the shrine of the Union. While the worst of the Cold Harbor fighting was going on, Welles communed with himself in his diary, seeing death and suffering as abstractions, remarking sagely that no man had been prepared for the extraordinary changes the war had brought. It often came to him, he wrote, that "greater severity" might well be invoked against the South—yet the thought had to be dealt with cautiously, for "it would tend to barbarism." And in his quiet study, where the night's peace was broken by no sound worse than the clatter of horse-drawn cabs on the paving stones outside the curtained windows, Welles reflected on the business of hanging one's enemies:

"No traitor has been hung. I doubt if there will be, but an example should be made of some of the leaders, for present and future good."

To be sure, the Southern leaders could be imprisoned or exiled, once the war was safely won, but that might not answer. People would try to rescue them, and parties would form to uphold their principles, and in the end these principles might revive and grow strong again. Perhaps ideas and emotions could be destroyed forever, if the men who held them were destroyed; and the thought led Mr. Welles to set down his conclusion:

"Death is the proper penalty and atonement, and will be enduringly beneficent in its influence."

But perhaps hangings would not be possible, since there is in man a deep tendency toward softness of heart. In such case, Mr. Welles felt, the Rebel leaders could at least be stripped of their wealth and families impoverished. The effect of this (wrote the good family man) would be wholesome. Yet it did not really seem likely that any of these stern things would be done, and he concluded regretfully: "I apprehend there will be very gentle measures in closing up the rebellion."[19]

Mr. Welles might be wrong about the inevitability of gentleness. In this year when blood-red fantasies danced against the clouded moon of war, men who had never seen the grotesque indignity of violent death could talk easily about the good fruits that might grow at the foot of the gallows tree, and devout Christians could wonder if something precious might not slip too easily through the loose meshes of Christian charity. At this moment, when casualties in the Army of the Potomac had averaged 2,000 men a day for a solid month, Abraham Lincoln was waging the hardest fight of his life to uphold the dream that peace could finally be made decently and justly, without malice or a desire to have revenge.

For of all the men who controlled and directed the war, Lincoln was the one who most deeply shared the spirit that moved across the steaming trenches at Cold Harbor—fight to the limit as long as the fighting has to go on, but strike hands and be friends the moment the fighting stops. Before the war even began, in that haunted springtime when its dark shape was rising, Lincoln had tried to warn North and South that they could never travel on separate roads. Win or lose, someday they would have to get along with each other again, and whatever they did before that day came had better be done in such a way that getting along together would still be possible. The soldiers had got the point perfectly, and they expressed it very simply: Hang a few troublemakers and we'll all go home. Mysteriously, the fighting seemed to be bringing them mutual understanding, and they may almost have been closer to each other, in spirit, than they were to their own civilians back home. Yet there was nothing they could do about it. They had not made the war and they would not end it. They could only fight it.

And the men who had made the war—the sharp politicians and the devoted patriots, the men who dreamed the American dream in different ways and the other men who never dreamed any dreams at all but who had a canny eye for power and influence—most of these, by now, were prisoners of their own creation.

The hospitals in Washington were full as never before, and every day steamers came up the river with more broken bodies to be unloaded, and it was easy for those who watched this pathetic pageant to be embittered by what had happened to these men rather than inspired by what they had dreamed of. It was hard to think clearly, and the act of embracing unmitigated violence could be a substitute for thought.

There was a colonel on Grant's staff who typified the trend perfectly. He could see that Southern resistance was still very strong, although he did not seem to be able to see anything else very clearly, and he was going about the tents these days smiting an open palm with a clenched fist and growling: "Smash 'em up! Smash 'em up!"[20] As a tactical slogan this had its faults, since logically it led to nothing better than Cold Harbor assaults, but it was a perfect expression of the growing state of mind behind the fighting fronts. Smash 'em up: the war cannot be settled, it can only be won; smash 'em up—and afterward, on the pulverized fragments, we can sit down quietly and decide what we are going to do next.

If the war was to be won, it was important that it be won soon. It had been born of anger and misunderstanding and it was breeding more as it went along. It was pushing men to the point where vengeance seemed essential, driving even a man like Secretary Welles to think well of the process of dangling a political opponent by the neck, with convulsive feet kicking at the unsustaining air. The longer the war lasted, the harder it was for people to think beyond victory, the more probable that victory when it finally came would have to be total and unconditional. What Lincoln and the soldiers wanted was a dream, and 2,000 casualties a day created an atmosphere in which dreams could not live.

So a Cold Harbor stalemate was unendurable, and among the people who saw this was General Grant. He had been commissioned to break the fighting power of the Confederacy, and he still hoped that it could be done by one bold stroke rather than by a slow process of grinding and strangling and wearing out. Before he even bothered to seek a truce so that dead men might be buried and wounded men brought back within the lines—they lay there, untended, for several days, bullets flying low above them—he set things in motion for a new move. The network of trenches grew deep and strong, but even as they took on their air of grim permanence the army that crouched in them was given a new objective.

From the moment he crossed the Rapidan, Grant's ruling idea had been to go for Lee's army without a letup—to keep that dangerous body of fighting men so everlastingly busy that it could never again seize the initiative, to compel it to fight its battles when and where Grant chose rather than by Lee's selection. The chance for decisive victory lay that way, and in the past month's fighting the army had come tolerably close to it two or three times. To stay in the Cold Harbor lines would be to give up all hope of decisive victory, for if anything was clear, it was that no offensive at or near Cold Harbor could possibly succeed. General Halleck was clucking like a worried mother hen, urging that the army stay put and conduct a siege, running no risks and counting on time and general military erosion to wear the enemy down.[21] But even though Grant had given the Army of the Potomac more trench warfare in a month than it had had in all of its earlier existence, he still believed in a war of movement. He had taken Vicksburg by maneuver and he had one maneuver left, and now he would try it.

Grant had a basilisk's gaze. He could sit, whittling and smoking, looking off beyond the immediate scene, and what he was looking at was likely to come down in blood and ashes and crashing sound a little later. Right now he was looking all the way across the James River to a peaceful, sleepy Virginia city named Petersburg, which lay on the southern bank of the Appomattox River, twenty-odd miles south of Richmond, near the point where the Appomattox flows into the James.

What Grant saw when he stared off through the mists toward Petersburg was the Confederates' problem of supply. The immediate vicinity of Richmond did not begin to produce enough food and forage to support either Lee's army or the

Confederate capital. An important part of this material came down from the Shenandoah Valley, over the Virginia Central Railroad and the James River Canal. Even more important, however, was what came up from the Deep South, and most of this came by railroads which ran through Petersburg. If the Federal army could seize Petersburg, the Army of Northern Virginia and the civil government which supported it would go on starvation rations. If, at the same time, the connection with the Shenandoah Valley could be broken, Richmond could no longer be defended.

Yet it was not Richmond itself which Grant wanted. He wanted to destroy Lee's army, and to do that he had to get it out of its trenches. The one way to compel it to move was to cut off its supplies. So he made his plans: seize Petersburg, block the line to the Shenandoah, and let hunger drive Lee's army out into the open. Once that happened there could be a finish fight, under conditions in which the Federal army's advantage in numbers ought to be decisive.

Within forty-eight hours of the failure of the June 3 assaults Grant was writing his orders, and by June 7 Sheridan had two of his cavalry divisions on the road, heading west for Charlottesville. At Charlottesville Sheridan was to meet an army under Major General David Hunter, who had replaced Sigel after that general's inglorious defeat at Newmarket. Hunter had the troops that had been Sigel's, another division which General George Crook had led east from West Virginia, and a good body of cavalry under Averell. With these men he had marched up the Valley to Staunton, crushing a small Confederate force which tried to delay him, and at Staunton he was turning east, burning and destroying as he came. Grant's idea was that Hunter and Sheridan would join forces and come down toward Richmond together, taking the Virginia Central Railroad apart as they came and rejoining the Army of the Potomac somewhere below the James River.[22]

Meade's engineers were building an inner line behind the front at Cold Harbor, and the army as a whole was shifting slowly to its left, with Warren's corps lining up along the Chickahominy. A fleet of transports had come up the Pamunkey to the base at White House, and warships, transports, barges, and a great number of pontoons were being assembled at Fortress Monroe, ready to go up the James on order. The arrangements were intricate but they were well directed, and finally, late in the afternoon of June 12, Grant and Meade struck their headquarters tents and rode down the north bank of the Chickahominy, past Despatch Station, to make a new camp beside a cluster of catalpa trees in a farmhouse yard. As night came on, the hot air was filled with dust as 100,000 soldiers began moving out of the positions which they had occupied for the better part of a fortnight.

It was risky business. This was no mere repetition of the sidestep which had been done so many times on the march down from the Rapidan. This time the whole army was marching directly away from its foes, gambling that it could disappear completely even though the two armies were in intimate contact along a five-mile front, their lines nowhere more than a few hundred yards apart. Once it got clean away—if it did—the Federal army had to make a fifty-mile hike and cross a tidal river which was half a mile wide and fifteen fathoms deep: a river which, unlike all of the little streams which had been crossed earlier, bore on its surface a number of formidable ironclad Confederate gunboats. There were Yankee gunboats, to be sure, to keep these in check, but if even one Southern warship managed to slip past these defenders, it could turn the projected river crossing into disaster.

Much worse than the danger of the gunboats, however, was the chance that Lee would find out what was going on and would move out to interfere. If he should catch the Army of the Potomac in the act of turning its back on him and marching down to the James River, what he and his soldiers might do to it would hardly bear thinking about. Two years ago he had detected McClellan making the same move on the same ground, and only the utter greenness of his staff and command arrangements had kept him from destroying McClellan's army. The greenness had long since been corrected.

Yet in making this move Grant was not simply gambling that Lee could be hoodwinked. Lee or any other general could be fooled briefly, in this country of obscure roads and concealing swamps and woods, but it was not likely that he could be fooled for very long. What Grant was really banking on was the belief that the terrible pounding of the last six weeks had taken something out of the Army of Northern Virginia—that it was no longer the quick, instantly responsive instrument that had made such deadly thrusts in the past, and that it would not lash out today as it had done in 1862, when it discovered its opponent in the act of making a flank march across its front. Those tawny gray legions were still unconquerable behind trenches, but they had lost the incomparable offensive power of the old days: that, in essence, seems to have been the bet Grant was really making.[23]

The different Federal moves were intricate, this night of June 12, but the timing was good. Hancock and Wright took their men back to the inner trench line as insurance against accidents. Smith led his XVIII Corps back to White House, where the transports were waiting. Burnside followed, turning off a few miles short of White House to follow a road down to the James. Wilson's cavalry, left behind by Sheridan, moved down to a Chickahominy crossing at Long Bridge—the bridge had long since been destroyed and the name merely designated a place—and went splashing across the river in the midnight dark, laying a pontoon bridge immediately afterward. Warren's V Corps promptly crossed on this bridge and marched boldly in the direction of Richmond along the fringe of historic White Oak Swamp.

By dawn of June 13 there was nobody left at Cold Harbor. Even the inner line was empty, for it needed to be held only long enough to protect the withdrawal of the rest of the army, and by daylight the VI Corps was following Burnside's men and Hancock was taking his corps down over the Long Bridge crossing. When Confederate skirmishers crept forward across the strangely silent rifle pits they found nothing but empty trenches and the indescribable unseemly refuse left behind by a departing army. Since the Yankees did seem to be moving toward Richmond below White Oak Swamp, Lee pulled his own army out of its lines and moved down to cover the capital, occupying roughly the ground that had been fought over so hard during the McClellan retreat in 1862, from Glendale to Malvern Hill. Meanwhile, Warren withdrew his own corps—he had moved forward simply to protect the rest of the army during the early stages of the march—and headed for a spot known as Charles City Courthouse, close to the James. Wilson's cavalry remained behind, holding all of the road crossings and driving back the inquisitive Rebel patrols. A curtain was drawn between the two armies, and for the first time in a month and a half Federal and Confederate infantry were out of contact.

Thoroughly delighted to get away from Cold Harbor, the men of the Army of the Potomac were also deeply surprised. For once, no camp rumor had warned of the move, and up to the last the men had been busy elaborating their trench system as if they were to stay there all year. Things had changed, one veteran mused, "and it was not now the custom to inform the rank and file, and the newspapers and the enemy, of intended movements." Another man was reminded by this march down to the river of the similar march two years earlier, under McClellan, and it seemed to him that everything was much better now than it had been then. Cold Harbor had been terrible, and what led up to it had not been much better, but morale was good and the men proved it by their looks and actions. On the earlier march they felt that they had been beaten, and were depressed; now they felt that they were on the way to victory, and they stepped out with a springy step.[24]

Late in the afternoon of June 13 the advance guard reached the James River, coming down to it past an impressive plantation once owned by the late President Tyler the "Tyler too" of the rowdy campaign song. The river was broad and it glinted in the afternoon sun, and it was the first really pleasant-looking body of water anybody had seen since the campaign began. Yankee warships were anchored in the stream, white awnings spread against the heat, small boats coming ashore with rhythmical dip and swing of dripping oars.

An officer on Meade's staff found himself blinking and gaping at these Navy people as they came ashore. There seemed to be something wrong about them, and at last he realized what it was. They were all clean, their persons washed, their uniforms whole, unfaded, and unsullied. The officer discovered that he had got to the point where he was suspicious of anyone who was not dirty and in rags. He was used to soldiers, and where soldiers were concerned, "the more they serve, the less they look like soldiers and the more they resemble day-laborers who had bought second-hand military clothes."[25]

Only the leading echelons of the army reached the river that evening. They included a swarm of engineers who immediately went to work to lay a pontoon bridge over to the southern shore. The army had never built such a prodigious bridge before. It would be nearly half a mile long and it would require more than a hundred pontoons, and three schooners had to be anchored in the deep water out in midstream to support the central section of the bridge. The sappers got to work without delay, tugboats and barges bringing men and material to each shore, and along the bank where the advance guard was camped there was a great chopping and shoveling, because a grove of huge old cypress trees had to be cut down and it was necessary to build a causeway across a swamp to provide an approach to the bridge. Other details went to work to put a half-ruined wharf in proper shape, a little upstream from the place where the bridge was being built, and the transports were anchored just offshore to take men aboard as soon as the wharf was repaired. As many of the soldiers as could get down to the water went in swimming, whooping and splashing as they began soaking off the sweat and grime of weeks of fighting.

A mile or so from the water, Gibbon's division was camped on the plantation of Tyler-too. The enemy was many miles away, and the officers announced that the camp need not be fortified. Nevertheless, as soon as the men had stacked their muskets they began to dig a long trench all across the western edge of the plantation, and before they went to bed they had the place in shape to resist a regular assault. Meade's assistant adjutant general looked on their handiwork and concluded that the enlisted man was convinced that a rifle pit was "a good thing to have in a family where there are small children."[26]

4. LIE DOWN, YOU DAMN FOOLS

Major General William Farrar Smith was a professional soldier who had nearly all of the qualities needed for success except a sense of the value of time and the ability to get along with his superior officers—to whom, as an admirer confessed, he was at times "a perfect Ishmaelite." His subordinates liked him immensely. He was kindly and courteous without condescension, he "looked after his men," in the army phrase, and his headquarters tents were a fabulous place to visit. Champagne was commonly served at dinner—it was so even at Cold Harbor, where Meade dropped in for lunch the day after the big assault and found things so pleasant he remained until dusk—and an overnight guest could expect to be awakened in the morning by a servant bearing a champagne cocktail. Yet with all of this, and the innumerable card games that were played, neither Smith nor his staff ever acquired the rake-hell reputation that clung about such a general as Joe Hooker.

Smith had been "Baldy" ever since his days as a West Point cadet, partly because of a thinned spot on his crown, but mostly, as a friend explained, because there were so many Smiths in the army that each one had to have an identifying nickname. Even men who did not like him—and, in the end, this included nearly all of the generals under whom he had served—admitted that he was brilliant. He ranked fourth in his class at the Academy on his graduation in 1845, he had gone into the engineers, and he had served for a number of years on the West Point faculty. On a tour of duty in Florida in the 1850s he had contracted malaria, from which he still suffered at times, and when the fever took him he was gloomy and morose. He had a sharp tongue and he never bothered to control it when he observed shortcomings in a superior officer, and this had done him much harm.[1]

In this war he had been up, and then down, and finally up again. He had organized and been first colonel of the 3rd Vermont Infantry, serving at the first battle of Bull Run and winning appointment as brigadier general and command of a division shortly thereafter. He fought well under McClellan on the peninsula, won promotion to major general and command of the IX Corps, which he led at Fredericksburg, and then he fell into trouble by giving vent to pointed public criticism of General Burnside.

Practically everybody was criticizing Burnside just then, but Burnside was backed by the powerful Committee on the Conduct of the War, which was suspicious of Smith anyway because he had been a close friend of McClellan. The upshot was that Smith lost both his corps command and his promotion, with the Senate refusing to confirm his nomination as major general, and for a time he dropped into obscurity. He showed up in Chattanooga in the fall of 1863 as chief engineer for the Army of the Cumberland, and in the dark days following Chickamauga he did a first-rate job of organizing and running the famous "cracker line" which saved the beaten army from starvation. (He had an extended row about this, later, with General Rosecrans, his commanding officer at the time, with both men claiming credit for the job.) When Grant moved in and put Thomas in Rosecrans's place he was highly impressed with Smith's capacities, and when Grant took command of all the armies he ordered Smith east and gave him an army corps under Ben Butler.

This brought Smith new troubles. It would have brought them to anybody, because serving under Butler was hard, but Smith was probably the last man in the army to adjust himself quietly to that officer's ruinous eccentricities. (To Grant, about this time, Smith burst out furiously, asking how he could retain in army command a man who "is as helpless as a child on the field of battle and as visionary as an opium eater in council.")[2] Since Butler was even more disputatious than Smith, and in addition possessed immense political influence, Smith's difficulties had been increasing by geometrical progression.

Probably no campaign in all the war was as badly mishandled as that of the Army of the James in the spring of 1864. While Grant was coming down through the Wilderness and Spotsylvania, Butler was taking his army up the James to menace Richmond from the south. He could have walked in and occupied Petersburg then almost without opposition, but apparently the idea did not appeal to him. Instead he wandered around the country, started for Petersburg and then turned back, lunged ineffectively toward Richmond, and wound up by letting a much smaller Confederate army lock him up in the formless peninsula of Bermuda Hundred—James River on the north and east, Appomattox on the south, and stout Rebel entrenchments running completely across the neck.[3]

When Smith was ordered to take his army corps away from there and help the Army of the Potomac at Cold Harbor, he went gladly, figuring that the fewer troops Butler commanded, the less harm was likely to result. But he found his reception in the clique-ridden Army of the Potomac lacking in warmth, and he was bitterly critical of the way Meade was running things, and when he brought his troops back to Bermuda Hundred he was not in a happy frame of mind.[4]

At Bermuda Hundred, however, new orders awaited him. Grant made a quick trip to see Butler, to outline the new campaign plans in person, and when Smith got his men off the transports he was told to take them over to the south side of the Appomattox and march on Petersburg without delay. Petersburg, he was informed, was held by a skeleton force and if he moved fast he could seize it, and the Army of the Potomac would follow to provide all necessary reinforcements. Smith's corps was badly thinned down—it had had heavy losses at Cold Harbor, there had been a great deal of straggling, and one division was to be left at Bermuda Hundred—and to bring him up to strength he was allotted a slim division of colored troops commanded by Brigadier General Edward W. Hinks.

These colored soldiers had been occupying City Point, a little steamboat landing on a low promontory on the south bank of the Appomattox at the point where that river flowed into the James. They had not yet been in any serious action, and most of the generals took it for granted that colored men would not make good soldiers, but Grant was in a hurry and there was no time to wait. So early on the morning of June 15 Smith's men crossed the Appomattox on a pontoon bridge a mile or two above City Point, picked up Hinks's soldiers, and set out for Petersburg. Altogether there were perhaps 10,000 men in the united column.

By an air line Petersburg was eight miles to the west. The ground was broken, with a series of north-and-south ridges coming down to the Appomattox, and the city might not be too easy to capture. If the Confederates could not spare many men for its defense, they had had plenty of time and abundant slave labor to fortify it, and a great semicircle of elaborate defenses ran all around it, starting in low ground by the Appomattox two miles east of town, cutting south in a great horseshoe curve, and coming up to the river again on the west. A few determined men could make these defenses very formidable, and after their experience at Cold Harbor Smith and his men were likely to be cautious when they saw Rebel trenches. Nevertheless, as the corps marched westward, raising an enormous cloud of dust and brushing Southern skirmishers out of the way, Smith was approaching one of the brightest opportunities an ambitious general could ask.

For the matter of that so was the Army of the Potomac, which was getting over to the south bank of the James as fast as it could, by pontoon bridge and by steamboat, in order to follow in his footsteps.

Never had the army been in a better strategic position than it was getting into on this fifteenth of June. Behind it were six weeks of the worst campaigning anybody had ever imagined, but all that had been endured might be justified by what lay just ahead. The army now was squarely in the rear of its opponent, the Army of Northern Virginia, which was still holding its trenches around Malvern Hill and Glendale, prepared to defend itself against an attack that was not going to take place. Grant had taken the army entirely out of Lee's reach, and in a few hours he would be able to strike where his enemy could not make an effective defense. Conclusive victory lay just ahead.

During the next few hours everything was going to be up to Baldy Smith and his 10,000. Smith took the men toward Petersburg, with his own divisions on the right and the colored troops on the left, and as the morning wore on the Rebel resistance grew stiffer, until at last Hinks had to move his men out into line of battle and storm a little hill where infantry and a couple of guns offered more than skirmish-line opposition. The colored boys went up the hill with a rush, driving away the defenders and capturing one of the guns, but the fight caused a delay and it was nearly noon when Smith's column came up against the main line of Confederate works.

These looked dangerous. The City Point Railroad ran half a mile or more

south of the river, and between the railroad and the river the ground was low
and the Rebel trench line slanted back toward the northwest, the ground in its
front covered by guns mounted on bluffs on the far side of the river. Just south
of the railroad the ground rose, and a long, uneven crest ran south of several
miles, and this high ground was covered with fortifications that appeared to be
stronger than anything that had been seen at Cold Harbor.

At intervals there were redoubts—square forts, solidly built, with embrasures
for artillery. The redoubts were connected by ponderous raised breastworks,
twenty feet thick at the base and six feet high. In front of the breastworks there
was a ditch, fifteen feet wide by six or eight feet deep, and a few yards in front of
the ditch there was an interminable slashing of felled trees anchored in place
with branches all interlaced. From end to end of the line the ground in front of
the slashing was open for half a mile so that it could be swept by fire from the
forest and trenches. Close to the slashing there were deep rifle pits for the skirmishers.[5]

All in all, it was no place to approach lightly. It seemed to Smith that the position was even stronger than the mountaintop line the Confederates had held at
Chattanooga. That line, to be sure, had finally been stormed, but no one quite
understood even yet how it had been done and one man who watched it wrote
that the victory looked like "a visible interposition of God." Smith had to form
his battle lines in deep woods and that took time, and it was two o'clock or later
before he had everything ready.

Even when the lines were formed Smith was not disposed to be hasty. It was
clear to him that if these Rebel trenches were held in strength, no attack could
possibly succeed. Potentially, the place was a worse deathtrap than Cold Harbor, and Smith was not going to order an attack until he had studied things very
carefully. He went out in front personally to do his looking, exposing himself to
dangerous sniper fire, and he spent two full hours making his survey, going from
end to end of the lines and studying the situation with the canny eye of a skilled
engineer.[6]

Now these Confederate works were just as strong as they looked, but they had
one glaring weakness: they contained hardly any soldiers.

Confederate commander here was the famous General Pierre Gustave Toutant Beauregard, a vain and theatrical personality, but at the same time a very
good soldier. He was responsible for the defense of everything south of the
James River, and after he had bottled Butler's army up at Bermuda Hundred he
had to send some of his best troops across the river to help Lee, and on this day
of June 15 he had no more than 7,000 soldiers in his command. Most of these
were in the Bermuda Hundred lines, which was where most of the pressure had
been so far, and in front of Petersburg there were barely 2,200 men, including
home guards and cavalry. With several miles of trench to occupy, these were
spread very thin, one infantryman to every four or five yards of trench. They
could kill a certain number of Yankees but they could not possibly beat off a
really determined attack, and no one knew it any better than Beauregard did.
He had been calling for help, and a division of the troops that had been sent to
Lee was on its way back to him, but it could not reach him until midnight or
later and until then he was strictly on his own.[7]

As he studied the lines Smith began to discover that there was a scarcity of
defenders, and he concluded that Rebel strength just now consisted mostly of
artillery. He would not assault with massed troops, which could be ripped apart
by the guns; instead he would use a succession of skirmish lines, against which
the guns would not be effective. If the trenches were held as lightly as he was
beginning to believe, the skirmish lines could carry them, and if he was wrong
and there were lots of Rebels in the trenches, then no attack would have a
chance anyway;[8] and by four o'clock, or such a matter, Smith finished his reconnoissance and ordered an attack.

Now came the first little hitch. Staff work had slipped, somewhere, and no one had warned the chief of artillery that a fight was imminent, so that officer had sent all of the artillery horses off to water. It seemed important to give the attacking troops plenty of artillery protection, and the guns could not be put into position until the horses got back. So there was a wait, and the afternoon died and evening came, and it was nearly sunset when everything was ready[9]—and north of the Appomattox, Confederate officers were driving lean columns down the roads, hurrying to get into the Petersburg lines before the war was lost beyond salvage.

Other troops were on the road, too—Union troops, two divisions of Hancock's II Corps, who had crossed the James during the night and now were struggling along to come up and give Smith's men a hand. Late in the afternoon, while he was waiting for the gunners to get their horses, Smith was told of their approach, and the news seems to have taken the edge off his eagerness. With strong reinforcements at hand, the delay in mounting the attack probably would not matter so much.

The artillery was moved forward at last and it began to smite the Confederate works, and around seven o'clock the Union lines rolled forward. The Confederates put up a good defense but their job was impossible. The Federal attackers simply swamped them, Hinks's colored troops going forward as stoutly as the rest, and by nine o'clock or a little earlier most of the formidable line was in Union hands, with sixteen guns and several hundred prisoners. The colored troops were exultant and they capered about their captured cannon with whoops of pride, and General Hinks was equally optimistic. Smith came riding over, and Hinks proposed that the entire command move boldly forward and march into Petersburg without further ado.

Night had come, but the moon was out and its clear thin light lay across the ridges and valleys and the empty roads to the little city. There were no more forts to storm, and the Confederates who had retreated were not even bothering to maintain a rear-guard fire. Hinks thought that the Federals could walk into Petersburg just about as they chose.

So did Beauregard. He wrote later that at that moment "Petersburg was clearly at the mercy of the Federal commander, who had all but captured it." But Smith did not think so. He told Hinks that Beauregard was going to be reinforced (which was true enough) and said that by the time the Federals could reach the town the defenders there would outnumber them (which was not true at all). He added that if they were not careful they would lose all that they had gained. It would be best to hold on where they were and wait for Hancock's men, and very likely something decisive could be done tomorrow. Smith sent Ben Butler a wire saying, "Unless I misapprehend the topography, I hold the key to Petersburg." Meanwhile, he ordered Hinks to make no advance."[10]

Hancock's men were just coming on the scene—two divisions, Birney's and Gibbon's, dusty and half-exhausted, but full of enthusiasm. They had had a very hard march, but they would have been on hand a great deal earlier except for a few little mistakes that had been committed here and there along the way. Altogether, these mistakes added up to nothing much except faulty staff work, and they would not be worth mentioning except that they helped to prolong the war by eight months.

The first mistake lay in the fact that somehow no one had told either Meade or Hancock that there was going to be a fight at Petersburg that day. Hancock's orders simply were to march to City Point, to wait long enough there to issue rations to his men, and then to march toward Petersburg and put his men in position at a spot where the City Point Railroad crossed something called Harrison's Creek. He was given a map showing all of the roads to Petersburg, and on this map his objective point was clearly marked. It was stated that the Federals already had field works there.

Hancock undertook to obey orders, but there were problems. The first was that there were no rations for him at City Point, and after waiting several hours he got impatient and had the column move on without them. The next trouble was that the map that had been given him turned out to be totally in error. Roads and streams did not run how or where the map said they did, and the troops were let in for a great deal of countermarching and backtracking. As the day wore on Hancock began to suspect that the spot he was going to did not exist; either the inhabitants of the region had never heard of any Harrison's Creek or they were refusing to share their knowledge with Yankees. (It turned out later that the designated place was well within the Rebel lines.) With all of this, the II Corps had a long day on the roads, and along toward 5:30 P.M. a message arrived from U. S. Grant telling Hancock to hurry because Smith had carried the outer works of the Petersburg defense system and needed help at once. A few minutes later Hancock got a similar note from Smith.

Thus, for the first time, Hancock knew that he was supposed to be marching up to take part in a fight. If he had known this at dawn he could have had his men up beside Smith's by midafternoon, bad maps or no: instead, as he wrote in his report, "I spent the best hours of the day ... in marching by an incorrect map in search of a designated position which, as described, was not in existence." As a result his men began to come up beside Smith's men after all of the fighting had stopped. Smith had made his decision, and when Hancock asked him, as the man on the spot, what was going to happen next, Smith simply suggested that Hancock have his men relieve Hinks's boys in the captured trenches. Tomorrow would be time enough to renew the attack.[11]

The II Corps of the Army of the Potomac was a battle-wise outfit, and during the last six weeks it had been hammered so hard that most of the spring had gone out of it. Nevertheless, it is recorded that for once in their lives the men in this corps made furious and profane objections when they were told that they would not immediately be rushed into battle.

During their march that day an electric sense of coming victory had gone through the ranks. The men had a fairly clear idea of what was going on, and they understood that at last a flank march had been fully successful. They had got ahead of their opponents, they were going to get to Petersburg before Lee's army could get there, and they were strategists enough to know what that was going to mean.[12] So they tramped along perkily, while the sun went down and the twilight faded into ghostly moonlight, and up ahead they heard firing. They came up through the backwash of Smith's battle, at last, and they passed some of Hinks's colored soldiers, gaily hauling brass cannon to the rear with long ropes, fifty men on a cannon, everybody shouting and laughing. The II Corps looked at this with interest and called out the obvious question: Where do you get those guns? Proudly the colored soldiers replied that they had just captured them from the Rebels.

The deduction which Hancock's veterans drew from this was not complimentary to Hinks's division, but it sent II Corps morale sky-high. If these colored troops had captured guns in prepared earthworks, Hancock's men figured, that could only mean that Lee's veterans had not yet reached Petersburg. The Army of the Potomac was winning the race! Up and down the moving column the men shifted their blanket rolls, moved cartridge boxes around to where they could get at them more easily, and remarked to no one in particular: "Put us into it, Hancock, my boy, and we'll end this damned rebellion tonight!"

But instead of going into line of battle and making an advance, they filed into the captured works, watched Smith's troops retire, ate their supper and boiled their coffee, and put out sentinels for the night. Slowly the men came to understand that there would be no fight that night, and one of them wrote afterward: "The rage of the enlisted men was devilish. The most bloodcurdling blasphemy

I ever listened to I heard that night, uttered by men who knew they were to be sacrificed on the morrow. The whole corps was furiously excited."[13]

So the II Corps went grumpily to sleep, and Smith's men went to sleep, and Beauregard's men stayed awake and worked hard. On a north-south ridge between the city and the works they had just lost, the Confederates were hard at it building new trenches and gun pits. During the night Hoke's division, which had been on loan north of the James, began to come in, and as the men were rushed out to the new defense line Beauregard took the last desperate step that was available: he ordered abandonment of the lines which held Butler's army immured at Bermuda Hundred, left a thin line of pickets there to watch the situation, and brought the men down to Petersburg. As a result of all of this, by morning he had 10,000 men or more in position to defend the town.[14] The odds against him were still long, but they were nothing like what they had been the day before, and it was just possible now that Beauregard could hold on until Lee's army could come down below the river and help.

Meade was busy, too. During the evening of June 15 he got word from Grant that Smith was fighting hard and that the rest of the army must come up as soon as possible, and so Burnside and his IX Corps crossed the river with orders to move up and take position on the left of Hancock's corps. The V Corps was to follow Burnside, artillery and trains and cavalry were to follow that, and Wright's VI Corps would hold the north bank of the James until everyone else was south of the river. Then the VI Corps would come up, the pontoon bridge would be removed, and everything would be south of the James with City Point as the new supply base.

Meade himself crossed the river on the morning of June 16, and as he rode up from City Point toward Petersburg, along toward noon, he met Grant, just returning from an inspection of the front. Grant was full of enthusiasm, and he told Meade: "Smith has taken a line of works stronger than anything we have seen this campaign. If it is a possible thing I want an assault made at six o'clock this evening."[15]

So ordered. Late in the day Hancock's and Burnside's troops were in line, the guns were in position in the captured works, and a great thunder of gunfire rolled out as the artillerists began to hammer the new Rebel trenches, which lay on the far side of a shallow valley. The sun was going down and the air was full of dust and smoke, and as Meade and his staff rode out to watch the fight there was a strange, coppery tinge in the atmosphere and on the landscape. Things looked posed and unreal, and one of Meade's party saw the gunners silhouetted against the unearthly light as they sponged out the guns and rammed the charges home and mused that they might have been lifted out of the old mezzotint engravings of Napoleon's battles which he used to see on the parlor wall of his parents' home.[16]

The Confederates had made good use of their time and the new line of works was strong. Hancock and Burnside sent their troops forward and there was bitter, inconclusive fighting. Gains were made, and the II Corps got in close around a commanding hill which anchored the left center of the Rebel line, but the Rebels lashed out with sharp counterattacks which made Meade think that Beauregard had a lot of troops in reserve, and in the end it was clear that the work could not be finished that day. The firing died out with a few spiteful rifle shots from the skirmish lines, and the hot guns on the ridge cooled as the sun went down, and Meade sent an officer back to City Point to give Grant a report.

This officer entered the general's tent and found Grant sitting on the edge of his cot, mostly undressed, just ready to go to sleep. He made his report, and Grant knew that Lee had only that afternoon begun to pull his troops out of the works north of the James to march for Petersburg; and he smiled a little and permitted himself a rare moment of self-congratulation, remarking: "I think it is pretty well, to get across a great river and come up here and attack Lee in the rear before he is ready for us." Then Grant went to bed and the staff officer returned to Meade, and everybody made ready for the next day.[17]

Next day ought to do it. Most of the army was up, by now—all of the II and V Corps, two divisions of Smith's corps and one of Wright's and three of Burnside's—in all, more than 80,000 fighting men. The men were very tired, for they had not yet had a chance to recover from six weeks' unbroken fighting and marching, and both Meade and Hancock noted that attacks now were not driven home as they used to be.[18] But morale was high, for the men sniffed victory in the air, and as June 17 dawned opportunity was bright.

Beauregard's trenches were strong, but the line was uneven. It ran south from the Appomattox for four miles, or thereabouts, and it had two principal strong points—the Hare house hill, around which Hancock's men had gained a foothold the night before, and a similar hill a mile or two south and a little east of there, crowned by the house of a man named Shand. This latter hill lay in front of Burnside, and it seemed likely that it could be flanked, and Meade considered that a hard joint attack by Hancock and Burnside ought to knock out both of these strong points and break the line wide open.

Farther south the prospects were even better. The Confederates months ago had built trenches completely encircling Petersburg, but they did not begin to have men enough to occupy all of them. Because the whole Yankee army was massed east of town, Beauregard had massed all of his troops there to meet the threat. On the south he was wide open. There was a country turnpike that dropped south from Petersburg, bearing the pleasing name of the Jerusalem Plank Road, and it and the country west of it held no Rebel troops at all, except for a thin cordon of cavalry pickets. Beauregard was painfully aware that he was defenseless in that quarter, and he wrote later that if Meade had put so much as one army corps over on the Jerusalem Road and told it to march due north, "I would have been compelled to evacuate Petersburg without much resistance."[19]

The army corps which might have made such a march was readily available—Warren's V Corps, which held the extreme left of Meade's line. It was the freshest outfit in the army, for it had not been involved in the hard fighting at Cold Harbor and had not, in fact, been heavily engaged since Spotsylvania. On June 16 Grant had wired Meade to get Warren over to the Jerusalem Road as fast as possible, and in a general way this was supposed to be Warren's objective on June 17. But Warren found Rebel skirmishers in his front and they were busy and seemed to be very bold and cocky, and Warren was cautious about pressing them too hard—and, in the end, nothing in particular was done and the empty country west of the Jerusalem Plank Road remained empty all day long.

On Warren's right there was hard fighting. Burnside dutifully moved up to attack the Shand house hill, where his men fought manfully but without intelligent direction. There was a ravine in front of the hill, and on the Yankee side the ground was full of gullies and patches of thick wood, which made it hard to form and move a line of battle. During the night Burnside's leading division, Potter's, struggled across this uneven ground. The going was hard, and the men had just made an all-night march after being under arms for thirty-six hours, and whenever a brigade or regiment was temporarily halted the men would drop where they were and go to sleep. When it was time to move on again they could be aroused only with much difficulty.

Line was formed close to the Confederate position. Orders were passed in a whisper, and the men were required to put their canteens in their haversacks so that they would not rattle. Just at dawn, with bayonets fixed, the division swept over the crest, plunged down into the ravine, and made for the Rebel position.[20]

The position was strong, but there were few Rebels in it, and Potter's tired men seized the hill, dug some rifle pits, and looked around for the support that had been promised. On their right a division of the II Corps had been told to make a simultaneous attack, but orders had gone sour somewhere and the attack was not being made. (One trouble probably was that Hancock had finally been disabled by his old Gettysburg wound and had had to turn the corps over to the senior division commander, General Birney; in any case, liaison had broken down and the support was not there.)

In the rear things were no better. Another of Burnside's divisions, Ledlie's, had been supposed to follow on Potter's heels, but through some incredible breakdown in staff work nobody had told Ledlie about it and he and his men were sound asleep when the attack was launched. For the time being Potter's men could do nothing but dig in and wait.

Birney finally got his attack moving and it was successful, swamping the Confederate defenses on the Hare house hill, from which position the II Corps might have made a sweep toward the south, taking in flank what was left of the Confederate line. But control of the fight seems to have slipped out of Meade's hands, and no unit commander up front was concerned with anything except what lay immediately before him, and although the Confederate line had been broken in two places before noon nothing effective was done to exploit the openings.

Several hours passed. Burnside finally got a second division forward and it charged through Potter's troops and attacked the new line with Beauregard had patched up there. The men had to cross a railroad cut and climb a steep slope and there was a Confederate battery placed so that it could fire down the length of the railroad cut, and the new division was broken up and forced to retreat with nothing accomplished. Toward dusk, Burnside brought up Ledlie's division, and it went slamming down into the railroad cut and up the far side in the face of a furious fire. There were confused attacks and counterattacks all up and down the slope, and men used bayonets and clubbed muskets in desperate fights for gun pits. The 39th Massachusetts won an advanced position, losing three color-bearers, and at last was forced back, leaving its colors on the ground. Its colonel asked for volunteers to go out and get the flags. A corporal and a private responded and ran out to get them, and suddenly—and quite unexpectedly—the Confederates stopped firing, allowed the men to pick up the flags, and as they went back to the regiment the Rebels waved their hats and raised a cheer. Night came, and Ledlie's men got to the crest of the slope, seized the Confederate works there, and then had to stop because they had run out of ammunition.

So once more the Confederate line had been broken, and Beauregard wrote afterward that it then seemed to him that "the last hour of the Confederacy had arrived." But the Union command system just was not functioning this day, and the story at twilight was a repetition of the story at dawn: it had occurred to no one to have troops ready to follow up a success, and there had not even been any routine arrangements for getting ammunition up to the firing line, and the strategy which had enabled the army to fight for Petersburg with eight-to-one odds in its favor was totally wasted. The day ended and the fighting ended, and in the darkness Beauregard retired his entire line to a final position within easy gunshot of the town.[21]

There was still a chance. Lee was getting his Army of Northern Virginia down to Petersburg with driving speed—lean men in faded uniforms or no uniforms hurrying on through the night, desperately in earnest and handled by a soldier who knew precisely what he was doing and how to do it—but he had not got there yet and he would not be able to get there until several hours after daylight on June 18. A dim awareness of this fact seems to have been astir in the headquarters tents of the Army of the Potomac, and during the night Meade issued orders for an attack all along the line at the moment of dawn.[22]

When light came on June 18 it brought only more confusion. The Federals now were posted on a long ridge, with the Hare and Shand house hills in their possession, and Beauregard's last line was on an opposite ridge, and the different Federal commanders seem to have felt that they ought to explore this new position with some care before they attacked. Up near the river Baldy Smith's troops seized a Confederate skirmish line, took a number of prisoners, and then halted. Birney found himself unable to get his men moving until nearly noon, when he attacked with one division and was quickly repulsed. Burnside managed to edge some men forward and consolidated the position he had won the evening before on the far side of the railroad cut, but he waited for Warren to go into action on his left and this wait turned out to be rather long.

Warren began to move at dawn, as ordered, with all four of his divisions abreast, and he had the power to go sweeping through to the Jerusalem Road, wheel toward the north, and break things up once and for all. But he ran into skirmish fire, found the ground unfamiliar, and at six o'clock halted his men and told them to dig in while patrols examined the ground in their front.

In the rear Meade was in a foul temper, which kept growing worse, and he emitted a furious stream of orders in a completely futile attempt to bring about the united attack which had been designed. Hours passed, and the breakdown in the command system became complete, and by early afternoon Meade was wiring to his corps commanders: "I find it useless to appoint an hour to effect co-operation . . . what additional orders to attack you require I cannot imagine. . . . Finding it impossible to effect co-operation by appointing an hour for attack, I have sent an order to each corps commander to attack at all hazards and without reference to each other."[23]

Late in the afternoon, the attacks were finally made. It was too late, by now, for Lee's veterans were in the trenches at last and the eight-to-one odds had vanished forever; this was Cold Harbor all over again, with its cruel demonstration that trench lines properly manned could not be taken by storm. The chance had gone, and an attack now could result in nothing but destruction for the attackers.

The soldiers knew this even if their generals did not. In mid-afternoon Birney massed his troops for a final attack. His principal column was formed in four lines, with veteran troops in the first two lines and oversized heavy artillery regiments, untried but full of enthusiasm, in the last two.

The men were lying down when the order to charge the Rebel works came in, and as the officers shouted and waved their swords the inexperienced artillerists sprang to their feet while the veterans ahead of them continued to lie prone. The veterans looked back, saw the rookies preparing to charge, and called out: "Lie down, you damn fools, you can't take them forts!"

One of the artillery regiments, 1st Massachusetts heavies, accepted this advice, lay down again, and made no charge. The other one, 1st Maine, valiantly stayed on its feet, ran forward through the rows of prostrate men, and made for the Confederate line. It was a hopeless try. The Confederate gun pits had been built low and the black muzzles of the guns that peered evilly out of the embrasures were no more than a foot or two above the ground, and when they fired the canister came in just off the grass so that nobody could escape. The whole slope was burned with fire, and in a few minutes more than 600 of the 900 men in the regiment had been shot down, the ground was covered with mangled bodies, and the survivors were running for the rear.[24]

In another part of the II Corps front, what remained of the veteran Excelsior Brigade of New York troops was moving up to the attack. The men passed through a line of artillery, and a gunner called out to ask if they were going to make a charge. A soldier answered him: "No, we are not going to charge. We are going to run toward the Confederate earthworks and then we are going to run back. We have had enough of assaulting earthworks."

The gunner who asked the question went to the rear shortly after this with a caisson to get more ammunition. He got his load and on his return he noticed that the road led over an open hill in such a way that he and his wagonload of explosives would be in the clear view of a distant Confederate battery. While he was reflecting that he would undoubtedly draw Confederate fire, he noticed that in a field on the reverse slope of the hill several hundred stragglers were lounging about little campfires, boiling coffee and enjoying themselves. He mused that these were the worthless bounty men and conscripts who had fled from the firing line, and whose mere presence in uniform weakened the entire corps, and he wished earnestly that something bad would happen to them: and just then the Rebel gunners caught sight of him, swung their guns in his direction, and let fly with salvo.

The range was long and their aim was imperfect, and the shells missed the caisson and skimmed down into the very middle of the coffee boilers, where they exploded and sent campfires and coffee pots up in flying dust and sparks and smoke. On the ground were screaming men, fearfully wounded, and those who had not been hurt were running desperately for the woods; and the gunner reined in to enjoy the scene, and hugged his knees and rocked in wild laughter, and when he got back to his battery he told his mates it was "the most refreshing sight I had seen for weeks."[25]

The afternoon's attacks came to nothing at all. Warren and Burnside finally sent their men forward at three o'clock—the morning's opportunity gone with the morning's mists—and the Army of Northern Virginia was waiting for them in secure trenches, and the men were repulsed with heavy loss. The day ended, finally, and Meade wired Grant that nothing more could be done. He added piously that "our men are tired and the attacks have not been made with the vigor and force which characterized our fighting in the Wilderness; if they had been, I think we should have been more successful."

Grant replied that they would make no more assaults: "Now we will rest the men and use the spade for their protection until a new vein has been cut."[26]

So the men huddled in their trenches, and after dark they could hear the mocking sound of the belfry clocks in Petersburg striking the hours, and a man in a Connecticut regiment wrote that "this was the most intolerable position the regiment was ever required to hold."[27]

The men were used to occupying trenches under fire, and in that respect the situation here was no worse than it had been at Cold Harbor or half a dozen other places. What made it truly intolerable was the realization, running from end to end of a tired, heartsick army, that the greatest chance of the war had been missed—and that, as a military critic expressed it years afterward, "the blame of the failure to take Petersburg must rest with our generals, not with our army."[28]

FOUR

White Iron on the Anvil

1. CHANGING THE GUARD

THE trenches ran south from the Appomattox for five miles, following the tops of the low ridges, and for all anyone could see the armies might stay there forever. There had been no rain for two weeks (nobody knew it, but another month would pass before there was as much as a light shower) and the dust was inches deep: a fine, powdery dust, like soiled flour, so light that every footstep sent up a cloud of it, and half a dozen men walking together along a trench or on open ground in the rear moved, invisible, in a choking mist of their own creation.

Sometimes the dust seemed to be the chief enemy. A Connecticut man wrote that taking a stroll was like walking in an ash heap, and he said that after a short time "one's mouth will be so full of dust that you do not want your teeth to touch each other." A gunner said that whenever a grasshopper hopped it raised so much dust that Rebel lookouts reported the Yankee army on the move, a New Yorker found the combination of 110-degree heat and 4-inch dust "is killing more men than the Johnnies," and a private from Michigan—remembering the cool pines and clear streams of his homeland—wrote despondently: "I think of the hottest days, in harvest time, away north in Michigan, and oh! how cool, compared with these." Every day men toppled over with sunstroke and were carried to the rear. Uniforms, faces, trees, shrubs, and grass were all a dull, ugly yellow gray. The air was heavy with the odor of unburied bodies, and the sun beat down day after day on men who cowered in deep slits in the earth.[1]

General Grant had said that they would use the spade, and they did. Each regiment in the line would dig a broad trench, and on the side facing the enemy there would be a solid wall of logs, with dirt banked up beyond it. Several yards in front of this there would be a ditch, six feet deep by ten feet wide, with the earth that came out of it added to the pile in front of the logs until the embankment was six or eight feet high and a dozen feet thick. Sandbags or logs would be arranged on top of the embankment, with slits or loopholes for men to stick their rifles through, and just behind the log wall there would be a fire step—a low ledge of packed earth, built so that a man who stood on it could put his musket through the loopholes. At intervals, leading to the rear, there would be covered ways, which were deep trenches zig-zagged to take advantage of the ground, built so that men could walk to the firing line from the rear without being exposed.

Out in front of the trenches, fifty or one hundred yards nearer to the enemy, there was an abatis. Much of the ground had been timbered, and the trees were felled with their bushy tops pointing toward the foe. The butts were embedded in shallow trenches to hold them in place, and the branches were sharpened and bound together so that it was almost impossible to get through them. In places there were several rows of these entanglements, with narrow lanes cut here and there so that pickets could go out to their stations. This abatis was supplemented very often by what were called *chevaux-de-frisl:* heavy logs laid end to end and

578

bound together with chains, bristling with six-foot stakes sharpened to a point and projecting in such a way that a man who tried to scramble over was certain to find his person or his clothing jagged and held fast.

On every hill or knoll there was a fort, a square enclosure of earth and logs with openings for the guns. These were arranged so that there was no place in front of the trenches that could not be reached by artillery fire. Farther to the rear there were pits like unroofed cellars where coehorn mortars were mounted. In these forts and pits, and adjoining all of the trenches, there were bomb-proofs—square holes in the earth roofed with logs and dirt, in which the men could hide when the enemy fired shells.[2]

That was the front. It was five miles long and the Rebel line was exactly like the Union line, and there was not the remotest chance that any part of either line could be taken by storm so long as a handful of defenders remained on duty and stayed awake. The dust and the sickening air and the killing sunlight lay on everything, and the sharpshooters and the gunners were always alert, and by day and by night there was intermittent heavy firing. A good many men were killed and wounded every day, to no particular end except to warn the survivors that they had better dig deeper and stronger trenches and hide in them every moment of their lives.[3]

On most of the line the trenches were not far apart, and in front of Burnside's corps there were hardly 150 yards between them, and the firing there was almost continuous. On each side sharpshooters with long-range rifles found vantage points a little behind the lines and kept their weapons trained on the firing slits in the opposing trenches, so that a man who looked out to see what he could see was quite likely to get a bullet in the face.

Toward the southern end of the line, however, where the V Corps was stationed, the works diverged. Here the Rebel trenches curved over toward the west and the Federal trenches continued in a southerly direction, and the rival lines were half a mile apart, and so there was much less shooting. Along here the pickets had made their usual arrangements with each other, and between the lines there was a little stream to which men from both armies came, in full light of day, to fill their canteens. When an officer came down the enemies would warn each other, because most officers had strong ideas about the need for keeping up a constant fire, and the general feeling was that officers were interlopers who ought to stay farther in the rear. One day the Union General Crawford came out to the picket line and stood up on a parapet and began examining the Rebel line through field glasses. A Reb scribbled something on a sheet of paper, wrapped the paper around a stone, and tossed it over into a Union rifle pit. The Federal soldier who picked it up found that the Southerner had written: "Tell the fellow with the spy glass to clear out or we shall have to shoot him."

When they were left to themselves the men in this particular sector faithfully observed the rules of their informal truce. There was a day when some recently conscripted Southerner was assigned to duty down here, and being full of the ideas his officers had drummed into him he leveled his musket and fired at the first Yankee he saw. The other Federals jumped into their holes and prepared to shoot back, but the Confederates called out: "Don't shoot—you'll see how we fix him." Thereafter, for the rest of the day, the ardent Southern recruit was seen pacing back and forth along the firing line ignominiously shouldering a fence rail, and the supposed enemies lounged on the grass, went for water, exchanged gossip, and kept a wary eye open for officers.[4]

But this was the exception. Along most of the line the two armies were playing for keeps, and it was considered certain death to expose oneself for more than a moment. Men cooked, ate, and slept in the earth, and when mortars were fired they ran for the bombproofs, although they soon discovered that most of these did not offer much protection against a direct hit by a shell of large caliber. On one part of the line certain Pennsylvania soldiers—time-expired members of the famous Bucktails, mostly, who had re-enlisted in another regiment when the Bucktails were paid off—found that it was highly amusing to fire ramrods at the enemy, because of the peculiar whirring noise and erratic flight of these iron arrows. Many men had been killed in this sector and there were discarded rifles all over the place, so the supply of surplus ramrods was large and some of the Pennsylvanians got so they could actually hit people with them. The fun was mostly in the noise, however, for the ramrods would go "whirling end over end, and every way, whipping out of the air a multitude of sharp screeches and cutting sounds."[5]

In some regiments men were under orders to fire a certain number of rounds per day, regardless. The more conscientious would try to find a good target before firing, but many of the men simply thrust their weapons over the parapet and fired at random."[6]

There did not seem to be any especial reason why this could not go on forever. Not even the major generals supposed any longer that Petersburg could be taken by assault, and it had become equally obvious that whatever else an army under Grant might do, it was not going to retreat. The strategy by which Grant had hoped to apply pressure elsewhere so as to compel Lee to retreat had fizzled out, so there was nothing for the Army of the Potomac to do but stay where it was, stand the hammering, and hope for the best.

Sheridan and his cavalry had got nowhere with the plan to team up with Hunter's forces at Charlottesville. Wade Hampton had gone in hot pursuit with Confederate cavalry, and he and Sheridan collided near Trevilian Station on the Virginia Central Railroad and had a desperate fight. Each general said afterward that he had beaten the other, but Sheridan had gone no farther west. He said this was because he had learned that Hunter was nowhere near Charlottesville and never would be, so that it was useless to go on. However that might have been, Sheridan rode north and east in a wide circle and got back into the Union lines.

Hunter had tried to go to Lynchburg instead of to Charlottesville, and he had bumped into a strong Confederate force led by the redoubtable Jubal Early. Hunter conceived that he did not have enough ammunition to carry him through a serious battle; conceived also, it may be, that Early and his men were pretty tough; conceived finally that he had best retreat, and did so, fleeing across the mountains into West Virginia, taking his command entirely out of the war for several weeks and nullifying this particular part of Grant's strategy as neatly as Lee himself could have wished. His departure left the Shenandoah Valley wide open, and Early promptly began to march down the valley toward the Potomac, taking a leaf from the Stonewall Jackson book of two years earlier.[7]

It was the railroads that made Petersburg important, and about the time the two armies settled down to unbroken trench warfare, Wilson was told to take his division of cavalry and ride far south to destroy the line that led to North Carolina. His men tore up much track, burned stations and freight cars, and wrecked bridges and culverts, but Sheridan's retreat from Trevilian had left Lee with a temporary surplus of cavalry and these rode hard and fast, overtaking Wilson, boxing him in, and coming close to destroying his entire command. He got back within the Union lines at last, minus his artillery and his wagons and a good many of his men, and his expedition looked like a flat failure. Actually, it had accomplished more than the Federal command quite realized. The break which it made in the vital Southern railway line was a bad one and it was not fully repaired for weeks, and while it lasted the Confederates were burdened with one of their worst supply problems of the war.[8]

There had been one other failure, and in some ways it was the worst of the lot. When Beauregard pulled his troops out of the Bermuda Hundred lines in order to save Petersburg, Butler's inactive army was released. For twenty-four hours the way was open for it to move forward, cut the railroad and highway from

Petersburg to Richmond, and sever all communications between Beauregard and Lee. Butler's front-line commanders saw the chance and tried to do something about it, and Grant saw it and sent Wright and two divisions of the VI Corps over to help, but Butler flubbed the shot completely. He hesitated and considered and then launched a spate of orders which looked good on paper but which served only to confuse the generals who had to do the fighting, and before he could get himself rounded up Lee sent Pickett's division in, shoved the irresolute Federals back, and closed the gap for good.

Somewhere, in the tangled mesh of politics that lay between Washington and the fighting fronts, Butler possessed influence that even the commander of the armies could not break. Grant tried to have him removed, and failed. Then he worked out a scheme by which Butler would retain his command but would do all of his work down at Fortress Monroe, where there was administrative routine to be handled, leaving all military operations to Baldy Smith, his second-in-command. That could not be done, either. Butler held his job and he held it on his own terms, although Grant warned Halleck that relations between Butler and Smith were so bad that if Butler stayed Smith probably would have to go.

In the end, Smith did go; and in the end, when he went, it was Grant who sent him away. While he fought his losing fight to get rid of Butler, Grant seems to have done a good deal of thinking about Smith's performance on June 15, when he captured the Confederate forts and then sent his soldiers to bed instead of into Petersburg. In the end Grant concluded that Smith was a man he could do without, Butler or no Butler, and when he came to this conclusion he acted on it. Smith was quietly removed and sent up to New York—indignant, protesting bitterly, writing long afterward that the real trouble was that Butler had got Grant drunk and then had used his knowledge of the fact as blackmail to make Grant do as Butler wished.[9]

The tale can be taken or left alone, at anyone's choice. The chief trouble is that it is too simple, explaining too much with too little. There is of course no reason to suppose that Butler would have been above blackmailing Grant or anyone else if it would have served his purposes, but something much more intricate than a threat to let one small cat out of a bag was unquestionably involved in the fact that Butler could not be fired. His political power had been moving mountains long before he had any opportunity to lay Grant under threat of exposure.

Everything about Butler was fantastic, beginning with his personal appearance: lumpy oversized body, arms and legs that looked as if they had been attached as an afterthought, eyes that refused to mesh. As a Democratic politician, he had in 1860 been an ardent supporter of the extreme Southern viewpoint; two years later the Southerners were announcing that Ben Butler was the one Yankee who, if captured by Confederate forces, would be shot without trial. Abolitionists made a hero of him and considered him a great friend of the Negro, although at the beginning of the war he had said that he would not interfere with slavery in a slave state, and when the idea of enlisting Negroes as soldiers was first suggested to him in New Orleans he turned it down flatly. A private in the 25th Massachusetts wrote that "as a military governor he is a none-such . . . but as a commander of troops in the field he is not just such a man as I should pick out."[10]

Butler was the archtype of the fixer, the influence man, the person on whom nothing much is ever proved but who is always suspected of everything. Devout Confederates believed that in addition to committing an illegal hanging and insulting Southern womanhood he had in New Orleans personally stolen silver spoons with his own hands. A Northern general who served under him for a time in Virginia reported that Butler had become a dictator who "made laws and administered them, dealt out justice and inflicted punishment, levied fines and collected taxes," and he added that the air about him was thick with rumors and hints of corruption. A good part of Butler's territory in the Norfolk–Hampton Roads area was a queer no man's land in which contraband trade seemed to flourish, with cotton shipped into the Union lines in return for war goods which went to support Lee's army. Nobody was ever quite sure just who got the rake-off, but it seemed obvious that someone must be getting a good deal. A tremendous scandal was always on the edge of breaking, but the break never quite came. There was always something soiled about the man, but he remained uncanny and untouchable.[11]

There were times when it was all but impossible for a good man to work under him. He could send a subordinate an order phrased so as to constitute the most cruel of insults; then, when the officer protested, Butler would write a smooth letter insisting that no insult was intended and that he had the highest personal and professional regard for the man he had insulted. A brilliant lawyer, he knew how to handle words, and none of the professional soldiers who tangled with him could match phrases with him.

Just at the end of the period when his troops might have broken out of the Bermuda Hundred lines he sent to General Wright a curt order to attack the Rebel troops in his front at once. The situation at the front was not at all as Butler imagined it and Wright wired back that the proposed attack was impossible, suggested an alternative approach, and asked further instructions.

Immediately Butler replied: "At 7:10 this evening I sent an order to you and General Terry to do some fighting. At 10:30 I get no fighting, but an argument. My order went out by direction of the lieutenant general." When Wright, somewhat baffled, protested against what he termed an unmerited reproach, Butler blandly replied: "No reproach is given; a fact is stated," and added loftily that victory could not be won if orders were not obeyed.[12]

In his campaign to keep his job this summer Butler held one prodigious trump card which Grant could not see. This was a presidential election year, and just when Grant was trying to rid himself of this incompetent general the leaders of the Republican party, very much against their will, were in the act of renominating President Lincoln for a second term. It was no time to rock the boat, and Butler was just the man who could rock it to the point of capsizing it.

From the beginning, Lincoln's real problem had been political. He had a war to win and he had to find generals who could win it, but above everything else he had to control the war—not merely the fighting of it, but the currents which would finally determine what it meant and what would come of it all. So far, the war had brought nothing but death: death by wholesale, death in all its forms, death in hospitals, in blazing thickets, on ridges swept by exploding shell, in ravines where dust and battle smoke lay thick and blinding. Unless the whole thing was no better than fever and madness, all of this death must finally be swallowed up in a victory that would justify the cost. The spirit that would infuse this victory must have infinite breadth, because the country was fighting no enemy: it was simply fighting itself. The death of a South Carolinian, brained by a clubbed musket butt in a fort in front of Petersburg, was fully as significant as the death of a Pennsylvanian killed by a Minié ball in a swamp at Cold Harbor. If what those men had bought, by dying, was to be principally hatred and smash-'em-up, then both deaths had been wasted and dust and ashes were the final truth.

There were strong men in the North who wanted revenge. The old technique of plowing up the site of a conquered city and sowing the ground with salt had fallen into disuse, since the fall of Carthage, but they would do the best they could with some modern variant. The Ben Wades and the Thad Stevenses and the Zach Chandlers had great capacity for hatred, and the South was not part of the country as they saw it. Lincoln stood in their way, and because they could not budge him they cried that he was soft and irresolute, and they would put one of their own kind in his place if they could. Standing with them were the men whose minds were laudably high but deplorably narrow—the abolitionists, the men who had taken scars in the long fight in the day when the odds were all against them and who now were disposed to judge a man by the iron which he was willing to put into the matter of punishment for the slave-owners.

There was something to be said on their side. They could remember Bully Brooks and his murderous assault on Sumner, and the taunts and jibes of men like Texas's Wigfall, who would have turned the Senate into a place where only an expert duelist could speak freely. If they were grim and implacable, it is at least possible to see how they got that way; and in addition they were that part of the Union cause which would never surrender or stop to haggle over costs. They provided a good part of the nerve and sinew which enabled the North to bounce back from Fredericksburg defeats and Wilderness casualty lists, and neither Lincoln nor any other Republican was likely to win the election if they went actively on the warpath.

What had kept them off the warpath so far was partly the fact that Lincoln did seem to have most of the people with him, and partly the old political truism: You can't beat somebody with nobody. To date, only nobodies had offered themselves against him, men like John Charles Frémont, who was heading a rickety third-party slate. But Butler was a somebody. Soldiers might know him as a cipher, but with abolitionists and bitter-enders he was a mighty hero. He had boundless ambition and a total lack of scruples, and he saw himself as a presidential possibility. If the army suddenly dropped him he would land in the arms of the political extremists. What that would mean, to the war and to the things that would finally come out of the war, was nothing good men could speculate about with easy hearts.

So the truth of the matter probably is that in the infinite, complicated economy of the Civil War it was better to keep Ben Butler a major general, even though soldiers were needlessly killed because of it, than it was to inject him back into the political whirlpool. Washington saw it so, at any rate, and Washington had to balance fearful intangibles when it made its decision. And although there was not, fortunately, anyone else quite like Butler, there were many other cases where similar intangibles had to be balanced—cases where the Administration had to ask, in effect: Where will this man do the least harm—as a general, or as a politician out of control? Often enough the wrong guess was made, but that was the kind of riddle the times were asking.

Halleck understood these matters, and when Grant first began suggesting that it would be easier to win the war with Butler a civilian, Halleck tried to explain to him that political considerations must at times override even the professional judgment of the general in chief. A little earlier, Halleck had frankly confessed in a letter to Sherman that "it seems little better than murder to give important commands to such men as Banks, Butler, McClernand, Sigel and Lew Wallace, and yet it seems impossible to prevent it."[13] Halleck was right. It was impossible to prevent it. The trouble was that the army had to carry these costly misfits on its shoulders.

But the political generals were only part of the story, as far as the army was concerned. As the army settled into its trenches after four days of battle in front of Petersburg—four days which cost, roughly, as many killed and wounded as had been lost in all twelve days at Cold Harbor—some of its professionals were giving cause for worry.

Meade was on the verge of removing Warren, just when Grant was sending Smith into exile. Warren was increasingly given to broad interpretation and spontaneous revision of his orders, and Meade could hardly fail to note that the all-out attack which he had told Warren to make at dawn on the crucial eighteenth of June had not actually been delivered until 3:30 P.M. At one time Meade had definitely made up his mind to send Warren away, but the trouble was reconciled somehow and by July 1 Assistant Secretary of War Dana wired

Stanton that "the difficulty between Meade and Warren has been settled without the extreme remedy which Meade proposed last week."[14]

Meade himself was showing the strain. His temper was always bad, but as June wore on into sultry July and frustration followed frustration he became as savage as a wounded grizzly, and Dana was presently telling Stanton: "I do not think he has a friend in the whole army. No man, no matter what his business or his service, approaches him without being insulted in one way or another, and his own staff officers do not dare speak to him unless first spoken to, for fear of either sneers or curses." Dana added that a change in command seemed probable.[15]

There was probably some exaggeration in this. Meade and Grant were never intimates, but in the main they got along well enough. Nevertheless, there was trouble. Meade had handled the Petersburg assaults about as ineptly as they could have been handled, and his angry complaint on the fourth day, that since he had found it impossible to co-ordinate attacks each commander should go ahead and do the best he could on his own hook, went far to merit the comment it got from General Wright—that the different attacks had been ordered "without brains and without generalship."[16] Grant seriously considered taking Meade out of the top spot and sending him up to the Shenandoah Valley, and he appears to have felt that if this happened Hancock was the man to take Meade's place.[17]

Yet that would hardly do, either. Hancock's wound still refused to heal. He returned to duty late in June, but a wound which remains open after nearly a year takes something out of a man, and Hancock's great days were over. Like Meade, he was getting irritable, and he was quarreling now with General Gibbon, who had been one of his best friends.[18] Worse yet was the fact that if Hancock was not himself his own immediate command, the famous II Army Corps, was in even worse shape.

The II Corps had been fought out and used up. It had been the most famous corps in the army. It had stormed Bloody Lane at Antietam, it had taken 4,000 casualties at Fredericksburg without flinching, it had beaten back Pickett's charge at Gettysburg, and it had broken the Bloody Angle at Spotsylvania. But now it was all shot to pieces, and instead of being the army's strongest fighting unit it was the weakest. Nothing but a long period of recruiting, drill, and discipline would bring it up to its old level.

Proof of this came in the latter part of June, shortly before Hancock returned to command, when the corps was sent out to the Jerusalem Plank Road in an effort to extend the army's left. Lee saw the move and sent A. P. Hill's veterans down to meet it, and these men caught the corps off balance, tapped at its flanks, crumpled it up, and sent it flying. The fight had not been a particularly hard one, and comparatively few men were killed or wounded, but the manner of the defeat was eloquent. No fewer than 1,700 men had been taken prisoner—more prisoners than the corps had lost at Antietam, Fredericksburg, and Chancellorsville put together—and whole regiments had surrendered without firing a shot. Among these were the remnants of regiments which had once been among the very best in the army. There was the 15th Massachusetts, for instance, which had had more than 300 casualties in the West Wood at Antietam but which, when forced to retreat from that doleful little grove, had proudly brought out not only its own flag but also the flag of a Confederate regiment with which it had come to grips. In this latest fight the 15th surrendered almost entire, flag and all, after no more than a token resistance. Also, the corps had lost four pieces of artillery, and its attempt to retake these guns had been very feeble.[19]

What had happened was clear enough. During the last two months almost all of the good men in the corps had been shot. The figures on Gibbon's division tell the story. This division crossed the Rapidan on May 5 with a total of 6,799 men in its three brigades. During May and June it had 7,970 casualties—more men, by a large margin, than the entire number under arms when the campaign began. It had received heavy reinforcements, to be sure, but its losses for the two months amounted to 72 per cent of its original strength plus all of the replacements. It saw forty regimental commanders killed or wounded, and, as Gibbon wrote, the losses showed plainly why it was that "troops which at the commencement of the campaign were equal to almost any undertaking, became toward the end of it unfit for almost any."[20]

Gibbon's division had had it worse than the other II Corps divisions, but only a little worse. Altogether, the corps had lost nearly 20,000 men in less than two months. More than a score of its brigadiers had been shot, and approximately a hundred regimental commanders. Naturally, the men who were lost were the best men—the officers who led the way, the enlisted men who ran ahead in a charge and were the last to leave when a position was given up. Numerically, most of the losses had been made good, but the new men were mostly substitutes and bounty jumpers, of whom a II Corps gunner said contemptuously that Lee's veterans could, if they chose, drown the lot by taking bean poles and pushing them into the James River.[21]

... There had been that dance for officers of the II Army Corps, in the raw-pine pavilion above the Rapidan on Washington's Birthday, and it had been a fine thing to see; and it had been a long good-by and a dreamy good night for the young men in bright uniforms and the women who had tied their lives to them. Most of the men who danced at that ball were dead, now; dead, or dragging themselves about home-town streets on crutches, or tapping their way along with a hickory cane to find the way instead of bright youthful eyes, or in hospitals where doctors with imperfect knowledge tried to patch them up enough to enable them to hope to get out of bed someday and sit in a chair by the window. There had been a romance to war once, or at least people said there was, and each one of these men had seen it, and they had touched the edge of it while the music played and the stacked flags swayed in the candlelight, and it all came down to this, with the drifting dust of the battlefields blowing from the imperfect mounds of hastily dug graves.

Famous old fighting units ceased to exist. At the end of June Gibbon's adjutant published orders consolidating what was left of the once mighty 15th, 19th, and 20th Massachusetts—there were about enough men left to make a slim battalion and thereafter they would serve as a unit, although separate regimental rolls would still be kept. The Philadelphia Brigade was broken up, the men in its five skeleton regiments being parceled out to regiments in other brigades. The survivors were angry, and jeered the next time they saw General Gibbon, and one man in the 106th Pennsylvania lamented that he and his comrades would no longer carry their prized regimental flag, which had been pierced (they had counted carefully) by thirty-nine bullets in its three years of service.[22]

The II Corps had been hit the hardest, but nobody had been on a picnic. General Lysander Cutler commanded what had been Wadsworth's division in the V Corps, and when he wrote his report for the campaign he explained why the report was going to be incomplete. Two regiments had been lost by expiration of their terms of service, he wrote, and one whole brigade had been transferred to another division. The regiments which still remained with the division had, when the campaign began, 3,742 enlisted men, and how they had 1,324, and the regiments which had been transferred had suffered in proportion. Furthermore: "The changes in the command have been so frequent, and the losing of nearly every original brigade, regimental and company commander render it impossible to make anything like an accurate report."[23]

In the 24th Michigan, which now had fewer than 100 men, there was one company with a total strength of two—one sergeant and one private—and on drill or parade a man remembered that "it afforded amusement to witness the evolutions of this little company." A man in the 12th New Hampshire said that his regiment had been under fire every day, and every night but one, over a period of seventy-two days, and a headquarters clerk in the V Corps wrote the age-old complaint of the soldier: "How often the words 'cruel war' are uttered, and how glibly people beyond the reach of its influence talk of the misery caused by it . . . but not one-thousandth part of the real misery is even guessed at by those who are not eye-witnesses of its horrors."[24]

Many men who had not been hit became unfit for service simply because they were worn out. Colonel Dawes of the 6th Wisconsin, appointed to a board to pass on officers' qualifications, recalled numerous cases of self-inflicted wounds. He remembered one captain whose fertile imagination led him to drink "a decoction of powdered slate pencils in vinegar" in order to unfit himself for further duty, and he reported sadly that "the excitement, exhaustion, hard work and loss of sleep broke down great numbers of men who had received no wounds in battle." Some men, he said, who had been noted for their bravery and leadership when the campaign began, became timorous, unstable, and all but useless toward the end of it. For a time the 150th Pennsylvania contained a unique detachment known as "Company Q," made up of line officers from other regiments who had been court-martialed and broken for cowardice but who were given the chance to serve as private soldiers and, if they could, redeem themselves. Company Q turned out to be a good fighting unit, and most of the men in it ultimately regained their commissions.[25]

Even the chaplains seemed to be showing the strain, and many of them quietly gravitated toward safe jobs far behind the lines. ("Undue susceptibility to cannon fever," a New England soldier complained, "ought to be regarded as a disqualification.") A surgeon in the 39th Illinois, on duty at a base hospital at Fortress Monroe, felt that the chaplains there were "pharisees who made it a business to pray aloud in public places . . . rotten to the core, not caring half as much for their souls' welfare or anybody else's as for the dollars they received." One chaplain ruined morale in his ward by coming in half a dozen times a day, sitting on the edge of some soldier's cot, and telling the man he looked bad and must prepare to die; a patient threw a plate at him one day and told him to go to the devil. The doctor added stoutly that he himself had "stood beside hundreds of soldiers when dying from disease or wounds, and he has never yet seen one manifest the least fear of death."[26]

In the 2nd Connecticut Heavy Artillery it was said that the chaplain got into a poker game one night and cleaned out an entire company, coming into regimental headquarters later to show a fat roll of bills and say, "There is my forenoon's work." An officer remembered seeing some dignified clergymen of the Christian Commission moving up toward the front, carpetbags in hand. They passed some soldiers, one of whom called out: "Hullo! Got any lemons to sell?" Gravely, one of the frock-coated contingent replied: "No, my friend, we belong to the army of the Lord." And from a blue-uniformed scoffer there came back: "Oh yes—stragglers! stragglers!"[27]

As usual, there were complaints that not all of the goods sent down for Christian and Sanitary Commission workers to distribute to the soldiers ever actually reached the men for whom they were intended. A soldier detailed as hospital orderly said that grafters and scroungers got most of these delicacies: "The articles to be distributed are first turned over to the surgeon in charge, he keeping out enough for himself and assistants, then the cooks take out enough for themselves and friends. The balance, should there be a balance, goes to the soldiers. I know the above to be true from personal observation."[28]

Underneath the grousing and the bills of complaint the army was trying to maintain a sense of the continuity of its own experiences and traditions. It had to do this, because actually this simply was not the army it used to be. Something like 100,000 combat men had come down across the Rapidan early in May (the flags were all flying and everything was bright and blowing and the dogwood blossoms lit the shadows in the woods) and 60,000 of them had been shot while many other thousands had been sent home as time-expired veterans, and so much the greater part of the men who had started out were not with the army any more. There were 86,000 men in the ranks at the end of June, and most of them were new men. What those who were gone had left behind them was the confusing raw material out of which a new morale would have to be made.

Always the army reflected the nation, and the nation itself was changing. Like the army, it contained many new people these days. The war had speeded everything up. The immigrant ships were coming faster, there were more factories and slums and farms and towns, and the magical hazy light that came down from the country's past was beginning to cast some unfamiliar shadows. The old unities were gone: unities of blood, of race, of language, of shared ideals and common memories and experiences, the very things which had always seemed essential beneath the word "American." In some mysterious way that nobody quite understood, the army not only mirrored the change but represented the effort to find a new synthesis.

What was going on in front of Petersburg was not the development of a stalemate, or the aimless groping of frozen men stumbling down to the last dead end of a cold trail. What was beginning meant more than what was ending, even though it might be many years before anyone knew just what the beginnings and the endings were. Now and then there was a hint, casually dropped, as the country changed the guard here south of the Appomattox River, and the choking dust hung in dead air under a hot copper sun. The men who followed a misty dream had died of it, but the dream still lived, even though it was taking another form.

There was in the 67th New York Infantry a young German named Sebastian Muller, who got off an immigrant ship in 1860 and walked the streets unable to find work because he could speak no English and because times in this land of promise were harder than he had supposed they would be. The war came and in 1861 a recruiting agent got him, and to his people back in the fatherland Muller wrote: "I am a volunteer soldier in the Army of the United States, to fight the rebels of South America for a sacred thing. All of America has to become free and united and the starry banner has to fly again over the new world. Then we also want to have the slaves freed, the trading of human beings must have an end and every slave should be set free and on his own time. . . . Evil of all kinds, thievery, whoring, lying and deception have to be punished here."

Muller served in the 67th and on June 20, 1864, the regiment's time expired and it was sent back for muster-out. But he had enlisted a couple of months late, and he and a few others were held in service and were transferred to the 65th New York to serve out their time, and two days after the 67th went back home Muller was a picket in an advanced gun pit on the VI Corps front, and a Rebel sniper drew a bead on him and killed him. A German comrade wrote a letter of consolation to Muller's parents: "If a person is meant to die on land, he will not drown. If death on the battlefield is to be his lot, he will not die in the cradle. God's dispositions are wise and his ways are inscrutable." The chaplain added a note saying that Muller had died without pain and had been given "a decent Christian burial."[29] That was that.

In the 19th Massachusetts there was an Irish sergeant named Mike Scannell—the same who won his chevrons by carrying the flag at Cold Harbor—and in the II Corps debacle over by the Jerusalem Plank Road Mike and his flag were out in front and were taken by the Confederates, one of whom came at Mike with leveled bayonet, ordering: "You damned Yankee, give me that flag!" Mike looked at the Southerner and he looked at the bayonet, and he replied:

"Well, it is twenty years since I came to this country, and you are the first man who ever called me a Yankee. You can take the flag, for that compliment."[30]

Nothing much had happened. A German who could not tell Virginia from

South America had seen a sacred thing in the war and had died for it, and an Irishman after twenty years of rejection had been accepted, at the point of a bayonet but in the language of his time and place, as a full-fledged American. The synthesis was taking place.

2. I KNOW STAR-RISE

The ravine was broad and it ran north and south, and along the bottom of it there were a little brook and what remained of the Norfolk and Petersburg Railroad. On the western crest, which was the side toward the Rebels, there was a line of Federal entrenchments, and the center of this line was held by the 48th Pennsylvania Veteran Volunteer Infantry.

The trench was high-water mark for the IX Army Corps—the extreme limit of the advance, the place where tired men who had fired all of their ammunition lay in the dark to build little breastworks out of earth scooped up with bayonets, tin plates, and bare hands.

Since the fight the line had been made very strong. There was a deep trench now, with a high parapet on the side toward the Rebels, and out in front there was a cunning tangle of abatis. A quarter of a mile in the rear, on the eastern crest of the ravine, there were gun pits, with artillery placed so that it could knock down any hostile parties that might try to storm the trench. The slope just behind the trench offered protection from Southern fire, and to make traffic toward the rear even safer, there was a deep covered way, which left the trench almost at a right angle, crossed the ravine, and ended behind the guns.

On the Confederate side things were much the same. The trench was deep and strong, and the point directly opposite the place where the 48th lived had been made into a fort, with brass cannon emplaced. Like the Federals, the Confederates had an abatis out in front, and covered ways leading to the rear, and batteries posted to beat back any attack. Five hundred yards behind the Confederate trench the ground rose to a long, rounded ridge, and just over this ridge was the Jerusalem Plank Road, which had once been an undefended avenue leading into Petersburg but which was undefended no longer.

As far as men could make them so, the opposing lines here were proof against assault. The soldiers who occupied them were always on the alert. They had to be, because the trenches here were closer together than at any other point along the front. Everyone kept under cover, and any man who exposed himself for an instant was immediately shot at—and usually was hit, too, for the sharpshooters were keen and the range was short. There were mortars back among the gun pits, and they were active. And although the trenches were deep and the men took care of themselves, it was very expensive to hold this part of the line and divisional losses could run to 12 per cent in one month just from sniper and mortar fire.[1]

The 48th Pennsylvania came mostly from Schuylkill County, up in the anthracite region, and it fancied itself a crack regiment. When the IX Corps was sent West, in the spring of 1863, the 48th was briefly assigned to provost guard duty in Lexington, Kentucky, and the men proudly remembered that they had done the job so smoothly, and had kept themselves looking so trim and neat, with well-shined shoes, polished buttons, clean uniforms, and white gloves, that the citizens petitioned Burnside to keep them in that assignment. Burnside was willing, and so the 48th spent nearly six months in Lexington, living comfortably and missing a great deal of hard campaigning, including the latter part of the siege of Vicksburg. When the 48th was finally ordered away, the whole town turned out to say good-by, and a band paraded the boys down the street to the tune of "Auld Lang Syne," while the girls on the sidewalks waved handkerchiefs and cried sentimentally and the soldiers said that leaving Lexington was harder than leaving home.[2]

Early in 1864 the regiment had gone back to Schuylkill County to "veteranize." The mine fields were supposed to be full of strong Copperhead sentiment, with coal miners demonstrating against the draft so violently that troops had to be sent in to keep order, but the 48th had no trouble getting recruits to fill its ranks. It mustered rather more than 400 enlisted men for duty nowadays, and about a fourth of these men had been coal miners before they enlisted.[3]

Coming from mining country and having many miners, the 48th knew a thing or two about digging in the earth. One day its commander, passing along the trench, came on a soldier who was peering through the firing slit at the Rebel works. The man stepped down, turned to a comrade, and said: "We could blow that damned fort out of existence if we could run a mine shaft under it."

The commanding officer was Lieutenant Colonel Henry Pleasants, and that was talk he could understand because he was a mining engineer himself and before being a mining engineer he had done railroad construction work, and he had tunneled under obstructions before now. Born in the Argentine, the son of a Philadelphia businessman who married a Spanish woman and spent many years in South America, he was thirteen before he was brought to Philadelphia for a North American education. Trained as a civil engineer, he worked for the Pennsylvania Railroad in the early 1850s and he had had a hand in driving a 4,200-foot tunnel through the Alleghenies. A few years before the war he quit the railroad for coal mining and made his home in Schuylkill County. He was thirty-one now—slim, dapper, dark, and bearded—and as he passed along the trench he kept thinking about what the soldier had said. A little later he went down the ravine to a bombproof where the regimental officers lived, and he introduced the subject to them by saying bluntly: "That God-damned fort is the only thing between us and Petersburg, and I have an idea we can blow it up."[4]

Not long after this, Pleasants passed the suggestion along, more formally, to his division commander, Brigadier General Robert Potter, and Potter sent a staff officer around to see what this was all about. Pleasants took the man to a place in the trench where they could get a good view of the Rebel fort. While they were looking over the parapet, the staff man unfortunately was hit in the face by a Confederate bullet, but after he had been carried away Pleasants drew a rough sketch of the terrain and sent it to Potter, and a few days later Potter sent for him and took him back to corps headquarters to see Burnside.

It was a sweltering hot night, and the two officers found Burnside sitting in his tent, coat off, bald head glistening in the candlelight, a long cigar cocked up at the side of his mouth. Burnside put the young colonel at his ease at once, and listened intently while the plan was explained, mopping beads of sweat off his forehead with a big silk bandanna while they talked.

Modestly enough, Pleasants admitted getting his idea from a chance remark dropped by an enlisted man. He then went on to explain how they could begin a tunnel on a sheltered spot on the hillside, forty or fifty yards behind their trench, where the Rebels would not be able to see what they were doing. The shaft would slant uphill, which would take care of the drainage problem, and although it would probably have to be more than 500 feet long, Pleasants thought he could devise a means of ventilating it.

Burnside liked the idea and he said he would take it up with Meade. Meanwhile, he said, Pleasants should go ahead with it. So the next day Pleasants organized his coal miners into details, led them to a spot on the protected side of the ravine, and put them to work. Lacking picks, they began by using their bayonets, and in no time at all they were underground.[5]

Meade took very little stock in the project, but he felt that it was good to keep the troops busy. Also, his engineers had just reported that "the new era in field works has so changed their character as in fact to render them almost as strong as permanent ones," and every professional soldier knew that the only way to take permanent fortifications was through the long, ritualized processes of siege warfare.[6] This involved an almost endless dig-and-fill routine—an advance by regular approaches, in military jargon—the general object of which was to inch one's own lines forward far enough so that heavy guns could be mounted where they could flatten the enemy's works at short range. The trouble was that the conditions which would make siege warfare successful simply did not exist here. Petersburg was by no means surrounded, and the Federals did not begin to have the necessary preponderance of force.

So when Burnside came in with this new idea, Meade was prepared to be receptive. The same could not be said for his engineers, who pooh-poohed the whole proposal and said it was clap-trap and nonsense. They said loftily that there was nothing novel about mining the enemy's works—it was standard operating procedure, once the besieging party had brought its own trenches up to within a few yards of the objective point—but they declared that no army on earth had ever tried to do it at anything like the distance involved on Burnside's front. A mine shaft of that length, they went on, could not possibly be ventilated and the men who had to dig it would all be suffocated, if they were not first crushed under falling earth. Besides, the Rebels would find out about it and would interfere. The army's engineers, in short, would have none of it.

Meade himself felt much the same way, but Grant was anxious to get on with the war and he was pressing Meade to see if there was not some way to break the Rebel front. Meade had to confess that there did not seem to be any way, but he did tell Grant that Burnside had some men digging a mine "which General B. thinks when exploded will enable him by a formidable assault to carry the line of works." So with this cautious endorsement, and largely because there was nothing else in sight, the Schuylkill miners suddenly began to be very important people.[7]

Pleasants began by getting from each of his company commanders a list of all the men who were actually coal miners. He organized these men into shifts, with a non-com named Harry Reese as mine boss, precisely as if he were going to mine for coal, and he put them to work round the clock, seeing to it that each man got a dram of commissary whisky when he finished his stint. Picks and shovels were supplied, and although the picks were not the kind used in coal mines, there were plenty of blacksmiths in IX Corps artillery units and Pleasants persuaded them to remodel the implements. The work went faster than he had anticipated, and in a short time he needed timbers to shore up the ceiling and walls.

At this point he found that the army was letting him do this job rather than helping him do it. Meade had promised Burnside to send a company of engineers and any other aid that might be needed, but the company never showed up and when Pleasants asked for some timber nothing seemed to happen. So Pleasants sent a detail from his regiment down into the ravine behind the lines, tore down a railroad bridge, and used those timbers as long as they lasted. Then he discovered an abandoned sawmill four or five miles to the rear. He got Burnside to issue a pass and provide some horses and wagons, and he sent two companies back to operate the mill and cut the necessary lumber.

Pleasants also needed handbarrows to carry the dirt out of the tunnel and dispose of it in some place where Rebel lookouts would not see it. Army headquarters had promised sandbags, but the sandbags never arrived, so Pleasants collected cracker boxes, reinforced them with iron hoops taken from pork barrels, nailed stout handles on them, and detailed parties to lug these in and out of the shaft.

After a week progress came to a halt when the miners struck a belt of wet clay and the ceiling sagged, breaking the timbers and nearly closing the tunnel.

Pleasants retimbered the shaft, shored up the ceiling with stouter props, and drove on. Next he struck a bed of marl which had a way of turning to rock soon after the air struck it. The soldiers amused themselves by carving tobacco pipes out of this in their spare time, but it was mean stuff to tunnel through and the colonel finally had to increase the tunnel's angle of climb so as to get into a softer earth stratum. He was making his tunnel five feet high, four feet wide at the bottom, and some two and one half feet wide at the top, and it was strongly timbered all the way—ceiling, both sides, and floor. Cutting and transporting all of this timber and getting it inside the mine, and taking all of the dirt out and concealing it in the ravine under fresh-cut bushes, kept calling for more and more hands, and before long practically the entire regiment was at work.[8]

When the shaft had gone a couple of hundred feet into the hillside, Pleasants felt that it was time to make some exact calculations about the spot where the powder magazine ought to go. (Obviously he would accomplish nothing if he dug past the Rebel fort or stopped short of it.) So he applied to the engineers for the instruments with which he could make the necessary triangulations. The engineers laughed this off, and a plea to Meade's headquarters was lost in the shuffle somewhere, and at last Burnside—who seems to have been the only important officer in the army who was disposed to be helpful—wired to a friend in Washington and had him send down a theodolite.

Pleasants had to take this into the front line to make his observations, and of course Rebel snipers were apt to shoot him while he was doing it. He got around this by having half a dozen soldiers put their caps on ramrods and raise them just above the parapet. While the sharpshooters peppered away at these, hitting them quite regularly and no doubt imagining that they were hitting human heads inside of them, Pleasants draped some burlap over his head and his instrument, got unobserved over the parapet level a few yards away, and made his observations.[9]

Farther and farther into the hillside went the tunnel. As the engineers had prophesied, ventilation was a problem, but Pleasants solved it. Close beside the tunnel, at a point just behind the main Federal trench, he dug a vertical shaft whose lower end opened into a little recess in the tunnel wall and whose upper end discharged unobtrusively into a clump of bushes. Then he built a square tube of boards, reaching from the mouth of the tunnel all the way to its inner end, and he prepared a door by which the outer end of the tunnel could be sealed shut, leaving the open end of the wooden tube protruding out into the air. The rest was simple: close the door and build a fire in the little recess at the bottom of the vertical shaft. The smoke and heated air went up this chimney, the resultant draft pulled the bad air out of the tunnel, and fresh air from the outside was drawn in through the wooden tube.

On July 17, three weeks after the job had been begun, the inner end of the tunnel was squarely beneath the Confederate redoubt, twenty-odd feet underground and 510 feet from the entrance, and the miners could hear Confederate soldiers tramping about overhead. Pleasants then had his men dig a 75-foot shaft running across the end of the tunnel; a diagram of his work now would look like a capital T with a very long shank, with the crossbar of the T running along directly beneath the Confederate works.[10]

Pleasants then reported that the mine was ready for its charge of powder—at which point further operations were temporarily suspended because the Rebels had discovered that the Yankees were digging a mine and were sinking shafts of their own trying to find it.

Confederate luck right here was bad. Their engineers misjudged the direction the tunnel was taking, and their countermining shafts failed to intersect it. When Pleasants had his men stop working, the Rebels in underground listening posts could hear nothing, and in the end all of their protective measures failed. Meanwhile, the Southern privates who were going about their business directly above the dark sinister gallery began to treat the whole affair as another camp rumor, and now and then they would call across and ask the Yankees when the big show was going to begin.[11]

After a pause, with the digging and timbering all finished, Pleasants went to work to lay the powder charges. Burnside wanted to use eight tons of powder, but the army engineers had one good suggestion here—the use of explosives in quantity was a subject they really knew something about—and they pointed out that a smaller charge would actually be more effective. In the end, Burnside settled for four tons, and Pleasants had his men build eight open-topped wooden boxes in the lateral gallery for magazines. The powder was delivered behind the lines in 320 kegs, each containing 25 pounds, and there was day-and-night work carrying these into the mind and pouring the charges into the magazines.

All of the magazines were connected by wooden troughs half filled with powder, and these troughs met at the place where the gallery crossed the inner end of the main shaft. The engineers had promised Pleasants a supply of wire and a "galvanic battery" to touch off the charge, but this was another delivery that was never made, so Pleasants got a supply of ordinary fuses, spliced them together, introduced one end into the powder in the trough, and strung the rest of the fuse back along the tunnel for about one hundred feet. As a final step, earth was solidly tamped into place, filling the main shaft for thirty-eight feet from the place where it met the lateral gallery. All that remained now was to light the outer end of the fuse.[12]

Pleasants never doubted that the mine would blow a big hole in the Confederate line, but the only other officer of any consequence who really believed in it seems to have been Burnside himself, and according to his lights Burnside did his best to make a success of the attack that would follow the explosion.

His army corps contained four divisions. Three of these had been in action more or less continually since the army crossed the Rapidan, and they had had a solid month of trench duty in front of Petersburg. Each of these divisions contained about 3,000 men, all of whom by now were very battle-weary. The fourth division had never been in action to speak of, having spent practically all of its time guarding wagon trains and doing other back-area jobs, and its 4,300 men consequently were fresh. Obviously, a fresh division ought to be used to spearhead the attack, and so—about the time Pleasants was beginning to dig the lateral gallery—Burnside brought this division forward and told its commander, Brigadier General Ferrero, to give it special training for the assault; it was the outfit that was going to break the Rebel line and march into Petersburg and win the war. (Burnside himself was so confident the attack would succeed that he had all of his headquarters baggage packed so that he could move right into Petersburg on the heels of his victorious troops.)

Burnside's plan was perfectly logical. The three divisions which had been holding the trenches were worn out—during the last ten days of June and the month of July they lost more than a thousand men, altogether, just from sharpshooter and mortar fire—and the men had adjusted themselves to trench life so completely that they looked on soldiering as being largely a business of getting behind a protective bank of earth and avoiding enemy bullets. If unbloodied troops were available it was only common sense to use them, and in picking Ferrero's division Burnside was exercising perfectly sound judgment.[13]

The difficulty was that an imponderable entered into things here, deep as the ocean and unpredictable as a tornado at midnight. Ferrero's division was made up entirely of colored soldiers.

The use of colored troops was an experiment to which the Administration had been driven partly by the demands of the abolitionists and partly by sheer desperation, the supply of white manpower having slackened. The implications of this experiment were faced by few people, and there probably would be time enough to worry about them after the war had been won. At the moment the great riddle was whether it was possible to turn colored men into good soldiers.

Most of these ex-slaves were illiterate, used to servile obedience, and living (presumably) in deep awe of Southern white men. They were husky enough, and yet they somehow lacked physical sturdiness and endurance,[14] and they had been held at the bottom of the heap for so long that they seemed to be excessively long-suffering by nature. Somewhere, far back in dim tribal memories, there may have been traditions of war parties and fighting and desperate combat, but these had been overlaid by generations of slavery, and most colored folk saw themselves as pilgrims toiling up the endless slopes of heartbreak hill—pilgrims whose survival depended on the patient, uncomplaining acceptance of evil rather than on a bold struggle to overthrow evil.

That was the sticking point. The average Northern white man of that era might refuse to associate with the Negro and hold himself to be immeasurably the Negro's superior—the superiority, of course, grew out of the natural order of things, and need not actually be proved—but there was a war on and the country needed soldiers, and if Federal corpses were the price of victory, it hardly paid to be finicky about the original color of the corpses' skins. The real trouble lay in the assumption that while it was all right to let the Negro get shot it was foolish to expect him to do any serious fighting first.

A young officer who left his place in a white regiment to become colonel of a colored regiment was frankly told by a staff officer that "we do not want any nigger soldiers in the Army of the Potomac," and his general took him aside to say: "I am sorry to have you leave my command, and still more sorry that you are going to serve with Negroes. I think it is a disgrace to the army to make soldiers of them." The general added that he felt this way because he was sure that colored soldiers just would not fight.[15]

Most men felt the same way. In support of the belief it was pointed out that in many years of American bondage there had never been a really serious slave revolt. Even John Brown himself, carrying fire and sword below the Potomac, had been able to recruit no more than a dazed corporal's guard of colored followers. Surely this proved that even though slaves might not be happy with their lot they had no real combativeness in them?

There might be flaws in the argument. It quite overlooked the fact that for many years the fabulous underground railroad had been relieving the explosive pressures the slave system had been building up, and had been in fact a great deterrent to slave revolt, for it took out of slavery precisely the daring, energetic, intelligent slaves who might have planned and led an uprising if they had been unable to escape.[16] The argument also overlooked the fact that if American slaves rarely made any trouble the people who owned them were always mortally afraid that they would do so some day. The gloomy island of Haiti was not far enough away to let anyone forget that black men there had risen in one of the most bloody, desperate revolts in human history, winning their own freedom and practically annihilating the master race in the process. Oddly enough, the general belief that colored men would not fight ran parallel with a conviction that they would fight with primitive viciousness if they ever got a chance.

Yet whatever prejudice might say, the hard fact now was that colored men were being enlisted as soldiers in large numbers and that there were times when it was impossible to avoid using them in combat. The use of Hinks's division was an example. They had stormed rifle pits and captured guns, and although Hancock's veterans saw in that fact nothing more than evidence that the Confederacy had only second-rate troops in line, Baldy Smith—who was far from being prejudiced in their favor—said afterward that Negro soldiers under certain circumstances might be as good as any.[17]

No matter how it might use them, however, the army certainly had not assimilated them. It had not tried to and if it had tried it would have failed, and it did not matter much anyway for it was no longer possible for this army to be homogeneous. It had become a representative cross section of an extremely mixed population; and now, as a final step, it contained long columns of colored men whose memories, as one of their officers said, were "a vast bewildered chaos of Jewish history and biography," the residue of chanted spirituals and the preaching of untaught plantation clergymen, men who in their innocence attributed every historic event to the doings of the great Moses.[18]

When Ferrero's dark battalions came up to the sheltered area just behind the front, they added a new dimension to army life and gave it a strange wild flavor. Always there had been groups of soldiers to sit around campfires in the evening, singing about their homesickness and the girls they wanted to get back to, about their comradeship, and, occasionally, about their patriotism, but when these black soldiers sang there was a haunting and a mystery in the air. For if the white soldier looked back with profound longing to something precious that had been left far behind, the colored soldier's homesickness seemed to be for a place where he had never been at all. He had nothing to look back to. Everything he could dream of lay ahead of him, and his dreams were apocalyptic, not to be expressed in ordinary words.

So when the colored troops met by the campfire to sing—and it was their favorite way to spend the evening—they sang made-up, spur-of-the-moment songs, which had never existed before either in words or in music, songs which grew out of the fire and the night and the dreams and hopes which hovered between fire and night forever.

All of the colored troops were officered by white men, and these white officers listened, fascinated, to the campfire singing, and when they wrote about it they tried to tell why it moved them so deeply. There would be a hundred men sprawled in a fire-lit circle, dark faces touched with fire; and one voice would go up, rich and soft and soaring:

> *I know moon-rise,*
> *I know star-rise——*

and half a dozen men would come in with a refrain:

> *——Lay dis body down.*

The singer would grope his way two lines nearer to the thought that was drawing him on:

> *I walk in de moonlight,*
> *I walk in de starlight——*

and now more voices would sound the refrain:

> *Lay dis body down.*

Finally the song would be finished, and a white officer who listened said that the chanted refrain would sound like "a grand creation chorus":

> *I'll walk in de graveyard,*
> *I'll walk troo de graveyard*
> * To lay dis body down.*
> *I go to de judgment in de evening of de day*
> * When I lay dis body down.*
> *And my soul and your soul will meet in de day*
> * When I lay dis body down.*[19]

They were men coming up out of Egypt, trailing the shreds of a long night from their shoulders, and sometimes they sang in the wild imagery of a despairing journey through parted waters to a land of promise:

> My army cross over,
> My army cross over—
> O Pharoah's army drownded—
> My army cross over.

> We'll cross de mighty river,
> We'll cross de River Jordan,
> We'll cross de danger water ...
> My army cross over.[20]

Most of the men were straight from the plantation. On many matters their ignorance was absolute. Yet they were men without doubts, and always their faith reached out to the future. A man in the VI Corps, talking to one of them, learned that men who could not read one word of Scripture could cite Biblical authority for their belief that the North would win the war. There was a prophecy, they said, which foretold that while the South would prevail for a time, in the end it would be overthrown. The VI Corps soldier searched his own Bible and at last concluded that the reference was to words in the eleventh chapter of the Book of Daniel:

"And in those times there shall many stand up against the King of the South: also the robbers of thy people shall exalt themselves to escape the vision; but they shall fall. So the King of the North shall come, and cast up a mount, take the most fenced cities; and the arms of the South shall not withstand, neither his chosen people, neither shall there be any strength to withstand."[21]

A Rhode Island soldier who had served along the Carolina coast remembered how a group of fugitive slaves had come within the Union lines after a harrowing nine-day flight through the swamps. One man explained his perseverance: "I seed de lamp of life ahead and de lamp of death behind," and another said that, on coming up to the Federal outposts, "When I seed dat flag, it lift me right up." Even before they left slavery, they had their own idea of what the war was about. A Pennsylvania soldier on that same Carolina expedition asked a slave if he knew why the Yankees had come, and the slave replied that of course he knew—"to kill Massa and set de darkeys free." A Wisconsin man who escaped from a prison pen in the Deep South took refuge in the hut of an aged slave who had never before seen a Union soldier, and he asked the old man if he would betray him. "No sah," replied the old man emphatically. "There's not a slave in South Carolina who would betray you." One officer discovered that before the war the Southern slaves had known about the Frémont campaign of 1856, and the campaign of 1860. Some of them told him that they had refused to work on March 4, 1861, expecting their freedom to date from that day.[22]

A Connecticut soldier who watched contrabands at work unloading ships at the Alexandria piers noticed that whenever there was a breathing spell some of the men would stretch out on the nearest pile of barrels or boxes, take out a spelling book, and laboriously study it. As a general thing, he said, they worked very hard: "All they want to encourage them is talk of freedom, and then the dirt will fly high and fast." They disliked to be called "contrabands," and when they were made soldiers they were intensely proud of their status as combat men. A white woman who visited her husband at army headquarters near Petersburg told about a meeting a wounded Negro soldier who was trudging along the road toward the base hospital at City Point, loaded down with his musket, cartridge box, and haversack. Her husband told him to throw his load away, but the man begged to be allowed to carry it all the way to the hospital: "I don't want de fellows at de hospital to mistake me for a teamster."[23]

A Regular Army enlisted man watched some of Ferrero's men marching up toward Petersburg and noted that many of them had taken off their shoes and were carrying them on their bayonets, going along barefooted. In the evening he went to their camp and observed evening roll call: "There were so many Jacksons and Johnsons that the first sergeant numbered them as high as 'Johnson Number Five.' They appeared to be very proud of being soldiers and serving with white troops."[24]

From the beginning it was realized that the effectiveness of colored troops would depend largely on the way the regiments were officered, and what would now be called an officer-candidate school was set up in Philadelphia. Non-commissioned officers and privates in the Army of the Potomac could apply for admission to this school, and if recommended by their own officers and approved by an examining board they would get thirty days of training and then would be commissioned to command colored soldiers. The rank and file seems to have been of two minds about this arrangement. Some felt that it was a good idea, that the standards were high and the training thorough—one man said he knew colonels in white regiments who could not get an examining board recommendation for a second lieutenancy—but others believed that the examinations and instructions "were not practical, but scholastic and theoretical," and that most of the men who were commissioned were not up to their jobs.[25]

Certain it was that these strange new regiments needed good leadership. They were reluctant to take orders from non-coms of their own color—it was common to hear the complaint, "I don't want him to play de white man over me"—and a company commander had to be careful to treat his sergeants with formal military courtesy, always addressing them by their titles and in general following precise Regular Army routine. The colored enlisted man who had a complaint or a problem was quite likely to try to by-pass his company officers and go direct to his colonel, and one of the colonels meditated on the reason for this: "The Negroes have acquired such a constitutional distrust of white people that it is perhaps as much as they can do to trust more than one person at a time." He added that in training and disciplining the men it was vital "to make them feel as remote as possible from the plantation," and said that the habit of obedience was worthless unless the officer managed to instill a stout feeling of self-respect along with it. An officer of polished manners could do better with colored troops than with white volunteers, who preferred a certain roughness of manner in their officers.[26]

In camp, the colored men made excellent soldiers. They picked up the drill quickly, learning it more easily than white recruits did. The different companies in a regiment would vie with each other for excellence on the parade ground, and sometimes would get into furious fist fights while arguing as to which company was the best. During that Carolina expedition, where local contrabands were organized into a regiment, there was one day a parade of colored soldiers through the city of Beaufort, with the band of a Maine regiment leading the way, and it was a big experience. A colored sergeant said afterward: "When dat band wheel in before us and march on—my God! I quit dis world altogedder!" And a private related: "We didn't look to de right nor to de left. I didn't see nottin' in Beaufort. Every step was worth half a dollar."

Some of the ordinary problems of army discipline seemed to be non-existent. Desertion was utterly unknown, and there was very little drunkenness. The men especially enjoyed practice on the target range. When one made a good shot there would be a gleeful chorus of "Ki! Old man!" and if an unskilled recruit fired his piece into the dirt there would be "such infinite guffawing and delight, such rolling over and over on the grass, such dances of ecstasy" that the colonel would remember it and put it in his memoirs.[27]

There were a few little subsidiary problems connected with the use of colored troops. The colonel of the 36th U.S. Colored Infantry told how a detachment from his regiment in the spring of 1864 was sent across from Point Lookout to the Rappahannock River area to destroy certain Rebel installations. One group, commanded by colored non-coms and with no white officers present, had a fight with some Confederates and did very well, capturing certain prisoners; and the problem was that the men wanted to kill all of the prisoners forthwith, being restrained only by their sergeant. On the other side of the ledger there was the example of Fort Pillow, a Mississippi River post held by colored troops, which had been stormed in recent months by Bedford Forrest's command. After the surrender some of Forrest's tough troopers got out of hand and turned the occasion into something like a lynching bee. The colored troops with the Army of the Potomac could read no newspapers and got their information of far-off events Heaven knows how, but every one of them knew about Fort Pillow. General Hinks, with colored men in his command, urged that all of them be armed with repeating rifles in place of the regulation muzzle-loaders. His men, he said, "cannot afford to be beaten and will not be taken," and ought to have the best arms the country could provide. His request was ignored, but the making of it was significant.[28]

As a general thing the Negro soldiers seemed to hold very little personal animus against their former masters. A white officer discovered, rather to his surprise, that they had neither hatred nor affection for the men who used to own them. They never mentioned their masters except as natural enemies, yet it was the class they hated, not the individuals in the class. They saw slavery, said this man, as "a wrong which no special kindnesses could right."[29]

When Ferrero's troops were brought up the Confederates in the Petersburg line quickly learned about it, and they despised the whole IX Corps because of it. On Burnside's front the fighting became vicious. There were no picket-line truces and no lulls in the fighting. Off to the left, where Warren's men held the line, tolerant Southerners might call, "Down, Yank!" before opening fire, but there was no more of that in Burnside's sector. Sharpshooters kept their pieces trained on the firing slit and they were shooting to kill.[30]

The men in Ferrero's division, meanwhile, were immensely proud of their new assignment. As they sat about their campfires in the evening they made up a new song:

> We looks like men a-marching on;
> We looks like men o' war—

and they sang it on every possible occasion. Ferrero drilled them in the maneuvers that would be expected of them. After the mine was exploded, they were to charge straight ahead. White divisions would follow them, wheeling to right and left to protect their flanks, but they were to go straight on and seize the long ridge that overlooked Petersburg. That would come very close to ending the war, and for these colored men it would be a new beginning, and the soldiers were buoyant and worked hard on their behind-the-lines rehearsals.[31]

Yet there was a doom over the men, and an extra sense seemed to tell them that things were not going to be simple. A prodigious thing was happening, and it could not happen easily. Here were men who had been held on a level with the mule and the ox, animated property with no rights which anyone was bound to respect, and now they were becoming men, and the very word "American" was taking on a new meaning. The war had changed. The soldiers were different and the country was different, and only the dream that had possessed them would go on. It was a dream that nobody could ever quite put into words, but it was growing as men died for it, and now it appeared that colored men could share in it.

But the road out of Egypt was long, and black men who were coming up to the unparted deep-sea waters looked ahead and made up a little campfire song to tell how they felt about it:

> For death is a simple thing,
> And he go from door to door,
> And he knock down some and he cripple up some
> And he leave some here to pray.[32]

3. LIKE THE NOISE OF GREAT THUNDERS

The ridge behind the Confederate trenches was not very high, and its slope was gentle and grassy, with dips and hollows here and there, and occasional clumps of trees. It lay naked under the July sun, and no one had ever climbed it (except for a few Confederate artillerists, who had parked some guns in the Jerusalem Plank Road), and it was like a mocking challenge to the Federal soldiers. If they could once reach the crest of that ridge, the war was over, for if they stood there they would be in rear of the entire Confederate line, and they would control Petersburg and everything that was in it, which meant that they could certainly capture Richmond and could probably destroy Lee's army. The crest was less than half a mile from the Union line, and between the crest and the Army of the Potomac there was nothing in particular except the Confederate trench which was about to be blown sky-high.

The Pennsylvania miners had brought the end of the war within whispering distance. Never before had there been a chance like this. A trench properly built and manned by a sufficiency of Southern riflemen and gunners could never be stormed, and by now everybody knew it; but if the trench and everyone in it could suddenly be obliterated the case would be very different, and if this business were handled right men could walk through and take the crest.

Grant finally saw it, and while he had certain doubts about this stunt of Burnside's, he was determined that it must at least be given a fair chance. He was commander of all the armies of the United States and he was not directly responsible for the tactics involved in an assault along half a mile of one front, but if strategy could insure success of this attack he proposed to use it, and so he laid a plan.

North of the James River, squarely in front of Richmond, there were miles of Confederate trenches held by a thin string of cavalry pickets. Potentially, this was the most sensitive part of Lee's entire line, and a Union attack there was certain to pull Confederate strength into the area just as fast as Lee could get it there. When Grant thought about ways to help Burnside's assault his mind naturally turned to those empty fortifications north of the river.

His plan was simple. He would send Hancock and the II Corps north of the James, accompanied by Sheridan and the cavalry. They would cross the Appomattox below Petersburg, march north back of Butler's lines, and cross the James by a new pontoon bridge at a place called Deep Bottom, and it would not hurt in the least if Lee saw them going. Presumably, Lee would take troops from the Petersburg lines to meet this threat. If Hancock and Sheridan could actually break the lines in front of Richmond, that of course would be all to the good. If they could not it would probably be because Lee had reduced strength in front of Petersburg in order to hold in front of Richmond. In that case Burnside's chance of success would be just so much better.[1]

So Grant planned and so it was ordered, and on the evening of July 26 the II Corps took the road north. The column got to the Appomattox bridge around midnight, and a newspaper correspondent on the north side of the river watched, fascinated, as the line of march wound past a huge bonfire which had been lit to show the way. The men came up out of the dark, passed through the pool of wavering light, and moved on into more darkness, marching steadily for the James River crossing, silent enough except when some brigade staff rode by with a jingling of scabbards and other equipment. Batteries rolled by now and then, firelight gleaming off the polished guns, and the reporter sat and watched for two hours, bemused by "that flow of men, like a river, passing, still passing, but never passed."[2]

Early on the morning of July 27 the corps crossed the James. Butler had laid two pontoon bridges at Deep Bottom somewhat earlier, and he had a detachment on the north bank to hold the bridgehead, and Sheridan took his cavalry over to strike the Charles City Road to Richmond, while the infantry fanned out along the banks of a little stream called Bailey's Creek. There was skirmishing all day long in the underbrush and forsaken fields by this brook, the Rebels apparently present in some strength with more coming up.

Back in front of Petersburg, Pleasants's men were carrying the kegs of powder down the long tunnel, each man stooping low under the ceiling and hugging the 25-pound keg against his belly. Over their heads the Confederates had stopped hunting for the rumored Yankee mine—partly, it seems, because Lee's engineers felt just the way Meade's felt: no soldiers could burrow 500 feet under a hill. A correspondent for the London *Times* who was visiting Confederate headquarters at the time helped to confirm this delusion. British army experience, he said, showed that 400 feet was the absolute limit for a tunnel of this kind.[3]

In any case, Grant's feint worked perfectly. Hancock's infantry and the dismounted cavalry gestured and skirmished and fought along a ridge back of Bailey's Creek and made threatening motions on the Charles City Road, and it looked as if a big attack was coming. One after another, Lee called veteran divisions out of the Petersburg lines, and by the morning of July 29 he had more than half of his army north of the James, leaving only 18,000 infantry to hold the five miles of line in front of Petersburg. More than a third of Hancock's people, meanwhile, had already gone back to Petersburg, and everybody else would go back as soon as the darkness came;[4] and Meade was sitting down with Burnside to draw up formal orders for the big attack, which was to begin at 3:30 o'clock the next morning, July 30.

By now, Meade was ready to support Burnside with everything he had. Burnside was to use his entire corps, and two army corps would be on hand to help him—Warren's corps, on the left, and Baldy Smith's old corps, now led by General E. O. C. Ord, on the right. A powerful mass of artillery had been quietly moved up into position during recent nights—eighty field pieces, eighteen huge 10-inch mortars, twenty-eight of the lighter coehorn mortars, and eighteen 4½-inch siege guns, all dug in where they could sweep the Confederate position.

Battle orders were precise. Burnside was to attack the moment the mine was sprung and he was to go straight for the crest of the ridge, pausing for no consideration whatever. The objective was a decisive break-through and final victory, and the only thing that counted was to get the troops up on the heights. They could get there only if they moved fast. Therefore they must be formed in columns of assault before the mine was exploded, and during the night Burnside's parapets and abatis must be leveled so that those columns could advance in line of battle. There must also be engineer parties at the heads of the columns, to remove Confederate obstructions and prepare a way for Yankee artillery to follow.

The plan was good, and it was about as Burnside had figured it. But Meade made one change in Burnside's original plan. He told Burnside that Ferrero's colored division must not be used as the first wave of the attack. The fight must be spearheaded by the white troops. If the colored troops were to be used at all they must go in later, as support.

Burnside objected, with heat, pointing out that Ferrero's was his biggest, freshest division and that it had been getting special training for weeks in the movements which would be involved in this assault. Meade refused to yield, and after a while Grant came in and Burnside appealed to him. Grant listened, and upheld Meade: the colored troops must not go in first. Profoundly disturbed, Burnside went back to his own headquarters to rearrange his plans and prepare new orders. The moment set for the explosion of the mine was now about twelve hours in the future.[5]

The Army of the Potomac was led to disaster many times, and there is a rather horrible fascination about tracing the steps by which, in each case, it reached that destination. Usually those steps seemed quite reasonable at the time, and they were generally taken with the best intentions in the world, and almost invariably they form a chain of events which might have been broken almost anywhere. So now.

It began with the decision not to put the colored division first. A little later Grant was to admit that this decision was a mistake, but it was made for what seemed excellent reasons. The battle that was coming up was a gamble at best. Nobody could be sure that the mine would actually have the effect Pleasants and Burnside believed it would have. If it did not, the troops that led in the assault would be butchered. If those troops happened to be colored men without combat experience it would immediately be argued that they had been sacrificed callously because no one cared what happened to them. (The argument would be made, incidentally, by some of the most vocal and determined arguers that ever lived, the abolitionists and the radical Republicans.) Neither Grant nor Meade felt that that was a proper risk to take.

But this decision started all of the trouble, because its effect was to deflate Burnside completely. Until now, Burnside had done what a good corps commander ought to do. He had seen merit in an unorthodox plan proposed by a subordinate, he had fought to get the idea approved, and he had supported it when higher authority failed to support it. But from this moment on he was as poor a general as a grown man can be, and both the army and the Union cause as a whole would have been much better off if he had taken to his bed, pulled the covers over his handsome face, and let someone else take charge.

First of all he had to pick another division to lead the attack, and he called in the commanding officers of his three white divisions. These were General Potter, to whom Colonel Pleasants had first suggested the mine, a capable man with a good record; General Orlando B. Willcox, a veteran who had been commanding a division ever since Antietam; and Brigadier General James H. Ledlie, a civil engineer without military training or experience when the war began, who had come into the army as major in a New York heavy artillery regiment and who had only recently risen to division command.

Burnside seems to have been pretty numb when he talked with these three generals. He explained that plans had been changed and one of their divisions would have to lead the attack. He confessed that he could not for the life of him see any reason to prefer one division or one general over the other two. Therefore, said Burnside, why should they not simply draw lots to see which division should go in first?[6]

Down under the fabulous whiskers and the kindly dignity, Burnside was a gambler. In the Mexican War he had almost been cashiered because of his weakness for risking everything on the turn of a card. This time he was gambling far beyond his means, and chance played him false. The luck of the draw, when they finally got down to pulling for the short straw, decreed that Ledlie's division must take the lead.

Why Burnside did not immediately call for a new deal is past understanding. Of all of his divisions Ledlie's was the weakest, and of all of his generals Ledlie was the most unfit. The whole division had grown notoriously gun-shy during the past month, and one of its two brigades was made up largely of heavy artillery regiments and dismounted cavalry. Although the heavies had turned into first-rate soldiers for the rest of the army, they were not highly regarded in the IX Corps. A few weeks earlier Burnside himself had said of them: "They are worthless. They didn't enlist to fight and it is unreasonable to expect it of them. In the attack last night I couldn't find thirty of them." But chance had put Ledlie's division in the lead and Burnside let it ride; and chance further decreed that when Ledlie formed his men for the charge it was the weak brigade that was put in front.[7]

The real trouble, however, was in Ledlie himself.

The army contained a good many poor generals, but it had very few who were ever accused of personal cowardice. Ledlie was one who was so accused. His subordinates knew him as a weakling. In the June 18 attack, while his men fought to carry a Rebel entrenchment, Ledlie had taken to the bottle, and at a climactic moment of the fight he had been stretched out on the ground in a safe place, the world forgetting and by the world forgot. His soldiers knew it and his junior officers knew it, but the IX Corps somehow was the kind of corps in which a thing like that could escape the notice of the commanding general, so Burnside did not know it. Burnside combined the great virtue of being loyal to his underlings with the terrible weakness of being quite unable to tell a good operator from a bad one, and now he was entrusting the supreme assault of the army's career to a soldier who was taken with palsy whenever it came time to go out where enemy bullets were flying.[8]

For good or for ill, the day ended and there was a stir all along the line. The secret of the mine had not been too well kept, and there had been gossip about it for days, but most Federals had at last begun to treat it as the Confederates did—as a rumor which someone had probably dreamed up over a jug of commissary whisky—and few people had taken it very seriously. Still, as June 29 drew to a close, there were omens for all to see. Sick men in the field hospitals were sent back to City Point. There was a great riding to and fro of staff officers and couriers, and practically every unit in the corps was being moved from one place to another. Ferrero's colored troops were brought forward, after dark, and lined up in the bottom of the ravine. They were full of enthusiasm, because in all of the excitement no one had thought to tell them that assignments had been changed, and they still supposed that they were going to lead in the attack. Indeed, they were the only division in the corps which believed that it knew what was going to happen.[9]

During the night Hancock's men came back from the north side of the James, and Meade and Grant got up early and went to Burnside's headquarters, half a mile behind the front—a convenient place, connected with other commands by telegraph, which Meade had designated as temporary headquarters for the army.

Burnside, meanwhile, went forward to a fourteen-gun battery that had been built on a hill a few hundred yards back of the entrance to the mine. The night wore away, silent except for the shuffling of thousands of men moving to their places, and a little after three o'clock in the morning Pleasants sent a man into the mine and shaft to set fire to the fuse.

Back on the hills behind the line the artillerists were ready. They had previously trained their pieces on their targets, and the guns and mortars were all loaded, and from three o'clock on the gunners were standing by, lanyards in hand, ready to fire at the word of command.[10] In the trenches, Ledlie's men were standing up, not knowing what was coming except that they realized they were about to be pushed into a big fight. On the slope behind them, Potter's and Willcox's divisions were waiting, similarly tense and ignorant. Back of all of them were Ferrero's colored men, massed at the bottom of the ravine, expecting at any moment to get word to go in and capture Petersburg. General Burnside stood in the battery, serene in his ineffable rectitude, conscious that his baggage was packed and that he could take up headquarters in the Rebel city on a moment's notice.

Half-past three came, with the high command fingering watches and staring off into the dark, and nothing happened. Another half hour went by, and half an hour more on top of that, and the silence was unbroken, except for the occasional discharge of some wakeful picket's musket. Grant got impatient, and at last he told Meade to have Burnside make his charge regardless: something had gone wrong with the mine, and there was no use waiting any longer.[11] In the east the sky was turning gray—and five eighths of Lee's army was north of the James River, with the full strength of the Army of the Potomac massed to smash through the fraction that was left.

Grant was impatient, and Meade was impatient, and probably even Burnside was getting a little restless; but the man who was really excited was Colonel Pleasants. About the time Grant was saying that the charge had better go ahead without the explosion, Pleasants called Sergeant Harry Reese, the mine boss, and told him to go into the tunnel and see what was the matter.

In went Reese, on as nerve-racking an assignment as the war could produce, groping forward all bent over along 400 feet of a dark tunnel, never sure that the solid earth ahead was not going to quake and heave and tumble to bury him forever. He got to the fuse, traced it, and found that the spark had died at a place where one fuse had been splied to another. He started back to get a new fuse, found Lieutenant Jacob Douty coming in, at Pleasants's direction, with the material he needed, and he and Douty went back to the splice and made a new connection. Then he lit the spark again, and he and Lieutenant Douty came out of the tunnel as fast as they could travel[12]—and the sky grew lighter in the east, so that ridges and trees and hillocks became dark shadows outlined against the dying night, and the whole Army of the Potomac stood by gripping its muskets, waiting for nobody knew just what.

Four forty-five: and at last it happened.

To the men who were waiting in the front line it seemed to occur in slow motion: first a long, deep rumble, like summer thunder rolling along a faraway horizon, then a swaying and swelling of the ground up ahead, with the solid earth rising to form a rounded hill, everything seeming very gradual and leisurely. Then the rounded hill broke apart, and a prodigious spout of flame and black smoke went up toward the sky, and the air was full of enormous clods of earth as big as houses, of brass cannon and detached artillery wheels, of wrecked caissons and fluttering tents and weirdly tumbling human bodies; and there was a crash "like the noise of great thunders," followed by other, lesser explosions, and all of the landscape along the firing line had turned into dust and smoke and flying debris, choking and blinding men and threatening to engulf Burnside's whole army corps.

Different men saw it and felt it in different ways. A soldier in the 36th Massachusetts wrote that "we witnessed a volcano and experienced an earthquake," yet an officer in Ferrero's division, standing not a third of a mile away from the explosion, recalled it as "a dull, heavy thud, not at all startling ... a heavy, smothered sound, not nearly so distinct as a musket shot." A man in Pleasants's own 48th Pennsylvania remembered it as "a magnificent spectacle," and another soldier recalled that a bronze cannon was tossed nearly over to the Union line. To one man the whole thing looked like "a waterspout as seen at sea," another felt it as "a heavy shaking of the earth, with a rumbling, muffled sound," and to men in Hancock's corps, waiting behind the artillery, it seemed that the solid earth went up "like an enormous whirlwind."[13]

The gunners had been waiting a long time, and some of them had their eyes fixed on the Confederate redoubt, and they jerked their lanyards as soon as they saw the ground begin to rise, so that the crash of their own guns rocked the air before the sound of the explosion reached them. There was a tremendous concussion from the artillery, with more guns beng fired than the Union army had fired in the great artillery duel at Gettysburg. An overwhelming cloud of white smoke from the guns went tumbling down into the ravine and overflowed the farther crest to mix with the hanging black dust and smoke from the mine, so that all along the Yankee line the air was dark as midnight, lit by brief stabbing flames as the shell began to go off.[14]

The troops which had been waiting to make the charge saw a hillside fly up in their faces, and it looked as if the mass of earth was going to fall on them, so that many men turned and ran, and it was five or ten minutes before the officers could get them reformed. Then the order for the charge was sounded and Ledlie's division started to make its attack—at which crucial moment the soldiers realized that nobody had prepared the way for them, so that the kind of charge which everybody had counted on was completely impossible.

In Meade's orders there had been a provision for leveling the parapet so that a line of battle could swing up out of the trench and go forward in fighting formation, but this assignment had dropped out of sight somewhere between "I ordered it done" and "Nobody told me to do it." Nothing whatever had been done. The leading brigade was standing in the bottom of an eight-foot ditch, and men who were loaded down with muskets and cartridge boxes and haversacks just could not scale the wall.

One officer, aware that time was a-wasting, had a squad improvise a ladder by jabbing bayonets into the log wall and holding the outer ends while their comrades climbed up and over. In another place, men tore down sandbags and piled them into a clumsy sort of stairway. Finally, with an additional ten minutes lost, a straggling line of men got up out of the trench and began to run forward by twos and threes—a thin trickle of wholly disorganized men, rather than the connected wave of a line of battle.[15]

Stumbling up the slope through dust and smoke, these men got to the place where the Confederate redoubt had been and found themselves peering down into a great smoking crater.

One hundred and seventy feet of the Confederate line had been blown up. In its place there was a huge chasm, 60 feet across and 30 feet deep. All around this crater, balanced on its rim and tumbled over the ground on every side, were big hunks of solid clay, broken timbers, dismounted guns, and lesser wreckage of every kind. Down at the bottom there was more of the same, including many human bodies. Some Southerners, still living, had been buried to their waists, some had only their heads above the earth. Others had been buried head downward, their legs protruding into the air. As the men of Ledlie's leading brigade came up they paused, stupefied by the sight; then they slid and scrambled down into the crater and began to uproot the buried Confederates. An officer got one squad together to dig out a couple of half-buried cannon.

Nothing could be seen very clearly, for smoke and dust still filled the air. To the rear the Federal guns kept up a furious bombardment, and there was no return fire. For 200 yards on each side of the crater the Confederate trenches were empty, the men who had inhabited them having taken to their heels when the mine blew up. Here and there a few stout souls began to fire their muskets into the haze about the crater, but half an hour would pass before their fire would have any appreciable effect.

Colonel Pleasants's little plan could not possibly have been more successful. Right in the middle of the impregnable Confederate chain of defenses it had created a gap 500 yards wide, and all the IX Corps had to do was march through and take the ridge. It would need to move briskly, because the gap was not going to stay open very long, but at five o'clock on this morning of July 30 decisive victory was less than half an undefended mile away.

But the one thing which Burnside's corps could not do that morning was to move briskly.

While one of Ledlie's brigades was getting down into the crater and acting partly like a rescue squad, partly like a salvage party, and partly like a group of sight-seers, his other brigade came dribbling out of the Federal trenches to support it. Those engineer parties which were to have cleared the way for the attacking columns had not materialized, and so the only gap in the abatis and *chevaux-de-frise* was right in front of the crater, where the earth thrown out by the explosion had buried the entanglements. This second brigade thus came forward through a funnel which led it straight toward the crater, and since the men were not coming up in regular formation—getting over the parapet was still a matter of every man for himself—and since nobody in particular was shooting at them, the men trotted up to the rim to have a look. While stray officers were urging everyone to continue the advance, most of the men slid down to the bottom of the crater, and presently almost all of Ledlie's division was jammed in there, a confused and aimless mob wholly out of control.

Not a vestige of military organization remained. Officers could not find their men and men could not find their officers, and there was a good deal of rather aimless activity. Along the farther rim of the crater, some industrious souls were trying to prepare a defensive line. The officer who had been digging up the buried cannon was putting men to work to horse them up to the rim where they could be fired—a difficult job, since the final feet of the crater wall were practically vertical—and he had other details hunting about to find the Rebel gunners' magazine. Half-entombed Confederates were still being dug up, and a few files of dazed prisoners were being sent to the rear. A few officers were yelling themselves hoarse, trying to get the men to climb up out of the crater and go on with the attack, but hardly anyone was paying any attention to them.[16]

This, of course, was the kind of situations which generals in charge of infantry divisions had been created to unscramble. Now was the moment for the division commander to take charge, restore order, pull the men out of the pit, form a coherent line of battle, and make his attack. But General Ledlie, who commanded this division, was snugly tucked away in a bombproof 400 yards behind the line, plying himself with rum borrowed from a brigade surgeon. From first to last he never saw the explosion, the soldiers, the crater, or the charge. Now and then reports would come back to him, and he would dispatch a runner with the order that everyone must move forward to the crest of the ridge. Beyond that he did nothing and was capable of doing nothing.[17] And General Burnside, back in the fourteen-gun battery, serenely unaware that anything was wrong, was busily ordering fresh troops forward.

The fresh troops were Potter's and Willcox's divisions. Time would have been saved if these troops had been lined up in brigade front just behind the front-line trench, but it was held that troops moving forward to the front ought to go up through the covered way—after all, that was what the thing had been built for—and so two infantry divisions were sent up a winding ditch that was wide enough for no more than two or three men abreast, colliding with stragglers, walking wounded, couriers, and other persons, and in due time they got into the front-line trench and scrambled up sandbag stairways, bayonet ladders, and what-not and went forward through the gap toward the crater. Their officers steered them off to the right and left, so that the empty Confederate trenches adjoining the crater could be possessed, and very slowly and with much confusion a trickle of Federal troops began to come up into line on each side of Ledlie's disorganized division.[18]

Meanwhile, the Confederates were rapidly coming to. On the right and left, regiments were being formed so that they could fire on the flanks of the attacking column. Between the crater and the ridge there was a shallow ravine—luckily, from the Southern viewpoint, it was out of reach of the Federal cannon—and an alert Confederate general put troops in it, and the fire from these men was beginning to be very heavy. The golden half hour in which the ridge could have been taken effortlessly was gone forever, and any advance that was made now would be made only after a hard fight.

After Potter's and Willcox's men had moved out into the empty trenches they began to go forward. The going was very bad. The ground beyond the trenches was a labyrinth of bombproofs, rifle pits, covered ways, and support trenches, and in many places the advance was a hoptoad business of jumping into a hole in the ground, scrambling out on the other side, jumping into another hole, and then repeating the scramble. The rising tempo of Confederate musketry did not make this kind of progress any easier.

Worse yet, Rebel artillery was coming into action, with power. A quarter of a mile north of the crater there was a four-gun battery, and the Southern gunners who had decamped when the mine was blown up came back to these guns and trained them on the Yankees who were trying to advance from the captured trenches. Federal artillery pounded this battery mercilessly, but it was well protected by solid earthen traverses and, although the shell dug up the ground all about until it looked as if the whole area had been plowed, the guns remained in action, putting canister right down the flank of the Federal battle line. On the other side of the crater the story was somewhat the same, with a battery posted so as to enfilade the Federal lines from the left. This battery also drew a storm of fire, but there was one gun that could not be silenced and it kept firing canister at deadly close range.

Up on the ridge west of the crater the Rebels put sixteen guns in line. The Federal gunners swept the ridge with overwhelming fire, but the Jerusalem Plank Road was sunken and offered a natural gun pit, and although ten of the sixteen guns were wrecked, the six that remained could not be subdued. In addition, the Confederates had mortars tucked away in hollow ground beyond the crater, and these began to toss shell into the dense jam of Federal soldiers.[19]

Minute by minute the situation grew worse. Potter's men gained ground on the right of the crater, but they were under a killing fire and their battle line was slowly pressed back. Mixed elements from half a dozen different commands crawled forward a few dozen yards from the crater itself in a valiant attempt to reach and silence the guns on the ridge, but the Rebels had a good second line in operation now and there were not enough men in this attack to break it. On the left of the crater Willcox's men could do nothing but cower in the captured trench and keep up an ineffective musketry fire.

Meade had been right: if the attack was to succeed at all it would succeed in the first rush. The first rush had failed, and the failure was both incredible and irretrievable. What could have been done easily at five o'clock had become a matter of great difficulty by six o'clock and by seven it had become virtually impossible. The fight now was just one more dreary repetition of the old attempt to capture entrenched positions. Most of the men in the attacking forces knew it perfectly well, and they hugged the ground. To all intents and purposes the battle was already lost.

But the high command did not know it. Both corps and army headquarters were helpless. Burnside's command post was a quarter of a mile behind the front and Meade's was half a mile behind that, and the fight was out of their hands. An officer might be sent forward to get news. He would spend five or ten minutes jostling forward along the covered way, and take his look around, and then spend another five or ten minutes getting back. By the time his report had been assimilated and orders had been started forward the situation would have changed completely—above all other battles, this one was fluid and every minute counted—and the new orders would be worse than useless.[20]

Burnside might well have been up at the crater himself. Grant said later that if he had commanded a corps in a fight like this, that was where he would have been[21]—but Burnside was a headquarters operator, and this was Fredericksburg all over again: reports coming in out of a blinding fog, orders going forward into the fog, nothing that was ordered having any relation to reality, the men who wrote the orders never once seeing the place where the orders were to be executed or the people who were to execute them; and all Burnside could do was to tell all and sundry to attack and keep on attacking. Meade might have gone forward, but he had announced beforehand that he could be reached at IX Corps headquarters and it seemed to him now that it would only cause more confusion if he left that spot. So he communicated with Burnside by telegraph, and he told Warren and Ord to get their own troops moving to help the attack; and nothing that happened up around the tangle of crater and captured trenches and broken earth was in the least as the officers in the rear thought it was.

Warren went to talk to Burnside about where the V Corps ought to go in, and Burnside suggested that he go forward and take a look, and Warren did so, and when he got back he and Burnside discussed the situation in some detail, after which Warren went over to his own headquarters and ordered Ayres's division forward.

Ord tried to advance, but the way was jammed with IX Corps troops and hardly more than a handful of his men were able to move. At 7:20 Burnside sent a wire to Meade saying that he was doing everything possible to push his men forward to the crest but that it was very hard work, and Meade lost his temper and sent an angry wire asking him what on earth was going on and snapping: "I wish to know the truth and desire an immediate answer." Then Burnside lost his temper and wired Meade that Meade had been "unofficer-like and ungentlemanly"; and up in front the Confederates stitched together a semicircle of fire around the attacking troops and the advance came to a hopeless standstill.[22]

At precisely which moment orders went down to the bottom of the ravine from corps headquarters telling Ferrero's division of colored troops to advance and seize the crest.

The colored boys had been under arms since dawn, and as far as they knew their original assignment was unchanged: charge straight across the place where the mine had exploded and take the high ground that overlooked Petersburg. Top authorities had said that they must not lead the charge lest they be sacrificed; now, with the battle lost beyond recall, they were being sent in for a job that was not even as good as a forlorn hope. They got into the covered way, struggled up to the front line, scrambled over the parapet and ran forward with a cheer. By now the Confederate defense was able to lay heavy fire on the ground between the Union trench and the crater, so that getting forward was costly. As the men advanced General Ferrero dropped off in the same bombproof that housed General Ledlie and borrowed a swig of his jug of rum, leaving his brigadiers to direct the fight.[23]

It was impossible to go through the crater, because it was full of white troops. The colonel of the leading regiment saw this difficulty and led the command off to the right. By this time most of Potter's men had been shoved out of the trenches they had seized, and the colored regiment found itself running along between the Rebel abatis and a trenchful of Southern infantry—so close to the trench that some of the men were bayoneted as they ran, and those who were shot bore powder burns from the flash of Rebel muskets. As soon as the tail of the regiment had cleared the crater the colonel gave the order: "By the left flank—march!" followed by "Charge!" and the men sprang into the trench, using bayonet and clubbed musket, taking prisoners and a stand of colors. A regimental officer had to intervene to keep the men from killing their prisoners.[24]

In the captured trench the colored troops re-formed for a further advance. It was not easy, because the trench was full of dead and wounded men of both armies, and from in front and from the right the Confederates were laying down a blistering fire. A colonel tried to organize a charge, but when he went over the parapet he could not get more than fifty men to follow him, and the hostile fire quickly knocked them back. Then, while officers were trying to figure out what to do next, a runner came up with a message from General Ferrero: "If you have not already done so, you will immediately proceed to take the crest in your front"—which may have sounded like a reasonable order to a man safely tucked away in a dugout far behind the front.[25]

Well, they tried. First the officers leaped up on the parapet, waving their swords and shouting, and most of these were shot before they took another step. Then a scattering of soldiers followed them—200 men, perhaps, from three regiments—and a thin little cheer went up, and the ragged line ran forward. They got almost to the hidden ravine where the Confederates were waiting, and the Rebels came out with a countercharge, and for a moment there was vicious combat rocking back and forth in the open. Then the charge broke, and the colored men came running back, most of their officers gone, regimental and company organizations wholly mixed up, furious Southern infantry on their heels. Such white troops as were on the ground were caught up in this retreat, and in another moment a disorganized mass of black and white soldiers in blue uniforms was running desperately for cover, diving into the trenches and rifle pits or streaming for the deep haven of the crater.

In the captured trenches there was a dreadful crush of men. An officer wrote afterward that people were packed in so tightly that he literally could not raise his arms from his side. The Confederates had followed close, and they poked rifles over the edge of the trench and fired into the huddle at three-foot range. Some of them jumped down in with bayonets, and men began to surrender, and the soldiers remembered hearing the Confederates crying: "Take the white man—kill the nigger!" There was a blind flurry of bitter fighting in the maze of trenches and rifle pits and dugouts, and eventually the whole section of captured trench was lost and the Union survivors got into the crater and prepared to hang on as long as they could.[26]

It was all over now, except for the killing. Grant had recognized failure and had told Meade to get the men back and call the whole operation off, and Meade had passed the word on to Burnside, but Burnside still thought that the attack somehow could be reorganized and made successful, and no recall was sounded. Hundreds of Union soldiers were jammed into the crater, most of them down at the bottom where they could do no fighting whatever. Men up along the rim were standing on a slope so steep that after a man fired his rifle he had to turn around, dig in with his heels, and brace his shoulders against the dirt in order to reload.[27]

Confederate mortars had the range and they were dropping shell into the crater on a helpless target that they could not miss; men who got out alive remembered a horrible debris of severed limbs and heads flying through the air after each shell exploded. The sun was high in the sky now and it beat down with unrelenting heat, terribly magnified in this steaming pit, and thirst seemed to be a worse foe than Confederate infantry. A Rebel countercharge came to the very edge of the crater, and Negroes lined the rim and fired and drove the attackers back, and the noise and all the heat and the exploding shell beat on men's brains and dazed them so that nothing was remembered very clearly afterward.

Here and there, officers were able to organize details to search among the dead and wounded for cartridges. Some men were ordered to run back to the Union line with a cluster of canteens to get water, and a few of them managed to make the round trip without being killed. More than 200 men dropped unconscious from sheer heat and exhaustion, and a captain in the 45th Pennsylvania wrote: "The loss of life was terrible. There was death below as well as above ground in the crater. It seemed impossible to maintain life from the intense heat of the sun." He noted that his regiment lost 67 of the 110 men who had gone in.[28]

Somehow, finally—long after noon—it ended. The men who could do so went back to the Union lines; the others stayed where they were and either died or went off to Confederate prison camps. Burnside continued to insist to Meade that the attack could still succeed, but Ord bluntly told Meade that it was non-sense, and defeat at last was accepted. Through it all, Colonel Pleasants had been standing on the parapet of the fourteen-gun battery where he could watch the proceedings, and he stormed and swore in unregimented fury, telling Burn-side that he had "nothing but a damned set of cowards in his brigade command-ers"; and one of the men in the 48th Pennsylvania recorded that "Pleasants was awful mad when he saw how things were going on."[29]

Mad Colonel Pleasants might well have been. Never before had the army met so completely ignominious a defeat. Grant summed it up by telling Halleck that it was "the saddest affair I have witnessed in the war," and he added: "Such an opportunity for carrying fortifications I have never seen and do not expect again to have." A man in the 36th Massachusetts wrote that this day had been "the saddest in the history of the IX Corps," and a boy in the 48th Pennsylvania wrote to his sister:

"I expected to wriite to you of one of the most glorious victories that was ever won by this army, but instead of a victory I have to write about the greatest shame and disgrace that ever happened to us. The people at home may look at it as nothing but a mere defeat, but I look at it as a disgrace to our corps."[30]

In the 115th New York, a sergeant blew his top from heat and fatigue, sprang up and cried, "We'll fight 'em 'till we die, won't we, boys?" and then dropped unconscious. And in Ferrero's division it was observed that the colored troops never again sang their song:

> We looks like men a'marching on;
> We looks like men o' war.[31]

As such things went, the great battle of the crater was not, perhaps, unduly expensive. When the butcher's bill was added up it recorded a loss of 3,798 men, more than a third of them in the colored division. Measured by the standards of the Wilderness and Spotsylvania, this was comparatively mild. Most of the cas-ualties occurred after Grant and Meade had ordered the attack given up, when the men were trying to do nothing more than get back to their own trenches.

Yet the casualty lists did not tell the whole story, which indeed was a good deal more complex than most of the participants were able to understand.

Since May 4 everything that had happened had been part of one continuous battle, a battle three months long, with advance and retreat and triumph and di-saster all taking place together, so that words like victory and defeat had lost their meaning. All that had gone before was no more than prelude. The nation itself had been heated to an unimaginable pitch by three years of war and now it had been put on the anvil and the hammer was remorselessly coming down, stroke after clanging stroke, beating a glowing metal into a different shape.

There would be change and the war was bringing it, even though it might be that the war could not bring victory. The war had taken on a new magnitude, and perhaps it was no longer the kind of struggle anybody could win. But it was moving inexorably toward its end, and when it ended many things would end with it, in the South and in the North as well. Some of these were things that ought to end because they shackled men to the past, and some of them were fit to be laid away in the shadowland of dreams that are remembered forever, but in any case they were being brought to an end. After that there could be a new beginning.

FIVE

Away, You Rolling River

1. SPECIAL TRAIN FOR MONOCACY JUNCTION

PRIVATE SPINK belonged to the 147th Regiment of Ohio National Guard Infantry, and in a modest and wholly innocent way he symbolized what was wrong with the defenses of Washington.

The 147th was doing a 100-day tour of duty, and it had been sent to Washington to help occupy the defensive lines so that the troops regularly in garrison could go down to fight the Rebels around Petersburg. Presumably Private Spink was a good soldier. He had recently been made acting ordnance sergeant, and with six other privates of the 147th he had been detailed to take charge of a battery of fieldpieces at the eastern end of the Chain Bridge, the farthest upstream of three Potomac River bridges which connected the District of Columbia with Virginia. This bridge had been guarded against Rebel intrusion ever since the early days of the war, and it was a key spot in the capital's defenses, and Private Spink and his detail cleaned the guns daily and swept the wooden gun platforms, and periodically they took the ammunition out of the magazine and exposed it briefly to the air so that it would not deteriorate. No one made any complaint about the way this duty was performed, but in July of 1864, when a Confederate army came north to menace the capital, it suddenly developed that cleaning the guns and airing the ammunition taxed the abilities of these seven guardsmen to their absolute limit.

Which is to say that not one of the seven knew anything at all about artillery. When an inspecting colonel from General Halleck's staff came out to look at the defenses he learned that neither Private Spink nor any of the men with him even knew how to load the guns, let alone fire them. This was quite natural, since they had been trained strictly as infantry, but the colonel wondered what they would do if the invading Confederates showed up across the river and tried to march over into the national capital. He asked the nearest officer—a Veteran Reserve Corps lieutenant, who with sixty-three men was responsible for this whole section of the defenses—and the lieutenant had a ready answer. In such case, he said, he would have his men remove the planks of the bridge flooring, and pile them up in a barricade at the Washington end. He would also close the gates which gave access to the bridge. He understood, further, that one of the western piers of the bridge had been mined so that it could be blown up, but when the inspector looked into it he found that this was not true.

It would have been unfair to blame any of this on the Reserve lieutenant or the acting ordnance sergeant, since neither men was in any way responsible. But the condition of things in their part of the line was fairly typical of the condition elsewhere. The next bridge downstream, for instance, was Aqueduct Bridge in Georgetown, and it was guarded by two dozen men under a Reserve captain. This man said that if attacked he wold close the gates of the bridge at the Georgetown end. He believed there were heavy bars lying around somewhere, although he had never tried them to see whether they would fit the staples in the

609

gate and stockade. The inspector took the trouble to find them and test them. They did fit. Comforted by that much, he went his way.

On the land front, the chief engineer of the Department of Washington reported with military horror that brush was growing all over the approaches to the line, in such quantities that attacking troops could easily get quite close to the parapet under cover. He urged strongly that details be assigned to cut this brush and provide the defense with a clear field of fire. At about the same time a War Department major general who had access to the White House told President Lincoln that the Rebels were really getting close and that "An enterprising general could take the city." He said that when he mentioned all of this to General Halleck he was told that the responsibility was Grant's and not Halleck's. This worried the major general, because Grant was quite busy down in front of Petersburg, and he told the President that Halleck seemed very apathetic. Mr. Lincoln nodded.

"That's his way," he said. "He is always apathetic."[1]

It was a bad time for apathy, because the approaching Confederates were under the command of Jubal Early, who was nothing if not enterprising. He had been moving down the Shenandoah Valley ever since General Hunter retreated from the vicinity of Lynchburg, and he had perhaps 15,000 men with him—veteran troops as good as any in the land, their number magnified by panic rumor to practically any figure which frightened imagination cared to think of.

The Washington defenses were extremely strong if there were men to hold them. Much time and money had been spent on them, beginning 'way back in the McClellan era, and they had been laid out according to the best military standards of the day. From the banks of the Potomac northwest of Chain Bridge, all the way around the city to the Potomac shore opposite Alexandria, the lines ran in a ponderous unbroken horseshoe, with a fort on every hill, trenches connecting the forts, and heavy guns posted to cover all the ground out in front. Over on the Virginia side it was the same, with another semicircle of works running from above Chain Bridge down to the lower edge of Alexandria. No one could approach the city from any direction without running into powerful fortifications. Yet fortifications needed soldiers in order to be effective, and now the soldiers were lacking.

If Grant had risked something by taking the soldiers away, the risk had been carefully calculated. What had thrown the calculations out of gear was the eccentric notion of strategy held by General Hunter.

While the Army of the Potomac remained on the offensive, Lee could not bring his own army up across the border as he had done in 1862 and 1863. The only danger would come from lesser detachments advancing down the Shenandoah Valley, and as long as Hunter and his troops were in the valley that way was barred. As far as the security of Washington was concerned it did not matter much whether Hunter was advancing, retreating, or sitting down. If he and his men were in the Valley, that was enough.

But when Hunter found Early ready to fight him in front of Lynchburg, and decided to run for shelter, he concluded for some incomprehensible reason that he had better run off through the West Virginia mountains instead of back down the valley toward Winchester and Harper's Ferry. That took his entire army out of the war for more than a fortnight, and it left the valley wide open for any use the Confederates wanted to make of it. Of this opening General Early promptly took full advantage.

Hunter could never see what was wrong with his move. He wrote to Stanton and he wrote to Lincoln, protesting that he had done everything for the best and complaining that he was unfairly blamed. Six months later he was still at it, writing to Grant, reciting all of his troubles with the undisciplined troops and unskilled generals he had inherited from the blessed Sigel and complaining that no one ever told him he had anything to do with the defense of Washington.

After the war he was obtuse enough to write to Robert E. Lee, asking if Lee did not agree that the retreat into the mountains had been strategically sound. Lee, who detested him, replied with dead-pan courtesy that he hardly felt competent to pass on Hunter's reasons for making that move, since he did not know what they were; but he said that the move itself had been a tremendous help to Lee personally and to the Southern Confederacy in general.[2]

An aging Regular with sagging cheeks, a stringy mustache, and a habit of writing ill-tempered letters, Hunter had had rather an odd career. In February of 1861 he had been one of four army officers assigned to guard Mr. Lincoln on the President-elect's trip from Springfield to Washington. Out of this experience Hunter got a dislocated shoulder, received when a crowd surged out of hand at Buffalo; but a little later, after Fort Sumter, he got a major general's commission, and when Frémont was removed from command in Missouri that fall it was Hunter who was put in his place. He did not last very long in that important job, and presently he was on the shelf in Kansas, with few troops and fewer responsibilities, and he complained about it so gracelessly that even Lincoln, who could put up with almost anything, told him it was hard to answer "so ugly a letter" in good temper.

Still later Hunter had been given command along the Carolina coast, where he had endeared himself to the radicals by proclaiming the emancipation of slaves some months before Mr. Lincoln was ready for such a policy. Naturally, he had been removed, and when the War Department this spring picked him to command in the Valley, Grant had approved on the simple theory that anybody would be better than Sigel.

His stay in the Valley had been brief enough and his exit had been disastrous, but in one way he had made his presence felt—by burning Virginia Military Institute and the home of Virginia's Governor Letcher. His troops took their cue from him and did a good deal of looting and house burning on their own hook, and when Early led his Confederates north of the Potomac the Southerners were not in a mood to be gentle with Northern civilians. One of Early's officers who surveyed the damage Hunter's troops had left behind them wrote that it was very hard to admit that vengeance belonged solely to the Lord.[3] So the Confederates levied heavy cash contributions on such towns as Frederick, Maryland, and when they seized horses and cattle and forage they were less urbane and polite about it than had been the case during the Gettysburg campaign. By the end of the first week in July they were destroying railroad bridges and other property in Maryland east of the great South Mountain ridge, and the long-suffering Baltimore and Ohio Railroad was asking the navy if it could send gunboats to protect railroad property in the upper reaches of Chesapeake Bay.

This call took Secretary Welles over to the War Department, where to his disgust he found that nobody knew anything about Early's army—"its numbers, where it is, or its destination." He wrote in his diary that an attack on Washington probably could not be resisted, and he predicted that such an attack would be made very soon. A couple of days later, on a Sunday, a Navy Department clerk hurried to Mr. Welles's office to tell him that Southern troopers had already crossed the district line and were prowling about in the outskirts of Georgetown. Welles had a low opinion of Halleck and Stanton anyway, and he wrote now that "on our part there is neglect, ignorance, folly, imbecility in the last degree."[4]

The War Department had not been quite as neglectful as Mr. Welles supposed. At the beginning of July Halleck had warned Grant that Early was becoming a menace, and Ricketts's division of the VI Corps had been sent up to Baltimore. There it joined a scratch contingent of miscellaneous troops pulled together by General Lew Wallace, the literary-minded soldier who eventually was to write *Ben Hur,* and Wallace took his command over toward Frederick, to fight the Rebels on the banks of the Monocacy. Early's veterans outnumbered him heavily and they pushed him aside without much delay, but the rest of the VI Corps was embarking on transports at City Point to come north and take a hand in the game, and ocean steamers were coming up the bay with veterans from Emory's XIX Corps, recently on duty in Louisiana. The situation would probably be all right if Early would just allow a few more days' grace.

Early was no time-waster, however. After routing Wallace's command he drove his men on mercilessly in mid-July heat, and by the morning of July 11 his weary advance guard was coming south through Silver Spring, its skirmishers creeping forward toward Fort Stevens, well inside the district line on the Seventh Street Road. Old Francis P. Blair's famous country home was occupied by Rebel officers, who took care not to damage the place unduly but did help themselves to the contents of Mr. Blair's excellent wine cellar. Not far away there was a house owned by Blair's son Montgomery, who was Postmaster General in Lincoln's cabinet, and this house the Rebels burned to the ground, leading Blair to remark bitterly that nothing better could be expected so long as "poltroons and cowards" had control of the United States War Department.[5]

To beat off Early's advance Halleck had very few troops, but he did have plenty of general officers. Among these was dignified Major General Alexander McD. McCook, temporarily without a command, and McCook was sent out to Fort Stevens and told to assume charge of the capital's defenses. He had very little to work with—a regiment of District of Columbia militia, some 4-F's from the Veteran Reserve Corps, a Maine battery, a few National Guard troops on 100-day dty, and a scattering of gunners in the different forts. He put these men in the trenches and had them begin shooting at Early's skirmishers. During the morning the military hospitals were combed out and a number of convalescents, representing nearly every regiment in the Army of the Potomac, was brought out the Seventh Street Road, together with some more Reserve Corps soldiers and odds and ends of dismounted cavalry. Meanwhile General Montgomery C. Meigs, the distinguished quartermaster general of the army, had donned his field uniform and was forming all of the clerks and detailed men of the Quartermaster Corps into a brigade and was marching them around to the arsenal to draw weapons. During the day he went trooping out to the scene of action with some 1,500 of these extemporized soldiers. At McCook's direction he occupied a mile or more of the trench to the right of Fort Stevens.[6]

The forts and trenches were good, and this assemblage of soldiers might do well enough if nobody pushed very hard. General Early—closer to the Capitol dome than any other armed Confederate during all of the war—was peering south from the high ground a mile north of Fort Stevens, getting ready to push just as soon as he could figure out just what was ahead of him.

He was a salty and a picturesque character, this Jubal Early, and a very dangerous opponent to boot. A West Pointer who had given up the Army for the law some years previously, he had been prosecuting attorney of Rockingham County before the war, and he was stooped and grizzled and sardonic, not greatly loved by other ranking Confederate officers because of his habit of blunt, sarcastic speech; an exceedingly capable soldier, grim as old Stonewall himself, a driver who could be counted on to get the last ounce of advantage out of the baffling, almost incomprehensible opportunity which faced him on this eleventh of July.

When General Lee sent him north, neither he nor Early had much hope that Washington could actually be captured. The idea was principally to make trouble and to joggle Grant's elbow. In former years the Lincoln administration had shown itself abnormally sensitive to any threat to the capital, and there was a chance that this thrust might force Grant to raise the siege of Petersburg and come back to save Washington.

If this could not be done it was just possible that Early could slide clear around Washington on the northern side, strike down southeast, and capture the prison camp at Point Lookout on the shore of Chesapeake Bay, releasing some thousands of Confederate prisoners of war. Failing that, he could at least make a great nuisance of himself, collect supplies in Maryland, and in general disarrange Federal strategy. Early's problem this morning was to determine exactly how much of an opening was in front of him now, while inexpert tacticians were assembling third-rate troops in the lines adjoining Fort Stevens.

The balancing of risks and opportunities was delicate and perplexing, and if "Old Jube" swore and bit off another chew of tobacco—as he very probably did—it could hardly be wondered at. He knew that the trenches before him were too strong to be taken if any number of regular troops occupied them. He also knew that even if he broke the line and got all the way to downtown Washington he could not hope to stay there very long, since the country in his rear was all swarming with Federal troops—Wallace's men, and Sigel's, and Hunter's dispirited army coming back from West Virginia—and in time the Yankees would undoubtedly form these into a compact mass that would bar the way home. Early's own army was small and very tired, and a hard fight might cripple it so badly that it could never return to Virginia, and Lee was so pressed for manpower that he simply could not afford to lose these men. The forces that made for caution were strong.[7]

But the possibilities also were good. No hasty collection of convalescents, casuals, and government clerks could hope to bar the way for the lean veterans of the Army of Northern Virginia—the prospect of looting the rich depots of Washington was enough to make these men fight like desperadoes—and the results that would flow from even a temporary occupation of the Federal capital might well be incalculable. If, after all that had happened this spring, a wing of Lee's army could actually seize Washington, the whole course of the war might be different. Anyway, Early was a slugger who never listened to the voice of caution unless he had to, and at last he decided to make the assault. He put sharpshooters into farmhouses to pick off gunners in the Yankee forts, and he wheeled his artillery forward and pressed his skirmishers in closer, and he began to get ready for a big fight.

In the forts and the trenches there were pallid men from hospital and office— "a mild-mannered set," as one observer felt, who looked as if "they would never hurt anyone, not even in self-defense," obviously uncomfortable in their unweathered uniforms, uneasy at the prospect of passing the night in the open air. Downtown there were nervous civilians in the streets, wondering what was going to happen next, listening to the fluttering, pulsing sound of the distant cannon, contemplating flight but not certain where to fly to or how to get there.[8]

But down by the Seventh Street wharf fat-sided steamers were coming up the river, tarred heaving lines snaking ashore to be taken by waiting longshoremen, mates busy about the decks, whistles grunting hoarsely, ships' timbers creaking against the pilings. Then the gangplanks were slung to the wharf, and long lines of tanned men in ragged, dusty, sun-bleached uniforms were coming ashore, forming up on the dock with elbow nudgings and right-dress craning of necks. Up Seventh Street they came, a solid column of soldiers with the Greek cross on their caps and their banners, men who slouched along casually without bothering about alignment, seeming to be in no hurry at all but somehow covering the ground very rapidly.

They were hard-boiled and unemotional, and as they tramped along they looked cynically at the people on the sidewalks, and made mental note of the locations of saloons; and they marched behind tattered, faded, shot-torn banners, and the people on the sidewalk looked at them and set up a sudden cheer, and called out to one another in elated relief: "The Sixth Corps! That's the Sixth Corps!"

From time to time the column would halt for a breather, and every time it halted a certain number of the veterans would slip away and head for a barroom and a glass of something cold, and one of the men who made the march said that not even "the military genius of a Napoleon" could have taken them out that dusty street on a hot July day without loss. The men who did not fall out made caustic remarks about militia and quartermaster clerks and well-fed civilians, and in midafternoon they got up to Fort Stevens and took charge. The amateurs could relax now; the professionals were taking over.[9]

General Wright had galloped on ahead, and General McCook received him with feelings of great relief, and as the head of the corps came up the men of the Army of the Potomac filed right and left into the trenches. One of Wright's men wrote that they found "a rattled lot of defenders, brave enough but with no coherence or organization," and he mentioned seeing a surplus of brigadier generals and a vast number of home guards whose skins looked strangely white and untanned. Out beyond the trenches, he said, he and his mates could see Early's Southerners—"as fine a corps of infantry as ever marched to the tap of a drum"—but the VI Corps was here now and the door was locked, and at the last minute of the last hour the Washington lines were occupied by men who knew how to hold them.[10]

After that it was all over, except for the incidental drama and excitement.

General McCook asked Wright to hold his corps in reserve but to relieve the picket line, and so several hundred of the VI Corps went out beyond the trenches to exchange shots with Early's skirmishers. The fire seemed hot and heavy to the clerks and 100-day militia, but Wright's veterans considered it light and scattering and they went out with nonchalant competence. One of them remembered, with an amused chuckle, that the troops that were being relieved were "astounded at the temerity displayed by these war-worn veterans in going out beyond the breastworks, and benevolently volunteered most earnest words of caution."[11]

Early's skirmishers were 600 yards away, and they were being supported by shellfire, and the veterans moved out and sparred with them, and after a while darkness came and the opposing armies settled down for the night. General Meigs, unused to field work, went along his line of trenches, saw that his men had rations and blankets, and himself went a few hundred yards to the rear, tied his horse to a tree in an apple orchard, and spread his poncho on the ground for a bed—feeling, one gathers, innocently thrilled and pleased with himself. Secretary Welles, who had come out to see what was to be seen, rode back to the city in his carriage, looking at the campfires and knots of lounging soldiers and groups of stragglers and musing: "It was exciting and wild. Much of life, and much of sadness."[12]

Next morning Early tapped harder, just to make certain that the reinforced defenses were as solid as they looked. The VI Corps sent a whole brigade out to meet him, and in Fort Stevens and nearby Fort De Russey the long-range cannon came to life, plowing up the slopes where the Rebel skirmishers were in line and knocking down the houses where the sharpshooters were hiding. The noise echoed and rolled across the open country north of the city, a blanket of ragged white smoke slid down into the hollows, and a trickle of wounded men began to flow back to the rear. Then a carriage pulled up by the barracks that had been built just behind Fort Stevens, and a tall man in frock coat and stovepipe hat got out—an unmilitary figure among all of these soldiers, but moving nonetheless with the air of one used to exercising command—and here was Abraham Lincoln, out to see for himself a little of the death and destruction which he had been living with for three years and more.

General Wright was in the fort, and he greeted the President; and without stopping to think, never imagining that the invitation would be accepted, he asked if Mr. Lincoln would care to get up on the parapet with him and watch the battle. The President said he would like to very much, and while Wright wished earnestly that he could recall his thoughtless words the President clambered up on top of the parapet. He was tall and gaunt, towering over everybody, an obvious target, standing right where Southern sharpshooters were peppering the place with Minié bullets.

Wright begged him to get down, but Lincoln refused, the idea of personal danger seeming not to enter his head. A surgeon who had got up on the parapet was struck, just a few feet away from where Lincoln was standing, and other bullets flicked up the dirt near him, and Wright in desperation moved around to stand between the President and the enemy fire. His entreaties having no effect, Wright at last bluntly told the President that he, General Wright, was in charge of operations here at the fort and that it was his order that the President get down out of danger; and when Lincoln still failed to move, Wright threatened to get a squad of soldiers and remove him by force. This seemed to amuse the President, and while Wright gulped at his brashness in threatening to arrest the commander in chief, Lincoln got down obediently and sat with his back to the parapet.

He was safe enough now, unless some Rebel gunner happened to burst a shell overhead, and Wright felt better. He noticed, however, that Lincoln was forever spoiling the effect by jumping up and peering over the ramparts for another look, and Wright later wrote to a friend: "I could not help thinking that in leaving the parapet he did so rather in deference to my earnestly expressed wishes than from any consideration of personal safety."[13]

Meanwhile the fight was getting warmer. Wright's infantry went forward, taking losses, and Lincoln saw men killed and watched while wounded men were carried to the rear. But Early realized that the situation was hopeless, and after a while he called in his skirmishers, and at dusk he ordered a retreat. He was in an acrid, festive humor, and as his troops fell into column for the march back to Virginia Early turned to an aide and remarked: "Major, we haven't taken Washington, but we've scared Abe Lincoln like hell!" The aide agreed that this was so, but he suggested that when the VI Corps line moved out to drive back Early's skirmishers there might have been a few Confederates who were equally scared. Early chuckled. "That's true," he said, "but it won't appear in history!"[14]

It had been a brisk scrap while it lasted, but one of Wright's veterans confessed that he supposed the Confederates had retired "more we think from the sight of the VI Corps flag than from the number assailing them." A man in the Vermont Brigade wrote that "the dignitaries in the fort returned to their homes, having witnessed as pretty and well-conducted a little fight as was seen during the whole war," and the War Department recorded that the whole business had cost the VI Corps some 200 in killed and wounded. General Meigs took his quartermaster details back to town, proudly writing that he had had command of a battle line two lines long containing 5,000 troops, and he presently got from Secretary Stanton a letter containing a brevet major general's commission and thanking him for his services. The Rebels drew off through Rockville, heading for the Potomac River fords, and some of General McCook's men advanced as far as the Sligo Creek post office, capturing a field hospital containing seventy-odd wounded Southerners plus a corporal's guard of surgeons and orderlies. Washington relaxed. The big scare was over.[15]

It was up to the VI Corps to pursue the enemy, and the pursuit was extremely vigorous. The Vermont Brigade remembered the first night's march out of Washington as one of the worst it ever made. The weather was hot and the roads were dusty, clogged with any number of stragglers and with obstructions which Early's men had thoughtfully left in their wake. By the time the veterans had seen the Confederates out of Maryland they were fully ready to call it quits and take a little rest.

The 2nd Connecticut Heavy Artillery came trailing back to Washington, and to its delight learned that it was to get back its original assignment as heavy artillery—it had been front-line infantry beginning with Spotsylvania Court House, and it had had fearful casualties—and it snuggled down in a fort near Tenallytown, dispossessing an Ohio National Guard outfit "with its gawky officers" and luxuriating in new uniforms, new shoes, and regular rations. It was especially delighted to get, at last, crossed cannon to put on its caps, for these insignia belonged to heavy artillery and the men felt that this made the new incarnation official. They looked fondly at the comfortable living quarters in the fort and told one another that they were going to sleep for a week. However, the very next morning orders were changed and the regiment was put back in the VI Corps infantry column, crossed cannon and all, and it went off on a grinding hike to the Shenandoah Valley to keep Early from launching a new invasion, and it never saw the Tenallytown fort again.[16]

For the VI Corps the next two weeks were a nightmare. The men forded the Potomac and went up through Leesburg and Snickers' Gap to the banks of the Shenandoah, and down at City Point Grant concluded that the danger was over and sent orders for the corps to come back to Petersburg. So there was a hard forced march, and just as the troops reached Washington and prepared to board the transports Early sent his cavalry riding hard up into Pennsylvania, where the men burned the city of Chambersburg—another little dividend on Hunter's depredations in the upper Valley—so once again orders were changed and the corps marched back to Harper's Ferry as fast as it could go, crossing the Potomac there and starting up the Valley again.

There was much straggling on this march, due to heat and general exhaustion and, as a brigade surgeon confessed, to "bad whisky from Washington." The corps had no more than started up the valley than orders were changed once more and everybody ahd to hurry back into Maryland. In the first days of August the men made a bivouac along the Monocacy River not far from Frederick, wondering bleakly what the people in Washington were going to think of next.

Corps morale was down at low-water mark for the war. Originally the men had been delighted to leave Petersburg and come up to Washington, and their appearance as saviors of the capital, the only troops who had ever fought under the eye of Lincoln himself, made them think very highly of themselves. But the marching since then had been harder than anything they had had in all their experience—it was even worse than the man-killing marches they had made in the Gettysburg campaign, which they had always supposed were the worst possible—and when they got to the Monocacy the men were so dead-beat that most regiments made camp with no more than twenty men around the colors. The series of aimless marches and countermarches showed clearly that Washington did not know what it was doing, and one veteran admitted that by this time "the Sixth Corps was, in army parlance, 'about played out.'" Another man wrote that "the thinking soldiers about their campfires felt a discouragement the gloom of the Wilderness had failed to produce."[17]

Still, the campsites by the Monocacy were pleasant, and for a few days there was rest, and with the rest men's spirits rose again. One of the 2nd Connecticut heavies, adjusted at last to the fact that the comforts of the Washington forts would be forever unattainable, grew almost lyrical when he considered the present bivouac:

"The clear, sparkling river ran along the lower edge of it, and the surrounding woods abounded in saplings, poles and brush, for which soldiers can always find so many uses. Regular camp calls were instituted, company and battalion drills ordered, and things began to assume the appearance of a stay." An officer died while the corps was camped here and he was given a full-dress military funeral, whereat all the men wagged their heads. They had seen so many men of all ranks put under the sod without any ceremony at all that this seemed to be an infallible sign that they would stay here for a long time, resting, drilling a little, and regaining their strength.[18]

Emory's men in the XIX Corps felt the same way. They had spent all of the war in the humid heat of Louisiana, and when they made camp by the Shenandoah a few miles from Harper's Ferry they felt that they were in a new world. One soldier wrote glowingly of "the bracing air, the crystal waters, the rolling wheat fields and the beautiful blue mountains," sick men in the field hospitals returned to duty, straggling diminished, and the men looked about them at the open country and the excellent roads and felt that marching in this region might almost be a pleasure.[19]

While the soldiers caught their breath and hoped for the best, Grant had been living through what were probably his most trying moments of the war. He was at City Point, and some sort of curtain seemed to have come down between his headquarters there and the War Department in Washington. He had a good many things on his mind—the tragedy of the mine and the attempted breakthrough came right when all of this frenzied, useless countermarching was going on—and when he sent orders north to govern the use of the troops that were supposed to be rounding up Early's army the orders had to go through Washington, and on their way through things happened to them.

The pursuit of Early had been ineffective because too many men were in position to give orders to soldiers like Wright and Emory. All lines of authority were crossed, and the War Department was buzzing and fretting and issuing innumerable orders, taking time along the way to modify, alter, or countermand the orders other people were issuing. Looking back long after the war, Grant wrote his verdict: "It seemed to be the policy of General Halleck and Secretary Stanton to keep any force sent there in pursuit of the invading army moving right and left so as to keep between the enemy and our capital; and generally speaking they pursued this policy until all knowledge of the whereabouts of the enemy was lost."[20]

The first step, obviously, was to put one competent soldier in charge of the whole operation with definite, overriding authority, and this step Grant took. He sent orders to pull Major General William B. Franklin out of retirement and give him command over everybody, and for a day or two he assumed that he had settled things. Then he got a fussy telegram from Halleck explaining that this just would not do. Franklin had been a McClellan man in the old days, and the grim Committee on the Conduct of the War considered that he was really responsible for Burnside's failure at Fredericksburg, and he was in very bad odor at the War Department—and Grant's order was nullified and Franklin was not appointed. It appeared that Halleck and Stanton were exercising a veto power over Grant's authority and substituting their own ideas of strategy for his.[21]

Now this was the old McClellan situation all over again, and in a sense it was the crisis of the war. This was a presidential election year and by every sign men could read the Northern people were tired and discouraged. Sherman had not taken Atlanta and Grant had not taken Richmond, casualty lists had been heavy beyond all previous experience, and now the Confederates had an army in the lower Shenandoah Valley, ravaging Northern towns and apparently quite as irrepressible as in the Stonewall Jackson days. Unless the general in chief could somehow regain control and put an end to the fumbling and meddling, the bottom might fall out of the whole war effort, with failure in the field leading to defeat at the polls, and with independence for the Confederacy coming along in due course.

In a very similar situation, McClellan wrote bitter letters to his wife, told his officers that Washington was villainously conspiring against him, and drifted on down to defeat. It remained to be seen what Grant would do.

On August 1—while he was still digesting the dismal story of the fiasco at the crater—Grant made his move. He ordered Phil Sheridan to go up to the Monocacy and take control of all the troops in that area, and he wired Halleck that he was instructing Sheridan to "put himself south of the enemy and follow him to the death."[22]

The emphasis here, of course, was on the instruction to get *south* of the enemy. Whenever the Confederates invaded the North they were actually offering the Federals a priceless opportunity, and the real job of the Federal commander at such times was not to repel the invasion but to destroy the invading army. Lincoln had always seen it so, but he could never make his generals see it, and both Antietam and Gettysburg had been barren victories. Now there was a general with iron in him, who saw things as Lincoln did; and yet the old viewpoint still prevailed in the War Department, and the War Department had muscled in between general and President, on the one hand, and opportunity, on the other.

Grant's order was not at all the sort of thing Secretary Stanton was apt to approve. Under all his bluster, Stanton was timid, and the idea of following a pugnacious enemy to the death was just too much for him. Also, he felt that Sheridan was too young for an important independant command, and it appears that he did not like him very much personally, and what would happen to Grant's order regarding Sheridan was likely to be very similar to what had happened to his order regarding Franklin.

But just at this moment President Lincoln took a hand. He had been reading all of the correspondence, and now he sat down to send a telegram of his own to General Grant.

Grant's instructions to Sheridan, said the President, were just exactly right, and what Grant wanted done was precisely what the President wanted done. But Grant was invited to look over all of the dispatches he had received from Washington, and to consider everything he knew about the way the War Department did things, "and discover, if you can, that there is any idea in the head of anyone here of 'putting our army south of the enemy' or of 'following him to the death' in any direction."

Mr. Lincoln closed with the blunt warning:

"I repeat to you it will neither be done nor attempted, unless you watch it every day and hour and force it."[23]

The whole history of the Army of the Potomac passes in review in Mr. Lincoln's brief dispatch: the history of the army, and the most exasperating problem of the war itself. Over and over the war had been prolonged because of the timid, restrictive caution that could paralyze action—the habit of mind that was always too busy weighing risks to grasp opportunities. It developed now that that habit of mind had never been eradicated because when all was said and done it had its final roots in the War Department itself. The War Department could not act and the President could not make it act. The most he could do was support a general who was bold enough to ram action down the department's throat.

Now Lincoln was giving Grant the final tip-off, just as he had so often and so vainly tried, two years earlier, to give McClellan a similar tip-off. Tables of organization and lines of authority meant nothing in themselves. In the end everything depended on the general, and it was up to the general to act. McClellan had never been able to rise to this challenge. Grant was the last chance.

Two hours after he had received this wire from President Lincoln, Grant was on a fast steamer, coming up the Potomac. When the boat docked at Washington he stopped off neither at the White House nor at the War Department. Instead he went directly to the railroad station and took a special train to Monocacy Junction, and as soon as he got there he went to see General Hunter.

Technically, Hunter commanded the military department in which all of these troop movements were going on, and so technically he was responsible for everything that was being done. Grant had no intention of letting Hunter have control over the attempt to destroy Early's army but he was quite willing to let him down easy. Hunter could shelve himself in a Baltimore office if he wished, retaining nominal command of the department while Sheridan did the actual work, and Grant told Hunter this in so many words. But Hunter had had enough. He was getting on in years and he was not much of a soldier, and there was something mean in him which had led him to burn college buildings and homes when he should have been fighting Confederate armies, but during the last fortnight he had been more sinned against than sinning. He told Grant frankly that he had been pulled and tugged around so much by War Department orders that at this moment he simply did not know where Early and Early's troops were—and, in short, he would prefer to be relieved outright and let Sheridan carry the whole load.

Grant wasted no further time. "Very well, then," he said. Hunter was relieved, and without even waiting for Sheridan to arrive Grant ordered all of the Union troops in the vicinity to move at once to Halltown, a little village at the lower end of the Shenandoah Valley a few miles away from Harper's Ferry. No matter where Early was, a concentration of Federal soldiers in the Shenandoah was something the Confederacy could not endure. Early would come back quickly enough, once blue-uniformed troops displayed themselves in force around Halltown.[24]

Sheridan reached Monocacy Junction the next morning, after most of the troops had moved. Grant met him, outlined the job he wanted done, and took off for City Point, with very few people knowing that he had ever left the place, and Sheridan took a one-car special train for Harper's Ferry and rode from there to Halltown to take over his new command. There was a great deal of work to be done and it was going to take Sheridan a month or more to get acclimated and learn how to do what he had to do, but from now on the road led upward. This was the beginning of the end.

2. TO PEEL THIS LAND

There may be lovelier country somewhere—in the Island Vale of Avalon, at a gamble—but when the sunlight lies upon it and the wind puts white clouds racing their shadows the Shenandoah Valley is as good as anything America can show. Many generations ago the Knights of the Golden Horseshoe climbed the Blue Ridge to look down on it in wonder, and ever since then it has been a legend and the fulfillment of a promise. There is music in its very name, and some quality in the region touched the imaginations of men who had never even seen it. The sailors on deep water sailing ships made one of their finest chanteys about it, and sent topsail yards creaking to the masthead in ports all over the world to the tune of "Shenandore":

> O Shenandore, I love to hear you—
> Away, you rolling river.

During the war it was known simply as the Valley: an open corridor slanting off to the southwest from the gap at Harper's Ferry, broad land lying between blue mountains with the bright mirror of a looped river going among golden fields and dark woodlands, pleasant towns linked along a broad undulating turnpike and rich farms rolling away to the rising hills.

Queerly enough, although it had been a vital factor in the war, in a way the war had hardly touched it. Stonewall Jackson had made it a theater of high strategy, and there had been hard fighting along the historic turnpike and near quaint villages like Front Royal and Port Republic, and most of the fence rails on farms near the main highway had long since vanished to build the campfires of soldiers in blue and gray. Yet even in the summer of 1864 the land bore few scars. East of the Blue Ridge and the Bull Run mountains the country along the Orange and Alexandria Railroad had been marched over and fought over and ravaged mercilessly, and it was a desolate waste picked clean of everything an army might want or a farmer could use. But the Valley had escaped most of this, and when Phil Sheridan got there it was much as it had always been—rich, sunny, peaceful, a land of good farms and big barns, yellow grain growing beside green pastures, lazy herds of sheep and cattle feeding on the slopes.

Originally, the Valley had drawn many settlers from Pennsylvania and the Cumberland Valley, and these were mostly Dunkers, with a sprinkling of Quakers, Mennonites, and Nazarenes: devout, frugal, and industrious folk who held firmly to a belief that war was sinful—a belief for which there may be a certain amount of backing, both in Scripture and in racial experience—and their religion forbade the faithful to take up arms. As non-resistants these people had been a problem to the Confederate government, since they would not volunteer and, because of the stubbornness with which they held to their faith, could not well be drafted. But before the war was very old they became an asset instead of a problem. The Confederate Congress in 1862 provided that they might be exempted from military service on payment of a $500 tax, and as a result the farms of the Valley had no shortage of manpower. And because the men were good farmers and the soil was fertile, the Valley became an incomparable granary and source of supply for Lee's soldiers. Rations might be short now and then, because of poor transportation and an incompetent commissariat, but as long as these sober pacifists continued to till their lands and raise their flocks and operate their gristmills, Lee's army could not be starved out of Richmond.[1]

An accident of geography made the Valley worth more to the South than to the North, strategically. Running from southwest to northeast, the Valley was the Confederacy's great covered way leading up to the Yankee fortress, the high parapet of the Blue Ridge offering concealment and protection. A Confederate army coming down the Valley was marching directly toward the Northern citadel, but a Yankee army moving up the Valley was going nowhere in particular because it was constantly getting farther away from Richmond and Richmond's defenders. Nor did a Confederate force operating in the Valley have serious problems of supply. The Valley itself was the base, and it could be drawn on for abundant food and forage from Staunton all the way to Winchester and beyond.

Both Lee and Grant were thoroughly familiar with these facts. In the spring of 1862 Lee had used them, sending Stonewall Jackson down the Valley in such a way as to bring the North to stunning defeat. In the summer of 1864 he had used them again, and Early's foray had caused more trouble. From the moment he took command Grant had had to take these facts into consideration. Until he solved the problem of the Valley, the Army of the Potomac was never safe from an attack in its rear.

When the 1864 campaign began Grant tried to solve it, and the solution then would have been fairly simple. All that he needed was to establish a Federal army in the upper Valley—at Staunton, say, or Waynesboro, anywhere well upstream. That would close the gate and the Confederacy's granary and covered way would be useless. But nothing had worked out as he had planned. First Sigel went up the Valley, to be routed at Newmarket. Then Hunter took the same road, only to lose everything by wild misguided flight off into West Virginia. So now the problem was tougher, and the solution that would have worked in the spring was no good at all in midsummer.

Grant studied the matter, fixing his eyes on the fields and barns and roads of the Valley, and he had a deadly unemotional gaze which saw flame and a smoking sword for devout folk whose way led beside green pastures and still waters. The war could not be won until the Confederacy had been deprived of the use of this garden spot between the mountains. If the garden were made desert, so that neither the Southern Confederacy nor even the fowls of the air could use it, the problem would be well on the way toward being solved.

Grant put it in orders. In a message to Halleck, sent before Sheridan was named to the command, Grant was specific about what he wanted: an army of hungry soldiers to follow retreating Rebels up the Valley and "eat out Virginia clear and clean as far as they go, so that crows flying over it for the balance of the season will have to carry their provender with them." He spelled this out in instructions for the Union commander: "He should make all the Valley south of the Baltimore and Ohio railroad a desert as high up as possible. I do not mean that houses should be burned, but all provisions and stock should be removed, and the people notified to get out."[2]

Sheridan got the point. A soldier in Torbert's division of cavalry remembered the orders that came down from Sheridan's headquarters: ". . . you will seize all mules, horses and cattle that may be useful to our army. Loyal citizens can bring in their claims against the government for this necessary destruction. No houses will be burned; and officers in charge of this delicate but necessary duty must inform the people that the object is to make this Valley untenable for the raiding parties of the rebel army."[3]

It could be written out concisely, and the telegraph instruments would click it off, and adjutants could read it before the troops at evening parade, with deep shadows dropping down through the rich dusk; and a grim eternity of war and the hardening of many hearts had gone into it, romance of war and knightly chivalry dissolved forever in the terrible acid of enmity and hatred, settlement by the sword coming at last to mean all-out war, modern style, with a blow at the economic potential cutting across the farmer's yard and dooming innocent people to the loss of a lifetime's hard-bought gains.

There was a young fellow in the 2nd Ohio Cavalry who presided over some of this devastation: a lad who had seen values beyond life glimmering on the edge of the war when he enlisted, and who wrote in his diary about a talk he had with a farmer on the western fringe of the Valley whose farm lay in the road of military necessity:

"He owned a farm, sterile and poor, of 200 acres in among the hills. Moved there 34 years since when all was a wilderness. Had never owned a slave. Had cleaned up the farm, built a log house and made all the improvements with his own hands. It made him almost crazy to see all going to destruction in one night—all his fences, outbuildings, cattle, sheep and fowls. An only son at home, an invalid. Had always been true to the government. Only wished that God would now call him, that he might be with his many friends in the church yard—pointing to it near by—and the aspect of suffering and starvation be taken from it."[4]

The war had grown old, and it was following its own logic, the insane logic of war, which had been building up ever since Beauregard's cannon bit into the masonry of Fort Sumter. The only aim now was to hurt the enemy, in any way possible and with any weapon; to destroy not his will to resist but his ability to make that will effective. The will might remain and be damned to it: if the will and the bitterness could be made impotent, nothing else mattered.

There was much bitterness abroad by now—everywhere, perhaps, except in the army itself—and kindly, God-fearing people were demanding that their enemies be made to suffer. An example of this feeling can be seen in a letter which President Lincoln received just about this time from the good businessmen who made up the Chicago Board of Trade.

The president and the secretary of this organization wrote to Mr. Lincoln to recite the terrible evils which were befalling Union prisoners in the great Confederate prison camp at Andersonville, Georgia. In that overcrowded pen men lived in an open field without tents or huts, exposed to the hot sun and the driving rain, unclothed and badly fed, dying miserably of disease and malnutrition, all but totally uncared for, none of their sufferings minimized by wartime propaganda. So the Chicago civilians were soberly urging that the Federal government set aside an equal number of Confederate prisoners and subject them to the same treatment: that is, throw them together in such a way that most of them would die and the rest would lose their health and their minds, do it deliberately and with calculation, in order that there might be a fair extension of pain and death.

"We are aware," wrote the Chicagoans, "that this, our petition, savors of cruelty"—but it was no time to be squeamish. There was a war on and they felt obliged to "urge retaliatory measures as a matter of necessity"; and, in sum, here was a black flag fluttering on the hot wind, a rallying point for any ill will which had not yet been properly organized.[5]

Admittedly, Andersonville had a record which even today cannot easily be read without horror and sick disgust. So did most of the other prison camps in the Civil War, in the Confederacy and in the Union as well, and the terrible things which happened in them seem to have taken place not because anyone meant it so but simply because men were clumsy and the times were still rude.

Even when they were camped in perfect safety behind their own lines, getting the best their governments had to give, the soldiers of that day got miserable food and defective medical attention, so that simply being in the army killed many more men than were killed in battle. Only when an army commander was a first-rate military administrator, willing and able to devote a large part of his time to such matters, did the lot of the troops become anything better than just barely endurable. Inevitably, prisoners of war fared a great deal worse. A certain combination of incompetence and indifference can cause almost as much suffering as the most acute malevolence.

One does not need to read wartime propaganda to get a full indictment of the prison camps. Each side indicted itself, in terms no propagandist could make much more bitter.

A Confederate surgeon, completing an inspection of Andersonville, reported to his superiors at Richmond that more than 10,000 prisoners had died in seven months—nearly one third of the entire number confined there. More than 5,000 were seriously ill. Diarrhea, dysentery, scurvy, and hospital gangrene were the chief complaints, and there were from 90 to 130 deaths every day. He found 30,-000 men jammed together on twenty-seven acres of land, "with little or no attention to hygiene, with festering masses of filth at the very doors of their rude dens and tents." A little stream flowed through the camp, and about it the surgeon found "a filthy quagmire" which was so infamous that a man who got a slight scratch on his skin, or even an insect bite, was quite likely to die of blood poisoning. A South Carolina woman, learning about similar conditions in the prison camp at Florence, wrote to the governor asking: "In the name of all that is holy, is there nothing that can be done to relieve such dreadful suffering? If such things are allowed to continue they will surely draw down some awful judgment upon our country."[6]

Thus in the South. In the North, an army surgeon inspected the camp for Rebel prisoners at Elmira, New York, and said that the 8,347 prisoners there exhibited 2,000 cases of scurvy. He asserted that at the current death rates "the entire command will be admitted to hospital in less than a year and 36 per cent die." Like Andersonville, the Elmira camp contained a stream, which had formed a dreadful scummy pond—"a festering mass of corruption, impregnating the entire atmosphere of the camp with the pestilential odors . . . the vaults give off their sickly odors, and the hospitals are crowded with victims for the grave." The camp surgeon had made repeated complaints but he could get no one in authority to pay any attention to them, and his requisitions for medicines had been entirely ignored.[7]

A little later, when the rival governments worked out a deal for the exchange of certain prisoners who were too ill to fight but not too sick to travel, a trainload of 1,200 such men was made up at Elmira and sent down to Baltimore to take a steamer for the South. Federal doctors who met this pathetic convoy at the dock wrote indignantly that many of the men were obviously unfit to travel. Five had died on the train and sixty more had to be hurried to hospital as soon as they reached Baltimore. There were no doctors, orderlies, or nurses on the steamer, and the whole setup indicated "criminal neglect and inhumanity on the part of the medical officers in making the selection of men to be transferred." The commander at Elmira, meanwhile, was writing that he had hoped that getting rid of his 1,200 worst cases would relieve overcrowding at the camp hospital but that somehow it had not. Overcrowding was as bad as ever, and "if the rate of mortality for the last two months should continue for a year you can easily calculate the number of prisoners there would be left here for exchange."[8]

There was a smoky moonlit madness on the land in this fourth year of war. The country was striking blindly at phantoms, putting scars on its own body. People can stand only about so much, and they had been pushed beyond the limit, so that what was monstrous could look as if it made sense. Ordinarily decent, kindly citizens could seriously propose that some thousands of helpless prisoners be condemned to slow death by hunger and disease, and the fact that the authorities rejected this mad scheme did not help very much because the reprisal was in fact already being inflicted.

That was what the climate of the war was like now. It was a climate apt to produce hard deeds by hard men, and some characters well fitted to operate in such a climate were beginning to come forward; among them, Major General Philip Sheridan, commanding the newly formed Army of the Shenandoah.

When he first got it, it was hardly an army. It was simply a collection of three infantry corps and three divisions of cavalry, totaling perhaps 36,000 men, of whom 30,000 or thereabouts could be classed as combat troops.[9] Its different units stood for widely varying traditions, and both time and leadership would be needed to turn them into an army.

At the bottom of the heap was the remnant of the army that had been led by Hunter. Now denominated the VIII Army Corps, it was led by George Crook, who was a very good man, and it needed new equipment, a good rest, much drill and discipline, and a thorough shot in the arm. An observer saw Crook's men as "ragged, famished, discouraged, sulky and half of them in ambulances." They had been overmarched and underfed and they had been ruinously beaten by the Rebels.[10] Someone would have to work on them before they would amount to much as fighting troops.

Much better were the two slim divisions of Emory's XIX Corps, just up from Louisiana. They were veterans of hard campaigning in the Deep South, and they had one asset, very uncommon among Union troops in the Virginia theater: they were used to victory rather than to defeat, and it never occurred to them to expect anything except more victories. It was only the army of Northern Virginia which bred an inferiority complex among Yankee troops, and that army the XIX Corps had never met.

Solid nucleus of Sheridan's new army was Wright's VI Corps. This was probably the best fighting corps the Army of the Potomac had, but at the moment it was a little worn and morose. It did not look the part of a crack corps. When it bivouacked, its regiments and brigades pitched their pup tents as the spirit of the individual dictated, instead of ranging them in formal rows with proper company and regimental streets. The men no longer kept their muskets brightly polished, preferring to steal clean ones from their neighbors. (An ordnance sergeant at this time confessed that as far as clean muskets were concerned, "we han't had one in our brigade since Cold Harbor.") There were regimental officers who freely admitted that although they had not exactly lost confidence in General

Grant they did have a good deal more confidence in General Lee, and even the famous Vermont Brigade was showing deficiencies in discipline, its historian confessing: "The regiments were organized somewhat on the town meeting plan, and the men were rather deferred to on occasion by the officers. . . . There was hardly the least rigidity, and camp life on the whole was of the easiest possible description."[11]

The VI Corps, in short, had had it, and how it would perform now might depend a good deal on Sheridan himself. The men were not very happy to see him. They did not know much about him except that he was supposed to be a hard and remorseless fighting man, and while they were willing to admire that quality from a distance they suspected that his assignment to command in the Valley meant that some very rough work lay ahead, and they had had about all of the rough work they wanted. When a general won a reputation as a fighter, these veterans understood perfectly well who it was that paid for that reputation.

They understood also, however, that the war was never going to be won by the aimless sort of maneuverings which had been going on during the last three weeks. Direct action might not be so bad if the man who was directing it knew what he was doing. As one man wrote, "We knew we were there for other purposes than a traveling procession, and the cause had been for a long time a failing one."[12]

So here was Sheridan, and they would see about him.

The first things they saw were the little things. When the army marched Sheridan was always up near the front, taking personal charge. If traffic jams or road blocks developed, the officer who galloped up to straighten matters out was Sheridan himself. Sometimes he stormed and swore, and sometimes, when others were excited, he was controlled and soft-spoken; either way, he struck sparks and got action. If infantry was ordered to march in the fields and woods so that wagons and guns could have the road, Sheridan got off the road too and went with the foot soldiers. Marches went more smoothly, and camp life ran as if someone was in charge again, and it began to dawn on the men that many of the pesky little annoyances of military existence were disappearing. Before long, VI Corps veterans were paying Sheridan one of the highest compliments they knew. Having him in command, they said, was almost as good as having Uncle John Sedgwick back.[13]

It was noticed, too, that army headquarters was managed without fuss and feathers. Headquarters in the Army of the Potomac had been elaborate and formal—many tents, much pomp and show, honor guards in fussy Zouave uniforms, a gaudy headquarters flag bearing a golden eagle in a silver wreath on a solferino background; the whole having caused U. S. Grant, the first time he saw it, to rein in his horse and inquire if Imperial Caesar lived anywhere near. Sheridan made do with two tents and two tent flies, and he had no honor guard. Instead he had a collection of two-gun scouts dressed in Confederate uniforms, who were probably the toughest daredevils in the army.

There were perhaps a hundred of them, the outgrowth of a small detail originally selected for special jobs from the 17th Pennsylvania Cavalry. They were a peculiar combination of intelligence operatives, communications experts, counterespionage men, and sluggers. They spent nearly as much time within the Rebel lines as in their own—they had "learned to talk the Southern language," as one of them put it, and they made themselves familiar with every regiment, brigade, and division in Early's army—and the biggest part of their job was to keep Sheridan at all times up to date on the enemy's strength, movements, and dispositions. If captured, of course, they could expect nothing better than to be hanged to the nearest tree, and they always ran a fair chance of being potted by Yankee outposts, since they did look like Rebels. They tended to be an informal and individualistic lot.[14]

In part, the existence of this group reflected one of Sheridan's pet ideas—that daring and quick reflexes were worth more than muscle. Standing by a campfire with his staff one evening, Sheridan remarked that the ideal cavalry regiment would consist of men between eighteen and twenty-two years of age, none weighing more than 130 pounds and not one of them married. Little, wiry men could stand the pounding better than the big husky ones, Sheridan felt, and a Pennsylvanian who heard him agreed. He had noticed that skinny little chaps from the coal breakers usually outlasted the brawny deer hunters and bear trappers who came down from the mountains. And only young bachelors were properly reckless.[15]

Even more, however, these scouts were the product of the kind of war that was developing in the Valley. Yankee soldiers here were not only up against Early's troops. They were also up against guerillas, some of them Colonel Mosby's, some of them answering to nobody but themselves, and guerilla warfare was putting an edge on the fighting that had been seen nowhere else in Virginia.

In modern terms, the Confederacy had organized a resistance movement in territory occupied by the hated Yankees; had organized it, and then had seen it get badly out of hand.

The Valley was full of men who were Confederate soldiers by fits and starts—loosely organized and loosely controlled, most of them, innocent civilians six days a week and hell-roaring raiders the seventh day. They owned horses, weapons, and sometimes uniforms, which they carefully hid when they were not actually using them. Called together at intervals by their leaders, they would swoop down on outposts and picket lines, knock off wagon trains or supply depots, burn culverts and bridges behind the Federal front, and waylay any couriers, scouts, or other detached persons they could find. They compelled Union commanders to make heavy detachments to guard supply lines and depots, thus reducing the number of soldiers available for service in battle. To a certain extent they unintentionally compensated for this by reducing straggling in the Federal ranks, for the Northern soldier was firmly convinced that guerillas took no prisoners and that to be caught by them was to get a slit throat.

So the guerillas gave the Federal commanders a continuing headache—and, in the long run, probably did the Confederacy much more harm than good.

The quality of these guerilla bands varied greatly. At the top was John S. Mosby's: courageous soldiers led by a minor genius, highly effective in partisan warfare. Most of the groups, however, were about one degree better than plain outlaws, living for loot and excitement, doing no actual fighting if they could help it, and offering a secure refuge to any number of Confederate deserters and draft evaders. The Confederate cavalry leader, General Thomas L. Rosser, called them "a nuisance and an evil to the service," declaring:

"Without discipline, order or organization, they roam broadcast over the country, a band of thieves, stealing, pillaging, plundering and doing every manner of mischief and crime. They are a terror to the citizens and an injury to the cause. They never fight; can't be made to fight. Their leaders are generally brave, but few of the men are good soldiers."[16]

Jeb Stuart, not long before his death, endorsed this sentiment, saying that Mosby's was the only ranger band he knew of that was halfway efficient and that even Mosby usually operated with only a fourth of his supposed strength, while Lee wrote to the Confederate Secretary of War strongly urging that all such groups be abolished, asserting: "I regard the whole system as an unmixed evil."[17]

The worst damage which this system did to the Confederacy, however, was that it put Yankee soldiers in a mood to be vengeful.

By this time the Union authorities had had a good deal of experience with guerillas and they were getting very grim about it. Much of this conditioning had been gained in states like Tennessee and Missouri, where neighbor was bitter against neighbor and barn burnings and the murderous settlement of old grudges went hand in hand with attempts to discomfit the Yankee invader, and most Federal generals considered guerillas as mere bushwhackers, candidates for the noose or the firing squad. An exception was generally (though by no means always) made in the case of Mosby's men, who were recognized as being more or less regular soldiers, but the attitude toward the rest was summed up by a Union general along the upper Potomac, who said: "I have instructed my command not to bring any of them to my headquarters except for interment."[18]

This attitude spread rapidly to the rank and file, particularly when the gueril-las took to killing any Union stragglers they could catch. Overlooking the fact that lawless foraging and looting by stragglers and bummers could easily pro-voke angry reprisals, the soldiers simply argued that if a Southerner wanted to fight he ought to be in the Confederate Army. If he was not in the Army, but fought anyway, they considered that he was outside the law. Since the guerillas could not often be captured—they usually struck at night, vanished in the dark, and became innocent farmers before the pursuit got well organized—the ten-dency was to take it out on the nearest civilians, on the broad ground that if they let guerillas operate in their midst they would have to take the consequences.

Most Federal soldiers would have endorsed the words and acts of a Union of-ficer in northern Alabama, where troop trains were fired on and railroad tele-graph lines were cut by anti-Unionists in a little country town. This officer assembled the townsfolk and told them that henceforth "every time the tele-graph wire was cut we would burn a house; every time a train was fired on we should hang a man; and we would continue to do this until every house was burned and every man hanged between Decatur and Bridgeport." He went on to put the army viewpoint into explicit words: "If they wanted to fight they should enter the army, meet us like honorable men, and not, assassin-like, fire at us from the woods and run." He concluded by warning that if the citizens let the bushwhackers continue to operate, "we should make them more uncomfortable than they would be in Hell." Having said all of this he burned the town, arrested three citizens as hostages for the good behavior of the rest, and went his way. He wrote that this action was spoken of "approvingly by the officers and enthusias-tically by the men."[19]

Now it should be remembered that ordinarily the soldiers were the least bloodthirsty of all the participants in the war. Secretary Welles might write fondly of hangings, and the Chicago Board of Trade might ask that Confederate prisoners be allowed to die of hunger or disease, and it could be washed off as part of the inevitable idiocy of superpatriotism in time of war. But when the soldiers themselves began to feel an interest in creating a hell on earth for enemy civilians the moon was entering a new phase. The tragic part about it now was that this was happening in an army one of whose functions was to ravage and lay waste a populous farming area until even a crow could not support himself in it. The hand that was about to come down on the Shenandoah Valley was going to be heavy enough anyway. What the guerillas did was not going go make it come down any more lightly.

It was mid-August, and the Army of the Shenandoah had marched more than a third of the way up the Valley. Lee sent reinforcements to Early, and the num-ber of them was exaggerated by rumor, and Sheridan—still feeling his way with his new command, and behaving with unwonted caution—decided to move back to Halltown and wait for a better time and place to strike. The army paused, and then it moved slowly back in retreat, and as it moved innumerable squadrons of Federal cavalry spread out from mountain to mountain in a broad destroying wave and began methodically and with cold efficiency to take the Valley apart.

They were not gentle about it. The chaplain of the 1st Rhode Island Cavalry wrote grimly: "The time had fully come to peel this land and put an end to the long strife for its possession," and he had found the precise word for it.[20] The cavalry peeled the Shenandoah Valley as a man might peel an orange. The blue tide ebbed, leaving wreckage behind it, pillars of smoke rising by day and pillars of fire glowing by night to mark the place where they had been.

The general idea was simple. All barns were to be burned, and crops were to be destroyed. Farmers were to be left enough to see themselves through the winter, although the definition of "enough" was left to the lieutenants and captains commanding the detachments which had the matches, and there was no right of appeal. Anything that could benefit the Confederacy was to be destroyed, whether it was a corncrib, a gristmill, a railroad bridge, or something that went on four legs. It was hoped that nobody would starve to death, and no violence was to be offered to any civilian's person, but the Valley was to feed no more Confederate armies thereafter.

The Rhode Island chaplain looked back on it, a dozen years later, and wrote: "The 17th of August will be remembered as sending up to the skies the first great columns of smoke and flame from doomed secession barns, stacks, cribs and mills, and the driving into loyal lines of flocks and herds. The order was carefully yet faithfully obeyed. . . . The order led to the destruction of about 2,-000 barns, 70 mills, and other property, valued in all at 25 millions of dollars." The chaplain went on to say that many guerilla bands had lived in this region and that it had finally been "purified" by fire: "As our boys expressed it, 'we burned out the hornets.' "[21]

A man in the 17th Pennsylvania Cavalry gave his picture of it: "Previously the burning of supplies and outbuildings had been incidental to battles, but now the torch was applied deliberately and intentionally. Stacks of hay and straw and barns filled with crops harvested, mills, corn-cribs; in a word, all supplies of use to man or beast were promptly burned and all valuable cattle driven off. . . . The work of destruction seemed cruel and the distress it occasioned among the people of all ages and sexes was evident on every hand. The officers and soldiers who performed the details of this distressing work were met at every farm or home by old men, women and children in tears, begging and beseeching those in charge to save them from the appalling ruin. These scenes of burning and destruction, which were only the prelude to those which followed at a later day farther up the Valley, were attended with sorrow to families and added horrors to the usual brutalities of war, unknown to any other field operations in the so-called Confederacy."[22]

Not all of the people quite got the point of what was being done. Even General Hunter had felt obliged to point out to his men, a month earlier, that there were in the Valley many people of stout Unionist sympathy, who sheltered Federal wounded men and did their best to aid the Union army; such people, he pointed out, ought to be given a little protection, which unfortunately his own army did not seem able to provide. Now the Pennsylvania cavalryman said that "the few Union people, old men, women and children, could not be made to understand the utility or necessity of the measure, while the outspoken Confederates heaped upon us maledictions. . . . The common hatred of open foes seemed to deepen, and to blot out forever all hope of future goodwill between North and South."[23]

The soldiers did not exactly enjoy their job. The historian of another regiment of Pennsylvania horse, the 6th, said that his regiment was lucky enough to avoid "the detail for this unpleasant duty," and said that he rode that day with the last element of the rear guard, marching in the wake of the men who had been swinging the torch. "The day had been an unpleasant one," he wrote, "the weather was hot and the roads very dusty, and the grief of the inhabitants, as they saw their harvests disappearing in flame and smoke, and their stock being driven off, was a sad sight. It was a phase of warfare we had not seen before, and although we admitted the necessity we could not but sympathize with the sufferers."[24]

A Michigan cavalryman remembered riding past a little home and seeing, in the gate of the fence by the road, an old woman, crying bitterly, blood flowing from a deep cut in one arm. He rode up to her and she told him that some soldier had struck her with his saber and then had taken her two cows. He wheeled and spurred after his regiment, found the officer in charge of the herd of confiscated cattle, recovered the two cows—or, at any rate, two cows which might have been the ones—and with the officer he tried in vain to find the man who had used the saber. Then he took the cows back to the woman, who thanked him in tearful surprise and told him that if he was ever captured by Mosby's men he should have them bring him to her home, and she would give testimony that would save him from being hanged.[25]

So the army made its way back down the Valley, leaving desolation behind it, and the war came slowly nearer its end in the black smoke that drifted over the Blue Ridge. The war had begun with waving unstained flags and dreams of a picture-book fight which would concern no one but soldiers, who would die picturesquely and without bloodshed amid dress-parade firing lines, and it had come down now to burning barns, weeping children, and old women who had been hit with sabers. In the only way that was left to it, the war was coming toward its close. Phil Sheridan passed the word, and his scouts laughed and went trotting off to spy on the Rebels and play a clever game with the threat of a greased noose; and the guerillas met in dark copses on the edge of the army and rode out with smoking revolvers to kill the cripples, and now and then one of them was caught.

It happened so with a group of Sheridan's scouts, who captured a Captain Stump, famous as a Rebel raider, a man they had long been seeking. He had been wounded, and when he was caught they took his weapons away and brought him to Major Young, who commanded the scouts, and Major Young had a certain respect for his daring guerilla, so he told him:

"I suppose you know we will kill you. But we will not serve you as you have served our men—cut your throat or hang you. We will give you a chance for your life. We will give you ten rods' start on your own horse, with your spurs on. If you get away, all right. . . . But remember, my men are dead shots."

Captain Stump was bloody and he had been hurt, but he was all man. He smiled, and nodded, and rode a few feet out in front of the rank of his captors—skinny young men, 130 pounds or less, unmarried, the pick of the Yankee cavalry. Major Young looked down the rank, and called out: *"Go!"*

A cavalryman wrote about it afterward:

"We allowed him about ten rods' start, then our pistols cracked and he fell forward, dead."[26]

3. ON THE UPGRADE

From the Shenandoah Valley to Chicago it is perhaps 500 miles, as one of General Grant's unrationed crows might fly, and the binding threads of war spanned these miles and tied valley and city together in an invisible bond.

In the Valley, as August came to an end, the winds from the mountains carried away the last of the smudge from charred barns and hayricks, and whether or not anybody could see it those winds came from the hour just before sunrise and there was a promise in them. In Chicago, the hour looked like the spectral twilight of collapse and defeat, and the passenger trains were unloading a large assortment of people who were prepared to stake a good deal on the belief that the great Union of the States was dying.

With that belief Abraham Lincoln himself felt a certain agreement. On August 23 he had somewhat mysteriously asked members of his cabinet to sign a curiously folded paper, which he then tucked away in his desk. None of the men who signed knew what was in the paper. If they had known they would have gabbled and popped their eyes, for in Lincoln's handwriting it contained his statement:

"This morning, as for some days past, it seems exceedingly probable that this administration will not be re-elected. Then it will be my duty to so co-operate with the President-elect as to save the Union between the election and the inauguration; as he will have secured his election on such ground that he cannot possibly save it afterward."

A pessimistic appraisal, which since then has often been considered far too gloomy, hindsight having made clear many things not then apparent. But men in wartime have to operate without benefit of the backward glance, and in the summer of 1864 the war looked very much like a stalemate. Many men had died and there was much weariness, and as far as anyone could see the people had had about enough—of the Administration and of the Administration's war.

Lincoln was not the only pessimist. Horace Greeley, whose progress through the war years was a dizzy succession of swings from fatuous optimism to profoundest gloom, had recently written: "Mr. Lincoln is already beaten. He cannot be re-elected." His pink cherubic face fringed by delicate light hair which always seemed to be ruffled by a faint breeze from never-never land, Greeley spoke for many Republican stalwarts when he wistfully hoped that Lincoln might somehow be replaced on the party ticket by Grant, or Butler, or Sherman. In such case, mused Greeley, "we could make a fight yet." With other prominent Republicans, Greeley had been working on a scheme to hold a national convention of radical Republicans at the end of September, so as to concentrate support "on some candidate who commands the confidence of the country, even by a new nomination if necessary."[1]

What was worrying Lincoln, of course, was not so much the prospect of his own defeat as the conviction that this defeat would mean loss of the war. In this judgment he may or may not have been correct. It is perhaps worthy of notice that one man who was very well qualified to form an expert opinion on the matter agreed with him thoroughly. When a visitor from Washington told General Grant that there was talk of running him for the presidency, Grant hit the arms of his camp chair with clenched fists and growled: "They can't do it! They can't compel me to do it!" Then he went on to show how Lincoln's leadership looked from the special vantage point of the commanding general's tent at City Point: "I consider it as important to the cause that he should be elected as that the army should be successful in the field."[2]

Grant was the man who fought all-out, with few holds barred and with the annihilation of the opposing armies as the end to be sought. Yet Grant was quite able to see that although the war must be won on the battlefields it might very easily be lost back home—in Chicago, for example. The same thought had occurred to many others, including Jefferson Davis, and as a result a number of Confederate spies and military agents were converging on Chicago just now in the hope that they could stir up a great deal of trouble.

The immediate magnet was the national convention of the Democratic party, convening on August 29 to nominate a candidate to run against Lincoln. Broadly speaking, this convention was bringing together practically everybody who disliked the way the war was being run, with the single exception of the dissident Republicans who felt that Lincoln was not tough enough. Among the assembling Democrats were stout Unionists who opposed the forcible abolition of slavery and the reduction of states' rights; among them, also, were others who wanted only to have the war end—with a Union victory if possible, without it if necessary. And there were also men who saw the war consuming precious freedoms and creating tyranny, who blended extreme political partisanship with blind fury against the war party and who at least believed that they were ready to strike back without caring much what weapon they used.

So the waters in Chicago were very muddy, and to the Confederate government it seemed likely that they might offer good fishing.

For many months the Confederacy had been getting ready to exploit just this kind of situation. It had assembled a large number of operatives in Toronto under the general leadership of Colonel Jacob Thompson, who bore the vague title of Special Commissioner of the Confederate States Government in Canada and who possessed a letter from Jefferson Davis guardedly instructing him "to carry out the instructions you have received from me verbally in such manner as shall seem most likely to conduce to the furtherance of the interests of the Confederate States of America." Thompson's people were trying to do a little bit of everything. Early in the summer they had put out peace feelers, briefly hoodwinking none other than Horace Greeley himself, and although nothing much came of this venture the apparatus was hard at work on many other projects, most of them involving some form of sabotage in the Northern states.

Thompson had a wild, devil-may-care crowd at his command. One of the most effective was a slim, black-haired, almost effeminate-looking Kentuckian named Thomas H. Hines, formerly a captain in John Hunt Morgan's cavalry— the man, in fact, who had engineered Morgan's spectacular and still mysterious escape from the Ohio penitentiary a year earlier. Hines was very tough indeed, and he had been sent to Canada from Richmond immediately after the Dahlgren raid, his mission being to round up all escaped Confederate prisoners of war who could find their way north of the border and to carry out with them "any fair and appropriate enterprises of war against our enemies" that might occur to him.

The ideas these men had ranged all the way from stirring up draft riots in the Middle West to the burning of Northern cities, the capture of Northern prison camps, and the seizure of U.S.S. *Michigan,* the Navy's warship which patrolled the Great Lakes. To a certain extent their program was frankly terroristic, and the papers which supposedly had been found on Colonel Dahlgren's body calling for the burning and sacking of Richmond were often mentioned as full justification for such a program.[3]

Colonel Thompson was an experienced politician well fitted for his shadowy role, and in Captain Hines he had as cool and capable a behind-the-lines operator as any fifth columnist could wish to have. Yet the results which these men obtained, from first to last, add up to nothing much more than a series of petty annoyances. Many of their operatives seem to have looked on the whole program as a glorified Tom Sawyer lark, with the sheer fun of conspiring and risking their necks offering a welcome outlet for restless spirits bored by the routine of ordinary army life. The whole operation was so effectively watched by Union spies that it had little chance to accomplish anything very sensational.

The really crippling thing, however, was that Thompson and Hines and everybody else made the same mistake which a number of good Republicans and Union generals were forever making: when they looked upon the vast body of supposedly militant Northern Copperheads, they took them seriously.

The Copperheads talked and at times acted as if they had both the means and the will to revolt against the Lincoln government, and they had grandiose plans for detaching from the Union various northwestern states and setting up a new confederacy actively friendly to the South. Their action arm was a mildly secret organization known as the Sons of Liberty, and their prophet was the famous Clement Laird Vallandigham, the former Ohio congressman whom Burnside in an excess of zeal had arrested in 1863 for seditious speechmaking and who had been rustled across the fighting lines and given to the Confederacy. Vallandigham had visited Richmond and had talked with government people there.

Then he had flitted north to Canada, and in June of 1864 Captain Hines met him at Windsor, across the river from Detroit. Vallandigham talked largely about the size and power of the Sons of Liberty. They had 85,000 members in Illinois, he told Hines, 50,000 in Indiana, and 40,000 in Ohio, and with such an organization it seemed likely that a great deal could be done.[1]

Soon after this Vallandigham donned a false beard and smuggled himself across the river, going thence to Ohio, dropping the beard, and beginning to make speeches. (The Lincoln government carefully looked the other way, figuring that as long as it did not officially know that Vallandigham had returned it would not have to make a martyr out of him all over again by re-arresting him.) In his speeches, Vallandigham expressed a vague menace. He warned the Lincoln tyranny that "there is a vast multitude, a host whom they cannot number, bound together by the strongest and holiest ties, to defend, by whatever means the exigencies of the times shall demand, their natural and constitutional rights as freemen, at all hazards and to the last extremity." At the end of August he went to Chicago to take part in the Democratic convention.

Captain Hines and sixty of his boys were in Chicago, too, dressed in civilian clothes and carrying revolvers. They had money and they knew where there were more weapons, and they had had a series of annoying, protracted, but apparently fruitful conferences with Copperhead leaders looking toward direct action. The modest Federal garrison in Chicago had recently been increased, and there were Democrats who felt that this could only have been done for the purpose of suppressing their convention and thereby ending the last of America's civil rights. County chairmen of the Sons of Liberty, accordingly, had been notified to alert their members and stand by to strike a blow for freedom, and the leadership assured Hines that they were "sure of a general uprising which will result in a glorious success."

Hines, meanwhile, reflected that there were 5,000 perfectly good Confederate soldiers locked up at Camp Douglas, near Chicago, and 7,000 more in another prison camp at Rock Island. He appears to have hoped that the Copperheads would create enough trouble and confusion so that those prison camps could be seized and the prisoners released and armed. Then, with 12,000 good troops loose in northern Illinois, he could make trouble for the Yankees on a really impressive scale.[5]

Unfortunately, as the time for action came closer the leaders of the Sons of Liberty grew more and more nervous. Talking nobly about taking up arms for the constitutional rights of free men was all very well, as long as it was just talk. The trouble was that this quiet, blue-eyed Kentuckian was in deadly earnest and so were the men he had with him, and they proposed to turn his talk into action in which many Sons of Liberty would probably get shot, with the gallows looming large in the background for those whom the bullets missed. Copperhead leadership began to have second thoughts, and it hedged and temporized, grossly exaggerating the number of Federal troops present in Chicago and dwelling long on the probability of failure.

By convention time, the Confederates could see that the Sons of Liberty simply were not going to rise in any substantial number. Disgustedly, Hines made a final proposal: if as many as 500 armed Copperheads would come together he could at least capture one of the prison camps, and he would play it alone from then on in. There were more conferences, more shiverings and headshakings— and, at last, the Confederates had to slip back to Canada, with nothing accomplished. The Copperheads could deplore and conspire and denounce, but they would not fight and the real fighting men whom the Confederacy had sent to Chicago could do nothing with them. Men who thought themselves bold had had to confront men who really were bold, and the meeting gave them a permanent scare.[6]

This fiasco was the surface indication that a crisis had at last been met and passed. The North might be divided by bitter passions and half paralyzed by the numbness brought on by a long war, but the nightmare that had been dimly visible in the background for two years was at last fading out. Whatever happened, it was now certain that the war would not be lost because of revolt at home. The attempt to crush secession would not fail because of a second secession.

Vallandigham might roam Chicago, conferring with leaders and orating to street-corner crowds, forcing the Democratic convention to adopt a platform deploring the "failure" of the war and calling for "immediate efforts" to end all hostilities. In the end there was just going to be another presidential election, not an armed uprising. The Chicago gathering remained an ordinary political convention, and it made an ordinary political bet—that general war weariness and discontent over a military stalemate could be made to add up to a majority at the polls.

In making this bet the convention played it both ways. It adopted the Vallandigham peace plank, to pull in all of the people who were tired of war or who had not believed in war in the first place; then, for its presidential candidate, it nominated a soldier—George B. McClellan, the enduring hero of the enlisted man in the Army of the Potomac, a leader whom Democratic orthodoxy considered a military genius unfairly treated by petty politicians in Washington.

Immediately after this, the roof fell in.

To begin with, McClellan would not stay hitched. On reflection he found the platform altogether too much to swallow. Accepting the nomination, he quietly but firmly turned the peace pledge inside out, saying that he construed it as a mandate to carry the war through to victory and remarking that to do anything less than insist on the triumph of the Union cause would be to betray the heroic soldiers whom he had led in battle.

Worst yet, William Tecumseh Sherman captured Atlanta.

Sherman had moved against Joe Johnston's Confederate army the same day Grant crossed the Rapidan. From the distant North his campaign had looked no more like a success than the one in Virginia. If it had not brought so many casualties, it had seemed no more effective at ending Rebel resistance. Wise old Joe Johnston, sparring and side-stepping and shifting back, had a very clear understanding of the home-front politics behind the armies. His whole plan had been to keep Sherman from forcing a showdown until after the election, on the theory that victory postponed so long would look to the people up North like victory lost forever, and his strategy had been much more effective than his own government could realize. To President Davis, Johnston's course had seemed like sheer faintheartedness, and he had at last dismissed Johnston and put slugging John B. Hood in his place. Hood had gone in and slugged, and Sherman's army had more slugging power—so now, with the Democrats betting the election on the thesis that the war effort was a flat failure, decisive success had at last been won.

First Sherman, then Sheridan: and in the middle of September Grant quietly went up to the Valley and had a talk with Sheridan, the two men walking back and forth across a little field, Sheridan gesturing with nervous hands, Grant chewing a cigar and looking at the ground. A leathery Vermont sergeant leaned against a rail fence, watching them, and he looked moodily at Grant's stoop-shouldered figure.

"I hate to see that old cuss around," said the sergeant at last. "When that old cuss is around there's sure to be a big fight on hand."[7]

The sergeant was quite right. The old cuss had been growing impatient and he wanted action. Sheridan had a big advantage over Early in numbers, and Grant believed that he ought to be able to move to the Valley Pike somewhere below Winchester, get south of the Rebel army, and at last do what Grant had demanded two months earlier—follow it to the death. Early had his army in position behind Opequon Creek, covering Winchester, and Sheridan felt that it was going to be hard to get at him. Still, he had held this command for six weeks now, the shakedown period was about over, and it was time for action.

So Grant and Sheridan finished their talk and Grant went back to City Point, and at two o'clock on the morning of September 19 Wilson's cavalry trotted down to one of the fords of the Opequon, went spattering across the shallows, drove in the Rebel outposts, and rode on to feel the main Southern defensive line, horse artillery banging away hard, dismounted troopers laying down a sharp fire from repeating carbines.

The Opequon fords lay perhaps six miles east of Winchester, and the VI Corps came over the water at dawn, the sun coming up behind their backs, dirty smoke piling up in the gray sky to the west. The veterans looked and listened, and one of them wrote that they "heard that sound which I believe strikes a chill through the bravest man that lives, and causes him to feel that his heart is sinking down, down till it seems to drop into his boots. I mean the dull rustling of air which is hardly more than a vibration, but which to the experienced listener betokens artillery firing at a distance. When one expects soon to join in the exercise, that signal is not inspiriting."[8]

According to Sheridan's battle orders the VI Corps was to come up on the heels of Wilson's cavalry, with Emory's and Crook's men close behind and the rest of the cavalry swinging in a half circle to come down on Winchester from the north. Speedy movement was essential. Early had scattered his forces, and most of his men were spread out somewhere between Winchester and Martinsburg. Perhaps a third of his infantry, supported by artillery and cavalry, was posted in the lines east of Winchester covering the road from the Opequon. If that infantry force could be smashed quickly, Early's troops north of town could be cut off and his army could be destroyed piecemeal. So the VI Corps pressed along and the offensive was under way at last.

Unfortunately, it was not under way very fast. Orders had gone awry somehow and there was an infernal traffic tie-up, and the army moved at a crawl. The road led up the length of a narrow valley, and in some way the whole baggage and supply train of the VI Corps, which was supposed to be sidetracked east of the creek, inserted itself into the line of march right behind the leading infantry divisions, with corps artillery behind it and all the rest of the army to follow. The infantry column thus was cut in half by miles of slow-moving wagons, ambulances, caissons, battery forges, and other lumbering vehicles, and the cumbersome procession could neither be parked by the roadside nor turned around and sent back, because road and valley were too narrow.

The foot soldiers left the road and tried to pass this tangle, but they found themselves scrambling along steep hillsides, through trees and underbrush, creeping up toward the fight at a rate not much better than a mile an hour. The slopes were clogged, as a man in the XIX Corps remembered, with "the hundreds of men who belong to an army but never fight—the cooks, the officers' servants, the hospital gangs, the quartermaster's people, the 'present sick' and the habitual skulkers"—not to mention various regiments of cavalry which had been told to wait by the road and let the infantry advance.[9]

The result was a bungled battle which nearly became a humiliating defeat. Early had plenty of time to pull his scattered divisions together, and when Sheridan finally attacked it was nearly noon, instead of 6 A.M. as he had planned. Even at noon he had only half of his infantry on hand, and a good deal less than half of his artillery, and his battle line had not gone far before it ran into trouble. The three divisions of the VI Corps were going in side by side, with one of Emory's divisions on their right, and somehow the two corps lost contact and let a gap develop, and the Rebels saw it and made a hard counterattack that stopped the VI Corps and sent Emory's men flying.

Emory's other division came up to check the rout, and Upton brought his brigade over to help plug the gap, and after a while the situation was stabilized. Nevertheless, by midafternoon the Federals were doing little more than hold their own, and they had had severe losses. Upton was knocked off his horse by a shell fragment and Sheridan told him to go to the rear and get into a hospital. Upton disobeyed—it was his theory that combat commanders ought to be up front with their troops—and after a doctor put a tourniquet on his wounded leg he got in a stretcher and made the stretcher-bearers take him along with the brigade through the rest of the battle.[10]

Meanwhile Sheridan was getting the mess straightened out. He was up and down the field in a fury, his dark face aglow, dripping perspiration, his eyes snapping, his black horse all flecked with foam. He had his staff officers take details and comb the woods for stragglers and shirkers, and these recruiting parties caught the spark and went through the underbrush with sabers swinging, herding their captives forward, making brand-new infantry companies out of them, and leading them into the fight with mighty saber thwackings for all laggards. A Connecticut officer who watched them chuckled that he had not seen so much spanking since he was a schoolboy.[11]

While the stragglers were being rounded up Sheridan demanded recapture of the ground which had been lost to the Rebel counterattack. This job fell chiefly to the 8th Vermont, a veteran regiment whose Colonel Stephen Thomas had once been a leading Democratic politician, stoutly opposed to all coercion of the South. Recently he had gone home on furlough and his former party associates had chided him for deserting the true faith. "Thomas, you've changed," they complained. "We haven't." A true Vermonter, Thomas replied: "Fools never do."

Now he was about to lead his regiment across a meadow and into a smoky grove full of embattled Rebels, and the prospect was not inviting. Thomas sized it up, then rode out in front of his regiment, color-bearers beside him, and in his powerful spellbinder's voice he thundered:

"Boys, if you ever pray, the time to pray has come. Pray now, remember Ethan Allen and old Vermont, and we'll drive 'em to hell! Come on, old Vermont!"[12]

The he wheeled about, his sword held high, and rode at a walk toward the Rebel firing line, without a backward glance. Old Vermont followed, cheering, and a regiment or two in the XIX Corps jumped up to join in the charge, and the Southern battle line began to draw back.

Sheridan went galloping over to the left of his own line, to where General Getty led a division of the VI Corps. Sheridan had at last got Crook's infantry out of the ravine and they were going into battle formation far over on the right, and beside them Sheridan's chief of cavalry, General Alfred Torbert, had two good mounted divisions ready to go, and Sheridan's army now formed a great crescent, five miles from tip to tip, far overlapping the Confederate left flank. It was Sheridan's idea that this crescent must now move forward, and when he came up to Getty—felt hat gripped in one hand, nobody riding with him but a lone orderly—he was all dust and sweat and fire, and he was shouting:

"General, I've put Torbert in on the right and told him to give 'em hell, and he's doing it! Crook too is in on the right, and giving it to 'em. Press them, General—they'll run!" He swore a tremendous oath and repeated: "Press them, General—I know they'll run!"[13]

And now it was late afternoon, and behind the piled-up battle smoke the sky was streaked with crimson and pale green and yellow in a wild autumn sunset. The Federal battle line was rolling at last, and there was a tumult of artillery and musketry and cheering men—and suddenly it was like the old days, and there was a color and a shine and a drama to combat once more, and if battle was as terrible as ever it had at least begun to sparkle again.

Now and then as the line advanced a check would develop somewhere. Then one of Sheridan's staff would come up at a pounding gallop, to ride the length of the line pointing with his naked saber at the Rebel battle line, all gesture and compelling movement, saying never a word, and the line would lunge forward again. To the north could be seen Crook's battle line—a whole army corps tramping along in perfect order, skirmishers out in front, battle flags leaning forward, the ranks closing faultlessly as wounded men fell out, no one firing yet, every man yelling at the top of his voice.

Upton on his stretcher brought his brigade over to help Colonel Thomas and Old Vermont, and they took the Rebel position, chasing the Southern marksmen out of the wood and away from the hilltop they had been holding. The Vermonters drew up behind a stone wall to catch their breath, and suddenly a company officer gestured with his sword and cried: "Boys! Look at that!"

Beyond the lower ground in their front and to their right, two or three miles away, distinct in the clear sunset light, they saw what one man recalled as "a sight to be remembered a life-time"—two divisions of Yankee cavalry massed in solid columns, drawn sabers flashing in the sun like streaks of flame, thundering down at a full gallop to strike the flank and rear of the Confederate line. Southern artillery fired desperately to break the charge, but the charge could not be stopped. The outflanked Confederate line curled up, and the cavalry took guns and flags and prisoners, the squadrons riding wildly over broken fields after fugitive Confederates.

From their hilltop the Vermonters saw it, and they started forward again, and suddenly Sheridan was riding ahead of them, while Rebel bullets searched the dusk. The men saw him and cheered madly, and he swung his hat to them and called back: "Boys, this is just what I expected!"[14]

Most of the Union soldiers who were in that fight actually got a firsthand, close-up view of Sheridan before the day ended. This was a new thing for a Yankee army, since the commanding general was usually an off-stage presence rarely seen in battle. Sheridan seemed to appear from nowhere, attended by the solitary orderly who carried Sheridan's personal battle flag—a little swallow-tailed banner, half red and half white, bearing the two stars of a major general.

The experience of the 12th Connecticut was typical. The regiment was drawn up in a field, waiting for fresh ammunition, when an officer rode up to ask why they were standing there. While a regimental officer was explaining, a shell burst almost directly over the head of the mounted man. He was unhurt, and as the smoke blew away he called out to the men: "That's all right, boys—no matter—we can lick 'em!" And up and down the line men passed the word: "That's Sheridan!" and they cheered and laughed and waved their caps. Sheridan waved, told them to move forward as soon as they got their ammunition, and then went cantering off.[15]

The last Confederate resistance ended and darkness came and the cavalry rode hard through Winchester, storming at the Rebel rear guard. Early got his men and most of his possessions away clean, and he was fully entitled to boast that he had fought well against heavy odds, inflicting more loss than he received and balking his foe's attempt to cut off his retreat and destroy his army. It was also true that during the first half of the day the Federal program had been handled with an absolute minimum of skill.[16] Yet somehow these facts were not in the least important.

What was important was that the war now was on the upgrade. Sheridan had taken Atlanta and sprightly old Admiral Farragut had broken into Mobile Bay, and now the jaunty Rebel army in the valley had been broken and sent streaming off in defeat; and here was the point of rebound for the whole war. The Chicago platform might bewail failure and call for immediate peace, but now the war very clearly was not a failure. Since spring the Confederacy's one hope had been that the people of the North would get tired and quit. After Winchester that hope no longer had any roots.

Sheridan followed up his victory. His army went along the Valley Pike, and just south of Strasburg, where a roll of high ground known as Fisher's Hill cuts across the Valley from mountain to mountain, the Confederates made a stand. Sheridan lined up his troops, telling them to keep up a heavy fire whether or not they saw anything to shoot at, and while he bluffed a frontal attack he swung Crook's corps far to the west and brought it in on the Confederate flank. The blow was struck at dusk on September 22, and the whole Rebel line collapsed, losing twelve guns and a thousand prisoners.

Once again the Federal storming columns going up the slope found Sheridan dashing across their front, orderly and battle flag at his heels, Sheridan's black bullet head bare in the breeze: and always he was waving the men on, calling "Come on! Don't stop!" Once he came on a brigade which was winded and had stopped to pant, and he reined up and gestured toward the retreating Confederates, shouting: "Run boys, run! Don't wait to form! Don't let 'em stop!" Some soldier piped up to tell him that for the moment they were just too bushed to run, to which Sheridan called back: "If you can't run, then holler!" And holler they did, while the general rode off to press the pursuit.

There was a note to all of this that these Union troops were not used to: a note of triumph assured, a driving flaming will to victory that would stop for no obstacles and accept no excuses. The men responded to it, and wherever Sheridan went now he was greeted by passionate cheers. A VI Corps veteran wrote that ever since McClellan's day it had been a point of pride with his outfit not to cheer any officers—but Sheridan was different, and "tumultuous hurrahs came unbidden from the bottom of every heart and conventional restraint was forgotten."[17]

While Early's main body had been trying to hold on at Fisher's Hill, the gray cavalry had been on the other side of the Massanutten Ridge, encamped at Front Royal. Sheridan sent in young General Wilson with his cavalry division to drive them out, and Wilson made his attack in the dense fog of an early morning, splashing through the Shenandoah fords and forming line of battle on the outskirts of the town.

No one could see thirty yards in the gray murk and Wilson was afraid his units would lose touch, so he passed the word that when his own buglers sounded the charge all of the other buglers in the division should pick the call up and repeat it. Since every battery, troop, regiment, and brigade in the division had its own buglers, this meant a lot of music; and the dripping quiet of early dawn was broken by the insistent notes of the charge, blown first by the men at division headquarters and immediately picked up all along the line, until 250 buglers were blaring away together, and the high imperious notes went echoing along the Blue Ridge until it sounded like the voice of ten thousand trumpets. Under it there was a great thunder of shod hooves on soft earth, and the Yankee cavalry went in on the gallop, sabers swinging, every man shouting with the jubilant confidence of an army that has begun to feel that it is invincible. Front Royal was taken and the gray troopers went back up the Valley, and Wilson's regiments reassembled in the town and agreed that it was a great day in the morning.[18]

4. NO MORE DOUBT

Thurlow Weed, Republican boss of New York State, told Secretary Seward that "the conspiracy against Mr. Lincoln has collapsed," and those who had been looking for a hard-war man decided to climb on the band wagon. Salmon P. Chase, convinced at last that destiny would not tap his shoulder this year, began to make speeches urging Lincoln's re-election. Michigan's Senator Zach Chandler, bitter-end abolitionist, moved to make a little deal; after which John Charles Frémont, petulant darling of the Republican radicals' lunatic fringe, withdrew his third-party candidacy for the presidency. By Chandler's deal or by sheer coincidence, within forty-eight hours Lincoln accepted the resignation of Postmaster General Blair, whom all of the radicals hated—accepted it, in fact, before Blair had even submitted it.

As September came to an end Lincoln told his old friend Ward Lamon that although "Jordan has been a hard road to travel" he was beginning to think that he would wind up on the right side of the river. Dour old Gideon Welles wrote in his diary that "we are, I think, approaching the latter days of the rebellion."[1]

So a new feeling was abroad in the land; an exciting, growing conviction that a mighty tide was flowing at last. The armies had created this feeling, and the armies shared in it. Sheridan's troops were driving on up the Valley, surging all over the landscape as they moved, a double file of artillery and battle wagons on the roadway, half a dozen parallel columns of infantry tramping along on either side. The days were cool and sunny and the haunting mellow light of the war's last autumn lay on the land, and the men saw the panorama which they themselves were creating and rejoiced in it. The war had turned a corner, and for the first time these soldiers were learning what it felt like to be victors.

"Our march had been a grand triumphal pursuit of a routed enemy," wrote a man in the VI Corps. "Never had we marched with such light hearts; and although each day found us pursuing rapidly from dawn till dark, the men seemed to endure the fatigue with wonderful patience."[2]

Far out on either side of the marching columns were the cavalry flankers, guarding against surprise. In front moved the line of skirmishers, trotting lightly across fields which had long since lost their fences—"skirmishing only enough," the veteran felt, "to maintain a pleasant state of excitement."

Through Mount Jackson the army marched, to Harrisonburg, and beyond that to Mount Crawford, and the cavalry roved on ahead to Staunton and Waynesboro. As it moved, the army picked up a number of Confederate stragglers. These professed deep interest in the Northern election, and to a man they hoped that McClellan would win. A Connecticut soldier told about this in a letter home, adding: "I would state that the 'hero of the seven days retreat' is fast becoming unpopular in the army. Not that the soldiers dislike the man so much as the company he keeps." Another man expressed the same view: "There are a good many soldiers who would vote for McClellan but they cannot go Vallandigham for support."[3]

Sheridan now had the Valley in his possession, and he believed that Early was not capable of further offensive operations. To Grant it now seemed that Sheridan could break out of the Valley at its upper end, cutting across through Gordonsville and Charlottesville on the thrust Hunter had tried to make three months earlier and rejoining the Army of the Potomac around Petersburg. Sheridan objected. The move would take him far from his base of supplies, and the Rebel guerillas were being more pestiferous than ever. It would be better, he felt, to finish the job of ruining the Valley, take position much nearer to the Potomac, and them send Wright's corps back to Grant. Reluctantly, Grant deferred to his judgment, and on October 6 the army faced about and started back for the lower Valley.[4]

Morale was still high, but the brief atmosphere of holiday soldiering was gone. Guerilla warfare made men savage, and when the partisan rangers swept in for a fight neither side gave quarter. Cavalrymen said they would rather go into battle than patrol the Valley roads. One of Sheridan's aides was found in a field with his throat cut, and in hot fury Sheridan ordered every house, barn, and outbuilding within five miles burned to the ground. Farther down the Valley, Mosby's men struck at a supply train and its cavalry escort. Among the killed was a young Union officer who had been shot after he surrendered—or so, at any rate, the Federal troopers believed. Men from the 17th Pennsylvania Cavalry and the 2nd Regulars rode out for revenge, captured six of Mosby's riders, shot four of them, and hanged the remaining two. Under the dangling bodies they left a sign: "Such is the fate of Mosby's men."[5]

As the army withdrew Sheridan had the men get the matches out again, and the upper Valley got the treatment which the area below Strasburg had been given earlier. A cordon of cavalry brought up the rear, and behind it there was a blackened waste. A gunner said that "clean work was done," and a newspaper correspondent wrote: "The atmosphere, from horizon to horizon, has been black with the smoke of a hundred conflagrations, and at night a gleam brighter and more lurid than sunset has shot from every verge." Orders were to burn no dwellings, but if a burning barn happened to stand close to a house the house usually went up too, and the correspondent admitted that all of this incendiarism could not take place "without undue license" by stragglers and bummers; so "there have been frequent instances of rascality and pillage."

Nearly all barns and stables were destroyed, he recorded, most gardens and cornfields were ruined, and more than 5,000 head of livestock were driven off. Stout Union man though he was, this correspondent felt that the devastation "fearfully illustrates the horrible barbarity of war." Sheridan's orders were to leave each family enough to avert starvation, but marauding stragglers often carried away the last morsel. The newspaperman summed it up:

"The completeness of the devastation is awful. Hundreds of nearly starving people are going north. Our trains are crowded with them. They line the wayside. Hundreds more are coming; not half the inhabitants of the Valley can subsist on it in its present condition."[6]

A Confederate officer on Early's staff left bitter testimony:

"I rode down the Valley with the advance after Sheridan's retreating cavalry beneath great columns of smoke which almost shut out the sun by day, and in the red glare of bonfires which, all across that Valley, poured out flames and sparks heavenward and crackled mockingly in the night air; and I saw mothers and maidens tearing their hair and shrieking to Heaven in their fright and despair, and little children, voiceless and tearless in their pitiable terror."[7]

Fully a year later, an English traveler wrote that the Shenandoah Valley looked like one vast moor.[8]

Heavy smoke, and blackened earth, and unending fires at night: and with the army as it moved there was an increasing stream of refugees, as if some strange emigrant train were off on an unimaginable journey. At many houses, as the cavalry approached, people were all packed and waiting. They could ride in army wagons, perhaps, and with the army there would be food, and if they were asked where they wanted to go they would reply: "Anywhere, to get out of this." Many of the Dunkers and Mennonites were setting out to join relatives in Pennsylvania, and there were scores and hundreds of contrabands who were departing for no one could imagine what goal. They had been told that the Yankees killed colored people, but with every barn for sixty miles going up in flames it seemed to them that they ought to leave.

These contrabands had many children, who looked in wide-eyed wonder at the odd things that were going on. The surgeon of the 77th New York reined in once by a rickety old cart drawn by an even more rickety horse. The cart seemed to be absolutely brimming over with small children, and the surgeon asked the bandannaed mammy who was driving: "Aunty, are these all your children?" She looked at him in mild surprise and protested: "They's only eighteen of 'em."[9]

Early pressed close behind the rear guard, and his cavalry struck whenever it found a chance. But things had changed since the early days of the war, when Confederate troopers could ride rings around the Yankees. The Rebel supply of horses was running out, and manpower was getting low, and the squadrons that came in on turnpike and field to harass the blue files no longer had the old advantage. A Confederate officer confessed glumly that Sheridan's cavalrymen nowadays "were more to be feared than their infantry—better soldiers all through."[10]

Sheridan grew irritated by the unending rear-guard actions, and at last he called in Torbert and told him to end the nuisance once and for all: "Whip or get whipped." On October 9 Torbert sent Custer and Merritt back for a head-on fight, and their seasoned divisions broke the Confederate mounted line to bits and chased the fragments up the Valley for twenty miles and more, capturing men and horses and eleven guns and inflicting, as one of the Southern riders confessed, "the greatest disaster that ever befell our cavalry during the whole war."[11] The Union army continued to retire at its leisure, smoke and flames still marking its passage, and by the middle of October Sheridan put it in position on a chain of low hills behind a little stream known as Cedar Creek, a little north of the town of Strasburg, twenty-odd miles south of Winchester.

For a few days the army rested in this camp. Early was not far away, but his army had been beaten twice in the past month and his cavalry had been thoroughly routed within the week, and the Yankees seem to have assumed that there was not much fight left in him—a risky assumption to make where Jubal Early was concerned, for he was as pugnacious a man as ever wore Rebel gray. And since there was a three-way disagreement between Grant, Sheridan, and the War Department as to what Sheridan ought to do next, Sheridan suspended the order transferring the VI Corps to Petersburg, put Wright in temporary command of the army, and went off to Washington for consultation. The situation of the rival armies seemed stable, and nothing much was apt to happen in his absence.[12]

Actually, the situation was highly unstable, principally because the destroying Yankee host had done its job so thoroughly. Early had perhaps 15,000 men with him, and the one thing these men could not do was stay where they were. The Valley had been so completely devastated that they could get no supplies of any kind from the surrounding country. Every mouthful of food for man and beast had to come up by wagon train, via Staunton and Waynesboro, and it was a hard pull for the worn-out Confederate transportation system. Early could either leave the Valley altogether, ceding the whole territory to the Yankees for the rest of the war—or he could attack.

To attack an army whose combat strength was twice his own would be, of course, to take fantastic risks. But the Confederate situation was desperate, and if fantastic risks were not taken the war was as good as lost. Early appears to have figured that Sheridan's force was not quite as solid as it looked anyway. The VI Corps was very good, but Confederate intelligence put a much lower estimate on the other two corps. Also, a good part of Sheridan's strength was in his cavalry, which did not ordinarily cut much of a figure in an infantry battle. Altogether, the odds could be worse.

In addition, there were two other encouraging factors. One was the obvious fact that nobody on the Federal side had any notion that the Confederates might take the offensive. The other was the position of the Union army.

Cedar Creek came down from the northwest to join the north fork of the Shenandoah River, and the chain of hills just behind the creek, on which the Federals were camped, ran from northwest to southeast. The VI Corps was on the Federal right, roughly a mile from where the Valley Pike crossed the creek and climbed through the higher ground. Next to it, north and west of the pike, was the XIX Corps. Southeast of the turnpike, anchoring the Union left, was Crook's corps. It was in a good position to knock down any force which tried to come up along the main highway, but there was open ground nearly a mile wide between its own left and the point where creek and river met. Since the river just there lay in what looked like an impassable gorge, it seemed unlikely that the Confederates would be able to get across and make any trouble for this exposed flank.

Unlikely, except to soldiers who had to take fantastic risks anyway—the desperate, fifty-to-one sort of gamble that led Washington to take his army across the Delaware to attack the Hessian camp at Trenton. To Jubal Early the exposed Federal left looked like opportunity. He studied the ground carefully, and it seemed that an army corps could be led along that impassable gorge if the man who led it was thoroughly familiar with the layout and did not mind marching his entire command within 400 yards of the Yankee picket line.[13]

To lessen the risk, Early sent his cavalry and part of his infantry over to the west, thrusting them forward as if he planned to attack the Yankee right flank. He put some more men in place where Wright's and Emory's men could see them, and he organized a third column to stand by for an advance directly along the turnpike. Then, with everything ready, he had General John B. Gordon take his army corps down into the gorge to get in behind the Federal left and open the attack. It meant an all-night hike, much of it in single file, and the men left canteens, cooking utensils, and everything except weapons and ammunition in camp so that no rattling or clanking of equipment would give them away.

So the army moved. Very early on the shivery, misty dawn of October 19, with fog hanging in the low places and the darkness lying thick in the graveyard hour between moonset and dawn, the Confederates rose up out of the gorge and came in yelling and shooting on the drowsy flank of Sheridan's army.

The day before, certain election commissioners from Connecticut had come into the Yankee lines to take the presidential vote of Connecticut soldiers, and they remained in camp overnight as special headquarters guests. They liked what they saw of army life, and to their hosts at supper they expressed regret that they could not see a fight before they went home. The officers who were entertaining them said they would like to accommodate them, but there just wasn't a chance: "it seemed very certain that Early would keep at a respectful distance."[14]

So here before reveille there was a popping and a racket off at the extreme left, and while nobody imagined it was anything except some little picket-line tussle there was a general stir in the Union camp, and the veterans began to cook breakfast on the theory that whether this was a false alarm or the real thing it would do no harm to eat and be ready. Then, suddenly, artillery began to pound, the infantry firing became sustained and intense, and a wild uproar came through the dark mist—and the election commissioners quickly found their clothes and ballot boxes and horses and took off for the North just as fast as they could go.[15]

Crook's corps was crumpled up in a twinkling, with Rebels coming in from the left and rear before the men even had time to grab their muskets. The corps had seven guns in line, and these were captured before they could fire a shot—to be spun about immediately by their captors and fired through the confusing mist into the middle of the Yankee camp. Crook commanded about 7,000 infantry that day, and in a matter of minutes those who had not been shot or captured were running for the rear, all 7,000 of them. For the next twenty-four hours, that corps did not exist as a usable military instrument.

Almost before the rest of the army realized that an attack was being made, Confederate Gordon had his infantry on the hill where Sheridan's headquarters had been—which meant that he was in rear of the entire army and that the men of Emory's and Wright's corps, who had as yet seen no Rebels, could do nothing on earth except retreat as speedily as possible. The surprise could not have been more complete.

General Wright came up from his own quarters, working to get troops over to the Valley Pike and check the rout. One of the men who went with him wrote that nothing was left of Crook's corps except "a disorganized, routed, demoralized, terrified mob of fugitives," and he sketched "the universal confusion and dismay" along the turnpike:

"Wagons and ambulances lumbering hither and thither in disorder; pack horses led by frightened bummers, or wandering at their own free will; crowds of officers and men, some shod and some barefoot, many of them coatless and hatless, with and without their rifles, but all rushing wildly to the rear; oaths and blows alike powerless to halt them; a cavalry regiment stretched across the field, unable to stem the torrent."[16]

Wright was in the middle of it, bareheaded, his beard all clotted with blood from a wound under the chin. He got the 2nd Connecticut heavies into line on a slope overlooking the highway, and as the men lay down to fire the sun came up and they found themselves looking directly into it, unable to see the Rebels, who were firing steadily: "We could see nothing but that enormous disk, rising out of the fog, while they could see every man in our line and could take good aim." The fog thinned, and more Confederates came in on the left and rear, and the regiment had to retreat, retreat turning quickly into a rout. General Emory brought over a brigade and sent it straight up the turnpike to break the Rebel charge and give time for a rally.

Federals and Confederates met head on and around the regimental battle flags there was furious fighting. A man in the 8th Vermont remembered that "men seemed more like demons than human beings as they struck fiercely at each other with clubbed muskets and bayonets," and at times it seemed that a dozen Confederates at once were reaching for each flagstaff. The colors tossed up and down in the dust and smoke. When they dropped the Southerners would cheer, and when they rose again the Northerners would cheer, and after a time the brigade got back out of the road and joined in the retreat. It still had all of its flags, but it had lost two thirds of its men.[17]

Step by step, the whole army retreated, and by the middle of the morning it formed a shaky battle line four miles north of its original position. This line stretched away to the west of the pike, and there was a lull in the fighting, and the men scooped up little breastworks and got ready to meet another attack. Crook's corps was gone, and plenty of men had vanished from the other commands too, and all of these fugitives, together with the usual concourse of coffee boilers, wagoners, ambulance drivers, and the like were stretched out in steady flight all the way back to Winchester.

This flight was not a headlong rush, because even a frightened man cannot run so very far without pausing for breath. After the first panic wore off the men settled down to a walk, carrying on their flight, as one officer said, "in a manner as systematic as if they had been taught it." Now and then they would stop to make coffee and talk things over. Then they would go on again, sauntering along without haste but also without any intention of making a real halt anywhere. It was noticed, in this as in all similar cases, that it was almost impossible for any officer to rally and re-form such fugitives unless they recognized him as belonging to their own regiment or brigade. They would obey no strangers. They might fall into ranks obediently enough for a strange officer, but the ranks would evaporate as soon as he tried to lead them back into action.[18]

The triumphant Confederates meanwhile had seized all of the Union camps, and had 1,300 prisoners and 18 of Sheridan's cannon in their possession. Ahead of them, perhaps a mile and a half to the north, they could see the last Federal battle line; it was nearly two miles wide, and swarms of cavalry were forming up on either flank, and as Early looked at it he was jocund and full of confidence.

Exactly one month earlier his army had been running away from the Yankees, at Winchester. Now it was the Yankees who were in flight, and Early was in high spirits. A good many of his soldiers were leaving their commands to despoil the captured camps, with especial attention to the good food their foes had not been able to take with them, but this absenteeism did not worry him. He declared that the Yankee battle line visible west of the turnpike was no more than a rear guard. It would go away before long and the victory would be complete.

General Gordon was of a different notion.

"That is the VI Corps, general," he said. "It will not go unless we drive it from the field."

But Early would not listen to him. The Yankees had been beaten and most of them had run away: the rest would run away before long and that was all there was to it. Still, to play safe he put his staff to work to round up the camp looters and get them back into formation.[19] From his headquarters post on a hilltop he continued to look north with deep satisfaction. Banks and Sigel, Hunter and Sheridan—they were all alike, when they collided with a Rebel army in the Valley!

. . . On a rise of ground just south of Winchester, about fifteen miles from the battlefield, the 17th Pennsylvania cavalry had been in bivouac. They had come down from Martinsburg, guarding trains against guerillas, and they had been ordered to wait here for General Sheridan, who had reached Winchester the night before on his return trip from Washington.

The day of October 19 began as usual for these troopers, with "Boots and Saddles" sounding before sunrise. As the men fed their horses and got their own breakfasts they could hear the mutter of gunfire, far to the south. Nobody thought much about it, since the word was that Wright was going to make a reconnoissance in force that morning to find out just where the Rebel army was, and it was assumed that that was the cause of the firing. The men finished their meal and stood by, waiting for the general.

Sheridan rode out about nine o'clock, a few aides riding with him. It was a sunny morning, bare fields rolling away to the hills and mountains which blazed with autumn colors, a warm Indian summer haze thickening the air. Off to the south there was that continued sound of firing, perhaps a bit louder now than it had been earlier. Sheridan seemed to be puzzled. As he picked up his cavalry escort he halted, dismounted, and bent over with his ear to the ground, listening intently. When he got back on his horse his swarthy face was clouded.

Down the road went general, aides, and cavalry, horses moving at a walk. After a mile or so they came upon a wagon train all in a tangle, wagons turned every which way, nobody moving. Sheridan sent his Major Forsyth trotting on ahead to see what was wrong, and presently Forsyth came back at a mad gallop. The train had been bound for the front, he reported, and at this spot had met an officer heading for Winchester bearing news that the army had been routed and was coming back in full retreat—on hearing which the teamsters had begun to swing their wagons around without waiting for orders.

Sheridan told Major Spera, the cavalry commander, to give him fifty of his best mounted men and to spread the rest across the road as traffic police: untangle the wagon train, round up fugitives, and in general see that everybody who thought he was going to Winchester turned and headed back for the place where the fighting was going on. Then with his chosen fifty Sheridan set off down the road, the horses moving at a walk no longer.

First they met wagon trains, coming back to escape capture, and these were told to park in the fields and await orders. Then they met the outriders of defeat—sutlers, camp followers of high and low degree, artillerymen without their guns, headquarters trains, battery wagons, caissons, and little knots of stragglers and walking wounded. A little farther on, they saw groups of men in the fields, clustering about campfires, boiling coffee, and they met increasing numbers of men walking along the highway. And always the sound of the firing grew louder.

Here and there Sheridan would rein up and call: "Turn back, men! Turn back! Face the other way!" Once he told a group of stragglers: "Face the other way, boys—if I had been there this morning this wouldn't have happened! You'll have your own camps back before night!"

Most of the time, however, he did not come to a halt but kept on at a gallop, swinging his hat in a great arc, now and then pointing toward the south, always calling: "Turn back, men! Turn back!"

The effect was electric. One group of coffee boilers, who had been stretched at ease around a fire, jumped up with a yell as he went past, kicked their coffeepots over, seized their muskets, and started back toward the battlefield. All along the way men sprang up and cheered. Those who were near the road turned and shouted, waving their arms in frantic signal, to attract the attention of men who were sauntering across fields a quarter of a mile away. They pointed to the speeding cavalcade in the road and at the top of their lungs they cried: "Sheridan! Sheridan!"[20]

The Valley Pike had been macadamized once, but in the war years it had seen many armies and no repairs, and its surface now was all pitted and broken, and a cloud of white dust rose as the mounted men galloped on, Sheridan in front, the rest trailing after him.

Sheridan was on his favorite horse, a tireless black named Rienzi, and it became a fable and a folk legend how Rienzi went a full twenty miles at a gallop without stopping. The legend outdid reality. There were a number of little halts, when Sheridan would pull up to ask for news, and at one halt he had Major Forsyth cut a little switch for him, with which he birched Rienzi into greater speed. Once he met a panicky man riding to the rear on a mule, and he asked the man how things were at the front. "Oh, everything is lost and gone," shouted the man, "but it will be all right when you get there"—after which the man got the mule to a gallop and kept on in the direction of Winchester. Once Sheridan stopped to look in on a field hospital, and talked to some of the wounded. Counting everything, Rienzi had a number of chances to catch his breath.

Yet the legendary picture is close enough to fact: black-headed man on a great black horse, riding at furious speed, his escort dim in the dust behind him, waving his arm and swinging his absurd flat little hat and shouting continually the order to turn around and get back into the fighting; a man followed for many miles by the cheers of men who spun on their heels and returned to the firing line because they believed that if he was going to be there everything would be all right again—and because the look of him, and his great ringing voice, and the way he moved and rode and gestured somehow made going back into battle with him seem light and gay and exciting, even to men who had been in many battles.

Major Forsyth wrote that every time a group of stragglers saw Sheridan the result was the same—"a wild cheer of recognition, an answering wave of the cap." In no case, he said, did the men fail to shoulder their arms and follow the general, and for miles behind him the turnpike was crowded with men pressing forward to the front which they had run away from a few hours earlier. And all along the highway, for mile on mile, and in the fields beside the road, there went up the great jubilant chant: "Sheridan! Sheridan!"

As they got closer to the front Sheridan became grimmer. Major Forsyth wrote: "As he galloped on his features gradually grew set, as though carved in stone, and the same dull red glint I had seen in his piercing black eyes when, on other occasions, the battle was going against us, was there now."[21]

They came at last to a ridge where there were batteries in action, dueling at long range; and up ahead, on the right of the road, they could see the ranks of the VI Corps, men standing in line waiting to be used. Sheridan came plowing up through the fainthearts and the skulkers, and his face was black as midnight, and now he was shouting: "Turn about, you damned cowardly curs, or I'll cut you down! I don't expect you to fight, but come and see men who like to!" And he swung his arm in a great inclusive gesture toward the VI Corps up ahead.[22]

These men had been waiting in line for an hour or more. As veterans, they knew that the army had been beaten in detail and not by head-on assault, and they were grumbling about it, making profane remarks about men who ran away—and then, far behind them, they heard cheering.

"We were astounded," wrote a man in the Vermont Brigade. "There we stood, driven four miles already, quietly waiting for what might be further and immediate disaster, and far in the rear we heard the stragglers and hospital bummers and the gunless artillerymen actually cheering as though a victory had been won. We could hardly believe our ears."

And then, while the men were still looking their questions at one another, out in front of the line came Sheridan himself, still riding at a swinging gallop—and the whole army corps blew up in the wildest cheer it had ever given in all of its career, and the roar went rocketing along the line as Sheridan rode on past brigade after brigade of the toughest veterans in the Army of the Potomac. The Vermont Brigade's historian wrote fondly:

"Such a scene as his presence produced and such emotions as it awoke cannot be realized once in a century. All outward manifestations were as enthusiastic as men are capable of exhibiting; cheers seemed to come from throats of brass, and caps were thrown to the tops of the scattering oaks; but beneath and yet superior to these noisy demonstrations there was in every heart a revulsion of feeling, and a pressure of emotion, beyond description. No more doubt or chance for doubt existed; we were safe, perfectly and unconditionally safe, and every man knew it."

All along the line went Sheridan, waving his hat, telling the troops: "Boys, we'll get the tightest twist on them they ever saw. We'll get all those camps back." To a colonel who rode up and said they were glad to see him, Sheridan replied: "Well, by God, I'm glad to be here!" And to another officer, still pessimistic from the morning's licking, who said that Early intended to drive them clear out of the Shenandoah Valley, Sheridan barked in fury: "What? Three corps of infantry and all of my cavalry; Jubal Early drive me out of the valley? I'll lick him like blazes before night! I'll give him the worst licking he ever had!"[23]

And that was the way of it, in the end. After Sheridan passed by the men in line retied their shoes, tucked pants legs inside their socks, tightened their belts, unfastened cartridge-box lids, slid ramrods down rifle barrels to make sure the weapons were loaded, and jerked their forage caps down lower on their foreheads. From the rear the returning stragglers came up in droves, wandering along the lines, finding their proper regiments and taking their places—to the tune of jibes from their comrades. Sheridan went to General Wright, who was lying on the ground, his throat and chin all swollen, blood on his coat. It was hard for him to talk, but he got up when Sheridan came, made his report, and prepared to go into action. Sheridan took plenty of time, waiting for his stragglers to come up, and it was nearly four in the afternoon when his battle line finally went forward.[24]

When it hit, it hit hard. Confederate ranks were thinned by the absence of men who persisted in foraging among what the Yankees had left, and if all of the absentees had been in line Sheridan still would have had more men than Early had. Anyway, this Federal army knew it was going to win, at last, and it rolled up to the Rebel lines with irresistible might.

One of Emory's men reported that the Confederates were retreating presently "in precisely the same kind of disorder we had exhibited that morning," and he wrote that they pursued eagerly because "the sight of so many rebel heels made it an easy thing to be brave." On a ridge, by and by, the Confederates made a stand, and with their heels no longer visible the joys of pursuit were not quite so overpowering; but Sheridan had a great mass of cavalry swinging in on the flank

like a scythe, and it sheared in behind the Rebel infantry and the whole line
gave way, and a disordered rout went southward as dusk came down.

Cheering madly, the Federal infantry pressed on, determined not to stop until
they had at least got past their old camping grounds. At times it seemed as if the
front were all flags, since the color sergeants were not loaded down with weapons and accouterments and so could run faster than the others. The infantry
pressed on so hard that George Custer once turned to his mounted men, pointing, and cried: "Are you going to let infantry get ahead of you?"[25]

It was the cavalry that made the victory complete. It cannoned into the Confederate wagon and artillery train, smashed a bridge near the town of Strasburg,
and went bucketing up and down and back and forth through the whole confused retreat. All of the Federal guns and wagons that had been lost that morning were retaken, together with twenty-five Confederate guns and any number
of wagons, and Early's army was ruined.

At times the cavalry was going too fast to take prisoners. Rebels who surrendered would be told, "You stay here!" while the captors rode off to get more—
after which most of the prisoners would disappear in the dark and try to rejoin
their comrades. A South Carolina officer who got away recalled that he had
surrendered five times during the retreat. The 5th New York boasted that one of
its troopers, a tough Montenegrin named Heiduc, had personally sabered the
two teamsters of a Confederate baggage wagon and had himself brought the vehicle back to camp.

Sheridan's word was good. The troops occupied their old camps that night,
and at least some of them found that hardly any of their things had been taken;
possibly fewer Rebels left the ranks for plunder than Early afterward alleged. A
field in front of Sheridan's headquarters was filled with captured matériel—guns
and ambulances and baggage wagons and stacks of muskets—and Sheridan's
hell-for-leather scouts equipped themselves with a score of captured Confederate flags and paraded wildly across the firelight with them. General Emory
watched Sheridan ride proudly by and he mused: "That young man has made a
great name for himself today."[26]

A few days after the battle a Connecticut soldier looked over the long files of
prisoners and wrote to his family that the Rebs were "smart healthy-looking
men," clad in neat gray uniforms and slouch hats. "They are very quick, walk
like horses," he added, and he found most of them quite cheerful, laughing and
joking all of the time. And all of them, he said, "from officers down to privates,
said they were tired of the war and that peace was worth more than the
C.S.A."[27]

SIX

Endless Road Ahead

1. EXCEPT BY THE SWORD

A LUMINOUS MIST of Indian summer lay on the desolate plains around Petersburg, and on the horizon the surviving woodlands were as remote and unreal as the memory of peace, magical with rich color, cool green of pines blending into the deep russet brown of oaks and the flaming red of maples and dogwood. Near the trees were thousands of tents and canvas-roofed huts, and across the fields and hills where there were neither tents nor trees were mile upon mile of trenches, scarring the earth with grotesque irregular patterns, the ground between them bristling with tangles of abatis and sinister sharpened stakes of *chevaux-de-frise*. Autumn sunlight sparkled on rifle barrels and bayonets, in the trenches and the skirmishers' rifle pits and the big square forts, and gleamed from the bright metal of the guns; and at night all the front glowed with flashing fires as the armies sniped and bombarded each other, and the great mortar shells climbed the sky in high slow parabolas, fuses burning red in the black sky.

The rival lines of forts and trenches ran for more than thirty-five miles. They began north of the James, at gloomy White Oak Swamp, and from the swamp they curved and twisted for eight miles to the north bank of the James. Along the river itself there was a four-mile stretch where Confederate artillery, mounted on the bluffs along the southern shore, barred the way against the Yankee monitors and gunboats. Then the trenches began again, running for five miles across the Bermuda Hundred neck to the Appomattox River, and here again, for four miles along the river bank, there was artillery. Then, below the river, due east from Petersburg and so close to the city that Yankee gunners could throw shells into warehouses and churches and dwellings if they chose, there were trenches once more.

These followed the battle lines that had been fixed in June, and they led south for four or five miles to the Jerusalem Plank Road—never very far apart, the men who occupied them always under fire, the hideous red wound of the mine crater lying just back of the Rebel parapets. Below the Plank Road the lines swung southwest, and here, early in the summer, they had ended, the Confederate system anchored by a work named Fort Mahone, the Yankee line tied to an opposing work named Fort Sedgwick. By day and by night, month after month, these forts dueled with each other, and the soldiers of the two armies had named the Federal work "Fort Hell" and the Confederate work "Fort Damnation."[1]

Always the lines had been creeping off toward the southwest. Since the day the mine was exploded the Federals had made no more frontal assaults. Grant resumed the old habit of edging constantly around by his left, looking always for a chance to strike in past the Rebel flank. There had been a series of moves of this kind during late summer and autumn, with Federal troops trying to get west from Fort Hell. None of these moves came to very much, and some had ended in humiliating defeat. The II Corps, for instance, was roundly whipped at a place called Reams's Station, men running in panic from a Rebel counterattack which the old II Corps would have beaten off with ease, Hancock riding among the routed troops waving his hat and crying: "Come on! We can beat them yet! Don't leave me, for God's sake!"[2]

Yet after each of these moves, somehow, the Union position was a little better and the Confederate position was a little worse. Lee was forever being compelled to stretch his line farther and farther, which meant that it was steadily growing thinner. While Confederate manpower was declining, he was being given more and more ground to hold. Month after month the Union army reached out, slowly but inexorably drawing closer to the railroad lines behind the Confederate right and rear which Lee must keep unbroken if his army and Richmond were to live.

Behind Grant's army was visible the enormous power of the North. City Point, which had been the sleepiest of riverside hamlets, had become one of the world's great seaports. Wharves lined the waterfront for more than a mile, with more docks extending up the Appomattox. An average day would see 40 steamboats, 75 sailing vessels, and 100 barges tied up or anchored along the waterfront. An army hospital that covered 200 acres and could accommodate 10,000 patients crowned a bluff above the river. There were vast warehouses for quartermaster, commissary, and ordnance departments; bakeries, blacksmith shops, wagon-repair shops, barracks for soldiers, quarters for civilian workers. Two steam engines had been set up to pump a water supply for this strange military city, and half a dozen sprinkling carts had been imported to lay the dust in its streets. The quartermaster general boasted that the facilities here were so extensive that he could easily supply an army of 500,000 men if he had to, and he had four passenger steamers providing daily service between City Point and Washington. (Very bad service, too, according to a newspaper correspondent, who found the boats dirty, crowded, and odorous and the food hardly fit to eat.)[3]

To connect this seaport with the army, the government had built a twenty-one-mile railroad, complete with freight yards, coal docks, roundhouse, repair shops, and all the rest. Nucleus of this was a prewar line which connected Petersburg with City Point, but of that seven-mile stub nothing much remained except the right of way; it had been a five-foot-gauge affair, and the military road was built to the standard four feet eight and one half inches. Branches had been built to run up and down behind the front, so that all of the military area below the Appomattox could be serviced by rail.

This railroad was enormously useful, since it meant that the fighting line could be kept supplied even in the worst weather, and it made the speedy reinforcement of any part of the line comparatively simple. The railroad amused the soldiers immensely. Even while it was contemporary, it managed to look quaint. It had been built in a great hurry and there had been almost no grading of the right of way, the tracks simply being laid on unprepared ground. As a result the railroad snaked up and down over hills and hollows, and it was said that watching a train go by was like watching a fly walk down a corrugated washboard. When a well-loaded train was at the top of a grade the engineer would open the throttle and go thundering down into the valley, hoping that the added momentum would get him up the opposite slope. If it did not he would back up and make a fresh start. If he carried troops, the men often would be ordered to get out and push.

The line had been built by railroad men. Army engineers had said that the road could never be operated—the grades would be too steep and cargo-carrying capacity would be too small. The railroad men knew better and went ahead with their program, and by fall the line was operating eighteen trains a day, with from fifteen to two dozen cars in each train, and was doing a fair passenger business besides.[4]

An Episcopal bishop from Atlanta, who had come north on a pass from General Sherman and who stopped off to visit Grant on his trip back south, was greatly impressed by the abundance of military supplies at City Point—"not merely profusion, but extravagance; wagons, tents, artillery, ad libitum. Soldiers provided with everything." He thought of the Confederate armies' lean rations and then looked in amazement at the comforts available to the Yankees. Bakeries were turning out thousands of loaves of fresh bread, sutlers' shops were everywhere, soldiers were forever buying extras to supplement their regular diet, and to him this reflected the wealth of the North.

The bishop believed that the consciousness of wealth and power had a direct effect on the mental attitude of the Northern soldiers and the Northern people. Everyone he talked to seemed obsessed with the greatness and destiny of the Federal Union. He found "a universal horror of rebellion," which made people feel that Rebels were almost "outside the pale of humanity," so that it was no sin to commit almost any sort of outrage on Southern people or property. It seemed to the good bishop that this was not merely a purse-proud complacency; it was something that looked far past the present, beyond the war to a future greatness for the whole country that would go beyond all present comprehension. He wrote: "Their idol is less the Union of the past than the sublime Union of the future, destined soon to overshadow all the nations."[5]

There was power in this sentiment, and as the fall progressed it seemed to overshadow everything else. It even dominated the one great emotional drive which had been bred into the very bones of the Army of the Potomac—the love which the army still felt for General McClellan. As election day approached there was much talk of McClellan among the veterans. A Quaker nurse at the City Point hospital wrote in September that "if it is left to the soldiers, his election is sure," and it was clear that the old affection for the handsome little general still ran strong.[6]

"Soldiers' eyes would brighten when they talked of him," one veteran recalled. "Their hard, lean, browned faces would soften and light up with affection when they spoke of him"—and yet, he continued, it was affection only. There was not, in the showdown, anything in it that would carry the election. Talking things over, the veterans agreed that they had been a better, stronger army in 1862, when McClellan commanded, than they were now in 1864, under Grant. Yet they also agreed that if Grant had commanded in 1862 the war would have been won in that year, while if McClellan had commanded in 1864 "he would have ended the war in the Wilderness—by establishing the Confederacy."

A man in the 20th Maine wrote that McClellan still was "almost worshiped" by the soldiers, but that very few would vote for him. By and large, they interpreted his candidacy much as the Confederates did: to vote against Lincoln would be to consent to dissolution of the Union. An officer in what was left of the Iron Brigade, musing about the election, put his thoughts on paper: "On one side is war, and stubborn, patient effort to restore the old Union and national honor; on the other side is inglorious peace and shame, the old truckling subserviency to Southern domination, and a base alacrity in embracing some vague, deceptive political subterfuge instead of honorable and clearly defined principles."[7]

And so, when election day came, the veterans voted by resounding majorities against McClellan, voted for Lincoln and for war to the bitter end—and, voting so, swung shut forever a door into their own past.

For McClellan had always been the great symbol. He was the trumpets these soldiers had heard and the flags they had carried and the faraway, echoing cheers they had raised: the leader of an unreal army which had come marching out of the horn gates with golden light on its banners, an impossible sunrise staining the sky above its path, and now it had gone into the land of remembered dreams. Everything that these men had, one supposes, they would have given to be again the army McClellan had commanded and to have him again for a leader, and yet they did not try to vote the past back into existence because they were fond young men no longer. They had come of age and they gave history something new to look at, not seen before in all the record of wars and men of war the sight, that is, of veteran soldiers who had long outlived enthusiasm and heroics walking quietly up to ballot boxes and voting for more war to be fought by themselves instead of voting for an end to it and no more fighting.

No one did any fancy talking about it, and it is probable that very little fancy thinking was done. It is even possible to doubt that many of the veterans were consciously voting for freedom and Union. At bottom, what counted most may have been nothing more than a simple refusal to admit that they could be beaten. An officer wrote that "they were unwilling that their long fight should be set down as a failure, even though thus far it seemed so," and that probably says it. The men were not quitters, and when it came time to vote they said so according to their understanding of the case. But it is not hard to agree with the New England soldier who, looking back after the war, remarked that the Army of the Potomac was never pluckier than when it voted by a big majority for Lincoln's re-election and the continuation of the war.[8]

Not long after the soldiers had cast their ballots the army was ordered to load all of its cannon, train them on suitable Rebel targets, and fire 100 rounds from each gun—a colossal salute in honor of Sheridan's victory at Cedar Creek. There had been many salutes of that kind this fall—salutes for Sheridan's army, and for Sherman's, and for victories by the Navy—and it seems to have occurred to no one that although this army was constantly firing salutes to celebrate somebody else's triumph, no one was ever firing salutes for the Army of the Potomac.

Its role was inglorious, as men then figured glory. It won no victories and earned no applause; its job was just to hang on and fight and make final victory possible. By election day the army had been in intimate contact with its foes for six unbroken months. During all of that time there had been two or three days when contact was maintained by cavalry alone. All the rest of the time, in sunlight and in darkness, infantry and artillery had been in action somewhere along the front. During August, September, and October—months when the front was relatively inactive—the army's siege artillery alone threw nearly six tons of shell every day into the Rebel lines.[9]

The Confederates gave as much as they received. A Pennylsvania soldier whose outfit was moved into Fort Sedgwick that fall wrote that "we are now in fort hell and it seems pretty much like it. On Tuesday of last week the Rebs threw 132 mortar shells into our camp . . . last Friday they threw 129 . . . every few days we have to practice on dodging shells to save our top knots." Artillerists on both sides had a way of firing any kind of scrap iron when there was work at close quarters, and a soldier who was wounded by such a salvo in a fight near Drury's Bluff explained: "the damned rebels fired a whole blacksmith shop over here, but nothing happened to hit me but the anvil."[10]

In such ways as they could the soldiers tried to make things easier for themselves. During daylight, the picket lines did little or no firing. When dusk came the men would call across to each other, "Get into your holes!" and the shooting would begin. In some parts of the line the rival marksmen agreed to fire high, and if someone accidentally put a bullet close to his enemies there would be an angry protest.

Even the IX Corps began to find trench life a little easier. Its colored division was transferred over to the Army of the James, and when the Confederates learned about it they dropped their old habit of shooting to kill every time a member of this luckless corps raised his head. When the corps was moved down to the left of the line, where there was a considerable distance between the trenches, one man wrote that "it was a great relief to be able to stand upright without the certainty of being shot," and another said: "It doesn't seem like war here. We can walk clear over to their picket line and trade coffee, tea, etc., for articles of theirs."

When the Irish Brigade found itself stationed opposite Mahone's Confederate division, which contained many Irish soldiers, it had a fine time and its historian reported: "The soldiers on both sides mingled freely, exchanged newspapers, coffee, tobacco and sometimes whisky." He added that this did not mean that the Rebels were losing any of their combativeness, for "when it came to actual fighting, they fought like bull-dogs."[11]

The comment was characteristic. The queer, upside-down comradeship which six months of battle-front intimacy had begun to create between the armies did not mean that anybody had ceased to fight hard. Being sensible men, the soldiers tacitly agreed to defang the day-to-day picket-line firing, which would not affect the outcome of the war very much if it went on for a century, but battles were going to be as grim and deadly as ever. A Michigan soldier in the II Corps remembered how his brigade got flanked and cut to pieces during a brisk little fight beyond the extreme left, late in October, and he commented drily: "Of course it would not be gallant to say that anybody run, but if there was any tall walking done during the war, we did it crossing that field."[12]

In December, Warren's corps and some cavalry were sent on a long raid aimed at Southern railroad lines and supply bases near the Meherrin River. The Weldon Railroad, which came up to Petersburg from the south, had long since been cut, but the Confederates were bringing up supplies on it to a point some twenty miles from Petersburg and then hauling them the rest of the way by wagon, and Grant wanted this traffic broken up.

It began like an enjoyable diversion. Once out of the trenches, the soldiers were in country which, at least by contrast with what they had been looking at, seemed untouched by war. It was nice to be in such country, even though a sleety December drizzle had set in, and one man felt that "the lowing of the cow and the tinkling of sheep bells suggested that quieter days than those that came to us still dawned upon the world." As a more tangible boon, there was good foraging, and the men ate many chickens and turkeys.[13] The Atlanta bishop had understood the matter: the Union soldier saw no wrong in taking chickens and turkeys owned by men who were in rebellion.

The big idea of this raid was to destroy so much of the railroad that it would no longer be practical for Lee's commissariat to run a wagon line to the end of the track, and once the infantry got into position the work of destruction began, soldiers working for miles up and down the right of way. The work went on far into the night, and a rookie in the 198th Pennsylvania saw it as strange and exciting: "As far as the eye could reach were seen innumerable glowing fires, and thousands of busy blue coats tearing up the rails and piling up the ties. It was a wild, animated scene, and the fatigue of the long day's march was forgotten."[14]

It was not all pure fun. Rebel cavalry hung around the fringes of the force, and irregular troops came into action as well, giving the V Corps a taste of guerilla warfare. Stragglers were waylaid and killed, and as the troops finished their work and began to move back to Petersburg they found stripped, mutilated bodies of their comrades lying in field and road. Just how many cases of this kind there actually were is not clear, nor can it be told now how many Union soldiers, if any, looked upon mutilated corpses and how many merely heard about them; but the news went through the army fast, and it raised murderous fury, and the command became a destroying host as it moved back northward. A man in the 9th Massachusetts battery saw many buildings on fire, and heard that every building in sight from the line of march was destroyed. "One thing is certain," he said. "The burning was approved by the commanders, and there was cause for it; probably murders were the cause of it. We believed it at the time."[15]

To a man in the Iron Brigade, this raid was "the most vindictive that the army had ever engaged in." He said the men had been infuriated by the work of the guerillas, but he admitted that "the destruction of the houses of peaceable women and children, though venomous in their Union hatred, cannot be justified," and he added proudly that "the Iron Brigade had no share in the vandalism."[16]

The year drew to an end: 1864, the year of the Wilderness and the Bloody Angle, of Cold Harbor and the Crater; the year that killed John Sedgwick and saw Abraham Lincoln under fire; the terrible year when war became total; the year of U. S. Grant. In the Shenandoah Valley snow drifted over black ruins, and what was left of Early's army huddled in a winter camp near Waynesboro, and Sheridan sent the VI Corps back to Petersburg. The people of the North put on a big campaign to give the soldiers a good Christmas dinner, and boxes and barrels of turkeys, doughnuts, mince pies, and cakes came down to City Point. The men in the huge hospital got an especially lavish turkey dinner, and a nurse reflected afterward that "there is not a class of persons in the world more cheerful than a ward full of wounded who are doing well." New Year's Day came in clear and cold, and below Fort Hell details went out to cut firewood from a stand of timber between the lines. They found Rebel details out on the same mission, and the woodsmen declared a truce, had a chat, and then pitched in together and cut wood until dusk, at which time they made a fair division of the firewood and went back to their respective lines.[17]

There was a severe winter that year, and life in the trenches was even less comfortable than usual. Army headquarters frowned upon idleness, and there were drills and work details for everybody, with brigade dress parades every afternoon for all except those actually on the firing line. Orders came through to comb out the non-combat details and get men back into combat roles, and a clerk in V Corps headquarters estimated that this would add fully 6,000 men to the army's combat strength. Discipline became sharper. Bounty-jumpers, draftees, and substitutes were going to be made soldiers in spite of themselves, and a special court was set up at City Point to give speedy trials to deserters. It hanged seven men in one day.

The army began to get back some of its old-timers. Some were men who had been wounded, earlier, recovered now and returning to their old regiments for duty. Others were men who had been mustered out when their enlistments expired, who had joined up again and were coming down to the front. Some of the new, high-number regiments were almost entirely made up of such veterans. These regiments would be as good as any the army ever had.[18]

Two generals the army had lost—two who had done much, for better or for worse, to shape its fate. One was Winfield Scott Hancock, still plagued by his Gettysburg wound, gone north now with some vague mission to recruit a new corps of time-expired veterans and bring it to the upper end of the Shenandoah Valley; a mission that somehow never came to much, and Hancock was out of the war. He had not been himself for months, had never really been the same since Gettysburg, but he had been one of the men who gave spirit and color to the army and he had been in the middle of its most desperate fights. The army would not be the same, without Hancock. In his place at the head of the II Corps went Andrew A. Humphreys, Meade's chief of staff, a hard fighter and the sternest of disciplinarians.

The other loss was sheer gain. Ben Butler had gone home, and although technically he had never belonged to the Army of the Potomac, it had had to pay for a number of his mistakes. In December, Army and Navy had mounted a big expedition to take Fort Fisher in North Carolina, the last seaport open to the Confederacy, and since the operation fell in his department Butler had elected himself commander of it. He had planned to destroy the fort by exploding a ship filled with powder as close to the ramparts as possible; did explode it, at dead of night, damaging the fort not at all, making in fact so little impression that the defenders vaguely supposed a Yankee boiler had burst. Butler then got troops ashore, grew discouraged, ordered them aboard ship again, and sailed away reporting that the fort could not be taken.

That was his last act. The admiral on this expedition was tough David Porter, who had been on intimate terms with Grant ever since the Vicksburg campaign, and Porter told Grant the fort could be had any time they sent a competent general to take it. The presidential election was over and the war was on the downhill slope, and it was suddenly realized that Butler no longer need be handled with tongs. So Grant relieved him of his command and sent him back to Massachusetts, and Lincoln sustained Grant, and the one man who ever bluffed those two citizens had lost all of his terrors.

Another expedition went out, Fort Fisher was captured, and the Confederacy was sealed away from the outside world. Sherman was beginning to come north from Savannah, and for the Army of the Potomac it was a winter of rising confidence. "There was hope in the air," wrote a veteran in the VI Corps. "All were beginning to feel that the next campaign would be the last."[19] Much of this was due to the realization that the men in the opposing trenches, the indomitable veterans of Lee's magnificent army, were themselves beginning to lose hope.

The Confederacy was visibly failing—in manpower, in rations, in equipment. A Union man in Fort Hell, peering through the wintry air, saw a stooped and ragged Confederate detail marching out to relieve the picket line and wrote that "I could not help comparing them with so many women with cloaks, shawls, double-bustles and hoops, as they had thrown over their shoulders blankets and tents which flapped in the wind." An officer of the day on the VI Corps front recorded that forty deserters had come into his lines in forty-eight hours, and he said that this was about average; "if we stay here, the Johnnies will all come over before the 4th of July." To another Union officer, the "starved and wan appearance" of the deserters proved that "the Confederacy was on its last legs."[20]

In the lines facing Richmond, Union pickets one night heard a great hallooing and cursing from a swamp out in front, and they crept out and rescued an indignant Rebel conscript who had got stuck in the mud while trying to desert. They took him to their campfire and found that he was fat and sixty, a man who ordinarily wore a wig, spectacles, and false teeth, but who had lost all three while floundering in the swamp. They dried him off and gave him coffee; he drank, looked about the circle, and then began to curse the Confederacy:

"He cursed it individually, from Jeff. Davis and his cabinet down through its Congress and public men to the lowest pot-house politician who advocated its cause; he cursed its army, from General Lee down to an army mule; he cursed that army in its downsittings and uprisings, in all its movements, marches, battles and sieges; he cursed all its paraphernalia, its artillery and its muskets, its banners, bugles and drums; he cursed the institution of slavery, which had brought about the war, and he invoked the direst calamity, woe and disaster upon the Southern cause and all that it represented; while the earnestness, force and sincerity with which it was delivered made it one of the most effective speeches I ever heard, and this together with his comical appearance and the circumstance of his capture made the men roar with laughter."

The Union man who told about all of this added, perhaps unnecessarily, that "the best element in the Southern army" did not desert.[21]

A New England private said that each evening the men in his company would speculate about the number of deserters who would come in that night: "The boys talk about the Johnnies as at home we talk about suckers and eels. The boys will look around in the evening and guess that there will be a good run of Johnnies." Heavy firing on the picket lines was always taken to mean that the enemy was trying to keep deserters from getting away. Many deserters were willing to enlist in the Union army, and before 1864 ended it was ordered that all such should be sent West to fight the Indians—it would go very hard with them if the army from which they had deserted should recapture them. When these men talked about the Southern cause, it was said, they would remark that it was a rich man's war and a poor man's fight.[22]

Yet there was always one striking point to remember. Confederate soldiers might be deserting in increasing numbers, but up to the moment of desertion they fought just as hard as ever. A VI Corps officer admitted that "the Army of North Virginia was still a most formidable foe," and when he studied the battle front he found that "their forts, with five lines of abatis in front, looked as if they could defy any attack." As the winter wore away the tension actually increased. Men felt that Lee would find some way to strike a blow before desertions crippled him, and it was agreed that when the blow fell it would come with savage force.[23]

At the end of January there was an odd, revealing incident.

Over the Rebel parapet near the old mine crater came a white flag, with a bugler to blow a parley, and a message came over for General Grant. As it happened, Grant was away just then, and there was a twenty-four-hour delay before the message reached him. During the delay, by the mysterious army grapevine, word went up and down the rival lines: the Confederacy was sending a peace commission to meet Lincoln and Seward to see whether they could not agree on terms to end the war.

The peace commissioners were men of note. One was John A. Campbell, former justice of the United States Supreme Court, now the Confederacy's Assistant Secretary of War. Another was Senator R. M. T. Hunter, former Confederate Secretary of State. The third was the Vice-President of the Confederacy, wizened Alexander Stephens, who had been in Congress with Lincoln and who, in 1848, made a speech which caused Lincoln to write to his law partner, Herndon, that "a little, slim, pale-faced consumptive man" had just made the best speech he had ever heard, a speech which moved him to tears. He and Stephens had been drawn to each other, somehow. Members of the Whig party, they had worked together in 1848 to help nominate Zachary Taylor.

Jefferson Davis once had used words of poetry to refer to Stephens as "the little pale star from Georgia." He would not use such tender language about him now, for he and Stephens had drifted far apart. Davis considered Stephens a defeatist, and Stephens considered Davis a despot, and said so in public; and now, against his will, Stephens was head of a mission sent to confer with Lincoln "for the purpose of securing peace to the two countries."

By the time Grant got the message, consulted Washington, and made arangements to get the commissioners through the lines, it was the afternoon of January 31. Both armies knew what was up, and when the carriages came out the Jerusalem Plank Road from Petersburg, bearing the three dignitaries and any number of anxious private citizens, the parapets of Union and Confederate trenches were jammed with soldiers as far as the eye could see.

There was an expectant hush. The commissioners' carriage turned and made for an opening in the Confederate lines—and suddenly all of the soldiers who could see it, blue and gray alike, swung their hats and raised a tremendous cheer. A gunner who looked on remembered: "Cheer upon cheer was given, extending for some distance to the right and left of the lines, each side trying to cheer the loudest. 'Peace on the brain' appeared now to have spread like a contagion. Officers of all grades, from lieutenants to major generals, were to be seen flying in all directions to catch a glimpse of the gentlemen who were apparently to bring peace so unexpectedly."

Slowly the carriage came through, jolting over the uneven ground. The cheering died down. Having yelled, the men seemed to be holding their breath in nervous anticipation. The Federal soldiers now saw something which they had never seen before, or dreamed of seeing—a large number of ladies, dressed in their frilly best, standing on the Confederate parapet.

The carriage stopped and the commissioners got out, tiny Stephens weighed down and made almost helpless with an enormous overcoat. The Confederates began to cheer again, and the three civilians walked across no man's land to the place where Grant had ambulances waiting for them. As they reached these a couple of soldiers helped Stephens climb in, and the Northern troops cheered. The ambulances drove away, and as they passed from sight a Confederate picket sprang out, turned to face his comrades, and proposed three cheers for the Yankee army. These were given, after which a Union man led his side in three cheers for the Confederates. When this shouting died down somebody proposed three cheers for the ladies of Petersburg and both sides joined in, and the ladies fluttered their handkerchiefs prettily.[24] Then the winter day ended, and the ladies went back to town, and the men climbed down from the parapets, and there was a quiet buzz of talk all up and down the lines. No soldier on either side seems to have asked what sort of peace terms were apt to come out of the conference. On this one afternoon, nobody was thinking of victory or defeat. It was enough to think that perhaps the war could end with no more killing.

For anti-climax, the conference came to nothing. One side insisted on an independent Confederacy and the other side insisted on a restored Union, and the conferees presently were reduced to nothing much more than an interchange of expressions of personal good will. It developed that Stephens's nephew, a Confederate officer, had for twenty months been a prisoner of war on Johnson's Island, in Sandusky Bay. Lincoln made a note of it, and a few days later that surprised young officer found himself called out of prison and sent down to Washington, where he was taken to the White House for a chat with President Lincoln; after which he was sent through the lines to Richmond. The Confederates returned the favor, picking at random a Union officer of the same rank, and so the 13th New Hampshire presently welcomed the return of its Lieutenant Murray, who was delighted and surprised by the whole business.

So the conference ended, and in the North the radicals reacted to it with bitter suspicion, shouting their fear that Lincoln was trying to revive "the old policy of tenderness toward the rebels." Congressman George W. Julian of Indiana, to whom, long ago, Burnside had confided that the real trouble with the Union soldiers was that they did not hate their enemies sufficiently, took the floor to warn that the sole purpose of the war now was subjugation, crying: "Both the people and our armies, under this new dispensation, have been learning how to hate Rebels as Christian patriots ought to have done from the beginning."

Lincoln meanwhile called a cabinet meeting and coolly proposed that the Federal government offer to the Southern states four hundred million dollars in six per cent government bonds, as compensation for the property values which would be destroyed by emancipation, on condition that the Southern states return to the Union within two months. The Cabinet was stunned and slightly indignant. In vain Lincoln pointed out that if the war lasted only another hundred days it would cost all of the money he was now proposing to spend. No one would agree that this was the way to get peace and reunion, and at last Lincoln put away the draft of his proposal, saying: "You are all opposed to me."

In Richmond, Davis addressed a patriotic rally, inviting all Southerners to "unite our hands and hearts" in the fond belief that before midsummer it would be the Yankees who would be crossing the lines to ask for terms. Stephens conceded that Davis made a brilliant speech, although he considered it "not much short of dementation," and when Davis asked what he proposed to do next the little Vice-President was blunt: "Go home and stay there."[25]

No peace, then, except by the sword, and the eerie light that had so briefly touched the winter sky faded out. It had been building up to this for four years, and here it was, visible and final: the war would end only when one side or the other had been pounded into helplessnes, for men had passed beyond the point where they could negotiate or compromise. It was up to the soldiers, after all.

The soldiers were hopeful, but sober, for the war had worked on them. In the Petersburg trenches and camps, no one was ever heard to sing "Tenting To-night,"once the favorite campfire song: "That song is especially dedicated to the brave and stalwart home-stayers." There was little horseplay, little joviality, few campfire jokes and pleasant yarns—not, as one man wrote, because men had grown discouraged, but simply because the wide range of a regiment's personal characteristic now "is narrowed to almost the definiteness of one special class: the steady and sober men." Yet there was little complaining, and very little self-pity: "The army laughs far more than it weeps."[26]

A Massachusetts gunner sat down and figured that in another 200 days his battery would reach the end of its enlistment and could go home, and he tried to write down what the rest of his term of service would amount to:

". . . only 200 more days of service, of which 33 are guard duty and the same of regular fatigue; three times mustered for pay—marching, fighting, perhaps; 2,000 hard tack, 75 pounds of pork, 125 pounds of beef to eat, 72 gallons of coffee to drink, part of it every day, and it will be done."[27]

2. GREAT LIGHT IN THE SKY

Fort Stedman was a square box of a place, with solid walls enclosing a space for the guns. Inside the enclosure were sodded mounds over the dugouts in which the soldiers slept and kept their stores. In front and on each side were the spiky entanglements of the abatis, and to right and left were the trenches which tied Fort Stedman into the main line of Federal works facing Petersburg.

The fort had stood there for nine months, and there was nothing in particular to distinguish it from several dozen other forts in the Federal lines except that it was in bad repair. It was less than 200 yards from the Confederate works, and that was easy range even for average marksmen, and so when the fort's walls settled that winter the authorities did not order them rebuilt because the men who worked on them would probably be shot. Behind the fort there was higher ground from which one could look into the fort, and there was no abatis in the rear, and all in all Stedman was one of the weakest spots in the whole Federal line. That did not matter much, however, for it seemed very improbable that the Rebels would ever make an attack. The New York heavy artillery regiment which held this part of the line kept pickets out in front—they were almost within handshaking distance of the Rebel pickets, the lines here were so close—but as long as these men stayed awake and the works behind them were adequately manned the weakness of Fort Stedman seemed nothing to worry about.[1]

This was sensible enough, as good sense goes in wartime. But the old balances were falling, and suddenly now the war was going to go with a rush and a roar toward the final smashup, all of the tensions built up in nine months of strained equilibrium letting go in one comprehensive explosion. For Stedman had been built across the path of Fate, and its imperfect walls enclosed the spot from which a man who looked sharply might see the beginning of the end.

It was four in the morning of March 25, 1865, black and still as polar midnight, with never a sound from the picket lines. Half a mile north of Stedman was another Union strong point, Fort McGilvery, and a sergeant in this fort peered off to the south, listened intently, and then went to rouse his commanding officer: "Captain, there is some disturbance on our left in the direction of Fort Stedman, but I can't make out what it is." The captain went to have a look, and the men could see a few pin-pricks of flame, and then they could hear scattered musket fire. Then they saw one of Stedman's cannon fired—not in front, toward the Rebel army, but off toward the rear.[2]

Several hundred yards south of Fort Stedman a Catholic chaplain had been saying predawn mass for sixty-odd communicants in Union Fort Haskell. He heard rifle firing, and the boom of cannon, and he got through the service as soon as he decently could, after which the worshipers took their weapons and ran to the parapets. And then there was a rising swell of firing, and the sound of men shouting, and there was a flashing of heavy guns in the Confederate lines—and Rebel infantry was past Fort Stedman, running out to seize Union trenches and batteries to right and left, and an assaulting column was swinging around to attack Fort Haskell while other troops were forming for a drive straight through to the Union rear.[3]

This part of the line belonged to the IX Corps. Burnside had gone home long since, the attack on the crater having been his final contribution, and the corps was in command of his former chief of staff, a pleasant-faced, competent general named John G. Parke. Parke was asleep at corps headquarters, well to the rear, when the fighting began. When he was roused and learned that he had a fight on his hands he also was told that Meade was temporarily absent and that, by seniority, he himself was in command of the Army of the Potomac. He notified the other commands that the Rebels were attacking, and got troops moving toward the danger area. Also, he brought up his own third division which had been in reserve and sent it in to mend the break.

This division was made up of six new Pennsylvania regiments, which had enlisted just before Christmas and were still under training. They seem to have contained good men—not all of the recruits were worthless bounty jumpers and substitutes—and they were commanded by a first-rate soldier, General John Hartranft, who as a colonel had led the successful attack on Burnside's bridge at Antietam Creek in one of the battles of the long ago. Hartranft took his men forward, and Federal artillery began to open a heavy bombardment as soon as dawn brought enough light to make targets visible.

The 200th Pennsylvania charged in against the Confederate advance, wrecking itself but blunting the spearhead of the Southern charge and forcing it to a halt. The garrison of Fort Haskell beat off the column that was attacking there, and in Fort McGilvery men hoisted cannon over the embankments by hand so that they could fire on the ground behind Stedman. Hartranft got a solid battle line strung out across the open country to the rear—and before long it was clear that the crisis was over. The Confederates had punched a clean hole in the Union line but they could not widen the hole enough to mount a new attack that would break the secondary defenses, and by eight o'clock Lee sounded the recall.[4]

Many of the Confederates never returned to their own lines. Yankee artillery was laying a heavy fire on the ground they had charged across and to retreat was as dangerous as to advance, and when Parke finally sent the Pennsylvanians smashing forward to recover Fort Stedman and the lost trenches and batteries hundreds of Confederates surrendered. In the end the attack cost Lee's army 4,000 men—twice the total of Union casualties—and the lines were as they had been before.

Meade got back from City Point just as the fighting died down, and he reasoned that Lee must have weakened his forces elsewhere to make this attack. He ordered the II Corps and the VI Corps, accordingly, to attack the entrenched Rebel picket lines in their front. They did so, seizing the lines, taking hundreds of prisoners, and gaining excellent positions from which to assault the main Southern defenses if that should ever seem advisable.[5]

The grimy Federals who cleared the recaptured trenches, sent wounded men and prisoners to the rear, and put the burial squads to work had had a bigger day than they could realize. They had beaten off the last great offensive thrust of the Army of Northern Virginia.

That army had struck at its Yankee antagonists many times—at Gaines's Mill and at Bull Run, at Chancellorsville and at Gettysburg, and on many other fields, and always it struck with terrible power, tough soldiers running forward under the shrill yip-yip of the Rebel yell, red battle flags sparkling above the flashing muskets, cold fury of battle lighting the eyes of the gray warrior who directed the blows. It would never happen again. It was a new war now, and the end was coming.

In the afternoon there were visitors on the battlefield—Abraham Lincoln and U. S. Grant, coming up by rattletrap military train from City Point, Meade and his staff officers going to meet them. Lincoln walked over the field, saw wounded men not yet removed to hospital, and dead men for whom graves were not yet ready. Grant had seen this many times and on many dreadful fields and Lincoln had never seen it at all except for a little at Fort Stevens; and these two men who were so very different were much alike in that neither one was ever able to forget the human cost of glorious victories, or his own responsibility for that cost. An army surgeon told how Lincoln once visited a hospital in Washington and afterward stopped to chat with the doctors. One of these was telling about a difficult operation just performed, in which a wounded soldier's arm had been removed at the shoulder joint, and he went into much technical detail, the other doctors listening intently. At last, as he finished, and the others were asking this and that about the operation, Lincoln burst out with the one question that interested him, the one question which no doctor had thought to ask: "But how about the soldier?"[6] Neither Lincoln nor Grant, who remorselessly held the country up to month after month of wholesale killing, ever got far away from that question.

Back to City Point went Lincoln and Grant, to talk by headquarters campfires, their shadows falling longer and darker over the dwindling borders of a fading Confederacy. Presently there came to join them another man who also cast a long and portentous shadow, a lean and wiry man with unruly red hair and a short stubble of a close-cropped beard, dancing lights in the alert eyes that peered out of a hard face—William Tecumseh Sherman, who had made his name terrible to the South, here now for a last conference before returning to the tough, devil-may-care army which he had left in the pine hills of North Carolina.

In a sense, Sherman was responsible for the attack on Fort Stedman. What remained of the Southern Confederacy was the ground that lay between his army and Grant's, and its doom was absolutely certain if he continued his relentless advance until the two armies made contact. If Lee could break away, get south fast, pick up the inadequate army with which Joe Johnston was opposing Sherman, beat Sherman by a quick, hard blow, and then turn to deal with Grant—if all of that could be done, then the Confederacy might survive. The blow at Fort Stedman had been an attempt to knock the Army of the Potomac back on its heels and cripple it just long enough to give Lee the start he would need on a move to the south.

The odds against the success of any such program were fantastically long, and both Lee and Grant knew it. But they also knew one other fact—that the people of the North were weary of the war with a deep, numb, instinctive weariness, so that one more major disappointment might be too much for them. Whether or not he could beat Sherman, Lee might at least prolong the war for six months if he could get away from Grant, and if he could do that there was a fair chance that the North would give up the struggle.

So Grant figured it, at any rate.[7] Lee may have reasoned in the same way, or he may have followed nothing more subtle than the born fighter's refusal to quit as long as he can stay on his feet and lift his fists waist high. In any case he was going to play out the string, and if the Northern generals did not watch him very carefully the triumph which was so near might drift off into nothingness like battle smoke blown down the wind. So Lincoln, Grant, and Sherman were taking counsel, in the armies' nerve center at City Point.

Yet they had not met just to discuss means of insuring victory. They had held the war firmly in their hands for nearly a year now; a few more weeks of vigilance and driving energy and it would all be over. They were thinking not so much about the ending of the war as about the new beginning that must lie beyond that. They were almost incredibly different, these three—Sherman quick, nervous, and volatile, Grant stolid and unemotional and relentless, Lincoln ranging far beyond them with brooding insights, his profound melancholy touched by mystic inexplicable flashes of light—but each held the faith that the whole country, North and South together, must ultimately find in reunion and freedom the values that would justify four terrible years of war.

The discovery of those values would by no means be automatic. Much hatred and bitterness existed, and there could easily develop a program of revenge and reprisal that would make real reunion forever impossible. There was talk of hangings and of proscription lists and of conquered provinces. There were powerful leaders in the North who meant to see these threats carried out in all their literal grimness, and it was not in the least certain that they could be kept from having their way. So the principal order of business for the President and two generals was not so much to checkmate the Confederacy as to checkmate the men who would try to make peace with malice and rancor and a length of noosed rope.

When the Southern armies surrendered the two generals would be the ones to say what the terms of surrender must be, and they would take their cue from Lincoln. If the terms expressed simple human decency and friendship, it might be that a peace of reconciliation could get just enough of a lead so that the haters could never quite catch up with it. On all of this Lincoln and Grant and Sherman agreed.

It was a curious business, in a way. The Confederacy had no more effective foes than these men. Lincoln had led the North into war, had held it firmly to its task, and had refused to hear any talk of peace that was not based on the extinction of the Confederate Government. Grant seemed to be the very incarnation of the remorseless killer, and Sherman was destruction's own self, his trail across the South a band of ruin sixty miles wide. Yet it was these three who were most determined that vindictiveness and hatred must not control the future. They would fight without mercy as long as there must be fighting, but when the fighting stopped they would try to turn old enemies into friends.

They spoke for the soldiers. The Northern and Southern armies had less bitterness now than they had had when the war began. On every picket line the cry "Down Yank!" and "Down Reb!" always preceded an outburst of firing. A veteran in the V Corps spoke for the rank and file when he said that the opposing troops in front of Fort Hell "decided that we would respect one another, as the lines at this point were very close and to keep up constant firing would make it very uncomfortable for one or the other."[8] These were the men who climbed on the ramparts to give three cheers for peace, and then gave three cheers for each other, and then returned to their fighting, and they did not need to be told that it would be well to make peace mean comradeship. All they needed was to see somebody try it.

So Lincoln and Grant and Sherman had their talk and agreed that it must be tried, and at one point there was a faint, ironic echo from the days of McClellan, forever critical of Washington. This came when Lincoln abruptly asked Sherman:

"Sherman, do you know why I took a shine to Grant and you?"

Sherman confessed that he did not know, and he added that he had received from the President kindness beyond his due.

"Well," said Lincoln, "you never found fault with me."[9]

Back to North Carolina and his restless, destructive army went Sherman, and as he went out Sheridan's cavalry came in, Phil Sheridan at its head, and the Army of the Potomac was ready to begin its last campaign.

Sheridan and his cavalry had wintered near Winchester, and as February ended they moved up the Valley to Staunton, two divisions of veteran mounted troops, 9,400 officers and men. The weather was vile, rain on the mountains and slush on the roads, every little stream over its banks, mud on everything, the burnt-out region looking more Godforsaken than ever. At Staunton, Sheridan learned that Early and a pitiful remnant of an army were entrenched on a knoll near Waynesboro, by the western entrance to Rockfish Gap, and he rode over there to get them. His men came into Waynesboro through a two-day rain, men and horses all dripping and plastered with mud, and Sheridan sent Custer's division up to obliterate the last Confederate force in the Shenandoah Valley.

Custer dismounted most of his men and attacked Early's flanks with carbines sputtering, and then he took the 8th New York and 1st Connecticut and drove them straight in on the middle of the line, charging in a galloping column of fours, bugles sounding in the raw March air. Straight over the breastworks went the mounted squadrons, and the flankers broke in the ends of Early's line, and all resistance collapsed, while the mounted men rode hard through the town of Waynesboro, sabering fugitives on the streets. Early and some of his officers and the merest handful of men hid out in friendly houses and escaped. When the fighting ended Sheridan counted 1,600 prisoners, 11 guns, 200 loaded wagons, and nearly a score of battle flags.[10]

Prisoners, guns, and wagons he sent back down the Valley, with a mounted brigade for escort. The battle flags he took with him, and as he rode into the Petersburg lines his band of scouts came cantering at his heels proudly bearing these trophies[11]—and if the North wanted a soldier who knew how to wear a conqueror's pride, perhaps Sheridan was the man for it. The Valley was dead, and Lee's army was half immobilized because the forage for cavalry and artillery horses that used to come from there was no longer available. Grant pulled the cavalry around to the extreme left of the long Union line and made ready to destroy the Army of Northern Virginia.

As always, that army was dangerous. Month after month it had been perfecting its defenses—raising parapets, digging deep ditches, mounting new guns and mortars, building double and triple lines of abatis, tying everything together with a crisscross of support and approach trenches—and when these lines were properly manned it was quite impossible to carry them by assault. But Lee had come to the end of his resources, and his lines were stretched to the very limit. His right flank rested along the marshy banks of a little stream called Hatcher's Run, eight or nine miles southwest of Petersburg in an air line, substantially farther by road. Grant's plan now was to send a strong force prowling around that flank. The chance was good that this would either induce Lee to pull his army out in the open for a finish fight—which Grant had vainly been trying to bring about for ten months—or compel him to stretch his thin line until it snapped.

There remained to the Confederates in Petersburg one vital railway line—the Southside Railroad, which ran west from Petersburg to Lynchburg, crossing the Richmond and Danville line at the junction town of Burkeville, fifty miles west of Petersburg. The Petersburg end of this line ran only a few miles in rear of Lee's outposts at Hatcher's Run, and a blow past the flank which broke the Southside Railroad would break Lee's principal supply line and force him to retreat.

Obviously, therefore, Grant's best move was to extend his left flank once more—a repetition of the move that had been made so many times since the army crossed the Rapidan. In preparation, Grant was shifting men about even before Sherman got to City Point.

In the Bermuda Hundred lines and directly before Richmond was the Army of the James, now under General Ord. This army was composed of two infantry corps, one containing three divisions of white troops and the other, three divisions of colored troops. Unnoticed by the Confederates Ord quietly took two white divisions and one colored division out of the trenches one evening and led them down to Petersburg on a grueling thirty-six-mile hike.

To occupy the lines facing Petersburg, Grant detailed Ord's three divisions plus the IX Corps and the VI Corps. For a movable force to menace Lee's flank he thus had two full army corps—Humphreys and the II Corps and Warren and the V Corps. He also had three superb divisions of cavalry under Sheridan, and from the moment he began to plan this move he seems to have concluded that the operation as a whole would be pretty largely under Sheridan's command.

He would start by sending Sheridan and the cavalry to the little hamlet of Dinwiddie Court House, half a dozen miles south and slightly west of the Hatcher's Run area. While Sheridan made this move Humphreys and Warren were to take their men up through the flat, wooded country closer to Hatcher's Run. They were not supposed to attack Confederate trenches there, but their presence might induce Lee to make a new extension of his line. At the very least it would cover Sheridan—who, from Dinwiddie Court House, could march northwest ten or twelve miles and strike the Southside Railroad. After that Sheridan might go on and break the Richmond and Danville road as well, and in the end he might even go down cross country and join Sherman. Plans were fluid. The chief idea was to shake things loose and end the long deadlock.[12]

It was March 29, at last, three o'clock of a clammy damp morning, with low clouds blotting out the stars, and behind the Union lines the grim columns began to move. Many times since they reached Petersburg different parts of the army had marched toward the left, and each time the result had been, if not an actual rebuff, nothing more exciting than a mere extension of the Union lines. But now men seemed to feel that the last act was beginning. Lincoln had been at City Point (was still there, as a matter of fact, to wait for news) and Sherman had been there, and Sheridan had come down from the Valley, and spring was in the air—and, altogether, perhaps this was it. A general in the V Corps wrote that men felt it so, and he said that as they took to the road it was almost as if, overhead, they saw "a great light filling the sky."[13]

Yet there were skeptics. A private in the 11th Pennsylvania wrote that "there was nothing borne on the wings of the wind" to hint that this move was going to be any different than all the earlier ones had been. "Four years of war," he said, "while it made the men brave and valorous, had entirely cured them of imagining that each campaign would be the last." Many times in the past high hopes had been disappointed. This morning as they moved out of winter quarters a soldier raised the butt of his musket to knock down the stick-and-clay chimney of one of the shacks. A contraband serving as company cook begged him not to destroy it: "We'll be back ag'in in a week, and I'll want to use it."[14]

The infantry reached their designated position, and had a sharp little fight with Confederate infantry which came down to see what the Yankees were up to. Farther west and south, Sheridan pushed Rebel skirmishers out of the way and put his men in bivouac near Dinwiddie, making his headquarters in a big frame tavern opposite the courthouse building. As evening came down it brought rain, the rain continued all night long, and there was no letup with the dawn. All of the country around Hatcher's Run and Dinwiddie Court House was low, covered with second-growth timber and seamed by many little brooks and creeks, and by noon of March 30 the whole area was a swamp. Sheridan put Custer's entire division to work corduroying the roads in rear of his position, the roads having become all but totally impassable for wagons and guns. A trooper remembered spending an atrocious night "with rations all soaked and blankets all wet, and spongy beds under leaking shelters."[15]

The rain refused to stop. Grant moved headquarters from City Point out to a waterlogged field near Gravelly Run, toward the left end of the line, and he remembered that the ground was so soggy that a horse or mule, standing quite motionless, would suddenly begin to sink out of sight and would have to be pulled out by a squad of soldiers. Men asked each other when the gunboats were going to come up and suggested that what the army needed now was Noah rather than Grant. The top echelons in the Army of the Potomac, remembering an occasion near Fredericksburg when the army had got hopelessly stuck in the mud, urged Grant to call everything off, get everybody back to camp, and start again a week or two later when the ground was drier. Grant himself seems to have wavered, for a time. First he told Sheridan to forget about the railroads and smash straight for Lee's flank and rear; then he sent another message suggesting that all forward movement be suspended until the weather improved.[16]

When he got this last letter Sheridan rode over to Grant's headquarters. The rain was still coming down and the mud was so deep that even Sheridan's horse could manage nothing better than a walk, sinking to his knees at every step, but Sheridan was all for action. To Grant's staff he expounded on the iniquity of delay—now was the time to move, Rebel cavalry could be knocked out of the way any time the commanding general pleased, and if Lee sent infantry out he was writing his own doom. Sheridan tramped back and forth in the mud and rain, striking his hands together. An officer asked how he would get forage for his 13,000 horses if the roads remained impassable.

"Forage?" echoed Sheridan. "I'll get all the forage I want. I'll haul it out if I have to set every man in the command to corduroying roads, and corduroy every mile of them from the railroad to Dinwiddie. I tell you I'm ready to strike out tomorrow and go to smashing things."

Staff suggested that Grant liked to hear that sort of talk, partly because it was so different from anything he ever got from top generals in the Army of the Potomac, and urged Sheridan to speak his piece to the lieutenant general. Sheridan demurred: Grant hadn't asked him to come over, he was just sounding off to relieve his mind. A staff officer, however slipped into Grant's tent and suggested that it would be good for him to talk to his cavalry commander, and in another moment Sheridan was repeating his little speech to Grant, strongly backed by impetuous Chief of Staff John Rawlins, with his pale cheeks and feverish burning eyes.

Grant made up his mind: the move would go on, bad roads or no bad roads, and it would not stop until there had been a final showdown. Long afterward he confessed that he believed the country to be so desperately tired of the war that unless the move to the left was a complete victory it would be interpreted as a disastrous failure.[17]

On March 31, therefore, with rain still falling and the country looking like the bottom of a millpond, the advance was resumed. Sheridan still had Custer's division at work behind Dinwiddie, fixing the bottomless road so that forage and provisions could be brought in, and he was holding most of a second division at Dinwiddie; and he sent the rest of the men marching north, and at a lonely country crossroads known as Five Forks they ran into the Rebels in strength.

Five Forks was nowhere at all, but it was important because it was where the road from Dinwiddie Court House to the Southside Railroad crossed the east-and-west road that led to Lee's right flank and rear. Lee's army could not stay in Petersburg if the Yankees held this crossroads, and so Lee had scraped his last reserves to make a fight for the place. Dug in behind temporary breastworks were five brigades of infantry under the legendary George Pickett. With the infantry was practically all of Lee's cavalry.

Up against this powerful force came one division of Yankee cavalry led by General Thomas C. Devin, a former New York militia colonel who had become enough of a soldier to suit the most exacting of Regulars. He had been a favorite of tough John Buford in the old Gettysburg days, and nowadays he was dubbed "Sheridan's hard hitter"—which, considering the general reputation of Sheridan's cavalry, was a fairly substantial compliment. This day he had his hands full. When his patrols reported Rebel infantry at Five Forks he dismounted his division and got ready to fight on foot. Pickett immediately obliged him, rolling forward a heavier battle line than Devin's men could handle, and before long the blue cavalry was in full retreat.

The Federals fought hard, withdrawing as slowly as they could manage and maintaining a steady fire, but they were heavily outnumbered and Confederate cavalry kept curling in around both flanks, and presently Devin had to warn Sheridan that he was badly overmatched and that they might have trouble holding Dinwiddie itself. He kept his fighting line dismounted because the men could put up a more stubborn resistance that way, and as they fought the area immediately behind the firing line was a howling madhouse.

All of the division's horses were here, four thousand and odd of them, one trooper to every four horses. The country was densely wooded, with few roads and many rail fences, and the air was full of smoke and bullets and shouting men, and the conditions under which one mounted man could easily lead three riderless horses did not exist. The horses became panicky and fractious, and they kept running on the wrong side of trees, or colliding with each other, creating fearful tangles of kicking, plunging animals and snarled reins and cursing soldiers—and, said one of the men afterward, the whole business was enough to make anybody understand why an exceptionally profane man was always said to swear like a trooper.[18]

While Devin's men gave ground Sheridan got the rest of his men strung out in line in front of Dinwiddie Court House, and at dusk the Confederates came storming up to drive the whole lot of Yankee cavalry back where it belonged. When Devin's men came in Sheridan put them into line with the rest, and he rolled forward all the guns he could lay his hands on. Then he rounded up all of the regimental bands and put them up on the firing line and ordered them to play the gayest tunes they knew—play them loud and keep on playing them, and never mind if a bullet goes through a trombone, or even a trombonist, now and then.

The late afternoon sun broke through the clouds, and all of these bands were playing, and there was a clatter of musketry and a booming of cannon and a floating loom of battle smoke. Sheridan got his little battle flag with the two stars on it and rode out in front of his lines, going from one end to the other at a full gallop, waving his hat and telling every last soldier—by his presence, by his gestures, and by the hard look in his black eyes—that nobody was going to make them retreat another step.

They held the line. At dusk Sheridan tried a counterattack, ordering Custer to make a mounted charge on a line of Rebel infantry. A man who saw him giving Custer his orders remembered Sheridan's emphasis: "You understand? I want you to *give* it to them!" Custer nodded, and he drove his squadrons forward—to a muddy anticlimax. The field across which the men tried to charge was so soupy with wet clay and rain water that the horses immediately bogged down, the charge came to nothing, and at last it was dark, with the Federals holding the town and the Confederates facing them just out of musket range.[19]

It looked like trouble, for these venturesome Confederates had more men than Sheridan had and they were well behind the left end of the main Union line. But Sheridan saw it as opportunity; it was Pickett's force and not his that was in trouble, the Rebels were isolated and they could be cut off, and if the business were handled right none of them should ever get back to Lee's army.

Off through the night to Grant went Sheridan's couriers with the message: Let me have the old VI Corps once more and I can really smash things.

The VI Corps Sheridan could not have, because it was too far off and with the roads as they were it would take two days to get it to him. Warren and the V Corps were available, however, no more than half a dozen miles away, and late that evening Warren was ordered to get his men over to Dinwiddie at top speed. Sheridan was told that they would show up at dawn, and they would be coming in from the northeast, behind Pickett's flank. Warren had much more infantry than Pickett had, and Sheridan had much more cavalry. Between the two of them they might be able to destroy his entire force.[20] Lee was so pinched for manpower that a loss of such dimensions would practically bankrupt him.

So Sheridan put his men into bivouac and waited impatiently for the morning. It was a restless night, since every square foot of open space behind the line was jammed with led horses and their grouchy caretakers, and it was an all-night job to get all of these straightened out so that the squadrons could be mounted next day if necessary. Trains of pack mules came up, bringing forage and rations, and the ambulances had got through—that work on the roads had been effective—and lanterns twinkled in the damp groves as stretcher parties went through, gathering up the wounded men.[21]

It was the last day of March 1865, and the Army of the Potomac had just nine more days of campaigning ahead of it.

3. THE SOLDIERS SAW DAYLIGHT

Major General Gouverneur Kemble Warren and his V Army Corps had been having a bad day. The corps had been in position, wet and uncomfortable, a little west of Hatcher's Run, presumably a trifle south of the extreme right flank of Lee's main line, and during the morning—while Devin's troopers were meeting Rebel infantry in front of Five Forks and were beginning their difficult withdrawal to Dinwiddie Court House—Warren sent one division forward to make a reconnaissance and find out just where the Rebels might be.

By ill chance this division began to advance just when Lee ordered a force of his own to move forward and pick a fight with the Yankees in order to protect the move which Pickett was making a few miles farther west. This force caught the Federal infantry division off guard and piled into it with savage vigor, and the Federals were driven back in disorder. In their retreat they ran through the bivouac of the second of Warren's three infantry divisions, and these troops were all gathered around smoky campfires trying to dry their clothing and their blankets, no one having alerted them to the fact that there might be action. So this second division was routed, too, and Warren had to send his third division and call for help from the II Corps, over on his right, in order to restore the situation.

By evening he had won back the ground that had been lost, but his men had had a hard all-day fight, with painful losses; and now, just as they were collecting their wounded and trying to get snug for the night, there came these orders to make a forced march over to join Sheridan.[1]

It was a foul night to move troops. It was so dark, as one soldier said, that it was literally impossible to see a hand before one's face. The rain had stopped, but the roads were deep with mud, every little creek had overflowed, and there was a completely unfordable stream flowing straight across the principal highway that the troops had to use. Warren's engineers tore down a house and used the timbers to build a bridge, but construction work at midnight with everybody exhausted was slow work.

Warren had received conflicting orders about the routes he was to take, so that there was a good deal of wearing countermarching for some units, and there

was much confusion about maps and place names. Also, at the time he got his
marching orders Warren's skirmish line was in contact with the enemy, and he
felt that he should use much caution in getting his men away. Some regiments
started on time but most of them did not, nothing that could conceivably go
wrong went right, and by five in the morning—the hour at which it had been
hoped that the whole corps would be taking position at Dinwiddie Court
House—two of his divisions were just beginning to move.[2]

Sheridan was furious. He met the head of the infantry column in a gray dawn
as the men came splashing up to the rendezvous, and he demanded of the brigadier commanding: "Where's Warren?" The brigadier explained that Warren
was back with the rear of the column, and Sheridan growled: "That's where I
expected to find him. What's he doing there?" The officer tried to explain that
Warren was trying to make sure that his men could break contact with the Confederates without drawing an attack, but Sheridan was not appeased. Later,
when Warren arrived, the two generals were seen tramping up and down by the
roadside, Sheridan dark and tense, stamping angrily in the mud, Warren pale
and tight-lipped, apparently trying to control himself.[3]

Wherever the fault lay, the early-morning attack that had been planned could
not be made. It was noon before the V Corps was assembled, and by that time
the Confederates were gone. During the night Pickett had got wind of the Yankee move, and around daybreak he took his entire force back to the breastworks
at Five Forks.

These works ran for a mile or more along the edge of the White Oak Road,
and they faced toward the south. At their eastern end, for flank protection, the
line made nearly a right-angle turn and ran north for a few hundred yards. With
his men in and behind these works, and cavalry patrolling both flanks, Pickett
seems to have taken it for granted that he was safe from assault for the rest of
the day. With a few other ranking officers he retired to a campfire some distance
in the rear to enjoy the pleasures of a shad bake.

As far as Sheridan was concerned, however, Pickett was in as much danger as
he had been in before. There was still a wide gap between his force and the rest
of Lee's army, with only the thinnest chain of cavalry vedettes to maintain contact, and in that gap Sheridan could see a dazzling opportunity. He had his cavalry maintaining pressure along Pickett's front, and he had a whole mounted
division waiting in reserve, ready to go slashing in around the Confederate right
at the proper time. If, while the cavalry held the Southerners' attention, he could
drive 16,000 good infantrymen into the open gap and bring their entire weight to
bear on Pickett's left flank, just where the Rebel breastworks angled back toward the north, the war would be a good deal nearer its close by nightfall.

The 16,000 good infantrymen were at hand, and a comparatively short walk
would put them into position. They were dog-tired. They had fought all of the
day before, and they had spent practically all of the night and morning on the
march, and while Sheridan and Warren discussed battle plans they were catching forty winks in some fields near a little country church. When Warren at last
came over to move them up to the jump-off line they were sluggish, and getting
them formed was slow work, and it seemed to Sheridan—watching the afternoon sun get lower in the sky, and reflecting that the whole situation might be
very different by tomorrow morning—that Warren was not doing much to make
things go faster.[4] But the men would fight well when the time came, because
they considered themselves a crack outfit and they had a great tradition.

The V Corps was one of the famous units of the whole Federal Army. Fitz-
John Porter had commanded it, and it had been McClellan's favorite corps, and
in general orders he had held it up as a model for the other corps to emulate,
which caused jealousies that had not entirely worn away even yet. (It caused
War Department suspicions, too, and promotion for higher officers in this corps

was harder to get, it was said, than in the rest of the Army of the Potomac.) The corps had been built around a famous division of Regulars, and in the beginning all of its ranking officers had been Regulars, mostly of the stiff, old army, knock-'em-dead variety. Its discipline tended to be severe, there was strict observance of military formalities, and the Regular Army flavor endured, even though many of the old officers and all of the Regular battalions had disappeared.[5]

This was the corps which Sheridan now was preparing to use as his striking force. When Grant first sent the corps out to operate on Lee's flank, he did two curious things. He detached it from Meade's command and put it entirely under Sheridan, promising to do the same with the II Corps if Sheridan needed it—which was a bit odd, considering that Sheridan was simply the cavalry commander, while Meade commanded the Army of the Potomac—and he specifically authorized Sheridan to relieve Warren of his command, if it seemed necessary, and to put someone else in his place.[6]

Grant's subsequent explanation of these acts was brief and vague, but what he was actually trying to do was to find a solution for the old, baffling command problem that had beset the Army of the Potomac from its earliest days.

Time and again the Army of the Potomac had missed a victory because someone did not move quite fast enough, or failed to put all of his weight into a blow, or came into action other than precisely as he was expected to do. This had happened before Grant became general in chief and it had happened since then, and the fact that Warren had been involved in a few such incidents was not especially important. What Grant was really shooting at was the sluggishness and caution that were forever cropping out, at some critical moment, somewhere in the army's chain of command. With the decisive moment of the war coming up Grant was going to have no more of that. Instinctively he was turning to Sheridan, Sheridan the driver—giving him as much of the army as he needed and in effect telling him to take it and be tough with it.

Sheridan was the man for it. As Warren's brigades struggled into position Sheridan was everywhere, needling the laggards, pricking the general officers on, sending his staff galloping from end to end of the line. He rounded up the cavalry bands, which had made music on the firing line the evening before, and he put them on horseback with orders to go into action along with the fighting men when the advance sounded. It was four o'clock by now, and there would not be a great deal more daylight, and at last the infantry began to move. Sheridan spurred away to send the cavalry forward too. There was the peal of many bugles and then a great crash of musketry, and thousands of men broke into a cheer, and the battle was on.

A skirmisher trotting forward a few hundred yards ahead of the V Corps turned once to look back, and he saw what neither he nor any of his mates had seen in a dreary year of wilderness fighting and trench warfare, and he remembered it as the most stirring thing he had ever looked upon in all his life. There they were, coming up behind him as if all of the power of a nation had been put into one disciplined mass—the fighting men of the V Corps, walking forward in battle lines that were a mile wide and many ranks deep, sunlight glinting on thousands of bright muskets, flags snapping in the breeze, brigade fronts taut with parade-ground Regular Army precision, everybody keeping step, tramping forward into battle to the sound of gunfire and distant music. To see this, wrote the skirmisher, was to see and to know "the grandeur and the sublimity of war."[7]

It was grand and inspiring—and, unfortunately, there was a hitch in it.

Warren was sending his men in with two divisions abreast and a third division following in support, and by some mischance he was hitting the White Oak Road far to the east of the place where he was supposed to hit it. Instead of coming in on the knuckle of Pickett's line, he was coming in on nothing at all. His men were marching resolutely toward the north and the battle was going on somewhere to the west, out of their sight and reach.

The left division in the first line was commanded by General Ayres, a hard-bitten survivor of the original old-army set of officers, and the left of his division brushed against the left flank of Pickett's force and came under a sharp fire. Ayres spun the whole division around, brigade by brigade, making almost a 90-degree turn to the left—hot enough work it was, too, with Rebel infantry and cavalry firing steadily and the ground all broken—and as he turned the rest of the corps lost contact with him. The division that had been advancing beside him was led by General Crawford, who fell a good deal short of being one of the most skillful soldiers in the army, and Crawford kept marching to the north, getting farther away from the battle every minute. Most of the third division followed Crawford, Ayres's men were for the moment so entangled in their maneuver that they could not do much fighting—and, in sum, instead of crunching in on the Rebel flank with overpowering force, the V Corps was hardly doing more than give it a brisk nudge.[8]

A confusing long-range fire, heavy enough to hurt, kept coming in from the left, and smoke fog was drifting through woods and fields. Warren had gone riding frantically on to try to find Crawford and set him straight, and entire brigades had lost touch with their corps and division commanders. One of these, presently, got into action, led by one of the most remarkable soldiers in the army, the hawk-nosed theologian turned general, Joshua Chamberlain of Maine.

Before the war Chamberlain had done nothing more militant than teach courses in natural and revealed religion, and later on in romance languages, at Bowdoin College. In 1862 he had been given a two-year leave of absence to study in Europe. Instead of going to Europe he had joined the army, and in a short time he showed up at Gettysburg as colonel of the 20th Maine Infantry, winning the Congressional Medal of Honor for his defense of Little Round Top. Since then he had been several times wounded—he had an arm in a sling today, as a matter of fact, from a wound received twenty-four hours earlier in the fight near Hatcher's Run—and he had twice won brevet promotions for bravery under fire. It was occurring to him now that since bullets were coming from the left there must be Confederates over that way, so he took his brigade over to do something about it.

Beyond a gully, Chamberlain could at last see a Confederate line of battle. He got his brigade into line, took it down into the little ravine, came out on the far side, and headed for the enemy. The fire was hot, now—and here, in the thickest of it, came Sheridan, riding up at top speed as always, his mounted color-bearer riding behind him. Sheridan pulled up facing Chamberlain, his dark face glowing.

"By God, that's what I want to see! General officers at the front!" cried Sheridan. He asked where Warren and the rest of the corps might be, and Chamberlain gestured toward the north, trying to explain what had happened. Sheridan interrupted, saying that Chamberlain was to take command of everybody he saw ir .ie immediate vicinity and press the attack—and then Sheridan rode off fast, looking for Warren and the missing infantry.[9]

All along the breastworks on the White Oak Road dismounted Yankee cavalrymen were attacking—looking, as a man who watched them said, with their tightly fitting uniforms, natty jackets, and short carbines, as if they had been especially designed for crawling through knotholes. Many of the carbines were repeaters, and at close range the troopers had terrific fire power, and a deafening racket went up from the narrow aisle in the woods. Around the angle Ayres's division and Chamberlain's brigade and fragments of other commands were still in some confusion, but they were beginning to get it straightened out now, and they were hitting the Confederates from flank and rear. Far to the north, the troops that had gone off at a tangent were at last being wheeled around so that they could cut across the Confederates' rear.[10]

Sheridan was all over the field. When a skirmish line met a severe fire, wavered, and seemed ready to fall back, up came Sheridan at a gallop, shouting to the men: "Come on—go at 'em—move on with a clean jump or you'll not catch one of 'em! They're all getting ready to run now, and if you don't get on to them in five minutes they'll every one get away from you!" An infantryman at his side was struck in the throat and fell, blood flowing as if his jugular vein had been cut. "You're not hurt a bit!" cried Sheridan. "Pick up your gun, man, and move right on!" The soldier looked up at him, then obediently took his musket, got to his feet, and staggered forward—to drop dead after half a dozen steps. Chamberlain came up to Sheridan once and begged him not to expose himself on the front line, promising that the rest of them would press the attack. Sheridan tossed his head with a grin which, Chamberlain felt, "seemed to say that he didn't care much for himself, or perhaps for me," and promised to go to the rear—and then dashed off to a sector where the fire was even hotter.

Finally the line was formed as Sheridan wanted it. In a boggy woodland, heavy smoke clouding the last of the sunlight, Sheridan looked down the shifting mass of soldiers, turned in the saddle, and called: "Where's my battle flag?" Up came his color-bearer. Sheridan took the flag from him, raised it high over his head, and went trotting along the front. The line surged forward and got up to the Rebel works, Sheridan put his horse over the breastworks, and the infantry went over in a riot of yelling jubilant men—and the Rebel flank was broken once and for all, and the men of the V Corps fought their way down the length of Pickett's battle line taking prisoners by the score and the hundred.[11]

By this time Warren had Crawford's errant division far around to the Rebel rear, rounding up fugitives and cutting off the line of retreat, and Warren sent his chief of staff over to tell Sheridan about it. This officer found Sheridan on the battlefield and trotted up proudly. But the great fury of battle was on Sheridan. Warren's corps had been late getting to Dinwiddie and it had been late getting into position at Five Forks, and when it attacked two thirds of it had gone astray and Warren had gone with it; Sheridan did not in the least care whether the reasons for all of this were good or bad, and he did not want to receive any more reports from General Warren.

"By God, sir, tell General Warren he wasn't in that fight!" he shouted. The chief of staff was dumfounded. Warren had been doing his best, no one in the Army of the Potomac ever spoke that way about a distinguished corps commander—but Sheridan was clearly implacable, his face black, his eyes flashing. The officer managed to say at last that he disliked to deliver such a message verbally—might he take it down in writing?

"Take it down, sir!" barked Sheridan. "Tell him by God he was not at the front!"

Warren's man rode away, stunned. The next to come up was General Griffin, ranking division commander in the V Corps—Regular Army to his fingertips, rough and tough and gifted with a certain magnetism—a man, in fact, cut somewhat after the Sheridan pattern. Bluntly, Sheridan hailed him and told him that he was now in command of the V Corps. Then he sent a courier to find Warren and deliver a written message relieving him of his command and ordering him to report to General Grant at headquarters.[12]

Pickett's force was wholly wrecked, by now, with the front broken in and victorious Yankees charging in from the flank and rear to make ruin complete. Yet Sheridan still was not satisfied. The enemy must be annihilated, all escape must be cut off, that railroad line must be broken, no one must relax or pause for breath as long as there was anything still to be accomplished. . . . He was in a little clearing in the forest, directly behind what had been the main Confederate line, and through the clearing went the road that led from Five Forks to the Southside Railroad, the railroad Lee had to protect if his army was to live; and just then there came up to Sheridan some now unidentified officer of rank, to report triumphantly that his command was in the Rebel rear and had captured five guns.

Sheridan gave him a savage greeting:

"I don't care a damn for their guns, or you either, sir! What I want is that Southside Railway!"

The sun was just disappearing over the treetops, and the clearing was dim with a smoky twilight. Many soldiers were in and about the road through the clearing, their weapons in their hands, conscious of victory and half expecting to be told that they had done a great thing and were very fine fellows. Sheridan turned to face them, and he suddenly stood up in his stirrups, waving his hat, his face as black as his horse, and in a great voice he roared:

"I want you men to understand we have a record to make before that sun goes down that will make Hell tremble!"

He waved toward the north, toward the position of the railroad, and he cried: "I want you there!"

He turned and rode to the north. Meeting Griffin and Ayres and Chamberlain, he called to them: "Get together all the men you can, and drive on while you can see your hand before you!"

While the officers formed the men into ordered ranks and prepared to move on, a pale, slight man rode up to Sheridan and spoke to him quietly: General Warren, the written order clutched in his hand, asking Sheridan if he would not reconsider the order that wrecked a soldier's career.

"Reconsider, hell!" boomed Sheridan. "I don't reconsider my decisions! Obey the order!" Silently, Warren rode off in the dusk, and Sheridan went on trying to organize a force to break through to the railroad.[13]

Actually, no more could be done that night. No more needed to be done. To all practical purposes, Pickett's force had been wiped out. Thousands of prisoners were on their way back to the provost marshal's stockades, and there were so many captured muskets that Sheridan's pioneers were using armloads of them to corduroy the roads. Some of the Rebel cavalry elements which had got away were swinging about to rejoin Lee's army, but the infantry that had escaped was beaten and disorganized, drifting off to the north and west, effectively out of the war. Sheridan could have the railroad whenever he wanted to march his men over to it, and he might just as well do it tomorrow as tonight because the force which might have stopped him had been blown to bits. There was no need to put exhausted troops on the road before morning, and in the end even Sheridan came to see it. Cavalry and infantry went into bivouac where they were.

Around General Griffin's campfire the new commander of the V Corps talked things over with division and brigade commanders. These men were deeply attached to Warren. They felt that his troubles today had mostly been caused by General Crawford, and it seemed very hard that Warren should be broken for mistakes and delays which had not, after all, affected the outcome of the battle. This was the first time in the history of the Army of the Potomac that a ranking commander had been summarily fired because his men had been put into action tardily and inexpertly. Sheridan had been cruel and unjust—and if that cruel and unjust insistence on driving, aggressive promptness had been the rule in this army from the beginning, the war probably would have been won two years earlier. . . .

As the generals talked, a stocky figure stepped into the light of the campfire—Sheridan himself.

He was in a different mood, now, the battle fury quite gone, and he spoke very gently: If he had been harsh and demanding with any of them that day he was sorry, and he hoped they would forgive him, for he had not meant to hurt anyone. But—"you know how it is; we had to carry this place, and I was fretted all day until it was done." So there was this apology for hot words spoken in the heat of action, and there was the general's thanks for hard work well done, and then Sheridan went away, and the generals gaped into the dark after him. General Chamberlain, who was one of the circle, reflected that "as a rule, our corps and army commanders were men of brains rather than magnetism"; but Sheridan, now—well, "we could see how this voice and vision, this swing and color, this vivid impression on the senses, carried the pulse and will of men."[14]

Several miles to the east, one of Grant's staff officers who had been with Sheridan this day finished a tiring ride over crowded, watery roads, and pulled up his horse by the open fire at Grant's headquarters. His fellow officers there crowded around him before he had dismounted, eager for news, and he shouted it to them in breathless sentences—complete victory, Rebels utterly routed, the way to Lee's railroad and Lee's rear wide open, roads all clogged with prisoners—and they shouted, tossed hats and caps in the air, slapped one another on the back, capering in wild enthusiasm; all but Grant himself, who stood in their midst impassive, cigar in his teeth, and as soon as he could make himself heard in the din asked the staff officer the question that seemed to be his private gauge for measuring a victory: How many prisoners? The officer said that the best estimate was about five thousand, and for a moment Grant looked pleased, almost enthusiastic. Then he went over to the telegraphers' tent, coming out a moment later to remark: "I have ordered an immediate assault all along the lines."[15]

Great things might have been done on the flank, but the Army of Northern Virginia still lay directly in front, and from the moment he crossed the Rapidan River Grant's basic idea had always been, not to make that army retreat, but to break it. Now the time had come when it could be broken. Yet "immediate" did not actually mean "right away." Orders had to go from Grant through Meade and Ord to corps and division commanders. Artillerists had to frame and distribute orders to batteries and gun pits. Orders for the infantry had to filter down from army to corps to division to brigade and regiment; and it was likely to be dawn, or close to it, before the assault could really be made.

On the right, where the lines were close together and where the Confederate defenses were most tightly knit, Parke would send his IX Corps straight in from their trenches. Farther around, west of Fort Hell, the big push would be made by the VI Corps, with Ord holding his men ready to follow the moment there was a sign of success. In this part of the front the lines were a mile or more apart, and in the counterblow after Fort Stedman the Federals had taken the Confederate picket lines; so in here there was a little room to maneuver, and around midnight the men of the VI Corps filed out of their trenches to go into position.

General Wright had gone out ahead of them to pick the target. There was comparatively high ground here, and along part of the front there was no water in front of the Confederate works. There were five lines of abatis to be crossed, very stout and formidable, but the pickets had reported a singular fact: there was a pathway through these entanglements, used by enemy details which came out to get firewood or go on picket duty, and at night the Rebels kept a bonfire alight toward the rear in line with this pathway. If the Federals who formed on the higher ground would simply guide their advance on this bonfire, then, they would get through the abatis and up to the trenches.

Wright formed his corps wedge-shaped, with the third brigade of the second division as the thin end of the wedge—1,600 men in six veteran regiments, the rest of the corps in echelon to right and left. With the advance there would be a detail of gunners with rammers and primers, ready to turn captured guns on the defenders. It was understood that the advance would begin as soon as a signal gun was fired from Federal Fort Fisher, in the rear.

The night was bewilderingly dark, and there was a mist that made the gloom even thicker. The VI Corps these days was known as the army's high-morale outfit—the men had shared in the great Shenandoah Valley victories, and they were cocky about it—but they were glum and silent as they left their trenches and took their places. The high command might know that when Lee detached troops to operate under Pickett at Five Forks he left his main line so badly undermanned that it could at last be broken, but the infantry knew nothing of this. All that the veterans understood was that these terrible fortifications which they had learned to consider unconquerable were at last to be attacked, and they took it for granted that the hour of doom had arrived.[16]

When company commanders read off the orders, soldiers here and there were heard to mutter: "Well, good-by, boys—this means death." As always, the men got ready for the fight in their different ways. Some scribbled hasty letters home, others threw away decks of playing cards, still others examined cartridge boxes and canteens to make sure that they were filled, a few put pipe and tobacco within easy reach. And tonight a good many did what they never did except when they figured they were about to be slaughtered. They wrote their names and addresses on slips of paper and pinned these to their uniforms, so that their bodies could be identified after the battle.[17]

Huddled close to the ground in the creepy no man's land between the armies, utter darkness and graveyard silence all around, the men waited nervously for the signal gun that would send them on their way. But once again there had been a mix-up in the arrangements. What finally came, jarring and stunning them and seeming to pin them down by sheer weight of violence, was not the report of one cannon but the crash of a tremendous bombardment, with every gun and mortar in the Federal lines opening fire.

There were miles upon miles of gun positions, all the way from the Appomattox to the works near Hatcher's Run, and from every weapon in this crescent there came the most intense and sustained volume of fire the gun crews could manage. Never before, not even at Gettysburg, had the army fired so much artillery so fast and so long. The whole sky pulsed and shuddered with great sheets of light. Jagged flames lit the horizon as the Confederate guns replied. In the blackness overhead the battle smoke piled up in monstrous thunderheads, fitfully visible in the flash of exploding shell.

A gunner wrote proudly of "a constant stream of living fire" pouring from the flaming gun pits, and a front-line infantryman said that the very ground shook and trembled with the concussion. Miles away to the west, men in the V Corps said the sky was lighted up as if by aurora borealis. How long it all lasted, nobody ever knew. After a time men realized that the Confederate batteries had stopped firing, and then the crash of the Union guns seemed definitely lighter— and now, as the bombardment slowly tapered off, staff officers from corps headquarters were going to brigade and regimental commanders asking why the men were not moving: the signal gun had been fired, somewhere in the midst of all of this uproar, and the attack should have been made ten minutes ago.[18]

Officers prodded men to their feet, and the smoky sky began to turn gray, although it was still too dark to see anything a hundred yards away, and presently the whole great wedge of infantry was moving. And then the guns stopped altogether, and there was silence on the battlefield, and in this silence an officer realized that there was a mysterious, pervasive noise that seemed to be the sound of a deep, distant rustling, "like a strong breeze blowing through the swaying boughs and dense foliage of some great forest." He realized at last that this was the noise made by 14,000 soldiers tramping forward over soft damp ground.[19]

Rebel pickets came to life and began to shoot, and then rolling volleys of musketry lit the main line of Confederate works, and the guns opened heavily. The VI Corps raised a cheer and began a run forward. The leading brigade lost sight of the path through the abatis, but the whole corps was running now, details with axes were smashing at the entanglements, sheer weight of numbers was breaking a dozen openings—and the tide flowed on, past the abatis and into the ditch, with the black loom of the fortifications rising just ahead.

Far to the rear, on the parapet of a Union fort, an army surgeon had been watching, and in the predawn gloom he could see a twinkling, flashing line of fire half a mile wide—the rim of the Confederate works, lit by musketry. As he watched he saw a black gap in the center of this sparkling line, and then there was another gap a little to one side, and then a third one, and as he watched these gaps widened and ran together, and suddenly the whole chain of lights was out and he knew that the line had been captured.

It was not done easily, for if the defenders were few they died hard, and there was hand-to-hand fighting along the works. Storming parties got over in squads, stabbing and clubbing muskets. There was no cheering—everyone was too much out of breath for that—but the men coming up in the support brigades realized that the trenches had been taken when they saw Confederate cannon reversed, firing toward the Confederate rear. In some cases Union infantry refused to wait for the parties of artillerists who had been sent over to work the captured guns, and tried to operate them themselves. The 11th Vermont claimed to have fired twelve rounds from one battery, overcoming the want of primers simply by discharging muskets into the vents of the loaded pieces.[20]

Dawn came at last, and the whole line of works was black with Union soldiers. Beyond the line lay the Confederate camps, with eager parties of VI Corps hot-shots pushing on through them, every man for himself—some of them running on to reach the unguarded rear areas, some looking through tents and huts for loot, some just going, kept moving by the excitement of victory. Far to the right, the IX Corps had stormed the whole first line of deadly trenches but met stubborn resistance on the second line, and the sound of artillery and musketry rolled across the pine flats. On the left, the entire line of defense had dissolved. Ord's troops, and the II Corps, were breaking through on the west, cutting the defenders' organizations into fragments and driving these broken units before them. By twos and threes and by disorganized squads, the Federals broke clear through past the railroad to the edge of the Appomattox. In a chance encounter by a bit of wood, some of these killed the famous General A. P. Hill.

In the Confederate camps the VI Corps made merry. One man remembered seeing a burly buck private outfitting himself in the tinseled gray dress-uniform coat which some Confederate officer would never need again, and another soldier was wrapping a Confederate flag about his shoulders as if it were a toga. The whole corps was up, now, overflowing the trenches, scampering around among bombproofs and huts and tents, staring out over ground which no armed Yankee had previously seen. Up into their midst came a group of mounted men, Grant and Meade and Wright trotting over to reorganize the storming columns and make the break-through complete.[21]

"Then and there," wrote a Connecticut soldier exultantly, "then and there the long-tried and ever faithful soldiers of the Republic *saw daylight!*" And the whole corps looked up and down the Petersburg lines—broken forever, now—and took in what had been done, and caught its breath, and sent up a wild shout which, the Connecticut man said, it was worth dying just to listen to.[22]

4. THE ENORMOUS SILENCE

The end of the war was like the beginning, with the army marching down the open road under the spring sky, seeing a far light on the horizon. Many lights had died in the windy dark but far down the road there was always a gleam, and it was as if a legend had been created to express some obscure truth that could not otherwise be stated. Everything had changed, the war and the men and the land they fought for, but the road ahead had not changed. It went on through the trees and past the little towns and over the hills, and there was no getting to the end of it. The goal was a going-toward rather than an arriving, and from the top of the next rise there was always a new vista. The march toward it led through wonder and terror and deep shadows, and the sunlight touched the flags at the head of the column.

For a long time the Army of the Potomac had wanted to enter Richmond, and it almost seemed as if that was the object of everything that it did, but when Richmond fell at last the army did not get within twenty-five miles of it—not until long afterward, when everything was over and the men were going home to be civilians again. Most of the army did not even get into Petersburg, which had been within sight but out of reach for so long. Instead the troops moved off on roads that led to the west, pounding along in hot pursuit of Lee's army—no victory was final as long as that ragged army still lived and moved.

Only the IX Corps entered Petersburg, and it did so chiefly because the town lay right across its path. It moved in on the morning of April 3 a few hours after the last Confederate soldiers had moved out. The corps came in proudly, flags uncased and bands playing, but the town was all scarred by months of shellfire, the cheers and the music echoed through deserted streets, and there seems to have been a desolate, empty quality to it all that made the jubilation sound forced and hollow. Officers and newspapermen who had breakfast in Petersburg hotels found the fare poor, as was natural in a starved beleaguered city, and noticed that the hotel proprietors would not accept Confederate money.

In the dwelling houses the blinds were all drawn, and here and there an expressionless face could be seen peering out through parted curtains. Men remarked that there was not a woman to be seen; only a few old men, and an occasional cripple, and of course an awed concourse of colored folk. One officer saw Grant standing in a doorway, gesturing with his cigar as he dictated orders to his staff, utterly matter-of-fact, displaying rather less emotion and pride than the ordinary brigadier would show at a routine review of troops, and looking "as if the work before him was a mere matter of business in which he felt no particular enthusiasm or care."[1]

In refusing to allow the army to relax and celebrate Grant was simply following common sense. From his viewpoint he had not actually won anything yet. From the moment when he headed down to the Rapidan fords, eleven months and many thousands of lives ago, he had had just one idea in mind: to destroy Lee's army. Now Richmond had fallen, and so had Petersburg, but Lee's army still lived and if it was to be destroyed it must first be caught. It would never be caught by pursuers who let days or hours go to waste: not that army, led by that general. So the Army of the Potomac would keep moving, and if there was to be a celebration it could come later.

Beaten and reeling in flight, the Rebel army was still dangerous. Proof that its men still wanted to fight came this morning at the prisoner-of-war stockade. Nearly 5,000 of the men captured at Five Forks were herded together there, and the Federal provost marshal had them paraded and made a little speech to them, pointing out that their cause was doomed and inviting everyone to step up, take the oath of allegiance, and then go home and fight no more. Out of the 5,000 present, fewer than 100 moved out to take the oath—and they were bitterly derided by all the rest, who profanely denounced them as cowards and traitors.[2]

So although the grim Petersburg trenches were empty and harmless, and troops from the Army of the James were in Richmond putting out the fires that threatened to destroy the whole city—the Confederate rear guard had fired arsenals and storehouses, and the flames had got out of hand—nothing had really been settled. The Army of the Potomac had not yet brought its adversary to bay, and it would have to march long and fast to do it.

There were certain advantages. Leaving Petersburg, Lee had gone north of the Appomattox River. Somewhere above that river he was picking up the troops that had come down from Richmond and was collecting the fragments that had been sent flying when Sheridan took Five Forks and the VI Corps broke the Petersburg line. With everybody assembled, he would try to join Joe Johnston in North Carolina, and to do that he would have to go west and south. The Army of the Potomac was nearly as far west as he was, and it was a good deal farther south. Properly handled it ought to be able to head him off because it had a shorter distance to travel.

The railroads were important. There were two lines that mattered: the familiar Southside Railroad, and the Richmond and Danville, which latter went slanting down into Joe Johnston's territory and bisected the Southside line halfway between Petersburg and Lynchburg. Lee's quickest route would put him on the Richmond and Danville at Amelia Court House, sixteen miles northeast of the point where the two railroads intersected.

If the Federals moved west by the shortest route, they should strike the Richmond and Danville road at or near the junction before Lee's people could get down there via Amelia Court House. If that happened, it would be impossible for Lee to meet Johnston. He would have only two alternatives: to stand and make a finish fight of it, a fight that could end in but one way, or to keep on going west in the hope that he could reach Lynchburg, where he might get supplies and win some sort of breathing space in the wooded folds of the mountains.

So the task was not to overtake his army but to get ahead of it. Every march was to be a forced march. Sheridan and his cavalry were leading the way. Meade and three infantry corps were following close behind, and Ord and three divisions from the Army of the James were moving on parallel roads just a little farther south. The men carried extra rations, for there would be no waiting for supply trains, and a thirty-mile hike—ordinarily a perfect prodigy of a march—would be considered no more than a fair day's work. Officers in the V Corps called out to the men: "Your legs must do it, boys!"[3]

Spring had come, and the world was turning green and white and gold with new leaves and blossoms. The cramping misery of the trenches had been left behind, and men's spirits were so high that even dogtrotting along in the wake of the cavalry did not seem a bad assignment. The rank and file was not entirely clear about just what had happened, but it was clear that the Johnnies were on the run at last. Grant summed it up in a telegram to Sherman: "This army has now won a most decisive victory and followed the enemy. That is all that it ever wanted to make it as good an army as ever fought a battle."[4]

They might be victorious, but the men were still cagey. Midway of the first day out, excited staff officers rode down the columns shouting the news—Richmond taken, the Union flag flying over the Confederate capital! The veterans perked up, and then they remembered that they had been had before. When an especially hard march was to be made, staff officers often circulated false announcements of good tidings just to keep everybody stepping along briskly. So the men jeered at each bearer of good news, calling out: "Put him in a canteen! Give him a hardtack! Tell it to the recruits!" But pretty soon the bands began to play, and the colonels formally announced the news to their own regiments, and up and down the line of march men began to realize that for once the good news was true.

"Stack your muskets and go home!" yelled one of Ord's men, when General Gibbon announced the fall of Richmond. As the army bivouacked that night, one veteran told another: "I feel better tonight than I did after that fight at Gettysburg."[5]

Far out in front, fantastic outriders of victory, went Sheridan's scouts. Sometimes they rode dressed as Confederate officers or couriers, and sometimes they wore faded jeans and rode decrepit horses or mules with makeshift bridles and saddles, pretending to be displaced farmers or roving horse doctors. Either way, they visited Rebel picket posts, rode blithely through cavalry cordons, ambled alongside Lee's wagon trains, paused to chat in Confederate camps. Most of them got back alive, and they kept Sheridan informed about where the enemy's people were and where they were going to be next.

As they did all of this, riding under no man's control, they appear to have found unheard-of opportunities for loot. They visited farms and plantations and collected much food for themselves, they got new horses when they felt that they needed them, and (as other cavalrymen reported enviously) they were not always above helping themselves to more substantial valuables, taking cash and jewelry from planters' homes and leaving their victims quite at a loss to say just who had robbed them.[6] They were a wild, lawless crew, carrying their own lives and other people's property in their naked hands, and they feared nothing in particular except the black scowl of Phil Sheridan.

They swarmed all around the head of the cavalry column, exploring the whole network of country roads and learning where every lane and cowpath led. Behind them came hard columns of questing cavalry, slashing through to nip at the flanks of Lee's moving army, driving Confederate troopers off the roads, harassing the plodding columns with quick thrusts and then pulling away fast to strike again a mile or two farther on. Back of these, in turn, came Sheridan and the main body of cavalry; and two days out of Five Forks Sheridan led his men into a country town called Jetersville, which place was important then for two reasons—it was on the Richmond and Danville Railroad and Lee and his army had not yet reached it.

Sheridan sent one division west and north to see what was to be seen and to cause as much trouble as possible for the Confederacy. The rest he led northeast, and after a few miles his men ran into Rebel cavalry patrols and drove them back. Then Sheridan called a halt and had his men build breastworks, and a little later General Griffin came up with the V Corps and threw his men into line of battle beside them, and the rest of the infantry was not far away. Meade himself was coming up, in an ambulance. He had taken ill, from indigestion and general nerve strain, after the fall of Petersburg, but he was coming along with the army regardless.[7] So here was the Army of the Potomac getting ready to fight its old antagonist, and for the first time in its history its battle line was facing toward the northeast. It had won the race and if Lee was to go any farther south he would have to fight.

Lee's army was at Amelia Court House, half a dozen miles short of the spot where Meade's infantry was going into line. It could not stay there because it had used up all of its rations and there was nothing in Amelia Court House for it to eat, and after surveying the Yankee line carefully Lee concluded that his army was not strong enough to fight its way through. Since the army could not retreat—there were Yankees in both Richmond and Petersburg now—only one move remained on the board: to go west, cross country, and strike the western part of the Southside Railroad. Provisions could be brought up from Lynchburg by this line, and if the army moved fast and had luck there was an outside chance that it could still slip around the Federal flank and get south. Failing that, it might at least reach Lynchburg and try to survive there for a time. There was nothing else it could even try to do.

Sheridan did not believe it should be given any leeway. His whole instinct was to attack before anybody got six hours older, and he seems to have feared that Meade would be content to wait for Lee to start the fight. At any rate, Sheridan wanted the boss; so one of his scouts, dressed like a Confederate colonel, took a note which Sheridan scribbled on tissue paper, folded the tissue paper in tin foil, concealed that in a wad of leaf tobacco, and shoved the tobacco in his mouth—after which he went trotting off cross country to find U. S. Grant.

Grant was with Ord that day, a dozen miles away, and the scout reached him toward evening, narrowly missing getting shot by Ord's pickets as he came cantering in. So Grant got Sheridan's message, which described the situation, suggested that Lee's army might be captured, and urged Grant to come and take charge in person. With his staff and a small mounted escort Grant immediately set out, guided by the gray-uniformed scout, following rambling country roads in the dark—with his staff wondering uneasily just what would happen to the war if the little party should blunder into the Confederate lines by mistake. It was late at night when Grant reached Sheridan's tent, and nothing could be done with the troops until morning.[8]

If Sheridan feared that Meade would sit down and wait for the fight to be brought to him, he was mistaken. Meade wanted to fight and he started the infantry toward Amelia Court House at dawn, but Lee was no longer there. He had put his tired, half-starved troops on the road for a night march, trying the last chance that was left to him, striking due west for the town of Farmville, on the Southside Railroad. When the flight was discovered Meade ordered pursuit, but Grant modified the order: let part of the infantry follow in Lee's rear, pressing him and making him stand and fight whenever it could, but let the rest follow the cavalry and get west as fast as possible, keeping always south of the Confederates. The idea still was to win a race, and if they could plant infantry across Lee's path just once more it would all be over.

So the foot race was on again and away they went, infantry and cavalry and the lumbering guns. It was April 6, and the Petersburg break-through was four days behind them, and some of the infantry units were doing thirty-five miles a day and more. In some ways it was like any other hard march—woods and swamps and wispy fields, muddy roads churned into quagmire by thousands of horses, a hard pull on the long hills and everybody too winded to say much. Yet now it was all different, because for all anyone knew the thing they had been marching toward for four years might lie just the other side of the next hill.

On every side there were multiplying signs of Confederate defeat, littering roads and fields like driftwood dropped by an ebbing tide: broken wagons and ambulances, guns with broken wheels, discarded muskets and blanket rolls, stragglers bedded down in fence corners or stumbling listlessly through the woods—and, every so often, "dropped in the very middle of the road from utter exhaustion, old horses literally skin and bones, and so weak as scarcely to be able to lift their heads when some soldier would touch them with his foot to see if they really had life." Every regiment had its congenital pessimists, as one soldier confessed, men who fought well but who always darkly prophesied ultimate Rebel victory; but now, this man said, "the utter collapse of the rebellion was so near that no one could fail to see it, and the croakers were compelled to cheer in spite of themselves."[9]

Humphreys was driving the II Corps in on Lee's rear guard, and the day was a long succession of savage little fights wherever the Confederates could find a defensive vantage point. On other roads the other corps struggled to gain ground, and up ahead and along the way there was the cavalry—always the cavalry, with Sheridan sending galloping columns in to skirmish, wheel, and dash away again, forcing weary Southerners to halt, form line of battle, and then go on with their march. He had three divisions doing this, probing always for a weak spot, slowing down the enemy's march, relentless and seemingly tireless. In midafternoon he found, at last, the opening he was looking for.

Custer spied a Confederate wagon train winding through hill country, the bleak woods glistening from the spring rains, and he whistled his squadrons in on the dead run with sabers swinging. Confederate infantry fell into line to repel the attack, but up ahead a gap developed in the moving column and Custer's men went pouring through it, stopping the wagon train, cutting the traces and driving the teams away, sabering drivers, breaking wagon wheels with axes, and setting fire to the wreckage. More and more cavalry went into the gap, and

Sheridan sent couriers back to bring up the infantry: here is a whole section of Lee's army cut off, come on up quick and we can bag the lot![10]

Nearest infantry was the IV Corps, which had marched all night and all day without food and was just filing into some fields to make coffee and eat bacon and hardtack when Sheridan's messengers came up. Down the lines went staff officers and colonels to tell the men the news: Sheridan is just ahead and he wants help, and we can all eat later perhaps. The men fell into ranks cheering and they stepped off eagerly, and before long they formed a battle line on a slope looking down to a little creek, on the far side of which there was a Confederate battle line. Sheridan rode up, and the VI Corps veterans who had followed him in the Valley pointed and told each other: "There's Phil! There's Phil!" and yelled their heads off. One of their officers mused: "The sight of that man on the field was more gratifying than rations, more inspiring than reinforcements."[11]

On the horizon was the burning Confederate wagon train. Straight in front was a fair piece of the Rebel army, brought to bay at last, the men dangerous as so many wounded panthers; and off to the left were four brigades of Yankee cavalry, moving forward at a walk as if passing in review, heading for the Confederate flank. For a minute or two everything seemed to hang in suspense, as if the army had gone to great pains to pose a dramatic picture. Then the wild high notes of the bugles sounded from end to end of the line, and everybody went forward on the run, cavalry and infantry alike, and there was a great shouting and the smoke from thousands of muskets banked up over the valley. Then the cavalry had broken through, and the infantry was tussling in the shallows, and suddenly there was no more Rebel battle line, nothing but groups of men throwing down their arms, cavalry ranging far and wide to round up fugitives, thousands of Confederates surrounded and surrendering—among them, picturesque one-legged General Dick Ewell, who had been Stonewall Jackson's lieutenant when the world was young. Far in the distance, Lee on a hilltop watched it all and told an officer beside him: "That half of our army has been destroyed."[12]

There was exaggeration in the remark, but not a great deal. What remained of two Confederate army corps had gone to pieces, with thousands of men taken prisoner, only a few escaping through the woods. The rear guard hung on until dark and then the Confederates followed their last fading chance to the north side of the Appomattox River, burning the bridges behind them. If they could keep the Federals south of that still unfordable river and go on with desperate forced marches it might yet be possible . . . just barely possible . . . to get away and join Johnston, or reach the mountains, or find somewhere a chance to rest and refit and make the war go on a little longer.

Along the creek where they had won their triumph the Federals cheered and danced. Someone found barrels of Confederate paper money in a headquarters wagon not yet burned, and the men went scampering about with handfuls of it, tossing it in the air, using it to kindle fires, offering great bundles of it to the gloomy prisoners. All of the ground was covered with the debris of the broken army, and as the VI Corps moved away the men found the road for two miles so littered with discarded muskets that it was hard to move without stepping on them. A major of the 65th New York was mortally wounded when someone's horse trod on one of these muskets and caused it to go off and shoot him.[13]

If the VI Corps found a few hours to relax, Humphreys kept the II Corps moving, and it got to one of the river crossings just as a Rebel rear guard was firing the last bridge. Barlow had the advance, and he sent his men down to the bridge a-running, fighting Confederate skirmishers and beating out the flames at the same time. In the end they saved the bridge and drove off the Confederate guards, and the whole army corps went pouring over to the north side of the river and pushed on to harry the rear of the Army of Northern Virginia and make any breathing spell impossible.

Two Confederate armies Grant had captured entire, in this war, and now the third and greatest of them was stricken, limping pathetically in its effort to get away from him. The increasing signs that the army was ready for destruction simply made Grant drive his own troops all the harder. Sheridan's cavalry ranged west, untiring, and Griffin's and Ord's troops followed as if the mounted men were pulling them on. North of the Appomattox, the II Corps continued to press the Confederate rear. Since this corps was miles away from the rest of the Union army, there was danger that Lee might turn suddenly and destroy it, and so Grant ordered the VI Corps to cross the river and march with Humphreys's men.

It was April 7 now, and Grant was in the little town of Farmville by the Appomattox. Evening had come, and the troops in Farmville had lighted bonfires all along the main street, and Grant was sitting on the veranda of the homely country hotel there when the head of the VI Corps came marching through on its way to the north side of the river. As they marched between the fires the men saw the unassuming little general on the porch, and they suddenly realized that this man was at last leading them to the victory they had dreamed of so long. They broke ranks briefly, seized brands from the bonfires and made torches, and then paraded past Grant, waving the burning torches and yelling hysterically. Brigade bands materialized, and the VI Corps marched by to music. Men who had no torches waved their caps, and the corps went on out of the firelight into the darkness, crossing the Appomattox. After they had passed, Grant went inside the hotel and wrote a formal note to be delivered to Robert E. Lee under a flag of truce, inviting Lee to surrender.[14]

Of this note the soldiers knew nothing. They knew only that in all of its existence the Army of the Potomac had never been driven as hard as it was being driven now. Wagon trains were left far behind, whole brigades and divisions marched without food, and every rod of the way the army dribbled stragglers. These stragglers found the foraging in this part of Virginia very good, since marching armies had not previously been here, but the land's plenty was of little help to the men who remained in the ranks. The army was moving too fast to bother with foraging details.

A soldier in the 20th Maine said that "we never endured such marching before," and another man in the V Corps remembered making a forty-two-mile march that went clear through from one sunrise to another. Whenever the column stopped for a five-minute rest, he said, men would drop in their tracks and go instantly to sleep, and when the column moved on many of the men stumbled to their feet, shouldered their muskets, and went lurching down the road would still be sound asleep. The very utmost men could do was demanded of them now, and the only reality was the road itself.[15]

It was a bad road to march on, like all the roads of war—deeply rutted, fouled by the march of the cavalry up ahead, by turns heavy with mud or deep with the dust that would make marching a gray choking agony. Yet this was the road the army had been marching toward from the very beginning, and many thousands of men had died in order that this road might at last be marched on; for this was the road to the end of the war, and on over the horizon to the unimaginable beginnings and endings that would lie beyond that. Also, and more intimately, it was the beginning of the long road home.

It was April 8, by now, and tomorrow would be Palm Sunday, and the land was rich and warm with spring. Below the Appomattox, that day, the road wound interminably through deep woods, so that dusk came down early. Ord's divisions were on the road, and all of the V Corps, together with much artillery, and the artillery was supposed to have the road while the infantry filed along on each side. But the road was very narrow, so that there was much crowding and confusion, and the men were very tired and quarrelsome, and some time after dark a tremendous fight broke out between infantry and artillery. Infantry complained that the gunners were driving their six-horse teams recklessly, forcing men off the road and causing injuries. Gunners declared that infantrymen were hitting artillery horses over the head with musket butts. Everybody was hungry, irritable, and half out of his mind with fatigue, and the yelling and cursing and hitting and general uproar went up from the dark lane for an hour or more.

When it was finally settled it was after midnight, and the troops were led off the road to make a supperless bivouac. They got very little rest—one regiment at the tail of the column complained that it was roused just fifteen minutes after it turned in—because couriers came riding in from Phil Sheridan, who was a few miles farther on, near a little place called Appomattox Court House. He had his cavalry squarely in front of the Rebel army, and he was writing that if the infantry could be there first thing in the morning they could probably wind the whole business up.[16]

Sheridan's scouts had come to him earlier in the day with word that several freight trains with food had pulled in at Appomattox Station, a mile or so from the courthouse town, and that Lee's wagons would presently be alongside, loading up. Sheridan sent Custer off at a gallop, and Custer's division took the Confederates by surprise, seizing the trains just as they were ready to unload. There were former railroad men among the Yankee troopers, and these flung themselves from the saddle and raced for the locomotives, climbing into the cabs with much clumping of heavy boots and clanking of sabers. They threw out the Southern train crews, blew whistles and rang bells, and bumped the trains back and forth in aimless celebration until someone finally had them run the cars up the track a few miles so that they would be out of reach of any Confederate counterthrust.

Custer took the main body of his troops on past the station, seized a big wagon park and artillery train, and chased fugitives eastward along a road that led uphill through deep woods. He came out into the open just at dark, and saw a rude breastwork cutting across the highway with gray-clad infantry behind it. Beyond, many campfires put a soft red glow on the sky. They were the campfires of Lee's army—and Custer's cavalry was due west of them.[17]

Sheridan came up soon after, with the rest of the cavalry. He sent hurry-up messages for the infantry, put half of his men in line, dismounted, facing the Rebel breastworks, and ordered the rest into bivouac near the railroad a mile to the south.

The road his cavalry was on was the main road to Lynchburg, which lay twenty miles to the west. Of all the world's roads, this was the only one that mattered now to the Army of Northern Virginia. If, when morning came, that army could knock the Yankees out of the way and march west on this road it might still hope to live for a while—a day or two, a fortnight, a few months. If it could not do that, it would cease to exist within twenty-four hours. Cavalry alone could not bar the way very long, but if the blue infantry came up in time then it would be taps and dipped flags and good-by forever for Lee's army.

Federal infantry was on the road in the dark hours before dawn, with very little sleep and no breakfast at all. The men were told that if they hurried this was the day they could finish everything, and this inspired them. Yet they were no set of legendary heroes who never got tired or hungry or thought about personal discomfort. They were very human, given to griping when their stomachs were empty, and what really pulled them along this morning seems to have been the promise that at Appomattox Station rations would be issued. Most of the men who made the march that morning, one veteran admitted, did so because they figured it was the quickest way to get breakfast. Even so the straggling was abnormally heavy, and there were regiments in the column which had no more than seventy-five men with the colors.[18]

It was Palm Sunday, with a blue cloudless sky, and the warm air had the smell of spring. The men came tramping up to the fields by the railroad station with the early morning sun over their right shoulders, and they filed off to right and left, stacked arms, and began collecting wood for the fires with which they would cook the anticipated rations. The divisions from the Army of the James were in front, Ord and John Gibbon in the lead, and the V Corps was coming up close behind. Gibbon and Ord rode to a little house near the railroad where Sheridan had his headquarters, and Sheridan came out to greet them and explain the situation.

The Lynchburg Road lay about a mile north of Confederate headquarters. It ran along a low ridge, partly concealed by timber, with a boggy little brook running along a shallow valley on the near side, and a couple of miles to the east it dipped down a little hollow and ran through the village of Appomattox Court House. In and around and beyond this village, with its advance guard holding the breastworks half a mile west of it, was what remained of the Army of Northern Virginia. Off to the east, out of sight beyond hills and forests but not more than six or eight miles away, was Meade with the II Corps and the VI Corps, coming west on the Lynchburg Road to pound the Confederate rear. In effect, the Federals occupied three sides of a square—cavalry on the west, infantry on the south, Meade and the rest of the army on the east. The Rebel army was inside the square, and although the north side was open that did not matter because the Confederates could find neither food nor escape in that direction. Their only possible move was to fight their way west along the Lynchburg Road.

So Sheridan explained it, warning the generals that he expected the Rebels to attack at any moment and that they had better get ready to bring their troops up in support.[19]

While he was talking the sound of musket fire came down from the ridge. It was sporadic, at first, as the skirmishers pecked away at each other, but it soon grew much heavier and there was the heavy booming of field artillery. The big push was on, and Sheridan sprang into the saddle, ordering the rest of his cavalry up into line and telling the officers to bring their infantry up as fast as they could. Then he was off, and the generals galloped back to put their men in motion.

The hopeful little breakfast fires died unnoticed, nothing ever cooked on them, and the infantry took their muskets, got into column, and went hurrying north to get astride of the Lynchburg Road. The crossroad they were on led through heavy timber and the men could see nothing, but the noise of the firing grew louder and louder as they marched. Then, for the last time in their lives, beyond the trees they heard the high, spine-tingling wail of the Rebel yell, a last great shout of defiance flung against the morning sky by a doomed army marching into the final sunset.

The Federals got across the Lynchburg Road, swung into line of battle facing east, and marched toward the firing and the shouting. As they marched, dismounted cavalry came drifting back, and the troopers waved their caps and cheered when they saw the infantry, and called out: "Give it to 'em—we've got 'em in a tight place!"[20]

In a clearing there was Sheridan, talking with Griffin and other officers of the V Corps; Sheridan, talking rapidly, pounding a palm with his fist; and the battle line marched on and came under the fire of Rebel artillery. One brigade went across somebody's farm, just here, and as the firing grew heavier a shell blew the end out of the farmer's chicken house, and the air was abruptly full of demoralized chickens, squawking indignantly, fluttering off in frantic disorganized flight. And here was the last battle of the war, and the men were marching up to the moment of apotheosis and glory—but they were men who had not eaten for twenty-four hours and more, and they knew Virginia poultry from of old, and what had begun as an attack on a Rebel battle line turned into a hilarious chase after fugitive chickens. The battle smoke rolled down over the crest, and shells were exploding and the farm buildings were ablaze, and Federal officers were waving swords and barking orders in scandalized indignation. But the soldiers whooped and laughed and scrambled after their prey, and as the main battle line swept on most of this brigade was either continuing to hunt chickens or was building little fires and preparing to cook the ones that had been caught.[21]

The Confederates had scattered the cavalry, and most of the troopers fled south, across the shallow valley that ran parallel with the Lynchburg Road. As the last of them left the field the way seemed to be open, and the Confederates who had driven them away raised a final shout of triumph—and then over the hill came the first lines of blue infantry, rifles tilted forward, and here was the end of everything: the Yankees had won the race and the way was closed forever and there was no going on any farther.

The blue lines grew longer and longer, and rank upon rank came into view, as if there was no end to them. A Federal officer remembered afterward that when he looked across at the Rebel lines it almost seemed as if there were more battle flags than soldiers. So small were the Southern regiments that the flags were all clustered together, and he got the strange feeling that the ground where the Army of Northern Virginia had been brought to bay had somehow blossomed out with a great row of poppies and roses.[22]

So the two armies faced each other at long range, and the firing slackened and almost ceased.

Many times in the past these armies had paused to look at each other across empty fields, taking a final size-up before getting into the grapple. Now they were taking their last look, the Stars and Bars were about to go down forever and leave nothing behind but the stars and the memories, and it might have been a time for deep solemn thoughts. But the men who looked across the battlefield at each other were very tired and very hungry, and they did not have much room in their heads for anything except the thought of that weariness and that hunger, and the simple hope that they might live through the next half hour. One Union soldier wrote that he and his comrades reflected bitterly that they would not be here, waiting for the shooting to begin, if they had not innocently believed that tale about getting breakfast at Appomattox Station; and, he said, "we were angry with ourselves to think that for the hope of drawing rations we had been foolish enough to keep up and, by doing so, get in such a scrape." They did not mind the desultory artillery fire very much, he said, but "we dreaded the moment when the infantry should open on us."[23]

Off toward the south Sheridan had all of his cavalry in line again, mounted now with pennons and guidons fluttering. The Federal infantry was advancing from the west and Sheridan was where he could hit the flank of the Rebels who were drawn up to oppose that infantry, and he spurred over to get some foot soldiers to stiffen his own attack. General Griffin told Chamberlain to take his brigade and use it as Sheridan might direct. Men who saw Sheridan pointing out to Chamberlain the place where his brigade should attack remembered his final passionate injunction: "Now smash 'em, I tell you, smash 'em!"

Chamberlain got his men where Sheridan wanted them, and all of Ord's and Griffin's men were in line now, coming up on higher ground where they could see the whole field.

They could see the Confederate line drawing back from in front of them, crowned with its red battle flags, and all along the open country to the right they could see the whole cavalry corps of the Army of the Potomac trotting over to take position beyond Chamberlain's brigade. The sunlight gleamed brightly off the metal and the flags, and once again, for a last haunting moment, the way men make war looked grand and caught at the throat, as if some strange value beyond values were incomprehensibly mixed up in it all.[24]

Then Sheridan's bugles sounded, the clear notes slanting all across the field, and all of his brigades wheeled and swung into line, every saber raised high, every rider tense; and in another minute infantry and cavalry would drive in on the slim Confederate lines and crumple them and destroy them in a last savage burst of firing and cutting and clubbing.

Out from the Rebel lines came a lone rider, a young officer in a gray uniform, galloping madly, a staff in his hand with a white flag fluttering from the end of it. He rode up to Chamberlain's lines and someone there took him off to see Sheridan, and the firing stopped, and the watching Federals saw the Southerners wheeling their guns back and stacking their muskets as if they expected to fight no more.

All up and down the lines the men blinked at one another, unable to realize that the hour they had waited for so long was actually at hand. There was a truce, they could see that, and presently the word was passed that Grant and Lee were going to meet in the little village that lay now between the two lines, and no one could doubt that Lee was going to surrender. It was Palm Sunday, and they would all live to see Easter, and with the guns quieted it might be easier to comprehend the mystery and the promise of that day. Yet the fact of peace and no more killing and an open road home seems to have been too big to grasp, right at the moment, and in the enormous silence that lay upon the field men remembered that they had marched far and were very tired, and they wondered when the wagon trains would come up with rations.

One of Ord's soldiers wrote that the army should have gone wild with joy, then and there; and yet, he said, somehow they did not. Later there would be frenzied cheering and crying and rejoicing, but now ... now, for some reason, the men sat on the ground and looked across at the Confederate army and found themselves feeling as they had never dreamed that the moment of victory would make them feel.

"... I remember how we sat there and pitied and sympathized with these courageous Southern men who had fought for four long and dreary years all so stubbornly, so bravely and so well, and now, whipped, beaten, completely used up, were fully at our mercy—it was pitiful, sad, hard, and seemed to us altogether too bad." A Pennsylvanian in the V Corps dodged past the skirmish line and strolled into the lines of the nearest Confederate regiment, and half a century after the war he recalled it with a glow: "... as soon as I got among these boys I felt and was treated as well as if I had been among our own boys, and a person would of thought we were of the same Army and had been Fighting under the Same Flag."[25]

Down by the roadside near Appomattox Court House, Sheridan and Ord and other officers sat and waited while a brown-bearded little man in a mud-spattered uniform rode up. They all saluted him, and there was a quiet interchange of greetings, and then General Grant tilted his head toward the village and asked: "Is General Lee up there?"

Sheridan replied that he was, and Grant said: "Very well. Let's go up."[26]

The little cavalcade went trotting along the road to the village, and all around them the two armies waited in silence. As the generals neared the end of their ride, a Yankee band in a field near the town struck up "Auld Lang Syne."

Acknowledgments

IT WOULD be harder to write this kind of book, and the final result would be poorer, if one did not get so much help from so many kindly people. In listing the sources from which material was drawn the writer must express his abiding gratitude for a great deal of generous assistance.

Of particular value has been the opportunity to study various collections of unpublished letters written by Federal soldiers. These letters not only provide useful source material; they leave one feeling that he somehow had personal friends in the Union army—and, now and then, give him the odd illusion that he actually served in that army himself.

The following manuscript collections were made available:

Letters of Edwin Wentworth, of the 37th Massachusetts Infantry, loaned by Miss Edith Adams, of Auburn, Maine. These letters provide a singularly appealing glimpse at the experiences and emotions of a typical New England soldier, and one feels a sense of personal loss upon discovering that the last letter in the collection is a note to next of kin announcing Private Wentworth's death at the Bloody Angle.

Letters of Lewis Bissell, of the 2nd Connecticut Heavy Artillery, loaned by Mr. Carl H. Bissell, of Syracuse, New York. Extremely valuable as an unrevised, day-to-day account of the experiences of a VI Corps veteran, these letters also provide a useful check on the formal regimental history of this Connecticut regiment, whose author is frequently mentioned in Private Bissell's letters.

Letters of Henry Clay Heisler, of the 48th Pennsylvania Veteran Volunteers, loaned by Mr. Donald M. Hobart, of Philadelphia. Written by a soldier in the regiment which dug the famous Petersburg mine, these letters shed a revealing light on that operation and on the reaction of Burnside's soldiers to Burnside's last battle. (Interestingly enough, this regiment apparently blamed the fiasco on Burnside's subordinates rather than on Burnside himself.)

Letters of Sebastian Muller, of the 67th New York Infantry: in the manuscript collection of the Library of Congress. Quaint and stilted in their formal, old-world phraseology, these letters show how the war looked to an immigrant who supposed he had enlisted to fight "the rebels of South America."

Manuscript diary of Corporal S. O. Bryant, of the 20th Michigan Infantry, loaned by Mr. Donald C. Allen, of Washington. In this diary another of Burnside's soldiers expresses himself about the war, and in a complaint about Spotsylvania foreshadows the disaster at the crater.

Letter of Sergeant George S. Hampton, of the 91st Pennsylvania Veteran Volunteers, loaned by Mr. J. Frank Nicholson, of Manassas, Virginia. Written some years after the war, this letter contains a priceless glimpse of men of the two armies at the moment of the cease-fire at Appomattox Court House.

The writer's especial thanks are due to Mr. Ralph Happel, historian, the Fredericksburg and Spotsylvania County National Military Park, for the loan of his excellent manuscript studies of the Wilderness-Spotsylvania battles, and for guidance in study of the terrain.

Dr. James Rabun, of the Department of History, Emory University, kindly forwarded a reprint of his article, "Alexander Stephens and Jefferson Davis," in the *American Historical Review*.

Major General U. S. Grant, III, was most helpful in recalling anecdotes and family recollections about his distinguished grandfather.

Colonel Charles G. Stevenson, state judge advocate, New York National Guard, provided interesting material on the history of the famous "14th Brooklyn" Regiment, and traced that regiment's lineal descent to the 955th Field Artillery Battalion recently active in Korea.

Finally, a substantial debt of gratitude for many acts of helpfulness is owed to various librarians—specifically, to Dr. David Mearns and Dr. Percy Powell of the Manuscript Division, Library of Congress; to Colonel Willard Webb of the Stack and Reader Division and to Mr. Legare Obear of the Loan Division in that library; to Mr. Paul Howard, librarian of the Department of the Interior, and to Miss Georgia Cowan of the History Division of the Public Library of the District of Columbia.

Bibliography

Chief reliance of course has been placed on the invaluable *War of the Rebellion: A Compilation of the Official Records of the Union and Confederate Armies,* published by the War Department in 1902. Unless otherwise noted, volumes cited in the footnotes are from Series I of this compilation. Reference has also been made to Appleton's *Cyclopedia of American Biography,* edited by James Grant Wilson and John Fiske and published in 1888, and to the more modern *Dictionary of American Biography,* edited by Dumas Malone and published in 1943. In addition, the following works were consulted:

GENERAL HISTORICAL WORKS

"Alexander Stephens and Jefferson Davis," by James Z. Rabun. *American Historical Review,* Vol. LVIII, No. 2.

Battles and Leaders of the Civil War, edited by Robert Underwood Johnson and Clarence Clough Buel. 4 vols. New York, 1884–87.

Campaigns of the Army of the Potomac, by William Swinton, New York, 1882.

Civil War Atlas to accompany Steele's American Campaigns: prepared by the Department of Civil and Military Engineering, U.S. Military Academy.

Confederate Operations in Canada and New York, by John W. Headley. New York and Washington, 1906.

The Crisis of the Confederacy, by Cecil Battine. London and New York, 1905.

Divided We Fought: A Pictorial History of the War, 1861–1865, edited by David Donald. New York, 1952.

Experiment in Rebellion, by Clifford Dowdey. New York, 1950.

Foreigners in the Union Army and Navy, by Ella Lonn. Baton Rouge, La., 1951.

The Generalship of Ulysses S. Grant, by Colonel J. F. C. Fuller. New York, 1929.

A History of Negro Troops in the War of the Rebellion, by George W. Williams. New York, 1888.

History of the Shenandoah Valley, by William Couper. 2 vols. New York, 1952.

History of the United States from the Compromise of 1850, by James Ford Rhodes. 9 vols. New York, 1899.

Lee, Grant and Sherman, by Lieutenant Colonel Alfred H. Burne. New York, 1939.

Lincoln and the War Governors, by William B. Hesseltine. New York, 1948.

Lincoln's War Cabinet, by Burton J. Hendrick. Boston, 1946.

The Long Arm of Lee, by Jennings C. Wise. 2 vols. Lynchburg, Va., 1915.

The Military Genius of Abraham Lincoln, by Brigadier General Colin R. Ballard. London, 1926.

Mr. Lincoln's Army, by Bruce Catton. New York, 1951.

The Northern Railroads in the Civil War, 1861–1865, by Thomas Weber. New York, 1952.

Numbers and Losses in the Civil War, by Thomas L. Livermore. Boston and New York, 1900.

Papers of the Kansas Commandery, Military Order of the Royal Legion of the United States. 1894.

Papers of the Military Historical Society of Massachusetts, edited by Theodore Dwight. 10 vols. Boston, 1906.

Photographic History of the Civil War, edited by Francis Trevelyan Miller. 10 vols. New York, 1911.

President Lincoln as War Statesman, by Captain Arthur L. Conger: Separate No. 172 from the Proceedings of the State Historical Society of Wisconsin for 1916.

The Rebellion Record: A Diary of American Events, edited by Frank Moore. 12 vols. New York, 1868.

Regimental Losses in the American Civil War, by Lieutenant Colonel William F. Fox, U.S.V. Albany, 1889.

Report of the Committee to Recruit the Ninth Army Corps, prepared by the Secretary. New York, 1866.

The Shenandoah Valley and Virginia, 1861 to 1865: A War Study, by Sanford C. Kellogg. New York and Washington, 1903.

The Shenandoah Valley in 1864, by George E. Pond. New York, 1885.

Statesmen and Soldiers of the Civil War, by Major General Sir Frederick Maurice. Boston, 1926.

The Virginia Campaign of 1864 and 1865, by Major General Andrew A. Humphreys. New York, 1883.

War Papers Read before the Commandery of the State of Wisconsin, Military Order of the Loyal Legion of the United States. Milwaukee, 1891.

AUTOBIOGRAPHIES, BIOGRAPHICAL STUDIES, MEMOIRS, ETC.

Abraham Lincoln, by Benjamin Thomas. New York, 1952.

Abraham Lincoln: the Prairie Years, by Carl Sandburg. 2 vols. New York, 1926.

Abraham Lincoln: the War Years, by Carl Sandburg. 4 vols. New York, 1939.

Army Life in a Black Regiment, by Thomas Wentworth Higginson. Boston and New York, 1900.

Campaigning with Grant, by General Horace Porter. New York, 1907.

Captain Sam Grant, by Lloyd Lewis. Boston, 1952.

Charles Francis Adams: An Autobiography. Boston and New York, 1916.

Correspondence of John Sedgwick, Major General. 2 vols. Privately printed. De Vinne Press, 1902.

Days and Events: 1860–1866, by Colonel Thomas L. Livermore. Boston, 1920.

A Diary from Dixie, by Mary Boykin Chesnut, edited by Ben Ames Williams. Boston, 1949.

The Diary of Gideon Welles, with an introduction by John T. Morse, Jr. 3 vols. Boston and New York, 1911.

Fifty Years in Camp and Field: Diary of Major General Ethan Allen Hitchcock, edited by W. A. Croffut. New York, 1909.

Following the Greek Cross; or, Memories of the Sixth Army Corps, by Brevet Brigadier General Thomas W. Hyde. Boston, 1894.

From Chattanooga to Petersburg under Generals Grant and Butler, by Major General William F. Smith. Boston and New York, 1893.

General Hancock, by Francis A. Walker. New York, 1894.

Gideon Welles: Lincoln's Navy Department, by Richard S. West, Jr. Indianapolis, 1943.

Gouverneur Kemble Warren: the Life and Letters of an American Soldier, by Emerson Gifford Taylor. Boston and New York, 1932.

"Grant Before Appomattox: Notes of a Conferate Bishop," by the Right Rev. Henry C. Lay. *The Atlantic Monthly,* March 1932.

Jeb Stuart, by John W. Thomason, Jr. New York, 1930.

Jefferson Davis: the Unreal and the Real, by Robert McElroy. 2 vols. New York, 1937.

Kilpatrick and Our Cavalry, by James Moore. New York, 1865.

Lee's Lieutenants, by Douglas Southall Freeman. 3 vols. New York, 1942–44.

Letters of a War Correspondent, by Charles A. Page. Boston, 1899.

The Life and Letters of Emory Upton, by Peter S. Michie; introduction by James H. Wilson. New York, 1885.

The Life and Letters of George Gordon Meade, by George Meade, Captain and Aide-de-Camp. 2 vols. New York, 1913.

The Life of John A. Rawlins, by Major General James Harrison Wilson. New York, 1916.

The Life of Ulysses S. Grant, by Charles A. Dana and Major General James Harrison Wilson, Springfield, Mass., 1868.

Major General Ambrose E. Burnside and the Ninth Army Corps, by Augustus Woodbury. Providence, 1867.

Memoir of Ulric Dahlgren, by Rear Admiral John A. D. Dahlgren. Philadelphia, 1872.

Military Memoirs of a Confederate, by E. Porter Alexander. New York, 1907.

Pemberton, Defender of Vicksburg, by John C. Pemberton. Chapel Hill, 1944.

Personal Memoirs of U. S. Grant. 2 vols. New York, 1885.

Personal Recollections of the Civil War, by Brigadier General John Gibbon. New York, 1928.

R. E. Lee, by Douglas Southall Freeman. 4 vols. New York, 1934.

Ranger Mosby, by Virgil Carrington Jones. Chapel Hill, 1944.

The Rebel Raider: A Life of John Hunt Morgan, by Howard Swiggett. New York, 1937.

A Rebel War Clerk's Diary, by J. B. Jones, edited by Howard Swiggett. 2 vols. New York, 1935.

Recollections of the Civil War, by Charles A. Dana. New York, 1898.

Recollections of War Times, by Albert Gallatin Riddle. New York, 1895.

Reminiscences of Winfield Scott Hancock, by His Wife. New York, 1887.

The Rise of U. S. Grant, by A. L. Conger. New York, 1931.

Robert E. Lee: The Soldier, by Major General Sir Frederick Maurice. Boston and New York, 1925.

Sheridan: A Military Narrative, by Joseph Hergesheimer. Boston and New York, 1931.

Sherman: Fighting Prophet, by Lloyd Lewis. New York, 1932.

South After Gettysburg: Letters of Cornelia Hancock, from the Army of the Potomac, 1863–1865, edited by Henrietta Stratton Jaquette. Philadelphia, 1937.

Ulysses S. Grant, by William Conant Church. New York, 1897.

Under the Old Flag, by Major General James Harrison Wilson. 2 vols. New York, 1912.

A War Diary of Events in the War of the Great Rebellion, by Brigadier General George H. Gordon, Boston, 1882.

A Woman's War Record, 1861–1865, by Septima M. Collis. New York, 1889.

REGIMENTAL HISTORIES, SOLDIERS' REMINISCENCES, ETC.

Annals of the 6th Pennsylvania Cavalry, by the Reverend S. L. Gracey. Philadelphia, 1868.

Army Letters, 1861–1865, by Oliver Willcox Norton. Chicago. 1903.

Army Life: A Private's Reminiscences of the Civil War, by the Rev. Theodore Gerrish. Portland, Me., 1882.

Berdan's United States Sharpshooters in the Army of the Potomac, by Captain C. A. Stevens. St. Paul, 1892.

A Brief History of the 100th Regiment, by Samuel P. Bates, Newcastle, Pa., 1884.

Campaigns of the 146th Regiment New York State Volunteers, compiled by Mary Genevie Green Brainard. New York, 1915.

Camp-Fire Chats of the Civil War, by Washington Davis. Chicago, 1884.

Civil War Echoes: Character Sketches and State Secrets, by Hamilton Gay Howard. Washington, 1907.

Deeds of Daring: or, History of the 8th New York Volunteer Cavalry, by Henry Norton. Norwich, N.Y., 1889.

The Diary of a Line Officer, by Captain Augustus C. Brown. New York, 1906.

The Diary of a Young Officer, by Josiah M. Favill. Chicago, 1909.

Diary of Battery A, First Regiment Rhode Island Light Artillery, by Theodore Reichardt. Providence, 1865.

Down in Dixie: Life in a Cavalry Regiment in the War Days, by Stanton P. Allen. Boston, 1888.

The Fifth Army Corps, by Lieutenant Colonel William H. Powell. New York, 1896.

First Connecticut Heavy Artillery: Historical Sketch, by E. B. Bennett. Hartford, 1904.

The 48th in the War, by Oliver Christian Bosbyshell. Philadelphia, 1895.

Four Years Campaigning in the Army of the Potomac, by D. G. Crotty. Grand Rapids, 1874.

Four Years in the Army of the Potomac: A Soldier's Recollections, by Major Evan Rowland Jones. London, 1881.

The Fourteenth Regiment Rhode Island Heavy Artillery in the War to Preserve the Union, by William H. Chenery. Providence, 1898.

Henry Wilson's Regiment: History of the 22nd Massachusetts Infantry, by John L. Parker and Robert G. Carter. Boston, 1887.

History of Durrell's Battery in the Civil War, by Lieutenant Charles A. Cuffel. Philadelphia, 1904.

History of the Corn Exchange Regiment, by the Survivors' Association. Philadelphia, 1888.

History of the 8th Cavalry Regiment, Illinois Volunteers, by Abner Hard, M.D. Aurora, Ill., 1868.

History of the 8th Regiment Vermont Volunteers, by George N. Carpenter. Boston, 1886.

History of the 87th Regiment Pennsylvania Volunteers, by George R. Prowell. York, Pa., 1903.

History of the 5th Regiment Maine Volunteers, by the Rev. George W. Bicknell. Portland, 1871.

History of the 50th Regiment Pennsylvania Veteran Volunteers, by Lewis Crater. Reading, Pa., 1884.

History of the 51st Regiment of Pennsylvania Volunteers, by Thomas H. Parker. Philadelphia, 1869.

History of the First Connecticut Artillery, by John C. Taylor. Hartford, 1893.

History of the First Regiment of Heavy Artillery, Massachusetts Volunteers, by Alfred Seelye Roe and Charles Nutt. Worcester and Boston, 1917.

History of the 19th Army Corps, by Richard B. Irwin. New York, 1892.

History of the Ninth Massachusetts Battery, by Levi W. Baker. South Framingham, Mass., 1888.

History of the 9th Regiment Connecticut Volunteer Infantry, by Thomas Hamilton Murray. New Haven, 1903.

History of the 150th Regiment Pennsylvania Volunteers, by Lieutenant Colonel Thomas Chamberlin. Philadelphia, 1895.

History of the 198th Pennsylvania Volunteers, by Major E. M. Woodward. Trenton, N.J., 1884.

History of the 106th Regiment Pennsylvania Volunteers, by Joseph R. C. Ward. Philadelphia, 1883.

History of the Philadelphia Brigade, by Charles H. Banes. Philadelphia, 1876.

History of the Sauk County Riflemen, by Philip Cheek and Mair Pointon. Privately printed, 1909.

History of the Second Army Corps, by Francis A. Walker. New York, 1886.

History of the 2nd Connecticut Volunteer Heavy Artillery, by Theodore F. Vaill. Winsted, Conn., 1868.

History of the 7th Connecticut Volunteer Infantry, compiled by Stephen Walkley. Southington, Conn., 1905.

The History of the 10th Massachusetts Battery of Light Artillery in the War of the Rebellion, by John D. Billings. Boston, 1881.

History of the 17th Regiment Pennsylvania Volunteer Cavalry, by H. P. Moyer. Lebanon, Pa., 1911.

History of the 3rd Pennsylvania Cavalry, compiled by the Regimental History Association. Philadelphia, 1905.

History of the 3rd Regiment of Wisconsin Veteran Volunteer Infantry, by Edwin E. Bryant. Madison, 1891.

The History of the 39th Regiment Illinois Volunteer Veteran Infantry, by Charles M. Clark., M.D. Chicago, 1880.

History of the 36th Regiment Massachusetts Volunteers, by Henry Sweetser Burrage. Boston, 1884.

History of the 12th Massachusetts Volunteers, by Lieutenant Colonel Benjamin F. Cook. Boston, 1882.

History of the 12th Regiment New Hampshire Volunteers, by Captain A. W. Bartlett. Concord, N.H., 1897.

History of the 24th Michigan of the Iron Brigade, by O. B. Curtis. Detroit, 1891.

History of the 29th Regiment of Massachusetts Volunteer Infantry, by William O. Osborne. Boston, 1877.

I Rode with Stonewall, by Henry Kyd Douglas. Chapel Hill, 1940.

In the Defenses of Washington: or, the Sunshine in a Soldier's Life, by Stephen F. Blanding. Providence, 1889.

The Irish Brigade and Its Campaigns, by Captain D. P. Conyngham. Boston, 1869.

The Iron-Hearted Regiment; being an Account of the Battles, Marches and Gallant Deeds Performed by the 115th Regiment New York Volunteers, by James H. Clark. Albany, 1865.

Journal History of the 29th Ohio Veteran Volunteers, by J. Hamp Se Cheverell. Cleveland, 1883.

The Last Hours of Sheridan's Cavalry, by H. E. Tremain. New York, 1904.

A Little Fifer's War Diary, by C. W. Bardeen. Syracuse, N.Y., 1910.

Meade's Headquarters, 1863–1865: Letters of Col. Theodore Lyman from the Wilderness to Appomattox; selected and edited by George R. Agassiz. Boston, 1922.

Memoirs of a Volunteer, by John Beatty, edited by Harvey S. Ford. New York, 1946.

Memoirs of Chaplain Life, by the Very Rev. William Corby, C.S.C. Notre Dame, Ind., 1894.

Military History of the Third Division, Ninth Corps, Army of the Potomac, compiled and edited by Milton A. Embick. Harrisburg, Pa., 1910.

Music on the March, by Frank Rauscher. Philadelphia, 1892.

Musket and Sword, by Edwin C. Bennett. Boston, 1900.

My Diary of Rambles with the 25th Massachusetts Volunteer Infantry, by D. L. Day. Milford, Mass., 1883.

My Life in the Army, by Robert Tilney. Philadelphia, 1912.

The Passing of the Armies, by Joshua Lawrence Chamberlain, Brevet Major General, U.S. Volunteers. New York, 1915.

Personal and Historical Sketches and Facial History of and by Members of the 7th

Regiment Michigan Volunteer Cavalry, compiled by William O. Lee. Detroit, 1907.

Personal Narratives, Second Series, the Rhode Island Soldiers and Sailors Historical Society. Providence, 1880–81

Personal Recollections of the War of 1861, by Charles A. Fuller. Sherburne, N.Y., 1914.

Personal Recollections of Distinguished Generals, by William F. G. Shanks. New York, 1866.

Recollections of a Private Soldier in the Army of the Potomac, by Frank Wilkeson. New York, 1887.

Record of Service of Company K, 150th Ohio Volunteer Infantry, by James C. Cannon. Cleveland, 1903.

Red-Tape and Pigeon-Hole Generals: as Seen from the Ranks during a Campaign in the Army of the Potomac, by a Citizen-Soldier. New York, 1864.

Red, White and Blue Badge: Pennsylvania Veteran Volunteers, by Penrose G. Mark. Harrisburg, 1911.

The Road to Richmond: The Civil War Memoirs of Major Abner R. Small, of the 16th Main Volunteers, edited by Harold Adams Small. Berkeley, Cal., 1939.

Reminiscences and Record of the 6th New York Veteran Volunteer Cavalry, by Alonzo Foster. Privately printed: 1892.

Reminiscences of the 19th Massachusetts Regiment, by Captain John G. B. Adams, Boston, 1899.

Reminiscences of the War of the Rebellion, by Colonel Elbridge J. Copp. Nashua, N.H., 1911.

Reminiscences of the War of the Rebellion, 1861–1865, by Major Jacob Roemer. Flushing, N.Y., 1897.

Sabres and Spurs: The First Regiment Rhode Island Cavalry in the Civil War, by the Rev. Frederic Denison. Central Falls, R.I., 1876.

Service with the Sixth Wisconsin Volunteers, by Rufus R. Dawes. Marietta, Ohio, 1890.

Shot and Shell: The Third Rhode Island Heavy Artillery Regiment in the Rebellion, by the Rev. Frederic Denison. Providence, 1879.

A Soldier's Diary: The Story of a Volunteer, by David Lane. 1905.

The Story of the 15th Regiment Massachusetts Volunteer Infantry, by Andrew E. Ford. Clinton, Mass., 1898.

The Story of the First Massachusetts Light Battery, by A. J. Bennett. Boston, 1886.

The Story of the 48th, by Joseph Gould. Philadelphia, 1908.

The Story of the Regiment, by William H. Locke. Philadelphia,1868.

The Sunset of the Confederacy, by Morris Schaff, Boston, 1912.

Ten Years in the Ranks, U.S. Army, by Augustus Meyers. New York, 1914.

Thirteenth Regiment of New Hampshire Volunteer Infantry in the War of the Rebellion: A Diary, by S. Millett Thompson. Boston and New York, 1888.

Three Years in the Army: The Story of the 13th Massachusetts Volunteers, by Charles E. Davis, Jr. Boston, 1893.

Three Years in the Sixth Corps, by George T. Stevens. New York, 1870.

Thrilling Days in Army Life, by General George A. Forsyth. New York, 1900.

The Tragedy of the Crater, by Henry Pleasants, Jr. Boston, 1938.

The Vermont Brigade in the Shenandoah Valley, by Aldace F. Walker. Burlington, Vt., 1869.

A Volunteer's Adventures, by John W. DeForest, edited by James H. Croushare. New Haven, 1946.

War Diary of Luman Harris Tenney. Cleveland, 1914.

War Years with Jeb Stuart, by Lieutenant Colonel W. W. Blackford. New York, 1945.

Notes

CHAPTER ONE: GLORY IS OUT OF DATE

A BOY NAMED MARTIN

1. The atmosphere of army dances during the winter of 1864 is well described in *A Woman's War Record, 1861–1865,* by Septima M. Collis, pp. 34–36. The II Corps ball is depicted in *History of the 106th Regiment Pennsylvania Volunteers,* by Joseph R. C. Ward, p. 193, and in *The Diary of a Young Officer,* by Josiah M. Favill, pp. 277–80, and the corps' battle casualties are listed in Francis Walker's *History of the Second Army Corps,* p. 397. There are references to the ball and to the entertainment of the women guests, in *South After Gettysburg: Letters of Cornelia Hancock from the Army of the Potomac,* edited by Henrietta Stratton Jaquette, p. 53, and in *The Life and Letters of George Gordon Meade,* by Captain George Meade, Vol. II, p. 167.

2. *Meade's Headquarters, 1863–1865: Letters of Col. Theodore Lyman from the Wilderness to Appomattox,* selected and edited by George R. Agassiz, p. 73.

3. *Under the Old Flag,* by James Harrison Wilson, Vol. I, pp. 369–73; *Meade's Headquarters,* p. 75.

4. *Civil War Echoes: Character Sketches and State Secrets,* by Hamilton Gay Howard, p. 214.

5. *Official Records,* Vol. XXXIII, pp. 170–72; *Kilpatrick and Our Cavalry,* by James Moore, p. 143.

6. Correspondence regarding the Butler fiasco, culminating in a tart interchange between Sedgwick and Halleck during the post-mortem phase, is in the *Official Records,* Vol. XXXIII, pp. 338, 502, 506–7, 512, 514–15, 519, 530, 532, 552 *ff.* The business is summarized in William Swinton's *Campaigns of the Army of the Potomac,* pp. 398–99.

7. *Memoir of Ulric Dahlgren,* by Rear Admiral John A. D. Dahlgren, pp. 1–66, 92–116; *The Rebel Raider: A Life of John Hunt Morgan,* by Howard Swiggett, p. 208.

8. *Memoir of Ulric Dahlgren,* pp. 159–62, 169, 185 *ff.,* 204–11.

9. *History of the 17th Regiment Pennsylvania Volunteer Cavalry,* by H. P. Moyer, p. 233; *Official Records,* Vol. XXXIII, pp. 170, 172–74.

10. Kilpatrick's report, *Official Records,* Vol. XXXIII, p. 183; *History of the 17th Regiment Pennsylvania Volunteer Cavalry,* p. 234.

11. *History of the 17th Regiment Pennsylvania Volunteer Cavalry,* p. 235.

12. *Personal and Historical Sketches and Facial History of and by Members of the 7th Regiment Michigan Volunteer Cavalry,* compiled by William O. Lee, pp. 28, 198; report of Captain Joseph Gloskoski, 29th New York Infantry, a signal officer attached to Kilpatrick's column, *Official Records,* Vol. XXXIII, p. 189; *History of the 17th Regiment Pennsylvania Volunteer Cavalry,* pp. 235–36.

13. *Personal and Historical Sketches . . . 7th Regiment Michigan Volunteer Cavalry,* p. 29; *Official Records,* Vol. XXXIII, pp. 184–85, 192.

14. *History of the 17th Regiment Pennsylvania Volunteer Cavalry*, pp. 242–44; *Personal and Historical Sketches . . . 7th Regiment Michigan Volunteer Cavalry*, pp. 30–31; *Official Records*, Vol. XXXIII, p. 193.

15. *The Rebel Raider*, p. 208.

16. *Campaigns of the Army of the Potomac*, p. 400; *Memoir of Ulric Dahlgren*, p. 214; *Official Records*, Vol. XXXIII, p. 195.

17. The best account of this period of the expedition is perhaps that of Captain John F. B. Mitchell, 2nd New York Cavalry, in the *Official Records*, Vol. XXXIII, pp. 195–96.

18. *Memoir of Ulric Dahlgren*, pp. 219–22; report of Lieutenant James Pollard, 9th Virginia Cavalry, *Official Records*, Vol. XXXIII, p. 208; *The Rebellion Record*, edited by Frank Moore, Vol. VIII, Part 2, p. 589.

19. There is a thoughtful analysis of the treatment accorded Dahlgren's body and effects in Swiggett's excellent *The Rebel Raider*, pp. 208–11. The photographic copies of the Dahlgren papers, forwarded by Lee to Meade, are now in the National Archives in *Union Battle Reports*, Series 729 of the Records of the Adjutant General's Office, Record Group 94. They are faded and are very nearly illegible, but it is fairly easy to see that the signature is misspelled—"Dalhgren" for "Dahlgren"—which would hardly be the case if it were genuine. The affair is discussed indignantly in *Memoir of Ulric Dahlgren*, pp. 225–35. The Bragg-Seddon-Lee correspondence is in the *Official Records*, Vol. XXXIII, pp. 217–18, 222–23.

20. *The Rebellion Record*, Vol. VIII, Part 2, pp. 572, 574, 581, 591–92; *Official Records*, Vol. XXXIII, pp. 178, 180.

21. *History of the 17th Regiment Pennsylvania Volunteer Cavalry*, p. 257.

TURKEY AT A SHOOTING MATCH

1. *Army Life in a Black Regiment*, by Thomas Wentworth Higginson, p. 310.

2. *Reminiscences and Record of the 6th New York Veteran Volunteer Cavalry*, by Alonzo Foster, pp. 102–04.

3. An interesting account of the adventures of Custer's men, and of the behavior of the contrabands who followed them, appears in *Annals of the 6th Pennsylvania Cavalry*, by the Rev. S. L. Gracey, pp. 228–29.

4. *History of the 17th Regiment Pennsylvania Volunteer Cavalry*, pp. 245–46.

5. Ibid., pp. 247, 251–52. The reference to the chalk line in the row of black faces is borrowed from this account.

6. *Journal History of the 29th Ohio Veteran Volunteers*, by J. Hamp Se Cheverell, p. 21.

7. *The Road to Richmond*, by Major Abner R. Small, p. 193. For an interesting depiction of a typical Army of the Potomac veteran early in 1864, see *Three Years in the Army: The Story of the 14th Massachusetts Volunteers*, by Charles E. Davis, Jr., p. 262.

8. An excellent analysis of the way the draft and bounty laws worked occurs in *Lincoln and the War Governors*, by William B. Hesseltine, pp. 290 *ff.* This writer points out that the draft actually brought in few new men; its chief effect was to compel the state governors to raise troops. See also the report of James B. Fry, provost marshal general, *Official Records*, Series III, Vol. V, pp. 599 *ff.*

9. *History of the 12th Regiment New Hampshire Volunteers*, by Captain A. W. Bartlett, pp. 152–53.

10. *Official Records*, Series III, Vol. V, p. 831; *Three Years in the Army*, pp. 131, 264. The report of Thomas A. McParlin, medical director of the Army of the Potomac (*Official Records*, Vol. XXXVI, Part 1, pp. 213 *ff.*) gives a horrifying account of the defective human material which came to camp in the winter of 1863–64.

11. *Three Years in the Army*, p. 270.

12. *History of the 12th Regiment New Hampshire Volunteers,* p. 155.

13. *History of the 2nd Connecticut Volunteer Heavy Artillery,* by Theodore F. Vaill, p. 45.

14. *Three Years in the Army,* p. 302. The gambling and fighting are described by Stephen F. Blanding in *In the Defences of Washington; or, the Sunshine in a Soldier's Life,* pp. 8–10.

15. *The History of the 39th Regiment Illinois Volunteer Veteran Infantry,* by Charles M. Clark, M.D., pp. 240–42.

16. There is a detailed and rather dreadful account of life on this island camp in *Henry Wilson's Regiment: History of the 22nd Massachusetts Infantry,* by John L. Parker and Robert G. Carter, pp. 359–60, 362–70.

17. *A Little Fifer's War Diary,* by C. W. Bardeen, pp. 261–62; *History of Durrell's Battery in the Civil War,* by Lieutenant Charles A. Cuffel, p. 167; *History of the 12th Regiment New Hampshire Volunteers,* pp. 156–57.

18. The reader who wants an extended account of one of these sea voyages is referred to Frank Wilkeson's *Recollections of a Private Soldier in the Army of the Potomac,* pp. 14–19—one of the most graphic and least romanticized of all the Civil War reminiscences, with a tone of bitter disillusionment which sounds almost as if it had come out of World War II.

19. *Ibid.,* pp. 1–14, 20. For the way the bounty men vanished on the way to camp, see *The Story of the 15th Regiment Massachusetts Volunteer Infantry,* by Andrew E. Ford, p. 290.

20. *Four Years Campaigning in the Army of the Potomac,* by D. G. Crotty, p. 141.

21. *Musket and Sword,* by Edwin D. Bennett, p. 200; *The Irish Brigade and Its Campaigns,* by Captain D. P. Conyngham, pp. 425–38. The writer of *History of Durrell's Battery in the Civil War* remarks (p. 168) that the 79th New York was the only IX Corps regiment which failed to re-enlist that winter. All regiments which re-enlisted were re-enforced by drafts of new recruits. See also the pamphlet, *Report of Committee to Recruit the Ninth Army Corps,* printed in New York in 1866.

22. *Official Records,* Series III, Vol. V, pp. 600, 669. In the summer of 1864 U. S. Grant wrote to Secretary of State Seward that not one in eight of the high-bounty men ever performed good service at the front. (*Official Records,* Series II, Vol. VII, p. 614).

23. *History of the 7th Connecticut Volunteer Infantry,* compiled by Stephen Walkley, p. 150.

24. *Recollections of a Private Soldier,* pp. 32–34.

25. *Four Years Campaigning in the Army of the Potomac,* pp. 117–18; *My Diary of Rambles with the 25th Massachusetts Volunteer Infantry,* by D. L. Day, p. 110; *Three Years in the Army,* pp. 302–3.

26. *History of the 5th Regiment Maine Volunteers,* by the Rev. George W. Bicknell, p. 296. The manuscript letters of Edwin Wentworth of the 37th Massachusetts, made available through the kindness of Miss Edith Adams of Auburn, Maine, show how the high-bounty system could affect a veteran's decision. Early in the winter, Private Wentworth was writing to his wife that he would not re-enlist: "There are plenty of men at home, better able to bear arms than I am, and I am willing they should take their chance on the battlefield and have their share of glory and honor." Later, however, he reflected that with the bounty he could buy a home and some land—"it will enable me to provide you a good home and a chance to live comfortably." In the end, Private Wentworth re-enlisted, and was killed at Spotsylvania Court House.

27. *A Brief History of the 100th Regiment,* by Samuel P. Bates, p. 21; *Service with the 6th Wisconsin Volunteers,* by Rufus R. Dawes, p. 235; *Official Records,* Vol. XXXIII, p. 776.

28. *Reminiscences of the 19th Massachusetts Regiment,* by Captain John G. B. Adams, pp. 79, 89.

FROM A MOUNTAIN TOP

1. *Music on the March, 1862–65,* by Frank Rauscher, pp. 122, 141, 145, 151; *History of the 3rd Pennsylvania Cavalry,* compiled by the Regimental History Association, pp. 409–11.

2. *Campaigning with Grant,* by General Horace Porter, pp. 15, 22, 28.

3. *Ibid.,* p. 30.

4. For various glimpses of Grant, see *Captain Sam Grant,* by Lloyd Lewis, pp. 99–100; *Campaigning with Grant,* pp. 45, 56; *Army Life: A Private's Reminiscences of the Civil War,* by the Rev. Theodore Gerrish, p. 324; *A War Diary of Events in the War of the Great Rebellion,* by Brigadier General George H. Gordon, p. 351; *Three Years in the Army,* p. 315; *Following the Greek Cross; or, Memories of the Sixth Army Corps,* by Brigadier General Thomas W. Hyde, p. 181.

5. *Meade's Headquarters,* p. 81; *Correspondence of John Sedgwick, Major General.,* Vol. II, pp. 177–78.

6. For soldiers' comments on Grant, see *Down in Dixie: Life in a Cavalry Regiment in the War Days,* by Stanton P. Allen, pp. 187–88; *Four Years in the Army of the Potomac: A Soldier's Recollections,* by Major Evan Rowland Jones, pp. 128–29; *The Road to Richmond,* p. 130.

7. *Campaigning with Grant,* pp. 46–47; an incident described to General Porter after the war by Longstreet himself.

8. Congressional doubts in regard to Grant's drinking, and the reliance placed on Rawlins, are touched on by General James H. Wilson, who was fairly intimate with both Grant and Rawlins, in *Under the Old Flag,* Vol. I, pp. 345–46. Dana's comment is cited in *Abraham Lincoln: The War Years,* by Carl Sandburg, Vol. II, p. 542. The whole question of the extent to which alcohol was a problem to Grant is carefully examined in Lewis's fine book, *Captain Sam Grant.* (His conclusion: that it wasn't nearly as big a problem as some people have assumed.)

9. References to heavy drinking among Army of the Potomac officers abound in regimental histories and personal memoirs. Specifically, see *Days and Events: 1860–1866,* by Colonel Thomas L. Livermore, p. 297; *South After Gettysburg,* p. 55; *Camp-Fire Chats of the Civil War,* by Washington Davis, pp. 284–85.

10. *The Life of Ulysses S. Grant,* by Charles A. Dana and Major General James Harrison Wilson, p. 185; *The Generalship of Ulysses S. Grant,* by Colonel J. F. C. Fuller, p. 210; *The Life and Letters of George Gordon Meade,* Vol. II, p. 201; *The Life of John A. Rawlins,* by Major General J. H. Wilson, pp. 426–27.

11. *Memoirs of a Volunteer,* by John Beatty, edited by Harvey S. Ford, p. 210; *History of Durrell's Battery in the Civil War,* p. 150.

12. *Recollections of a Private Soldier,* pp 36–37.

13. *Down in Dixie,* pp. 180–82.

14. *Letters of a War Correspondent,* by Charles A. Page, p. 110; *Musket and Sword,* p. 198.

15. There is a good pen picture of Sheridan in Gerrish's *Army Life,* p. 249, and Sheridan's crack about the bob-tailed brigadiers is to be found in *Personal Memoirs of John H. Brinton,* p. 267. For the cavalryman's complaint about hard work, see *Deeds of Daring: or, History of the 8th New York Volunteer Cavalry,* by Henry Norton, pp. 106–7. Other details are in the *Official Records,* Vol. XXXIII, p. 711, and *Under the Old Flag,* Vol. 1, pp. 331, 374–75.

16. *History of the 10th Massachusetts Battery of Light Artillery in the War of the Rebellion,* by John D. Billings, pp. 37–38. (Incidentally, this book contains a good account of the assignments and duties of members of a Civil War gun crew, pp. 18–19.) See also *Recollections of a Private Soldier,* p. 22.

17. *Official Records,* Vol. XXXIII, p. 907.

18. *Memoirs of Chaplain Life,* by the Very Rev. William Corby, p. 357; *Reminiscences of the 19th Massachusetts Regiment,* pp. 84, 86.

19. *Three Years in the Army,* p. 316; *Serevice with the 6th Wisconsin Volunteers,* pp. 241–42.

20. *Reminiscences of the War of the Rebellion,* by Major Jacob Roemer, p. 30; *The Diary of a Line Officer,* by Captain Augustus C. Brown, p. 11; *History of the First Regiment of Heavy Artillery, Massachusetts Volunteers,* by Alfred S. Roe and Charles Nutt, pp. 124–36; *History of the 12th Massachusetts Volunteers,* by Lieutenant Colonel Benjamin W. Cook, p. 126; manuscript letters of Carl Bissell, of the 2nd Connecticut Heavy Artillery.

21. *History of the 2nd Connecticut Volunteer Heavy Artillery,* p. 81; *Official Records,* Vol. XXXVI, Part 3, p. 110.

22. *The Road to Richmond,* p. 195.

23. *Official Records,* Vol. XXXIII, pp. 638–39, 688, 717; *History of the Second Army Corps,* p. 400. Soldiers of the Army of the Potomac usually identified themselves first with their regiment and next with their army corps. Brigades and divisions generally (with a few striking exceptions) claimed less of their loyalty.

24. *Correspondence of John Sedgwick, Major General,* Vol. II, pp. 168, 175; *Personal Recollections of the Civil War,* by Brigadier General John Gibbon, pp. 209–10. One of the most fascinating might-have-beens of the Civil War is this move which almost put Sedgwick in charge of operations in the Valley. If he had been there instead of Sigel, the story in 1864 would have been very different. Meade planned to give John Gibbon command of the VI Corps.

25. Brigadier General Hazard Stevens, in *Papers of the Military Historical Society of Massachusetts,* Vol. IV, pp. 178–79 (referred to hereafter as *M.H.S.M. Papers*).

26. Francis A. Walker, in *M.H.S.M. Papers,* Vol. X, pp. 51, 53, 56–57.

27. For Warren, see *Gouverneur Kemble Warren: The Life and Letters of an American Soldier,* by Emerson Gifford Taylor, pp. 5 *ff.; The Road to Richmond,* p. 126; *Days and Events,* p. 304; *Three Years in the Army,* p. 349.

28. *South After Gettysburg,* p. 73; *History of the 87th Regiment Pennsylvania Volunteers,* by George R. Prowell, p. 117.

29. *Three Years in the Army,* p. 309; *History of the 8th Cavalry Regiment, Illinois Volunteers,* by Abner Hard, pp. 292–93; *A Little Fifer's War Diary,* p. 168.

30. *Down in Dixie,* pp. 165–66.

31. *The Road to Richmond,* pp. 129–30.

CHAPTER TWO: ROADS LEADING SOUTH

WHERE THE DOGWOOD BLOSSOMED

1. *Following the Greek Cross,* p. 182; *Recollections of a Private Soldier,* pp. 42–43; *Meade's Headquarters,* p. 180; *Army Life: A Private's Reminiscences,* pp. 156–57; *The Road to Richmond,* p. 130.

2. *Down in Dixie,* p. 206.

3. Discussions of the courses open to Grant at the beginning of the 1864 campaign in Virginia are practically without number. A good brief summary of the alternatives can be found in *The Virginia Campaigns of '64 and '65,* by Major General Andrew A. Humphreys, pp. 9–12. (This book is authoritative, comprehensive, and unfortunately rather dull; it is cited hereafter as Humphreys.) For an extended study, see *The Generalship of Ulysses S. Grant,* pp. 209 *ff.* Grant discusses the matter in some detail of the *Official Records,* Vol. XXXVI, Part 1, pp. 12–18. I am greatly indebted to Ralph Happel, historian, Fredericksburg and Spotsylvania County National Military Park, for the loan of his manuscript account of the Battle of the Wilderness, which contains an excellent analysis of the strategy of the Wilderness campaign and its relation to the grand strategy of the final year of the war.

4. *Down in Dixie,* p. 210.

5. Campaigning with Grant, pp. 42–43.

6. *Recollections of a Private Soldier,* pp. 43–46; *M.H.S.M. Papers,* Vol. IV, p. 185; *The Road to Richmond,* p. 131. Note the comment by Brigadier General Rufus Ingalls, chief quartermaster: "Our troops are undoubtedly loaded down on marches too heavily even for the road, not to speak of battle. . . . Our men are generally overloaded, fed and clad, which detracts from their marching capacity and induces straggling." (*Official Records,* Vol. XL, Part 1, p. 39.)

7. *Campaigns of the 146th Regiment New York State Volunteers,* compiled by Mary Genevie Green Brainard, p. 176; *Down in Dixie,* p. 176.

8. *Recollections of a Private Soldier,* pp. 49–51: *The Story of the Regiment,* by William Henry Locke, p. 323.

9. *Campaigns of the 146th Regiment New York State Volunteers,* p. 179.

10. *Army Life: A Private's Reminiscences,* pp. 217, 345–46.

11. *Campaigns of the Army of the Potomac,* pp. 420–22; *M.H.S.M. Papers,* Vol. IV, p. 188; *Following the Greek Cross,* p. 183.

12. *Campaigning with Grant,* pp. 50, 64–65.

13. *Army Life: A Private's Reminiscences,* p. 161.

14. *The Fifth Army Corps,* by Lieutenant Colonel William H. Powell, pp. 608, 610.

15. Colonel Theodore Lyman, in *M.H.S.M. Papers,* Vol. IV, pp. 167–68; also in *Meade's Headquarters,* pp. 90–91.

16. Report of Emory Upton, *Official Records,* Vol. XXXVI, Part 1, p. 665.

17. *History of the Corn Exchange Regiment,* by the Survivors' Association, p. 400; *Four Years in the Army of the Potomac,* p. 129; *Three Years in the Sixth Corps,* by George T. Stevens, pp. 309–10; *Army Life: A Private's Reminiscences,* p. 170.

18. *Campaigns in the Army of the Potomac,* p. 422; *Three Years in the Army,* pp. 329–30; *Official Records,* Vol. XXXVI, Part 1, p. 614; *Campaigning with Grant,* p. 72.

19. There is a good account of Wadsworth's and Crawford's advance in the *M.H.S.M. Papers,* Vol. IV, pp. 127–32. For a glimpse of Crawford, see *The Road to Richmond,* p. 149.

20. *Campaigns of the 146th Regiment New York State Volunteers,* p. 195; *Official Records,* Vol. XXXVI, Part 1, pp. 601, 610–11, 614.

21. *M.H.S.M. Papers,* Vol. IV, pp. 189–94; General Getty's report, *Official Records, Vol. XXXVI,* Part 1, pp. 676–77.

22. *M.H.S.M. Papers,* Vol. IV, pp. 192–93.

23. *Official Records, Vol. XXXVI,* Part 1, pp. 696–98; *Recollections of a Private Soldier,* pp. 66–67.

24. *A Little Fifer's War Diary,* pp. 110–11, 302; *M.H.S.M. Papers,* Vol. IV, pp. 142, 193–94. For a good discussion of Federal difficulties in adjusting to woods fighting, see *The Crisis of the Confederacy,* by Cecil Battine, p. 382.

25. *The Road to Richmond,* p. 133.

SHADOW IN THE NIGHT

1. *Reminiscences of the 19th Massachusetts Regiment,* pp. 87–88; *Official Records,* Vol. XXXVI, Part 1, pp. 218–19; *History of the Corn Exchange Regiment,* p. 403; *M.H.S.M. Papers,* Vol. IV, pp. 101–2; *The Road to Richmond,* p. 133.

2. *Recollections of a Private Soldier,* pp. 52–54.

3. *Meade's Headquarters,* pp. 93–94; *Official Records,* Vol. XXXVI, Part 1, pp. 320–21, 667.

4. The classic account of this, of course, is Douglas Southall Freeman's, in *R. E. Lee,* Vol. III, pp. 286–88.

5. *Four Years in the Army of the Potomac,* p. 130; *Official Records,* Vol. XXXVI, Part 1, p. 403; *The Diary of a Line Officer,* p. 35; Humphreys, p. 56.

6. *Recollections of a Private Soldier*, p. 201.

7. *Ibid.*, pp. 57, 206; *Army Life: A Private's Reminiscences*, p. 170; *A Little Fifer's War Diary*, p. 86.

8. *M.H.S.M. Papers*, Vol. IV, p. 196; *History of the Second Army Corps*, pp. 428–29.

9. *Official Records*, Vol. XXXVI, Part 1, p. 438; *M.H.S.M. Papers*, Vol. IV, p. 151.

10. *History of the Second Army Corps*, pp. 417, 422.

11. Brigadier General Alexander Webb in *Official Records*, Vol. XXXVI, Part 1, pp. 437 *ff.*; also in *Battles and Leaders of the Civil War*, Vol. IV, pp. 159 *ff.*

12. "Battle of the Wilderness and Death of General Wadsworth," by Captain Robert Monteith, in the *War Papers Read before the State of Wisconsin Commandery, Military Order of the Loyal Legion of the United States*, Vol. I, p. 414; *Official Records*, Vol. XXXVI, Part 1, pp. 477, 934.

13. *History of the Philadelphia Brigade*, by Charles H. Banes, p. 231; *Meade's Headquarters*, p. 95; *Official Records*, Vol. XXXVI, Part 1, p. 488.

14. *M.H.S.M. Papers*, Vol. IV, pp. 154–55, 200; *Official Records*, Vol. XXXVI, Part 1, p. 624; *History of the 150th Regiment, Pennsylvania Volunteers*, by Lieutenant Colonel Thomas Chamberlin, pp. 187–88.

15. Hancock discusses all of this in some detail in his report, *Official Records*, Vol. XXXVI, Part 1, pp. 320–23, 325. After the war a sharp argument over the misunderstanding developed between Hancock and Gibbon; Gibbon tells about it in his *Personal Recollections*, pp. 387 *ff.*

16. *History of the 106th Regiment Pennsylvania Volunteers*, pp. 201–2; *Official Records*, Vol. XXXVI, Part 1, p. 514; *Recollections of a Private Soldier*, p. 73. For a very vivid account of this phase of the battle, see *The Crisis of the Confederacy*, p. 385.

17. Grant's *Personal Memoirs*, Vol. II, p. 201.

18. *Campaigning with Grant*, p. 59.

19. *Ibid.*, p. 52. For glimpses of Grant's earlier relations with Hays, see *Captain Sam Grant*, pp. 128, 172.

20. *Meade's Headquarters*, p. 98; *History of the 5th Regiment Main Volunteers*, p. 305; *Following the Greek Cross*, pp. 186–87; *History of the 3rd Pennsylvania Cavalry*, p. 419.

21. *Letters of a War Correspondent*, p. 57; Colonel Theodore Lyman, in *M.H.S.M. Papers*, Vol. IV, p. 105n.; *Campaigning with Grant*, pp. 69–70.

22. *Four Years in the Army of the Potomac*, p. 131; *Following the Greek Cross*, p. 188.

23. The extent to which Grant was shaken, and the way in which he concealed his alarm, are set forth by this firm admirer, General Wilson, in *Under the Old Flag*, Vol. I, pp. 390–91.

24. *Campaigning with Grant*, p. 74.

25. *History of the Philadelphia Brigade*, p. 235; *Reminiscences of the 19th Massachusetts Regiment*, p. 88; *Annals of the 6th Pennsylvania Cavalry*, p. 237.

26. *The Road to Richmond*, p. 134; *Campaigning with Grant*, p. 79; *History of the 3rd Pennsylvania Cavalry*, p. 421.

27. *Recollections of a Private Soldier*, p. 79. Major General U. S. Grant, III, grandson of the Civil War general, says that as a young lieutenant just out of West Point he served under an elderly officer who had been an enlisted man in the Army of the Potomac. This officer one day remarked that the most thrilling moment of the whole war, to him, came when his column turned south at the Chancellorsville crossroads and the men realized that they were advancing instead of retreating. As Historian Ralph Happel says, in his manuscript study previously referred to, Grant's decision to continue south after the Wilderness was "one of the most important decisions in American history."

28. *Following the Greek Cross*, p. 189.

ALL THEIR YESTERDAYS

1. *Following the Greek Cross,* pp. 189–90.

2. *History of the 3rd Pennsylvania Cavalry,* pp. 421–22. In General Warren's journal entry for May 7 (*Official Records,* Vol. XXXVI, Part 1, p. 540) there is reference to a delay caused by Meade's cavalry escort. Major Small refers to it in *The Road to Richmond,* p. 135, and General Webb mentions it in *Battles and Leaders,* Vol. IV, p. 164. It should be added, of course, that various other factors delayed the move to Spotsylvania Court House, the most important probably being the job done by the Confederate cavalry under Fitzhugh Lee.

3. *History of the 12th Massachusetts Volunteers,* p. 129.

4. There is an excellent description of the approach, assault, and repulse of Robinson's division, by Brigadier General Charles L. Pierson, in the *M.H.S.M. Papers,* Vol. IV, pp. 214–16, supplemented by Colonel Theodore Lyman, pp. 238–39. See also the *Official Records,* Vol. XXXVI, Part 1, pp. 594, 597, 619; *The Story of the Regiment,* p. 333; *Military Memoirs of a Confederate,* by E. P. Alexander, pp. 510–12.

5. *Campaigning with Grant,* p. 84; *Meade's Headquarters,* pp. 105–6n.

6. *Down in Dixie,* p. 316; "Sheridan's Richmond Raid," in *Battles and Leaders,* Vol. IV, p. 189.

7. *Down in Dixie,* pp. 276–77.

8. The handling of the Wilderness wounded is treated in detail in the report of Surgeon Thomas A. McParlin, Medical Director of the Army of the Potomac, in the *Official Records,* Vol. XXXVI, Part 1, p. 220. See also *Down in Dixie,* p. 276; *Red-Tape and Pigeon-Hole Generals,* by a Citizen-Soldier, p. 242; *Army Life: A Private's Reminiscences,* p. 171.

9. Surgeon Edward B. Dalton, chief medical officer of Depot Field Hospital, in *Official Records,* Vol. XXXVI, Part 1, p. 270; also Surgeon McParlin's report, in that volume, p. 234; *South After Gettysburg,* pp. 85–86, 88; *Three Years in the Sixth Corps,* p. 343.

10. *Three Years in the Sixth Corps,* pp. 344–45.

11. Report of Surgeon McParlin, *Official Records,* Vol. XXXVI, Part 1, pp. 227 *ff.*

12. *Ibid.,* pp. 235, 271–74.

13. *History of the First Regiment of Heavy Artillery, Massachusetts Volunteers,* p. 151.

14. *South After Gettysburg,* pp. 88, 90.

15. *Army Life: A Private's Reminiscences,* p. 177; *Recollections of a Private Soldier,* p. 88; *History of the Corn Exchange Regiment,* p. 410.

16. *Following the Greek Cross,* pp. 191–92; *Campaigning with Grant,* pp. 89–90; *Correspondence of John Sedgwick, Major General,* Vol. II, p. 210; *Battles and Leaders,* Vol. IV, p. 175.

17. *Abraham Lincoln: The War Years,* Vol. III, p. 47.

18. *Campaigning with Grant,* p. 83.

SURPASSING ALL FORMER EXPERIENCES

1. *The Life and Letters of Emory Upton,* by Peter S. Mitchie, pp. 1–9, 12–37, 51–68.

2. *Ibid.,* pp. 96–98. Upton's formal report on this assault is unusually detailed and graphic. It is in the *Official Records,* Vol. XXXVI, Part 1, pp. 665–68.

3. *Military Memoirs of a Confederate,* p. 517; *Official Records,* Vol. XXXVI, Part 1, pp. 667–68.

4. *History of the Philadelphia Brigade,* pp. 242–43.

5. *Ibid.,* p. 244; *M.H.S.M. Papers,* Vol. IV, p. 436.

6. Upton's report, *op. cit.,* p. 668.

7. *War Diary of Luman Harris Tenney, 1861-1865,* p. 115; *Meade's Headquarters,* p. 110.

8. *Official Records,* Vol. XXXVI, Part 1, p. 230; *Battles and Leaders,* Vol. IV, p. 170.

9. *The Long Arm of Lee,* by Jennings C. Wise, Vol. II, pp. 787-88.

10. Hancock's report, *Official Records,* Vol. XXXVI, Part 1, p. 334.

11. *Ibid.,* p. 335. General Barlow described the movement of his division in the *M.H.S.M. Papers,* Vol. IV, pp. 245-270. His article has been drawn on liberally in the preparation of this chapter.

12. *Personal Recollections of the War of 1861,* by Charles A. Fuller, pp. 9-10; *The Irish Brigade and Its Campaigns,* by Captain D. P. Conyngham, p. 474; *Mr. Lincoln's Army,* by Bruce Catton, pp. 209-10.

13. Barlow's account, *M.H.S.M. Papers,* Vol. IV, p. 247. See also, in the same volume, the article by Lieutenant Colonel William R. Driver, p. 277.

14. *Official Records,* Vol. XXXVI, Part 1, pp. 409-10,.

15. *History of the 106th Regiment Pennsylvania Volunteers,* p. 206; *Official Records,* Vol. XXXVI, Part 1, pp. 335, 470; *History of the Second Army Corps,* p. 470.

16. *History of the Philadelphia Brigade,* p. 246; Barlow, in *M.H.S.M. Papers,* Vol. IV, pp. 251-52; *The Long Arm of Lee,* Vol. II, pp. 789-90; *Military Memoirs of a Confederate,* pp. 519-20.

17. *Lee's Lieutenants,* by Douglas Southall Freeman, Vol. III, pp. 404-6; *Service with the 6th Wisconsin Volunteers,* p. 268; *Official Records,* Vol. XXXVI, Part 1, pp. 373-74; *M.H.S.M. Papers,* Vol. IV, pp. 281-82.

18. *Military Memoirs of a Confederate,* p. 522; *Reminiscences of the 19th Massachusetts Regiment,* p. 91; *History of the Philadelphia Brigade,* p. 247.

19. *Military Memoirs of a Confederate,* p. 522; Barlow's story in *M.H.S.M. Papers,* Vol. IV, pp. 254-55; *History of the Philadelphia Brigade,* p. 248; *History of the Second Army Corps,* p. 473.

20. *Brigadier General Lewis A. Grant,* in *M.H.S.M. Papers,* Vol. IV, p. 269. This fighting is graphically described by G. Norton Galloway in *Battles and Leaders,* Vol. IV, pp. 170-74. See also *Following the Greek Cross,* p. 202. Incidentally, it may be well to emphasize that the famous "bloody angle" was here, and not at the tip of the salient where Barlow's men first broke the line.

21. *Battles and Leaders,* Vol. IV, pp. 171-72; *Official Records,* Vol. XXXVI, Part 1, pp. 537, 539; *History of the 150th Regiment Pennsylvania Volunteers,* pp. 196-97.

22. *History of the 24th Michigan of the Iron Brigade,* by O. B. Curtis, p. 243; *History of the Second Army Corps,* p. 475.

23. *Reminiscences of the 19th Massachusetts Regiment,* p. 91; *History of the 106th Regiment Pennsylvania Volunteers,* p. 207; *Service with the 6th Wisconsin Volunteers,* p. 266; *Following the Greek Cross,* pp. 200-1.

24. *Following the Greek Cross,* p. 200; report of Brigadier General Lewis Grant, *Official Records,* Vol. XXXVI, Part 1, p. 704; *Reminiscences of the 19th Massachusetts Regiment,* p. 92; *History of the 24th Michigan in the Iron Brigade,* p. 244.

25. *The Road to Richmond,* p. 141; *Campaigns of the 146th Regiment New York State Volunteers,* pp. 205-6.

26. *Recollections of a Private Soldier,* pp. 83-86; *M.H.S.M. Papers,* Vol. IV, pp. 297-98; *Letters of a War Correspondent,* p. 72; *History of the First Regiment of Heavy Artillery, Massachusetts Volunteers,* pp. 152-58. It might be noted that veteran troops called up to stand in support of the heavies in this fight put in a profitable afternoon looting the knapsacks which the green troops had piled in a row before going into action.

27. *My Life in the Army,* by Robert Tilney, p. 53.

CHAPTER THREE: ONE MORE RIVER TO CROSS

THE CRIPPLES WHO COULD NOT RUN

1. Grant's report of the final year's operations, *Official Records,* Vol. XXXVI, Part 1, pp. 20–21; *Campaigning with Grant,* pp. 124–25.
2. *Recollections of a Private Soldier,* pp. 91–93.
3. *Recollections of the Civil War,* by Charles A. Dana, p. 199.
4. *Four Years in the Army of the Potomac,* p. 190.
5. *Three Years Campaigning in the Army of the Potomac,* pp. 132, 134.
6. For these incidents involving punishment for cowardice, see *The Story of the 48th,* by Joseph Gould, pp. 177–78; *Reminiscences of the War of the Rebellion,* p. 200; *Reminiscences of the 19th Massachusetts Regiment,* p. 94; *Berdan's United States Sharpshooters in the Army of the Potomac,* by Captain C. A. Stevens, p. 355.
7. *Musket and Sword,* p. 169; *A Little Fifer's War Diary,* p. 119.
8. *History of the Philadelphia Brigade,* p. 247.
9. *The History of the 10th Massachusetts Battery,* p. 181.
10. The point is emphasized in Humphreys, p. 118.
11. *Army Life: A Private's Reminiscences,* pp. 187–90.
12. *Down in Dixie,* p. 86.
13. *History of the Corn Exchange Regiment,* p. 426; *History of the 51st Regiment of Pennsylvania Volunteers,* by Thomas H. Parker, p. 555; *Letters of a War Correspondent,* p. 81; *Official Records,* Vol. XXXVI, Part 1, p. 405; *The Story of the First Massachusetts Light Battery,* by A. J. Bennett, pp. 153–54; *The Road to Richmond,* p. 200.
14. *Musket and Sword,* p. 238.
15. *Three Years in the Army: The Story of the 13th Massachusetts Volunteers,* p. 132.
16. *History of the Philadelphia Brigade,* pp. 255–56.
17. *Meade's Headquarters,* pp. 99–100; Gibbon's *Personal Recollections,* p. 229.
18. *History of the Sauk County Riflemen,* by Philip Cheek and Mair Pointon, p. 110.
19. The organization of the Veterans Reserve Corps, and the amazing adventures of the regiment as described in the text, are fully covered in the report made at the end of the war by Captain J. W. De Forest, acting assistant adjutant general, to Brigadier General James B. Fry, provost marshal general. It is found in the *Official Records,* Series 3, Vol. V; pp. 543–55.
20. *Four Years Campaigning in the Army of the Potomac,* p. 140; *History of the 12th Massachusetts Volunteers,* p. 142; *History of the 24th Michigan,* p. 241.
21. *M.H.S.M. Papers,* Vol. VI, p. 389.

JUDGMENT TRUMP OF THE ALMIGHTY

1. The enlisted men of the Army of the Potomac referred to this constant shift to the left as "the jug-handle movement." (*History of the Corn Exchange Regiment,* p. 432.)
2. *Three Years in the Army; The Story of the 13th Massachusetts Volunteers,* pp. 356, 364; Major William P. Shreve in *M.H.S.M. Papers,* Vol. IV, p. 316; *Service with the 6th Wisconsin Volunteers,* p. 279; manuscript letters of Lewis Bissell: *History of the 51st Regiment of Pennsylvania Volunteers,* p. 548. Note the sentiment expressed in *History of the 50th Regiment Pennsylvania Veteran Volunteers,* by Lewis Crater, p. 62: "Notwithstanding the regiment had lost fully 330 men killed, wounded and captured during the month, the very best feeling was exhibited, from the fact that all felt that some progress was being made and that the end of the rebellion was prospectively drawing near."
3. *In the Ranks from the Wilderness to Appomattox Courthouse,* by the Rev. R. E. McBride, p. 62.

4. *M.H.S.M. Papers,* Vol. V, p. 3; *Following the Greek Cross,* p. 214.

5. *M.H.S.M. Papers,* Vol. IV, pp. 326–28.

6. *Following the Greek Cross,* p. 208; *Three Years in the Sixth Corps,* p. 350; *History of the 2nd Connecticut Volunteer Heavy Artillery,* pp. 54–55.

7. Grant to Halleck, dispatch of May 22, *Official Records,* Vol. XXXVI, Part 1, p. 7; Grant to W. F. Smith, *Official Records,* Vol. XXXVI, Part 3, p. 371; Smith to Rawlins, *ibid.,* p. 410.

8. *History of the 2nd Connecticut Volunteer Heavy Artillery,* p. 58.

9. *Ibid.,* pp. 60–62, 65–66; *Three Years in the Sixth Corps,* pp. 352–53; *Official Records,* Vol. XXXVI, Part 1, pp. 662, 671.

10. A brief summary of the reasons for attacking at Cold Harbor is given in Humphreys, p. 181. See also *Lee, Grant and Sherman,* by Lieutenant Colonel Alfred H. Burne, p. 50. For a detailed account of the battle, strongly critical of Grant, see "Cold Harbor," by Major General Martin T. McMahon, in *Battles and Leaders,* Vol. IV, pp. 213 *ff.*

11. An extensive discussion of the way the rifle-trench combination had revolutionized tactics by 1864 can be found in Fuller's *The Generalship of U. S. Grant,* pp. 51–52, 57–58, 61.

12. *Official Records,* Vol. XXXVII, Part 1, pp. 761, 775, 778, 831–32; Humphreys, pp. 75–76.

13. *History of the 36th Regiment Massachusetts Volunteers,* by Henry Sweetser Burrage, p. 189; *M.H.S.M. Papers,* Vol. V, p. 9.

14. *Meade's Headquarters,* p. 138.

15. *History of the Second Army Corps,* p. 506.

16. *Meade's Headquarters,* p. 139.

17. *Official Records,* Vol. XXXVI, Part 3, pp. 482, 489, 491–92, 505, 506; Humphreys, pp. 176–78, 182; *History of the Philadelphia Brigade,* p. 269; *Recollections of a Private Soldier,* pp. 127–28; *History of the 106th Regiment Pennsylvania Volunteers,* p. 219.

18. The point is stressed by Captain Charles H. Porter in *M.H.S.M. Papers,* Vol. IV, p. 339.

19. *Letters of a War Correspondent,* p. 96.

20. *Battles and Leaders,* Vol. IV, p. 217.

21. *Recollections of a Private Soldier,* p. 129; *History of the 10th Massachusetts Battery,* p. 200.

22. *Reminiscences of the 19th Massachusetts Regiment,* pp. 98–99.

23. Hancock's report on Cold Harbor is in the *Official Records,* Vol. XXXVI, Part 1, pp. 344–46. See also Gibbon's report, in that volume, p. 433, and Barlow's, p. 369. Humphreys' account, accurate but somewhat prosy, is in his book, pp. 182–85. There are graphic glimpses of the II Corps assault in *History of the Philadelphia Brigade,* pp. 270–72, and *History of the 106th Regiment Pennsylvania Volunteers,* pp. 220–21. See also *Following the Greek Cross,* p. 211, and *Meade's Headquarters,* p. 144.

24. *Army Life: A Private's Reminiscences,* p. 194. The very weight of Confederate fire seems actually to have kept the VI Corps from suffering as many casualties as Hancock's men had, by pinning the assault waves down from the very beginning. Reading the reports of division and brigade commanders in this corps leads one to believe that June 1 was a worse day for the VI Corps than June 3. Emory Upton's report, for instance, disposes of the June 3 assault with the simple statement that "another assault was ordered, but being deemed impracticable along our front was not made." For the VI Corps reports, see the *Official Records,* Vol. XXXVI, Part 1, pp. 662, 671, 674, 680, 689–90, 708, 720, 727, 735, 739, 744, 750, 753. Most of these reports contain little indication that June 3 was especially different from any other day at Cold Harbor.

25. *History of the 12th Regiment New Hampshire Volunteers,* pp. 202–8. The account of Cold Harbor in this regimental history is one of the best contemporary battle descriptions in Civil War literature.

26. Offhand, it would seem both difficult and unnecessary to exaggerate the horrors of Cold Harbor, but for some reason—chiefly, perhaps, the desire to paint Grant as a callous and uninspired butcher—no other Civil War battle gets as warped a presentation as this one. It is usually described as a battle in which the entire Federal army attacked "all along the line," losing 13,000 men thereby. Actually, the 13,-000 casualties are the total for nearly two weeks in the Cold Harbor lines, and the June 3 assault involved only part of the army. The V Corps did not attack at all on that day and the IX Corps did little more than drive in the Confederate skirmish lines. The VI Corps, as mentioned above, fared worse on June 1 than on June 3, and the real weight of the June 3 attack was born by two of Hancock's divisions and one—Martindale's—of Smith's. In those three divisions, of course, the loss was genuinely frightful.

27. *Campaigning with Grant,* p. 109; manuscript letters of Lewis Bissell.

SECONDHAND CLOTHES

1. *Official Records,* Vol. XXXVI, Part 3, pp. 672, 870.

2. For trench life at Cold Harbor immediately after the June 3 attacks, see *History of the 106th Regiment Pennsylvania Volunteers,* pp. 223–24; *Army Life: A Private's Reminiscences,* p. 195; *History of the 12th Regiment New Hampshire Volunteers,* p. 214; *In the Ranks from the Wilderness to Appomattox Courthouse,* p. 54; *Three Years in the Sixth Corps,* pp. 357–58.

3. *Recollections of a Private Soldier,* p. 120; *History of Durrell's Battery in the Civil War,* pp. 190, 229.

4. *Official Records,* Vol. XXXVI, Part 1, p. 365.

5. *Official Records,* Vol. XXXVI, Part 3, p. 647.

6. There is a good discussion of this point by Major William P. Shreve in *M.H.S.M. Papers,* Vol. IV, p. 316.

7. *Diary of Battery A, First Regiment Rhode Island Light Artillery,* by Theodore Reichardt, p. 139.

8. *History of the 12th Regiment New Hampshire Volunteers,* p. 214; *History of the 106th Regiment Pennsylvania Volunteers,* p. 224; *History of the Corn Exchange Regiment,* p. 469.

9. *Service with the 6th Wisconsin Volunteers,* pp. 277, 284–85; *Meade's Headquarters,* p. 147.

10. *Campaigning with Grant,* pp. 107–8.

11. *Following the Greek Cross,* p. 211.

12. *The Life and Letters of Emory Upton,* pp. 108–9. In view of the violent criticism that has descended on Grant because of Cold Harbor, it might be noted that Upton is specifically blaming the army's troubles there, not on Grant, but on the various generals of the Army of the Potomac.

13. *Under the Old Flag,* Vol. I, p. 400.

14. *Four Years Campaigning in the Army of the Potomac,* p. 151.

15. *The Iron-Hearted Regiment,* by James H. Clark, p. 131.

16. A Connecticut soldier in the VI Corps, at about this time, declares himself in respect to civilians: "I suppose that all those miserable hounds who stay at home, that have no more courage than a chicken, who do all they can to encourage others to enlist but stay at home themselves, are marrying all of the smartest girls up there and leave the soldier boys without any or of the poorest quality." (Manuscript letters of Lewis Bissell.)

17. *History of the 12th Regiment New Hampshire Volunteers,* p. 208; *Letters of a War Correspondent,* p. 99.

18. *M.H.S.M. Papers,* Vol. V, p. 15; *Reminiscences of the 19th Massachusetts Regiment,* p. 100; *History of the Corn Exchange Regiment,* p. 469; *The Diary of a Line Officer,* p. 68.

19. *The Diary of Gideon Welles*, Vol. II, pp. 43–44.

20. *Under the Old Flag*, Vol. I, p. 445.

21. Humphreys, p. 194.

22. For diametrically opposite verdicts on Grant's strategy up to this point the reader is referred to two studies in Vol. IV of the *M.H.S.M. Papers*—"Grant's Campaign in Virginia in 1864," by John C. Ropes, which is highly critical, and "Grant's Campaign Against Lee," by Colonel Thomas L. Livermore, which is very laudatory.

23. Grant's plans and the reasons assigned for them are set forth in his dispatch to Halleck dated June 5, *Official Records*, Vol. XXXVI, Part 1, pp. 11–12.

24. *History of the 2nd Connecticut Volunteer Heavy Artillery*, p. 69; *History of the Philadelphia Brigade*, pp. 277–78.

25. *Meade's Headquarters*, p. 163.

26. Colonel Theodore Lyman in *M.H.S.M. Papers*, Vol. V, p. 21.

LIE DOWN, YOU DAMN FOOLS

1. *Following the Greek Cross*, p. 117; *Meade's Headquarters*, p. 148; *Days and Events*, p. 372; *Under the Old Flag*, Vol. 1, p. 271. There is a good sketch of Smith's career in the *Dictionary of American Biography*.

2. *Official Records*, Vol. XL, Part 2, p. 595.

3. Butler's moves are briefly summarized in Grant's report, *Official Records*, Vol. XXXVI, Part 1, pp. 20–21. There is a good picture of the way this fumbled campaign looked to the men in the ranks in *History of the 12th Regiment New Hampshire Volunteers*, pp. 171–85.

4. *From Chattanooga to Petersburg Under Generals Grant and Butler*, by Major General William Farrar Smith, p. 36.

5. This description is taken from Colonel Livermore's *Days and Events*, p. 369.

6. *M.H.S.M. Papers*, Vol. V, p. 89.

7. "Four Days of Battle at Petersburg," by General Beauregard, in *Battles and Leaders*, Vol. IV, p. 540.

8. *M.H.S.M. Papers*, Vol. V, p. 56.

9. *Ibid.*, p. 90

10. *Ibid.*, p. 68; *Battles and Leaders*, Vol. IV, p. 541; *Official Records*, Vol. XL, Part 2, p. 83.

11. Hancock's report, *Official Records*, Vol. XL, Part 1, pp. 303–5; Grant's report, *Official Records*, Vol. XXXVI, Part 1, p. 25; *M.H.S.M. Papers*, Vol. V, pp. 64–72, 93–96; *Days and Events*, pp. 361–62; *History of the Second Army Corps*, pp. 527–32.

12. *Recollections of a Private Soldier*, p. 157: "We were in high spirits. . . . We knew that we had out-marched Lee's veterans and that our reward was at hand."

13. *Ibid.*, pp. 158, 160, 162.

14. *Battles and Leaders*, Vol. IV, p. 541.

15. *M.H.S.M. Papers*, Vol. V, pp. 28–29; *Official Records*, Vol. XL, Part 2, p. 86.

16. Colonel Theodore Lyman in *M.H.S.M. Papers*, Vol. V, p. 30.

17. *Ibid.*, p. 31. See also *History of the Second Army Corps*, pp. 532–36. For a detailed and judicious critique of the operations of mid-June, see "The Failure to Take Petersburg on June 16–18, 1864," by John C. Ropes, in *M.H.S.M. Papers*, Vol. V.

18. *Official Records*, Vol. XL, Part 2, pp. 91, 117.

19. Letter of General Beauregard to General C. M. Wilcox, printed in *M.H.S.M. Papers*, Vol. V, p. 121.

20. Ropes, *op. cit.*, pp. 167–68; Humphreys, pp. 217–18.

21. Ropes, *op. cit.*, pp. 169–72; *History of the 51st Regiment of Pennsylvania Volunteers*, pp. 564–70; *History of the 29th Regiment of Massachusetts Volunteer Infantry*,

by William H. Osborne, pp. 304–5; *Battles and Leaders,* Vol. IV, p. 543; *History of the Second Army Corps,* p. 539; Humphreys, p. 219; manuscript letters of Henry Clay Heisler.

22. *Official Records,* Vol. XL, Part 2, p. 120.

23. *Ibid.,* pp. 167, 179, 205; *Battles and Leaders,* Vol. IV, p. 544.

24. *History of the First Regiment of Heavy Artillery, Massachusetts Volunteers,* pp. 173–75; *History of the Second Army Corps,* pp. 541–42.

25. *Recollections of a Private Soldier,* pp. 166–67, 180–81.

26. *Official Records,* Vol. XL, Part 2, pp. 156–57.

27. *History of the 2nd Connecticut Volunteer Heavy Artillery,* p. 74.

28. Ropes, *op. cit.,* p. 184.

CHAPTER FOUR: WHITE IRON ON THE ANVIL

CHANGING THE GUARD

1. Manuscript letters of Lewis Bissell; *History of the 10th Massachusetts Battery,* pp. 228–29; *The Diary of a Line Officer,* p. 91; *A Soldier's Diary: The Story of a Volunteer,* by David Lane, p. 177; manuscript letters of Henry Clay Heisler; *M.H.S.M. Papers,* Vol. V, p. 29.

2. *A Soldier's Diary: The Story of a Volunteer,* p. 225; *Musket and Sword,* p. 291; *Campaigns of the 146th Regiment New York State Volunteers,* p. 230; *Army Life; A Private's Reminiscences,* pp. 203–4.

3. *Days and Events,* p. 377; *Ten Years in the U.S. Army,* by Augustus Meyers, p. 323.

4. *Meade's Headquarters,* pp. 181–82.

5. *The Story of the 48th,* p. 281; *In the Ranks from the Wilderness to Appomattox Courthouse,* pp. 93–94; *Thirteenth Regiment of New Hampshire Volunteer Infantry in the War of the Rebellion: A Diary,* by S. Millett Thompson, p. 259.

6. *In the Ranks from the Wilderness to Appomattox Courthouse,* p. 97; manuscript letters of Lewis Bissell.

7. Humphreys, pp. 230–35, 243; *Battles and Leaders,* Vol. IV, pp. 233–39.

8. *Under the Old Flag,* Vol. I, pp. 457–82.

9. *From Chattanooga to Petersburg under Generals Grant and Butler,* pp. 5, 52–53, 174–78: *Official Records,* Vol. XL, Part 2, pp. 558–59.

10. *My Diary of Rambles with the 25th Massachusetts Volunteer Infantry,* p. 109. Theodore Lyman described Butler as "the strangest sight on a horse you ever saw . . . with his head set immediately on a stout, shapeless body, his very squinting eyes, and a set of legs and arms that look as if made for somebody else and hastily glued to him by mistake." (*Meade's Headquarters,* p. 192.) For an understanding of what Colonel Lyman had in mind the reader is urged to study the photograph of Butler in *Divided We Fought,* edited by David Donald, p. 95.

11. *A War Diary of Events in the War of the Great Rebellion,* by Brigadier General George H. Gordon, pp. 359, 365.

12. *Official Records,* Vol. XL, Part 2, pp. 131–32, 188.

13. *Official Records,* Vol. XXXVI, Part 3, pp. 332–33. For an illuminating exchange of letters between Grant and Halleck on the general subject of politics and military appointments, with especial reference to General Banks, see that same volume, pp. 252–53, 293, 316, 332, 409–10.

14. *Official Records,* Vol. XL, Part 1, p. 28.

15. *Ibid.,* p. 35.

16. *Recollections of the Civil War,* p. 227.

17. Grant to President Lincoln, *Official Records,* Vol. XXXVII, Part 2, p. 433. It should be pointed out that in suggesting Meade as commander in the Valley Grant

warmly endorsed him: "With General Meade in command of such a division I would have every confidence that all the troops within the military division would be used to the very best advantage from a personal examination of the ground."

18. Gibbon's *Personal Recollections,* pp. 243–44, 248–51.

19. *History of the Second Army Corps,* pp. 544–47; *Official Records,* Vol. XL, Part 2, pp. 304, 330, 468. The corps' historian calls this "perhaps the most humiliating episode in the experience of the Second Corps."

20. Gibbon's *Personal Recollections,* pp. 227–28; *Official Records,* Vol. XL, Part 1, p. 368.

21. *History of the Second Army Corps,* p. 556; *Recollections of a Private Soldier,* p. 194.

22. *Official Records,* Vol. XL, Part 2, pp. 444–45; *History of the 106th Regiment Pennsylvania Volunteers,* p. 232.

23. *Official Records,* Vol. XL, Part 1, p. 474.

24. *History of the 24th Michigan,* p. 275; *History of the 12th Regiment New Hampshire Volunteers,* p. 229; *My Life in the Army,* p. 95.

25. *Service with the 6th Wisconsin Volunteers,* pp. 299–300; *History of the 150th Regiment Pennsylvania Volunteers,* pp. 197–98.

26. *Musket and Sword,* p. 183; *History of the 39th Regiment Illinois Volunteer Veteran Infantry,* p. 208.

27. Manuscript letters of Lewis Bissell; *Meade's Headquarters,* p. 232.

28. *A Soldier's Diary: the Story of a Volunteer,* p. 150.

29. Manuscript letters of Sebastian Muller, Library of Congress.

30. *Reminiscences of the 19th Massachusetts Regiment,* p. 105.

I KNOW STAR-RISE

1. Burnside's testimony at the Court of Inquiry on the Petersburg Mine, *Official Records,* Vol. XL, Part 1, p. 60; the three white divisions in the IX Corps lost 1,150 men between June 20 and July 20, and on the latter date mustered 9,023 enlisted men for duty. See also *Major General Ambrose E. Burnside and the Ninth Army Corps,* by Augustus Woodbury, pp. 420–21.

2. Manuscript letters of Henry Clay Heisler.

3. *The Story of the 48th,* p. 160: *The Tragedy of the Crater,* by Henry Pleasants, Jr., p. 35.

4. *The Tragedy of the Crater,* p. 32; *The 48th in the War,* by Oliver Christian Bosbyshell, pp. 163–65.

5. *The Tragedy of the Crater,* pp. 34–37.

6. Report of Major Nathaniel Michler, Corps of Engineers, *Official Records,* Vol. XL, Part 1, p. 291.

7. *The Tragedy of the Crater,* p. 41; *Battles and Leaders,* Vol. IV, p. 545; *Official Records,* Vol. XL, Part 1, p. 45; Part 2, p. 619.

8. Manuscript letters of Henry Clay Heisler; *The 48th in the War,* pp. 167–68; *Official Records,* Vol. XL, Part 1, pp. 556–58; Part 2, pp. 396–97, 417; *The Tragedy of the Crater,* p. 38.

9. *The Tragedy of the Crater,* pp. 44–45; Colonel Pleasants' report, *Official Records,* Vol. XL, Part 1, p. 558.

10. *Official Records,* Vol. XL, Part 1, pp. 557–58. Cross sections, diagrams, and general plans of the mine shaft, magazines, and ventilating shaft can be found in that volume, pp. 559–63, and in *Battles and Leaders,* Vol. IV, p. 548.

11. *History of the 36th Regiment Massachusetts Volunteers,* p. 228; *Grant's Personal Memoirs,* Vol. II, p. 314; *The Long Arm of Lee,* Vol. II, p. 846.

12. *Official Records,* Vol. XL, Part 1, p. 557.

13. *Major General Ambrose E. Burnside and the Ninth Army Corps,* p. 430; *Meade's Headquarters,* p. 201.

14. *Official Records*, Series III, Vol. V, p. 669.

15. *Personal Experience of a Staff Officer at Mine Run and Albemarle County Raid*, by Brigadier General H. Seymour Hall; *Paper of the Kansas Commandery, Military Order of the Loyal Legion of the United States*, p. 11.

16. This point is made in *A History of Negro Troops in the War of the Rebellion*, by George W. Williams, p. 170.

17. *Ibid.*, pp. 235–36.

18. *Army Life in a Black Regiment*, p. 36—one of the most fascinating books, incidentally, in Civil War literature.

19. *Ibid.*, p. 74; *The Negro in the Late War*, by Captain George E. Sutherland; *War Papers, Wisconsin Commandery, Military Order of the Loyal Legion of the United States*, Vol. I, p.183.

20. *Army Life in a Black Regiment*, p. 274.

21. *Three Years in the Sixth Corps*, pp. 275–76.

22. *Shot and Shell: the 3rd Rhode Island Heavy Artillery Regiment in the Rebellion*, by the Rev. Frederic Denison, pp. 214, 229; manuscript letters of Henry Clay Heisler; *Service with the 6th Wisconsin Volunteers*, p. 296; *Army Life in a Black Regiment*, p. 31.

23. Manuscript letters of Lewis Bissell: *A Woman's War Record*, p. 56.

24. *Ten Years in the U.S. Army*, p. 327.

25. *Memoirs of a Volunteer*, p. 231; *Musket and Sword*, p. 315; *Official Records*, Vol. XXXIII, p. 898.

26. *Army Life in a Black Regiment*, pp. 39, 71–72, 350.

27. *Ibid.*, pp. 14–15, 80; *The Fourteenth Regiment Rhode Island Heavy Artillery in the War to Preserve the Union*, by William H. Chenery, p. 18.

28. *Official Records*, Vol. XXXIII, p. 1020; Vol. XXXVII, Part 1, pp. 71–72; *A History of Negro Troops in the War of the Rebellion*, p. 238.

29. *Army Life in a Black Regiment*, p. 335.

30. *Major General Ambrose E. Burnside and the Ninth Army Corps*, pp. 420–21; *M.H.S.M. Papers*, Vol. V, p. 216.

31. *Battles and Leaders*, Vol. IV, p. 563; *Personal Experience of a Staff Officer*, p. 16.

32. *Army Life in a Black Regiment*, p. 286.

LIKE THE NOISE OF GREAT THUNDERS

1. Humphreys, pp. 247–48; Grant's *Personal Memoirs*, Vol. II, p. 310; *History of the Second Army Corps*, p. 559.

2. *Letters of a War Correspondent*, p. 190.

3. *The Long Arm of Lee*, Vol. II, p. 846.

4. *R. E. Lee*, Vol. III, p. 466; *History of the Second Army Corps*, pp. 565–66.

5. Meade's orders are in the *Official Records*, Vol. XL, Part 1, pp. 43–44. His testimony at the court of inquiry, pp. 44–58, tells how he overruled Burnside on the use of the colored troops and how Grant upheld him. The plan of attack, as finally approved, is well outlined in *M.H.S.M. Papers*, Vol. V, p. 229.

6. Burnside's testimony at the court of inquiry tells about the drawing of lots; *Official Records*, Vol. XL, Part 1, p. 61. There is a full account of his meeting with the division commanders in *Major General Ambrose E. Burnside and the Ninth Army Corps*, pp. 432–34.

7. *Meade's Headquarters*, pp. 168, 199. It is interesting to note that during the fighting around Spotsylvania Court House, two and one-half months earlier, a IX Corps private was writing in his diary that "the regiment on our left, the 14th N.Y. Heavy Art., ran for life at the first fire, leaving our left flank entirely exposed." (Manuscript diary of Corporal S. O. Bryant, 20th Michigan Infantry.) This heavy artillery regiment was in the first assault wave at the Petersburg crater.

8. Brigadier General Stephen M. Weld, *M.H.S.M. Papers*, Vol. V, p. 218: "He was a drunkard and an arrant coward. In every fight we had been in under Ledlie he had been under the influence of liquor." See also the testimony of Surgeon H. E. Smith, 27th Michigan, at the court of inquiry; *Official Records*, Vol. XL, Part 1, p. 119. In his *Personal Memoirs* (Vol. II, p. 313), Grant remarked: "Ledlie, besides being otherwise inefficient, proved also to possess disqualification less common among soldiers."

9. *History of the 51st Regiment of Pennsylvania Volunteers*, p. 573; *History of the 36th Regiment Massachusetts Volunteers*, p. 233; *Personal Experiences of a Staff Officer*, pp. 16–17.

10. *Official Records*, Vol. XL, Part 1, pp. 600, 609.

11. *Ibid.*, p. 47.

12. *Ibid.*, p. 557; *Battles and Leaders*, Vol. IV, p. 551n.

13. *Major General Ambrose E. Burnside and the Ninth Army Corps*, p. 437; *History of the 36th Regiment Massachusetts Volunteers*, pp. 234–35; *Battles and Leaders*, Vol. IV, p. 564; *The Story of the 48th*, p. 230; *History of the 29th Regiment of Massachusetts Volunteer Infantry*, pp. 312–13; *Reminiscences of the War of the Rebellion, 1861–65*, p. 246; *M.H.S.M. Papers*, Vol. V, p. 246; *Official Records*, Vol. XL, Part 1, p. 323.

14. *Official Records*, Vol. XL, Part 1, p. 324; *Letters of a War Correspondent*, p. 195; *The Diary of a Line Officer*, p. 102.

15. *Battles and Leaders*, Vol. IV, p. 561; *The Story of the 48th*, p. 230; *M.H.S.M. Papers*, Vol. V, p. 208; *Musket and Sword*, p. 293.

16. *Battles and Leaders*, Vol. IV, p. 562; *Major General Ambrose E. Burnside and the Ninth Army Corps*, p. 438; *M.H.S.M. Papers*, Vol. V, p. 209; *The Story of the 48th*, p. 231.

17. Humphreys, p. 255. (General Humphreys declares flatly: "Had the division advanced in column of attack, led by a resolute, intelligent commander, it would have gained the crest in 15 minutes after the explosion, and before any serious opposition could have been made to it.")

18. *Official Records*, Vol. XL, Part 1, pp. 78, 84, 92, 121–22, 701.

19. Humphreys, pp. 256–57; *Major General Ambrose E. Burnside and the Ninth Army Corps*, pp. 439–40; *Official Records*, Vol. XL, Part 1, pp. 280–81, 567, 574. There is a good account of the work done by the Confederate artillery in *The Long Arm of Lee*, Vol. II, pp. 865–75.

20. For testimony on this point, see *Official Records*, Vol. XL, Part 1, p. 122.

21. *M.H.S.M. Papers*, Vol. V, pp. 214–15.

22. *Official Records*, Vol. XL, Part 1, pp. 48, 55, 80–81, 142–43.

23. *Ibid.*, p. 119.

24. *Personal Experiences of a Staff Officer*, pp. 18–19, 31; *Battles and Leaders*, Vol. IV, p. 564; *Official Records*, Vol. XL, Part 1, p. 104.

25. *Ibid.*, p. 105; *Battles and Leaders*, Vol. IV, p. 565.

26. *M.H.S.M. Papers*, Vol. V, pp. 210–11.

27. *Official Records*, Vol. XL, Part 1, pp. 49, 57, 144; *The Story of the 48th*, p. 239.

28. Report of Captain Theodore Gregg, 45th Pennsylvania, an unusually vivid picture of the situation in the crater, *Official Records*, Vol. XL, Part 1, pp. 554–56. See also *History of the 36th Regiment Massachusetts Volunteers*, p. 238; *Reminiscences of the War of the Rebellion*, p. 249.

29. Manuscript letters of Henry Clay Heisler.

30. Grant to Halleck, *Official Records*, Vol. XL, Part 1, p. 17; *History of the 36th Regiment Massachusetts Volunteers*, p. 240; manuscript letters of Henry Clay Heisler. Accurately enough, this young private remarked that the trouble was due to "a mismanage by some of the Brigadier Generals in our corps."

31. *The Iron-Hearted Regiment*, p. 154; *Battles and Leaders*, Vol. IV, p. 564.

CHAPTER FIVE: AWAY, YOU ROLLING RIVER

SPECIAL TRAIN FOR MONOCACY JUNCTION

1. Details as to Private Spink and his crew, the befuddled guard at Aqueduct Bridge, and the heavy growth of brush on the approaches to the defenses, are in the *Official Records*, Vol. XXXVII, Part 2, pp. 61, 83. For Lincoln's remark about Halleck, see *Fifty Years in Camp and Field: Diary of Maj. Gen. Ethan Allen Hitchcock*, edited by W. A. Croffut, pp. 463–64.

2. *Official Records*, Vol. XXXVII, Part 2, pp. 339–41, 365–67; *R. E. Lee*, Vol. IV, pp. 240–41.

3. *Official Records*, Vol. XXXVII, Part 1, pp. 555–56, 607; *I Rode with Stonewall*, by Henry Kyd Douglas, pp. 288, 290.

4. *Diary of Gideon Welles*, Vol. II, pp. 70–71, 73.

5. *Official Records*, Vol. XXXVII, Part 1, p. 259; *Diary of Gideon Welles*, Vol. II, p. 84.

6. *Official Records*, Vol. XXXVII, Part 1, pp. 231, 254–55.

7. *Ibid.*, pp. 346–47. Need it be remarked that any reader who has not yet allowed Douglas Southall Freeman to introduce him to Jubal Early, through the three volumes of *Lee's Lieutenants*, should get on with the ceremony at once?

8. *Personal Memoirs of John H. Brinton*, pp. 280–81. There is an artless story of the adventures of one of the 100-day militia outfits in *Record of Service of Company K, 150th Ohio Volunteer Infantry*, by James C. Cannon.

9. *Following the Greek Cross*, p. 222; *History of the 2nd Connecticut Volunteer Heavy Artillery*, p. 83; *Three Years in the Sixth Corps*, pp. 375–76.

10. *Following the Greek Cross*, pp. 222–23.

11. McCook's report, *Official Records*, Vol. XXXVII, Part 1, p. 231; *The Vermont Brigade in the Shenandoah Valley*, by Aldace F. Walker, p. 29.

12. Meigs' report, *Official Records*, Vol. XXXVII, Part 1, p. 259; *Diary of Gideon Welles*, Vol. II, p. 75.

13. Letter of General Wright, printed in *Three Years in the Sixth Corps*, p. 382.

14. *I Rode with Stonewall*, pp. 295–96. It should be noted that when Early made his remark about scaring Abe Lincoln he did not know that Lincoln had been present at Fort Stevens during the fighting.

15. *Following the Greek Cross*, p. 224; *The Vermont Brigade in the Shenandoah Valley*, p. 30; *Official Records*, Vol. XXXVII, Part 1, pp. 232–33, 247, 259–60, 276–77.

16. *The Vermont Brigade in the Shenandoah Valley*, p. 37; *History of the 2nd Connecticut Volunteer Heavy Artillery*, pp. 86–88.

17. *Three Years in the Sixth Corps*, pp. 383–87; *The Vermont Brigade in the Shenandoah Valley*, pp. 38–48; *Following the Greek Cross*, p. 228.

18. *History of the 2nd Connecticut Volunteer Heavy Artillery*, p. 90.

19. *History of the 19th Army Corps*, by Richard B. Irwin, p. 367.

20. Grant's *Personal Memoirs*, Vol. II, pp. 315, 317.

21. *Official Records*, Vol. XXXVII, Part 2, pp. 374, 408.

22. *Ibid.*, p. 558.

23. *Ibid.*, p. 582.

24. For Grant's move to Washington, his talk with Hunter, and his order moving the troops to Halltown, see his *Personal Memoirs*, Vol. II, pp. 318–20.

TO PEEL THIS LAND

1. *The Shenandoah Valley and Virginia, 1861 to 1865: a War Study*, by Sanford C. Kellogg, pp. 214–15; *History of the Shenandoah Valley*, by William Couper, Vol. I, pp. 140–47, 217–26; *M.H.S.M. Papers*, Vol. VI, pp. 62, 156.

2. *Official Records*, Vol. XXXVII, Part 2, pp. 301, 329.

3. *Annals of the 6th Pennsylvania Cavalry*, p. 286.

4. *War Diary of Luman Harris Tenney, 1861–1865*, p. 136.

5. *Official Records*, Series 2, Vol. VII, pp. 1014 15.

6. *Ibid.*, pp. 976, 1012–13.

7. *Ibid.*, pp. 1092–93.

8. *Ibid.*, pp. 892–94, 997. As late as the winter of 1865, Senator Ben Wade was urging Congress to adopt a joint resolution prescribing retaliatory treatment on Confederate soldiers in Northern prisons. After much debate, the measure was watered down so that it simply condemned alleged mistreatment of captured Federals and enjoined humane measures on the men in charge of Northern prisons. (*Recollections of War Times*, by Albert Gallatin Riddle, p. 326.)

9. This particular estimate is from *The Vermont Brigade in the Shenandoah Valley*, p. 51. It can hardly be repeated too often that the numbers reported "present for duty" by Federal commanders seldom bore very much relationship to the number that would actually be put into action. Two examples may be cited. The morning report of one regiment in this summer of 1864 showed 708 enlisted men present for duty; but the regimental historian explains that only 472 would go into action. The other 236 would be accounted for by the infinity of details, and by the "present sick." A less extreme case is shown by a Pennsylvania regiment which reported 343 "present for duty" at Gettysburg but which put only 300 into the fight there. (*History of the 2nd Connecticut Volunteer Heavy Artillery*, p. 118; *History of the 106th Regiment Pennsylvania Volunteers*, p. 169.)

10. *A Volunteer's Adventures*, by John W. De Forest, p. 163.

11. *Ibid.*, p. 165; *The Vermont Brigade in the Shenandoah Valley*, p. 23.

12. *The Vermont Brigade in the Shenandoah Valley*, p. 50; *Following the Greek Cross*, p. 228.

13. For the reaction to Sheridan, see *Three Years in the Sixth Corps*, p. 391; *The Vermont Brigade in the Shenandoah Valley*, pp. 54–55; *History of the 19th Army Corps*, p. 367.

14. *History of the 17th Regiment Pennsylvania Volunteer Cavalry*, pp. 219–22; *Army Life; A Private's Reminiscences*, pp. 249–50.

15. *History of the 17th Regiment Pennsylvania Volunteer Cavalry*, p. 188.

16. Rosser to Lee, *Official Records*, Vol. XXXIII, p. 1081.

17. *Ibid.*, pp. 1082, 1120–21.

18. Telegram from General E. B. Tyler to Lew Wallace, *Official Records*, Vol. XXXVII, Part 2, p. 55.

19. *Memoirs of a Volunteer*, pp. 108–9.

20. *Sabres and Spurs: The First Regiment Rhode Island Cavalry in the Civil War*, by the Rev. Frederic Denison, p. 381.

21. *Ibid.*, p. 381.

22. *History of the 17th Regiment Pennsylvania Volunteer Cavalry*, pp. 211–12.

23. *Ibid.*, p. 212.

24. *Annals of the 6th Pennsylvania Cavalry*, pp. 286–87.

25. *Personal and Historical Sketches . . . of the 7th Regiment Michigan Volunteer Cavalry*, p. 263.

26. *History of the 17th Regiment Pennsylvania Volunteer Cavalry*, p. 228.

ON THE UPGRADE

1. *Lincoln's War Cabinet*, by Burton J. Hendrick, pp. 453–59; *Abraham Lincoln*, by Benjamin P. Thomas, pp. 441–42.

2. *Abraham Lincoln: The War Years*, Vol. III, p. 218.

3. There is a good account of this Confederate program in the North, and of Captain Hines's activities, in *Confederate Operations in Canada and New York*, by John W. Headley, pp. 214–20. See also *The Rebel Raider*, pp. 123–26, 132, 157–58,

167–73. The projected raid on the Johnson's Island prison camp is voluminously covered in the *Official Records,* Series 2, Vol. VII, pp. 842, 850, 864, 910–6.

4. Headley, *op. cit.,* p. 222.

5. *Ibid.,* pp. 223–28.

6. *Ibid.,* pp. 229–30. Swiggett (*The Rebel Raider,* p. 132) remarks that Hines was "by all odds one of the two or three most dangerous and competent men in the Confederacy."

7. *A Volunteer's Adventures,* p. 172.

8. *Battles and Leaders,* Vol. IV, pp. 506–7; *History of the 8th Regiment Vermont Volunteers,* by George N. Carpenter, p. 177.

9. *A Volunteer's Adventures,* p. 173; *Battles and Leaders,* Vol. IV, p. 507.

10. *Under the Old Flag,* Vol. I, p. 554; *Three Years in the Sixth Corps,* pp. 401–3; *Official Records,* Vol. XLIII, Part 1, pp. 173–74, 197, 222.

11. *A Volunteer's Adventures,* p. 186. This engaging book contains a first-rate account of the battle of Winchester by a Federal participant.

12. *History of the 8th Regiment Vermont Volunteers,* pp. 181, 255–56.

13. *Three Years in the Sixth Corps,* p. 404.

14. *History of the 8th Regiment Vermont Volunteers,* p. 183; *A Volunteer's Adventures,* pp. 187–90; *Battles and Leaders,* Vol. IV, pp. 509–10.

15. *A Volunteer's Adventures,* p. 189; *Official Records,* Vol. XLIII, Part 1, p. 189.

16. There is an odd similarity between Sheridan's handling of the battle of Winchester and Stonewall Jackson's conduct of the battle of Cedar Mountain. In each case a general of high reputation, enjoying a great numerical advantage over his opponent, put his troops in maladroitly, was rocked hard by an unexpected enemy attack, and for a time was in danger of outright defeat—winning out, finally, because his own driving energy at last made his numerical advantage effective. For a good critique of Sheridan's campaign in the Valley, see "The Valley Campaign of 1864: A Military Study," by Lieutenant L. W. V. Kennon, in the *M.H.S.M. Papers,* Vol. VI, pp. 39 *ff.*

17. *The Story of the First Massachusetts Light Battery,* p. 179; *The Vermont Brigade in the Shenandoah Valley,* p. 105.

18. *Under the Old Flag,* Vol. I, pp. 558–59.

NO MORE DOUBT

1. Thomas's *Abraham Lincoln,* p. 449; *Lincoln's War Cabinet,* by Burton J. Hendrick, pp. 45–47; *Diary of Gideon Welles,* Vol. II, p. 158; *Abraham Lincoln: The War Years,* Vol. III, pp. 237, 244, 246.

2. *Three Years in the Sixth Corps,* p. 413; *History of the 2nd Connecticut Volunteer Heavy Artillery,* p. 108.

3. *Three Years in the Sixth Corps,* p. 414; manuscript letters of Lewis Bissell; *History of the 2nd Connecticut Volunteer Heavy Artillery,* p. 108.

4. *M.H.S.M. Papers,* Vol. VI, pp. 48 *ff.*

5. *History of the 17th Regiment Pennsylvania Volunteer Cavalry,* pp. 135, 217–18; *History of the 2nd Connecticut Volunteer Heavy Artillery,* p. 109; *Sabres and Spurs,* p. 407; manuscript letters of Lewis Bissell.

6. *The Story of the First Massachusetts Light Battery,* p. 182; *Letters of a War Correspondent,* pp. 269–70.

7. *I Rode with Stonewall,* p. 315. Note that even the historian of the 17th Pennsylvania Cavalry, normally troubled by few qualms, wrote: "If ever troops found an incentive to strike vigorous blows for their 'homes and firesides' it was those who fought Sheridan's destructions from the 6th to the 9th of October, for we do not think the annals of civilized warfare furnishes a parallel to these destructive operations . . . the blackened face of the country from Port Republic to the neighborhood of Fisher's Hill bore frightful testimony to fire and sword." (*History of the 17th Regiment Pennsylvania Volunteer Cavalry,* p. 216.)

8. *History of the Shenandoah Valley,* Vol. II, p. 954.

9. *History of the 2nd Connecticut Volunteer Heavy Artillery,* p. 109; *The Story of the First Massachusetts Light Battery,* p. 182; *Three Years in the Sixth Corps,* pp. 415–16.

10. *I Rode with Stonewall,* p. 313.

11. *Battles and Leaders,* Vol. IV, p. 513; *Lee's Lieutenants,* Vol. III, p. 597.

12. *M.H.S.M. Papers,* Vol. VI, pp. 48, 97.

13. Early's narrative about all of this in *Battles and Leaders,* Vol. IV, p. 526. There is a description of the Union position in *A Volunteer's Adventures,* pp. 205–6—whose author, incidentally, draws the parallel between Early's audacity at Cedar Creek and Washington's at Trenton.

14. *History of the 2nd Connecticut Volunteer Heavy Artillery,* pp. 119–20.

15. *Ibid.,* pp. 120–21.

16. *The Vermont Brigade in the Shenandoah Valley,* pp. 136–40.

17. *History of the 2nd Connecticut Volunteer Heavy Artillery,* pp. 121–3; *History of the 8th Regiment Vermont Volunteers,* pp. 215 18. For descriptions of the confused fighting in the heavy fog, and the unavailing attempt to stem the fugitives and their pursuers on the turnpike, see the *Official Records,* Vol. XLIII, Part 1, pp. 215, 233, 245, 267, 284. General Wright's report on the battle is in that volume, pp. 158–61.

18. *Personal Recollections of Distinguished Generals,* by William F. G. Shanks, pp. 340–41; *Battles and Leaders,* Vol. IV, p. 518; *A Volunteer's Adventures,* pp. 210–11, 213–14, 220. The latter work speaks of the flight as taking place "with curious deliberation." For accounts of the rallying of the soldiers who did not panic, see the *Official Records,* Vol. XLIII, Part 1, pp. 197, 209–11.

19. *Lee's Lieutenants,* Vol. III, pp. 603–4.

20. *History of the 17th Regiment Pennsylvania Volunteer Cavalry,* pp. 115–17; *Thrilling Days in Army Life,* by General George A. Forsyth, pp. 135–38.

21. *Thrilling Days in Army Life,* pp. 140–43; *Battles and Leaders,* Vol. IV, p. 519.

22. *The Story of the First Massachusetts Light Battery,* p. 189.

23. *The Vermont Brigade in the Shenandoah Valley,* pp. 147–48; *History of the 17th Regiment Pennsylvania Volunteer Cavalry,* pp. 117–18; *Official Records,* Vol. XLIII, Part 1, pp. 251, 309.

24. *Thrilling Days in Army Life,* pp. 155–56, 159–60.

25. *History of the 2nd Connecticut Volunteer Heavy Artillery,* pp. 126–27; *The Vermont Brigade in the Shenandoah Valley,* p. 152, *History of the 8th Regiment Vermont Volunteers,* p. 223; *A Volunteer's Adventures,* p. 227.

26. *A Volunteer's Adventures,* pp. 228–29. Sheridan probably got a better reputation out of Cedar Creek than he really deserved, and it has often been argued that General Wright and Getty would eventually have pulled the victory out of the fire even if Sheridan had not reappeared at all. Sheridan provided the dramatics and the spur, which had long been missing from the experience of men in the Army of the Potomac. The most unrestrained enthusiasm and admiration came to him from the VI Corps itself, which provided most of the casualties at Cedar Creek, lost the fewest men captured, did most of the fighting—and, all in all, seems to have been quite willing to give to Sheridan the credit which might well have been claimed for its own generals.

27. Manuscript letters of Lewis Bissell.

CHAPTER SIX: ENDLESS ROAD AHEAD

EXCEPT BY THE SWORD

1. For a moving description of the autumn landscape at Petersburg, see *Letters of a War Correspondent,* pp. 275–76. The account of the fortified lines follows Humphreys, p. 310.

2. *History of the 10th Massachusetts Battery of Light Artillery,* p. 253.

3. *Official Records,* Vol. XL, Part 1, pp. 270–71; Series 3, Vol. V, pp. 70–71; *Letters of a War Correspondent,* pp. 155–59.

4. *Official Records,* Series 3, Vol. V, pp. 70, 72–73; *History of Durrell's Battery in the Civil War,* p. 209; *History of the 2nd Connecticut Volunteer Heary Artillery,* p. 133; *Battles and Leaders,* Vol. IV, p. 708.

5. "Grant Before Appomattox: Notes of a Confederate Bishop," by the Right Rev. Henry C. Lay, in the *Atlantic Monthly,* March, 1932.

6. *South After Gettysburg,* p. 144.

7. *Recollections of a Private Soldier,* pp. 191–92; *Army Life: A Private's Reminiscences,* p. 209; *Service with the 6th Wisconsin Volunteers,* p. 309.

8. *The Passing of the Armies,* by Major General Joshua Chamberlain, p. 12; *Army Life: A Private's Reminiscences,* p. 209. Interestingly enough, one veteran wrote that it was the new regiments, plus the shirkers and bummers who never got on the firing line, who provided most of the vote for McClellan. (*History of the 150th Pennsylvania Volunteers,* p. 244.)

9. Report of Colonel Henry L. Abbot, *Official Records,* Vol. XL, Part 1, pp. 664–65.

10. Manuscript letters of Henry Clay Heisler; *History of the 12th Regiment New Hampshire Volunteers,* p. 427.

11. *History of Durrell's Battery in the Civil War,* p. 228; *History of the 36th Regiment Massachusetts Volunteers,* pp. 246, 277; manuscript letters of Henry Clay Heisler; *The Irish Brigade and Its Campaigns,* p. 510.

12. *Four Years Campaigning with the Army of the Potomac,* p. 160.

13. *The Story of the Regiment,* pp. 367–68.

14. *History of the 198th Pennsylvania Volunteers,* by Major E. M. Woodward, p. 25.

15. *Ibid.,* p. 27; *History of the Ninth Massachusetts Battery,* by Levi W. Baker, p. 155.

16. *History of the 24th Michigan,* p. 283.

17. *South After Gettysburg,* pp. 163, 165; *History of the 87th Regiment Pennsylvania Volunteers,* p. 218.

18. *My Life in the Army,* pp. 135–36; *Music on the March,* pp. 203–4; *History of the 7th Connecticut Volunteer Infantry,* p. 176; *M.H.S.M. Papers,* Vol. VI, p. 413; *In the Ranks from the Wilderness to Appomattox Courthouse,* p. 97; *The Passing of the Armies,* pp. 21, 23. For the recruiting and training of an entire new division of first-rate troops, see *Military History of the 3rd Division, Ninth Corps, Army of the Potomac,* by Milton A. Embick, pp. 1–5.

19. *Following the Greek Cross,* p. 238.

20. *Ibid.,* p. 240; manuscript letters of Lewis Bissell; *History of the 2nd Connecticut Volunteer Heavy Artillery,* p. 144.

21. *Thirteenth Regiment of New Hampshire Volunteer Infantry in the War of the Rebellion,* pp. 533, 537–38.

22. Manuscript letters of Lewis Bissell; *Musket and Sword,* p. 303.

23. *Following the Greek Cross,* p. 240; *History of the 2nd Connecticut Volunteer Heavy Artillery,* p. 148.

24. *History of Durrell's Battery in the Civil War,* pp. 232–34; *History of the 51st Regiment of Pennsylvania Volunteers,* pp. 602–5. For early glimpses of Stephens and Lincoln, see *Abraham Lincoln: The Prairie Years,* by Carl Sandburg, Vol. I, pp. 378, 382 *ff.*

25. There is a good discussion of the peace mission and the Davis-Stephens relationship in "Alexander Stephens and Jefferson Davis," by James Z. Rabun, in the *American Historical Review,* Vol. LVIII, No. 2. See also *Abraham Lincoln: The War Years,* Vol. IV, pp. 39–46, 48, 58–60; *Jefferson Davis: The Unreal and the Real,* by Robert McElroy, Vol. II, pp. 435–40; *Diary of Gideon Welles,* Vol. II, p. 237. There is a mention of the return of Lieutenant Murray from his Southern prison in *Thirteenth*

Regiment of New Hampshire Volunteer Infantry in the War of the Rebellion, p. 534.
26. *Ibid.,* pp. 447, 520, 542.
27. *History of the Ninth Massachusetts Battery,* p. 160.

GREAT LIGHT IN THE SKY

1. *History of the 1st Connecticut Artillery,* by John C. Taylor, p. 154; *Major General Ambrose E. Burnside and the Ninth Army Corps,* p. 476.
2. *Reminiscences of the War of the Rebellion,* p. 262.
3. *Memoirs of Chaplain Life,* p. 335.
4. *Military History of the 3rd Division, Ninth Army Corps, Army of the Potomac,* pp. 1–4, 14–16; *Battles and Leaders,* Vol. IV, p. 584 *ff.* Hartranft's report on the fight is in the *Official Records,* Vol. XLVI, Part 1, pp. 345–49.
5. Grant's *Personal Memoirs,* Vol. II, pp. 433–34; Humphreys, pp. 320–21; *Official Records,* Vol. XLVI, Part 3, pp. 141–42, 171.
6. *Personal Memoirs of John H. Brinton,* p. 265.
7. Grant's *Personal Memoirs,* Vol. II, p. 425.
8. Manuscript letter of Sergeant George S. Hampton, 91st Pennsylvania Veteran Volunteers, in the possession of Mr. J. Frank Nicholson of Manassas, Virginia.
9. *Sherman, Fighting Prophet,* by Lloyd Lewis, p. 524.
10. Sheridan's report, reprinted in Moore's *Rebellion Record,* Vol. XI, p. 634 *ff.*
11. *Army Life: A Private's Reminiscences,* p. 251.
12. Humphreys, pp. 322–25; *Official Records,* Vol. XLVI, Part 1, pp. 50–51.
13. *The Passing of the Armies,* p. 34.
14. *The Story of the Regiment,* p. 381.
15. *Annals of the 6th Pennsylvania Cavalry,* p. 330; *Last Hours of Sheridan's Cavalry,* by Henry Edwin Tremain, pp. 19–24.
16. Grant's *Personal Memoirs,* Vol. II, p. 439; *Battles and Leaders,* Vol. IV, p. 709; Moore's *Rebellion Record,* Vol. XI, p. 644; *The Life of John A. Rawlins,* pp. 309–10.
17. Horace Porter describes the meeting between Grant and Sheridan in *Battles and Leaders,* Vol. IV, p. 710. See also *The Passing of the Armies,* p. 62; Grant's *Personal Memoirs,* Vol. II, p. 437.
18. There is an engaging description of Devin's movements, with particular reference to the difficulties of the horse holders on the retreat to Dinwiddie Courthouse, in *Last Hours of Sheridan's Cavalry,* pp. 37–45.
19. *Ibid.,* pp. 50–55; Sheridan's report, Moore's *Rebellion Record,* Vol. XI, p. 644; *Battles and Leaders,* Vol. IV, p. 711.
20. Grant's *Personal Memoirs,* Vol. II, p. 442; *Battles and Leaders,* Vol. IV, p. 711; *Official Records,* Vol. XLVI, Part 1, p. 380.
21. *Last Hours of Sheridan's Cavalry,* p. 56.

THE SOLDIERS SAW DAYLIGHT

1. *The Passing of the Armies,* pp. 65–78; *The Fifth Army Corps,* pp. 781–83; Humphreys, pp. 330–34; *Official Records,* Vol. XLVI, Part 1, pp. 337, 817–18.
2. *Campaigns of the 146th Regiment New York State Volunteers,* p. 292; *History of the Corn Exchange Regiment,* p. 574; Humphreys, pp. 337–40; *The Passing of the Armies,* pp. 90–96; *Official Records,* Vol. XLVI, Part 1, pp. 820, 822. In his report on Five Forks Warren explained that since his troops were so close to the enemy it was impossible to summon them out by drum or bugle; verbal orders had to pass down a long chain which began at corps headquarters and ended with non-coms arousing individual soldiers by shaking them. For the confusing series of orders Warren got that night, see the volume just cited, pp. 365–67, 410, 419–20.
3. *The Passing of the Armies,* pp. 104, 121.
4. Humphreys, p. 356; *Battles and Leaders,* Vol. IV, p. 723.
5. *The Passing of the Armies;* introduction, pp. xii–xiv.

6. Grant's *Personal Memoirs*, Vol. II, p. 445.

7. *In the Ranks from the Wilderness to Appomattox Courthouse*, pp. 193–94.

8. *The Fifth Army Corps*, pp. 800–4; Humphreys, pp. 346–48; *M.H.S.M. Papers*, Vol. VI, pp. 249–52.

9. *The Passing of the Armies*, pp. 129–30.

10. *Battles and Leaders*, Vol. IV, p. 714.

11. *Ibid.*, p. 713; *The Passing of the Armies*, pp. 133–34.

12. Very loyal to Warren but impressed by Sheridan in spite of himself, General Chamberlain describes all of these exchanges in *The Passing of the Armies*, p. 142. There are very extended descriptions of the battle of Five Forks, with particular reference to the movements of the V Corps, and with strong defense of Warren's actions, by Captain Charles H. Porter and Brevet Lieutenant Colonel William W. Swan, in *M.H.S.M. Papers*, Vol. VI, pp. 211–34, 237–55, 259–408.

13. Chamberlain, *op. cit.*, pp. 143–44, 151.

14. *Ibid.*, pp. 152–53.

15. *Battles and Leaders*, Vol. IV, pp. 714–15.

16. *Following the Greek Cross*, pp. 249–50; Humphreys, p. 364; "The Storming of the Lines at Petersburg," by Brevet Brigadier General Hazard Stevens, in Vol. VI, *M.H.S.M. Papers*, pp. 412–13, 418. The latter work has an exceptionally good description of the formidable Confederate defenses.

17. General Stevens, *M.H.S.M. Papers*, p. 422; *Red, White and Blue Badge*, by Penrose G. Mark, p. 321.

18. *Following the Greek Cross*, p. 252; *History of Durrell's Battery in the Civil War*, pp. 241–42; manuscript letters of Lewis Bissell; *History of the Corn Exchange Regiment*, pp. 282–83

19. *M.H.S.M. Papers*, Vol. VI, p. 423.

20. *Ibid.*, pp. 426–28; *History of the 5th Regiment Maine Volunteers*, p. 344; General Wright's report, *Official Records*, Vol. XLVI, Part 1, pp. 902–4.

21. *Following the Greek Cross*, p. 253; *History of the 5th Regiment Maine Volunteers*, p. 345; *Battles and Leaders*, Vol. IV, p. 717.

22. *History of the 2nd Connecticut Volunteer Heavy Artillery*, pp. 159–60. The break-through of the VI Corps was by no means inexpensive, the corps losing 1,100 men in fifteen minutes. The Confederate works at Petersburg were all but literally invulnerable, despite the extreme attenuation of Confederate manpower, and General Wright said later that the spot his corps attacked, which was the weakest place in the entire Confederate line, was the only place where an assault could possibly have succeeded. See Humphreys, p. 365.

THE ENORMOUS SILENCE

1. *Letters of a War Correspondent*, pp. 308–10; *Days and Events*, pp. 439–40.

2. *Music on the March*, p. 227.

3. *History of the 198th Pennsylvania Volunteers*, p. 53.

4. *The Story of the Regiment*, p. 394; *Last Hours of Sheridan's Cavalry*, p. 115; *Official Records*, Vol. XLVI, Part 1, p. 510.

5. *Army Life: A Private's Reminiscences*, pp. 247–48; *History of the Corn Exchange Regiment*, p. 583; Gibbon's *Personal Recollections*, p. 302; *The Story of the Regiment*, p. 395.

6. *Last Hours of Sheridan's Cavalry*, pp. 97–101.

7. *Meade's Headquarters*, pp. 345–46.

8. *Battles and Leaders*, Vol. IV, pp. 719–20; *The Generalship of Ulysses S. Grant*, p. 351.

9. "A Recruit Before Petersburg," by George B. Peck, Jr. from Rhode Island Soldiers and Sailors Society, Personal Narratives, Second Series, p. 52; *History of the 2nd Connecticut Volunteer Heavy Artillery*, p. 160.

10. *Last Hours of Sheridan's Cavalry*, pp. 133, 149–52.

11. *Four Years in the Army of the Potomac*, p. 199.

12. *Following the Greek Cross*, pp. 262–63. There is an unforgettable glimpse of what Lee himself saw of this disaster in *R. E. Lee*, Vol. IV, pp. 84–86. For Meade's anger at what he considered Sheridan's attempt to assume sole credit for this victory, see *Meade's Headquarters*, p. 351.

13. *Days and Events*, p. 449; manuscript letters of Lewis Bissell.

14. *Battles and Leaders*, Vol. IV, pp. 729–30; *History of the Second Army Corps*, pp. 681–83.

15. *Army Life: A Private's Reminiscences*, pp. 251–52; *In the Ranks from the Wilderness to Appomattox Courthouse*, p. 212; *History of the Corn Exchange Regiment*, p. 587. Looking back from his old age, Grant wrote glowingly that "straggling had entirely ceased" (*Personal Memoirs*, Vol. II, p. 481), but the men who did the marching made no such claim.

16. *Army Life: A Private's Reminiscences*, p. 253. This unpretentious book has a very good description of the march to Appomattox, the final scene there, and the surrender ceremonies. The artillery-infantry fight on the dark road is also depicted in *History of the Corn Exchange Regiment*, p. 587.

17. *Last Hours of Sheridan's Cavalry*, pp. 214–18, 228 *ff.*; *History of the 17th Regiment Pennsylvania Volunteer Cavalry*, p. 315.

18. *Army Life: A Private's Reminiscences*, p. 254; *The Fifth Army Corps*, p. 849; *In the Ranks from the Wilderness to Appomattox Courthouse*, p. 213.

19. *The Sunset of the Confederacy*, by Morris Schaff, p. 214; Gibbon's *Personal Recollections*, p. 315.

20. *Ibid.*, pp. 316–17; *Sabres and Spurs*, p. 456.

21. *Army Life: A Private's Reminiscences*, p. 255–56.

22. *The Sunset of the Confederacy*, p. 215.

23. *Army Life: A Private's Reminiscences* p. 257. The author of *Last Hours of Sheridan's Cavalry* says (p. 427): "We were too sleepy to move rapidly. We were too cross to be shoved by bullets."

24. *The Sunset of the Confederacy*, pp. 219–20; *History of the 198th Pennsylvania Volunteers*, p. 57; *Last Hours of Sheridan's Cavalry*, pp. 252–53.

25. *Thirteenth Regiment of New Hampshire Volunteer Infantry in the War of the Rebellion*, p. 587; manuscript letter of Sergeant George S. Hampton, of the 91st Pennsylvania. For an interesting account of the presentation of the flag of truce, and a postwar letter from the Confederate officer who carried it, see *History of the Corn Exchange Regiment*, pp. 589–91.

26. *Thrilling Days in Army Life*, p. 187. The reference to the playing of "Auld Lang Syne" is from *History of the 198th Pennsylvania Volunteers*, p. 58.

Index